SALISBURY

By the same author

'The Holy Fox': A Life of Lord Halifax (1991)
Eminent Churchillians (1994)
The Aachen Memorandum (1995)

SALISBURY

Victorian Titan

Andrew Roberts

Weidenfeld & Nicolson

LONDON

First published in Great Britain in 1999 by
Weidenfeld & Nicolson

© 1999 Andrew Roberts

A catalogue reference for this book is available
from the British Library

ISBN 0 297 81713 2

Typeset by Selwood Systems, Midsomer Norton

Printed in Great Britain by Butler & Tanner Ltd, Frome and London

Weidenfeld & Nicolson

The Orion Publishing Group Ltd
Orion House
5 Upper Saint Martin's Lane
London, WC2H 9EA

To Margaret Thatcher
Thrice-elected *'illiberal* Tory'

Contents

Illustrations and Maps

The Cecils, some in fancy dress, outside the North Front of Hatfield House[1]
Some of Salisbury's 1895 Cabinet[7]
Four generations of monarchs: Queen Mary, King Edward VIII, Queen Victoria,
    King George V, King Edward VII[2]
Salisbury preaching rejection of the Second Irish Home Rule Bill in Ulster
    in 1893[1]
A stroll in the park at Hatfield with Joseph Chamberlain[1]

Between pages 650 and 651
As Chancellor of Oxford University, by George Richmond, 1870–2[1]
Tsar Nicholas II[6]
The Chinese Viceroy visits Hatfield[1]
Salisbury with his grandchildren Robert and Beatrice about 1895[1]
God Save the Queen: Queen Victoria arriving at St Paul's Cathedral
    by John Charlton[8]
President Paul Kruger of the Transvaal[2]
Cecil Rhodes[2]
Sir Alfred Milner in Johannesburg, October 1900[2]
General Sir Redvers Buller[6]
Field-Marshal Lord Roberts: Commander-in-Chief in South Africa[2]
General Lord Kitchener[6]
Crowds celebrating the relief of Mafeking on the night of 18th May 1900
Lord Salisbury at Walmer Castle, 1896

Sources
1 Reproduced by kind permission of the 6th Marquess of Salisbury. Photographed by John
    Bethell.
2 Weidenfeld & Nicolson Archive
3 National Portrait Gallery
4 Author's collection
5 *Punch* (9 April, 1887)
6 Mansell/Time Inc
7 Illustrated London News
8 Royal Collection Enterprises Ltd
9 The Public Records Office of Northern Ireland

MAPS (by John Gilkes)
The Balkans 1878   188
Central Asia 1878   210/211
The Balkans 1885   338
Africa 1892   516
Sudan 1898   634
South Africa 1899   712/713

ENDPAPERS
Front: Hatfield House, North Front, 1875
Back: Hatfield House, South Front, date unknown

The Cecil Family Tree

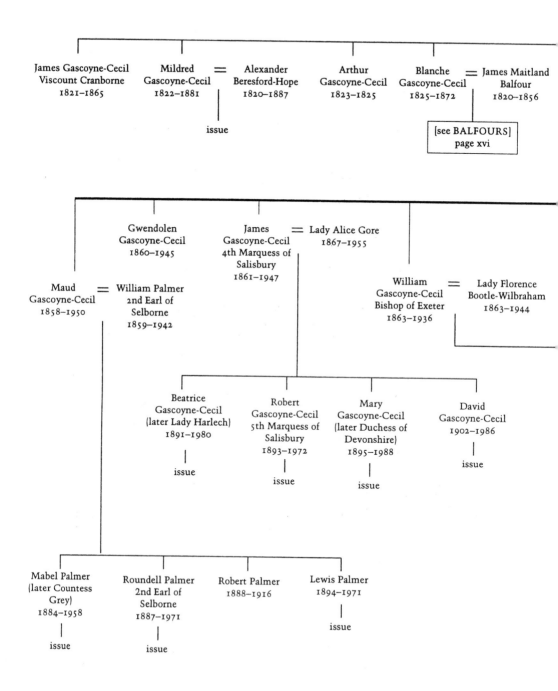

James Gascoyne-Cecil
Viscount Cranborne
1821–1865

Mildred
Gascoyne-Cecil
1822–1881
=
Alexander
Beresford-Hope
1820–1887

issue

Arthur
Gascoyne-Cecil
1823–1825

Blanche
Gascoyne-Cecil
1825–1872
=
James Maitland
Balfour
1820–1856

[see BALFOURS]
page xvi

Gwendolen
Gascoyne-Cecil
1860–1945

James
Gascoyne-Cecil
4th Marquess of
Salisbury
1861–1947
=
Lady Alice Gore
1867–1955

William
Gascoyne-Cecil
Bishop of Exeter
1863–1936
=
Lady Florence
Bootle-Wilbraham
1863–1944

Maud
Gascoyne-Cecil
1858–1950
=
William Palmer
2nd Earl of
Selborne
1859–1942

Beatrice
Gascoyne-Cecil
(later Lady Harlech)
1891–1980

issue

Robert
Gascoyne-Cecil
5th Marquess of
Salisbury
1893–1972

issue

Mary
Gascoyne-Cecil
(later Duchess of
Devonshire)
1895–1988

issue

David
Gascoyne-Cecil
1902–1986

issue

Mabel Palmer
(later Countess
Grey)
1884–1958

issue

Roundell Palmer
2nd Earl of
Selborne
1887–1971

issue

Robert Palmer
1888–1916

Lewis Palmer
1894–1971

issue

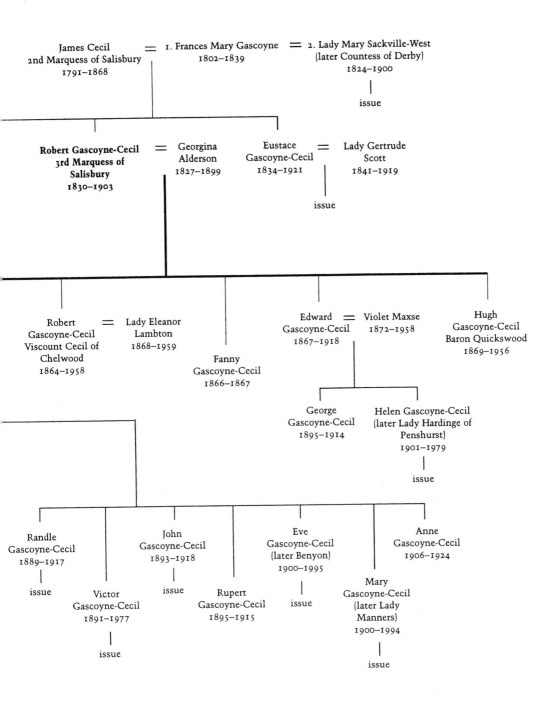

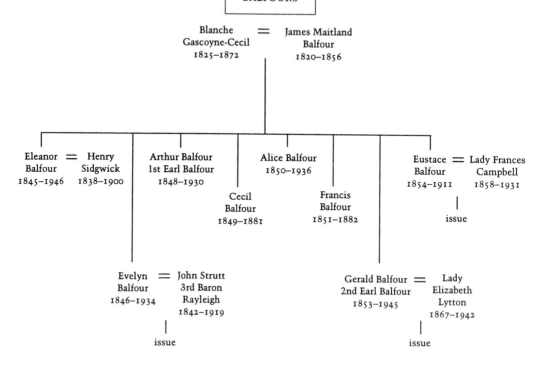

BALFOURS

Blanche
Gascoyne-Cecil   =   James Maitland
1825–1872   Balfour
                        1820–1856

Eleanor = Henry   Arthur Balfour   Alice Balfour   Eustace = Lady Frances
Balfour   Sidgwick   1st Earl Balfour   1850–1936   Balfour   Campbell
1845–1946   1838–1900   1848–1930   1854–1911   1858–1931

                                    Cecil   Francis
                                    Balfour   Balfour   issue
                                    1849–1881   1851–1882

Evelyn   = John Strutt   Gerald Balfour = Lady
Balfour   3rd Baron   2nd Earl Balfour   Elizabeth
1846–1934   Rayleigh   1853–1945   Lytton
              1842–1919   1867–1942

        issue   issue

Family Nicknames

'Baffy'	Lady Blanche Dugdale (née Balfour)
'Bob'	Lord Robert Cecil, Viscount Cecil of Chelwood
'Bobbety'	5th Marquess of Salisbury
'Fanny'	2nd Marchioness of Salisbury (i.e. mother of 3rd Marquess)
'Fish'	Lord William Cecil
'Fluffy'	Lady William Cecil (née Bootle-Wilbraham)
'Fran'	Lady Mildred Beresford-Hope (née Cecil)
'Geordie'	Lord George Hamilton
'Georgie'	Lady Salisbury
'Jem' or 'Jim'	4th Marquess of Salisbury
'Linky'	Lord Hugh Cecil
'Mima'	Beatrice Edith Cecil, later Lady Harlech
'Moucher'	4th Marquess's daughter, Mary, later Duchess of Devonshire
'Nelly'	Lady Robert Cecil, Viscountess Cecil of Chelwood
'Nigs'	Lord Edward Cecil
'Packy'	E. Packington Alderson, Lady Salisbury's brother
'Pete'	Eustace Balfour
'Poey' or 'Pooey'	Louisa Alderson
'Pom'	Sir Schomberg McDonnell
'TT' or ' Tim'	Lady Gwendolen Cecil
'Wang'	Mabel Palmer
'Widow, The'	Queen Victoria
'Willy'	William Palmer, 2nd Earl of Selborne

Acknowledgments

'No one reads old speeches any more than old sermons', wrote Lord Rosebery in his biography of Lord Randolph Churchill. 'The industrious historian is compelled to explore them for the purposes of political history, but it is a dreary and reluctant pilgrimage.' It has not been so for me. Not only have the several hundred of Lord Salisbury's speeches been a source of genuine pleasure over the past five years of research, but his two million words of journalism are as intellectually stimulating today as they were when they were written a century and a half ago. I have an unpleasant suspicion that, aged thirty-six, I will never again find so congenial a subject.

In one sense the subject found me, because I was fortunate enough to be commissioned by the 6th Marquess of Salisbury to write the life of his great-grandfather, and so try to fill the largest historiographical gap left in modern British political biography. For his original choice and his subsequent encouragement I am enormously grateful. Lord and Lady Cranborne and other members of the Cecil family have also been tremendously supportive of the project, for which I thank them.

To have been allowed free access to the Archive at Hatfield House, where so much of the raw material of British history rests, has been an enormous privilege. The Librarian there, Mr Robin Harcourt Williams, is a prince amongst archivists; he has made my task a great deal easier by placing his huge knowledge and scholarship at my disposal. I am much indebted to him for his sage advice and generosity with his time on the dozens of visits that I made over the years. I still blush at the schoolboy howlers – Cardinal Wolseley! – which he spotted in my first draft.

Although I once met a woman who remembered celebrating Mafeking Night, the distance of time has meant that no interviews were possible for this book, so it has almost all depended on documents of various kinds. Owners of private papers who have given me access to their family archives, and in some cases generous hospitality as well, include Sir William Benyon, the Duke of Devonshire, Lord Hambleden, the Earl of Harrowby, Mrs Diana Makgill, Lord Rockley, the late Duke of Rutland, and the Hon. Guy Strutt. I should like to thank them very much indeed, and should also like to acknowledge the gracious permission of Her Majesty the Queen to quote from material in the Royal Archives.

Mr Stephen Parker painstakingly produced scores of potted biographies for me, which were extremely useful. A master of esoteric pieces of information, he has made my task both simpler and far more enjoyable. Both he and Robin Harcourt Williams read through the entire first draft, making many invaluable suggestions, as too did Mr Alan Bell, Lord Blake, Lord and Lady Cranborne and Mr Simon Heffer. Busy people all, it was tremendously kind of them to work through so long a script, greatly improving it in the process. Other parts were also read by Mr Bruce Anderson, Mr John Aspinall, Prof. Paul Bew, Mr Alistair Cooke, Prof. Maurice Cowling, Dr Niall Ferguson, Mr Michael Gove, my father-in-law Roger Henderson QC, Dr John Mason and Prof. John Vincent, for which I heartily thank them all. With Prof. Vincent I have enjoyed a long and very fruitful correspondence on many aspects of Salisburiana, for which I am most grateful.

In the preface to *Lord Salisbury: The Man and his Policies*, Robert Blake and Hugh Cecil wrote in 1987 that they hoped their collection of essays would 'ease the burden of a future biographer, struggling through the vast mass of documents in the Hatfield House Muniment Room'. It certainly has, for which I thank them both. Dr David Steele also very kindly allowed me a preview of his fine revisionist study, *Lord Salisbury: A Political Biography.*

Translations from German and Latin were kindly undertaken for me by Mrs Joseph Godson, Hubert Picarda QC and the late Rt Hon. J. Enoch Powell. Mr John Gross explained the more obscure of Salisbury's literary allusions. Other very useful help and advice were kindly given by Mr Timothy Baker-Jones, Dr Correlli Barnett, Mr Robin Birley, Mr Michael Bloch, Mr Michael Bosson, Dr Piers Brendon, Mr Michael Cockerell, Lady de Bellaigue, Lord Dunluce, Mr Eamon Dyas, Prof. Ronan Fanning, the staff at GCHQ and readers of *The Times* literary pages who attempted to decipher Lady Gwendolen Cecil's 1888 coded diary entry, Mr David Huddleston, the unfailingly obliging staff at The London Library, Miss Grania Lyster, Mr John Major of the Sandringham Estate, Dr Anthony Malcomson, Mr Charles Noble at Chatsworth, Dr Thomas Otte, Dr S.G. Roberts of the Royal Commission on Historical Manuscripts, Mr Kenneth Rose, Prof. Richard Shannon, Dr J.S.G. Simmons of All Souls College, Oxford, Mr Hugo Vickers and Miss Lucy Whitaker of The Royal Collection Trust.

My thanks must also go to Mr Ion Trewin at Weidenfeld and Nicolson, who has loyally supported this project despite it running a year over schedule, and to my editor Miss Linda Osband who has brought her inimitable expertise to the script.

   This book was written at the Hamptons home of Mr and Mrs Daniel Masters over eight weeks in the summer of 1998. In giving me, my wife Camilla and our one-year-old son Henry the run of their house, Blythe and Dan were fantastically generous. Hail to the Mæcenases of Long Island!

   Camilla and the Great Marquess entered my life at roughly the same time. Britain's most over-qualified secretary, she was responsible for typing up these 400,000 words about the man she affectionately nicknamed 'Old Eeyore'. Although this particular book is formally dedicated to another strong-willed lady barrister, in a sense everything I write is dedicated to Camilla.

Andrew Roberts
Tite Street, Chelsea
July 1999

Introduction

Queen Victoria's Diamond Jubilee

London: Tuesday, 22nd June 1897

'Scarlet and gold, azure and gold, purple and gold, emerald and gold, white and gold, always a changing tumult of colours that seemed to list and gleam with a light of their own, and always blinding gold,' recorded a spectator. 'No eye could bear more gorgeousness.' Field-Marshal Lord Roberts VC, the diminutive hero of the Second Afghan War, led the procession on the famous white Arab pony which had seventeen years earlier borne him from Kabul to Kandahar. His baton resting on his right thigh, Roberts rode at the head of more than forty-six thousand men, the largest military force ever assembled in London. Queen Victoria had been on the Throne for sixty years, and the units taking part were chosen to emphasise the breadth of her Empire, which stretched over a fifth of the world's land surface and comprised a quarter of mankind.

There were broad-chested lancers from New South Wales, *zaptiehs* from Cyprus in red fezes, militiamen from Malta, hussars and dragoons from Canada and artillerymen from Trinidad. The *dyak* policemen from Borneo had black-and-white feathers on their scabbards; one of them, so *The Times* reported, had hunted thirteen heads in his former occupation. There were Ceylonese light infantrymen, baggy-trousered *hausas* from the Gold Coast, slouch-hatted carabiniers in khaki from Natal and Cape Colony, frontier policemen from Sierra Leone and a Chinese detachment from Hong Kong and the Straits Settlements who wore large, conical coolie hats. Even eighty years later, Queen Victoria's granddaughter, Princess Alice of Athlone, could recall the dyed red hair of the fierce Fijian warriors.

There were Sikhs and Malays and 28-stone Maoris and a camel corps belonging to the Maharajah of Bikaner. The South Australian Mounted Rifles wore spiked pith helmets, the British Guiana Police white *képis* and the Royal Niger Constabulary large red epaulettes. The most admired of all were the Indian cavalry regiments, in particular the

Bengal Lancers. Their dark beards, upright carriage and strange and rich uniforms made them the sensation of the procession. The brightly coloured turbans, nine-foot beflagged lances and the proud martial bearing of these elite corps thrilled the million Britons who packed the six-mile route of the procession.

There was much to celebrate. In the last three decades of the nineteenth century, the Empire had expanded by four million square miles. The Royal Navy, whose policy it was always to be larger than the next two navies combined, patrolled the oceans in protection of the world's greatest trading nation. London was the most powerful financial centre on earth. Even the French newspaper *Le Monde* was enviously but favourably comparing Britain's *imperium* to that of Ancient Rome.

Peoples as diverse as the Romans, Macedonians, Mongols, Turks, Spanish, French and Americans have had their moment in History's limelight – a time when the rest of the world watched their imperial progress with admiration, or fear, or both. On that glad, confident Tuesday morning it was Britain's turn to know such glory, to be the object of global awe and envy.

The 3rd Marquess of Salisbury and his wife waited on the steps of St Paul's Cathedral during the procession, together with the Cabinet, two military bands, the Corps Diplomatique, senior clergy, 500 choristers, a detachment of Yeomen of the Guard and the Gentlemen at Arms. After the Queen's carriage drew up in the bright sunshine, accompanied by a cavalcade of thirty-six princes and 100 courtiers, the *Te Deum* and the *Hundredth Psalm* were sung. When the Archbishop of Canterbury called out 'Hip, Hip, Hurrah!', the three great volleys of cheers could be heard all the way to Trafalgar Square. 'It will live in history as a unique and unexampled demonstration of the attachment which has grown more and more in intensity between the sovereign of a vast Empire and her subjects in every clime,' the Prime Minister wrote to the Queen that evening.

Lord Salisbury had guided the destinies of the Empire, nurturing and massively extending it, for almost nine of the previous twelve years, and he was to carry on the task for a further five. He knew there were times of great trial approaching: disputes with France on the White Nile, with Russia in the Orient, with the Dervishes of the Sudan, with the United States over commerce, with Imperial Germany and her new High Seas fleet, with Chinese nationalists and with the two small but pugnacious Boer republics in South Africa. 'The dangerous temptation of the hour', he warned a political meeting soon after the Jubilee, 'is that we should consider rhapsody an adequate compensation for calculation.' Even as the crowds were rhapsodising their time in the imperial sun, Lord Salisbury was calculating how to keep it from setting.

TORY TRIBUNE

ONE

Early Life

The Cecils – Eton and Oxford
– The Grand Tour

1830 to 1853

'Perhaps a phoenix may arise.'

Lord Robert Arthur Talbot Gascoyne-Cecil was born at Hatfield House in Hertfordshire on Wednesday, 3rd February 1830, the second surviving son of the 2nd Marquess of Salisbury. 'Robert' was a family name, in honour of the 1st Earl of Salisbury, the Secretary of State to both Queen Elizabeth I and King James I. 'Arthur' was a tribute to the Prime Minister, the Duke of Wellington, who stood godfather. Another god-father was the 16th Earl of Shrewsbury, whose Talbot family were long-standing allies and kinsmen of the Cecils. 'Gascoyne' was the maiden name of Lady Salisbury, whose Liverpudlian commercial fortune had nine years earlier bought the honour of hyphenation with the great Tudor name of Cecil.

The Cecils originally hailed from Wales, their name an anglicised form of the Old Welsh 'Sitsilt' or 'Seissylt', hence the pronunciation to rhyme with 'whistle' rather than 'wrestle'. His ancestry mattered to Lord Robert and was invaluable to him politically. His physical similar-ity to his great forebear, Lord Burghley, Queen Elizabeth I's tall, bearded adviser, provided an irresistible comparison for sentimental late-Victorian profile-writers.

Ever since David Cecil left Wales to fight for King Henry VII, the Cecils have been politicians. After fighting at the Battle of Bosworth in 1485 and becoming a Yeoman of the Guard, David Cecil settled in Stamford in Lincolnshire and sat for the borough in Parliament. His son Richard became a Gentleman of the Privy Chamber and Sheriff of Rutland. It was Richard's grandson, William, who was appointed Secretary of State by Elizabeth I, her first act after being informed of her accession when sitting under an oak in the park of the then Crown property of Hatfield. 'He had a cool temper, a sound judgment, great powers of application', wrote Macaulay, 'and a constant eye to the main chance.' Created Lord Burghley in 1571, William Cecil counselled the Queen cautiously and sagaciously until his death in 1598, gaining honours, titles and land in the process.

Burghley's son by his first wife became the Earl of Exeter and inherited the Burghley estate in Stamford. His son by his second wife, Robert Cecil, took his father's place as chief minister and managed the smooth succession from the Tudor to the Stuart dynasty. 'A statesman's statesman,' he has been described, 'a figure intimidating, aloof and formidable.' So Machiavellian was he that he has even, probably unfairly, been accused of having managed the Gunpowder Plot for his own political ends. He was certainly responsible for the Plantation of Ulster, which transplanted thousands of Protestant Scots into the north-eastern part of Ireland in the early seventeenth century. Created Earl of Salisbury, he too collected titles and land and, after swapping his home, Theobalds, with the King, he built a beautiful Jacobean palace at Hatfield, dying just before its completion in 1612.

The family's political genius then went into virtual hibernation for a century and a half, when, as the 3rd Marquess's daughter and biographer Lady Gwendolen Cecil put it, 'the general mediocrity of intelligence which the family displayed was only varied by instances of quite exceptional stupidity'.[1] This is slightly unfair to the 2nd Earl, who somehow contrived both to sit in Cromwell's regicide parliament and get his grandson appointed a page of honour at Charles II's Coronation, but was probably true of the 4th Earl, who became a Roman Catholic and imprudently raised a troop to support James II at the time of the Glorious Revolution. 'Oh God, I turned too soon, I turned too soon!' he was reputed to have exclaimed on hearing of William III's success, and his inexpert sense of timing cost him four years in the Tower of London.

The family motto, '*Sero Sed Serio*', translates as 'Late but in Earnest'. It was the courtier and politician James Cecil, the 7th Earl, who was raised to the marquessate in 1789. 'Now my lord,' King George III said to him, 'I trust you will be an English marquess and not a French marquis.' A Tory MP, Fellow of the Royal Society and Lord Chamberlain from 1783 to 1804, the 1st Marquess rejected the Foxite Whig embrace which enveloped so many of his class. From almost the earliest days of the political philosophy, therefore, the Cecils were Tories.

~

James Cecil, the 2nd Marquess, was born in April 1791. Prevented by his father from joining the army because he was an only son, he found commanding the Hertfordshire Militia and South Hertfordshire

Yeomanry a poor substitute. A tough landowner, he interested himself in country sports, the local magistracy and his role as Middlesex's Lord Lieutenant, as well as representing Hertfordshire's interests in the House of Lords. He was a fatalistic, old-fashioned Tory who opposed parliamentary reform and detested railways (while nevertheless winning excellent terms from the company which built one close to his estate). Particularly interested in the operation of the Poor Law, he had some influence on the ideas of Edwin Chadwick, the Secretary of the Poor Law Commissioners. When Wellington's younger brother, Lord Cowley, married one of his sisters, Salisbury was irritated not to find office in the Duke's brief 1834 ministry. After opposing Sir Robert Peel's repeal of the Corn Laws, he served in two of the 14th Earl of Derby's short-lived ministries, as Lord Privy Seal in 1852 and as Lord President of the Council in 1858–9. He seems to have exerted little influence beyond providing landowning, and thus protectionist, ballast.

In 1821, the 2nd Marquess massively augmented the Cecil fortune in the traditional aristocratic manner, when he married the nineteen-year-old heiress Frances Mary, only daughter of the late Bamber Gascoyne, a merchant prince whose Essex and Lancashire estates more than complemented the Cecils' own in Hertfordshire and Dorset. Fanny Gascoyne's father and both grandfathers had been members of Parliament, and she was passionately interested in politics. Attractive, witty and high-spirited, she softened her husband and entertained on a large scale, partly in order to advance his career. The Duke of Wellington, who gave her away at her wedding, was so close a friend that he had to write to her in 1837 to discourage her from visiting him at Walmer Castle without her husband, for fear of a scandal, adding the (quite untrue) protestation: 'I am beyond the age to afford any ground for it.'

An heir, James, Viscount Cranborne, was born nine months after the Salisburys' wedding. Two daughters, Mildred and Blanche, followed in 1822 and 1825. A second son, Arthur, died aged sixteen months, and Cranborne developed a disability which soon led to blindness, possibly as a result of his mother suffering German measles during her pregnancy. It therefore became vitally important that the next baby should be a healthy male. When a baby was born two months premature and greatly underweight, Lady Salisbury exclaimed to the wife of the Hatfield rector: 'Oh Mrs Faithfull, pray don't let them kill it, especially as it is a boy.'[2] Robert survived, and at his christening on 1st May 1830 a 'sumptuous' dinner and rout was held at Hatfield, attended by nine dukes, but not by Princess Mary, another godparent, owing to the mortal illness of her brother King George IV.

Little is known of Robert Cecil's very early years, other than that he was sleeping in a four-poster bed in the south-east wing at three, and could write his Christian name at four. When he was five his grandmother, the eccentric widow of the 1st Marquess, burned herself to death in a famous fire which devastated the west wing of Hatfield House on the evening of 27th November 1835. Although she had hunted into her late seventies, by eighty-six she should not have been left alone with a lighted candle in her room. As the dowager Marchioness's ashes could not be distinguished from the rest of the debris, they simply scooped up those closest to a ruby ring she was known to have been wearing and put them in an urn. The ring had been taken out of pawn for a forthcoming party. (In *Oliver Twist*, published two years later, one of those who helped extinguish the flames was the villain Bill Sikes, on the run from London after having killed Nancy.)

When staying at Hatfield during Christmas 1835, Wellington was fond of 'taking Bobby on his knee and putting questions to him upon the different things he learnt'. Everything changed, however, in October 1836, when, aged six, the boy was sent to the school run by the Rev. Francis Faithfull, the rector of Hatfield and the 2nd Marquess's former tutor. 'My existence there', recalled the doleful victim years later, 'was an existence among devils.' The boys were woken at 6 a.m., given no food until 10 a.m., worked seven hours a day, beaten with shaving straps, 'and naturally learnt nothing'. He told his niece, Lady Rayleigh, sixty years later, that they regularly fell ill, 'but nobody minded'. According to Cecil's younger brother, Lord Eustace, who was born in 1834 and who also had to endure Mr Faithfull: 'My father's idea was that the more boys roughed it in every way, the stronger and better they grew up.'

The children were never allowed flannel next to skin or a greatcoat in winter. Pneumonia struck regularly, as they were not protected from draughts. 'When I required purgative medicine,' remembered Eustace, 'I was given green apples!' They slept on mattresses on the floor, rode without saddles and, until Lord Salisbury finally put a stop to it, were forced to endure Mr Faithfull's 'Methodistical tenets, discouraging every innocent amusement' on Sundays. No worse regime could have been devised for a shy, slight, introverted child, and Robert Cecil was to suffer regular severe bouts of illness and depression over the next three decades.

He was much happier when he attended the Berryhead, Devonshire, school of the Rev. Henry Lyte, the author of the hymns *Abide with Me* and *Praise, my Soul, the King of Heaven*, who encouraged his early interest in science and botany. He was also allowed to avoid the riding and field sports which he said brought him misery. In June 1838, Wellington asked 'my friend Bobby' to be his page at the Coronation of Queen Victoria, but he was found to be too small for the uniform. He went to the ceremony as his father's page instead, and found it interminably long. At the supreme moment when the Crown was placed on the Queen's head, however, a kind neighbour lifted him up on his shoulders. The child forever afterwards remembered 'an abiding vision of gorgeous colour and light centred upon one slight lonely figure'.

'I do not think I have ever met so promising a boy,' Lyte reported to Lord Salisbury on 3rd October 1839, 'and I have no doubt of his distinguishing himself hereafter in life. His constitution is, I fear, a little delicate, and he requires a stimulus to induce him to take exercise.' Within a fortnight of that report, at 7 a.m. on Tuesday, 15th October 1839, Frances, Lady Salisbury, died of a pancreatic disease associated with diabetes, in those days known as 'the dropsy'.[3] Her distraught husband recorded how at midnight on the 14th 'a violent spasm came on which we thought would carry her off. After some time she revived a little. She knew us all, and desired to see the children and blessed them in a faint voice.... Asked for scissors and endeavoured to cut off some hair for us, which she gave us when she cut it...she expired without a groan.' A week later Salisbury noted how, at her large Hatfield funeral, Robert, then only nine years old, 'behaved well and with calmness'.

At precisely the time when he most craved affection, the young boy found himself starved of it. His elder brother was an invalid who spent much of his life abroad, his sisters were eight and five years older than him and both married young. His brother Eustace was four years younger and unaccountably antagonistic. His domineering father would occasionally hear his history lessons and correct his essays, but was following a political career that kept him in London for much of the year. 'Outside the limits of his family', his *Times* obituary was to observe in 1903, 'he never really had an intimate friend.' Instead his boyhood consisted of what his nephew Algernon later called 'a pathetic loneliness', living amongst the forty indoor servants at Hatfield, studying alone in its well-stocked library. As a result, he became sensitive, solitary, highly strung and phenomenally well read. Of acute shyness he later wrote: 'Nobody pities the unfortunate victim to it.... Most people who do not happen to be afflicted in that way look upon it as a deliberate offence against themselves, planned for their especial annoyance.'

Both his sisters' marriages were to be important to the young Cecil. In 1842, Mildred married Alexander Beresford-Hope, the very rich heir to a Dutch diamond fortune and a British field marshal's estates. A right-wing, High Anglican Tory MP as well as a novelist, poet and founder of the *Saturday Review*, Beresford-Hope supported many of the causes Cecil came also to champion. Blanche married another Tory MP, the equally rich Scottish landowner James Maitland Balfour of Whittinghame, in 1843. Although he died in 1856 aged only thirty-six, they had had eight children, including Arthur and Gerald, both of whom were to serve in their uncle's ministries.

~

The Eton of the 1840s was the worst possible place to have sent an eleven-year-old with anything but the most robust mental and physical constitution. It was then a monument to child's inhumanity to child. Cecil's housemaster there, the Rev. W.G. Cookesley, doubled as his tutor. His sharp academic brain entirely failed to atone for his naïve myopia about the brutal bullying that was rampant in his house. His reports to Lord Salisbury depict a child whose intellect and learning placed him in sets three years ahead of his age group, but also a housemaster who failed to appreciate the dangers this might involve.

Although he tended absent-mindedly to lose his hats, clothes and books, Cecil was 'industrious, amiable and endowed with a fine understanding'.[4] By 1843, his letters to his sister Blanche were written in fluent French and sometimes German, which he had asked to be taught extra-curricula. He disapproved of Eton's over-emphasis on the Classics, 'the eternal verse-making' system which he later complained 'makes Horace and Virgil all in all, while it ignores Dante and Goethe and Corneille'. By 1861, he believed that 'nothing is taught at Eton which people wish their sons to know', but he excelled there intellectually nonetheless. His exams were written in a 'very remarkably superior way', and he was recommended as a candidate for the Newcastle Scholarship. Beneath these academic laurels, however, lay much misery. Cecil's refusal to do Latin and Greek verses for his far older and dimmer classmates spelt purgatory.

Having begun in earnest in the summer of 1843, by May 1844 the bullying had become so vicious – especially after Troughton *major* with ten pints of beer inside him had burnt Cecil's mouth with a candle so badly that he could not speak for the rest of the evening – that Cecil decided to 'sneak' to his father. 'I know that you do not like complaints,' he wrote, 'and I have tried to suppress them and conceal all this, but you are the only person to whom I can safely confide these things. Really now Eton has become perfectly insupportable. I am bullied from morning to night without ceasing.' He described how four boys, each larger than himself, would regularly kick and thump him, seven more had pelted him throughout breakfast, and someone else had just spat in his face. 'Then when I come into dinner they kick and shin me and I am obliged to go out of dinner without eating anything... I have no time to learn my lessons. I know this is very little interesting to you, but it relieves me telling it to someone.' He considered merely acceding to the bullies' demands, but the precedent of a boy who had been withdrawn from school the previous year suggested it would not have appeased them. Because the unsympathetic Cookesley was both his housemaster and his tutor, Cecil had no independent mentor amongst the beaks who could intervene for him, and he also knew that any official investigation might only make the bullying worse.

On his father's inquiry he named the ten worst bullies – all three years older and 'considerably bigger' – begging him not to mention them to Cookesley 'so as in any way to implicate me or them'. The best his father could do was make the common but contentious assertion that 'bullies are always cowards, and it is not unlikely that you will succeed against one' if he challenged the next boy to a fight on the playing fields. Later that month, Cecil returned to his room to find his clock smashed, butter stamped into his new carpet and a valuable book thrown into the fireplace with its cover torn off. As he was writing the closing paragraphs of a letter to his father, a boy came in, 'kicked me and pulled my hair and punched me and hit me as hard as ever he could for twenty minutes, and now I am aching in every joint and hardly am able to write this'. He ended by begging his father not to let the bullies suspect that he had sneaked, but simply to take him away from 'this horrid place'.

Salisbury hamfistedly complained to Cookesley, who made equally clumsy inquiries in the house and reported back that: 'I have never detected or suspected them being the worse for drinking.' He even went so far in his complacency as to send Salisbury a copy of the prayers which he read to his boys at night, in order to show 'how earnestly I endeavour to inculcate mutual forbearance amongst them'. Myers *minor*, Cookesley admitted in a later letter, had 'shoved him about… but I seriously believe in a <u>playful</u>, not an <u>angry</u> manner'. It was not until December that the house-master finally had to admit: 'I have no doubt that Robert has been coerced,' but even then he added: 'I wish to act as gently and mildly as I can.' It was not until July 1845 that Salisbury finally withdrew Robert from Eton, when he saw that his son's physical and nervous health was on the verge of collapse.

His schooling profoundly influenced Cecil's outlook upon life. His pessimism about human nature, his assumptions about the cowardice of the silent majority, the cruelty of the mob and the vulnerability of the rights of the individual were instilled in him by his Eton experiences. 'I think the human heart naturally so bad', he wrote to his sister Blanche while still at school, 'that if not checked by true religion, the bad principle will in most cases predominate over the good.' He refused all invitations to return, and his sole visit there, to introduce his two eldest sons, he found such a painful experience that he refused to repeat it for the younger ones. He only sent them there because he had been assured that it had changed for the better, which indeed it had, but when his son Edward fared badly in his Sandhurst exams, he automatically blamed the school. 'He would never talk about his school life,' reminisced one of his daughters to another, 'I remember trying to get him to, but quite unavailingly. He only said he was thoroughly miserable.'⁵ Even when a Member of Parliament, if Cecil saw a school contemporary approach in the street, he would duck down a side alley, preferring a circuitous route to his destination to one that risked unnecessary social contact with an Etonian.

~

After two and a half years of successful tutoring at Hatfield by the Rev. Arthur Starkey of St John's College, Oxford, Cecil matriculated as a gentleman-commoner at Christ Church, swearing his belief in the Thirty-Nine Articles in December 1847. His time there was spent with the brightest and most high-minded undergraduates, men such as the 4ᵗʰ Earl of Carnarvon, Henry (later Canon) Liddon and Henry Acland, who went on to become Oxford's Regius Professor of Medicine. He avoided physical exercise, read very widely in German literature, the Classics and modern history, and delivered papers to a college secret society, the Pythic Club.

Victorian Oxford was the home of High Anglicanism and High Toryism, and Cecil imbibed deeply of both. He enthusiastically attached himself to the Tractarian wing of the Church of England, which was founded in the belief that in a time of increasing scientific inquiry and social licence, the Church of England was in danger and 'a great effort must be made to stem the threatening flood'. Inaugurated by John Keble's famous sermon, 'National Apostasy', delivered at St Mary's, Oxford, on 14ᵗʰ July 1833, which attacked the Whig Government's proposed suppression of ten Church of Ireland bishoprics, the Movement attracted the most brilliant Oxford theologians and preachers of the day, including John Henry Newman, A.P. Percival, Richard Hurrell Froude and William Palmer.

In September 1833, the first of a series of *Tracts for the Times*, reiterating High Anglican doctrine, was distributed, and by the end of 1834 Dr Edward Pusey, the great Oxford divine, had joined what became known as the Oxford Movement. Described by Dean Church as 'clear, brief, stern appeals to conscience and reason, sparing of words, utterly without rhetoric, intense in purpose', the *Tracts*, which eventually numbered ninety, could have been written specifically with Cecil in mind. For a conservative-minded young man with a feeling for history, Tractarianism was an intoxicating force, preaching a traditional creed with clarity and conviction and it was to provide the main spiritual and intellectual influence on Cecil's life. The Movement attempted to appeal to the educated classes through the intellect, leaving emotion to the evangelicals. Thus tract No. 84, published in 1840, was entitled: 'Whether a Clergyman of the Church of England be

Now Bound to have Morning and Evening Prayers Daily in his Parish Church?' (concluding that he was) and No. 87 was 'On Reserve in Communicating Religious Knowledge'.

When Cecil arrived in Oxford in 1847, the Movement was staggering under the tremendous blow of Newman's secession to Roman Catholicism two years earlier, which seemed to confirm all that its enemies had been warning about how the *Tracts'* homilies tended to lead towards Rome. Pusey, Palmer and Keble remained, however, and helped to mitigate the blow. (Canon Pusey himself resided in the south-west corner of Tom Quad of Christ Church when Cecil's rooms were in the north-west.) Newman's book, *Parochial and Plain Sermons*, had provoked 'supreme admiration' in Cecil, but, rather than wishing to unpick the Reformation, Cecil instead wanted to regenerate the Church of England, and he had little time for those who converted. When setting up Pusey House in 1882, he spoke of 'the church of eighteen centuries', in the Prayer Book sense in which the Church of England is that part of Christ's Holy, Catholic and Apostolic Church established by law in England. He did not accept for example that the administering of the Last Rites made any difference in the next world, and classed it with the laying-on of hands and the necessity of baptism as 'reducing the whole thing to the level of a lawyer's deed or a chemical reaction, rather than the ruling of an intelligent being'.

Cecil also found time to take revenge on the type of hearty boors who had made such a misery of his life at Eton. Anticipating a surprise 'ragging' attack on the set of rooms occupied by one of his intellectual friends, he led the defence in beating them off. After the vicissitudes of his unhappy childhood, the concepts of fun and playfulness were largely alien to him, and he only really discovered them once he was married with a family. In contrast to most people, the older he grew the less priggish and earnest he became, until one of his closest Cabinet colleagues remarked that as Prime Minister there was nothing that he did not find a fit subject for teasing and humour, except of course Christianity.

Cecil's rooms were in one of the two turrets on the corner of St Aldate's, reached through the gateway below Tom Tower and then turning sharply left. The young undergraduate could hardly have missed the slogan 'No Peel' which had been burnt into a door in 1829 at the time of Catholic Emancipation. It was a sentiment with which he entirely sympathised, and in an inelegant phrase to the Oxford Union, Cecil declared that, for splitting the Conservative Party over the Corn Laws in 1846, the former Conservative Prime Minister 'should be left to lie in the grave of infamy which his tergiversation had dug'.

Cecil had discovered High Toryism before leaving Eton. In a discussion there upon the relative political merits of Sir Robert Peel and Lord

John Russell, he was remembered to have said: 'I am an *illiberal* Tory,' refusing even to take sides because he 'had a peculiar pleasure in taking higher ground still'. By the time he left Oxford, Cecil's Toryism was so High it regularly spilled over into pure reaction. To attack the Conservative Party from the Right was a habit it took thirty years and two spells in government to dispel, and on some subjects, such as his nephew Gerald Balfour's 1890s Irish Land and Irish Local Government Bills, he even criticised the Party's policies when he himself led it.

Coming at the sensitive ages of fifteen and sixteen, when great events can determine political views far after adolescence, the actions of Peel in 1845 and 1846 had an enormous influence on Cecil. Decisions taken during the Irish Home Rule controversy forty years later can be traced back to the disgust Cecil felt over Peel's willingness to split the Conservative Party by granting taxpayers' money to the Catholic Irish seminary at Maynooth in 1845, and by repealing the protectionist Corn Laws. In letters to Blanche in April and May 1845, Cecil denounced Peel for 'supporting idolatry', subsidising 'heresy' and trampling on his former principles, concluding that 'there must be something wrong at the root'. The argument that the largely Catholic Ireland should be treated differently from Protestant England drew his analogy that one might as well allow rural Essex to have Protection whilst industrial Lancashire could enjoy Free Trade.

Beneath these debating arguments lay Cecil's assumption that Ireland was a potential enemy, that the Maynooth Grant was the thin end of the wedge of Irish nationalism and that England faced great dangers there. 'You give the priests education and learning,' he complained to his family, 'powers of sophistry and argument, and you cultivate their talents and intellects which you know afterwards will be employed in biting the hand that nursed them, in promoting revolution and destroying the English.' In 1848, as the Year of Revolutions progressed on the Continent, Cecil became if anything more reactionary still. 'Their Celtic blood indisposes the inhabitants to all bodily industry,' he wrote to his father of the Irish poor as the famine abated in 1849, 'and their religion deadens the mental energy which is otherwise a peculiarity of the race.' His preferred solution was mass emigration, one which by then, of course, hundreds of thousands of Irishmen had already discovered for themselves. By December 1850 he was writing of 'my hero Strafford', despising Charles I for betraying 'Black Tom Tyrant'. Cecil's complaints contain the kernel, once toned down and put into language palatable enough for a mass electorate, of the arguments with which he was to wreck Irish Home Rule forty years later.

Cecil was not a natural orator at the Oxford Union Society, tending to look down and sideways as he spoke. The height he had desperately needed at Eton had come too late, and by the time he left Oxford he was

6'4". The Union was an acknowledged nursery for would-be parliamentarians. When the Society celebrated its fiftieth anniversary in 1873, it could boast no fewer than seven former Presidents in Gladstone's Cabinet. The society's debates there were small, a typical division might be 29 to 25, with Cecil invariably taking the most reactionary line in them. In June 1849 he spoke against the removal of Jewish political disabilities, and in November in favour of 'sufficient restraint on the liberty of the Press'. As well as speaking against Henry VIII's dissolution of the monasteries, Free Trade and 'the endowment of the Romanish priesthood', he stood for elective office, becoming Secretary in November 1848 and Treasurer in the Easter Term of 1849. One of his few schoolfriends, the Earl of Dufferin, had been President the year before Cecil matriculated. The President when Cecil was Secretary was Frederick Lygon, later 6th Earl Beauchamp, who later served in his second ministry.

Cecil's time as a Union Society office-holder brought him down to the petty level of politics, at a time when he was receiving high praise in his termly reports for his work on Sophocles and Theology, Trigonometry and the Epistles. The minutes he kept as Secretary cover such mundane matters as the auditing of accounts, use of the reading room by honorary members, blackballing, sub-committees, five shilling fines for missing committee meetings and whether the President should have an ordinary as well as the casting vote. The very triviality of university politics is part of what can make it absorbing, and Cecil learnt valuable lessons about human political behaviour in the committee's debates on whether the library should economise on subscriptions to The Times, the Spectator or the Daily News. (The Calcutta Review and the Railway Gazette survived the purge.)

Before he could stand for more senior Union offices, however, Cecil left Oxford. His ill-health, which he blamed on Eton, allowed him to stay up only for six terms and in 1850 he graduated with an honorary fourth in Mathematics, a special pass degree then available to the scions of noble families. Rather than face the strenuous mental competition of Oxford's class lists, in which Acland and Carnarvon both took firsts, Cecil was advised by his doctor to build up his strength through travel. After half-heartedly joining Lincoln's Inn in April 1850 and discovering the Bar not at all to his taste, the twenty-one-year-old left for Cape Town aboard the Maidstone on 9th July 1851.

The classic Grand Tour usually covered Florence, Venice, Paris and Rome. Possessing little æsthetic sense but some adventurousness, Cecil planned a journey around the major British colonies in the southern hemisphere, with South America also included if money and time permitted. The twenty-three months he spent touring Cape Colony, Australia, Tasmania and New Zealand, and on the long journeys in

between – his return voyage involved 110 days at sea – tended to
confirm him in the low view of human nature and society that he had
already formed. South Africa in the Kaffir Wars, Gold Rush Australia
and New Zealand during the Maori Wars could hardly have been
expected to have done anything else.

If Oxford had taught Cecil what he liked – High Anglicanism, High
Toryism and the political and social status quo – his time in the
colonies demonstrated to him just as effectively what he despised –
atheism, 'ephemeral plutocrats' and democracy. From an entirely shel-
tered social background, this sickly, fastidious and still shy young man
was plunged into a heaving world of ex-convicts, prospectors, bootleg-
gers, soldiers and settlers. On the journey out to South Africa, when he
was not being seasick (a lifelong complaint), Cecil for the first time
encountered serious drinking and swearing, sailors flirting with female
'steerage' passengers, 'vulgarians and bores', as well as a missionary's
wife who 'was more revoltingly, loathsomely vulgar than you can fancy
even in a dream'. Despite 'all my practised bearishness' during the
sixty-one days at sea, he had to sit opposite her on the way out, and he
found himself 'quite unequal to putting down the impudence of this
woman'.[6]

Once he landed in Cape Town in September 1851, Cecil covered a
great deal of ground. Before leaving South Africa on 13th December he
had visited Robben Island, Protea, Constantia, Rondebosch, Somerset
West, Caledon, Zuurbrak, Montagu's Pass, Hartenbosch, Wynberg and
Riversdale. His comments on people, vouchsafed to a diary as well as in
letters home, were invariably rude. One vicar was 'an abominable prof-
ligate', a Mr Bray was 'very vulgar in manner and mind', a Mr Baker was
'weak, illogical and shallow', a Dutchman was described as 'indolent'
and another woman he put down as 'a garrulous old twaddler, given to
"deary me" and "ecstatics"'. It was some time before Cecil recognised
that rather different types of Victorians chose to make their living in the
colonies than in Hertfordshire. Travelling on mail carts in all weathers,
listening to his Hottentot drivers, Cecil heard how the Boers were 'so
stupid you could not talk to them'. By September he was telling his
father that free institutions and responsible government should not be
extended to Cape Colony because the Boers outnumbered the British
three to one, and 'it will simply be delivering us over bound hand and
foot into the power of the Dutch, who hate us as much as a conquered
people can hate their conquerors'.

Cecil took cynical pleasure from the story of the emigration of fifty
'distressed' needlewomen, a scheme which the Peelite minister Sidney
Herbert had helped to arrange and finance. 'Before they got to the Cape',
Cecil reported to his sister, 'the surgeon, captain, mate and a couple of
passengers had seduced – if such a term is applicable – nearly all of

them. When they came here they took to the streets and, as Herbert had consigned them to the Bishop's care...they were called the Bishop's women. So much for philanthropic efforts.' Missionaries were always another bugbear; the London Missionary Society he denounced as 'a dreadful set of Radicals', telling his father to 'beware, for they lie like troopers'.

In contrast to his dislike of the Boers, whom he regarded as in-bred, dishonest, brutal, illiterate, stubborn slave-drivers, Cecil considered the Kaffirs 'a fine set of men – whose language bears traces of a very high former civilisation', which he thought not unlike Italian in its melody. He thought the Kaffirs 'an intellectual race, with great firmness and fixedness of will', but 'horribly immoral' as they lacked all idea of theism. By October 1851, his diary was sardonically recording tales of settlers' adultery and incest, as well as the social torture of 'tiffin with Lady Smith', the wife of Cape Colony's Governor, the Peninsular War hero Sir Harry Smith, of whose campaigns against the Kaffirs Cecil held a particularly low opinion. The jagged corners of Cecil's diffident personality were slowly being rubbed down by contact with one of the roughest parts of the British Empire, to be replaced with an ironic detachment and a sceptical banter which were to stay with him for the rest of his life. In his letters and diary he also honed a written style which was to stand him in good stead before the end of the decade. Staying with the Bishop of Cape Town in December, he noted how: 'The ladies sat in a row and the gentlemen huddled into a corner, and people dropped solemn jokes at long intervals, like minute guns.'

Social intercourse with women was especially irritating for someone who preferred to discuss the minutiæ of High Church liturgy with the local clergy. Cecil was never happier than when talking about the prospects for Puseyism and the Tractarian movement, even out in the South African bush. Although what passed there for society – in towns where often the only three stone buildings were the church, the prison and the public house – was keen to lionise a marquess's son, he was always far more interested in whether an archdeacon's font or reredos was ecclesiastically correct, or whether curtaining off the vestry at the western end of some outback church was objectionable on religious grounds. He was merely irritated when taken out to see 'views', let alone wildlife. 'I found the general love of scenery to be the greatest nuisance in the world,' he wrote in his diary on 15th October. 'The more I protest my apathy the more they urge me to visit some hackneyed lion ... [or] go into ecstasies at some landscape which I wish all the time at the bottom of the sea.' In the end, he thought, he ought to get a certificate sent out from Hatfield 'to testify to the real nature of my tastes'.

Leaving Cape Town on board the *Amazon* on 13th December, Cecil arrived at Adelaide in South Australia on 30th January 1852, stepping ashore in a white top hat, a garment which was to excite some ribald comment when he wore it at the goldfields. There was a 'frightfully vulgar' woman on the long and rough passage with her 'thoroughbred squaller' children, and he joked that his time in South Africa had taught him 'to endure vulgar society with less repugnance. When I get home – as Charles II could eat only bad oysters – I shall like no other.'

Gold-mania meant that with all the able-bodied men absconding to the goldfields it was hard to find service in Adelaide, so Cecil made his way to Melbourne in the company of an Irish baronet and MP, Sir Montagu Chapman. March 1852 saw them at Golden Gully in the Bendigo field, going down mines and viewing the valley, which they found 'honey-combed with holes'. The nuggets he watched being prised out of the quartz-clay conglomerate varied in size from a pin's head to a flattened pea. Staying with the local police commissioner, Cecil was present at the smashing of an illegal 'sly grog shop', heard diggers' 'bush language' and tales of violence, but witnessed little actual lawlessness at the goldfields themselves. It was only when he visited Melbourne that he came across mass drunkenness, occasional gunfire, street prostitution and other scenes of burlesque far removed from the refined debates of the Oxford Union Society.

Cecil was struck by the way that whereas in Melbourne the streets were 'thronged with ephemeral plutocrats, generally illiterate, who were hurrying to exchange their gold nuggets for velvet gowns for their wives and unlimited whisky for themselves', a process which sometimes led to crimes of 'audacious violence', in the actual Bendigo goldfield itself 'there is not half as much crime or insubordination as there would be in an English town of the same wealth and population'. Four men armed with two carbines policed 10,000 diggers at Bendigo, and at Mount Alexander 200 policemen protected 30,000 people, almost all of them armed, where over 30,000 ounces of gold were mined per week. 'During my stay there,' he reported home, 'I found generally far more civility than I should be likely to find in the good town of Hatfield.' He drew the Tory moral that order derived from the fact that 'the government was that of the Queen, not of the mob; from above, not from below. Holding from a supposed right (whether real or not, no matter) and not from "the People the source of all legitimate power".' The product was a fine degree of civic obedience, where otherwise there would have been anarchy.

After a further trip to Melbourne, where, as he told the Marquess of Lothian, 'all the foulest words we used to hear at Eton are here household words at which nobody is surprised', Cecil sailed to Tasmania. On landing, he witnessed an anti-Tractarian protest meeting in Hobart, one of his first experiences of democracy in action. 'Of course they are grossly abusive and very ignorant,' he commented of the protesters and he left predictably scornful of 'the mob's supremacy'. The bishop who had inflamed this opposition by supporting a priest's decision to allow his communicants to confess, further impressed Cecil because he 'forgets all the little etiquettes which the sensitive dignity of the *nouveaux riches* requires'. Hobart was therefore, he reported home, the only place he had so far left with reluctance.

On the issue of the transportation of convicts, Cecil fully admitted that 'no island can be the better for the yearly admixture of two thousand select villains to its population', but he thought the system about as reformatory 'as a non-religious system can be, for I have no faith in paper schemes of conversion, or reformation by Act of Parliament'. A completely theological state might work, he thought, 'but of course the nineteenth century is much too enlightened for this'. To an Oxford acquaintance, the Rev. Charles Conybeare, he asked rhetorically: 'Can anything exceed the absurdity of punishing a man by giving him a *gratis* passage to a goldfield?', neglecting to point out that prison walls separated one from the other.

The then crime of sodomy horrified Cecil, especially when he discovered that in one Tasmanian prison no fewer than seventy inmates were being treated for diseases in relation to it. Despite the fact that it 'supersedes all the less revolting forms of lust, and deadens and brutalizes (so the clergy say) the whole nature, to an extent unknown in any more ordinary sin', it was impossible to 'rouse the epicurean indifference of the Colonial Office' to what was going on. Disgusted that the rape of young men, the 'filthiest depravity' and the 'depths of degradation' could exist in a Christian country, Cecil placed the blame squarely if illogically on Lord Stanley, the Under-Secretary for Foreign Affairs and the son of the Tory Prime Minister Lord Derby. Cecil believed Stanley's 'high character happened to be negligent or too facile' to deal with the abuses.

Sydney found Cecil plagued by mosquitoes which lurked at the bottom of his lavatory. Newcomers to the city, he told his father, were instantly recognisable from 'a remarkable tendency to scratch the least honourable part of their persons, and an extreme unwillingness to sit down'. He was thus happy to be able to sail for New Zealand, arriving in Auckland in mid-July 1852. As in South Africa, he instinctively sympathised with the local black population, who were then fighting against rapacious European settlers. 'The natives seem when they have converted', he wrote back to Hatfield from Wellington on 1st September, 'to make much better Christians than the white man.' A Maori chief called Katana generously offered Cecil five acres of land to settle near Auckland, but with his health by then restored, Cecil abandoned plans to visit South America and returned to England, arriving at Plymouth on 29th May 1853.

Writing to his father from Wellington the previous September, Cecil had broached the subject of his future career. He admitted to the 'great horror' he felt at returning to London's social conventions and Season, 'to be stewed and bored at dinners and parties'. (He only reluctantly shaved off the beard he had grown.) The House of Commons was a sphere in which 'a man can be most useful: but my chances of getting in are, practically, none'. Holy Orders was another possibility, but Cecil rejected them because of his 'inaptitude for gaining personal influence', i.e. persuading other people. His father's original idea of the Bar was anathema. 'The barrister is at best a tolerated evil,' he explained. 'He derives his living from the fact that the law is unintelligible.' Cecil concluded that even eking out a living writing for newspapers was preferable to the horrors of practising the law.

His first choice turned out to be not so impracticable as he thought. The borough of Stamford had survived the Great Reform Act of 1832 and remained in the pocket of the Marquess of Exeter, the descendant of Lord Burghley's eldest son. One of his two nominee MPs, J.C. Herries, wanted to retire, and so, within ten weeks of stepping off the boat, Lord Robert Gascoyne-Cecil was elected unopposed for Stamford. He only visited the town after the mayor had moved the writ on Thursday, 16th August, and the returning officer had announced that the election would take place the following Monday.

Cecil's election address was a masterpiece of patriotic generalisation. He opposed class-based income taxes and the secularisation of education. He believed in religious tolerance, but would oppose any 'ultramontane' interference with the Established Church which was 'at variance with the fundamental principles of our constitution'. He had no objection to 'cautious change' *per se*, but would resist 'any such tampering with our representation system as shall disturb the reciprocal powers on which the stability of our constitution rests'.[7] The religious parts of his election address were virtually dictated to him by his ultra-Protestant patron Exeter, and he also had to state that he would not support the reintroduction of Protectionism, which by then was not a likelihood. These fine-sounding but rather platitudinous sentiments were unlikely to present Cecil with any future hostages to fortune.

The only real interest in the poll shown by Cecil's constituents, reported the *Lincoln, Rutland and Stamford Mercury* after he was elected, was the customary scramble at the close of poll for the timber from which the hustings were made. The whole proceeding, from opening speeches to the declaration, took less than an hour. Nor was Cecil opposed in any subsequent election in the fifteen years he sat in the House of Commons. This was just as well, because he held a low opinion of his electors. When in 1867 his brother Eustace, then Tory MP for South Essex, complained that he had been addressed by some of his constituents in a Brittany hotel, Cecil commiserated: 'A hotel infested by influential constituents is worse than one infected by bugs. It's a pity you can't carry around a powder insecticide to get rid of vermin of that kind.'

Salisbury agreed to pay all Cecil's (very low) election expenses and settle on him £300 per annum, the interest on £10,000 which was earmarked for him from his mother's estate, adding £100 per annum from his own pocket. Aged twenty-three, Cecil was in Parliament, sitting in the interest of what the month before his birth had been christened the Conservative Party. Here was his opportunity to fulfil Horace Walpole's prediction, prematurely made on the succession of the 7th Earl in 1780: 'As the ashes of the Cecils are re-kindling, perhaps a phoenix may arise.'

TWO

Rebellions

*All Souls – Faith – Parliament
– Marriage*

1853 to 1857

'If he will work, and he has a working look, I will soon make a man
of him.'

Soon after his election to Parliament, Cecil sat the examination for a
Prize Fellowship to All Souls College, Oxford. There were sixteen
candidates for two vacancies, six of whom Lygon told Cecil were
'formidable'. 'My own chance of All Souls – never high – has sunk to
zero,' a despondent Cecil told his family on being appraised of the odds
in November 1863. He added that 'the fact that "no Lord" has ever been
elected' would further count against him. This suspicion of an anti-
aristocratic tone to the College could not have been more wrong. In fact,
of the 274 fellows elected in the century after 1753, forty-eight were the
sons of noblemen. Furthermore, Cecil counted as Founder's Kin, being
related to the brother of Archbishop Chichele, who founded the College
in Henry V's memory in 1438, through Catherine Howard, the wife of
the 2nd Earl of Salisbury. Of the 113 fellows elected between 1815 and
1857, no fewer than seventy-eight were Founder's Kin, meaning that the
College was not only an intellectual power-house but also a giant
system of indoor relief for Chichele's brother's extended gene pool.

After Thomas Chichele wrote to *The Times* in November 1853
announcing that Lord Robert Gascoyne-Cecil MP and a Mr A.G.
Watson of Balliol had been elected, the Radical *Mercury* newspaper
commented that the former hardly represented the class of 'poor
students' for whom fellowships were designed. Yet there is no indication that Cecil's background, rather than his fine intellect and
examination results in Classical languages and an English essay,
explained his success.

When Cecil had written to his father about Parliament being the sphere in which 'a man can be most useful', he was not referring to something primarily secular, or even political. He went to his grave with a profound disbelief in the capacity of legislation to affect the state of the human soul, which was in itself the only thing that truly mattered in life. He meant instead that in Parliament he could take his place in the Anglican Church's rearguard action against the forces of atheism, agnosticism and disestablishmentarianism, which he believed were welling up in Victorian Britain and threatened to smash civil society.

Cecil's Christian faith was total and unquestioning. According to his grandson, Lord David Cecil, he 'underwent a momentous spiritual experience' as a teenager, which 'involved an intimate sense of what he believed to be the living and personal presence of Christ'. The only hint of this strange but possibly seminal event from his daughter Gwendolen's writings appears in a single sentence in the first volume of her 1921 biography of her father: 'The unique appeal which Our Lord's revealed personality makes to the heart may well have been emphasised to the lonely child whose craving for affection was so meagrely fed in his human surroundings.' Exactly where or when this 'momentous spiritual experience' took place we cannot now know. Nonetheless, it seems profoundly to have affected the nature of his faith.

'The light is too dazzling for our weakened eyes,' he wrote to his sister Blanche from Cape Town about the doctrines of Original Sin and the Fall of Man; 'we must turn from it, lest it blind us. At the proper time we may logically test these doctrines, and if true accept them. But as a habit we must not think of them.' Yet for Cecil there never was a proper time. He preferred to take the view that the ways of God were too unfathomable to be explicable to man, that no human experience could possibly come close enough to His to make any attempt to employ reason or logic worth while. 'God is all-powerful, and God is all-loving and the world is what it is!' he would say to his children when they attempted to apply logic to their faith: 'How are you going to explain *that*?'

Cecil's Christianity was both so monolithic and so personal to him, possibly because of his teenage spiritual experience, that he never felt the need to discuss his faith with anyone else. When one of his children told him he found it useful to talk about important subjects with other people, he 'expressed surprise and almost incredulity'. The solitary childhood spent in the library at Hatfield had left him spiritually and intellectually self-sufficient, and he almost took solace from the very inexplicability of his faith. 'We live in a small bright oasis of knowledge surrounded on all sides by a vast unexplored region of impenetrable mystery,' he stated in a lecture in Oxford on Evolution in 1894, and for him the author of that mystery was God.

The very idea that mankind could even so much as guess anything useful about the ways of God struck Cecil as profoundly pretentious. During the American Civil War, he ridiculed the Liberal politician W.E. Forster's contention that if the Confederacy won it would shake his faith in Providence. Cecil thought that this showed:

> a want of mental perspective – an outrageous exaggeration of the dimension of the things which happen to be close to us. We cannot shake ourselves free from the arrogant idea that our own planet, our own race, our own generation, our own corner of the earth is the culmination of the Creator's work, and that in the events which pass through our field of view the final issues of Creation are being fought out. If we could better preserve our sense of proportion we might recognise the humiliating fact that the events of our day, visible from our point of view, are but an infinitesimal atom in the great whole. No one to whose mind this truth was present would dream that, from the mere fragment of the vast drama that falls under his view, he can grasp its real meaning, or conjecture the intentions which it is accomplishing.[1]

For all that it was 'humiliating', this knowledge had its comforts for Cecil. He feared a future avalanche of infidelity, an onslaught of agnosticism and atheism which would deluge Christianity. He regularly predicted 'widespread unbelief' and in 1867 a neighbour at lunch at Hatfield reported that 'he thinks we are rapidly approaching a state of religious chaos, what will come after it is hard to say'. Fortunately for Cecil's febrile state of mind there was an answer, a salvation for England from the horrors which such an atheistic world threatened: the Oxford Movement.

In December 1900, in a characteristically oblique mood, his nephew Arthur Balfour remarked of his uncle that 'the key to [his] character is contradictoriness and that is why he is a Christian. In his youth – at Oxford – his contemporaries who thought at all were not all religious – and therefore he became religious.' This was unfair; Cecil was attracted to Tractarianism at Oxford for the best of scholarly and spiritual reasons. Reverence for the sacrament, frequent services, high standards of clerical life and dignified ceremonial were its hallmarks. Cecil worshipped every day in the chapel at Hatfield and twice on Sundays. When he was Prime Minister, he treated the appointment of bishops as seriously as that of government ministers, and he fought unyieldingly throughout his political life in defence of the rights and privileges, as well as the tithes, Church Rates and endowments, of the Church of England. Some colleagues believed that defending the Established

Church motivated him more than anything else in politics, including the direction of foreign policy. Although an impulse for perversity undoubtedly did play a part in Cecil's general psychological make-up, it played little or no part in his genuinely profound religious faith.

Religious life in Victorian Britain consisted of an unending struggle between sects, and Cecil threw himself into the fray with partisan gusto. Attacking a Papal Encyclical in 1865, he wrote that the Jesuits were once 'a homage to the powers of intellect, and a recognition of the vital importance of its aid to the cause of religion. But now Rome ... is content to base her power upon the credulity of women and of peasants.'[2] The Broad Church tradition of the Church of England he decried as 'a religion without dogma', while the Low represented 'haziness and undefinedness'. On Sir Morton Peto's 1862 Bill to allow nonconformist ministers to conduct burials on Established Church land, Cecil said that since Welsh land was cheap, 'let them procure a plot of land in each district where they can bury them in their own fashion without troubling their neighbours'.

Balfour recalled how, when it came to Presbyterianism, his uncle 'respected the history of the church...hated its services and the Covenanters'. Missionaries, Cecil warned the Archbishop of Canterbury in 1899, 'may have the ultimate result of giving a powerful and enduring stimulus to race-hatred on both sides'. Nor did Evangelicalism in general escape a pen-lashing. Cecil considered it had:

> never made much way with the higher class of intellects. But it has stood its ground because it has always been popular with children, with women, and with half-educated men. The plumpness and almost juridical precision of its statements make it eminently suitable for minds that are too blunt for subtle distinctions, and both too ignorant and too impatient to be satisfied with half-truths.

It was, however, in criticising ultra-Protestant intolerance that Cecil most regularly vented his highly productive spleen. When in 1861 a civil servant was ejected from the Record Office because he was a Roman Catholic, Cecil attacked 'the pure and perfect bigotry' of the Protestant Defence Association, which had been behind it. 'Who would have thought that Popery could lurk in pigeon-holes,' he mocked, 'or heresy be propagated by catalogues?' Squires who believed themselves to be defending Protestantism by throwing High Churchmen out of their livings he denounced as 'those agricultural divines who are so fond of turning their ploughshares into swords'. Such fanaticism, he believed, only 'succeeded in placing intellect in hostility to faith', and as a result talented and intelligent men such as Shaftesbury, Bolingbroke, Hume, Gibbon and Adam Smith 'have been driven by this disgust for religious vandalism to fight in the ranks of infidelity'.[3] As

Prime Minister he appointed Henry Matthews to the Cabinet, the first Roman Catholic to serve there since the reign of James II. He also appointed the first Catholic Ambassador since the Glorious Revolution and the first Jewish Lord-Lieutenant. If a tolerant High Anglican fundamentalism is not doubly oxymoronic, it defines Cecil's lifelong faith.

Fortunately such a religious stance fitted perfectly with the philosophy of Toryism which Cecil was simultaneously developing. Over almost all the great questions where there was friction between Church and State – such as tithes, the abolition of compulsory Church Rates, disestablishment, the excision of the Athanasian Creed, allowing marriage with a deceased wife's sister and especially over denominational education – Cecil was always found ranged solidly behind the main traditions of the Church of England. If the late-Victorian Church of England was 'the Tory Party at prayer', this was partly because Cecil resolutely defended the Church's interests when he was its Leader. For him, the two institutions were intricately intertwined. When the nonconformist Liberation Society almost converted the Liberal Party to disestablishment in the mid-1880s, he hoped every Anglican parson would double as a Tory election agent.

In Parliament, Cecil soon won a name as a peppery, caustic speaker with a habitually vituperative tongue. *Punch* called him 'a vinegar merchant', but, for all the friends his rhetorical rudeness lost him, it won him the attention of the House. Never fundamentally believing in the efficacy of debate, Cecil used speeches primarily to sledge-hammer his enemies and embolden his supporters, but only very rarely ever to try to change people's minds.

Cecil's maiden speech, in opposition to the second reading of the Oxford University Endowment Bill on 7th April 1854, was on a subject tailor-made for his talents and views. The Derby Government had fallen in December 1852, to be replaced by Lord Aberdeen's Whig–Peelite coalition. The Cabinet minister and former Prime Minister, Lord John Russell, wished to amend the University's statutes in order to allow money to be diverted to modern uses from the often arcane endowments their donors had, sometimes centuries earlier, originally stipulated. A Royal Commission had reported in favour of altering the statutes, but Cecil attacked this on several grounds. Ignoring founders' wishes, he argued, would discourage future bequests. Cecil was sceptical of the utility of the reforms themselves and, on a more basic level, it was the founders' money, not the University's (and still less the State's), so their original wishes should be respected.

There was also the argument of the thin end of the wedge, one that he used constantly throughout his political career. What would prevent a future House of Commons one day confiscating private property on much the same principle? He even argued that 'if the will of the founder was to be overturned, let the property return to the heir in the natural course of law'. Although he himself considered the speech 'a failure', it pleased his father and impressed the Chancellor of the Exchequer, William Gladstone, who called this first effort 'rich with future promise', but who warned against indulging in too much hyperbole.

Someone else who was impressed was Benjamin Disraeli, the Conservative former Chancellor of the Exchequer and leader of the Party in the Commons, who wrote to Lord Salisbury 'a hasty line to tell you that your son made a most satisfying debut last night in the Commons.... His voice is good, and he showed debating power, taking up the points of preceding speakers, and what he had prepared was brought in naturally.... If he will work, and he has a working look, I will soon make a man of him.' Nor was this simply typical charm towards a colleague, because to John Mowbray, a veteran MP who later became Father of the House, Disraeli said that despite the fulsome congratulations accorded to the Hon. G.C.H. Byng ('letters from all the duchesses and countesses in London') for his maiden speech in the same debate, it was in fact Lord Robert Cecil 'who made his mark as a natural debater, and will become a considerable man'. Within a month, Disraeli was suggesting that Cecil should speak in a forthcoming debate on the malt tax. 'I know nothing whatever of the subject,' Cecil wrote to Hatfield, asking for his father's views on it, 'so I shall probably make a great hash.' In the event, he was saved from having to perform when the debate was unexpectedly brought forward.

Cecil's negative reaction to his own maiden speech performance, which by any objective standard had been a success, was actuated partly by modesty, but also by a deep sense of pessimism, brought on by what was almost certainly clinical depression. When the 1st Earl of Salisbury's wife died, his mother warned him during his prolonged mourning against becoming 'a surly, sharp sour plum, no better than in truth a melancholy mole and a *miseranthropos* hateful to God and man'. The 2nd Marquess was also liable to intense despondency and laboured under an unalterable conviction that the country was going to the dogs. He detected a growing contempt for law and order, and when his wife read out items of news from the newspapers at breakfast he used to say: 'All very bad – depend upon it, the end of the world is coming.' He was only really happy when smashing up the theodolites of the surveyors sent by the railway companies.

Cecil found his own depression 'lays me up and makes me incapable – sometimes for days – without any sort of warning'. His daughter recorded how what he called his 'nerve storms' alternated between mental agitation and physical exhaustion, and 'they could be accompanied by an overwhelming depression of spirits and also by great bodily lassitude and by a morbid acuteness of the senses of touching and hearing. The slightest physical contact became painful to him when in this state.'[4] Writing about depressives, Cecil gave some idea of his pain:

> Their physical condition sharpens every little sting they undergo, by giving a preternatural sensitiveness to their power of suffering.... Men who are really ill are allowed for, but 'delicate' men are not, nor are 'depressed' men. There is no bigotry in existence so complacent, so absolutely self-satisfied, as the bigotry of robustness.

In defence of an MP who voted in a division despite being under medication and recently released from a lunatic asylum, Cecil wrote: 'He is no more mad than Oliver Cromwell was, or than any man is who is subject to fits of extreme depression.' When changes in the lunacy laws were proposed in 1872, he wrote to Gladstone in warm support of the sufferers' rights. As soon as he became Prime Minister with a working majority, Cecil supported two Bills to codify the lunacy laws and prevent men who were not dangerously insane from being incarcerated in asylums. There was more than simple humanitarianism in this concern for the rights of the mentally unstable; there is also a certain sense of 'there, but for the Grace of God ...'.

Just as Eton had been the worst place for a sensitive eleven-year-old, so the House of Commons, with its cheering and jeering and late nights, was disastrous for Cecil's still delicate physical and mental condition. Writing to his typically unsympathetic father in April 1855, turning down the offer of a commission in the Hertfordshire Militia, he pointed out how 'the House of Commons work especially exposes me to these nerve attacks and I know by sad experience that unless I obey when it does attack me, the incapacity of a day may be turned into a week'. Ill-health was reducing his parliamentary career to 'a sham', and the thought of taking on fresh commitments – let alone something as hearty as soldiering – 'gave me a stomach ache all morning'. There was a criticism implied in his parting line: 'I have a naturally weak constitution; and I have been brought up as though it was a strong one.'

Though hardly medical, the connection between depression and extreme pessimism is well established and was tremendously powerful in Cecil. At Oxford in February 1850, in a Union debate on Protection, he gloomily observed: 'We are not the same people that we have been in our social characteristics, in our patriotic sentiments, or in the tone of our moral and religious feelings.' This, just as Britain had put its louche

Regency past behind it and was beginning to embrace mid-Victorian values. Cecil's Hobbesian view of human nature was if anything reinforced by events in the Maori and American Civil Wars, which, he wrote, 'furnish instructive evidence of the small extent to which civilisation has power to tame the natural savagery of mankind'. His daughter remembered the 'peculiar horror' with which he contemplated the very concept of optimism, a state which he regarded as 'essentially cowardly'.

Another reason for refusing his father's offer of a commission in the Militia was that Cecil opposed the war that had been going on since the Allies landed in the Crimea in August 1854. 'Has the regiment volunteered for foreign service? If so, all hesitation is at an end. I have no vocation for fighting.' In February 1853, Tsar Nicholas I had told Sir Hamilton Seymour, the British Ambassador in St Petersburg, that he would understand if British interests required the annexation of Cyprus and Egypt, and offered in effect a pre-planned dismemberment of the Ottoman Empire. 'We have a sick man on our hands, a very sick man,' said the Tsar. 'It would be a pity if he slipped away before we had made arrangements for his funeral.' Lord John Russell, the incoming Foreign Secretary, instead reappointed the Turcophile Lord Stratford de Redcliffe to the Embassy at Constantinople, thereby wrecking the chances of any partition deal. For the rest of his life, Cecil believed this to have been a tragically missed opportunity.

Cecil detested the Crimean War from its start, and denounced it in Parliament in June 1855. On the fifth night of a debate on its prosecution, he depicted the peace terms as ridiculously harsh on Russia, and asked whether the Allies genuinely intended to hold Sebastopol once it had fallen, equating it to 'placing a lot of Dutchmen in the Isle of Wight, and telling them to hold it in the teeth of England'. In July, he went so far as to second an amendment of the Tory MP General Jonathan Peel, the former Prime Minister's brother, which allowed the Liberal Government to survive a Tory motion of censure. At a meeting on 16th March 1857 at the George Hotel in Stamford, he 'contended that the seventy-six millions of money and the enormous sacrifice of life in the Black Sea, had been thrown away', and he defended his votes and speeches against the war 'on the broad ground of humanity and justice'.[5] By then the animosities had faded, however, and Cecil found himself facing a far more dangerous adversary than mere constituents, in the person of his own father.

~

In 1847, the fifty-six-year-old 2nd Marquess of Salisbury had married for a second time. Lady Mary Sackville-West, daughter of the 5th Earl De La

Warr, was twenty-three, and the couple proceeded to have five children, bringing Salisbury's total to ten. The new Lady Salisbury 'was certainly not gifted with tact', according to a bitter account of the burgeoning feud written half a century later by Cecil's younger brother Eustace. It took all their tact to remain on speaking terms when it was discovered that Salisbury was using Gascoyne money left to them in their mother's will to make large settlements on his new wife and their children. Cecil's elder brother Lord Cranborne understandably found it 'a constant source of irritation', and over the years Lady Salisbury's overt preference at Hatfield for her own children created what Eustace was later to describe as a 'climax of squabbling, distrust and suspicion in the family'.

By 1856 the situation had calmed, although Cranborne was effectively estranged from his stepmother. Into this uneasy stalemate stepped Georgina Alderson, a friend of the Sackville-Wests. She was the intelligent, gregarious and strong-willed daughter of Sir Edward Alderson, Baron of the Court of Exchequer, a senior Tractarian layman and committed High Tory. Georgina too was a keen Tractarian and, to Lord Salisbury's irritation (as he was not one), Miss Alderson was befriended by the fellow-Tractarians Lady Salisbury and Mildred Beresford-Hope, gaining regular invitations to Hatfield in 1855 and 1856. It is easy to see what the intelligent, earnest Robert Cecil saw in her; nearly three years older than him, she wrote verses and short stories and was interested in church architecture and ecclesiology. She was something of a blue-stocking, but was also capable of lifting Cecil out of his 'black dog' depressions. He fell in love with Georgina, something Eustace suspected she had carefully engineered.

Sir Edward Alderson was a distinguished and respected lawyer, but he was also irredeemably middle class, and his daughter could bring no fortune to the marriage. When the twenty-six-year-old Robert Cecil announced his engagement to Georgina in November 1856, Lord Salisbury ignited in anger, as did his wife, who claimed her friendship had been betrayed. 'My intelligence is brief, though possibly startling,' Cecil wrote to Eustace asking for his support. 'I wish to marry Miss Alderson and My Lord kicks vehemently. At present we – My Lord and I – are in no amicable temper with each other – the matter may end in a grand family row.' Cecil had no idea whether he would receive his share of any of his mother's fortune. Eustace, whose own livelihood also depended on their father's largesse, replied that he hoped that there would be 'no grand family row', but avoided giving any intimation of support.

Salisbury's insistence that his son should marry someone rich, so as not to prove a drain on the Hatfield estate, drew Cecil's ire. After his father had written of the social and financial privations he must inevitably face as a younger son if he married into the middle classes, Cecil replied on 27th November 1856 with a letter which deserves extensive quotation:

'Privation' means the loss of something I enjoy now. If the privation in question is the want of food, warmth, clothing, I am not prepared to face it. But I cannot enjoy anything else I now enjoy, for the simple reason that I do not enjoy anything. Amusements I have none.... The persons who will cut me because I marry Miss Alderson are precisely the persons of whose society I am so anxious to be quit. My marriage therefore cannot entail upon me any privations. I have considered the matter for very many months, anxiously and constantly.

I have come to the conclusion that I shall probably do Parliament well if I do marry, and that I shall certainly make nothing of it if I do not. In the latter case, therefore, it will be useless to worry myself with so arduous a life. I have further come to the conclusion that Miss Alderson suits me perfectly. Heiress-hunting – which you suggested for three years on the chance that I might find one suiting equally well – is a profession to which my pride will scarcely bow. I have therefore decided to marry Miss Alderson if I can. It is, I believe, the universal custom, when a mother is wealthy, to secure something to the younger children: but in the present case the practice was, I think I have heard you say, departed from in deference to your remonstrances. My resolution is necessarily contingent on your furnishing me with the requisite means. I have agreed to a six months' separation for the purpose of testing my resolution: but the demand I believe is not a usual one. But as I never remember to have receded from a resolution once deliberately undertaken, I do not anticipate much from my present trial: and I think it strange that you should have taken a different view of my character. However, I have promised – though it seems to me a needless source of irritation – not to set eyes on Miss Alderson till May, except on one occasion specially reserved for Holy Communion.

I am exceedingly sorry that my adherence to this marriage should cause you annoyance: but my conviction that I am right is too strong for me to give it up: and it is my happiness, not yours, that is at stake. I cannot resist the feeling that through my life, you have erred in dealing with me as though our tastes and temperaments were similar when in truth they are diametrically opposite. I am quite sensible that if you were in my place this marriage would be a very unwise one.

This could be read as an accusation that Salisbury had married his mother solely for her money – something that was widely though wrongly assumed at the time – and it drew a furious response from his father. Cecil had to write back quickly to apologise, but added: 'It was a fault in style...if I said what I meant – I might possibly appear disrespectful. You say I am strangely ignorant of my position. I was fully aware of it as you describe it, namely that I am utterly at your mercy.'

The Marquess was not disposed to clemency and let Cecil know that he would prevent the marriage by blocking access to his mother's fortune. In this Trollopian situation, made more dramatic by his married sister Lady Mildred Beresford-Hope's supporting him against the opposition of Cranborne and Eustace, Cecil was not bluffing. 'You speak of my attachment as one that under no possible circumstances "could end in marriage",' Cecil wrote to his father on 23rd December. 'This might seem to imply that, in case you should finally resolve to give me no aid, the marriage could thereby become an impossibility. I do not think this is quite the case. Of course it would enormously increase the difficulty: but I think I can see contingencies, by no means visionary, under which that difficulty might be overcome.' He went on to mention entering the Church, saying that he had a number of friends who were patrons of livings, and added: 'the world in disputes of this kind, is apt, rightly or wrongly, to side with the younger disputants'. Then there might be a change of government, in which he could be offered 'some small permanent office'. Finally, as he rather unsubtly put it, there was always the chance 'that Cranborne should die'.

By May, Salisbury had gone so far as to instruct his solicitors to see whether it was possible to get Cranborne to cut off the entail of the family estates away from Robert and towards Eustace in the event of Cranborne's death without issue. 'You have hinted to me yourself,' Cecil wrote to his father, 'and conveyed to me still more directly through others, that in case of my marriage with Miss Alderson, and in case of Cranborne's dying without children, you would leave the family estates over my head.' Even this prospect of a lifetime of relative poverty failed to deter him. He told his father on 7th May that even in the event of his refusing to hand over the capital his mother had left, the marriage 'will take place in any case', although it would 'materially increase my comfort' if he could invest the £10,000 himself, as he felt sure of being able to obtain better than the present 3 per cent return.

Eustace hoped to usurp his elder brother's fortune and later wrote that 'my brother's mind was poisoned against me, and the estrangement between him and me (though never openly avowed) increased and was never allowed to die out by his wife'. If there was really an estrangement, which is doubtful, it was primarily Eustace's own fault. From his papers it is clear that he intended that Cranborne's letter refusing the wedding invitation should be even ruder than the one finally sent. Cranborne had written that 'I most fully concur with my Lord in disapproving the step you are about to take.' However, had he sent Eustace's original draft letter, it would have added that the marriage was 'an imprudent match, one as ruinous to your prospects as it is little in accordance with your rank and position'.[6] Eustace's own letter was equally unconciliatory: 'My Lord's expressed disapprobation, and the rupture of all communication between the two families, leave me no alternative but to decline most positively, your very kind and affectionate invitation.'

Although Cecil invited his father, stepmother and brothers to the wedding at 8 a.m. on Saturday, 11th July 1857, at St Mary Magdalene, Munster Square, none attended. Only Alexander and Mildred Beresford-Hope braved the family boycott to attend. As Baron Alderson had died on 27th January and the family were still in mourning, it was to be solely a family affair, so the absence of Cecil's relations was felt all the more. The rupture took seven years to heal, the young couple not visiting Hatfield again until July 1864. It was hardly surprising, therefore, if Georgina Cecil held a grudge against Eustace, although from the constant invitations he received to her receptions and dinners when her husband was in the Government, he could hardly complain of 'estrangement'.

After the ceremony, the couple honeymooned in Switzerland and on the Baltic island of Rügen. They returned to live with Georgina's widowed mother for a few months in Park Crescent, and then moved into a small house at No. 21, Fitzroy Square. So unfashionable was the area that one would-be acquaintance refused to visit them because she 'never left cards north of Oxford Street'. Later in life, Cecil admitted that he had hated the small rooms there, and the fact that he could not afford good doctors for his family. In the course of the next eight years, they were to move to No.11, Duchess Street and No. 1, Mansfield Street, and were never completely financially secure. On top of his original £400 per annum, Georgina managed to contribute £100 per annum. It was only by writing articles for newspapers and reviews that Cecil managed to pay for the upkeep of his growing family. Maud was born in 1858, Gwendolen in 1860, James in 1861, William in 1863, Robert in 1864, Fanny in 1866, Edward in 1867 and Hugh in 1869. By the time Robert was born in September 1864, Cecil was earning enough money from journalism to rent a small country house called The Oaks, in Headley on the Hampshire–Surrey border.

Cecil found in Georgina somebody who could lift him, albeit gradually, out of the debilitating state of neurotic depression into which he sometimes fell. 'She knew his secret mind,' wrote Lady Frances Balfour, a niece-in-law, 'and understood how outward things affected it...

between them there was an understanding not of words, but of the very being of human existence.' She soothed him, enthused him and provided the domestic tranquillity he needed to be able to concentrate on his writing and politics. When he doubted himself in his early years in Parliament, a friend, Lady Airlie, later reminisced, it was Georgina's loyalty and faith in him which gave him courage.

Georgina had a sense of humour as sharp as her husband's, except, one visitor recorded, 'when she does not wish to make acquaintance or desires to snub people, when she becomes hopelessly impenetrable'. Totally dedicated to the furtherance of her husband's interests, she was invaluable to him on occasions such as at the Queen's birthday dinner at the Foreign Office when she somehow managed to steer both the Prince of Bulgaria and the Austrian Ambassador into dinner with her, though each refused to recognise the other. The scale of her activities on her husband's behalf can be judged from a letter she wrote to her son Robert in May 1886: 'I am giving a party, buying a house, opening a bazaar, raising money for a church, furnishing a house, besides a few other trifles too numerous to mention such as receiving 200 colonists at Hatfield, arranging a monster Conservative demonstration and buying a wedding present.'

The man who at twenty-seven was about to embark on making a living from his pen, whilst simultaneously pursuing a parliamentary career, was as unlike the archetypal Conservative grandee politician as it was possible to be. He had already begun to stoop; he was short-sighted, still hyper-tense, highly intelligent (in what John Stuart Mill later famously dubbed 'the stupidest party'), almost devoid of small-talk, and utterly devoid of optimism and sentimentality. In society he acquired the nickname 'the Buffalo'. He never hunted, shot, fished or raced, and guarded his privacy as though it was his honour. 'To take a walk with him through any frequented place', wrote a daughter-in-law years later, 'was to realise with some accuracy what must be the feelings of a criminal escaping from justice.'

Utterly uninterested in clothes, he once told his nursemaid he wished he had been born a cat as he would not be expected to change his coat. If his dress-sense had been deliberate he might have been considered Bohemian, but he was a sartorial misfit through negligence rather than intent, and one commentator assumed he must have had a tailor and valet as little interested in clothes as himself. The fashion-conscious Lord Ribblesdale complained of his 'shiny broadcloth of the Early Victorian Period', and the courtier Sir Frederick Ponsonby said that he had 'such ill-fitting breeches that they looked like ordinary trousers'.[7] To his and his family's huge amusement, he was once refused admittance to a Monte Carlo casino for being 'unsuitably attired', by a doorman who failed to recognise the British Prime Minister.

When, during a great international crisis, the Prince of Wales upbraided him for wearing the trousers of an Elder Brother of Trinity House with a privy councillor's coat, he tried to excuse himself on the grounds that his valet was away. The Prince, a stickler over sartorial solecisms, said that he found it extraordinary that he had not noticed the mistake himself. 'It was a dark morning,' answered the Prime Minister with a hint of acidity that most people would have noticed, 'and I am afraid at the moment my mind must have been occupied by some subject of less importance.'

For all his massive intellect he entirely lacked æsthetic taste, and rather revelled in the fact. Welcoming his artistic future daughter-in-law Violet to his home for the first time, he proudly announced: 'Hatfield is Gaza, the capital of Philistia.' He enjoyed Brahms because it was 'noisy', but otherwise disliked musical evenings. When in August 1893 the celebrated Mrs Austin Lee came to sing at Hatfield, Lady Salisbury made 'the most visible signs to Lord Salisbury to induce him to ask Mrs Lee to sing again, but he only smiled'. The only advantage of going to concerts, he thought, was that 'you pay for it in money rather than in the dearer coin of reciprocal civilities'. The opera involved 'four hours' hard sitting, besides the loss of your dinner, and a very fair probability of bronchitis'. Other than occasional French plays and Shakespeare – he liked *The Winter's Tale*'s trial scene – he avoided the theatre as far as possible, though he liked the concepts of theatre and ballet as they tended 'to neutralise that money-worshipping grovelling materialistic spirit so rapidly increasing amongst us'.[8]

He liked Byron, Goethe and Pope, but blithely admitted to 'hating' Wordsworth, Keats, Milton and Shelley, although he eventually came round to the last. 'Lord Salisbury's want of understanding of things he does not like is very curious,' noted a daughter-in-law during a stay at Hatfield in 1901. 'He thinks that people who read poetry (except Pope), go to concerts, or look at pictures, are either hypocrites or idiots.' In literature, when he was not reading Greek, Latin or German for relaxation, he enjoyed middle-brow popular fiction. He also liked French fiction, establishing a large collection of French novels at Hatfield. His favourite author was Jane Austen, and he preferred Scott to Dickens, whom he regarded as a 'vulgarian' but nevertheless still read and to whose works he would allude in speeches and letters.

For the eight years after his 1857 marriage, however, it would be writing that would concern Cecil and his reading was concentrated on the thousands of books he reviewed, while he penned nearly two million words in order to pay for the luxury of defying his father and marrying the woman he loved. In so doing, he left as complete an exposition of his political philosophy as we have from any British Prime Minister. As a corpus of Tory thought, taken together and shorn of the extraneous articles on crinolines and chaperonage, it is a route map for the views he was to attempt to convert into a political programme over the next forty-five years. There, in black and white, lie his principles and his prejudices.

THREE

Journalism: Foreign Policy

Colonialism - The Schleswig-Holstein Question
– The American Civil War

1857 to 1866

'If we do not mean to fight we ought not to interfere.'

Samuel Johnson, a fellow Tory depressive, famously pronounced that no man but a blockhead wrote except for money, and when Cecil threw himself into journalism he accepted pretty much any and every offer, producing an astonishing output in both quantity and quality. He began in December 1856, when it seemed, a month after his engagement, that money would be tight, and only stopped after Cranborne's death in 1865, when he came into his brother's inheritance and prospects. Very occasionally thereafter, as a favour to a friend, a holiday diversion or in order to announce a major policy initiative, he would again put pen to paper, but the great mass of his output was undertaken directly in order to provide for himself and his family.

Cecil wrote for small-circulation reviews influential in the areas of life he knew – colleges, clubs, country houses and rectories. He wrote prolifically, for cash and on every conceivable topic. He rarely spoke about his new trade and resented others attempting to discuss it with him, both for reasons of privacy and because journalism was hardly a gentlemanly calling, although Disraeli had written in *The Times* and Peel and Palmerston in the *Courier*. His work was almost all published anonymously, despite his belief that a signed article attracted thrice the readership of an unsigned one. Cecil appreciated the way that anonymous writing 'disarms the native flunkeyism of the true-born Briton'.

Reviewing a book on the sources of the Nile in November 1860, Cecil accused the author of giving 'an occasional parenthetical snarl', yet a large proportion of his own work consisted of snarling denunciations of many aspects of life, especially modernity in all its forms. One Tory historian has called his journalism 'as powerful and reasoned a protest against modern thinking as Burke had made in the 1790s'. Judges, Protestant bigots, schoolmasters (unsurprisingly), Irish nationalists, Emperor Napoleon III, 'progress', democracy, sentimental lady novelists, the Radical politician John Bright, philanthropy, optimism and America were the favourite targets of his witty, scathing prose. It is in the nature of bileful weekly journalism that it is easier to distinguish what the columnist opposes than what he supports, but the Church of England, Elizabeth I, Lord Castlereagh, William Pitt the Younger and 'the ancient constitution' rarely came off badly.

Cecil's acerbic, restless dissatisfaction with the status quo is more commonly found in revolutionaries than reactionaries, but even before he was twenty-seven his mature intellect was working at full throttle, denouncing very many aspects of society and politics. 'This book is a model to students of composition', he wrote in a review in April 1863, 'who desire to know how the most biting sarcasm may be lavishly employed in controversy without the slightest transgression of good taste.'[1]

In a discursive article on 'the use of ridicule in public controversy', Cecil explained how its indiscriminate use in attacking concepts such as Relativism, Sociology or Logical Positivism was not a serious danger, in fact, 'it is only by the unsparing use of ridicule that such follies can be dispelled. Elaborate and solemn argument is wasted upon them.... There is no alternative – one must either believe in M. Comte or laugh at him. As a tireless propagandist for privilege, who used irony, paradox and epigram rather than any statistics, his writing inverts C.P. Scott's worthy dictum – for Cecil, comment was sacred, facts were free.

The anonymity attaching to his work – although *cognoscenti* could sometimes spot which pieces were by him – allowed Cecil occasionally to indulge in rampant nepotism, such as when he praised his brother-in-law Alexander Beresford-Hope's plans for protecting the hop trade, or when he reviewed Cranborne's book of travel articles and historical essays extremely favourably. To the biography of Sir Edward Alderson he also give a kind notice; Cecil felt under no obligation to state that the subject was his wife's father, or indeed that the author was his own brother-in-law.

Cecil was astonishingly eclectic in his book reviewing. Thousands of children's books, travel guides and novels, as well as books on history, linguistics, botany, social anthropology, ethics, Church history and geology were judged by him. He also wrote the *Saturday Review*'s German column, where he would review a dozen books of German history, philosophy and literature at a time, once a month for nine years. Cecil was *au fait* with the works of Bentham, Burke, Mill, Hegel, Montesquieu, Gibbon, Rousseau, Locke, Humboldt, Madison, de Tocqueville, Froude, Carlyle, Macaulay and a score of other thinkers.

Didactic novels, however, rarely failed to draw his coruscating ire: 'The crime of binding up a sermon as a three-volume novel is hardly less than that of an Eton boy who brings into chapel a novel bound up as a prayer book,' he said of one. A book on Australia he similarly swatted aside as 'the unpremeditated scribblings of an occasional leisure hour'.

On Christmas Eve 1856, Cecil told his fiancée that his first piece, a review of *The Letters of Henrietta Maria*, would appear in the *Saturday Review* two days later. The thirty-page, sixpenny weekly magazine had been founded in November 1855 by Beresford-Hope, and for the next nine years Cecil contributed articles to it, sometimes at the rate of two or three per week. From 1861 to 1864 he wrote 422 articles for that publication alone. In all, he wrote 608 articles for the *Saturday Review*, each of around two thousand words.

The *Saturday Review* featured some of the best writers of the day, including Walter Bagehot, James Fitzjames Stephen, Charles Kingsley, Max Müller and Dante Gabriel Rossetti. J.A. Froude was on the staff, as was John Morley, who was once sent to one of Baroness Burdett-Coutts's donkey-shows for 'copy'. Published on a Saturday in time for the weekend trains, it was an immediate success, the weekly circulation jumping from 2,000 in November 1856 to 5,000 by March 1858. The editor, J.D. Cook, called it 'a weekly review without news but with reviews of all the stirring subjects'. It doubled Cecil's income during the period of his greatest activity. He would write on any subject, from Mormonism to the most recent poisoning case, from interior decoration to the dangerous inflammability of crinolines ('The British Suttee').

The leading intellectual journal of the day was John Murray's *Quarterly Review*, which ran long, 18,000-word articles on weighty topics. Lord Acton, Matthew Arnold, William Gladstone, François Guizot and John Ruskin were occasional contributors. We know from Gwendolen Cecil's meticulous list of all her father's magazine journalism that, of the twenty-six issues of the *Quarterly Review* which appeared between the spring of 1860 and the summer of 1866, all but three carried anonymous articles by Cecil. These covered major political topics, and each was written in his distinctive, often vituperative style. In addition to his work for the reviews, Cecil regularly wrote leaders for the *Standard*, which had been founded as a Tory evening paper in 1821 to oppose Catholic Emancipation, but which by the 1860s, relaunched as a morning daily, had become a competitor to *The Times*. Having worked in the *Standard*'s office in Shoe Lane, Cecil found it very difficult, even decades later, to shake off the suspicion that he still directed its editorial policy.

Cecil was a founding co-editor of another journal, *Bentley's Quarterly Review*, along with J.D. Cook and the Rev. William Scott, which according to the July 1858 minutes in his handwriting was intended 'to

be progressive in politics, moderate and unobtrusive in religion'. He was
to be paid £62 10s per issue by Dickens's former publisher Richard
Bentley. The publication folded after only four issues, three of which
carried extremely unprogressive, immoderate and highly obtrusive
anonymous attacks by Cecil on Disraeli's attempts to outmanoeuvre
the Whigs by appealing to the Radicals, something he always viewed as
anathema.

Sadly for Cecil, the late 1850s and early 1860s presented few great
domestic issues over which the young writer could break his literary
lance, in the way that the 1830s had Reform and the 1840s had the Corn
Laws. There was a mild Reform Bill in 1859 which he could fulminate
against, but otherwise mid-Victorian England concentrated on enrich-
ing itself, under the hegemony of a Liberal Party which was in a
parliamentary majority for almost the whole period after Peel's fall in
1846. Cecil was acutely aware of the relative peacefulness of the political times and had to content himself with attacking the Whiggery of
Palmerston and Lord John Russell, and warning of the dangers of the
oncoming democratic onslaught.

~

Russell's foreign policy drew Cecil's anger, especially for what he
dubbed its 'tariff of insolence' to smaller powers, whilst refusing to face
up to stronger ones. Cecil was dismissive of Russell, 'a born schoolmaster accidentally elevated to the Foreign Office', who was under five feet
tall. 'There is always something comical about the indignation of a very
small man,' he had written on another subject, and he tried to draw
Russell out by attacks that became progressively ruder and more
personal. Over British policy towards Denmark during the Schleswig-
Holstein Question, Poland's subjugation by Russia, and the
non-recognition of the Confederacy during the American Civil War,
Cecil believed he could detect a pattern of what he called Russell's
'sequence of snarling remonstrance, officious advice, treacherous
encouragement, and shameless abandonment'.[2]

The fledgling MP accused the veteran former Prime Minister of
'always being willing to sacrifice anything for peace ... colleagues, principles, pledges', of following a policy of 'cowardice' and 'bluster', of 'a
portentous mixture of bounce and baseness', but above all of being
'dauntless to the weak, timid and cringing to the strong'. In his defence
it must be added that Cecil was equally discourteous on the floor of the
House of Commons as in his anonymous *Saturday* and *Quarterly
Review* articles. Describing Russell's policy over Brazil as that of 'an
angry old maid', his 'insolence' to the King of Denmark, his rudeness to
Japan and his quixotic offer to the Pope to live in Malta if ousted from

the Vatican by the Risorgimento, Cecil accused the Foreign Secretary of 'making up for weak action with valorous words'.[3]

In his analysis of Russell's tenure of the Foreign Office, Cecil drew out a few vital principles which served him well when he himself presided over that department. The first was not to listen too much to the Opposition or the press, otherwise:

> we are to be governed…by a set of weathercocks, delicately poised, warranted to indicate with unnerving accuracy every variation in public feeling. A gentleman from the office of *The Times* will do it for a tenth part [of Russell's £5,000 salary] and probably do it better… If the functions of a Minister are reduced to those of a head clerk, it will be difficult to induce anyone but head clerks to assume them.

The second lesson was that foreign policy was about raw *Realpolitik*, not morality. 'No one dreams of conducting national affairs with the principles which are prescribed to individuals. The meek and poor-spirited among nations are not to be blessed, and the common sense of Christendom has always prescribed for national policy principles diametrically opposed to those that are laid down in the Sermon on the Mount.' Grand talk by politicians about the rights of mankind and serving humanity, rather than purely the national interest, were, for Cecil, simply so much cant.

The third principle he drew from Russell's policy was about how far Britain could or should be the 'candid friend' of other countries, involving herself in their domestic political arrangements. When the British minister in Florence, Lord Normanby, intervened in Italian domestic politics, Cecil reminded his fellow legislators how:

> The assemblies that meet in Westminster have no jurisdiction over the affairs of other nations. Neither they nor the Executive, except in plain defiance of international law, can interfere with the brigandage of Italy, or the persecutions in Spain, or the teaching of the schools in Schleswig. What is said in either House about them is simply impertinence…. It is not a dignified position for a Great Power to occupy, to be pointed out as the busybody of Christendom.

He went on to aver that anything Britain was likely to say about governmental misdeeds in Italy might equally be used by foreign countries against the British administration of Ireland.

Finally, Cecil considered that giving 'unasked advice or impotent scolding', not backed up by the ultimate threat of force, merely irritated Britain's friends and encouraged the scorn of her adversaries: 'Quixoticism was acceptable only so long as it did not falter at the sight of a drawn sword.' The fact that Russell usually backed down when faced with the prospect of war provoked Cecil's contempt: 'A willingness to fight is the *point d'appui* of diplomacy, just as much as a readiness to go to court is the starting-point of a lawyer's letter. It is merely courting dishonour, and inviting humiliation for the men of peace to use the habitual language of the men of war.'[4] Few better initiations into the art of Great Power diplomacy, at which Cecil was to become Europe's prime master after the fall of Bismarck, could be devised than having carefully to analyse the conduct of foreign affairs for a weekly column on which his livelihood depended.

In his writings on colonialism, the Lord Robert Cecil of the 1850s and 1860s seems an entirely different person from the Lord Salisbury who as Prime Minister added two and a half million square miles to the territory of the British Empire four decades later. 'A genuine Empire is a very grand thing,' Cecil admitted in an article in June 1864, on the 'little wars' that were being fought against the Ashanti Kingdom in West Africa – present-day Ghana – and against the Maoris in New Zealand. 'But a sham Empire, consisting chiefly of titles and professions of allegiance heavily paid for in hard cash, is a rather parvenu counterfeit of the real thing.' Thinking the British army 'most unfitted' for bush wars, he was 'simply sickened' by the news from the Ashanti campaign, and hoped there would be 'no more New Zealand wars' at all.

Cecil's was essentially an eighteenth-century, utilitarian attitude towards colonisation, one that would have been easily recognisable by earlier Prime Ministers such as Lord Melbourne. He was extremely reluctant for Westminster to accept direct responsibility for administering the huge areas of Africa and Asia which the European Powers were beginning to acquire. He subscribed to what was later called the 'fit of absence of mind' theory of colonial acquisition, and blamed traders, land sharks, prospectors, missionaries and settlers for occupying the areas and subsequently forcing ministers in London to annex them as colonies, rather than allow anarchy or foreign conquest. The missionary he defined as 'a religious Englishman with a mission to offend the religious feelings of the natives'. When he was Prime Minister and missionaries requested protection for their evangelical work in central China, he refused. 'It is all very well to have the Gospel of Christ at your head,' he minuted, 'but your influence will be greatly diminished if you must be followed by gunboats at your tail.'

Despite having visited far more colonies than the average Briton, Cecil was not particularly interested in them, describing their settlements as 'very like a second-rate English town, with some addition in energy, and some deduction in morality'. He considered that it required 'the courage of a literary martyr, or the despair of a seaside lodger, to open a book of colonial facts'. Of his 608 *Saturday Review* articles, only twenty-two covered colonial issues, of which the vast majority were written in support of the Maoris whom he considered viciously ill-used. In the House of Commons, his nine speeches on colonial affairs between 1853 and 1866 were fewer than those he delivered on the American Civil War.

Cecil's scepticism about the use of colonies sprang primarily from their cost to the British taxpayer. He was one of those Tories who saw income tax as William Pitt's emergency wartime imposition, which sadly no one had yet got around to abolishing. The £1¼ million spent annually on imperial defence in 1860 struck him as merely 'an expenditure which enables us to furnish an agreeable variety of station to our soldiery, and to indulge the sentiment that the sun never sets on our Empire'. He was nonetheless furious when colonies made secessionist noises, however timidly, considering them mere blackmail. Reviewing a book about Australia's complaints about the mother country in January 1860, he observed with satisfaction that 'four sloops of war could at any time bring the four colonies to their knees'.[5]

Cecil blamed what he called the Empire's 'prodigal sons' – those local Governors who indulged in semi-authorised military expeditions such as Sir Harry Smith's against the Kaffirs in Cape Colony – for unnecessarily violent and costly 'little wars'. He wrote a series of philippics against Sir Thomas Browne, the Governor of New Zealand, whom he accused of precipitating the war against the Maoris and abrogating their 'scrupulously reserved' land rights as prescribed in the 1840 Treaty of Waitangi. Browne's crushing of the Maoris, 'a sovereign nation who voluntarily entered into an agreement to live under our flag under specified conditions', struck Cecil as 'flagrantly unrighteous' and not really warfare so much as 'man-stalking'. The New Zealand Government he dismissed as nothing 'but a firm of Auckland attorneys', and settlers in general as 'incorrigible, plausible scapegraces' whom Westminster should not continue to subsidise.

Cecil thought part of the problem lay in the low quality of the 'prodigal sons', because the Government insisted on using governorships as 'convenient almshouses in which political incapables may be cheaply boarded and lodged'. As a result, rather than saving money, their incompetence involved Britain in wars which in the Cape cost £500,000, and in New Zealand twice that, with no discernible profit to Britain deriving from either. Racial arrogance – what he called 'the "damned nigger" principle with which we are so familiar in India and the United States' – was generally growing, he thought, using 'a thin veil of commonplace professions', such as 'the advance of civilisation'. This would one day pose a serious danger, when the natives developed better military strategies than that of merely 'testing our Armstrong guns'. He held

Governor Browne up as 'one of the most striking instances of the "nigger-despising" temper' which he described as 'the bane of our colonial policy'.

Fearing that there would be a European scramble for Japan after the revolution there, Cecil wrote in January 1863 that it was 'easy to philosophise about the vanity of extended territory', but, should other countries such as France and Russia be seen to profit, 'the instinct of the nation will never be content without a share in the booty which it sees its neighbours greedily dividing'. Although deeply sceptical about the 'hopeless mess' which he believed characterised British colonial policy, Cecil opposed John Bright's anti-imperialism, which he described as 'the simple process of cutting the colonies adrift'. He accepted that they were 'worth maintaining', if only on the utilitarian grounds of protecting trade. The ultimate objective must be to 'lay the foundations for great, durable and friendly nations', but he believed that this could and should be done without the extermination of tribal peoples.[6]

Lord Palmerston's famous trio who understood the Schleswig-Holstein Question – Prince Albert who was dead, the Danish statesman who had gone mad, and Palmerston himself who had quite forgotten all about it – ought in fact to be a quartet. Robert Cecil made it his business to master the complexities of the Blue Books (the official Government reports to Parliament), Salic law, the lineage of the duchies' rulers, and the historical, linguistic and religious background of that notoriously complicated issue. He was the first to admit that 'the mere vocables in which the dispute must be conducted, such as Schleswig-Holstein and Augustenberg Glücksburg, Dannerwerrke and Rigsraad, are not such as any man would wish to pronounce except when his powers of concentration are in first rate order'.

His studies convinced him that the Prussian and Austrian claims upon the Danish duchies were based more on German nationalism and 'irrepressible patriotism' than upon any inherent legal right. He blamed the pan-Germanic Nationalverein's desire for naval expansion, and argued that only by standing up to its early manifestations could 'the extravagant and flagitious demand of the Germans' be halted. Otherwise, he warned, the crisis would both establish the existence of a German Bund and furnish 'a harmless and bloodless gratification to the martial imaginations of the Prussians'. He did not, however, advocate direct British intervention on Denmark's side, and condemned Russell for seeming to offer it before backing down in front of the Central Powers.

In the House of Commons in February 1864, Cecil described Austria, which that month had invaded the duchies in alliance with Prussia, as 'that hypocritical power, which, with one foot on Venetia and another upon Hungary, turns northward and calls herself the champion of nationalities'. In identifying German nationalism as the new, dynamic threat to European peace, Cecil showed Themistoclean prescience, especially as Prince Otto von Bismarck had only been Prime Minister of Prussia since September 1862. Cecil's anti-nationalist stance was also directed against Hellenism, pan-Slavism and the Italian Risorgimento. He called a united Italy 'a student's dream if there had been no misgovernment to warm it into life' and ridiculed the 'artificial and premature freedom' won by the Greeks at the Battle of Navarino in 1827.

Cecil declared that by sabre-rattling in support of Denmark and then stepping back from a clash with the Central Powers when challenged, 'England, under pretence of serving and defending Denmark, is in reality betraying her.'[7] In Parliament and the press he rammed home the point that Russell's policy of 'friendly bystanding' actually harmed Danish interests, by encouraging a vain and naïve policy of resistance. 'If we do not mean to fight we ought not to interfere. If we did not attempt to carry out by arms our threats and measures, we must abstain from the luxury of indulging in them.' His foresight deserted him, however, when he consoled his readers that Napoleon III, 'who, in the matter of breaking treaties and rectifying frontiers is perfectly ready to mete out to them the measure they mete out to others', would one day bring Nemesis upon German designs.

Reviewing a book about Arminius, who had visited the Varian disaster on three Roman legions in 9 AD, Cecil expounded on the need for hero-worship in the German national character. Their reverence this obscure, flawed figure who also fought other Germans produced a paradox: 'There are no people who venerate antiquities like the Americans; there is no place where trees are so much admired as in Holland; and so there is no nation that reveres a national hero like the German.'

Except as the future vanquisher of Teutonic hubris, Cecil had little time for what he called Napoleon III's 'democratic cæsarism'. Deeply suspicious of France's foreign policy, especially towards Italy and Mexico, he worried that her 'unscrupulous worship of military glory' might eventually lead to war with Britain. He also noted how the Emperor was 'the only Frenchman who is perfectly free to speak', and the suppression of free speech had been achieved in 'a masterpiece of dexterity' through universal suffrage. 'So long as the Emperor preserves his subjects from the demon of *ennui*,' he predicted, 'he may do what he likes with the liberty of the Press.' Cecil's own experience of earning a living had obviously made him more jealous of press freedom than when he had spoken up for censorship at the Oxford Union.

It was just as well for Cecil that his journalism was anonymous, and thus in the final recourse deniable, otherwise his remarks about Austria in 1862 would have severely embarrassed him once he became Foreign Secretary. Phrases such as 'supposing the Austrians were lucky enough to get rid of [Emperor] Francis Joseph', or 'a monarchy which is at once the most blundering and most priest-ridden in Europe', or 'hereditary tyrants' would have been quoted with painful effect when he was attempting to bind Austria into his anti-Russian entente sixteen years later.

If pan-Germanism worried Cecil, it was the peril from across the Atlantic that terrified him. This derived not from the United States' military might but from her ideological *raison d'être* – Democracy. The threat was so apocalyptic for him that it gave him nightmares and severely aggravated his 'nerve-storms'. Cecil disliked America and most Americans, despite never having been there. 'The Yankee,' he wrote in an article ridiculing America's belief in her 'manifest destiny', 'whose life is one long calculation, appears to have bombast for his mother tongue.' After reading Charles Dickens's 'pungent' *Martin Chuzzlewit* in 1843, he wrote to Blanche that in the United States, money-lust 'prevails universally and operates to the exclusion not only of literature and refinement but to the destruction of good faith, honour, gentleman-liness, high feeling, and in fact all those substitutes for Christianity which until Christianity itself supersedes them, it is so necessary to maintain'.[8] He believed Americans to be instinctively anti-British, not from calculation but out of 'hearty, genuine feeling', and he despised the way that British liberals held up American democracy, republicanism and classlessness as a model for the rest of the world.

It was thus with a powerful sense of *Schadenfreude* that, once the Civil War broke out in April 1861 and important civil liberties began to be suppressed, Cecil relished pointing out that the idea that somehow Americans 'were sagacious and long-headed, much too far in the vanguard of civilisation to be deluded by martial passions or dreams of empire' had been shown to be 'utterly untrue'. Part of his passionate, lifelong anti-Americanism sprang from his anti-Puritanism. He denounced the hypocrisy of the Founding Fathers professing to escape the rigours of a State church only to set up one yet more rigid them-selves. 'They were no evangelists of religious liberty,' he wrote in 1859, but instead 'the most intolerant generation of the straitest of all sects'. Instead of attempting to convert the Red Indians, Cecil reminded his readers, 'they sought to Christianise the country by the simple expedient of slaughtering all who were not Christians'.

Curiously for one who wanted the Confederacy to be recognised by Britain, another animus against America was the 'eminently wasteful and inefficient' system of slavery, which 'habitually tears wife from husband, and child from mother, which rules by cruelty and spreads by prostitution'. In an article entitled (with deliberate irony) 'A Word for Slavery', Cecil refused to accept such a concept as the inalienable rights of man, but he also assumed that because 'you cannot flog them into ingenuity, or care, or diligence', slavery was a doomed institution. 'Isolated acts and cruelty are no more an argument against slavery than against omnibus-driving,' he nonetheless argued in 1857, but a system which 'bred slaves like cattle, only treating them worse,' could not be right. He was quick to point out that for all the championing of the negroes by the North, they were still made to feel unwelcome in most white hotels, churches and schools there.

When the Confederacy seceded from the Union and attacked Fort Sumter, Cecil supported it, in part because he believed 'the best chance for the alleviation of the slave's condition lies in the increased wealth and prosperity of the South', which he convinced himself, if not necessarily many of his readers, would lead to a transitional period of 'modified and alleviated slavery' on the road to emancipation. 'The wickedness of slavery', he argued, was no more a reason for Britain not to recognise the Confederacy as an independent country 'than the fact that a baby squints would prove that it had not been born'.

Cecil did not anyhow believe that Abolitionism was the primary cause of the war. Democratic triumphalism was to blame for the Northern majority forcing its will on the Southern minority, just as it had been responsible for thrusting Free Trade on to a Southern economy which was better suited to Protection. A mature Constitution such as Britain's would have been able to hammer out a compromise without recourse to war. 'The omnipotence of the majority, imperious as any king, greedy as any court-mistress or court-confessor,' he argued, 'has bred the revolution.' This revisionist analysis condemned Northern aggression in general and Abraham Lincoln in particular. Calling for British recognition of the Confederacy in the *Quarterly Review* in October 1862, Cecil argued that it was only after 'a gradual process, in which the Negro's culture and his freedom shall increase together, that emancipation is either desirable or safe'. Britain was friendly with and recognised Brazil and Spain, in whose empires slavery still survived, and in the Crimean War she fought for the integrity of Turkey, where the slave trade flourished. With famine threatening Lancashire for want of blockaded Southern cotton, it was anyhow wrong, he contended, to be so 'squeamish' about America's domestic institutions.

Cecil reserved his sharpest invective for those British liberals who opposed recognition, comparing it to 'the sympathy of our kinsmen for anyone, whether Tsar or sepoy, whose conduct was embarrassing for England'. In a February 1864 Commons debate over the *Alabama*, a Confederate raiding ship built in Britain but captured and impounded by the Union Navy, the pro-abolitionist W.E. Forster told his wife how he was amused to see Cecil 'glaring up at me with his dark eyes from under his hat'. Forster had accused Cecil of supporting the Confederacy because the aristocratic, landowning Southerners were 'the natural allies of the noble Lord and of the order to which he belonged'. Cecil answered that Forster was 'a fanatic about slavery', a charge which Forster readily accepted. Washington's claims against Britain for the damage done by the *Alabama*, *Florida* and *Shenandoah* were eventually settled, to Cecil's fury, when the Gladstone Government paid a $15.5 million indemnity to America eight years later.

Out of Forster and Cecil, it was in fact probably the latter who was the more fanatical about events in America. Just as Cato the Elder concluded every speech on every subject with a call for the destruction of Carthage, so Cecil slipped the dangers of American democracy into almost everything he said and wrote during this period. Reviews of books on German nationalism, Professor Jowett's theology, historical anecdotes, even an article about Anglican bishops condemning Sunday excursion trains, all had at least a passing reference to the evils of American democracy or the 'despotism' of Lincoln's Government.

John Bright said that Cecil bore 'unsleeping ill-will' towards the Americans, but in fact it even continued on into his subconscious. Georgina Cecil worried for his state of mind and told her daughter Gwendolen how alarmed she had been when she woke one night to see him standing at the wide open window of their second-floor bedroom, fast asleep, but in a state of extreme perturbation. He was, she thought, 'preparing to resist forcibly some dreamt-of invasion of enemies – presumably Federal soldiers or revolutionary mob leaders'. She told her daughter that 'never in her knowledge of him did he suffer such extremes of depression and nervous misery as at that time'.[9]

Such total identification with the protagonists in a war over three thousand miles away led Cecil into wild hyperbole, to the point that he even compared the Federal forces during General Sherman's admittedly brutal march through Georgia with those of 'Genghis Khan and Tamerlane'. Cecil could hardly believe civilised Christians could act as Generals Sherman's and Butler's troops had. He partly blamed the 'singularly barbarous instincts' of the Federal troops on the supposed fact that 'a large proportion of Red Indian blood must have entered into the composition of the people of the Northern States'. There had been few white women in the original thirteen colonies at the time of their greatest expansion, he contended, so miscegenation probably explained the 'traits of monstrous ferocity which accord but little with the character of the European races from which the Yankees are ostensibly descended'. Whilst fully admitting that 'war is not made with rose-water', he nevertheless accused General Butler's army in New Orleans of employing systematic rapine as a method of terrorising the women of the South. 'The history of Christendom will be ransacked in vain for another instance of a general who has avowedly utilised the lust of his men for the purposes of military terrorism,' thundered Cecil.

Yet it was not solely humanitarianism that animated Cecil against the North, nor the fear he often reiterated of an attack on Canada as soon as the Confederacy was crushed. Rather he saw events in America as a sinister portent of what might happen in Britain should democracy triumph. 'As soon as real danger touches her,' he wrote of the American system of government, 'the surface gloss of liberty falls off, and the latent image of despotism develops itself with startling directness.' For those liberals who preferred American democracy to British constitutional and representative (albeit strictly numerically limited) government, Cecil thought that 'the weary search for a political ideal must be commenced afresh'.

Cecil's admiration for the Confederate President Jefferson Davis's 'good taste and high moral feeling' contrasted with his view of Abraham Lincoln's 'personal nullity'. He thought that Lincoln had only 'done what all weak and timid rulers do' when he arrested his political opponents and closed opposition newspapers. Lincoln's suspension of *habeas corpus* and subsequent internment of 14,000 people without trial was, in Cecil's view, as unconstitutional and despotic as anything that was happening in Warsaw, Paris or Naples at the time, except that it was being done in the name not of an avowedly absolutist regime, but of 'The People'. 'The French Emperor himself,' wrote Cecil, 'under threat of assassination, never did anything to rival this.'

The United States Chief Justice, Roger B. Taney, believed that only Congress, and not the Executive, could suspend *habeas corpus*, but he was overruled by Lincoln, so Cecil had a reasonable legal point. By arresting elected members of the Congress and even a Supreme Court judge, introducing conscription and suppressing Opposition newspapers, Lincoln had indeed assumed virtually dictatorial powers. Of the famously despotic King Ferdinand VII of Naples, Cecil asked: 'What did Bomba do that Lincoln has not done?' Yet the circumstances were entirely exceptional in America, and Cecil was widely thought to be indulging in hyperbole when he argued that tyranny was the inevitable result of democracy. 'Gradually, but surely, the elaborate fabric devised by Washington is crumbling away, and the well-known outlines of a military despotism are shaping themselves in its place.' This was the gravamen of a large number of Cecil's articles in the *Saturday Review* from that time.

In his portrait gallery of heroes at Hatfield, alongside men such as Lord Castlereagh and Pitt the Younger, hangs a print of General 'Stonewall' Jackson dated January 1864. By the end of that year, however, Cecil had lost hope in the Confederates' ability to secure even an acceptable truce. His bitterness at their final defeat showed when, after a *pro forma* condemnation of Lincoln's assassination, he wrote in May 1865 that John Wilkes Booth had shown 'not only courage, but the hardihood of desperation', and argued that the murder was 'very little different' from a legitimate act of war. Writing seven years later, he still felt 'the whole of our conduct towards the Yankees is too disgusting to think calmly of....If we had recognised the South ten years ago, America would have now been nicely divided into hostile states.'

One lesson Cecil had learnt from the conflict was that the nature of modern warfare had entirely changed. After discussing the possibility of a new type of missile that could smash through armour plating, he wrote that events in America had 'wholly falsified the doctrine that such facilities, by sharpening war, also shorten it'. His daily study of the struggle convinced him that railways, trenches, barbed wire, 'an aerial ship', long preliminary bombardments and mass mobilisation would be the hallmarks of future wars. At the annual dinner of the 5th Lincolnshire Volunteer Corps at Stamford in October 1862, he predicted that 'armies like that with which Napoleon invaded Russia will be the normal armies of future wars'. Might Cecil have also foreseen the tank? In a *Saturday Review* article of October 1863 entitled 'Scientific Warfare', he predicted the eruption on to the world's battlefields of 'moveable iron forts, containing men and guns, which should have travelled as easily over the land as the gunboats do upon rivers...an army of traction engines whose flanks could never be turned, and which would be equally invulnerable before as behind'.

Cecil also predicted what has been called 'the American century'. In March 1902, on the verge of retirement, he wrote to his son-in-law about the news that the American financier J.P. Morgan was about to acquire a predominating influence in Cunard, White Star and other transatlantic shipping lines:

> It is very sad, but I am afraid America is bound to forge ahead and nothing can restore the equality between us. If we had interfered in the Confederate War it was then possible for us to reduce the power of the United States to manageable proportions. But <u>two</u> such chances are not given to a nation in the course of its career.[10]

FOUR

Journalism: Domestic Policy

*Ireland – The Class Struggle – Parliament
– William Gladstone*

1857 to 1866

'The quaint antics of pygmies in power.'

Cecil did not believe in fate. His rejection of historical determinism, by which 'great men ... are treated as mere clips indexing the course of the stream along which they float, but which they cannot guide', was best adumbrated in his reviews of the works of Leopold von Ranke, whom he admired in everything except the fact that 'his historical theory is of the necessitarian, not the free-will type'. In Cecil's opinion it was human agency operating through free will, with people taking responsibility for their actions, which explained historical development. He listed the exploits of Elizabeth I, Cromwell, Wolfe, Nelson and Wellington as supporting the 'great men' theory for the creation of the British Empire, rather than any concept of 'the destined expansion of the English race'.

Cecil denied that there were 'currents', 'tendencies', 'elements', 'impulses', 'developments' and 'fermentations' that drove history along predestined courses, and, because God did not take sides, civilisation was not embarked upon any onward march, but could dawdle, take blind alleys or even slip backwards at certain periods. When Forster made his Bradford speech saying that a Confederate victory would make him doubt his belief in an 'overruling Providence', Cecil retorted that had Forster been living in Carcassonne during the Albigensian crusade, or Rome during the fall of the Republic, or the Levant 'when the blight of Mohammedan conquest was passing over', he would presumably have doubted his faith then also.

Some historical periods were thus more worthy of study than others. Reviewing the letters of Horace Walpole, whom he thought 'as malicious as a mannekin', Cecil described the reign of George II as not affording fitting material for a historian, as it was merely 'a petty,

stagnant, pulseless age.... The King had no one salient point of character, except a love of ugly mistresses. Political contest was a sheer
struggle for the then golden prize of place.' Cecil was just as stern a
moralist when it came to the historian's duty, which was 'to trace the
action of political principles, the growth of ideas, the rise and the effects
of widespread feelings, not the disconnected results of selfish intrigues'.
Those were the property of gossips like Walpole, who 'wander by choice
in the dirty lanes and crooked alleys of history', in order to record 'the
quaint antics of pygmies in power'. Nor did he approve of biography,
writing in the *Saturday Review* in January 1859 about a life of Bishop
Wilson: 'A place in history is the reward of great men – a biography is
the fitting commemoration of those who are remembered more for the
love and respect they earned from their friends than for the mark they
have left on the destinies of their fellow men.'

A true bibliophile, Cecil would always have two or three small books
in his voluminous pockets wherever he went, so he would never have to
waste time on railway journeys, picnics or waiting for people. 'I want to
know what happened,' he would complain about over-authored history
books, 'not what the man thinks.' He distrusted the use of the anecdote,
suspecting that the phenomenon it was employed to illustrate was
often the exception but was too often quoted as if it was the rule. He
criticised Carlyle, Macaulay and J.A. Froude, 'our most eminent historians', for using 'the great blemish' of anecdotes, and argued that a
historian of the future might one day cite the various assassination
attempts on Queen Victoria in order to substantiate the claim that she
was 'a bloody-minded tyrant'.

It was largely anecdotal information, rather than statistics or facts, that
Cecil employed in his own writings on the subject of Ireland. The 1848
humiliation of the nationalist revolutionaries in the Widow
McCormack's 'far-famed cabbage garden' was a favourite theme, to
which Cecil returned whenever he wished to conclude that Irish
patriots were cowards at heart and 'a sound whipping – stinging but not
injurious – administered once a week for six months is the prescription
[and] the world will have heard the last of Fenianism'.[1]

It is impossible to escape the conclusion that, because of their
perceived rebelliousness, Catholicism, nationalism and refusal to
respect the rights of property on which he believed civic order to be
based, Cecil simply could not stand the Irish. He readily accepted that
Ireland had been subjected to gross historical wrongs, he rejected the
intolerance of the Orangemen, and he attacked absentee landlordism,
but the evidence of his journalism can only lead to the conclusion that

Cecil also intensely disliked Ireland and the Irish. 'England knows Ireland as well as a man knows the corn that has afflicted his spirit from early youth,' he wrote in 1857, reviewing a travel book. 'She has given us foreign invasions, domestic rebellions; and in quieter times the manly sport of landlord shooting.' He believed that 'the extirpation of Irish landlords is the Irish peasant's one idea of political Utopia', and that 'taste for deeds of violence has become almost a national characteristic of the lower orders of Irish'.

Because Cecil believed that 'there is no firm resting place between interference with the rights of property and confiscation', he was opposed to all forms of Irish tenant-right, ridiculing the proposals that tenants could be compensated for improvements they had made on their landlord's property. When a peasant 'puts up some ricketty shanties... which he calls farm buildings', or 'allows a pig to wander in search of refuse [and] informs the bailiff that he has manured it with his stock', or 'digs a hole in the earth at several intervals ... and tells the landlord he has drained the land' he had not genuinely improved it, but when the landlord refused to pay compensation, there was 'a howl from every priestly and parliamentary agitator.... The Saxon is trampling upon the Celt.' In December 1861 *The Nation* newspaper complained at the growing number of evictions, but Cecil sarcastically remarked that they were taking place 'for no other offence but that they omitted to conform to the purely Saxon custom of paying the rent on which they had agreed'.

Cecil argued that the central problem was 'the absolute want of capital' in Ireland, money which if the killings ceased would pour into the island because of its 'virgin soil', 'magnificent harbours' and 'vast mineral wealth'. Only the lack of capital to drain marshes, construct mills and work mines held Ireland back. The sole reason for this under-investment was that 'capitalists prefer peace and 3% to 10% with the drawback of bullets in the breakfast room'. So capital instead migrated to Brazil and Asia Minor. The problem was not so much isolated crimes, 'the chance outbreak of individual passion', which scared off the prospective investor, but 'organised murder, in which the whole peasantry are accomplices'. As a result, 'the peasantry will not be able to flatter themselves that the Irish famine, when it comes, is a mysterious visitation from God. It will be the direct and legitimate consequence of systematised crime.' Cecil further considered Irish emigration a matter for 'unmixed congratulation', frankly saying 'the sooner they are gone the better'. He hoped that when he departed for Canada or America, the Irish peasant 'leaves a place behind him to be filled up by a Scotchman or Englishman over whom the vicious tradition has no power'.

Cecil considered the Orange tradition to be quite as vicious as the Green. 'An Orangeman values his religion', he wrote in 1864 in words that had they not been written anonymously would have severely embarrassed him on his anti-Home Rule campaign thirty years later, 'chiefly for the opportunity it gives him of making his natural enemies uncomfortable.' After dozens of people were killed and wounded in eleven days of rioting in May 1865, Cecil blamed 'the special fanaticism of Ulster' and the gross partiality shown by the Protestant-dominated local authorities there. 'An Orangeman believes he is the agent of the Protestant world', he wrote indignantly in July 1865, 'to see the Irish Catholic properly bullied.' He denounced the Protestant Ascendancy as incapable of understanding concepts such as impartiality and justice.

Despite all the acknowledged problems involved in keeping Ireland within the Union, Cecil never wrote or spoke so much as a sentence, even in the most hypothetical way, to suggest that the island would be better off as an autonomous political entity. His heroes Pitt the Younger and Castlereagh had forced through the Act of Union in 1800, and Irish wishes were not as important as the considerations of prestige, grand strategy and fidelity to the Ulster settlers which Cecil always believed should take precedence. Ireland had to be kept, he wrote in the *Quarterly Review* in 1872, 'like India, at all hazards: by persuasion, if possible; if not, by force'. He was the first to admit that it was England's 'evil work of many centuries' which had made the Irish question so intractable, but it seems never to have so much as crossed Cecil's mind simply to accord the nationalists the freedom from Westminster rule that they were demanding.

The Irish Catholics had been, he stated in 'The Condition-of-Ireland Question' in the *Saturday Review* in April 1864,

> governed by men of an alien race and alien creed, persecuted because they clung to their fathers' faith and avowed the blood that flowed in their veins; stripped of their property by the invaders, fettered in their trade that their masters might prosper, crushed by unequal laws, harnessed by degrading disabilities, galled, depressed and disheartened by the open, never-abating scorn of the race that had conquered them.

All these were 'sins for which England has socially, if not politically to answer'. Financially also, and Cecil supported 'any fitting opportunity of giving back to Ireland a portion of the wealth which she has mistakenly taken from her'.

Yet at no stage did he advocate any form of Home Rule, despite stating that 'exceptional injuries require exceptional reparation'. Increased trade and inward investment, not self-determination, were his answer to Ireland's problems. It could not be southern Ireland's religion which condemned her to poverty, he argued, as the Catholics of Belgium were rich. Nor could it be the fact that they were Celts, because Cornwall, Wales and Brittany did not suffer 'monstrous and abnormal misery'. The climate and natural conditions could not be to blame either, because Ulster thrived under the same ones. The problem lay in Ireland's 'political history', and for that it was incumbent upon the rest of Britain to make 'some effort to atone for the wrong which the errors of our ancestors have wrought'.[2]

Because trade and investment could only be achieved by the crushing of agrarian outrage, Cecil advocated 'a strong and merciless hand' in Ireland. If the authorities hanged a Catholic priest for every murder committed in a district, he wrote somewhat histrionically in June 1863, 'we should have very little more of agrarian outrage in Ireland'. No 'pedantic theories' should be allowed to stand in the way of 'the vigorous extirpation of agrarian crime', and a reconstructed police force should scare the Irish peasant 'with prompt, rough vigour' into renouncing 'that "wild justice of revenge" which is the source and origin of all the evils that are special to Ireland'.

Cecil's draconian views on law and order were not confined to Ireland. He believed that people should be allowed to witness public executions, 'not that they may learn holiness or purity, but that they may learn to fear the law.... It teaches, not an abstract truth, but a plain fact which it commends to the attention of spectators – that, if A cuts B's throat, A's neck will be wrung.' Uncompromising on issues of prison discipline, Cecil was clearly writing rhetorically in January 1863 when he asked 'whether a criminal should be made to suffer, or whether a gaol is a mere House of Solomon for conducting experiments in planting and cultivating exotic virtues in unnatural and uncongenial soils'. Without at least two hours' hard labour daily, he wrote, prison 'deprives punishment of its most important element – that of personal suffering'.

Cecil's writing was not all harsh and doom-laden; he also wrote much about the absurdities of Victorian high society, holding the manners and morals of his class up to the most unforgiving of lights. The Belgravian 'marriage-market', the trials of a younger son in heiress-hunting, the 'huge white lie' of politeness and the artificiality of compliments were all fit subjects for the satire of 'the Buffalo'. He would dilate wittily on dinner-party mores, the practice of leaving visiting cards (he was against it), quadrille-dancing, bathing machines and whether women should be allowed to model nude at the Royal Academy (he was in favour of it). Public dinners were 'saturnalias of humbug', gossip was 'cheaper than a lawsuit, and safer than an attempt at horse-whipping', and hostesses who insisted on party games were 'social Torquemadas'.

Another favourite bugbear was the International Exhibition held at

Brompton in 1862, which afforded Cecil no fewer than five opportunities to mock its advertising ('The Palace of Puffs'), its building
('Dishcovers and Dripping Pans') and everyone connected with the
exercise. He made great jest of the fact that one of its sponsors, Mr
Harper Twelvetrees, a haberdasher who had stood for Parliament for
Marylebone supported by someone called the Rev. Jabez Inwards, had
once used the following jingle for one of his products:

> Fat bugs at midnight always prowl,
> And make you rise with hideous growl,
> Resolving that you'll be a buyer
> Of Harper Twelvetrees' bug-destroyer.

Cecil railed at the ceremony to inaugurate the Exhibition, calling it 'the
solemn and religious opening of a gigantic joint-stock showroom', and
taunted the Exhibition commissioners for making an exhibition of
themselves, accusing them of gross jobbery into the bargain. When the
Liberal Lord President of the Council, Earl Granville, agreed to attend,
Cecil recommended that he walk down Regent Street wearing a sandwich board instead. He could not conceal his glee when one of the
backers went bankrupt and was later discovered to have received an
'introduction' fee from one of the exhibitors. Altogether, Cecil's
campaign was harsh, often unfair, unusually snobbish against commerce,
and very funny indeed.

Cecil reviewed dozens of novels, arguing that: 'Whatever a man has to
communicate to the world, he has no hope of its being read unless he
dresses it up as a novel.' He could be merciless; Archdeacon Hare's
posthumous philosophical work *Guesses at Truth* drew forth the observation: 'He was a victim of that mania to which so many clever men are
subject, of liking that work best which they do worst. The infatuation
which induced Johnson to write poetry and Newton to descant upon the
Apocalypse hardly surpassed that which induced Hare to guess at truth.'
Witty though this cornucopia of scorn was, he considered it little more
than a comic turn, and one can almost sense the relief when he could
return to a serious subject. For Cecil the most serious of them all, even
dwarfing the American Civil War in comparison, was parliamentary
Reform.

On 19th January 1861, Cecil reviewed a pamphlet entitled *Herr Vogt*,
which he described as:

> the invective of a refugee who lives in London against a refugee who lives
> in Switzerland. One of them has accused the other of being Napoleon's spy;
> and the other retorts, among other abuse, with cutting observations on his

adversary's personal appearance. It will add something to the secret history of 1848, and much to the vocabulary of any Englishman desiring to learn the art of German imprecation.

Although at first sight Cecil might not seem to have much in common with the pamphlet's author, Karl Marx, in fact he fully agreed that a class war was being fought. The only philosophical difference between Marx and Cecil was that the former believed the triumph of the proletariat to be desirable and inevitable, whilst the latter emphatically denied both. Their numerical superiority did not imply to Cecil that the proletariat had any inherent right to dominate the bourgeoisie.

'The struggle between the English Constitution on the one hand,' Cecil wrote in the *Quarterly Review* in April 1860, 'and the democratic forces that are labouring to subvert it on the other, is now, in reality, when reduced to its simplest terms and stated in its most prosaic form, a struggle between those who have, to keep what they have got, and those who have not, to get it.' Marx could also just as easily have written Cecil's dictum: 'The distribution of property and the distribution of political power are inseparably connected. If power is not made to go with property, property will, in the long run, infallibly follow power.'

'The suffrage is not a red riband to be given to classes who have behaved well,' wrote Cecil in 1864 in answer to a speech from the Radical democrat Henry Fawcett. 'It is an article in a deed of partnership, to be arranged on strict business principles.' The working classes, then largely denied the franchise, should not be accorded it, for the simple reason that because their numbers exceeded all the other classes combined, 'they would no longer have a share in the government of the country, but would govern it altogether'. This would be disastrous because 'every class, high and low, habitually and invariably uses whatever legislative power it possesses in order to protect and promote its interests as a class'. To prove this he cited the way Irish MPs voted for subsidies to Ireland, squires stayed up all night (very much against their normal inclinations) to vote for anti-poaching legislation, manufacturers agitated for commercial treaties and landowning MPs voted for the abolition of the malt tax.

Cecil had an apocalyptic vision of what would happen if the working man 'succeeded to uncontrolled power' and then pursued his own self-interest. Unlike the present ruling class, which knew they could not strain their supremacy too far if those under them were not to assert themselves and shatter the artificial fabric of power 'by one blow', the working class would not be held back by any such scruples. 'They will be at liberty so to adjust taxation that the whole weight of it shall fall on those who do not depend on weekly wages, and they shall be exempt.' The working class would very soon 'divide the lands of the rich among them'. Poor relief, local taxation, master–servant relations, the legal obligations between Capital and Labour, 'will be equally at their unfettered disposal'. Cecil believed that should the proletariat triumph, as it inevitably must under universal suffrage, then mass confiscation and redistribution of property through taxation would be the ultimate result.

If somehow the working classes refrained from using their new political power in order to serve their own interests, they would 'differ much from all other types of humanity, and may be regarded as nothing less than angels in fustian'.[3] To prevent them getting the opportunity to subject the rich to exceptional taxation was, he said, in another unconscious comparison with Marx, 'a matter, not for arguing, but for fighting'. Once the franchise battle was lost and the constitutional palisades had been stormed, Cecil assumed that there could be no going back. In an exposition entitled 'The Theories of Parliamentary Reform', published in a book called *Oxford Essays* in 1858, Cecil boiled his argument down to the fact that 'the poor voters are numerous, the rich voters are few; and the few voters are absolutely and entirely at the mercy of the many'. Under democracy, he wrote elsewhere, eight workers would have seven Rothschilds at their mercy.

Because of his utilitarian belief that the enfranchised voted according to their financial self-interest 'in its lowest and least mitigated form', the idea that the working classes would not do exactly the same was to be 'found chiefly in Utopia'. Radical politicians would bribe the hugely enlarged new electorate with the money of the rich through taxation, and the horrific result would be equality of outcome, despite 'the enormous danger to freedom and property that it would involve'. Any *a priori* constitutional checks 'to fetter the Frankenstein' would soon prove worthless once 'the lower classes ... hastened to confirm their monopoly of power'.

Cecil constantly referred to the American experience, where 'regularly every four years the whole administrative expenditure of the country is converted into an electioneering bribe' on a scale far larger than 'the shy and covert corruption of the Old World'. Worse still, the bribes offered were with the taxpayers' own money, rather than that of the corrupt parliamentarians. 'We do not care to scrutinise too closely', Cecil wrote in February 1861, 'the moral boundary which separates a reckless hustings pledge from premeditated fraud.' Reform would merely elevate the bribery of the electorate from an endemic evil into an approved system of government. 'A philosopher may draw a distinction between the pecuniary benefits which will result to you, as one of a class, from the adoption of a political measure, and the coarser forms of pecuniary benefit which results from the insertion of a five-pound note into your pocket. But the elector cannot be expected to exercise so subtle a discrimination.'

Cecil's argument against enfranchising the working class was not based on snobbery; he did not argue that the rich were necessarily better human beings, as his criticisms of clubland and Mayfair society made clear. But he did believe that the leisure and education which the rich could afford, as well as the pecuniary disinterest they could show, made them more likely to be better legislators and choosers of legislators. 'Always wealth, in some countries birth, in all intellectual power and culture, mark out the men whom, in a healthy state of feeling, a community looks to undertake its government,' he wrote in the *Quarterly Review* in 1862. 'They have the leisure for the task, and can give to it the close attention and the preparatory work which it needs. Fortune enables them to do it for the most part gratuitously, so that the struggles of ambition are not tainted by... sordid greed.' After a long day's work, he argued, mechanics had little opportunity to develop the intellect and political knowledge necessary to make informed decisions. Ridiculing a Radical MP, Edward Baines, who argued in January 1862 that the working classes should be enfranchised because of their 'good behaviour', Cecil said that the socio-political equipoise of the nation should not be upset simply because the working classes were 'universally well-conducted, buy an abundance of penny tracts, and, when they are admitted to the Crystal Palace, do not break the curiosities'. Just because John Bright 'had been cheered in half a dozen music halls', Cecil did not believe the victory of Reform was inevitable, or much more than the latest manifestation of 'the coarse and grovelling materialism of the Manchester School'. When a private member's Reform Bill was defeated in the Commons, Cecil claimed it was because 'English gentlemen will scamper off at the first sound of a demagogue's bluster as quickly as an English mob at the first sight of a red-coat.'[4]

He was over-sanguine, and when Gladstone proclaimed himself in favour of universal suffrage in 1864, famously declaring that the working classes must be brought within 'the pale of the Constitution', Cecil knew that the battle he had long anticipated was just about to commence. He automatically assumed, however, that Derby, Disraeli and the Conservative Party would be staunch on the issue. They, surely, could be relied upon to recognise how, taken to its logical conclusions, Reform was only likely to stimulate what he called 'the love of a good dinner which animates the garotter'. At least the Party of property could be trusted to remember that, as Cecil put it at its mildest, 'the laws of property are not very safe when an ignorant multitude are the rulers'.

Quite why Cecil should have had such a faith in the political mettle of the Conservative Party is hard to understand, considering the contempt he exhibited for the vast majority of politicians. Much of his most waspish journalism was directed against his fellow MPs, such as this report of the speech of the Radical MP George Hadfield in February 1862:

> A shrill sound, like the dissonant wail of an oil-less door, is all that meets the ear.... If he had been a general in French uniform announcing that a French army was encamped at Blackheath, or another Cromwell taking away the new bauble, or even an errand-boy shouting 'Fire', he could not have produced a more general rush to the door.

Most MPs' 'style of oratory is quite safe from deterioration', and their lack of dignity was such that 'if a Member of Parliament were obliged to dance upon his head for the amusement of his constituents, it is probable that men of fortune and independence would be found to do it, and to assure the spectators that the time devoted to the feat was the proudest moment of their lives'. (In his early days in politics, Cecil considered it 'an impudence' to be asked to speak outside his own constituency.)

He thought the average MP a 'dull ornament to a drawing room, painfully addicted to talking shop', but also 'as greedy of applause as a public singer'. Committees of Supply had degenerated, since the days of the Long Parliament, into 'an exercise ground for convicted bores' where 'the graces of Metropolitan diction are the order of the day – the letter "h" is put under the table with the mace – most people sleep, some snore, a few talk, nobody listens'. Cecil blamed 'the shopocracy and the ploughocracy – the men who smirk behind counters and the men who speculate in beans' for lowering the tone of Parliament. Just because nine-tenths of MPs would not read the laws they pass, or nineteen-twentieths understand them, it did not matter, because the British Constitution, so long as Parliament remained unreformed, was 'the subtlest, and the most complicated science in which the mind of man is conversant'.

His particular parliamentary *bêtes noires* were the non-Party independent MPs – 'members upon whom nobody can depend' – and MPs who represented large metropolitan seats, whom he thought 'exist in an incessant canvass'. Nor did he have much time for dim, know-nothing Tory squires. He was conscious of the quality of Members declining as 'seats are falling to local attorneys, pushing tradesmen and contractors of various kinds, to whom a seat is an advertisement that well repays the cost'. It was all a terrible portent of what would happen after Reform, when 'men refined by thought and education will not stoop to pay this revolting tribute' and would refuse to 'supply in any abundance that bombastic and gross adulation which tickles the unfastidious vanity of the uneducated and rude'. Instead, electorates would prefer a representative who 'will swallow with the plumpest acquiescence any political formula or cry which will be put before him'. He feared that, when Reform came, 'the transient orgy of misrule in which whips govern and statesmen cringe would become the permanent order of parliamentary subordination'.

Private members' Bills were a regular butt of Cecil's mockery. 'On the wickedness of the mosquito net it is needless to enlarge,' he wrote of Lord Raynham's annual attempt to pass an animal welfare Bill. Cecil claimed that under its provisions, a free-born Briton could be consigned to gaol for three months 'for cracking fleas'. MPs who asked questions about foreign countries' internal affairs were another favoured target; he claimed that they threatened to turn the House of Commons into 'a debating society for the discussion of evils which it has no power to allay'. But somehow the mystical genius of Parliament always managed to rise above the selfish, scrabbling, ignorant boors who inhabited it, for to Cecil 'the dignity of Parliament is a subtle, impalpable essence, which it is not given to eye to see, or the mind of logician to define. Like a saint, its existence is principally known by the invocations that are addressed to it. Like a ghost it is invulnerable to all worldly weapons of attack.'

For Cecil, the only thing worse than speeches at Westminster were 'extra-parliamentary utterances', the debasing duty of speechifying at public dinners or the hustings. How could one produce something 'warm and slipshod enough to elicit the cheers of farmers who have dined', yet, when it was reported in the newspapers the following day, 'calm and polished enough to extort the admiration of readers who have not breakfasted'? Cecil believed that there were two separate languages politicians used in Parliament and at the hustings, and 'nobody likes to be overheard in the practice of those little "economies" which are necessary for the purpose of making a man intelligible to the minds of those who are his inferiors in education'. It involved 'a lavish use of superlatives in which he only half believes' and generally amounted to nothing less than 'a voluntary self-abasement'. It had to be done, however, and in the autumn Recess 'men will read even the speeches of county members at county dinners, as men will eat shoes in a siege'. One day, he hoped, farmers might find a way 'to show fat pigs against each other without thinking it necessary to conclude the ceremony by boozing and listening to bad speeches for six hours. But this is Utopian.'

The pain of Cecil's shyness and offended fastidiousness can be glimpsed at his outburst, irate by even his choleric standards, against the necessities of electioneering at all, and especially the way it involved:

days and weeks of screwed-up smiles and laboured courtesy, the mock geniality, the hearty shake of the filthy hand, the chuckling reply that must be made to the coarse joke, the loathsome, choking compliment that must be paid to the grimy wife and sluttish daughter, the indispensable flattery of the vilest religious prejudices, the wholesale deglutition of hypo-critical pledges.[5]

All this from a man who became Prime Minister without once having to fight a single contested election for any political post.

Cecil believed statesmanship to be the rare ability to govern without dishonouring oneself or ignobly leaping through the hoops held up by the electorate. The true statesman, he felt, was being subjected to more and more humiliations: 'He stands in a kind of voluntary pillory, in which it is his business to smirk and to bow with ever-increasing suavity; while the dead cats of slander and the rotten eggs of sarcasm fall thicker and thicker round his head.' If this was permitted to continue, the best men in society would soon abjure the political life altogether. 'To be obliged to utter exaggerations against which your heart and intellect revolt, to be counselled on all occasions to reiterate untenable or unmeaning formulas which in your innermost soul you utterly despise, are self-degradations to which the higher class of intellects find it very difficult to stoop.'

Reviewing a book of the Duke of Wellington's despatches, Cecil praised another of his heroes, Lord Castlereagh, for his contempt for 'whipper-in statesmanship' and the way he made 'petty parliamentary tactics appear infinitely despicable'. Cecil felt contempt for the Party Whips, calling the job 'an admission that the aspirant does not feel himself equal to a political career'. Of the duties involved, 'a gorilla of a docile character, who could be taught to articulate "Hear, Hear", would be able to perform them quite as effectively'. It was not a view he retained once he became Prime Minister.

Despite Palmerston being the leader of the Liberal Party, and no mean 'whipper-in' politician, Cecil accorded him the laurel crown of states-manship. He admired Palmerston for precisely the opposite reasons from everyone else. The general opinion was that his 'gunboat diplo-macy' foreign policy was magnificent, whereas his resistance to Reform was reprehensible. Cecil thought his and Russell's foreign policy mere bluster, but admired the way that in domestic affairs this octogenarian Whig held up parliamentary Reform. He lauded Palmerston as one of those 'cynical philosophers who look upon Parliament as more useful for what it prevents than what it performs', and many years later he told a friend that Palmerston had been the model of 'an astute and moderate leader'.

Cecil would genially criticise Palmerston's 'government by bam-boozle' and promotion of incompetent peers who had 'no conceivable recommendation except the handle to their names'. He would joke that it was not because Palmerston was a fine orator but because he was eighty years old that crowds came out to hear him, rather as they gathered 'in thousands to see Blondin cook an omelette on a tightrope'. Palmerston's easy carriage of power, however, his 'muscular accomplishments and animal spirits', but above all his 'determined immobility' over extending the franchise, engendered genuine admiration in the thirty-five-year-old MP.

'The axioms of the last age are the fallacies of the present,' Cecil wrote about his ultimate political hero, William Pitt the Younger, 'the principles which save one generation may be the ruin of the next. There is nothing abiding in political science but the necessity of truth, purity and justice.' Cecil admired Pitt because 'he was far too practical a politician to be given to abstract theories, universal doctrines, watchwords or shibboleths of any kind'. He also liked Pitt's 'calm complacency' and the lack of triumphalism with which he 'announces his victories over the Coalition in the same unimpassioned tones in which he announces that he has been to the Duchess of Bolton's'. Of Pitt's ultra-conservative reaction to the abuses of rotten boroughs and Catholic Emancipation, Cecil wrote that he accepted that 'concession must be made, but he wished to strip it of all its terrors'.

Incorruptible, unflappable, Pitt was admired by Cecil as much as his enemies, such as Charles James Fox, Richard Sheridan and the Prince Regent, were despised. 'No man was ever so yielding without being weak, or so stern without being obstinate.' Pitt's 1801 resignation over Catholic Emancipation struck Cecil as the highest point in his statesmanship. His action to protect the Sheldt in 1792 amounted to 'a war of self-defence, not a crusade', the product of the 'crucial maxim of British policy to protect Antwerp'. No one could have been better placed to combat 'the rapidity, the contagiousness, the appalling results of the disease' of Jacobinism, which 'were new to the experience of mankind'. Insofar as a man of Cecil's utter independence of spirit can be said to have had a political rôle model, his was the Younger Pitt.

Cecil's views on the relief of poverty were predictably unsentimental; he told the Hertfordshire Quarter Sessions, as its Chairman in April 1871, that: 'The state did not relieve the poor on the ground of philanthropy, but on the ground of general order, because it was found to be impossible, in a country like England, to maintain general order unless some relief was given to those who needed it.' He believed relief under the Poor Law should be administered efficiently, rather than haphazardly through private philanthropy. 'Relieving distress is a profession,

just like any other,' he told his *Saturday Review* readers in 1863.
Amateurs tended to bungle it, lose interest in the less fashionable areas
or, worst of all, lecture the poor, an attitude which he found intolerable.
Some of his most passionate journalism was directed against those Poor
Law Guardians who ran 'mean' workhouses, and he argued for a single
Poor Law rate across the capital, rather than one which varied from
parish to parish. The diseases to which some of the poorest were susceptible were, he wrote, 'a disgrace to our civilisation, and a rebuke to the
boastful generosity of our land'.

Cecil believed protection for property, rather than pure charity, was
the ultimate point of poverty relief, which was why he castigated those
Poor Law Guardians who tried to evade their legal responsibilities and
turned paupers away from their workhouses, leaving them 'to live on
air, or mud, or any other substance which he might be able to obtain
gratis on the streets'. This amounted to an invitation to burglary and
petty theft: 'Vice offers him a good dinner at a moment's notice; virtue
offers him a bad dinner in a week's time.'

In an article entitled 'Casual Shepherds', Cecil attacked the practice
of middle-class amateurs visiting the slums to try to do good.
Clergymen and professionals who knew the individual cases involved
might genuinely help, but the well-intentioned benevolence of
outsiders was worse than useless, he argued. Cecil likened the activities
of part-time do-gooders to the action of the Governor of Jamaica who, in
order to exterminate snakes on the island, paid for each head brought to
him, thereby succeeding only in encouraging snake-breeding. 'It is the
same with all efforts to root up any evil by the expenditure of money.
To attach a money value to the existence of an evil, even for the purpose
of extirpating it, can have no other end than that of multiplying the
evil.' Cecil never believed in 'bribing vice to be virtuous', however
much it might be 'a soothing amusement to philanthropists', not least
because it would never work. 'If chastity and short commons are to be
pitted against vice and victuals, it needs no prophet to foretell the
issue.'

Yet Cecil was equally pessimistic about Christianity's chances of
improving the moral character of the very poor:

> In ancient times, the poor are recorded to have been eminently the most
> forward to receive the truth; in modern times, it is necessary that a district
> should be made tolerably comfortable before there is any hope that the
> clergyman can be successful....Christianity forced its way up from being
> the religion of slaves and outcasts, to become the religion of the powerful
> and rich; but somehow it seems to have lost the power of forcing its way
> down again.

Salisbury entirely denied that there was anything inherently noble about poverty. The State had a duty to ensure that the poor never turned revolutionary, but poverty itself was an unfortunate part of the human condition which it was quite outside the capacity of anyone to eradicate.

One aspect of poverty that produced a surprising response from Cecil was prostitution. Society, he argued, had closed its eyes to the way that 'soiled doves' had become a 'formidable nuisance' in central London, leading to falling rents in some once-fashionable areas. Prostitutes, he said in February 1862, 'have seized upon the West End like an army of occupation. We might almost as well refuse to recognise a flight of locusts, or the fleas on an Italian bed, or the touters on the pier at Boulogne. The principal streets are in their hands. The pavement in the Haymarket they rule with a sway that no prudent passenger will come to challenge after the sun has fallen.' Unsolicited advances from prostitutes were commonplace in Regent Street, Pall Mall and Regent's Park, French prostitutes promenaded in Portland Place, yet 'still we flatter ourselves that our national morality is benefited by the fact that we recognise them only in the newspapers, and are absolutely silent about them in the Statute Book'.

Such classically Victorian hypocrisy about prostitution elicited a maverick response from Cecil. Instead of harsh police action, as one might have expected from the rest of his stance on law and order, in June 1862 he proposed that the Government should attempt to 'arrest the progress of a plague' of venereal disease by having the sex industry 'duly catalogued and registered', as it was in Paris, Berlin, Vienna and Hong Kong. Pretending 'to check the growth of this vice ... would be ridiculously futile', but it should be made less dangerous medically and removed from the streets. No longer should 'the half-tipsy, half-amorous sirens of the pavement' be allowed to make the 'raven-like croak in which their endearments to the passer-by are conveyed'. Once again, this was not really presented out of social altruism: 'The modesty of landlords has endured a great deal; but when it comes to the falling of rents, they must speak out.'[6] In his attitude to both poverty and prostitution, Cecil's underlying lack of faith in the perfectibility of mankind was powerfully manifest.

Cecil admired Gladstone's High Churchmanship, learning and obvious high character, and he was starting to share his distrust of Disraeli. 'The struggles of so powerful a wrestler, whether they succeed or fail,' wrote Cecil in an article entitled 'The Future Prime Minister', three years before Gladstone reached No. 10, 'will shake the arena on which they take place.' Cecil's respect for Gladstone's talents never diminished, but by the mid-1860s he thought he had given too much away to the Radicals in his Party, a suspicion which grew with the years until he was convinced that Gladstone had himself actually converted to Radicalism.

At the time of Gladstone's masterful 1860 Free Trade Budget, Cecil reported that 'throughout the whole four hours of intricate argument neither voice nor mind faltered for an instant', despite the Chancellor's 'impressive' bronchitis. It was 'one of the finest combinations of reasoning and declamation that has ever been heard within the walls of the House of Commons', a judgment that history has subsequently confirmed. The Budget itself was 'pure Gladstonism – that terrible combination of relentless logic and dauntless imagination...we soar into the empyrean of finance'. Cecil opposed Gladstone's policy of remitting and abolishing hundreds of tariffs, whilst transferring the burden from indirect duties to direct tax. The great advantage of placing duties upon imported luxuries was that they were essentially voluntary. Gladstone's changes confirmed his fears that taxation would become 'the vital question of modern politics', to be used increasingly as the primary weapon in the class war.

Although its Peelite formulæ delivered mid-Victorian prosperity, Cecil opposed Gladstone's reforms on grounds of precedent, arguing that 'we have now entered upon the descent of the smooth, easy, sloping path of popular finance, on which there is no halting-place to check our career short of confiscation'. He nevertheless had to admire Gladstone's financial mastery in devising, explaining and forcing the Budget through, although he came close to using unparliamentary language when he described the remission of duties on paper, which would aid Gladstone's allies in the burgeoning Liberal local press, as a 'dodge'.[7]

When the Chancellor reduced the tariffs on 440 items to just forty, Cecil ascribed it to 'the abstract love of symmetry which belongs to a worshipper of the beautiful'. He noted 'the amoeban ode of mutual compliment' between the rivals Gladstone and Bright, but accused the Chancellor of cheese-paring over Civil Service pay and using the philosophy that 'unless your driver grumbles a little, you may be sure you have overpayed him'. These were intended as little more than glancing blows. When Gladstone encountered effusive public adulation on visits to Middlesbrough and Gateshead in the autumn of 1862, Cecil commented that 'to most people so greasy a dish would have been nauseous', but then he himself took personal modesty to absurd lengths. Cecil had a weak stomach for compliments, which he considered 'discreditable to the utterer, and odious to the receiver'. Gladstone was, as he wrote a week later, 'a hippopotamus....He is something to walk around, to stare at, to poke up.'

Cecil's reportage in describing Gladstone's great parliamentary clashes with Disraeli featured some of the best of his writing. Disraeli, at his most ferocious over Gladstone's 1862 Budget, fired a 'volley of sarcasms' at the surprisingly thin-skinned Chancellor:

> Every shot obviously tells. As the attack goes on, [Gladstone's] colour grows whiter and whiter, his eyes flash and his lips curl, and his whole expression alters with the nervous tension of the muscles on his face. He keeps himself still with difficulty, and if a chance offers, he interrupts with some sharp and snappish contradiction.

The result was that, after 'the single combat of the two embittered chieftains', Gladstone came off worst, having 'hit about him wildly, like an infuriated rustic fighting with a professional'. Cecil's inheritance, and the weaker calibre of the opposition provided by the Liberal front bench in the House of Lords, sadly meant that he himself was denied the chance ever to be pitted against a worthy opponent in one of those great Victorian gladiatorial contests.

By 1863, Cecil's high view of Gladstone had started to change: for 'Whatever is recondite and circuitous, and ingenious, and paradoxical – whatever is the reverse of plain and simple,' he wrote that July, 'he has an irrepressible hankering.' Although Cecil saw no competition for Gladstone as Palmerston's successor, and admitted that he was the most brilliant orator of his day, he felt obliged also to mention 'the schoolmaster tone', 'his many political failures', and the way in which the House of Commons could be 'offended by the extreme superciliousness of manner'.

It was, however, on 11th May 1864, when Gladstone announced his support for universal suffrage, that Cecil's stance towards him entirely altered. 'The kaleidoscopic effect of his parliamentary life would be incomplete without this latest vagary,' he had written the previous month. By May, Cecil was denouncing Gladstone's 'theories which would have satisfied the most violent Chartists' and predicted, correctly as it turned out, that 'the future wanderings of a meteor so wayward' would one day include an attempt to end the veto powers of the House of Lords. Cecil believed Gladstone should have 'arrived at a time of life when "phases of opinion" should cease', but in fact the Grand Old Man's long trek towards Radicalism still had a long way to go. In September 1865, Cecil predicted that if Gladstone 'persists in making himself the master of democracy, he will have raised against himself a phalanx of powerful interests and tenacious animosities against which no displays of talent will avail'.[8] When two decades later this prediction came true, the leader of that phalanx was none other than Cecil himself.

FIVE

Politics

The House of Commons – The Oaths Bill – Competitive
Examination – Education – Parliamentary Reform

1857 to 1866

'His motto in politics and religion is: "No surrender!"'

Cecil's journalism covered a myriad of other subjects: the House of Lords, trade unionism, the Poor Laws, Civil Service competitive examinations, the French Revolution and so on. Whilst he wrote these slashing, witty, dyspeptic pieces, Cecil was simultaneously pursuing an active parliamentary career. His speeches and votes – against the 'revolutionary measure' to abolish the Church Rate, against Sir John Pakington's education schemes which he denounced as 'the secular system in disguise', and even against a Bill to decommission superfluous City churches which was supported by the bishops – won him a prominent place on the right wing of the Conservative Party, despite his relative youth.

When Palmerston's ministry fell on 26th February 1858, Cecil wrote to Lord Derby to apply for office, either in the Government or in the colonies: 'I venture to make this direct solicitation because I find that everyone believes that the son of a very wealthy father must be well off.' In fact, as he told the incoming Conservative Prime Minister, he was 'in difficulty about the means of support'. Although MPs were unpaid, ministers received large salaries, and Georgina was pregnant with their first child, Beatrix Maud, who was born on 17th May. Derby replied politely, but said: 'I do not see how it is to be done.' Considering Cecil's criticisms of Disraeli in recent articles as 'damaged goods' and as dull an orator as 'a village schoolmaster lecturing a form of ploughboys', it is difficult to see how Derby could possibly have obliged.[1] The reason for Cecil's hostility to Disraeli was the former Chancellor's willingness to damage the Palmerston Whig Government by appealing to the Radicals to Palmerston's left, especially over the issue of Reform.

Benjamin Disraeli had been writing novels since Cecil was two years old and had been an MP since Cecil was seven. He had known Cecil's grandmother and was a friend and Cabinet colleague of his father. A week before applying for office in the Government in which Disraeli was the presiding genius, as well as Chancellor of the Exchequer and Leader of the House of Commons, Cecil had expressed his distrust of the 'vague moralisations' and 'mysterious views' of Disraeli's novels. He had read *Coningsby* whilst at school, but what he thought of the rhapsodic gush about the 'bowery meads of Eton' – the first spoken words of the novel are 'Floreat Etona!' – sadly went unrecorded. It was, however, an early intimation that Disraeli and the truth were at best on nodding acquaintanceship.

Cecil believed, not without justification, that Disraeli, who had flirted with Radicalism early in his political life, was 'one whose Conservative convictions were an accident of his career'. He also thought that, during Palmerston's lifetime, Tory principles were probably better served by having a Whig government in power than a Conservative one which was constantly bidding for Radical support. In temperament and outlook, therefore, Disraeli and Cecil were likely to have clashed politically. But the personal, searing bitterness, at least on Cecil's side – Disraeli was extraordinarily tolerant throughout – was not preordained.

When in May 1858 Lord Exeter complained to Cecil about a remark he had made about Disraeli, his reply to his parliamentary sponsor had to be couched in fulsome language: 'I have a great deal to thank you for, and am very anxious that everything I do so long as I am in the House of Commons should be quite satisfactory to you,' he began. As to the central accusation, he claimed to have been 'curtly quoted', but 'though, in common with many Conservatives, I cannot in private quite approve of many things which Mr Disraeli has said and done, I have never had any other intention than to give the Government all the support in my power in the House of Commons', if not, he implied, in the *Saturday Review*.

By July, in need of his £118.8s.1d Stamford election expenses, Cecil wrote to his father to say that Disraeli, who was stung but not hurt by his criticisms, 'has intimated to me that he proposes offering me an Under-Secretaryship shortly. To what extent I can look on that as a promise I do not know – but it has had the effect of altering my plans materially.' With a young family in the offing, Cecil needed a larger house, and Disraeli's semi-offer of preferment persuaded him not to move out of London. He wanted to take a £1,600 lease on a property, but with his severe lack of capital he needed his mother's £10,000 to secure it. His father sent a cheque for only £200, and the following month Cecil had to admit: 'I understand Mr Disraeli's promises of offering me an Under-Secretaryship were entirely a mistake on his part.'

Instead, it was a far less attractive Commissionership of the Inland Revenue which fell vacant. Cecil thought seriously about taking the job for its regular salary, although as 'an office of profit under the Crown' it would require leaving Parliament. Writing to his father again, he shrewdly dropped the demand for his mother's money and instead emphasised that 'all I am asking for is sufficient information as to my own future to guide me in the present instance.... I do not think you would wish me to shelve myself now by seeking permanent place.' He asked his father for an early answer, which is all he did get: 'I lose no time in anwering your letter. You have placed yourself in a position with reference to me which makes it impossible for me to offer you advice, whatever interest I may take in your welfare.' Disraeli himself was predictably suave – 'my vexation is not inferior to your own...the Government have been deprived of abilities which I highly appreciate' – but it was Derby's son, Lord Stanley, who came out best from the distressing incident, in which Cecil almost became a taxman instead of a statesman. He advised Cecil not to sacrifice his political prospects for a pecuniary advantage which though immediate was small. It was advice he was one day to have cause bitterly to regret.

Cecil opposed the 1858 Jewish Oaths Bill; he even disliked the idea of Roman Catholics and nonconformists belonging to the House of Commons, which he considered was not primarily a secular assembly. As with Oxford, which he looked upon as a type of seminary for Anglicans, he wanted Parliament to be true to what he saw as its original statutes and the Church–State connection, and refuse to admit non-Anglicans. Cecil was too intelligent and rational to be ideologically anti-Semitic, although occasionally disparaging remarks about Jews do crop up in his correspondence, in the same way that they do about the Americans, Greeks, Boers, Portuguese, Italians, Montenegrins and especially the Irish. Ridiculing an essay by a German author in November 1863, who claimed that the Jews were becoming masters of the world, Cecil asked why other, respectable contributors to the book in question had not refused to appear in his literary company? 'It is very rarely that money will induce a Jew to lend himself to a false oath,' he wrote in a review of a book about German crime and punishment, and blamed the Germans for the fact that the Jews formed 'the nucleus of the outlaw and criminal population' there.

Cecil wrote to Carnarvon of Disraeli's 'Hebrew tricks' when describing his tactical wiliness, and when Foreign Secretary he brushed off Jewish deputations demanding full civil rights for the Jews of Romania with talk of eastern European instability. Although he appointed Lord

Rothschild as the first Jewish Lord-Lieutenant in 1889, two years later
he refused to allow Sir Robert Morier, Britain's first Ambassador to St
Petersburg, to remonstrate with the Tsar about Russia's pogroms. He
argued that the Lord Mayor of London might forward a protest through
any channel he liked, but the British Ambassador 'ought not to touch it
with a pair of tongs', for fear of impairing the all-important Anglo-
Russian relationship. The following year Salisbury went further, and
privately asked Morier whether he could take any steps to stop Jews
emigrating to Britain, not placing the request in a formal despatch
'because it is evidently so delicate'.

In the debate on the Oaths Bill on 22nd March 1858, Cecil pointed out
that the House of Commons was the guardian of the Church of England
and the questions which excited the most political interest were those
of a religious nature, which was undoubtedly true at the time.
Controversial political issues such as Church Rates, the endowment of
the Irish Catholic seminary at Maynooth, Sunday openings at the
British Museum, denominational education and the perennial question
of whether to legalise marriage with a deceased wife's sister were all
based on religious belief. Of the fifty divisions taken before the Easter
recess, twenty-six had been on secular and twenty-four on religious
questions. 'The insincere Jew will only legislate according to his own
interests, and in order to make political capital, like any other member,'
Cecil said in the debate. 'It was the sincere Jew who has pledged to
legislate against Christianity.' One of the 'insincere' Jews Cecil doubtless had in mind was otherwise the Anglican-baptised but racially
Jewish Disraeli, who had referred to 'my Lord and Saviour' in a speech
supporting the removal of their disabilities in 1847.

In a subject which temporarily split the Conservative Party – four
Cabinet ministers voted against the measure, as well as the Chief Whip
and Sir Hugh Cairns, the Solicitor-General – Cecil had made his mark.
His stance had brought round Lord Exeter, who, when Disraeli wrote at
Christmas asking whether one of his vacant parliamentary seats could
go to Lord Henry Lennox, replied that it was being kept warm for Cecil
in case Disraeli's Reform Bill should abolish Stamford as a separate
constituency.[2]

Exeter had a good eye for parliamentary talent, and on 28th April 1859
Stamford returned Cecil to Parliament in the General Election along
with a baronet called Sir Stafford Northcote. The polling in the town
hall was attended by only forty-four people. After a brief speech from
Cecil supporting Church Rates, opposing Reform – 'the effect would be
to swamp property and intelligence' – and a sideswipe against warring
Austria and Sardinia – 'both sides were in the wrong' – the two men
were elected unopposed. A month earlier Cecil had turned down the
offer of the Governorship of Moreton Bay in Australia because, although

it would have paid him £2,500 per annum, he had to finance his own expenses. 'I am afraid it would not pay in a commercial point of view,' he assured the Colonial Secretary, Sir Edward Bulwer-Lytton, 'and to the commercial point of view I am compelled to pay a very humiliating regard.' To a disappointed father he explained that he 'must be in a very bad way before I should undertake an office, out of which I could only screw a profit by doing it badly'.

Apart from promoting, in vain, a scheme to introduce postal ballots, the rest of 1859 was spent attacking Disraeli for supporting a Reform Bill which offered 'fancy' franchise qualifications. These attacks began in earnest in *Bentley's Quarterly Review* in March, where Cecil lambasted Disraeli's 'serpentine' career, arguing that 'hostility to Radicalism, incessant, implacable hostility, is the essential definition of Conservatism', whereas Disraeli was only out to buy 'Radical support in the enterprise of ousting the Whigs'. That same month in the *Saturday Review*, he observed how in introducing his Reform Bill to a packed house,

> Disraeli always on such occasions seems to be arranging his attitude to suit a possible photographer in the gallery. He throws back his coat, makes a theatrical pause, eyes the Gentile rabble in front of him for a moment with supreme contempt, and then, remembering that meekness is the fitting emblem of conscious genius, drops his head and begins in an inaudible murmur. For the first hour, like all Mr Disraeli's exordiums, the speech was intolerably dull.

The Reform Bill itself was tame, only fifteen seats redistributed and not one borough disenfranchised, nor did Cecil oppose it outright but only tried to amend it in committee, but he hated the fact that the Tories were undertaking it at all, especially through bidding for Radical support. 'There is no escape on earth', he wrote, 'from taxes, toothache or the statesmanship of Mr Disraeli.'[3] Cecil claimed that a snap division Disraeli had called in June 'savoured more of the *legerdemain* of a thimble-rigger than of the tactics of a parliamentary chief'. What was really only smart parliamentary footwork in avoiding a damaging Commons defeat drew forth Cecil's pent-up (and surely libellous) invective against his Commons Party leader:

> The truth is that his life, from his first appearance in the journalist's world down to the present hour, has been spent in dodging, and he cannot leave it off.... He has reached the *delirium tremens* stage of treachery. Everybody knows half a dozen people in whom the taste for lying is so developed, that they will live for the mere pleasure of the thing, even when the lie is certain to be found out. The present leader of the House of Commons is a victim of the same sort of possession. He is bewitched by the demon of low dodging.

The next month, July 1859, saw Cecil attack Disraeli's 'oriental cunning', 'the foulness of his language in [denouncing Peel in] 1846', and his 'ceaseless intrigues and unscrupulous invective'. Of his Tory supporters, whose 'guide is self-interest and their moving power spite', Cecil also blamed 'the obtuseness of the bucolic mind'. This article, entitled 'The Artless Dodger', and the previous one in *Bentley's Quarterly Review* in which Cecil had called Disraeli 'the grain of dirt that clogs the whole machine', drew an angry letter from Salisbury in defence of his 'distinguished Cabinet colleague'. It made the reasonable point that Cecil's voting record of support for Disraeli in the chamber 'must therefore lead to the conclusion that your avowed opinions are greatly at variance with those of which you entertain anonymously'.

This stung Cecil's sense of honour. 'I am wholly unconscious of the discrepancy,' he answered the following day. 'I have never concealed my opinion of Mr Disraeli, and lapse of years has rather strengthened than improved it.' He added that he was even ruder in private conversations than in his journalism, adding that it was perfectly possible to be a Conservative in the Commons without having to trust the Conservative leader there, and that plenty of other Tory MPs agreed. The barb at the end of Cecil's letter was unmistakable: 'It must be remembered that I write for money. Various concurring circumstances have left me with no other means of gaining money.... I must write in the style that is most likely to attract, and therefore to sell.' Although it was popular enough with other Tories on the Right, such as his brother-in-law Alexander Beresford-Hope and his brother Eustace, such ostentatious disloyalty brought opprobrium from many other Conservatives. Years later, he referred to himself in this period as having been 'an Ishmaelite', referring to Genesis chapter 16 verse 12: 'His hand against every man and every man's against him.' During the Church Rates controversy, Palmerston told a friend: 'Beware of that young man, he possesses one of the secrets of success, for instead of defending himself and his cause, he attacks the other side.'

Having never made more than a total of five speeches a year in the House of Commons in his first four years, and only three each in 1858 and 1859 when the Earl of Derby was briefly in office, Cecil spoke thirteen times in 1860, a rate he was to keep up for almost the whole of the rest of his time there. These orations were just as slashing as his prose. Gladstone's attempt to replace the duty on paper with a penny increase in income tax he denounced as 'plundering finance' intended to subsidise out of the Exchequer the cheap newspapers belonging to his new allies. When the House of Lords rejected Gladstone's Paper Duties Bill, Cecil applauded their stalwart defence of their class and political interests, only to find Gladstone putting his measures in his Budget, which then passed the House of Lords in June 1861.

Cecil sent the Commons into uproar when he denounced Gladstone's action as 'more worthy of an attorney than of a statesman'. This was considered unacceptable parliamentary language, as attorneys were not necessarily gentlemen. A few days later he got up and, having used the terms that usually led up to an expression of contrition, he said he wanted to apologise. Just as the House was murmuring its approval he added, 'to the attorneys'. The indignant Commons roared its anger and refused to hear the rest of his speech, but for all his rudeness Cecil had unmistakably made his name as one of its foremost controversialists.

One of the reasons Cecil opposed the remission of paper duties was that he did not believe it 'could be maintained that a person of any education could learn anything worth knowing from a penny paper'. When it was observed that at least they reported parliamentary debates, Cecil retorted: 'Well, would that contribute to their education?' In his *Saturday Review* round-up of the year 1860, he wrote that Gladstone 'will continue to be the universal solvent of Administrations, with eloquence enough to shatter any from which he is excluded, and crotchets enough to split up any to which he belongs'.

On the issue of competitive examinations for civil servants, hitherto appointed almost entirely through jobbery, nepotism and patronage, Cecil was as witty as he was reactionary. Merciless was the ridicule he directed against those hapless reformers who wished to rationalise the archaic process, arguing that theirs was simply a plan 'for the bestowing of appointments not upon persons who are qualified for them, but upon those who had shown their fitness for something else'. Examinations, he felt, were 'at best a sorry test for discovering the qualifications that are fittest to govern men', and the idea that candidates could prove their ability to govern India by asking them to turn Goethe's *Iphigenia* into tragic trimeters struck him as ludicrous. In the Foreign Office, the duties of a junior attaché in foreign missions would 'be far better performed by a dandy to whom William the Conqueror was a myth... than by any professor in either university.... To submit a man whose most important duty is to dangle about at parties and balls to any intellectual test, except that of a knowledge of French, is to ignore the real objects of his profession.'

Cecil denounced the way that 'a clique of theorists' had decided to impose professionalism even on the army, despite the fact that Wellington or Marlborough 'would have been floored by a request to make impromptu quotations from the Greek tragic poets'. The result would be 'battalions of mooning, narrow-chested, blear-eyed bookworms whom modern progress will place at the head of our troops'. He put in a word for patronage, asking: 'Why should favour and friendship, kindness and gratitude, which are not banished by men from private life, be absolutely excluded from public affairs?' To appoint someone whom you know and trust was surely better than some clever stranger; after all, 'Sir Robert Walpole's bribery saved his country: Necker's purity ruined his.' Just as one did not choose a Chancellor of the Exchequer for his moral character – a clear dig at Disraeli – or a boot-maker for his religious principles, which would 'generally end in financial embarrassment and sore feet', so the Civil Service would only be filled 'with pedants and malcontents' if bureaucrats were chosen simply on intellectual merit.

The exams themselves were fantastically hard, and Cecil made great play in pointing out how hopeful Colonial Office candidates were required to state concisely David Ricardo's theory of rent, Inland Revenue officials had to know 'on which side of the Himalayas were the sources of the Indus, the Ganges and the Brahmapootra', and Customs and Excise officers had to list six of the principal mountain ranges in Europe, stating the countries to which they belonged, their extent, height, directions and most striking physical features. 'Only if ships were in the habit of clearing the Alps or Carpathians,' wrote Cecil, would 'these questions be very pertinent to the duties of a custom-house clerk.'[4]

Meanwhile the assault on Disraeli continued, as Cecil likened his career to that of Napoleon III, calling him a 'vulture', 'shameless' and possessing 'unrivalled powers of conducting his Party into the ditch'. On Disraeli's political dexterity over Reform, and especially his attempts to attract Radical support, Cecil declared that: 'An Englishman half asleep may be coaxed into giving away what the same man threatened and aroused would rather die than yield.'

When Salisbury wrote his son a curt letter refusing to finance any further election expenses, Cecil replied that if forced to decide between his parliamentary seat and his journalism he would have to choose the latter: 'I shall earn a deal more by my pen than I should ever get by my tongue,' and wondered aloud whether 'the House of Commons is not a sheer waste of time'. The result of 'Your driving me from Parliament would not tend to stop my writing... only that I should be more free and have more leisure.' As for his father's colleague:

> I have ceased to condemn Mr Disraeli because he has ceased to deserve it. Much as I dislike and despise the man, I should abstain from attacking him needlessly, for the sake of the party to which he is unfortunately attached.... I have merely put into print what all the county gentlemen were saying in private.... I cannot change my convictions to suit his intrigues.

Yet, as Gwendolen wrote later of this period, if Cecil 'entertained any

undue sense of his importance as a mutineer', it must have been effectively dissipated when he met Disraeli by accident at a country house
one weekend. 'Robert, ah Robert, how pleased I am to meet you!' said
Disraeli, enveloping his embarrassed antagonist in his arms.

When a son was born to the Cecils on 23rd October 1861, Cranborne
wrote a rare letter to his younger brother asking that the child should be
named James 'after my Lord', their father, a request to which Cecil
readily agreed. He only received a frigidly polite letter of congratulations from Salisbury in acknowledgment. If there was no immediate
reconciliation, there was at least the abatement of hostilities, because,
as Cecil wrote to Carnarvon on 31st March 1861, 'Dizzy, converted from
evil ways, has behaved like an angel' in supporting Palmerston against
Bright on all possible occasions. Cecil had nevertheless not altered his
opinion that 'if a Government is to depend on Liberal support I think it
is much better for the reputation of public men that it should be one
calling itself Liberal and not one calling itself Conservative – though the
names are great trash'.

By 1862, relations had improved with his father enough for him to be
able to send on the £122.16s.1d bill for his Stamford expenses, which
included subscriptions for a footbridge to commemorate the Prince
Consort, who had died the previous December, as well as for the county's
agricultural show at Burghley Park. 'The Stamford people are getting very
shameless in their begging, and we [Cecil and Northcote] disregard as
many applicants as we can,' he told his father. 'It is a consolation to
reflect that Prince Albert cannot die next year again, and that the
Northamptonshire Agricultural Association will not meet at Stamford.'

The doorkeeper of the House of Commons, William White, wrote of
Cecil in his diary in March 1863:

> He is haughty and proud, of an intractable temper. He cannot submit to
> party discipline…he is too Conservative for modern times. He is a High
> Churchman. In politics he is a Tory. His motto in politics and religion is
> "No Surrender!"… In short he is a man of a past age, has no sympathy with
> the life, the stir and growth of the present, and no belief in the future.

Cecil himself would doubtless have agreed with every word. At a dinner
to found the Oxford Conservative Association that July, and to support
the local candidate Gathorne Gathorne-Hardy against Gladstone, Cecil
declared: 'Every Churchman must be a good Conservative, and every
Conservative a good Churchman,' which caused much controversy,
especially when he repeated it in the House of Commons. Once again,
however, it did nothing to harm his prospects on the Tory Right.

In January 1864, Derby told his son Lord Stanley that he expected to form a government that year and that he would send Cecil to the Foreign Office as Lord Malmesbury's Under-Secretary. A week later, Cecil was invited to an eve-of-session dinner at Disraeli's house, where a dozen senior Tories discussed the Queen's Speech. Cecil had been in the Commons for ten years and had to be taken seriously by the Party leadership, despite his rebellious barbs. At dinner with Disraeli at Bellamy's, the famous Westminster restaurant, on 19th February, Stanley heard how Cecil, 'though mollified by hopes of office', belonged to the party of Tory malcontents who only numbered about twenty-five, but who 'had the sympathies of many more'.

Stanley, a Tory Radical, believed the malcontents damaged the Party; he likened them to Bright's position in the Liberal Party. When on 6th May 1864 Cecil was 'cheered from all sides' for his vehement speech in support of the Danish duchies, Stanley was convinced that Cecil did the Tory cause 'more harm than good: for he made it appear as though he wished us to go to war', which he later assured Stanley was not his intention at all, thinking it 'too late and useless'. Rebellion was of course a well-established way to achieve junior office, but that was not primarily what motivated Cecil.

When in July 1864 he submitted his £137.11s.3d bill for Stamford (girls' school: 15 shillings, soup kitchen: 10 shillings, agent's bill: £70), Cecil and his wife, who was seven months pregnant, were invited to visit Hatfield for the first time since their marriage in 1857. Disraeli and Stanley were also present, and the latter recorded how: 'It was curious to see Robert in his own home looking around at the improvements, of which there were many.... Both he and Lady Robert were evidently nervous and ill at ease.' Relations were re-established and by September 1864, Salisbury was writing to his son as 'My dear Robert' once again. With his black beard, premature baldness, stoop and serious demeanour, photographs of the time depict Cecil as a man who looked considerably in excess of his thirty-four years.

Because he thought education to be a crucial issue of the age, the arena where atheism must be fought, it was always in the first rank of political questions in which Cecil interested himself. He admitted it to be 'unromantic', but flung himself into the subject nonetheless, stalwart in the defence of Anglican denominational education. Even the moderate Education Rate proposed in 1856, by which local authorities took over education funding from the Privy Council grants system, he had denounced as 'the thin end of the wedge of disestablishment'. Believing that 'the middle classes are the powerful and ruling classes of the country', who therefore needed 'enlightened knowledge', Cecil became Senior Trustee of the Rev. Nathaniel Woodard's movement to build a series of independent schools to be run on Tractarian principles. At the public meeting to launch the movement, held at Brighton Town Hall on 2nd December 1856, the nonconformists organised an anti-Puseyite demonstration, and Cecil, Beresford-Hope and the Bishop of Winchester had to try hard to make themselves heard above catcalls, insults, hissing, groans, foot-stamping and incessant interruptions.

Over the following decades, under the direction of Woodard, the movement was responsible for the establishment of Hurstpierpoint, Ardingly, Lancing, King Alfred's Taunton and several other High Church schools. At the inaugural meeting in Brighton Woodard had failed to distance himself from the doctrine of auricular confession, for which Cecil nearly resigned, as 'I dislike the Roman doctrine too heavily to suffer myself willingly to seem to approve it.' As he told his friend Charles Conybeare some years later, confession might do some good in some special cases, but 'as a general practice it is, at its best, fatal to moral vigour, at its worst an instrument of corruption or ambition'. By 1857 this potential schism was patched up, and in 1872 Cecil wrote to Woodard, then organising a series of public dinners to raise money for further schools, enclosing a cheque but refusing the invitation with the excuse that: 'Dying by slow indigestion is an exquisite form of martyrdom which never occurred to the pagans.' Years later when a junior minister was promoted to the Education department, he consoled him that 'dull as the work of keeping parsons in good humour is, you are on a higher official level'.[5]

As well as bridge-building with his father, 1864 also saw Cecil take the scalp of perhaps the cleverest minister in the Government, when he forced Robert Lowe to resign as Vice-President of the Council, the Education portfolio. An albino intellectual who had spent much of his life in Australia, Lowe was as unlike the archetypal Liberal Cabinet minister as Cecil was unlike the archetypal Conservative politician of the day. Cecil discovered that several of Her Majesty's Inspectors of Schools had sent reports to the Privy Council chastising the Government's new Revised Code for Education – which Cecil had long denounced as 'violent and doctrinaire' and 'the last of the imported Yankee "notions"' – but that these had not been published in the Blue Book. 'From Mr Lowe's proceedings,' Cecil wrote in the *Saturday Review* whilst simultaneously bringing up the matter in Parliament, 'it is evident that Blue Books are meant, not for the information of those who read them, but for the recreation and solace of those who write them.'

Using documents leaked to him by disaffected inspectors, Cecil accused Lowe on 12th April 1864 of having doctored the Blue Books, claiming that 'the mutilation of the reports ... are violations in and tend entirely to destroy the value' of what the inspectors had originally written. Whilst Lowe was actually on his feet denying that his department had underlined certain passages for censorship, Cecil started to circulate the leaked report with its underlined passages. The near-blind Lowe, who could not see what was happening, was 'disconcerted by the hum and laughter moving along the benches'. When Lowe had got up to speak, many of the Government front bench, expecting a dull, prolonged debate, had gone off for dinner, so the House was lightly attended. Seizing his opportunity, Cecil called for a snap division. Palmerston and Gladstone managed to get back from their meals just in time, but the Government was defeated by 101 to 93. A dozen Liberals voted with Cecil and the House roared with laughter when it heard the result. Lowe resigned six days later, and although a Select Committee accepted his explanation that he had no personal knowledge of what had gone on, he was not reappointed.

His personal involvement did not prevent Cecil from anonymously writing the story up in the *Saturday Review* that weekend, referring to himself in the third person and arguing that it should have been Lord Granville, the Lord President of the Council, who resigned, rather than the estimable Vice-President. Palmerston reported to the Queen that: 'Lord Robert Cecil, who never loses an opportunity of saying or doing an unhandsome thing, lost a fair opportunity of taking a handsome and generous line, and alone cavilled at and criticised Mr Lowe's statement.' The doorkeeper was also unimpressed by Cecil's success, writing that: 'There is not another member of the House that we know who carries on now in this fashion.' Whatever the rules of politeness dictated, Cecil had taken the scalp of a brilliant senior minister and proved himself a dangerous political force.

On the morning of Wednesday, 14th June 1865, during a debate on the Oxford Tests Bill, Cecil was called out of the Commons chamber to be informed of the death of his elder brother Lord Cranborne, who was forty-two. His death certificate gives the cause as congestion of the lungs, after two days of illness. Unfortunately, such was Cecil's natural reserve that we can only speculate as to his reaction to the news, as with other family bereavements. 'A great change in his position and future,' noted Gathorne-Hardy in his diary the next day, 'which affects our party much.' Cecil's succession to the courtesy title of Viscount Cranborne, and more importantly to the direct succession to Hatfield, came almost as a relief to their father, whose 'strongest feeling is attachment to his family as an institution – and wish that its importance should continue'. The Cecils, now Lord and Lady Cranborne, were by then on 'good and friendly terms' with the Salisburys and regular visitors to Hatfield.[6] Before his brother's death, Cecil had written 589 pieces for the *Saturday Review*; after it he only wrote nineteen, mostly on political issues in which he was personally involved. Now heir to Hatfield, the days of writing for a living about the combustibility of crinolines were over.

When in July 1865 a serious plague in cattle was first diagnosed, the Royal Veterinary College reported to the Privy Council that the cows were dying from a malignant disease then unknown to science. In September, a Royal Commission was appointed to stamp it out, under the Chairmanship of the 5th Earl Spencer, a distinguished Liberal. Robert Lowe, the chemistry professor Lyon Playfair and the new Lord Cranborne also sat on it. After quickly taking scientific and agricultural evidence, its report only a month later advocated draconian measures concerning the export, transport and slaughter of cattle. These were attacked by farmers and in the press, but once Parliament had adopted them the following February the disease was swiftly defeated. Cranborne and Spencer were appointed to protect the landed, farming interest, but they supported the recommendations, and, although in February 1866 18,000 new cases had been reported, by the end of April they were down to 5,000. In November, there were only eight new cases and the country was offically declared plague-free by 1867.

On 18th October 1865, Lord Palmerston died in office. Cranborne had admired him for providing what he called 'the resistance of a sandbag' and for doing the 'most difficult and most salutary [thing] for a Parliament to do – nothing'. He was one of the few leading Opposition MPs to attend Palmerston's funeral and had good reason to regret his passing. Cranborne feared that, with Palmerston gone, the issue of Reform would soon raise its head, and he was right. Palmerston was replaced by Lord John Russell, who had become Earl Russell in 1861, as Prime Minister, with Gladstone as Leader of the House of Commons and Cabinet places for George Goschen, the financier, and soon afterwards the Marquis of Hartington as Secretary for War.

By February 1866, Cranborne was being spoken of as a future Cabinet minister, should a group of about fifty right-wing Liberals led by Robert Lowe split from Lord John Russell's Government over the comprehensive Reform Bill that Gladstone was promoting, and 'fuse' with the Conservatives. Just turning thirty-six, Cranborne was even being discussed as a future Foreign Secretary, although his hawkish behaviour over the Schleswig-Holstein Question and the American Civil War persuaded Disraeli that this was wildly premature.

Cranborne was impressed by Disraeli's tough rejection of Gladstone's franchise proposals and by the strong speech he had made to the parliamentary Party in mid-March at Lord Salisbury's home in Arlington Street, St James's, where he proposed the rejection of the second reading of Gladstone's Bill. 'The meeting was most cordial and unanimous,' recorded Northcote. Although Cranborne was still writing in April 1866 in the *Quarterly Review* that 'Party allegiance is but a means to an end; it can never determine the decision of questions more important than itself', he was very content with the anti-Reform stance adopted by his own Party.

Cranborne had not set his face against all franchise reform in all circumstances. In his 1865 election address, he said that he would welcome changes to the provisions of the 1832 Reform Act that would expand the electorate without giving undue weight to any single class. Postal ballots, changes in registration procedure and a limited redistribution of seats all found favour with him. Gladstone's 1866 Bill, however, by enfranchising £14 per annum property-renters in the country and £7 per annum in the towns – i.e. the lower-middle classes – would have added 400,000 voters to the electorate, bringing it up to 2.23 million (out of an adult male population of 13.6 million). To understand, in those pre-democratic days, the horror with which such a proposal struck MPs like Cranborne and Lowe, one would have to imagine a present-day proposal to give the vote to twelve-year-olds. In meetings both public and private, Cranborne was impressed by Disraeli's stance of 'uncompromising resistance' to Gladstone's measure.

Meanwhile, Robert Lowe along with Lord Elcho created a 'Cave of Adullam', as it was nicknamed by John Bright after a phrase in the Book of Samuel about 'where the distressed and discontented gathered'. Liberals who were nevertheless prepared to vote with the Conservatives to halt democracy, they filled Cranborne with admiration. It was a rebellion, he wrote, 'against the superstition that there is anything "liberal" in the desire to commit the rule of the British Empire to the least enlightened and least responsible class'. He emphasised that it was not because they were the lower, but because the proletariat were the most numerous class that mattered. 'They may not be vicious or foolish, but they are human.... It is their numbers, not their vices, that we fear.' The Adullamites, together with the Conservatives, managed to defeat Gladstone's Reform Bill by 315 to 304 on 18th June.

When Russell resigned eight days later, Derby offered Cranborne an important seat in the Cabinet. It is not known which one, but it was subsequently withdrawn and on 3rd July he was given the lesser post of India Secretary instead, which nonetheless greatly pleased him. He had leapt from *enfant terrible* to Cabinet rank without the intervening stage of lobby-fodder, or even that of under-secretary. Although Pitt and Disraeli had become Chancellors of the Exchequer without any previous government experience at all, it was still unusual. Cranborne suddenly found himself with the Secretary of State's salary of £5,000 per annum, a figure that had been instituted in 1831 and was to last, incredibly, until 1965. He was also at last able to stretch out his immensely long legs. The backbenches had been uncomfortable; he believed that when Sir Charles Barry had drawn up his plans for the Commons chamber, he had omitted to make any allowance for the fact that MPs might be tall. *The Times* was surprised by his appointment, which at thirty-six years old it considered was 'a notable achievement, even for a clever Cecil', adding that his lack of prudence and moderation could soon be corrected.

In July 1865, Cranborne had written that: 'No one becomes a Member of Parliament, at great cost and trouble, in order that he may sit in judgment upon roads and waterworks; but he does these subordinate duties because they are incident to the condition of a member of Parliament, which he has been anxious to obtain for other reasons.'[7] A year after writing that, he held sway over the lives of 250 million Indians. On 6th July 1866, he took a special train to Windsor with the other thirteen members of the Cabinet. As they went upstairs to kiss hands with the Queen, they met the outgoing ministry coming down, and everyone shook hands. On the journey home Disraeli, the new Leader of the House of Commons and Chancellor of the Exchequer, missed his seat in the saloon carriage and fell to the floor. A more apposite omen would have had it happen to Cranborne instead.

SIX

Secretary of State for India

India – the Second Reform Bill – Resignation

July 1866 to July 1867

'Is Robert still doing his sums?'

During his brief stint as Secretary of State for India, Cranborne only had time to lay down the outlines of the policy he was to adopt when he returned to the post later for a longer sojourn. The Mutiny had only been put down eight years before and British administrators, led by the Viceroy, Sir John Lawrence, were cautiously building the Raj of the Crown where the rule of the East India Company had been. One of the results of the effective nationalisation of the Company in 1858 had been that the old Board of Control was replaced by an India Council, whose duty was to advise the Secretary of State. With his individualist's suspicion of committees, Cranborne disliked having to work with these old India hands, despite the fact that several were great experts and they included some of the most distinguished veterans of the Mutiny. In the *Saturday Review*, he had described the new Council as 'only a machinery for soiling white paper with elaborate protests it is nobody's business to read', and in office he soon complained that the Council's financial powers held the Secretary of State 'in tutelage'.

With characteristic thoroughness, Cranborne threw himself into his office, even studying the Koran in order to help him understand Islam. (He was surprised to find it 'by no means an unsympathetic subject'.) He was an unabashed supporter of the 'divide and rule' policy, which, as he wrote to Lawrence in December 1866, 'followed the despotic trend of employing our soldiers as much as possible at a distance from their birthplace', and wondered if it could not be more widely employed in India. 'Would the Mahometan Afghans be as dangerous in the South of India – or even in Ceylon – as in the North-West Frontier? Would a Sikh be as formidable to his masters at Calcutta as he is in his own country?'

It was 'a resource which has recommended itself to conquerors in every age – Roman, Russian, French – and which on the whole has ensured their purpose well'. Better still would be to employ soldiers 'with neither caste nor Koran to defend nor deposed rulers to avenge', and suggested recruiting in Burma, Ceylon, Nepal and Borneo for troops to serve in India.

Cranborne extended much the same principle to taxation, advising Lawrence to increase it in such a way that 'it is split up into a number of small local grievances and directed at different times against subordinate local offices, [so] it can never constitute a serious political danger'. Over grand strategy, Cranborne agreed with Lawrence that since money was tight – £35 million of India's annual revenue paid for £16 million military expenditure, with only £19 million left for civil administration – and the threat from Russia unrealistic, it was impolitic at that time to meddle in Afghanistan. 'We are strong enough to give them a warm reception when they come,' he wrote to a generally supportive Lawrence, 'and there seems to be no need to disturb ourselves prematurely on that subject.' The day would indeed come, but in the mid-1860s Cranborne refused 'to look on those alarms even seriously', not least because it would be 'sheer wantonness' for Russia to march south when so much remained to be conquered east of Bokhara.[1] He added that he 'would as soon sit down' upon the frontier town of Quetta as 'upon a beehive'. He advised the Foreign Secretary, Lord Stanley, to give Sir Henry Durand, the former Indian foreign minister at Calcutta who suggested taking Quetta, a consignment of blue pills for Christmas.

Cranborne won plaudits for his presentation of the Indian Budget less than a fortnight after coming to office. He was aided by the fact that debates about the sub-continent were notoriously ill-attended. As Cranborne had written in the *Saturday Review*, Indian questions were 'richly endowed by that centrifugal force which scatters Parliamentary atoms abroad into the infinite space of the West End'. As few divisions were taken, constituents could not tell whether MPs were there or not, and Indian names were 'an intolerable complexity' for many MPs. The Secretary of State for India, Cranborne had once written, 'ought to fight as the cuttle-fish fights. It ought to fly, leaving the waters behind him so impenetrably and so unpleasantly turgid as both to blind and to disgust his pursuer'. That Cranborne was so pleased to have been offered the India portfolio was surprising, as in his writings he had rightly said it gave little scope for parliamentary distinction and was 'not, therefore, a position which a man who desires to rise will willingly accept', but instead was 'more often given to satisfy long-standing claims than to provide employment for genuine capacity'. In the major crisis of his first India Office tenure, however, Cranborne failed to show his own capacity, to his sincere and lasting regret.

'The day I took office', Cranborne reminisced a decade later, the former Governor-General of India, Lord Ellenborough, 'wrote to me warning that there were indications of a terrible famine, and urging me to take measures in time. I was quite new to the subject and believed that if any precautions were necessary, the local Government was sure to take them. I did nothing for two months. Before that time the monsoon had closed the ports of Orissa – help was impossible – and – it is said – a million people died. The Governments of India and Bengal had taken in effect no precautions whatever.... I never could feel that I was free from all blame for the result.'[2]

Cranborne was over-harsh on himself, although as Secretary of State he must bear the ultimate responsibility for the tragedy. He could only work on the information his officials gave him, however. He did make inquiries about reported food shortages in eastern India as soon as he came to office, but the men on the spot failed to appeal to the Government even when they saw the people starving. Indeed, as Cranborne stated later, they seemed 'more inclined to look at starvation merely as a question of police'. He demanded irrigation schemes to be put in place 'without further delay', but he was dealing with a Lawrentian administration which was itself, in the estimation of an Indian historian, 'tardy and inadequate', due to the Viceroy being constantly overruled by his own Council in Delhi. Lawrence's own attempts to get grain imported into famine areas were blocked by the Council on grounds of political economy.

Sir Cecil Beadon, the Lieutenant-Governor of Bengal, to Orissa's north, was ill in Darjeeling at the time the reports were coming through, which Cranborne likened to the Home Secretary's living in John O'Groats for six months of the year. Beadon failed to appreciate the scale of the coming catastrophe, and informed Lawrence that the situation was not as serious as rumours suggested. A hitherto extremely competent official, Beadon's assurances were accepted by Lawrence, and Cranborne in turn accepted Lawrence's.

By the time Cranborne discovered the ghastly truth it was too late. He fumed, appointed a Committee of Inquiry, raised finance from the Cabinet and forced through large-scale irrigation schemes on the eastern seaboard. 'It is not a subject on which time ought to be lost' was his constant refrain, but as he had written four years earlier, 'there is nothing to check the Secretary of State except an India official's unlimited powers of procrastination'. With two Councils, two finance ministers and two local Governors, Cranborne's efforts against the famine, though strenuous, were largely unavailing. He even attempted to divert large amounts from the sums to be spent on India's defence, in order to prevent 'the periodic loss of vast numbers of human beings'. Setting up a new Department for Irrigation in December 1866, Cranborne encouraged Lawrence to spend more and he promised that 'every technical and dilatory obstacle to a prompt commencement and energetic execution of those works will be put aside with a strong hand'.[3] By then, however, it was largely an exercise in stable door-locking.

When the Orissa famine came to be debated in the Commons on 2nd August 1867, Cranborne delivered a philippic against experts and political economy in general and the Government of Bengal in particular, which received 'an enthusiastic, hearty cheer from both sides of the House'. John Stuart Mill crossed the floor of the Commons to congratulate him, and even the sceptical doorkeeper admitted that although Cranborne 'used to be caustic, acrimonious and uncharitable ... now ... we have seriousness, solemnity, earnestness, stern independence'. Quoting from Blue Books, Cranborne showed how, especially as there had been a famine the year before, officials such as Beadon had been 'walking in a dream ... in superb unconsciousness, believing that what had been must be, and that as long as they did nothing absolutely wrong, and they did not displease their immediate superiors, they had fulfilled all the duties of their station'.

Those officials worshipped political economy 'as a sort of "fetish"', he said, and because they believed supply and demand would always square themselves, they 'seemed to have forgotten utterly that human life was short, and that man did not subsist without food beyond a few days'. He considered at the time that around three-quarters of a million people had died, largely because Beadon and the local administrators chose 'to run the risk of losing the lives than to run the risk of wasting the money'. He defended the Viceroy, who had been told by Beadon 'that no supplies of rice were necessary', and who had not found out the truth until it was too late.[4] In the days before direct telegraphic communication with India, when despatches took at least six weeks to send, Cranborne was hardly personally blameworthy, and the House of Commons exonerated him. Nonetheless, the experience left him with a profound and lifelong distrust of experts of all types. In the photograph albums at Hatfield, amongst the pictures of smiling Cecil children in 1866–7, are two haunting images of skeletal, famine-struck Indian children.

One area in which Cranborne had made himself an acknowledged expert, immersing himself in the statistics until it became something of a joke amongst his less swottish colleagues, was the electoral mathematics of franchise reform. During the 1866 debates which had wrecked Gladstone's Bill, he had painstakingly mastered all the detailed intricacies, based on census returns, of how each clause would affect the electoral situation in each constituency. He was convinced that reform would lower the quality of MPs, because 'First-rate men will not canvas mobs: and mobs will not elect first-rate men.' In September 1866, he was writing to 'My dear Disraeli', to support the idea of a modest Bill to disenfranchise corrupt boroughs, but warning that Lowe's support for the Conservative Government was conditional on no Bill being brought in during the session due to start in February 1867. There were no fewer than twelve Cabinet meetings held in November 1866 on the question of Reform, and at none of them did Cranborne suspect what was germinating in the minds of Derby and Disraeli.[5]

On Boxing Day 1866, Disraeli wrote to Cranborne from his country seat of Hughenden in Buckinghamshire to say of Reform: 'I have, throughout, been against legislation, and continue so. Lord Derby, about the time you were here, thought it inevitable, but, as you know, his views are now modified. It's a difficult affair, but, I think, we shall pull thro' – the Whigs are very unanimous in wishing the question settled – but you and I are not Whigs.' Nonetheless, Disraeli wanted to steal the Liberals' most popular electoral 'cry'. He wanted to enfranchise a section of the population which Cranborne assumed would vote first Liberal and eventually socialist, but whom Disraeli believed could be persuaded to vote Conservative.

For two decades, most of Disraeli's political life, the Conservatives had been only capable of forming three short minority administrations, and had not looked like the natural party of government since 1846. Rather than stay in opposition forever, Disraeli was preparing for a bold political *volte face*, one which Cranborne, quoting Thomas Hobbes's last words, was later to dub 'a leap in the dark'. Disraeli intended nothing less than to regain the initiative for the Government by proposing in 1867 a Reform Bill yet more radical than the Gladstonian one which he had been instrumental in wrecking only the previous year. Exactly what it contained he did not much mind; that he should be its sponsor was the great thing.

Lady Salisbury, Cranborne's stepmother, was the first person to suspect this, when Disraeli did not discuss the subject of Reform at a house party at Carnarvon's home, Highclere, over the New Year. Cranborne scorned her intuition at the time, but later confessed to his wife, when Disraeli finally showed his hand: 'My Lady's murder is out. She was quite right. She is the sphinx.' It was also his stepmother who subsequently effected a reconciliation between Cranborne and her friend Robert Lowe. This was to lead to a close alliance between the

Tory Right and the Adullamites, who voted with the Liberals against Disraeli's Bill, versus the mainstream Conservative Party and the Radical Liberals, who voted in favour of it. Lowe, Lord Elcho and around forty other Adullamites agreed with Cranborne that 'the great danger of democracy is that it places supreme power in the hands of those who might be misled by hunger into acts of folly or wrong'.

Throughout January 1867 Cranborne was entirely ignorant of Disraeli's plans, writing to him about how Lowe was cursing the Government 'with bell, book and candle' because he had learned from *The Times*' editor John Delane that it was intending to bring in a Reform Bill, albeit one which Cranborne believed would be a mere tinkering measure. As Queen Victoria had agreed to open the Houses of Parliament in person on 5th February 1867, only the second time since Prince Albert's death, there was a good attendance despite bad weather. They heard the non-committal, even platitudinous sentence dealing with Reform in the Speech from the Throne, read out by Lord Chelmsford, the Lord Chancellor: 'Your attention will again be called to the state of the representation of the people in Parliament, and I trust that your deliberations, conducted in a spirit of moderation and mutual forbearance, may lead to the adoption of measures, which, without unduly disturbing the balance of political power, shall freely extend the suffrage.'

The Cabinet meeting the next day displayed 'considerable division of opinion' for the first time. As Carnarvon, Northcote, Gathorne-Hardy and the First Commissioner of Works, Lord John Manners, all kept diaries or memoranda during this period, and the correspondence of many of the protagonists is also extant, it is possible to discern the way in which Disraeli and Derby hoped to bounce the Cabinet into accepting a very wide measure of franchise extension, and how Cranborne led the increasingly dogged resistance to it. The first dissident, however, was Major-General Jonathan Peel, the former Prime Minister's brother and a highly respected Secretary for War, who on 9th February threatened to resign if Disraeli's speech two days later so much as mentioned household suffrage. When Disraeli stood up in the Commons, 'Lord Cranborne sat with his eyes cast down upon the floor and his countenance overshadowed by his hat' as he heard that resolutions would be presented shortly, at the end of which 'the number of electors from counties and boroughs in England and Wales ought to be increased', but carefully not specifying by how much.[6]

In Cabinet on Saturday, 16th February, Disraeli unveiled his proposals more fully, but still by no means completely. Cranborne still kept his opinions under his hat, as he tried to amass the necessary statistics to put them into context. Starting by congratulating the Cabinet on being 'homogeneous and effective', the Chancellor proposed a plan for plural voting in which individuals would receive a second vote according to different criteria, namely the payment of £5 per annum in rates, an educational qualification, savings bank investments or the payment of direct tax. The figures Disraeli presented were compiled by the parliamentary lawyer, political author and statistician Robert Dudley Baxter. They seemed to show that about 330,000 newcomers would be added to the electoral roll, all but 60,000 of whom would gain extra votes through the other franchises. Not now one to accept an expert's conclusions unquestioningly, Cranborne carefully checked Baxter's figures. General Peel, who was averse to any significant widening of the franchise, announced, after 'a long and painful conversation', his intention to resign.

By 1 p.m. on Tuesday, 19th February, Derby was able to announce to the Cabinet that Peel had waived his opposition, that the House of Commons was thought to be in favour of the resolutions as they stood, and that the Queen – who had brought pressure to bear on Peel – believed 'the security of her throne was involved in the settlement of this question'. With Peel's threat withdrawn, the Cabinet discussed plurality, residential qualifications and the level of payment of direct taxation at which voters would be enfranchised. A £10 ratepaying franchise was also discussed.

Cranborne was troubled. In the gloom of the evening of Thursday, 21st February, he met his old Oxford friend and closest political ally Carnarvon, the Colonial Secretary, at the far end of the House of Lords library. As Carnarvon confided to his diary:

> He is firmly convinced now that Disraeli has played us false, that he is attempting to hustle us into his measure, that Lord Derby is in his hands and that the present form which the question has now assumed has been long planned by him. On comparing notes it certainly looks suspicious. My own suspicions have been for some time roused in this direction though I hardly perhaps admitted them as fully as he did. The conclusion was a sort of offensive and defensive alliance on this question in the Cabinet.

This alliance was intended to 'prevent the Cabinet adopting any very fatal course'. They had both seen how, in Carnarvon's words,

> the system of separate and confidential conversations which Mr Disraeli had carried on with each member of the Cabinet from whom he anticipated opposition had divided them and lulled their suspicions; whilst the pre-arranged decision of the interior Cabinet, and the weakness of the general Cabinet had so strengthened Mr Disraeli's hands that the individual in question stood in an isolated and thus powerless position.[7]

Both men greatly regretted having gone along with the Cabinet decision of 16th February, Carnarvon adding that he had mistakenly trusted that Disraeli was acting in good faith.

On the night of Thursday the 21ˢᵗ, Cranborne spent three hours working through Baxter's figures. He wrote to Carnarvon the next day to say that, although Baxter assumed 30 per cent of the £10 ratepayers who qualified would not register, this was 'true in the lump; but it is untrue as respects the smaller boroughs. There the register is well looked after, and ... ninety [per cent] or even more register.' It was a dangerous lacuna in Disraeli's logic, so the same day, Friday, 22ⁿᵈ February, Cranborne wrote to Derby urging him to accept ten shillings rather than Disraeli's twenty shillings for the direct taxpaying franchise qualification. 'The taxing franchise is our counterpoint,' he argued. 'Now above 10 shillings you won't get in the large mass of the £20 householders. At 20 shillings I fear you won't get more than 150,000 double voters; instead of the 270,000 on which we counted. And I fear this will tell horribly on the small and middle-sized boroughs.' It was there that household suffrage would bring in the largest number of voters and the richer plural-voters would be fewest, and yet it was upon winning the small boroughs that the Tories had long depended. The large urban working-class boroughs rarely returned Conservatives, so the smaller ones were crucial to the Party's success. 'We are making a very dangerous experiment and we must take every security we can get,' Cranborne warned the Prime Minister.

At the Saturday, 23ʳᵈ February, Cabinet meeting, with the Monday the 25ᵗʰ deadline for meeting Parliament with agreed resolutions fast approaching, Disraeli recapitulated his figures, describing Baxter as the ablest statistician of the age. The business was hurried through as Derby said he had to leave early. An anti-bribery Bill and also a redistribution of seats Bill were also discussed cursorily, although Cranborne complained at the eleventh-hour nature of their introduction. According to Carnarvon, 'Cranborne muttered his discontent in very audible tones,' and Stanley recorded that 'Cranborne made objections, but all the rest assented without difficulty.'[8] The Cabinet, after this rushed, unsatisfactory meeting, had therefore officially committed itself to rated residential (i.e. household) suffrage, duality of voting and what were being called 'fancy' franchises, along the lines of the original 16ᵗʰ February Cabinet agreement. Derby was due to explain this to a meeting of the whole parliamentary Party at 2 p.m. on the following Monday, with Disraeli announcing it in the Commons later that same day.

On Sunday, 24ᵗʰ February, Cranborne, having had another chance to revisit Baxter's statistics in minute detail, using census returns and other statistical information, tried to work out borough by borough the likely effect of Disraeli's scheme on the psephological map of Britain. He discovered that Baxter had only taken the totals of new voters across the board and not differentiated between the types of borough in his statistics. The actual distribution of new voters in small boroughs of under twenty thousand population tended to suggest to Cranborne that the 'counterpoise' fancy franchises for direct taxpayers and dual voting in these crucial seats would be not quite equal to the addition of new working-class voters in each constituency. He visited Carnarvon's house in Grosvenor Street that evening, where they went through the figures together several times, always coming to the same result. 'A complete revolution would be effected in the boroughs,' such as Stamford, because the new working-class voters who were expected to vote Liberal would outnumber their richer, multiple-voting neighbours who were expected to vote Conservative.

Cranborne's first reaction was to send the statistics to Derby along with his resignation. Carnarvon persuaded him instead to exercise his right as a Cabinet minister to call a Cabinet meeting. One was arranged for lunchtime the next day, just before Derby and Disraeli had to announce the policy to the Party at 2 p.m. and Parliament at 5 p.m. Carnarvon promised to support him. After Cranborne returned home, Carnarvon tried to rally support by visiting Gathorne-Hardy in Grosvenor Crescent and persuading him to visit Cranborne. They then both drove to Cranborne's house at Mansfield Street near Portland Place, where Gathorne-Hardy found him in 'a very disturbed state of mind, but clearly set in his resolution not to be a party to the Bill.... I foresee future difficulties, for clearly Cranborne will not long act with Disraeli, that is at the bottom of it.' The three men discussed the matter until 11 p.m., but Cranborne and Carnarvon failed to persuade Gathorne-Hardy to join them. Carnarvon then left again, this time for Peel's house in Park Place, where 'bare-legged and dressing gowned', the General 'declared that if either Cranborne or I left the Government he would at once resign'.

Cranborne's letter to Derby, written on Sunday night and left in the letter box at his St James's Square residence overnight, went straight to the cardinal point. 'I trust you will believe me that it gives me great pain to have to say what I am going to say,' he began, before explaining that close examination of Disraeli's 19th February franchise scheme had shown him:

> that its effect will be to throw the small boroughs almost, and many of them entirely, into the hands of the voter whose qualification is less than £10. I do not think that such a proceeding is for the interest of the country. I am sure that it is not in accordance with the hopes which those of us who took an active part in resisting Mr Gladstone's Bill last year raised in those whom we induced to vote for us.

Cranborne went on to show how most of the Conservatives representing boroughs of fewer than twenty-five thousand inhabitants – a

majority of the boroughs in Parliament – would be far worse off under
Disraeli's Bill than even under Gladstone's. He went on to criticise the
tempo of the arrangements since 19th February, when they had been
announced 'to my extreme surprise; and though, since that day, I have
devoted every spare moment to the study of the statistics, it was not
until today that I obtained the leisure, from heavy departmental work,
in order to go through them borough by borough'. He added that,
although he and Carnarvon requested a special Cabinet to be held the
following day, he could not promise to support any alternative proposals there, as 'the error of attempting to frame a Reform bill during the
week previous to its production is one that, in my opinion, cannot be
redeemed'. He claimed that he would have preferred not to embarrass
the Government in this way, 'But if I assented to this scheme, now that
I know what its effect will be, I could not look in the face those whom
last year I urged to resist Mr Gladstone. I am convinced that it will, if
passed, be the ruin of the Conservative party.'[9]

The people Cranborne had urged to resist the 1866 Reform Bill were
principally those Adullamite followers of Lowe and Elcho with whom
he had been in close consultation, and with whose anti-democratic
creed he entirely concurred. If possible he would have liked the
Adullamites to have 'fused' permanently with the Conservatives,
providing some anti-Disraelian ballast to the Party. Writing to Elcho on
Monday, 25th February, he repeated his belief that, though not massive,
the overall addition to the electoral roll would be uneven enough to
threaten small boroughs despite all the deductions and counterpoises.
Three other considerations weighed heavily with him. Would the Bill's
counterpoise clauses survive the committee stages and three voting
stages of parliamentary scrutiny and Liberal attack? Were Disraeli's
basic figures even accurate? If Disraeli could pull this trick, fulfilling
all Cranborne's earlier suspicions, was there any point in serving in
government with such a man anyhow?

Derby's initial reaction to Cranborne's letter was to panic. 'Utter
ruin,' he wrote to Disraeli at 8.45 a.m. after reading both it and a separate letter from Carnarvon also requesting an emergency Cabinet:
'What on earth are we to do?' Disraeli came over at once and they
discussed the matter along with Stanley. The emergency Cabinet was
called for 12.30 p.m., to be held at St James's Square rather than at
Downing Street, in order to avoid publicity. The meeting was, in
Derby's words to the Queen, 'of a most unpleasant character'.
Carnarvon remembered 'a very angry discussion', made all the worse for
him because Cranborne only received his summons late and did not
arrive until after 1 p.m.

When Cranborne entered the room 'with reams of paper in his hand',
he started to read out figures, but was interrupted and told of a proposal

by Stanley that since there was so little time they should fall back on a £6 borough rating franchise rather than full residential suffrage and a £20 rather than a £50 county franchise. With Derby due to chair the Party meeting at 2 p.m., the row continued almost until the minute he had to leave. No attempt was made to dispute the statistical accuracy of Cranborne's case, but Disraeli 'white as a sheet' and Derby 'very angry' instead attempted to browbeat the three recalcitrant ministers into submission.

Sir John Pakington, the First Lord of the Admiralty, 'vehemently' urged Cranborne to give way altogether, and, when Cranborne refused, he proposed to the Cabinet that the three resignations be accepted and the original plan proceeded with regardless. This was overruled and instead Stanley reiterated his compromise, which doubtless had already been agreed with his father and Disraeli that morning. After further protests from the Duke of Buckingham, Lord Chelmsford, Gathorne-Hardy, Northcote, Manners and Pakington again, this was adopted. Pakington, whose education schemes in the early 1860s had been the butt of several Cecilian sallies, two days later described the moment to Peel as 'that distressing and unparalleled scene'. The meeting was so acrimonious that another minister who arrived late initially thought that the Cabinet was discussing the suspension of *habeas corpus*.

It was only within ten minutes of the Party meeting that a compromise was finally reached. Derby announced its outlines at 2 p.m. and Disraeli in more detail to the House of Commons at 5 p.m. Both assemblies were distinctly unimpressed. Most of the Cabinet regretted the withdrawal of Disraeli's bolder scheme. They were furious at Cranborne for having agreed on Saturday to something he refused to accept on Monday morning, and complained that the 'extreme suddenness of the act' had left them no room to manoeuvre. The bouncers had been bounced. Cranborne had also admitted that he had been in discussions with non-Cabinet members, probably including Lord Elcho whom he had met on 23rd February, thus further irritating his colleagues. After what Carnarvon called 'a very painful scene', nobody was satisfied with the resulting Stanley compromise. Manners described it as a 'poor and miserable *pis aller*'. A second round was inevitable.[10]

On the following day, Tuesday, 26th February, 'great gloom and personal irritation prevailed' at Cabinet. Cranborne, Peel and Carnarvon said little, and the meeting agreed to Disraeli's plan to introduce a Bill in a week's time, the exact nature of which would be the result of further negotiation. Meanwhile, Disraeli was acting quickly to mobilise backbench Tory opinion, as well as writing to the Queen to say that Peel and Cranborne 'have acted in a complete ignorance and misapprehension of the real feeling of the Conservative Party', oleaginously adding that 'the Chancellor of the Exchequer is confident that Her Majesty will not be disturbed'. The same day he wrote to Derby trying to goad the Prime Minister into taking tougher action against the dissidents. Disraeli did not much care about Carnarvon, whom he nicknamed 'Twitters', leaving the Government, and Peel might be persuaded to stay so as not to split the Party, but he correctly identified Cranborne as the man who was spoiling his 'great plan' to steal the Liberals' clothes.

Disraeli sent Derby reports of the views of the Home Secretary, Spencer Walpole, who had sat virtually speechless throughout the crucial meeting, as well as two senior backbenchers and the Chief Whip, Gerard Noel, who was getting up support in the Carlton Club. He tried to steel the Prime Minister to accept the three resignations if necessary. Nor was he deterred by a letter from Baxter himself on 28th February, which admitted that on further examination he had realised that Cranborne's figures were correct, and 'the larger scheme of rating household suffrage and duality...would...hand over all those small boroughs to the working class'.

That same day a meeting of around one hundred and fifty backbench MPs at the Carlton Club – over half the Party in the Commons – came out in support of the leadership's line. When Disraeli reported this meeting to the Queen, he said that 'there was only one feeling, that Lord Derby should be allowed to fall back on his own policy, and that the measure he seemed forced to introduce was not equal to the occasion'. This was untrue. An annotation made by his biographer G.E. Buckle, the editor of *The Times* and of Queen Victoria's letters, points out that in fact 'this was the feeling of the majority, but there was a minority in favour of a more moderate measure'.

Cranborne and Carnarvon agreed on 28th February that 'a strong pressure is to be put on us', not least by the Tory press, and the next day Disraeli sent Northcote to Carnarvon to try to 'detach' him from Cranborne, saying that Derby was now prepared to accept the resignations, but Carnarvon could save himself by an eleventh-hour apostasy.[11] The Cabinet meeting at 3 p.m. on Saturday, 2nd March, passed in better temper than Monday's had. Two hours were spent in trying to persuade the three ministers not to relinquish office, but once Cranborne had 'announced his intention of resigning...Peel and Carnarvon, with evident reluctance, followed his example'. Gathorne-Hardy thought that Peel would have stayed if one of the others had, and Manners wrote that 'Carnarvon cut a sorry figure and it all turned on Cranborne, who remained unmoveable.'

Derby, finally seeing it was useless to persevere further, closed his red box with a heavy sigh and got up, saying 'The Party is ruined!' Cranborne also stood up and as he did so, in a last-ditch attempt to save the situation, Peel said: 'Lord Cranborne, do you hear what Lord Derby says?' But Cranborne took no notice. The three ministers then left the room, 'and so ended a painful scene'.[12] The Cabinet, now denuded of the sceptics, went swiftly ahead with Disraeli's original, bolder scheme for large-scale franchise reform.

The reconstruction of the Government was swift, with two dukes – Richmond and Marlborough – joining the Cabinet and the India Office being taken by Sir Stafford Northcote. Stanley assumed that the Government would fall, and the loud cheers during the resignation speeches of Cranborne and Peel on 6th March tended to confirm his fears. When Derby met Lady Cranborne socially soon afterwards, he chaffingly asked: 'Is Robert still doing his sums?' She assured him that he was indeed, and 'he has reached a rather curious result – subtract three from fifteen and nothing remains'. For all the wit of her riposte, she spoke too soon. The Conservative Party's instinct for self-preservation easily outweighed its desire for consistency, and, crucially for his later leadership prospects, Cranborne made little attempt to split the Party, despite keeping up a powerful rearguard action against the provisions of the Bill.

His resignation speech was, according to Carnarvon, 'moderate and in good taste – a sufficient justification for us who seceded and yet no disclosure of the frequent changes of policy in the Cabinet'. It was not, however, a call to arms to try to bring down Derby and Disraeli, as Lowe had brought down Russell and Gladstone in 1866. Cranborne hoped the Government would fall, but did not want to be seen on the clifftop when it happened, and only contacted Gladstone via Carnarvon over the following months. Lord Burghley, who had recently succeeded as Marquess of Exeter, approved of Cranborne's course at the time, so his place in Parliament was safe.

At a Party meeting on 15th March, only Beresford-Hope and Sir William Heathcote, Cranborne's two closest supporters in the Commons, opposed Derby's policy, and three days later Disraeli introduced the first reading of his new Bill, designed to give the vote to all rate-paying householders of two years' residence, plus dual voting for university graduates, or members of a learned profession, or those with £50 in government funds or the Bank of England or a savings bank. Just as Cranborne had predicted, these 'fancy franchises' were gradually surrendered over the forthcoming months, duality going in March, the compound householder vote in April and the residential qualification being reduced in May. The county franchise was eventually given to all householders rated at £12 per annum, the redistribution clauses were hugely widened, and all the other extra votes such as that for those paying £1 per annum or more in direct taxation completely disappeared. When finally the Act received Royal Assent, the Duke of

Buccleuch quipped that nothing remained of the original Bill except its first word, 'Whereas...'.

Social ostracism was employed in the lobbies against those Tories who spoke for or threatened to vote with Cranborne, but, as John Bright's biographer pointed out, 'it was not possible to treat Lord Cranborne in this fashion', which anyway he would have in most cases welcomed. Lady Cranborne retaliated with her own brand of social ostracism when she and Lady Alice Peel, the General's wife, cut the poor, entirely non-political Mrs Disraeli at a Buckingham Palace party.[13] Cranborne's disgust with Disraeli and the Government deepened as it became clear in early April that they were telling the Radicals one thing and their backbenchers quite another about how much of the Bill they were willing to sacrifice. By 4th April, Cranborne was writing to Carnarvon that the Whigs' 'hatred of Gladstone almost exceeds, if that be possible, our hatred of Dizzy'.

He resented those who ascribed ambitious motives to his actions, telling J.A. Shaw-Stewart, an Oxford contemporary: 'I have opposed it because I think it a bad and dangerous Bill. I am not "testifying" or any nonsense of that kind, I am trying to kill the Bill.' He went on to say that: 'My connection with the Conservative Party has been purely one of principle – for as you know I have no feelings of attachment to either of the leaders. But what kind of principle can there be now? After having for years opposed every Reform Bill on the ground that it admitted too many of the working class, the very moment they get into office they introduce a measure admitting far more than it was ever proposed to admit before.' Of truckling to Radicalism, he continued: 'It is evidently their settled plan of political warfare – their notion of a good Parliamentary strategy.... I cannot do what is inconsistent with my own sense of honour – and that appears to be an indispensable condition of political prominence – at least on our side of the House.'[14]

A letter from Cranborne to Elcho of 21st March shows the way his mind was working at this time: 'Everything seems to me as gloomy as possible.... A Gladstone reform bill seems to me preferable to the present thing, 1st because it will admit fewer voters, 2nd because it will be in the hands of an honester man and 3rd, that it is of the greatest importance that if such changes are to be made, the Conservatives should be in Opposition when they are made. But it is a bad workout anyhow.'

On 24th April 1867, in the midst of the struggle over the wording of the Bill, just as it was clear that the Adullamites themselves were splitting down the middle and the Radicals were turning Disraeli's measure into just the kind of comprehensive legislation he dreaded, Cranborne's fourteen-month-old daughter, Fanny Georgina Mildred, died of influenza and pleurisy after a three-week illness. Georgina was six months pregnant at the time. For all his overt political passion, Cranborne kept a tight rein on his personal feelings, exercising the utmost reserve. He once said that 'to talk about deep things, or to discuss the hidden things of the heart, was as indecent as to go about without clothes, and it made him sick'. He considered reserve and a stiff upper lip to be important attributes of Englishness. 'I write a line by Georgie's desire to tell you that she is getting on very well,' Cranborne reported to Lady Salisbury a fortnight later. 'She is a good deal worn and shaken – and now that all occasion for effort has passed away, it begins to show. But she is getting better, and I have no doubt will soon be strong again.'

On 6th May, during the Recess, a vast pro-Reform demonstration of working men took place in Hyde Park. The Home Secretary, Spencer Walpole, failed to exercise his right to ban it, possibly because Disraeli needed Radical votes for his Bill. Five years earlier, Cranborne had doubted whether Walpole was really up to 'the sport of political eel-catching', and his doubts were confirmed when the Home Secretary, on being told that the crowd were pulling down the iron railings on the outskirts of the Park, burst into tears. He later resigned over his mismanagement of the affair. The pressure on Parliament for a broader measure was growing.

The third reading of the Representation of the People Bill took place on 15th July 1867. The result was a foregone conclusion and Cranborne, who spoke first, said he would not even press for a division, but only asked to be heard. In possibly the greatest oration of a career full of powerful parliamentary speeches, Cranborne stood at the end of the Opposition front bench below the gangway and, occasionally pointing at Disraeli with his long finger from his great height in what *The Times* called an 'ungainly but effective action', he mercilessly exposed the way in which the Bill, which on its second reading had 'bristled with pre-cautions, guarantees and securities', had been progressively denuded of them all one after another, usually at John Bright's bidding. He went through each of the ten qualifications which had been stripped away from the original measure, and said:

> If ever you come to a question between class and class where the interest of one class are pitted against those of another, you will find that all those securities of rank, wealth and influence, in which you trust, are mere feathers in the balance against the solid interest and the real genuine passion of mankind … and, I may add, the interests of enlightenment and of progress will suffer fatally from the power you have given.[15]

On summing up, Cranborne changed tack entirely, away from the issue of the franchise altogether and on to an *ad hominem* attack on Disraeli, though not deigning to mention him by name. As Gathorne-Hardy had perceptively observed when he had been taken to Cranborne's house by Carnarvon on the Sunday night back in February, his 'abundant bitterness' against Disraeli had been one of the driving forces behind Cranborne's course of action. It was not by then so much a question of preventing the urban working classes from voting, as of protecting his personal honour from Disraeli. In 1866, apparently on grounds of principle, Disraeli had prevented Gladstone from bringing in a Reform Bill less radical than the one which he himself had introduced in 1867, a course of action which Cranborne believed was profoundly dishonest. The peroration of Cranborne's speech is worth quoting in full:

> I desire to protest, in the most earnest language which I am capable of using, against the political morality on which the manoeuvres of this year have been based. If you borrow your political ethics from the ethics of the political adventurer, you may depend upon it the whole of your representative institutions will crumble beneath your feet. It is only because of that mutual trust in each other by which we ought to be animated, it is only because we believe that expressions and convictions expressed, and promises made, will be followed by deeds, that we are enabled to carry on this party Government which has led this country to so high a pitch of greatness.
>
> I entreat honourable Gentlemen opposite not to believe that my feelings on this subject are dictated simply by my hostility on this particular measure, though I object to it most strongly, as the House is aware. But, even if I took a contrary view – if I deemed it to be most advantageous, I still should deeply regret that the position of the Executive should have been so degraded as it has been in the present session: I should deeply regret to find that the House of Commons has applauded a policy of *legerdemain*; and I should, above all things, regret that this great gift to the people – if gift you think it – should have been purchased at the cost of a political betrayal which has no parallel in our Parliamentary annals, which strikes at the root of all that mutual confidence which is the very soul of our party Government, and on which only the strength and freedom of our representative institutions can be sustained.

SEVEN

Life Outside Politics

The Great Eastern Railway – The Marquessate –
Life at Hatfield – Experiments

1867 to 1874

'The dodge has ridiculously failed.'

When a son was born on 12th July 1867, three days before his speech on the third reading of the Second Reform Act, Cranborne asked Carnarvon to stand godfather, 'both for auld lang syne and political sympathy.... Shall we call him Benjamin *in memoriam* of this year's campaign? Or Ichabod?' (after Eli's grandson in the Old Testament, whose name meant 'the glory has departed from Israel' after their defeat by the Philistines). He was in fact christened Edward. 'The baby was very like Dizzy,' Cranborne told Lady Salisbury, "till it was washed.'

After the Second Reform Bill passed, the rest of 1867 was spent in a cathartic state of freedom. 'A politician finally relinquishing the ties of party and the prizes of ambition', he had written three years earlier in the *Saturday Review*, 'enjoys something of that exemption from early hopes and wishes which gives value to the evidence of the dying.' Praise came from John Bright in August, who, although he had disagreed with everything Cranborne said, stated that he 'has been perfectly consistent in everything he has done on this question'. September saw Cranborne writing to Eustace convinced that Derby and Disraeli had intended to dish the 'Anti-Democrats' as early as June 1866: 'If it had been money instead of political support they had been dealing with there is not a jury in the country that would not have found them guilty of getting it upon false pretences.' But he did not mean to be uncharitable to the Government, so long as that 'does not imply trusting them again'.

A little charity was evident in 'The Conservative Surrender', his *Quarterly Review* account of the events of 1867, published that October. 'It is the duty of every Englishman, and of every English party, to accept a political defeat cordially, and to lend their best endeavours to secure the success, or to neutralise the evil, of the principles to which they have been forced to succumb.' His criticism of Derby, that he had 'obtained the votes which placed him in office on the faith of opinions which, to keep office, he immediately repudiated....He made up his mind to desert these opinions at the very moment he was being raised to power as their champion,' was more representative of his true feelings. As for Disraeli, Cranborne wrote that history could find no precedent for his betrayal, at least in the period of modern parliamentary government. Charles Fox's recklessness, Henry Fox's venality, Walpole's cynicism; none was so bad. Historians, he thought, would have to go back to the Glorious Revolution for a precedent, 'to the days when Sunderland directed the Council, and accepted the favours of James when he was negotiating the invasion of William'. Disraeli meanwhile also used historical precedents in his speech at Edinburgh, in which he invoked Bolingbroke and Pitt the Younger in his defence, and described Cranborne as 'a very clever man who has made a very great mistake'.[1]

The total votes cast in the 1865 Election, which Palmerston won, had been 854,856 for 922 candidates, of whom 303 were unopposed. In the 1868 Election, once the Reform Act was in force, 2,333,251 people voted for 1,039 candidates of whom only 212 were unopposed. Compared to that revolution, Gladstone's original 1866 Bill would have enfranchised only 400,000 extra electors. Instead of confiscating the Reform issue from the Liberals altogether, as Disraeli had hoped, agitation soon began for a further extension of the franchise, this time to the rural proletariat, just as Cranborne had predicted. The watershed year 1867 taught Cranborne a number of important lessons, not least that it was not enough to be right about the facts and details if one loses the central argument.

Yet, despite Cranborne's gloomy prognostications, Reform did not lead to confiscations, the dictatorship of the proletariat or the extirpation of civilisation and enlightenment. He had failed to appreciate how the working classes might be willing, at least until the foundation of the Labour Representation Committee in 1900, to range themselves deferentially behind the established Liberal and Conservative banners, still largely waved by a social elite.[2] For all Salisbury's fears of Jacobinism in 1867, the Cecils still own Hatfield House today. The central lesson of 1867 was that he and the Conservative Party, rather than retreat hermit-like into black reaction, would have to improvise new techniques and 'cries' to win the allegiance of the enlarged electorate.

When a life-threatening attack of gout forced Derby's resignation on 25th February 1868, the Queen called for Disraeli, without any consultation with the Conservative Party. The news, according to the Speaker of the House of Commons' journal, was received in silence 'not broken by any expression of opinion, one way or the other'. Cranborne told Carnarvon, 'there is a good deal of grumbling about it, and the temper of his followers is anything but hearty'. When Northcote was sent by the new Prime Minister two days later to offer Cranborne the India Office, he informed the emissary that he 'had great respect for every member of the Government except one – but that I did not feel my honour was safe in the hands of that one'.[3] Undeterred, Disraeli offered Eustace Cecil, MP for South Essex, a government post, but he recognised the implied criticism of his brother if he accepted it, and he had anyhow been as anti-Reform and personally rude about Disraeli as Cranborne himself. Cranborne was amused by the response of Lord Chelmsford, whom Disraeli summarily replaced with Hugh Cairns as Lord Chancellor, who, when asked whether he would like the GCB to ease him on his way, replied: 'He might as well offer me the Victoria Cross.'

Cranborne's venom against Disraeli, in public and in private, did not abate. Over Gladstone's March 1868 proposals to disestablish the Irish Church, he broke ranks in refusing to accept Stanley's amendments and instead called for a forthright rejection of the resolutions. 'Dizzy intends to pursue the old game of talking Green in the House and Orange in the Lobby,' he told Carnarvon, and Gathorne-Hardy thought his speech on the subject 'sneering as regards us all, venomous and remorseless against Disraeli'. Lord Cairns believed that Cranborne was simply using the issue as a stick with which to beat Disraeli, his 'ardour' for the Irish Church having lain pretty dormant until then. To the Queen, Disraeli coolly described Cranborne's speech as 'a very bitter attack on the ministry. Nothing could have been more malignant, but it wanted finish.'[4]

Cranborne's resignation dealt him a harsh financial blow, just at a time he could ill afford it. He had invested heavily in the prestigious firm of bill-brokers and discount bankers Overend and Gurney, which in May 1866 suddenly went spectacularly bankrupt. He could probably have borne the losses on their own, but in 1864 he had been forced to pay part of the initial promotion costs of the Adelaide Railway Company of which he was a director, and he had also tied up further capital as a backer of the National Provincial Aereated Bread Company. He was forced to ask his father for £1,500, but added that he should not have to go into debt because of his ministerial salary. When in July 1867 another of his major investments, the Imperial Mercantile Credit Company, also went into liquidation, Cranborne no longer had his £5,000 per annum salary, and so he went back to Salisbury with a begging bowl for a further £1,250. 'It's a horrid mess,' he readily admitted.

In January 1868, partly in order to help repay his father, Cranborne accepted the offer of the railway magnate Sir Edward Watkin to become Executive Chairman of the Great Eastern Railway, whose application to borrow £1.5 million had recently been refused by Parliament and was thus facing bankruptcy. Cranborne soon showed commercial skills in managing the railway which he clearly lacked as a financial speculator. He demanded the right to put his own accountants into the firm, finding two Board of Trade auditors for the task. He also turned down Watkin's initial salary offer of £1,400, taking only £700 on the grounds that 'a highly-paid chairman is a luxury which should be reserved for the return of a good shareholders' dividend', something that had been absent for some years.

Cranborne quickly mastered the complexities of the railway industry, with its arbitrations, interlocking compromises, gargantuan ambitions and regular bankruptcies. Asking Gladstone to arbitrate in a dispute over the Bishops Stortford Railway in February 1868, Cranborne explained the kind of difficulty he faced: 'The Great Eastern is forbidden by Act of Parliament to distribute any dividend till that line is opened. The contractor refuses to open it until his bill is paid, and the Great Eastern is forbidden by Act to pay his bill.' From his offices at Bishopsgate Station, Cranborne, who had once criticised the 'slowness, unpunctuality and discomfort' of the Great Eastern in the *Saturday Review*, undertook deep-seated reforms. He made redundancies, abandoned plans to build potentially unprofitable lines, convinced bankers, petitioned Parliament, sacked the managing director, arranged deals with other companies for handling through-freight and on 15th July 1868 successfully issued £1 million of debenture stock, persuading the larger debtors to take preference shares in lieu of cash. The official receiver was discharged, and a proud and relieved Cranborne could at last remove the labels which denoted which locomotive would go to which creditor in the event of liquidation.

Cranborne constantly warned the shareholders against being seduced 'by engineers, by solicitors, by persons whose minds are strung to a very sanguine degree', displaying a combination of his natural pessimism and his suspicion of experts. A profound distrust for the estimates of engineers also led him to refuse to sign an address to Napoleon III asking for his support for the building of a railway tunnel under the English Channel, which, as he suspected, would eventually turn out to cost much more and take far longer than the experts had budgeted. By the time he finally resigned from the Great Eastern in 1872, it was back on a sound financial footing and paying a reasonable dividend, and the shareholders presented him with a vast gothic silver-gilt table centre-piece with sugar vases emblazoned with the coats of arms of the Cecil family and the Great Eastern Railway.[5]

Shortly after six o'clock on the evening of 12th April 1868, all Cranborne's money worries ceased when his father, the 2nd Marquess of Salisbury, died aged seventy-seven. Because it was Easter Sunday there was no telegraph service. Early on Monday morning, the new Lord Salisbury left the house he rented in Hampshire to attend a meeting in Manchester, and had the 'terrible shock' of reading about his father's death in *The Times* at Guildford railway station.

'The sudden translation of such a statesman to the House of Lords', commented *The Times'* first leader on 14th April, 'must influence the course of our future political history.... Mr Disraeli is relieved of an immediate rival in the House of Commons, without the necessity of having recourse to a Canadian Governorship.' Astonishingly, the 3rd Marquess at first hoped that he could somehow stay in the House of Commons, and was even advised by Earl Grey to continue sitting there and simply ignore the writ to attend the House of Lords. His solicitor informed him that there could be a difficulty in finding his father's marriage and his brother's death certificates. It would have been a bizarre undertaking, not least because he would effectively have declared his own illegitimacy, but it illustrates how reluctant he was to enter the House of Lords. He soon saw the conceit (as well as the deceit) involved in such a line of action. 'It would amount to a modest announcement on my part that my own presence in the House of Commons was so important as to justify a departure from the unbroken tradition of centuries,' he shrewdly observed to Carnarvon. 'Whether I succeeded or failed I should be making myself ridiculous.'[6]

Once translated from the green to the crimson leather benches, Salisbury scarcely ever returned. On only two occasions – for W.E. Forster's resignation speech of 1882 and a statement by Arthur Balfour in 1899 – did he deign to appear in the Commons gallery. Nor, as the veteran parliamentary reporter Sir Henry Lucy remembered, was he ever seen chatting in the lobby with political supporters. Whenever he was compelled to refer to the Lower House in debates, 'he managed to throw into his tone a note of contempt that greatly aroused the Commoners thronging the Bar, or privy councillors standing on the steps of the Throne'. As Prime Minister, Salisbury exhibited 'small respect for the opinions of the House of Commons, and constantly chafed against his obligations to support in the Lords proposals to which his colleagues in the Commons had been obliged to agree'.

'At least', Salisbury was told on joining the House of Lords, 'it's a place from which one can get to bed.' Sittings began at 5 p.m. and were often concluded by 7 p.m., whereas in the Commons late nights were common. Attendance in the Lords plummeted after the Glorious Twelfth, and Salisbury soon found that the place lived up to all his *Saturday Review* criticisms of it as 'the Paradise of Bores'. Salisbury's answer to the threat of the Lords 'dying of inanition' was to insist on its rights and ceaselessly to talk it up as the constitutional equal to the Commons, arguing, as he did in June 1868 over the Bill to disendow the Church of Ireland, that for the Lords to become 'a mere echo and supple tool of the House of Commons was slavery'. In order to justify this defence, Salisbury supported the creation of life peers – 'we belong too much to one class. We want more representatives of diverse views and more antagonism,' he wrote, and he put down an amendment to make all Appeal Court judges *ex officio* peers, like the senior bishops.

For all the constitutional heroism Salisbury hoped to map out for it, he had to admit that the House of Lords debates were tedious, although, as he put it in 1871, 'not much duller than a perpetual Committee of Supply in the House of Commons would be'. Replying to a letter of commiseration on his father's death from Sir John Coleridge, the Solicitor-General, Salisbury readily admitted: 'My opinions belong to the past; and it is better that the new principles in politics should be worked by those who sympathise with them heartily.'[7]

It would have taken Job's saintliness for Salisbury not to have felt a twinge of *Schadenfreude* when Disraeli lost the November 1868 general election by 271 Conservative seats to the Liberals' 387, especially as the most severe losses were, exactly as he had predicted, in the small boroughs. 'When I first heard that they had such a majority,' he told the Lords three years later, 'I was glad there was a party which could take a definite position and put an end to a state of things which, in my opinion, had proved injurious to the standing of public men in this country.' He had refused to help any Conservative candidate, even Eustace, telling his brother that he preferred 'to abstain altogether from taking any part in reference to those contests'.

Gladstone was actually staying at Hatfield in the second week of December when he formed his first Government. Having gone to Windsor on Saturday, 12th December, he walked five miles with Salisbury the following Monday to visit Palmerston's octogenarian widow at Brocket Hall. *The Times* reported that the Liberal

Government had offered Salisbury the Viceroyalty of India, which he contradicted as 'idiotic', but in fact, unbeknownst to him, Gladstone had approved of Granville's suggestion as 'excellent', except that Lord Mayo's appointment had already been announced. (As Mayo was assassinated by a lunatic in 1872, it was probably for the best.) 'The "dodge" has ridiculously failed,' Salisbury exulted in his last *Saturday Review* article on 28th November, writing about the Conservative defeat. 'To have gone through all this dirt in order to make their political condition exactly twice as bad as it was must be irritating,' he added, indulging in some sparingly employed but exquisite understatement.

In January 1869, Salisbury's contempt for Disraeli increased, if that were possible, when Delane told Carnarvon that back in the winter of 1866/7 he had been shown a printed draft Reform Bill, proving, as Carnarvon noted, 'that an interior Cabinet was carrying out a pre-arranged scheme of policy to be kept back for the moment from the majority of the Government, for fear of prematurely alarming them'. Perhaps Salisbury's anger at this discovery of Disraeli's stratagem was naïve; one does not after all reveal one's hand in politics until the right moment. The caption to the caricature of Salisbury by 'Ape' in *Vanity Fair* read: 'He is too honest a Tory for his party and his time.'[8] It was a fine epithet, but the events of 1867 taught him that wiliness, rather than outraged innocence, would serve him better in the future.

Salisbury was determined that the home life of his children should be as far removed as possible from the internal exile of his own boyhood. Canon Edward Lyttelton of Haileybury said that the education of the Cecil family violated every convention on the subject, only with the happiest results. In contrast to other Victorian families, the young Cecils were expected to be both seen and heard. Their appearance, punctuality or even cleanliness mattered hardly a jot, but their Christianity, intelligence, conversation, honesty and sense of humour were all-important. Nor were they expected to be respectful in front of distinguished visitors; polite disputation was encouraged so long as they were able to define their terms concisely. 'My father always treats me as an ambassador,' said Robert as he reached his twenty-first birthday, 'and I do like it.'

Hatfield, without rules, but with a firm moral example set by their parents, was an exhilarating place in which to grow up, and the fact that amongst the seven surviving children there were no serious disputes, either between each other or with their parents, is testimony to the success of the experiment. The two girls, Maud and Gwendolen – nicknamed 'the Salisbury plains' because of their unprepossessing looks –

were particular favourites of Disraeli when he stayed at Hatfield after the quarrel with their father was eventually patched up. 'Lord Beaconsfield has rarely met more intelligent and agreeable women,' he wrote to the Queen in April 1878, 'for they are quite women though in the wild grace of extreme youth.' He awarded them his Order of the Bee, a brooch otherwise only given to Princess Beatrice and his confidantes, Ladies Bradford and Chesterfield.

When Lord Esher visited Hatfield for the first time in the 1890s, he found the Prime Minister playing with his grandsons, 'seated in a fur rug being drawn around the great hall by a band of romping boys'. Salisbury always encouraged the presence of plenty of children at Hatfield – those of friends, cousins and neighbours – and his son Robert remembered a 'very cheerful and crowded family life' in a particularly close and loving environment. 'It never occurred to the younger members of the household', a distinguished historian has written, 'that they should not play rowdy games of billiard fives in a room lined with seventeenth-century panelling, or ride iron-wheeled tricycles down the marble floor of the armoury or use Charles I's cradle for charades.'9 Salisbury took up billiards himself, and played to win; he would be heard to mutter 'Bulgaria' when his careful aim did not come off. For all his children's iconoclastic games, however, Salisbury was proud of the house and its antiquity. When asked by a French diplomat whether he still possessed a particular portrait of a sixteenth-century French ambassador, Salisbury replied that indeed he did, and it was 'hanging from the same nail on which my ancestor hung it'.

Occasionally the informality which Salisbury encouraged with grown-ups could be taken too far, as when Hugh, aged five, told Gladstone that he was a very wicked man. 'My dear boy, what would your father think if he heard you say that?' inquired the Grand Old Man. 'He thinks you are, too,' came the reply, 'and he is coming to kill you in a quarter of an hour.' Robert remembered how his siblings were 'never pushed in the ordinary sense of the word' and were never physically chastised because a look from their mother was usually enough to quell bad behaviour. That only worked when she was there, however. Once when she was away, Salisbury reported to her that one of their sons, 'Having tried all the weapons in the gun cupboard – some in the riding school and some, he tells me, in his own room – and having failed to blow his fingers off, he has been driven to reading Sydney Smith's *Essays* and studying Hogarth's pictures.' Lady Salisbury's comment was that her husband 'might be able to govern the country, but he is quite unfit to be left in charge of young children'.10 By encouraging their children to read modern French novels, and discouraging them from going to church until they were old enough to consider it a privilege rather than an obligation, the Salisburys turned Victorian child-rearing mores on their head.

Hatfield was managed by Lady Salisbury, and her husband's appreciation of his own lack of æsthetic sensibility meant that he rarely interfered with her decisions about decoration. It was she who ran the 127-room house, the stables and gardens, she who looked after the estate tenants and their dependants, and organised the vast amount of entertaining. With her county duties, cottage-building, philanthropy in a slum parish of Westminster, and the education and entertainment of seven children, it was a huge task, but one to which Lady Salisbury was more than equal. A great-niece described her in later life as 'a big woman, [who] moved ponderously with immense dignity. Her hair was grey and rippled from the parting in the middle of her broad forehead; her face was florid; her mouth was large and firm, widening often into laughter.'

The days of poky London houses and scrimping in order to afford good doctors now over, Georgina Salisbury came into her own at Hatfield. Anecdotes abound of her overturning sleighs into ditches, calling on all the ambassadresses, 'but not those of the South American republics or any others of the people who live up trees', and telling the Prince of Wales, when he commented that he had seen her dress before: 'Yes, Sir, and you will see it very often again.' The story was also told of when, curtseying to the Royal Family at a ball in a satin crinoline and the Cecil diamonds, she momentarily disclosed the grey woollen stockings and sensible walking shoes she was wearing underneath. She was big-hearted, highly opinionated and, in her niece's recollection, 'very outspoken in her opinions on every subject'. If she wanted to drive through a neighbour's park, she thought nothing of ordering her coach-men to lift his gates off their hinges. She was very unpunctual, and Salisbury claimed that he had read the whole of the Church Fathers in the time spent waiting for her.[11]

Occasionally the ghost of one of his 'abominably wicked' ancestors would drive a phantom coach up the main staircase, only to disappear once Salisbury had dressed to greet what he had thought were unexpected visitors. For all Salisbury's reputation as a 'Buffalo' and social misanthrope, entertaining at Hatfield was undertaken on a massive scale. Bishops were a speciality, minor royalties a necessary chore; generals, diplomats, writers, proconsuls, poets, painters, politicians and, when he was Prime Minister, visiting heads of state such as the Kaiser of Germany and the Shah of Persia, as well as the Crown Princes of Italy and Germany, all came to stay. 'Celebrities' such as Sir Richard Burton, John Delane, J.A. Froude, Lewis Carroll, Robert Browning, the Chinese viceroy Li Hung Chang, Matthew Arnold and Lord Kitchener also visited. Salisbury stood by what he called the 'great cause of Guest Emancipation', by which everyone was allowed to amuse themselves in their own way, rather than being dragooned by their hosts.

Salisbury was normally scrupulously courteous, but he also had a good line in occasional put-downs. After he had been monopolised all dinner by one woman, his hostess Lady St Helier asked if he had had an agreeable evening. 'I have had a highly educational one,' he replied. At a large dinner party at Hatfield a bumptious young man teased an elderly squire, implying that he was 'a Philistine'. When the squire, a neighbour of Salisbury's, inquired as to the meaning of the word, Salisbury defined it as 'a gentleman who is assailed by the jaw-bone of an ass'. Lady Randolph Churchill recalled how Salisbury 'had the happy knack of seeming vastly interested in one's conversation, whatever the subject, and however frivolous – there was no condescension about it'.[12] (Had there been, it is doubtful she would have had an inkling of it.) Lady Salisbury, on the other hand, was famed for her ability to employ a glacial *froideur* when necessary.

'The family learnt everything by discussion,' wrote the wife of one of Salisbury's nephews. Politics, religious dogma and foreign affairs 'were discussed in every passage and doorway of the house'. The subjects covered at one entirely typical dinner in November 1892 included headaches, pretty women, dogs, music, waxworks, poetry, sculpture and tortures. The family motto, 'Late but in Earnest', certainly applied to their mealtimes, the pre-prandials of which were scheduled at what Lady Salisbury called 'easy eight', which could mean any time between 7.30 p.m. and 8.30 p.m. When the Cecils finally appeared, the 'talk flowed freely ... always conducted on a basis of mutual equality'. Over the notorious Mrs Maybrick, the half-American doyenne of the great Victorian husband-poisoners, Salisbury 'informed' himself about the subject over dinner with his family and argued in Cabinet that she ought to be released three years early, partly in order to please American public opinion. He was overruled by the Home Secretary.

Cecilian opinion was not always so lenient. 'The family are greatly excited about the infant murderers at Liverpool,' Lady Salisbury wrote to 'Nigs' (Edward) about one family discussion, 'Tim [Gwendolen] and Nelly [Lady Robert Cecil] think they are not so much worse than other boys. Jem [James, Lord Cranborne] says he hopes they won't put them in prison. Bob [Robert] says it is all the fault of the Roman Catholics (why, I cannot imagine). I am for hanging their parents. Linky [Hugh] has a general view of five years' penal servitude for all concerned. All agree in beginning with a flogging. The head of the family inclines for painless execution.'

In a manner that harked back to an earlier age, Salisbury's sons went into the Law (Robert), the Church (William), the Army (Edward) and Parliament (Hugh), leaving the eldest (Cranborne), who also entered Parliament, to inherit the title and estates. Maud married the Liberal Unionist MP William Palmer, Lord Wolmer, the heir to the earldom of

Selborne. 'Willy has what one might call an early English sense of humour,' wrote Maud's sister-in-law Violet, 'simple, hearty and unwearied by repitition!' Maud herself was wise and resourceful. 'Never take a reference from a clergyman,' was one of her maxims. 'They always want to give someone a second chance.' Not everyone appreciated the constant, exuberant, free-range arguments. '*Chiffon* women are dull and tiresome,' wrote Robert's wife Nelly in February 1897, 'but they don't try to knock one down over a difference in the weather!' When the subject got on to Ritualism, Lady Salisbury reported to her daughter-in-law: 'Fish [William] unreasonable to the last extent and paradoxical to madness – His Lordship humble and silent as he always is among his sons.'[13]

As well as 'Goose', Salisbury's family nicknamed him 'Citizen Salisbury' and 'Danton' as a tease on his lack of interest in the social and county obligations that went with his rank. He accepted an honorary rank in the Hertfordshire Militia in May 1868 on the condition that it did not impose on him 'the slightest military duties or responsibility whatever', as he was 'so utterly unfit' for them. He also took on the chairmanship of the Hertfordshire Quarter Sessions, which he carried out conscientiously until he became Prime Minister. It allowed him one of his few, if inevitably skewed, personal insights into working-class life, and did little to raise his estimation of human nature.

Having hitherto self-confessedly not known 'the difference between a horse and a cow', Salisbury suddenly had to administer an estate of over twenty thousand acres. He learnt about scientific farming techniques and kept a close eye on the accounts. When in the agricultural depression of the late 1870s some of his tenant farmers went bankrupt, the land had to be worked by Salisbury through bailiffs. It was a challenge, but when he was in opposition in the 1880s and able to concentrate on them properly, his farms paid their way. His annotations to his estate Labour Book show how sharp-eyed he was over his outgoings. Of the 153 men, twenty women and forty boys he employed for outside work at Hatfield in one typical week in October 1882, one man, called Marling, was being paid a half-day's wages at two shillings and fourpence for replacing thatch in field number 224. 'There is no rick in this field,' noted Salisbury in the margin. Every farthing was accounted for out of a weekly grand total of £210.11s.10d, down to the nightwatchmen's beer money, the two shillings paid to the rat-catcher for two dozen rats, and the wages of a boy called Pales who spent the whole twelve months flattening molehills.

'I do not believe that rich people have more responsibility than poor people,' Salisbury once casuistically reasoned. 'This doctrine would make responsibility to depend upon the effect of your acts, not on the intention.' Nevertheless, he was more of a caring, paternalistic employer than many others who did not deny their moral obligations. When he took over the estate, Hatfield was not on the list of good landowners published by the Royal Commission on the Employment of Women and Children in Agriculture, which had toured the cottages of estate workers throughout the country. Owning about a third of the town of Hatfield, but almost all the surrounding land, Salisbury set himself the task of rebuilding all the cottages of his labourers. A large proportion of his total expenditure between 1868 and 1877 was devoted to this, and in the last ten years of his life no fewer than 218 sanitary, unornamental and comfortable cottages were built, all with good ventilation and running water.[14]

Salisbury also built a cottage hospital, Church Army hall, boys' school, post office, waterworks and a new rectory. Amongst the building projects he first undertook when he inherited the estate was the restoration of Hatfield church, which involved completely rebuilding the nave. He also totally altered the interior of the private chapel at Hatfield. He did not interfere, as other Victorian landlords often tended to, in the moral welfare of his tenants. If they paid their rent and behaved discreetly, their personal conduct was left between them and the rector of Hatfield, who after 1888 was his son William. Salisbury adopted a similarly *laissez-faire* attitude towards his forty indoor staff, some of whom he knew stole from him. He reasoned that 'if you keep too tight a rein on the household your guests suffer'. He had a limit beyond which he did not allow expenditure to rise, but when warned of a tipsy old housekeeper, whom one of his daughters-in-law suspected was drinking some of the beer which every autumn was rubbed into the oak panelling, his uncharacteristically meek response was that he knew, but could not prevent it. This is doubtful; in September 1880, Salisbury noted that in 1879 they had consumed 2.76 bottles of claret a day at their French holiday home in Puys, near Dieppe.

Lady Salisbury thought the answer to the epigram that no man was a hero to his valet should be: 'That is because he *is* a valet,' and she described stupid or chippy remarks as 'valetisms'. In his *Saturday Review* column, he had written how servants were a necessary evil and looked forward to 'the happy day when steam substitutes should have been invented'. They stole, gambled, disturbed one's privacy and sold gossip, because 'bits of information are a perquisite as substantial as dripping'. The Cecils made it a rule to keep general talk for the main part of the meal, but confidential, political discussions only took place once the servants had left.[15]

Because in his youth dogs had not been allowed at Hatfield due to two cases of hydrophobia, Salisbury never developed much of an affection for them, although he did have a huge boarhound 'Pharaoh', so called because 'he won't let people go'. Lady Salisbury was proud of their horses, the famous 'Salisbury blacks', which pulled their many barouches and carriages. The Hatfield Abstract Book for September 1894 lists stabling for Squib, Spice, Samson, Swift, Strongbow, Stamp, Striker, Spirit, Swallow, Skylark, Soldier, Saladin, Suffolk, Scotia, Swindler and Simpleton. Soudan, Sir Garnet, Sauerkraut and Sambo were to follow later, and by 1900 Sirdar and Suakim, after Lord Kitchener and a victory in the Sudan.

∿

Salisbury was fascinated by technical innovations. In 1869, Hatfield became one of the first houses in Britain to install electric bells and five years later it also boasted a form of electric lighting. The county ball held there in January 1874 was the first occasion for a successful experiment, with two powerful arc lamps placed in specially-made sentry boxes near the flower beds on either side of the house's south front. As the carriages drew up in the evening, the house was illuminated by means of huge batteries. In 1881, an estate labourer working in a part of the park where the cable had fallen on to the wet grass, touched the wire and became the first person to die by electrocution. By 1883, the drawing room of Salisbury's London house was lit with electricity, and he spent a good deal of time and money on the invention.

In 1891 another tragedy nearly struck in the library, when, as a family member recorded, 'suddenly eight lamps went smash bang, and in a second the ceiling was on fire in three places. They all took it quite quietly, and put it out by shying cushions up, but if it happens when the room is empty some day, goodbye to the house.' Lady Salisbury had been 'voluble' in support of her husband's efforts as he and various Balfour nephews chucked the cushions at the flames, and the incident was made into a family joke, but the memory of the great fire of 1835 was always there.[16]

The telephone, which was also viewed with suspicion by many households in the late 1870s, was immediately welcomed by Salisbury. 'Nothing would give me greater pleasure than to infringe Prof. Bell's patent by manufacturing my own telephone,' he told his fellow experimenter Professor Herbert McLeod in 1877. McLeod was a distinguished chemist and Fellow of the Royal Society who specialised in the measurement of gases at low temperatures and invented the Sunshine Recorder. By 1877, Salisbury had covered the floors of Hatfield's principal rooms with the cords of the new telephone invention, which Robert Lowe tripped over and declared 'a great bore'. Visitors to Hatfield would be startled, recalled Gwendolen, by hearing Salisbury's voice 'resounding oratorically from selected spots within and without the house, as he reiterated with varying emphasis and expression: "Hey diddle diddle the cat and the fiddle; the cow jumped over the moon"'.

Salisbury quickly appreciated the political implications such an increase in the speed of communications might have. When he was staying at the home of one of his MPs, Sir William Forwood, in February 1893 prior to switching on the world's first full-gauged electric railway in Liverpool, the house was connected up to the chamber of the Commons. 'I can hear someone talking about Uganda,' Salisbury announced delightedly. He later told his host: 'I hate political functions; but this was a very different occasion. It was one of the most interesting twenty-four hours I have passed.' He did not trust the telephone altogether, however, and told the Queen's assistant private secretary that he disapproved of it as a medium for transacting official business, 'as there was nothing to vouch for its genuineness'.[17]

Salisbury's interest in science extended far further than mere technical innovations and gadgetry, a hobby along the lines of Chamberlain's orchid-growing or Gladstone's tree-felling. 'The great mark of difference which distinguishes this age from all that have gone before it, is its advance in physical science,' he wrote in the *Saturday Review*. Whereas art, poetry, philosophy, political theory, 'the love of freedom and the passion for strong government' had changed little over the centuries, and mankind had hardly improved at all morally in that period either, he believed the recent advances in the knowledge of the physical sciences were 'palpable and undisputed'.

New scientific precepts could only be discovered through diligent experimentation with logical, observable phenomena. Salisbury despised what he called the 'intuitive' school of scientific endeavour, believing only in reason and verifiable statistics. Reviewing a book on botany which attempted to argue for a teleological pattern in nature, using dreams, imaginations and a 'spiritual eye' instead of hard data, Salisbury wrote that 'all the gifts of all the Muses cannot save a man from writing like a lunatic when once he betakes himself to promulgating his "intuitions"'. Addressing the Chemical Society in 1891, Salisbury said he liked chemistry because it offered so little play to 'scientific imagination' and so much to verifiable knowledge. Although he was elected a Fellow of the Royal Society for his chemistry in 1869, it was the physical sciences which most attracted him. A room in Hatfield's east wing directly below his study was converted into a laboratory. Lord Rayleigh, who married Blanche's daughter Evelyn and won the Nobel Prize for discovering argon, was shocked by how Salisbury, who had little taste for *objets d'art*, happily drove a nail into an intricately marquetried table in the course of one of his experiments there.

It was primarily in the field of electricity and the observation of gases and light at low temperatures that Salisbury experimented, even publishing a paper in *The Philosophical Magazine* in April 1873, entitled 'On Spectral Lines of Low Temperature', in which he noted that:

> If a thermometer be fixed on an insulated metal plate connected with one of the secondary poles of a powerful inductorium, the discharge produces a green light in the vacuum above the mercury in the thermometer tube. This light, though accompanied by only the slightest possible development of heat, is sufficiently strong to admit of spectroscopic study.

Other, full-time scientists were to use this and similar discoveries to invent neon lighting.

As well as light there were experiments in magnetism and electricity, with Salisbury writing over one hundred letters to McLeod about thermo-electricity and electro-magnetism. 'In science I am an iconoclast and love to see popular theories overthrown,' Salisbury stated in August 1875. He was also interested in botany, but as he told his friend Janetta Manners, Lord John's wife, in 1879, 'politics brutalize and degrade the mind – and I have forgotten all I ever knew'.

Although it is not true that, as Lord Randolph Churchill told Lord Rosebery, Salisbury was 'never happy out of that damned laboratory at Hatfield', he did derive great intellectual stimulation from the time he spent there, and he took his respect for facts and statistical information into his political life. One of his reasons for admiring photography was that it was 'never imaginative, and it is never in any danger of arranging its records by the light of any preconceived theory'. Salisbury foresaw the possibilities of microphotography, colour photography and photography's uses in criminal investigations, but he hated having his picture taken. 'If you listen to the photographer's admonition to smile,' he told his *Saturday Review* readers in 1862, 'you come out upon the plate with a horrible leer, looking like the Artful Dodger in the act of relating his exploits.' But if to smile was ridiculous, 'to look solemn is more so. You desire to look intelligent, but you are hampered by a fear of looking sly. You would wish to look as though you were not sitting for your picture; but the effort to do so only fills your mind more completely with the melancholy consciousness that you are.'[18]

No. 20, Arlington Street, in St James's, had been a Cecil residence since the late eighteenth century, but in 1870 Salisbury spent two years and up to £60,000 extensively renovating it. By 1878, the Salisburys could entertain over a thousand people there. It was five storeys high, 230 feet long by 34 feet wide, with a first-floor ballroom that was seventy feet long (roughly the area of a championship tennis court). The family complained of the house being stuffy and ill-ventilated, but since the whole Conservative Party of both Houses could meet there, it served its purpose well. It also had a laboratory on the ground floor, with a special flue to expel noxious gases.

In 1870, another residence was built on the cliffs above the small coastal village of Puys, two miles from Dieppe. Châlet Cecil was a large, hideous red-brick building with wooden balconies and conical turrets, somewhere between a Swiss chalet and a gothic castle. Fortunately they had not yet put on the roof when the Prussian army commandeered all the other major houses in the area during the Franco-Prussian War. This holiday home, very close to the English coast and serviced by packet boat from Newhaven, was regularly used by the family between 1872 and 1895. Salisbury did not take the direct Newhaven–Dieppe route himself; he was a bad sailor and preferred to take the shorter Dover–Calais crossing, munching on dry biscuits. He was not therefore present in 1890 when an over-officious customs inspector stopped Salisbury's family carriage at Newhaven on suspicion of smuggling tobacco.

The Cecils excited many apocryphal stories amongst the Dieppois, such as that of Lord Salisbury personally collecting the whisky off the Newhaven boat each week. Lady Salisbury, who swam in the Channel in all weathers, was grudgingly respected amongst the local tradesmen for her habit of hard bargaining at the market, rather than leaving it up to her cook. The sight of the family marching down the hill to the small All Saints' Anglican church in rue de la Barre each Sunday ended only in 1895 when a house called La Bastide was built above Beaulieu in the far warmer south of France.[19] Salisbury was never a believer in tourism *per se*, perversely thinking that 'the more the facilities of travelling bring the two nations into contact the less goodwill is likely to be generated'. Other than the occasional visit to a Swiss spa town for his health, and one diplomatic mission to Constantinople, he never travelled beyond France, Germany and Italy in the last fifty years of his life.

As the year 1869 dawned, Salisbury's relationship with the Conservative Party was still undefined but uncomfortable. He had had no doubts whatever about his actions of 1867 and felt no romantic attachment to the Party, seeing it solely as the vehicle most likely to advance his particular brand of High Toryism. Should principle force him to leave it altogether, he said, he would happily walk out of the Carlton Club for the last time without so much as a regretful thought or backward glance. When the three ministers had returned their seals, Peel was in tears, Carnarvon was 'dreadfully distressed' but Cranborne had handed them back 'with scarcely a word' to or from the Queen. His attitude to the future was summed up in a letter to the Marquess of Bath in November 1868: 'So long as Disraeli is leader of the party in the Commons, we in the Lords must follow the course which seems honest without much reference to the action that may have been taken by the Conservatives in the other House.'[20] A recipe for confusion in government, this had more of a chance of working now that, largely thanks to Disraeli's Second Reform Act, the Conservatives were once more in opposition.

EIGHT

The Politics of Opposition

*The Oxford Chancellorship – The Franco-Prussian
War – The Irish Land Act – Relations
with Lord Derby – Joining the Ministry*

1868 to 1874

'I wish party government was at the bottom of the sea.'

'Matters seem very critical,' Salisbury wrote to the anti-democrat Tory
MP, G.M. Sandford, in May 1868, 'a woman on the Throne and a Jew
adventurer who found out the secret of getting round her.' After Derby
had retired in February, the leadership of the Conservatives in the
House of Lords had been taken by the former Foreign Secretary, Lord
Malmesbury, but only acting as a stop-gap. For a single session starting
in February 1869, Disraeli's ally, the very Low Church former Lord
Chancellor Lord Cairns, took on the leadership, hoping to keep it.
Salisbury had been considered for the post by the Dukes of Marlborough
and Richmond, but was rightly suspected of being incapable of working
with Disraeli. 'I could not accept any quasi-official position,' he told
Lord Bath that month, 'which involved in any form or degree the
acknowledgment of Disraeli as my leader.'

When Derby died on 23rd October 1869, Salisbury's name again
emerged as a potential leader of the Conservatives in the Lords, especially amongst those such as Carnarvon and Gathorne-Hardy who were
anxious for the Party to reunite. But so also did that of Stanley, now the
15th Earl of Derby, who as a former Foreign Secretary and the golden boy
of the Conservative Party, as well as a close friend of Disraeli, could
stake a stronger claim. Salisbury had little time for Cairns, whom he
thought 'honest though weak', writing to Eustace that 'Dizzy was too
much for him.' There might also have been class considerations at
work. 'To call Lord Cairns a member of the aristocracy', Salisbury wrote
to Lord Stanley of Alderley, 'and not to call Mr Gladstone, is ridiculous.'

When Cairns, who had already made tactical errors in his short leadership, was encouraged to resign, the contest seemed to be between Derby and Salisbury. Gathorne-Hardy thought Salisbury was standing aloof, and Derby's diary recorded the widespread opinion amongst peers that: 'Salisbury's energy and talent are admired, but he is thought rash, and not entirely trusted: and there is also the drawback that he cannot, or rather will not, act with Disraeli.'[1] Carnarvon was in despair about effecting a reconciliation, especially when Salisbury agreed to attend a farewell dinner for Cairns only out of politeness and 'without any reference to any organisation in the House of Commons'. Salisbury and Carnarvon instead threw their support behind Derby. Carnarvon's original hope that Salisbury might have been able 'to take a sort of independent Lords lead not communicating with Disraeli' was considered impractical.

Derby was new to the House, had a weak speaking voice and several Radical opinions. He refused the offer, and then Salisbury almost immediately afterwards did likewise. He also turned down Derby's offer to mediate with Disraeli for him, saying that he supposed 'a personal interview between the two, of a confidential nature, would not be agreeable to either'. To Disraeli's evident relief they settled on the Duke of Richmond, a former President of the Board of Trade. In accepting the leadership, Richmond, whom everyone liked but few respected for his intellect, 'begged, as a personal favour, that Salisbury and Carnarvon would take their seats on the front bench', instead of sitting in the traditional place of internal opposition below the gangway. Salisbury 'took occasion to say in a rather pointed way, that he was not to be reckoned as a follower of Disraeli', but reluctantly agreed, as, more readily, did Carnarvon. Carnarvon still feared that his friend might prove a 'wild elephant', but at least he would now be one that faced in the same direction as the official Tory leadership in the Lords.[2]

On issues such as W.E. Forster's educational reforms, especially the Bill to allow an Endowed Schools Commission to modify the trust deeds of charitable bequests, Salisbury was in his slashing element. On the greatest political issue of 1869, however, the disestablishment of the Church of Ireland, he shocked everyone by voting in its favour, despite having denounced the measure regularly over many years. Salisbury had never thought much of a church which he described in the *Saturday Review* as 'a blunder unworthy of the genius of Elizabeth' and which 'appears to combine, in happy proportions, the lowest bigotry of the Scottish Free Church with the laxest view of clerical duty that was prevalent in England fifty years ago'. It was not on its own merits that this minority Protestant church in a majority Catholic land was sacrificed by Salisbury, however. His rationale was that because the 1868 general election had been fought primarily on the issue of disestablishing the Church of Ireland, Gladstone had a clear mandate against which the House of Lords should not stand.

It was a principled stance, especially considering the incomprehension of his dimmer supporters who found it hard to credit when he and thirty-one other Conservative peers trooped into the Government lobby in support of the second reading on 19th June 1869. It was, after all, on precisely this issue that Tractarianism had been founded. The *Spectator* believed that Salisbury's speech in the debate provided the main influence which induced the Conservatives to desert their Party's cause. It also implied the reverse precedent, however, one that Salisbury was keen to establish, that the House of Lords did have the right to veto legislation for which it felt the Government had no electoral mandate. Salisbury was playing a longer game than many of his detractors appreciated.

As the Bill passed by only 179 to 146, his intervention had indeed been crucial. Immediately after the division he said to the Liberal leaders, Lords Kimberley and de Grey, that they had won by more than he wanted, having only intended a Government victory by seven or eight votes. During the debate, Salisbury argued that it was for the Lords to decide 'whether the House of Commons does or does not represent the full, the deliberate, the sustained convictions of the nation'. Although he had to admit that 'the will of the nation' was in favour of Irish disestablishment, over the following years he would be able to deny that it supported many other key planks of Liberal policy, especially as unpopular governments staggered towards the end of their terms.[3]

The death of the 14th Earl of Derby, who had been Chancellor of Oxford University, also afforded another great opportunity for Salisbury, and this time not one he would pass up. Ever since his maiden speech, Salisbury had spoken and lobbied for Oxford's rights and privileges. His name had also been mentioned in connection with the University's parliamentary seat. Salisbury had a previous record of heartfelt political support for the University, especially his 1854 and 1863 attempts to preserve swearing to the Thirty-Nine Articles before matriculation and before taking the MA. If elected, at thirty-nine Salisbury would be the youngest Chancellor of Oxford since the Glorious Revolution.

He played the situation perfectly, putting Carnarvon's claims as High Steward before his own and modestly pointing out that he had not even taken honours, 'and have never taken any prize of any sort – except the fellowship of All Souls'. As the University Vice-Chancellor, Dr F.K. Leighton, was also Warden of All Souls and his greatest supporter, it was an exception which carried some weight, and the College endorsed his candidacy the moment Derby was buried. Some of the most consummate academic politicians of Oxford worked for his election, such as the ultra-Tory Balliol professor Henry Wall. Salisbury also found solid support from his own college, Christ Church, which at that time was almost a prerequisite for victory.

Other candidates, such as Sir Roundell Palmer (later 1st Earl of Selborne) and Carnarvon himself – both godparents to Salisbury's children – were persuaded to endorse Salisbury. Northcote was abroad. No former Prime Ministers were serious contenders and the Prince of Wales was known not to be interested. After his disestablishment of the Irish Church, his break with Pusey over the nomination of bishops, and his failure to be elected Burgess in 1865, Gladstone, the only man who could have significantly split the important Christ Church vote, decided not to take the risk of losing. At seventy-one, Lord Harrowby was only thought capable of being a stop-gap Chancellor. So when the poll opened in Convocation on 12th November 1869 and closed three-quarters of an hour later, Salisbury was elected by thirty-seven to one rogue vote cast for Carnarvon.

The Installation took place in the 166-foot Long Gallery at Hatfield on the evening of 23rd November. The Cecils, their servants and some guests, including Gathorne-Hardy, the Bishops of Rochester and Oxford, Sir William and Lady Heathcote, the painter George Richmond RA and Lord Chelmsford, watched in the wings as the Vice-Chancellor, three University beadles with maces, proctors, doctors, Earl Bathurst and Sir John Mowbray conducted the ceremony, including a long Latin speech from the University orator lamenting the late Chancellor. Salisbury's speech in reply was considered 'a good specimen of Latinity'. They then sat down for a huge celebratory banquet.

When the following May, Dr Pusey objected to Charles Darwin being awarded an honorary doctorate, Salisbury wrote to say that 'it is not desirable that the Church and those who represent her should condemn scientific speculations when they are only inferentially and not avowedly hostile to religion'. He complained to Leighton about Pusey's 'intemperate' letter, which had stated that he now wished he had never voted for Salisbury as Chancellor: 'As I neither asked for his support nor expressed any wish for it, he is scarcely entitled to send one his lamentations upon his mistake.' Three other prospective honorary doctors, Admiral Keppel (because he was alleged to have seduced a governor's wife on board his flagship), Judge Cockburn (because of his three illegitimate children) and Sir George Grey (because he was separated), also had to be withdrawn, to Salisbury's disgust. 'To admit Palmerston, Rawlinson and Layard – and then, on the score of chastity, to object to Cockburn, is to strain at the gnat and swallow the camel,' Salisbury complained. He did however manage to honour the uxorious General Peel, and made sure he was on hand to confer the degree himself.

At his first Encænia in June 1870, Salisbury's own nominees, Henry Liddon and Matthew Arnold, were awarded honorary doctorates. Liddon effected an introduction for the Reverend Charles Luttwidge Dodgson, a mathematics don at Christ Church, who wanted to photograph the Cecil children. 'They seemed a very pleasant and good-natured family,' he noted in his diary after photographing Salisbury, Cranborne and Robert Cecil in their robes as Chancellor and train-bearers, 'and their children very charming.' Dodgson, who later found fame as the writer Lewis Carroll, was a gifted story-teller and was regularly invited to Arlington Street and Hatfield to amuse the younger Cecils. 'I fancy *Wonderland* had a great deal to do with my gracious reception,' he wrote after one visit. Carroll stayed at Hatfield over several New Year holidays as the Cecil children grew up and the early chapters of his book *Sylvie and Bruno* are believed to have taken the house and children as his inspiration.

Oxford could not have chosen a better Chancellor, and the University had a determined champion at or near the seat of government for the next third of a century. Salisbury promoted a Royal Commission in the spring of 1876 to strengthen the University against the colleges, created additional professorships in physics, was partly responsible for the foundation of Hertford College and conducted a holding operation against non-resident fellowships, which he dubbed 'idle fellowships'.[4] Defending Oxford was the only reason, other than war or forming a government, for which he would cut short a holiday, as in August 1881 when he returned early from Puys to speak against the Liberal Government's Universities Bill.

Salisbury opposed the abolition of religious tests in 1870–1, warning that: 'You are absolutely severing the connection between the University and the Church. You are turning what for centuries has been an institution for the education of youth in the principles of the dominant religion into a simple instrument for grinding Latin and Greek into young brains.' He feared that tutors would begin to teach anti-Christian doctrine to impressionable youths, and although dissenting undergraduates had been allowed at Oxford since 1854, there had been a method to prevent practising atheists being elected fellows, until Gladstone reluctantly did away with it. As Kimberley noted in his journal when the measure passed on 13th June 1871: 'All the Tory leaders except Lord Salisbury were against further opposition to the Bill, but were forced by him to make a fight. They supported him in a very half-hearted manner.' As Salisbury complained to the Liberal Lord Ripon, the Government's behaviour had 'an unpleasant appearance of playing fast and loose – in short a flavour of Dizzyism'.

Speaking to the Church Congress at Leeds in October 1872, Salisbury raised the spectre of Oxford becoming 'a nucleus and focus of infidel teaching and practice', which, like the German universities, would then play its part in 'the de-Christianisation of the upper and middle classes' with the ultimate result that 'infidel teaching' would spread to the Bar, the press, Parliament, the Cabinet and eventually even into the Church itself. Parents would need to exercise greater vigilance over their children's moral guidance, he said. When a young, untried peer called Lord Rosebery argued that exclusively clerical fellowships might expose poor scholars to the temptations of taking holy orders simply for the posts, he was intemperately slapped down by Salisbury, who said that there were three types of Oxford gossip – common-room, undergraduate and scouts, and that Rosebery's facts derived from the last.[5]

Salisbury refused all further offers from other seats of learning to confer honorary doctorates and posts upon him, believing that the Chancellorship of Oxford scarcely required garnishings. When in 1864 Lord John Russell won an election for the Rectorship of Aberdeen University, Salisbury had been predictably caustic, writing that: 'He might as well apply to the Belgravian young ladies, or the Greenwich pensioners, or any other body equally discerning and well-informed, for a certificate of political distinction.'

In the Franco-Prussian War, despite his distaste for Napoleon III, Salisbury's sympathies lay entirely with France and against the worrying new face of German nationalism. He had first spotted the danger when reviewing German books in the *Saturday Review* a decade earlier, and then more directly during the Schleswig-Holstein War. In his essay on Castlereagh in January 1862, he had ridiculed what he called 'the philological law of nations', by which 'no two people speaking different languages ought to be under the same government', arguing that the British Empire comprised, 'without any consent of the peoples whatever, more nationalities than she can comfortably count'. Equally, the mere fact that one people happened to speak the same language should not qualify them for statehood, as the pan-Germanic movement suggested.

In the *Quarterly Review* in October 1870, whilst Paris was under siege, Salisbury explained how Bismarck used war and nationalism to shore up his own rule, because 'it adjourns all internal controversies'. His response to Prussia's demand for Alsace-Lorraine, ostensibly to protect herself from France, was sarcastic:

> At the head of six hundred thousand men, under the walls of a beleaguered Paris, Count Bismarck has the courage to pretend that peaceful, idyllic Germany needs to be protected against her formidable and intolerant neighbour. The allegiance of a couple of millions who detest her is the safe-

guard which her feebleness requires against the overwhelming power of France.

Salisbury believed that the concept of a pacific Germany was 'a new diplomatic commonplace' which there was nothing in Germany's history to justify. The bacillus of German nationalism was immune to 'the highest education, the most advanced civilisation', and in his *Quarterly Review* article entitled 'The Political Lessons of the War' the salient one was that 'if you scratched the cultivated German professor you will find the nature which made...the marauders of the Thirty Years War'.

Salisbury visited Paris in one of the first trains allowed into the capital once the Commune had been defeated in 1871, only a few weeks after King Wilhelm I of Prussia had been declared Kaiser (Emperor) of Germany in the Hall of Mirrors at the Palace of Versailles.[6] He made a detailed study of the Commune, building up a large collection of contemporaneous pamphlets and books on the subject, to join his collection on the French Revolution which he had bought in second-hand bookshops – 'my gin-shops'. He was thus present only days after the births of both Communism and German hyper-nationalism, the twin terrors of the next century. Unlike many intellectuals and statesmen of his day, however, Salisbury vigorously opposed both from the start.

Gladstone's Irish Land Bill, which sought to control the rents landowners could charge their tenants through a Commission, evoked a predictably uncompromising response from Salisbury, who saw it as an assault on freedom of contract. As usual, the rest of the Tory leadership in the Lords was inclined to be conciliatory. In a two-hour meeting to discuss amendments to be made in committee, with Richmond, Buccleuch, Marlborough, Cairns, Derby and Carnarvon present, 'the tone of the meeting was moderate and prudent, the only exception being Salisbury'. But even he was not about to try to persuade them to go to the last ditch in opposition to the Bill, as it was clear to him that the Irish landlords themselves were 'not capable of holding their own in the open fight of politics'.

Salisbury contented himself with pointing out that the difference between commercial recession in Ireland and elsewhere was 'that in England we put up with loss of bread, and in Ireland they shoot.... A paternal Parliament, therefore, compensates the Irish to induce them not to shoot their landlords.' Privately, Salisbury regretted not challenging the Gladstone Government over the Bill, telling Carnarvon that he feared that if they did not soon exercise the vetoing powers of the Lords, 'our future position in the Constitution will be purely decorative'. His view of the Irish problem was entirely unaltered by Gladstone's victory. 'The optimistic view of politics assumes that there must be some remedy for every political ill,' he wrote in October 1872. 'But is not the other view barely possible? Is it not just conceivable that there is no remedy that we can apply for the Irish hatred of ourselves?'[7] Instead, Salisbury blamed Britain's ceaseless attempts at political and financial initiatives, which constantly raised Irish expectations and thus helped cause the very problems they were intended to solve.

~

On 5th July 1870, two years after the 2nd Marquess of Salisbury's death, his widow Mary married Lord Derby in the Chapel Royal. The Salisburys, Beresford-Hopes, Eustace Cecils and Sackville-Wests attended the ceremony. It was a strange and new twist to the delicate relations which had always existed between Salisbury and Derby, the two most able Tory aristocrat politicians of their generation. Salisbury's earliest recorded mention of Derby came in February 1847, when he asked his sister Blanche: 'Do you know Lord Stanley's son? Is he clever or does he only want to seem so?' He was indeed very clever, as his firsts in Classics and Mathematics and his numerous prizes at Cambridge showed. Derby was something of a social misfit; he was sent down from Eton, reputedly for kleptomania. His father called him 'Grandpapa' for his obsessive interest in dull, esoteric questions and he is thought to have been the model for Trollope's Plantagenet Palliser (whose own fetish was for decimal currency). Peel had praised Stanley's maiden speech in March 1848 for its radicalism and toleration, neither attributes likely to impress Salisbury. Furthermore, Stanley thought John Stuart Mill's liberal tract *On Liberty* to be 'one of the wisest books of our time'.

When still up at Oxford, Salisbury had seen the then Lord Stanley, MP for King's Lynn, walking towards him along the terrace at Hatfield. 'Here', he murmured to a fellow undergraduate, Frederick Meyrick, through half-closed eyes, 'comes the future leader of the Conservative Party.' Meyrick said he doubted it if John Bright's saying about him – 'A very promising young man: he hates the bishops and despises his father' – were true. 'Ah,' replied Cecil, 'but he is his father's son.' Widely travelled after Cambridge, Stanley had visited North America, the West Indies and Ecuador for two years, before entering Parliament aged twenty-two, only to turn down Palmerston's offer of the Colonial Office and oppose the Crimean War. The similarities with Salisbury's early life are striking, and in August 1855 the two men toured Wales together for a week.

Something seems to have happened between 1855 and the early 1860s to make Salisbury turn against his travelling companion, and write a number of unflattering remarks about him in the *Saturday Review*, such as that he 'usually marches in the direction in which he thinks general opinion is likely to follow...looks upon statesmen only as straws in the wind, and resigns himself very contentedly to the dignified position of being such a straw'. Back in 1853 he had (quite unfairly) blamed Stanley for the unbridled buggery then prevalent in Tasmanian gaols, and in 1862 and 1863 he levelled a series of anonymous attacks against him, portraying him as a Radical in Tory clothing, only a Conservative because of his patrimony, whilst despising the Party of squires and Churchmen 'among whom fortune has perversely cast him'. He wrote that Stanley's speeches were 'absolutely colourless' and platitudinous, and unsound over poaching, Reform, ecclesiastical questions and the admittance of Dissenters to university.[8] Salisbury's hostility might, of course, be entirely explicable on political grounds alone – or it might be, as the editor of his voluminous lifelong diaries suspects, that Derby had an affair with Salisbury's stepmother whilst she was still married to Salisbury's father.

Another possible explanation is provided in the hitherto secret autobiography, *Apologia Pro Vitâ Suâ*, written by Eustace Cecil in 1909. A short, attractively bound, blue linen-covered book, embossed with the Cecil coat of arms and privately printed by Chiswick Press of Chancery Lane, *Apologia* was written as a posthumous bombshell, intended to offend as many of the Cecil and Balfour family as possible. In 1914, Eustace wrote a letter of intentions to his son Evelyn, then an Unionist MP, to say that he wished the sixty-four copies of this most unapologetic *Apologia* to be distributed to all of Salisbury's children, nephews, nieces and their in-laws, and authorising full publication of any extract from it.

Very rarely are cover-ups successful for over three-quarters of a century, but in July 1921, when his father died, Evelyn Cecil, later 1st Baron Rockley, wrote a memorandum explaining why he had instead burnt all but six of the books. One copy he placed in his library and the remaining five he wrapped up in brown paper, tied up with string and placed in a black metal box in the attic of his country house, Lytchett Heath in Dorset, where they lay undisturbed for seventy-seven years. Evelyn Cecil had an active political career, and, although he admitted it troubled him, he was not about to infuriate his colleagues and cousins, and especially Arthur Balfour, by indulging his father's posthumous and somewhat malevolent whim. 'To have distributed this book round the family would have permanently estranged our happy relations with all the Salisbury cousins,' wrote Rockley, 'and it would have alienated the Balfours.' Furthermore, 'it would have much irritated all the descendants of "My Lady"', Mary, Countess of Derby.

Bearing in mind how much of the *Apologia* was motivated by bitterness against his perceived mistreatment by Mary Derby and Georgina Salisbury, its evidence, written fifty years after the events it describes, cannot be taken as proof positive. Eustace also laboured under a lifelong grudge against and inferiority complex towards his elder brother. After half a century such reminiscences, however seemingly well remembered, tend to get embroidered. Lord Eustace Cecil does however state categorically that in the period covering 1856–7 Georgina Alderson 'did her best to marry Lord Stanley (the 15th Earl of Derby). Her suit, however, was not reciprocated, and she then turned her attention to my brother Robert, with whom she eventually became engaged.'[9]

If Salisbury had the slightest inkling either that Stanley had been his wife's first choice, or that Stanley had seduced his stepmother during his father's lifetime, it is easy to see why a distance, despite their overtly friendly political correspondence, would have developed between them. Serving in Stanley's father's ministry from 1866 to 1867 there was a certain degree of amiable banter between the two men, as for example when Salisbury asked Derby what he should do with a bearskin, 'which stinks horribly', given by a Hindu official from Oudh province whose pension he had increased. It was also Derby's £6 rating franchise compromise that had, albeit temporarily, saved the day at the frenetic Cabinet meeting of 25th February 1867.

Derby's 1869 diary makes reference to 'past differences' with Salisbury, and in 1870 to the fact that 'we shall never, I think, be on intimate terms again'. But it does not state exactly why not. When Salisbury congratulated him on his engagement to his father's widow, Derby noted that 'in the circumstances I am glad of it'. Despite Derby, who in 1863 had refused the offer of the throne of Greece, being one of the richest landowners in the country – owning 68,000 acres of Lancashire, Cheshire, Kent and Surrey – Salisbury still had to pay a large annuity to Lady Derby until her death, under the terms of his father's will. In 1887, this amounted to his third largest item of expenditure.[10] As well as simple political rivalry and a chasm between their High Tory and Radical Tory philosophies, therefore, there might well have been personal and financial reasons which aggravated the uneasy relationship, and helped to create the situation which in 1878 was to flare up into a bitter lifelong feud.

~

In 1871, Disraeli again put out feelers to Salisbury and Carnarvon to see whether they would reconsider serving under him, but once again the two men refused, Carnarvon largely because Salisbury insisted. An example of Salisbury's highly practical Toryism came early in the session of 1871 when a General Holiday Bill came before the House of Lords to add Easter Monday, Whit Monday and the first Monday in August to the two existing national holidays of Good Friday and Christmas Day. Salisbury, never given to Utopian redistribution schemes for working-class advancement but always receptive to ideas that might genuinely ease their lot, fought for it in committee against governmental scepticism, suggesting that they be renamed 'Bank Holidays'. The first one to be observed fell on Whit Monday 1871, and they have since given pleasure to millions.

Salibury's major campaign of 1872 was against the Army Regulation Bill, the abolition of the system whereby army officers could purchase their commissions. When the Secretary for War, Edward Cardwell, argued that abolition would encourage 'seniority tempered by selection', Salisbury retorted that it would actually result in 'stagnation tempered by jobbery'. He urged the Lords to reject the Bill and tell the Commons: 'We snap our fingers in your face against your decision, and will decide for ourselves in spite of you.' Once again the Conservative leadership in the House of Lords did not want to go down Salisbury's route of deliberately clashing with the Lower House, especially in so reactionary a cause, and they repudiated Salisbury's pugnacious stance. He was left to argue that Lord Granville 'has been the instrument – I have no doubt the most reluctant instrument – of insulting the Order to which he belongs.... He thinks that the whole duty of the House of Lords is to obey the House of Commons.'

Derby thought that Salisbury's opposition was merely 'gratifying an unhappy temper', but Lord Kimberley wondered whether other, more Machiavellian motives might be behind his hopes for a collision between the two Houses. 'Can it be', he asked his journal in August 1871 soon after abolition of army purchase had passed, 'that he wishes to destroy the Lords in order to be himself again eligible for the Commons?'[11] Both that analysis and the one by which Salisbury was angling for a split in the Conservative Party because of 1867 are wide of the truth. Yet nor could he bring himself to look forward to another Disraeli Government. 'I don't think he knows what truth means,' he told Eustace from his holiday in Lucerne in August 1871, and 'in the midst of this mountain scenery' the very idea of another Disraeli premiership seemed 'like the half-effaced recollection of a tiresome nightmare'.

~

Despite several ideal opportunities – such as Disraeli's high-sounding but essentially empty speeches at Manchester and the Crystal Palace and an anti-Disraelian conclave of senior Conservatives at Burghley

House – Salisbury deliberately avoided making further trouble for the Conservative leader in 1872. As Derby, his close contemporary, was the likeliest alternative leader in the event of a successful *coup*, this might have been prompted by tactical self-interest. In the October issue of the *Quarterly Review*, another chance to attack Disraeli was almost ostentatiously passed up. Instead, Salisbury wrote that when the Conservatives had another opportunity to go into minority office, as in 1852, 1858–9 and 1866–7, they should refuse it. Sure enough, when in March 1873 Gladstone resigned, Disraeli refused to drink from what he called 'the poisoned chalice'.

Although Salisbury had promoted a Bill for postal ballots in 1857, by the time the Gladstone Government proposed a Bill for secret balloting in 1872 he had come to believe that it would discourage the respectable classes from voting and 'proportionately increase the powers of busybodies, enthusiasts and party wire-pullers'. He was, however, once again the only senior Conservative in the Lords who wanted the Party there to oppose the second reading of the Bill. Still determined to force a clash between the Conservative majority in the Upper House and the Liberal majority in the Lower, Salisbury wished to provoke a constitutional crisis which would force a general election which he now felt sure Gladstone would lose. 'Salisbury destroys by violence the effect of his undoubted ability,' thought Derby in July, after he had insisted 'that the House of Commons is the expression of the opinion of the nation is a constitutional fiction'. Salisbury's scheme to embolden the House of Lords to throw out any Liberal legislation which had not got a direct electoral mandate was, he told a doubting Carnarvon, 'theoretically sound, popular, safe against agitation, so rarely applicable as practically to place little fetter upon our independence'.

Speaking to 400 members of the Bournemouth Conservative Association, presided over by Sir Henry Drummond Wolff, who was nursing the Christchurch constituency, Salisbury said that the Lords should be 'trying to aid, assist, and if need be, to control the House of Commons in interpreting the deliberate wishes of the nation'. To become 'the mere servile echo' of the Commons would mean that 'it will deserve and will speedily meet with its overthrow'.[12] They were sound, ultra-Tory sentiments, but Salisbury could not fasten them practically on to the Ballot Act, any more than he could on abolition of army purchase or the Irish Land Bill. When Disraeli refused office in March 1873, Salisbury grudgingly approved his decision, but assumed (wrongly) that it had been forced on him by Derby and Gathorne-Hardy. When Disraeli and Derby corresponded about the make-up of a future Government, they agreed that Carnarvon could be found a place at the India Office, but Salisbury had to be left in the wilderness.

On 17th October 1873, Salisbury presided at a large public dinner at the Corn Exchange in Hertford, where his nephew, Blanche's eldest son Arthur James Balfour, had been adopted as Conservative candidate with Salisbury's assistance. Three hundred and fifty Hertfordshire noblemen and gentlemen were present to hear a rumbustious, all-encompassing denunciation of the Gladstone ministry. Banners on the walls proclaimed such High Tory slogans as 'The Church, the Throne and the Cottage', 'Thoughtful Progress', 'No Sensational Legislation' and 'Reduction of Local Taxation'. A band played *The Roast Beef of Old England*, and Salisbury, on taking the chair, was 'much cheered'. Proposing the toast, 'Our Conservative Member and our Future Conservative candidates', he went through the whole lexicon of criticisms against the Liberal Government, which for the last five years had pushed through an unprecedented programme of administrative reform, and promised more, including, temptingly enough, the abolition of income tax.

Salisbury described it as 'a ministry of heroic measures', and, to cheers and laughter, explained why although their measures might be heroic, the Government itself was not. General Sir Garnet Wolseley had set off on an expedition against King Koffee of the West African Ashanti kingdom, which had ended in the razing of the capital, Kumasi. Salisbury mocked the way the Government 'turn the left cheek to Russia and America and demand the uttermost farthing from the Ashanti'. The disestablishment of the Church of Ireland had been solely 'in order to acquire the goodwill of a priesthood noted throughout the world for its arrogance'. The 1870 Irish Land Act 'places the landlord in an absolute wardship and tutelage of the police magistrate as to how he should manage his property'. Gladstone's great reform programme meant that 'if a year has gone by and nobody is despoiled and no institution is smashed, we say the Session has been wasted'. Government, he argued, 'ought to look upon Parliament as an impartial arbiter of their differences, and not as an instrument for carrying into effect a class of sectarian hatreds of those who may chance to get the majority at the poll ... the feeling of the people is that this heroic age of legislation must cease.'[13] He was right, and by early 1874 the British people had tired of Gladstone's seemingly permanent reforming.

In January 1874 the Cecils wintered at Sorrento, owing to Hugh's ill-health. It was there that a telegram was received, reporting that Gladstone had dissolved Parliament on the 24th and would be going to the polls on 1st February. Salisbury returned to England on Saturday, 7th February, to find a Conservative majority certain. The election campaign itself seemed to confirm much of what Salisbury and Carnarvon had predicted in 1867. 'Gladstone offers a bribe of £50,000 in the shape of remission of taxation, and Disraeli at once caps it,' Carnarvon noted, adding that he and Salisbury had always warned that 'the Constitution would be put up to auction at each general election.' The Conservatives, despite gaining 1.09 million votes, fewer than the Liberals' 1.28 million, won 350 seats to the Liberals' 242. A new Irish Nationalist parliamentary party demanding Home Rule had won sixty seats, which, although not large enough to threaten Disraeli's majority, was a grave portent for the future.

Salisbury's dilemma – perhaps the hardest of his life – was whether, if he was invited, he should join Disraeli's Government. As soon as he landed in England he talked matters over with Carnarvon, who clearly wished to go in. As Salisbury wrote to his wife, who had stopped in Bordeaux with Hugh, a conversation with Carnarvon had concluded that 'if I remained outside I should be a perfect cypher – which is entirely true; but slavery may be a worse evil than suicide. I urged that coming back into the same Cabinet with Disraeli as dictator would be practically a submission.' At dinner with the Derbys that evening, Salisbury urged Derby to challenge Disraeli for the premiership. Derby did not bring up the subject of Salisbury's joining the Government, 'but my impression is that he will prefer to remain a free lance'. On 9th February, *The Times* counselled that Salisbury and Carnarvon should 'condone the past and return', and the Marquess of Bath and the Duke of Northumberland wrote to Carnarvon pleading that he and Salisbury ought to go in to prevent the Cabinet being staffed entirely with Disraelian yes-men. (Disraeli once defined an agreeable person as 'someone who agrees with me'.)

Although almost seven years had passed since his resignation, the extravagant language he had used against Disraeli, albeit not for the last two, put Salisbury in a difficult position. What has been described as the Cecilian 'hair-trigger conscience' was never more delicately cocked. It is of course a mark of Disraeli's magnanimity that he still continued, after so many rebuffs, to make the effort to bring Salisbury on board when he had a Commons majority of nearly fifty and little chance of losing divisions in the Lords either. On 9th February, Disraeli told Derby that if he himself took the premiership and the Exchequer, Derby the Foreign Office, Carnarvon the India Office and Manners the Colonies, 'Admiralty remains for Salisbury's acceptance (but he will certainly refuse),' after which it could be offered to the Duke of Somerset.

The fact that Salisbury had returned from Italy at all was interpreted as a positive sign by the canny Gathorne-Hardy. The seventy-two-year-old Sir William Heathcote seems to have been an important figure in persuading Salisbury to accept office. Heathcote was one of the very few men whose political judgment Salisbury respected, having been Carnarvon's guardian and a High Tory and High Church MP since 1826, sitting for Oxford University between 1854 and 1868. They had been through many Oxford and Reform political battles together, and, on the evening of 9ᵗʰ February, Heathcote argued that the new famine in Bengal meant that if Salisbury refused the India Office he 'shall be held to have run away from emergency'. Salisbury told Carnarvon that Heathcote's arguments had come 'down upon me like a sledge-hammer'. As he also wrote to his brother Eustace: 'You could not think much of a lieutenant who declined to go into action because his colonel had cheated at cards or even had run away from a former battle.'

The opportunity of mitigating by resolute action his responsibility for the Orissa tragedy of 1866 was naturally a powerful element in his final decision. 'I am quite alone,' he told Carnarvon. 'I feel in despair – for I know it is unwise, and hardly right, to act on so perfectly isolated an opinion. I can only hope that Disraeli's arrogance may stand my friend – and that he may either not make the offer – or make it in such a way that we must refuse....I wish party government was at the bottom of the sea. It is only insincerity codified.'[14]

Salisbury had tended to despise go-betweens in private life, believing that quarrels usually healed themselves 'by the natural curative of time, until some peacemaker comes in by constant discussion to engrave our grievances ineffaceably on our minds'. By choosing Lady Derby as his go-between, Disraeli, who did not expect Salisbury to accept his offer, found someone who was keen to patch up family as well as political differences, and who worked hard to persuade Salisbury to accept. Both Beresford-Hope and Drummond Wolff later claimed to have been influential in Salisbury's eventual decision, and Carnarvon, Eustace, Heathcote, Lady Derby and Lady Salisbury all had their say too, but in the end it was only Salisbury's judgment that mattered.

Lord Eustace Cecil was unimpressed by articles in *The Times* and the *Pall Mall Gazette*, saying of the famine that 'one man pre-eminently, if not one man only...is despatched by ability and experience for this... present emergency in which minor differences should give way to the claims of public duty'. He thought them likely to have been 'inspired at [Disraeli's home of] Hughenden and in [Derby's home in] St James's Square and that there is a strong desire in certain quarters to destroy any independent power of criticism that you might have – in other words to shut your mouth and shelve you'. Eustace ended his letter by saying it was mere flattery to suppose that only Salisbury could be India Secretary, and anyhow 'the lieutenant is <u>not</u> responsible for the acts of a colonel who cheats at cards', which had not at all been Salisbury's point. In his answer to his brother, Salisbury admitted that the famine was already probably past anyone's help, but his best hopes of hindering bad Disraelian measures might be from inside the Cabinet rather than without. 'I know the House of Lords: my influence there, severed from my own party, will be zero....I am afraid either way it is a choice of impotence.'[15]

On Saturday, 14th February, Salisbury visited Derby at St James's Square to hear the deal that Disraeli proposed. Derby denied that the Government intended to produce a Bill restricting labour to nine hours per day, and Salisbury apparently showed little interest in franchise questions or even income tax rates. He was, however, anxious that 'though disliking the Ritualist party…no step should be taken against them that might lead to a breaking up of the Church'. Salisbury himself was no Ritualist, believing that devotion to Romish practices could be taken to ludicrous lengths. He feared that any legislation that could be framed to suppress Ritualism might also cover the High Church, however, and he also found distasteful the ultra-Protestant intolerance which he thought gave the anti-Ritualist movement much of its impetus. Derby referred Salisbury to Disraeli on religious questions, 'saying they were not in my line'. He purposefully avoided expressing any personal preference at all as to Salisbury's eventual decision, 'partly because with his temperament, I know that the expression of a desire that he should do a certain thing would probably drive him in the opposite direction'.

Salisbury wrote to his wife on Sunday, 15th February: 'The prospect of having to serve with this man again is like a nightmare.' With the famine in Orissa, however, 'to shrink from even an apparent post of duty is not to set a good precedent.' Still concerned about the likelihood of legislation against the extreme High Church Ritualist movement, Salisbury had a further meeting at St James's Square. On the way to stay with the Beresford-Hopes at Bedgebury, he called in on Disraeli at No. 2, Whitehall Gardens, but was quite relieved to find him not at home. When he arrived at Bedgebury, he received a letter from Disraeli tentatively inviting him to:

> have some conversation on the state of public affairs. The high opinion which, you well know, I always had of your abilities, and the personal regard which I entertained for you, and which is unchanged, would render such a conversation interesting to me, and, I think, not disadvantageous to either of us, or to the public interest.

Disraeli went on to offer to visit Salisbury at Arlington Street, or to meet at a third place, whichever he preferred.

Salisbury's answer was equally polite and encouraging, arranging to call at Whitehall Gardens at 6 p.m. on Wednesday, 18th February, saying that it 'would certainly be satisfactory for me to hear your views upon some of the subjects which must at present be occupying your attention – the more so that I do not anticipate that they would be materially in disaccord with my own'. The discussion at their meeting, their first proper face-to-face conversation for seven years, centred on Ritualism. 'Disraeli was very strong in language indeed. I must take it for what it is worth,' Salisbury told his wife; 'he pledged himself that the Government would introduce or, as a Government, support no measures against the Ritualists, but said that in his patronage to give fair representation to all schools in the Church.'

They also discussed whether Salisbury's younger brother should become his Under-Secretary. Salisbury thought that having two brothers in the India office might look ridiculous, so instead Eustace became Surveyor-General of Ordnance, a more junior post. 'I never got over this gratuitous humiliation which my brother Robert had he chosen might, by a word, have prevented,' fumed Eustace in his *Apologia*. He blamed Lady Salisbury, who 'showed by her rudeness (then proverbial in Society) to my wife and in other ways, that she was not inclined in any way to push me on'. As a result, he moaned, 'my political career suffered from the fact that I was never a favourite with my brother, and never thoroughly in his confidence'. Considering the way Eustace had behaved at the time of his brother's engagement, such indignation seems misplaced. His own diaries, showing how very often he and his wife visited Arlington Street in the 1870s, also tend to contradict his complaints.

Salisbury accepted Disraeli's offer of the Indian portfolio, though with very little love lost. 'Disraeli is sublimely ignorant' was his only personal comment after the interview. He knew that he would have only the High Churchmen Carnarvon and Gathorne-Hardy to rely upon in Cabinet should there be a struggle over Ritualism, but he obviously thought them enough. Disraeli wrote to the Queen that Salisbury had 'readily consented' to join his Government, and she answered that she 'highly approved', as Disraeli made sure to tell Salisbury soon afterwards. When on the evening of 18th February Salisbury dined again with the Derbys, he was in 'good humour, seemingly quite indifferent about politics, and chiefly concerned to know what sort of bishops Disraeli is likely to make'.

Salisbury inevitably came under criticism for his decision, from both the Right and the Left. Sir Rainald Knightley, the reactionary Tory MP, put down Salisbury's action to 'love of office and fear of being left out in the cold', although Lady Knightley believed it to be 'inspired by the longing to try and save India from this fearful famine'. The Liberal propagandist Frederick Dolman later wrote: 'In 1874 his ambition for public life, and his desire for office overcame his wounded pride, and he accepted office under the politician he had charged in 1867 with the violation of every type of political friendship. He suffered present humiliation, in the hope of obtaining future honour.' The fact that *The Times*, the *Daily News*, the *Spectator* and the *Pall Mall Gazette* had all urged him to join meant that Salisbury was subjected to far less public obloquy than he had expected, although he privately described their generous remarks as mere 'puffing'. It was Lord Rosebery's explanation, made in a valedictory speech unveiling Salisbury's bust in the Oxford Union thirty years later, that best explains his decision. It was neither naked ambition, nor a desperation to save India's starving, that finally made up Salisbury's mind, but the realisation that: 'He was living in a world, not of abstract principles, but of practical work; and, if he had ever to apply his high abilities to the public service, it was now or never.'

On the train journey which the new Government took together to Windsor to receive the seals of office, Gathorne-Hardy, the new Secretary for War, noted how 'Salisbury and Disraeli seemed quite harmonious', as though everyone had expected a row to break out in the carriage. Salisbury's own impression, as vouchsafed to Lady Salisbury, was that 'Disraeli's mind is as enterprising as ever and that therefore the experiment will be a trying one', but as he pointed out to McLeod: 'It is not permissible to decline work of this kind – however much I may wish that events had left me with pursuits which I like better.'[16] Salisbury's attitude is reminiscent of Frederick the Great's remark about Maria Theresa during the partition of Poland: 'She wept, but she took.'

NINE

A Careful Start

The Famine – Ritualism – Relations with Disraeli – Northbrook as Viceroy

February 1874 to April 1876

'He is a great master of jibes, and flouts, and jeers.'

'The language that has been used about the famine rather puts me in the position of a Portuguese sailors' saint,' Salisbury wrote to his wife the day after receiving his seals of office. 'I am frantically appealed to stop the tempest; of course the tempest will go on, and I shall be taken down and cuffed.' In fact although the famine, which had started long before he came to office, did continue, his exertions to relieve it began as soon as he arrived at the India Office, unlike eight years earlier when he had trusted his officials. The stocks of grain in Orissa and Bengal were large enough; the problem was money to pay for its transport to the affected areas. On his third day in the job, Salisbury asked the Cabinet for a loan of between £6 million and £10 million, a staggering sum, to meet the crisis, and he got it. (Only £8 million, by contrast, was spent by the United Kingdom to counter the effects of the Irish potato famine in the 1840s.)

The Viceroy was the Whig former Home Secretary, Lord Northbrook, who had taken over after Mayo's assassination in 1872. Salisbury wrote to him of his 'recollection of the horrors of the Orissa Famine of '66' and urged upon him the importance of suspending all food exports from India. Northbrook did not do this, yet still brought the famine under control in the most effective act of his Viceroyalty. He instituted large public works programmes in which workers were paid in food. Salisbury ensured the necessary funds arrived, and he wrote scores of letters to the efficient Bengal Famine Commissioner, Sir Richard Temple, encouraging him to spend as much as he wished. 'Even if it should turn out that you have made too large a provision,' he told him in June, 'it will be much better than to have lost life by the slightest deficiency in supply.' He reported that the Lord Mayor of London's famine fund had been ailing because of Temple's success. 'If we could only have some stirring news,' the Lord Mayor told Salisbury in a classic instance of horse–cart substitution, 'a few deaths for instance, the subscriptions would come in splendidly.'

Salisbury's moral sense was stirred by the famine, and he told Temple how 'the disbelievers in famine find no representatives in England, and their inhumanities only awaken repugnance in those who read of them'. He also believed that it had required the unique combination of autocracy and high-mindedness of the British administration in India to deal with the problem so effectively. 'No European system could have produced such results in the face of such an emergency,' he told Temple once it was over; 'the free governments could not have formed the machinery: the strong governments could not have found the men.'[1] The machinery included specially built famine steamers, which could reach those areas not served by railways or roads.

Salisbury next turned his attention to an issue which threatened to end his Secretaryship of State almost before it had begun. In contradiction of what he understood to be the undertaking Disraeli had given him on 18th February, the Government threatened to support the Archbishop of Canterbury's Public Worship Regulation Bill, intended to suppress the Ritualist movement in the Church of England. Salisbury had for many years been fearful of the threat of 'civil war' between what he called 'the Sacramental, the Emotional, and the Philosophical Schools' in the Church of England, by which he meant the High, Evangelical and Broad traditions. He believed that legislating on precisely which Church rituals were permissible might precipitate just such a clash. Yet the Queen, who disliked sacramental religion in general, Disraeli, the two Archbishops, Derby and the Low Church Lord Chancellor, Cairns, all agreed upon the need for legislation, with only Carnarvon, Gathorne-Hardy and Salisbury speaking up for the status quo.

'Romish practices', including altar lights and incense, genuflection and confessionals, had been slowly on the increase in the Church of England, and the bishops and courts had no legal power to stop them. Issues such as the reredos, the eastward-facing Eucharist, the timing of Holy Communion and the use of hymns provoked passionate argument in Victorian society, and the more excitable Protestants such as the Queen (who at one point threatened to go into exile on the issue) easily convinced themselves that the Ritualists were about to deliver the Church of England over to Rome by the back door. On 13th and 14th

January 1874, the Anglican bishops had met and agreed on a Bill to give themselves the legislative power to ban certain ceremonials, on pain of eventual imprisonment. Disraeli, who once described himself as the blank page between the Old Testament and the New, faced the break-up of his Cabinet less than six months after forming it.[2] As early as 23rd February, Disraeli was writing to Salisbury predicting 'religious sand-banks and shallows' for the Government.

The year 1874 was the last in which an entire parliamentary session was mainly spent discussing religious matters. When the Cabinet and Party debates became heated, Salisbury did what he had failed to do in 1867 – he stayed and fought to modify the unwelcome legislation from within the Government. He allowed Cairns to take over the official business relating to the Bill in the Lords, and even reluctantly gave up the parliamentary time in July which had been reserved for his pet Endowed Schools Bill. Salisbury tried to broker a compromise with Archbishop Tait by which the status quo should be preserved, and only new Ritualist practices outlawed, but it was not taken up.

Salisbury's personal lack of enthusiasm for the Public Worship Regulation Bill was made evident when it was introduced in the House of Lords on 11th May, and he stated that the Government 'do not hold ourselves responsible for its introduction'. In the committee stage on 25th June, he added that 'it was impossible to speak too lightly' of the measure. Derby was astute when he wrote to Disraeli to say that Salisbury was not a Ritualist,

> in fact he makes no secret of his opinion that that party are bringing the cause into contempt by their follies: but he sympathises with a great deal of what they teach, and (like Gladstone) he attaches more importance, personally, to that class of question than to all political and national considerations. His feeling in that respect seems to me exactly what it was when he left Oxford.

Although Salisbury regularly interrupted Cairns in Cabinet when discussing the Bill, and said in Parliament that he thought it all an intolerant overreaction, he did not actually vote against it. That he was keen not to fall out with Disraeli again – sensing that a second resignation from the Cabinet, within months of its formation, might look absurd – is proved by his invitation to the Prime Minister to stay at Hatfield after the crucial 11th July Cabinet on the issue. That was the meeting at which Disraeli had said that the House of Commons, the bishops and the Queen were passionate for a Bill which would stamp out auricular confession and prayers to the Virgin Mary, and the Cabinet agreed that Government time should therefore be afforded it in Parliament.[3] Wholly unexpectedly, Salisbury said that although he personally disagreed, 'he would not contend against the unanimous opinion of his colleagues'. Disraeli, who had earlier said that he was unwilling to act without a united Cabinet, was jubilant, and wrote to the Queen that he had 'passed the Rubicon' and 'the country is with your Majesty'.[4]

Having thus turned it into a Government measure, Disraeli proposed the Bill in the Commons, aggressively describing it as intended to 'put down Ritualism', which he described, in an ill-considered pun, as 'mass in masquerade'. Worse, the Cabinet then strengthened the Bill against Salisbury's wishes, so much so that on 24th July he wrote to Carnarvon: 'I feel that the matter is too small to resign upon, but my position is very disagreeable.'[5] When an MP called J.M. Holt passed a Commons amendment strengthening it yet further, Salisbury's patience snapped. He had long been trying to persuade their Lordships to assert their independence *vis-à-vis* the Commons and it was that, as much as the inherent demerits of the Holt amendment, which led to his outburst in the Lords on 4th August. 'Much has been said of the majority in "another place",' said Salisbury, in typically pugnacious mood. 'There was a great deal of that kind of bluster when any particular course had been taken by the other House of Parliament.' The word 'bluster' was therefore intended to refer to those peers who wished to conform to the Commons' view, not to the Commons itself. Salisbury went on that he, 'for one, utterly repudiated the bugbear of a majority of the House of Commons. It was their Lordships' duty to take the course which they deemed to be right.' They did, and rejected Holt's amendment by 44 to 32.

The next day, 5th August, the Liberal former Solicitor-General, Sir William Harcourt, called on Disraeli to defend the honour of the House of Commons against 'the ill-advised railing of a rash and raucous tongue', and, to general astonishment, Disraeli did just that. In an epigram that was to hang around Salisbury's neck for decades, Disraeli agreed with Harcourt and said of Salisbury: 'He is not a man who measures his phrases. He is a great master of jibes, and flouts, and jeers; but I do not suppose there is anyone who is prejudiced against a member of Parliament on account of such qualifications.' It was left for Gladstone to point out that Salisbury had not in fact described the House of Commons as a 'blustering majority', but Disraeli's pungent words were out. At last, after a decade and a half of suffering insults from Salisbury – who in 1860 had called Disraeli a 'great master of sarcasm' – the biter had been very publicly bitten.

Within two hours Salisbury had received an apologetic letter from Disraeli, saying that he had intended to give 'a playful reply' to Harcourt's invective, but what had come out was 'ill-conceived' and 'was, I fear, ill-executed, and knowing what figure that style of rhetoric makes in "reports", I write this line to express my hope that you will not misconceive what I may have been represented as saying – or believe for a moment that I have any other feelings towards you but those of respect and regard'. Salisbury immediately replied to 'My dear Mr Disraeli' that he feared he must infer that in the next morning's papers he would:

> find myself the subject of a severe castigation not only from Harcourt but from you. If so I do not doubt that I deserve it: and I am much too accustomed to speaking my own mind with very little restraint to complain if others in the course of their argument find it necessary to fall foul of me.... Parliamentary life would be unendurable if people took such incidents in bad part.

He was not so generous when that evening he wrote to Carnarvon: 'What impertinence he has been saying about me I can't conceive.'

Seeing shades of another 1867, Gathorne-Hardy begged Eustace, who had not been present during Disraeli's speech, to ask Salisbury to view the remarks not as offensive but as 'mere chaff'.[6] Eustace put his own negative interpretation on the situation, saying that he could 'only surmise that however funny and sarcastic Disraeli may have been at your expense he now repents it'. Salisbury answered his brother saying, 'I don't think I can admit you to the dignity of a Cassandra on this occasion... hard words break no bones.' Overall, although the 1874 session had been 'disagreeable', Salisbury was tolerably satisfied, if characteristically downbeat: 'I think I have been able to prevent more mischief in office than I should have been able to prevent out of it. Perhaps that is not saying much.'[7] By not resigning over the progress of the Act, and even giving up the most contentious clauses of his Endowed Schools Bill to provide parliamentary time for it, Salisbury showed he had learnt the political lesson of 1867.

After the 'jibes' incident, relations with Disraeli generally improved, with gossipy letters beginning to be exchanged and Salisbury gradually being introduced into Disraeli's inner cabinet of Cairns, Derby and Northcote. It almost required Disraeli to deliver a public admonition to Salisbury to settle the long overdue account between them. 'Since the Public Worship Bill,' Salisbury wrote to the Marquess of Bath in February 1876, turning down an offer to intrigue against Disraeli's leadership, 'we have worked together without friction of any kind.'

Friction was, however, increasing exponentially between the High Tory Secretary of State for India and the Whig Viceroy. The laying of the Red Sea cable in 1870 had brought Whitehall into much faster communication with India than had been possible in 1866–7. 'I do not regard myself as a departmental officer,' a chagrined Northbrook told Salisbury when London went into matters he felt lay solely within his jurisdiction, 'and must judge for myself.' Salisbury's and Northbrook's philosophical outlooks on the British Raj were diametrically opposed, and for all Salisbury's early politeness and professed regard for Northbrook, clashes soon began. Whereas Northbrook believed the British could become popular in India by good works such as famine relief, Salisbury primarily saw fear, awe and respect for the law as the key to British rule there. 'One thing at least is clear,' he wrote to Northbrook in May 1874, 'that no one believes in our good intentions. We are often told to secure ourselves by their affections, not by force. Our great-grandchildren may be privileged to do it, but not we.' To Sir Philip Wodehouse, the Governor of Bombay, he was even more blunt. 'India is held by the sword,' he wrote in June 1875, 'and its rulers must in all essentials be guided by the maxims which befit the government of the sword.' Even sixteen years later, the Mutiny was still fresh in his mind.

Salisbury had an aversion to according significant powers to any public bodies on which Indians sat. 'I have the smallest possible belief in "Councils" possessing any other than consultative functions,' he wrote in June 1874. Giving the Viceroy's Council too much independence would be, he argued the following month, setting a dangerous precedent. 'For it could in the end mean appealing to native opinion in India against the English government.' The fault lay originally with what he called 'the deadly legacy' of Thomas Macaulay, who had introduced Western education to the Indian middle class. Instead of primary vocational and industrial training that could have given millions a chance to raise themselves from poverty, he argued, the Whig historian and politician had instituted university education in the liberal humanities, which 'only manufactures a redundant supply of candidates for the liberal professions in a country where the demand is small: and in a by-product turns out a formidable array of seditious article writers', as well as an Indian elite which could never be 'anything else than an opposition in quiet times, rebels in times of trouble'.[8]

Over his favoured area of improvement – irrigation projects – Salisbury also clashed with Northbrook, especially over the appointment of a 'public works' member to the Viceroy's Council. In his first letter to Northbrook, he spoke of 'a special impulse' being given to irrigation schemes, but Northbrook was against having an Act of Parliament to place a special member on his Council. Salisbury overruled him and passed the Act, but nevertheless attempted to be conciliatory. One supporter in his irrigation campaign, who soon became a nuisance when she involved herself in a score of other Indian issues, was Florence Nightingale. Her high-pitched, bossy, precise accent has been captured on phonograph, and in the India Office a letter from her was described as 'another shriek from Miss Nightingale'. Salisbury always kept an even temper, despite her ever more importunate demands for direct Whitehall intervention over everything from Bombay's sanitation to the Madras death-rate, areas which he considered to be well within the Viceroy's jurisdiction. [9]

A major subject for disagreement with the Viceroy arose over Disraeli's and the Queen's desire that she become Empress of India, a title which struck Northbrook, as it did many Liberals, as an inglorious, unnecessary, un-British aping of foreign autocracies. Salisbury was also privately unimpressed with Disraeli's flashy stunt, with the City sheriffs proclaiming the latest addition to the Queen's titles, 'Indiæ Imperatrix', on the steps of the Royal Exchange to a flourish of trumpets. His initial reaction had been one of surprise: 'I know nothing about the "Empress of India",' he wrote to Disraeli on first being appraised of her wishes, 'what <u>does</u> the Queen mean?' He thought it enough that she should be called Empress of India on a few formal documents in India, rather than go to the politicised bother of officially altering her title. If it had to happen, he reasoned, it should be 'gaudy enough to impress the orientals, yet not enough to give hold for ridicule here'. It later emerged that the Queen wanted it partly because Germany had declared herself an Empire in 1871, so there was a danger that her daughter Vicky, who had married the Crown Prince of Prussia, would take precedence over her. The Tsar's 1874 State Visit, following the marriage of his daughter to the Duke of Edinburgh, is also thought to have encouraged the Queen to think imperially.

Salisbury complained how the Royal Titles Bill had 'brought to a head, and has given expression to, much latent feeling against the Queen on account of her retired life', as well as against the Prince of Wales for his fast private life. But he was determined to see it through, not least because it might impress the Indian princes who ruled one-third of the sub-continent. By 1880, Salisbury was insisting that in formal treaties the words 'and Empress' should always appear after 'Queen', and when Prime Minister in February 1892 he ensured that 'Ind. Imp.' would be minted on the British coinage as part of the Queen's title, which happened after he returned to power in 1895. [10]

One point on which Salisbury and Northbrook did agree was in refusing to subscribe to any master-race theory. 'There is no prejudice so catlike in its vitality as the prejudice of race,' Salisbury had written in the *Saturday Review* in January 1860, later adding, somewhat contradictorily, 'there is no sounder test for a high and true civilisation than its dealings with a race of helpless savages'. Like Queen Victoria, Salisbury assumed that although Europeans – particularly the British – were indeed superior to native Africans and Asians, it was both rude and impolitic ever to say so.

The surest way to inflame the Empire's subject peoples was to treat them as inferiors, he thought, so when Salisbury addressed the prize-giving day at the Royal Indian Engineering College at Cooper's Hill, Staines, the training centre for future Indian administrators and engineers, he always made a point of encouraging them to eschew racial arrogance. 'The vast multitude of Indians I thoroughly believe are well contented with our rule,' he told them in July 1875; 'they have changed masters so often that there is nothing humiliating to them in having gained a new one.' He said he deplored 'that "John Bull" spirit which led men to look down with contempt on every country but their own, and which broke out on the natives of India in anger'.

References to coloured people in his private correspondence differed little, however, from those expressed by anyone else of his era and background. When in 1876 the Foreign Secretary, Derby, wanted him to see Malcom Khan, the Persian envoy, Salisbury refused because, as he put it, 'it is better for the public interest that you should wallop your own niggers. Don't you think so?'[11]

Salisbury's attitude towards the Indian princes was just as mistrustful as to the multitudes of India. He had told the Viceroy, Sir John Lawrence, eight years earlier that they 'will certainly cut every English throat they can lay their hands on whenever they can do it safely'. So when Northbrook took the highly unusual step of deposing the Gaekwar of Baroda for gross misgovernment in April 1875, Salisbury supported him, partly *pour encourager les autres*. The Gaekwar, Mulhar Rao, had allegedly poisoned his British Resident, Colonel Phayre, and Northbrook appointed a tribunal to try him. Its three British judges found him guilty but the three Indians found him not guilty, and the Maharajah of Jaipur's casting vote went with the latter, to the Government of India's extreme embarrassment. Northbrook, who was convinced of his guilt, had the Gaekwar rearrested, bundled on to a special train and taken to Madras. He was later dethroned for 'notorious misconduct, gross misgovernment, and incapacity to introduce reform'.

Salisbury, who, in a sign of the times, had heard the result of the trial from Baron Paul Reuter's news agency three hours before learning it officially from Northbrook, supported the action but criticised the Viceroy for allowing anyone but British lawyers on the tribunal in the first place. He also wanted Mulhar Rao's entire family exiled, Baroda partitioned and a minor installed as the next Gaekwar, of which only the last recommendation was acted upon. Salisbury had even been prepared to find the Gaekwar guilty solely on the British judges' findings, 'though I know it to be utterly untenable in argument'. His reasoning was that the Raj was not based on legal argument but upon power, and that, if the Gaekwar escaped punishment no British Resident would be safe. With princes in general, as he told Northbrook, it was good to allow them plenty of ceremonial grandeur as 'it is often possible to pay them in shadows for the substantial power of which we are increasingly compelled to deprive them'.[12]

Although in general Salisbury preferred the princely states to be allowed to retain their own social customs, and he was loath to allow missionaries to proselytise in them, when in December 1874 the Maharana of Udaipur died, Salisbury was able to report to Queen Victoria that the practice of *suttee*, by which a widow joined her dead husband on his funeral pyre, had been prevented for the first time in that state. Describing it as 'this horrible crime' to the Prince of Wales in June 1876, Salisbury was proud of his part in trying to stamp it out.[13]

The Prince's visit to India in 1875 had involved Salisbury in some very delicate negotiations, especially as the Queen had not wanted it to take place at all. Salisbury hoped that it might improve the Prince's standing both in England and India, as well as strengthen the Crown's connection with the native princes. Much discussion took place about the status of the Prince in India *vis-à-vis* the Viceroy; whether or not the Princess of Wales should be included – to her irritation she wasn't; whether his high-spirited friend Lord Charles Beresford should go – to his delight he did; and who should pay for it. In the triangular haggling between Calcutta, Whitehall and Windsor, Salisbury and Disraeli drew closer, and finally had their views grudgingly accepted. Disraeli found £112,000 from Parliament and Salisbury squeezed over £100,000 out of the Government of India.

Salisbury insisted that India must finance a large part of the outlay, telling Disraeli in July 1875: 'It was time to put a stop to the growing idea that England ought to pay tribute to India as a kind of apology for having conquered her: and you have done it effectually.' Anything less would be 'a species of international communism to which I cannot subscribe'. All presents given by Indian princes would be sold to avoid a public outcry at the Prince making a profit from the tour. When, staying at Balmoral, Salisbury heard the preacher bless 'the objects of the mission', he quipped to the Queen's private secretary, Sir Henry Ponsonby, that he was probably referring to the tigers. Tigers were indeed shot, but serious work was also done and by the end of the four-month, highly successful tour, the Prince had also met the survivors of the Lucknow siege, held a grand review at Delhi, visited Nepal and met a large number of the more important Indian princes. Furthermore, contrary to the Queen's predictions, there had been no scandals involving what Salisbury called '*zenanas* escaladed on ladders of ropes' by Lord Charles Beresford.[14]

Although Northbrook was an orthodox Free Trader and Salisbury was not, over the issue of Indian duties on imported British cotton goods their roles were reversed. Northbrook wanted to nurture a domestic Indian cotton industry, and defended the 5 per cent import duty on finished cotton imported from Britain which raised £800,000 per annum in revenue for the Indian Government. Salisbury came under heavy political pressure from the Lancashire manufacturers to have the duty removed. In February 1874, Northbrook adamantly refused the Government's request to remit the duty and argued that the money it raised would require another tax to replace it, which would be a blatant act of 'sacrificing the interests of India to those of Manchester'. A commission was set up by the Viceroy that spring which reported, not surprisingly, that the tax was unobjectionable.

Meeting a deputation of leading Tory Lancastrian manufacturers at the India Office on 4th November 1874, Salisbury said that he believed them to be in the right and he hoped to be able to abolish the duty. The scene was set for a struggle that continued throughout Northbrook's Viceroyalty. At first it was good-tempered and moderate, but it turned antagonistic after 5th August 1875, when Northbrook announced a surprise Budget without informing Salisbury, which left the cotton duties intact while cutting revenues and spending in a way he had previously declared impossible. Salisbury despatched Sir Louis Mallet, the Permanent Under-Secretary at the India Office, to 'set the tariff right in the sense desired by Lancashire', but when Mallet arrived in India he fell ill. Salisbury felt that Northbrook never appreciated his political predicament and begged him to 'pay more attention to the guidance of English rather than Indian opinion. If Indian opinion goes wrong you can always disregard it; but if English opinion goes wrong it takes the form of a vote in the House, which pushes you inestimably into a line of action that may be pernicious.'

Although in general the Commons was not interested in the affairs of the sub-continent – 'India is like a bagged fox,' Salisbury had written, 'only turned out when there is no other' – there was always a residuum of MPs who did not go off to dinner during Indian questions, but tried instead to trip up the Government. Whereas Northbrook saw things primarily from Calcutta's point of view, the British Cabinet had to fit Indian policy into overall imperial and international grand strategy. Over cotton tariffs in particular, Salisbury believed that since 'native consciousness is only half awakened' on the issue, it could be largely disregarded, but the cotton duties stayed in place until Evelyn Baring, Northbrook's cousin, finally abolished them during the Viceroyalty of Lord Ripon in the 1880s.

~

Although the cotton duties issue had not helped, it was Northbrook's refusal to acquiesce in Salisbury's plans for India's north-west frontier that led to his taking early retirement in April 1876. Salisbury was no Russophobe; in a review of a book on the Lebanon by the famous former diplomat David Urquhart, he had diagnosed Russophobia as a form of lunacy and prescribed camomile to 'relieve Mr Urquhart of the frightful malady of Russia on the brain'. Arguing that Russia was governed rather as Irish estates used to be managed, incompetently and not in the proprietors' best interests, he discounted the danger she supposedly posed, just as he had opposed the Carthaginian peace some politicians had demanded after the Crimean War. In his first stint as India Secretary, Salisbury had followed the Lawrentian policy of abjuring any unnecessary clashes with Russia. In the intervening eight years, the Russian juggernaut had driven south-eastwards, however, crushing the hitherto independent khanates of Turkestan which separated Russia from Afghanistan. In the late 1860s, the Russians had taken Tashkent and Bokhara, and in 1873 they captured Khiva.

By the time Salisbury returned to the India Office in February 1874, therefore, the strategic situation was far less secure than when he had left it seven years earlier. He demanded far more accurate information about Russian activities in Central Asia, and in particular from the buffer state of Afghanistan, than Northbrook was able to give from sporadic reports from British spies operating there. An enthusiastic player of the Great Game who rarely begrudged the Intelligence Service funds, Salisbury had written in the *Saturday Review* that 'it is no reproach to a general on active service that he has used either bribes or spies in furtherance of his operations against the enemy', and he advocated the extensive employment of both in Central Asia. As he told Northbrook, his fear was not so much that Tsar Alexander II wished to harm British India, but 'that he is not rigorous enough to prevent his officers doing it in spite of him'. Northbrook, who had concluded a treaty with the Amir of Afghanistan, Sher Ali, in 1873, was completely opposed to Salisbury's idea of demanding a permanent British presence in Kabul. Northbrook's military advisers harked back to the disastrous experience of 1842 when a British expeditionary force had been massacred in a retreat from the Afghan capital.

Salisbury wrote to Northbrook on 26th March 1875 to complain that British policy towards Afghanistan was becoming 'dangerous and humiliating'. He asserted that, although Britain supported the Amir, she had not yet asked for representation in his country, despite insisting upon it from every other ruler in the world. The British agent stationed there was an Afghan friend of the Amir, who 'naturally tells us nothing'. Salisbury suspected that the Amir was either disloyal, or pro-Russian, or both, or possibly 'too feeble to be worth cultivating'.

As was his wont in everything he undertook, from reform of the franchise to the Great Eastern Railway, Salisbury made as full and intensive a personal study of all the relevant records and statistics available. India Office papers on every aspect of Central Asia were relayed to Hatfield, and by October he knew almost as much about the technicalities of the various political issues as the officials who had served there for years. But recent information from the three parts of Central Asia that most mattered, Kabul, Herat and Merv, was patchy and unreliable.

The received wisdom was that, should Merv fall to Russia, it would be a dangerous blow to British prestige in a region where, with hundreds of unreliable tribal chiefs holding sway over their own fiefdoms, prestige was all. This anxiety, inevitably dubbed 'Mervousness', grew steadily throughout Salisbury's time at the India Office. Although he never suffered from it himself, nor did he trust the Amir or any of his lieutenants. What he most disliked was the lack of accurate information, especially about Russian intentions. 'Your intelligence department is inadequate,' he bluntly told Northbrook in May 1874, encouraging him to get secret agents into Herat and Kabul as soon as possible. Salisbury continued writing in this vein for six months, becoming progressively more concerned that Northbrook had no plans about how to react when the Russians took Merv. In mid-December, he told the Viceroy of reports reaching the India Office that hawkish elements in the Russian army in Turkestan were likely soon to persuade the Tsar of a 'Forward' policy, and that he still had no reliable reports on what was happening in Afghanistan, telling him that 'arrangements to obtain them ought to occupy your earliest attention'.

On 22nd January 1875, Salisbury gave the Viceroy a direct order to request the Amir to accept British agents in Herat and if possible also Kandahar, for the first time since the 1842 catastrophe. Northbrook replied that fears of Russian designs upon India were based upon a chimera. Salisbury generally agreed, but argued that 'without a Resident Englishman upon the Afghan frontier you cannot know what is going on'. His own hope, which turned out to be justified by events, was that 'the Russian avalanche is moving on by its own weight', but due east through Central Asia, not towards India:

If it keeps north of the Hindu Kush, it may submerge one dynasty of Muslim robbers after another, without disturbing our repose. It will at last break itself harmlessly over the vast multitudes of China. If any frontier ever gave safety, we may surely contemplate with equanimity what goes on north of the Himalayas.[15]

Supported by Sir Henry Rawlinson, the former political agent at Kandahar and First Afghan War hero, and Sir Bartle Frere, the legendary former Governor of Bombay, on his Council, Salisbury kept up the pressure on Northbrook for formal diplomatic representation with the Amir. 'Afghanistan is undoubtedly our responsibility. We cannot conquer it – we cannot leave it alone,' he wrote to the Viceroy on 5th March. 'If we only have a fair start and plenty of information, we ought to be able to keep our moral hold on the Afghans.' Salisbury made it clear that he would not mind Northbrook 'creating' a pretext for action with Sher Ali, a word the fastidious Viceroy baulked at and was later to use against Salisbury. Stalling for time, Northbrook waited for four months before even replying to Salisbury's direct instructions of 22nd January. In the meantime, Salisbury attempted unsuccessfully to prevent Rawlinson publishing his bestseller, *England and Russia in the Near East*, a Russophobe book which described Sher Ali as untrustworthy, 'petulant', 'spoilt' and 'perverse'.

The Amir of Afghanistan, caught between the world's two largest expanding empires, was meanwhile trying to maintain his independence. He happily accepted bribes from both as he attempted to play each off against the other. Salisbury believed that Great Power *Realpolitik* abhorred a vacuum, and as he told Northbrook on 30th April, 'the idea of neutral territory is fundamentally impossible'. To Northbrook's complaints that Rawlinson's book was paranoiac and likely to anger the Amir, Salisbury replied that 'an indiscreet friend who goes about whispering that you have a very bad temper and are a dead shot has his uses', but he indicated that he had tried to get Rawlinson to tone down some of the passages relating to the Amir.

On 20th May, Northbrook finally replied to Salisbury's January despatch, saying that 'all those best qualified to form an opinion' believed that the Amir would refuse the request, adding that he could not himself recommend the policy.[16] Because Northbrook disliked Salisbury's method of communicating through private letter rather than official despatch, this view was repeated officially to the India Office on 7th June. The most the Viceroy would concede would be to send a friend of the Amir's, Nawab Gholam Hassein Khan, to sound him out. The complacent, even patronising tone of the letter, saying that suspicions of Russian designs on Merv 'are not confirmed by any one of authority here', might almost have been designed to raise Salisbury's hackles about the value of experts' opinions.

Salisbury told Northbrook in mid-October that when Russia got to Merv, 'for thither she will inevitably go', a British 'sit still' policy would ensure that 'the Amir will tender his faithful allegiance to the Tsar in a panic'. This was a far cry from his analysis of the summer of 1874, when he had told Northbrook that Britain had 'no power or interest to prevent' Russia taking Merv. As for Lord Lawrence, who had served in India since 1830: 'He is like a man who has seen a ghost in early life: he cannot get 1842 out of his mind.' Finally, after over a year of prevarication and opposition from Northbrook, Salisbury sent secret instructions specifically ordering him on the authority of the Cabinet 'to make the effort to obtain the consent of the Amir to the residence of an European Agent in Afghanistan'. This was to help prevent 'Russia being materially or diplomatically mistress of Afghanistan'. If that ever happened, he warned, Russia might either invade India herself, or more likely encourage India to be attacked by tribesmen keen on looting northern Hindustan. The fall of Afghanistan might also 'excite our subjects to revolt', and if it became a Russian satellite it would require a large British permanent force to guard the North-West Frontier, something she could financially ill afford.[17] Northbrook, by then believing Salisbury was bent on war, would not even agree to establishing 'listening posts'.

One of them had to give way. Northbrook had in fact written asking to resign on 12th September, citing his need to look after his young family (a reason Disraeli thought feeble). A month later Salisbury discovered it was not an empty threat and suggested to Disraeli that Northbrook be awarded an earldom, to kill the rumour that the Government wished to sack him, as 'people are looking around for a tin kettle to tie to the tail of the Government'. Disraeli did not think Northbrook deserved it, 'but you deserve anything – and therefore if, on reflection, you wish it, he shall have five balls'. Northbrook left India in April 1876, and his viscount's coronet was duly upgraded on his return.

There was no obvious replacement. Lord Powis and Lord John Manners declined the viceroyalty outright, as did Carnarvon, who had motherless children whom Salisbury advised him he ought not to leave. The Queen disliked Derby and so put his name on the list, which struck Salisbury as 'a charming touch of nature. It reveals a world of untold suffering – and desperate hope.' In the end, the position was offered to 2nd Baron Lytton, the son of Disraeli's friend the novelist Edward Bulwer-Lytton. Salisbury had known his Hertfordshire neighbour Lytton since boyhood. Knebworth, the family seat, had been built in 1490 when Sir Robert Lytton was a privy councillor to King Henry VII. Tory, literary and forty-four, Edward Lytton was only the minister at the Lisbon Legation when he became Viceroy, the Government's fourth choice.

The appointment was well received, and it was generally thought that he would work better with Salisbury than had Northbrook. In the meantime, as Salisbury told Lytton in May, Northbrook was on his way home, 'with an invective against me: but his invectives do not flow very glibly and I expect that his purpose will cool as he approaches our foggier sky'. In a debate on India in late March 1875, Salisbury had easily seen off the combined attacks of the two Liberal former Secretaries of State for India, the Duke of Argyll and Lord Halifax . He expected little trouble from Northbrook, whom he called his 'aggrieved Cæsar'.[18] For all his witty, charming, occasionally brilliant weekly correspondence with Lytton, and their family friendships and connections, it turned out to be Lytton whose cæsarism was to cause Salisbury and the Government far more trouble than ever had Northbrook's dour obstructionism.

TEN

Senior Plenipotentiary

The Eastern Question –
The Constantinople Conference

1875 to 1877

'Seasickness, much French and failure.'

'A strong and painful apprehension has been gradually stealing over the minds of English statesmen for some time past', Salisbury had written in the *Saturday Review* in November 1861, 'that the enormous efforts which England has made to uphold the Turkish Empire will not avail to avert its fall.' It was a *sine qua non* of British strategic thought that the Ottoman Empire, which had been declining ever since it was turned back from the gates of Vienna in 1683, by the third quarter of the nineteenth century was tottering dangerously. Although Conservatives and Liberals disagreed about what could or should be done about it, nearly everyone accepted the overall, doom-laden analysis. 'No false hopes can conceal from us the real state of the "sick man",' Salisbury observed. 'To all outward appearances, he is sinking fast; and the terrible calamities that must follow his dissolution are already casting their shadow over Europe.'

For Britain, the worst of these was that Russia might so capitalise on the collapse of Ottoman rule that by taking Constantinople she would be able to cut Britain's lines of communication with India and sail her Black Sea fleet into the Mediterranean. Were France to extend her Syrian interests further in the Near East, Britain's communication and trading lines might also be vulnerable. The Eastern Question for Britain was thus essentially a defensive issue, concerned with protecting her status as a Great Power by shoring up Turkey against the dreaded day of eventual, inevitable collapse. (In the event, of course, the Ottoman Empire lasted for just as long as the Romanov, Hapsburg and Hohenzollern Empires which had so patronised it.)

Salisbury would ideally have liked Britain to have accepted Tsar

Nicholas I's offer to Sir Hamilton Seymour of 1853, and partitioned Turkey peacefully and harmoniously between the European Powers in such a way as to give Britain enough strategic outposts to prevent Russia and France from cutting her routes to India. Occasionally, to the exasperation of his colleagues, Salisbury would propose this iconoclastic solution, but he could never find the support, either amongst Tories at home or in chancelleries abroad, for overturning decades of British Turcophile policy and cynically dividing up the Empire for whose integrity she had gone to war in the Crimea.

In July 1875, the Christian populations in Bosnia and Herzegovina, two of Turkey's provinces in Europe, rose against Ottoman maladministration and religious persecution. 'The Turks seem too hopelessly bankrupt to subdue Herzegovina,' Salisbury wrote to Northbrook in mid-November, predicting that if the two provinces were allowed their independence it might provoke such internal disorder in Turkey as to overthrow the Sultan, Abdul Aziz.

On 26th November, Disraeli dramatically purchased 176,602 of the 400,000 shares in the Suez Canal, an act of which Salisbury approved but considered to be 'a declaration of policy which may very possibly hasten the *dénouement* of the Oriental drama'. With his ability to think far ahead strategically, Salisbury appreciated how a British-dominated Egypt, albeit nominally under the control of the Sultan's vassal, the Khedive, the shares' vendor, might eventually take Turkey's place as the main conduit for Indian trade and communications, making the risks undertaken in British support for Turkey no longer necessary.

For the time being, however, Salisbury accepted that Britain had to act towards Turkey within her historical traditions. When in December 1875 Count Julius Andrássy, the Hungarian statesman and Foreign Minister of Austria, sent what became known as 'The Andrássy Note' demanding religious reforms in European Turkey, Salisbury advised Derby not to support it, because by so doing 'we should be, not protesting bystanders, but assenting parties' to the coercion of Turkey. The Note proposed the establishment of religious liberty, fairer tax gathering, a change in the Bosnian and Herzegovinan governments, and a mixed Christian–Muslim commission to oversee reforms. In themselves they were all very laudable objects, but Salisbury felt that to support them would sacrifice British influence at 'the Sublime Porte' (the name given to the Ottoman seat of government at Constantinople – present-day Istanbul). He also feared that Britain would gradually find that Turkey would become 'a protected principality' of Austria, Russia and Germany. Salisbury thought that Britain should herself demand almost identical reforms, but not agree to the Andrássy Note itself. 'It cannot be left as a no-man's land,' he wrote of the Ottoman Empire in January 1876. 'But the division of that kind of jetsam is particularly difficult. If the Powers quarrel over it, the calamities of a gigantic war must be undergone. If they agree, people call it a partition and denounce it as immoral.'[1]

Although Abdul Aziz agreed to adopt the Andrássy Note reforms at the end of January 1876, the insurgents in Bosnia and Herzegovina, scenting victory and independence, continued their revolt. When the mainly Christian Serbians and Bulgarians also then attempted to break away from Ottoman rule, the Sultan sent in Circassian Muslim irregular troops, called 'Bashi-Bazouks', to put down the unrest, which they started to do with horrific brutality in May. There was not much that was sublime about the Porte in the spring and summer of 1876, when its soldiers committed gross outrages upon as much of the Christian population of the Balkans as they could terrorise. In Britain the press, in particular the Liberal *Daily News*, carried harrowing reports of the massacres, which continued unabated even though on 10th May the liberal Turkish politician Midhat Pasha formed a new ministry in Constantinople, which later that month deposed and probably assassinated the Sultan, replacing him with his nephew, Murad V.

When questioned in Parliament, Disraeli and Derby expressed disbelief in the reports of what Britain's ally was doing in Bulgaria. The extreme Turcophile British Ambassador to Constantinople, Sir Henry Elliot, tended to play down the tales, blaming them on the exaggerations of *agents provocateurs*. Disraeli went a quip too far when he dismissed the talk of massacres as just so much 'coffee-house babble'. He even told the House of Commons, in one of his last speeches before becoming Earl of Beaconsfield, that he doubted the stories of widespread torture were true because: 'Oriental people usually terminate their connection with culprits in a more expeditious fashion.'

The stories of atrocities were largely true, however, and Gladstone, sensing a moral issue on which he could turn public opinion against the Disraeli ministry, published a pamphlet in September entitled *The Bulgarian Horrors and the Question of the East*, which became an overnight bestseller. Thanking the publisher John Murray for sending him a copy, Salisbury wrote: 'It certainly is the most eloquent thing he has written for some time. But he seems to forget that it was he who first took these charming Turks under the English protection.' When in a speech on Blackheath Gladstone called for Turkey to be turned out of Europe 'bag and baggage', the Conservative Government belatedly recognised that they had a full-scale political as well as strategic crisis on their hands.

On 30th June, Serbian nationalists declared war on Turkey, followed two days later by the Montenegrins. What had hitherto been a localised insurgency campaign had turned into a full-scale Balkan conflict. On 31st August, Murad V was deposed and his brother Abdul Hamid II was proclaimed Sultan. The Turks defeated Serbia at the Battle of Alexinatz on 1st September and started to win back some of their lost territory. With Russian soldiers privately volunteering to fight for their fellow Slavs against Turkey, and Russia herself in danger of being drawn into the conflict, the atmosphere of crisis worsened. As India Secretary, Salisbury was more closely involved with policy towards Russia than most other ministers. He warned Derby that should yet another Sultan – the secular leader of all Muslims – be overthrown by forces which were seen to be abetted by Britain, then 'a Mahommedan rising in India is a real danger'. To Lytton he cynically pointed out a welcome by-product of the agitation: 'Happily the public, supping its fill of Bulgarian atrocities, is enjoying all the secret excitement of a bull fight: and is in no mood to trouble itself with the depreciated rupee.'

On 3rd September, Beaconsfield wrote to Salisbury from Hughenden: 'Affairs are most critical. Had it not been for those unhappy "atrocities", we should have settled a peace very honourable to England, and satisfactory to Europe. Now, we are obliged to work from a new point of departure, and dictate to Turkey, who has forfeited all sympathy.' Salisbury generally agreed, but the fact that the Prime Minister still put quotation marks around the word 'atrocities' shows how far he was from Salisbury's view, who deplored the massacres and intensely disliked his insouciant approach. Salisbury has been accused of heartlessness for not expressing more openly his disgust at the Turkish atrocities. His response came in a speech at the Mansion House that November: 'Those who are in office have their feelings like other men; but they hold the resources and power of England not as owners, but as trustees.' It should not be doubted that for all his occasional cynical comments, his anger against the persecution of Christians was genuine.

Three years later, Carnarvon recorded how Salisbury's 'antagonism to Turkey was of the strongest, not to say the bitterest kind, and I understood and believed him to consider the case of the Christians to be one of absolute, essential, vital importance – in which morals as well as politics were involved – and on which no real sacrifice could be accepted without a personal sacrifice of honour and right from our point of view'. He further recalled how when they spoke about the Government's misreading of public opinion on the atrocities' issue, Salisbury 'was not sparing in his expression of feeling against Disraeli'.

Salisbury's attitude towards Turkey was well expressed in a letter to Lytton of 5th September, in which he wrote:

> Foreign affairs are in an unintelligible condition. Serbia's senseless rashness is as mysterious as Turkey's vitality. Turkey, a despotism without a despot, is governed absolutely by a set of officials who have no title to their places except that they were appointed by the man they murdered: is fighting a very costly war without money and without credit: and is

maintaining with success a desperate struggle for national existence without the aid of a single man of conspicuous ability, against the hatred of more than half her subjects, and against the growing ill will of the greater part of Europe. I shall begin soon to believe in the Hindu legend that the elephant which bore the world stood on the tortoise – and the tortoise stood on nothing in particular.

His stance against Turkey hardened through September 1876, and on the 13th he wrote to Carnarvon from Puys with penetrating prescience. Reporting that Beaconsfield's policy in Constantinople was to press for a Serbo-Turkish armistice, he concluded:

If we fail I presume Russia will act; and an entire change of scene will take place. If we succeed there will of course be a Conference, and the instructions given for the Conference will be of primary importance. Elliot is evidently disposed to make everything pleasant to Turkey. No advantage to England can result from such a policy now, and their alliance and friendship is a reproach to us. The Turk's teeth must be drawn, even if he be allowed to live.... I hold that all our troubles come from Elliot's stupidity and caprices; and I have been preaching against him privately and in Cabinet for the last two years.

Not only did Turkey pose a problem in the region but so too, in Salisbury's view, did Austria, which jealously watched both Russia and Turkey in south-eastern Europe and which prevented firm action being taken against Turkey for fear of opening a vacuum that Russia might fill. Salisbury showed he was quite capable of thinking both strategically and in an intensely Machiavellian style when, on 23rd September, he wrote two letters, one to Beaconsfield and the other to his Permanent Under-Secretary, Sir Louis Mallet. To the former he said that Austria's existence would indeed:

be menaced if she were hedged on the south by a line of Russian satellites. But her existence is no longer of the importance to us that it was in former times. Her vocation in Europe has gone. She was a counterpoise to France and a barrier against Russia: but France is gone, and the development of Russia is chiefly in regions where Austria could not, and if she could, would not help to check it. We have no reason, therefore, for sharing Austria's terrors.

Instead, he urged that Britain should come to 'an early understanding with Russia' to bring peace to the region, in the shape of an agreement that would squeeze out of Turkey guarantees for Christians throughout the Ottoman domain, over and above those paper promises made at Paris at the end of the Crimean War, which were being so flagrantly broken. The European Powers, he suggested, should prepare their own lists of potential governors of Bosnia, Herzegovina and Bulgaria, from which the Sultan could choose. Salisbury's fear was that 'we should make that result impossible by hanging on to the coat-tails of Austria'. Beaconsfield could therefore have been under no illusions about Salisbury's anti-Turkish and anti-Austrian stance.

In his reply from Hughenden, Beaconsfield wrote of the untrustworthiness of Russia, his own efforts through Elliot to get an armistice, and with some approbation for Salisbury's idea about the Turkish governorships. The Prime Minister was on weaker ground when he tried to argue that the new Sultan, Abdul Hamid II, had some promise, on the grounds that he had got W.E. Forster's speech on 'atrocities' translated and had taken a Belgian wife who had once sold him gloves and somewhat unromantically replied to his marriage proposal with the words '*Pourquoi non?*' For all Beaconsfield's obvious keenness to persuade Salisbury, the word 'atrocities' was still placed between quotation marks.

In his contemporaneous letter to Mallet, Salisbury was frank to the point of terseness:

> I deplored the Crimean War – and I heartily wish the Turks were out of Europe. But as far as I can see at present the difficulties seem to me insuperable.... The obstacle to any reasonable arrangement is Austria: and by that unlucky Treaty of Paris we are bound – to Austria among others – to respect the integrity of Turkey.

He even went so far as to contemplate outmanoeuvring both Austria and Germany in a bold stroke in support of Russia against Turkey in the Balkans. Three days later, in a letter to Lytton, he made it clear that he believed that no arrangement would work which did not in some degree detach the administration of the revolting provinces from the Porte. 'There is no doubt that the British lion – whose nerves are not as good as they were – has been driven half mad by the Bulgarian stories: which indeed are horrible enough in all conscience.'

After Cabinet on 4th October, Salisbury wrote to his wife to say that the Government was strongly in favour of a more active foreign policy, despite the recalcitrance of the Foreign Office. After much discussion the Cabinet had agreed to refuse Russia's proposition that she occupy Bulgaria, and instead Elliot was instructed to demand a six-week armistice and then an international conference. If this was refused, he was ordered to leave Constantinople and inform the Porte that Britain would start direct negotiations with Austria and Russia for imposing a solution on Turkey. If Russia carried out her threat to occupy Bulgaria, however, the Cabinet agreed that Britain would occupy Constantinople, although Salisbury doubted that Derby had really assented to that, 'but all the rest were against him, especially Great Cat [Cairns], who was very much for action'.

By 24th October, Russia's sabre-rattling against Turkey and Britain's diplomatic defence of Turkish interests, while attempting all the time to persuade her to institute genuine and far-reaching reforms to protect Christian minorities, had brought the crisis to such a head that Salisbury was writing to Lytton warning him that within three weeks war might be declared, and wanting to know how India could strike 'a rapid and effective blow' against Russia. Lytton's reaction was so belli-cose that Salisbury had jokingly to tell Beaconsfield: 'I am telegraphing hastily back to prevent the immediate annexation of Central Asia.' On 31st October, Russia demanded a six-week armistice between Turkey and her European vassals, which was accepted by all the combatants.

A conference of the six Powers who were signatories to the 1856 Treaty of Paris at the conclusion of the Crimean War – France, Piedmont (now Italy), Prussia (now Germany), Britain, Russia and Austria – was proposed to explore ways to pressurise Turkey into adopt-ing reforms, and thereby prevent Russia from declaring war on her. On 2nd November, Beaconsfield and Derby agreed that Salisbury would be the man to send to the Conference, which was to be held at Constantinople. Beaconsfield reasoned that Salisbury, as a leading Cabinet minister, could speak with more authority than a diplomat, and furthermore 'he is able, and capable of holding his own, not liable to be easily talked over'. Salisbury would be able to defend his actions in Parliament on his return, and the other plenipotentiary, Sir Henry Elliot, would not feel aggrieved if superseded by a superior 'not merely by rank but by official position'. Beaconsfield did not add that, because there was very little chance of the Turks agreeing to the Powers' propos-als, whoever was sent out would probably be considered to have failed. Although Salisbury had long preached against intervention in other countries' domestic quarrels – 'there is no practice which the experi-ence of nations more uniformly condemns, and none which governments more consistently pursue' – he was now about to practise precisely that.[2]

A scribbled note in Cabinet from Beaconsfield, 'I want you to go. That is my idea – a great enterprise and would not take much time. B', was the first Salisbury heard of the plan, and he replied: 'Of course I will do what the Cabinet wishes – but it is essential that your policy should be settled first.' Above all he wanted precise instructions as to how far he could go in coercing the Turks into accepting a settlement. Although he was given the instruction to demand administrative autonomy for the insurgent provinces, he was not allowed to threaten that Britain would accept a Russian occupation of Bulgaria if this was not granted. As a result, Salisbury described the mission to his wife as 'an awful nuisance – not at all in my line – involving seasickness, much French and failure'.

Support for Salisbury's appointment came from an unexpected source when Gladstone publicly welcomed it in a meeting at St James's Hall in Piccadilly. In private he was just as generous, writing:

> He has little foreign or Eastern knowledge, and little craft. He is rough of tongue in public debate, but a great gentleman in private society; he is remarkably clever, of unsure judgment...has no Disraelite prejudices, keeps a conscience, and has plenty of manhood and character. In a word, the appointment of Lord Salisbury to Constantinople is the best thing that the Government have yet done in the Eastern Question.

On 3rd November, when Derby finally proposed that Salisbury should go, the Foreign Secretary used the arguments Beaconsfield employed, as well as saying 'your tendencies are not supposed to be pro-Turkish', but 'your Indian experience will have shown you that Russians are not exactly the self-sacrificing apostles of a new civilisation which our Liberals seem inclined to consider them'. In his acceptance letter Salisbury was pessimistic, saying: 'I am afraid that there will not be much reality in the Conference. I doubt the possibility now of Russia being content with any terms to which Turkey can reasonably be expected to submit,' but promising: 'I will take my part in the comedy with all solemnity.' He first wished to settle 'the limits of deviation' and discover from Derby precisely how far he could go in trying to coerce the Turks into an agreement.[3]

Three years after his return, Salisbury told Arthur Balfour that before leaving for Constantinople he had 'constantly urged on his colleagues that it would be little use his going unless it was previously decided exactly what should be done in the event of the Turks refusing the propositions of the Powers. "Oh! but they won't refuse" was the only answer he could ever get; and with that he had to be content.' Whereas Cairns, Carnarvon, Northcote, Richmond and Salisbury himself were generally in favour of coercing Turkey into an agreement on reforms, the most important Cabinet members, Beaconsfield and Derby, were adamantly against it. Throughout the Conference itself, Salisbury suspected that Derby and Beaconsfield were sending the Sultan messages via Sir Henry Elliot advising him to refuse the demands which Salisbury was busy formulating with the other plenipotentiaries.

Beaconsfield announced Salisbury's appointment at the traditional Prime Minister's speech at the Guildhall banquet on 9th November 1876. The following day he wrote in avuncular vein, saying it 'is a momentous period in your life and career. If all goes well you will have acquired an European reputation and position which will immensely assist and strengthen your future course. You should personally know the men who are governing the world, and it is well to know them in circumstances which will allow you to gauge their character, their strength, and their infirmities.' It was reminiscent of the character of

Sidonia in *Coningsby* who, 'when he had fathomed the intelligence which governs Europe, and which can only be done by personal acquaintance, he returned to this country'.

Even before setting out on what he described to Lytton as 'this futile mission of mine', Salisbury attempted to outline the reforms he would demand. The *valis* (governors) of Turkish provinces should be appointed for long fixed terms, provincial assemblies should have taxing and spending powers, and Christians should be appointed to the police and militia in the same proportion as their overall numbers in the population. Submitting amendments to the instructions drawn up by the Permanent Under-Secretary at the Foreign Office, Lord Tenterden, Salisbury complained to Derby that 'their effect is to give Elliot discretion to vary while they tie me up'. Ever since late October, Salisbury had been complaining that Elliot's 'feebleness and prejudice have been our stumbling block', because 'instead of looking on and keeping his head clear, [he] is in the thick of the mêlée'. On 18th November, Salisbury's proposed instructions caused the Cabinet to 'differ more than we have done hitherto'. Cairns and Carnarvon wanted Salisbury to be able to threaten Turkey with a Russian military occupation of Bulgaria, whereas Derby and Beaconsfield stood out firmly against any such policy. According to Derby, Salisbury was 'moderate and sensible' through it all, but that did not help him to get his way.

On Monday, 20th November, a large concourse of people assembled at Charing Cross to say farewell to the Salisburys, who took their son Cranborne and daughter Maud along with them. Derby regretted Lady Salisbury going, as 'she will certainly quarrel with the staff, and say and do the most imprudent things: having great cleverness, great energy, and not a particle of tact'.[4] They also took four secretaries, including Stafford Northcote's son Henry, and a junior diplomat suggested by Tenterden called Philip Curry. That evening, Salisbury met the French Foreign Minister, Duc Decazes, in Paris, who seemed to suggest simply giving Bulgaria to Russia, Macedonia to Britain and Bosnia to Austria. Salisbury replied with what he called the Cabinet's 'consecrated formula', that Britain could not accept Russian military occupation of Turkish territory, but that she wanted to arrange guarantees for good government of the Christian minority populations.

The next stop was Berlin, where Salisbury met Prince Otto von Bismarck at 10 p.m. on 21st November, when 'he lectured me for more than an hour'. The man who was later famously to remark that the whole of the Balkans were not worth the healthy bones of a single Pomeranian grenadier took a predictably dismissive stance, arguing that 'what we were trying to do in Turkey was hopeless – you could not set it on its legs'. Bismarck's overall aim was to appease the Russians, who believed they had vital political and even spiritual interests at stake in the region. Salisbury found that Bismarck's view of the prospects of peace was very gloomy, but he looked forward with 'eminent satisfaction' to Russia getting into difficulties with Britain and Austria over Bulgaria. He further said that he doubted Russia's ability to defeat Turkey in the coming war, and that Britain should take Egypt or even occupy Constantinople if necessary.

The next day, Salisbury and his entourage met Kaiser Wilhelm I, the Crown Prince and Princess Friedrich, and Bismarck again. Of the latter, Maud wrote home to Gwendolen: 'Papa looks quite small beside him. His face is very ugly, the features all put on anyhow, they look more as if they had been caused by a volcanic eruption, like granite mountains ... [he] has a habit of darting a look at the person he is talking to as if he could see right through them.'

Lady Salisbury kept a daily diary throughout the Conference, providing an invaluable source in addition to Salisbury's formal despatches and telegrams home. In it, she recorded how at dinner on the 23rd Bismarck 'ate more enormously than I ever imagined a man could eat. He also talked all the time.' The British Ambassador in Berlin was Lord John Russell's nephew, Lord Odo Russell; he told the story of Bismarck eating a dozen snipe, 'beaks, bones and all'. The subjects covered at dinner included the German ultramontane party, the fortunes of the German Reich, 'the true story of the Lourdes miracle' (all based on sex), the cleverness of the Russian Ambassador in London, Count the General Pyotr Schouvaloff, and how Count Nikolai Ignatiev, the Russian Ambassador in Constantinople, negotiated like a horse-dealer. The Crown Princess, Salisbury told Derby, 'is shrewd, behind the scenes, and hates Bismarck like poison'.

On the 24th, the final wording of his formal instructions was cypher-telegraphed to Salisbury on his way to Vienna. 'You will not however suppose that we look upon the possibility of military occupation [of Turkish territory] by Russia', it read, 'in any more favourable light than that of an alternative which might in some circumstances be preferable to war.' It hardly clarified matters, and it gave Salisbury very little room to threaten the Porte. Because he did not trust Disraeli or Derby, Salisbury organised a special telegraphic code so that Carnarvon could keep him informed of the movements of opinion in the Cabinet while he was away.

At Vienna, Salisbury dined with the Emperor Franz Josef and spoke at length with the Foreign Minister, Andrássy, whom he found 'was exceedingly talkative and not very coherent'. At their first meeting Andrássy said that he assumed the Conference would fail and that

Russia would occupy Bulgaria. He also did not even want to waste time discussing the proposed reforms as he thought they would not be agreed. Yet the very next day Salisbury found that Andrássy was willing 'to discuss reforms and to assume that the Conference would succeed'. In the event of war, Andrássy hoped that Britain would occupy Constantinople and said that Austria must annex Bosnia. 'His language and reasoning were so similar to Bismarck's that I am convinced they are in concert,' Salisbury reported to Beaconsfield on 26th November. At one point, asked by Salisbury why he was seemingly indifferent to a Russian occupation, Andrássy stood up and walked silently to the map of the Balkans and, 'with a dramatic gesture, laid his finger upon the neck of land which separates Hungary from the Black Sea'. With Austrian troops pouring from Transylvania to the sea, he intimated, Russia's lines of communication could be cut off with ease.

The next stage of Salisbury's whistle-stop tour of the European capitals, which covered no fewer than four in eight days, was Rome, where he met Agostino Depretis, the Prime Minister, Signor Melagari, the Foreign Minister, as well as King Victor Emanuel II and his heir Prince Umberto. Salisbury found the politicians as pacific as the royals were bellicose, which he thought far preferable to the other way around. 'In the course of my travels,' Salisbury told Derby on 30th November, 'I have not succeeded in finding the friend of the Turk. He does not exist. Most believe his hour has come.'5 On 2nd December, the family boarded the specially chartered *Aurora* at Brindisi. At 9 a.m. on the 5th, they arrived off Constantinople at the Pera landing place. The first *coup d'œil* disappointed the family, the city being flatter than they had expected. Pera was the European and diplomatic quarter, and the Embassy *caique* was sent out with ten rowers in red and white tunics to row them ashore. The party took seven bedrooms and four drawing rooms at the Hotel Royal in Pera, pointedly not staying with the Elliots at the Embassy.

Almost as soon as he landed, Salisbury entered into direct negotiations with Ignatiev, who had attended the Peace of Paris in 1856 and had been Russian Ambassador at Constantinople since 1864. A charming rogue, Ignatiev had the reputation, in a heavily contested field, of being the most accomplished liar on the Bosphorus. The Salisburys quickly took both to him and to his bright, pretty wife. 'General Ignatiev is an amusing man without much regard for truth', Salisbury wrote to Gwendolen, 'and an inordinate vanity which our Embassy takes every opportunity of wounding.' Maud wrote that he 'is a broad man, not tall, dark red moustache and hair and eyes to match. He is very amusing with a sort of slap-bang manner.'

When the two plenipotentiaries were soon seen walking arm-in-arm down the main street of Pera, despite being warned of brigand attacks on unaccompanied, unarmed Europeans, rumours flew that Salisbury had fallen under the spell of the heavily-moustachioed magician. As he needed above all else to convince Turkey that Britain would not fight for her if she rejected the reforms, such talk worked greatly in Salisbury's favour. Only two days after disembarking he felt able to report that 'an accommodation will be quite possible. I am puzzled on its smoothness – and naturally look for a snare.'

It soon presented itself in the form of Sir Henry Elliot, a career diplomat since 1841 and Ambassador to Turkey since 1867, who had, in Salisbury's view, 'gone native'. Elliot immediately took against the man appointed above his head to coerce the Porte into reforms which for nearly a decade he had failed to persuade them to implement. In his autobiography he accused Salisbury of being 'ignorant of [the Turks'] character and of the temper prevailing amongst them', and of having 'put himself so entirely into General Ignatiev's hands' that he accepted all the Russian proposals without any independent inquiry. 'The Elliots are stiff, extra proper, not over goodlooking and madly philo-Turk' was Maud's estimation, and very swiftly a *froideur* was established between Lady Salisbury and Lady Elliot, who had for years loathed the young, attractive Madame Ignatiev with whom Lady Salisbury seemed to prefer to spend her time.

Elliot was later to complain that 'I found myself without one word of explanation, simply ignored as if I did not exist.' Salisbury's first task was to sideline Elliot and the equally Turcophile British business community of Pera if he was to convince the Turks, who reputedly had spies in every embassy, of the seriousness of British intentions. His major problem was that Elliot was able to inform the Porte that Salisbury did not speak for a united Cabinet. 'As soon as the Conference was over I went home where I found the Cabinet divided into two parties,' Elliot later recalled, 'and neither Lord Beaconsfield nor Lord Derby concealed from me how thoroughly they had shared my views.' Hobbled like this from the start and from the very apex of the Government, it was inevitable that Salisbury's mission would fail.

Salisbury, Cranborne and two of the secretaries were formally presented to Sultan Abdul Hamid II at Yildiz Kiosk, one of his four palaces, on 10th December 1876. He was, in Salisbury's account to Gwendolen,

> a poor frightened man with a very long nose and a short threadpaper body. Fortunately they don't use doors in a Turkish palace – otherwise an incautious slam would certainly have blown him away. We were all presented by a great fat man called the *Dragoman* of the Porte and afterwards (having sent Jem and clerks away) I had a conversation with His Majesty through the medium of the said fat man. He was all the time in a ridiculous terror. Any time he began a sentence of any kind he made a grotesque reverence

which consisted of three movements – first bending down as if to scoop up ashes, then punching himself in the stomach and then pouring the ashes on his head.... He wriggled, perspired, panted, gasped – in fact made such an image of himself that I had the greatest difficulty in getting out my sentences for laughing.

At the meeting, Salisbury tried 'to bring His Majesty to a sense of the seriousness of his situation', but had few illusions about the result.

Sultans of Turkey lived on the grand scale, some compensation for their occasionally short life expectancy. As well as his sweaty *dragoman*, Abdul Hamid II employed four chief chamberlains, twenty-three *aides-de-camp*, five professional talkers, an official buffoon, eighty *odalisques*, 120 black eunuchs, 300 cooks, 200 waiters, ten pipe servants, twenty valets and a brass band, at an annual cost of £2.2 million for his palaces alone.

The Salisburys disliked the squalor and dirt of Constantinople, but readily acknowledged that, as Cranborne told Gwendolen, 'on a bright day when you look down on Constantinople with all its mosques and minarets glittering in the sunlight it is very pretty'.[6] Lady Salisbury was more angry than shocked at the *seraglio* culture, allowing Maud to smoke a cigarette with 'a melancholy princess' in a harem. A row with the Elliots ignited on 12th December when Lady Elliot 'got very angry and made quite a scene when she discovered that Madame Ignatiev had been invited on a tour of the city walls'. Lady Salisbury tried to soothe her, she recorded, but her husband, 'being instigated by the Evil One made cutting sarcasms and drove her nearly mad. So she went off in a rage', pretended to be ill, refused to let her daughter go on the trip and, as Cranborne told his sister two days later, 'consequently we are thrown very much into Madame Ignatiev's hands'.

In the hectic pre-Conference bartering, Salisbury had meanwhile won important concessions from Ignatiev, informing Carnarvon on 14th December that they had got rid altogether of the proposition of Russian soldiers being allowed into any Turkish provinces, but instead a 5,000-strong *gendarmerie* of Belgians or Swiss would be deployed to keep the peace in regions which would pay a fixed revenue to the Sultan but not be ruled directly by him. They were significant concessions from a Russian Government which did not want to go to war, but would do so if necessary to protect Christian fellow-Slavs.

Salisbury received strange instructions from Beaconsfield on 10th December, 'by private and trusty hand', saying that he should try to get the Conference to accept a proposal for Britain to put the Turkish army entirely under British control, and then allow 40,000 British troops to occupy Bosnia and Bulgaria. Salisbury dealt with this ludicrous suggestion by the time-honoured diplomatic method of ignoring it altogether. At Birmingham, John Bright had made a speech attacking Salisbury's 'hearty unwisdom', but adding that 'he may do great good' if he did not act as 'the subservient representative of his chief'. Salisbury had no intention of it, especially as his chief was fundamentally unsympathetic to the Conference's aims of coercing Turkey.

A more worrying development was the way that he occasionally received more accurate reports of what was taking place in British Cabinet meetings from Ignatiev than from Derby. As Carnarvon was to learn on 14th December, Salisbury was 'rather disturbed' at the way Schouvaloff, a former head of the Russian secret service, and the man who in 1874 had arranged the marriage between Queen Victoria's son the Duke of Edinburgh and Tsar Alexander II's only daughter, seemed to be receiving sensitive British secrets. Salisbury suspected the hand of Lady Derby, who was friendly with Schouvaloff. Although Gwendolen Cecil suppressed the fact in her 1921 biography of her father, Beaconsfield agreed that Lady Derby was to blame. 'It puts me in a very awkward and difficult position,' Salisbury complained with commendable understatement. Meanwhile, Carnarvon fought Salisbury's corner in Cabinet, with varying degrees of support from Cairns, Northcote and the Home Secretary Richard Cross.

In his letters to Derby in mid-December, Salisbury argued in favour of a semi-autonomous Bulgaria, the detailed borders of which he was daily thrashing out with Ignatiev and the other plenipotentiaries. He saw her having a relationship with Turkey rather like America had with Britain before 1776, except that Turkey could claim her share of the Bulgarian revenue without trouble. He was hoping not to have to create a Bulgarian parliament, 'having no personal passion for assemblies'. If the six Great Powers could agree on the form a future Bulgaria might take, it would be hard for Turkey to refuse. Beaconsfield and Derby reluctantly agreed to Salisbury's idea of a temporary, neutral, probably Belgian *gendarmerie* in Bulgaria, and Gathorne-Hardy wrote to assure Salisbury that 'we put the greatest trust in your freedom of action'.

Derby, even while agreeing in Cabinet that the Conference proposals should be put to the Turks, privately hoped that they would be rejected. He thought Salisbury over-hasty in supporting Russia's views, although he admitted that he had managed to modify them. Beaconsfield agreed, and told his confidante Lady Bradford on the 20th that Salisbury had 'succeeded in all the great points of his mission as regards Russia', including the splitting of Bulgaria into two provinces, no Russian occupation, no withdrawal of Turkish troops and no disarming of the Christian population, 'which would create civil war'.[7] Nonetheless, he expected the Turks to turn the proposals down. When the Turks did exactly that, arguing that the scheme would 'compromise their "dignity"', Salisbury told Derby: 'It's like a street sweeper complaining that he has been splashed.'

Salisbury thought the reason was the Porte's 'belief that England will fight for them in the long run: and on this belief no amount of counter protestations appears to have the slightest operation'. He complained of the British Turcophile 'fanatics' in Constantinople, such as a certain Mr Butler-Johnstone who was claiming to be Beaconsfield's secret emissary and who was doing great harm by encouraging the Turks to resist. Ever since Salisbury had landed, Constantinople had lived up to its former name as the home of Byzantine intrigue, with two conspiracies exposed while he was there – one to kidnap the ex-Sultan Murad V, and the other to assassinate Midhat Pasha.

In order to 'squeeze the Turk' into changing his mind, Salisbury begged the Cabinet for tougher sanctions than the vague ones mentioned in his instructions. He argued that the moment was critical for preventing a Russo-Turkish war, which once begun 'cannot be localised' and which could easily turn into the general European conflagration he had long feared. Salisbury had won a major concession from Russia in getting Bulgaria split into two provinces, keeping the southern half well away from the Aegean Sea to avoid the possibility of a Russian port being established there with access to the Mediterranean.

On 22nd December, he indicated to Disraeli that 'if one can succeed in getting these Bulgarian populations decently content', they would probably, like the former Turkish populations in Romania, Greece and Serbia, eventually turn against Russia, whose path to Constantinople would then 'lie for six hundred miles through a hostile population'. Salisbury was convinced such a deal 'furnishes as strong a security against Russia as we are likely to obtain in any circumstance', and begged Beaconsfield to give him 'the strongest means of pressure' for forcing the Turks to agree to this reorganisation of their empire in Europe. The power he wanted was that of calling up to Constantinople the British fleet stationed at the Bosphorus, but Derby and Beaconsfield never so much as contemplated allowing him so potent a force.

The negotiations over the delineation of what were called 'the two Bulgarias' were tough and highly detailed and required from Salisbury an intimate knowledge of the geography of the region. As the senior Ambassador, Ignatiev was custodian of the map, and one morning Salisbury noticed that a frontier which had been agreed upon the previous night had been minutely shifted by the morning. Salisbury immediately spotted the alteration and drew it to Ignatiev's attention, to which the Russian replied: 'Your Lordship is so quick, one can hide nothing from you.' Instead of anger, Salisbury was 'convulsed with laughter' at Ignatiev's subterfuge. The frontier was then replaced to its original state.

On Saturday, 23rd December, three things happened. The Conference opened officially for its first plenary session. When the Turkish Foreign

Minister Safvet Pasha referred in his opening speech to the atrocities as 'événements relativement insignifiants', Salisbury 'in a few strong words protested against this description', and was seconded in this by Ignatiev. There was a slight pause, when cannon-fire was heard. This turned out to be a salute announcing that the Sultan had granted a modern, westernised constitution, the text of which was later read out in the pouring rain in front of Midhat Pasha, the newly-appointed Grand Vizier, and a large crowd. It promised a bicameral legislature, complete civil and religious equality, and 'the blessings of liberty, justice and equality. That evening, huge crowds bearing torches marched in front of the European embassy compounds in Pera shouting 'Long live the Constitution!' On the same day, the Cabinet met in London and agreed that Salisbury would only be allowed to use 'strong moral pressure' on the Turks: 'no coercion by arms, no assistance in time of war' was to be the avowed policy.[8]

By refusing to allow Elliot to send Derby reports critical of his negotiating stance, Salisbury hoped the Ambassador would request leave to return home 'on health grounds', but Elliot did not. Whether he was more dangerous to Salisbury in London or Constantinople was debatable, but the fact of his recall might have influenced the Porte positively. On Christmas Day, Salisbury telegraphed Carnarvon to say that, once the Turks had officially refused the Conference's demands, he would ask the Cabinet for the right to denounce the 1856 Treaty of Paris which had guaranteed Turkey's independence and integrity. Carnarvon used their cypher to warn that he was 'extremely anxious' that Disraeli was bent on war with Russia. He added that Derby was 'drawn along at his chariot wheels as if fascinated', and that he was now entirely isolated in Cabinet in his support of Salisbury.

Salisbury was irritated by the way the Turks preferred 'backstairs gossip' as their sources of information to what he had repeatedly told them face to face, that 'we shall leave them to their fate'. He saw his task, now that he had induced the Russians to yield what he had wanted in Bulgaria, as one of 'thumping and bribing' the Turks. But in his second interview with the Sultan – 'a wretched feeble creature who told me he dared not grant what we demanded because he was in danger of his life' – he made little headway. 'He is frightened by this nest of divinity students,' Salisbury wrote to his son Robert, 'who whenever the ministers wish to influence him are sent howling through the streets. They are very picturesque – but not in the least dangerous.' To the reports that Ignatiev was bribing the Sultan's ministers to support peace, Salisbury said he hoped it was true: 'It is a great thing to get other people to do the dirty work – if dirty work has to be done.'

Lady Salisbury had meanwhile learnt to enjoy Constantinople, watching 'whirling dervishes' perform a dance she likened to the

Highland fling, and buying Persian carpets for the Long Gallery at Hatfield. British society at Pera she found 'overdressed and underbred' and their gossip an exaggerated version of the Bennett family's in *Pride and Prejudice*. She was amused when one grand Turkish lady advised her to tell her husband to poison Midhat: 'I do not see the harm. A cup of coffee and then one man less in the world. That is all.' The Persian minister's wife, a former slave-girl who was reputed to have cost him £700, Lady Salisbury sniffed was 'cheap at the money'. Maud, too, had a good line in put-downs. When proudly told that the road on which they were travelling had been built by the Emperor Constantine in the fourth century, she inquired whether anyone had mended it since.[9]

Beaconsfield's and Derby's cynicism towards the mission was perfectly illustrated on Boxing Day 1876, when the latter wrote in his diary of their irritation that the Opposition were praising Salisbury for being more anti-Turkish than the Government.

> D[israeli] dwelt on the awkwardness of allowing this impression to prevail. I agreed, but pointed out on the other hand that the mission would almost certainly fail, that we had foreseen this from the first, and that what was of the most importance was to take from Salisbury's special partisans the possibility of saying that he had failed because thwarted at home. The more certain the Conference was to end in nothing, the more it behoved us to be able to prove that we had given it every chance of succeeding.

They again refused to allow Salisbury to bring the fleet then stationed at Besika Bay up to Constantinople. On the same day, Salisbury wrote to Eustace saying that he was 'convinced that we must look for our securities elsewhere than to a Turkish alliance. It is a vain support.'

By 29th December, Salisbury was begging Derby to recall Elliot, who had still not left Constantinople. The other plenipotentiaries from the Great Powers 'have all separately urged me most earnestly to procure Sir Henry's absence, as a most important addition to our chances of peace … he allows it to be seen that his sympathies are with the Turks, and against the proposals of the Powers'. As that was also Derby's and Beaconsfield's true stance, nothing was done, even though Salisbury used the strongest language, writing that the Cabinet 'should know in how false and difficult a position I stand. All that I can do is undone, effectively but unconsciously, by the man who is supposed to represent the views and wishes of the English Government.'[10] He was not asking for Elliot's dishonourable discharge, merely that he 'should be induced to come away for a short time'.

Beaconsfield was entirely unsympathetic, telling Derby that

'Salisbury seems most prejudiced, and not to be aware that his principal object, in being sent to Constantinople, is to keep the Russians out of Turkey, not to create an ideal existence for Turkish Christians.' In the same week, Ignatiev and Midhat signed a two-month armistice, but Turkey still showed no sign of willingness to accede to the Great Powers' demands. When finally the Conference received a counter-proposal from the Porte, it omitted all the guarantees that they had installed, such as fixed-term *valis*, militias open to Christians and the appointment of *valis* by agreement with the Great Powers. The Powers regarded the Turkish reply as an intentional insult. The Porte had also rejected amnesties for prisoners, local languages on the same footing as Turkish and the cantonment of Turkish troops, as well as the Powers' taxation and immigration proposals. Salisbury proposed, and the Conference agreed, to give the Porte one more opportunity to deliver a more satisfactory reply without delay.

The Conference staggered on for another three weeks, with Derby and Beaconsfield refusing to recall Elliot, ostensibly because the Russians had asked them to. Salisbury let the Turks know he had telegraphed to Admiral Drummond to send a ship to collect him, after which he would leave the city to its fate. 'Convincing the Turk is about as easy as making a donkey canter,' Salisbury wrote to Derby, blaming in part the 'fanatics, oddities and all the *déclassé* scoundrels' who made up the British community in Constantinople and who, in the hope of future defence contracting profits, were urging the Turks to resist the Powers to the utmost, even if it meant war with Russia.

More despatches and telegrams were sent to and fro, but with increasing despair and suspicion on Salisbury's part. On 6th January 1877, he wrote to Derby that somehow the British Government's proposed concessions to the Porte had been leaked to the Turks: 'Indiscretion very mysterious: somebody is playing foul. I fear the result will be to make Turks refuse to concede anything.' Derby denied that he was in any way involved, and blamed Decazes's ill-advised language in Paris, but Salisbury still suspected that Lady Derby was to blame. On 9th January, Salisbury dropped his demand for Elliot's recall as the 'enormous evil' he had done 'may not be reparable now'. Two days later, he stated his regret at ever having taken on the mission while Elliot was still *en poste*, but he blamed the British policy of blind support for Turkey ever since the Crimean War more than the Ambassador.

When on 14th January all the Great Powers' Ambassadors said that they would leave Constantinople if the Turks rejected their new, greatly reduced proposals, Elliot refused to promise to join them. Salisbury wrote to Derby saying that this 'will create the greatest scandal', and immediately justify all the rumours that 'the British Government does not support me'. At last Beaconsfield gave some tangible support, ordering Elliot to follow Salisbury out of Constantinople if and when he went. As to policy after the collapse of the Conference, Salisbury wrote to Derby to urge that Britain come to terms with Andrássy and the Russian Chancellor and Foreign Minister, Prince Alexander Gortschakoff, for a regulated occupation of Bulgaria and Bosnia as the safest future course to avoid a direct Anglo-Russian clash.[11]

On 20th January, the Porte formally refused the Powers' final, watered-down terms, believing that Russia would not defeat them in the inevitable war and that Britain must in the end support them or lose her Asia Minor route to India. Salisbury believed that the suspicion that he did not really represent the British Government had certainly increased 'the obstinacy of the Turk'. He took the initiative in closing the Conference and getting agreement that all the plenipotentiaries would leave on 22nd January. As he told the Conference:

> I am charged to declare formally that Great Britain is resolved to give her sanction neither to bad administration nor to oppression, and if the Porte, through obstinacy or inertness, resists the efforts which are being made at present with the object of placing the Ottoman Empire upon a more secure basis, the responsibility for the consequences which will follow will rest solely on the Sultan and his advisers.

That evening the Salisburys went to the French Embassy, 'where we found all the world dancing so we danced too and forgot the sorrows of the world'. Bismarck's and Andrássy's predictions had been vindicated. Salisbury was at least spared a final audience with the Sultan, who pleaded diplomatic toothache rather than bid farewell to the Powers' plenipotentiaries. Returning to London via Athens, Brindisi, Naples and Rome, Salisbury took his time, 'for I am very tired'. To make matters worse, a storm in the Bosphorus caused him to fulfil his original prediction of 'seasickness, much French and failure'.

Salisbury expected a hostile reception on his return, but in fact received a warm one. *Punch* produced a cartoon of him pushing the sick man of Turkey's bathchair, above a ditty which rhymed 'in Asia' with Turkey's 'euthanasia'. Another cartoon, published on 27th January, had Mr Punch asking the British lion: 'If you didn't mean to back him up, why did you send him?' With his black beard, high brow and ubiquitous privy councillor uniform, Salisbury started to become identifiable to a wider public in caricature, an important point in any politician's career.

The Conservative Party had never wanted to see Turkey forced into a corner anyhow, and Salisbury's supporters, such as Lord Bath, put it about that his failure was due 'to his being overruled at home by Dizzy and other and higher authorities', meaning the Queen. She herself was 'very civil', the Cabinet greeted him 'quite enthusiastically', and he was cheered louder than Lord Beaconsfield when he walked into the House of Lords chamber to take his seat.[12] Gladstone's opinion, vouchsafed to his wife, was that 'Salisbury (for the second time in his life, the first in 1867) [was] proving his manhood.'

To be able to witness for himself the complexities and realities of the most important international question of the age was to prove invaluable for Salisbury when he became Foreign Secretary. As well as appreciating Bismarck's cynicism – 'such a man's friendship you can never trust … all the result of a Jesuit education' – and having reiterated the truth that force is all when it came to negotiations, Salisbury left Constantinople, as he told Carnarvon, with an ineradicable belief in 'the task of devising some other means of securing the road to India'. As in 1867, Salisbury had failed, but he had learnt.

ELEVEN

Cabinet Crises

A Fractured Ministry – 'Jingoism'
– The Russo-Turkish War –
The Fall of Lord Derby

February 1877 to March 1878

'If our ancestors had cared for the rights of other people,
the British Empire would not have been made.'

Salisbury arrived at Charing Cross at 6.30 p.m. on Wednesday, 6th February 1877, having taken a special train from Dover that left half an hour earlier than Sir Henry Elliot's. He was met at the station by Sir Stafford Northcote and, ironically enough, Lady Derby, and then drove to Arlington Street for dinner with Carnarvon, who had taken over the day-to-day running of the India Office in his absence. The two men talked until midnight, and two years later his colleague remembered how he appeared 'to have but one feeling – viz; a rooted belief in Disraeli's untruthfulness, and a dread of the policy which he thought Disraeli intended to pursue'.

A letter from Beaconsfield was waiting for him at Arlington Street expressing the hope that 'you will not permit the immediate result of the Conference unduly to depress you', and announcing a Cabinet meeting for the next morning at noon. The Prime Minister thought it was 'a compliment to Lord Salisbury though I dare say he would rather remain in bed'. Although it was a 'most harmonious' meeting, Salisbury harboured a rumbling suspicion that he had been let down in London. Had he seen Derby's diary entry about Sir Henry Elliot, ('I am…determined to uphold him'), and had known that Derby and Beaconsfield planned Elliot to return to Constantinople as soon as possible, those suspicions would have been confirmed. Telling Derby that 'the kind of criticism which I fear is that which would charge us with insouciance and inactivity', Salisbury served notice that he fully intended to take a central part in the forthcoming Cabinet debates on the Eastern

Question. In a speech to the Associated Chambers of Commerce, he argued that the Conference had not been a complete failure; although common sense had not been infused into the Turks, the Powers had at least shown that they could work together.[1]

Because the Balkan roads were impassable before spring, there was a lull before the Russo-Turkish War broke out. Salisbury was highly sceptical of Europe brokering an agreement in the meantime, and feared that Bismarck might use the opportunity to attack France. 'If things go wrong,' he told Lytton, 'we may be fighting for Holland before two years are out.' His growing criticism of Derby – he used to say that contending with him in Cabinet was 'like fighting a featherbed' – was based on the Foreign Secretary's refusal to 'provide ourselves with a *pied à terre*' in the Near East upon which Britain could fall back in an emergency. Instead, as he told Lytton with irritation: 'English policy is to float lazily downstream, occasionally putting out a diplomatic boathook to avoid collisions.'[2]

Salisbury wanted an active policy to pursue 'some territorial re-arrangement', such as the acquisition of Crete or the Dardanelles, as he believed the old policy of sustaining the Ottoman Empire was no longer practicable. With an aggressive France, and Germany threatening to become a great naval power, Salisbury argued that Britain needed more Mediterranean security than hitherto, probably at Turkish expense. At the time, Beaconsfield called such radical strategic thinking 'immoral', and Gwendolen well remembered how her father would reminisce about this in later life 'with a grimly ironic smile', once Germany had built her High Seas fleet.

Salisbury was perfectly prepared to conduct his own foreign policy, and even sent his wife to Paris to meet Ignatiev secretly on 8th March. Ignatiev said that Schouvaloff was about to present a Protocol to Turkey, 'the last and only chance of averting the catastrophe', and hoped Britain would lend her support. When Germany came out in support of the Protocol a few days later, Salisbury wrote to Beaconsfield to argue that if Britain rejected it, 'We shall have brought on a war by this isolation.' Britain, he argued, should not refuse a Protocol which bound her to nothing to which she was not pledged already and which was, in his opinion, extremely moderate.

On 15th March, Ignatiev arrived in Britain to stay at Hatfield, and Salisbury asked for a Cabinet meeting to get a final decision on the Russian Protocol before seeing him, for otherwise he feared 'things will be said which had better not have been said'.[3] Beaconsfield thought the visit 'inopportune' and said he could not call a Cabinet 'without interfering discourteously with Lord Derby'. The shades of the events of exactly a decade before were obvious to all, with Derby taking the part of his father. The fiercely Russophobe Queen Victoria reacted with 'dismay' at Ignatiev's presence in Britain, and Derby was privately indignant at this virtual commandeering of foreign policy by Salisbury.

Staying at Hatfield, Madame Ignatiev summed up English country-house life as: 'Eat and dawdle, dawdle and eat', but on that particular weekend serious business was done by her husband, albeit largely with the Opposition because the senior Conservatives, led by Beaconsfield and Derby, all declined Salisbury's invitation. Lord Hartington, then acting leader of the Opposition in the House of Commons, and W.E. Forster were invited to Hatfield to meet Ignatiev, and were shocked to be given confidences about how to attack the Conservative Government's position in Parliament. It struck them as not 'quite the thing to be intriguing against a man in his own house'. More usefully, Ignatiev told Forster how badly Elliot had undermined Salisbury at Constantinople. Derby was mystified by the whole unorthodox proceeding, writing that Ignatiev 'is not a gentleman, and I can't understand why or how Salisbury should have taken to him'.

On 23rd March the Cabinet, with Salisbury assenting only 'in deference to the opinion of the majority', resolved not to sign the Protocol without an *a priori* Russian promise of demobilisation, which was obviously not going to be forthcoming. Beaconsfield's recapitulation of the crisis made it quite clear that he blamed Salisbury and Carnarvon for preferring what he called 'the policy of crusade…a nation indulging in sentimental eccentricity', to 'the imperial policy of England'. This reference to the High Churchmen's assumed sympathy with the Orthodox Slavs was a clear invitation to both men to resign again, but, as Beaconsfield described the moment to the Queen,

> there was a pause, and then Lord Salisbury spoke: low but clear and with becoming seriousness…he said, however strong, or the reverse, the party of crusade were in the country, he hoped that the Prime Minister did not believe there was a crusader in the Cabinet. But the religious sentiments of bodies of our countrymen could not be disregarded, nor could our own convictions be set aside.[4]

Writing to Carnarvon the day after the incident, Salisbury said that Beaconsfield's attack had put him in mind of Norfolk's advice to Buckingham about Cardinal Wolsey in the opening scene of Shakespeare's *King Henry VIII*:

> You know his nature,
> That he's revengeful, and I know his sword
> Hath a sharp edge; it's long and, 't may be said,
> It reaches far, and where 'twill not extend,
> Thither he darts it.

Carnarvon also believed that the Prime Minister wanted to get rid of

him and Salisbury, but no Prime Minister had actually dismissed a
Cabinet colleague since Russell sacked Palmerston in 1851.
Nevertheless, the close-run episode persuaded Salisbury that 'we must
be cautious till the crisis comes'. He thought it unlikely that Disraeli
would risk looking like a warmonger, for 'whatever change may come
when they see blood, the people are in no humour for war at present'.

Although diplomatic activity continued, and a Joint Protocol was
sent from London on 31ˢᵗ March calling on the Sultan to introduce
reforms, Salisbury and Carnarvon stayed relatively quiet, waiting like
everyone else for the Russo-Turkish War to break out. On 18ᵗʰ April,
however, Beaconsfield suggested to Salisbury a plan to take Gallipoli,
because the experts in the War Office had said it might only take nine
weeks for the Russians to capture Constantinople after the outbreak of
hostilities. By occupying the peninsula of Gallipoli, fortifying it further
and promising to restore it at the end of the war, Beaconsfield argued
that they would save time and box the Russians into the Black Sea. A
memorandum from the Intelligence agent, Colonel Robert Home, in
January had argued that the 500 square miles could be defended by a
20,000-strong garrison on both the European and Asiatic sides for £2.63
million, and would 'completely deny the use of the Dardanelles to men
of war or vessels of any kind'.

Salisbury strongly objected to the proposal, 'insisting that such a
course would be in effect an alliance with Turkey'. He questioned the
experts' prognostications, arguing that getting enough heavy artillery
down the Balkans to besiege Constantinople would take the Russians
far longer than nine weeks. If they did reach the Turkish capital, and
Salisbury doubted that was even Russia's ultimate intention, the Royal
Navy could easily act in time. Furthermore, any earlier action would
correctly be interpreted by St Petersburg as a provocation and the
Government would be blamed for protecting Turkish interests in
Bulgaria.

When Salisbury said this, Beaconsfield almost admitted that that had
been his idea all along. 'I was with him for an hour,' Salisbury reported
to Carnarvon afterwards, 'and when he saw he could make no impression on me, he was almost rude. Of this I took no notice and left him.'⁵
At Cabinet three days later, Manners proposed the Gallipoli plan and
Cairns suddenly advocated it too, which Carnarvon suspected was a
prearranged attempt to isolate him and Salisbury. Undeterred, they both
'spoke strongly against helping Turkey in any way'. Derby sided with
Salisbury and Carnarvon, which he himself found 'singular', by pointing
out that it might be taken as a signal for 'a general scramble – which is
not our policy'.⁶

On 24ᵗʰ April, Turkey formally rejected the London Joint Protocol, so
Russia declared war on her and invaded Bulgaria. Derby announced

Britain's neutrality on 6th May, with the *caveat* that she would fight if her interests on the shores of the Persian Gulf, at the Suez Canal, in the navigation of the Straits, or at Constantinople itself were threatened. Far from nine weeks, it took nine months before any of these applied. 'I cannot go very far with those who dread the Russians,' Salisbury wrote to Lytton from the India Office on 27th April 1877:

> Except the size of the patch they occupy on the map, there is nothing about their history or their actual condition to explain the abject terror which deprives so many Anglo-Indians, and so many of our military party here, of their natural sleep.... Their military history (except against Poland and barbarians) has been one long record of defeat. Their only trophies (Poltava and 1812) were won only after a series of defeats. Their national history simply does not exist. Their finances, never good, are now desperate; their social condition is a prolonged crisis threatening at any moment of weakness, socialist revolution. Their people are unwarlike – their officials corrupt – their rulers only competent when borrowed from Germany.... And yet we are asked to believe that their presence on the Black Sea or the Bosphorus would be a serious menace to England.

Salisbury did not deny that Britain would probably have to protect Constantinople in the end, but for reasons of oriental prestige rather than sound strategy. Should it fall, he feared, 'every Arab, Kurd, Persian and Afghan would think Russia stronger than England', with disastrous future consequences for the Raj. But in itself he did not even think Constantinople worth fighting over. Derby's foreign policy of 'never making a plan beyond the next move' filled Salisbury with 'sadness and apprehension', despite signs that Derby was slowly coming around to his point of view. The Foreign Secretary's policy, he thought, was 'an emasculate, purposeless vacillation', but he was not about to resign in protest over it.

Of his own Machiavellian scheme to partition Turkey, Salisbury told Lytton that Tsar Nicholas I's 1853 proposal had been 'practicable, though harsh, but it was not adopted. The commonest error in politics is sticking to the carcasses of dead policies. When a mast falls overboard, you do not try to save a rope here and a spar there, in memory of its former utility; you cut away the hamper altogether.' To that end, Salisbury was hoping Britain might take some place far further than the most eastward of the present British Mediterranean possession, Malta. His eye rested on Egypt or Crete for 'securing the waterway to India' once the 'obliteration of Turkey' became inevitable.

On 16th May, Romania joined the war against Turkey. When Carnarvon argued that he and Salisbury should resign rather than contemplate an 'unnecessary, impolitic and criminal' war against Russia, Salisbury reminded him of the events of 1867, saying: 'This was a card that could not be played twice by the same persons.'[7] Two years later Carnarvon thought he could identify a shift by Salisbury during the summer of 1877, for 'as Derby's opposition to a war policy became plainer, Salisbury seemed to draw somewhat closer towards Disraeli. In looking back calmly on the time, I think the two events synchronised – how far they bore on each other it is harder to say.' Carnarvon, Derby and some historians have effectively accused Salisbury of spotting his opportunity to become Beaconsfield's successor, ditching his principled opposition to a Russian war in the process, and sidling up to Beaconsfield's and Queen Victoria's dangerously bellicose stances for personal advantage.

These accusations are misplaced; Derby's political suicide was merely a felicitous by-product of Salisbury's policy, not its *raison d'être*. Salisbury had long despised Derby's inability even, as he contemptuously put it, to contemplate the annexation of the Isle of Wight. The fluidity of the Cabinet crises of 1877 and 1878 allowed him to pursue the one plan he had always believed in, that of securing for Britain a permanent anchorage to the east of Malta from which the route to India could be protected, without having to shore up, at possibly vast expense in blood and treasure, the doomed Ottoman Empire.

If Beaconsfield's hawkish policy permitted such a policy, without too much danger of a catastrophic re-run of the Crimean War, then Derby's pacific conscience and fastidious qualms about territorial aggrandisement were not going to be allowed to stand in Salisbury's way. But, until Constantinople came under serious threat, Salisbury thought it premature to be too bellicose. 'It has generally been acknowledged to be madness to go to war for an idea,' he told a dinner for the Merchant Taylors' School on 11th June, 'but if anything it is yet more unsatisfactory to go to war against a nightmare.' This brought a knuckle-rap from Beaconsfield, who said that 'it is but ingenuous to tell you, that the Queen is "greatly distressed" about the very wavering language of Lord Salisbury, which will encourage Russia and the Russian party'. She threatened to abdicate no fewer than five times during the crisis; at one point Beaconsfield feared for her sanity, recalling that she was after all the granddaughter of King George III.

On 16th June, Derby protested vigorously against Salisbury's idea of seizing an Egyptian base. The Cabinet, which had many long, increasingly acrimonious meetings throughout the period, was splitting into ever smaller and mutually antagonistic groups, each urging that Britain should act differently in different contingencies. In late June, Salisbury agreed to a £2 million vote of credit being taken in Parliament for emergency military use, but on 10th July the Russians suffered their first major reverse when the Turkish army in Bulgaria under Osman Pasha won the Battle of Plevna.

Salisbury could not see how an Anglo-Russian war would actually be fought, quoting Andrássy as saying it would be like 'a fight between a shark and a wolf. They may show any amount of natural animosity – but after snapping at each other they could do nothing more than pass on.'⁸ The British army was one-fifth the size of Russia's, and it could hardly threaten Russia directly. Other than 'the barbarism of burning Odessa', Salisbury found it hard to see what the Royal Navy could achieve, especially as the Crimea was by then properly defended. In the Crimean War, virtually the whole of Europe sent contingents against Russia; this time it might just be Britain and Turkey.

At the crucial Cabinet meeting of 21st July to discuss contingency planning in the event of the Russians threatening to take Constantinople, Salisbury surprised many by supporting Beaconsfield's contention that this should in fact be regarded as a *casus belli*. Anyone reading his letters to Lytton would have known that this had long been his (most reluctant) view. Carnarvon sarcastically recorded Salisbury's support for despatching the fleet to Constantinople, if invited by the Sultan, as 'this marvellous conversion' which 'turned the balance of the parties'. Derby also recorded his surprise, as well as his own opposition to the despatch of the fleet, on the grounds that if Gallipoli were subsequently occupied by the Russians, the fleet might be cut off in the Black Sea.

Salisbury explained his apparently Damascene conversion to Carnarvon, who had spent the Cabinet meeting looking intensely miserable, on the grounds that 'war was necessary to blow up the whole unsound foreign policy of this country'. His old colleague understandably found this an 'extravagant and rash proposition'. It certainly sits ill with Salisbury's overall attitude until then and does not really ring true. In fact, war against Russia over the Balkans was never his preferred option, although he was willing to bluff. Someone else who carefully noted Salisbury's new-found bellicosity, however, was Beaconsfield, who delightedly told the Queen that the Government had agreed, 'no one stronger and more decided than Lord Salisbury, that the Cabinet should advise your Majesty to declare war against Russia' in the event of a Russian occupation of Constantinople, should conditions about withdrawal not be agreed beforehand.⁹

As the Cabinet disintegrated into ill-tempered factions, with 'everybody talking at once' and much mutual recrimination, Salisbury's seeming conversion to Beaconsfield's hawkish point of view over the period from 21st to 31st July left him in prime position to pick up Derby's mantle, should the Foreign Secretary ever actually carry out one of his resignation threats. Only that February, Derby had referred to himself in his diary as Beaconsfield's natural successor, planning to refuse to serve under Richmond or Salisbury if by some misfortune the succession were offered to them instead. Yet only five months later he was ready to resign from Beaconsfield's Government altogether. His 31st July resignation threat was not put in so many words, because Derby thought 'menaces of that kind to be in bad taste, but I let it be seen clearly that I did not mean to be overturned in my own department'.

Salisbury believed there was no great desire in Britain for war; indeed, he thought the public was feeling 'more and more peaceful', and he gave Lytton the strongest orders not to allow any Afghan incidents to inflame the situation. Even in October, Salisbury did not think war with Russia 'rises nearly to Income Tax point' in the priorities of the British electorate. The Renfrew by-election victory in October 1877 did not seem to have been predicated on foreign policy at all, although, as Salisbury complained to Sandford, 'one of the nuisances of the Ballot is that when the oracle has spoken you never know what it means'. (The same was true, he said on a different occasion, of general election results, which, 'unlike legal proceedings, do not admit of a clear answer being given by the deciding authority to different questions'. It was a defect in the Constitution, he thought, that merely by winning an election victory a political party could claim a mandate for the measures in spite rather than because of which they were elected.)

Returning specially from Puys for a Cabinet meeting on 5th October, Salisbury was able to halt a scheme by Beaconsfield for British intervention should Plevna and Kars fall to Russia in the second campaign of the war, which was expected in December. Salisbury told his wife he thought the initiative 'had the air of a Scotch intrigue', a reference to the Queen and Beaconsfield in conclave at Balmoral. When Salisbury, Carnarvon and Derby declared themselves against Beaconsfield's plan, and Northcote, Gathorne-Hardy, Cross and the new First Lord of the Admiralty, W.H. Smith, also proved unenthusiastic, if more generally supportive of the Prime Minister, the idea was shelved.[10]

'In a Cabinet of twelve members there are seven parties, or policies,' Beaconsfield told the Queen in early November 1877. The war party consisted of Gathorne-Hardy, Manners and the Chief Secretary for Ireland, Sir Michael Hicks Beach. Cross, Smith and Richmond wanted war if Russia did not undertake not to occupy Constantinople. There was Salisbury, who, Beaconsfield stated, was 'the party that is prepared to go to war if, after the signature of peace, the Russians would not evacuate Constantinople'. Then 'the party of "peace at any price" is represented by the Earl of Derby'. Northcote wished to involve other Powers, and Carnarvon, Beaconsfield stated somewhat satirically, thought that the Russians should have Constantinople. 'The seventh policy is that of your Majesty, and which will be introduced and enforced to his utmost by the Prime Minister.' It was fairly facetious stuff, but it did explain, albeit in caricature, the Cabinet's deep fissuration.

Salisbury's support for tougher action against Russia than Derby or Carnarvon would countenance came not out of any regard for Turkey, which he despised, still less from any animosity towards Russia, which he felt to be impotent. It was, as he told Gathorne-Hardy after a long talk on 6th December, because: 'He is bent upon England having a share if there should be a break up in the East and evidently has no desire that Turkey should stand.' If the Russians could be kept out of the Turkish capital, the division of the Ottoman spoils would be fairer between the Powers. Salisbury thus became more bellicose the closer the Russian army came to the prize. On 10th December, Plevna finally fell to the Russians and the road to Constantinople lay open. On the 14th, supporting Derby's verbal warning to Russia that even a temporary occupation of Constantinople must 'seriously endanger' peace, Beaconsfield asked for the immediate recall of Parliament in the first week of January, to vote for another £5 million supply of credit for the army and navy. To this the whole Cabinet except Salisbury, Carnarvon and Derby agreed, in what the latter described as the 'least harmonious meeting we have had yet'. In the face of the three refusals, they broke up without any policy being agreed.

As in the past, the Chancellor of the Exchequer, Sir Stafford Northcote, was sent to Salisbury by Beaconsfield to try to find a *via media* before the Cabinet met again. On 15th December, Salisbury wrote Northcote two letters explaining his opposition to the recall of Parliament, saying that there was plenty of time, the winter had just begun and Constantinople was not yet in serious danger, whereas 'A call to arms, hasty and urgent, may have the effect … of involving us in a war to uphold Turkey.' In his second letter, he summed up his view of the Eastern Question, one that has often been wilfully misconstrued:

> An active policy is only possible under one of two conditions – that you shall help the Turks, or coerce them. I have no objection to the latter policy: or to a combination of the two. With the former alone, I cannot be content. But as you know, neither the Queen nor the Prime Minister will have anything to do with the latter.[11]

It was only after Beaconsfield also threatened to resign at the Cabinet held on 17th December that the next day he won approval for the recall of Parliament on 17th January 1878, an increased vote of credit and the instruction to Lord Augustus Loftus, the British Ambassador in St Petersburg, to initiate Turkish peace talks with the Tsar. For his part, the Prime Minister backed down over the demand to regard the occupation of Constantinople, however temporary, as a *casus belli*. Salisbury was content with the compromise, thinking the postponement of Parliament's recall by a month would 'take all the sting out of the proposition'. He also knew that the Queen's alliance with Beaconsfield

– the closest in British politics at the time – meant that his resignation threats were more theatrical than serious.

A new phenomenon was starting to manifest itself in music halls, the places of popular entertainment where a beery form of super-patriotism was developing. The chorus of a favourite ballad sung by audiences went:

> We don't want to fight but by Jingo if we do,
> We've got the ships, we've got the men, we've got the money too,
> We've fought the Bear before, and while Britons shall be true,
> The Russians shall not have Constantinople.

For all its defects in scansion, the ballad spawned a new political soubriquet. 'Jingoism' became a powerful force, one for which Salisbury conceived a lifelong loathing but which was to work to his political advantage at several crucial stages of his career.

Writing to the Russophile High Tory, the Marquess of Bath, on 19th December, Salisbury assured him that Derby's 6th May neutrality despatch, and not the 'impudent pretensions' and 'ravings' of the pro-war *Daily Telegraph*, *Morning Post* and *Pall Mall Gazette*, was still Government policy. For the Opposition to claim that those newspapers represented Government policy, Salisbury described as 'only one of what I may call the legitimate injustices of party warfare'. He reiterated his own fear of the 'danger of sliding insensibly into an alliance with the Turk'.

Had it not been for the prestige implications for the Empire, Salisbury would not have particularly baulked at Constantinople being occupied. By now, however, Derby was convinced, as he told Salisbury on 23rd December, that the Prime Minister was bent on war because 'He believes thoroughly in "prestige", as all foreigners do', which was an 'intelligible' view, but 'not mine nor yours'. If Derby thought that this sideways reference to Beaconsfield's Jewishness might help convince Salisbury, he gravely misjudged his rival. As Secretary of State for India, where British power depended to a large degree on prestige rather than actual resources employed, Salisbury disliked the word but fully understood the concept. He was one of the first people to appreciate quite the extent to which militarily the British Empire was a gigantic bluff. Derby, an isolationist in European politics, wanted British foreign policy to emphasise Empire, trade and peace, and to avoid getting involved in events in south-east Europe.

On Christmas Eve, Beaconsfield made a direct plea to Salisbury for more support in Cabinet, for 'unless we make an effort to clear ourselves from the Canidian spells which are environing us, we shall make shipwrecks alike of our own reputations and the interests of our country'. (Canidia was a Neapolitan courtesan beloved of Horace whom, when she deserted him, he held up to contempt as an old sorceress.) In the same letter he let Salisbury know that Colonel Frederick Wellesley, the Military Attaché in St Petersburg, was warning that Russia had been receiving accurate reports of British Cabinet meetings, and thanked Lady Salisbury for 'expressing her sentiments to the great culprit', Lady Derby. But the reports did not cease despite Beaconsfield mentioning it to Lady Derby himself, and it was one of the underlying issues which helped precipitate Derby's fall. Lady Derby had struck up a close friendship with Schouvaloff and learnt about Russian opinion, information which she passed on to her husband. It is reasonable to assume the flow was two-way; Salisbury certainly deeply disapproved of Derby's practice of keeping notes at Cabinet meetings.

The Queen and Beaconsfield were also not above conducting their own non-official diplomacy, instructing Wellesley to warn the Tsar on 30th August 1877 that, although Britain did not want war, her neutrality could not be relied upon in all circumstances. These secret contacts through Wellesley were not vouchsafed to Derby or Salisbury, but only came out in his autobiography decades later. Despite being the Iron Duke's great-nephew and the son of the veteran Ambassador to Paris, Earl Cowley, Wellesley was a curious choice as a confidential agent. Although the Tsar liked him and asked him to be in attendance at the Battle of Plevna, he was only thirty-four, had a fascination for the 'night-houses' of the Haymarket, and was a keen aficionado of opium dens, and public executions.

With both sides begging for Salisbury's support, and British neutrality policy essentially the same since May, it is small wonder that the Liberal former Foreign Secretary Earl Granville reported to Gladstone on the 25th that 'Salisbury is in high spirits, and considers the position [to] be exactly in accordance with his views.'[12] Salisbury told Derby that Britain should not encourage the Turks in any way, and Beaconsfield that a war would be unprofitable, unpopular and probably unwinnable. Yet when much the same sentiments were expressed publicly by Carnarvon to a deputation from South Africa at the Colonial Office, and reported in *The Times* on 3rd January 1878, a bitter Cabinet row ensued. Salisbury and Derby regarded the speech as ill conceived, but they defended him. Carnarvon offered to resign, but was placated. 'I have a general fear of the undefined evil', Salisbury wrote to Lytton on the day of the Cabinet meeting, 'which results from stirring up a dirty puddle.' In the forty-four Cabinet meetings held to discuss the Eastern Question in the first three months of 1878, Beaconsfield was undoubtedly highly frustrated, feeling that with public opinion behind him he was being cheated of his firm policy by only three men.

Carnarvon's intention to resign over Beaconsfield's rudeness was slapped down by Salisbury:

Have you a right to take that course because a man, noted during a long life for unrestrained language, has given rein to his sharp tongue for a moment? It is not constitutional. You are a member of a Cabinet not a servant of the Premier.... Providence has put in our hands the trust of keeping the country from entering a wrongful war. Do not renounce such a task on account of a rude phrase by a man whose insolence is proverbial.

Carnarvon fancied he had also been called a coward by the Queen, and Derby had to step in to restrain him from resigning, despite finding Carnarvon 'weak, vain, and fussing in his personal relations, though a good administrator'. Salisbury, in a meeting with Beaconsfield, also tried to smooth the matter over, privately thinking that since the untimely death of his beloved wife in January 1875 Carnarvon had become 'very irritable and unmanageable'.

Salisbury's success in excising the pro-Turkish passages from the forthcoming Queen's Speech was, Carnarvon reminisced, 'the last time that Salisbury acted with Derby and myself. After this he was acting openly and consistently with the Prime Minister.'[13] This was an over-simplification, but nonetheless there was a moment in the second and third weeks of January 1878 when Salisbury saw his chance to replace Derby as Foreign Secretary. Believing he could give British foreign policy a positive impetus that Derby would not, whilst simultaneously restraining Beaconsfield from declaring war, he took it. To make matters easier, the issue which Salisbury knew Derby would resign over was precisely the one on which he had a long record of support, that of taking an eastern Mediterranean outpost, a *'pied à terre'*, from which the Royal Navy could protect the route to India should Turkey collapse. Crete, Scanderoon (also called Alexandretta), Gallipoli and various Egyptian ports had all been mentioned in this context, although in the event it was to be none of these. Salisbury has been accused, then and since, of putting his ambition before his original, principled opposition to war when he helped Beaconsfield to displace Derby as Foreign Secretary. Yet, as in 1874, he only took office because he felt that he could make a positive difference; ambition in so talented a man is but an expression of sincerity.

The second campaign of the war went badly for Turkey. On 3rd January, she had been defeated at Sofia and six days later an entire army corps surrendered at the Shipka Pass. Constantinople was now within Russia's grasp, and on 12th January a climactic Cabinet meeting was held at which Derby, obviously not now considering it to be in such bad taste, threatened to resign over the proposal to send an expedition to occupy Gallipoli. Salisbury, declaring the Cabinet splits 'insurmountable', threatened to resign with him. The meeting ended after two and a half hours with a compromise formula from Salisbury, that the new minister at Constantinople, Sir Henry Layard, should ascertain from the Sublime Porte whether an application to protect the Dardanelles would be favourably received. Salisbury had protected Derby, but knew that the situation was certain to be reactivated later whatever the Sultan decided. He did not wish to be seen to be edging the Foreign Secretary out of office, a man who after months of continual crisis was suffering from acute nervous tension.

By Tuesday, 15th January, Derby was too ill to attend the Cabinet, and since no answer had been heard from the Porte, the despatch of the fleet to the Straits was agreed upon. Carnarvon resigned. A message was received later that day from St Petersburg to say that Russia had agreed not to occupy Gallipoli, so the order to the fleet was rescinded, as was the resignation. Once again it was Salisbury who stamped his will on the Cabinet, articulating his long-held policy of 'no assistance to the Turks, but resistance to Russian encroachment'. He was losing patience with his old friend Carnarvon, who at the Cabinet meeting had effectively called Beaconsfield a liar. 'I was struck by Salisbury's resolution today,' wrote Gathorne-Hardy.[14] In Derby's temporary absence, Salisbury was establishing his claims for the succession and attempting to arrange Austrian support for a possible British occupation of Gallipoli if it became necessary.

On 17th January, with the Russians still advancing towards Constantinople and their Commander-in-Chief, the Grand Duke Nikolai, in communication with Turkish peace emissaries, Parliament met in a state of high excitement. Although they knew of the Cabinet split, most MPs and journalists assumed that Salisbury was still of the peace party. 'My acquaintance with the newspapers is not so great that I can say whether the *Morning Post* abuses me or not,' Salisbury told the House of Lords with becoming *sang froid*, 'but if it wants to abuse me, I hope it will continue to do so.' Mocking the idea of a 'war of liberation', Salisbury took a utilitarian line against war, saying: 'It has accumulated in nine short months more misery than would result from generations of Turkish government.'

With Beaconsfield scrupulously avoiding any pro-Turkish sentiment in his own speech, the scene was being carefully set by both men for a momentous political *rapprochement*, albeit one entirely lacking in trust on Salisbury's side. Salisbury's speech made it clear how little 'crusading' and how much the national interest mattered to him, and distanced him from Gladstone's moralistic, sermonising stance: 'I am not prepared to accept the new gospel which I understand is preached – that it is our business for the sake of any populations whatever to disregard the trust which the people of this country and our

Sovereign have reposed in our hands.'[15] Derby approved when he read it in bed, though it sounded very much like the speech of a prospective Foreign Secretary.

On 20th January, the Russians captured Adrianople – present-day Edirne – and at the Cabinet meeting the next day Salisbury supported Beaconsfield's idea of a mutual defence treaty with Austria, which Derby thought provocative to Russia. 'Salisbury is quite gone around,' he wrote in his diary, 'and is hot for Austrian alliance, of which last summer he used to talk with marked contempt.' The difference was that the previous summer Russian artillery was not drawing up virtually to the walls of Constantinople. Indeed, a Russian observation corps was actually on its way to Gallipoli when the Cabinet met for yet another crucial meeting on 23rd January.

Beaconsfield called for a military credit vote of £6 million, an agreement with Austria and the ordering of the fleet to the Dardanelles regardless of the consent of the Sultan. 'Salisbury was very warlike,' noted Derby that day, 'his natural tendency to pugnacity is thoroughly roused, and considering the Turk as now destroyed, his religious zeal does not interfere with his hostility to Russia.' In fact, religious sensibilities seemed to have played next to no part in Salisbury's calculations, which were primarily concerned with grand strategy and prestige. He in turn was prepared to ascribe outside influences to Derby, telling Arthur Balfour that the Foreign Secretary was 'between overwork, alcohol and responsibility, in a condition of utter moral prostration, doing as little as was possible, and doing that under compulsion.... I believe [Cairns] during that period wrote many of the critical despatches for him and, so to speak, put the pen in his hand and made him sign!' When the Cabinet supported the Beaconsfield–Salisbury proposals, Carnarvon and Derby made it clear they would resign.

Although Salisbury privately looked forward to Derby's departure, he was unhappy at Carnarvon's. Years later he recalled how they had 'paced together for an hour and a half round and round St James's Square, in the frozen sleet of a bitter January evening, while he urged in vain for a continuance of the old comradeship', but to no avail. The Queen accepted Carnarvon's resignation on 24th January.[16] Salisbury told Carnarvon that 'the necessity of parting has given me as severe a pang as ever I felt in my life ... it has left me with little interest in politics. But politics are not all one's life – and may form a very small part of it.' Beaconsfield meanwhile crowed to the Queen: 'Lord Salisbury also is detached from his intimate friend.'

Salisbury was appointed in Derby's place on 25th January, and Gathorne-Hardy took over the India Office. He wrote to Lytton that day to apologise for a short letter because 'we are, as my telegram will have told you, *en pleine crise* ... my time is more than engrossed with it!' On the surprise news that the Turks had agreed to an armistice – a painful one for them with a pecuniary indemnity, large cessions of Asian territory, the promise of self-governing principalities and a new, autonomous 'Big' Bulgaria – three ministers went to Beaconsfield at No. 10 to beg him to countermand the order to the fleet. He agreed, and the new orders reached it just as the ships were about to enter the Dardanelles.

Salisbury, who was not present and did not approve of the change of policy, years afterwards 'expressed the conviction that, had the ships gone up at that time, the Russians would never have advanced to Constantinople nor pressed the extravagant claims to which that achievement incited them'. This second withdrawal of the fleet did not affect Carnarvon's decision to go, but it did mean that Derby could be invited back. To prevent the Government splitting at such a critical time, Beaconsfield asked him to return. 'I am very glad Derby has come back,' Salisbury wrote to the Prime Minister as he returned to the India Office on the 27th, after two days as the acting Foreign Secretary. 'At this juncture his secession would have exposed us to all kinds of wild suspicions.'

Privately, however, Salisbury thought the return a mistake, and his suspicions could not have been lessened by Derby's pointed refusal to sit in his old seat next to the Prime Minister, but in the chair Carnarvon had vacated instead.[17] To those friends who accused him of turning his coat, Salisbury pointed to the entirely altered circumstances that were prevailing in the last days of January 1878:

Russia will not give us any unambiguous promise about Constantinople and the Dardanelles.... The Russians are within a day's march of Gallipoli and I believe of Constantinople ... contrary to her pledges. I do not see how – acting as a trustee – I should be doing my duty if I did not join in recommending precautions.

Rumours of Russian bad faith, some valid, others later proving false, continued to arrive in London from Layard in early February, when the Russian army was poised at the very outskirts of both Constantinople and Gallipoli. The armistice had failed to halt the advance, and on 7th February Russian troops were (falsely) reported actually to have entered the panic-stricken city. On 6th February, under Salisbury's urging, orders were telegraphed to Besika Bay for the British fleet to enter Turkish waters. Grand Duke Nikolai threatened that the arrival of British warships in the Bosphorus would be taken as a signal to enter the Turkish capital, and the Sultan begged for the ships to be withdrawn. When they arrived at the Dardanelles, they were warned that the Turkish Governor had orders to bombard any attempt at passage. A

British fleet had not forced the Straits since 1807, and although
Salisbury advised Beaconsfield to attempt it, Derby, Cairns and
Northcote all opposed the action.

'It is the most critical moment we have yet passed through,' Salisbury
wrote to Beaconsfield on 10th February, adding that Britain would be a
European laughing-stock if the fleet was once again ordered to return to
Besika Bay. 'We shall disgust our friends in the country, and lose all
weight in Europe,' as well as confirming doubts in the Sultan's mind
about British 'timidity'. His view prevailed, and the Russian and
Turkish bluff was called. The fleet sailed through the Sea of Marmora
unopposed and, five days later, twelve British ironclads, with their
massive offensive ordnance, were anchored off Constantinople at the
Golden Horn. Once there, they concentrated Russian and Turkish
minds wonderfully.

The fleet stayed in position for over six months, facing the Russian
army and allowing Layard to speak with hugely increased authority in
Constantinople. 'Salisbury talks recklessly and is all for fighting,'
recorded Derby, but in truth it was paradoxically due to Salisbury's
bellicosity that fighting was averted. The next evening, the Salisburys
gave a fête for 500 people at Arlington Street in honour of the Crown
Prince and Princess of Austria. The grand staircase was festooned with
laurel and adorned with flowers, as were the corridors and principal
rooms. The Austrian, German and Russian Ambassadors were there and
the party lasted until 4 a.m.

Derby lauded Beaconsfield's 'entire absence of vindictiveness' in
offering Carnarvon the Governor-Generalship of Canada the following
week. A cynic might have discerned an element of 'my language fails,
go out and govern New South Wales' in the proposal, which Carnarvon
promptly refused. Derby also marvelled at how the Prime Minister
'works with Salisbury as cordially as though they had never quarrelled',
which he ought to have spotted earlier as a potential danger to his own
highly exposed position. Beaconsfield was actively setting up his
Foreign Secretary for a fall. On 26th February, he wrote privately to
Derby to say that 'after consulting the naval authorities, he had satisfied
himself that an island would be of no use as a station', and by 6th March
he added that any such occupation would have to be temporary and
consensual.

Yet on the very same day the War Minister, Gathorne-Hardy, found
Beaconsfield 'bent' on the occupation of an island, 'and seems to disregard military considerations'. Since Salisbury had been calling for
Britain 'to seize an island somewhere' ever since 27th February, it is not
difficult to spot what Beaconsfield was planning.[18] Derby's arguments
against seizing anywhere, put with increased force in the Cabinets of
early March 1878, were that it would be a violation of international law,

that Malta was good enough, that it could set a dangerous precedent for the other Powers, that the Russians might use it as an excuse for attacking Constantinople and Gallipoli, and that it would make a peaceful settlement – with Bismarck now suggesting that he host an international congress – virtually impossible. Salisbury was not convinced.

On 3rd March 1878, a Russo-Turkish peace treaty was signed at San Stefano, the Turkish village housing the Russian headquarters near Constantinople. As Salisbury had predicted, its provisions were far more draconian for Turkey than the demands the Great Powers had made at the Constantinople Conference back in January 1877. The Treaty provided for an autonomous 'Big' Bulgaria stretching from the Aegean to the Danube and from the Black Sea to Albania, thereby including much of Macedonia, which Russia claimed the right to occupy for two years. Romania, Montenegro and Serbia were to become independent. Turkey had to pay a 700 million rouble indemnity and surrender Ardahan, Kars, Batoum and Bagazid to Russia, retaining only Adrianople. Ignatiev's pan-Slavist 'Big' Bulgaria would contain large Serb and Greek minorities. The Treaty of San Stefano, signed by the Turks under maximum duress, thus ripped up the Treaty of Paris and created a large Russian satellite state of Bulgaria that would dominate the Balkans.

Britain protested strongly against the proposals, hoping to persuade the Russians to discuss them at the great international congress which Bismarck proposed to hold at Berlin. Meanwhile, the Cabinet hawks, now led by Salisbury, were calling for the seizure of the Aegean island of Mitylene as a material guarantee should the Congress not award Britain a naval station. When Manners, at a Cabinet on 8th March, opposed this on the grounds of international 'right', Salisbury 'treated scruples of this kind with marked contempt, saying ... that if our ancestors had cared for the rights of other people, the British Empire would not have been made. He was more vehement than anyone else for going on.'

Despite Andrássy's sweeping gesture to Salisbury in Vienna back in December 1876, the Austrians did not seem to be any keener to provoke Russia than were the French, Italians or Germans, and by 18th March 1878 Beaconsfield heard that Schouvaloff did not believe there would even be a congress. On 21st March, the San Stefano terms appeared in the British press, to universal condemnation. On the same day, Salisbury wrote to Beaconsfield to say that 'we ought to prepare ourselves, in case there is <u>no</u> congress, to state which are the articles of the treaty to which we specially object'. The letter was in part a job application, both men assuming that Derby would take little effective part in coercing Russia into dropping San Stefano. It also sent the warning to the Prime Minister: 'I am, as you know, not a believer in the possibility of setting the Turkish Government on its legs again, as a genuine reliable Power.'

Salisbury set out in detail his belief that San Stefano, as it stood, was absolutely unacceptable to Britain, for under it the Russians would 'menace the balance of power in the Aegean', threaten the Balkan Greeks 'with extinction', endanger the Straits and reduce Turkey 'to vassalage', which was in itself a violation of British interests. The alternatives he sought were to split Bulgaria into two, obtain effective guarantees for the control of the Straits, win two naval stations for Britain such as Lemnos and Cyprus, and lastly secure a reduction in the Turkish indemnity. Salisbury blatantly affirmed that he would be equally satisfied 'with a war or negotiations which ended in those results'. These *desiderata* so closely approximated to Beaconsfield's own that Salisbury was as good as telling him that, the moment Beaconsfield felt himself strong enough to get rid of Derby, he would find no great policy differences with his new Foreign Secretary.

The break came less than a week later, in circumstances that were later to cause controversy and subsequent accusations of sharp practice. Minutes were not then taken at Cabinet meetings, but from letters, diaries and circumstantial evidence it is reasonably clear that the meeting at noon on Wednesday, 27th March 1878 discussed but did not actually agree to the despatch of Indian troops to Malta and to the capture of a small port on the North Syrian coast called Scanderoon, or Alexandretta – present-day Iskenderun – in Turkey. The questions of simply seizing Cyprus, an island over which the Sultan had sovereignty, and of calling up the Army Reserves, were also discussed. Derby's diary recorded how Beaconsfield had opened the meeting by saying that 'peace is not to be secured by "drifting"', which might have been taken as a reference to Derby's vacillations.

The Prime Minister then spoke of Russia's financial and military weakness, and how San Stefano would upset the delicate Mediterranean balance of power. 'He proposed to issue a proclamation declaring [an] emergency,' Derby recorded, 'to put a force in the field and simultaneously to send an expedition from India to occupy Cyprus and Scanderoon.' Salisbury and Cairns then supported Beaconsfield but Derby 'declared my dissent in a brief speech...and agreeing with an expression that had fell from Salisbury, that we must now divide, and that no compromise was possible.... It was understood that my resignation was to follow.'

Two years later, a memorandum by Northcote made it plain that the Cabinet had not in fact agreed to Beaconsfield's proposition. When Salisbury had written a note to Northcote at the meeting asking him to sign a statement promising that the British Exchequer pay for the Indian force being sent to Scanderoon and Cyprus, Northcote wrote back that the Cabinet had not agreed to send the troops, but agreed that if it did, then it would certainly have to bear the expense.[19] It was as tenuous as it was legalistic, but it was to prove a crucial let-out afterwards, for if the Cabinet had not decided to seize part of the Sultan's domain, Derby could not have resigned in protest at it, as he later claimed to have done.

Another of Northcote's memoranda, drawn up in September 1880, made it clear why Beaconsfield chose Salisbury as Foreign Secretary over Northcote's suggestion of the veteran diplomat Lord Lyons: 'Salisbury had undoubtedly broken with Carnarvon, and given his adhesion to an anti-Russian policy – having shaken himself free of the influence which Ignatiev seemed to have gained over him at the time of the Constantinople Conference... the Queen, too, inclined to him.' It was a biased and in many ways ridiculous reading of the situation, but it helped win Salisbury the Foreign Office, then the second position in the Government, at a time when Beaconsfield had no obvious successor.

Beaconsfield said that losing his old friend and colleague Derby was the bitterest moment of his public life, but he had spent the best part of a month manoeuvring for that outcome and he lost no time in confirming Lord Salisbury as Foreign Secretary, and asking the Queen to tell Derby not to mention the Indian expeditions in his House of Lords resignation statement. As a result, the public assumed that Derby had resigned over the calling out of the Reserves, which had also been agreed at the Cabinet meeting. Gathorne-Hardy took over the India Office and was raised to Viscount Cranbrook and, to Derby's chagrin, his own brother and heir, Colonel Frederick Stanley, took Cranbrook's place as Secretary of State for War. This was Beaconsfield's way of trying to salvage as much of Tory Lancashire as possible after Derby's departure.

Salisbury knew that his stewardship at the Foreign Office would be judged by the alterations he was able to make in the Treaty of San Stefano, and the extent by which he could arrest the perceived drift in British foreign policy. Accordingly, after returning from a dinner party to Arlington Street at 11 p.m. on Friday, 29th March 1878, he went to his study and, without data, advice or help from anyone else, he wrote what became known as 'The Salisbury Circular', a despatch to all the Great Powers setting out Britain's objections to the Treaty of San Stefano and her determination to alter it. By the time he rose from his desk at 3 a.m. the next morning, he had written what is generally regarded as one of the greatest State Papers in British history.

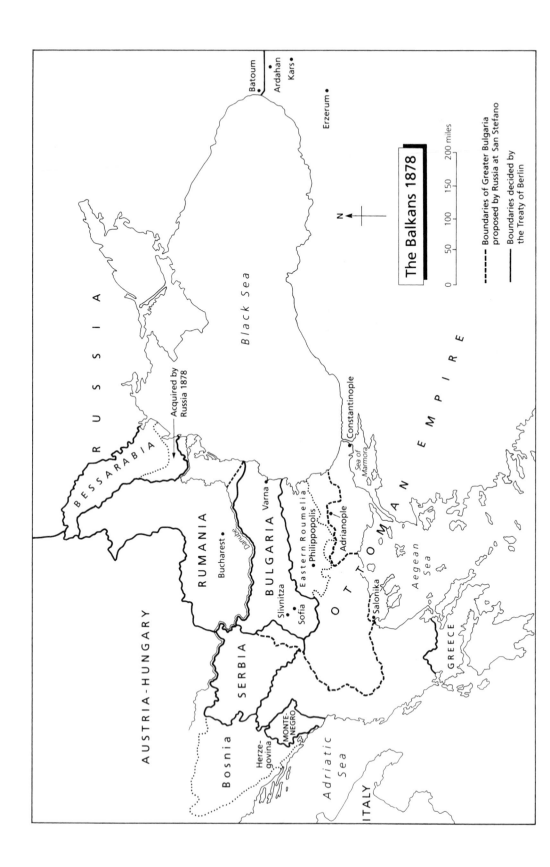

The Balkans 1878

- - - - - Boundaries of Greater Bulgaria proposed by Russia at San Stefano

——— Boundaries decided by the Treaty of Berlin

0 50 100 150 200 miles

N

RUSSIA

Batoum

Ardahan

Kars

Erzerum

Black Sea

Constantinople

Sea of Marmora

Acquired by Russia 1878

BESSARABIA

RUMANIA

Bucharest

Danube

Varna

BULGARIA

Eastern Roumelia

Philippopolis

Adrianople

Slivnitza

Sofia

Salonika

SERBIA

AUSTRIA-HUNGARY

Bosnia

Herze-govina

MONTE-NEGRO

Adriatic Sea

ITALY

Aegean Sea

OTTOMAN EMPIRE

GREECE

TWELVE

The Congress of Berlin

'Peace with Honour' (and Cyprus)

March to July 1878

'To become K.G. with a Cecil is something for a Disraeli!'

At breakfast on the morning of Saturday, 30th March 1878, Salisbury was 'tired but satisfied'. In his clear, vigorous, tightly argued style he had shown how the San Stefano Treaty effectively revoked the 1856 Treaty of Paris and that, therefore, all the original signatories to that Treaty must now be recalled to reach a new settlement. 'I was only picking up the china that Derby had broken,' he was later modestly to remark, but the Circular had a huge and immediate effect once the Cabinet had accepted it in its entirety. Hicks Beach told his daughter that the only alteration they had made to the text was the omission of a superfluous 'it'. As Lord Rosebery said years later, the Salisbury Circular bestowed upon its author an European reputation at a blow.

Circulated to the Great Powers on Monday, 1st April, it explained how San Stefano would 'suppress, almost to the point of entire subjugation, the political independence of the Court of Constantinople'. The crucial passage read:

> It is in the power of the Ottoman Government to close or to open the Straits which form the natural highway of nations between the Aegean Sea and the Euxine. Its dominion is recognised at the head of the Persian Gulf, on the shores of the Levant, and in the immediate neighbourhood of the Suez Canal. It cannot be otherwise than a matter of extreme solicitude to this country that the Government to which this jurisdiction belongs should be so closely pressed by the political outposts of a greatly superior Power that its independent action, and even existence, is almost impossible. These result not so much from the language of any single article in the Treaty as from the operation of the instrument as a whole.

Andrássy, calling San Stefano 'an Orthodox Slavic sermon' and despairing of a peaceful outcome, seized on the Circular as a way of avoiding war with Russia. He believed a congress held in Berlin would flatter Bismarck's pretensions to be Europe's 'honest broker'. France and Italy, concerned at being sidelined, would be included because they were signatories to the 1856 Paris Treaty. In the Cabinet it was 'universally admired', and, most important of all, its conciliatory language allowed the doves in St Petersburg to hail it as 'an instrument of peace', as it called for the radical modification, but not the complete scrapping, of San Stefano. Dean Church had described the Oxford Movement's *Tracts for the Times* as 'clear, brief, stern appeals to conscience and reason, sparing of words, utterly without rhetoric, intense in purpose'. The Circular was just such a tract for Salisbury's times, and Europe recognised it as such.

'We object to Russia under the mask either of Slav or Turk,' Salisbury told Lord Odo Russell, the British Ambassador in Berlin, 'dominating on the various coasts, Persian, Arabian, Syrian, Greek, where we have now friends, clients and interests. How that domination is to be met, whether by diminution or counterpoise – is another question.' It was through German good offices, discreet and tactful, that a mutual military and naval stand-down was negotiated. By 13th April, Salisbury could write to Queen Victoria, who was always suspicious of Bismarck, that 'the Russians desire an excuse for peace, and will welcome the Chancellor's interference as saving their *amour propre*'.

Beaconsfield worked hard to encourage the Queen to appreciate Salisbury, saying, 'He is a man of feeling, and some imagination, and can, therefore, appreciate your Majesty, which the cold blooded, or the dull, cannot,' which sounds far more like a compliment to Victoria than Salisbury, but was helpful nonetheless. So far the Queen and Salisbury had clashed far more than they had agreed. She had supported Germany over the Schleswig-Holstein Question, Disraeli over the Reform Act, Archbishop Tait over Ritualism and Derby over the invitation of Ignatiev to Hatfield. 'I am afraid we shall never see much of him here,' the Queen's private secretary, Sir Henry Ponsonby, wrote from Balmoral in September 1874, 'he is too independent and speaks his mind too freely to be acceptable.' But the Queen was coming round to Salisbury, and noted in her journal when he visited Osborne the following January that he was 'particularly agreeable and gentle, and who one could not believe could be so severe and sarcastic in debate'.[1]

In order to get Russia to the negotiating table, Salisbury had to coax Austria. The new Ambassador to Vienna was none other than Sir Henry Elliot, his place in Constantinople having gone to Sir Henry Layard, the former Liberal MP and excavator of Nineveh, whom Salisbury soon suspected, like Elliot, of having 'gone native' in Constantinople. Salisbury wrote to Elliot urging on him the difficult task 'of inducing this insincere, unready [Austrian] Government to pledge itself to some definite line of action'. The French and Italians, though sympathetic, were not inclined actively to interfere. The Germans were not about to threaten Russia over a theatre which Bismarck always considered peripheral. So it came down to Andrássy, and Salisbury urged him to stop showing 'the insincerity that belongs to weakness' – not a phrase he used directly – and held out the prospect of an Austrian annexation of Bosnia and Herzegovina as a reward for his co-operation.

Meanwhile, Salisbury bluntly told the Russians, via the German Ambassador to London Count Münster, that the whole of the San Stefano Treaty needed to be laid open immediately. Prior understandings could be entered into beforehand, as 'it was of no use to go into Congress while the ideas of the principal persons engaged were so divergent that a hostile conclusion of it was almost inevitable'. Salisbury believed secret, pre-congress diplomacy was essential, and soon afterwards Count Schouvaloff, the Russian Ambassador, made his first approach. On 10th April, at Schouvaloff's suggestion, he and Salisbury talked of the general outlines of an agreement that Russia and Britain might be able to reach before either side so much as set foot in Berlin that June. By 29th April, Schouvaloff was beginning 'in a very cautious and circumspect manner' to negotiate the major questions of San Stefano, such as the very existence of a 'Big' Bulgaria.

Writing continually to Russell, Layard and Elliot, Salisbury kept up the pressure for a congress to discuss all the outstanding Eastern Question issues, but only one at which the most serious ones had already been decided to the mutual satisfaction of Britain and Russia. It was during these tense, detailed negotiations that Salisbury came into his own, his intellect working at full power to construct a genuine settlement which might both bring peace and decouple British Eastern policy from its decades-old, inherently unstable, pro-Turkish foundations. To find Russia an honourable, even attractive, route of retreat from San Stefano, yet without endangering Turkey, was a delicate problem. Yet it was one on which Salisbury, very unusually, allowed himself to feel glints of optimism. Writing on 30th April to the Home Secretary Richard Cross, who was just off on a speaking tour of the provinces and wanted some hints on the correct line to take, Salisbury summed up his thinking: 'For myself, I do not think there will be a war, but this result can only be obtained by maintaining an attitude in word and deed, which, first, shall show no flinching in our resolution.'[2]

Writing to Layard, Salisbury said that talk of Turkey's independence and integrity had been a sham in 1856 and 'would be a pure mockery now'. He ought therefore to sell to the Turks the idea of a British guarantee against any further Russian encroachments against their Asian territories. Although Salisbury did not actually mention Cyprus by name as Britain's *quid pro quo* for such a guarantee, he was whetting Turkish appetite for a comprehensive protection deal in the east. By 12th May, the Cabinet had adopted his proposals in principle. Time, as Salisbury told W.H. Smith, was worth more to Britain, which was 'rich and unprepared than to Russia exhausted and armed to the teeth'. Russia's losses in the recent fighting had been huge, and her memories of the Crimean War were unhappy.

By 16th May, the Cabinet had approved a draft Anglo-Turkish agreement, known as the 'Cyprus Convention', which was sent off to Layard. It was only to come into effect if Russia retained Kars and Batoum, and would involve Britain guaranteeing Turkey's Asian borders if there were assurances of good government of Asiatic Christians – a clause Salisbury thought necessary to avoid 'divisions at home' – and if Britain could occupy Cyprus, whose proximity to Asia Minor and Syria made it an ideal operational base in the event of a Turkish collapse. It was thought the other Powers would have protested against a mainland European territorial acquisition, such as Gallipoli.

When rumours grew of a Russian *coup de main* in the Bosphorus in mid-May, Salisbury's phlegmatic style was displayed at its best. When ministers asked him to instruct the Ambassador in St Petersburg to investigate them further, he answered that, if the stories were true, a question would not elicit anything, but if not it would look timid to have asked. As for Admiral Hornby, who was demanding that war preparations be stepped up, Salisbury wrote to Smith: 'If Hornby is a cool-headed, fearless, sagacious man, he ought to bring an action for libel against his epistolary style.'[3]

When on 23rd May, Schouvaloff returned from St Petersburg, after direct consultations with the Tsar, Salisbury could at last see the way ahead. The Russians wanted to keep Bessarabia, Montenegro, Kars and Batoum, but conceded that non-Slav populations could be shaved off Bulgaria. In other words, there could be a small rather than Ignatiev's 'Big' Bulgaria. Other demands were made relating to terms of occupation, Turkish provincial good government, communications and policing. Salisbury said nothing definite at the time, but there was clearly the basis for an agreement emerging. The garrisoning of fortresses was likely to be a difficult issue, with a 'very long and at times animated' discussion about the exact role of Turkish troops in the putative southern Bulgarian state, but, after all, there had to be something semi-substantive left over to discuss at the Congress.

Once Salisbury had ascertained that Russia was not about to insist on hanging on to all her Asiatic conquests, he instructed Layard to give the Sultan only twenty-four hours to agree to the Anglo-Turkish Convention, and, if refused, to hint that Britain would allow the Russian advance to continue and look favourably at an agreed partition of Turkey instead. Viscount Sandon, who had that month joined the Cabinet as President of the Board of Trade, recorded how on Friday, 24th May, Salisbury and Beaconsfield urged it as 'absolutely necessary' to adopt very pre-emptory language with the Porte. Afterwards, the whole Cabinet handed their copies of Salisbury's memorandum on the issue back to him; he then lit a match and burned them all in the Cabinet room's fireplace.

The Porte's reply would either bloodlessly win Cyprus for Britain, or allow the Russians into Constantinople, which could possibly bring down the Government. As Salisbury hosted the Queen's birthday reception at the Foreign Office on 25th May, 'no sign of anxiety or even of preoccupation could be detected in him.... A slight and apparently rather pleasurable excitement was the only feeling of which he ever showed external symptom in moments of crisis.'[4] For a man who found much of politics tiresome and was so prone to ennui, cathartic crises of this kind fully engaged his interest, and gave him the opportunity to excel at public displays of *sang froid*. The news that Russia was purchasing ships, possibly for use in war, he dismissed as mere 'painted cannon'.

When word of the Sultan's adhesion to the Cyprus Convention arrived the next morning, Salisbury authorised Elliot to conclude an agreement with Austria stating that the two countries would work together for a 'small' Bulgaria, with 'sufficient military and political supremacy of the Sultan' in the south and south-west Balkans. In return, Britain would support Austria's annexation of Bosnia and Herzegovina. Signed on 6th June 1878, this agreement was not officially acknowledged until 1926. Meanwhile, Salisbury was busily trying to prepare public opinion in favour of an Asian protectorate and 'England's need of taking a local position' in the Mediterranean, planting an anonymous but authoritative article in *The Times* to that effect.

On the night of 30th May 1878, Salisbury also signed an agreement with Schouvaloff in which the Russians agreed to a partitioned Bulgaria, only the northern part of which would be autonomous. Russia was to keep Kars and Batoum, but surrender the Alashkert Valley route to northern Persia. With the Erzurum Pass in the Shah's hands, it would keep Russia far from the Tigris, Euphrates and Persian Gulf. Sandon recorded how at the meeting in which the Cabinet was informed of the Anglo-Russian Convention, Salisbury again burned all their copies before they left the room.

These three almost simultaneous bilateral agreements with Turkey, Austria and Russia were secret, interlocking, advantageous to Britain and in the interests of peace. They made the great issues of the Berlin Congress foregone conclusions even before it was officially summoned. Critics have since complained about the secret methods by which

Salisbury sewed up the Congress of Berlin, but Salisbury implicitly believed in the efficacy of secret diplomacy.

Not surprisingly therefore, the Government, and especially Salisbury himself, were profoundly embarrassed when an accurate *précis* of the Anglo-Russian Convention was published in a London evening paper, the *Globe*, the very next day. A copying clerk called Charles Marvin, who was on secondment from outside the Foreign Office, had been given the Convention to copy by the Treaty Department and had leaked it to the *Globe* for £40. (He later made out that he had done it in the interests of open government.)

When Andrássy and other Foreign Ministers telegraphed to inquire about the veracity of the *Globe*'s report on Saturday, 1st June, they were told that it 'was incorrect'. Had it been confirmed as genuine to the Chancelleries of Europe, the Congress might have collapsed out of anger at a carve-up which allowed Russia to keep Kars and Batoum before the Powers even had a chance to discuss the matter. Salisbury therefore had little choice, and when questioned on the subject in the House of Lords on 3rd June by Earl Grey, he stated categorically that: 'The statement to which the noble Earl refers, and other statements that I have seen, are wholly unauthentic, and are not deserving of the confidence of your Lordship's House.'

It was not true, and when the *Globe* published the entire text of the Convention on 14th June, just as the Congress opened, everyone knew it. Only the most serious *raison d'état* would have induced Salisbury to tell so blatant a falsehood, but protection of the Anglo-Russian Convention was just such a circumstance. He never believed an individual statesman's reputation for truthfulness to be as important as European peace. 'No one is fit to be trusted with a secret who is not prepared, if necessary, to tell an untruth to defend it,' he had written in the *Saturday Review* in 1862, 'for, in the presence of an acute questioner, falsehood and betrayal are his only two alternatives.'[5]

Excuses have been made for Salisbury's conduct, arguments have been put that the *Globe*'s report had some small errors, or that the Convention was 'unauthentic' as the Congress had not yet opened, but these are casuistic and unconvincing. Put crudely, Salisbury lied for his country and lost no sleep over it. 'Sharp lines between right and wrong are convenient fictions,' he once wrote in an article entitled 'White Lies' about 'the delicacy of the gradations by which right and wrong fade into each other'. The *chiaroscuro* of Salisbury's *Globe* lie might be debated, but it kept the process of European conciliation on track.

At the Cabinet meeting on Saturday, 1st June, Beaconsfield proposed that he and Salisbury should represent Britain at the Congress, and said that he himself 'should only go for the beginning...but believed Salisbury would be kept long'. There had been a certain amount of behind-the-scenes negotiation over the composition of the delegation, with the Prime Minister's private secretary, Montagu Corry, canvassing Cabinet opinion and discovering that Smith and Cross were against Beaconsfield attending at all. In Cabinet, however, Salisbury:

> said he thought it very important, as it would stop all the gossip of Europe and England as to he and Lord Beaconsfield representing different policies, and that you must have men from the Cabinet who knew all the ins and outs of the recent negotiations, and that he and Lord Beaconsfield respectively would satisfy the two different views – and that as 'in England, people were very much guided by authority', the philo-Turks would accept necessary concessions to Russia from Lord Beaconsfield which they would not from him. He spoke most strongly in favour of Lord Beaconsfield going with him.

It was decided that the British plenipotentiaries to Berlin would be Beaconsfield, Salisbury and Odo Russell, 'the former only attending at the commencement to show perfect unity of opinion', according to Cranbrook's diary. The detailed negotiations would be left to Salisbury.

In contrast to the period before April, Cabinets were good-humoured affairs, with Sandon's journal mentioning 'much laughter' at Salisbury's dismissive references to minor Powers such as Serbia and Romania. Draft telegrams were read out and rewritten at the table, with everyone allowed to contribute suggestions as to their wording. There was a scare when an order to Admiral Hornby not to attack the Russians at Constantinople somehow omitted the word 'not' in transmission, but correctly worded duplicates had fortunately been sent to others, who warned him in time.

That weekend, the Salisburys entertained the Crown Prince and Princess of Germany at Hatfield. On Sunday the 2nd, Count Münster handed Salisbury the official invitation to the Congress. Only hours later, the celebratory mood was shattered by a telegram which announced an assassination attempt on the Prince's father, the eighty-one-year-old Kaiser Wilhelm I. A special train was ordered for the royal guests, who returned to Berlin by midnight the next day.

The most salient feature of the Congress was, despite its being a famous and colourful European occasion, its relative unimportance. The major outlines of the deals had been agreed in the three secret bilateral agreements concluded by Salisbury beforehand. As Salisbury saw it, the British people would be unwilling to go to war over Kars and Batoum alone, any more than Parliament would vote a shilling to fight for Montenegro and Serbia.

On 4th June, the penultimate part of the jigsaw puzzle clicked into place when the Cyprus Convention was formally signed, committing Britain to protecting Turkey's Asia Minor territories in return for

Cyprus and administrative reforms to safeguard Turkey's Asiatic Christians. The clause which only put the agreement into effect if Russia retained Kars and Batoum at the Congress was a foregone conclusion, as the Anglo-Russian Convention of four days earlier had already agreed that outcome. Whether Salisbury ever really expected the Sultan to institute the necessary reforms, at great danger from his Muslim domestic opponents, is debatable. The important point was that the commercial route through Asia Minor had been secured.[6] When the Anglo-Austrian Convention was signed on 6th June, it was at last safe for the Congress to begin. At the final Cabinet before the plenipotentiaries left for Berlin, Sandon recorded: 'Friendly parting with Salisbury. Though we had our jokes – all, though cheerful, felt it sad and solemn.'

When the Congress of Berlin opened, with port and biscuits at Bismarck's Radziwill Palace at 2 p.m. on 13th June 1878, Salisbury was accompanied by Cranborne and his parliamentary private secretary, his nephew Arthur Balfour. At Beaconsfield's request uniforms were worn. Germany was represented by Bismarck, the Congress President, as well as Prince Hohenlohe and Herr von Bülow; Austria by Count Andrássy, Baron Haymerle and Count Károlyi; Russia by Prince Gortschakoff, Count Schouvaloff and Baron D'Oubril; Italy by Count Corti and Count Launay; and France by William Waddington, the Comte de Sainte Vallier and M. Desprez. The Turks, delayed at sea, had sent Pasha Karathéodory and Mehemed Ali. (Midhat Pasha had been dismissed as Grand Vizier in the early days of the war, prior to his banishment to Syria and eventual strangulation.) When they arrived, it turned out the Turkish delegation had no instructions about Bosnia or Asia Minor, and seemed not even to know of the Anglo-Turkish Convention. The Sultan, it was assumed, intended to use them as a mere telegraph office. Matters were made worse by Bismarck's loathing of Mehemed Ali, who in his youth had deserted from the Prussian army.

    Although the details of the settlement, especially the exact borders of the two new Bulgarian states, had to be fine-tuned over four weeks of tough but generally good-humoured negotiations, the outlines were all already there. The Congress was an opportunity for the men who would be controlling the destiny of Europe, and increasingly of Africa and Asia as well, to meet and entertain one another incessantly.[7] All the British needed to ensure was that everyone stuck to the spirit as well as the letter of the three Conventions. The night before the Congress opened, Andrássy, spreading maps all over the floor in front of Beaconsfield and Salisbury, tried to haggle over the terms of the Austro-British Convention which had been signed a week earlier. One of the junior diplomats attached to the British delegation, Francis Bertie, reported to the Foreign Office that the Austrian Chancellor reminded him of 'a clean looking knock'em down man at a fair on Epsom Downs'. Andrássy was unsuccessful in squeezing any revisions out of the British plenipotentiaries.

At the Congress's opening ceremony, Salisbury said that Beaconsfield made 'rather a good' speech. It was delivered in English because Odo Russell had persuaded the Prime Minister that the delegates all wanted to hear English spoken by 'its greatest living master', flattery which actually masked embarrassment at the Prime Minister's inelegant French. Salisbury himself spoke what Schouvaloff dismissively referred to as 'Foreign Office French'. Prince Gortschakoff, the octogenarian Russian Foreign Minister, who had held the post since 1856 and had also been Imperial Chancellor since 1866, seemed to Salisbury 'a little insignificant old man – full of compliments – but otherwise having evidently lost his head'. Gortschakoff was to consider Berlin his greatest diplomatic failure.

Schouvaloff told Andrassy that 'the old man is full of obscurity and vanity, and would spoil everything' by his tough insistence on Russia's rights. Salisbury agreed, and told Cross, who was minding the Foreign Office for him back in London, that 'if some kindly fit of gout would take him off we should move much faster'. Instead, Gortschakoff marched out of meetings, refused to attend the sitting at which the Bulgarian terms were passed, and provided numerous diplomatic *bêtises*. Lord Frederick Hamilton, a former embassy official, remembered him as 'a little, short, tubby man in spectacles; wholly undistinguished and looking for all the world like an average French provincial *notaire*'. He was not, however, allowed to upset the proceedings.

The Congress allowed Beaconsfield to play to perfection a favourite role, that of the brilliant Sidonia, the Great Diplomatist. The story has been told, but never verified, that when the Russians attempted to back-track on the 30th May Convention, Beaconsfield let it be known that he had summoned a train to take him back to London to prepare for war, at which the Russians relented. He certainly impressed Bismarck, who was supposed to have said to Count Münster: 'I think nothing of their Lord Salisbury. He is only a lath painted to look like iron. But that old Jew means business.'[8] Another version goes: '*Das alte Jude, das is der Mann.*' Although Bismarck denied ever making the lath remark, both remained part of the Congress legend. Bismarck was also reported as calling Salisbury 'obstinate', 'maladroit' and 'a clergyman'. For his part, Salisbury told the 'not very edifying' story of Bismarck's answer during the Franco-Prussian War to a question of whether a captured *franc-tireur* should be shot: 'I believe in a future life, so I don't see why I should object.'[9]

The relationship between Salisbury and Beaconsfield was far more complex than the hate-then-love one commonly described. A creative tension existed in which both men, Salisbury grudgingly and Beaconsfield far more readily, came to recognise that they had more to gain than lose from a closer alliance than Salisbury would ideally have preferred. In denouncing his Party leader for lack of principle in the 1860s, Salisbury had after all only attempted unsuccessfully to do what Disraeli himself had managed to do to Peel twenty years earlier. They constitute two rare examples of politicians who both wielded the knife and also wore the crown. *Coningsby* set out a vision of brilliant young aristocrats ruling Britain, and the author's crashing snobbery – 'this comes of giving office to a middle class man', Disraeli bemoaned of Cross soon after appointing him – certainly helped the Marquess with the Tudor ancestry and Jacobean seat.

By January 1875, only five months after the 'jibes' remark, Salisbury was starting his letters 'My Dear Disraeli', for the first time since 1867. 'It is impossible for anyone to be more cordial!' their recipient told Lady Bradford. Over a Madras gubernatorial issue in May 1875, Disraeli told Queen Victoria that 'Lord Salisbury has no petty views on these matters, and is quite superior to any personal considerations.' When he wrote to ask Salisbury's advice on whether to take a peerage in July 1876, Salisbury – perhaps recognising Derby as the most likely successor – had begged him not to retire altogether. As for joining the Lords, 'you would give life to the dullest assembly in the world... as one of the shades who is on the wrong side of the stream, I must honestly say that I think you will regret the irrevocable step when you have taken it'. The advice went unheeded but the generosity did not.

For all the traditional pleasantries of a close and mutually advantageous working relationship there was little genuine friendliness between the only two bearded premiers, not least because Salisbury had never yet recanted his view of Beaconsfield's actions in 1867. A satirical play written by the eleven-year-old Edward Cecil on his father's Foreign Office paper, entitled *The Eastern Question* and set at the Constantinople Conference, opens in Downing Street with Beaconsfield telling his factotum, Montagu Corry, 'I thank Hibraic fathers for teaching me the value of a scapegoat.' Beaconsfield is portrayed as a cynical, posturing hack and pickpocket who sings, to the tune of *The Vicar of Bray*:

> Because I steadfastly resolved,
> Since first I was a novice,
> That whatsoever creed might rule,
> I'd always be in office.

The skit was dedicated to Edward's elder brother Cranborne, and it is not known whether it was actually performed at Hatfield, but the Foreign Office writing paper implies an anti-Beaconsfield feeling still prevailing in the family into 1878.[10] The persona of the pickpocket might have been a reference to 'The Artless Dodger', one of Salisbury's harshest *Saturday Review* articles on Beaconsfield.

Certainly Salisbury's waspish comments from Berlin to Hatfield bear out the thesis that for all Beaconsfield's *politesses*, there was still little love lost. 'What with deafness, ignorance of French and Bismarck's extraordinary mode of speech,' Salisbury told his wife on 23rd June, Beaconsfield had 'the dimmest idea of what is going on – understands everything crossways – and imagines a perpetual conspiracy.' To Cross he complained that 'the Chief seemed to have forgotten the various agreements we had made, and wanted a constant flapper [memorandum] for him to remind him of them'. When the two plenipotentiaries visited the Empress Augusta, Salisbury wrote to his wife: 'She was very foolish and Beaconsfield's compliments were a thing to hear!' On yet another occasion, Salisbury wrote that Beaconsfield 'is not exactly false, but he has such a perfect disregard for facts that it is almost impossible for him to run true'. The Prime Minister, ignorant of these criticisms, thanked Salisbury for his 'consummate mastery of detail' at Berlin, and told Gwendolen: 'Your father is the only man of real courage that it has ever been my lot to work with.'

It took some courage to deal with the further publication in the *Globe*, on the second day of the Congress, of the entire text of the Anglo-Russian Convention. Jingoes attacked Salisbury's concessions to Russia in Asia, Liberals contrasted it with the high-sounding principles of his Circular, and Layard pointed out the fury in Turkey at the revelation that the British Government had been from the first in league with Russia 'for the division of spoils'. Salisbury's official denial, that 'as an explanation of the policy of the Government, it is incomplete, and, consequently inaccurate', persuaded few and reassured none. In fact, it was reported to Salisbury that the *Globe*'s version was correct in all but fifteen words.[11] Indeed, so close was the report to the original that Salisbury privately blamed the Russians for leaking the document *in toto*, hoping thereby to have their claim to Kars and Batoum set in stone. It was not until 26th June that Marvin was arrested and the truth revealed. With no Official Secrets Act in existence, it was discovered that he had broken no actual law and had to be released. When her husband was criticised for not entrusting the copying to safer hands, Lady Salisbury retorted that he knew no more about the individual clerks at the Foreign Office than he did about the housemaids at Hatfield.

Rather than being nonplussed or defensive, Salisbury immediately tried to use it as further leverage over Turkey. On 15th June, the very day after it appeared, he telegraphed Layard asking for the Porte's permission to navigate the Straits, since Russia would have Batoum. The Grand Vizier came up with the suitably Byzantine suggestion that only token resistance should be offered, with blank cartridges being fired at the British fleet. Nothing came of this farcical notion.[12] In order to propitiate Andrassy over the *Globe*'s revelations, Salisbury agreed to propose to the Congress that Austria occupy Bosnia, thereby saving Andrássy from having to do it.

The issues at Berlin were discussed in descending order of difficulty, with Bulgaria coming first. Highly detailed negotiations requiring close knowledge of the frontiers, rivers, populations and especially the defensive mountain ranges saw the well-briefed Salisbury, ably advised by a fortifications expert General Simmons, winning important points off the Russians. It was at this stage that the laziness and ignorance of some other negotiators came to the surface. When Bismarck suggested that in the southern Bulgarian province the Sultan should only employ Christian troops, thus allowing the Tsar to retain his favoured soubriquet of 'Liberator of the Balkans', Salisbury's response was that it was an admirable idea, only, as he told Cross on 15th June, the Sultan did not have any as Christians were excluded from military service in the Ottoman Empire.

On 17th June the Congress got down to the meat of the Bulgarian question, with Salisbury proposing that Bulgaria be split into an autonomous principality north of the Balkan mountain range, whilst the territory south of it would be called the province of Eastern Roumelia and left under the military and political control of the Sultan, with protective guarantees for non-Muslim minorities. Andrássy asked to be included in the negotiations, prompting Schouvaloff to remark that if his foot had to be amputated it mattered little to him if there was one surgeon present or two.[13] Nomenclature did matter though; the Russians wanted the province to be called 'South Bulgaria', to emphasise the partition. Salisbury insisted on it being called 'Eastern Roumelia'. Discussions continued over the right to fortify the mountain ranges and sea coasts, over the exact nature of the Sultan's *de jure* but not *de facto* sovereignty in the north, and over almost every frontier.

Back in Britain, Jingo fever was running high against Russia. Northcote warned Salisbury that if the Anglo-Russian Convention was finally authenticated and it was discovered that Batoum, which even *The Times* was describing as crucial to Britain's communications with India, had been voluntarily ceded to Russia, 'we should be out before you could get home'. Salisbury's somewhat self-serving answer was to say that Beaconsfield should return home anyway, as 'the Jingoes require to be calmed in their own language and he is the only one among us who speaks it fluently'. Beaconsfield stayed, and Jingoism became a language whose cadences Salisbury was to learn to speak fluently, however much he might privately have disliked its vocabulary.

By 22nd June, with or without Beaconsfield's threat to leave, the Russians had given way on the most important Bulgarian points. But as Salisbury wrote to his wife that day: 'Batoum is a great bother. Its real importance is not very large, but the mass of people are so ignorant about it that a few strenuous Jingoes have continued to persuade the world it is a great matter.' Using a family code about 'Richardson' (Russia) and the colour of the Puys morning room (which was green and therefore meant Turkey), Salisbury was also able to keep Gwendolen in Dieppe in touch with the latest developments. Nor was the Congress all work; Salisbury had the opportunity to meet and quiz Professor Hermann Helmholtz, who held the chair of Physics at Berlin University and specialised in the field of electrical conduction.

Beaconsfield's attitude to Northcote's jitters was rationalised in terms of class. 'They are all middle class men,' the genuinely classless Prime Minister told his Foreign Secretary about his Cabinet, 'and I have always observed through life that middle class men are afraid of responsibility.' Only Beaconsfield could have so written off a Cabinet which included the Duke of Richmond, Viscount Sandon and Lord John Manners, the heir to the dukedom of Rutland. Northcote, said Beaconsfield, 'had early been made a bureaucrat and had never lost the feeling'. This was a little hard on the Eton- and Balliol-educated eighth baronet, but might have been a reference to Northcote's stint as Gladstone's former private secretary and campaign manager.

With Beaconsfield playing the more amenable role and charming the royalties as well as Bismarck and even Gortschakoff, Salisbury could concentrate on being the hard man of the team, simultaneously squeezing the maximum security for Eastern Roumelia out of the Russians and the maximum protection for its Christians and Orthodox minorities out of the Porte. 'Heat here is extreme – the place detestable,' Salisbury complained to his wife. At the Kaiser's residence at Potsdam there were mosquitoes, but at Berlin 'there are minor Powers. I don't-know which is worse.'

Late June saw a serious fear lest the news of the Anglo-Turkish Cyprus Convention had also been leaked. Its provisions were hinted at in a German newspaper, the *Tages-Blatt*, and alarm bells rang in London and the British Embassy in Berlin lest any Power tried to prevent Britain occupying Cyprus at the end of the Congress. Salisbury telegraphed to Admiral Hornby to be ready to sail to the island at any moment, 'to avoid accidents'. The Sultan was to issue a *firman* (proclamation) for the British occupation of Cyprus to Layard, which was then to be taken to Cyprus by Northbrook's cousin and former private secretary, Evelyn Baring, who would take immediate formal possession of the island in the name of the Queen. In the emergency, however, Salisbury was willing to cut corners, saying that once Baring was ordered to move, if the *firman* was still not ready 'a simple note from the Grand Vizier would probably suffice'.[14] Salisbury appreciated that possession of an island protected by the Royal Navy would probably constitute nine parts of international law.

Salisbury had to walk warily between his increasingly nervous colleagues who feared 'violent indignation' over Batoum, Schouvaloff's desire for the port, Beaconsfield's love of drama, Turkey's resentment of anything smacking of Christian imperialism and French jealousy of further British territorial acquisition in the eastern Mediterranean. He flippantly put the 'violent revulsion of feeling in our own party' down to the hot weather, but he was concerned lest the settlement he had carefully set in place should not be welcomed when finally it 'oozed out' in London. 'Our torpedo must explode now in a very few days,' he warned London on 3rd July, but until it did, he could not be sure whether it would blow up in their faces. Politeness dictated that he inform the French plenipotentiary, William Waddington – the son of an Englishman who had become a French citizen – the day before his Cypriot *fait accompli*, but no earlier in case France seriously protested. In early June, Salisbury had told the Cabinet that 'he expected some shrieks from Waddington, but that he would soon get over it'.

When the *firman* had still not been issued by a more than usually dilatory Sultan by 4th July, Salisbury instructed Layard to strong-arm the Porte by threatening British support of Bismarck's plan to give Thessaly, Epirus and Crete to Greece. 'Inform Sultan and spare no efforts or threats to get *firman* issued at once,' he told Layard, who duly had it in his hands three days later. On 6th July, Salisbury informed Waddington about the Cyprus Convention, describing it as 'purely conditional in its tenor'; another case of testing the elasticity of the truth.[15] With the granting of the *firman* on 7th July, Baring and a Turkish pasha left Constantinople in a warship bound for Cyprus. A naval squadron under Lord John Hay went with them to ensure a suitably respectful reception from the local population, which they duly received on taking formal control.

The *Daily Telegraph* announced the Cyprus news on 8th July, but at 6.25 p.m. that day Cross telegraphed to say that 'all still very anxious to know about Batoum final arrangements'. There, too, Salisbury had some good news, in that although it was to remain in Russian hands,

James Gascoyne-Cecil, 2nd Marquess of Salisbury

Fanny Gascoyne, his Marchioness, who died when her son Robert was only nine

Lord Robert Gascoyne-Cecil MP aged 27

Georgina, Lady Salisbury in 1876: he married for love in the teeth of bitter family opposition

Viscount Cranborne, Lord Robert's half blind invalid elder brother who died in 1865

The new Lord Cranborne in 1866; striking a statesmanlike pose as Secretary of State for India

Salisbury's hatred for Benjamin Disraeli (later the Earl of Beaconsfield) was eventually transformed into a close working relationship

Salisbury said of William Ewart Gladstone: 'His hypocrisy makes me sick'

The 4th Earl of Carnarvon: Oxford friend, Cabinet ally, political scapegoat

The 15th Earl of Derby, the former rival whom Salisbury denounced as a liar in the House of Lords

Otto von Bismarck gave Salisbury this
photograph on the day they both signed the
Treaty of Berlin

Sultan Abdul Hamid II of Turkey: 'sick,
sensual, terrified,' but a consummate
survivor

William Waddington was an Old Rugbeian
and Cambridge rowing blue who became
Prime Minister of France

Count Nikolai Ignatiev, Russia's
Ambassador to Constantinople and 'the
greatest liar on the Bosporus'

Tsar Alexander II of Russia, Salisbury's opponent in the Great Game on India's North-West Frontier

Sir Stafford Northcote, 1st Earl of Iddesleigh, who Salisbury outmanoeuvred for the premiership. He later died in Salisbury's arms

As Viceroy of India, the 1st Earl of Lytton launched the Second Afghan War without Cabinet permission

Gathorne Gathorne-Hardy, 1st Earl of Cranbrook

Lord John Manners, 7th Duke of Rutland

Richard Cross, 1st Viscount Cross

Lord Salisbury as Prime Minister in 1886

Adversaries

Lord Randolph Churchill, whose sensational resignation in December 1886 was intended to destroy Salisbury, but which dramatically backfired

Kaiser Wilhelm II might have dressed up as Frederick the Great, but he had not a particle of his ancestor's genius

Charles Stewart Parnell, romantic leader of the Irish Nationalist Party

Salisbury as Sisyphus, from *Punch* in April 1887

Châlet Cecil, Salisbury's gothic holiday home at Puys, near Dieppe

they had agreed for it to be *'essentielement'* a free, open, 'commercial' port, without naval installations. The frontiers would also be redrawn to repatriate 100,000 Muslims to Turkey. Beaconsfield had inadvertently allowed Gortschakoff to write *'essentielement'* in the agreement instead of *'exclusivement'*, as Salisbury had requested when he passed negotiation on the issue over to the Prime Minister. 'The old wretch knew that Beaconsfield was short-sighted and ignorant of detail,' Salisbury complained to Cross on 10th July, 'and took the opportunity of substituting another line. Schouvaloff acknowledges we were done.... Chief has been – and remains – bad with his asthma – and was not able to attend Congress today.'[16]

With the Union Flag hoisted at Larnaca on 11th July, the French press underwent a characteristic Anglophobic spasm, but Waddington himself stayed calm. The explanation only seeped out years later. Salisbury liked Waddington, a half-English archaeologist who had been to Rugby and had rowed in the Cambridge eight, and he wanted to placate French anger. As far as an accredited plenipotentiary can ever speak privately, Salisbury informed Waddington that Tunis, nominally a Turkish dependency but ruled by a Bey, was France's for the taking. Britain had no interests there, so, as Salisbury told Lord Lyons in Paris, if 'France occupied Tunis tomorrow we should not even remonstrate'. After the Conference ended, Waddington asked for written confirmation of the *'procès verbal'* from Salisbury, and much to the future Liberal Foreign Secretary, Lord Granville's, outrage three years later, he got it. The exact phrase used by Salisbury had been: '*Prenez Tunis, Carthage ne doit pas rester aux barbares,*' and Beaconsfield also used much the same language, thinking Waddington 'an *épicier*, but a good man'. What Salisbury later called 'the policy, if it be practicable, of giving her Tunis to gnaw at', meant that France was far less troublesome over Cyprus than she might otherwise have been.[17]

With a light white feather quill, which can today be viewed in the Long Gallery at Hatfield, Salisbury signed the sixty-four-clause Treaty of Berlin in the Radziwill Palace at 2.30 p.m. on Saturday, 13th July 1878, in time for Bismarck to go on his annual visit to the Kissingen baths. When Beaconsfield signed, the title 'Prime Minister', which had originated, as so many political soubriquets, as a term of abuse, was used officially for the first time. In 1863, Salisbury had written of a European conference proposed by Napoleon III that each plenipotentiary 'will appear at the Congress with the fullest intention of treading on his neighbour's toes, and the fullest consciousness that his own are full of corns'. The final protocols made it clear that Salisbury had done more than his fair share of treading. As the Congress ended, Salisbury was hugely amused to hear that the Sultan had awarded his wife the Turkish Order of Chastity (Third Class).

Russia's San Stefano pretensions to domination in the Near East had been reversed. Bulgaria had been trisected into a Russian satellite in the north, the autonomous province of Eastern Roumelia, and a southern part below the Balkan mountains which remained part of Turkey-in-Europe. Austria acquired Bosnia and Herzegovina. The Greeks secured only promises of future negotiations over Ottoman-held Epirus and Thessaly. Russia was ceded Kars, Batoum, Ardahan and the part of Bessarabia taken from her in 1856, but received nothing else from her victorious campaigns except the warm feeling of having liberated their fellow Slavs north of the Balkans. Batoum was to become a demilitarised Russian free port, if only essentially rather than exclusively.

The laws regarding navigating the Straits remained unchanged from the 1841 status quo, whereby all warships were forbidden passage when Turkey was at peace, and passage was *de facto* the Sultan's choice when at war, thereby keeping the Russian navy out of the Mediterranean, a prime British *desideratum*. The principles of full religious and political equality and freedom were officially accepted by Turkey, but Salisbury recognised the extreme difficulties that lay ahead in their implementation. As her *pied à terre*, Britain had won Cyprus, with its fine harbours and strategic position close to Egypt, Syria and the proposed railway route to Baghdad.[18] As a general European conflagration had also been averted, it was little wonder that London erupted into celebration on Beaconsfield's and Salisbury's triumphal return.

The steamer put alongside Admiralty Pier at Dover at 2.40 p.m. on Tuesday, 16th July, where a large crowd cheered loudly and a band struck up *Home, Sweet Home*. There was of course an element of political stage-management to the welcome, which was partly organised by the chief Tory wire-puller, the Marquess of Abergavenny, to make it seem so national a celebration that the Opposition's criticisms of the Treaty would look unpatriotic, but overall it was massive, good-hearted and spontaneous. At their meeting three days earlier, the Cabinet agreed that Montagu Corry should 'be told that Salisbury should come at the same time so as to share the reception'. They were not about to allow the Prime Minister to hog all the limelight.

Dover and its shipping were arrayed in bunting for the homecoming. At the quayside, Beaconsfield told the crowd: 'We have brought a peace, and we trust we have brought a peace with honour, and I trust that will now be followed by the prosperity of the country.' The phrase 'peace with honour' stuck. Charing Cross Station was decorated with flags, arches, Union Flags, shields, trophies and vast displays from the Queen's florist, John Wills of South Kensington; a total of 10,000 plants in all. Beaconsfield was conspicuous in a long white overcoat and 'was visibly affected' (i.e. tearful) when mobbed by ladies desperate to shake his hand.

On the way to Downing Street, Beaconsfield insisted that Salisbury be offered a seat in Lady Abergavenny's open carriage. As it carried the two plenipotentiaries through the dense, cheering crowds, people hung on to the railings of St Martin-in-the-Fields and climbed up the statues of Trafalgar Square for a better view. 'The compact black mass of heads in one line hundreds deep', recorded *The Times* the next morning, 'impressed the imagination most.' Balconies, roofs and windows along the short route were packed with cheering people waving hats and scarves. The carriage was met on the threshold of No. 10 by the Queen's private secretary, Sir Henry Ponsonby, bearing flowers from her. The street itself was thronged with crowds of well-wishers shouting 'Duke of Cyprus!', and Beaconsfield waved and cried once more. Salisbury, with his instinctive distrust for the fickleness of crowds and his powerful reserve, merely smiled and occasionally doffed his top hat.

After Beaconsfield had repeated his 'peace with honour' line, there were calls for Salisbury, who came to a front window at No. 11 and, eschewing his Chief's hyperbole, confined himself to saying: 'I thank you heartily, and I gather from this assemblage that you will always support a Government which supports the honour of England.' *Rule Britannia* was sung, Salisbury said a few words more, and after a further long interval of cheering the crowd dispersed as ambassadors and minor royalties arrived to pay their respects. Salisbury had 'protested to his utmost' against this public reception in London, basing his opposition not only on his distaste for personal advertisement, but also because he feared it would cause a backlash both at home, where it might alienate support for the Government, and abroad, where it could make further diplomatic successes over Russia and Turkey more difficult. He was ignored by the Tory Party managers who laid on the spectacle with glee, but Gladstone's later successes in denouncing the flashier excesses of 'Beaconsfieldism' might be taken to justify his kill-joy stance.

At the first Cabinet meeting after their return, held the following day, Beaconsfield seemed 'pale and worn' from his Congress-induced gout. Salisbury, on the other hand, looked 'remarkably well'. On the question of which department of state should govern Cyprus, Salisbury pressed for the India Office, on the grounds that it would remind France that 'we were an Asiatic not Mediterranean power', but also because if it was administered by the Colonial Office, the Liberals would 'infallibly give it a constitution, which would be fatal to the whole scheme, whereas the India Office, under every Government, hated constitutions'.

Writing to Professor McLeod on 18th July, Salisbury acknowledged that he thought 'we have got as good a settlement as could fairly be expected – without bloodshed. But we have not settled the Eastern Question. That will not be done for another fifty years to come.' The Opposition agreed, and three days later, Gladstone denounced the occupation of Cyprus as an 'act of duplicity' and 'an insane covenant', repeating an adjective used by Derby in the House of Lords three days earlier. Carnarvon described secret treaties *per se* as contrary to the British tradition, and argued that Turkey had been partitioned and left defenceless, all to burnish the Government's 'glamour'.[19]

Salisbury had considered the Order of the Garter, which had been awarded to both his father and grandfather as well as the early Cecils, as 'a very useful institution. It fosters a wholesome taste for bright colours, and gives old men who have good legs an excuse for showing them.'[20] He was a middle-aged man with bad legs who had started to put on a good deal of weight, but he nonetheless accepted the Queen's offer on 22nd July. 'To become K.G. with a Cecil is something for a Disraeli!' exclaimed his brother knight. It laid the two men open for an inevitable quip from the Radical MP Wilfred Lawson about obtaining 'peace with honours', but it was the only one Salisbury ever accepted from Queen Victoria, refusing many others throughout his career, including two offers of a dukedom. He had flicked away Beaconsfield's offer of a GCB in April, and with the Garter star on his breast he understandably felt that little else signified.

On 8th April 1878, Salisbury had set out what has since become the classic definition of the doctrine of Cabinet responsibility, when he laid down that:

> For all that passes in a Cabinet, each member of it who does not resign is absolutely and irretrievably responsible, and that he has no right afterwards to say that he agreed in one case to a compromise, while in another that he was persuaded by one of his colleagues.... It is, I maintain, only on the principle that absolute responsibility is undertaken by every member of a Cabinet, who, after a decision is arrived at, remains a member of it, that the joint responsibility of ministers to Parliament can be upheld, and one of the most essential conditions of Parliamentary responsibility established.[21]

Lord Derby had liberated himself from that responsibility, and on 18th July 1878 he launched an attack on Salisbury which was so strong, and was repulsed so aggressively, that Salisbury was plunged, as he had been with his father over his marriage and with Disraeli over the Second Reform Act, into an icy enmity which lasted for years. In the debate on the Berlin Treaty, Derby claimed he had quitted the Cabinet because of its decision to seize and occupy Cyprus, together with a port on the Syrian coast, regardless of the Sultan's consent. 'I could not reconcile it to my conscience,' he told their Lordships, 'either as a matter of justice or of policy, to be a party, in time of peace, to the seizure of part of the territory of a friendly Power, without the consent of the rightful owner.'

Salisbury was furious. 'Those who know him intimately could recognise the sombre gleam in his eyes,' recalled Gwendolen, 'the shadow which darkened his face.' Barely restraining his temper, he unleashed the full power of his sarcasm at the man who, he was convinced but could not publicly say, had allowed his wife to leak Cabinet secrets to the Russians and whose inactivity and pusillanimity had, he believed, brought Britain to the edge of catastrophe:

> This is the third speech which my noble Friend has made since he left the Cabinet, and every one of them has contained an instalment of the fatal tale. The same objection was made to Dr. Oates, when he brought forward his successive fragments of his disclosure. When taunted with the fact, he said that he did not know how much the public would endure.

To equate Derby with Titus Oates, one of history's most infamous perjurers, whose lies led to the judicial killing of thirty-five people, was in itself a vicious jibe, but Salisbury did not stop there in his assault on his former colleague and his step-mother's husband:

> Any person who hereafter serves with him in the Cabinet must be prepared to have anything that passes, or is supposed to pass there, produced ultimately, in spite of the rule which privy councillors have hitherto observed. But in the present case, the statement which my noble friend has made, to the effect that a resolution had been come to in Cabinet... is a statement which, so far as my memory goes, is not true.

Cries of 'Order!' from their Lordships at this accusation brought Salisbury to amend the sentence, saying: 'well, is not correct.' Derby leapt to his feet: 'I must ask my noble Friend, whether he intends to impute that I made an untrue statement?' Granville got up to beg Salisbury not to use unparliamentary language. Salisbury tried to explain that 'the language I have used does not necessarily impugn the veracity of the speaker'. Lord Selborne exclaimed in disbelief: 'What! To say it was "not true"!' Salisbury: 'I have substituted the words "not correct". What I wish to say is, that I was not relying on my own memory.'

He was, he added, also relying on the memory of Beaconsfield, Cairns, Cranbrook, Northcote, Smith and others, who all agreed that Derby's statement was 'not correct'. Salisbury was fortunate that the Cabinet peers were present, shaking their heads, and Northcote and Smith were standing on the steps of the Throne saying, 'It's perfectly untrue!' and

'What does he mean?', loud enough to be overheard.[22] Northcote later confirmed that no decision had indeed been reached on the subject, although a conversation had taken place about it. It was, as *The Times* put it, 'a mode of controversy which fifty years before would have meant pistols and Wimbledon Common'. Salisbury himself thought duelling 'as ridiculous as the man in armour in the Lord Mayor's show', but he was indeed fortunate that its days were over.

The day after the clash, Salisbury wrote to Northcote propagating the line that 'no resolution of the Cabinet was come to except that the Indian troops should be brought to Malta: and it was on that (as we understood it) and the calling out of the reserves that he resigned'. It was of course not really up to Salisbury to state why Derby had resigned, and on the same day Derby showed Granville a memorandum he had written at the time which supported his assertions. Gladstone urged that Derby should publish this document as soon as possible, as the general view was the one Beaconsfield had propagated in the House of Lords on 28th March, the day after the resignation, that it had been over the far less controversial calling up of the Reserves that Derby had gone. Salisbury wrote to Eustace to say how damaging Derby's 'imaginings' might be abroad, adding that the fact that his denial was 'not agreeable to Derby's feelings was under the circumstances a very secondary consideration. His proceeding is quite unintelligible on very ordinary principles of honour.'[23]

Derby was not the only person Salisbury slighted in the House of Lords on 18th July. In a lighter vein, when Granville questioned him closely about Cyprus's climate and soil, attempting to make out that the island was a worthless acquisition, Salisbury answered: 'If the noble Earl will consult the *Encyclopædia Britannica* when he gets home, he will get all the information he desires.' Just as he could not write a boring sentence, so Salisbury was also incapable of uttering a commonplace or canting remark. Lord Rosebery once wrote that reading old political speeches was as dull as drinking decanted champagne. Salisbury's *extra brut* speeches are the exception, and of a vintage that is still effervescent.

Beaconsfield and Salisbury were easily able to rebut criticisms of the Berlin Treaty in the House of Lords debate. But in their speeches at the banquet given by the Carlton Club at the Duke of Wellington's Riding School – now Knightsbridge Barracks – on 27th July, they went further. It was the famous occasion on which Beaconsfield described Gladstone as 'a sophisticated rhetorician, inebriated with the exuberance of his own verbosity'. After nine courses of twenty-nine dishes, Salisbury got up and proclaimed that the Government was striving 'to pick up the broken thread of England's old imperial traditions'. He contrasted the way in which the Russians in Asian Turkey and the Austrians in

Muslim Bosnia were being resisted by the local populations, whereas the Cypriots had greeted the British with enthusiasm. When other Powers, he said,

find out what our policy really is, that we are there merely to extend to others the blessings we ourselves enjoy; when they find that we welcome their competition; that we invite every trade, that we grudge success to no nationality; that the one object we have in mind is that peace and order should be maintained, and that races and creeds which for centuries back have lived in feud shall henceforth live in amity and goodwill, then I believe all idea of jealousy will vanish and that they will heartily co-operate with us in our civilising mission.[24]

R U S
• Bokhara

Caucasus

Caspian
Sea

• Kizilarvat

Oxus

• Merv

• Teheran

Penjdeh
Zulficar Pass • •

PERSIA

• Herat

AFGHANISTA

N

Maiwan •
• Kandaha

S E I S T A N

Helmand

Central Asia 1878

0   50   100   150   200 miles

BALUCHISTA

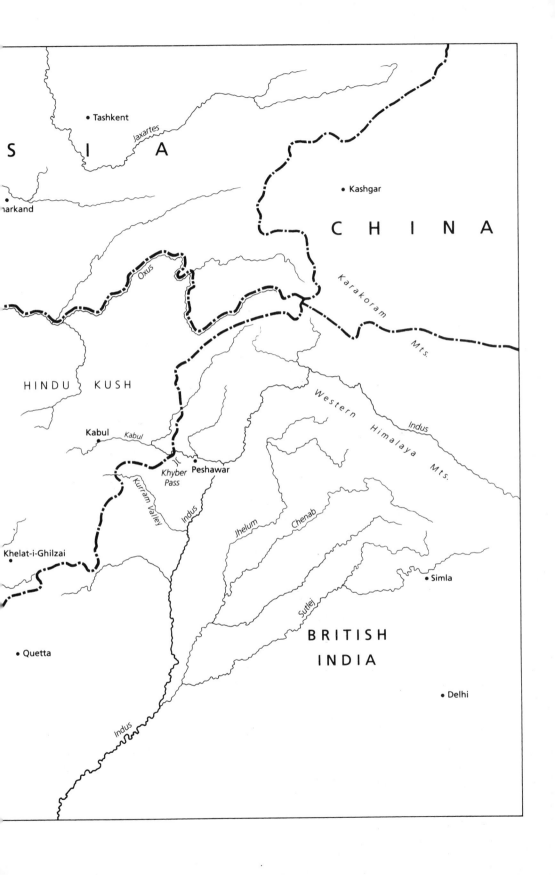

THIRTEEN

Lytton as Viceroy

The Second Afghan War

1876 to 1880

'No lesson seems to be so deeply inculcated by the experience of
life as that you should never trust experts.'

If Salisbury's diplomacy was lauded for avoiding a war in the Near East,
it was soon accused of precipitating one in Afghanistan. Responsibility
for the Second Afghan War is still disputed by historians, but Salisbury
is among the prime suspects. The confluence of a war in Afghanistan,
another in Zululand, strong-arm tactics in Egypt and what Salisbury
was to call 'governing the Porte by diplomatic thunderstorms', which
included the temporary suspension of diplomatic relations, seem to
add up to a 'Forward' foreign policy. In his famous campaign to
win the Scottish seat of Midlothian, Gladstone denounced it as
'Beaconsfieldism', the immoral, bullying acquisition of territory and
influence, almost for its own sake. Yet taken individually and in
context, Salisbury was largely innocent of the charge of sponsoring such
a policy.

It is true that he had a low opinion of the average Afghan, who, he
said, 'looks upon an Englishman in two lights – first, as a person who is
an infidel, and next as a person who has money. In the first character he
is anxious to kill him, in the second he is anxious to rifle him.' It was
because of this perceived untrustworthiness that, even before he arrived
in India, Lytton was instructed by Salisbury to ask the Amir of
Afghanistan to receive a permanent British mission. If it was refused,
'His Highness should be distinctly reminded that he is isolating
himself, at his own peril, from the friendship and protection it is his
interest to seek and preserve.' It amounted to a fairly blatant hint from
the paramount regional power, and as soon as Lytton arrived in India he
asked the Amir to accept the residence of a senior official, Sir Lewis
Pelly. This was rejected.

In his original orders, which Lytton read on the boat out to India, Salisbury had said that the Amir was slowly being 'brought within a steadily narrowing circle between the conflicting pressures of two great military empires, one of which expostulates and remains passive, whilst the other apologises and continues to move forward'. Salisbury believed that the Russian Empire was a juggernaut forced always to enlarge itself in order to survive: 'It is an internal necessity to move on – directly her frontier becomes fixed her political troubles begin.' The policy of the Government of India should be so to reflect this internal dynamic as 'not to offer the slightest obstacle to her walking over other people's hedges, so long as those hedges do not lie in our direction'.

Fundamentally, Salisbury never believed a direct Russian invasion of India via Afghanistan was likely, not least because he could not see how they could get the necessary heavy equipment, artillery and ammunition over passes sometimes 15,000 feet above sea level.[1] The occasional pieces of information from Central Asia gleaned from undercover agents there fascinated him; he likened them to reading a novel in a weekly periodical. 'Though the course of true love will not necessarily run smooth,' he wrote to Lytton on 26th May, 'I trust that a consoling and blissful third volume awaits us.' The next day, Lytton telegraphed to say that the Amir had refused the Pelly mission on the grounds of 'great danger to British officers from fanatics or opponents of [the] Amir', and also the fact that assent to a British mission would involve accepting a Russian one as well. Salisbury interpreted this as 'the feminine view that flirting with two lovers is pleasanter than marrying one of them'.

Salisbury's view of the relationship between the Secretary of State and the Viceroy was that ultimately all power resided in London, but the maximum possible amount of leeway should be accorded to the man on the spot. 'Whenever they really trust each other,' he told Lytton in early June, 'the relationship is a very easy one to work. When they do not, no amount of sound doctrine can make things go smooth.' The problem was that, in contrast to Northbrook, Lytton turned out to be another imperial 'prodigal son', who felt himself to be on a mission to expand the Empire by whatever means. Despite their personal friendliness and the mutually charming and witty correspondence, Salisbury's trust in Lytton's judgment was ebbing. In the early period, however, Salisbury was just as keen as Lytton to get listening posts, spies and missions into Afghanistan, taking a far more 'Forward' view than he had in 1866–7. Faced with the prospect of sitting next to his old collaborator Lord Lawrence in a two-hour Indian Council meeting, Salisbury wrote to Lytton that he could hardly bring himself to speak charitably to the former Governor-General, 'when I thought of all the mischief his masterly inactivity has caused'.

Northbrook, whom Salisbury described as 'a curious compound of tough little prejudices', later ascribed the Second Afghan War to Lytton's refusal to take the Amir's initial 'No' for an answer. Instead a second, more forceful request was sent on 8th July 1876. Salisbury supported Lytton, but as 'you do not address advice to a billiard player at the moment he is about to strike', he left the exact form of threat up to the Viceroy. The main lines of policy had been agreed in March and, 'as long as you do not step outside them, I should only embarrass you by interposing'.[2] It was a hands-off policy he was to come to regret. Occasionally he would write with specific advice on the key strategic points in the Great Game ('protect Khelat – it is your queen'), and he always supported surveillance operations in Herat, Merv and Seistan as well as efforts to win greater influence in Baluchistan, but initially he tried not to interfere with Lytton overmuch.

The close personal connection between Secretary of State and Viceroy was emphasised when Salisbury agreed to stand godfather to Lytton's eldest son, Victor Alexander George Robert, Viscount Knebworth, the last Christian name given in his honour. His friendly, easy correspondence with Lytton was stuffed with epigrams. Of the Viceroy's Council: 'They enjoy the protection of absolute obscurity.' Of a Colonel Malleson at Mysore: a 'very untrustworthy type of man...journalist broidered on the official'. On another occasion: 'Philosophy can be very useful to those who have to command: but a fatal siren to those who have to obey.' On the bimetallism problem facing the rupee, Salisbury thought that all would be well once the purchasing power of the Indian peasant returned to 1868 levels, and 'he resumes that process of accumulating bangles which appears to be the final cause for which men labour with brains and hands in the Nevada mines'.

Salisbury was no more expectant of Indian loyalty in 1876 than he had been ten years before: 'To expect political support as a consequence of good Government is an optimist's dream. Good government avoids one of the causes of hate: but it does not inspire love.' When the Indian Government claimed its 'rights' against the Home Government, Salisbury put his response in terms the owner of Knebworth would appreciate:

> You know the feelings of a landowner. He is content his neighbours should enjoy the utmost liberty of going through his park, so long as they do not set up a right: but if they do that, he begins to think of his rights, and the claims of his estate, and his duty to his successors.... The Government of India has no 'rights' strictly speaking, except those which are given to it by Act of Parliament.[3]

Salisbury was not insensible to Lytton's Russophobia, telling the Permanent Under-Secretary at the India Office, Sir Louis Mallet, that he thought it 'more literary than anything else. When he has to write an effective paper, he cannot help laying on the colours artistically.' But he believed he could keep an effective rein on it, especially as he by then had the total support of the Prime Minister. 'My confidence in you is complete,' Beaconsfield had written over the question of the reorganisation of administration on the North-West Frontier on 3rd September 1876, 'whatever you decide on, I shall uphold.' Lytton also seemed to appreciate Salisbury in the early days, writing to John Morley, the historian and Liberal MP, that same week: 'It is impossible to do business with him and not love him. I can't conceive how he ever acquired the reputation for being overbearing. I find him singularly considerate, most sympathetic and most loyal in supporting me through my difficulties.'

Lytton's proclamation of Queen Victoria as Empress of India on New Year's Day 1877 was planned minutely. A durbar was held at Delhi with sixty-three ruling princes and 100,000 people present, to hear the Viceroy read out a message from the Queen-Empress. The celebrations across India were huge, comprising military reviews, medal investitures, a 101-gun salute, fireworks, three days of addresses, a massive State banquet, pensions increases, the restoration of decommissioned mosques to religious use, amnesties to release thousands of prisoners, and the cancellation of all debts of under 100 rupees. Schools were renamed, statues erected and large sums were donated to famine relief. Salisbury insisted on as much 'local colour' as possible, to make it clear that this meant 'not the Anglicizing of India, but the enthronement of the Queen as an oriental potentate'.

Writing from Rome on his way to Constantinople, Salisbury advised Lytton that Indians were generally 'fond of the colours of oratory, and pardoning exaggeration more easily than coldness'. A special rank of 'Councillors of the Empire' was created on Lytton's advice (though they were never subsequently asked for their counsel), but Salisbury turned down his proposal to appoint some of the princes to his Legislative Council, likening it to making Garter knights honorary members of the Metropolitan Board of Works.

Lytton's romantic imagination and Salisbury's amused cynicism merged to create a truly spectacular pageant, ignoring the carping of those Liberal 'kill-joys' in England whom Salisbury characterised as 'frigid, cautious, Quakerish, philistine, only considering a composition faultless when it has been divested of all richness and all force'. Lytton put on a spectacle which achieved the two criteria Salisbury had set him six months earlier, of being 'gaudy enough to impress the orientals, yet not enough to give hold for ridicule here', and furthermore a pageant which hid 'the nakedness of the sword on which we really rely'.[4]

Although Salisbury still felt another Mutiny to be 'our one great danger', and wished to see the army arranged in 'mutiny-tight compartments' with regiments kept as separate and diverse as possible, he did not believe that the promotion of natives to responsible positions in advance of their abilities would propitiate native feeling. 'Sooner or later natives must be promoted to offices of high trust,' he wrote to Delane, the veteran editor of *The Times*, contradicting a report that he was encouraging a 'fast-track' process for natives, 'but the change must be introduced tentatively and with much caution.' His private feeling about that class of minor notaries from which many of the nationalists sprang was predictably harsh. As he told Mallet, 'I can imagine no more terrible future for India than that of being governed by competition-baboos,' the clerks who owed their places to competitive examination.

Salisbury regularly opposed those who wished to push the Indian peasantry into modern Western society too precipitately. 'If Mr Weld had been a Protestant fanatic, instead of a sanitary fanatic, people would have seen it at once,' he wrote of someone who had wished to institute sanitation reforms. 'To the people it is obviously the same thing whether their feelings are trampled on in the name of some ancient religion, or of some brand new scientific dogma.' Salisbury's High Tory respect for custom and tradition extended to the Indian peasant, whom he feared would revolt sooner than accept over-hasty Westernisation, as in 1857. He stood out against the Whig ethos propagated by Macaulay and others that Britain's duty was simply to prepare the Indians for eventual self-government. In Salisbury's view, India was a prize that should remain Britain's until it was forcibly wrested from her.

Whilst at Constantinople, Salisbury had hoped to enter into detailed negotiations with Ignatiev over Central Asia. He was ready to offer to abandon British influence in Kashgar and Bokhara, both of which were falling within the Russian ambit anyhow, in return for the neutralisation of Merv and Kabul. It would have been a fine deal had it come off, but the Conference ended too soon. The untrustworthiness of the Russians was proved when Schouvaloff assured Derby that General Constantin von Kaufmann, the Russian Governor of Turkestan, had not been communicating with the Amir. 'This is cool,' wrote an amused Derby in his diary, 'for we have copies of the correspondence in our possession.'[5]

By March 1877, Lytton had lost patience with the Amir's temporising and broke off diplomatic relations. 'We must completely, and unflinchingly, support Lytton,' wrote Beaconsfield on hearing the news, 'we wanted a man of ambition, imagination, some vanity and much will – and we have got him.' But Salisbury was starting to worry whether they had after all got the right man, telling Mallet that Lytton's father's literary romanticism – he wrote *The Last Days of Pompeii* – and the son's German education biased his judgment, even though 'he means it all in a spirit of the purest patriotism'. In June 1877, Salisbury began reining

Lytton back, blaming his hawkish advisers in Delhi for his enthusiasm to contest areas with Russia as far away as Erzurum and Kizil Arvat, when, in Salisbury's view, 'nobody pretends that it matters to us whether they are held by Hottentots or Esquimos'. Their doubtful utility to Russia would not be worth the cost of 'a gigantic war' with her, one that Salisbury estimated would cost £200 million and put threepence in the pound on income tax 'for ever'. Salisbury went to great lengths to calm Lytton, who was sending ever more excitable telegrams about deposing the Amir by force.

The Great Game suddenly seemed not so playful. On 11th June 1877, Salisbury wrote to Beaconsfield to say: 'If I understand Lytton's policy aright, he wants to plunge Afghanistan into war in order to turn the edge of its sword from us. This is quite a new policy of which 'till now I have never had a hint.' The dangerous situation in the Near East – in the same month that the Russians crossed the Danube – meant that a proxy war being fought in Central Asia would be likely to ignite precisely the Anglo-Russian conflict that Salisbury always dreaded, but which he also suspected Beaconsfield wanted. '"Unofficial" war on the Atteh or the Oxus', he told the Prime Minister, 'can produce nothing but embarrassment and discredit.'

That same day in the House of Lords, in reply to Lord De Mauley who had moved for a consul to be sent to Central Asia, Salisbury made one of his most celebrated remarks. De Mauley had cited the adventurer and spy Colonel Frederick Burnaby's recently published book, *A Ride to Khiva*, to prove that Russia's progress towards India was 'slow, silent and certain', and that one day 'hordes of Cossacks would swarm like locusts over our frontier'. Salisbury's *sang froid* was affected neither by the paranoia nor by the clichés. 'The noble Lord will forgive me if I say that his notice hardly prepared me for his references to Napoleon the First, the Tsar Peter, the pertinacity of Russian policy, and the general rapacity of the Russian nation,' he began, pointing out that there were deserts to be traversed between Russia and India and the nearest point of the Caspian Sea from which supplies could be gathered was over a thousand miles from the Indian frontier.

I cannot help thinking that in discussions of this kind, a great deal of misapprehension arises from the popular use of maps on a small scale. As with such maps you are able to put a finger on India and a finger on Russia, some persons at once think that the political situation is alarming and that India must be looked to. If the noble Lord would use a larger map – say one on the scale as the Ordnance map of England – he would find that the distance between Russia and British India is not to be measured by a finger and thumb, but by a rule.

The strongest man in the British army, Colonel Burnaby was a physical giant who could reputedly pick up a pony under each arm. A favourite party trick was to vault across a billiard table. He was an unlikely man for undercover work, but he undertook a solitary, 1,000-mile midwinter expedition across Central Asia to try to ascertain Russian intentions there. Salisbury approved of Burnaby's various missions and appreciated being sent his journal before it was printed. 'I cannot see any reason for interfering with the natural right of a Briton to get his throat cut when and where he likes,' he told Lytton as Burnaby set off for freelance intelligence work. His prediction proved eerily accurate; on 17ᵗʰ January 1885 Burnaby was killed, speared in the throat by a dervish on the expedition to relieve Gordon in Khartoum, to which he had attached himself without permission.

Four days after his 'small maps' speech, Salisbury penned a despatch to Lytton which also contained a phrase which became celebrated:

> I think you listen too much to the soldiers. No lesson seems to be so deeply inculcated by the experience of life as that you should never trust experts. If you believe the doctors, nothing is wholesome: if you believe the theologians, nothing is innocent: if you believe the soldiers, nothing is safe. They all require to have their strong wine diluted by a very large admixture of insipid common sense.[6]

Common sense told Salisbury that Lytton was wrong when he telegraphed from Simla on 16ᵗʰ June that the Russian occupation of Kizil Arvat rendered their occupation of Merv inevitable in two or three years, 'if not prevented by counter measures'. When a few days later Salisbury discovered that Lytton had been encouraging Layard in Constantinople to send a Turkish mission to Kabul, he warned Beaconsfield of their latest 'prodigal son': 'Lytton is burning with anxiety to distinguish himself in a great war – and if you allow him to direct Layard's movements I warn you that serious danger will be the result.'

Salisbury made it a central feature of his policy to calm Lytton, answering his Kizil Arvat telegram by saying: 'You foreshorten the vista of the future, and crowd up into the next few years, or less, events which will take a generation to complete.' In September, he described the prospect of a Russian attack as the 'shadow of a shade'. In fact, Merv fell to Russia in 1884, but Salisbury was right in deprecating an imminent Russian assault on India herself, as none transpired. As their official relationship deteriorated over policy towards Afghanistan, Lytton started criticising Salisbury to friends. He told Salisbury's Eton and *Saturday Review* contemporary, the distinguished lawyer James Fitzjames Stephen, that Salisbury was 'so contemptuously regardless of the fact that our Indian Empire is a great Mahommedan power and can never be anything else, that his letters fill me with dismay and alarm'.

This was unfair, as only the previous month Salisbury had written to Lytton saying that to allow Muslims to demonstrate in favour of the Sultan in India would be as reasonable as 'to expect the porter in a powder factory to encourage bonfires'. Salisbury merely believed that Indian policy should fit into overall British foreign policy, whereas successive viceroys acted as though the reverse were true.

'India may lay aside her terrors for the present,' Salisbury wrote to a sceptical Lytton in July 1877, assuming that Russia would be too poor after the Russo-Turkish War to engage in any Afghan or Persian adventures. The Viceroy was categorically told that 'you will not stir a soldier beyond the frontier (treating Khelat as within it) without obtaining our view on the matter first'. Over the previous twenty-eight years Britain had undertaken no fewer than twenty-eight local expeditions against the Afghan and Pathan tribes on the North-West Frontier, to pre-empt plundering raids into the Punjab, so this was a more constricting ordinance than it sounds. Salisbury believed Lytton was out of touch with pacific British opinion and warned him that 'the dominant feeling around you in Simla has no relation or similarity whatever to the English feeling'.[7]

A new tone of asperity had entered their correspondence. When Lytton criticised the timidity of his policies in mid-August, Salisbury consoled himself with the thought that as *The Times* and Lord Hartington were attacking him from the opposite viewpoint, 'I can only be half as black as I am painted.' Although he reported that his Council in London almost unanimously opposed Lytton's hawkish policy, he did admit that 'they are really compounded half of sentiment, half of suspicion. These men have the feelings towards the Punjab of an Old Etonian or Old Harrovian towards their schools. It is not patriotism – it is a far fonder and less rational feeling.'

Salisbury, unencumbered by any such fond feelings for his old school, let alone the Punjab, also took a more rational view of Lytton's actions dragging Britain into a war about a Central Asian sideshow, just as the Near Eastern crisis was reaching danger point. He condoned British spies being sent to investigate and inquire about conditions near Merv and Kizil Arvat, but expressly forbade any instigation of the local tribes against Russia and entirely repudiated all armed action. In early September he was forced to reiterate to Lytton that 'your whole proceedings on the North-West Frontier crave wary walking'. The issue of whether Britain should take Quetta on the Baluchistan–Afghan border was splitting expert opinion in London: 'The whole Indian world here is divided into Quettites and Anti-Quettites who hate each other with all the fever of Big Endians and Little Endians – and at present the Quettites are much in the minority.'

When famine hit Madras in September 1877, Salisbury's advice to

Lytton was the same as to Northbrook in 1874, encouraging him 'not to shrink from the extraordinary expenditure that is necessary'. A total of £11 million was spent, and the suffering was averted as successfully as nineteenth-century communications would permit. Past mistakes were not repeated, but the shadow of the tragedy was still with Salisbury, who reminded Lytton how: 'In 1866 we simply let a million people starve.'[8]

For all his excellent management of the famine, Lytton's very sanity was soon being called into question after he circulated a long memorandum in early October 1877 in which he denounced the Government for allegedly attempting to create an Anglo-Franco-Russian coalition against Germany, about as absurd a contention as it was possible to make at the time, even from the distance of Simla. In Cabinet, Salisbury explained the Viceroy's ravings by admitting that he was 'a little mad'. It was known that both Lytton and his father had used opium, and when Derby read the 'inconceivable' memorandum, he concluded that Lytton was dangerous and should resign: 'When a man inherits insanity from one parent, and limitless conceit from the other, he has a ready made excuse for almost any extravagance which he may commit.' Salisbury contented himself with rapping the Viceroy's knuckles – 'whatever you do, keep clear of the printing press' – and advised him to keep 'the swashbuckling school' of his military experts under tighter control.[9] It was Salisbury's misfortune that whereas Northbrook's military advisers had been over-cautious, Lytton's were not cautious enough.

On giving up the Indian portfolio in April 1878, Salisbury wrote to Lytton that their 'two offices are so placed towards each other, that they tend naturally to friction'. At least *sotto voce*, there had been plenty between the two men in recent months. To his successor Lord Cranbrook, Salisbury warned that Lytton's 'mind tends violently to exaggeration'. After the Berlin Treaty, all eyes shifted eastwards for the next focus of Anglo-Russian tension. Only a fortnight afterwards, the news arrived in Calcutta that the Amir had welcomed a Russian mission to Kabul under General Stolietev, whilst continuing to refuse to accept a British one. Cranbrook, a brilliant administrator and very hard-working politician, had not Salisbury's mettle in holding back Lytton's impulsiveness. Imperial *amour propre* and prestige had been insulted by the Amir's action, and this time Lytton was not about to be cheated out of a war.

On 8th September 1878, Lytton issued a communiqué announcing that the commander of the Madras army, General Sir Neville Chamberlain, would be leaving Peshawar for Kabul on 17th September, taking 1,000 men through the Khyber Pass. A month earlier the Government in London had remonstrated about the Stolietev mission, and the India Office had not yet officially heard back from St Petersburg. Staying with Beaconsfield at Hughenden on 9th September, Salisbury agreed that no precipitate action should be taken. He backed this up with a letter to Beaconsfield on the 13th, pointing out that Russia could easily finance 'some allied barbarians' to attack Afghanistan, which would be 'likely to force us into some costly inglorious tribal war'.

'Pray let me know your feelings without scruple about mine,' he wrote to Cranbrook on 14th September about postponing the Chamberlain mission; 'in such grave affairs frankness ought never to do harm.' He could see how Lytton's rashness might easily unravel overnight the delicate European settlement he had spent months building and cementing at Berlin. The previous day, Cranbrook had specifically ordered Lytton to do nothing and 'await orders'. Furthermore, the mission had to be sent to the second city in Aghanistan, Kandahar, and not via the legendarily treacherous Khyber Pass.

On 15th September, to Lytton's fury, the London Government ordered him to halt Chamberlain's mission, only two days before it was due to set off. Yet entirely in contravention of these direct Cabinet instructions, Lytton sent Chamberlain's heavily armed 'diplomatic mission' against the Khyber Pass on Friday, 20th September, where it was humiliatingly repulsed by a large Afghan force. Salisbury, who only ever considered Afghanistan as a buffer state, appreciated that the Raj had now suffered a dangerous loss of prestige, and all because Lytton had acted without authorisation from London. His letter to Beaconsfield from Puys of 24th September was unequivocal:

> Lytton has disobeyed his orders twice: and the results have not been happy. He was told to send his mission by Kandahar, and he has sent it instead by the Khyber, where he has been stopped. He was told to wait 'till we had received the Russian communication, and given him orders to go on. He has now got a snub which I fear will make active measures inevitable.

Salisbury hoped that Lytton might now occupy Kandahar unmolested and not get into the sort of difficulties the Austrians were experiencing in their contested occupation of Bosnia. His pessimistic prediction to Northcote, who had to find the money to pay for the expedition, was that since Lytton had so flagrantly disobeyed orders, he would now conduct operations 'so as to achieve the most brilliant results – lose the greatest number of men – and spend the largest amount of money'. In his continual letters to Beaconsfield, Northcote and Cranbrook, Salisbury emerged as the dove of the crisis, willing to countenance Kandahar being taken as a 'material guarantee' but loath to expand the operations into a general war against the Amir.[10] British policy had never been to stir up sedition against a lawful ruler who was neither misgoverning nor even actively threatening British interests, he argued. It was a new departure that Salisbury deprecated, believing that the right place to act against the Stolietev mission was at St Petersburg, not Kabul, and still less the Khyber.

Beaconsfield was also sound on the Afghan issue, declaring on 3rd October that no real *casus belli* existed. Salisbury complained that Cranbrook, for all his other qualities, failed to understand 'the gaudy and theatrical ambition which is the Viceroy's leading passion'. He warned Beaconsfield that Lytton's policy might be the thin end of the wedge, and ended his letter with a prescient warning that 'without vigilant supervision he will land us certainly in vast expense – possibly in a vast disaster'. By 22nd October, Salisbury was still saying that 'my counsel is to minimize both the action and the splash', advocating only the occupation of the Kurram Valley. In a Cabinet meeting held on 25th October, Salisbury inveighed against Lytton's gross insubordination and the way it was upsetting the Government's foreign policy as far afield as Turkey and Egypt. But Cranbrook defended Lytton and supported an invasion of Afghanistan.

After much debate over the following five days, and a resignation threat from Cranbrook, it turned out that most of the Cabinet were as bellicose as he and Lytton; they also believed that a Second Afghan War would be popular with the electorate. Salisbury once again chose not to push his opposing view to the point of resignation. An ultimatum was despatched to Kabul stating that if by 20th November the Amir had not agreed to a permanent mission, and moreover had not apologised for having initially repulsed the Chamberlain mission, Britain would regard him as an enemy. No reply was received, so at dawn on 21st November 1878 three British columns invaded Afghanistan and the prospective British agent, Major Louis Cavagnari, the naturalised son of a Napoleonic general, began negotiating agreements with the Khyber tribes for their Pass to be sold to the Government of India.

Parliament was recalled on 5th December to debate the campaign. Gladstone denounced it as 'this evil war' and Northbrook said it 'was unnecessary and ought with the exercise of a little common prudence to have been avoided'. Despite privately agreeing with him, Beaconsfield of course defended Lytton as, with more reluctance, did Salisbury. On 20th December, Salisbury heard from Schouvaloff that the Russian Foreign Minister, Nikolai Giers, had sent the order to Kabul to withdraw Stolietev, who left two days later.[11] One of the three columns, under the command of General Sir Frederick Roberts, occupied the Kurram Valley and then routed a vastly larger Afghan army, forcing Sher Ali to flee to Turkestan. When Kabul fell to Roberts in early

January 1879, the Amir's friendly correspondence with the Russians fell into British hands. Salisbury managed to restrain Cranbrook and others from publishing it, because although it would have embarrassed the Opposition, which had tended to play down the Afghan–Russian connection, it might also have tempted the Tsar to intervene in Afghanistan more openly.

Sher Ali died on 21st February and was succeeded as Amir by his eldest son Yakub Khan, who had been in rebellion against his father since 1870. On 8th May, Yakub was received by Cavagnari at Gandamak to negotiate a peace treaty, which was signed on the 26th. This provided for the Khyber Pass to be ceded to India for a subsidy, and Cavagnari to be welcomed to Kabul under the protection of the new Amir. Salisbury wrote warmly to congratulate Lytton on what he had to admit had been a faultlessly executed campaign, but only received a cool reply for, as Lytton complained to his daughter, 'he had received no help from Salisbury'.

Salisbury's pessimism was vindicated on 3rd September 1879, when Cavagnari and the rest of the British Legation in Kabul were massacred by Afghan fanatics. When the news reached Britain six days later, Beaconsfield telegraphed the Viceroy giving permission for Roberts to occupy both Kabul and Kandahar, which was achieved soon afterwards. Salisbury thought it not enough. To protect the British Residents in other 'half-barbarous countries', he thought that 'almost any severity' would be justified, such as the wholesale razing of Kabul or the execution of every senior officer in the Afghan army. He admitted that there might be some difficulty 'in reconciling public sentiment at home to such measures', but his first concern was for British prestige abroad. The Liberal MP Mountstuart Grant Duff launched an attack on Salisbury for the Kabul massacre, telling his Elgin constituency that: 'The blood that had been shed has been really shed by him as if he had slain with his own hand the unhappy men who had been massacred. His obstinate, wicked folly had been their death-warrant.'

Salisbury shrugged off the hyperbole, preferring privately to place blame where it was properly due. Writing to Beaconsfield on 10th October, he said: 'Lytton has the insight, but also the impatience, of a poet. What he wants to do in one year, will take twenty.... There is no hurry. We can reach [the passes of the Hindu Kush] when we please – the moment we hear Russia is advancing.' Meanwhile, he wanted to concentrate on protecting the communications, taming the tribes and building the railways on those parts of the Afghan frontier already conquered. Far from being the monkey to Beaconsfield's organ-grinder, as *Punch* had unfairly portrayed him in August 1878, Salisbury was sceptical about both 'Beaconsfieldism' and the 'Forward' policy, seeking to use his influence to concentrate it in areas where it might do genuine good, such as Egypt, rather than where it would spend itself to no very useful purpose, such as in Afghanistan or Zululand.

Writing to Lord Dufferin, the Ambassador in St Petersburg, on 4th February 1880, Salisbury produced an article of oriental strategy that might also have doubled up as an exposition of his Toryism: 'It is a fallacy to assume that within our lifetime any stable arrangement can be arrived at in the East. The utmost we can do is to provide halting-places where the process of change may rest awhile.' His duty, he concluded, was to 'assume the probability of change, and so shape our precautions that it shall affect no vital interest of ours'.

Nothing like stability was achievable in Afghanistan, at least in the short term. Having captured Kabul on 11th December 1879, Roberts was besieged there for a fortnight. When he broke the siege the insurgency seemed to be over, and the British recognised Abdur Rahman as the new Amir, setting him up against Yakub Khan. But in the summer a new revolt ended in the massacre of almost a whole British brigade at the Battle of Maiwand on 27th July 1880. Kandahar seemed to be in danger, so Roberts led a column from Kabul which relieved the city on 31st August, defeating a larger Afghan force the following day. He then pacified the country, avenged Maiwand, was awarded a baronetcy and became a national hero. The Gladstone Government evacuated Afghanistan the following year, leaving it in the fairly capable hands of Abdur Rahman. It continued to be a bone of contention between the Liberals, who accused Salisbury of presiding over an immoral and aggressive policy, and the Conservatives, who derided Gladstone for throwing away such a hard-won prize.

FOURTEEN

'Beaconsfieldism'

The Zulu War – Egypt
– Turkish Obstructionism
– Germany Offers an Alliance
– The General Election

July 1878 to April 1880

'The English voter, like the English footman, likes "a change".'

Salisbury had long found Sir Bartle Frere, the Indian Mutiny hero and former Governor of Bombay, 'quarrelsome and <u>mutinous</u>'. Back in 1866, he had noticed how 'Impatience of control is a common defect in men of his able and fearless character and his impetuosity of disposition.' It was the Government's ill fortune, just as it was faced with a 'prodigal son' in India, also to be landed with another in the shape of Frere directing policy towards the Zulus. As soon as he arrived at the Cape as Governor-General in 1877, Frere had begun preparing for a war with the strongest native military power on the African continent, a proud warrior nation which as yet posed no threat to the British settlers, but rather was a useful counterpoise to the Boers.

As early as 18th October 1878, Salisbury was holding meetings at the Foreign Office of ministers whom he felt might oppose this extension of the 'Forward' policy into areas of Africa the British were not yet ready to subdue. As Secretary for the Colonies, Carnarvon had appointed Frere to the Cape without even consulting Salisbury, despite Salisbury's former connections with Frere on the India Council. After his resignation in February 1878, Carnarvon was succeeded as Colonial Secretary by Sir Michael Hicks Beach, 9th baronet and MP for East Gloucestershire since 1864. Tall, dark, tough and obstinate, 'Black Michael' had an infamous temper. 'Hicks Beach is the only man I know who habitually thinks angrily,' wrote a colleague. A sympathiser with Salisbury over Reform in 1867, Hicks Beach possessed 'a tongue that was a terror to pretentious busybodies'. His qualities went down well in the House of Commons, where he was never popular but where his clear, persuasive manner was appreciated. For all his tough talking, however, Hicks Beach was no match for Frere's precipitate proconsulship, and on 11th December 1878 an ultimatum was sent, once again without Cabinet sanction, to the Zulu king Cetewayo, including the ludicrous demand that he disband his army.

Salisbury later told Balfour that 'Bartle Frere should have been recalled as soon as the news of his ultimatum reached England. We should then have escaped in appearance, as well as in reality, the responsibility of the Zulu War. So thought the majority of the Cabinet, so thought Dizzy himself.' But, just as Cranbrook had supported his Viceroy over Afghanistan, so too did Hicks Beach defend Frere, and three columns of troops marched into Zululand on 12th January 1879. Against Salisbury's inclinations, Britain was again plunged into an unnecessary and dangerous war.[1]

When in the early hours of 11th February the news reached Britain that an entire column of the British invasion force had been wiped out at the Battle of Isandhlwana on 22nd January, with the loss of 1,329 men, the British Empire recognised it had suffered its most costly military defeat at the hands of a native army. The Cabinet received the request of the Commander-in-Chief, Lord Chelmsford, for three more regiments and instead authorised five to be despatched forthwith. The financial and foreign policy implications were discussed: Salisbury brought up the possibility of recalling Frere, but was overruled in favour of a Court of Inquiry. Beaconsfield's speech in the House of Lords on 13th February dwelt on the astounding bravery shown by a small detachment of the 24th Regiment of Foot near Isandhlwana at Rorke's Drift, and the award of their eleven Victoria Crosses was suitably staggered at intervals over seven months between May and November to maximise public appreciation. Nonetheless, the war proved a godsend for an Opposition keen to attack 'Beaconsfieldism' for its rashness, incompetence and immorality.

When on 27th May the Conservative MP for Midhurst, Sir Henry Holland, decided to vote for a Liberal motion of censure on Frere, the Whips sent him to Salisbury to be discouraged. 'Are you concerned that it is your duty to state your views in the House, and to support the motion?' Salisbury asked him. 'I am,' answered Holland. 'Then, I advise you to do your duty, and may I add, for your personal information, that I concur largely with your view of the action of Sir Bartle Frere.' What the Whips Office made of this candour is unrecorded, but Lady Salisbury's comment was: 'So like Robert.' Salisbury thought that defending Frere, as he told Beaconsfield on 11th March, was a waste of political capital, and wanted him swiftly replaced with Lord Napier, the former Commander-in-Chief in India. But he found on visiting Windsor in mid-

March that the Prince of Wales, who had been accompanied by Frere on his 1875 Indian tour, was very much a supporter of the errant Governor-General, as was the Queen.[2]

In the five Cabinet meetings held on the subject between 22nd and 28th May, Salisbury was unable to get the policy changed, so Frere, by then the hero of the Jingoes, stayed in office. 'Oh! that Bartle Frere,' Salisbury wrote to Northcote in mid-June after a notorious murderer had been hanged, 'I should like to construct for him a gibbet twice the height of Haman's.' Nor could Salisbury quite understand why the Queen wanted Prince Louis Napoleon Bonaparte, Napoleon III's son, to go out to Zululand to serve with the Crown forces there. 'I am as puzzled as you are,' he wrote to Beaconsfield. 'Every way it seems to me a mistake.' The Prince Imperial, whom Beaconsfield privately called 'that little abortion', was nevertheless allowed to go off to the war, where he was promptly surprised by a Zulu detachment on 1st June and killed. They stripped his corpse and all that was found near it the next day was his dead terrier and a single blue sock embroidered with the letter 'N'. His body was brought back and buried alongside his father in Kent. The Napoleonic epic that had begun a century earlier in Corsica thus came to an end in Chislehurst.

Salisbury had feared that the removal of the Zulu threat would merely encourage Britain's true enemies in the region, the Boers. Sure enough, once the Zulu army was smashed at the Battle of Ulundi on 4th July 1879, it only took six months before a Boer republic was proclaimed in the Transvaal. This was the real threat, a source of frustration and danger that was to last over twenty years and which was eventually to take much of the sheen off the reputation of the British Empire. Salisbury had lost all patience with the Empire's 'prodigal sons'. When in November a British local governor ran up the Union Flag in a territory in Dahomey claimed by France, Salisbury wrote to Lyons: 'Really, these proconsuls are insupportable,' and he successfully implored the Colonial Office to have the man recalled. In September 1885, he himself recalled the over-zealous General Sir Charles Warren from the command of an expedition to the Bechuanaland protectorate, where he had managed to anger both the Cape and Pretorian Governments. 'His continuance in power was a real danger,' Salisbury explained. 'He belonged to the Gordon–Frere type of official: who thinks it is his mission to save a short-sighted Government at home in spite of itself.'

~

Derby characterised 'Beaconsfieldism' as 'occupy, fortify, grab and brag', and although Salisbury's policy in Egypt was guilty of none of these, he was attacked for an overbearing policy towards the Cairo authorities.

Because the Khedive of Egypt was *de jure* a vassal of the Sultan, Egyptian issues were run from the Foreign Office. The *de facto* reality was that Egypt was run by International Boards which were largely controlled by Britain and France, between whom there was a festering rivalry. Because Egyptian bonds were a favoured investment vehicle throughout Europe, vast financial interests were involved. Gladstone himself had 37 per cent of his total personal equity portfolio invested in them.

One of Salisbury's first decisions on becoming Foreign Secretary had been to instruct Hussey Vivian, the British Consul-General in Cairo since 1876, to ensure that the payment of the half-yearly interest on Egypt's public debt was honoured, despite complaints from the Khedive, Ismail Pasha, that Egypt could not afford it. 'It is clear that, unless the Khedive's administration is put under some restraint,' he wrote to Vivian proposing a new inspector-general of taxes in early May 1878, 'he will go on oppressing his subjects more and more – but will also defraud his creditors more and more.' Egypt's two finance ministers were the Anglophile Egyptian Nubar Pasha and Sir Charles Rivers Wilson, who had been appointed to ensure that the bonds paid their interest in full, despite 85 per cent of the country's total revenue leaving the country to service the debt. Salisbury believed that 'the only motive that will reconcile France to our supremacy would be the belief that, without our intervention, the interest would not be paid, and that with it, it would be'.

In January 1879, the Khedive led a nationalist revolt, and with the help of 2,000 disaffected Egyptian soldiers he ejected Nubar Pasha, whilst leaving Rivers Wilson undisturbed. When Rivers Wilson and Vivian clashed over policy it was the latter who was recalled, but Salisbury told his successor, Frank Lascelles, formerly the Secretary of the Legation at Rome, to let Rivers Wilson know that 'he has practically no physical force behind him, and he is acting as if he were the master of many legions'. With the British legions hard pressed in Afghanistan and Zululand at the time, Egypt could not be occupied, but neither could the French be allowed to step in.

On 7th April, the Khedive sacked both Rivers Wilson and his French counterpart, M. de Blignières. Although Salisbury initially thought the best response might be to threaten Egypt with bankruptcy, the financial interests at stake were enormous, not least in the Suez Canal Company, 44 per cent of which was owned by the British Government. Despite wishing to steer clear of any further direct foreign entanglements, Salisbury was conscious that the Khedive could not be allowed to insult Britain, and, as he told Northcote, 'we must be abreast of France' at all costs. His answer was to ask the Sultan to depose Ismail Pasha and install the Khedive's son Tewfik Pasha in his place. The *coup d'état* was efficiently carried out in late June 1879, with Britain playing as shadowy a role as possible in order not to inflame nationalist or Muslim sensibilities. 'The Musselman feeling is still so strong', Salisbury told Lyons the day before Ismail received his *firman* of deposition from Constantinople, 'that I believe we shall be safer and more powerful as wire-pullers than as ostensible rulers.'

Three weeks later, after the transition had been smoothly effected and Ismail was packed off into exile, never to return, Salisbury explained further this preference for 'informal' empire. 'The only form of control we have is that which is called moral influence, which in practice is a combination of nonsense, objuration and worry,' he told Lyons; 'we must devote ourselves to the perfecting of this weapon.' The country was henceforth to be run under Anglo-French dual authority, Salisbury told Evelyn Baring, who was sent out as a Commissioner for the Debt, whilst leaving to the new Khedive only 'the externals of authority'.

Of the three courses open to Britain in her behaviour towards France in Egypt – renouncing, monopolising or sharing power – Salisbury had no doubt which was best. 'Renouncing would have been to place the French across our road to India,' he told Northcote. 'Monopolising would have been very near the risk of war. So we resolved to share.' He was not worried that this policy might lead to future clashes, having told George Goschen, who represented the British bondholders, that he 'had faith in the English influence in Egypt drawing ahead; a result which in my belief depended, not on any formal acts, but on the natural superiority which a good Englishman in such a position was pretty sure to show'.

Salisbury believed implicitly in national stereotypes; when Italy attempted to insinuate herself into the Egyptian situation, he wrote to Sir Augustus Paget, the Ambassador in Rome, that the Italians 'have very much the huffiness which you see occasionally in the governess of a family. They are always thinking themselves slighted.' The other alternative to dual authority, an international commission to rule Egypt, struck Salisbury as the worst of all outcomes. 'The resources of obstruction are endless,' he told Baring in September. 'It is like the *liberum veto* of the Polish Diet without the resource of cutting off the dissentient's head.'³ So for the next three years an uneasy Anglo-French combination exercised *de facto* power through the new Khedive.

Salisbury was under no illusions, when he returned from Berlin, about how difficult the implementation of the Turkish reform programme would be. It had to be forced upon a reluctant Sultan by a vigilant and insistent Layard. The settlement of the Greek frontier would be another difficulty, and keeping the Russians up to their Berlin promises to evacuate their armies from Turkey-in-Europe yet another. The delicate manoeuvre of a staged British withdrawal of the fleet from the Black Sea, coinciding with the Russian evacuation of Turkish territory, was undertaken between August 1878 and, after several stallings and threats of reversal, 3rd August 1879, when the last Russian soldier left. The occupation, taxation and administrative reform of Cyprus also had to be regulated, as did reforms on Crete. From July 1878 until the general election in March 1880, these and other Berlin-related problems took up what time Salisbury had left over from Afghanistan, Zululand and Egypt.

Salisbury's original post-Berlin intention was to launch a 'pacific invasion of Englishmen' into Turkey, as 'good government means government by good men'. By inserting British officers into key positions in the police, judiciary and finance ministries, he hoped to run the Turkish provincial administration in much the same way as Egypt was soon to be run, disinterestedly and efficiently by Europeans who nevertheless did not carry ultimate political responsibility. But the pasha class turned out to be too strong for him and for Layard, and the good intentions of August 1878 for a type of informal empire in Turkey were gradually disappointed. Salisbury also feared that Layard's long sojourn in the Orient had made him 'go native', tending to sympathise more with the Porte than a British ambassador ought to do. 'It is curious how entirely eastern minds subjugate a western mind when they establish any hold over it,' he was later to write, citing a case of a Resident with an Indian prince who had 'become the mere creature and instrument of the prince he is sent to control'.

Salisbury's hopes for a Scanderoon–Baghdad railway, with an £8 million loan to Turkey repayable at 3 per cent interest over thirty years as the bait, were, along with a trans-Asian telegraph, two of the grand projects which ran into the sand once the Treasury refused to help underwrite them. Over the failure to secure the loan, Salisbury consoled himself that the Sultan would doubtless have only spent it on 'ironclads and palaces'. In April 1880, the Foreign Office drew up a memorandum surveying the state of the Berlin reforms on the ground in Asiatic Turkey. Only three Europeans had been appointed as financial inspectors in the seven *vilayets*, of whom only one, a Frenchman, held a senior post. Incompetence and corruption were rife in the judiciary and British officers had been obstructed from taking up posts in the police force. Only Salisbury's plans to turn Cyprus into a showpiece for British good government in Asia Minor had come to fruition.[4]

Salisbury sought to follow as pro-Austrian a line as the Cabinet and Beaconsfield would allow. He discouraged the Sultan from covertly assisting resistance to the Austrian occupation of Bosnia and Herzegovina, in appreciation of Andrassy's refusal to join another *Dreikaiserbund* (Three Emperors' League) with Germany and Russia. When the British Consul-General in Sofia was discovered to be supporting the Liberal pan-Slavist party there, Salisbury promptly reassigned him to Bangkok. There were occasional war scares, and the 50,000 Russian troops had to be coaxed out of the Balkans frustratingly slowly, but Salisbury's patience and constant pressure paid off. When, in November, Romania seemed to be about to accord Russia the right to march through her country, Salisbury ordered William White at the Budapest Legation to threaten 'a new disposition of Roumanian territory' if it went ahead. It did not.

White was an exceptional diplomat with an unconventional career, much of it assisted by Salisbury. Born in 1824 and educated on the Isle of Man, he could not take up his Trinity College, Cambridge, degree because he was a Roman Catholic. After years in the consular service he made the rare switch to the diplomatic, and became Agent in Belgrade. At Constantinople during the Conference, Salisbury conceived a high regard for this tall, stout, sturdy, highly intelligent man whom the Turks nicknamed 'The Bosphorus Bull'. Salisbury was to appoint him to a series of important Eastern posts, and he was to become the first Catholic to be appointed a full Ambassador since the Glorious Revolution.

Only once did Salisbury display his indignation at Russian intransigence during the painstaking evacuation process. In early April 1879, after the British fleet had been withdrawn from Constantinople, the Tsar announced that he was 'generously pleased' to allow the Turks to occupy Bourgas. Salisbury expostulated to Lord Dufferin, the new Ambassador to St Petersburg:

> As this is an unofficial communication, I may be excused for saying Confound his impudence! The Turks have a treaty right to go to Bourgas: and as it is by the seaside we have the material power of seeing that they enjoy it. I am afraid that another sight of that fleet which he detests may be necessary to induce His Imperial Majesty to admit that he has anything in common with the Treaty-holding mass of mankind.

Salisbury had a practical view of the diplomatic use of the Royal Navy: 'A ship lying at anchor long in one port is of little value for political purposes. A big fleet going from place to place – if it was only seen in each place every two years – would have twice the effect.'[5]

The combination of reassurances, promises and threats by which Dufferin persuaded the Russians to fulfil their Berlin commitments was masterly, and directed by Salisbury from London at every step. 'Partly from inherent slipperiness, partly from the disjointed character of their administration,' he advised his schoolfriend, 'you always have to deal with the Cabinet of St. Petersburg as you might have dealt with the firm of Quirk, Gammon and Snap.' By use of 'the fear of any unnecessary reappearance of the hated fez', Salisbury hoped the Russians could be kept up to the mark. Mistrust was ever present, however, as is shown by Salisbury's advice to Smith about not mentioning the Russians in a forthcoming speech: 'If you blame them the Tsar is angry: if you praise them Count Andrassy becomes suspicious.'

When Prince Alexander of Battenberg was elected Prince Alexander I of Bulgaria on 29th April 1879, Salisbury was reasonably content, because he had made private promises to get rid of his Russian advisers and officials as soon as possible. To the Queen, who adored 'Sandro', Salisbury was complimentary, saying that he hoped the Prince might bring peace to that 'unhappy peninsula'. To Beaconsfield he wrote that Alexander was 'a typical Lifeguardsman – much perplexed at being a reigning Prince. All his sentiments quite unexceptional.' The British Commissioner for the reorganisation of Eastern Roumelia was the maverick Conservative MP Sir Henry Drummond Wolff, whom Salisbury contrived to keep out of Britain for much of his career. In reply to a doubtful Beaconsfield in September 1879, Salisbury employed a rare equestrian analogy and agreed that, 'Your [unflattering] estimate of him is I think correct: unfortunately in our profession the good horses have bad mouths.' Reining Drummond Wolff back was to be a recurrent problem for Salisbury, but it was felt that he could do less damage in the Balkans than in Parliament.

On 4th August 1879, the day after the last Russian troops vacated the Sultan's domains, Salisbury delivered a speech in the park at Hatfield to over a thousand members of the London and Westminster Working Men's Constitutional Association, an organisation founded to ensure that the Conservative metropolitan working classes registered for the vote. Salisbury attacked Liberal 'obstructiveness' of his foreign policy and rhetorically asked:

> Supposing one hundred and fifty years ago a school had arisen…who had persuaded the English Government that such things as the conquest of India, or of Canada, or Gibraltar, or Malta, or the Cape of Good Hope – that these things were unimportant, and that the one thing was to look at home at our own parochial politics. Suppose this had been said one hundred and fifty years ago, do you imagine you would now be the great, the numerous, the prosperous nation that you are?

No such occasion would be complete without an attack on Gladstone, the mere mention of whose name never failed to elicit hisses and boos from the audience. 'The treadmill and the crank are a mere trifle compared with what Her Majesty's ministers in the House of

Commons have to undergo,' said Salisbury at Hatfield, complaining of the *de facto* alliance between the Liberals and the Irish Nationalists who were practising parliamentary obstructionism. 'The name of Mr Gladstone it is not necessary to mention. Of all possible statesmen who have ever occupied a great position, probably he is the only man who would ever have seen in the tactics of the Obstructives something which could fortify his own position.' After reading the speech, Granville laconically remarked to Gladstone: 'How strong the old Saturday Reviewer is in him.' Though long on polemics, it had been noticeably short on legislative substance, and together the Liberals surmised, correctly, that the Government would not announce any new policy initiatives before the General Election.[6]

One major initiative which Beaconsfield would have liked to have attempted, but which Salisbury prevented, was to accept Bismarck's proposal for an outright Anglo-Austro-German alliance. In early September 1879, Andrassy suddenly and inexplicably fell from power, to be replaced by Count Eduard Taaffe, an Irish 11th viscount, whom Beaconsfield thought 'a red-taper' but nonetheless a man of integrity. That month also saw war scares and rumours on supposedly good authority that Russia and France were planning to attack the Central Powers. It was in part to scotch these that William Waddington, who in February had become Prime Minister of France, visited Salisbury at Puys. Salisbury liked Waddington and appreciated the advantages of having 'a French minister who works on principles intelligible to the English mind'. Although Francis Bertie had thought that 'he looks the cheesemonger all over', Waddington could not have been so unimpressive, for in January 1880 he wounded a journalist in a duel on the Franco-Belgian frontier.

At the Puys meeting on 19th September, the entire gamut of Anglo-French relations was discussed. These included Newfoundland fisheries, Egyptian bonds, Romanian religious intolerance, Tahitian territorial claims, Eastern Roumelian reforms, Turkish finance, Greek frontiers, Serbian railways and West Africa (where Salisbury had refused to fall out with Waddington in April over Matacong, which he told Lyons was just 'a desert island at the mouth of a pestilential river'). Waddington was 'earnest and indignant' in his denials of any plot to attack Germany and Austria, a war which he described as 'causeless and unjustifiable'.[7]

So when, exactly a week later, Count Münster stayed at Hughenden and presented Bismarck's scheme for a full alliance with the Central Powers, it was not out of any hankering for splendid isolation that

Salisbury looked so sceptically at the proposal, but simply because he did not believe in the threat that it was supposedly intended to offset. Nor did he believe that Germany, which had a vast indefensible frontier with Russia, would really help Britain in the event of war. Once Beaconsfield had repeated the proposal to Salisbury and Queen Victoria, including Bismarck's argument that the Russian obsession with pan-Slavism meant that war would one day be inevitable, Salisbury could properly dissect and expose what he described to Beaconsfield as this 'startling' offer.

Salisbury's critique of the German alliance proposal was based on the fact that they could not tell whether Russia 'is really seeking a quarrel: or whether Bismarck is forcing the offensive on her – as he did in Denmark, Austria and France'. It seemed to Salisbury that Germany, not Russia, was the more likely aggressor against European peace, for 'if Bismarck wishes to rectify his eastern frontier – over which he often laments – the present time has many favourable circumstances. Russia is weakened. France is still disinclined for action, Austria and England are in a temper which makes them lean to him, and makes it impossible they should work with Russia.' Salisbury saw no reason for British blood and treasure to be wasted in an unnecessary war against Russia, let alone against France – or both – especially as it would be a war designed by Bismarck to thrust the borders of Germany hundreds of miles to the east. 'On what nation', Salisbury wondered to Dufferin, 'will his experienced medical eye next discern a necessity for depletion?'

The furthest Salisbury wished to go was to influence France and Italy to observe neutrality in the event of a war between Russia and the Central Powers, in which Britain would be sympathetic to the latter but neutral. Beaconsfield, however, looking for an election 'cry', thought that a German alliance would 'probably be hailed with something like enthusiasm by the country'. By 13th October 1879, Münster seems to have thought better of the whole proposal, and in a conversation with Salisbury, 'he never advanced beyond vague generalisation and expressions of "tendency"'. Salisbury's analysis to Beaconsfield was that, having signed a five-year dual alliance with Austria on 7th October, Bismarck 'may need us no longer. If so, we are well out of it, and he would have thrown us aside in any case.' It was the first of five separate occasions on which Salisbury blocked an Anglo-German alliance, with distrust of Bismarck, and later Kaiser Wilhelm II, also playing a significant part in the decisions of 1889, 1895, 1898 and 1901.

The furthest Salisbury was willing to go, in a meeting with Münster at Hatfield on 15th October, was to assure him that a French attack on Germany through neutral Belgium would not be tolerated, and that Britain would offer 'our goodwill and assistance' if Germany were attacked by Russia, without specifying what that assistance would consist of, beyond encouraging other countries also to observe neutrality. Having really done nothing much more than restate the existing commitment since Britain's 1839 guarantee of Belgium in the Treaty of London, Salisbury watched the German offer disappear as suddenly as it had arrived.

On 18th and 19th October, Salisbury spoke to a dinner of 700 at the Manchester Chamber of Commerce in the Free Trade Hall, and to a massive rally in the Pomona Gardens in Manchester. It was fine, knockabout stuff. 'Sir William Harcourt tells us that we should have relied on a friendly Afghanistan,' he said to gales of laughter (which recurred twenty-four times in his short speech). 'We should have relied for our deepest interest of our Indian Empire on the proposed friendship of the most perfidious nation that has existed on the earth.' His bias against isolation, and sarcasm about 'masterly inactivity', were very marked, but the significant moment came when he said to loud cheers that the press had reported that a defensive alliance had been signed between Austria and Germany: 'I will only say to all who value the peace of Europe and the independence of nations – I may say it without profanity – it is "good tidings of great joy".'[8]

In the light of later events, it might seem injudicious that a British Foreign Secretary should have so ecstatically and publicly welcomed the coalition that caused so much carnage thirty-five years later. But until Germany began building her High Seas fleet, British interests were impinged upon far less by her than by France and Russia, whilst Austria's interests and Britain's coincided in the Balkans and clashed nowhere else. To an almost exaggerated extent Salisbury never allowed personal considerations to affect his *Realpolitik*. He owned houses in France, spoke and read French fluently, and generally preferred the company of French politicians and diplomats to that of any other foreigners, yet he realised that French envy of the British Empire, the large areas where the tectonic plates of the two empires rubbed against one another, and the Anglophobia of the French press, made a truly cordial *entente* unlikely in his lifetime.

When the Austrian Ambassador, Count Károlyi, called at the Foreign Office on 27th October 1879 and twice read out the secret terms of the Austro-German defensive alliance, Salisbury expressed his 'great gratification' at the news. 'As neither Count Károlyi nor Count Münster asked for anything but our approval of the policy the two Empires were pursuing,' Salisbury told the Queen, 'England is in no way engaged or committed.' In 1879, and for many years afterwards, it seemed to be a guarantee of peace that Russia's aggression in the Balkans would inexorably draw Germany and Austria down upon her. What no one could possibly have predicted in 1879 was that it would instead be Austrian sabre-rattling in the Balkans, aided and abetted by Germany, which would ultimately trigger Armageddon.

November 1879 saw Gladstone emerging from semi-retirement for the second time to reclaim the leadership of the Liberal Party, delivering a series of speeches in Scotland known as the Midlothian campaign. His 3,620 electors were treated to six long orations and more than twenty shorter ones, which denounced 'Beaconsfieldism' in all its manifestations. 'Remember', he told a Dalkeith audience, 'that the sanctity of life in the hill villages of Afghanistan among the winter snows is as inviolable in the eyes of Almighty God as can be your own.' Although his son Herbert later said that Salisbury's foreign policy had 'written the theme of the Midlothian orations', Gladstone concentrated his most telling attacks on the Prime Minister.

The emotions aroused by the Eastern Question had meant that Gladstone had not visited Hatfield, and invitations to Balfour to stay at Hawarden were similarly suspended. Feelings even ran high enough for the Whig Duke of Argyll to worry whether his daughter Frances should marry Salisbury's nephew Eustace Balfour (which she nonetheless did in May 1879).[9] In his answer to the Midlothian rhetoric about Afghanistan and Zululand, Salisbury said that Gladstone's:

> pulpit style of eloquence, admirable and beautiful as it is as a testimony of the moral feelings of the speaker...is in danger of leading the country very far astray if it induces you to think that the considerations which are true and just as applied to your civilised neighbours can safely be taken as a guide to policy on the frontiers which are threatened by barbarians.

Over the Sultan's refusal to budge on the Greek territorial dispute, Salisbury surmised that he was 'probably activated by a fear of the resentment of his Mahomedan subjects', who had killed his uncle Abdul Aziz and deposed his brother Murad. The Queen also believed Layard had 'gone native' in Constantinople, and Beaconsfield reported to Salisbury that her language became quite 'Billingsgate' about him at times. Writing to Major Trotter, the Consul-General in Kurdistan, a province Salisbury believed to be populated by 'mere brigands', the Foreign Secretary lamented that the Turks were 'so well accustomed to mere threats that they are perfectly callous to them'. Neither was a palace coup desirable, as the Sultan's heir was believed to be imbecilic. Unlike Amir Sher Ali or Khedive Ismail, Sultan Abdul Hamid II could not even be deposed safely.

On 6th November, Salisbury announced to Layard that, with their reforms having been stalled and the railway and loan plans having fallen through, 'our responsibility for Turkey is at an end'. Threats of using Hornby's fleet to force the Porte to accept a British soldier, Valentine Baker, as Inspector-General of Reforms did work, but as a despairing

Salisbury wrote to Layard a week later, they were only pushing Turkey closer to revolution in order to make her see sense, and that was 'rather like burning down a house to procure roast pork'. The only effect of the British reforms in Turkey, he thought, was that they made 'virtue so disagreeable while vice is so very pleasant' for a whole new generation of Turks.[10]

~

Although Indian, Near Eastern and, latterly, global affairs had dominated his official life since 1874, Salisbury did not confine himself solely to them. He would speak on most subjects in Cabinet, such as master–servant relations, the law of conspiracy and the desirability of an Act to protect official secrets. In January 1875 he attempted to introduce a Bill against the pollution of rivers, for which the Government could find no parliamentary time. The same month he wrote to the great philanthropist Lord Shaftesbury to say that the Lunacy Commission's order that male and female corpses should be sent to separate mortuaries was 'grotesque'. The following May found him attempting, in support of the medical profession, to thwart Carnarvon's anti-vivisection legislation.

In late January 1880, Salisbury's health, which was never particularly strong and often laid him low, completely collapsed in what Beaconsfield told Lady Bradford was 'a feverish attack which always frightens me'. He melodramatically begged her to tell no one, 'or the enemy will triumph'. After six years in office, several of them spent in almost perpetual political crisis, Salisbury's health had finally given way. He was diagnosed with an acute kidney disease and ordered by his doctors, including Sir William Jenner who was sent by the Queen, to stay in bed at Hatfield without work for several weeks. This could not be kept quiet, and from 27th January *The Times* issued regular health bulletins, fourteen of them in all. These at least quashed the rumours that he was suffering from typhoid.[11]

Salisbury was not a good patient; he resented having to take very hot baths and even more having to hand over the Foreign Office to Richard Cross. Although the Lancastrian had previously been close to Derby, he was generally supportive of Salisbury's Eastern Question policy. A hard-working, middle-class Tory Democrat, Cross's worth as a legislative draftsman came to be appreciated by Salisbury. He had not made any errors at the Foreign Office when Salisbury was at Berlin, and although they were never close, and Salisbury did not allow him into his innermost counsels, Cross was subsequently promoted to important posts as a loyalist and possessor of those most useful political extremities, 'a safe pair of hands'.

Salisbury, whose health raised 'grave anxiety' for his life at one point, subsequently put on a great deal of weight after three months without much exercise and eating a diet designed to strengthen him. He was able to work but not to receive people, so on 6th March the Cabinet met at Arlington Street to decide on the immediate dissolution of Parliament. Cranbrook described Salisbury as 'much better but looking rather worn and wearied'. Egypt, Zululand and Afghanistan were all relatively quiet. The Party agents' reports were positive. By-elections since February 1874 had resulted in sixteen seats lost, eleven gained and sixty-three unchanged, and the November 1879 municipal election results had not been too bad. It was thus without any great sense of foreboding that the Cabinet recommended a dissolution, and Salisbury left for Biarritz for further recuperation. Beaconsfield stayed at Hatfield to await the election results. It was considered constitutionally improper for peers to take an active part in elections for the House of Commons; indeed, Cranbrook was shocked when Derby broke this unwritten rule in 1880 by writing a public letter to his agent for communication to his tenants and allowed Lady Derby to canvass openly for the Liberals against Cross. With Beaconsfield, Salisbury and Cranbrook all absent from the campaign, the Tory cause was seriously disadvantaged.

Salisbury was not the only minister on whom six years of office had started to tell. In late January 1880, Cairns was suffering from asthma, Northcote was in bed with influenza and Beaconsfield was 'unable to move' for gout. Had a Cabinet been held, no fewer than six ministers would have had to have pleaded absence. Back in August, Salisbury had written to Dufferin that the Prime Minister 'gets tired as night advances and has on one or two occasions left out important sentences in his intended speech'. In 1872, Disraeli had famously described Gladstone's Cabinet as a 'range of exhausted volcanoes'; by 1880 the epithet could just as accurately have been applied to his own. Salisbury later candidly told Charles Conybeare that he was personally reconciled to a change of government, 'for I was hardly equal to another term in office'.

The election results telegraphed to Biarritz by Arthur Balfour were disastrous, and, as Salisbury told Sir Augustus Paget, they came as 'a complete surprise to most of us; for there was no premonitory sign of such a revolution'. A glance at the state of the economy could have afforded them one, however, as a profound agricultural depression and decline in industrial rates of growth had coincided to produce a serious economic downturn. In August 1878, when the Government was running a £2.6 million revenue deficit, Salisbury was one of the ministers who had warned Beaconsfield that the economy would be an issue 'of life and death to the Party and the Government', but no action had resulted.

There had been bad harvests in 1873, 1875, 1876 and 1879.

Cranbrook's own rent roll at Hemsted Park in Kent (today Benenden School) confirms that the 1878–81 depression caused large numbers of rent arrears in 1878 and forced him to allow a 20 per cent rent remittance in 1880, and a further 10 per cent in 1881. As President of the West Hertfordshire Agricultural Society, Salisbury had spoken on the depression at the Watford Corn Exchange on 9th December 1879. He held out small comfort for the farmers, insisting that 'when the stress of the present pressure should have passed, landlords and tenants alike would look back upon this evil time as one that stimulates their energies'.[12] To be so surprised when the electorate punished them at the polls for what Salisbury admitted was an 'evil time' seems myopic of the Government, even in an age when economic cycles were not always blamed on traditionally non-interventionist governments.

Only 237 Conservatives were returned to the Commons, against 352 Liberals and 63 Irish Home Rulers, giving Gladstone an overall majority of 52, and a majority over the Conservatives alone of 115. Although the Salisburys and the younger Cecils were at Biarritz, Cranborne and William stayed at Hatfield with Beaconsfield. The Prime Minister was served Château Margaux 1870, but on Salisbury's specific orders the *premier crû* was not given to anybody else. 'I feel awkward,' Beaconsfield told a friend, 'but forget my embarrassment in the exquisite flavour.' As the election results came through he remarked to Cranborne: 'This is an incident in your life. It is the end of mine.'

Gwendolen Cecil claimed that Salisbury took the defeat very heavily, regarding it as primarily a personal verdict on his foreign policy. Yet his comment to Beaconsfield on 7th April 1880, 'I suppose bad harvest and bad trade have done the most,' is hardly a *mea culpa* and the Prime Minister's analysis was no different. He described it, in a letter to Salisbury thanking him for the use of Hatfield, as 'a discomfiture alike vast and without an adequate cause. "Hard Times", so far as I can collect, has been our foe.' His further comment about how the smaller boroughs had voted in a 'capricious' and 'insensible' way must have prompted rueful thoughts in Salisbury. Organisational difficulties in getting out the vote were also widely blamed. Lady Salisbury, trying to buck Beaconsfield up, told him that 'the moral of the story seems to be that the English voter, like the English footman, likes "a change"'.

Balfour was disappointed that Gladstone had won Midlothian, albeit only by 211. He too put the results down to 'bad times, the fickleness of the multitude – supplemented as they have been by Gladstonian lies'.[13] Salisbury advised Beaconsfield to resign before meeting Parliament so as not to emphasise the scale of the defeat in a formal division. He wondered whether the result might have a larger portent than a mere electoral blip. 'The hurricane that has swept us away is so strange and new a phenomenon that we shall not for some time understand its real meaning,' he wrote to Balfour. 'It may disappear as rapidly as it came: or it may be the beginning of a serious war of classes. Gladstone is doing all he can to give it the latter meaning.' If it had been his diplomacy that was being criticised, then, under democratic control, 'England must abandon all idea of influence upon the world's affairs.'

As time went on Salisbury's gloom deepened. Admitting to Lord John Manners that during the first two days of bad results he had felt that five Cabinet ministers had so needed a rest that the results 'did not affect me much', after the sheer scale of the defeat became apparent it made him think it 'a perfect catastrophe and may I fear bust up the party altogether'. He also wondered whether a 'sulking' clergy might have been responsible, angry at the Government's opposition to temperance reform, its passing of the Public Worship Regulation Bill and its failure to protect the Eastern Christians. Despite his daughter's informed insider statement that he was racked with doubt and guilt about his own role in the defeat, for having pursued an unpopular and hawkish foreign policy, little evidence exists in his contemporary correspondence to substantiate her view.

Gladstone believed that his victory must 'have given joy, I am convinced, to the large majority of the civilised world'. Driving to Leatherhead with the Treasury official Edward Hamilton after lunch on 19th April 1880, he dilated on the subject of the Cecil family, and said 'that, though it was not generally known, he believed that there was a doubt as to the parentage of Lord Salisbury caused by the undue intimacy of his mother with Lord Melbourne (father of the Prime Minister)'. For all the pleasing symmetry of Queen Victoria's first and last premiers having been natural brothers, it is highly unlikely to have been true. Quite apart from the fact that the 1st Viscount Melbourne died over twelve months before Salisbury was born, the 2nd Viscount Melbourne, whom Lady Salisbury hardly knew, was in love with someone else at the time Salisbury was conceived. Melbourne anyhow preferred sleeping with Whigs to Tories, and the Salisbury–Gascoyne marriage had been a love as well as a dynastic match. It does, however, rather explode the myth that Gladstone was never malicious about Salisbury.

At Beaconsfield's 'rather conversational' last Cabinet on 21st April 1880, Cairns, Northcote and Cross spoke of their pride in serving under him, and Salisbury 'added a few words... saying that there was never a cloud between him and the Prime Minister through all their arduous work'. As to the future, Salisbury and Smith undertook to look into the problem of Party organisation, 'to redeem our position'. There were no tears, as at Gladstone's lachrymose farewell Cabinet, just a sense of foreboding about what the future held. 'Before this Parliament is over,' Salisbury predicted to Richmond, 'the country gentlemen will have as much to do with the government of the country as the rich people in America have.'[14] Full-scale class war was on the horizon, he believed, and so he was pleased to see some extreme Radicals amongst the newly elected Liberal MPs, for, as he told Beaconsfield, 'many of our friends want frightening'. Over the next five years, Salisbury adopted a deliberate policy of trying to scare them out of their wits.

FIFTEEN

The Dual Leadership

The 'Fourth Party' – 'Suzerainty'
– Oratory – 'England' –
The Death of Beaconsfield –
The Irish Land Act

April 1880 to November 1881

'The terror of the English name has disappeared.'

Enjoying leisure for the first time since 1874, Salisbury returned to his scientific experiments and corresponding regularly with Professor McLeod. He renewed his lapsed Chairmanship of the Hertfordshire Quarter Sessions and once again took up amateur botany, collecting many different types of seaweed at Puys. He also investigated the sorry state of Conservative Party organisation, and reappointed John Gorst, MP for Chatham, who had been principal agent until the 1874 election and Secretary of the National Union until 1878. Gorst was energetic but impulsive, with a particular gift for making people detest him. A Central Committee was set up under W.H. Smith's chairmanship in August 1880, with Lord Eustace Percy and Arthur Balfour joining it the following year. Although the Conservatives used their majority in the House of Lords to reject the Compensation for Disturbance (Ireland) Bill, Gladstone's measure to help evicted tenants, other Liberal measures such as the Hares and Rabbits Bill and Burials Bill passed smoothly. 'I have ceased to understand much about British politics,' Salisbury wrote to a favourite correspondent, Lady John Manners, in July, 'only I have a dim apprehension that we shall none of us have any rents, rabbits or religion when the Session is over.'

Lady Salisbury again wrote to try to cheer up Beaconsfield, saying that she had seen Lord Hartington, the new Secretary for War and leader of the Whig faction of the Liberal Party, at Ascot, where he had complained that Beaconsfield would 'soon be back again', as the

Liberals were 'such a lot of cantankerous loons!!!' There were cantankerous Conservative loons too, and soon after the election the
thirty-one-year-old third son of the Duke of Marlborough, Lord
Randolph Churchill, MP for Woodstock since 1874, joined Sir Henry
Drummond Wolff, John Gorst and the thirty-two-year-old Arthur
Balfour to form themselves into what *The Times* in September nick-
named the 'Fourth Party'. It was a tiny but vociferous Tory group
intended to ginger up the half-hearted official Opposition in the
Commons then being provided by Northcote. In late April, Frederick
Stanley had spoken anxiously to Northcote, on behalf of Smith and
Sandon, 'against any step being taken which would seem to imply that
Salisbury was to inherit the lead of our party'.[1] The jockeying between
Northcote and Salisbury to succeed Beaconsfield, who was ill and
hardly up to another period in office, was infinitely subtle and carried
on entirely by proxies on both sides, allowing the principals to work
together harmoniously.

In this *sotto voce* duel between the former Foreign Secretary and the
former Chancellor of the Exchequer, Arthur Balfour played an important
role as the unacknowledged conduit between Salisbury and the Fourth
Party. In late August, as Salisbury was convalescing in Dieppe after a
bout of cholera, Balfour wrote to complain that Northcote was 'a source
of weakness rather than of strength'. Gladstone agreed, telling the Dean
of Windsor that although Northcote was more able than Cross, his only
Commons rival for the post as shadow Leader of the House, 'he is much
less straightforward, less courageous and less strong'.

Yet Salisbury knew that Northcote was popular on the Conservative
backbenches and that his leadership, though faltering, was trusted in a
way that his own perceived rashness was not. Northcote was also able
to cross swords with Gladstone in a way that Salisbury's place in the
Lords precluded. Furthermore, there was no real need for a single
Opposition leader for at least five years of that Parliament. Any attempt
to usurp the post, especially during Beaconsfield's lifetime, would
smack of an ambition which most politicians have but few wish to be
seen to have. 'We must have patience,' Salisbury shrewdly answered
Balfour from Puys, 'and make up our minds to wait for some time.'
Richmond agreed, telling Salisbury's other supporter Cranbrook that,
'Whenever the necessity arises whatever is done must be done, I
conclude, in a formal manner.'[2]

The very existence of the Fourth Party, consisting of some of the most
talented Conservatives in the Commons (though also the least manage-
able), was a standing reproach to Northcote, especially when they took
more popular and extreme stances in opposing Gladstone than him.
Over the issue of the atheist MP for Northampton, Charles Bradlaugh,
who asked to affirm his allegiance to the Queen rather than swearing it

by religious oath, the Fourth Party made most of the Tory running, out-
distancing the more moderate, tolerant Northcote. Because Balfour was
his nephew, Salisbury was unavoidably connected to the Fourth Party,
but he publicly distanced himself from these turbulent freelances when
they proved a potential embarrassment.

Balfour thought Northcote 'no more a match for Mr Gladstone than a
wooden three-decker would be a match for a dreadnought', and in the
days when Tory leaders emerged rather than were elected, the Fourth
Party deliberately set out to embarrass Northcote and expose him for
deferring overmuch to Gladstone. The best parliamentary sketch-writer
of the day, Sir Henry Lucy of *Punch*, described Northcote as 'pre-
eminently a man blessed (or cursed) with the faculty of seeing both
sides of a question with equal clearness'. It was not the most useful
attribute for a Leader of the Opposition.

In the five-year covert war for the Party leadership, Salisbury had an
inestimable tactical advantage over his rival in the Commons.
Northcote wished to woo the Whigs away from the Liberal Party, which
since its foundation in 1859 had always been an uneasy amalgam of
anti-Tory political viewpoints. As the Liberal Party moved towards
Radicalism, the Whigs became progressively more disenchanted. The
Tory problem of the 1880s was how to get them to secede altogether.
Salisbury, who thought that the Whigs would come over to the
Conservatives only when Gladstone forced them to, and not as a result
of anything the Conservatives might say or do, believed in opposing
Gladstone to the uttermost, emboldening Conservatives in the country
and provoking constitutional crises whenever possible. Northcote
wanted a gentler approach, coaxing the Whigs over by showing moderation and a toleration of Liberal views.

This dichotomy in outlook allowed Salisbury to pursue a more
distinctive, vigorous and ultimately more popular stance than
Northcote. In the meantime, Salisbury was content to wait. Time was
on his side, because although Northcote seemed the most likely successor to Beaconsfield in 1880/1, his lacklustre Commons performances
were increasingly being contrasted unfavourably with Salisbury's far
more hard-hitting ones in the Lords. Northcote's consensus politics and
absence of charisma started to tell, and both were cruelly emphasised by
the increasingly insubordinate activities of the Fourth Party.

Beaconsfield himself was predictably mischievous over his succession, dropping broad hints to both men. In April and July 1880, he spoke
on two separate occasions to Northcote about what would happen
'when you come to form a ministry'. Yet that October, Salisbury was
also persuaded that 'the Chief' had chosen him, and letters with
remarks such as 'you would be leading Her Majesty's Opposition' did
little to disabuse him of the notion.[3]

As the Bradlaugh affair was primarily a House of Commons question, Salisbury left it to the *enfants terribles* of the Fourth Party, who leapt upon it with obvious opportunism, as none of them (except perhaps Balfour) was particularly known for his Churchmanship. Salisbury made *pro forma* criticisms of Drummond Wolff's 'great impudence' towards Northcote, but never attempted genuinely to hold them back from criticising his colleague, the man with whom he had once sat for Stamford. By late October 1880, Salisbury was canvassing for himself in a very tentative way, telling Cranbrook that he was 'willing to place himself at the disposal of the party if Northcote's feelings are respected'.

Little respect for them was evident when Lord Randolph Churchill made what he described as 'an audacious request' for Salisbury, then staying at Blenheim Palace, to speak at a meeting intended almost as a public launch for the Fourth Party at Woodstock on 30th November 1880. This caused great interest in political circles, not so much for what Salisbury actually said there as the fact that his very presence implied approbation of the group, prompting rumours that the Fourth Party was really a Cecilian front organisation. In fact it was primarily a vehicle for thrusting Lord Randolph forward, but as Churchill wrote to the rich landowner and keen Master of Foxhounds, Henry Chaplin, MP for Mid-Lincolnshire, when he heard that Beaconsfield was unwell: 'the Fourth Party are strongly in favour of Lord Salisbury as opposed to the Goat. What do you think on this matter?' Chaplin's presence at the Woodstock meeting, along with that of a Northumberland MP called Sir Matthew Ridley and an ambitious and brilliant young man freshly down from Oxford called George Curzon, confirmed Cranbrook's belief that 'a cave exists and will grow'.

Salisbury was particularly adroit at Woodstock, praising Churchill's 'energy and ability', but also the 'sagacious guidance' of Northcote in the Commons, which he claimed had produced an 'energetic and thoroughly united party' there. Eyebrows were raised at the specific mention of the House of Commons, thus indicating to the *cognoscenti* that Salisbury did not recognise Northcote's claims to any general leadership of the Party.[4] Northcote admitted to Cross that he was 'secretly uneasy lest they should receive a little too much encouragement from quarters which I need not mention', but there was little he could do about it. Salisbury had taken Churchill's measure perfectly, telling Beaconsfield the day after the Woodstock meeting that there was no real danger of his breaking away from the Party altogether; 'But he must be watched and humoured – for he is not a man who calculates consequences when his temper is moved.' Whilst Churchill was a threat only to Northcote, Salisbury was happy to watch and humour him. Once he became a threat to Salisbury himself, this inability to calculate consequences was used against Churchill to devastating effect.

Charles Stewart Parnell, a tall, handsome twenty-nine-year-old Irish Protestant, had entered Parliament in 1875 as the Home Ruler MP for County Meath. In 1878, he was elected President of the Irish National Land League, a radical pressure group for the protection of tenants' rights. During the 1880–5 Gladstone Government he emerged as the principal spokesman for Ireland's discontents, eloquently putting the case for Irish Home Rule, which was simultaneously being promoted by others who employed less constitutional means. In September 1880, for example, the Galway landowner Lord Mountmorres was shot only a hundred yards from his home.

Salisbury's most significant legislative activity in the 1880 post-election session was to urge the House of Lords to throw out Gladstone's Bill for compensating those Irish tenants evicted for the non-payment of rent. When Derby pointed out how popular it was in Ireland and in the Commons, Salisbury said that he refused 'to ask with the noble Earl what would be thought of the action of the House of Lords out of doors. The matter for the House of Lords should be "Be just and fear not", and be sure that if you fear you will not be just.' The Lords rejected the Bill by 282 to 51. The Whig landowner the 5th Marquess of Lansdowne resigned the Under-Secretaryship of the India Office in protest at the measure, and more Liberal peers, including Robert Lowe (now Lord Sherbrooke), had voted against than for it.

Speaking to the Hackney Conservative Club in November, Salisbury claimed that 'terror reigns in the West of Ireland' and he denounced the 'branding, tarring and feathering of men turned out on a winter midnight by the roadside'. Arguing that there were now two governments in Ireland, and that the rule of law was being superseded by 'the reign of the secret societies which Parnell has set up', Salisbury said that the House of Lords' 'duty was to represent the permanent as opposed to the passing feelings of the English nation', and they should thus throw out the measure altogether, which he claimed only encouraged the non-payment of rent. He called on the Whigs to resist Gladstone's increasing Radicalism, saying that his Government was nothing like that of Lord Palmerston. Privately he was forced to admit that the Irish landowners had no stomach for the fight, even though he hoped that this time the Whigs' resistance might 'be something more than a Brooks's pout'.

As for Gladstone himself, Salisbury wrote to Balfour that 'there are marks of hurry which in so old a man are inexplicable. I suppose he still cherishes his belief in an early monastic retreat from this wicked world – and is feverishly anxious to annihilate all his enemies before he takes it.'[5] The phrase 'old man in a hurry' was years later used by Churchill with great effect to describe Gladstone, but, as so often with telling Victorian political phrases, the patent was Salisbury's. Drawing on his journalistic experience, Salisbury was an inveterate phrase-maker, experiencing all the pitfalls of that small, clever but accident-prone band. Gladstone's references to Salisbury were also becoming less charitable, and he told Sir Edward Hamilton of 'the marked manner in which Lord Salisbury's character has suffered of late', especially once he discovered the secret agreement over Tunis that Salisbury had made with Waddington at Berlin. Somewhat self-righteously, Gladstone said that Salisbury's 'good faith used to be regarded as part of the national estate', but could be no longer.

~

The ambushing of Major-General Sir George Colley at the hands of the Boers at the Battle of Laing's Nek on 28th January 1881, followed by his defeat and death at the Battle of Majuba Hill the following month, were themselves followed by the Pretoria Convention which granted the Transvaal a large degree of independence, albeit under the overall nominal 'suzerainty' of the British Crown. Salisbury thought the Convention a disgraceful capitulation to the Boers. It helped convince him that Gladstone's foreign policy was pusillanimous and it was to form a staple part of his denunciation of the Government in all future foreign policy speeches. Salisbury believed implicitly in the politics of prestige and vengeance; the Pretoria Convention left him aching to reverse the Empire's humiliation in South Africa.

In the Preamble to the Pretoria Convention, which was ratified by the Volksraad on 25th October 1881, it stated that 'complete self-government, subject to the suzerainty of Her Majesty, her heirs and successors, will be accorded to the inhabitants of the Transvaal'. Salisbury immediately denounced the way that the Gladstone Government had accepted defeat at the hands of 'the successful armed rebellion of an insignificant minority' and told the House of Lords that 'a suzerainty over a Republic is, I believe, merely a diplomatic invention. The suzerainty contains no atom of sovereignty whatever. The truth is that this is merely a device to cover surrender.' He likened it to Turkish suzerainty, which 'has sometimes been employed to cover the loss of power by the Sultan', presumably with Cyprus, Egypt and Bulgaria in mind.

When in March 1883 Derby, by then Colonial Secretary again, allowed the British military contingent in South Africa to fall to a mere 7,100 men, at a time when the Boers were making incursions into Bechuanaland in breach of the Pretoria Convention, Salisbury returned to the attack. 'Encroachment has been their very life,' he said of the Boers.

'They have been engaged in a perpetual career of filibustering.' Derby's speech in the debate he described as 'pathetic and melancholy' and as likely to prevent the Boers advancing further as to 'persuade the wolves, in some woodland impossible of access, to abandon the habit of feeding on sheep'. Once again he denigrated the concept of 'suzerainty', claiming: 'It served its purpose at the moment in hoodwinking the public opinion of England. It covered a retreat which otherwise would have been too disgraceful even for the tolerant public opinion of England.'

When in 1884, in order to avoid further conflict in South Africa, the Liberals signed a further Convention with the Boers, this time in London, the 1881 Preamble was not prefixed to the opening passages. In the departmental papers, Derby had even struck out the 1881 Preamble in the draft document for the 1884 Convention. The 1884 Convention had a Preamble of its own, although not dignified with the title, and the Boers understandably later argued that this superseded the 1881 one altogether, excising any British claim to suzerainty over the Transvaal. Salisbury spotted what had happened and vigorously denounced it at the time, but it was not until much later that the full implications of the ceding of 'suzerainty', itself a nebulous concept, became fully apparent.[6]

'Power is more and more leaving Parliament and going to the platform,' Salisbury wrote to Cranborne in February 1881, when his twenty-year-old eldest son began seriously to consider a political career, 'and in the next generation platform speaking will be an essential accomplishment to anyone who wishes to give effect to his own political opinions: especially if those opinions happen to be on the unpopular side. It is – to my mind – a peculiarly difficult and unattractive form of public speaking: and therefore the earlier you begin to practise it the better.' Salisbury always disliked 'stump' oratory, or what he dismissively called 'my "starring" in the provinces'. Yet after Gladstone's Midlothian campaign it became obvious how important the mass public meeting, often held in the open air, had become. With full verbatim reports appearing the next day in the newspapers, which recorded 'laughter', 'cheers', 'hear hear', 'loud cheers', 'renewed laughter' and so on, Salisbury could reach an audience far larger than the five or even ten thousand who might turn out for a rally. John Morley believed five or six thousand people was 'commonly understood to be the limit of possible hearers in the open air', but loyal supporters known as 'shouters' were sometimes employed to convey the speaker's words to the crowds beyond.

'The necessity of making these excursions', Salisbury complained to the Queen as he was about to leave for three days of speaking engagements in Edinburgh, 'is an odious addition to the burdens of political life in modern times. The bad fashion was introduced by Mr Gladstone.' Salisbury believed these extra-parliamentary speeches might have an effect in persuading people to vote Tory, telling his niece-in-law that even St Paul had 'stood on a tub' when making conversions. Despite loathing the whole process and considering it personally demeaning, Salisbury realised that the advancing democratic tide meant that he could not allow Gladstone to monopolise British platform oratory. Between 1880 and 1886, Salisbury appeared more than seventy times all over the country, and although he told Lady Rayleigh in 1889 that 'the prospect of having to make a speech oppresses his spirits with a dull leaden weight', he was to excel at platform oratory.

Salisbury had written in the *Saturday Review* how modern statesmen 'share with Wombwell's Menagerie and Cooke's Travelling Circus the honourable mission of pleasingly exciting the provincials'. He mocked the conventions of public speaking, saying, 'Patriotism, faintly tinged, but in no way modified, by humanity, is the dominant feeling of a provincial audience after dinner', and specifying that the 'peroration must always be serious, and should, if possible, wind up with a general panegyric upon religious education and the nineteenth century'. For all his satire, he was to stick to these rules rigidly himself, only substituting the British Empire for religious education.[7]

Salisbury's speeches attracted and held vast audiences not by any great oratorical fireworks like Churchill's or Gladstone's, but through his ability to speak cogently and sometimes brilliantly, with constant use of wit and metaphor, often for over an hour and without recourse to notes. People came not only to see a celebrity, but to hear at first hand his almost conversationally-delivered thoughts. What he described as 'the prospect of death' concentrated his mind before a big speech. He was able to discard notes because in his youth he had realised that his eyesight would not be strong in later years, so he trained himself to depend on his memory for both the substance and the arrangement of his speeches. He spoke without any gesticulation and never attempted to strike rhetorical poses, keeping his sentences short and his sentiments earth-bound. Having determined the general outline of a speech in his mind, he never learnt phrases, but relied on his natural capacity for epigram to see him through, which it always did. Occasionally there were slips of the tongue; he was mortified in 1866 when the Commons collapsed with laughter when he accused Gladstone of having 'burned his breeches behind him'.

In the House of Lords, Salisbury entirely abjured flourishes of all kinds, and Sir Henry Lucy remembered his explanation of a particularly complicated history of negotiations with the Portuguese in Africa in which the obscure history, geographical terms and difficult names were all made perfectly clear 'to the perception of the dullest lord in the assembly'. Nor would he talk down to audiences. Speaking to a banquet at the annual conference of the National Union of Conservative and Constitutional Associations (NUCCA) in Newcastle in October 1881, he said: 'Mr Gladstone's complaint of Mr Parnell for preaching the doctrine of public plunder seems to me a strange application of the old adage that Catiline should not censure Cethegus for treason,' which reference to first-century BC Roman politics was greeted with cheers and laughter by the 700-strong audience.[8] Lord Ribblesdale had an attractive theory that Salisbury's feel for language came from his mother having read him Joseph Addison and other *Spectator* essayists between the ages of seven and nine.

On the rare occasions when Salisbury did employ a note, he would laboriously take a small piece of paper out of his waistcoat pocket, instantly capturing any attentions that might have wandered, and would read out a statistic, a quotation from an opponent's speech, or a line from a letter from some great potentate such as the Shah of Persia or the Sultan of Turkey. All gestures or demagogic tricks he despised, and he hardly ever used the first person singular. Although he did not believe he was particularly successful at making himself heard outdoors he persevered, and his great height and stature must have helped as he bellowed his message to thousands in all weathers.[9]

What a colleague called his 'unfailing instinct for spotting the weak point in his adversary's argument, and [his] pungent and concise power of expression and sarcasm' made Salisbury a formidable debater. By avoiding all sentimentality, but adopting instead the conversational style that Curzon said made it 'seem a mere accident that the reflections were conducted audibly and in public rather than in the recesses of the library at Hatfield', Salisbury managed to win the public's trust, if not their love. 'He talked of things which interested him,' wrote an impressed Liberal opponent, 'but whether or not they interested his hearers he seemed not to care one jot.' However it might have looked, this was not really the case. In fact, Salisbury always tried to keep his message as close to his listeners' real concerns as possible, for as he explained in 1881: 'To those who have found breakfast with difficulty and do not know where to find dinner, intricate questions of politics are a matter of comparatively secondary interest.'

Salisbury's total lack of declamatory display fitted in perfectly with his nature. It skilfully emphasised his image of English reserve and unostentatious grandeur. Caricaturists were at a loss; where Gladstone had his huge collars, Randolph Churchill his vast moustache and Joseph Chamberlain his orchid and monocle, Salisbury affected no recognisable props; he was simply himself. They simply hoped his beard and a Garter star would make him recognisable.

Curzon, who was no mean judge, considered Salisbury 'the ablest and most polished speaker in England'. The slowness of the sentences, sometimes delivered with long gaps in between, the sonorous deepness of his voice, the outward forms of 'a philosopher meditating aloud', were largely successful in producing a public image of Salisbury which a closer knowledge of his depressions would never have engendered. As Curzon wrote: 'His massive head, bowed upon his chest, his precise and measured tones, his total absence of gesture, his grave but subtle irony, sustained the illusion.'[10] The only indication of nervousness came when, preparing to get up to speak, his right leg would jog up and down at great speed, which Lucy estimated as 'at a pace equivalent to ten miles an hour on a level track'.

The multitudes who turned out to hear him imply that, even despite the lack of alternative mass entertainment in those pre-television days, he was an impressive crowd-puller, but Salisbury never enjoyed public-speaking, saying it was 'like dancing on a tight-rope – an exercise which palls on you'. Occasionally he fell off the rope. His lack of notes meant that he would sometimes make a serious political gaffe, particularly when he was tired. 'I am very glad when Lord Salisbury makes a great speech,' joked the Liberal MP John Morley, 'it is sure to contain at least one blazing indiscretion which it is a delight to remember.' They were not such a delight for the Party agent Richard Middleton: 'There go twenty seats!' he would exclaim when Salisbury made a gaffe. Because epigrams came easily to him, and he was never more comfortable than when on the offensive, his career produced a large number of famous hostages to fortune. 'I am afraid of not being dull enough,' he told Gwendolen after yet another momentary lapse in self-restraint, 'if I speak when I am tired I always shock people.'

In the *Saturday Review*, he had written that ministerial indiscretions usually appeared in the spring, 'with the nightingales and green peas', but with him they were perennial. In 1862, he once wrote of Palmerston's annual speech at the Guildhall dinner that:

> Statesmen are but human after all, and bad wine is generally strong. Then, endurance of three hours of oppressive weariness creates an intense desire to relieve the nerves by some vigorous display of energy, which will show itself in the phrases even of a practised orator.... Even experienced speakers are not apt to drop expressions of which they have preferred, in cold blood, to modify the force.... There will always be a tinge of recklessness in the phrases even of a calm and sober speaker, when he is addressing an excited, hallooing, thumping, half-drunk mob of guests.... It has been under the combined influence of municipal wine and municipal bores, that several of our foremost statesmen have made some of their leading blunders.[11]

As might be expected for a man as prone to ennui as Salisbury, he proved no exception to this rule.

Salisbury's use of the word 'English' in speeches to describe what might properly be taken to mean 'British' was no slip of the tongue, but the product of a considered policy. He explained this to a Scot, Lord Balfour of Burleigh, who had complained about it in 1899, and as it illustrates Salisbury's view of the Union of the United Kingdom, it deserves extensive quotation:

> The advantage of the use of the words 'England, English and Englishmen' is that it has not any strict geographical interpretation, but is generally used for any inhabitants of these islands. Its use is traditional and based on a long course of history. It has followed the development of our literature. The language in which we all speak is without contest called the English language. The practice of using the words England, English and Englishmen is convenient, it carries a clear idea to anybody's mind, and it rests not upon the interpretation of a statute, but upon a long established custom, it raises no jealous question of honour or pre-eminence among the various populations of the two islands. While agreeing that the formal phrase 'United Kingdom of Great Britain and Ireland' should be employed in all documents of a strictly formal character, I do not think any advantage would be gained by attempting to modify the laxer practice which is instinctively followed by writers and speakers upon public questions, in designating either the territory of the United Kingdom, the adjective formed from it, or the inhabitants who dwell in it.

Salisbury moreover thought the word Briton 'carries with it a slight flavour of ridicule', and thought that Great Britain 'is not capable of being inflected so as to be used as an adjective, or for the purpose of designating an inhabitant of the country.' Quite what he had against the obvious choice 'British' he did not explain, but his attitude is testament to his belief in English hegemony within the United Kingdom.

On 19th April 1881, Beaconsfield died of bronchitis with asthma complications, in a room filled with primroses sent from Osborne. He had told Cranborne at Hatfield that the election defeat meant the end of his life, and for once he was as good as his word. In his House of Lords panegyric, Salisbury caught the public mood, which was to convert Beaconsfield into a legendary figure almost overnight, and spoke of his 'patience, his gentleness, his unswerving and unselfish loyalty to his colleagues and fellow labourers', and how 'zeal for the greatness of England was the passion of his life'. Salisbury said Beaconsfield's social reforms, of which he had never entertained a high opinion, were 'of secondary interest compared with this one great question – how the country to which he belonged might be made united and strong'.

As the Beaconsfield myth progressed, and even his more unfocused remarks about creating One Nation out of the rich and poor were turned into the talismans of a political movement that Churchill soon attempted to monopolise, Salisbury realised that it was better to play up his connections with his old chief than to play them down. In his commiserating letter to the Queen, he showed that he had learnt at least one lesson from Beaconsfield, writing: 'It is a long time since any sovereign has lost so devoted a subject.'

Soon after the 1880 defeat, Salisbury had told Balfour how Beaconsfield's statesmanship was greatly misunderstood:

> As a politician he was exceedingly short-sighted though very clear-sighted. He neither could nor would look ahead, or attempt to balance remote possibilities: though he rapidly detected the difficulties of the immediate situation and found the easiest if not the best solution for them. As the head of a Cabinet his fault was lack of firmness ... a statesman whose only fixed political principle was that the party must on no account be broken up and who shrank from exercising coercion on any of his subordinates.... The Eastern policy of the Cabinet suffered much through having at the head of affairs a man who with all his great qualities was unable to decide on a general principle of action or to ensure that when decided on it should be carried out by his subordinates.[12]

It must be added in Beaconsfield's defence that, had he exercised co-ercion on his Cabinet subordinates, Salisbury himself could never have survived the turmoils of 1876–8.

The two men had little more than a sardonic sense of humour in common, but Salisbury appreciated the way that by 1878 he was increasingly being consulted by Beaconsfield on wider issues than just his department's. Over foreign policy the two men had been unchallenged in Cabinet, sitting opposite each other at the centre of the table and entirely dominating the arena. Lady Salisbury would tell the Prime Minister that 'if the sun should come out and you would like to talk a little nonsense and walk up and down the gallery among the flowers we shall be enchanted to see you', invitations that were fully reciprocated at Hughenden, which Disraeli called 'an hotel for you whenever you like'. From the deepest rancour on Salisbury's part, their relationship metamorphosed into a congenial political alliance, though never true friendship. Salisbury respected some of Beaconsfield's instincts, however, and Gwendolen remembered how, even when Beaconsfield was not able to give any reasons to support a policy, her father would remark appreciatively that 'with a man of his age it is the opinions for which no reasons can be given that are dangerous to neglect'. Salisbury always respected instinct and prejudice, which, as Burke wrote, never leaves one hesitating at a moment of crisis.

Salisbury was fully alive to the 'very severe' political implications of the loss, writing on the day of Beaconsfield's death to Lord John Manners that he 'has been so long associated with the Tory Party, and of late his popularity has risen so much that the party will hardly believe in its own existence without him.... One can hardly talk of the death of a man of seventy-six as if it were a strange and unexpected event – yet now that it has come it fills me with sadness and helplessness.'[13] His sister Mildred had died on 18th March aged fifty-eight and Salisbury himself had been seriously ill until shortly before Beaconsfield's death. It was not surprising, therefore, that aged only fifty-one this third blow should have hit Salisbury hard.

Northcote did not immediately press the leadership question on Beaconsfield's demise, but agreed to Salisbury's suggestion that it be split between them in the Lords and the Commons. Articles appeared about this dual leadership system, the *Standard* supporting Salisbury, the *St James' Gazette* calling him 'rash, headstrong, incautious, prejudiced', and the *World* alleging that Richmond disliked him intensely. Salisbury wrote to Northcote on 29th April, only three days after they had attended Beaconsfield's primrose-strewn funeral at Hughenden, to agree 'that it is best to take no notice' of the coverage. To Richmond he said that the Duke had been more indulgent 'than my uneven temper sometimes deserves', and it would be 'a considerable evil' not to treat the editor of the *World* with contempt.

On the morning of 5th May 1881, Northcote was summoned to Buckingham Palace with the 'injunction that I was not to mention the subject'. The Queen spoke of Beaconsfield and said: 'I must now look to you, dear Sir Stafford, to take his place,' adding that Beaconsfield had often told her that he was to be his successor. She furthermore said that, if it would be of use to Northcote, she 'could let it be known that, she "looked to him" as the real leader'.[14] Northcote said he was perfectly happy to have Salisbury as the Leader of the House of Lords, but came away under the understandable impression that the premiership would devolve upon him when eventually the Conservatives formed another government.

When Cairns, Cranbrook and Richmond stood aside for Salisbury to take the now vacant place as Conservative Leader in the Lords, Northcote was not overmuch concerned, accepting Cairns's formula that, 'should any need arise in our time for the formation of a

Government on our side, that question must be solved when the emergency arises'. On their way to the meeting of Conservative peers at the Marquess of Abergavenny's house in Dover Street, Richmond remarked to Cranbrook that, had he been married to Lady Salisbury rather than the Duchess, he would not have been allowed to stand aside. Although Abergavenny was 'troubled' about Salisbury's nomination, Beauchamp 'very hostile' and Pembroke, who wanted an early fusion with the Whigs, 'very strongly against', Salisbury was elected *nemine contradicente* on 10th May. Cranbrook believed that, if Richmond had announced his intention of standing against him, the majority of the 104 peers present would have supported him, because despite the Duke's clear deficiency in intellect he had none of Salisbury's perceived rashness.

Commenting on the news that Richmond had been persuaded to stand down, Sir Edward Hamilton made the acute prediction that 'practically this will mean [Salisbury is] leader of the party, for he must absorb Northcote... whatever objections there may be to him, there will be <u>one strong man</u>'. Salisbury's own attitude to the leadership question was made clear to his brother Eustace in a letter the following year:

> I am the last person who can stir in this matter. I have never secured any kind of 'mandate' from members of the House of Commons – and therefore, it would be an impertinence in me to meddle with their affairs. I know that if Northcote is incapacitated they will be in some difficulty: and, if I am wanted, I shall be happy to give what help I can: but it will only be 'if wanted' – for the task will be neither pleasant nor easy. My imprisonment in the House of Lords makes me very powerless.[15]

His remedy was the bold one of attempting to make the House of Lords itself more powerful, by encouraging it to exercise its veto against the Gladstone Government's legislative programme.

Salisbury took a very active line defending his foreign policy against what he regarded as Gladstone's reversal of it. When Gladstone threatened to join the Great Powers in forcing Turkey to abide by the Berlin promises to Montenegro, and it was revealed that the British fleet had no authority to land troops or fire guns, Salisbury told a banquet in Taunton in October 1880 that 'they might for all practical purposes have just as well sent six washing tubs with flags attached to them'. As for the Montenegrins, whom Gladstone had praised as the most high-minded race in Europe, Salisbury said that in fact they were 'very much what half-civilised mountaineers generally are. In peace they are caterans and cattle-lifters: in war they are heroes,' albeit heroes who thought nothing of mutilating captured prisoners. The Hellenophile Gladstone's hopes of stripping Thessaly and Epirus from Turkey and donating them to Greece, Salisbury denounced as 'mere partition', unjustified by international law. Salisbury said the Greeks, who had 'the advantage of a most admirable and excellent monarch, whom I am afraid they did not rear themselves', were only favoured by Gladstone out of a 'half-romantic, half-literary romanticism' about what their civilisation had represented five centuries before Christ, but no longer did.

In February 1881, Salisbury returned from Nice to take part in the debate on the Government's policy over Afghanistan, which he thought weak and 'evidently the price we pay for the advantage of having Mr Bright in the Cabinet'. Writing to his vicar friend Charles Conybeare four days before, he said that Gladstone's Midlothian theories about how Liberal sentiments might bring peace to the world were receiving a rude shock: 'I wish the English army may be equal to all the work his peace-loving policy has given it.'

The embarrassing publication by Granville in May 1881 of Salisbury's *carte blanche* to Waddington over Tunis three years earlier meant that too vigorous a denunciation of Government policy in that region was difficult, but in southern Africa the battle of capitulation after Majuba Hill provided a source of reproach. 'When our military fortunes were at their lowest,' he told the Middlesex Conservative Registration Association banquet in Willis's Rooms in King Street, St James's, 'this unlucky Quaker curb is put on. A discreditable peace was signed, and now the loyal inhabitants of the Transvaal, who invested their capital and staked their fortune on the promises we made and the security we offered them...call upon us to help them out of their distress.' All the Prime Minister gave them was 'a disheartening sermon in reply'. The Government's failed attempts to get a British right of way to the Transvaal through the Portuguese port of Lourenço Marques would, he told a diplomat, 'only have italicised our disaster'.[16]

Gladstone's attitude to the Turks was hardly rational, calling them 'the one great anti-human specimen of humanity', and his anti-Turkish policy towards Montenegro and Greece, in contrast to Salisbury's more hands-off approach, encouraged Austria to rejoin the *Dreikaiserbund* halfway through June 1881. It left Britain in dangerous strategic and diplomatic isolation. All this was being done for Montenegro, somewhere that Britain had no significant interests. Salisbury mocked Gladstone's attempted revival of the concert of Europe as 'a Concert of Europe directed against us'.[17]

The dual Party leadership imposed social duties on Salisbury which he disliked, and underwent as plaintively as his Foreign Office ones before. Lady Salisbury threw four large receptions at Arlington Street in June and July 1881, and *The Times* reported how 'all the leading members of the Diplomatic Corps and a large number of the principal members of the aristocracy attended. Large numbers of Tory MPs and their wives were also invited.' It was an arena in which Northcote, who had a far smaller house at No. 30, St James's Place and resented the fact that the Shadow Cabinet met at Arlington Street, could not compete.

The need to keep in touch with the Party also encouraged Salisbury to engage Henry Manners, the twenty-nine-year-old son of his friend Lord John, as his private secretary. His job was to deal with 'matters of delicacy in which I have difficulty in one sort or another in acting myself'. The future 8th Duke of Rutland turned out, except for one embarrassing *faux pas*, to be a fine additional pair of political eyes and ears for Salisbury, who acknowledged that 'my engagements – and to some extent my idiosyncrasies – make it difficult for me to know as much as I ought to know what people in the party are thinking on pressing questions'. Manners's baptism of fire was to be over the greatest issue of 1881, indeed of the whole Liberal ministry, the Irish Land Act.

For all Gladstone's avowal of a 'mission' to 'pacify' Ireland in 1868, the six years of his first ministry had done little to achieve this, and by 1881 civil order was in grave danger there. That year saw 2,500 agrarian outrages and over a hundred thousand cases of pauperism in Ireland, with over two thousand evictions. By 1882, this had risen to 5,201 outrages and 3,432 evictions. As Gorst told Salisbury after a visit there in 1881, the resident magistrate with whom he was staying had the Riot Act pasted into the crown of his hat so he was always ready to read it in an emergency.

Throughout the autumn of 1880, Parnell led the agitation to 'keep a firm grip on the land', organising seventeen vast public meetings such as the one at Cork on 3rd October, at which he addressed 30,000 people. Later that month, four men who had been arrested for Lord Mountmorres's murder were discharged for want of evidence. The Irish Land League leaders were prosecuted in early November, but were acquitted in January 1881 when the jury could not agree on a verdict. A new form of aggression against landowners, named after Lord Erne's land agent Captain Boycott of County Mayo, was instituted against Irish landowners, who pleaded with the Viceroy (or Lord-Lieutenant), Earl Cowper, for coercion legislation. On 28th November, Parnell was elected leader of the Irish Nationalist parliamentary party.

It was into this dangerous situation that Salisbury launched his attempt to derail the Gladstone ministry, with a call for uncompromising resistance to the Land League. Speaking of 'the ignorant peasantry of Ireland' at the Taunton banquet, he sarcastically described 'the amiable practice to which they were addicted of shooting people to whom they owe money'. He argued that the Irish had no more excuse to kill landowners because of old grievances than Highland tenants could break the law because the Duke of Cumberland 'misbehaved himself very much after Culloden'. As he was speaking in Taunton: 'I should be sorry to think that in going home tonight I should...run the risk of getting a bullet from some discontented descendants of one of Judge Jeffreys' victims.'

Salisbury's attitude was ruthless, hoping that the Irish landlords, whom he never trusted to protect their own interests aggressively enough, would not capitulate. 'It is very inexpedient that they should be allowed to give way,' he had written to Beaconsfield on 1st December 1880. 'Both for the sake of the party, and their own sake, they should hold their pretensions as high as possible. It is very desirable now that many of them should proceed to eviction, which will alone bring about a collision, and force the Government either to act or confess its incapacity.' None of Salisbury's own 20,000 acres lay in Ireland; indeed, in December 1881 he gave notice to all the tenants on his estate that the half-year's rent had been entirely remitted.[18] 'Like all landowners, I find tenants just now are a weariness to the flesh,' he told his confidante, Janetta Manners. 'How pleasant it must be to have nothing but Consols.' Believing that any Radical legislation against Irish landowners would one day become applicable to the mainland, however, he saw the campaign in Ireland as merely the precursor for a general class struggle over the rights of property.

'I am very anxious to see how Gladstone means to get out of this Irish mess,' he wrote to Eustace on 22nd December. 'It looks very like a revolution. We shall have to reconquer Ireland, if we mean to keep her: and is there stuff and fibre in the English constituencies – at present composed – for this? I doubt it.' Salisbury was instinctively hostile to the proposals to institute the powers of parliamentary clôture, by which debate was foreshortened and votes automatically taken, thinking it hardly in the interest of Conservativism 'to grease the wheels of all legislation'. He wanted the new powers of guillotining debates confined to questions of supply, mutiny and public order. In his last letter to Beaconsfield, he expressed delight that 'the Chief' was also against clôture, saying that if applied to ordinary Bills, 'we should have a press of democratic legislation thrown up to the House of Lords which would strain our powers of resistance'.

This silencing of the minority by the majority was denounced as illiberal and un-British by the Conservatives, but after the Irish continued to employ parliamentary rules to obstruct various important Bills of the Irish Secretary, W.E. Forster, clôture was introduced on 3rd February 1881. Forster's Coercion Bill, which gave the Government emergency powers and suspended *habeas corpus*, was introduced on 24th January, and after the maximum possible obstruction by Irish MPs it was passed using the clôture guillotining procedure on 2nd March. So far, Salisbury was impressed by Gladstone's tough response to the breakdown of law and order in Ireland, which was not far removed from the introduction of martial law.

On 7th April, an Irish Land Bill was introduced in the House of Commons to give tenants what were soon nicknamed 'the three F's' – fixity of tenure, 'fair' rent and free sale. As well as establishing durability of tenure, it set up judicial tribunals to settle rent levels in Ireland. Salisbury argued that this would destroy freedom of contract, in a way that had not been mentioned by the Liberals on the election hustings and for which the Government therefore had no mandate. 'We can but die like gentlemen,' conceded a gloomy Beaconsfield after reading the Bill. Salisbury disagreed, and vigorously criticised the Bill's principles and methods of application, and argued that it would not pacify Ireland either.

'Loot, pure loot, is the sacred course for which the Land League has summoned the malcontents to its standard,' Salisbury declared in the *Quarterly Review* in April 1881. By discouraging capital investment in land and establishing a nebulous form of joint-ownership of it, the Bill made future proprietor–tenant conflict inevitable. 'This will be long remembered in our constitutional history as the year in which the argument of "land hunger" was invented,' he warned at the Merchant Taylors' Hall in mid-May, and it was just the thin end of the wedge. If it surrendered to 'land hunger', he argued, why should not governments give way in the future to 'house hunger', 'consols hunger' or even 'silver plate hunger'?

Unfortunately for Salisbury even the Ulster Tories, usually the most stalwart, recognised that the Bill would eventually be passed and that anarchy was the alternative. They preferred to receive reduced rents rather than none at all. Salisbury's aggressive speech against the second reading of the Bill sounded like a clarion call to reject it, but in fact his colleagues had agreed to let it pass and instead try to amend it in committee, which was achieved with a couple of notable successes. When Gladstone accepted a few of the amendments, Salisbury drew up more to test him further, but the Conservative former Attorney-General for Ireland, Sir Edward Gibson, along with Northcote and Carnarvon, tried to rein him back.[19]

On 9th August 1881, Salisbury was delighted to find that, at a meeting of Conservative peers he had called at Arlington Street, a large majority of them agreed with him against compromise and wished to insert the further amendments. Amid rumours of dissolutions, resignations and Lords–Commons conflict, Gladstone accepted several of them, to the fury of his Radicals. Cranbrook was delighted that due to Salisbury's

firmness, against the advice of almost all his colleagues, they had introduced important modifications to the Bill and mitigated the landlords'
apprehensions. On 15th August, at a Shadow Cabinet meeting, someone
remarked that Gladstone should be humoured because he was 'so
impulsive and excitable that in some ways he must be regarded as some
kind of lunatic'. Salisbury answered, to general laughter, that: 'If it is
such an advantage to the Government to be able to use that argument,
we should have a lunatic too. I offer myself for the position.'

When, later that day, Gladstone agreed to the most important of
Salisbury's amendments, the crisis was over. Salisbury advocated acceptance and Lord John Manners wrote to him to say that his actions 'have
completely vindicated the position of the House of Lords before the
country, and established yours in that Assembly and the party'. By
presenting himself as the tough, intransigent negotiator who could
force Gladstone into important concessions, when Northcote had advocated a more moderate and less confrontational response, Salisbury had
come out well from the incident. The Colonial Secretary, Lord
Kimberley, wrote to the Viceroy of India, Lord Ripon, that Salisbury had
been 'insolent and defiant to the House of Commons, and if Gladstone
had not behaved with admirable tact and temper he might have brought
on a serious conflict between the two Houses'.[20] It was exactly such a
conflict that Salisbury, hoping to detach the Whigs from Gladstone over
Ireland and strengthen the constitutional position of the House of
Lords, was to spend much of 1882 attempting to engineer.

Immediately after the Irish Land Act passed, Salisbury went to Puys
for a nine-week holiday, pointing out to Balfour when asked to speak in
Glasgow that: 'As a rule I observe that the places where we win seats are
the places where no Tory Leader has spoken.' He reverted to his old
view that the ideal political arrangement was a moderate Liberal
government with a strong Conservative Opposition, such as existed
under Palmerston. 'That is undoubtedly the condition of things under
which the wearing away of the Constitution is most nearly suspended,'
he told Conybeare.

On one of his brief returns during the long holiday, he spoke to the
700 members of the NUCCA Conference in Newcastle, and to 4,000
people in a public meeting the next day. Appearing with Northcote each
time, he preached a characteristically forceful, uncompromising
message. He claimed that it was due to the support of Parnell and the
Irish vote in mainland constituencies that Gladstone was Prime
Minister, citing the case of the pro-Home Rule Liberal minister Lord
Ramsay, who sat for Liverpool in the Commons. Salisbury claimed
their idea was to reduce landowners to mere 'mortgagees and debenture-
holders'. Forster's Coercion Act, he said, had only locked up
'second-rate personages', and nothing like enough of them.

'The Liberal conscience is a wonderfully constituted mechanism,' Salisbury said of Gladstone's 1870 Land Act.

> However carefully it is cleared – and it was thoroughly cleared eleven years ago – if it happens to be driven into the damp shades of Opposition a film creeps over its spotless surface, and it has to be cleared again. The Liberal conscience differs from our conscience, in that most people are taught to clear their conscience by themselves making sacrifices. The Liberal's conscience is always cleared by cutting off a bit of the landlord's property and giving it to the occupier.

If Britain could not rule Ireland, he argued, 'what right have we to go lecturing the Sultan as to the state of things in Armenia or in Macedonia?' In Afghanistan, where the late Government's policy had got the Russians 'hunted out of the country', the new Government was 'abandoning bulwarks and neglecting precautions'.

In the Transvaal, he said, 'to put it in a terse Oriental phrase, they have eaten dirt in vain'. A favourite theme, and a blatant appeal to the Whigs, was how unlike the Liberal Party of the Midlothian campaign was from that of Palmerston and Grey. Another was how the Government fomented discontent in the Empire and between different classes in the country, until 'so highly artificial and multifarious an empire as ours' must split up, or be strained until it was 'a mere bundle of conflicting classes and nationalities, bound together only by the slender tie of a decaying tradition'. Salisbury's speech was cheered longer than Northcote's, and it hit home amongst Liberals too. Gladstone called it 'the worst speech he had ever known delivered by the leader of a party', and in Glasgow Harcourt denounced it for language which 'the better sort of pagans would be ashamed of.... Lord Salisbury's doctrine is that the honour of a nation consists in the vengeance which it exacts.'[21] To encourage supporters and anger opponents was his old *Saturday Review* formula, and Salisbury returned to Puys content.

SIXTEEN

Reaching the Nadir

Ireland – Egypt – 'Disintegration'
– The Primrose League

October 1881 to October 1883

'It will be very interesting to be the "last of the Conservatives."'

The arrest of Parnell on 13th October 1881 for incitement to intimidation under the Suspects Act, and his subsequent imprisonment in Dublin's Kilmainham Gaol, shocked Salisbury. 'If I were Parnell I would never forgive it,' he told his family. Midnight raids, arson, punishment beatings, mutilation of livestock, boycotting and intimidation had led the Government to intern 1,300 people, using soldiers as well as police. Salisbury took the opportunity of Parliament opening on 7th February 1882 to say that 'without trial or proof of guilt' one could not hold the men 'simply on the authority of a minister', and that the conciliatory policy of the Land Act had now been proved to have failed.

The Times often printed brief replies from Party leaders to loyal addresses from local associations. Usually these were anodyne thanks for support, but by mid-March Gladstone's private secretary Edward Hamilton was complaining how Salisbury 'has been letting out most frantically in short epistolatory ejaculations, attributing directly to Mr Gladstone all sorts of sinister motives'. One such, appearing in the paper on 23rd March under Salisbury's name, answered the Honorary Secretary of the Camberwell, Peckham and Dulwich Conservative Club on the issue of clôture: 'The efforts of the Government to repress discussion in the House of Commons and inquiry in the House of Lords are portions of the same dictatorial policy that has introduced the machinery of the Caucus into our elections. They should awake the solicitude of all who value the ancient freedom of our institutions.' When later that day Granville rebuked Salisbury for this hyperbole in the Lords, Hamilton saw Salisbury wince. After the debate he crossed the floor of the House privately to assure Granville that the composition had been that of his secretary, 'an inexperienced youth'. Hamilton laconically noted that Manners was thirty years old.[1]

Salisbury's policy of outbidding Northcote, who was twelve years his senior and often ill, continued in the speeches both men made over three days in Liverpool in mid-April 1882. In the first, laying the corner-stone of the new Conservative Club in Dale Street, Salisbury declared that Gladstone had inaugurated 'a new theory of property' with his 1870 Land Act, and asked: 'Why is it that even this tremendous bribe has failed of its effect? Simply because they have been taught by the past conduct of their ministers and by the past history of their country to expect something more.' He likened it to 'the teaching of Robin Hood', because 'Radicalism feeds upon the discontent of classes'. Northcote invoked Disraeli's name, reminding everyone that he had been the great man's closest lieutenant, and spoke of his memories of serving in Derby's 1859 Government, which of course had not included the then renegade Salisbury. He then gave a large number of economic statistics and sat down without having produced a single stirring, thought-provoking sentence. Historians are divided as to whether Northcote was nicknamed 'the Old Goat' for his thick, yellowish-brown beard or for what has been called his 'mild cud-chewing disposition'.

The next day, Salisbury spoke to 5,000 people at the fourteenth annual meeting of the Liverpool Working Men's Association. When he quoted Gladstone as likening the Irish tenants to 'slaves', someone shouted out 'His father!', a reference to John Gladstone MP, a Liverpudlian merchant part of whose fortune had been made from the slave trade. Salisbury immediately responded by pointing out that at least Gladstone's father had enjoyed generous compensation from Parliament when the slave trade was abolished. What would Gladstone's father have thought, he asked the crowd, had the level of compensation been set by 'some frantic abolitionist, or actually some slave himself', claiming the Irish land courts were run by biased, anti-landlord sub-Commissioners. 'Of course there must be change,' he conceded:

> Nothing is stable, nothing is permanent in this world. Changes are going on about us and changes will work themselves into our national life, but let them be changes worked by the slow process of persuasion, by the natural growth of our institutions ... this practice of setting class against class is new within the memory of the present generation.

Edward Hamilton denied that this was the case, saying that Salisbury had conveniently forgotten the agitations against tithes of half a century earlier. Like most political speakers, Salisbury employed exaggeration, cursory quotation and an occasional blind eye to inconvenient facts, but he did it with a sledgehammer technique which appealed to the large, often working-class audiences he addressed. His quick wit and sardonic humour always made him ready to take on hecklers from the crowd, who rarely worsted him. His passionate belief in the Constitution, national institutions, the rights of property and the greatness of Britain was transparently sincere. His belief in the class system was also absolute, writing to Richmond, who had twice been President of the Royal Agricultural Society and was the primary spokesman for the farming interest in the Cabinet: 'I hope we shan't sweep away the gradation of tenantry – and leave nothing but big capitalist farmers with big hedgeless farms, who go in for radical politics because their wives are not admitted to county society.'[2]

The sudden release of Parnell on 2nd May 1882, in return for a promise to use his influence to end the land war, shocked Salisbury even more than the arrest had done. Salisbury called a meeting of the ex-Cabinet to discuss the 'astonishing circumstances' before the Party met at the Carlton Club on 5th May. They suspected that Gladstone had also offered a substantial measure to help Irish tenants with arrears of rent, to be paid for out of the British Exchequer. W.E. Forster, the Chief Secretary, and Earl Cowper, the Irish Viceroy, both resigned over what was soon nicknamed the 'Kilmainham Treaty'. The very day after the Conservative Party had expressed its outrage at the deal, yet worse news hit London.

On 6th May, Lord Frederick Cavendish, who had earlier that day been sworn in as the new Chief Secretary for Ireland, and the veteran Under-Secretary for Ireland, Thomas Henry Burke, were set upon in Phoenix Park by four assassins belonging to a terrorist organisation known as the 'Invincibles' and stabbed to death with surgical knives in broad daylight. Cavendish, the son of the Duke of Devonshire and younger brother of Lord Hartington, left a widow, Lucy, who was Gladstone's niece. 'Uncle William, you must never blame yourself for sending him,' Lucy said as he was about to leave after his consolation visit. 'Oh no,' the Prime Minister replied, 'there can be no question of that.' Someone else present at the time records his words as: 'I don't regret sending him. I was right to do it.'[3]

(Salisbury could be equally insensitive. When Frank Balfour, a Cambridge professor and Blanche's third son, died in an Alpine mountaineering accident aged thirty in July 1882, his sister-in-law, Lady Frances Balfour, mused about what a loss it was to Science. Salisbury's reply, which Frances thought 'almost scornfully expressed', was: 'Science, like any other truth, never suffers from the loss of any individual.' Equally harsh was his estimation of vagrants, whom the same month in the House of Lords he described as 'perfect pests.... Formerly the great mainstay of the British Constitution with regard to the vagrant was washing him. It used to be thought that if they washed him frequently, and made the water cold enough, they would drive him away; but that resource has failed, and the vagrant went to his bath with the utmost courage.')

Attacking Gladstone's Irish policy in public meetings over the ten days following Cavendish's assassination was liable to offend sentiments and backfire, and in any case Salisbury told his family he could not do it. But in answer to the resolution of the Cheltenham Conservatives which ascribed the killings to 'the feebleness of the Government', Salisbury did let the following letter appear in *The Times* of 17th May: 'The resolutions appear to me to be thoroughly right, not only in the horror they express at the crimes committed in Dublin, but also in the close connexion they trace between those crimes and the policy which has caused them.' This was as good as blaming Gladstone personally for his nephew-in-law's death. On 5th June in the House of Lords, Salisbury pointed out the essential contradiction inherent in the Kilmainham Treaty. If Parnell controlled the criminal activities that were taking place, he should be in gaol; if he did not, he should not be, but there was no point doing deals with him either, let alone by relieving tenants in arrears of rent. 'Where there is a suspicion or a strong belief that your conciliatory measures have been extorted from you by the violence which they are meant to put a stop to, all the value...is taken away.'

It was a violence that endangered Salisbury personally. When the Chief Constable of Hertfordshire received a letter in early August threatening to kill Salisbury and W.H. Smith the following Monday, Salisbury sent it to his colleague with the rejoinder: 'My dear Smith, the enclosed might interest you. I am afraid I am, in point of superficies, the biggest mark of the two. Sincerely, Salisbury.'4

September 1881 saw the system of Anglo-French dual control in Egypt placed in jeopardy when a Muslim uprising under the nationalist Colonel Arabi Pasha seized power from Khedive Tewfik. Arabi refused to collect taxes and therefore pay interest to the bondholders. A joint note from Britain and France, inspired by Léon Gambetta's incoming French Cabinet, was published in early January to support the Khedive against Arabi, but, true to Third Republic form, Gambetta fell on 27th January. Three weeks later, Tewfik was forced to appoint a nationalist ministry.

Gladstone dithered, hoping first that Turkey would take action, then that he could obtain 'the authority of Europe' before intervening. According to Lord Sherbrooke, Gladstone wanted Parliament to give Ireland its undivided attention and thus underplayed the importance of the Suez Canal, even remarking that 'it seems to be forgotten by many that there is a route to India round the Cape of Good Hope'. To the fury of the First Lord of the Admiralty, Northbrook, and the India Secretary, Hartington, Gladstone made every effort to avoid taking any firm action against Arabi. 'Egypt for the Egyptians', he said, was 'the only good solution of the Egyptian question'.

On 11th June 1882, 200 Europeans, including four Britons, were killed in Arabi-inspired riots in Alexandria. It took another month, and the threatened resignations of Northbrook and Hartington, before Gladstone permitted the bombardment of Alexandria in retaliation. Salisbury discounted the tales of Gladstone threatening to resign, telling Janetta Manners on 14th July that it was too early to look at assigning Cabinet places after a dissolution. 'Cutting up the bearskin is an agreeable occupation for optimistic and "narcissian" minds, but the bear is lively yet.' It was with relish that Salisbury pondered the 'curious destiny for John Bright – to be a member of the first ministry that – in the old world – has ever bombarded a commercial port', but in fact Bright resigned the following day.[5] The value of Egyptian bonds jumped 32 per cent on the news that Britain was to undertake a full-scale invasion of Egypt. The French declined to take part.

When on 13th September Sir Garnet Wolseley destroyed Arabi Pasha's army in a brilliant night action at Tel-el-Kebir, killing 2,000 nationalists for the loss of fifty-four men, the Conservatives had to formulate their response to what was already a very popular operation. Writing to Northcote, Salisbury suggested that they give full credit to the Government for the campaign, concentrating on Northbrook and the War Secretary Hugh Childers rather than on Gladstone, whilst arguing that it would all have been unnecessary had they followed the 1879 policy of toughness and swift action. Salisbury had deposed Khedive Ismail eleven days after his defiant proclamation, whereas Gladstone had allowed Arabi to sow sedition and riot for fifteen months before intervening. At a speech at Hatfield in early August, Salisbury contrasted Gladstone's Midlothian Campaign pacifism with the bombardment of Alexandria, and argued that the riots and retaliations that had taken place afterwards would have been unnecessary had Gladstone pursued a tough policy from the start. Overall, however, he had privately to admit that Gladstone had achieved a success that was to help him in the crisis over the coming Irish Arrears Bill.

When Arabi was captured by British troops in mid-October, Salisbury was insistent that he 'should not be condemned unless he is found guilty by English methods and according to English notions'. Handing him over to Tewfik's doubtful mercy was deemed unacceptable, and in the end he was banished to Ceylon and eventually pardoned by Salisbury in 1901. 'You have not held up the Khedive; you have picked up the Khedive,' he told the House of Lords. 'He must be sustained by that which is the only thing left upright in that land – namely, the power of Great Britain.'[6] A far greater *pied à terre* even than Cyprus, Egypt was increasingly to be seen by Salisbury as the future fulcrum of his Near Eastern policy, and the Suez Canal as Britain's principal route to India.

~

The debacle over the Arrears Bill in August 1882 proved a watershed for Salisbury, setting back his leadership hopes and dealing a devastating blow to his strategy of permanent, uncompromising opposition to Gladstonian Liberalism. Salisbury assumed the Bill's proposals – that the State should share the loss of rent with the landlord where genuine poverty could be shown by tenants in arrears – were inimical to the laws of contract, rights of property and economical tendencies of the House of Commons, and that therefore the Conservatives should oppose it outright. The suspicion that it had been part of Gladstone's secret Kilmainham Treaty with Parnell, which less than a week later had been followed by the assassination of Cavendish, only confirmed him in this opinion.

Salisbury did not visit Ireland until 1893. 'Moreover there is the four hour sea passage,' he told Northcote when turning down an invitation to go there in September 1882. Because agrarian outrages were growing in number and seriousness, Salisbury assumed that the Conservative Party would follow him willingly in making Ireland an election issue. But, far from being in a robust mood to defend great principles and interests, most Conservatives in the House of Commons were loath to undergo the expense, effort and risk of fighting a general election over the Lords' rejection of the Arrears Bill. Neither were the Conservative peers, most of whom did not own Irish land, as stalwart as Salisbury hoped them to be, especially once Richmond and Cairns, both still somewhat resentful at being passed over for leader, came out in favour of compromise.

Even Irish landowners such as the Marquess of Waterford, who was one of the thirty-four Britons in 1881 who owned more than one hundred thousand acres, were lukewarm about provoking civil war on their estates. Some others were frankly delighted at the idea of the British Exchequer helping to subsidise their tenantry's rent arrears. With the Queen and Northcote all for compromise as well, Salisbury made a serious error of judgment when he advocated all-out resistance to Gladstone's measure. 'On what principle of justice', he asked the South Essex Conservative Registration Association in Stratford Town Hall on 24th May 1882, 'is the money of the people of Essex to be taken to pay the debts of the Irish tenant-farmer, while the tenant-farmer of Essex has been left to face ruin as best he may?'[7] Salisbury's miscalculation was made because at the start of the controversy all the running was made by Tory die-hard opponents of the Bill. Unfortunately, he mistook verbal opposition at the opening stages of a long struggle for hard commitments of support once the Government had retaliated with threats of dissolution.

At a Shadow Cabinet meeting held at Arlington Street on 19th July, it was agreed to recommend to the Party, which was due to meet two days later, that the Bill should be read a second time in the Lords. In committee, however, two of Salisbury's amendments would be inserted into the Bill which Cranbrook believed 'could hardly fail to wreck it'. The first would make the landlord's consent necessary for the Bill's provisions to be triggered. The second would take into account the value of the tenant right itself as an asset when assessing the tenant's state of destitution. Both of these 'stiff amendments', as Salisbury described them to an absent Cairns, were approved on the understanding that many Conservative peers probably wished to go still further and throw out the Bill altogether on the second reading. Also present at the meeting were Edward Gibson, for his expertise in Irish law, Rowland Winn, the Conservative Chief Whip in the Commons, and the Duke of Abercorn, the spokesman of the Irish landowning peers. At that first steering meeting Winn, Northcote, Cross, Smith and Salisbury all expressed 'the opinion clearly' that a dissolution over Arrears would be 'a good thing'.

Two days later, just as the Bill passed its third reading in the Commons, ninety-nine Conservative peers met in Salisbury's ballroom at Arlington Street in a 'very warlike mood'. With only Lords Leitrim, Beauchamp and Hereford expressing dissent, they showed their willingness to reject the Bill on its second reading, but were persuaded to consent to Salisbury's proposal to pass the two amendments and stick to them come what may. Salisbury took the opportunity of 'pledging myself that, if they forbore to oppose the second reading and carried the amendments, I would, in any event, vote for them to the end'.

Sure enough, on 31st July, Salisbury's two amendments were carried in the Lords, and sent back to the Commons for their consideration. Gladstone made it clear that he would dissolve Parliament and fight a general election on the issue sooner than accept the first amendment, although he offered a compromise formula for the second. This move split the Conservative Party. Most of the MPs in the Commons agreed with Lord George Hamilton, Abercorn's son, who told Salisbury that they did not want a general election only two years into the ministry, and with Gorst, who estimated that they would fare no better at the polls than they had in 1880. When the Lords' amendments were rejected by the Commons on 8th August and another vote was fixed for the 10th, Salisbury found his support ebbing away fast.

The bombardment of Alexandria looked robust and had been immensely popular with the public, as was the passing of a tough new Peace Preservation Act for Ireland. As well as the obvious risk of losing their seats, elections were very expensive for MPs and their patrons. The Queen communicated to Abercorn her hope that the peers would now pass the Bill unamended. With another bad harvest in prospect and a total of 79,455 'fair rent' applications pending under the 1881 Land Act, and with agreements for fixed rents running at 11,364, Cairns and Richmond began to consider leaving Salisbury high and dry. On 6th August, Cairns had made it clear, to Cranbrook's surprise, that he was not prepared to support Salisbury. The day before the vote, Northcote himself complained to Cranbrook of Salisbury's 'personal sense of what is due to his party and to himself' and predicted that the next day the Party would be 'leaving him, like Uriah, in the front of the battle'.

Salisbury himself dismissed the Government's threat of resignation as 'a rhetorical trope'. Answering Lord George Hamilton, he pointed out how categorical had been the assurances he had given the peers at the meeting on 21st July: 'They say a Council of War never fights. This Council at all events was an exception.' He further argued that the next Reform Bill, which they feared would equalise the county with the borough franchise won in 1867, would be better altered by a Conservative Party which had been tough over Arrears than one that had shown itself to be weak. He also raised the spectre that

with his present majority which on such a question will be intact, [Gladstone] can easily so manipulate these arrangements as to efface our party for a generation: and the House of Lords will have to submit to that result, or to appeal to the country on the Reform Bill – a very dangerous cry for such an operation. If a dissolution happens now, he must lose considerably – and we shall be in a position to make our influence really felt in the discussions on the Reform Bill.

Salisbury acknowledged that he might not be able to muster his men, but if that were the case, 'it will be entirely their responsibility after the full assent they gave to my programme at the party meeting'. To Cairns, who announced his intention to go to Scotland to avoid the meeting on the 10th, he icily replied that had he known earlier of his views, he would have simply opposed the second reading altogether: 'it will be a warning to me in future.' That was true of the whole disastrous episode. At the meeting of Tory peers in the ballroom at Arlington Street on Tuesday, 10th August 1882, Salisbury opened with a short speech putting the case for standing by his amendments. 'Then the Irishmen got up one after the other and advised surrender,' he wrote to his wife about the speeches of Abercorn, Waterford and Longford, 'some qualifying it by saying that, if I insisted, they would vote against me'. Richmond then put the case for concession. Carnarvon and Cranbrook said they would vote with Salisbury, but thought it better to capitulate to the majority rather than risk splitting the Party, as the Bill was now certain to pass. Salisbury insisted on a division there and then, however, and roughly twenty peers walked with him to one side of the room, the remaining sixty or so staying put. 'This is a tremendous smash,' he candidly admitted. He was nonetheless not willing to compromise. 'I will not eat dirt,' he told Cranbrook.

'The Irish landowners'...notion of self defence', he fumed to Northcote later that day, 'is that you should fight for them under the condition of not causing them the slightest agitation of mind by your blows.' Instead of proposing any compromise, or attempting to gain any concession, Salisbury simply walked down to the House of Lords and denounced the measure, winding up by saying:

> I intend to incur no responsibility in respect of one jot or tittle of this Bill....I believe it to be a most pernicious Bill; that it is an act of simple robbery; and that it will bear the gravest fruits as a legislative precedent for the future. Those are my opinions. I have had the opportunity this morning of conferring with the noble Lords who form a majority of your Lordships' House, by whom the amendment was carried...and I find that the overwhelming majority of their Lordships were of opinion that in the present state of affairs...it is not expedient that the Arrears Bill should be thrown out. If I had the power I would have thrown out the Bill. I find myself, however, in a small minority, and, therefore, I shall not divide the House.[8]

Punch reported how, during the debate, Salisbury was 'all the time sitting with his head well up, staring solidly at the roof', an attitude which prompted one spectator, the Liberal MP for Walsall Sir Charles Forster, to remark that Salisbury reminded him of the wise man in scripture who had dug a pit for his enemy and then fallen into it himself. Instead of a division a voice vote was taken, with Salisbury, Cranbrook, Carnarvon, but precious few others, calling out 'Not content'. One Tory peer later remarked that the majority of peers who had so embarrassed Salisbury looked and felt 'like a pack of whipped hounds'. As Lord Sandhurst wrote to the new Irish Viceroy, Earl Spencer: 'What a snub for him!! Then he came down to the House and delivered a speech I have never heard surpassed for venom and bitterness. He appeared very angry indeed.'

Watching closely, Cranbrook 'felt much for Salisbury as I saw that the iron entered his soul and no doubt he was badly used by being pressed unanimously to one course and almost as unanimously deserted when the time of trial came'. In writing to explain his stance to the Queen, who thoroughly disapproved of it, Salisbury emphasised the Reform angle, hoping to make her flesh creep at the idea of a perpetual Gladstone premiership, and arguing that a dissolution before a Third Reform Bill would have been preferable for the Conservatives to one 'after the passage of a Reform Bill framed so as to <u>secure</u> the mass of electoral power to the [Liberal] Party'.

A week after the debate, amid press comments that he had shown as much rashness in the Lords as Northcote had shown statesmanlike sagacity in the Commons, Salisbury left for Dieppe and two weeks of recuperation and wound-licking. Made to look reactionary and isolated in the most public way possible, Salisbury had reached the nadir of his leadership of the Tories in the Lords, indeed of his whole post-1867 career. 'Like the feather-end of the weather vane,' he had written of John Roebuck MP in September 1862, 'he always points to the quarter from which the wind is not blowing.'[9] Two decades later, Salisbury seemed to be emulating him. Pessimism descended; on 10th December, a bad by-election result had him writing to Janetta Manners: 'It will be very interesting to be the "last of the Conservatives". I foresee that will be our fate.'

In January 1883, Salisbury asked Henry Manners to send him the statistics for Irish outrages for the last three years, as 'my own impression is that the calm is chiefly due to the coercive – and not to the "remedial" measures', meaning the Crimes Act rather than the Arrears and Land Acts. At 9.01 p.m. on 15th March, a terrific Fenian explosion at the ground-floor offices of the Local Government Board in Parliament Street, so forceful it shook the floor and galleries of the Commons chamber, allowed him to view an outrage at first hand. He went with Cranbrook the next morning to see the 'signs of the frightful power employed', and it reinforced his belief in coercive rather than remedial measures for Ireland.

At a speech in Birmingham on 28th March, Salisbury likened the struggle in the Liberal Party between the Whig Lord Hartington, the new War Secretary, and the Radical Joseph Chamberlain, the President of the Board of Trade, as 'a perpetual zigzag...rather like one of those Dutch clocks which we used to see in our infancy, where there was an old woman who came out of one door, and an old man who came out of another'.[10] Chamberlain had been Mayor of Birmingham between 1873 and 1876 and was that city's acknowledged political master. The well-drilled 'caucus' he set up there regularly won the vast majority, and sometimes all, of the city's dozen parliamentary seats. His slightly sing-song voice was the one that called the political shots in Birmingham, and for Salisbury to go there to denounce the caucus, and in particular the way it was intended 'to make the House of Commons itself the pliant tool of a tyrannist organisation', was to invite retaliation.[11]

The Liberal politician Herbert Asquith once said that Chamberlain had 'the manners of a cad and the tongue of a bargee', and two days after the Birmingham speech Chamberlain described Salisbury as:

> The spokesman of a class – of a class to which he himself belongs – who toil not neither do they spin, whose fortunes, as in his case, have originated by grants made in times gone by for services which courtiers rendered kings – and have since grown and increased while their owners slept, by the levy of an increased share on all that other men have done by toil and labour to add to the general wealth and prosperity of the country of which they form a part.

Salisbury called this attack 'the Jacobin theory pure and simple', but forbore to point out that Chamberlain himself owned equities which certainly also produced unearned income. His only public response was made to the banquet of the Kingston and District Working Men's Conservative Association when he said, to loud cheers: 'I believe that I am not myself to be entirely excluded from the category of working men.' Lady Rayleigh noted in her diary that Chamberlain's speech had been 'somewhat off the mark as Lord Salisbury has almost a diseased appetite for work, and is certainly not arrayed like the lilies of the field'. Randolph Churchill agreed, and told a meeting at Blackpool that 'as a matter of fact, Lord Salisbury from his earliest days has toiled and spun in the service of the state and for the advancement of his countrymen in learning, in wealth and in prosperity'. The Queen was furious with Chamberlain's jibe, believing that both he and Sir Charles Dilke, the President of the Local Government Board, were republicans.

Far from being pleased by Churchill's support that month, however, Salisbury was deeply embarrassed by it. Although he could sometimes be privately slighting about Stafford Northcote, telling Janetta Manners that 'the advice he actually follows is that which he gets from his next neighbours at the moment of decision', Salisbury could not approve of public attacks on him. Yet on 29th March a letter appeared in *The Times* from 'A Tory' which complained about how Northcote, not Salisbury, had been invited to unveil a new statue of Beaconsfield, and that there was a plot afoot amongst Northcote's adherents to grab him the Party leadership.

Commenting on the letter in its leader column, *The Times* concluded: 'There are two parties in the Conservative ranks, whose relations to one another singularly resemble those alleged by Lord

Salisbury to subsist between Whigs and Radicals.' Churchill's second letter to *The Times*, this time sent under his own name and appearing on 2nd April, was even more blunt. It blamed Northcote, though not quite by name, for 'neglected opportunities, pusillanimity, combativeness at wrong moments, vacillation, dread of responsibility, repression, and discouragement of hard-working followers, jealousies, commonplaces and want of perception'. Nor did he stop there: 'All the malignant efforts of envious mediocrity' were directed against Salisbury, Churchill alleged, who was the only man capable of replacing Gladstone. This monumental lack of subtlety immediately backfired, and even Winston Churchill in his most filial biography had to admit that, in the Commons that day, his father sat 'alone and abandoned, hunched up in his corner seat' while Northcote received a 'tremendous ovation'.

After Northcote unveiled the statue in Westminster Abbey Green (now Parliament Square) on 19th April, the anniversary of Beaconsfield's death to be known as 'Primrose Day', Churchill wrote an article in the May issue of the *Fortnightly Review*. Entitled 'Elijah's Mantle', it argued that the Conservatives needed a leader who 'by all the varied influences of an ancient name can move the hearts of households...a statesman who fears not to meet, and knows how to sway, immense masses of the working classes'.[12] It was widely suspected that in the author's own mind that 'ancient name' was probably Spencer-Churchill rather than Cecil, but all Churchill managed to do was embarrass Salisbury, and lose Gorst and Balfour from the Fourth Party in the process.

By August 1883, Gladstone was nicknaming Salisbury 'Prince Rupert', for the way he misled his Party, always at the charge. 'Despite his intellect', he told Edward Hamilton, 'he is absolutely devoid of any political nous.' He was not alone in thinking it, and in the same month Drummond Wolff was writing to Churchill to say that Salisbury was 'a broken reed', only to be tolerated because the alternative Conservative leader in the Lords, Richmond, was 'too goaty and afraid'. Little had gone right for Salisbury since the Arrears Bill, and at a meeting of the County Down Association held in Belfast on 3rd October, Abercorn actually introduced Northcote by saying that 'when an election came around they would see their distinguished guest in his right place as head of the Government'.

Later that month, a small group of senior Tories met at the Marquess of Abergavenny's country seat, Eridge Castle in Kent, to confer on 'the future', by which the Marquess meant Salisbury's future. His three sessions as Leader in a chamber dominated by the Conservatives had seen three failed attempts to take on the Liberal majority in the House of Commons with Gladstone's Irish Land Act passing in 1881, the Arrears Act in 1882 and, thanks to Richmond's support for the measure, the Agricultural Holdings Act in 1883. Cairns called for 'a more consistent plan of action than Salisbury has hitherto pursued' and accused him of 'swagger'. Cranbrook supported Salisbury at the meeting, but Abergavenny stayed neutral. However brave a face he put on it, Salisbury's leadership was clearly on probation. When he complained late in the session of 'this parliamentary goose-step' which the Liberal legislative programme had occasioned, it was almost a confession of failure in holding up any but the most insignificant measures.[13] Furthermore, men like Cairns and Richmond, who had let him down, were now busy blaming him.

Had Salisbury's detractors at Eridge Castle needed to remind themselves of his intellectual calibre, they need only have read the current edition of the *Quarterly Review* which appeared in mid-October 1883. More than any other article he wrote, 'Disintegration' provided Salisbury's political credo. It was also to be the last of his *Quarterly Review* articles, because, to his anger, his name leaked out as the author. Other than for the *National Review*, a Tory quarterly which he was instrumental in setting up in 1883, he wrote no more articles, but 'Disintegration' was a splendid swan-song. 'Like Achilles emerging from his tent,' *The Times* commented, 'he is evidently determined his followers as well as his adversaries shall be reminded, by contrast, of his prolonged absence from the field.' A *tour d'horizon* whose themes encompassed Ireland, class antagonism, the Empire, collectivism, the atomisation of society and how to deal with the coming age of democracy, it pointed out in forty pages the dangers facing the constitutional status quo. Of change he admitted that 'it is as useless to repine at this process, as to repine because we are growing older', but instead he made a passionately forthright attempt to summon forth forces that might yet save those things about Britain which he believed were worth saving.

'Things that have been secure for centuries are secure no longer,' he warned, but implacable opposition to all social and political change was no answer for Tories. 'In the first place the enterprise is impossible. In the next place there is much in our present mode of thought and action which it is highly undesirable to conserve.' What was needed was 'that spirit of the old constitution' which had the power to hold the nation together, 'instead of splitting it into a bundle of unfriendly and distrustful fragments'. Looking far into the future, Salisbury believed:

> The dangers we have to fear may roughly be summed up in the single word
> – disintegration. It is the end to which we are being driven, alike by the
> defective working of our political machinery, and by the public temper of

the time. It menaces us in the most subtle and in the most glaring forms – in the loss of large branches and limbs of our Empire, and in the slow estrangement of the classes which make up the nation to whom the Empire belongs.

The House of Commons, far from being able to arbitrate judiciously between the competing interests of the State, was becoming 'an assembly which is itself the very field of battle on which the contending classes fight out their feuds', a process which he likened to 'civil war with gloves on'. Even worse, some politicians twisted in the prevailing winds:

> The idea that the convictions of politicians are never stable, that under adequate pressure every resistance will give way, every political profession will be obsequiously recast, is fatal to the existence of either confidence or respect. Neither trust nor fear will, in the long run, be inspired by a school of statesman who, whatever else they may sacrifice, never sacrifice themselves.

Many historians have since seen the 1880s as the time when British commercial supremacy was first effectively challenged by the American and German protected economies. For a contemporary accurately to spot these dangers was remarkable. Egalitarianism and envy politics, deepening class consciousness and antagonisms, the radicalisation and syndicalisation of the British Left, Salisbury identified and analysed them all. He was writing only seven months after a three-inch obituary, tucked away at the bottom of the last column of page thirteen of *The Times*, had recorded the death of a German philosopher and journalist whose 'chief work was *Le Capital*, an attack on the whole capitalist system'.

On the Irish question, 'Disintegration' was absolutely adamant about the Union, and it is worth quoting him at length to refute those who claim that only two years later Salisbury was willing to flirt with Home Rule:

> One issue there is which...is absolutely closed. The highest interests of the Empire, as well as the most sacred obligations of honour, forbid us to solve this question by conceding any species of independence to Ireland; or in other words, any licence to the majority in that country to govern the rest of Irishmen as they please. To the minority, to those who have trusted us, and on the faith of our protection have done our work, it could be a sentence of exile or ruin. All that is Protestant – nay, all that is loyal – all who have land or money to lose, all by whose enterprise and capital industry and commerce are still maintained, would be at the mercy of the adventurers who have led the Land League, if not of the darker counsels by

whom the Invincibles have been inspired.... It would be an act of political bankruptcy, an avowal that we are unable to satisfy even the most sacred obligations, and that all our claims to protect or govern anyone beyond our own narrow island were at an end.[14]

The most cogent critique of 'Disintegration' came from T.H.S. Escott in the *Fortnightly Review* in August 1884, who complained that Salisbury was the sort of man who 'rendered the French Revolution possible' and who left 'a certain deposit of bitterness' in public life. 'He is completely detached from the majority of his own party,' he analysed. 'Such a man is out of place in the party struggles of Parliament,' he added, correctly, before entirely spoiling it by saying that Salisbury should retire, predicting that his career 'can yield no harvest of success'. For within a year, Salisbury had embarked upon the longest series of premierships since the Napoleonic Wars.

The secular canonisation of Beaconsfield, whatever Salisbury might privately have thought about it, was clearly something that needed to be harnessed to the Party's advantage. When a Beaconsfield Club was proposed, Salisbury wrote to Northcote: 'I believe there is a great deal of Villa Toryism which requires organisation,' and he proposed that they should both speak in its support. The suburbanisation of London, with ribbon development creating large middle-class communities in its outskirts from the 1870s onwards, provided fertile new ground for Conservative activism, and Salisbury was determined that when they inevitably gained their own parliamentary representation by sheer weight of numbers, these new suburbs should return Conservatives.

One of the primary instruments in winning them over was the Primrose League, an organisation which Salisbury at first thought absurd and unlikely to succeed, but which in fact, with well over a million enrolled members by 1910, was to become the largest voluntary mass movement in British political history. Hatfield had happily complied with the mythification of Beaconsfield as early as the first anniversary of his death. Flowers were customarily brought round to all guests' bedrooms each evening, and on the night of 19th April they were primroses; the dinner table was decorated with them as well. Even Lady Frances Balfour, the Whig Duke of Argyll's daughter, wore one that evening, rationalising it on the basis of 'When in Rome ...'

The Primrose League was founded by Tory Democrats in the card room of the Carlton Club on 17th November 1883, and was intended to embrace everyone 'except Atheists and enemies of the British Empire'. It was set up by the Fourth Party, which thought the Conservative and Constitutional Associations had failed to attract the public. It was not officially affiliated to the Conservative Party until 1914. With Churchill, Gorst and Drummond Wolff as its founders, it inevitably prompted suspicions that it was intended to be a caucus within the National Union. Since the 1883 Corrupt Practices Act, which forbade large-scale spending on elections, both political parties needed armies of unpaid constituency activists who would canvass, register voters, distribute propaganda and get supporters to the polls. Salisbury swiftly recognised how such voluntary effort would be crucial, and when in December 1883 Churchill sent him the Primrose Tory League's constitution, he replied: 'Its objects are most excellent...a great advantage to the party.' On the same day he wrote to Northcote: 'I doubt the Primrose League coming to anything: there is too much unlimited obedience to suit English tastes.'

It was in fact its inclusiveness – accepting women, working people, non-voters, Roman Catholics and occasionally even Liberals – which made the League so popular. Its branches (called 'habitations') organised tea parties, dances, lectures, dinners and excursions. Eight countesses joined in December 1883 alone. For a 'tribute' (subscription) of only threepence a year, anyone could rub shoulders with an aristocracy that in the Victorian age enjoyed all the glamour that movie stars do today. 'Of course it's vulgar,' said Lady Salisbury, 'that's why we are so successful.' At smoking concerts, musical soirées and fêtes, the energy and organisational ability of women was unleashed on to the British political scene. Using slides, posters, exhortation and propaganda, middle-class female platform speakers urged a mainly working- and lower-middle-class audience to vote Conservative, with astonishing success.

Another feature was the colourful titles they gave one another, which Salisbury naturally found ludicrous. Churchill started out as the Ruling Counsellor, and there were different gradations of Knights, Priors, Precepts, Dames, Masters, Chancellors, Grand Chancellors and so on. The habitations themselves drew on a combination of freemasonry, Disraeliana, patriotism and the novels of Sir Walter Scott for names such as 'King Athelstan' (Malmesbury), 'The Coningsby' (Brighton), 'The Pitt' (Hampstead), 'The Loyal' (Burnham-on-Sea) and 'King Arthur's Round Table' (Port Isaac). 'It does seem very hard', Salisbury had written in 1865, 'that if the Hospital for Diseases of the duodenum, or the Society for the conversion of Qushimaboo is in want of funds, they should not be content with having for their chairman anyone but some hard worked Minister, who has other things to do besides spending an evening in the distribution of vigorous compliments. But such is the stern law of modern popularity-hunting.'[15] It was a law to which Salisbury dutifully conformed when in November 1884 he agreed to become a patron of the League, on the condition that the same honour was also offered to Northcote. 'But I suppose we shall have no common-place name,' he teased Drummond Wolff. 'What do you say to Vavasours?' They became Grand Masters, a position Salisbury was to hold for life.

The following month, thanking the League for its electioneering work in Hackney, Salisbury wrote: 'I cannot say that I know exactly very much about the character of the Primrose League. I believe it was set on foot by those who are familiar with the mysteries of another craft to which, unhappily, I do not belong.' The chivalric language and pseudo-masonic ritual, the lantern shows and bazaars, the medals and Knights Harbinger and diplomas and long-service badges, and the oath on enrolment about the 'maintenance of Religion, of the Estates of the Realm and of the Imperial Ascendancy of the British Empire', all nonetheless had a serious purpose, especially once the organisation grew enormously. It provided a mass movement which would canvass the electorate for the Conservative Party in between, as well as simply during, general elections, something that had never really happened before in British politics.

Salisbury entered into the spirit of it once, as Drummond Wolff snidely concluded, 'the League had become a success'. The Cecils became involved; Gwendolen going on to the Divisional Council, Robert becoming a Ruling Counsellor and Hugh a Treasurer. 'You are', Salisbury told a Grand Habitation (i.e. mass rally) in the Albert Hall in 1886, in an attempt to define their relationship with the Conservative Party, 'rather the preaching friars of the message that you have to convey than the regular clergy attached to each particular district.'[16] He sagely forbore to tell them of Gladstone's conviction that Beaconsfield had never even particularly liked primroses, or that in his novel *Lothair*, one of the characters, Lord St Jerome, remarks that 'they say primroses make a capital salad'.

SEVENTEEN

Opposition and Renewal

*Laissez-Faire – Whitehall
– Housing – Tory Democracy
– The Mahdi*

November 1883 to May 1884

'The first of duties is to be pachydermatous.'

Except in one important area, Salisbury's credentials as an economic libertarian were impeccable. 'By a free country,' he told the Kingston and District Working Men's Conservative Association in June 1883, 'I mean a country where people are allowed, so long as they do not hurt their neighbours, to do as they like. I do not mean a country where six men may make five men do exactly as they like.' His attitude towards freedom of contract was fundamentalist: 'When it is a question of what men should commercially gain or lose by a bargain, Parliament had better let grown-up men settle with each other their own bargains,' he pronounced in Edinburgh in November 1882, adding that, although the Whitehall civil servant generally believed 'he himself is the best person to decide', he was often wrong, and over-centralisation of power was inimical to liberty.

'You can no more act against the operation of great economic laws than you can act against the laws of the weather,' was his *laissez-faire* philosophy, believing that 'all Parliament can really do is to free the energies and support the efforts of an intelligent and industrious people'. Such support should not include large-scale social reform unless the need was obvious and overwhelming. Leasehold reform was an abomination to him, for, as he told a correspondent, he could 'see no reason for forcing A to sell his freehold to B simply because B wishes to have it'. He feared that such a principle might set a dangerous precedent. 'He hated all factory acts and Temperance laws,' recalled one of his daughters-in-law, 'believing that no one had a right to prevent anyone else from getting drunk.' He did support laws against child labour, however, on the grounds that abuse had indeed been shown to be happening and children were by definition too young to enter into a meaningful contract with employers.[1]

During the 1860s, Salisbury spoke of how 'that great moral teacher, Mr Punch, some years ago proclaimed a society which he called "The Anti-meddling-in-other-people's-business Society,' which he hoped the Government would join. When Sir Charles Burrell introduced a Bill intended to lessen the number of accidents to servants from falling off windows when cleaning and repairing them, Salisbury asked facetiously: 'Does he propose to repeal the law of gravitation by Act of Parliament?... If, while he is about it, he will insert a clause forbidding the dirt to accumulate on the window-panes, he will be conferring a real service on the metropolis.' Another Bill to provide chairs for shop assistants and housemaids had him asking whether Parliament was 'prepared to have an army of inspectors to examine the house of every householder to see that there are a number of chairs placed at stated intervals, so that at each moment of exhaustion the housemaid may sit down in comfort?' He argued that putting such 'impediments' in the way of retail traders would only diminish the market for women's labour. 'I have a profound distrust of government inspectors,' he told the Rev. Nathaniel Woodard in 1871, 'and am generally disposed to find them wrong.'

These views could be taken to extremes, as when Salisbury opposed an important clause of Lord Rosebery's Bill to protect young women from pimps, or when he described as 'repulsive' the idea 'that the State should undertake the responsibility of seeing that all, or any one, of the classes which form the nation are well educated'.[2] To a correspondent who recommended that pleasure cruising should be regulated by law, Salisbury admitted that lives might be saved, but added: 'It runs counter to the time-honoured right of the Englishman to take any risk he fancies,' which was of greater importance. As a magistrate, he was zealous in protecting the civil rights of suspects when questioned by the police.

When in April 1889 the Under-Secretary at the Foreign Office reported that fraudulent agents were purporting to organise emigration to Argentina, without having any genuine knowledge of the country, Salisbury declared that for the Government to undertake to caution people could be the thin end of the wedge. 'If you warn them against dishonest emigration agents, why not against dishonest promotion of companies – or dishonest vendors of medicine?' he asked, arguing that it was not the duty of the State to teach people the common-sense precaution of making proper inquiries before they parted with money. Writing to the Tory MP Sir Henry Peek about the 1888 Pigeon Bill, Salisbury stated that: 'On general grounds I object to Parliament trying to regulate private morality in matters which only affects the person who commits the offence.' This disbelief in 'victimless crime' was a highly advanced opinion to hold at the time.

Salisbury's support for a minimal State arose partly from his profound suspicion of government's ability to do good. 'As a general rule,' he had written in the *Saturday Review*, 'it is almost as bad to stimulate prosperity as to depress it, by artificial means.' What Balfour called his 'contradictoriness' and love of paradox left him a lifelong believer, as he told the Associated Chambers of Commerce in March 1891, that 'Parliament is a potent engine, and its enactments must always do something, but they very seldom do what the originators of these enactments meant,' and therefore most legislation 'will have the effect of surrounding the industry which it touches with precautions and investigations, inspections and regulations, in which it will be slowly enveloped and stifled'.[3]

As well as an ideological preference for liberty on its own merits, Salisbury was convinced of the inherent incompetence of bureaucracy in general and in particular the way that Whitehall 'will create business for itself as surely as a new railway will create traffic'. One of the reasons he disliked Prussia was for its 'despotism of officials' and he was determined that over-centralisation and a lack of vigilance should not allow the bureaucracy to impose itself on Britons in the same way. His two worst bugbears were the Treasury and the Service departments. The officials of the former he described as 'imbecile punctilios' and complained that the only way of extracting anything from them was to 'cultivate the style of a Vali reporting to the Grand Vizier, or of Archbishop Manning arguing with the Pope'. He particularly hated its cheese-paring nature and 'the damage to England's reputation' which 'this unscrupulous straining after minute economy has caused'. When it came to providing even very small amounts of money for non-essential expenditure, Salisbury told Professor McLeod in 1885 that the Treasury was 'a deity as inexorable as Pluto. They look upon the arts and sciences merely as so many excuses for extravagance.'[4]

Similarly, although Salisbury's strong points were never military or naval strategy, the War Office and Admiralty regularly came in for Salisburian rebuke. Hicks Beach believed that this dislike amounted to 'distrust', because Salisbury constantly suspected that the experts were attempting to entice the politicians into unnecessary conflict and expenditure. Furthermore, as he complained to Baring, 'that mania for paper piling, which is the endemic pest of the British Departments', opened up 'endless temptations to pedantry and circumlocution'. He thought that admirals were particular victims of professional 'hallucination', spotting Admiral 'Jackie' Fisher as one such, and he lampooned the way that the Admiralty would always 'follow the progress of science at a respectful distance, always arriving at an appreciation of each successive invention just soon enought to find that it is obsolete, and never yielding their adhesion to anything new until the time has come to defend it against the claims of something newer'.

Salisbury's patience and persistence helped turn him into an unusually effective, grizzled old inter-departmental warrior, who established a primacy for the Foreign Office in Whitehall which took many decades to unfasten.[5] When, after years of being lobbied, Salisbury finally in 1889 bowed to pressure for a Board of Agriculture to be set up, the minister in charge, Henry Chaplin, was not allowed a financial grant, a parliamentary under-secretary, or even a departmental building, let alone a seat in the Cabinet.

The one great exception to Salisbury's otherwise pure *laissez-faire* principles was in the area of working-class housing. Having emerged from his tent with his 'Disintegration' article in the *Quarterly Review*, Salisbury then wrote a long, signed, detailed and surprising article in the November 1883 issue of the *National Review* entitled 'Labourers' and Artisans' Dwellings'. This advocated limited State intervention in the financing of slum clearance and the building of cheap but decent new working-class accommodation. Because 'the grave injury, both to morality and to health, is more generally recognised' than in earlier times, he argued that 'this misery and degradation, which casts so terrible a shadow over our prosperity' must now be addressed by public action. 'These overcrowded centres of population are also centres of disease,' he warned his readers, 'the successive discoveries of biologists tell us more clearly that there is in this matter an indissoluble partnership among all human beings breathing in the same vicinity.' Victorian London's worst rookeries, such as housed Fagin's lair, were situated cheek-by-jowl with middle-class neighbourhoods, and Salisbury explained that the rich were in danger simply because of their physical proximity with the poor. Salisbury had long been interested in housing reform, having mentioned it as long ago as his first electoral address, as well as in *Saturday Review* articles and speeches.

'*Laissez-faire* is an admirable doctrine,' Salisbury argued, 'but it must be applied on both sides.' Because Parliament had sanctioned new London streets, railways, viaducts, law courts, the Thames Embankment (which he had opposed) and other improvements which were built where poor people once lived, it was also responsible for 'packing the people tighter'. The result was that by 1883:

thousands of families have only a single room to dwell in, where they sleep and eat, multiply, and die.... It is difficult to exaggerate the misery which such conditions of life must cause, or the impulse they must give to vice. The depression of body and mind which they create is an almost insuperable obstacle to the action of any elevating or refining agencies.

Highly sensitive to accusations of promoting socialism, Salisbury cited Peel's irrigation loans to landowners as his precedent. These had been made at an interest rate which repaid the State in full, but which was lower than the landowners could have obtained privately. If a cottage cost £150 to build, at 6 per cent interest the rent would have to be £9 per annum, more than the average labourer could afford, so Salisbury argued that limited State intervention was necessary. The model he took was the clean and comfortable central London tenements run by the Peabody Trust, whose non-profit-making dwellings earned only 3 per cent on capital employed. The Trustees charged lower rents and had the great advantage of not having 'to meet a roomful of sanguine shareholders twice a year'.

'Something has to be done,' wrote Salisbury, to encourage Parliament to authorise loans for similar schemes to house its own employees in the Post Office, police force and Customs and Excise, and set an example to other large-scale employers. Shorn of his usual journalistic fireworks, entirely free of cynicism and mockery, the article was a considered plea for lower rents through large-scale house building, for a suspension of speculative suburban jerry-builders, for factories to provide employees' accommodation, for twenty-year government loans set at low interest rates, and for cheap suburban transport to take commuters to and from work and thus relieve congestion in the inner city. Enlightened quasi-public bodies were to be the agents for this change. It was a heartfelt, intelligent response to one of the most pressing social problems of the day.[6]

Salisbury was simultaneously attacked on all fronts: for hypocrisy because he was himself a landlord, for crypto-socialism by the 10th Earl of Wemyss (the former Lord Elcho) and his Liberty and Property Defence Association, by the left-wing press for not going far enough, for plagiarism by the Fourth Party, for political opportunism by Joseph Chamberlain, and for trying to force 'the urban ratepayers to pay for the squires' privilege of depopulating the agricultural districts' by the *Daily News*. The fact that it easily fitted into Salisbury's long-held view, that working-class interests were better defended by Conservatives gradually reforming proven abuses than by socialists promoting Utopian schemes, was ignored in the stampede to denigrate his contribution to the debate. The *Pall Mall Gazette* said Salisbury had entered 'the turbid waters of State Socialism', the *Manchester Guardian* called his article 'State socialism pure and simple' and even *The Times* announced that

Salisbury was 'in favour of state socialism', all of which represented a total misreading of Salisbury's proposals. Coming as it did a month after the anonymous publication of *The Bitter Cry of Outcast London*, a bestselling attack on overcrowding in which the words 'Incest is common' shocked the Victorian conscience, Salisbury's article engendered huge public controversy.

T.H.S. Escott of the *Fortnightly Review* sent a former war reporter, Archibald Forbes, to Hatfield in the hope of finding Salisbury's own labourers' cottages in bad repair. 'Lord Salisbury keeps a brothel among other sweet things,' Forbes reported back. Escott sensibly engaged another reporter, the notorious libertine Frank Harris, to Hatfield to double-check, presumably on the basis that if Harris couldn't find a brothel in a strange town, nobody could. When he discovered that Forbes had made everything up and that Salisbury was a model landlord at Hatfield, Chamberlain congratulated Escott on his narrow escape from what would have been an extremely expensive libel.[7] In the December issue of the *Fortnightly Review*, Chamberlain wrote a detailed critique of Salisbury's article, saying he 'has not arrived at a clear conception of the duty of the State in this matter', and asking whether he would now support free schools and trade unions as well. Chamberlain knew about public housing from his time as Mayor of Birmingham, and when he said that Cross's 1875 Artisans' Dwellings Act had only timidly been put into effect he was right, but that was more a criticism of Cross and Beaconsfield than of Salisbury, who was at the India Office at the time.

Salisbury turned down the offer to reply to Chamberlain, saying that he wanted to keep the issue 'away from the field of party or class controversy', not because he was not usually more than happy to engage in both but he believed it more likely to secure legislation if the issue was perceived to be cross-Party. After another speech of Chamberlain's against the great landowners in November 1883, Salisbury asked Manners: 'Is it not time we went at the great screw-owners? I think they ought to get to work at Central Office to find out how the Chamberlain firm lodge their "hands" and how they treat them.' Nothing came of it, but it showed how personal the Salisbury–Chamberlain duel had become.

In the Lords debate on housing on 22nd February 1884, Salisbury tried to separate the sanitary from the overcrowding elements of the question, making it clear that he would find sanitary legislation alone not enough. He put in a word for the ground landlord, who, he said, 'like everyone else, has to sell the goods he possesses in the open market for the price he can obtain for them, and it is ridiculous to blame him for obtaining the best price he can'. He was keen to 'at once say that I do not favour any wild schemes of State interference', but was also ready to slap down Wemyss's dogmatic opposition to all action, saying that 'he must bear in mind there are no absolute truths or principles in politics.... If there be a material evil, disease will follow, and the contagion of that disease will not be confined to those amongst whom it arises, but will spread over the rest of the community. And what is true of material evil is true of moral evil too.'[8]

If the Government had not themselves proposed a Royal Commission on the Housing of the Working Classes, Salisbury and Cranbrook agreed that they would do so, but on 4th March 1884 one was set one up under the efficient chairmanship of Sir Charles Dilke, with an unusually powerful and impressive membership. The Prince of Wales sat on it, attending nineteen of the fifty-one meetings, signing the Report at the end. Cardinal Manning, the Liberal trade unionist Henry Broadhurst MP, George Goschen, Jesse Collings, the Bishop of Bedford, Richard Cross and Salisbury himself were also members, along with three builders, a rural property-owner, a Local Government Board official and half-a-dozen others. Dilke was proud of the way it had 'fewer fools on it than is usual on Royal Commissions'. There were also fewer Tories; Salisbury only counted three out of twenty, but he considered the issue too important to boycott the Commission out of political bias.

Salisbury had been cynical about Royal Commissions in the past, telling Henry Acland in 1868: 'They are useful to a weak Government, because they postpone questions, and because they enable a Government in that way to silence or at least to pledge, and so to disarm, some of its opponents. But all the information they collect can be procured far more rapidly by the Home Office.' This one, he felt, was different. The Commission met twice a week in the spring and summer of 1884; it heard witnesses, asked 18,000 questions, visited the worst areas and interviewed doctors, policemen, Poor Law Board officials, school visitors, clergymen, government officials and vestry sanitary committee chairmen.

The Report, published in 1885, was an amalgam of Salisbury's programme of national subsidies and loans and the more collectivist Dilke–Chamberlain approach of increasing local authorities' powers. Salisbury's central thesis that overcrowding, rather than bad sanitation, was the central problem was fully acknowledged. Salisbury dissented from that part of the Report which he thought looked too much like Chamberlainite 'expropriation' and produced a minority Report with important and dramatic recommendations of his own. To his surprise he got on well with Dilke, and proposed him for membership of the political dining club, Grillions.

When Dilke presided over the last meeting of the Commission on 20th July 1885, there had been a change of Government, and his political career lay in ruins as a result of his having been named the previous day as a co-respondent in a divorce case. But on 24th July Cross introduced the Housing of the Working Class Bill in the Commons and Salisbury in the Lords. It made available Treasury loans to county districts on the security of the rates. The Local Government Board was empowered to compel local authorities to close unhealthy houses, making landlords personally liable for the health of the inhabitants. It also became illegal for landlords to let dwellings which did not conform to elementary sanitation standards. Salisbury's own scheme for the Metropolitan Board of Works to convert into dwellings the forty-two acres of the three central London prisons, Coldbath Fields, Pentonville and Millbank, was blocked by Goschen and the Treasury.

Salisbury was not accustomed to being attacked from the Right, but Wemyss condemned the Bill as 'class legislation', and asked whether the Government would now take it upon itself also to house the police and Foreign Office clerks. He claimed the Bill would be 'strangling the spirit of independence and the self-reliance of the people, and destroying the moral fibre of our race in the anaconda coils of state socialism'. This was too much for Salisbury. 'Do not imagine', he told Wemyss during the debate, 'that by merely affixing to it the reproach of Socialism you can seriously affect the progress of any great legislative movement, or destroy those high arguments which are derived from the noblest principles of philanthropy and religion.'[9] The Bill received Royal Assent in mid-August, and was followed by a consolidating measure in 1890 which allowed local authorities directly to build and maintain working-class housing. 'It is a great nuisance that this charge of socialism is flung at the head of anyone who wishes to do anything for the poor,' Salisbury wrote to Janetta Manners, 'for Socialism is a very real danger. However the first of duties is to be pachydermatous.'

Had Mr Escott sent his investigators to the Strand and St Martin's Lane, rather than to Hatfield, he might have found a better story for his journal. In early December 1883, Salisbury told a deputation from the Amalgamated Society of Riverside Workmen that 'his property was very small and within a very small area, and not in any of the districts where those unsanitary, overcrowded buildings existed', and that 'streets that were called Salisbury Street and Cranborne Street' should not necessarily be supposed to be his property, because although they belonged to his family 200 years ago, 'some of his ancestors were thriftless'. Yet in Dilke's autobiography Salisbury's 'courts in the neighbourhood of St Martin's Lane' were named as amongst the worst in London, and he did in fact own much of Salisbury Street and Cecil Street south of the Strand, as well as Cecil Court between St Martin's Lane and Charing Cross Road, which in 1880 his agent had warned him was well on the way to becoming a slum. When long leases fell through, he made no conditions about overcrowding before selling new ones.

Although he was not 'a bit of a slum landlord', as he has been described by one historian, he indisputably treated his Hatfield tenantry far better than those who lived in London. The latter, because they were not also employed by him, were seen primarily as a source of income. One alteration he did make, as soon as his attention was drawn to it, was to strike out the condition in the leases which excluded Jews.[10]

One esoteric upshot of the Housing Commission concerned the formal social position of Cardinal Manning in relation to Salisbury. Should a cardinal take precedence over a marquess? The Prince of Wales thought so, because Manning was a 'Prince of the Church'. Sir William Harcourt thought that since Manning's was a foreign appointment, Salisbury should take precedence. The Prince of Wales's private secretary, Francis Knollys, was sent to Salisbury to discuss it and found him 'far too sensible and too much of a gentleman to have any feeling on a matter of this sort and at once said that there could be no doubt that Cardinal Manning should come first'. Salisbury did not have much time for Manning, writing in 1864 that 'he has won little fame as a preacher, except by his sermons to well-born ladies', but had already accorded him social precedence at the fiftieth anniversary celebrations of the Oxford Union in 1873.

When the issue arose again in 1890, Salisbury claimed he had forgotten all about it, but nevertheless a long and heated debate on his precedence ensued in *The Times*, between anonymous correspondents such as 'Corvus', 'Cantabrigiensis' and 'A Clergyman'. His true opinion on the matter was finally vouchsafed in 1896, when he told the Archbishop of Canterbury after a Royal Academy dinner at which the Prince of Wales had placed Cardinal Vaughan below the Lord Chancellor but above the Anglican bishops and the Cabinet, that 'this is only by courtesy and really Cardinal Vaughan has no rank or precedence whatever – simply none. It does not matter to dukes or marquesses, whose rank is personal, where they come ... but it is quite a different thing with Bishops who hold an office and are trustees for it.' As always with Salisbury, the privileges of the Established Church took priority, and as its thirty-seventh Article stated: 'The Bishop of Rome hath no jurisdiction in this realm of England.'[11]

Arthur Balfour once famously remarked that he would sooner listen to his valet for political advice than to the Conservative Party Conference. Although after 1902 this proved a vainglorious statement, when successive Party Conferences helped wreck his premiership, before that time they had little appreciable influence over Party policy. The reason was Salisbury's determination not to allow the voluntary sector of the Party, and least of all its executive arm, the Council of the National Union, to exercise any real power. His staple criticism of the Liberal Party was of the way in which its extra-parliamentary caucus, the National Liberal Federation, sought to direct what MPs did in Parliament, and he was not about to allow the same thing to happen to the Conservatives.

When Lord Randolph Churchill emerged as the leader of the movement for Party democracy in 1883 and 1884, Salisbury set his face against anything that he considered liable to fetter the complete independence of parliamentarians, as famously enunciated in Edmund Burke's 1774 address to the electors of Bristol. He was not about to allow parliamentary sovereignty to be circumscribed by caucuses of Party bureaucrats, let alone rank-and-file Party members. Control of Parties from outside Parliament both seemed to Salisbury impractical, as it could not take into account the fast-moving mood swings of the Commons chamber, and repugnant in a Constitution in which an MP was expected to represent his whole constituency, not just that part of it which voted for him. There were therefore philosophical as well as practical considerations why Salisbury and Churchill were set upon a collision course.

As his 'cry' to the constituency associations, Churchill devised a concept he called 'Tory Democracy', something Salisbury always found an oxymoronic 'phantom', especially as it claimed its inspiration from Disraeli's novels. Even Churchill himself found it difficult to define. In conversation with Wilfrid Scawen Blunt in April 1885, he said: 'That is a question I am always in a fright lest someone should put it to me publicly. To tell the truth, I don't know myself what Tory Democracy is, but I believe it to be principally opportunism. Say you are a Tory Democrat and that will do.' When finally he was forced to define it publicly, in Birmingham in April 1888, Churchill came out with the following explanation: 'What is the Tory Democracy? The Tory Democracy is a democracy which supports the Tory Party...because in the excellence and soundness of true Tory principles...it invokes the idea of a Government who...are animated by lofty and liberal ideas. That is Tory democracy.'[12]

The unscrupulous and mercurial Churchill, for all his brilliant platform oratory and energetic parliamentary performances, would not have recognised a 'true Tory principle' if it horse-whipped him in the street, but Salisbury knew that the Conservative front bench in the Commons was singularly free of men of talent and leadership qualities. Churchill was also credited with having an appeal outside Parliament that would be useful electorally in winning over working-class voters from the Liberals. Perhaps Salisbury also saw in Churchill a young Cecil of twenty years earlier, brilliantly making his name with sharp phrases, extreme views and an unwillingness to defer to his Party leaders.

Churchill's daring scheme, as unveiled to his lieutenant Drummond Wolff in September 1883, amounted to nothing less than 'the transference of all executive power – all financial control, from the nominees of the Leader, to the Council of the National Union'. The next month Churchill was elected Chairman of the key seven-man Organisation Committee of the Council, and at the annual meeting of the National Union a motion was passed demanding 'legitimate influence in the party organisation', code for the abolition of the Central Committee. In the opening negotiations between Churchill and Salisbury in December, Salisbury insisted that nothing be agreed until Northcote was present, and as he had royalty staying at Hatfield over Christmas it was impossible to arrange such a meeting before January. In the meantime, Balfour worked hard over the New Year trying to assess the relative strengths of the two sides, Party establishment versus Tory Democrats, should the situation deteriorate.

After a short meeting in January, where it became clear that Salisbury and Northcote held an entirely different view of the role of the voluntary sector from that of the Organisation Committee, there followed a coup on 1st February 1884, when Churchill captured the Chairmanship of the Council of the National Union from Earl Percy, a Party stalwart who had been Chairman since 1879, by seventeen votes to fifteen. Salisbury nevertheless continued to communicate with the Council through Percy, a Tory MP since 1868 and the future Duke of Northumberland, which Churchill understandably took as a slight. On 29th February, Salisbury and Northcote sent a message to the National Union, saying that it had an important role in stimulating the exertions of the local constituency associations, furnishing them with advice, money and lecturers, organising voter registration, co-ordinating volunteers, and indeed doing everything apart from actually deciding Party policy. The letter was intended to be as non-specific as possible, but the Organisation Committee instead 'hailed it as their charter' and demanded the means to put the tasks into effect, entirely ignoring the crucial *caveat*.

Concerned that they might have given a hostage to fortune, Salisbury and Northcote wrote again on 6th March, making it quite clear that the National Union was not going to be allowed to replace the Central Committee, which was 'appointed by us, and represents us: and we could not in any degree separate our position from theirs'. Churchill replied the same day with the observation that: 'In a struggle between a public body and a close corporation, the latter, I am happy to say, in these days goes to the wall.' A meeting of the Council on the 14th saw Percy suffering another defeat – this time by nineteen votes to fourteen – when he failed to reject the Organisation Committee's new definition of its own powers, even after reading out a letter from Salisbury opposing it.[13] Undeniably rattled by the course of events, Salisbury and Northcote then sent Churchill, via the principal Central Office agent, G.C.T. Bartley, an ultimatum, threatening to have the National Union ejected from Conservative Central Office altogether, 'to avoid any confusion of responsibility'. As the National Union had been faithfully paying its £175 per annum rent ever since 1872, Salisbury and Northcote were on doubtful ground legally, and relations merely worsened further. After a letter from Salisbury to Churchill asking for a meeting to discuss 'the limits of the work to which the National Union should address itself', relations became glacial.

On 2nd April 1884, after Salisbury had offered to withdraw what he called the 'notice to quit' in return for the Party Whips joining the Council as *ex officio* members, Churchill and three other members of the Organisation Committee, including Gorst and the intrepid Colonel Burnaby, wrote a letter which accused the leadership of 'vague, foggy and utterly intangible suggestions', such as the 'extravagant and despotic demand' about the *ex officio* Whips, which they claimed was intended to emasculate the National Union and leave it 'completely and forever reduced to its ancient condition of dependence upon, and servility to, certain irresponsible persons, who find favour in your eyes'. There was even a slighting reference to 'the aristocratic and privileged classes', as though Lord Randolph Spencer-Churchill MP were just any other inhabitant of Woodstock. Salisbury's laconic comment to Cranbrook, when in early May Churchill published his insolent letter of 2nd April, was that it was 'not such as one is accustomed to receive'.[14]

Percy's attempts to prevent the letter from being sent had been defeated, after an unedifying row, by six votes. Although at one point it looked like direct negotiations might have worked, Churchill then suddenly resigned the Chairmanship of the Council on 2nd May after a minor vote went against him. 'The bone of contention', Edward Hamilton perceptively reported from the other side of politics, 'is really the question of introducing the most abused "caucus" into the Conservative Party, which Lord Salisbury will not have at any price.' Writing of the Sudanese leader who had destroyed a 6,000-strong Egyptian army under Hicks Pasha, Salisbury joked to Janetta Manners: 'Randolph and the Mahdi have occupied my thoughts about equally. The Mahdi pretends to be half mad, and is very sane in reality: Randolph occupies exactly the reverse position.'

The 1884 NUCCA Conference opened on 23rd July in the Cutlers' Hall in Sheffield, and resulted in an overwhelming personal victory for Churchill, who came top of the Council poll with 345 votes, with his senior supporter, Arthur Forwood, coming second with 296 votes and Percy only eighth. Henry Manners was not even elected. As Churchill's majority on the Council had nonetheless fallen, there was room for a compromise, and at the Prince of Wales's garden party at Marlborough House on 26th July Salisbury and Churchill discussed the outlines of a peace deal.

The previous November, Richmond had complained to Cairns that Salisbury was 'much too rash and hot-headed and did not seem to know the meaning of the word "compromise"'. But at Marlborough House he came to an arrangement with Churchill, giving way on several ephemeral issues while refusing to accept the concept of a central caucus with the power to direct national policy. The Primrose League was to be officially recognised, a dinner was to be given by Salisbury at Arlington Street for the Council to publicise the reconciliation, Hicks Beach was to be the future Chairman of the National Union and the Central Committee was to be abolished. Balfour and Aretas Akers-Douglas would meanwhile join Gorst as Vice-Chairmen of the National Union. Akers-Douglas, MP for East Kent, was deputy Chief Whip and a shrewd, occasionally ruthless, manager of men, whose large estates and unhappy marriage gave him the time and inclination virtually to live in the House of Commons, becoming Salisbury's agent there. By August, Salisbury and Churchill were appearing together on the same platform.[15]

In the same week as the garden-party compact, a 'monster' Reform demonstration took place in Hyde Park, and Salisbury wanted the Party united in case of a forced dissolution. Churchill's four-month tour of India in the winter of 1884/5 suggested to his son Winston that although no documentary proof existed of it Salisbury had actually mentioned the post Churchill might expect to receive in a future Conservative ministry if he co-operated. Whatever the sweetener might have been, Churchill, who realised that with an election due in the next couple of years he could not rebel forever and also expect a Cabinet post, loyally returned to attacking Gladstone, and the spectre of the voluntary sector influencing Conservative Party policy was seen off. Salisbury had dealt with the danger, Churchill had shown his strength, and Northcote had, as was increasingly the case, taken a back seat.

In attacking the Government's foreign policy during 1884, Salisbury's main aim was to drive home the fact that, as he told an audience at Devonport on 4th June, 'Mr Gladstone has never been able heartily to take up the sceptre of English power. He has always held it as if it burnt his fingers.' He would then, in speech after speech, give five separate examples to illustrate this 'one long record of failure'.

The first was South Africa. After the Transvaal President, Paul Kruger, visited London in February 1884, a new Convention was signed which restored the name of the 'South African Republic'. It also made no reference to the Crown's 'suzerainty' which had been present in the 1881 Pretoria Convention. Indeed the Colonial Secretary, Lord Derby – who had joined the Liberals a year after Salisbury's Titus Oates remark – had struck out the Preamble which contained the disputed word. The new 1884 Convention had demoted the British Resident in Pretoria to a Consular Officer, had reduced the Transvaal's war debt to £250,000 and had ended British attempts to alleviate the ill-treatment of the black population. For Salisbury the last issue was the most disgraceful, and on successive public platforms he denounced the way that fewer than 50,000 Boers 'have almost made slaves' of 400,000 blacks. He called Majuba a 'defeat that was never avenged' and almost admitted in so many words that suzerainty had been given away, something he was vehemently to deny when he himself came to avenge the defeat fifteen years later.

On the civil war in Zululand, 'which we had pacified', Salisbury shed what a cynic might have thought were crocodile tears over the 'miserable death' of Cetewayo, whose visit to Britain after the Zulu War had made him something of a hero in the paradoxical affections of his Victorian hosts. In Egypt and the Sudan, Salisbury said the Government's policy 'fills me with shame'. The victory of the Mahdi over General Hicks Pasha at the Battle of El Obeid – 'six thousand corpses which are bleaching in the neighbourhood of Suakim' – was bad enough, but Gladstone's subsequent decision to evacuate the Sudan led Salisbury 'to believe that some foreign, craven race has forced its way into the House of Commons'. The Quakerism of John Bright was in fact 'a policy of blood' when it led to retreat in the face of fanatical Dervish hordes. 'We should, in every sense, govern Egypt,' Salisbury reiterated.

Salisbury was the first politician to latch on to the possibility that General George Gordon, who had been sent to Khartoum to organise the evacuation of the Sudan, might prove to be a huge embarrassment for Gladstone and the Liberal Government. As early as 30th January 1884, less than a fortnight after Gordon had been sent out, Salisbury argued that the General needed more than the £40,000 he had been granted, and should have been given an army to take the place of the one massacred at El Obeid. 'I feel this is a matter which we shall hear much more about, and it is possible that counsels may be offered which would involve this country in a disgrace deeper than that which we have already undergone at the other end of the African continent.' Accusing the Government of 'not impolicy, but imbecility', as well as 'impotency', Salisbury kept up the pressure over Gordon, even though his categorical orders were not to defend Khartoum but to evacuate it. By mid-May, Salisbury was saying that the 'unhappy and splendid hero' had been 'abandoned', and 'nothing could be more contemptible than the course which the Government has pursued, except, perhaps, the excuses by which they defend themselves'.

Salisbury's fourth area of attack was over the Government's evacuation of Kandahar, and the Russian annexation of Merv in February 1884. With a Russian railhead at Saraks, only 200 miles from Herat, the 'Forward' school were in uproar. In the House of Lords debate on 10th March, Northbrook called Merv 'a few mud hovels in the desert', whereas in 1877 Lytton had described it as 'undoubtedly the most important spot in Central Asia'. Although Salisbury had tended towards the former view while at the India Office, believing it could take a generation before Russia got there, he was not about to pass up the opportunity to fit Central Asia into his general denunciation of Gladstone's foreign policy. 'The terror of the English name has disappeared since the Government retreated from Kandahar,' he announced at Manchester on 16th and 17th April; 'they will not learn that these tribes, these vast uncivilised multitudes, are not governed merely by the sword. They are governed by the imagination. They are governed by their fears.'

What was true of Afghanistan went for India too; the 250,000 Britons who held an Indian empire of 250 millions were only able to do so because 'your greatness is acknowledged', but if that reputation was lowered or power weakened, 'do not for a moment delude yourselves with the belief that any benefits which you have conferred or any benefits which you can promise will lengthen by a single day your empire in that peninsula'. It was a harsh and uncompromising message, far removed from the one Gladstone had preached at Midlothian. It opened Salisbury to accusations of war-mongering, but it also addressed the warrior sentiments of an imperial caste and, as such, his speeches attracted as many people as they repelled.

Salisbury did not pretend there was a direct Russian military threat to India, something in which he had never believed, but he did hope, in the debate on the Russian annexation of Merv on 10th March, to capitalise upon the fears which even senior figures in the Government were privately expressing. 'The real danger', Salisbury argued, came from intrigues and rebellions fomented by Russia, from 'the gradual weakening of the respect for English arms' and the 'crumbling away of our responses before Russia has struck a blow against our frontier'. Because of this he felt justified in describing the fall of Merv as 'the gravest that has happened in respect to our Empire in the East'.

As well as the Transvaal, Zululand, the Sudan and Central Asia, Salisbury cited Gladstone's appeasement policy towards the tenantry of Ireland, which he said had 'absolutely paralysed' the land market there, as proof that the Liberal Government could not be trusted to uphold the Empire. It was a formidable indictment, presented in characteristically uncompromising language. In the sheer number of platform speeches across the country, to audiences often numbered in several thousands, it almost amounted to a Midlothian Campaign in reverse.[16] 'Give us your programme!' a heckler had shouted during a speech to the Chelsea Conservative Association on 12th March. 'Our programme is a very simple one,' he bellowed back, 'and can be summed up in four words, it is: "Appeal to the people".' Beyond winning the next election, Salisbury had no detailed policies. He believed that manifesto pledges merely encouraged what he called 'heroic measures'; his business was to pitch Gladstone out, not to specify areas of future action which might alienate groups of voters whose support he needed.

He enjoyed teasing the Whigs in the Liberal Party with the accusation that they had surrendered to the Radicals' programme, saying in April:

> You know that in old Pagan times there was in the winter a festival called Saturnalia, in which slaves represented themselves as the equals of their masters. At first Lord Hartington disposed himself as the man who could combat the opinions of Mr Chamberlain; but December has gone by, the winter is passing away, the Saturnalia is over, and Lord Hartington is seen humbly carrying the legislative baggage of Mr Chamberlain.

Salisbury's concentration on foreign policy gave him an edge over Northcote, who had been Chancellor of the Exchequer in the last Government, and his attacks on Gladstone and willingness to personalise the issues left Northcote, who could not hide his personal respect for the man he had once served, floundering behind. It was not in the country, however, but in Parliament that Salisbury knew he had to build up the support in order to wrest the diadem from his rival. In the summer of 1884, the ideal issue presented itself, one that would allow him to show his toughness, intellect and brinkmanship to advantage, but also his ability to compromise. It would furthermore give him the opportunity to exorcise the doubts raised by his 1867 resignation and the Arrears debacle. As in 1867, the issue was Reform.

EIGHTEEN

Provoking Constitutional Crisis

The Third Reform Act

June 1884 to February 1885

'Gunpowder and Glory.'

'The classes that represent civilisation, the holders of accumulated capital and accumulated thought,' Salisbury had written in *Bentley's Quarterly Review* a quarter of a century before, 'have a right to require securities to protect them from being overwhelmed by hordes who have neither knowledge to guide them nor stake in the commonwealth to protect them.' That battle had been lost in 1867, and by 1884 his main concern was to ensure that the coming enfranchisement of approximately two million rural working-class voters would not eclipse the Conservatives electorally. To his surprise and delight, Salisbury found that far from attempting to confiscate Hatfield, the newly enfrachised voters tended to eschew Radicalism. Indeed, in the seventeen years after the Reform Bill came into effect, Salisbury was to be Prime Minister for all but four.

In his speaking tour of the western counties in June 1884, Salisbury described the House of Lords as 'an ambassador or an agent' with a mission 'to see that no great change shall take place in the institutions of the country without the full knowledge and consent of the people whom they concern'. In effect this was a threat to reject a Gladstonian Reform Bill. Gladstone's private secretary Edward Hamilton described the speeches as 'Gunpowder and Glory'. For all his swashbuckling talk, however, Salisbury was privately uncertain that his colleagues would be any sounder over Reform than they had been over Arrears. 'A parapet which gives way when you lean upon it', he told his family at Hatfield, 'is more dangerous than no parapet at all.' The line he and Northcote agreed to adopt was an acceptance of the principle of Reform, but only if a simultaneous redistribution measure was attached. Stage one would be unacceptable without stage two. Large-scale geographical redistributions of seats had been attached to both the 1832 and 1867 Reform Bills, so this time the precedent was with Salisbury. 'Do not forget to give the Franchise Bill a good parting kick,' he told Northcote as the third reading in the Commons approached.

Nor would he make the same mistakes as during the Arrears debacle. This time he persuaded Cairns to propose the wrecking amendment to the Bill's second reading, which was passed by the Lords by 205 to 146 on 8th July. 'All sober-minded Conservative peers', Gladstone had claimed to Lord Tennyson two days earlier, 'are in great dismay at this wild proceeding of Lord Salisbury's.' In fact, one of the most sober-minded of them, Cairns, had actually proposed the effective rejection of the Bill, ably supported by the other Arrears backslider, the Duke of Richmond. On the first day of the debate, Wemyss announced that a survey by the Universal Knowledge and Information Office of Bloomsbury had disclosed that only a third of all Liberal candidates had alluded to Reform in their election addresses in 1880, and so the Government had no legitimate mandate for it. Salisbury's own peroration the next day set the scene for the controversy which was to rage throughout the preternaturally long and hot summer of 1884:

> Now that the people have in no real sense been consulted, when they had, at the last General Election, no notion of what was coming upon them, I feel that we are bound, as guardians of their interests, to call upon the Government to appeal to the people, and by the result of that appeal we will abide.

Salisbury's speech was, as Carnarvon acknowledged, 'an election manifesto...we are now in the open sea of war'.[1] After the Lords rejected the Bill, Parliament was prorogued for ten weeks of national campaigning and public meetings.

Salisbury had been instrumental in refusing compromises before the Bill was wrecked, but, according to Hamilton, Richmond 'was evidently working behind Lord Salisbury's back, and begged that nothing might on any account be said to Lord S.' about his hinting that 'some arrangement might still be made'. Carnarvon also went to Arlington Street to try to persuade Salisbury of the need for compromise two days after the debate, but he got short shrift. Mocking Gladstone's proroguing of Parliament, which had meant dropping the popular cross-Party Bill to create a Scottish Office, Salisbury likened the Prime Minister to a medieval pope, who, when he failed to extract something from a monarch, placed an interdict on all the religious services in his kingdom.

Salisbury was outwardly very calm about the impending crisis. To the High Churchman Canon Malcolm MacColl, who was trying to set himself up as a mediator between Salisbury and Gladstone and who had urged moderation in order to secure the Party leadership, Salisbury demurred: 'To be the leader of a large party – still more to be the leader of anything resembling a coalition, requires in a large measure the gifts of pliancy and optimism, and I, unfortunately, am very poorly endowed in either respect.' On the threat of his Party throwing him over yet again he was equally philosophical:

> I do not think such an issue by any means impossible, but the idea is not a deterrent: on the contrary it is a soothing prospect to dwell upon, like a mirage in the desert...to those who know English politics well, they are not attractive – their highest rewards confer no real power. The strongest men...have to carry out ideas that are not their own...they fill up your life with an incessant labour which to those who are not blessed with optimism leaves behind it the feeling of an almost unmingled waste of time.[2]

Gladstone's offer of enfranchisement without redistribution would lead to 'the absolute effacement of the Conservative Party. It would not have reappeared as a political force for thirty years. This conviction... greatly simplified for me the computation of risks.'

There was an element of calculation in his letter. Salisbury knew that MacColl was in close communication with his friend Gladstone, so if he could convince the cleric that he was serious about putting his demand for a dual Bill before even his own political future, he might be able to persuade the Prime Minister to back down from the policy that had been announced to the Liberal Party at a meeting at the Foreign Office the day before, which was to press ahead with the Franchise Bill that autumn without a dissolution but after a campaign of massive demonstrations in favour of the Bill and against the Lords. As Hamilton's diary of 12th July contains an exact *précis* of Salisbury's letter to MacColl, his suspicions were obviously justified. Lady Salisbury adopted the same stratagem, openly saying that her husband had nothing to gain by the existing constitution of the House of Lords and would prefer to be back in the Commons. 'If it went,' she was reported by Hamilton as having said, 'he might find arrayed against himself some metal worthier of his steel.'

'I fear nothing but irresolution,' Salisbury told a Lancashire supporter, F.W. Freston. 'I will stand to the principle that the new franchise shall not come into operation without redistribution. But will others stand by me?' He found out at the Party meeting of peers and MPs held at the Carlton Club on 15th July, where he put his scheme for forcing the Government to put a Seats (or Redistribution) Bill through the Commons whilst simultaneously holding up the Franchise Bill in the Lords. The unspoken but clear threat was that Salisbury would resign if he were not supported this time, and although it was not unanimous and some dissatisfaction was expressed, Northcote supported him, albeit 'in more moderate terms', and the policy was agreed. Carnarvon, who was not called upon by Salisbury to speak at the meeting, complained in his diary that in the Lords there was 'considerable excitement' over Salisbury's intemperate language and the general expectation was that 'with all his ability he will end by making some great mess'.[3]

With Parliament prorogued, attention turned to the platforms, press and political meetings, which were supposed to give an indication of the people's wishes. A *Punch* cartoon on 19th July entitled 'Noblesse Oblige!' featured Salisbury trying to shove his coronet into the mouth of a cannon labelled 'Public Opinion'. On 21st July, a well-behaved meeting was held in Hyde Park, where somewhere between twenty-five and sixty thousand people heard speeches in favour of Reform. 'The employment of mobs as an instrument of public policy', Salisbury replied via *The Times*, 'is likely to prove a sinister precedent.' It was during one such huge procession that Lady Frances Balfour had ample opportunity to make a survey of the faces of Salisbury and Balfour, as they sat unrecognised in a hansom cab in a traffic jam, as the bands and marchers crossed Waterloo Bridge on their way to Hyde Park. Salisbury 'looked infinitely bored, and somewhat puzzled', while his nephew 'looked aloof and remote, and yet as if he was benevolently interested'.

The Conservative counter-offensive began in Sheffield on 23rd July, where Salisbury told a crowd of 8,000, with thousands more having tried in vain to gain admission, that the Government 'imagine that thirty thousand Radicals going to amuse themselves in London on a given day expresses the public opinion of the day … they appeal to the streets, they attempt legislation by picnic'. The laughter and cheers were, according to *The Times*'s report, 'again and again renewed' at this jibe. Gladstone had adopted Reform as an electoral manoeuvre, declared Salisbury, because he needed a 'cry' to avoid being judged on his foreign or economic policies at the next election. Furthermore, it was 'the most servile House of Commons – servile to the ministers, servile to the caucus – that the Palace of Westminster has ever seen'.

It was therefore up to the House of Lords to protect the Constitution by insisting on no extra enfranchisement without the second stage of simultaneous redistribution: 'I do not care whether it is an hereditary chamber or any other – to see that the representative chamber does not alter the tenure of its own power so as to give a perpetual lease of that power to the party in predominance at the moment.' Salisbury told Janetta Manners that the Drill Hall where he had spoken in Sheffield had 'a more filthy atmosphere than ever before it was my lot to breathe – eight thousand very unwashed and enthusiastic persons – only two or three panes broken in the roof for ventilation!'

When two days later a pro-Reform demonstration of 40,000 people met in Leicester, Salisbury was accorded the signal honour of being burnt in effigy. One of the banners quoted Shakespeare's *Henry VI*: 'Old Salisbury – shame to thy silver hair, Thou mad misleader.' Another meeting in Bournemouth turned into a free fight, with the audience only pausing at 9 p.m. to sing *Rule Britannia* and *God Save the Queen* before carrying on brawling.[4] It was in this atmosphere that, not wishing to be attacked on both flanks, Salisbury concluded the Marlborough House compact with Churchill, who then swiftly fell into line. Salisbury considered publishing a pamphlet against Reform, but found the dual leadership with Northcote an obstacle. 'Have you ever composed a document of any kind in conjunction with anyone else?' Salisbury asked an ally on 24th July. 'Are you satisfied with the result? Such composites have a hybrid air about them – and retain only the worst characteristics of both parents.' Any such document might also contain unnecessary pledges, misconstruable phrases or language which could divide their followers, so it was shelved.

In the ten weeks after Parliament was prorogued, no fewer than seven hundred political meetings were held, which an aggregate of two million people attended. Most were held by Liberals in favour of Reform, but the Conservatives ensured that a significant minority representation made itself heard. At the Manchester demonstration on Saturday, 9th August, where admission was ticketed but free, the numbers who enjoyed the sunshine and came to hear Salisbury and Churchill speak were reckoned at over one hundred thousand. Salisbury again offered to pass a franchise Bill into law, but only if simultaneously attached to a redistribution Bill.

A article in the *Fortnightly Review* calling Salisbury 'a foe' of 'the people' raised his ire. In a letter to MacColl he wrote:

> Mr Hutton's interpolation is a curious case of survival of expressions. That impersonation of 'the people' as a thing you can love or hate – or be the 'foe' of – belongs to the dialect of the French Convention. It means nothing. However unchristian he may think me, does he imagine I hate the people who vote Tory as well as the people who vote Radical – the people who cheer me as well as the people who hoot me? The only restraint I should like to impose on the liberty of the press would be to make political abstractions penal.[5]

By early September Salisbury was concerned, as he told the Tory Chief Whip Rowland Winn, that some senior Conservatives, such as Wemyss, Churchill or Lord Jersey, might try to break ranks and attempt 'compromises, bridges, open doors and the rest'. He admitted that 'this is the danger I am most afraid of – some cunning half measure which surrenders everything, which may seem to the obtuser lords to save their dignity'. He openly admitted that his plan was to 'checkmate the

Government and bring about a crisis', because he believed that the Liberals would not win a general election, or at least not by so large a majority as in 1880.

So when in mid-September the Duke of Argyll offered a compromise whereby the Lords would pass the Franchise Bill after a Seats Bill had been laid on the Commons table, Salisbury rejected it in favour of waiting for the Seats Bill to pass the Commons, as 'we should look unutterably foolish' if the Government then let the Seats Bill fall or get hopelessly amended in the Lower House after the Franchise Bill had passed all its stages in the Upper. 'I think the Government are in a hole,' Salisbury wrote to Drummond Wolff on 20th September. 'It is not our business to pull them out.' Instead, in the middle of the crisis, he nonchalantly left for a week in Dieppe, hoping that Gladstone would blink first.

On his return, Salisbury made a 'stumping' tour of south-west Scotland, with a break at the Duke of Richmond's Gordon Castle to consult on future tactics with Cairns and his host. On his way up he did not put his head out of the window to acknowledge the crowds at the railway stations, still less did he give them 'impromptu' uplifting addresses like Gladstone, 'but sat touching his hat with a ghastly grin in the furthest corner' of the compartment, loathing every second of the intrusion. When he arrived at Glasgow station at 8.10 p.m., on 30th September, however, between ten and twelve thousand people were there to greet him. The din of cheering under the arched roof meant that few could hear his speech, and there were fears that the platform on which the senior luminaries of the Grand Orange Lodge of Scotland were standing would collapse. 'We wish that the franchise should pass,' was his message, 'but that before you make new voters you should determine the constitution in which they are to vote.'[6]

The October issue of the *National Review* carried an immensely detailed psephological article by Salisbury entitled 'The Value of Redistribution: A Note on Electoral Statistics', which showed how the Conservatives 'have no cause, for Party reasons, to dread enfranchisement coupled with a fair redistribution'. Analysing the 1880 results almost constituency by constituency, Salisbury estimated that the net loss to the Conservatives of enfranchisement without redistribution would be forty-seven seats. Gladstone saw nothing in the article to 'startle or repel' him, and enough in favour of good boundary divisions, fairer representation and even possibly single-member constituencies to be a future basis for a compromise.

In the meantime, however, and in the face of *The Times*'s constant opposition in what it called this 'unprofitable contest', Salisbury stumped on through Scotland, arguing in speeches that rarely took longer than an hour that the Liberals, in the fifth year of a Parliament, did not have the legitimate authority radically to alter the Constitution without first appealing to the people. 'I should have thought that anyone who had studied the history of the world,' he declared on 1st October, 'and could read the signs of the times, would know that if freedom runs any dangers it is certainly not from any possible revival of the powers of the aristocracy.' Instead, the danger to freedom would come from 'those who shelter under the cover of its forms, and who speak its language with unparallelled eloquence and vigour'. Centralisation of power through the caucus, he argued, was the greater threat to liberty than the House of Lords.

He did not confine all his speeches to the Reform issue, and managed at St Andrew's Hall in Glasgow on 3rd October to touch on the disestablishment of the Scottish Church, the future of the Concert of Europe, the slavery practised by the Boers, the betrayal of General Gordon and that 'silliest possible display', the bombardment of Alexandria. Even the hapless Montenegrins came in for another tongue-lashing: 'They are a people whose fate matters as much to us as the people of Mongol Tartary. They are excellent mountaineers, they have a great love of independence, and I fancy accompanying it, as you often find in the early development of a mountaineer nation, they have a great love of other people's property.' When speaking of 'English rule' he was interrupted by cries of 'British', to which Salisbury answered: 'If I may interpose a moment I should say that Scotland, which has practically annexed England, ought not to be bashful about the word England being mentioned.'

At Gordon Castle from 8th to 10th October, Salisbury had to defend his uncompromising policy to Richmond and Cairns, especially in the light of political gossip about the Queen being asked to create enough Liberal peers to force Reform through the Lords. 'Here I am in a very ugly place, where everyone talks salmon-fishing,' he told Janetta Manners, 'and there is no Moselle.' Despite discovering that Richmond had been in contact with the (as ever pro-Reform) Queen, and that Cairns had been speaking privately to Hartington, he was not too put out. 'I left my two wise counsellors in the north in a very poor frame of mind,' he wrote to his wife, 'they will give me trouble in the future – but I hope to pull through.' He had managed to persuade them that the Government feared a dissolution, and that the Queen would not create peers without one.

On 10th October, Sir William Harcourt delivered a blistering attack on Salisbury, placing all the blame for the Reform impasse on him. Despite being a Cecil, Harcourt intoned,

> Lord Salisbury has nothing of the masculine confidence in the fibre of the English people that distinguished the councils of Elizabeth: his statesmanship belongs to a later period and is founded upon the model of the Stuart type. His statecraft is that of Laud and his temper that of Strafford.... He

never sees a voter, especially a Liberal voter, added to a constituency
without thinking that he is going to have his pocket picked or that he is
going to be robbed of some darling privilege.

Speaking at Kelso the next day, Salisbury observed of this *ad hominem*
assault: 'The plaintiff's attorney is only abused when there is no case.'[7]

It was always Salisbury who was at the centre of the struggle, both
delivering and receiving the heaviest blows. Northcote was merely kept
in touch by Salisbury about developments such as the Gordon Castle
meeting. On 11th October, Salisbury informed him that the policy to
give the Franchise Bill a second reading in the Lords, and then hold it up
until a redistribution Bill reached them, remained unchanged.
'Decidedly, as long as the G.O.M. lives,' he said of the Grand Old Man,
Gladstone, on his journey back south, 'Scotch railway stations are
places to be avoided.' Salisbury's vigorous policy was not without its
critics, especially once public meetings began to turn violent. At Aston
Park on 13th October, a Conservative gathering was gate-crashed by
Radicals with forged tickets. A wall was pushed down and Balfour later
said that Northcote had been in fear of his life. A large number of chairs
were thrown by roughs, prompting jokes about the redistribution of
seats, and it encouraged Conservatives to worry whether Salisbury was
not risking social upheaval through his obstinacy. But when Canon
MacColl wrote to warn him of another whispering campaign against
him, Salisbury answered: 'I regard such conspiracies as you mention
with much philosophy. *Cantabit vacuus coram latrone.*[8] [Someone
without possessions has nothing to fear from a highwayman.]'[9]

The Duke of Buccleuch, whose son the Earl of Dalkeith had lost
Midlothian to Gladstone in 1880, chaired a meeting of 4,500 people at
Dumfries on 21st October, where Salisbury denounced the Aston riots,
slightly damning Northcote with faint praise by calling him 'so moderate and careful a statesman' that he had not deserved his meeting being
'broken up by Liberals'. If Chamberlain, whose attacks on Salisbury
were becoming so aggressive that Gladstone ordered him to calm down,
had been responsible for inciting the disturbance, Salisbury said that in
future: 'I hope that he would head the riot, when I was pretty confident
that his head would get broken.' The rest of the meeting was a fairly
standard discussion of Free Trade versus Protection, with the extra
point that to offer the franchise to the unemployed of Glasgow was 'like
offering a stone to those who are asking for bread'. Stones were thrown
at Salisbury when he left the meeting, one weighing over a pound
smashed through the window of his carriage where he sat with his two
daughters. They were unharmed, and he used it at Hatfield for a paper-
weight. The mob also broke a number of the windows of the King's

Arms Hotel where he stayed that night.[10] Anything Northcote could do, Salisbury showed he could do better.

When Parliament met again in late October, Gladstone made an attempt at 'turning Salisbury's flank', as he put it, by offering Carnarvon and some other worried Tories a compromise just short of the joint enfranchisement-plus-redistribution measure that Salisbury demanded. 'There is nothing in reason which you could ask that would not readily be granted,' the Prime Minister wrote to a potential Tory backslider, Lord Norton. The Queen, advised by Richmond, attempted to induce Salisbury to compromise and talk to Hartington, but after a brief meeting held largely to humour her, Salisbury regretfully reported that they could not agree. 'Something must be done,' she noted in her journal on 29th October, 'and if Lord Salisbury won't do what is right, then someone else must take the lead.' It is possible, though unlikely, that Salisbury would not have minded a royal coup against him at that time. 'Politics stand alone among human pursuits in this characteristic,' he told a correspondent on the 30th, 'that no one is conscious of liking them – and no one is able to leave them. But whatever affection they may have had they are rapidly losing. The difference between now and thirty years ago when I entered the House of Commons is inconceivable.'

It is hard to escape the conclusion that Salisbury, conscious of the untrustworthiness of the House of Lords as a parapet, was mentally preparing himself for yet another defeat, a re-run of the Arrears Bill. This time, however, it would result in his leaving politics altogether. The very extremity of his position, despite being backed up by his speeches and statistics, was a test for the Conservative Party to back him or sack him, and letters like the one to Rev. James Baker quoted above, or to Canon MacColl at the time of the initial rejection of the Bill, were self-justificatory defences written with possible future defeat and resignation in mind. Had Gladstone succeeded in his efforts to detach Cairns, Carnarvon, Churchill, Hicks Beach, Richmond or worst of all Northcote from Salisbury's hard-line position in November 1884, Salisbury would have been at best a footnote in the political history of the last quarter of the nineteenth century, rather than one of its three giants.

It was close run. On 7th November, Carnarvon met Northcote and told him of the 'widespread belief that Salisbury is "riding for a fall" and is quite reckless as to the destruction of the House of Lords'. Northcote believed that the Liberals 'disliked him so much and were so anxious to damage him' that they were even willing to accept worse terms over redistribution in order to be rid of Salisbury. He 'admitted that it was very disastrous', but did not betray his colleague, and nor did Hicks Beach when Hartington suggested they meet on 8th November.[11]

On 11th November 1884, the Franchise Bill had its third reading in the

House of Commons and a date was set for its second reading in the Lords. At a meeting of the Conservative leaders the next day, Salisbury found himself heavily outnumbered. Lord John Manners and Rowland Winn supported his hard line, but Carnarvon, Cross, Smith, Sandon and Northcote were 'in favour of coming to terms if good ones could be had'. With Cairns and Richmond coming down from Scotland, Salisbury had little time to win the trick, and even his faithful ally Cranbrook was talking of compromise. Behind Salisbury's back, Northcote was also giving the Government signs of wanting a compromise, but Salisbury was convinced that the closer they pushed towards a dissolution, the more they would gain when Gladstone eventually caved in.

When on 13th November Canon MacColl came up with the idea of Salisbury meeting Gladstone secretly at Glamis Castle, he turned the offer down on the grounds that he might be able to get there incognito, 'but not Mr Gladstone. His face is known at every railway station in the kingdom [and] to meet publicly would breed suspicions and resentments on both sides.'[12] Salisbury anyhow doubted any genuine desire on Gladstone's part to negotiate, suspecting 'there is only a desire to have the credit of negotiation'.

So long as he was not let down by any of his colleagues, Salisbury was confident of success. There were doubts about his ability to get the Conservative peers to follow him, but he was convinced that Gladstone, fearful of a dissolution, would crack if only no Tories started a splitting action. When Northcote had an interview with Gladstone on 14th November, Salisbury refused to allow him to agree to Gladstone's terms. 'Lord Salisbury can't let the Franchise Bill go out of the hands of the House of Lords until they get the Seats Bill for the Lower House!' noted Edward Hamilton. 'If only Pembroke and his friends have the pluck to stand up against Lord Salisbury, Lord Salisbury must give in or be left in the lurch.'

The drama of Monday, 17th November 1884, when Salisbury won all he had wished for, more than made up for the humiliation of the Arrears Bill two years before. The morning papers had hinted that, if the Conservative leaders gave 'adequate assurance' that the Franchise Bill would pass the Lords by Christmas, the Government would promise to carry a simultaneous Seats Bill which could receive its second reading in the Commons as the Franchise Bill went into committee in the House of Lords. The dual passages through Parliament would thus be closely choreographed. Salisbury immediately expressed his willingness to discuss such an arrangement, but only if the Franchise Bill did not come first. A Party meeting was held where Salisbury repeated this condition to his fellow peers at the Carlton Club.

A letter from Gwendolen to her brother Robert takes up the (slightly embroidered) tale:

The three arch-funkers Cairns, Richmond and Carnarvon cried out declaring that he would accept no compromise at all as it was absurd to imagine the Government conceding it. When the discussion was at its height (very high) enter Arthur [Balfour] with explicit declamation dictated by G.O.M. in Hartington's handwriting yielding the point entirely. Tableau and triumph along the line for the 'stiff' policy which had obtained terms which the funkers had not dared hope for. My father's prevailing sentiment is one of complete wonder...we have got all and more than we demanded.[13]

After four years, Salisbury's 'No Surrender' policy had finally paid off. The scene was set for face-to-face meetings between the Party leaders, encouraged by the Queen's offer of mediation.

The meetings at Downing Street found Salisbury and Gladstone working together surprisingly well, considering that at the beginning of the month Sir Henry Ponsonby had predicted that after being 'locked up together nothing would be found but a beard and a pair of collars next morning'. They got on in a very workmanlike way, and the Queen even joked with the Lord Privy Seal, Lord Carlingford, that 'the way that Gladstone and Salisbury buttered each other, one does not see how she is to have an Opposition again'. The first meeting was held between Gladstone, Hartington, Granville and Dilke on the Government side and Salisbury, Northcote, Richmond and Cairns for the Opposition. Granville privately described Richmond and Cairns as 'tame elephants' in the Tory camp. Salisbury readily admitted to Cranbrook that 'a great many indications combined to prove that ice was cracking all around us', before the Government caved in – so it was in both sides' interests that the talks should prove fruitful. His handling of the conference, which although Northcote was present was entirely led by Salisbury, helped him to emerge as the putative Party leader.

Salisbury soon found the eight-man committee far too unwieldy – and probably suspected that Cairns and Richmond were potential saboteurs – so the next meetings were attended solely by Northcote, Hartington, Dilke and himself. 'Hartington took a kind of bored external interest in the whole affair,' Salisbury reported to Gwendolen, 'while Dilke brimming over with details is the businessman of the party.'[14] Because details were the essence of these negotiations, and Salisbury and Dilke had fully mastered them constituency by constituency, it was they who dominated the discussions, and the good rapport they had built up together during the Housing Commission proved invaluable in the give and take of negotiation.

Schedules, maps, census returns, county divisions, boundary changes, memberships of the various Boundary Commissions, all were discussed amicably. Gladstone intervened on the most important policy questions and after one of the last meetings, on 26th November, he told Hamilton how 'Lord Salisbury, who seems to monopolise all the say on his side, has no respect for tradition. As compared with him, Mr Gladstone declares he is himself quite a Conservative. They got rid of the boundary question, minority representation, grouping and the Irish difficulty. The question was reduced to ... for or against single member constituencies.'

The 'Arlington Street Compact' was finally drawn up by Dilke on 28th November 1884. It put the arrangements into black and white, along with a number of alterations and addenda written by Salisbury. It was agreed that the details should be kept secret. 'I trust we shall be fortunate enough to escape a Marvin,' Salisbury told Gladstone the next day, thanking him for 'the courtesy and consideration with which you have conducted our abnormal conferences'. The haggling had been tough and the results were correspondingly dramatic. For the first time in history, most of the 670 parliamentary constituencies were split into roughly equal sizes of population to be represented by a single member each. A mass franchise was established which lasted in the same form until 1918. Boroughs of fewer than 15,000 population were mingled with the neighbouring county districts. Areas of between 15,000 and 50,000 people were represented by one member. Those between 50,000 and 165,000 retained the old two-member system. Towns of over 165,000 inhabitants, and all counties, were split into divisions which returned a single member each.

Scores of new suburban constituencies were thus created, which proceeded to return Conservatives, and because the Boundary Commissions were instructed to 'have regard for the pursuits of the population' even hitherto Liberal-dominated cities returned some Conservatives after the 1885 election as well. The electorate itself was increased by over two million, but for a multitude of reasons the number of people actually voting increased only from 3.359 million in 1880 to 4.368 million in 1885.[15] Single-member constituencies meant a political revolution in themselves; where once Liberals were able to share seats between Whigs and Radicals, now only one or the other could fight the Conservative. It therefore encouraged the antagonisms which were growing within the Liberal Party. During the consultative process every political idea was considered, even proportional representation. Salisbury, surprisingly, did 'not despair' of the idea 'establishing itself at a later period', as he told a correspondent on 3rd December. 'But it cannot be at a time when one party is in strong predominance, and only dreams of perpetuating its rule. If ever parties are so balanced that each is nervous about its future, they will be in a mood to listen.'

To those Ulster landowners who complained about being swamped by single-member constituencies, Salisbury admitted that 'I have little comfort to offer them. If I had been allowed to make a crisis of the

Arrears Bill we might have put off this trouble for several years. But given the Franchise Bill – there was nothing to be done for them – they labour under the disease of paucity of numbers.' Chamberlain assumed the Third Reform Act would be a triumph for the Liberals. If he were a Tory, he told the lawyer and Liberal MP Henry James, he would poison Salisbury's rum and water. 'If he had been in the pay of the caucus what more could he have done to destroy his party and give up everything for which it has hitherto existed?'

He was not alone in thinking that Salisbury had made a terrible error. On the Tory Right, Eustace Cecil later wrote in his *Apologia*, 'that my brother should have been one of the principal parties to the betrayal of all he fought for in 1867, <u>distressed</u> and <u>disgusted</u> me beyond measure'. Because Salisbury had not attempted to stop the enfranchisement of agricultural labourers, Eustace – and a few others including Lord John Manners and James Lowther in the Commons – suspected, in Eustace's hyperbolic words, 'Principles no longer existed! They were simply made to be changed according to the weathercock of expediency and personal ambition.' Eustace retired from the House of Commons at the next election, unwilling to continue to have his brother pay his electoral expenses and commenting bitterly that Salisbury had done nothing to encourage him to remain.

Parliament adjourned in December, and Salisbury travelled to the French Riviera and Italy with his family. Gladstone had said during the Reform negotiations that Salisbury played the 'mother hen' to Northcote's 'chick'. Less kind commentators contrasted Gladstone, the Grand Old Man, with Northcote, the Grand Old Woman. Until the Queen made her choice, however, Salisbury still needed to find another great cause in which his superior capacity for denouncing the Liberal Government could be displayed to the full.[16] While holidaying at Naples on 7th February 1885, he received a telegram reporting that Khartoum had fallen to the Mahdi and that General Gordon was dead.

NINETEEN

The Path to the Premiership

*Gordon of Khartoum – The Press
– The Queen*

February to June 1885

'Anything but a matter for congratulation.'

With his mental instability, religious fanaticism and complicated sexual orientation, General Gordon was perhaps an archetypal Empire-builder, but he was also, in Salisbury's estimation, 'the last possible man to be entrusted with any form of diplomatic mission', let alone a major evacuation. Employed as a general in China in the early 1860s, he had then explored the Equatorial Nile and been the Khedive's Governor of the Sudan between 1877 and 1880, before interfering in Irish land law reform, serving in Mauritius and visiting Palestine. 'They must have gone quite mad!' was Salisbury's response when in January 1884 the Government suddenly despatched this unruly, self-advertising firebrand to oversee the delicate operation of withdrawing the Khedive's forces from the Sudan in the face of the advancing Mahdi.

Arriving in Khartoum in February, soon after Baker Pasha's attempt to relieve the Egyptian garrisons in Sudan had been routed, Gordon failed to persuade the Mahdi to negotiate and by May he was trapped in the Sudanese capital with only Nile steamers capable of breaking the siege. Although it was Gordon's vanity and insubordination, and perhaps also a form of death-wish – 'Better a ball in the brain than to flicker out unheeded,' he wrote in his journal – that had stranded him in Khartoum, it was still the Government's duty to rescue him. Evelyn Baring, Egypt's greatest proconsul, put the date at 27th June when even 'the most indulgent critic' thought that an expeditionary force should have been sent to relieve the siege, for that was the day the news was confirmed in London that the Dervishes had captured Berber a month earlier.

Yet for a further six paralysing weeks Gladstone, despite coming under the greatest pressure from Hartington and others, did nothing. 'The Nile expedition was sanctioned too late,' wrote Baring many years later in his book *Modern Egypt*, 'and the reason it was sanctioned too late was that Mr Gladstone would not accept simple evidence of a plain fact which was patent to much less powerful intellects than his own.' Finally, an expedition was sent under General Sir Garnet Wolseley, whose steamers reached Khartoum on 28th January 1885. They were two days too late. In the early hours of the 26th, Khartoum had fallen after an heroic 317-day siege.

Salisbury had for months been making what turned out to be astonishingly accurate predictions, almost from the moment Gordon had been sent out. He had been asking parliamentary questions since February 1884, and on 4th April, before Gordon was even cut off in Khartoum, he delivered this jeremiad to the House of Lords:

> I fear that the history of the past will be repeated in the future; that, just again, when it is too late, the critical resolution will be taken; some terrible news will come that the position of General Gordon is absolutely a forlorn and hopeless one; and then, under the pressure of public wrath and parliamentary censure, some desperate resolution of sending an expedition will be formed, too late to achieve the object which it is desired to gain; too late to rescue this devoted man whom we have sent forward to his fate; in time only to cast another slur on the statesmanship of England and the resolution of the statesmen who guide England's counsels.

When later in April it was suggested that £200,000 should be raised, Salisbury told a correspondent that what Gordon needed was not money, but men.[1] So when on 7th February 1885 he received the 'terrible news' in Naples, Salisbury was in a prime position to deliver his greatest philippic since the speech at the third reading of the Second Reform Act eighteen years earlier. Moving a vote of censure in the Lords, only days after the Government had survived in the Commons by just fourteen votes, Salisbury fitted Gordon's death into his general theory of Gladstone's vacillation and indecision on imperial matters. The point he had been trying to hammer home at countless meetings, in parliamentary speeches and in letters – that the Liberals could not be trusted with the stewardship of the Empire – had now been publicly and vividly illustrated.

In what even the normally unappreciative *Punch* described as a 'speech of great vigour, hugely cheered' – and which was widely contrasted with Northcote's notably lacklustre performance in the Commons – Salisbury at last repaid Gladstone in kind for the taunts of the Midlothian Campaign:

> Now the terrible responsibility and shame rests upon the Government, because they were warned in March and April of the danger to General

Gordon, because they received every intimation which men could reasonably look for that his danger would be extant, and because they delayed from March and April right down to the fifteenth of August before they took a single measure to relieve him. What were they doing all that time? It is very difficult to conceive. I suppose some day the memoirs will tell our grandchildren, but we shall never know.

Some people think there were divisions in the Cabinet, and that after division after division, a decision was put off, lest the Cabinet be broken up. I rather incline to think that it was due to the peculiar position of the Prime Minister. He came in as the apostle of the Midlothian campaign, loaded with all the doctrines and all the follies of that pilgrimage.... It was the business of the Government ... to see that those who were surrounded, who were only three Englishmen among such a vast body of Mahommedans, and who were already cut off from all communications with the civilised world by the occupation of every important town upon the rivers, were really in danger, and that if they meant to answer their responsibilities they were bound to relieve them.

Northbrook turned to Carlingford during the oration and murmured: 'I can't answer this,' but eventually spoke 'with difficulty' in Gladstone's defence.[2] The Government lost the division by 198 to 68. Rarely for him, Salisbury received an adulatory press the next day.

'The manipulation of intelligence became a warlike weapon of the most deadly efficiency,' Salisbury had written decades earlier in a *Saturday Review* notice of a book about the American Revolution. 'The fortunes of the struggle depended in no small degree on the false fears or the false hopes that could be installed into the American population.' For someone who had himself worked in Fleet Street, Salisbury had a strangely ambivalent relationship with the press, one that shifted between despising the inky trade, investing in it and occasionally pretending to be aloof from it altogether. He had supported French press freedom under Napoleon III, where it had been 'gradually tormented and worried into a semi-animate prostration', and he appreciated that for all its power, 'without the shield of [public] opinion, the press is at the mercy of a corporal's guard'.

Salisbury was consistently misquoted in the newspapers, but, as he advised a colleague in 1899, 'I have always followed Dizzy's sound rule, never to reply to the press, except in correction of an evident misstatement.' In January 1883 when on holiday in the South of France, it was reported in various newspapers that Salisbury had been to Nice for Léon Gambetta's funeral, that he had been boar-hunting (which was far less likely), that he had been on a cruise, that he was due to go to Portsmouth and that he had been to a ball at Valescure. All were completely untrue. 'I have not left Cannes for my villa in Antibes', he informed Janetta Manners about one such misreport, 'seeing that I have not been at Cannes, and I have not got a villa at Antibes.'

In 1891, a story went around that Salisbury had employed an Italian priest as a butler, which he had to explain 'is an idiotic fabrication from beginning to end. Italian priests do not accept positions as butlers, which they would probably be incompetent to fulfil, and I have never had an Italian, whether priest or layman, in my service as a butler.'[3] Overall, however, as a secretary explained, Salisbury preferred not to correct newspaper reports, because errors were so frequent that if he corrected some it would justify the inference that the reports not corrected were accurate. Furthermore, 'if he were to answer all the libels published about him he would have nothing else to do. He thinks that they do no harm, and may be safely let alone.'

Because of his earlier anonymous connections with the press, rumours abounded that he had written, or at least inspired, various important articles. Although he thought newspapers 'make the task of constitutional government much easier than it would be otherwise, by signalling hidden rocks', he was often embarrassed by the assumption that he had been behind stories damaging to colleagues. In October 1875, for example, he had to deny to Northbrook, who had been attacked by the *Globe*, that he even knew who the editor, proprietor or writer were, or even that he had known the article had appeared in the first place. Salisbury thought it absurd for politicians to be over-sensitive. 'As the bee to the flower,' he told Lytton in 1877,

> so flies the sleepy distracted article writer to the statesman whose activity promises to supply his material for the copy which within the next two hours must be inexorably rendered.... These gentlemen of the press much exaggerate their own power.... They bear much the relation to a man's unpopularity that flies do to a wound. If the wound exists, they can aggravate it and make it malignant, but they do not make the wound.

Only a year later, however, Marvin's revelation in the *Globe* severely wounded Salisbury.

While affecting to be superior to the press – one of his best-known quips was that the *Daily Mail* was a newspaper 'written by office-boys, for office-boys' – Salisbury read it avidly, spending no less than £62.4s.5d on newspapers in 1887 (at W.H. Smith's, naturally), more than the £57.14s.10d he spent on books that year. The floor of his railway carriage would be covered by papers he had read and discarded in his voracious quest for information. Yet he would not allow *The Times* to send a reporter to his Party meetings, telling Buckle that he did not want MPs' words 'immortalised in an authentic report'. He was also very reluctant to confer honours on newspaper editors, calling it 'an entirely new proceeding' likely to provoke 'the utmost jealousy'. By 1896 he had tossed a baronetcy to George Armstrong, proprietor of the *Globe*, however, and a barony to Henry Gibbs, the Conservative MP who founded the *St James' Gazette*. When in 1895 Sir Algernon Borthwick, the Tory MP and proprietor of the *Morning Post*, became the 1st Baron Glenesk, Salisbury apologised to Hartington, explaining that 'the Queen is very fond of him'.

Salisbury was keen that rich Tories should buy newspapers, and put £500 into the *Western Gazette* himself. The principal Conservative agent, Captain Richard Middleton, who had taken over after G.C.T. Bartley resigned over Salisbury's handling of the Reform issue, was assiduous in trying to find buyers for Liberal newspapers, however minor, which could then be 'turned'. He once attempted (unsuccessfully) to interest Salisbury in investing in the *Crewe and Nantwich Advertiser*.[4]

In his evidence to a Select Committee on parliamentary reporting in 1881, Salisbury complained that misreporting had often embarrassed him, but blamed the bad acoustics in the Lords rather than the reporters. By 1886, he would stand with his back to the Woolsack for important speeches and direct his voice straight at the reporters' gallery. The worst misreporting he believed came from the news agencies, particularly that of Baron Reuter, whom he considered having the secret service attempt to bribe. 'I can't affect the least surprise that you were deceived by the news spread abroad by the telegraphic correspondents,' he told the newspaperman W.T. Stead in 1897. 'I have never had experience of a more imaginative body of men.'

Over one newspaper, the *Standard*, Salisbury did have some influence, though far less than his enemies imputed, through the activities of an acolyte called Alfred Austin. Minute in stature yet vain as Cicero, Austin was a leader-writer who also penned execrable, ultra-Jingoistic verse. He is credited, perhaps unfairly, with these deathless lines on the illness of the Prince of Wales in the winter of 1871/2:

> Across the wires the electric message came:
> 'He is no better, he is much the same.'

As well as penning doggerel, the walrus-moustachioed Austin defended Salisbury's interests, attacked his rivals within the Party, put a positive gloss on his defeats and even allowed Salisbury occasionally to rewrite his copy, sometimes with the knowledge of the editor, W.H. Mudford. Although nominally Tory, Mudford's *Standard* reserved the right to cause trouble to the Party leadership, especially over the Irish land question. In his struggles against Northcote and Randolph Churchill,

Salisbury nevertheless found the *Standard* a useful ally.

In late October 1882, a group of rich Tories, led by Carnarvon, had set up the *National Review*, to be jointly edited by Austin and W.T. Courthorpe. Salisbury hoped that it might 'give something of a scientific shape to the mass of Conservative thought which lives at the bottom of most educated men's minds'.[5] The first issue appeared in March 1883, and it soon reached an average quarterly sale of 1,300, which Salisbury thought not bad, 'especially when it's distinctive political colour is considered'. In July 1883, Salisbury had to renege on his promise to write for it immediately – 'my days have been all snipped up into little bits' – but, in November, 'Labourers' and Artisans' Dwellings' appeared there and 'The Value of Redistribution' the next year.

Alfred Austin's correspondence with Salisbury, and occasional invitations to Hatfield, helped the unctuous hack to turn into a monster of conceit, writing of Salisbury in the second volume of his autobiography that 'our minds, if I might venture without vanity to say so, were cast in somewhat the same mould... my concern in Politics was for the welfare of the State, not my personal advantage'. When asked for an autograph in later life, Austin appended the uplifting but in his case otiose motto: 'Humility is the Window of the Heart.' He was, however, useful to Salisbury during the Reform agitation; Salisbury told him of his fellow peers that 'having no constituents they are very sensitive to opinion – especially of papers of their own side'. In 1889, Salisbury wrote to congratulate Austin on the success of the *National Review*, saying that he liked the way the articles lacked 'ardour', because 'there is a feeling of relief in escaping from the elephantine earnestness affected by Radical writers'.

During the problems with Randolph Churchill over the National Union, the *Standard* also took a distinctly pro-Salisbury stance. But overall Salisbury was being accurate when he told the Queen, on the news in March 1887 that the Sultan took his view of English politics from the columns of the *Standard*, that 'occasionally it will put in what it is asked to put in: but that is very rare. The paper is quite independent: but we have to bear the brunt of its proceedings.' Even as late as April 1895 Salisbury was complaining to his son-in-law, Lord Selborne, who had married Maud in October 1883, that he was never able to persuade either foreign ambassadors or Joseph Chamberlain 'that I did not write the whole paper'.[6]

'Defy England and England will astound the world by her cowardice,' announced the *Kölnischer Zeitung* in 1885, and Salisbury feared that with Gladstone still in power this was perceptive advice. When on 30th

March the Russian commander General Komarov successfully attacked and occupied Penjdeh in Afghanistan, inflicting heavy losses on Abdur Rahman and breaking a delimitation agreement signed less than a fortnight before with Gladstone's Government, a full-scale international crisis developed. The Cabinet applied to Parliament for £11.5 million of war credits and called up the Army Reserve. Sharp falls on the Stock Exchange greeted each new item of bad news.

Opening a new Conservative Club in Wrexham on 21st April, Salisbury joked that during the Midlothian campaign Gladstone's 'observations were conveyed in that voluminous form which requires his matchless intonation to make it tolerable', and argued that the evacuation of Kandahar had been disastrous. 'The name of England no longer commands the respect it did,' he told 6,000 people. 'A name is a precious inheritance in the guardianship of a nation.' On the train journey from Wrexham to Welshpool the next day, a clergyman and several ladies entered Salisbury's carriage and showered him with cluster of primroses, a combination of Disraeliana and invasion of privacy that amounted to purgatory for him, but which he acknowledged politely.

It was at Hackney on 5th May, in a speech opening a new Conservative clubhouse, that Salisbury made one of what Morley called his famous 'blazing indiscretions'. Admitting that Russia might be sincere when she made promises after the Penjdeh incident, he said that 'whether swindler or bankrupt, you are very careful about trusting him the next time'. Elsewhere in the speech he added: 'I rather dread that word *prestige*. It is a French word which is connected with conjuring...but it expresses an idea of the utmost importance to the people of this country.' By stigmatising Russia as a 'swindler or bankrupt', Gladstone thought Salisbury had used 'strong language in reference to a friendly Power' and the press agreed. Salisbury had to give a personal explanation in the House of Lords a week later, saying that he had merely employed 'a commercial analogy', but it was nonetheless thought to have damaged his position severely *vis-à-vis* Northcote. Gladstone even hoped 'that this speech makes it almost impossible for the Queen to send for Lord Salisbury'.[7]

Over the previous year, Northcote had been slipping back in the leadership stakes. 'If he could hardly be said to lead the Conservatives in the House of Commons', wrote one Tory backbencher, he 'at all events strolled in front of them and was recognised as their nominal chief'. Salisbury had acknowledged as early as October 1882 that 'an electioneering atmosphere hangs around us'. Despite that, the two families stayed at St Raphaël together for a week the following February. Northcote's tour of Scotland in Gladstone's wake in September 1884 had been a flop, drawing far smaller crowds than Salisbury attracted

later that month. The argument put by Northcote's supporters, such as
W.H. Smith, that the House of Commons was now too important a
political arena for Prime Minister to be absent from it, seemed to be
contradicted by the Reform question which had centred almost entirely
on the actions of the Lords. By mid-April 1885, Northcote was ill, be-
leaguered by Churchill and complaining at the way the press 'daily and
monthly seems to take for granted the leadership of Salisbury'.

Northcote was of course, entirely *au fait* with the disloyalty of the
Fourth Party, and indeed kept a file amongst his papers with the title
'*Incedis per ignes suppositos cinere doloso 1883-4*', a quotation from
the Odes of Horace which translates: 'You are walking over fires that lie
concealed beneath deceitful ashes.'[8] Salisbury stayed resolutely aloof
from the fray, telling Churchill, who had again tried to draw him into
an anti-Northcote plot in late April 1884, that 'I am bound to Sir S.N. –
as a colleague – by a tie, not of expediency; and I could not take part in
anything which would be at variance with entire loyalty to him.' He
did, however, obliquely acknowledge that there was a problem of leadership in the Commons, and suggested that Churchill assist Northcote
rather than attempt to supersede him there.

The final choice between Salisbury and Northcote lay not with the
Shadow Cabinet, the Carlton Club, or even the press, still less with
Tory MPs or the Party at large, but with Queen Victoria. As the Party
would not decide whom it preferred, her decision on whom to choose to
form the next administration would end the uncertainty. She had on
several occasions told both her private secretary Sir Henry Ponsonby
and her confidant Lord Rowton, Beaconsfield's former private secretary
Montagu Corry, that Northcote would be the man. It was always
against the odds that Salisbury would emerge as the successful candidate, considering how often he and the Queen had disagreed in the past.

Salisbury had taken a predictably utilitarian view of royalty in the
Saturday Review, considering it an invaluable political, social and
constitutional instrument but utterly refusing to flatter the individuals
concerned, let alone employ Beaconsfield's recommended trowel. 'In
the case of royalties,' he had written in 1860, 'the boundary line
between adulation and affection is very narrow, and a writer of delicacy
will jealously guard himself from approaching its extremist border.'
Salisbury respected the Prince Consort's ability, and genuinely regretted
his death, not least for the way it tipped the scales of royal favour
against Gladstone and towards Disraeli. Although he generally thought
constitutional history was 'trash', Salisbury wrote an article in the
Quarterly Review in April 1862 that was remarkable for its echoes in

Walter Bagehot's hugely influential book, *The English Constitution*, five years later.

> We have eased the descent from a monarchy that once was absolute to the indefinable balance of power with which we at present live by the convenient help of constitutional fictions. Our theory, as it stands, is that the sovereign exerts all the power of the executive, while her minister bears all the responsibility. Of course, in its literal sense this never has been true, and never can be.

When Queen Victoria's son, Prince Alfred was offered the Greek throne in 1862, Salisbury merely mocked, saying that it looked as if 'a fearful famine of royalties has just set in', for whereas fifty years ago 'the great German supply was as then almost untapped, and was believed to be ample for all contingencies', now Europe had to resort to British princes. When the Queen retreated to Windsor after Albert's death, Salisbury criticised her for her 'unfulfilled duty' to her people, writing in the *Saturday Review* in 1864: 'Seclusion is one of the few luxuries in which Royal personages may not indulge.... Human affections will not fasten upon abstractions.'

It was as well for his future career that the Queen did not know it was he who had attacked 'the calamity of a reclusive Sovereign' and warned that 'we cannot live on the loyalty inspired by the Court Circular'.[9] Over the Schleswig-Holstein Question, Salisbury had supported the Danes when the Queen sympathised with her German cousins and son-in-law. He pointed out to his readership that when, as in the reigns of Charles I, William III and the first two Georges, sovereigns were thought to be influenced by the advice of foreign relations, they came to grief, because 'the national will must necessarily be supreme in the last resort'.

'I am very much obliged to you', Salisbury wrote to Derby in September 1866, 'for having got me off the Scotch trip.' Although he had first met the Queen in October 1846 when she and Prince Albert visited Hatfield, it was not until March 1866 that Salisbury was officially presented at Buckingham Palace by his father. Within a year the Queen was receiving back Cranborne's ministerial seals in stern silence. He intensely disliked staying at Balmoral, which he referred to as 'Siberia', and resented the length of time it took to get there and back. When Prime Minister, his rooms had to be heated to a minimum temperature of sixty degrees Fahrenheit before he went up. 'He refused to walk out,' Ponsonby recalled of a reluctant Salisbury visit to Balmoral in 1875, 'and did not conceal his entire abhorrence of the place and the life here. He positively refused to admire the deer which [the Queen's lady-in-waiting] Lady Ely pointed out to him.' It was hardly behaviour likely to endear him to a sovereign who so loved the Highlands.

Nor did their religion unite them. The ever-practical monarch regarded different sects in the Church of England as 'very unnecessary', and she had been one of the driving forces behind the Public Worship Regulation Act which Salisbury had thought both unwelcome and potentially schismatic. Beyond demanding that the Star of India should not be 'too common', she had little to do with his second period in office as Secretary of State for India, although she tried to block his idea of sending the Prince of Wales there.[10] When speaking of possible future leaders of the House of Lords with Cranbrook in September 1875, she 'doubted of Salisbury but evidently likes him'.

Queen Victoria's sympathies were so violently anti-Russian and pro-Turkish over the Eastern Question, partly because of her memories of the Crimean War, that Beaconsfield even told Derby in January 1878 that he doubted 'whether there is not in all of this a beginning of insanity'. The Queen believed that Russia posed a direct military threat to India, which Salisbury did not. Salisbury also suspected that the Cabinet crisis of October 1877, when Beaconsfield seemed to want to push him and Carnarvon to resignation, 'had all the air of a Scotch intrigue'.

All the conditions were present, therefore, for at best a stand-off and at worst actual bad relations. Yet as Foreign Secretary Salisbury had developed a genuine toleration of, and then a great trust of, the Queen, even paying her the accolade of saying that talking foreign affairs with her was like talking about them with a man. He found her assessment of her nephews' and cousins' characters extremely useful, especially considering how much of Europe they ruled over. The Queen ran an intelligence service based on her wide and ideally placed cousinage that was in many ways superior to that of the Foreign Office. When the Austrian Crown Prince committed suicide at Mayerling she was able to put Salisbury right about the lovelorn, unpolitical circumstances.

Like many Victorians, the Queen derived a *frisson* of pleasure from being shocked, and Salisbury was no prude either. When in 1879 the natural daughter of the British Consul-General in Siam, Miss Fanny Knox, ran off with Phra Phri Cha, a Siamese provincial governor and embezzler, and became one of his wives, Salisbury spared the Queen no detail of the salacious tale. 'He persuaded her to elope and to sleep one night with his other wives, of whom he has a large number, on board his steam yacht,' he reported. The Consul-General had even attempted to call up a British man-of-war to chastise the Siamese Government for having had his reprobate future son-in-law flogged thirty times for his misdemeanours, both financial and sexual.[11]

The myth that Queen Victoria was in any sense an unbiased constitutional monarch has long since been exploded. In the early part of her reign, she had shown great prejudice against the Tories, but by the

1880s Gladstone was almost right when he told Edward Hamilton that there was 'no greater Tory in the land'. She was quite ready to ask Salisbury's opinion on Gladstone's Cyprus policy even when Salisbury was in opposition, and during the Irish Home Rule crisis she was to do far worse than that. Over the Arrears Bill she wanted Salisbury to capitulate before he damaged the House of Lords, and her sympathies were all with Richmond, Cairns and the 'arch-funkers' during the Reform crisis in 1884. It would have easily been within her power to call for Northcote to form a ministry, as she had privately told him she would, and neither Salisbury nor any of his supporters could have done anything much about it.

When her Highland servant John Brown died in 1883, the Dean of Windsor, Randall Davidson, managed, after strenuous discussion with her, to dissuade the Queen from writing his biography. During that anxious period he wrote a sentence in his journal that was edited out of his 1938 biography: 'There is a good deal more difficulty in dealing with a spoilt child of sixty or seventy than with a spoilt child of six or seven … the vagaries or follies on the part of people who had the extreme disadvantage of being free all their life from the wholesome influence of their equals.'[12] Davidson also stated that the Queen only respected people who showed themselves capable of standing up to her. It was a category into which Salisbury certainly fell, and this did him no harm when she came to make her choice in 1885.

In the event, Queen Victoria threw Northcote over with scarcely a backward glance. Salisbury had emerged as the man best placed to save her from her ultimate political nightmare – five more years of William Ewart Gladstone. After a quarter of a century of finding themselves on opposite sides, there was at last something, or in this case someone, where the Queen and Salisbury could agree. After she made her choice there was little on which they disagreed, and by the time of her death sixteen years later, she named Salisbury as her best Prime Minister, superior even to her beloved Disraeli.

$$\sim$$

'Matters are gloomy – I never saw them gloomier,' Salisbury wrote to Cairns on 3rd March 1885. 'We have differences amounting to very serious tension with France – Russia – and Germany which carries Austria. Add to that Egypt, Ireland and a crushing Budget in prospect, and trade which will not revive. I can't be thankful enough to those fourteen gentlemen who stand between us and such an inheritance as that. But can the Government go on?' He was equally pessimistic with his brother, and blamed democracy: 'All this is the mere flowering of the bed which was grafted in 1867. I expect the House of Commons will be mainly filled by tradesmen trying to secrete gentility...you will every day congratulate yourself that you are out of it – for there is little honour to be won in the politics of the future.' Matters were not improved by the resignation in late March of the Party's principal agent, G.C.T. Bartley, who, to Salisbury's disgust, wrote to *The Times* to publicise his action, saying the co-leaders were 'not in harmony and touch with the great body of Conservatives' and that 'simple criticism, obstruction, mild platitudes and abuse...will not now form an Opposition which can command the respect and confidence of the Party'.

It was understood that there would be a general election in November, as soon as the register of the new electorate was ready; the only question was whether the Liberals would be in Government or Opposition when it took place. For the reasons given in his letter to Cairns, who died of pneumonia on 2nd April, Salisbury originally wanted Gladstone to be Prime Minister when it came, and thus more visibly to blame for the foreign policy reverses of the previous five years. 'Our chance in November will be all the better for our not winning now,' he also told Churchill. The Irish Coercion Act was coming up for renewal, and with relative peace in Ireland non-renewal was thought to be popular with Irish voters in the United Kingdom as well as with Parnell's Home Rule MPs. In early June rumours abounded that the Government was split over the decision, taken on the 5th, to renew the Act after all. Hicks Beach wrote to Salisbury on Sunday the 7th to say that, after a long talk with Churchill that evening, they both thought 'that we could keep the peace in Ireland until a General Election was over, without the renewal of the Coercion Act', but that the Conservative Party would need convincing and Salisbury was 'the only man who could persuade them'.

Northcote had a bad cold, and Salisbury advised him not to bother coming down to the House of Commons for the Budget vote on Monday, 8th June. 'Nothing would be more intolerable than a ministerial crisis just now,' he told Janetta Manners, 'and nothing would be harder on the Tories. To have to govern six months with a hostile but dying Parliament is the very worst thing that can happen to us.' Her husband had experience of serving in Derby's three minority governments and Salisbury felt sure 'his recollection of it will not be cheering'. There was loud cheering, nonetheless, led by Randolph Churchill, when at 1.45 a.m. on Tuesday, 9th June, Hicks Beach's amendment to the Budget's increases on beer and spirits duty and succession tax passed by 264 to 252, the Irish Nationalists having voted with the Conservative Opposition. Later that morning, Gladstone rose to announce that he had forwarded 'a dutiful communication to her Majesty', and the House adjourned.

For all Churchill's jubilation, Salisbury was unimpressed. He sent Akers-Douglas to find out how the Government majority could possibly have collapsed so badly, suspecting that the Liberals had deliberately organised it in order to be able to fight the November election as the underdogs. Akers-Douglas reported that seventy-six unpaired Liberal MPs had been absent from the division. 'No member was seen in the Central Lobby during the division – sixteen Liberals who did not vote were in the House earlier in the evening.' (Small wonder, with such a level of accuracy, that he acquired the nickname 'the Prince of Whips'.) 'The prospect before us is very serious,' Salisbury wrote to Cranbrook on Wednesday the 10th. 'The vote on Monday night was anything but a matter for congratulation.'[13]

The first man for seventeen years to become Prime Minister who was neither Disraeli nor Gladstone, Salisbury was on the verge of what he had once quoted Macaulay as calling 'the closely-watched drudgery, mocked by the name of power'. When Disraeli had become Prime Minister in 1868, he famously exulted that he had 'climbed to the top of the greasy pole'. Equally as flamboyantly, Gladstone had laid down his axe at Hawarden later the same year and grandly intoned: 'My mission is to pacify Ireland.' It was supremely characteristic of Salisbury's pessimism and modesty that, on the very threshold of his first premiership, his instinctive reaction to the vote that won him power was that it 'was anything but a matter for congratulation'.

TWENTY

'Elijah's Mantle'

The Ministerial Crisis – Cabinet-Making

June 1885

'An indiscreet admirer is a far more intolerable nuisance than an
acrimonious enemy.'

'It has been a week of conclaves and conspiracies,' Salisbury had written
in the *Saturday Review* in February 1860, 'of pulse-feeling and thumb-
screwing, of slippery intrigues and abortive stratagems.' June 1885 saw
an entire month incorporating all of those and more, as Salisbury
changed his mind about going into Government, screwed concessions
out of Gladstone not to use his preponderant majority in the Commons
to make Conservative governance impossible before the election, and
reconciled Churchill and Northcote to serving in the same Cabinet
together. It was by no means certain that the Conservatives should take
office at all. Salisbury had approved when Disraeli had refused
Gladstone's 'poisoned chalice' in March 1873, forcing the similarly
damaged Liberal ministry into the 1874 defeat. He was highly suspicious of what he saw as Gladstone's manoeuvre in losing the Budget
vote, and worried whether the Conservatives would do better in the
November elections after five months of Government than if they
stayed in Opposition.

On Tuesday, 9th June, after Gladstone's announcement, Northcote
visited Salisbury at Arlington Street and Hicks Beach arrived during
their discussion. Northcote recorded how Hicks Beach was 'much disinclined to take office, Salisbury hesitating: I strongly in favour,
considering that, with all its disadvantages, it was the only honourable
course open to us, after our action in turning out the present
Government'. The Liberals' taunt that the Conservatives had 'no policy
and no men' could only be rebutted by taking office, he argued. The
problem of whether to renew the Peace Preservation Act, by which
Ireland had been governed since 1882, would now become Salisbury's

rather than Gladstone's, and he was not at all keen to take it on. But, as Ponsonby informed the Queen on Wednesday the 10th, Salisbury was 'ready to, and will, form a Government if honoured by command'. Years later, Hicks Beach averred that it had only been the Queen's tears which induced Salisbury to take office.

Hicks Beach wrote to Salisbury on the 10th to say that Churchill wanted a place in any ministry formed, but, not wanting to look like a place-hunter, he hoped Salisbury would invite him to Arlington Street to discuss it. 'You know what a creature of impulse he is, and how he fancies neglect, etc, without cause.' Hicks Beach added that no Government could be formed 'without the man who is far and away the most popular Conservative in the House of Commons'. Salisbury knew it, but he also knew how deeply Churchill was disliked by Northcote, whose *amour propre* was about to receive a terrible blow from the Queen.

According to one account, Salisbury was experimenting on wires in his laboratory at Arlington Street when the telegram arrived from Balmoral. It was at a little after six o'clock in the evening, but it summoned him there that same night. 'This is "being sent for" with a vengeance,' he wrote to the Liberal India Secretary, Lord Kimberley, as he prepared to catch the 9 p.m. mail train. In the meantime, Salisbury sent Cranborne to St James's Place to break the news to Northcote and ask him to visit Arlington Street. When Northcote arrived, Hicks Beach was also there, and Salisbury sketched out a scheme whereby he would become Prime Minister and Foreign Secretary, making Northcote First Lord of the Treasury and Leader of the House of Commons, thus almost splitting the premiership with him. It would be the first time since the Elder Pitt that the first minister in the Government would not also be the First Lord of the Treasury. Northcote would have the government patronage and appointments, but Salisbury would see the ambassadors. As the architect of the Congress of Berlin, Salisbury could hardly be refused this, but Northcote did prevent Cross becoming Chancellor of the Exchequer, for, as he told his diary, 'I could not stand Cross's fussiness, and constant desire to push himself forward.'

When Hicks Beach suggested that Balfour should go to Ireland, Salisbury said he wanted him for the Local Government Board, as 'I must have someone there with whom I can be in close relations.' The mask of joint leadership had slipped, and Northcote recorded how 'I noticed to myself this little indication of the intention to grasp at everything.' Northcote asked to see all the Foreign Office telegrams, 'otherwise we may be exposed to serious trouble' in the Commons, to which Salisbury readily agreed. At lunch earlier that day, Salisbury had told Lord John Manners that he wanted Cross to be Chancellor of the Exchequer, Churchill to be Secretary for India and Gibson to be Home

Secretary. So far only one of those arrangements had been made impossible by Northcote.[1] In order to avoid the reporters, whom he called 'touts', at the railway station, Salisbury went to Balmoral alone in a third-class compartment. 'It's evidently a mistake!' he had the satisfaction of hearing one of them shout from the platform. 'He's certainly not on the train.'

Northcote had been mortified at the way the Queen had let him down, and, it was said, became so emotional that he had to leave the room after Cranborne broke the news to him. He decided the next day to raise the price of his accession to the Government, suspecting that he had sold himself short the previous evening. Although he seemed to Manners to be 'content with, or rather resigned to, Salisbury's primacy', he started making conditions and telegraphing them to Balmoral. He wanted to have 'regular direct communication with the Sovereign', close involvement in the selection of Treasury ministers and civil servants, and a 'scientific frontier' formally agreed between his political role and Salisbury's. He evidently felt a form of dual leadership could continue in Government as it had in Opposition, but Salisbury had other ideas.

Up at Balmoral, Salisbury asked the Queen to telegraph Gladstone asking him to reconsider his resignation, which she duly did. 'I am sure he will not take office unless he is absolutely forced to,' Lady Salisbury told Lord Bath of her husband that day. Gladstone declined. So why, without any cast-iron assurances from Gladstone that he would not harry his ministry, did Salisbury then agree to go in? Hicks Beach believed that it was the Queen's tearful insistence that the dangerous international situation, with Bismarck threatening to 'Europeanise' the Egyptian Question and Austria announcing her neutrality in the event of an Anglo-Russian war over Penjdeh, made it imperative that Salisbury rather than Gladstone should direct foreign policy. Politicians who say they do not want the premiership always have to be taken with a pillar of salt, but Salisbury's belief that it would harm his November election chances was genuine. If becoming Prime Minister for five months in June would damage his prospects for the next five years, such doubts were justified. Although Ponsonby, who had a ringside seat and was in a good position to know, thought Salisbury was 'very pleased' to take office, Churchill and Balfour believed that without such a pressing foreign situation he would have refused it.[2]

When told of the general wish, expressed at the Carlton Club, that he should go to the Upper House, Northcote wryly noted in his diary on Sunday, 14th June: 'With some of them it is a wish to get rid of me; with others it is anxiety for my health.' The same day, on returning to Hatfield from Balmoral, Salisbury wrote to him to say that he had 'of course, told the Queen, as I had previously told Ponsonby, that if she preferred that you should form the Government, I should acquiesce very willingly in the arrangement, but that was a matter purely for her independent decision'. Cranbrook hoped that Northcote had not been too hurt by the Queen's choice of Salisbury, 'but for more than a year events have given the latter a clear precedence in and outside the party'.

On Sunday the 14th, Salisbury was still hoping for an undertaking from Gladstone, expressed via the Queen, that the Liberals would support the necessary legislation for finding, by loans if necessary, the money required to undertake their own votes of credit and Estimates. 'Otherwise we shall be put in an impossible position,' Salisbury told her. Gladstone was understandably reluctant to give Salisbury any such clear run, and a long, detailed and relatively ill-tempered correspondence ensued in which Salisbury tried to obtain Gladstone's assurance that his Government would not be pitched out before the November election, while Gladstone tried to retain complete freedom of action. Meanwhile, the Chief Whip, Rowland Winn, invited himself to Arlington Street when Salisbury arrived there on Monday morning to discuss a 'very real danger…of a rupture in our ranks'.[3] Undisguised hostilities over the spoils of office had broken out between the supporters of Churchill and Northcote.

At 12.30 p.m. on Monday, 15th June, Salisbury called a meeting of the Shadow Cabinet, which was attended by Northcote, Cross, Smith, Manners, Cranbrook, Richmond, Carnarvon, Sandon (by then the Earl of Harrowby), Gibson, Hicks Beach and George Hamilton. Frederick Stanley was detained in Lancashire. Churchill was invited, but refused to attend if Northcote was to be given the Leadership of the House and Cross was going to be in the ministry at all. All but two present were of the opinion that Salisbury should take office, on the understanding that Gladstone would allow them to wind up the uncontroversial but indispensable business of government. Hicks Beach and Hamilton were against going in without Churchill, and when Hicks Beach went so far as to complain that Salisbury had not tried to urge upon the Queen the necessity of forcing Gladstone to reconsider his resignation, Salisbury, with an unaccustomed *coup de théâtre*, produced from his pocket a telegram which the Queen had sent Gladstone, at his request, as well as Gladstone's telegram of refusal in reply.

Salisbury wound up the discussion 'by declaring that in honour he could not abandon the Queen, and that if he had to do so owing to the desertion of his colleagues, he should abandon public life'. It was a well-timed threat, and united everyone except Hicks Beach. Churchill's explanation for his non-attendance, that 'he did not like some of Lord Salisbury's friends', was generally thought to be 'preposterous', but Northcote recognised that without Churchill, who represented the younger, dynamic, Tory Democrat section of the Party, Salisbury could not form a viable ministry or fight a credible election campaign, and so he agreed to accept a peerage. 'I have not much heart in the matter,' he wrote in his journal that day, 'the Queen's passing me over without a word of sympathy or regret is not pleasant.'[4]

The Shadow Cabinet agreed to meet again at noon on Wednesday the 17th, by which time Salisbury would have attempted to break the Churchill boycott. Using Balfour as his intermediary, he contacted Churchill to arrange a meeting. 'Though I fear I must draw an unfavourable inference from your absence, I still venture to express a hope that you will allow me to put down your name for the India Secretaryship on the list which I must submit to the Queen on Wednesday,' Salisbury wrote in a letter which ignored Churchill's demands about Northcote and Cross.

That Monday evening there was an extraordinary scene in the House of Commons, when Drummond Wolff, a Churchill ally, moved the adjournment of a debate on the Lords' amendments to the Redistribution Bill. Dilke pointed out that the amendments had the support of both Salisbury and Northcote, which the latter publicly confirmed. Nevertheless, Gorst, Churchill and even Hicks Beach, along with thirty-one other Conservative MPs, voted for Drummond Wolff's overtly disloyal motion. The interpretation given to this act of insolence against the Party hierarchy was that it was the Churchillites' way of showing their power, embarrassing Northcote yet again and, in Sir Edward Hamilton's opinion, 'protesting publicly against revival of the old Tory Cabinet – the "Old Gang" as [Churchill] calls them'. He concluded that 'of course if Lord Salisbury cannot arrange the personal differences, his game will be up and we shall have to be back again'.

Hicks Beach later protested that he had been an unwitting accomplice in the vote, but it might just as easily have been his own way of putting a shot across Salisbury's bows. Only hours prior to his meeting with Salisbury, Churchill had eloquently demonstrated the impossibility of governing without him. According to Eustace, the group had also included 'orthodox' Tories (i.e. non-Churchillites) who had acted 'purposely to accentuate the apparent division of the party in the eyes of the public – and render its return to office impracticable'. These people wanted to fight the election out of office rather than in it and force Gladstone to stagger on in office for another six months. Salisbury himself suspected that they might be right. 'It is an evil world', he wrote to Eustace that day, 'is this political world.'

The next day, Tuesday, 16th June, Salisbury saw Churchill for an hour between eleven and noon at Arlington Street. Churchill had dismissively quipped that Salisbury 'can form a ministry if necessary with waiters from the Carlton Club' if he wished to exclude him, but at the meeting he accepted the India Office and demanded places for his supporters, Gorst (who became Solicitor-General) and Drummond Wolff (who became a privy councillor). Although Salisbury stood by Cross, he accepted Churchill's terms about Northcote's removal to the Lords, something a cynic might think suited him also, by removing his major rival's power base. As for Churchill, Salisbury hoped 'that the India Office would be a padded room for that restless being' for, as he told Northcote, 'he could be prevented from doing mischief by the Council at one end and [the Viceroy] Lord Dufferin at the other'. So, like Salisbury himself, Churchill became India Secretary aged thirty-six without having held any subordinate post.

It is possible that Salisbury also promised Churchill that Coercion would not be renewed in Ireland, although with Ireland quiescent and having no Commons majority in a Liberal-dominated Parliament, that might have been taken as a foregone conclusion. Churchill had been involved in secret talks with the Parnellites over the Coercion legislation, and on 11th June Cranbrook believed that he 'has evidently some assurance from some of the Irish. Can he trust them?'[5] The real question was whether the Conservatives could trust Churchill, because while waiting nervously for Salisbury to contact him he had even spoken to Rosebery about joining the Liberal Party if Salisbury's offer never came. Rosebery had offered to open negotiations for his admittance.

Telegraphing the Queen after the Churchill problem was removed, Salisbury said that Cross and Churchill would serve, but Northcote might have to go to the Colonial Office with a peerage. The Queen ciphered back, angry that the man about whom she might have had a guilty conscience had been so marginalised. Northcote's peerage was the origin of the political phrase 'kicked upstairs' to denote someone raised to the Lords in order to emasculate them politically. The Queen told Salisbury that she did not think Churchill 'should be allowed to dictate entirely on his own terms, especially as he has never held office before'. She furthermore said that she was 'ready to do anything' to facilitate a pledge of support from Gladstone for the survival of the ministry over the technical and financial votes still before the Commons. Arthur Balfour, whom Gladstone liked, had been sent that morning to ascertain whether the Liberal leader would allow Supply and Ways and Means Bills to pass the House smoothly. Gladstone answered, when also pressed on this by the Queen, that he would not 'embarrass' the new Government.

Meanwhile, Salisbury began filling up the junior posts. 'Are you disposed to join in our administrative cruise?' he asked Sir Henry Holland, offering him the Financial Secretaryship of the Treasury. 'It may not last long: and the weather will be rough. And it is certainly not to be looked upon as a pleasure party. But it will be pleasanter and more profitable if you are with us.' Holland accepted. Salisbury offered Richmond the Presidency of the Board of Trade, a post he had held fifteen years earlier and a significant demotion for the man who from 1870 to 1876 had been Leader of the House of Lords. To loyal Cranbrook he awarded the Lord Presidency of the Council.

It was all fitting neatly into place, especially once he had warned the Irish Tory leader, Edward King-Harman that he would probably not be reintroducing Coercion, and found it accepted. Irritated by gossip that he had been forced out of the Commons by Churchill and Hicks Beach, however, Northcote soon threatened to upset everything. Writing on 16th June about his 'gradual declension', he said that he did not want to take office at all. 'I cannot but feel that the position assigned to me is not what I might fairly have expected,' he wrote, adding that it was 'best for all' if he retired altogether. Salisbury, knowing how bad this would look to the Conservative backbench loyalists, replied: 'Your letter is very painful to me – more painful than I can say.' He pointed out that he would not have asked Northcote to give up the Leadership of the House of Commons unless he himself had suggested it only the day before.

Salisbury denied that Churchill had anything to do with the decision, but 'in view of the chaos of rivalries, and divisions that exist among our men in the House of Commons it would be better for your own useful-ness and peace of mind' if Northcote became Lord President of the Council (the post Cranbrook had accepted the day before), adding: 'But do not leave us altogether.' As a postscript to the letter, Salisbury said that if Northcote wanted to see him, 'I will come at any time.' Northcote's reply was pure pique: 'Is it not sufficient that I should leave the House of Commons and clear the way for others who are preferred to me?' In the end he was propitiated with an earldom, becoming Lord Iddesleigh. A document was even drawn up and signed by both men delineating precisely the powers he was to have over patronage and appointments, and he was given No. 10, Downing Street, the official residence of the First Lord of the Treasury. This was a small sacrifice for Salisbury, who anyhow had no intention of leaving his large town house in St James's for a terraced one in Whitehall. It was difficult to escape the conclusion, however, as Joseph Chamberlain joked in a speech in Islington the next day, that Churchill had 'his foot on Lord Salisbury's neck'.[6]

Wednesday, 17th June was spent attempting to get Gladstone to produce a more concrete promise than simply not to 'embarrass' the new Government. Winn told Salisbury that the rumours that the Liberals intended blocking ordinary Commons business were untrue; they would only vote down contentious legislation. As Salisbury told the Queen, he was unwilling to take office without a specific undertak-ing from Gladstone that he would be allowed to wind up the business of the session without opposition. Because the Reform Bill was just about to become law, there were new boundaries for constituencies but no new register of electors, so a dissolution could not take place until November under any circumstances. If Salisbury was to take over what was already being derisively called a 'caretaker' ministry, he needed to know that the Appropriations Bills would be passed and the day-to-day business of government allowed through the Liberal majority. Churchill, in a memorandum written four years later, acknowledged that in those anxious June days, 'Lord Salisbury was most reluctant to form a Government.'[7]

The shadow-boxing continued throughout Thursday the 18th. Gladstone and Rosebery went to Windsor and actually wrote out in the Queen's presence the headings of a memorandum which might reassure Salisbury. Gladstone did not want to give pledges which might tie his hands in the future, but understood, as he told the Queen, that Salisbury could not form a government without such a pledge 'at a juncture when an appeal to the constituencies is legally impossible'.[8] 'The hitch continues,' noted Edward Hamilton in his diary the next day, 'Lord Salisbury is not satisfied.' There was even talk that Salisbury's proposed new Lord Chancellor, Sir Hardinge Giffard, was asking for the legal briefs which he had turned down on the expectation of office to be sent back to him.

The hitch continued throughout Friday and Saturday, with Salisbury going so far as to refuse to proceed with passing the Seats Bill without a specific promise from Gladstone to 'concur in the measures which are indispensable for winding up the business of the session'. It is possible that he hoped that this loophole might allow him to slip out of the need to form a government altogether. *The Times* reported who entered and left Arlington Street, including Ponsonby, who stayed for much of Saturday morning. A Shadow Cabinet, with Northcote and Churchill at last sitting around the same table, was held at 4.30 p.m. An amused Northcote recorded in his diary that evening that 'we are pestered by reporters, who cross-question the servants. Smith (the butler) was asked the other day what office I was to have. "After much consideration the Cabinet had offered me the private secretaryship to Lord Randolph Churchill".'

Droll butlers aside, some sharp business was going on. Rowland Winn was another of the visitors to Arlington Street, and a memorandum he wrote Salisbury that Saturday the 20th shows the extent of the co-operation that was being negotiated between the Conservatives and the Irish Nationalists. Winn had spoken to Richard Power, the County Waterford MP and Parnellite Whip who had given him a list of possible future Chief Secretaries from which Salisbury could choose if he wanted Nationalist support in the forthcoming general election. Sir Henry

Holland, Robert Bourke, Sir William Hart Dyke and Arthur Balfour were on the list, with Gorst, Sir David Plunkett and Henry Raikes as runners-up. The only man they would not take was the ultra-Unionist Henry Chaplin. Furthermore, Parnell wanted two minor and relatively uncontroversial Bills passed, the first diminishing election expenses in unopposed constituencies and the second extending the time labourers could pay for land deals. In return he promised: 'If we can get these [we] will assist you all we can both now and at the general election,' claiming that the Irish vote could influence fifty mainland seats. Power undertook to furnish Winn with the names of those seats in which 'we will throw our influence to the Conservative side'.[9]

Churchill also held some equally off-the-record conversations with Parnell at this time, promising him that the Conservatives would not renew the Coercion Act, to which Parnell allegedly replied, 'In that case, you will have the Irish vote at the next election.' As Rosebery later commented on Churchill's denial that this constituted an actual agreement with Parnell: 'This may not have been a compact, but it is remarkably like one.'

Between noon and eight o'clock on Sunday evening, Ponsonby had gone backwards and forwards between Salisbury and Gladstone 'three or four times' with Salisbury's various modifications to a letter Gladstone would send the Queen. Edward Hamilton complained of 'so much haggling' over the content, and then more over exactly which letters should be made public, all of which led Gladstone to consider Salisbury's behaviour 'nothing short of impudence'. On Monday, 22nd June, Salisbury's patience and determination finally paid off. He wrote to the Queen asking her to write back to him a letter saying that 'he may reasonably accept [Gladstone's] assurances as a security that the new Government will receive the support necessary to enable it to complete the financial and other business of the session'. Armed with that, he called an inner Cabinet of Cranbrook, Manners, Richmond and Hicks Beach, and showed them the Queen's letter, which also asked him to form a government and offered to make her interpretation of Gladstone's undertakings public.

At the Monday meeting, Hicks Beach, who had hitherto been doubtful about going into government, said the Party should do so if Gladstone's letter were made public. A *précis* of the deal was published the next day in *The Times*. 'He has been ill to deal with,' Gladstone complained of Salisbury when it was all over, 'requiring incessant watching.' Cranbrook recorded how in forming his first ministry Salisbury was 'weary of the self-seekers, the beggars, the impracticable, and, above all, of one forced on him who plays such pranks', meaning Churchill.[10]

Salisbury submitted his list of ministers to the Queen at Windsor on

Tuesday, 23rd June. Iddesleigh became First Lord of the Treasury; Giffard (who became Lord Halsbury) re-returned his briefs and became Lord Chancellor; Gibson became Lord Chancellor of Ireland, taking a peerage as Lord Ashbourne; Salisbury himself was Prime Minister, Foreign Secretary and Leader of the House of Lords. In the Commons, Hicks Beach became Chancellor of the Exchequer and Leader of the House, Cross survived Iddesleigh's ire to become Home Secretary, Sir Frederick Stanley took the Colonial Office and W.H. Smith was Secretary of State for War. Lord George Hamilton had complained that he himself could not do the job, as having only been a Guards' ensign he could hardly push through military reforms against the formidable figure of Field Marshal the Duke of Cambridge, the Queen's cousin and Commander-in-Chief, so he was appointed First Lord of the Admiralty instead.

Lord John Manners became Postmaster-General, a not unimportant post in Victorian Britain as the Post Office was a large employer, and Edward Stanhope, the man who had run the Central Committee during the clashes with Randolph Churchill, took over the Education portfolio as Vice-President of the Council. With Churchill himself as Secretary for India it made a Cabinet of sixteen, the largest ever. Outside the Cabinet were Aretas Akers-Douglas, who at thirty-three took over from Winn as Chief Whip, and Arthur Balfour, who became an undistinguished President of the Local Government Board.

It was a 'Fair Trade' Cabinet, six of whom had spoken in favour of trade protection or retaliation. The Ulster Tories were very well represented, holding seven Government posts in all, thereby consoling them for the non-reintroduction of Coercion.[11] 'All the high political offices in the House of Lords are occupied by those who have had Cabinet office in the government of 1874,' Salisbury told a disappointed Lord Beauchamp. 'If we survive there must be gaps and consequently new arrangements.' The *Spectator* complained that it was a singularly aristocratic Cabinet, with all but three members either peers or sons of peers. It was also accused of being a landlords' Cabinet, but, as Salisbury only had to bring in an interim Budget and abstain from making any great changes in Egypt, the press thought he would be quite safe until the election.

The other important business of Monday the 22nd was to learn from Carnarvon, the new Viceroy of Ireland, whom he wished to have as his Chief Secretary. Carnarvon turned down the idea of Chaplin because he was 'personally disliked by the Irish members', and chose the former Chief Whip Sir William Hart Dyke. This was fortunate as Salisbury already knew from Winn, who retired and was created Baron St Oswald, that Parnell would accept him and not Chaplin. Hart Dyke was nevertheless to be outside the Cabinet, leaving Carnarvon in overall control of Irish policy. The appointment of Carnarvon surprised *cognoscenti*.

This was not because he did not have a *prima facie* right to high office – he had after all been a frontbencher for as long as Salisbury – but because, as Salisbury admitted to his family: 'I am not easy about Carnarvon – he is getting so very "green".'

Salisbury had been alerted to Carnarvon's pro-Home Rule tendencies earlier that year when they had dined together at the Travellers' Club and his friend had eulogised the ideas of Sir Charles Gavan Duffy. This moderate Irish nationalist and former premier of Victoria, Australia, had written an article entitled 'An Appeal to the Conservative Party', in the most recent edition of the *National Review*. This argued that, since Peel had established parliamentary government in Canada and Derby had established it in Australia, Ireland could be safely given Home Rule within a British imperial federation by the Conservatives. Of the propertied and Protestant minorities, Duffy – who had been a revolutionary in 1848 – argued that 'it is practicable to provide securities which would satisfy the most timid'. In his stint at the Colonial Office between 1874 and 1878, Carnarvon had enthusiastically worked the federal constitutions of Canada, Australia and South Africa, and he believed the same could be put in place for Ireland. Salisbury, however, believed that Ireland's unhappy historical links with England so contrasted with the other colonies as to invalidate the analogies.

Salisbury nevertheless knew that to encourage the belief that he was genuinely interested in such a solution might help reconcile the Parnellites to supporting the Conservatives for the next five months, and particularly at the coming general election. He was entirely unconvinced by the federal approach to the Irish Question; the very furthest he had been willing to go was to say in a letter to Carnarvon on 10th February: 'It is possible that such a scheme as you hope for may be devised, which would give us all requisite guarantees for the interests which we are bound in honour not to abandon, and yet would satisfy the separatists' feeling.'

This has often been quoted to suggest that Salisbury was willing to consider limited self-determination for Ireland, but the rest of the letter makes it quite clear that he was interested in stringing the Irish along, not in satisfying the nationalist aspirations that he had spent a lifetime decrying, and which in 'Disintegration' he had specifically refused to consider. 'I am not hopeful,' he told Carnarvon,

for I have been unable to think of any provisions which would satisfy the above requirements. But even if such a scheme were produced, it could only be accepted as an agreement by plenipotentiaries in the strict sense of the word – that is by those who can answer for the Irish party of movement on the one side, and those who can answer for the English Parliament on the other.... From that point of view I think we have plenty of time for reflection before us.

To extrapolate from this and from future events, as several historians and politicians have done, that Salisbury was in any way genuinely interested in enacting Home Rule himself, or was engaging with the Parnellites in earnest, is to misinterpret what he was trying to do in the early days of his first, minority premiership. He appointed Carnarvon, whom Parnell knew to be a convert to Home Rule ideas, in order to win support from the Irish for as long as he could, before they realised that he would never accord them anything substantive. Five days after the Travellers' Club dinner, Salisbury made it clear to Carnarvon that the proposed securities for the Protestant loyalist landowning minority in an all-Ireland state:

> do not seem to me of a precise or practical character. If you are handing over legislative power to a body you mistrust, and desire to insure any particular class or interests from a misuse of that power, you can only do so by establishing some controlling authority which you can trust, with sufficient jurisdiction, and sufficiently backed by material force.... In the case we have in our hands, no security of any kind could be allowed without some sort of Supreme Court. I do not see how even that could stand up against some popular outbreak of land-hunger.[12]

Without the physical power to force the Irish to accept the rulings of a British supreme court, the estates of people like Waterford and Abercorn could not be protected from a ravenous, confiscatory Dublin government. Issues of Ireland's own economic good, and of Britain's security should Ireland ally herself with an enemy, were other considerations in his thinking. Salisbury's most fundamental sticking point, however, was a profound disbelief in any long-term safeguards which would protect the Protestant clients of England whom his namesake, the 1st Earl of Salisbury, had planted in Ireland in the early seventeenth century. He also believed the Ulster Protestants would fight a civil war rather than submit to majority Catholic rule from Dublin. Yet if the Parnellites could be persuaded not to oppose him, or even to advise Irish mainland electors to vote Tory in the belief that constitutional concessions might come, he was more than willing to keep up the pretence of being interested in such a solution, and his letters to Carnarvon and others should be read in that light. It was perhaps cynical, but it was politics. It also worked spectacularly well.

What he might also have guessed, not least because the Queen (most unconstitutionally) told him, was that Gladstone himself was starting to consider embracing Home Rule. This was just the issue that might at last allow Salisbury to detach the Whigs from the Liberal Party. If Gladstone could be persuaded to think that the Conservatives were not fundamentally opposed to some kind of Irish separatism, he might be encouraged to come out in public with some actual proposals. Thus when Power spoke to Winn in late February 1885, he was told that Salisbury would not diminish the Irish representation of 103 seats at Westminster, even though the post-Famine population could not proportionally justify the retention of so many. The Parnellites' votes were being actively bought by Salisbury, although, as Winn insisted after a second meeting, 'no arrangement, compact or agreement was come to between us, nor was anything of such a nature either asked for or alluded to by either of us'. This is because it did not have to be; nods and winks were all it took.

Carnarvon made his views perfectly clear when he agreed to take on the Viceroyalty. Refusing to serve if Salisbury renewed Coercion, he wrote that the 'old methods of government of Ireland' were no longer applicable. The British Government, he said, had to 'run certain risks and make certain sacrifices' and what was needed was 'a full and permanent settlement of the Irish relations with England'. Because of the climate and his health, Carnarvon only agreed to take on the job for the six months until the general election, and hoped that 'when I resign it at the appointed time there may not be the slightest feeling that I give it up from any difference of opinion with yourself or the Party'.[13] With views like his in a Cabinet like Salisbury's, it was always a vain hope.

～

The business of ministry-making left Salisbury profoundly depressed. When George Buckle, the editor of *The Times*, visited Arlington Street after it was over, he was greeted warmly by the new Prime Minister:

> You are the first person who has come here to see me in the last few days who is not wanting something at my hands – place, or decoration, or peerage. <u>You</u> only want information. Men whom I counted my friends, whom I should have considered far above self-seeking, have been here begging, some for one thing, some for another, till I am sick and disgusted. The experience has been a revelation to me of the baser side of human nature.

This was something from a man who had witnessed the Great Australian Gold Rush.

On Wednesday, 24th June 1885, the whole Cabinet (except Richmond who had hurt his foot), along with five other senior ministers, took a special train to Windsor to kiss hands and receive their seals of office from a delighted Queen. It was a hot midsummer's day and through the open windows over the terrace garden, with Windsor Great Park beyond, they could see hay-making in progress. Manners enjoyed the 'exquisite and refreshing' view from the Castle as Salisbury kissed the monarch's hands as Prime Minister.

Salisbury had never had to canvass for himself. His parliamentary seat, the Leadership of the Lords, the Chancellorship of Oxford, the Party leadership and now the premiership itself had all come to him without once having to undergo the indignity of vote-grubbing. Some critics believed this was a misfortune, because it meant he never developed any personal knowledge of the ordinary elector, but his capacity for winning general elections – three out of five, each by a landslide – did not seem to suffer.[14] His perceived aloofness and obviously disinterested character might even have helped in those more socially deferential days to engender the feeling of trust, especially over foreign policy, that the British people were increasingly to feel in Salisbury's competence. Those commentators with a sense of history pointed out that once again a tall, stooping, brilliant, grey-bearded Cecil was chief counsellor to a great Queen at a time of much expansion, confidence and consequent danger.

As Rosebery later pointed out, the Conservatives had at last got a genuine Tory for a leader. Canning had been repudiated by the Tories, Wellington was entirely unideological, Peel was excommunicated by them, Derby had been a Whig minister and Disraeli had spoken in favour of Chartism in his early career. Here, by contrast and at long last, was a true believer in philosophical and practical Toryism, someone who since his schooldays had declared himself 'an *illiberal* Tory'.

Salisbury was fifty-five when he became Prime Minister for the first time, and at the height of his intellectual powers. His huge high forehead, thick greying beard, great height and bulk gave him an impressive physical presence. He also weighed eighteen stone according to the scales upon which the Prince of Wales weighed his guests at Sandringham. Salisbury was compounded of idiosyncrasies, such as a refusal to allow his family or friends ever to give him presents: 'I know it is odd: but I was brought up so.' He thought popular applause 'humbug', and suspected that people came to listen to his speeches from the same motives as 'those which drew them round the last monstrosity in a showman's booth'.

Salisbury had a genuine, unstudied modesty rarely seen in his calling. When asked to autograph a photograph of himself, he would usually sign it over the face. The idea of unveiling a bust of himself for the Edinburgh Conservative Association struck him as so 'insupportably ridiculous' that he 'rebelled'.[15] When Orangemen in Liverpool asked to name their Loyal Orange Lodge number 311 after him, he refused, but they went ahead anyway. Compliments gave him an almost physical pain. 'However kindly and sincerely meant,' he told Janetta Manners 'they are to me always intensely disagreeable. I dislike hearing them said by other people, one to another: and naturally much more do I dislike them being said to myself.'

Once when visiting his Dorset estate, Cranborne Manor, he saw the local band assembled on the railway platform to greet him. He stayed on the train for an extra stop to avoid them and doubled back by cab. 'An indiscreet admirer', he had written in the *Saturday Review*, 'is a far more intolerable nuisance than an acrimonious enemy.' His detection of personal vanity in Disraeli, Churchill and latterly in Gladstone also was a powerful motivation in his disapproval of all three. 'His clothes hung upon him anyhow,' recorded the dapper counsellor at the French Embassy, J.J. Jusserand, 'he seemed to be satisfied with any sort, provided they were not the fashion; his top hat always had the appearance of having been purposefully brushed the wrong way.' One political journalist believed that Salisbury's hat looked battered because of the brusque way he used to shove it under his seat in the House of Lords.

Not everyone agreed about Salisbury's lack of vanity. The Liberal Chief Whip in the House of Lords, the 4th Baron Ribblesdale, was once at Penhaligon's, the barber's shop in St James's Street, when he noticed the Prime Minister having his beard cut. Salisbury 'proved himself appreciative of his fine appearance. "Just a little more off here", and he indicated the exact spot.' Coming from the subject of John Singer Sargent's famous 'swagger' portrait, in which the jodhpured peer sports a top hat and long black cape and holds a riding crop as he poses beside a vast pillar in his country seat, such accusations of self-regard are rich indeed.[16]

Shyness was regularly ascribed to Salisbury, but the truly shy do not speak to audiences of 8,000 people. The genuine diffidence of his youth had instead metamorphosed into a love of privacy whenever he could find it. 'The owner of a fine park, or an old house,' he bemoaned in 1863, 'had better emigrate if he has a taste for seclusion,' because privacy for gentlemen was a mere matter of history, 'a luxury like hawking, of which they may study the pleasure in the descriptions of their ancestors, but which they must never hope to enjoy'. By middle age the prudery and self-consciousness of his adolescence had vanished, and contemporaries agreed that the way Salisbury gave himself far fewer airs than many under-secretaries was one of the most attractive facets of his personality. In a former Speaker's opinion, Salisbury 'was averse from public appearances or display and never attempted the minor arts of obtaining popularity'. This was entirely natural and not, as so often, a pose to win popularity by inverse means. He had the true aristocrat's utter lack of interest in what others thought of him. Having forgotten to take his skull cap to church at Hatfield during the winter, he once placed a grey woollen glove on his bald patch throughout the service.

One critic was the tutor who gave the Cecil children French lessons in Puys one summer and who noticed in Salisbury, '*la petite pointe de malice qui se montre dans les yeux et aux coins de sa bouche*'. Malice is a hard accusation for a statesman to refute, considering how many lives he has the ability to affect. It is easy enough to discern a touch of it in Salisbury's refusals when he considered people were pushing for honours. But other than a natural love of hearing gossip, and a suffused delight in refusing thrusting would-be baronets, Salisbury cannot be called a particularly malicious man.

Nor was he a prude, despite living such an exemplary private life. When Dilke was named as a co-respondent in a sensational divorce case, which featured a mother and her daughter and (separately) troilism, he was still reluctant to strip him of his privy councillorship. After Colonel Valentine Baker had been found guilty of making unwelcome advances to a lady in a railway carriage, Salisbury supported the most lenient of the various dismissal options available. (He eventually commanded the Egyptian police force.)

Victorian decorum often struck Salisbury as simply amusing; when Lord Stanley of Alderley demanded his intervention when a public gallery proposed to exhibit a nude portrait of St Elizabeth of Hungary, on the grounds that maid-servants might visit it, Salisbury remarked in the House of Lords that he was:

> wholly unable to enter into the discussion to which the noble Lord invites me, until he can lay down for me some canon as to the course artists should pursue in dealing with the question of clothes or no clothes. Artists take a very different view of the subject from that taken by the majority of mankind, and some of the matters which they represent as wholly innocuous, and, indeed, praiseworthy would, if translated into ordinary life, attract the attention of the police.

He considered a public exhibition better for St Elizabeth than a private gallery, as he thought fewer people went to them.

'The utter freedom from pomposity, formality and self-assertion,' wrote the Liberal politician G.W.E. Russell, 'and the agreeable clash of genuine cynicism which modifies, though it does not mask, the flame of his fun' was what made Salisbury a most un-Victorian Victorian statesman, who in certain things was almost a left-over from the reign of George IV which had ended five months after his birth.[17] Victorian high politics are not automatically associated with 'fun', but those who knew Salisbury well certainly thought him tremendously good fun; indeed, Gwendolen was taken to task by Lord George Hamilton for not making enough of her father's 'playfulness' in her biography. 'He loves to laugh,' said the veteran Russian Ambassador, Georges de Staal. Everyone and everything was a fit subject for Salisbury's ironic humour, said one of his few close advisers, Philip Currie, except of course 'the Christian religion as by law Established in England'.

The way in which Cabinet business was easily expedited, at least after Randolph Churchill's departure, was aided by Salisbury's dry, very English wit, which survives in his correspondence and marginalia. His eccentricities, witticisms and jotted notes generated a huge collection of anecdotes about him, which were then refracted throughout the political scene, acquiring the embellishments which tend to accrue to good stories. No less a master of the English language than Lord Randolph's son paid tribute to the quality of Salisbury's letters, saying they:

> have a character and interest apart from and even superior to the events with which they deal. A wit at once shrewd and genial; an insight into human nature penetratingly comprehensive, rather cynical; a vast knowledge of affairs; the quick thoughts of a moody, fertile mind, expressed in language that always presents a spice and flavour of its own, are qualities which must exert an attraction upon a generation to whom the politics of the '85 Government will be dust.

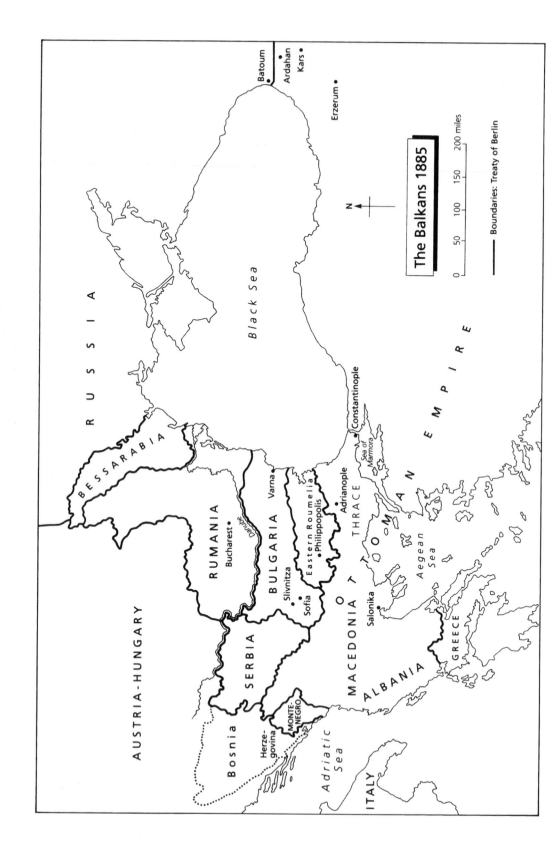

The Balkans 1885

Boundaries: Treaty of Berlin

0   50   100   150   200 miles

Batoum
Ardahan
Kars
Erzerum

Black Sea

RUSSIA

BESSARABIA

AUSTRIA-HUNGARY

RUMANIA
Bucharest
Danube

SERBIA
Sofia
Slivnitza

BULGARIA
Varna

Eastern Roumelia
Philippopolis

Adrianople

Constantinople

Sea of Marmora

THRACE

OTTOMAN EMPIRE

Bosnia

Herze-govina

MONTE-NEGRO

Adriatic Sea

ITALY

MACEDONIA

ALBANIA

GREECE

Salonika

Aegean Sea

TWENTY-ONE

The 'Caretaker' Ministry

The Zulficar Pass –
The Drummond Wolff Mission –
The Carnarvon–Parnell Interview –
The Bulgarian Crisis –
The Newport Speech

June to November 1885

'I danced my egg-dance with fair success.'

Salisbury's bitter joke, that the Liberal Government had 'achieved their desired Concert of Europe, they have succeeded in uniting the continent of Europe – against England', had more than a hint of truth. Britain was more isolated in June 1885 than she had been for decades. With the risk of war with Russia over Penjdeh and the Zulficar Pass, Britain had lost the friendship of Bismarck, who had attacked the Gladstone Government in the Reichstag on 2nd March and seemed happy, in return for a resuscitation of the *Dreikaiserbund*, to let Russia have a free hand in Asia. The Sublime Porte had been entirely alienated by the obsessively Turcophobic Gladstone Government, and would have closed the Straits against any significant blow the British navy might have been able to strike against Russia in time of war. France, furious at the way dual control in Egypt had been replaced in 1882 by unilateral British military occupation, was agitating for a European grouping to redraw global colonial boundaries at Britain's expense. Perhaps worst of all, Austria, which Salisbury had taken great pains to woo during his Foreign Secretaryship, was drawing closer to Russia out of fears, as the Ausrian Foreign Minister Count Gustav von Count Kálnocky confirmed at the time, that Granville was about to conclude an agreement with St Petersburg.

With the Mahdi victorious in the Sudan and now threatening southern Egypt, Russian generals plotting to annex Herat and Britain isolated internationally, Salisbury could hardly have inherited a worse situation. But as he told a meeting of the Conservative Party in the Carlton Club soon after kissing hands, 'a timorous policy would be an unwise, if not a fatal one'. At his very first Cabinet meeting, Salisbury therefore cancelled Gladstone's arbitration agreement with Russia over the Zulficar Pass and telegraphed Wolseley to halt the evacuation of Dongola in the Sudan. He meant to show Russia and the Mahdi that Britain would fight if her stategic interests in Afghanistan and Egypt were further threatened.

In claiming to the Party meeting that the Liberals had been unwilling to return to government, the *Spectator* said that Salisbury 'overshot the truth', but in presenting his premiership as fulfilling a duty of honour to the Queen, it worked well. Without a Commons majority, he also needed no legislative programme. The only significant domestic items on his agenda were transferring Scottish education to a new Scottish Office and the setting up of a Royal Commission to report on the depression of trade and industry. The Government would tread water until the election, and by early August Salisbury could reply to the Queen that the only business before the House of Lords was a Bill to enable pleasure parties on the Thames to moor their boats opposite the lawns of people who had houses on the river.[1]

The situation was entirely different abroad. Reported Russian troop movements around the Zulficar Pass in Afghanistan were worrying the Government of India. The Viceroy, Salisbury's schoolfriend the Earl of Dufferin, feared that Afghanistan's status as a buffer state was in danger. The crisis had to be dealt with jointly by Salisbury and Churchill, and throughout the new Prime Minister treated his India Secretary with great courtesy. By the time Salisbury became Prime Minister, he was writing to Churchill as 'My dear Randolph', a rare privilege. Had he not been quite so ambitious, Churchill could easily have become Salisbury's heir apparent, despite his unrivalled capacity for putting people's backs up. His cleverness and oratorical ability might have prevailed over his rashness, rudeness and utter lack of principle.

The Zulficar Pass, at least to the 'Forward' school of India strategists, was the place through which the Russians, who were at Merv and thus closer to Herat than the British at Quetta, could bypass the difficult terrain of the Hindu Kush and march into India. General Sir Frederick Roberts, by then Commander-in-Chief in Madras, had written to Salisbury on the day the Gladstone Government lost the Budget vote in the Commons, warning that the Russians were 'at the gates of Herat' and saying that Britain needed to recapture Kandahar as soon as possible to counter the threat, should Herat fall. A paper he had written urging the British garrison in India to be increased from 65,000 to 80,000 men presented a 'domino' theory, whereby if Russia's influence were to be felt in Kabul, it would gradually extend through Chitral, Yasin, Gilgit and Kashmir to India herself. Salisbury replied, agreeing that the doctrine of a 'friendly Afghan' had 'pretty well broken down', but he did not consider such a large-scale military commitment necessary. 'Our people require to have it driven into their heads that if they will not submit to a conscription they must submit to a corresponding limitation of their exploits.'

After the experience of Lytton's Afghan adventure, Salisbury's strategic philosophy on the North-West Frontier was based on containment. To Churchill he went further, and in his typically iconoclastic way remarked of the British guarantee to Afghanistan: 'The quarrel seems very small and unimportant. I don't see where the Zulficar Pass leads to. The only awkward circumstance is the promise to the Amir. We shall have to keep our word to that diseased barbarian.' Salisbury wanted a commission despatched to discover what they called a 'scientific frontier' with Russia, with the proviso that the Amir would allow a British officer to reside near Herat. When the Russian Ambassador, Georges de Staal, proposed on 9th July that ownership of the Pass itself could be decided upon later, Salisbury refused, saying that Russia had been allowed to keep Penjdeh only on the understanding that she ceded the Pass to the Amir. During the negotiations there were (false) rumours that the Russians were advancing in force on the Pass, which caused nervous falls on the Stock Exchange.

So far Salisbury was able to bring Churchill along with him. There were occasional disagreements, usually over Ireland where Churchill refused to countenance tough action against the National League. A disobliging article about Churchill in the *Standard*, wrongly attributed to Austin, was blamed on the Prime Minister by the India Secretary. But, in a row over whom to have as the new Commander-in-Chief in India, Salisbury loyally supported Churchill's choice of Roberts over Wolseley, in an area in which the Queen believed she should not only be consulted but should actually have the final say.[2] So solicitous was Salisbury of Churchill's opinions that Lord Coleridge was prompted to remark to the Governor of Madras, Sir Mountstuart Grant Duff, that 'with such a man as Salisbury at the head of affairs, dominated (he is always dominated by some one) by such a flibbertigibbet as Randolph Churchill, we may wake some morning at war with half the world'. This represented about as complete a misreading of the true political situation as it was possible to have.

There was a good chance of war, and Salisbury made every effort to ensure that Britain could not be blamed. 'It is our business to take care that the challenge comes from their side,' he emphasised to Churchill on 31st July. Through constant contact with de Staal, tough negotiating over every aspect of border policy, attempting to involve Bismarck, and deferring whenever necessary to Churchill's idiosyncrasies, Salisbury managed to steer a path towards eventual settlement. He was not helped by a painful and debilitating attack of eczema, which spread over almost his whole body, but he was helped by Iddesleigh's quiet acceptance of his diminished role, who appreciated the earlier hours kept by the Lords and his new-found ability 'to dine peacefully at home'.

On 14th August, Churchill submitted the first of several resignation threats. The day before, Salisbury had told Richmond that 'Randolph has been specially unmanageable' and four days later he reported that he 'has been giving me such a dance lately'. Churchill had opposed the appointment of the Queen's favourite son, Prince Arthur, Duke of Connaught, to be Commander-in-Chief in Bombay, despite Dufferin and Roberts both having agreed to it. The resignation threat was withdrawn when Salisbury agreed to postpone the appointment until after the general election, when he strongly suspected he would not have to deal with it himself. He indulgently put the tantrum down to Churchill's bout of bad health which, 'having taken calomel', as he told the Queen, ended as quickly as it had begun.[3]

The Zulficar crisis started to abate on 20th August, when Salisbury saw de Staal in a waiting room at King's Cross Station and agreed a basis for a commission to draw up a 'scientific' frontier. He was characteristically sceptical of its chances of success, about whether the map de Staal produced was 'honestly drawn', and even whether the various British and Indian authorities and departments would accept it. On one point he was adamant. When Hicks Beach suggested that Churchill be invited to be present at Salisbury's meetings with de Staal, the Prime Minister flatly refused, saying that it would set a dangerous precedent. He argued that de Staal would expect another Russian to be present and the Colonial and War Offices would then want to attend also, turning every meeting from a mutually useful *tête-à-tête* into a mini-conference.

At the end of August, suddenly and without warning, the doves overcame the hawks in St Petersburg. Assessing motives and power struggles in nineteenth-century Russian politics is as difficult as in the days of Soviet 'Kremlinology', but Salisbury's determination not to allow the balance of power in Afghanistan to shift in Russia's favour without war was probably the central factor in the Tsar's pacific decision. On 7th September 1885, a protocol was signed which delineated the borders. It incorporated mutual concessions, but it kept the Russians out, and it reduced the tension in the Central Asian theatre for the rest of the century.

Simultaneously with his Afghan negotiations, Salisbury was busily defending Britain's position in Egypt, both militarily against the Khalifa, who had succeeded to the Dervish leadership after the Mahdi mysteriously died in July, and diplomatically and financially against the rest of Europe, which resented Britain's having occupied the country despite the protection it gave their bondholders' investments. The Great Powers, and especially France, disbelieved British claims to be willing to evacuate Egypt as soon as she safely could. They suspected, with some justification, that, despite Salisbury's protestations of a willingness to evacuate, Albion was being perfidious and Egypt was to be a British client state, part of her 'informal' empire, although nominally ruled by the Khedive under the suzerainty of the Sultan of Turkey. Although it had been generally acknowledged to be a military necessity, Britain's occupation of Egypt had not been officially recognised either by Turkey or the European Powers.

Although Salisbury had not supported Gladstone's 1882 invasion of Egypt, still less the bombardment of Alexandria, he was not about to return Egypt to the Egyptians without a number of cast-iron guarantees. In April 1884, he had told an audience in the Manchester Free Trade Hall that the independence of Egypt was 'a screaming farce', and on 26th February 1885 he had said in the House of Lords, 'It is the road to India. The condition of Egypt can never be indifferent to us...we have a right and it is our duty to insist upon it, that our influence shall be predominant in Egypt.' He wanted to end the Egyptian slave trade and 'do much to prevent the <u>cruelty</u> of Government' by the Khedive, but primarily the British would be there for British strategic interests. A believer in informal empire, Salisbury disapproved of 'the plan of moulding the Egyptians to our civilisation'.

With invasion and anarchy threatening southern Egypt, Salisbury, via Evelyn Baring, the Agent and Consul-General in Cairo, pledged Britain to uphold Khedive Tewfik, raised money to pay his army and sent officers to organise the defence of the country. Egypt herself could not afford a full-scale war against the Khalifa, who was allowed to keep his conquests until the finances were healthy enough to settle the score over Gordon. Meanwhile in August, Salisbury sent Sir Henry Drummond Wolff to Constantinople to negotiate with the Sultan over Britain's future in Turkey. By choosing one of Churchill's friends for the task, Salisbury ensured that his India Secretary would not repudiate the outcome.[4] Drummond Wolff had served with Goschen on an official inquiry into Egyptian finance in 1876, and between August 1876 and June 1879 he was the British commissioner for the organisation of

Eastern Roumelia after the Berlin Congress. In that capacity, he had sent no fewer than 266 despatches, testing even Salisbury's penchant for detailed information.

In his instructions to Drummond Wolff on 13th August, Salisbury wrote that:

> The end to which I would work is evacuation, but with certain private reservations e.g. a Treaty right to reoccupy Alexandria when we pleased and predominate control of Egyptian railways. These terms might be hard to obtain but I would not cut myself off from them until the state of Europe has cleared up.... I do not see my way to bind myself to a fixed date for evacuation.

Salisbury had set Drummond Wolff an almost impossible task, but knew that he would be far too vain a plenipotentiary to turn the commission down. If the Sultan, who was nominal suzerain of Egypt, could be encouraged to help garrison Egypt's border with the Sudan, so much the better, proving to the Porte that Britain did not want sovereignty over Egypt. (Britain never established formal sovereignty, but her troops did not finally leave Egypt until 1954.)

Salisbury always intended one day to conquer the Sudan and destroy the Khalifa, but it would have to be done cautiously and at no great financial cost. Until then, as he told Sir Edwin Egerton, the Secretary at the Constantinople Embassy, the reoccupation of the Sudan was 'wholly out of reach of our present penury'. He insisted that Drummond Wolff should not set an evacuation date, as 'relief from our hated presence is the one bribe we have to offer'. Meanwhile, he told Drummond Wolff that he was pressuring the Turkish Ambassador in London, Musurus Pasha, with 'perpetual' threats, hoping they would therefore send soldiers to help in Egypt's defence. The major sticking points, he thought, were 'Turkish apathy and French jealousy', the twin constants of that era of Great Power diplomacy.[5]

To no one's great surprise (or regret), Drummond Wolff only managed to get the Sultan to agree to a special Turkish commissioner, Moukhtar Pasha, being sent out to Cairo to reorganise, along with Drummond Wolff and the Khedive, the Egyptian administration and army. Because the Sultan suspected that Salisbury's Government might fall at any moment, and would probably anyhow lose the general election in November, Salisbury likened Drummond Wolff's task to 'the difficulty a man has in getting credit from the neighbouring tradesmen, when he is only staying at an hotel'. Salisbury knew all about sending a plenipotentiary to Constantinople with impossible instructions, to urge upon a recalcitrant Sultan a policy in which the London Government did not wholly believe. Drummond Wolff's Privy Councillorship had been forced on Salisbury by Churchill in June 1885, so it was hardly an act of unbridled malice to have saddled him with this doomed mission.

When he became Prime Minister, Salisbury had the use of a private train with a single carriage, to be permanently available to take him from Hatfield to King's Cross and back. He also had a private waiting room built at Hatfield Station. After his step-down bath (to save himself having to heave his great bulk over the side), morning worship in the chapel, brisk walk, breakfast, estate business and light luncheon, the train would be ready to take him to London at 1.50 p.m. 'As soon as the carriage stopped,' recalled the Great Northern Railway porter at Hatfield, 'down jumped his little page boy, who was seated on the box beside the coachman, and opened the door and out stepped his Lordship, and walked leisurely on to the platform.... I never remember hearing him speak to anyone and he did no fuss.' A pheasant was distributed to each railwayman every Christmas.

Salisbury enjoyed racing from the Foreign Office back to King's Cross, his record time being seventeen minutes. A footman would be ready with his greatcoat, another would open the door of the single-horsed brougham, which would set off the moment it closed. Horse Guards Arch, Whitehall, Trafalgar Square, Charing Cross and Bloomsbury would then be negotiated at speed by his coachman, Henry Hooker. On one occasion, a stranger entered his railway carriage at King's Cross to travel back to Hatfield with him. Assuming him to be a guest of his wife's whom he failed to recognise, Salisbury nodded to the man and then dozed on the journey. It was only at Hatfield, once he had given the man a lift in his brougham to the house and had been addressed on the subject of the existence of God, that he realised that he had, as he informed a footman, 'left a madman in the front hall'.

Identifying Russia and France as Britain's probable future enemies, it was only natural for Salisbury, who never considered isolation to be splendid, to attempt to befriend the Central Powers, Germany and Austria, as soon as he took office. Within a fortnight of coming to power, he had written to Bismarck about Kandahar and Egyptian loans, and asked Paget, then in Vienna, 'to counteract as far as possible the evil effect upon our negotiating power produced by the presumed transitoriness of our tenure of office'. Hoping that the Queen would insist on Rosebery becoming Foreign Secretary rather than Granville should the Liberals win the election, Salisbury tried to instil in Károlyi's mind the idea that the 'possible' new Liberal ministry might adopt a more 'Palmerstonian' (i.e. anti-Russian) policy than Gladstone's Turcophobic one.

At the end of July, Philip Currie was sent to see Bismarck in Berlin, to discover whether any arrangements could be reached over Zanzibar, where, in what Salisbury called 'an unwise display of swagger', the Germans were claiming the coastline and interior. 'He is rather a Jew,' Salisbury complained about Bismarck's tough negotiating stance, 'but on the whole I have as yet got my money's worth.' Bismarck was biding his time, however, and like the Sultan and the Austrians, he was waiting until the British electorate had spoken.[6]

Salisbury 'loves the Foreign Office', his wife told Lord Cranbrook at a ministerial banquet on 11th August, 'and would gladly have a Prime Minister over him, but not give it up'. She was satisfied his eczema was improving, was anxious he should have his three weeks' holiday at Royat in the South of France, and said the thing he 'abhors' most about the premiership was 'patronage and its exhibition of littleness'. In Iddesleigh's case such littleness had even been taken to the limit of having to draw up an official, signed memorandum delineating which areas of patronage each man would control. The Prime Minister would decide all political offices, the two Viceroyalties, bishops, Chapters, deans and honours. Meanwhile the First Lord's fiefdom would include 'royal bounty, civil list pensions, church livings, political pensions, permanent civil offices (generally speaking)'.[7]

Back in August 1882, in Maamtrasna, an isolated part of Connemara, a father, mother and their two childen had been murdered in a local feud. Lord Spencer, Gladstone's tough Irish Viceroy, had upheld the capital sentences on the alleged killers, which Parnell and the Fourth Party had at the time passionately contested. Nearly three years later, in July 1885, the controversy was disinterred by Parnell, despite the Government having finally announced on 6th July that they were proposing not to renew the Coercion legislation, despite the fact that, as Salisbury admitted to the Queen, boycotting and intimidation were on the increase in Ireland. The re-emergence of the attempt to overturn Spencer's death sentences was a test set by Parnell of the goodwill of the Salisbury Government. Both Churchill and Hicks Beach wished to support Parnell's motion, both to appease the Irish party and because they had attacked Spencer at the time of the original sentencing.

Salisbury, however, was immovable, telling Hicks Beach: 'We shall lose confidence if we seem to allow parliamentary tactics to interfere with the administration of the criminal law.' In the debate on 17th July, Churchill repudiated Spencer's refusal to reopen the case and was supported by Hicks Beach and Gorst, with the latter even attacking 'reactionary Ulster members'. Salisbury's view of this insubordination was that, although Hicks Beach's speech had been 'harmless', it was also 'incompetently blundering', whereas Churchill's had been 'objectionably ill-advised' and Gorst's insults to the Ulstermen were 'indefensible'. He was irritated at having now to praise Spencer more than he thought he deserved, and pessimistically reported to Henry Manners on 19th July that 'if we hold together "till the prorogation, it is as much as we can do'. Salisbury wrote to the Queen explaining that he entirely agreed with her that the Parnellites could not be trusted and that 'any bargain with them would be full of danger'.[8] On 21st July, he dutifully praised Spencer's 'high and manly courage' in the House of Lords, saying, to loud cheers, that 'he administered his functions with the fairest and most equitable intentions'. The following month he let his real views be known, privately saying that Spencer was 'a stupid, narrow-minded, second-rate man'.[9]

Meanwhile, after a director of the Munster Bank embezzled £70,000, converted it into gems and promptly disappeared, Carnarvon had stepped in to offer to guarantee half the Bank's deposits, effectively pledging the credit of the Bank of England without prior Cabinet authorisation. Small farmers and tradesmen in the already very poor south-west of Ireland were the main victims, and Carnarvon's primary aim was to relieve their distress. He also wanted to avoid a general banking crash, as the Hibernian and the National Banks were also far from strong. 'How is England to be made to swallow measures the Irish authorities consider necessary for Ireland?' Salisbury asked Carnarvon on 22nd July, as he repudiated the promise of assistance, to the Viceroy's great embarrassment. By 12th August, Salisbury was telling Carnarvon that as Irish matters were so problematic they would not even be mentioned in the Queen's Speech.

If the depositors of the Munster Bank felt let down by Salisbury's ministry, Irish would-be peasant proprietors had cause to thank it. The Ashbourne Land Act, which made a £5 million Treasury grant available to tenants to borrow the full monetary value of their land purchases from willing landlords, was introduced on 17th July and rushed through to receive Royal Assent within a month.[10] The idea was that they would pay back the entire purchase price at 4 per cent over forty-nine years, with a security of 20 per cent deposited with the Irish Land Commission, which oversaw the measure. Salisbury, who had denounced Gladstone's Land Act as 'a threat to the very foundations of civilisation', saw this as the start of a process which would give the Irish peasant, as a proprietor and owner of land, a stake in the Union and rights of property. It also facilitated landlords who wished to sell out. As the tenant's holding was forfeit if he defaulted, there was also financial security for the State. Parnell welcomed the measure as it helped to relieve the constipated Irish land market and all legal fees were picked up by the Commission. Because it contained no anti-landlord clauses about rents, Salisbury justified it to himself and others as a Tory measure, merely a rural Irish version of what he had proposed for housing reform for the urban working classes.[11]

The Ashbourne Land Act, non-introduction of Coercion and the amendment of the Labourers' Act were not, however, enough to win the Irish support at the elections. There were going to be two million extra voters under the 1884 Reform Act, and every effort had to be made to detach Irish Nationalists from the Liberals at the forthcoming polls. So Salisbury reluctantly sanctioned an astonishingly risky venture, one that was to cause him enormous embarrassment over many years as well as hugely vexatious misunderstandings that were to provide a staple line of attack for generations of Liberal and Irish Nationalist politicians, journalists and historians, even up to the present day.

'A well-dressed lay-figure in the centre of a mimic court', Salisbury had called the post of Irish Viceroy in the *Saturday Review* in 1861, a position for which 'the want of intellectual power would be a positive recommendation'. But times had changed and resurgent nationalism had made it a crucial post in any 1880s Government. Salisbury's choice of his oldest ally, the intelligent and idealistic 4th Earl of Carnarvon, surprised many who knew the secret of his conversion to Home Rule. Ireland was a comparatively recent interest for Carnarvon; even as late as January 1884 Salisbury advised him not to miss out on a holiday early in the session, as 'you do not much care about' the Irish question.[12]

On 6th July 1885, Carnarvon had announced the Government's new non-coercive Irish policy in the House of Lords, saying that as there had been only 762 agrarian crimes in 1884 – and no murders – as against 4,439 agrarian crimes in 1881, 'I believe for my part that special legislation of this sort is inexpedient.' It was 'a memorable scene' for Lord Rosebery, because Salisbury, breaking with precedent, did not speak in favour of the policy himself but handed over the whole task to Carnarvon.[13] 'No one who was present on that occasion will ever forget it, or can have carried away the belief that this Irish policy was congenial to the head of the administration.'

A meeting that morning between Carnarvon and the Irish Nationalist MP Justin M'Carthy at M'Carthy's home had resulted in Carnarvon learning that Parnell only wanted self-government for Ireland in a manner 'not quite equal to that enjoyed by a State in the U.S. Union'. A direct personal meeting between Carnarvon and Parnell was suggested, and not rejected out of hand. In his subsequent conversation with Salisbury, prior to his Lords' announcement, Carnarvon had reported

M'Carthy's remarks. Salisbury said he thought that the Conservative Party might accept a policy of provincial councils in Ireland, but totally repudiated any central body. He would not, he said, play the part Sir Robert Peel had in 1829 and 1845 over Catholic Emancipation and the Corn Laws.[14]

Salisbury nonetheless did agree to a secret interview taking place between Carnarvon and Parnell to ascertain the latter's intentions, so long as Ashbourne was also present, nothing was written down and there was maximum possible deniability. Writing to Salisbury on 26th July, asking him (clearly in vain) to destroy the letter, Carnarvon told Salisbury that it was 'only common sense' to discover Parnell's wishes, that it would merely be an 'exchange of views', but that he had reason to believe Parnell might agree to 'an actual alliance' at the general election in return for a promise to deliver 'a very large measure, though not an extreme one' in the next Parliament if the Conservatives and Irish together won a majority.

Any such meeting was liable to massive misinterpretation, but Salisbury resolved to risk it nonetheless. With Ashbourne, an Irish Tory and lifelong opponent of Home Rule, present at the meeting, Salisbury assumed that little rash talk would take place. The Cabinet and Queen were not to be informed, so nobody had to be squared beforehand. Salisbury's secret diplomacy had fixed the Congress of Berlin successfully, so might it not again work over Ireland? Salisbury, as his experience of life in Beaconsfield's Cabinet showed, did not think that Cabinet collective responsibility entirely excluded individual enterprise by ministers, and if Carnarvon wanted to take the risk he felt it was up to him. The prize of defeating Gladstone with the help of the Irish vote in November, with absolutely no commitment to enact any of the Irish demands, was too tempting for Salisbury to pass up.

On Saturday, 1st August 1885, Carnarvon met Parnell alone – Ashbourne was not present – in the dust-sheeted drawing room of No.15 Hill Street, a large townhouse off Berkeley Square which was being mothballed because its owner, Carnarvon's mother-in-law and Beaconsfield's confidante, the Countess of Chesterfield, had died just four days earlier. Carnarvon and Parnell spoke for seventy-five minutes, after having agreed that everything that passed between them would be kept entirely secret. They also agreed that 'no sort of bond or engagement' would be entered into, but simply 'a mere interchange of opinion'.[15]

Parnell assumed that Carnarvon was speaking on behalf of the Cabinet, rather than just for himself, and his interlocutor crucially said nothing to disabuse him of the notion. They then fell to discussing constitutional safeguards for the property of the Protestant minority under a separatist Irish constitution, which led Parnell to suggest statutory provisions over issues such as taxation. He went so far as to say that even land questions could still be decided at Westminster. On the question of a Dublin parliament, Parnell said that 'some form of central body, council or Board was essential' for reasons of 'sentiment', but a body which simply dealt with education, railway regulation, drainage and fisheries might be initially acceptable.

'He was, in fact, singularly moderate throughout the whole discussion, and was not as absolutely cold as I had expected,' Carnarvon reported to Salisbury, having found Parnell 'apparently anxious to find common ground'. For Parnell, who knew that with their in-built Lords majority only the Conservatives could really pass such a quasi-Home Rule proposal, it was an obvious tactic to ask for the bare minimum and offer extensive safeguards, only to agitate for the remainder and shave away the guarantees over the following years and decades. His gradualist agenda was transparent, but Carnarvon was impressed, and after more talk about internal migration to relieve congested districts, how much Parnell was doing to fight the 'extremists' on his own side, and protection for nascent Irish industries from Manchester, the two men parted on good terms. 'You will be interested to know that I have had a remarkable conversation which lasted for 1¼ hours,' Carnarvon reported to the absent Ashbourne afterwards, 'and that I shall hope to give you all details on my return.'

Salisbury was deeply dismayed when he first discovered that Ashbourne had not been present, and Carnarvon's memorandum on the full extent of the subjects that had been discussed shocked him still further. They had talked in so many words about a legislative body in Dublin, exactly what Pitt's 1800 Act of Union had brought to an end. Carnarvon went to Hatfield to report on Sunday, 2nd August, where Salisbury utterly rejected his suggestion of telling the Cabinet and the Queen about the meeting. By keeping the interview secret, but assuming that Parnell would leak the substance of it to Gladstone, Salisbury possibly hoped that the Liberal leader might be encouraged into thinking that the Tories were secretly planning to trump him and pass a comprehensive Home Rule measure themselves, as Disraeli had done with the Second Reform Act. This in turn might entice Gladstone to announce his own conversion to Home Rule, a move Salisbury believed could be suicidal for the future cohesion of the Liberal Party.

So at the Cabinet meeting on Monday, 3rd August the subject of Ireland was not brought up. After it, Salisbury was placed in the cringe-making position of having his close colleague Cranbrook complain to him about Churchill's relations with Parnell – 'There is nothing tangible but I dread his secret action and believe it to be wrong and dangerous' – when far more dangerous had been Carnarvon's and Salisbury's own secret actions.[16]

Salisbury's personal beliefs were entirely unchanged by Carnarvon's stratagems. Writing to Henry Howorth, a parliamentary candidate, on 10th September, he emphasised that 'whatever happens I do not believe that the mass of the Tory party will ever consent to any measures savouring of separation'. Critics of Salisbury who claim that he would have instituted some form of Home Rule had he won the November 1885 election, and in the event only opposed it out of selfish and myopic reasons once Gladstone had proposed it, have failed to spot the far more risky and devious game Salisbury was playing. This was to lure the Liberal leadership into a trap from which it could not escape, thereby emasculating it whilst protecting the Union which he always believed Britain had a debt of honour to defend.

In a letter to Ponsonby of 29th November 1885, in response to a letter from Carnarvon to the Queen about a legislature being established in Dublin, Salisbury made his own position abundantly clear.

> My opinion is that a Central Parliament for Ireland is practically Home Rule: that is to say, it will involve either at once or in a very brief space so much independence as to reduce the connection between England and Ireland to a personal union exercised in H.M.'s sovereignty. In every other respect the two kingdoms will be independent. In my opinion, this result would be principally hurtful in that it would expose the Loyalists – the classes who have made themselves unpopular by backing the policy of England – to utter ruin. Their properties would be taken from them. Such a result seems to me scarcely consistent with the honour of an English Sovereign, or of English Statesmen.... It could only be carried out, now, at the cost of a great disruption of parties, and an entire loss of honour among public men.

Salisbury was working a fourteen-hour day, and on the same day that he wrote to Howorth about Ireland, for example, he also wrote (by hand) to the poet and traveller Wilfrid Blunt about Egypt, Mr Staveley Hill about public appointments, a Mr Lake about a Gordon memorial in Melbourne, Sir Peter Lumsden about India, Mr Hugh O'Donnell about a Chinese alliance, Sir Julian Pauncefote about Zanzibar and the Lord Mayor of London about South Africa. Most of these letters were fairly businesslike, but he would regularly exercise his powerful written charm. In choosing the first Secretary of State for Scotland in August 1885, for example, Salisbury at first invited the 9th Marquess of Lothian, who had initially sponsored the creation of the department, but he would not take it. After three other people were considered, the choice fell on the Duke of Richmond and Gordon, to whom Salisbury wrote: 'I think you seem pointed out by nature to be the man....It really is a matter where the effluence of two dukedoms and the best salmon river in Scotland will go a long way.'[17]

Just when Salisbury might have been forgiven for expecting a quiet run to the general election, another full-scale crisis with Russia broke out, the third in seven years. A fortnight after the signing of the agreement on the Zulficar Pass, a revolution in Philippolis, the capital of Eastern Roumelia, expelled the Turkish Governor-General and offered Alexander of Battenberg, the Prince of Bulgaria, the Regency. In effect, this was a popular movement for the scrapping of the Berlin Treaty's provisions against a 'Big' Bulgaria, and for the unification of the two states which Salisbury had striven so hard to split in 1878. 'There have always been many more small German princes than there have been thrones to put them on,' Salisbury had written in 1863, but now Alexander, a twenty-eight-year-old, impulsive, handsome prince, whom Salisbury found 'not very wise – but he is stubborn', had two thrones to himself, which he hoped to unite into one.

Salisbury's initial reaction, despite Prince Alexander's 'violent antipathy' to Tsar Alexander III, who had succeeded after the assassination of his father Tsar Alexander II in 1881, was to send a circular to Berlin, Vienna and Rome to protest against the *coup d'état* and stand by the Treaty of Berlin. But events overtook him, and on Sunday, 20th September, Prince Alexander suddenly arrived in Philippolis, accepted the Regency and declared the union of the two countries. The Turks, who had failed to garrison the Eastern Roumelian frontier when the Russians left in August 1879, despite the restoration of their nominal sovereignty at Berlin, were powerless to resist. Salisbury's contempt for Turkey's lack of response was evident from a letter to White in Constantinople four days later: 'If the Turks had had a spark of vitality left they would have marched in all the force at their command and stamped out this insurrection at once....That Turkey has not done this spontaneously, proves that Turkey is dead.'

Salisbury's old fears of a general Balkan maelstrom were revived when Serbia mobilised immediately against Bulgaria. In Vienna, the King of Greece told the British Ambassador that he could now 'liberate' Crete, on the basis of 'What's good for the Prince of Bulgaria is good for me!' London, Paris and Berlin all begged Kálnocky to stop the war, but Serbia knew an attack on their traditional enemies had to be made before Alexander could weld the two Bulgarias into a single nation.

Rather than break up the *Dreikaiserbund* over the question, Bismarck told Count von Radowitz, the German Ambassador in

Constantinople, that he wanted to 'drown the question in ink'. He was doubtful about Alexander's chances of success, having told him personally that having been monarch of a united Bulgaria 'might prove an interesting episode to look back on'. Having sent off his protesting circular, Salisbury sat back, content at the lack of response. It had been an entirely *pro forma* exercise, intended to show he stood by the Treaty of Berlin in principle. In practice, however, he was happy to see this particular part of it repudiated, so long as the whole edifice did not crack.

Since it was signed, far from becoming a satellite state of Russia as everyone had automatically assumed in 1878, Bulgaria had become very anti-Russian, resentful of the officers, administrators and advisers that Russia had sent there. Despite Prince Alexander of Bulgaria's father having been the brother of Tsar Alexander III's mother, the two men disliked one another intensely, and suddenly Prince Alexander's stubbornness and independence seemed as though they might provide a new strong buffer state between Russia and Constantinople. In a complete reversal of their 1878 roles at Berlin, therefore, Salisbury now did favour a 'Big' Bulgaria, whilst St Petersburg preferred the partitioned Bulgaria of two states, with the southern part under the Sultan rather than Prince Alexander.

Salisbury was very averse to fighting Russia over Bulgaria, telling Sir Robert Morier in St Petersburg that the Tsar 'is really his own minister, and so bad a minister that no consequent or coherent policy is pursued'. Even if it had been, Russia's practical invulnerability to military attack meant that at all costs Britain must 'avoid if we can a crisis which must lead to such terrible calamities'. Russia was so poor that 'we must lead her into all the expense that we can, in the conviction that with her the limit of taxation has been almost reached, and that only a few steps further must push her into the revolution over which she seems to be hanging'.

On 22ⁿᵈ September 1885, only four days after the events in Philippolis, Salisbury was telling the French and Turkish Ambassadors and the *chargés d'affaires* of Italy, Germany and Austria that he considered 'the time for restoring the status quo had passed, and that the object now must be to reduce to the smallest possible point the necessary alteration in the Treaty of Berlin'. He proposed to do this by accepting the union of the two Bulgarias, but only as 'a personal union' under the Prince, rather than a full-scale constitutional alteration. This obvious fudge pleased the Queen, who adored the equally Russophobic 'poor Sandro' and who hoped he would marry one of her daughter Vicky's children. 'Balmoral has got a telegraphing fit on just now – ', Salisbury complained to Henry Manners a week later, 'which is a great aggravation to the trials of life.'

Salisbury was as practical as ever about Britain's ability to protect Alexander from a Russian or even a Serbian invasion, telling the Queen: 'The country being practically wholly inland, Your Majesty's Government has very little power in the matter.'[18] In the meantime, he told her the most important thing was to cleave to Austria and not allow the flame of rebellion against Turkey to ignite Macedonia. If Britain were to be seen assisting in the tearing up of the Treaty she had concluded with such a flourish only seven years before, 'her position would not be honourable and her influence would be much diminished'. Salisbury's major fear, as he vouchsafed to Sir William White in Constantinople, was that Bulgaria herself might become strong enough to pose a threat to Turkey. White was concerned about another potential danger: if a pan-Slavic coup against Alexander succeeded, it might lead to a pro-Russian 'Big' Bulgaria, the original fear of 1878.

Salisbury's overall stance at the end of September was to hope that the Great Powers would not act, but to give them reluctant support out of deference to the Berlin Treaty if they did so. Chamberlain lost no time in declaring that the events in the Balkans showed the hollowness of Beaconsfield's and Salisbury's 'triumph' in 1878. 'The Treaty of Berlin has broken down', crowed the *Daily News*, 'precisely on those provisions for which the government of Lord Beaconsfield and Lord Salisbury, as its Foreign Minister, were most directly responsible.'[19] Meanwhile, Gladstone and Granville expressed their private delight that the crisis had not occurred during their time in office. 'It is very tiresome of the Eastern Roumelians revolting at such unseasonable times,' Salisbury wrote to Janetta Manners on 29th September. 'Every Minister, ambassador, consul and Secretary of State of every country was quietly reposing himself when comes this thunderclap and sends us all back from our holidays.'

By 15th October 1885, Salisbury was forced to come out in his true colours. The Austrian Foreign Minister, Count Kálnoky, issued a circular to the Great Powers, proposing a conference to force Alexander to withdraw beyond the Balkan mountain range separating Bulgaria from Eastern Roumelia, with Turkey given a free hand to intervene militarily in the southern state if he refused. Salisbury demurred, saying 'the wish of the people of Bulgaria' should now be consulted. With a general election looming in a matter of weeks and Alexander extremely popular with the British public opinion, he could hardly have taken any very different stance, but it was one he had followed, whatever his diplomatic pronouncements to the other Great Powers, since the revolution on 18th September. 'The situation is a delicate one because we are bound to be fervent for the exact fulfilment of the Treaty of Berlin,' he explained to Lyons in Paris on 16th October. 'On the other hand the proposal is obviously intended to upset Prince Alexander and, if we acquiesce, we may find ourselves with a big Bulgaria under a Russian Prince.'[20]

Lord Randolph Churchill took a divergent course from Salisbury, complaining that the Prime Minister's action was exasperating the Russians in Central Asia. Having had minor surgery on his hand, Salisbury asked Balfour to write to Churchill on 29th October, pointing out that 'it would not do for us, just at this time, and in the face of the Elections, to appear to be dragged at the chariot wheels of the Three Emperors and at their bidding to crush with Turkish troops the "infant liberties" in Roumelia and promote Russian influence in the Balkans'. When finally forced into the Great Powers' Conference, Salisbury refused to allow White to make any substantial concessions, despite also not really being able to intervene in any significant way. 'Essentially he was bluffing,' one historian has correctly surmised, 'as it turned out, very successfully.'[21]

At the Ambassadors' Conference in Constantinople on 7th November, White pressed the Powers to recommend that the Sultan should not send troops to Eastern Roumelia if Prince Alexander did not pursue anti-Muslim policies there, and only to alter the Treaty of Berlin to make Alexander Eastern Roumelia's Governor-General-for-life, but not to oust him. 'I am doing my best to prevent the Conference from simmering over,' Salisbury reported to Churchill on 12th November, 'but the difficulty of reconciling Imperial wrath with English opinion is considerable.' It finally broke up on the 25th, without Russia having been able to persuade the other Great Powers to return to the *status quo ante*.

When the Serbians invaded Bulgaria on 13th November, they were defeated by Alexander at the Battle of Slivinitza six days later. The following day, Salisbury told a jubilant Queen that this meant it was probably now impossible for Russia to separate the two Bulgarias. It also encouraged the Italians to change sides on the question of Turkish military intervention, and the French also swung round to Salisbury's point of view. In declaring an early armistice in late November, Alexander shrewdly precluded Austria joining the Serbs, an outcome which Salisbury told the Queen would have left the Prince 'quite helpless'. Sir Robert Morier said that as neither Austria nor Russia would allow military force to be used by the other in Bulgaria, and Russian public opinion would probably not allow the Turks to repress the Bulgarians either, some form of status quo might develop. 'The great thing as [Bismarck] says', Salisbury told the Queen on 3rd December, 'is to gain time.'

By then, however, Salisbury had himself run out of time, having lost November's general election. Partly because of the Bulgarian situation, he decided to stay in office until Parliament met in January 1886.

During that time he put pressure on the Greeks not to attack Turkey and the Turks to negotiate directly with Prince Alexander. With Rosebery, the new Foreign Secretary, following the general lines of Salisbury's policy, a Turkish–Bulgarian agreement was signed on 6th April 1886 which recognised Alexander's rule in Eastern Roumelia, albeit under nominal Turkish suzerainty.[22] Another Balkan crisis had been settled without a conflict between the Great Powers, an achievement for which Salisbury's steady and cautious diplomacy was largely responsible.

Because Salisbury did not believe in issuing written election manifestos, thinking them 'rather an interference on the part of a peer' in elections to the Lower House, he instead delivered a speech at Newport in Monmouthshire on 7th October which was intended to present his programme. George Curzon, who was sitting five feet from where Salisbury stood, later recalled how the Prime Minister spoke for one and three-quarter hours, the longest speech he ever gave, without a single note but only an extract from a speech by Chamberlain written on a card in his pocket. To 'a perfect hurricane of applause', Salisbury told the standing crowd of 8,000 people that the Roumelian rising had not actually restored the 'Big' Bulgaria of the San Stefano armistice, but anyhow 'treaties do not affect to overrule the general impulses of populations'.

He attacked Chamberlain, calling his most recent speech 'a baseless libel'. Over local government he proposed that County Boards, later called County Councils, should take the place of the old Quarter Sessions. Over the issue of temperance reform Salisbury was adamant:

> If I like to drink beer it is no reason that I should be prevented from drinking it because my neighbour does not like it. If you sacrifice liberty in the matter of alcohol you will eventually sacrifice it on more important matters also, and those advantages of civil and religious liberties for which we have fought hard will gradually be whittled away.

There were other, more mundane promises: to make land transfer cheaper, to reduce elementary school fees, and oppose the 'lifeless, boiled down, mechanical, unreal religious teaching which is prevalent in Board schools'. Salisbury also raised the old bogey of disestablishment – 'Our Party is tied up with the Established and Endowed Churches of this island' – implying that the Liberals were planning it, which Gladstone denied the following week. He was keen to dampen expectations of a Conservative programme. 'People imagine that where an evil exists, the Queen, the Lords and the Commons should stop it,' he chaffed. 'I wonder they have not brought in an Act of Parliament to stop unfavourable weather on the occasion of political demonstrations.'

By far the most important, closely watched and widely misunderstood part of the speech was his reference to Ireland. His remark about his desire 'to cherish and foster strong self-sustaining nationalities' was made entirely in reference to Bulgaria and the Balkans. But the rest of his speech managed somehow simultaneously to raise Irish nationalist hopes and yet not excite Unionist suspicions. On the thorny question of extending local government to Ireland, Salisbury said: 'This is a difficult question, I admit. Our first principle, on which we have always gone, is to extend to Ireland so far as we can all the institutions in this country,' which obviously did not include a separate parliament but only County Boards. He also made it clear, to prolonged cheers, that:

> We look upon the integrity of the Empire as a matter more important than almost any other political consideration that you can imagine, and we could not regard with favour any proposal which directly or indirectly menaced that which is the first condition of England's position among the nations of the world.

Coercion, he said, had not prevented the growth of the National League or boycotting, which was 'more like the excommunication or interdict of the Middle Ages than anything that we have now'. So it would not be renewed. At Newport, Salisbury went as far as he possibly could towards appeasing the Irish nationalists, taking refuge in ambiguity. To anyone hoping that he might offer anything in the nature of Home Rule, there was nothing of comfort, however much some people have attempted to convince themselves otherwise.[23] Parnell's assessment, that the speech 'suggested much and proposed nothing', was accurate enough, but the later claim by the Irish Nationalist MP Timothy Healy, that 'Salisbury used language consistent with the grant of Home Rule', or that 'he foreshadowed a Central Government in Ireland', is untrue.

It was because Salisbury had not adopted his usual dismissive tone, but instead showed a willingness to discuss local government ideas, that his comments attracted such attention, far more than was warranted by what he actually said. By describing Parnell's idea of a federation on the Austro-Hungarian model as 'remarkable', rather than anything actually rude, Salisbury had cleverly given a hint, but not one which committed him to anything whatever.[24] He had managed simultaneously to satisfy and stimulate almost all sects of non-Liberal opinion. When Churchill congratulated him, Salisbury answered that it was 'very satisfactory to know that you think I danced my egg-dance with fair success'. It was not, however, quite successful enough.

TWENTY-TWO

The 'Hawarden Kite'

The General Election –
Gladstone's Conversion to Home Rule –
Upper Burma Annexed –
Leaving Office

November 1885 to February 1886

'It has transformed a chimera into a burning issue.'

With two million extra voters, a redistribution of boundaries, election expenditure restricted by the 1883 Corrupt Practices Act, and a trebling of the Irish vote in mainland Britain owing to the enfranchisement of agricultural labourers, the outcome of the general election, which opened on 23rd November and continued for three weeks, was exceedingly difficult to predict. Salisbury supported the idea of encouraging what would be called Conservative Labour candidates, proletarian Tories who could contest the new working-class seats for the Conservatives. 'My impression is that on most questions you will find them voting much straighter than some more cultured persons,' he told Akers-Douglas, but nothing came of it. Salisbury's huge contribution of £2,000 to the election fighting fund was used by the Party fund-raiser, Lord Kintore, to encourage other peers to stump up for the cause. Lord Harrowby was also touched for the same amount.

When Salisbury spoke to 5,000 people at the Victoria Hall in Lambeth's Waterloo Road on 4th November, he attempted to dispose of the Liberals' claim that he was planning to reintroduce the Corn Laws, and thus the dear loaf, calling it 'a downright thumping lie' designed to scare the agricultural labourer. He did, however, take the opportunity to ridicule 'the fetish worship' of 'the holy doctrine of Free Trade', preferring to retaliate against those countries which protected their produce from British competition. He proposed 'raising duties on their produce to bring them to a better state of mind'. Salisbury spoke as if

Chamberlain's radical and collectivist 'Unauthorised' Programme was official Liberal policy. Once more raising the prospect of disestablishment, Salisbury pointed out that in the 1865 election Gladstone had denied wishing to disestablish the Church of Ireland, yet just four years later he had done exactly that. 'Gladstone must be interpreted by Gladstone,' he scoffed, 'and by no other interpretation.'

It was fine, knockabout, electioneering stuff. 'Can you fancy their inner councils,' he joked of Goschen and Hartington, 'the Egyptian skeleton and Rip Van Winkle trying to make up each other's minds, and Lord Derby steadily pouring cold water upon both?' To laughter from the crowd he said that 'the function the Whigs perform in the Liberal camp is to cling about the legs of the Radical combatants and prevent them from advancing to the charge. I should not like myself to have that part in political life assigned to me.' He likened the Whigs 'to those fine names that you sometimes see upon the prospectus of a doubtful company' whose respectability lulled the gullible into investing. In answering Granville's attack on him for using 'passionate' language defending the Church of England's privileges, Salisbury countered that Granville himself 'was never guilty of passionate language in defence of anything in his life'.[1]

The Liberals raised their own *canards* too, and Salisbury found himself having to deny that he banned Jews from taking tenancies in his London property and that he had ordered Northbrook 'to find or make a pretext for the Afghan war'. He dismissed both accusations and wrote to *The Times* to say that the idea that there might have been any arrangement with Parnell during the election was 'too absurd to be worth further contradiction'. Cranbrook thought Salisbury looked tired and preoccupied during the journey from Paddington to Windsor for the dissolution on 18th November. He acknowledged the cheering crowds at both stations, but on the train he was 'absorbed in thought most of the time though ready to enjoy a laugh at some of the things we told him'.

'It is very hard that everyone gets colds except G.O.M.,' Salisbury wrote to Churchill on 17th November as the irrepressible Leader of the Opposition stumped the country, speaking to vast audiencies. The first returns came in on 24th November, and as the English constituencies tended to report earlier they started off well for the Conservatives, who captured fifty-four out of the eighty-seven newly created English seats, doing especially well in the virgin lands of suburbia. Two days before the polls opened, Parnell had issued a manifesto to all Irishmen living in mainland constituencies. Drafted by T.P. O'Connor, it urged them not to vote for the Liberals, calling them 'the men who coerced Ireland, deluged Egypt with blood, menaced religious liberty in the schools, the freedom of speech in Parliament, and promise to the country generally a repetition of the crimes and follies of the last Liberal administration'. It is thought that this pronouncement might have cost the Liberals between twenty-five and forty seats. For all the embarrassments to Salisbury in store, the Carnarvon secret interview with Parnell had delivered the electoral goods.

Salisbury allowed himself a rare moment of tempered optimism as the polls opened, telling Carnarvon: 'This is very curious – and we look forward with something like dismay to the possibility of our remaining in office.' He was soon disabused though, for except in Tory Kent the agricultural workers tended to vote Liberal, partly in gratitude for the new franchise. Scotland and Wales went heavily Liberal, but in Ireland the fourteen Liberal seats were wiped out altogether. Had Salisbury not raised the 'Church in Danger' fear, the result might have been much worse for the Conservatives. It was a violent election, with riots in Dundalk, Armagh and Penzance, as well as in the less likely Maidenhead and Guildford. At Hertford, Radicals stormed the Tory platform, which, as Salisbury's assistant private secretary affectionately recalled, 'afforded us the excitement of a free fight with them, our weapons being the broken legs of chairs, tables and other articles of furniture'.

Mud flew as well as furniture, and on the last night of the campaign Salisbury spoke to a dinner of 240 members of the St Stephen's Club. 'Mr Gladstone has been subject to illusions lately,' he viciously remarked. 'He is under the impression that the night he went to the theatre when Khartoum fell there was no rumour of the death of General Gordon.' It was a low blow but true; Gladstone had indeed gone out to watch *The Candidate* at the Criterion the same day that Gordon's death had been reported, telling his diary it was 'capitally acted'. Salisbury's aggression was a product of his fears, however. Despite outwardly acting as if he could hardly care less about the result, in fact, as Gwendolen told Robert, 'he was in reality only too anxious'.[2] By 3rd December, with results still coming in, Salisbury was hopeful that, as he told Churchill, 'we may be above low-water mark – i.e. Tories + Parnellites = Liberals'.

The result finally came to rest exactly upon the low-water mark. The Conservatives won 249 seats, the Liberals 319, with an extra 16 Liberal Independents who were for all practical purposes to be counted with the Gladstone Liberals at the time, and there were 86 Home Rulers. In an extraordinary fluke, therefore, in a House of 670, the Parnellites added to the Conservatives exactly equalled the number of Liberals, at 335. Parnell therefore precisely held the balance and could deliver the premiership to either Salisbury or Gladstone. The actual polling figures were hugely unrepresentative of the result: 3.31 million people voted Liberal, against 2.02 million Conservative and only 310,000 Irish Nationalist. The Reform Act had therefore worked much as Salisbury had hoped.

Churchill wrote to Salisbury on 30th November offering to resign his place to the Liberal MP George Goschen if it might bring over enough Whigs from the Liberal Party to allow Salisbury to form a coalition. 'They hate me as much as they hate you,' was the reply, 'and if retirements are required for the sake of repose and Whig combinations I shall claim to retire with you in both respects. The time for a coalition has not come yet – nor will, so long as G.O.M. is to the fore.'[3] The Queen, 'much distressed she must say at the unsatisfactory way the Elections have taken', asked Salisbury 'not to desert her', but to meet Parliament before resigning just in case a reconstitution of Parties was possible. She was particularly keen that Hartington and Goschen should join 'a coalition of all moderate and intelligent people' to protect her from Gladstone and Granville, who 'are both utterly unfit'. As for Chamberlain and Dilke, they were 'impossible' because of their cryptorepublicanism. Salisbury answered the next day that he would 'have no objection to serve under Lord Hartington; it is Lord Hartington who would refuse to serve under Lord Salisbury'.

Salisbury informed the Queen that he was pessimistic about the chances of his Conservatives remaining in office, as it would depend upon the Irish, 'with whom they have nothing in common'. However, he was not crushed by the result in the rural divisions. As in 1832 and 1867, the 'new voters have always begun with a Radical fling,' he told Lord Bath, but 'it by no means follows that they will continue to be as unmanageable hereafter'. Carnarvon, writing from Viceregal Lodge in Dublin Castle, urged that 'we must govern by and through the Irish'. Salisbury foresaw how the Viceroy's conversion to Home Rule could soon produce another ministerial crisis.[4]

In a letter to Churchill on 9th December, Salisbury said that he thought the state of the Parties meant that the Government should meet Parliament rather than resigning immediately. 'In making the Queen's speech I entirely agree that our leaning must be to the moderate Liberals – and that we can have nothing to do with any advances towards the Home Rulers. The latter case would be quite contrary to our convictions, and our pledges, and would be quite fatal to the cohesion of our party.' When the time came for fusion with the moderate Liberals, Hartington's supporters, the Tories would have to 'recognise the political necessity of admitting a somewhat stronger ingredient of Liberal policy into our measures'. It would not therefore do to display undue Liberalism in the Queen's Speech: 'If we are too free with our cash now, we shall have no money to go to market with when the market is open.'

To Mr W.J. Harris, who had lost Mid-Devon by 1,250 votes because the agricultural labourers had wanted the 'three acres and a cow' offered in Chamberlain's Unauthorised Programme and feared the return of the 'dear loaf', Salisbury pooh-poohed the idea of changing the

Conservative Party's name to win popularity: 'Names grow, and are not made, and cannot be given by the agency of man to any body of men.' (This was a good Tory sentiment, although it would have surprised the southern Bulgarians, whom Salisbury had for entirely political purposes ordained should be called East Roumelians.)

By mid-December, Carnarvon, whose resignation had been demanded by Churchill for his increasingly open pro-Home Rule views, was considering leaving the Government for a number of reasons. His Hampshire rents were down by 75 per cent, he had only promised to serve until Parliament met, and he claimed to Cranbrook that his health was not good. It was primarily for political reasons that he wished to go, however. At two Cabinet meetings on 14th and 15th December, he proposed setting up a committee to draft a separatist Irish constitution, which the Cabinet rejected on both occasions. The embarrassment of a public split just as Parliament was about to meet led Salisbury and Cranbrook to persuade Carnarvon to hold his resignation up until the whole Government fell in January.[5] By then, however, the entire topography of the issue, indeed of British politics, had changed, due to the most momentous political announcement since four decades earlier Sir Robert Peel had stated his intention to repeal the Corn Laws.

On Saturday, 12th December 1885, there appeared in the fourth column of page six of *The Times* a two-inch, 162-word letter from Gladstone's son Herbert. Dated 4th December and postmarked from Gladstone's country seat, Hawarden Castle, it was to alter the face of British politics for a generation. 'Nothing could induce me to countenance separation,' wrote Herbert, presumably writing on his father's behalf, 'but if five-sixths of the Irish people wish to have a Parliament in Dublin, for the management of their own local affairs, I say, in the name of justice, and wisdom, let them have it.' As 86 Parnellites had been elected out of the 103 Irish seats, Gladstone believed that the time had come to accede to their demand for Home Rule. Salisbury said of this letter, which he called 'the Hawarden Kite' because it was flown to test Liberal reactions: 'It has transformed a chimera into a burning issue.'

Not only was such a move not mentioned in his election address to his constituency, but neither had Gladstone spoken much about Ireland during the campaign. In fact, his recorded public pronouncements tended to the opposite conclusion, as when he said in 1871 that as Irish Home Rule would lead to similar Scottish and Welsh movements, it would thus be 'making ourselves ridiculous in the sight of all mankind'. Gladstone had never visited Ireland, which made his sudden conversion all the more unexpected. When his Cabinet had discussed setting up

Irish County Boards that February, which the Parnellites and Radicals hoped might be a stepping-stone towards a Dublin legislature, every peer in the Cabinet opposed it save Granville, and every commoner supported it except Hartington (who as heir to the dukedom of Devonshire was a very uncommon commoner). No clearer sign could have been afforded to Gladstone that the Whigs needed careful wooing on the issue. Yet, without educating the Liberal Party for such a huge *volte face*, Gladstone also somehow expected the Conservatives to aid him in a policy they despised, and then went on to heap contumely upon them for selfishness and short-sightedness when they refused.

Just because he himself had served and admired his hero Peel, Gladstone seemed to imagine that Salisbury would act in the same way, splitting his Party for the profoundly un-Tory principle of Irish separatism. He entirely misjudged his man, and not least over Salisbury's well-known view of Peel's legacy. Dining at Brooks's on the night of Salisbury's Newport speech, Gladstone told his former private secretary, Sir Algernon West, that he thought Home Rule 'a matter for serious consideration before ten years were over'. Having read 'Disintegration' he should have known that Salisbury would never have supported him over it. In his own private papers are also the handwritten notes Gladstone had taken of Salisbury's Mansion House speech on the subject of the Union, delivered on 9th November 1885, at which Salisbury said of Ireland: 'The traditions of our party are known. The integrity of the Empire is more precious to us than any possession we can have. We are bound by motives, not only of expediency, not only of legal principle, but by motives of honour, to protect the minority.' Here was not a man who was about to endorse Gladstone's brainstorm, which, Salisbury believed and had countless times stated, would lead to the disintegration of the Empire.

It was not only Peel, but his own godfather the Duke of Wellington whom Salisbury had attacked for the inconstancies of 1829 and 1832. 'The politician who "yields" to public opinion is simply a dishonourable man,' he had written in the *Saturday Review* in October 1863. 'No "voice of the people", however distinct and powerful, can absolve a man from the guilt of professing doctrines in which he does not believe.' There was nothing wrong in a politician losing a battle and later choosing not to re-fight it, as over the Second Reform Act. What Salisbury found unforgivable was to change one's own opinion simply because of the number of people who held an opposing one. This is what he believed Gladstone had done over Home Rule, and that Gladstone should expect him to follow him in his apostasy he found personally insulting. His view of Gladstone's transparent attempt to split the Conservatives over Ireland, rather than run the risk of splitting his own Party, was bluntly summed up in a letter to Churchill on Christmas

Eve: 'His hypocrisy makes me sick.'

Yet Gladstone seemed genuinely to have believed that Salisbury could be persuaded to embrace a separate parliament in Dublin, or at least allow a Liberal Government to set one up without serious opposition. W.E. Forster once said that Gladstone 'could convince most people of most things and himself of anything' and the Grand Old Man's reasoning did have a certain internal logic. Not only had the Tories passed Catholic Emancipation, the repeal of the Corn Laws and the Second Reform Act, but Salisbury had shown his ability to work out a compromise solution twelve months earlier over Reform. Parnell's lover, Mrs Kitty O'Shea, was a regular political go-between and probably informed Gladstone about Parnell's secret interview with Carnarvon. The Radical Liberal MP, Henry Labouchere, had also told him, via Herbert Gladstone, of Carnarvon's meetings with the Irish Nationalist MP Justin M'Carthy. Gladstone could have been forgiven for assuming that the Conservative Cabinet had known and approved of what had taken place. The Newport speech had been seemingly ambiguous about Irish provincial government, and then there was the further intervention of Canon Malcolm MacColl.

Having helped to let Gladstone see what Salisbury wanted him to see of his opinions during the Reform Bill controversy in 1884, Salisbury allowed MacColl, a friend and acolyte of Gladstone's, to play a similar part over Irish Home Rule. It is not impossible that Salisbury deliberately led MacColl into thinking that he was more willing seriously to consider the issue than he in fact was, in order to lure Gladstone into flying the Hawarden Kite.[6] Before the Kite was flown, MacColl had written to Gladstone: 'I found Lord Salisbury...prepared to go as far probably as yourself in the question of Home Rule, but he seemed hopeless as to the prospect of carrying his party with him.' Once the Kite was airborne, MacColl was forced to explain to Gladstone on 28th December that 'All I told Lord Salisbury – indeed all I knew – hardly went beyond your public utterances on the subject of Ireland. The impression that you left on my mind was that you were not in favour of a Parliament in Dublin.'

Salisbury did not need to lie to MacColl, because no one but Gladstone knew the Liberal leader's mind on the issue, but he might have knowingly misled them both into thinking he could countenance a larger degree of separation than was in fact the case. Along with all the other indications, and with an unhealthy dose of wishful thinking, Gladstone somehow came away with the impression that Salisbury's mind was open on the question of Irish legislative separatism, which it never was. Something of a socially ambitious busybody who saw himself as an inspired amateur go-between, there are also indications that MacColl might have exaggerated Salisbury's interest in order to increase his own influence with Gladstone.[7]

In fact, as Winston Churchill was later to write of Salisbury: 'No English statesman in the nineteenth century was less likely to split his party or to lead some forlorn, uncalculated crusade of enthusiasm and adventure,' adding that the very idea of Home Rule was 'not even mentioned for the purpose of being dismissed' in the correspondence between Salisbury and his father. Salisbury had long seen the Act of Union as a bulwark of property rights and law and order. The 1st Earl of Salisbury had been instrumental in the wholesale confiscation of land in Armagh, Cavan, Derry, Donegal, Fermanagh and Tyrone between 1607 and 1609, and selling it in lots roughly the size of parishes to Scottish and City businessmen for settlement. His descendant was not now about to sell out their descendants.

Randolph Churchill, who was an inveterate leaker, told Labouchere (who told Chamberlain) that: 'The aim of the Conservatives will be to keep in a short time with [Irish] aid, then to quarrel with them, and to seek to hold their own against the Irish and the Radicals by a combination with the Whigs.' This was indeed precisely Salisbury's plan, and always had been. It was also exactly what happened. That Chamberlain's Radical Imperialists came over too was merely an unexpected but hugely added bonus.

Salisbury used to say that the British electorate always chose honour above prosperity. Believing that any serious measure of Home Rule would be bound to lead directly to Irish independence, that it would encourage other parts of the Empire also to demand their separation, that it would mean the abandonment of both Protestant and Catholic supporters of the Act of Union, that it would betray his hero Pitt's legacy, that it would be an ignoble surrender to the threat of violence, and that strategically it could prove advantageous to a future Continental enemy, Salisbury would never have supported it. 'The common tendency of mankind is not towards union, but secession,' he had written deploring America in the *Quarterly Review* in January 1862. 'The promptings of neighbourly jealousy find a readier ear than the dull suggestions of statesmanlike policy.'

Charles I's betrayal of Strafford, Peel's 'tergiversations', above all Disraeli's *volte face* over the Second Reform Act, all disgusted Salisbury, and he made it abundantly clear on many occasions, private, public and in print, that he would never have anything to do with foisting another such betrayal on the Party. Unlike so many Conservative leaders before and since, Salisbury was a true, dyed-in-the-wool Tory, entirely lacking in either middle-class guilt or ideological doubt. That did not, however, preclude him from practising the ancient political art of misleading his opponent and attempting to entrap him.

Salisbury believed that Gladstone was following the Radical direction that had actuated him ever since forsaking the Tory Right for the Peelites half a century before. 'Many men allow their interests to overbear their convictions,' he had written in the *Quarterly Review* in July 1866:

> A still greater number are biased by their interests in forming their convictions, and half-consciously drive their reason to conclusions to which it would not otherwise guide them. But such a description is not applicable to Mr Gladstone. He is never, even half-consciously, insincere.... His ambition has guided him in recent years as completely as ever it guided any statesman of the century; and yet there is not even a shade of untruth in the claim made for him by his friends, that he is guided wholly by his convictions. The process of self-deceit goes on in his mind without the faintest self-consciousness or self-suspicion. The result is that it goes on without check or stint.

By adding Parnell's eighty-six MPs to the 335 Liberals, Gladstone hoped that, even given a number of pro-Union Liberal rebels voting with the Conservatives, he could pass a Home Rule measure that could subsequently be muscled through the House of Lords in a tougher version of the 1884 Reform agitation. It had happened between 1830 and 1832 over Reform; if the Tories refused to co-operate, he reasoned, it could happen again, even though Queen Victoria was not William IV. The repeal of the Act of Union would be his new crusade of progress and principle, his greatest victory to date, dispelling the suspicions both that the Party was falling to Chamberlain's Birmingham caucus and that aged seventy-six he was no longer up to great challenges. If he could also split the Conservative Party into the bargain, it would be better still, so on 15th December Gladstone met Arthur Balfour at Eaton Hall, the Duke of Westminster's Cheshire seat, to offer Liberal support for any Home Rule legislation passed by the Conservative Government. 'I think it would be a public calamity if this great subject should fall into the lines of party conflict,' he wrote to Balfour. 'I desire specially on grounds of public policy that it should be dealt with by the <u>present</u> Government.'[8]

Salisbury was 'wholly contemptuous' of what seemed to him nothing more than 'a crude attempt to draw a veil of disinterested patriotism over a contemplated surrender to the Parnellite vote'. Gladstone wrote to Balfour again, concerned at the lack of reply to his original letter and worried that he was losing time to explain his position to his supporters, to whom he was, incredibly, absolutely silent despite his son's open discussions of Home Rule with the National Press Agency on 16th December. Along with Gladstone's letter, Balfour sent Salisbury the news that Hartington had publicly distanced himself from Gladstone's *démarche*, Goschen was 'firm' against it and Chamberlain was 'only with difficulty restrained from denouncing the G.O.M. in his last speech'.

Salisbury was at last witnessing the disintegration of the Liberal Party before it had even met Parliament to expel his own Government. With regard to Gladstone's second letter to Balfour, Salisbury's view was unchanged since the days of Palmerston: it was more fitting that radical measures should be advanced by Radicals and opposed by Conservatives. That was, after all, the very reason he had resigned in 1867. He wrote to Churchill to say that Gladstone was 'practically announcing that if we don't bring forward a plan for Government of Ireland, he will: which is as it should be'. After Christmas he told Lord Bath that he 'never admired the political transformation scenes of 1829, 1846 and 1867; and I certainly do not wish to be the chief agent in adding a fourth to the history of the Tory Party'.[9]

Salisbury already knew the views of the moderate Liberals because the Queen was, without their writer's knowledge, passing on the letters Goschen sent her. Salisbury hoped the Liberal Party might implode without his even entering the fray and he feared any intervention on his part could only tend to reunite them. 'Joe did not conceal at all his hatred of Hartington and Goschen,' Churchill reported to Salisbury in January about Chamberlain, 'and snarled awfully at both many times.' Although Hartington and Goschen were politically close, and Hartington and Chamberlain were not, it was not relations between them that mattered so much as the increasingly arctic relations between all three men and Gladstone.

Hartington looked upon the Irish question primarily as one of defending property and landowning rights. This authentically Whig stance was also coloured by the fact that Lord Frederick Cavendish had been his younger brother. Goschen, the financier, thought Home Rule would be economically disastrous for both Ireland and the rest of Britain. Chamberlain was actuated by imperialist beliefs quite as strong as his Radical ones. Each man had a significant body of support in the Liberal Party, and their secession from it, let alone adhesion to the Conservatives, would open the prospect of a consummation of Salisbury's hopes for 'fusion' which he had entertained ever since the days of Lowe's Cave of Adullam thirty-five years earlier.

In his eve-of-poll speech to the St Stephen's Club, Salisbury had described the Liberal Party as:

> an artificial confederacy of men who are united by motives and opinions of a very different kind ... but whom false shame and old association and other sophistries of the kind prevent from assuming in the face of the world the responsibility of the convictions which they entertain. Depend upon it a hollow fiction of this kind cannot last.

Yet it had lasted since 1859, and, although Radicalism was making headway, there was no good reason before the Hawarden Kite was flown why its four decades of hegemony should end. To split the Liberal Party, which had held power for the vast majority of time since 1846, needed an issue which went to the heart of Victorian imperial and national self-perception. The Kite provided just such an issue.

Gladstone's high-handed manner of appraising his Party of his thoughts also provided Salisbury with a new angle for attack. 'He had somehow or other entirely omitted to inform any of his colleagues of what was going on,' Salisbury joked to a large audience at the Edinburgh Corn Exchange three years later, 'and during the whole of that time, I have no doubt with the utmost sincerity, he used language and made eloquent speeches which conveyed, unfortunately, to the world the exact reverse of the truth.' By mocking 'the peculiar, phenomenal, and I have no doubt magnificent workings of Mr Gladstone's mind', Salisbury was able to plant the suspicion that other equally radical ideas were 'generating in the recesses of that teeming brain'.

For all his hopes of a Liberal split, Salisbury's own Party looked as fractious as ever. On 16th December 1885, Churchill made another of his resignation threats, this time over the issue of reforming parliamentary procedure. The Cabinet had not wanted to make promises on the question, but Churchill said that he was 'pledged up to the neck' on it and was unwilling, as he put it to Salisbury, to 'eat more dirt than ever, before those holy men Iddesleigh, Cross, John Manners and Co'. Salisbury was soothing, offering to hold Cabinets in his room at the Foreign Office, 'and then when the holy men are too much for you, you can seek solace from a cigarette in the little room at the side. I am sure many Cabinet difficulties are owing to that filthy, small, close room' at No. 10, Downing Street. He asked Churchill not to resign, but said that 'to do our duty to those behind us, we must go on in spite of many disagreeables for a few weeks longer'. On being asked what it was like to have two great offices of State, Salisbury quipped: 'In fact I have four – the Prime Ministership, the Foreign Office, the Queen and Randolph Churchill – and the burden of them increases in that order.'

Economic circumstances were not working in the Government's favour. In mid-December, Salisbury and Hartington's father, the Duke of Devonshire, acknowledged the severity of the agricultural distress by allowing their tenantry 15 per cent and 10 per cent off their half-yearly rents respectively. 'His Grace', *The Times* additionally reported, 'has also made large grants of manure.'

Salisbury felt that if his ministry resigned before meeting Parliament they would be admitting their inability to govern, which would hamper them in Opposition, whereas being turned out by the House of Commons was different.[10] Disraeli had ended the old constitutional convention that Parliament rather than the electorate dismissed governments when he resigned on losing the December 1868 election, but, realising how hard Gladstone might find it to form a government in January 1886, Salisbury resuscitated the older tradition. He might have elongated his rule further, as sessions usually began in February (except in 1878 and 1881 when it was January). In 1874 and 1880, they had not begun until March. With the 1886 session not ending until September rather than in August, that year's struggle over Home Rule was to be one of the longest and toughest in the history of Parliament.

On 1ˢᵗ January 1886, the British Government formally annexed Upper Burma, a kingdom larger than Britain, which had been conquered by Colonel Harry Prendergast VC with the loss of twenty men. When he had been at the India Office, Salisbury had approved of ingesting Burma into India, but did not have the money for a campaign. He was insistent, however, that no other Power (by which he meant France) should be allowed to interpose herself there. He did not think Burma important for herself, so much as a useful future communication route with western China. 'At this distance I can only form guesses, not opinions,' he had written to Lawrence in December 1866. 'Do whatever you think right in this matter and I will support you in whatever it is.'

At the time of his second India Secretaryship, Salisbury was willing to avenge the murder of Mr Margery, an interpreter and civil engineer who had been killed by Chinese tribesmen in February 1875. This was not because he wanted to extend British influence in Burma, so much as the fear that not avenging him might set an unhappy precedent: 'The lives of future envoys to semi-civilised powers will be in great danger.' By September 1879, Salisbury believed that Burma had to be annexed to prevent her falling under French influence, but this was put off until after the 1880 election, which was then lost.

When in 1885 King Theebaw of Burma rejected Dufferin's remonstrances against the negotiation of a convention with France, Churchill acted swiftly and ruthlessly. A force of 3,000 British and 6,000 Indian troops was collected by 14ᵗʰ November, which three days later routed the Burmese army with the loss of one British officer and three men. By 27ᵗʰ November, Mandalay was captured and Theebaw had been taken prisoner. To propitiate the Chinese, a Buddhist Lama was established there, despite Salisbury's belief that 'the Chinese Empire is no more Buddhist than Chartist'. On 1ˢᵗ January 1886, Churchill issued this single-sentence proclamation:

> By command of the Queen-Empress, it is hereby notified that the territories formerly governed by King Theebaw will no longer be under his rule, but have become part of Her Majesty's dominions, and will during Her

Majesty's pleasure be administered by such officers as the Viceroy and Governor-General may from time to time appoint.

It was the first of Salisbury's many additions to the British Empire.

New Year's Day 1886 also saw the Cabinet reject the idea of supporting Gladstone's Home Rule plans. It was agreed unanimously, Carnarvon being in Dublin. Shrewdly it decided to leave Gladstone guessing about their intentions until the Queen's Speech was forwarded to him just before it was formally read. On 4ᵗʰ January, Balfour finally wrote Gladstone a bland acknowledgment in reply to his letters.[11] Home Rule had virtually no other senior advocates in the Conservative Party other than Carnarvon. Salisbury has often been accused of putting the unity of the Tory Party and the Empire before the happiness and well-being of the Irish people. He would have rejected the charge, as he did not believe the Irish could be better off under Home Rule, but if pushed to a choice it is true that their aspirations would not have rated on a par with what he was increasingly coming to see as Britain's greatest contribution to civilisation and mankind, her Empire. To accord self-government to a province so close to Westminster would, he feared, encourage separatism in other possessions around the globe, and this consideration weighed heavily on someone who believed so implicitly in the importance of maintaining prestige.

'I am feverishly eager to be out,' Salisbury wrote to Carnarvon on 3ʳᵈ January. 'Internally as well as externally our position as a Government is intolerable.' The paragraph in the Queen's Speech dealing with Ireland posed a dilemma: how to reconcile a separatist Viceroy with a solidly Unionist Cabinet? With the Queen's Speech being delivered on 21ˢᵗ January, Salisbury managed to get the Duke of Abercorn to move the Address in the House of Lords, which he hoped 'would greatly comfort the Loyalists in the North'. As a far greater coup, he persuaded the Queen to open Parliament in person, for the first time since she did it to help Beaconsfield in 1877, and, as it turned out, the last time ever. Here was yet another unmistakable indication of whose side she favoured, and Salisbury thanked her for 'the very great advantage and assistance which such a step' rendered his ministry.[12]

On 15ᵗʰ January, the Cabinet split over demands for strong action against Parnell's National League. With 1,200 branches across Ireland by 1885, it was ostensibly a legitimate political movement, but in some areas of southern and western Ireland it doubled as an organiser of boycotting and fomentor of violence and intimidation. It was in effect the Land League, which had been banned in October 1882, in another guise, and was loosely connected in some places – but by no means all –

with secret 'courts', cattle-maiming and the setting up of almost an alternative government in Ireland, something which Salisbury had long denounced and was keen to crush.

It was proposed, before even meeting Parliament, to proscribe the movement, arrest its prominent members and seize its offices and documents, asking Parliament to indemnify them retrospectively for this breach of *habeas corpus*. Cranbrook and Lord George Hamilton supported these draconian measures. Iddesleigh and some others wanted a Bill passed first, and then much the same action taken. Salisbury wanted a secret committee to look into where the existing law fell short, and Manners (along with the Irish Government) wanted the existing law vigorously exercised. Churchill and Hicks Beach, both firm Unionists, nevertheless believed themselves to be pledged to Parnell not to introduce Coercion, and vigorously opposed it. Carnarvon just wanted to resign, choosing to interpret the whole discussion as a criticism of his rule in Ireland.

The next day, with the majority of the Cabinet still keen on at least one repressive paragraph in the Queen's Speech about the National League, Carnarvon resigned for the third and last time in his career. It was agreed that the true reason for the resignation would not be made public, but instead his health, and his original intention only to serve for one session, were cited. The letter he had written in June 1885, accepting the office for the 1885 session only, was made public, but few were convinced.[13] In a memorandum he wrote later that year, Carnarvon stated that over his views in favour of a Dublin legislative body: 'I am bound to say that [Salisbury] was consistent in his refusal to entertain them.'

Salisbury now, as he told Churchill on 16th January, absolutely insisted upon 'a policy which will show that we do not shrink from the duty of Government, and that we mean to stand by the Loyalists'. He put out a statement saying that there had been no disagreement within the Cabinet over Carnarvon's past policy, neatly sidestepping the chasm over his present and proposed future ones. It was the end of an alliance which went back nearly twenty years, but Salisbury still had favours to ask of Carnarvon and he still received them. Meanwhile, the Irish Viceroyalty was left vacant and W.H. Smith succeeded Hart Dyke as Chief Secretary.

On 18th January, the Cabinet met in Salisbury's room at the Foreign Office, both because Salisbury 'could not bear the want of air in the small room' at No. 10, Downing Street, but also because he said he suspected that their deliberations there three days before had been overheard. (The Irish *Freeman's Journal* had reported late on 15th January that the proclamation of the National League had been discussed.) In the course of the discussions on the 18th, there were 'doubts generally

expressed whether the room on the other side of the folding doors of
[the] old Cabinet room might not be used for over-hearing – general
feeling better to meet at F.O.' Edward Hamilton, dining with Goschen,
Stanhope and George Hamilton, was told that 'there had been leakages
which were believed to be due to the overhearing of their deliberations',
especially if one of the double doors of the old Cabinet room was left
open. The simple precaution of ensuring that the doors were shut and
guarded does not seem to have occurred to them, or that the *Freeman's
Journal* 'leak' might have been an inspired guess, or even a deliberate
leak by the Churchillites. Whatever the truth, the resulting move to the
Foreign Office was convenient for Salisbury.

When the Queen opened Parliament in person on 21st January 1886,
Salisbury, bearing the Sword of State in the procession, 'looked most
gloomy' in the opinion of Archbishop Benson.[14] He had good reason, for,
as he told the Queen, the paragraph on Ireland in her Speech 'was only
adopted to prevent the secession of the two leading rulers of the House
of Commons', Churchill and Hicks Beach. Rather than any direct
mention of suppressing the League, it merely stated that the
Government was, in relation to the Act of Union, 'absolutely opposed
to any disturbance of that fundamental law', which was at least unambiguous. In the subsequent debate, Salisbury blamed statements 'by
leading statesmen' about Ireland for having 'enormously added to our
difficulties' there. When Granville disingenuously asked him whom he
meant, Salisbury specified 'the declarations which have appeared in the
newspapers. They seemed to be authentic, and they were not distinctly
contradicted…the kite that has flown, the pilot balloon that was sent
up.' Like 'leap in the dark', 'puppet state', 'horny-handed sons of toil'
and 'old man in a hurry', Salisbury's fertile journalist's mind had coined
another evocative political expression.

'Oh! for a good adverse division!' Salisbury wrote to Janetta Manners
on 24th January. 'It will not be long coming if all tales be true. We have
had great troubles – and our internal condition is unsatisfactory.' Party
agitation and demands for firm action from Smith in Dublin had built
up pressure on Churchill and Hicks Beach, and finally on 25th January
the Cabinet agreed to present a Coercion Bill for Ireland. As the Home
Rulers would vote against it was clearly doomed, but Salisbury thought
that, if his Government was going to be turned out anyway, it should
happen on an issue that showed uncompromising vigour.[15]

So, recognising that they were likely to be defeated that evening,
Hicks Beach announced in the Commons that as soon as Smith
returned from Dublin, he would introduce 'a Bill for the purpose of
suppressing the National League, and giving the Government larger
powers for the protection of life, property and public order in Ireland', to
be followed by 'a more extensive' Land Bill than even the Ashbourne

Act. Salisbury told the Queen that day how he 'deeply laments the appearance of vacillation' not having had such an announcement in her Speech. Now it was on the table and constituted a standing invitation for the Parnellites to help Gladstone expel his Government. Indeed, when Hicks Beach announced the programme, 'there was a howl from the Irishmen that spoke of coming triumph'.

Sure enough, on the night of Tuesday, 26th January 1886, Salisbury's Government was defeated on an amendment proposed by the Radical Liberal Jesse Collings. Irritatingly for Salisbury, it was not over Coercion that his Government fell. The actual amendment was over Chamberlain's promise of providing 'three acres and a cow' to every agricultural labourer, as set out in his Unauthorised Programme. Yet Coercion was of course, as Rosebery recalled, 'the issue on which every mind was silently fixed, while the audible talk was of the area necessary to support a cow'.

The Parnellites, thrilled by the implications of the Hawarden Kite, voted solidly with Gladstone, who won the division by 329 to 250. Eighteen Liberals, including Hartington and Goschen, voted with the Conservatives however, neither supporting the Radical amendment itself nor wanting Gladstone to form a pro-Home Rule administration. Even more ominously for Gladstone, no fewer than seventy-six others abstained or were absent. The Irish cheered the fall of the Government, but otherwise, as Lewis Harcourt, Sir William's son and private secretary recorded, 'never were victors less triumphant or vanquished less depressed'. Churchill remarked to his friend Rosebery after the result was announced: 'Well, it is over, but it has not been bad fun.' To which Rosebery, with his intimate knowledge of Napoleana, replied: 'Just what Fleury said of the Second Empire.'[16]

The next morning the Cabinet unanimously resolved to resign. Cranbrook even found a cause for satisfaction in Gladstone's relatively small majority of seventy-nine on Collings's amendment, which was totally dependent on the eighty-six Irish Nationalists. The 'Caretaker' Government had done its duty, he thought. In his conduct of foreign policy, 'Salisbury has established a European reputation,' adding that Gladstone had told the Duke of Westminster that he could not find anything about it to which he would object. (When the Prince of Wales asked Cranbrook to pass this on, Salisbury's response was: 'I fear I must have done something wrong.') The Queen refused to accept Salisbury's resignation until she had seen him in person, telegraphing him from Osborne that she could 'not see what other Government can be formed', her pathological antipathy once more blinding her to her obvious constitutional duty to call for Gladstone.

Salisbury impishly played along with this, even suggesting that she send for Goschen instead. At their meeting at Osborne at 7.30 p.m. on

Thursday, 28th January 1886, the Queen 'lamented greatly what had occurred'. Salisbury blamed Hicks Beach and Churchill for the omission of Coercion in the Queen's Speech, and agreed with the Queen in hoping that Gladstone might not form a government. 'He heard he was greatly changed,' said Salisbury, who warned of another dissolution and election soon. Salisbury then set about advising her whom she should and should not accept in Gladstone's Cabinet. He advised her not to refuse Chamberlain or Morley, the former because it would martyr him, the latter because he was clever. When she said she would refuse Granville as Foreign Secretary, Salisbury 'said I would be "perfectly justified" in doing so, and thought Lord Rosebery would do very well.... Lord Kimberley would not do'.

After dinner, Salisbury told her that Ashbourne and Carnarvon had done badly in Ireland, and the latter had damaged the Government and Party and could not be entrusted with any important post again. 'What a dreadful thing to lose such a man as Lord Salisbury for the country, the world, and me! V.R.I.' she ended her memorandum of the conversation. In a part of the memorandum cut by Buckle from the edited version of her published papers, Salisbury even told the Queen that Edward Levy-Lawson, the proprietor and editor of the *Daily Telegraph*, had told him that Gladstone would end 'in a dreadful smash', which the Queen said she thought 'he deserves'.[17]

Salisbury, having offered to serve under Hartington but having been refused by the nevertheless flattered Liberal rebel leader, returned to Arlington Street. There he found a telegram from his son Edward: 'I hear turned out. Many congratulations.' He was, perhaps apocryphally, 'visibly irritated' to find that the wire he had been experimenting on when called to office in June 1885 had in the meantime been mislaid.[18] On 30th January, Hartington also refused to serve in Gladstone's Cabinet and was joined in the wilderness by Derby, Northbrook, Selborne and Carlingford, all members of the last Liberal Cabinet. Bright and Goschen were also opposed to Home Rule and refused office. Chamberlain and George Otto Trevelyan only joined the Cabinet on the basis of there being an inquiry into the implications of Home Rule before any legislation was tabled. Gladstone was followed by Granville, Spencer, Kimberley, Rosebery (as Foreign Secretary), Morley, Hugh Childers and Henry Campbell-Bannerman. The anti-Home Rule Sir Henry James refused the Lord Chancellorship, which was taken by Lord Herschell, and Gladstone's Chancellor of the Exchequer was Sir William Harcourt.

On 31st January, Salisbury turned down the offer of a dukedom from the Queen. Like Disraeli before him – and Lansdowne and Winston Churchill afterwards – he used financial considerations to refuse. Thanking her profusely, he said 'his fortune would not be equal to such a dignity', although he was in fact just as rich as some other dukes of the day. 'The kind words in which your Majesty has expressed approval of his conduct', he trowelled, 'are very far more precious to him than any sort of title.' The realisation that after only seven months of caretaking it was too munificent a gift might also have played its part. In the same letter, Salisbury told the Queen that Hartington's refusal to serve under Gladstone would mean that 'a coalition is certain to take place before long', especially as he suspected that 'the Parnellites will find moderation a tiresome game to play'.[19]

For all the anguish that the loss of control over foreign affairs gave him, Salisbury believed that he could look forward to being in a stronger position to influence events and protect the Union as Leader of the Opposition than he had been as Prime Minister of a minority administration. His 'administrative cruise' was over; a bitter seven-year struggle was about to begin for the unity of Great Britain and ultimately, he believed, for the integrity of her Empire as well.

TWENTY-THREE

Apotheosis

*The Liberal Split – The First Irish Home Rule Bill –
The General Election*

February to July 1886

'Rightly or wrongly, I have not the slightest wish to
satisfy the national aspirations of Ireland.'

On the day Salisbury's Cabinet surrendered their seals, Saturday, 6th February 1886, there was a very hard frost at Osborne. 'The Queen sat alone at the great gilt table with its black marble top,' recorded Harrowby after he placed the Privy Seal upon it. She left them under no illusions about their duty to fight what she saw as an irreversible measure which also ran counter to her Coronation Oath. 'We must agitate,' she told Cranbrook. 'I do not like agitation, but we must agitate every place small as well as large and make people understand.' At the 'cheerful' luncheon afterwards, the Cabinet were 'all very bright', except Churchill who said he feared Gladstone would last six years in office. Salisbury was 'in good spirits and looking much better'; he talked of obliging Gladstone to show his hand immediately over Home Rule. Before taking his leave of her, Salisbury assured the Queen that 'in whatever position he was, he would do anything to help'.

'He feels so much for me,' the Queen wrote in her journal that evening, 'and for my being alone, so cut off.' Salisbury was deftly setting up an entirely unconstitutional line of communication, which, however much Sir Henry Ponsonby might tut over it, stayed open and proved of enormous value to him throughout the coming crisis. Within a week, Salisbury started to receive 'very confidential' letters from the incorrigible monarch, even enclosing letters she had received from Gladstone, her elected Prime Minister, who of course believed he was writing to her in confidence.

Salisbury in turn kept her informed of the meetings he was holding with Goschen, offering him the possibility of the Conservatives not standing against him and his supporters at the next general election, should they make a definite break with Gladstone over Ireland. Salisbury has been criticised for not having referred the Queen sternly to her new Prime Minister, but to expect such a course is to misunderstand the man for whom the ends of defeating Home Rule easily justified the unconstitutional means involved.[1] It is debatable just how much Gladstone told the Queen about his most private thoughts and plans, but as a conduit of information, and later as a method of advising the Queen when a dissolution would be of most use to him, Salisbury's regular secret contact with her proved immensely helpful.

Salisbury also managed to use the Queen to put his views to Rosebery about foreign affairs in a way that the confrontational nature of politics, let alone professional pride, might otherwise have precluded. There survive twenty-three letters from the Queen to Salisbury when he was in Opposition, which sometimes enclosed her letters from Goschen and Granville as well as from the Prime Minister. Beaconsfield's former factotum, Lord Rowton, was also a verbal conduit of messages and advice. The subjects covered were not confined to Ireland, but ranged over policy towards Greece, the danger of Alexander of Bulgaria being assassinated, Rosebery's attitude to France, the refusal of Whig peers to accept Household appointments, Labouchere, dissatisfaction with Lord Spencer for accepting office under Gladstone and her loathing of the Ambassador to St Petersburg, Sir Robert Morier, whom she thought was attempting to engineer an Anglo-Russian *entente*.

None of these leaks was published in Buckle's edition of the Queen's letters, although from three of Salisbury's letters to her which were published it is discernible that they were in close communication. In 1888, Salisbury confessed to Gwendolen that he had even advised the Queen to go ahead and allow the publication of her 1885 commiseration letter to General Gordon's sister, in which she had written of the 'promises of support' which she had 'frequently and constantly pressed' upon the (unnamed) statesman 'who had asked him to go'.

The lengths to which Salisbury was prepared to go to resist Home Rule can be discerned from an after-dinner discussion at Churchill's home on 16th February, where Sir Henry James, the Liberal former Attorney-General, noted that Salisbury's 'mind seemed full of a put-your-foot-down policy'. The son of a Hereford surgeon, James was a cricketing enthusiast and friend of Churchill's. As the port was being passed, Salisbury said 'the blow' should be struck sooner rather than later. James asked what 'the blow' meant. Salisbury answered: 'Oh, both in the House and out of it.' James said: 'That means civil war.' To which Salisbury replied: 'I think not, but if it does, I cannot help it. We must not desert the loyal people of Ulster.'

He was no more compromising in his first speech as Leader of the

Opposition the following day. To a large dinner at the Hotel Metropole in Northumberland Avenue given for the four Hertfordshire Conservative MPs, Salisbury set out the basis of the arguments he was to use throughout the anti-Home Rule campaign. He claimed his ministry had fallen because they were about to insist upon 'a strict obedience to the law and of exterminating every organisation that pretended to set up its authority against the Queen's government'. His old scorn was on full display; in response to the argument that many Irish people were writing letters to MPs in favour of Home Rule, he said: 'There are five millions of inhabitants of Ireland: and if you say that one Irishman in five has a grievance and is prepared to support it with copiousness and aptitude of diction...[Gladstone] has called into existence a million of correspondents.' He predicted that over Home Rule, Gladstone would give the oysters to his new Parnellite allies and leave the moderate Liberals with only the shells, albeit 'properly decorated and illuminated'.

The Home Rule Bill, he predicted, would 'bristle with securities' for the Protestants, but these would be merely a 'paper barricade' because 'once set up a legislature at Dublin...will make an independent nation'. Whole flotillas of the Royal Navy would be needed to guard against the fact that 'In time of war you will have on your western side an island controlled, filled, possibly prepared and equipped, by a Government that hates you bitterly.' He asked his audience to think of the effect on the Indian Raj if 'the Loyalists of Ireland will be flung aside like a sucked orange'. He said the Loyalists faced ruin because they were unpopular, precisely because 'they had the folly to take your side'. It was not a question of loss, embarrassment or perplexity 'which we have to meet, we have to meet something that is infinitely more dreadful, and that is dishonour'.

Yet he was entirely trumped in his militant Unionism by a speech Randolph Churchill delivered in the Ulster Hall in Belfast on 22nd February. Despite having only recently written to Salisbury that 'those foul Ulster Tories have always ruined our party', Churchill played what was called 'the Orange card' in a manner that was at the least blatantly inflammatory, and if taken literally might even have been an incitement to civil war. The Churchills had impeccable Protestant credentials going back to the Glorious Revolution and Randolph had been his father's private secretary when the Duke of Marlborough had been Beaconsfield's Irish Viceroy. When he told the Loyalists 'most truly that in that dark hour there will not be wanting to you those of position and influence in England who would be willing to cast in their lot with you and who, whatever the result, will share your fortunes and your fate', he was trying to imply that the seventeen Unionists elected for Ulster, out of the total of 103 MPs from Ireland, had a right of veto over Home Rule more powerful than the Constitution. The Liberals' argument, that many more Irishmen wanted Home Rule than did not, was hardly one that would be likely to commend itself to Salisbury, for whom a popular majority in favour of something almost automatically suggested to him that it was likely to be wrong-headed.

Salisbury wrote to Churchill as soon as he had read his inflammatory speech, calling it 'singularly skilful. You avoided all shoals, and said nothing to which any Catholic could object.' Churchill, who was privately worried whether the Orange card he had played would turn out to be the two of trumps rather than the ace, answered that 'If I am put upon my trial for high treason, I shall certainly rely on your evidence that at any rate up to the second of this month my action was constitutional.' In May, writing in a public letter to a Liberal Unionist in Glasgow, Churchill went on to pen the fateful phrase: 'Ulster will fight; Ulster will be right.'[2]

Salisbury used his 3rd March speech at a dinner of 1,300 in Crystal Palace to celebrate Tory victories in Lambeth and to rebut various allegations made about him and Home Rule. The Chief Secretary of Ireland, John Morley, he called 'a very distinguished literary man, but he had no other title to fame'. He described Herbert Gladstone as 'a vehicle for half the political slanders that are uttered'. Of the accusation that a secret deal had been done with Parnell in May 1885 over Coercion, Salisbury said: 'It is absolutely untrue. We conveyed no intimation to the Parnellite party.' He ignored the Carnarvon–Parnell conversations, which were not strictly on that subject, and the Winn–Power ones, which involved Parnell and himself at one remove but which had not specifically mentioned Coercion either. However, Churchill's promise to Parnell not to go into government if Coercion was to be renewed also went unmentioned.

Salisbury then claimed that the Bill to repress the National League was not 'invented at the last minute', which was allowing maximum elasticity to the truth, considering he had only sent Curzon to the library to look up its precedents on the morning that his Government fell. Of Gladstone's contention that Salisbury could be as statesmanlike as Wellington and Peel had been over Catholic Emancipation and the repeal of the Corn Laws, Salisbury did 'not dispute that a man who had gained office by promising to oppose them, had any right to remain in office by passing them'. Gladstone's insinuations that Salisbury and Hicks Beach had favoured Home Rule, possibly as a result of a garbled and misunderstood account of the Carnarvon–Parnell conversation, Salisbury called 'absolutely false. I speak in the presence of colleagues who would despise me if I did not state the absolute truth, and I tell you that I have never, to anybody or in any Cabinet, given the slightest encouragement to the delusion of Home Rule.' It was the truth but not the whole truth. Those Cabinet ministers present – except Ashbourne – did not know of the Carnarvon–Parnell meeting, which had certainly encouraged Parnell in that 'delusion'.

Salisbury then gave his dystopian vision of what a self-governing Ireland would be like, saying that any funds invested there would be 'as though they had been subscribed to the maintenance of the Mexican republic'. In an intellectual version of a phrase that was becoming popular, 'Home Rule is Rome Rule', Salisbury averred that 'the worst government in the world is the government by priests'. Because Roman Catholic priests had been closely involved in the National League in some areas of Ireland, Salisbury, despite the Duke of Norfolk being present, attacked the Catholic Church in Ireland for having 'wantonly descended' into the political arena. In his peroration, after a warning that Morley would revive the agitation against the Lords if it rejected Home Rule, Salisbury said: 'In this political saturnalia through which we have passed, we have seen rights that never before were contested treated as open questions, and we have seen political truths which nobody before opposed, treated as matters suitable for open discussion.' The theme of his 'Disintegration' article being acted out as he predicted.

One favoured line Salisbury now abjured was that of goading the Whigs for political cowardice in not throwing Gladstone over. This was because he was due to meet Hartington the following day in the second of the several minuets he was to dance in a most protracted, nine-year wooing process. Beyond their shared social class, Salisbury had little in common with the hunting, racing clubman, who was conducting an affair with the Duchess of Manchester. He had been dismissive of 'Rip Van Winkle' in the past, calling Hartington's speeches 'delightful; they seem like a foretaste of that millennium when there shall be no controversies and parties shall be at an end…but unfortunately he has not the slightest influence on his colleagues'. In the Liberal schism, Salisbury recognised the influence Hartington held over wavering members. The Cavendish name lent a respectability to the anti-Home Rule Liberal camp, who were starting to be called Liberal Unionists, during the painful process of severing their links with the Party which the Whigs had been instrumental in founding.

When they met for an hour at Arlington Street on 4th March, just before Salisbury left for Beaulieu for the Recess, he and Hartington agreed that there was no obstacle to their acting together to resist Home Rule, but anything in the nature of a more formal alliance was not, at least until an election loomed, 'within the field of practical politics at present'. Negotiations did, however, continue between Goschen and Akers-Douglas over an electoral armistice between his followers and the Conservatives in certain seats. 'It was said of the Peelites in 1850', Salisbury wrote to Churchill from Monaco on 16th March, as he recovered from a bout of bronchitis, 'that they were always putting themselves up for auction, and always buying themselves in. That seems to be the Whig idea at present.'

Meanwhile, Salisbury calmed Churchill's concerns that he might be the impediment to a coalition, saying that Hartington's oratorical public references to Salisbury's own 'rashness' made him 'suspect that I am more the difficulty than you'. Salisbury, ever irritated by Whig hauteur, now thought it best that the next moves should come from them rather than him. He ended his letter with his best wishes to 'one of your sons', whom he had been told was suffering from pneumonia in Brighton. In fact the boy, Winston, had a closer brush with death then than at any other stage in a life crammed with such encounters.[3]

Despite rumours of Chamberlain's resigning and even eventually joining a coalition with the Tories, Salisbury resolutely stayed in Monte Carlo until, as he told Cranbrook, Gladstone tabled a Home Rule measure and 'generously allows us to do business'. He was enjoying himself in Monaco, and bought the land on which a new house was to be built at Beaulieu. 'I don't hear of any terrible tales of ruin,' he gossiped to Janetta Manners, 'and I have not come across any suicides hanging from the olive trees, but I am told it is only the Italians who commit suicide: and they do not come here 'till the summer.'

After a particularly blatant indication from Chamberlain, Balfour predicted to his uncle that 'we shall find in him a very different kind of ally from those lukewarm and slippery Whigs whom it is difficult to differ from and impossible to act with'. They were prophetic words, and on 20th March both Joseph Chamberlain and the Scottish Secretary, George Otto Trevelyan, resigned from the Cabinet over the plans for Home Rule. Still Salisbury put off his return until his 'internal machinery' was up to the three-day journey. His hope was to form a government of national unity – perhaps under Hartington – where 'the right wing of the Liberals can be fused with the Tories... But I see little hope of it.' The libertarian in him deprecated Chamberlain's recent calls for 'strong government', remarking to Balfour that: 'With us the feebleness of our government is our security – and the only one we have against revolutionary alterations of our law.' He was pessimistic that Home Rule would stir up much popular excitement at the next election: 'The instinctive feeling of an Englishman is to wish to get rid of an Irishman. We may gain as many votes as Parnell takes from us: I doubt more. Where we shall gain is in splitting up our opponents.'

Writing to his wife on 3rd April, Salisbury played down the idea of a purely Hartingtonian ministry supported by the Conservatives from the outside, thinking it must lead to quarrels. Far better to have a dissolution on Home Rule, where the Liberal Unionists would be forced into an electoral understanding with the Conservatives. On 6th April, a month after their previous meeting, Salisbury saw Hartington at Devonshire House and they agreed to parliamentary co-operation for the session. It was a deal Hartington was to stick to conscientiously, contacting Salisbury on all important matters in both Houses. Salisbury meanwhile informed the Queen that he did not wish to take office, 'for it would re-unite all the Liberals of all shades' just as the Liberal Unionists were taking their first tentative steps towards Party apostasy.[4]

On 8th April 1886, Gladstone moved the (traditionally unopposed) first reading of the Irish Home Rule Bill in his grand, slightly lilting tone, in a speech lasting three hours and twenty-five minutes. Although Salisbury stayed in close contact with Hartington during the debate, discussing amendments and tactics, it was not until Monday, 14th August, that they appeared together on the same public platform at Her Majesty's Theatre, the opera house in the Haymarket. It was the first manifestation of what Churchill was already calling 'The Unionist Party', the alliance which was to govern Britain for seventeen of the next twenty years.

The doors had to open half an hour early because of the huge press of people who then packed the house. Two vast Union Flags adorned the back of the stage. Hartington began by saying how 'noble and honest' Gladstone was, but his name and that of Parnell only drew groans and hisses. It was a very Tory and highly emotional audience, which almost persuaded the fastidious Whigs to drop the public experiment of joint meetings altogether. Salisbury's speech was along the same lines as his other attacks. 'We are suddenly confronted by a great danger to the Empire,' he warned, and hammered home his central point that 'there is no middle term between government at Westminster and independent and separate government at Dublin'. The federal option he dismissed as 'not within our political horizon' because advance in science and communications 'has abolished distance'. Consolidation was the general political norm for the future, not severance. When Turkey allowed Romania, Serbia and Bulgaria the semi-autonomy similar to that which Parnell demanded for Ireland, complete independence was soon the result, but whereas 'Turkey is a decaying Empire; England, I hope, is not.'

It was not what Salisbury said, so much as the fact that he said it in the political company of Hartington and Goschen that mattered. Lady Ponsonby had attended, discreetly parking her Royal Household carriage away from the front door, and Salisbury soon received orders from the Queen to organise many more such 'admirable' events.[5] 'We hope to succeed in smashing the old lunatic,' Lady Salisbury wrote about Gladstone on 19th April, with the Cecils now translating G.O.M. as 'God's Only Mistake'. To Gladstone's daughter Mary, however, she wrote to thank her for a medical prescription saying: 'Because we differ about the horrid Irish question, why should that destroy the friendship of a life? It does not with me, and I assure you, it never will!'

Writing to a supporter in Lancashire, Salisbury explained how, despite the natural objections of the local Conservative associations to withdrawing their chosen candidates, it would be important not to split the anti-Gladstonian vote in the next general election. But he was equally irritated by the Whigs' attitude: 'Their view seems to be that in allying themselves with us they are contracting a *mésalliance*: and though they are very affectionate in private they don't like showing us to their friends, till they have had time to prepare them for the shock.'

To the Queen's annoyance, Salisbury went silent after the Haymarket speech, explaining that he was 'loth to run the risk of repelling a single Radical or Liberal auxiliary' on the approaching second reading in the Commons. He did not want to present his own manifesto, and he was increasingly worried that Carnarvon was about to make a formal denial of any agreement with Parnell, which would bring the fact of the interview into the public arena. Visiting Windsor he found the Queen in bellicose mood. His highly placed mole was now producing less and less useful information about Gladstone's intentions, having presumably been rumbled by her Prime Minister. As Rowton told Salisbury on 30th April, the Queen now 'knows nothing of Mr Gladstone's mind or intentions'. She was, however, entirely in Salisbury's hands with regard to any future dissolution which Gladstone might request. She evidently understood how unconstitutional was her behaviour, because she sometimes asked Salisbury to correspond with her via her lady-in-waiting, the Marchioness of Ely, using a Bond Street hotel as the cover address.

'A retired statesman working in a Welsh castle', Salisbury told the Merchant Taylors' Company on 10th May, 'resolving by himself, apparently without any support from others, has resolved that this vast change shall be. He turns the machine, and straightway colleagues change their opinion, men of unblemished fame change their coats.'[6] Salisbury had finally broken his silence, and it was on 15th May 1886, in a speech to the NUCCA dinner in the St James's Hall, Piccadilly, that he made the most notorious 'blazing indiscretion' of his career, in a speech of such calculated virulence that it deliberately made it harder, rather than easier, for Hartingtonians and Chamberlainites to come over to the Tories, and once they had crossed the Rubicon it made it almost impossible for them to go back.

Speaking to 600 delegates at the end of their one-day conference at the Westminster Palace Hotel, Salisbury cited maintenance of the Act of Union as the unbroken tradition of Pitt, Castlereagh, Canning, Peel and Beaconsfield. He said of Gladstone that 'he is not dishonest, but his assurances cannot be trusted'. He argued that any central Parliament in

Dublin would be the thin end of the wedge, leading to a 'step by step' reduction of 'English power to the lowest point'. Unfortunately for Tories, he said, the arguments against Home Rule were harder to put, because 'Nobody argues now. They give you an opinion neatly expressed in a single sentence, and that does the work of argument. My belief is that a fallacy in two lines will carry you further than a mathematical demonstration in two pages.'

Such fallacious vocabulary included Parnell's use of the word 'nation' in relation to Ireland, when it had no history, no traditions, no common interests or sympathies which united all Irishmen. Salisbury argued that the island of Ireland was only a nation in the sense that it 'means a certain number of individuals collected between certain latitudes and longitudes'. Otherwise, 'Ireland is two nations ... two deeply divided and bitterly antagonistic nations.' The next fallacious word he examined was 'confidence', and it was then that Salisbury made a remark which was to dog him for a decade.

Commenting on the nationalist line that 'we are to have confidence in the Irish people', Salisbury said:

> Confidence depends upon the people in whom you are to confide. You would not confide free representative institutions to the Hottentots, for instance. Nor, going higher up the scale, would you confide them to the Oriental nations whom you are governing in India – although finer specimens of human character you will hardly find than some who belong to those nations, but who are simply not suited to the particular kind of confidence of which I am speaking.... This which is called self-government, but which is really government by the majority, works admirably well when it is confided to the people who are of Teutonic race, but it does not work so well when people of other races are called upon to join in it.

After pointing out that Cromwell was not exclusively an Irish phenomenon, but someone who did great damage in England too, Salisbury came out with his own programme for Ireland:

> My alternative policy is that Parliament should enable the Government of England to govern Ireland. Apply that recipe honestly, consistently and resolutely for twenty years, and at the end of that time you will find that Ireland will be fit to accept any gifts in the way of local government or repeal of coercion laws that you may wish to give her. What she wants is government – government that does not flinch, that does not vary.

Not content with just that, he also suggested that if the Government 'could only emigrate another million of the Irish people ... to Manitoba, the result would be magical upon the social conditions of the Irish people', because wages in Ireland would rise and rents would fall. For good measure, he accused the Irish priesthood of being 'singularly exposed to the temptation of misusing an organisation meant for high spiritual ends', and wound up by urging the Liberal Unionists to 'put country before party on every occasion'.

The speech was pure *Saturday Review* polemic, and it was also partly the reason that he rather than Iddesleigh was Party leader. The backlash was fierce; for months afterwards no Liberal platform speech was complete without a reference to what John Morley nicknamed the 'Manacles and Manitoba' speech, which was accused of polarising the issues between Protestants and Catholics and introducing 'Ulsteria' into British politics. For all of Salisbury's denials that 'twenty years' of 'resolute' government necessarily meant he wanted twenty years of Coercion, it was the seeming equation of Irishmen with Hottentots which rankled most. Salisbury was still defending himself against what he called this 'stupid calumny' six years later, and his nephew Gerald Balfour even tried in a Commons debate in 1896 to explain how Salisbury had in fact been somehow praising the Irish. Salisbury's sanguine remarks about Teutonic democracy have also been ridiculed in the light of later experience, as though any statesman could have foreseen the events of more than a quarter of a century in the future.[7]

There were more justifiable criticisms, such as from Cranbrook, who thought the expressions 'imprudent' and a gift for Liberal retaliation. 'They give a handle to the unscrupulous, an excuse to the waverers,' he complained. All this was true, but they also helped to close the avenues of return when Hartington finally came over. For on the same day as his speech, Salisbury wrote to the Queen that 'there appears now to be no doubt as to the defeat of the Bill'. In discussing whether there should be a dissolution afterwards, he held out for her the prospect that a Liberal defeat at the polls would probably involve Gladstone's retirement. Salisbury did not want her to call on Hartington to form a government, which would allow Gladstone to raise issues other than Ireland, over which he might 'regain the allegiance of numbers who are falling away from him now'. His opinion was that a coalition government between Tories and Liberal Unionists, regardless of who led it, would not last long with Ireland as their only point of agreement. Salisbury therefore advised the Queen to let Gladstone have his dissolution the moment the Home Rule Bill was defeated in the Commons.

To the Grand Habitation of the Primrose League on 19th May, Salisbury rebutted various misinterpretations of his St James's Hall speech and announced, to great cheering, 'that no Liberal shall suffer in his electoral prospects by reason of the part he has taken in the defence of the unity of the Empire'. He further made it clear that 'our desire is to unite with them as far as they will unite with us'. It was an offer of a free run in their constituencies to any Liberal Unionist who voted against the Home Rule Bill. Only the Radical but also imperialist

Liberal MP for Chelsea, Sir Charles Dilke, who was involved in his scandalous divorce suit and was, moreover, as Salisbury told Lord Brabourne, an 'enemy of all we care about', failed to have the offer extended to him.

During the Commons debate on the second reading of the Irish Home Rule Bill on the evening of 7th June, Parnell revealed that a senior minister of the Salisbury Government had secretly offered him a statutory parliament with power to protect Irish industries. It caused a sensation, especially once the *Pall Mall Gazette* had named the minister as Lord Carnarvon. It did not, however, affect the outcome of the debate, which the Government lost by 311 to 341, not including the two tellers on each side. Hartington, Chamberlain, Bright, Goschen, James, Trevelyan and Collings – leading 103 Liberals in all – failed to vote for Gladstone's measure.

The post office at Hatfield was kept open so that sixteen-year-old 'Linky' (Hugh) could bring the news when the result was announced after one o'clock in the morning of 8th June. 'The note of triumph in his shouts as he ran up to the House with the paper was the first intimation they had of what had happened,' wrote one eyewitness. Salisbury emerged from his study with Bul-Bul, his big Persian cat, perched on his shoulder. '"It's too good," he observed when presented with the voting figures. "They might resign on that. I want them to dissolve." And repeating "I want them to dissolve", he went to bed.'8

Despite the jubilation at the Carlton Club, and the Ulstermen who carried Hartington shoulder high through the Commons Central Lobby, Salisbury saw a dangerous situation developing over the Carnarvon–Parnell interview. Although in July 1885 Parnell had written a public letter denying Herbert Gladstone's accusation that there was an 'alliance' between Tories and Irish, 'for parliamentary purposes and for the purposes of the General Election', a year later he was keen to cause the Conservatives maximum embarrassment over just that. By 10th June 1886, the day that Gladstone announced that Parliament would be dissolved and fresh elections fought, Carnarvon resolved to come clean about the whole incident. 'Pray make it as dry as possible without any sentiment,' requested Salisbury. 'I shall be very short and simple, but I always eat my bread with butter,' Carnarvon replied. Carnarvon then publicly admitted meeting Parnell, denied Parnell's account of his having offered a statutory Dublin parliament, claimed that it had been his duty as Viceroy to obtain information and, more convincingly, said that he had 'no authorisation' from the Cabinet for his actions, and thus could have given no promises, assurances or understandings. 'Both of us left the room as free as when we entered it,' he stated.

Salisbury was neither mentioned during Carnarvon's statement nor did he open his mouth afterwards. When four years later Carnarvon complained to Salisbury about his conspicuous lack of support on that occasion – 'a few words from you confirming what I said would have practically closed the matter' – Salisbury answered that Carnarvon had ended his speech with 'eloquent expressions of your desire to satisfy "the national aspirations of Ireland"'. This was too much for Salisbury: 'Rightly or wrongly, I have not the slightest wish to satisfy the national aspirations of Ireland; and I remained silent, because if I had spoken I must have spoken to some extent against you, which in the circumstances I was exceedingly anxious not to do.'[9] For years afterwards, Salisbury had to choose his words extremely carefully when rebutting allegations about the Carnarvon–Parnell interview and the Winn–Power discussions. In answer to Justin M'Carthy's claims in January 1888, for example, he wrote to Sir Frederick Milner: 'There is no truth in the statement that I ever sent anybody to make assurances on the subject of Coercion to Mr Justin M'Carthy or any other Irish members.' Once again, it was strictly true, but nothing approximating the whole truth.

By May 1888, Carnarvon was willing to implicate Salisbury in the meeting, but until then Salisbury merely blocked all inquiries, including outraged ones from the Queen and members of his Cabinet who assumed he had not known about the meeting. It was a bruising saga, but, as it had led Parnell to deliver to the Tories the crucial number of seats necessary to defeat the second reading by thirty votes, it was ultimately well worth it. Herbert Gladstone always believed that if the Conservatives had won the 1885 general election they would have adopted 'some form of autonomy in lieu of coercion'. He thought that Salisbury was negotiating via Carnarvon in earnest, and that all his father had done was to put into practice Salisbury's intended policy. He was wrong in this, because like his father he took at face value the various indications Salisbury had given in order to wrong-foot the Liberals.

With less than three weeks to go before the polls opened, a formal electoral pact needed to be concluded immediately with those ninety-three Liberals who had voted against the second reading (a further ten had abstained or were absent). In his *Saturday Review* days, Salisbury had scoffed that the Whigs consisted, like the *antebellum* American militia, 'mainly of generals and colonels' but very few foot-soldiers. Now there were no fewer than ninety-three constituencies where the Conservative candidates had to be persuaded not to stand. In all but six of those constituencies the local Conservative candidate was prevailed upon to renounce the opportunity of entering Parliament, and instead to campaign for the sitting MPs, whom in many places they had hitherto been working for years to unseat. Constituency associations were far more autonomous than they are today, and the job of strong-arming them was left to Akers-Douglas and Middleton, who managed it with remarkable success. In this they were supported by Salisbury, who would write to association chairmen when required to point out their patriotic duty.

After the election, the Liberal Unionists, who eventually turned down the alternative names of 'Loyalists', 'Constitutionals' and 'Unionist Liberals', sat on the same side of the House as before, beside the Gladstonian Liberals. They even shared the same front bench and despatch box, an uncomfortable situation for all concerned. Far more jarring for Salisbury was the fact that the Liberal Unionist leader in the House of Lords was none other than the Earl of Derby, who since the 'Titus Oates' remarks of 1878 had not been on speaking terms with him. Lord George Hamilton told the story of arriving at Grillions one Monday night with John Morley and finding 'two big, very confused figures standing in the remotest corners of the room, and each ignoring the other's presence. No one else came to dinner, so we sat down four.... The conversation was at first somewhat strained.' Hamilton and Morley discovered that 'if one of the two belligerents addressed a question to a neutral, the other would reply to it through the other neutral. So we progressed.'[10] It was hardly an ideal working arrangement for the leaders of two allied Parties in the House of Lords.

Derby had disapproved of Hartington going into coalition with the Conservatives at all, because he said that Salisbury was too untrustworthy. Even when Salisbury visited Liverpool on speaking engagements he did not meet Derby, and of the ninety-nine letters from Derby in Salisbury's papers at Hatfield, only one dates from after 1878, and that is a formal one concerning London University. Gladstone's Hawarden brainstorm had thrown up the unlikeliest of bedfellows. The situation was only alleviated when the Duke of Devonshire died in 1891 and Hartington took over as the Liberal Unionist leader in the Lords.

Salisbury had long believed in electoral pacts in certain constituencies, advising Disraeli in January 1867 that it should be stated that 'any Whig who stands by us against Bright will not be molested in his seat'. A 'fusionist' since the earliest days, he nonetheless privately despised the Whigs as 'a dwarfed race, amiable and cultivated, animated by all the honesty which thorough narrowmindedness can confer, but possessing no trace of originality or of mental energy'. He had been particularly rude about Hartington in the *Saturday Review*, whom he had dismissed, fortunately anonymously, as 'distinguished by that surly and tedious mediocrity which, conjoined to high rank, is looked upon as a valuable qualification for office in this country'.

Salisbury reassured Churchmen worried about the nonconformity of Chamberlain, he calmed the personal antagonisms in the constituencies, and he banged recalcitrant and over-ambitious heads together elsewhere. He was under no illusions that the alliance would produce a watered-down version of his own brand of High Toryism once in office, but at least until Gladstone departed the political scene he resigned himself to that. 'It is the first lesson of statesmanship', he had written in February 1860,

> to be ready to surrender a portion of his convictions to those with whom he acts; and as he has fifteen colleagues and three hundred and fifty supporters, the necessary surrenders multiply in proportion. The microscopic residuum that is left after all those demands are satisfied will probably have to be given up for the purposes of satisfying the Opposition. It is hard, therefore, since greatness has been so clipped and pared, to envy it the one privilege that remains to it. If it can do little in these days and suffers much, at least it can stop everything.[11]

If Irish Home Rule were to be stopped, the election needed to be won, and Salisbury ditched the convention by which peers stayed aloof from elections to the Lower House. His campaign began at Hatfield speaking to a mass rally from a wooden platform in the courtyard on the south front of the house. 'The wooden roof formed an admirable sounding-board,' reported *The Times* the next day, 'and an audience of many thousands assembled and stood noiselessly on the large area.' To deaden the sound of feet on the gravel, the front of the house was strewn with tan for the occasion. Hoping to rebut the criticism that because Australia and Canada had semi-autonomous federal systems so could Ireland, Salisbury bluntly stated that Ireland was only four hours away, and whereas Britain was friendly with Canada and Australia, 'a large proportion of the Irish people hated us'.

Meanwhile, Carnarvon was coming under great pressure to reveal whether or not Salisbury had known in advance about his interview with Parnell. Challenged by Gladstone to deny it, Carnarvon asked Salisbury what to do. The same day, 18th June, Salisbury spoke to 5,000 in Leeds Coliseum and ridiculed Gladstone's 'spasmodic ejaculations' about the Parnell interview, calling them 'mere gossip'. He went on to praise Hartington's and Chamberlain's 'fibre and robustness and honesty'. The next day he wrote to Carnarvon saying that he 'must protest most earnestly against your making any statement of what passed between yourself and me when we were Cabinet ministers together, upon official business. It is against all rule and practice.' He argued that should Carnarvon say anything at all during the election campaign, 'it will be impossible to stop at the simple statement you propose to make'.

So Carnarvon stayed silent and Salisbury stayed safe, at least for a while. He was hardly grateful, telling the Queen that Carnarvon 'has acted impulsively, and with little foresight. Lord Salisbury does not think that Lord Carnarvon realised the shifty character of the man with whom he was dealing.' At no point in the letter was it made clear even to her that Salisbury himself had approved the whole proceeding before it took place.[12] To Lord Brabourne he went so far as to say that he did not 'know exactly what Carnarvon thought about Home Rule during our term of office. His language was always vague.' Salisbury then met Carnarvon and tried to agree a line on what could be said about what had taken place the previous August.

'No one could suggest that I coquetted with Home Rule,' Salisbury protested, knowing that that was exactly what the Liberals were hoping to imply, just as the polls were about to open. 'If a conversation is to be repeated, it should be recorded,' he told Carnarvon on 27th June. 'If it is not recorded, it should not be repeated.' Salisbury wanted Carnarvon to confine himself to denying Parnell's 'inventions' about the meeting, 'and abstain from disclosing any communications that have passed between us'. A document was actually drawn up, complete with Salisbury's corrections specifying in red ink what Carnarvon could say.

In a speech to the annual dinner of the Constitutional Union at St James's Hall on 29th June, Salisbury admitted that 'Lord Carnarvon treated me absolutely without reserve, and I know – he informed me – what passed at that interview with Mr Parnell, and his statement, which was made two or three days afterwards, absolutely agreed with what he stated the other day in the House of Lords.' Salisbury entirely failed to mention that he had prior knowledge of the interview, let alone that he had encouraged it. He also denied that Carnarvon had resigned over differences with his colleagues, saying that ill-health was part of the reason, as was his original intention to stay on only until the November 1885 election. 'I really am ashamed that I have spent a quarter of an hour on this matter,' he said, but 'no electioneering weapon is too monstrous for partisans to despair to use'.

Carnarvon's death in June 1890 did not end the speculation about what the Prime Minister had known and when he had known it. Until well into the 1890s, Salisbury was having to put out various denials about the exact nature of his involvement. The 'smoking gun' just kept on billowing. When in July 1893 Balfour told the Primrose League that Carnarvon had 'acted without the knowledge of a single one of his colleagues', Salisbury had to write to him to admit that 'that statement goes a little beyond the facts'. Lord St Oswald – formerly Rowland Winn – sailed even closer when he claimed that: 'I never had any interview with Mr Parnell on behalf of the Conservative Party or otherwise in reference to any question concerning the Government of Ireland.' A note from Winn exists at Hatfield recording the two meetings he held with Richard Power, who spoke for Parnell, about the proposed size of Irish representation in the post-election Commons. 'In politics, as in business,' Salisbury wrote to a correspondent on the issue in 1892, 'it is often necessary to see people of whom one may not think very highly.'[13]

In his 29th June speech to the Constitutional Union, Salisbury pointed out how the process of unification in Italy, France, Spain, Germany and Austria-Hungary had made each of those states more progressive and powerful, whereas Turkey, going the opposite way, was on 'the road to decay'. Gladstone, 'the hero of the policy of scuttle', was merely displaying 'the impatience of those who mistake the narrow span of their own lives for the long life of nations'.[14] Many Radicals, including Chamberlain, agreed with Salisbury that the whole tenor of recent European history was moving towards closer bonds between political entities, rather than weaker ones.

July saw Salisbury visit the spa town of Royat in the Auvergne, with the general election still underway, to try to counteract the eczema which had spread all over his body. His complaint aroused Gladstone's sympathy, although he also said that Salisbury was 'so foul mouthed' and 'is one of those men, like the old Derby, whose courage overboils in Opposition and only simmers in office'. On 6th July, Gladstone admitted to his diary that the election perturbed him, but consoled himself with the thought, 'but One ever sitteth above'. This time even the Liberal Almighty did not assist, however, and Salisbury won the first of his three landslide election victories. As the results came in, Salisbury shed crocodile tears for those Liberal Unionists who had refused to share platforms with Conservatives and had 'systematically snubbed us', and who had therefore lost Conservative support without attracting the necessary anti-Tory voters to counteract them. Overall the results were splendid, however, with 316 Conservatives and 77 Liberal Unionists returned, against 192 Gladstonian Liberals and 85 Home Rulers. In a House of Commons of 670, the Unionists had a 116-seat majority, at least on matters relating to Ireland.

Whereas 4.638 million people had voted in November 1885, only 2.974 million had bothered the following June, the agricultural labourers not being as interested in the Irish question as they had been in each being provided with three acres and a cow. Summer elections brought fewer labourers out to vote because of the harvest anyhow, and the novelty of voting for the first time had by then worn off. Another important factor was that, whereas only fifty-eight Conservative seats were left uncontested by Liberals in 1885, this figure had more than doubled the following year, whilst the Conservatives continued to contest the same number of Liberal seats. The Conservatives and Liberal Unionists together took 51.4 per cent of the vote: their compact had worked well. At Darwen in Lancashire, Cranborne won his seat by 726 votes – not safe, but far better than the majority of five he had had before. 'I hope the old wretch won't resign till my baths are over,' Salisbury wrote to Henry Manners in mid-July, but a little over a week later Gladstone did, and the Queen sent for Salisbury at once.

'We must give all loyal support to the Conservatives,' Chamberlain wrote to Hartington on 16th July, 'providing they do not play the fool either in foreign policy or in reactionary measures at home.' Salisbury considered whether to offer Hartington the premiership, again, as a way of tying the Liberal Unionists into a steady coalition rather than have his own Government dependent at every division on Liberal Unionist support. Many of his closest colleagues were against the Liberal Unionist tail wagging the Tory dog, however, and Akers-Douglas calculated with his unerring precision that a coalition with the Conservatives would drive twenty-nine Liberal Unionist MPs back into Gladstone's camp.[15]

Returning to London on 23rd July, Salisbury resolved that he nevertheless would offer Hartington the premiership the following day. If he accepted, Hartington would be the virtual prisoner of Salisbury, who could take the Foreign Office whilst also effectively running the Government. Even if he refused, he could hardly fail to be flattered by this second offer and might consider that the coalition held out a better future prospect than a return to the Liberal camp. Salisbury was concerned about the lack of Tory front-bench strength in the Commons, something Derby had also identified as a weakness. Writing on 21st July, Derby had told Hartington that the Conservatives were without a first-rate speaker, 'unless Churchill is entitled to that credit: and he is as uncertain as hereditary madness can make him'.

'I went to Hartington this morning,' Salisbury reported to Hicks Beach from Osborne on 24th July,

> and laid out before him as clearly as I could the reasons which induced us to think that the new ministry should be formed by him and not by me.... He combated my arguments in his normal sleepy manner – but he evidently has made up his mind: for he ended by pulling out a manuscript and reading out a considerable extract setting out his reasons for refusing. I declined to take any immediate negative – and remained arguing with him till I was forced to catch the train.

Salisbury had tried to persuade Hartington to talk to the Queen, but he had 'strongly deprecated any such summons'. He summed up Hartington's subsequent long letter of refusal by explaining that 'if he joined us Chamberlain would be left with so small a following that he would have no choice but to slide back into Gladstonianism'. Salisbury had refused to offer anything to Chamberlain because including such a hard-line Radical would both have angered his Tory followers and diluted any vaguely conservative political programme his coalition might try to pursue.

After consulting with his three leading supporters, Sir Henry James, Northbrook and Derby, none of whom was well disposed towards Salisbury, Hartington wrote to say that 'the difficulties in the way of my forming a Government are so insuperable that it would be useless for me to attempt it'. It would be seen as a Tory-dominated administration and would split the Liberal Unionists, he argued. Instead, he offered them an 'independent but friendly support'.[16] Goschen, Selborne and Argyll wanted to go in, with Goschen suspecting that he might even make a good coalition premier himself. As Salisbury refused to take Chamberlain, it has been suggested that the whole offer was a Machiavellian scheme to affect disinterestedness and self-abnegation, while in fact only stroking Hartington's ego. This is unlikely, not least because he could not be certain that Hartington would not accept, but also because a Tory fusion with Whiggery against Radicalism was a cause Salisbury had promoted all his political life. He tried not to make a habit of offering offices to people in the expectation that they would refuse, citing Ripon's Viceroyalty of India as an example of how the practice could backfire.

A solution which left Salisbury with the Foreign Secretaryship, control of four-fifths of the ministerial Party in the Commons and Hartington making the Guildhall speech, taking the publicity and staying at Balmoral would have been close to his ultimate ideal. Instead, Salisbury kissed hands as Prime Minister for the second time on Sunday, 25th July 1886. 'It is an office of infinite worry', he told his son Cranborne, 'but very little power.'

TWENTY-FOUR

Enduring Randolph

Cabinet-Making – A Coup in Sofia
– Churchill's Private Diplomacy

July to December 1886

'The time is not yet.'

'One half of our lives is employed in trying to cut the friends which the other has been employed in making,' Salisbury had written in 1862. 'Eternal friendships belong to the mythical age of human sentiments.' Salisbury's first task after kissing hands was to write from Osborne to disabuse Carnarvon of any notion that he might find a place in his new ministry. After the 1878 resignation, so his daughter Gwendolen believed, Salisbury's friendship had been merely 'a shell of habit' rather than a living organism. 'I am representing more than anything else', Salisbury wrote to Carnarvon, 'the mandate of the country to resist Home Rule. The country does not understand nuances; the new Government will have to do its best to maintain the law, while refusing any satisfaction to "national aspirations".... The point on which we differ has become the paramount question of the day.'

That done, Salisbury offered the Irish Viceroyalty to the Marquess of Londonderry, saying that it had 'the attraction of being exercised in very critical times, and will be of historical importance'. His Chief Secretary would be Sir Michael Hicks Beach, whom Salisbury originally wanted to stay on as Leader of the House of Commons but who had stated in respect of Churchill that 'the Leader in fact should be the Leader in name'. Hicks Beach, who had been opposed to Coercion, was a moderate on Irish matters and was respected by the Liberal Unionists. His was a shrewd appointment; any indication by Salisbury of an overtly repressive policy might have offended the now all-important Liberal Unionist opinion.

So Churchill took Hicks Beach's posts as Leader of the House and Chancellor of the Exchequer, an appointment the Queen much disliked as 'he is so mad and odd, and has also bad health'. Churchill's meteoric promotion was much resented by those Conservative politicians whom he sneered at as 'Marshalls and Snelgroves', after the frumpish London department store. 'It shows that Lord Salisbury is a weaker man than I believed him to be,' Gladstone's former private secretary Edward Hamilton noted. Cross, who Salisbury believed had 'lost all command of the House of Commons' and who could never have served as Churchill's deputy anyhow, was edged out of the Home Office, awarded a viscountcy and sent to the India Office. Despite Henry Raikes wanting the Home Office, and only accepting the Post Office 'with a growl', a barrister called Henry Matthews QC, a relative newcomer to politics but a protégé of Churchill's, was promoted to Home Secretary. The Queen accepted the appointment of Matthews, the first Roman Catholic Cabinet minister since the reign of James II, 'without a word', as Salisbury told Churchill. Cranbrook took his old place as Lord President of the Council, annoyed not to have been offered the Colonies.[1]

Without any Liberal Unionists in his Government, Salisbury told Alfred Austin that Cabinet-making was a 'task of making bricks without straw – but if I fail my taskmasters will only say "You are idle!"' Salisbury told the Queen that his 'sole object has been to strengthen the front bench in oratorical power', and Matthews was also known to be a strong supporter of the Union. Henry Chaplin was offered only the Presidency of the Local Government Board and, on being told it did not have Cabinet rank, he 'flounced indignantly out of the room'. So it went instead to a former Dundee jute trader, C.T. Ritchie, Tory MP for Tower Hamlets since 1874. Otherwise there were few surprises. Sir Frederick Stanley got a peerage and the Presidency of the Board of Trade, Smith and Lord George Hamilton returned to the War Office and the Admiralty respectively, and Edward Stanhope became Colonial Secretary.

Ashbourne went back to the Lord Chancellorship of Ireland, a post he was to hold in every Unionist ministry until 1905. Lord John Manners became Chancellor of the Duchy of Lancaster, irritated at the seeming capitulation to Churchill. 'Ministries to a great extent make themselves,' Salisbury explained to Harrowby, for whom he was unable to find a place. There were felt to be too many peers in the Cabinet, seven out of fourteen, so the Privy Seal went to Earl Cadogan outside it. Balfour, who became Secretary of State for Scotland on Richmond's retirement, was also not included.

Salisbury reluctantly felt that, at least until the Government was steady, he had to relinquish his own favoured post. 'I like the Foreign Office,' he told Lord Harrowby, 'but this double duty is quite intolerable.' He sent Philip Currie to Paris to offer the post to Lord Lyons, the

Ambassador there, but at sixty-nine he was in failing health and indeed died the next year after a stroke. Cranbrook's French was not considered good enough for the post. Iddesleigh's relative ignorance of foreign affairs was felt to be no bar to his appointment; indeed, it might even be an asset because Salisbury had every intention of keeping ultimate control himself. The Queen was fearful that, at sixty-eight, Iddesleigh's health would not stand the work, a view shared by Salisbury. At their first Cabinet, Iddesleigh both mumbled and was hard of hearing, a frustrating combination for the other thirteen people around the table. Churchill's chain-smoking also irritated some, including Cranbrook. [2] It was not a strong Government, as Salisbury was the first privately to admit.

Placating Lord Randolph Churchill was to be the *leitmotif* of the next five months. George Curzon, whom Salisbury had agreed to take on as an assistant private secretary in the next session should the Government somehow survive, was staying at Hatfield in early January 1886 at the same time as Churchill. The contrast, he noted in his diary, between Churchill – 'a great swell, he will scarcely look at his subordinates, and the barest civility is all one can expect' – and his host could not have been greater. 'His affability is almost embarrassing,' he wrote of Salisbury. 'He pays as much attention to the words of a boy of twenty-one as to those of a statesman of seventy.' Holding two key Cabinet posts aged thirty-seven, Churchill could easily have become Salisbury's heir apparent had he been able to show half the patience that Salisbury had shown when reluctantly entering Disraeli's Cabinet in 1874.

A vivid account was written by Eustace Balfour's daughter, Blanche, of the occasion when Salisbury visited Hertford to thank the constituency for its support in the 1886 general election:

An open carriage, high on its springs, and drawn by four fine horses with huge rosettes of pale blue satin at their ears, is bowling along a country road. On the near-side horses, two postilions in cockaded hats and white buckskin breeches, wearing the same rosettes on their dark blue livery coats. On the lofty box of the carriage sit coachman and footman similarly decorated.... Inside the carriage sits the great Lord Salisbury with his square grey beard, his massive figure shrouded in a voluminous grey cloak. Beside him his wife, a no less majestic form. Opposite them sits my mother, and the fourth place is occupied by my six-year-old self.... As we enter the town of Hertford, people are gathered on the pavements, and a crowd fills the market place. They cheer, and my great-uncle and -aunt acknowledge their salutations. I do my best to copy their dignified inclinations to right and to left. Mama whispers that the plaudits of the people are meant for Uncle Robert, not for me. I ignore the remark, which seems to strike a discordant note on an occasion which otherwise exactly fufils one's ideals of how life should be.

Salisbury's second ministry began cautiously, with the setting up of two Royal Commissions to investigate the land and local government situation in Ireland, and a friendly talk with Hartington on 6th August. 'Until the Liberal Party becomes Unionist,' Salisbury reported to the Queen, 'he will support the present Government on all critical occasions.' The most pressing problem for this *ad hoc* alliance, all three acknowledged, would be their relations with Chamberlain. When the question arose of the Duke of Argyll defecting to the Conservatives, Salisbury actively discouraged it, saying that the moderates needed bolstering 'to prevent Hartington slipping more and more to Chamberlain'.

The rest of the session was spent winding up business, passing Estimates, organising which ministers should visit Balmoral once a fortnight and calming Churchill, who tended to alarm the rest of the Cabinet with his visionary schemes to increase taxes on luxuries whilst slashing government spending. Meanwhile the Queen 'found Salisbury's tone and way with her most acceptable'.[3] So towards the end of August 1886 the Queen was squared, the middle classes were quite prepared for eventual tax cuts and Salisbury was considering getting over to France to finish the eczema cure that had been interrupted by his call to office the previous month. He had time to let Eustace know that he would be delighted to allow the Dorset Natural History Club to visit Cranborne Manor, although 'I do not know what they will find there in their line. I expect some very fine rats – and some interesting specimens of dry rot in the beams.' Then suddenly Bulgaria exploded again.

In the *coup de main* which inspired Anthony Hope's *The Prisoner of Zenda*, a shadowy pro-Russian pan-Slavist junta surrounded the royal palace at Sofia and kidnapped Prince Alexander of Bulgaria on 20th August 1886, spiriting him away by steamer to Keni Russi in Bessarabia. The following day, a provisional government in Sofia declared him deposed. 'It is a cruel end to all Prince Alexander's efforts and sacrifices,' Salisbury wrote to the Queen the next day. 'A more flagrant display of popular ingratitude is not on record. There is something sickening in the treachery of the troops whom he had led to victory...turned against him on the instigation of Russian agents.' Whether St Petersburg was actually behind the coup was not known for certain at the time, but the circumstantial evidence for it seemed overwhelming. Salisbury now perceived 'a serious danger to Europe' in the Russification of the two united provinces, exactly the danger of which White had warned. Salisbury feared that an anti-Turkish rising was to be expected in Macedonia, which might suck in Greece and Austria, and so destabilise the Ottoman Empire and threaten European peace.

On 24th August, Salisbury followed up his original letter to a by now distraught Queen with the opinion that this 'lamentable catastrophe' will have 'lost the bulwark against Russian aggression which has been built with so much care'. It was a care which Rosebery had faithfully continued, following Salisbury's pro-Austrian Near Eastern policy to the letter, to the fury of Radicals like Labouchere who complained that Salisbury's foreign policy was put into effect whether he was in office or not. By 27th August, the Intelligence services could still not locate Alexander, nor could they find any definite proof that the Russians were behind the 'simply piratical' coup. Salisbury desperately wished 'to bring English counsels to bear upon him', in order to prevent Alexander either abdicating or encouraging a rising in Macedonia.

On 29th August, in response to the Queen's indignation at the 'infamous outrage' against 'poor Sandro', Salisbury was forced to point out how his Government had to labour 'without money, without any strong land force, with an insecure tenure on power, and with an ineffective agency'. With only £15,000 per annum available for bribery ('a sum so small as to be practically worthless'), the system of Buggins's turn at the Foreign Office throwing up 'not able men', 'no army capable of meeting even a second-class Continental Power', let alone Russia, and a Cabinet of fourteen 'usually ignorant of [foreign policy] and seldom united in their views', Salisbury disabused her of any prospect of early success. 'Lord Salisbury <u>will</u> succeed,' she answered. 'I feel pumped out,' he replied on 2nd September.

On 7th September, Alexander suddenly reappeared in Sofia and formally abdicated. On the same day, a Cabinet revolt against Salisbury's Balkans policy was led by the now Russophile Churchill and supported by the two Service ministers, Smith and Hamilton. At an unpleasant Cabinet meeting, Churchill attacked Iddesleigh – and also, by implication, Salisbury – accusing him of allowing Britain to drift towards a European war in support of Prince Alexander and Bulgarian self-determination. 'How we shall hold together for twelve months I cannot conceive,' Salisbury told his wife the next day. Churchill's alternative policy was to abandon Bulgaria to Russia and concentrate British influence and troops on Egypt, Cyprus and Afghanistan instead.

Intellectually, Salisbury had been wedded to this stance since Churchill was an infant. Politically, however, he recognised the danger to any ministry in power at the time of the Russian capture of

Constantinople, the best bulwark against which was an anti-Russian 'Big' Bulgaria lying in its path.[4] Also, as Friedrich von Holstein, the influential director of the Political Department of the German Foreign Ministry, noted in his journal on 14th September, 'the English, unless they are mad, cannot allow the Sultan, who as Caliph wields authority over eighty five million Indian Mohamodans, to become a vassal of Russia, or else her rule in India will soon be over'. The danger of Austria fighting Russia in the Balkans, thus dragging in Germany and precipitating a general European conflict, also bulked large in Salisbury's thoughts.

On top of the Bulgarian crisis came Franco-German war scares, so serious that Balfour urged Salisbury to take Iddesleigh's place at the Foreign Office, 'and soon'. When the news arrived of Alexander's abdication, Salisbury's attitude was that it was 'very vexatious – but I suppose we may treat him as history now'. German diplomatic documents released after the First World War make it clear that Churchill was speaking without Salisbury's authorisation to the German Ambassador, Count Hatzfeldt, attempting in effect to conduct his own foreign policy behind the backs of Iddesleigh and Salisbury. In Iddesleigh's case this was not difficult, for, as he himself told Malet, he could not 'pretend to fathom the secrets and understand the abstruse diplomacy of the day'. With Salisbury, however, it was a gross betrayal, although no worse than that of which Salisbury had himself been guilty with Ignatiev a decade earlier.[5]

Salisbury was unwilling to copy the error he had denounced when it was committed by Lord John Russell, and told the Queen that 'we would lose rather than gain authority by uttering a useless protest'. He phlegmatically explained that he wished to reserve his expressions of public indignation until they could influence events effectively. Meanwhile, Churchill was letting it be known in the chancelleries of Europe that the Salisbury Cabinet was utterly split over Bulgaria. On 24th September, Hatzfeldt reported to Bismarck a 'chance conversation' he had had with Churchill, in which the second man in the Government said that, as an Asiatic rather than an European Power, Britain should allow Russia a free hand in the Balkan peninsula.

From de Staal's correspondence it is clear that the Russians had also learnt from Churchill that Egypt now mattered far more to Britain than Constantinople. 'I am puzzled at Hatzfeldt's proceedings,' wrote Salisbury to Churchill on 28th September, in what might have been a shot across the bows. 'He tells more to Rothschild than he does to you: he tells more to you than he does to me; and he tells more to me than he does to Iddesleigh – the person to whom it is his business to speak. I wonder what he is at.' After Salisbury had received a letter from Churchill refusing to agree to his plan to fortify the Dardanelles should a Russian army threaten Constantinople, he replied with less patience than he usually reserved for his talented but increasingly insubordinate *enfant terrible*:

> You are naturally sarcastic on my Dardanelles. I hope the matter will not come up in our time. But the possession by Russia of Constantinople will be an awkward piece of news for the Minister who receives it. The prestige effect on the Asiatic population will be enormous and I pity the English party that has this item on their record. They will share the fate of Lord North's party.

Salisbury had every excuse for exasperation when Churchill replied: 'I feel sure that our present niggling meddling intriguing fussy policy is gaining for us the contempt and dislike of Bismarck every day.' Yet, in his answer from Puys on 1ˢᵗ October, Salisbury kept his patience:

> A pacific and economic policy is up to a certain extent very wise: but it is evident that there is a point beyond which it is not wise either in a patriotic or party sense – and the question is where we shall draw the line. I draw it at Constantinople. My belief is that the main strength of the Tory party both in the richer and poorer classes lies in its association with the honour of the country.... I am afraid you <u>are</u> prepared to give up Constantinople: and foreign powers will be quick enough to find that divergence out.

Owing to Churchill's insubordination, they already had.

Writing to Morier in St Petersburg the next day, Salisbury set out his views on Russia in typically robust language. He dismissed the talk of a Russian advance on Kandahar, which, even if it did take place, 'will only incur a hot version of the retreat from Moscow'. As so often, Salisbury suspected that his man in St Petersburg had gone native, proposing an Anglo-Russian settlement across the board. 'You can have an entente with a man or government but no one except Canute's ever tried to have it with a tide,' he wrote, arguing that the same military-religious impulses 'which moved the hosts of Mahomet and those which moved the hosts of Attila' were now operating on Russia, forcing her to overspill her borders in a quest for 'faith and glory'. No meaningful *entente* was possible with a country that 'can promise nothing with respect to Afghanistan except that she will eat Constantinople first'.

Salisbury described his policy towards Russia as 'Fabian', after the Roman general Quintus Fabius Maximus who wore down Hannibal by guerrilla attacks rather than a frontal assault. 'In proportion that we can delay the ultimate issue we shall have the advantage of them,' he wrote to Morier. Any number of setbacks might befall Russia before Britain needed to engage her militarily, including a war with Austria or Germany or both, a Nihilist revolution, internal secessions, Turkish regeneration under a strong leader or another Alexander of Bulgaria figure uniting the Balkan nationalities against her. A *modus vivendi* with Russia now would merely smooth her path, so Salisbury advocated 'a dilatory diplomacy' to draw Russia's strength and gain Britain time.[6]

The major obstacle to an active Balkans policy, besides Churchill's increasingly open opposition, was Salisbury's fear that he did not have a Commons majority for it. Over Ireland, he told Cross, they had a good majority but no policy as yet. But in defending Turkey they had a policy but no majority, unlike in Disraeli's time. 'We had staked all our hopes on Alexander,' he commented ruefully, 'and he has been driven away.' The careful handling of the crisis was made yet more difficult by an absurd expedition Churchill undertook to the Central Powers in October.

Travelling under the hardly impenetrable incognito of 'Mr Spencer', yet sporting one of the most famous handlebar moustaches in Europe, it was inevitable that he would be recognised and that the Continental press would assume some perfidious British intrigue was afoot. In the course of the trip he met the Austrian Commander-in-Chief in Vienna, and, entirely unauthorised, promised Kálnoky the support of the Royal Navy, should Austria work in concert with Germany in the Near East. Yet more confusion was caused when Salisbury replied to an official Foreign Office cypher telegram signed 'Iddesleigh', only to discover the next day that it had actually been sent by Churchill.

The Bulgarian stand-off carried on throughout October, with Russia saying and doing nothing actually at variance with the Treaty of Berlin. Bulgaria herself was now ruled by a strong-man Regent, Stephen Stambulov. 'If we step forward in a perfectly isolated condition and use defiant language,' Salisbury once more explained to his impatient monarch, 'it may make us ultimately ridiculous, as we have no intention of resorting to force by ourselves in the case of the occupation of Bulgaria.' The Queen was hardly mollified, bemoaning: 'We are nothing any more, and I cannot say what I feel and suffer.' For the monarch of History's largest empire to tell her ever-indulgent Prime Minister that 'we are nothing any more' is rich in unintended irony, and pure Queen Victoria. Salisbury replied that of course Britain would protest if Russia actually invaded Bulgaria, but, as there was no chance of obtaining the Porte's permission to send the fleet into the Black Sea, there was very little that could practically be done.[7]

This pragmatic, unheroic wait-and-see policy was adhered to in Salisbury's Guildhall speech, traditionally delivered on 9th November, in which he made pro-Austrian remarks and accused the officers who had abducted Alexander as having been 'debauched by foreign gold', though not directly mentioning Russia by name. The sensitive balancing act between the Queen's bellicosity and Churchill's passivity, between encouraging Austria, warning Russia and threatening Turkey, was wearing Salisbury down, but continued European peace was his ultimate prize and it was worth the constant effort.

Salisbury's careful calculations were continually upset by Churchill's maverick private diplomacy. On 24th November, Hatzfeldt wrote to Holstein in Berlin that Churchill was 'the man, as things stand now, who may be expected to take positive and far-reaching action', and it was his opinions, rather than Salisbury's or Iddesleigh's, which were relayed in detail to Kaiser Wilhelm I. 'Salisbury is getting to the position where he will be pressed no more,' Lord George Hamilton warned Churchill on 25th November, to no appreciable effect. By 19th December, Salisbury was at the very end of what had been an astonishingly long tether. Writing to the Queen about policy in the Black Sea, and the possibility of one day forcing the Porte to allow a British fleet through the Dardanelles, he had to admit that he doubted 'whether, with the present Cabinet, it is in his power to infuse into the action of the Government the vigour which Your Majesty has a right to expect. He is not speaking of Lord Iddesleigh, but of other difficulties; and he looks to the future with some anxiety.'[8]

If Churchill chastised Salisbury's foreign policy with whips, he was simultaneously chastising his domestic policy with scorpions. The story of the first five months of his second ministry was, in Salisbury's rare musical analogy to Cranbrook, one of attempting to conduct an orchestra where the first fiddle was constantly playing a different tune. Salisbury was willing to give his Chancellor of the Exchequer good advice, such as not abolishing the half-sovereign, because there was 'nothing so dangerous [as] to meddle with the currency – because change inconveniences everybody just a little', but Churchill seemed always to be spoiling for a clash.

On 2nd October 1886, Churchill spoke to an audience in Oakfield Park, Dartford, estimated at fourteen thousand, where he unveiled his personal manifesto. Not only had it not been previously cleared by the Cabinet, but it contained several measures which he knew the majority of them actively opposed. He called for the creation of small-holdings and allotments for agricultural labourers, large-scale reform of local government, the abolition of primogeniture in intestacy, a large reduction of taxation, closer ties with the Central Powers, parliamentary clôture by a simple majority, and further enfranchisement of leaseholders and copyholders. Despite his later claims that it was 'a mere ventilation of the programme of Lord Salisbury at Newport', Churchill was in fact baiting his colleagues with a 'Tory Democracy' agenda, trying to force the pace of reform in a generally leftwards direction. The Parnellite MP T.P. O'Connor, thought the Dartford speech Churchill's 'golden hour', when 'the retiring and almost hermit-like habits of Lord Salisbury' meant that in two years Churchill would 'bundle Lord Salisbury out of the Premiership'.

Salisbury stayed calm, and even seemed to support some of the clôture proposals. He put up with Churchill's self-pity – 'I certainly have not the courage and energy to go on struggling against cliques, as poor Dizzy did all his life' – and on 7th November he gave sound advice to the man who could so easily have been his protégé and successor:

> The Tory party is composed of very varying elements; and there is much trouble and vexation of spirit in trying to make them work together...we have so to conduct our legislation that we shall give some satisfaction to both classes and masses. This is specially difficult with the classes – because all legislation is rather unwelcome to them, as tending to disturb a state of things with which they are satisfied.... Your role should be rather that of a diplomatist trying to bring the opposed sections of the party together – and not that of a Whip trying to keep the slugs up to the collar.

Sadly, Churchill was in no mood to listen to advice about how 'We must work at less speed and at a lower temperature than our opponents. Our Bills must be tentative and cautious; not sweeping and dramatic.' Lord Rosebery, who had been an Oxford and Bullingdon Club contemporary of Churchill's, believed it possible that the syphilitic attacks which eventually killed him in 1895 were already influencing Lord Randolph's behaviour from as early as 1885, leaving him capable of acting in a way that was 'unbalanced and almost unhinged'.

The Cabinet ministers who clustered around Salisbury after his Guildhall speech, and who urged him to take a strong line against Churchill, were, as he remarked to his wife in the carriage journey back to Arlington Street, exactly the same men who had urged appeasement of Churchill back in August. 'But they are wrong now,' he told her, 'the time is not yet.'[9] With his premiership dependent on the support of Liberal Unionists, Salisbury was not about to take on Churchill until he had manoeuvred his errant lieutenant into a position from which his resignation or expulsion from the Cabinet would cause the minimum possible danger to his ministry.

When on 17th November Salisbury announced to the Cabinet that 'in view of the fact that much of our impending legislation had a Scotch side' he intended to invite his nephew Arthur Balfour to join them, it was 'very cordially received'. Churchill immediately leaked the news to Buckle, but Salisbury asked that *The Times* not announce it until he had obtained the Queen's permission for the appointment. Buckle withheld the information for Salisbury, a favour the implications of which

Churchill would have done well to have dwelt upon. It was Churchill's untrustworthiness and undermining of his foreign policy to which Salisbury objected, not his pushiness. Churchill was thrusting and impatient, but, as Salisbury told Eustace in reply to a particularly self-pitying letter in mid-November, that aspect of modern politics was just:

> one of the known, and most evil characteristics of democracy. But there it is – no one can doubt the fact. In that competition, 'pushing forward' is an essential qualification. I have practised what I preach – and if I had waited for 'encouragement', I should have waited a very long time.... No doubt the state of things which has established itself in America will gradually prevail here.[10]

'You must forgive me for saying that you have too much self-renunciation for a Prime Minister,' complained Cranbrook on 23rd November over the question of Irish local government, on which he and most of the rest of the Cabinet felt Salisbury had let Churchill get away with too much. 'The position requires your distinct <u>lead</u> and your just self assertion.' Salisbury took an entirely utilitarian approach in his answer to Cranbrook: 'What you call my self-renunciation is making an effort to deal with an abnormal and very difficult state of things. It arises from the peculiarity of Churchill.' As the only possible Leader of the House of Commons, Hicks Beach having refused the post, Churchill had to be humoured, and 'his ability is unquestionable'. But Salisbury admitted that 'the machine is moving along with the utmost friction both in home and foreign affairs. My self-renunciation is only an attempt – a vain attempt – to poor oil upon the creaking and groaning machinery.'

In the afternoon of 25th November, Salisbury met Hartington again to discuss the business of the next session, especially the deadlock over both Irish and mainland local government. The entire Cabinet except Churchill wanted to put off that part of English local government legislation which concerned the Poor Law, for the simple reason that it would allow the majority of electors – agricultural labourers in many areas – to impose charges on the rich. 'A lavish and demoralising administration of outdoor relief would be the probable consequence,' Salisbury warned the Queen.[11] Salisbury fought for compromise, however, writing to Churchill in this sense on the 28th. But privately his tone was 'desponding' about the chances of placating his restless lieutenant. Churchill even broke ranks over the signing of an agreement with France about the free passage of the Suez Canal in time of war, wanting a postponement of the convention that had been promised the previous year. 'The problem is a difficult one,' Salisbury told Henry Manners, 'for the state of the Union makes it unusually difficult for us to resign. Randolph can always put before us the dilemma of accepting his views, or endangering the Union with Ireland: and this gives him a strong position.'

The alternative, simply to accept one of Churchill's regular resignation threats and carry on regardless, was assumed to be too dangerous, despite the precedent Derby had set with Salisbury himself in 1867. It was feared that enough of Churchill's Tory Democrat supporters, as well as Radical friends such as Chamberlain, might split off in sufficient numbers to threaten the Unionist majority in the Commons. To Churchill himself Salisbury lamented: 'I wish there was no such thing as local government.'[12] As though all the other disagreements with the Cabinet were not enough, Churchill was also planning an eye-catching Budget. Edward Hamilton, who had been Gladstone's principal private secretary until June 1885, and then became the head of the Treasury's Finance division, was well placed to record how Churchill 'evidently wants to make a coup by a popular Budget – a general remission all round: a great reduction of the income tax, also a reduction of the tea and tobacco duties'. Other proposals included a uniform death duty, a graduated house tax and a reform of local taxation. 'I expect he will "fly too high",' was Hamilton's perceptive comment.

When the War Office submitted its spending Estimates for 1887/8, its officials were asked by the Treasury to review their proposals, because Churchill needed every penny he could save for his Budget hand-outs. On 14th December, Smith wrote to Churchill politely refusing to do so. The following day, Churchill told Salisbury that he had to insist on savings in the Army Estimates. 'The Cabinet, happily, not I will have to decide the controversy between you and Smith,' Salisbury replied. 'But it will be a serious responsibility to refuse the demands of a War Minister so little imaginative as Smith: especially at such a time.' Salisbury added that Wolseley had been critical of Smith for already retrenching too much, and that he was personally surprised that Lord George Hamilton at the Admiralty had been able to reduce the Naval Estimates as much as he had. It was the clearest possible warning to Churchill not to press that particular matter at that time. Not only was the Bulgarian crisis still simmering, but persistent rumours of war between France and Germany were depressing the stock market. Now, Salisbury was making patently clear to Churchill, was no time to stint on defence.

'We are not a happy family,' Salisbury admitted to the Queen on 16th December. A long-term advocate of high defence expenditure, Salisbury believed that the differences could only be 'patched up for a time'.[13] When the next day, Friday, 17th December, Churchill put his Budget proposals before his Cabinet colleagues, they were received in silence. 'The barque looks crazier and crazier,' Salisbury wrote to Balfour the next day, 'the chances of her floating diminish day by day.'

Lord Rothschild warned Churchill that 'Salisbury, if driven too hard, might jib,' but he took no notice and instead planned yet another resignation threat to see his Budget over the hurdle of the Service department. Lord George Hamilton had also sent similar warnings about the limits of Salisbury's endurance. In her *Reminiscences* published many years later, the beautiful Jenny Churchill, Randolph's wife, remembered 'hearing Lord Salisbury say that a man who could not be vindictive was not a strong man. I often quoted this without effect to Randolph.'

TWENTY-FIVE

Breaking Randolph

Churchill's Resignation
– Goschen Accepts Office

December 1886 to January 1887

'Coldness of manner may be an excuse for an erring wife,
but not for an overbearing colleague.'

The story of Lord Randolph Churchill's shock resignation, or more accurately Salisbury's shock acceptance of yet another Churchillian resignation threat, has attracted the myths which encrust all sensational political events. The first inkling Salisbury had of trouble came on Tuesday, 14th December 1886, when Churchill wrote to him to say that he and Smith could not agree on the Army Estimates for his Budget, the War Secretary flatly refusing to drop his requirements below those of the previous fiscal year. On Monday, 20th December, Smith wrote to Salisbury to say that after a two-hour meeting with Churchill at the War Office, they had still been unable to agree on a diminution of the Estimates and that Churchill was threatening to resign. 'He gave me to understand it was not simply on Estimates or expenditure that he should go but on general policy – a bad programme and an undecided Foreign Policy. It comes to this – is he to be <u>the</u> Government. If you are willing that he should be, I shall be delighted, but I could not go on, on such conditions.'

Churchill had left the War Office after the meeting to go to Windsor by train, sharing a compartment with Lord George Hamilton, to whom he also blithely confided his intentions. Hamilton had actually reduced his Naval Estimates, but had used an accounting technique that produced little in the way of real savings. It was a piece of financial *légerdemain* which Churchill – who had a good financial brain despite referring to decimal points as 'those damned dots' – easily spotted.

Churchill had used the resignation threat successfully in the past, and had actually carried it out in May 1884 during the NUCCA controversy.

Using Windsor Castle writing paper, he fired off to Salisbury what he possibly thought was just the opening shot in yet another struggle with the Prime Minister, but which turned out to be a shot through his own political temples:

> Dear Lord Salisbury, the approximate estimates for the army and navy for next year have been communicated to me by George Hamilton and Smith ... the total thirty-one millions for the two services which will in all probability be extended is very greatly in excess of what I can consent to. I know that on this subject I cannot look for any sympathy or effective support from you, and I am certain that I shall find no support in the Cabinet. I do not want to be wrangling and quarrelling in the Cabinet: and therefore must request to be allowed to give up my office and retire from the Government. I am pledged up to the eyes to large reductions of expenditure, and I can't change my mind on this matter. If the foreign policy of this country is conducted with skill and judgment our present huge and increasing armaments are quite unnecessary and the taxation which they involve perfectly unjustifiable.[1]

Whether it was this insolent last sentence which persuaded Salisbury not to back down this time, or the fact that Parliament was not due to meet for over three weeks, or Smith's quasi-resignation threat, or the belief that the increased expenditure was justifiable at a time of war scares and Balkan crises, or simply the accumulation of three years of irritation with his youngest and most irrational colleague, Salisbury reckoned the time had finally come to take Churchill on, despite the risk of his Government falling and a Home Rule ministry taking its place. 'In many ways,' he told a niece years later with a high degree of hindsight, 'he had found Randolph very attractive.' The threat he posed to his own control of foreign, and latterly also domestic, policy however now made his excision imperative.

On their return journey to London by the earliest possible train, Churchill and Hamilton found that they had no small change between them to pay for their newspapers at Windsor Station. The newsagent told Churchill he could 'pay next time you come back, my Lord'. As the train left, Churchill joked to Hamilton: 'He little thinks that I shall never come back again.' He had a jay-like laugh which Lord Rosebery described as weird and discordant, but nonetheless 'merriment itself'. Having successfully cheated a trusting tradesman out of threepence, Churchill went home. Meanwhile, Hamilton went straight to the War Office to tell a 'much surprised' Smith what had happened. To the end of his life, Hamilton believed that Churchill resigned over 'a sudden and ungovernable impulse' rather than over any serious disagreement over the Estimates, and that this would seem to indicate mental instability.

Salisbury had meanwhile written out at least two copies of

Churchill's letter in his own hand. He sent one to Hicks Beach in Dublin and the other to Balfour. Hicks Beach, who was Churchill's closest friend in the Cabinet and a supporter of both his Irish and his Bulgarian stances, was the third key figure in this crisis. If Hicks Beach, who crucially had not been squared beforehand by Churchill, had supported his Cabinet ally, the Government probably could not have survived. The previous day Salisbury had written of Hicks Beach that 'the influence R.C. exerts over him is very perilous', and it was Salisbury's top priority to negate it.

Writing to Hicks Beach on Tuesday, 21st December, Salisbury reported that Smith and Churchill had failed to agree on the Estimates, and that Hamilton agreed with Smith. 'In the present state of Empire,' he wrote, 'it is absurd to say that Estimates which are somewhat smaller than those of last year, are extravagant. But, if R.C. insists, as he may probably do, we shall have to consider our position.... But I sorely need some talk with you on the subject. Is there any possibility of your coming over next week? Or the week after?'

This letter totally failed to convey either a sense of immediate crisis, or Salisbury's actual intention to accept the resignation. It implied that Hamilton supported Smith, which at that time was not certain, and Hicks Beach's reply, that he would speak to Churchill over Christmas and try to 'bring him straight', made it clear that he did not appreciate the imminent seriousness of events. Indeed, on Boxing Day, Hicks Beach complained to Smith that the announcement of Churchill's actual resignation 'came absolutely without previous warning to me', so little importance did he attach to Salisbury's anæsthetising message, even though it had arrived with a copy of Churchill's resignation letter enclosed.

Churchill's remark about not expecting sympathy from Salisbury over defence cuts was well founded. Salisbury was always acutely conscious of the diplomatic weakness arising from the tiny size of Britain's standing army, and regularly regretted the way that the Services always tended to be slimmed down to the bare minimum in peacetime. In the *Saturday Review*, he had attacked the way the army was 'looked upon as a sort of luxury, like a private gentleman's carriage, which is naturally "put down" when times are bad'. He had blamed the 1853 military expenditure cuts for the early disasters in the Crimea and warned in 1862 that 'the evil days of retrenchment are coming on us fast'.

In 1871, Salisbury told the House of Lords that whereas Germany and Austria could put over a million men into the field and the Russians one and a half million, the utmost strength for a British expeditionary force was 100,000. (Bismarck had scoffed that if the British army ever landed on the north German coast, he would send the local police force to arrest it.) Although he supported low taxation, Salisbury had long believed Britons thought it 'a mere waste of time to rail at military expenditure'.[2] Philosophically as well as pragmatically, politically and personally, therefore, Salisbury was on the side of his Service ministers.

'New sensation!' Salisbury reported to Balfour at Whittinghame on Wednesday, 22nd December:

> Randolph meets Smith on Monday – & after two hours discussion goes down to Windsor from whence he writes me a letter of which I enclose you a copy. I have replied expressing effusively my very deep regret – but stating that I fully concurred with Smith and Hamilton: & that I should regard it as the gravest responsibility to refuse in the present state of Europe, the funds necessary for protecting our ports and coaling stations.

Salisbury replied to Churchill by the afternoon post on Wednesday 22nd December, the letter arriving as Drummond Wolff and Churchill were dining at the Carlton Club prior to watching *The School for Scandal*:

> In this unfortunate state of things, I have no choice but to express my full concurrence with the view of Hamilton and Smith, and my dissent from yours – though I say it, both on personal and public grounds, with very deep regret. The outlook on the Continent is very black. It is not too much to say that the chances are in favour of war at an early date: and when war has once broken out we cannot be secure from the danger of being involved in it. The undefended state of many of our ports and coaling stations is notorious: and the necessity of protecting them has been urged by a strong Commission: and has been admitted on both sides in debate.... The issue is so serious that it thrusts aside all personal and party considerations. But I regret more than I can say the view you take of it; for no one knows better than you how injurious to the public interests at this juncture your withdrawal from the Government may be. In presence of your very strong and decisive language – I can only again express my very profound regret.[3]

The rough draft of this letter shows how it originally contained the words 'disastrous' and 'formidable' to describe Churchill leaving the Government, but Salisbury crossed the words out. In what was clearly now going to be a war to the knife, it did not do to display weakness. Although he kept several key supporters, such as Balfour and the Lord Chancellor, Lord Halsbury, closely in touch with events, Salisbury took the actual decision to accept Churchill's resignation without reference to anybody else. Balfour, who was ultimately the greatest beneficiary of Churchill's political eclipse, had told his uncle that he hoped: 'If R.C. leaves us he does so on some point with regard to which he does not carry the sympathy of any considerable section of the Party.' Defence cuts were just such an issue. Retrenchment and cost-cutting were more a Gladstonian than a Tory cry; Churchill had chosen the ground of his challenge as badly as his timing.

Salisbury's letter came as no surprise to Churchill, who had lunched with Smith at the Carlton Club that day. He wrote back immediately, sending his reply straight to Hatfield by special messenger:

> I believe myself to be well-informed on the present state of Europe, nor am I aware that I am blind or careless to the probabilities of a great conflict between European powers in the coming year. A wise foreign policy will extricate England from continental struggles and keep her outside of German, Russian, French and Austrian disputes. I have for some time observed a tendency in the Government to pursue a different line of action which I have not been able to modify or check. This tendency is certain to be accentuated if large estimates are presented to and voted by Parliament.... I decline to be a party to encouraging the military and militant circle of the War Office and Admiralty to join in the high and desperate stakes which other nations seem to be forced to risk.
>
> Believe me I pray you that it is not niggardly cheeseparing or Treasury crabbedness, but only considerations of high state polity, which compel me to sever ties in many ways most binding and pleasant.... I take leave of your Government and especially of yourself with profound regret but without doubt or hesitation.[4]

A county ball was under way at Hatfield when Churchill's second letter arrived at a quarter past one in the morning. Princess Mary, Duchess of Teck, and her daughter Princess May (later Queen Mary) were the guests of honour. Also present were the Duchess of Marlborough, Churchill's mother and close political confidante, and her daughter Lady Sarah Spencer-Churchill, Lord Randolph's sister. Salisbury was sitting on a sofa with Princess Mary watching the dancing when the red box containing the letter was brought up. The Princess 'used often afterwards to make reproachful fun of the deceptive suavity with which, having glanced at the contents, he continued their conversation with apparently unbroken interest'. If Churchill managed to combine with Chamberlain, and possibly Hartington, Salisbury's political career might be over in a matter of days, but his *sang froid* always coursed best in crises.

When they awoke later that morning, Thursday, 23rd December, Lady Salisbury suggested that she and her husband get up in time to say goodbye to those of their guests, including the Duchess of Marlborough, who were leaving by the early train. 'Send for *The Times* first,' Salisbury told his wife. 'Randolph resigned in the middle of the night and, if I know my man, it will be in *The Times* this morning.' Sure enough, at the interval of *The School for Scandal*, and telling his wife and

Drummond Wolff that he was going to his club, Churchill had gone off to Printing House Square to show his correspondence with the Prime Minister to George Buckle, authorising him to publish the scoop of his resignation. A bitter row ensued when Buckle refused to publish the private correspondence.

'We have this morning to make the startling announcement that the Chancellor of the Exchequer has placed his resignation in the hands of Lord Salisbury,' *The Times* announced the next morning. The paper came down unreservedly on Salisbury's side, stating in the editorial that,

> In view of the condition of affairs in Europe, which becomes from day to day more ominous, the Premier has found himself unable to interfere with the discretion of the Secretary for War and the First Lord of the Admiralty, and has preferred to face the inconveniences which no one is better able than himself to appreciate. His decision is wise and patriotic, and we have no doubt will be so regarded by the nation at large.[5]

When, taking breakfast at one of several small tables in the dining room at Hatfield, the Duchess of Marlborough read the news, she let out what one spectator, Lord Charles Beresford, later described as 'a shriek ... followed by a fit of hysterics'. According to Lady Alice Gore, Cranborne's future wife, who was also present, she burst into tears, crying to her daughter: 'Oh Sarah, *why* are my sons so unlike other people's sons?' As only four months earlier she had told the young diplomat Cecil Spring-Rice, that Salisbury 'was a child about everything but foreign politics and that he had to be advised about the smallest things', she was forced drastically to revise her opinion.

The Duchess was indignant that the Salisburys had neither told her the news the previous night nor bid her goodbye before she left, but as almost anything they said would be liable to misinterpretation, their slightly impolite course – they claimed to have overslept – was doubtless the most sensible. George Curzon, who was also present, claimed years later that he could 'remember the thanksgivings and hosannas that went up' at the news on the night of the ball. As Salisbury told no one about it that night, not even his wife, this must be incorrect, although the Cecils were certainly masters at putting on brave public faces, which they all did the next morning.[6]

Salisbury's patience had been 'very much strained during the past three or four months', recalled George Hamilton, 'the whole Cabinet was groaning and creaking from the wayward and uncontrolled language and action of one member, and I was certain that Salisbury would be only too pleased to accept that colleague's resignation.' With no general election due for another six years, and not resigning on a particularly 'Tory Democrat' issue either – although he subsequently tried strenuously to widen the issue from simply defence expenditure to the whole range of Government policy – Churchill had chosen his moment disastrously. As Balfour gloated in his reply to Salisbury on the 23rd, 'he could not do so on any question, or at any time, more convenient to us'.

By the time Salisbury telegraphed the Queen with the news at 9.28 a.m. she had already seen the announcement in *The Times*. She was furious that a journalist had been informed of the resignation before her, and also that Churchill had used Windsor Castle writing paper on which to pen his resignation letter. Ponsonby was sent to Hatfield to coordinate the official response. Reporting the news to Janetta Manners that day, Salisbury wryly wrote: 'Not much, I am afraid, around us, of "peace and goodwill".' He pronounced himself astonished that Churchill 'never breathed a word to the Queen, talked of his proceedings in the coming session as if nothing had happened: and then sat down and wrote this letter to me. Politics is a weary pursuit.'

Meanwhile, at his home at No. 2, Connaught Place, Churchill put on a brave face to his wife. Apart from a Delphic remark the previous night to say that he did not expect them to be hosting a large government reception (ironically enough to be held at the Foreign Office) that she was busy organising, he had given her absolutely no inkling of his intentions. When she came down for breakfast with *The Times* in her hand, she 'found him calm and smiling. "Quite a surprise for you" he said. He went into no explanation, and I felt too utterly crushed and miserable to ask for any, or even to remonstrate.'

Middleton, Akers-Douglas, Balfour and the Whips Office quickly got to work putting the resignation in as black a light as possible. It was emphasised that with the *revanchist* General Georges Boulanger becoming War Minister in France, Smith and Hamilton both being very moderate and unmilitaristic men, and soldiers like Wolseley attacking the Estimates for being too low, Churchill was merely irresponsible and had simply succumbed to a 'freak of temper'. Churchill later complained to Chamberlain that Salisbury had 'jumped at [his] resignation' and had been preparing for it for weeks, 'and possibly courting the crash?' Gwendolen Cecil agreed, arguing that her father had assumed another resignation threat was in the offing and had been carefully labouring to 'provide as unsympathetic background as possible for the central figure'.

If so, he was enormously helped by Churchill himself. By the time MPs and the lobby had been confidentially briefed on Churchill's pique, hubris and flounces, the Party – not wanting a third general election in fourteen months – stayed loyal. Akers-Douglas was able to report to Smith that he was finding 'the greatest unanimity of feeling among our party, all are against R.C.... Many of his particular friends have told me they think his conduct insane.... I have had heaps of letters today from MPs regretting the present crisis but all asking me to assure the Government of their support.' Instead of throwing in his lot with Churchill, Joseph Chamberlain stayed non-committal, while making noises that were wrongly interpreted by some as indicating a desire for re-fusion with the Liberals. He did not hide his admiration for Salisbury, who, he told his friend Lord Esher on 23rd December, 'is a bold man and is no doubt prepared for all the consequences. The old combination is irretrievably smashed. I hardly know what new ones may be possible in the future.'[7]

It was in pursuit of a drastic new combination that Salisbury wrote a typically phlegmatic letter to Hartington (who was in Rome) on Christmas Eve, offering him the premiership for a third time:

> My dear Lord Hartington, I am very sorry to disturb you with tiresome affairs of State during your Christmas trip – but Randolph's ways are inconvenient. His resignation brings up again under new circumstances and in a new shape the question I ventured to put to you last July.... Our front bench power in the House of Commons is so weak, now, that we run a very great risk of being broken to pieces in the chance medley of the House of Commons. And if we are defeated, a separatist ministry must follow us, for by constitutional usage we should be disabled from coalescing there. We could not, after having been defeated, take office in any Government, until our adversaries had been tried. See the precedents of 1855, 1851 and 1839.

Salisbury admitted this third offer was 'a persistence – to which you may well object as bordering on importunity'. He also played the Unionist card, saying that 'interests very much larger than those of any party in the State are at issue. Pray do not decide it wholly with reference to the future of the Liberal party.'

Hartington, who was being advised by Esher that Chamberlain was holding out an olive branch to Gladstone, took soundings amongst his friends. Although Salisbury had purposely not gone into policy details, Churchill believed, as he told Chamberlain the same day, that it would be impossible for Hartington to join the Salisbury Government as 'their innate Toryism is rampant and irrepressible'. For their part, Smith and Akers-Douglas were concerned that Hartington's presence in a Cabinet might affect policy on local government and allotments, but overall the major worry was how to keep out Gladstone.

Meanwhile, the letters Churchill was receiving from MPs and peers showed that few understood his action and even fewer supported him over it. His sallies into the Carlton Club met with little response, and some overt shunning. The Prince of Wales spoke for many when he asked him to reconsider. Only Esher told him that the Government 'is smashed' and that Churchill would soon be forming the next one. Lord

Dunraven offered to resign in sympathy, but when even Churchill's own Woodstock constituency association asked him to withdraw the resignation, as though it was a slip of the tongue that he could apologise for and then forget, Churchill must have appreciated how isolated he was.[8]

Churchill desperately needed to get the private correspondence between himself and Salisbury, which Buckle had refused to publish, into the public domain as soon as possible. It would show that he had left the Government over more than simply defence spending. This led to a sharp exchange of telegrams with Hatfield. Asking for permission to publish the letters exchanged on 22nd December, Churchill said it would 'clear away a great deal of misconception to the position of all parties interested'. Salisbury, in whose favour the misconception was working, answered: 'I cannot agree. It would be entirely at variance with the accepted practice according to which such explanations should be reserved for Parliament. You clearly cannot do it without the Queen's leave.' Churchill replied: 'Very well of course as you wish. I only asked [because] obviously correspondence had been shown to [the] *Standard*.' Salisbury replied: 'No. Your supposition is incorrect. The letters referred to have not been seen by anybody.'

In fact, Salisbury had shown the correspondence to several ministers, but not directly to any newspapers. Considerable off-the-record briefing of journalists had taken place, however, and the *Standard* had published the story of Churchill's not having informed the Queen of his intentions before talking to the editor of *The Times*, something Lewis Harcourt, who assumed the leak came from Hatfield, viewed as 'most monstrous and discreditable' behaviour by Churchill. Salisbury also wrote to W.T. Stead, who edited the *Pall Mall Gazette*, explaining in some detail what had happened, and saying that Churchill had 'not before alluded' to his dissatisfaction with the Government's broader legislative intentions 'in connection with his resignation'. Although he told Stead that he could publish that fact, he added: 'do not say, or let it be seen, that I have been in communication with you'.[9] Churchill's caddish abuse of the Queen's hospitality was a recurring theme in the London press's attacks on him, a detail attributable to Hatfield's deft news management.

Christmas Day, which fell on a Saturday, saw Salisbury writing to Cranbrook and Hamilton in unflappable tone, explaining why he had taken the action he had and saying that Churchill's original idea of opening Parliament on 13th January should be postponed for a fortnight at a Cabinet to be held on Tuesday, 28th December. 'You must bear in mind that Randolph's interference was incessant,' he told Hamilton, and only his anxiety to keep the Cabinet united meant that he 'deferred to him as much as I possibly could. The result was a rather composite policy.' He also pointed out how dangerous Churchill's isolationist and pro-German stance had been for his conduct of foreign policy, even though he still denied that Churchill's decision to resign was over anything more than defence expenditure.

Each letter Salisbury wrote from Hatfield during Christmas and the New Year subtly emphasised to each recipient the aspect of events most likely to encourage them to forsake Churchill. To Drummond Wolff he floated the idea of a Hartington ministry in which both he and Churchill might serve. To Cranbrook he wrote that he had answered Churchill's initial letter by 'arguing with him', which was hardly the case. To right-wingers he raised suspicions about Churchill's closeness to Chamberlain. To Unionists he emphasised the likelihood of another Home Rule Bill should the Government fall and Gladstone take their place. Smith was drumming up support too, and it was unlikely to have been coincidental that Henry Howarth, then a regular visitor to Hatfield, wrote a letter to *The Times* on 23rd December suggesting that 'Goschen is the man' to take Churchill's place as Chancellor, even offering to give up his South Salford seat to the Liberal Unionist who had lost his in the 1885 election.

On Christmas Day, the *Morning Post*, an influential Tory paper, came out for Salisbury, saying that 'sober-minded people will be inclined to ask themselves why the withdrawal of a statesman who previous to the summer of last year had never held any office whatever should wreck a Cabinet and plunge a great political party into despair'. Much more serious was Hicks Beach's letter, which stated that he would try to attend the Cabinet meeting on the 28th, but he thought it best for the Government to resign at once if Hartington refused to join a coalition. This was both because Chamberlain would support the Churchillites and because there was no one else, other than Hartington himself, capable of leading the House of Commons. He was wrong; Chamberlain showed no sign of throwing in his lot with Churchill, and where were the Churchillites?

On Christmas Day, Esher went to visit Churchill at Connaught Place and found him 'lying on the sofa in his large grey library, smoking cigarettes and completely prostrated by the excitement of the last two days. He said he was shunned like a pest and no one had been near him, not even those who owed everything to him.'[10] In Esher's journal (but not the published edition), Churchill added that he had resigned because he suspected Salisbury had been intriguing to get rid of him. He also blamed 'the women at Hatfield' for inspiring the negative articles about him in the *Standard*: 'Lady Salisbury he thinks a clever fool and he described her as "Ashmead-Bartlett in petticoats",' wrote Esher. Churchill could hardly have been ruder; Ellis Ashmead-Bartlett, the Brooklyn-born Suffolk MP, was famously vain, loud, pretentious and something of an adventurer.

Salisbury's supposed domination by 'female influence' was a theme regularly used by Churchill over the forthcoming months to explain why the Prime Minister had accepted his resignation. It is true that after the Duchess of Marlborough's carriage had left, Lady Salisbury had openly remarked of her son: 'Anyhow, an open enemy is better than a false friend,' but all Salisbury's actions would have been identical whatever the female members of his family felt. Churchill complained that when he had presented his proposed Budget to the Cabinet, Salisbury had been 'very satirical and carping', while the majority of the Cabinet approved it. This was far from the truth, but he might have been closer to the mark when he also complained that Salisbury was 'the incarnation of pessimism, and thinks the democracy certain to ruin the country'.

On Boxing Day, as Lord Beauchamp complained to Smith that the Prime Minister was only being 'properly punished' for over-promoting Churchill in the first place, Salisbury wrote to Akers-Douglas to say that Churchill's conduct could only be explained 'on the theory that the work has upset his nerves, and when his nerves go, his judgment goes altogether'.[11] These mitigating circumstances would not be allowed to save him. At the Cabinet meeting on the 28th, the first since the crisis began, Salisbury kept the subject matter on the Estimates and 'no lamentations were wasted over R.C.'. Hicks Beach did urge that the Government should resign, but Salisbury said he would not 'throw up the sponge' just because of one man, and suggested that Goschen might be asked to join the ministry as Chancellor of the Exchequer in Churchill's place. The Cabinet also approved Salisbury's request for Hartington to join, but the great majority did not want him to replace Salisbury as Prime Minister.

The way in which Churchill had dropped the National Union as soon as it had served his purpose meant that neither it nor the Primrose League, which he had founded, came to his support. Instead, as Salisbury told the Queen on the 28th, 'the excitement at his resignation was beginning to subside'. Nevertheless, the recall of Parliament was cautiously put back a fortnight to 27th January 1887. At Salisbury's request, the Queen wrote a personal letter to Goschen begging him to join the Government, just the sort of appeal which an ambitious politician could use to justify on patriotic grounds the course that he was always intending to take anyhow.

'The fact is', wrote Cranbrook of Churchill in his diary after the Cabinet meeting, 'that he was a growing rival of the Prime Minister, and wished to wrest the lead from him.' Salisbury had little choice but to destroy Churchill, and bringing a leading Liberal Unionist into his coalition would allow his Government to survive. Goschen adamantly refused to become a Conservative himself by joining the Carlton Club or becoming Leader of the House of Commons. 'I have observed that in Ministerial crises', Salisbury wrote to Henry Holland, who had offered to resign the Vice-Presidency of the Council if his place were needed, 'the people who are most ready to give up their places are always the people whom no Minister would part with willingly. I do not get similar offers from the other sort of people.'

Should he fail to get any Liberal Unionists to join, Salisbury had nevertheless resolved to face Parliament and the attacks of Churchill and Chamberlain in the Commons, and to 'fight on for the cause entrusted to us, till the power of doing so is taken from us. But I by no means despair.' He had good reason not to; Akers-Douglas and Middleton were already telling Salisbury that 'the party are loyal to you as a man'. They even thought that resigning in Hartington's favour would show a dangerous loss of face, and would only 'magnify the position of Churchill'. Manners also believed that substituting Hartington for Salisbury would wreck the Party's morale, not least because Hartington's views on everything other than Ireland and the Empire were too liberal for the Tory rank-and-file.

Salisbury was careful to let Buckle, who sympathised with the idea of a Hartington premiership, know the opinions of the Party about 'submission to a Liberal who only brings forty votes'.[12] If no Liberal Unionist accepted office under him, Salisbury intended to appoint Smith to Churchill's two vacant posts, because nobody could replace Hicks Beach in Ireland, and anyhow Hicks Beach himself had refused them. Despite his mediocre oratory, 'Old Morality' Smith might, through his modesty and very contrast to Churchill, be able to reassure the Conservatives that solidity had returned.

Salisbury allowed his sense of irritation with Churchill to emerge on 30th December, when he replied to a letter from the Oxford contemporary, High Court judge and former *Saturday Reviewer* Sir James Fitzjames Stephen, who had had a long talk with Churchill in which he alleged that Salisbury's 'coldness and indifference' had been major factors in his resignation. Salisbury began his response with a studied understatement – 'His opinions on several subjects were not those of his colleagues, and he did not urge them in a manner to make them more acceptable' – but then he wrote:

> Whether my coldness of manner aggravated these difficulties of course I cannot judge. To my own eyes, I have been incessantly employed for the last five years in making things smooth between him and others, both by word and act. But, after all, coldness of manner may be an excuse for an erring wife, but not for an overbearing colleague.

As well as citing the danger of losing Smith and Hamilton, and the inherent merits of the Estimates issue itself, Salisbury mentioned

Churchill's 'friendship for Chamberlain which made him insist that we should accept that statesman as our guide in internal politics', as another reason for his having let his Chancellor quit.

In an almost schoolmasterly report, Salisbury summed up Churchill in terms which killed any hopes Stephen might have entertained of being an instrument for effecting Churchill's early return to the Government:

> His character, moreover, is quite untrained: both in impulsiveness and variability, and in a tendency which can only be described by the scholastic word 'bully', he represents the characteristics of extreme youth. Whether there is any growth left in him I do not know, but unless he can develop more proportion in his views, and more consideration for others in carrying them out, he will not be able to work in office with any ministry, no matter from what school of politics it is drawn.

At the same lunch party at which Churchill had complained to Stephen about Salisbury's 'coldness', he had also joked to the political hostess Mrs Jeune, when she inquired about the possibility of Goschen taking over the Treasury: 'I had forgotten Goschen.' It became a line Churchill used regularly, both belittling Goschen – who was not even an MP at the time – and also displaying a rare spark of self-deprecation. The German-born George Joachim Goschen was educated in Germany, then at Rugby and Oriel, where he took a first in Greats. A director of the Bank of England at twenty-seven, he was MP for the City of London by thirty-two. The author of *The Theory of Foreign Exchanges*, Goschen was an orthodox economist who had held high office in successive Liberal Governments since 1866, until as an opponent of Home Rule he lost his East Edinburgh seat in the 1886 general election.

For Churchill, who was in correspondence with Goschen over currency matters on the very day of his resignation, to have 'forgotten' the former financier as a potential replacement Chancellor of the Exchequer was unlikely. Yet Goschen had an impressive track record for refusing office, having turned down the Viceroyalty of India in 1880, the War Office in 1882 and the Speakership in 1883. Nor would his politics be allowed to pose an insuperable problem. 'It certainly does seem absurd that he should shrink from calling himself Conservative,' Salisbury told the Queen on 30th December. 'All his opinions are those of the Conservatives. No Liberal constituency in the country will have him, however much he may profess himself a Liberal.'[13]

Writing to his mistress the Duchess of Manchester, Hartington said that he had consulted Goschen, Chamberlain, Lord Rothschild, the deputy Speaker Leonard Courtney, George Buckle 'and heaps of others' about Salisbury's offer of the premiership, but although finding it 'a very difficult point indeed to decide on', he found the sticking point to be the opposition of the Tory backbenchers to the idea. So when he, Salisbury and Smith met on Friday, New Year's Eve, the best he could offer was that Goschen should be asked once again. Hartington said that his friends had unanimously told him 'that he could not without losing all influence over the Liberals in the country either join a Conservative Government or form a coalition Government'. But the refusal was not categorical; he could conceive a situation in which he might become Prime Minister in order 'to avoid a dissolution or if the Conservatives by resignation declared that they were unable to carry on the Government, but in no other case'. Salisbury refused 'a confession that would not be true and which would be humiliating', but they agreed that Goschen might be asked again, with Salisbury offering him a Conservative seat in the Commons.

Akers-Douglas was sent to Goschen later that day to reassure him that the Tory rank-and-file 'would cordially welcome him'. Goschen made it clear that he would only accept the Chancellorship, not the Leadership of the House, and wanted a Liberal Unionist peer to join him if he did so. Salisbury agreed readily to both conditions, suggesting Northbrook or Selborne as possible candidates. Salisbury then renewed his offer of the Leadership of the House to Hicks Beach, who again refused. According to a memorandum drawn up by Robert Cecil only three weeks later, obviously on his father's testimony, although Hicks Beach was doing well in Ireland and had not been very successful previously as Leader, the refusal was because he hoped to be able to compel the Government to resign and thus force Hartington into the premiership, 'a result which he had very much at heart'.

On New Year's Day 1887, under strong if somewhat hypocritical urging from Hartington to join, Goschen was cautiously considering whether to save Salisbury's Government. 'There is much laughter here', Frances Balfour wrote to her brother-in-law Gerald Balfour from Hatfield, 'over Hartington's action in making poor Conservative-hating Goschen go over, when he [himself] won't.' Salisbury asked the Queen to telegraph Goschen yet again, which she readily did. She was 'very animated' in support of a coalition when Cranbrook saw her that day, but when he got the subject on to a recent murder case she was just as animated about that too. 'If a woman dances around her husband, and abuses him,' she opined, 'that is hardly a justification for cutting her throat.'

Churchill, in a letter to Akers-Douglas on 1st January, seemed to be severely limiting his options when he promised of Salisbury: 'I shall make no further attempt to defend my action, lest by any such attempt I might even by one iota, increase the difficulties which surround him; but recognising to the full my great fallibility of judgment, shall watch silently and sadly the progress of events.' This was not entirely true, as he still had his resignation speech to make when Parliament re-assembled. Chamberlain remarked two days later: 'When a man says that in no case will he return a blow, he is very likely to be cuffed.'[14]

On Sunday, 2nd January, Goschen let it be known that at an interview with Salisbury the following day he would accept the Chancellorship of the Exchequer, but not the Leadership of the House of Commons, although he might even be willing to take that on too after an interval. Salisbury told Hartington, through whom almost the entire negotiation had been conducted, that it was entirely up to Goschen 'to determine in what language he will describe his own political connections: it is not a matter on which the Conservative party are likely to give any trouble'. He arranged to meet Hartington at 12.30 p.m. on Monday the 3rd to arrange 'the other questions', meaning policy details.

Salisbury wrote to Hicks Beach to say that Goschen wanted a 'temporary' Leader of the Commons, 'a friend in the Lords', i.e. a Liberal Unionist peer as an under-secretary at the War Office or Colonial Office, and that he would not call himself a Conservative. All these demands were conceded. To mollify Hicks Beach, Salisbury wrote that he felt 'it is absolutely impossible to spare you in Ireland and that Ireland is the first consideration', even though only days earlier he had said he wanted him to take the Commons Leadership. There were other problems. According to Robert Cecil's memorandum, and there seems no reason why Salisbury should have misled his son, 'before anything was definitely settled Mr Goschen declared that he was strongly averse to joining the Government unless Lord Iddesleigh were removed from the Foreign Office'. As this came at the same moment that Smith declared his proposed Leadership of the House to be incompatible with his tenure at the War Office, Salisbury clearly had a large-scale government reconstruction on his hands. Despite all this, however, for the first time since Churchill exploded his mine on 20th December, the ministry looked secure.[15] The Cecil motto, 'Late but in Earnest', certainly applied to the breaking of Churchill.

'Lord Salisbury regards the attainment of this result as a matter of enormous importance at this juncture,' he informed the Queen about Goschen's joining the ministry. He put it more colloquially at dinner at Hatfield that evening: 'We have hooked our fish.' To the Duchess of Marlborough's letter begging for an interview, Salisbury advised her not to turn up at Arlington Street as: 'I am watched as if I was a Fenian and your name would be sure to get into the papers.' They did meet, however, at the Duchess's London home where she begged Salisbury 'as a father' to forgive her son, Churchill's own father having died in 1883. Salisbury could not, to her lasting, bitter regret, oblige.

On 11th January, Salisbury wrote to the Duchess again in warm terms about her son, saying that he was amiable, fascinating and agreeable to work with, 'as long as his mind is not poisoned by any suspicion'. He even wound up by suggesting that Churchill's promising career had not been seriously injured by what had occurred. The best construction to be placed on this generous letter is that Salisbury was indulging a tearful mother, rather than relating the precise truth. His real attitude to Churchill's re-employment was perfectly summed up in one of his most cutting remarks: 'Did you ever hear of a man who having got rid of a boil on the back of his neck ever wants it back again?'[16]

With Churchill's departure from the ministry, and Goschen's adherence which guaranteed its survival, Salisbury could at last embark on the second phase of his political career – the one in which he was in command. Hitherto he had been a Tory tribune, setting out his beliefs as forthrightly as anyone in Victorian politics, but always hedged about by opponents, from both sides of politics, who were in the majority. As 1887 dawned, however, with Churchill gone and a large Unionist majority at his back, he could now finally come into his own. A century after Horace Walpole's prediction, the Cecilian phoenix had arisen.

TORY TITAN

TWENTY-SIX

Reconstruction at Home and Abroad

Reconstruction – The Death of Iddesleigh
– The Mediterranean Agreements –
Bulgaria – Egypt – 'Diplomaticus'
– Private Finances

January to April 1887

'I felt that politics was a cursed profession.'

On Monday, 3rd January 1887, Salisbury and Goschen met to discuss the various domestic and international issues of the day, and fortunately found themselves in substantial agreement. There would have to be an extensive Government reconstruction and the man left standing when the music stopped was Iddesleigh. On 30th December, the Foreign Secretary had written a letter to Salisbury offering up his post, more as a polite gesture than in the serious expectation of being taken up on it. 'I need not say that if you want places for any combination,' Iddesleigh had inadvisedly said, 'I am only too ready to make way.'

Salisbury, who had already taken Churchill at his word, proceeded to interpret Iddesleigh's offer equally literally. Underlining in red ink the words 'for any', he proposed to take full advantage of his old colleague's *pro forma* exercise in self-abnegation. Telling Iddesleigh that W.H. Smith could not be Leader of the House from the War Office, Salisbury explained that his own post of First Lord of the Treasury must therefore go to Smith, whilst he himself was 'absolutely compelled, without the possibility of escape, to accept your very kind and frank offer of making way, and take refuge in the Foreign Office'. He of course added that he hoped it might be temporary. Here was Salisbury at his most ruthless. 'I must go somewhere,' he told Frances Balfour, but that 'somewhere' just happened to be his favourite place in government. For all his talk of the inescapable logic of Smith's move to the First Lordship, Salisbury's hands had been itching to take back the reins of foreign policy.

Salisbury had telegraphed Iddesleigh on the afternoon of 4th January, because that morning the *Standard* had carried an authoritative leak, announcing that 'it is not the first time Lord Iddesleigh has stepped aside in the interest of what he deemed the public good'. Salisbury had told Austin what was about to happen, who had told his editor W.H. Mudford, who in turn had printed the story and Austin's leader on the subject, despite such prior disclosure having been strictly forbidden by Salisbury. Mudford claimed to have heard it from a separate source, but his excuse rang hollow. Salisbury's eagerness to have a positive twist put on the removal of his old colleague had led to the news getting out prematurely. Austin, who was privately claiming to have been instrumental in persuading Goschen to join the ministry in the first place, had blundered badly, and Iddesleigh's humiliation was only equalled by Salisbury's embarrassment and fury.[1]

Although Salisbury was angry with Mudford – 'whose views on morality are not infrequently overridden by his inclinations as editor', as Robert Cecil put it – he was philosophical and could see little point in making an enemy of the powerful editor. Austin returned Mudford's cheque for the article, hoping the incident would soon blow over. Salisbury could not see why Austin had done so, 'but that is no business of mine'. He told Austin that because of their known connection, 'The *Standard* possesses an authority when speaking of Conservative proceedings not possessed by any other paper. It was certain, therefore, that when Iddesleigh saw that paragraph...he would think I had inserted it; before communicating it to him: which would seem to him a great brutality.'

Iddesleigh was indeed deeply hurt and refused all subsequent offers, including the Colonial Office and the Lord Presidency of the Council, with terse one-sentence telegrams. 'Perhaps you will not be sorry of a little rest,' Salisbury replied soothingly, because Iddesleigh was known to be in some ill-health. Although Iddesleigh replied that 'though I leave the Foreign Office with regret, I accept your decision cheerfully', he was in fact extremely bitter at his treatment after twenty years' service on the Conservative front bench. On 6th January, Salisbury asked Iddesleigh to reconsider the offer of Lord Presidency of the Council. It was again rejected, Salisbury believed under family pressure. The Northcotes thought it merely 'a tardy concession to public opinion'. When the Marquess of Lansdowne, then Governor-General in Canada, and Northbrook refused the Lord Presidency, Salisbury complained to Hartington about how the offers had been leaked to *The Times*.[2] The reconstruction was generally starting to look badly mismanaged.

'As to Iddesleigh it was merely a question of doing a very painful thing in the least painful way,' Salisbury told Austin. 'I hate the whole business.' The Queen criticised Salisbury sharply over it, but although

Marquis of Lothian | Count Hatzfeldt | Duke of Rutland | William Waddington | Rustem Pasha

Lord Eustace Cecil

Spanish Ambassador

Lady Salisbury

Prince of Wales

Sir Henry Drummond Wolff

Sir Henry Rawlinson

Lord Salisbury | Shah of Persia | Malcom Khan | Princess of Wales

The Shah of Persia visits Hatfield in July 1889.

George Goschen, the Liberal Unionist who saved Salisbury's Government

'Old Morality': WH Smith, millionaire bookseller and Salisbury's 'beloved colleague'

Joseph Chamberlain at the time of the disastrous Jameson Raid: Why did Salisbury save his former rival's career?

The 5th Earl of Rosebery: the Liberal Prime Minister who nonetheless faithfully carried out Salisbury's foreign policy

Schomberg McDonnell, Salisbury's private secretary from 1888 to 1902

Sir William Harcourt

Sir Henry Holland, 1st Viscount Knutsford

Evelyn Baring, 1st Earl of
Cromer: The strong-willed
de facto ruler of Egypt for 24
years

Lord
Selborne

Lord
Hugh

Lord
William

Lord
Cranborne

Lord
Salisbury

Lady Selborne
(Maud)

Lady
Cranborne
(Alice)

Lady
Gwendolen

Lady Salisbury
(Georgina)

Lord
Edward

Lady Robert
(Eleanor)

Lord Robert

The Cecils,
some in fancy
dress, outside
the South Door
of Hatfield House

Lady
William
(Florence)

Lady Edward
(Violet)

LORD SALISBURY'S NEW CABINET.

Photo by Russell and Sons.

MR. JOSEPH CHAMBERLAIN,
SECRETARY FOR THE COLONIES.

Photo by Russell and Sons.

THE MARQUIS OF SALISBURY,
PRIME MINISTER AND FOREIGN SECRETARY.

Photo by Russell and Sons.

MR. G. J. GOSCHEN,
FIRST LORD OF THE ADMIRALTY.

Photo by Russell and Sons.

MR. A. J. BALFOUR,
FIRST LORD OF THE TREASURY.

Photo by Russell and Sons.

LORD HALSBURY,
LORD CHANCELLOR.

Photo by James Bacon.

SIR MATTHEW WHITE RIDLEY,
HOME SECRETARY.

Photo by Russell and Sons.

EARL CADOGAN,
LORD LIEUTENANT OF IRELAND.

Photo by Davenor.

THE DUKE OF DEVONSHIRE,
LORD PRESIDENT OF THE COUNCIL.

Photo by Russell and Sons.

LORD GEORGE HAMILTON,
SECRETARY FOR INDIA.

Photo by Russell and Sons.

VISCOUNT CROSS,
LORD PRIVY SEAL.

Photo by Russell and Sons.

MR. HENRY CHAPLIN,
PRESIDENT OF THE LOCAL GOVERNMENT BOARD.

Photo by Bender and Co.

MR. C. T. RITCHIE,
PRESIDENT OF THE BOARD OF TRADE.

Right Four generations of monarchs: Front row: Queen Mary, King Edward VIII, Queen Victoria. Back row: King George V, King Edward VII

Opposite Some of Salisbury's 1895 Cabinet

Below Salisbury preaching rejection of the Second Irish Home Rule Bill in Ulster in 1893

A stroll in the park at Hatfield with Joseph Chamberlain (right)

the newspapers took up Iddesleigh's case warmly, the Tory back-benchers crucially did not. Even his younger son Henry Northcote, the Surveyor-General of Ordnance, failed to resign from the Government, and was tossed a baronetcy for his placidity. Nor did the Liberal Unionists seem to mind, for, as Rosebery wrote to Gladstone on 11th January, they were in the position of Roman allies to Roman citizens: 'they may bear any amount of burden and heat, but are not qualified to receive the rewards. Surely this must leave a rankling sore in the [Liberal] Unionist relations to the Tories.' It did not, because although they refused the rewards of office Salisbury ensured that they were liberally sprayed by the fountain of honours.

'I have been rather worried', Salisbury wrote to Janetta Manners on 12th January, 'not by Randolph – but by Iddesleigh. It is very painful to hurt the feelings of a man you like and admire, without meaning it.' Later that day, Salisbury was to feel far worse when his ex-colleague, having wrapped up his business good-naturedly in the Foreign Office, walked over to see him at Downing Street at 2.45 p.m. to discuss his forthcoming speech to the Imperial Institute at the Mansion House. Having walked upstairs to the anteroom of Salisbury's office, he sank into a chair, his groans attracting the attention of Henry Manners in the next room. Manners got him on to a sofa and doctors were sent for, but at 3.05 p.m. Iddesleigh expired of a heart attack in the presence of Salisbury, Manners and the doctors.

Cranbrook, who saw Salisbury shortly afterwards, found the Prime Minister alone and 'deeply grieved'. The Queen also noted that day how Iddesleigh's death had dealt Salisbury 'a serious blow'. When Churchill wrote the following day to say that 'never in public life did any man have a truer friend and colleague than Lord Iddesleigh had in you', Salisbury suspended their differences in his heartfelt reply:

> I have never happened to see anyone die before – and therefore even apart from the circumstances the suddenness of his unexpected death would have been shocking. But here was, in addition, the thought of our thirty years companionship in political life: and the reflection that now, just before the sudden parting, by some strange misunderstanding which it is hopeless to explain, I had, I believe, for the first time in my life, seriously wounded his feelings. As I looked upon the dead body stretched before me, I felt that politics was a cursed profession.[3]

Realising, correctly, that Salisbury would somehow be criticised for Iddesleigh's death – 'the only dramatic personal incident in a placid life', as Henry Lucy cruelly but accurately described it – Henry Manners quickly drew up a memorandum to show how good-humoured and relaxed Iddesleigh had been earlier in the day. Evidence was obtained from the Under-Secretary, Sir James Fergusson, and others at the Foreign

Office, that Iddesleigh had been in 'good spirits' when taking his leave. It was also noted how Doctors Langston and Hebbert had applied 'suitable remedies'. Dr Mortimer Granville, who had also been called, attached a memorandum to say that the 'melancholy event... has been anticipated by his medical attendants'. For all the malicious talk, the only public criticism of Salisbury came in Iddesleigh's official biography published in 1890, which included the pointed remark that 'if any persons sinned, or seemed to sin, in the official affairs of his closing days they may make their own confessions'.[4]

The question arose of whether Salisbury would be welcome at Iddesleigh's funeral. If Smith attended to represent the House of Commons, Salisbury told Janetta Manners he must go too, in order to represent the peers. But the next day the Northcotes made it clear that they did not want either man to attend, stating that the ceremony at Upton Pynes 'would be as private as possible'. Instead, they hoped that 'the late Earl's colleagues should be content to attend the service in Westminster Abbey'. Salisbury was thus to be treated as a colleague rather than as a friend. He waxed almost lyrical when describing the scene in the packed Abbey to the Queen: 'A strange dense fog came on just before the service began, making the windows absolutely dark. It lasted till just the end of the service – and lent a strange unearthly gloom to the scene.'

Yet, far from a private service, the funeral at Upton Pynes was a large affair. Seventy private carriages brought, in the words of *The Times*, 'most of the nobility of Devon and representatives from county bodies and political associations', until 'the little church and graveyard were crowded to overflowing'. Although it was carefully reported that wreaths had been received from Lady Salisbury and her two daughters, and 'a letter was received full of kind sympathy from the Marquess of Salisbury', the snub was made pretty clear.[5]

'They have now only one really able man,' Carnarvon noted about the Government now devoid of Churchill and Iddesleigh, 'all the rest are cyphers in popular estimation.' This was almost true, although as well as Salisbury they could now also boast Goschen, a formidable economist. Yet Salisbury was relatively relaxed about the meetings that were being proposed between Chamberlain, Trevelyan, Morley and Harcourt to see whether the Liberal Party could be reconstituted, correctly assuming that Home Rule would continue to prove an insuperable difficulty. Churchill's long-awaited resignation speech was delivered on the day that Parliament reconvened on 27th January 1887. From his corner seat below the gangway, he attempted to broaden the reasons for his resignation into general dissatisfaction with national policy, but it made little impression. In the House of Lords debate on the Estimates, Northbrook supported the Government, while Salisbury reported with satisfaction to the Queen that 'the universal impression is that Lord Randolph's speech ... produced no impression in his favour'.

The press reaction was also subdued, the *Spectator* speaking for most when it said that Churchill had been 'imprudent to make so headlong and premature a stand'. Churchill might have 'forgotten' Goschen, but the political world quickly forgot him. He instructed his wife not to go to parties at Arlington Street, especially after Salisbury had delivered the ambiguous compliment that 'Randolph's brain works so quickly that it must wear out his nervous system.'[6] In mid-February Lord Dunraven, the Under-Secretary at the Colonial Office, resigned out of sympathy with Churchill and Tory Democracy. It changed nothing, and his place was swiftly filled by the Earl of Onslow.

Churchill's initial stance was to make constructive criticisms of the Government from the sidelines, writing regularly to Smith to set him right on War Office questions. He blithely continued putting people up for baronetcies and asked to be nominated for important committees. He even visited the Tsar in January 1888. Privately he announced that 'Lord Salisbury would rather sink the ship than recognise in any effectual manner the new – and better – school of Tory politics.' He also told his wife: 'What a fool Lord S. was to let me go so lightly.' In his turn, Salisbury calmed the Queen's fears that Churchill might be invited back, let alone as Viceroy of India. When Hicks Beach asked for Churchill to be readmitted to the Government, Salisbury told him that his friend's 'variable and impulsive nature was like that of a woman: and that he could never manage women'. As his general paralysis brought on by syphilis, took hold, the question of Churchill's further employment receded.[7]

Salisbury refused to consider Churchill for the Paris Embassy, and in 1889 he told Chamberlain that a particular scheme of Churchill's 'would reduce political life very far below the level it occupies in any other country – even the United States'. In his retirement, Salisbury enjoyed reminiscing about Churchill, and explained the reason for his exit as having been 'because having agreed to buy guns, he absolutely refused to sanction the purchase of ammunition', which was as unfair as retirement reminiscences often are. More convincingly, in January 1903 Salisbury 'dwelt on Randolph Churchill's great unscrupulousness and violence and said it was a most intolerable time ... and that the relief of Goschen was hardly to be believed'.[8]

The relief was not immediate, however, as Goschen still had to get into Parliament. He inadvisedly stood for the Exchange division of Liverpool, and at their eve-of-session dinner the Cabinet were disappointed to learn that he had lost by eleven votes. The Budget had to be postponed until Goschen was finally returned for St George's, Hanover Square on 9th February 1887, which was a safe Conservative seat obligingly vacated for him by Lord Algernon Percy. The Budget which Churchill never had an opportunity to deliver was later found and hung on the wall in his son's study at Chartwell. Although not in fact adding up in the income column, it showed a large surplus of income (£94.5 million) over expenditure (£82.0 million). Salisbury had thought Churchill, as he told the Queen, 'a most selfish statesman, not caring for the good of the country, for commerce, etc. provided he could make his Budget popular!' Instead, Goschen moved a far more sober measure and by 24th March the Bank Rate stood at the relatively low figure of 3 per cent.

'As to politics generally,' Salisbury admitted to his brother, 'I do not see my way in the future. I look upon my present mission as consisting in the duty of keeping G.O.M. out of office by all legitimate means. But what is to happen when he goes I cannot guess.' As the Liberal leader had another seven years in active front-bench politics, Salisbury did not have to worry too much about the post-Gladstonian political topology; and as for staying in office himself, the most difficult fence had been successfully jumped.[9] By the time Churchill died in January 1895 (owing the Rothschilds £66,902), he had long been, in Rosebery's cruel phrase, 'the chief mourner at his own protracted funeral'.

'The prospect is very gloomy abroad,' Salisbury wrote to the Queen on 24th January 1887, 'but England cannot brighten it....We have absolutely no power to restrain either France or Germany: while all the power and influence we will have will be needed to defend our influence in the south-east of Europe.' General Boulanger, an adventurer who modelled himself on Napoleon and wanted to recapture Alsace-Lorraine, was Minister of War in Paris, and a Franco-German war looked probable. Salisbury listened to reports of Bismarck's private conversations and the opinions of the Rothschilds and feared the worst. He was principally worried that, should such a war break out, Russia would take advantage of Germany's preoccupation in the west to launch an attack on Bulgaria. If that happened, he suspected, Austria 'would probably be involved in it, and would probably be overthrown'.

Salisbury hoped that the Tsar, 'a passionate but slow-witted man', would stay calm, for he was 'in his cooler moments hesitating and helpless, and nervous as to the political effects of war on his own country'. For all Labouchere's criticisms of Salisbury as 'the great perturbator of the peace of Europe', he was in fact constantly slapping down belligerent advice from the British military attachés abroad and doing everything in his power to discourage another war. Every Great Power except Austria impinged on the British Empire somewhere, be it Germany in Zanzibar and Samoa, Russia in Asia and Afghanistan, or France in Egypt, West Africa, the Pacific and Indo-China. For Salisbury, diplomacy represented an intricately interconnected Chinese puzzle of ambitions, rivalries, fears and strategic imperatives, all underlined by the need to avoid war with other Great Powers. A movement in one direction in one part of the globe might affect events thousands of miles away, in ways not immediately apparent to brains slower than those of Salisbury and Bismarck. As Foreign Secretary, acting free both of Iddesleigh and Churchill, Salisbury could at last play the game unhampered.

On 1st February 1887, Count Francesco Corti, the Italian plenipotentiary at Constantinople in 1876–7 and now Ambassador to London, came to Salisbury with a proposal for an alliance in case of war against France. Salisbury refused it on the grounds that 'England never promised material assistance in view of an uncertain war of which the object and cause were unknown.' Nonetheless, he left open the possibility of an agreement for Anglo-Italian co-operation to maintain the Mediterranean status quo, especially in the Aegean, Adriatic and Black Seas and along the North African littoral. The Cabinet agreed to the general policy the same day, after which Salisbury took the whole matter into his own hands, not even informing the Foreign Office of what was about to happen.[10] A few trusted lieutenants such as Philip Currie, William White and Evelyn Baring were told what was going on, but Salisbury point-blank denied the rumours to others, such as Sir Robert Morier in St Petersburg. Salisbury's overview was that England, Germany and Austria were 'satisfied' powers, whereas France and Russia were 'hungry' ones. 'Italy, it is true, is eminently a hungry Power: but the objects of her hunger are no great matter to us,' because they largely lay in areas of north Africa in which Britain was uninterested.

A pact with Italy and Austria to defend the Mediterranean status quo held out many attractions for Britain. Italy had 'far too large a seaboard to make a deadly enemy of England', and she opposed both Balkan pan-Slavism and French adventurism. Salisbury had described Austria as 'England's ancient and true ally, and bound to her by the only bond of union that endures, the absence of all clashing interests'. Together they would discourage any Turkish *entente* with Russia. It had to be secret because, if the Sultan got wind of the way his freedom of action was being circumscribed, he might react adversely. As so often with Salisbury's secret diplomacy, although much was suspected, nothing could be proven, and despite Labouchere's detective work and some awkward parliamentary questions, even eleven years after the

Mediterranean Agreements, as they became known, were signed, Chamberlain told Hatzfeldt that he had no inkling that anything had been formally agreed back in 1887.[11]

The Mediterranean Agreements were deliberately nebulous and never quite a formal alliance as such. In the past, Salisbury had denounced such uncodified leanings, 'sympathies' and *de facto* but not *de jure* understandings. Defending the Cyprus Convention in the House of Lords on his return from Berlin in July 1878, he had said it was a 'Convention of Defensive Alliance' very unlike 'those misty and shadowy guarantees which bound you to everything in theory, and which turned out, in practice, to bind you to nothing'. Such semi-alliances he had denounced as 'anything but honourable to the character of European diplomacy', yet it was precisely such an understanding that he proposed in February 1887.

Realising that because of the huge contrast in the sizes of the armies of Russia and Britain, 'England can never, therefore, take the place of Russia in Prince Bismarck's calculations or induce him to take any course which will forfeit the goodwill of Russia,' Salisbury had to construct a form of *entente* whereby no Power was formally committed actually to going to war against Russia or France in any particular circumstances. Meeting Corti and Hatzfeldt on 5th February, Salisbury reiterated that Britain could not promise any assistance to another country until it first knew the *casus belli*, but he said that Britain would 'co-operate heartily' to prevent Russia or France from increasing 'their dominion over the shores of either the Mediterranean, the Aegean, or the Black Sea'. To the Queen he justified what might otherwise be seen as an encirclement of France in terms of insuring against a situation in which Britain found herself isolated, and he reiterated that no formal treaty would be signed, although 'some informal understanding will be arrived at'.

Hatzfeldt called it a '*Wendepunkt* [turning point]', and asked for written details for Bismarck to consider. Salisbury took Goschen into his confidence, emphasising the benefits of Austrian and Italian financial support in Egypt. 'The French are inexplicable,' he wrote to Lord Lyons in Paris. With France acting aggressively over Newfoundland fisheries, New Hebrides sovereignty, threats to Tangier, 'sheer cussedness' in Egypt and the 'studied insult' of a French naval officer planting the *tricoleur* in Dongorita on the coast of British-protected Somaliland: 'One would have thought that under the present circumstances it was not necessary to make enemies – that there were enough provided for France by nature just now.'[12]

On 12th February, the draft *entente* with Italy was agreed by the Cabinet. Salisbury emphasised to the Queen that it had been:

so drawn as to leave entirely unfettered the discretion of Your Majesty's Government, as to whether, in any particular case they will carry their support of Italy as far as 'material co-operation'. But short of a pledge upon this subject, it undoubtedly carries very far the *relations plus intimes* which have been urged upon us. It is as close an alliance as the parliamentary nature of our institutions will permit.

Under it, Italy could not depend on automatic British military assistance if she took part in an aggressive war against France. The argument Salisbury used with the Queen might surprise those who persist in seeing him as the champion of 'splendid isolation': 'If, in the present grouping of nations, England was left out in isolation, it might well happen that the adversaries, who are arming against each other on the continent, might treat the English Empire as divisible booty, by which their differences might be adjusted: and, though England could defend herself, it would be at fearful cost and risk.' To Paget he described the exchanged despatches as 'more effusive perhaps than precise', but they were a definite statement of policy, and one that was to serve Britain well for almost a decade.[13]

A similar exchange of despatches was effected with Austria on 24th March 1887. Fergusson meanwhile quelled foreign press speculation by stating in the House of Commons that no engagements had been made with any other Powers to give material assistance to anybody, which was as literally accurate as it was intentionally misleading. Salisbury indulged in his own bout of misleading the Lords; when asked by Lord Stratheden whether there was an alliance between Italy and the German powers, he answered that he was 'wholly unaware', had no information and did not even know if any could even be obtained. The fact that only days earlier Britain, Austria and Italy had formed an *entente* for mutual support, which Germany externally encouraged, he felt under no obligation to divulge.[14]

At least at Dongorita the situation was eased when, as Salisbury reported to Lyons in April, 'the two flags were flying side by side; but a provident Somali who passed that way thought it would simplify the situation to carry them both away. So now the place is desert.' Unfortunately, the same thing was unlikely to happen in Zanzibar and Samoa, where Salisbury despaired of Germany's capacity for paternal imperialism. 'I can never get them to show any decency in their treatment of the wretched native sovereigns whom they despoil,' he complained to Sir Edward Malet. 'Their treatment of [the Anglophile Samoan Chieftain] Malieotoa and the Sultan of Zanzibar is atrocious.'

'Spite is not, I think, the whole of Prince Bismarck's motive,' Salisbury told the Queen, 'though doubtless it is part.' He thought that Bismarck's policy was to try to entice the Russians into a war with

Austria and Britain over Bulgaria, thus preventing the Tsar from interfering in any Franco-German conflict. Bismarck was as interested in
inciting trouble in the Balkans as Salisbury was in keeping the peace
there, but the German Chancellor had better materials at his disposal as
the Bulgarians had still not chosen their ruler. 'He is very particular
about the cut of his fingernails,' Salisbury wrote dismissively to Currie
about one of the leading contenders, Prince Ferdinand of Coburg, on
22nd December 1886, 'and he goes to St Petersburg periodically to have
them cut as St Petersburg is the only place where a sufficiently skilful
operator can be found. But no-one – except the poor prince-famished
Bulgarians – takes his candidature seriously.'[15]

When in early April 1887 Salisbury suspected that Bismarck had
attempted to bribe Russia with a free hand in Bulgaria if she would
stand aside while Germany and Italy crushed France, he described the
Iron Chancellor's 'main principle' as 'employing his neighbours to pull
out each other's teeth'. Prince Alexander's threatened return to power
in May, and declaration of complete Bulgarian independence from the
Porte, Salisbury described as that country's 'ingenious combination for
leaving themselves in an absolutely helpless condition', certain to infuriate Russia and Turkey simultaneously. When the Queen proposed
to pay off Alexander's debts, Salisbury had to block the scheme by
reminding her of the basics of constitutional practice, which Lord
Melbourne is generally credited with having taught her at the start of
the reign half a century earlier: 'The Government could not without
parliamentary authority spend sixpence.... It would have to be included
in a bill in the usual manner, and read three times in each House.'[16]

On 4th July 1887, the well-manicured Prince Ferdinand of Saxe-
Coburg, known to history as 'Foxy Ferdy', was elected to the throne of
Bulgaria by the Grand Sobranje, in succession to Prince Alexander of
Battenberg. On entering the palace at Sofia on 11th August, he told his
Bulgarian tutor that he noticed Prince Alexander's smell, an odour he
said he could remember from the Tsar's Coronation six years earlier.
(The tutor had no difficulty in believing it, as Ferdinand's nose was 'a
veritable chimney'.) The election had been arranged by Stephen
Stambulov, who would continue to rule Bulgaria *de facto* along with his
'regents', but Russia refused to recognise Ferdinand. 'We have got back
to the dangerous period of the year when Ministers go to baths, and
revolutions take place in the Balkan peninsula,' wrote an outwardly
calm Salisbury to Sir Augustus Paget in Vienna, asking about Austrian
intentions under various different scenarios for the unfolding Ferdinand
drama. Salisbury's greatest fear was that Russian-encouraged anarchy in
Bulgaria might induce St Petersburg to pressurise the Turks to intervene in Bulgaria, which would thereafter lead to a Russian occupation,
ostensibly to restore order.

Salisbury emphasised to Sir William White on 23rd August the disadvantages to Britain of such an outcome, which he said would undoubtedly lead to 'some serious loss of territory' to the Porte. His hope was for Ferdinand to become popular in Bulgaria and for the Great Powers to range themselves peacefully against Russia's plots to oust him. Characteristically pessimistic, Salisbury told White that he thought the likeliest outcome was for Ferdinand to be deposed and for Turkey, Austria and Russia to fight one another in the vacuum. Britain would not actively intervene, and he ordered White to be generally 'dilatory and negative' in negotiations with the Russian and other ambassadors at Constantinople. 'Whatever happens will be for the worse, and therefore it is in our interest that as little should happen as possible,' he wrote, in what might be taken as a neat encapsulation of his whole political philosophy as much as a comment on the Balkan situation of August 1887.

Bismarck would be no help in the coming conflict, as Salisbury warned Sir Nicholas O'Conor, the Consul-General in Sofia: 'The Germans never can forget that Russia is looking at them.' When in October Bismarck began urging Italy, Austria and Britain to take a tougher stance against Russia in the Balkans, Salisbury suspected that he wanted 'a nice little fight between Russia and the three Powers, he will have leisure to make France a harmless neighbour for some time to come. It goes against one to be one of the Powers in that unscrupulous game.' Salisbury was perfectly willing to join in a close understanding with the other two Powers, but not in a way which provoked war. 'Prince Bismarck is urging the three powers to lift a weight which he will not touch with one of his fingers,' he told the Queen later that month.

The crisis continued through to February 1888, with Russia still attempting to get the signatories of the Treaty of Berlin to organise a protest to the Sultan about Ferdinand remaining on the Bulgarian throne. Russia was overtly supported by Bismarck in this, but the refusal of Austria, Britain and Italy to agree eventually led to the project petering out. Later that month, Salisbury was amused by the attempts of Count Herbert Bismarck, then visiting London, to explain how his father's policy of supporting the Russian proposals himself, whilst simultaneously urging the Tripartite Powers to reject them, was somehow 'not open to the charge of duplicity'. Ferdinand remained on the throne of Bulgaria, declared his independence from Turkey in 1908 and only abdicated after supporting the Central Powers in the First World War. The man whose throne he took, Prince Alexander, died in 1893 as the result of a bite from his pet monkey.

Duplicitous or not, Salisbury did not think Bismarck was about to risk, as he put it in a letter to Alfred Austin on 7th March 1888, 'the edifice which he has had the glory of constructing, and all the fame he has gained, on a venture where he cannot gain more than he has already. I can believe he means to end his days in peace if he can.' He was right. Indeed, all the leading figures in Europe at that time – Bismarck, Tsar Alexander III, Emperor Franz Josef, Sultan Abdul Hamid II and Salisbury – were committed to avoiding a general European conflagration, in which they all recognised they would be likely to lose far more than they could gain. Only two days after Salisbury wrote that letter to Austin, however, Emperor Wilhelm I of Germany died, and by the end of the year there was a new German Emperor, someone who was anything but a man of peace and who had no patience for the intricate, delicate, mutually respectful diplomacy by which European peace was carefully preserved.

~

Salisbury equated the permanent British occupation of Egypt with what he called 'permanent disagreement with France and Turkey which may at any moment take an acute form', but he saw little realistic alternative to it, and he blamed France for 'pouring out upon us the hatred which they dare not show to Germany'. In January 1887, he again sent Sir Henry Drummond Wolff to Constantinople to negotiate a convention with the Sultan, but, as he told Malet in Berlin, because the French wanted either to quarrel with Britain over Egypt or to force her out, 'therefore our negotiations must be circumspect, slow, and a little hazy and ambiguous'. To Salisbury's surprise, the French Government was even willing to oppose strictly technical and apolitical improvements in the Egyptian economy simply in order to embarrass Baring's regime there, despite the concomitant ill-effects it would have on French holders of Egyptian bonds. Although he called Gladstone's commitments in Egypt 'a disastrous inheritance', which allowed Bismarck to ask for unreasonable terms for his continued refusal to join an anti-British coalition with France and Russia, Salisbury never really contemplated evacuating such a strategically vital point on the route to India, especially as Russian intrigues might at any time have opened up the Bulgarian road to Constantinople.

'I heartily wish we had never gone into Egypt,' he frankly told Drummond Wolff on 23rd February 1887. 'Had we not done so, we could snap our fingers at all the world. But the national, or acquisitional feeling has been roused, it has tasted the fleshpots and it will not let them go.'[17] When Smith complained that the Commons had not been kept properly informed of Drummond Wolff's progress in Constantinople, Salisbury answered that: 'All negotiations, and Turkish ones especially, must be conducted on the principle of salmon-fishing.

The length of time during which you must play your fish depends upon <u>his</u> choice, not on yours. Even the omnipotence of the House of Commons cannot prescribe that a fish shall be caught in a fixed number of minutes; and they will find that catching Turks is a more uncertain matter still.' Should the angler not even genuinely want to catch his fish, as was possibly the case with Salisbury, the enterprise would be yet more uncertain.

The negotiations came to a head in May 1887 over the time limit before a British evacuation had to come into operation. With the French Ambassador in London insisting on three years and Drummond Wolff calling for five, Salisbury 'inferred that four years was the right thing'. A three-year stipulation, he told Drummond Wolff, would cause 'some considerable storm in our own party. There are a number of Jingoes who on all questions between foreign countries and us or our colonies, take the most extravagant view as a matter of course... they may give us an evil quarter of an hour.' In a further explanation to Baring in Cairo on 6th May, Salisbury admitted that ideally he would prefer to remain in Egypt for fifteen years, 'But the political position caused by our occupation of Egypt is one of great difficulty. It places us a great deal at the mercy of the German Powers, who only have to guarantee France from interference on their part to cause us a formidable amount of trouble, and we are perpetually being reminded of this liability.' Further, the Gladstone Government had given pledges on eventual evacuation which Salisbury felt bound him 'hand and foot'.

The influence of Germany in the matter had been demonstrated only the previous week, when Bismarck had demanded the dismissal of the energetic British Consul-General in Zanzibar. 'I could not censure a man who, in my judgment, had done no wrong,' Salisbury intoned to the British Chargé d'Affaires in Berlin on 28th April. When only days later the German Ambassador in Constantinople, Count von Radowitz, told Drummond Wolff that Berlin had ordered a suspension of all German support for Britain in his negotiations with the Sultan, the Foreign Office quickly had to promise to promote the Consul-General elsewhere. 'It is not worth quarrelling with Bismarck,' a chastened Salisbury told the Chargé. 'It is only Egypt that puts us in this difficulty, for otherwise Bismarck's wrath would be of little moment for us. It is heartily to be wished we were delivered from this very inconvenient and somewhat humiliating relation.'

On 22nd May 1887, Drummond Wolff signed a Convention providing for a complete withdrawal of British troops from Egypt after three years, with the crucial proviso that this would be deferred in the event of any external or internal danger to Egypt at the time. Britain and Turkey would subsequently both have the right to send a force back into Egypt to protect her or to restore order. Salisbury insisted that the Convention also carry the Declaration that if any one of the Mediterranean Great Powers refused to accept the Convention, it would fall, as this would constitute the 'appearance of danger from without'. Although the Germans, Austrians and Italians proclaimed themselves satisfied with the Convention, the French and Russians were angered at the re-entry provisions and threatened the Porte that it could lead to the partition of Turkey itself. Under great pressure, the Sultan begged Salisbury to rene-gotiate the re-entry clauses of the Convention, which Salisbury adamantly refused to do. Abdul Hamid II then regretfully refused to ratify the Convention, and Drummond Wolff left the Golden Horn on a British man-of-war on 15th June.

Salisbury could now blame Britain's continued presence in Egypt on France and Russia, something that might well have been his intention all along. On 3rd July, he told Austin that 'for all practical purposes, Turkey has become the "janitor" of Russia. France has acted very shiftily. She is an insupportable neighbour.' To Lord Lyons he went further: 'Can you wonder that there is, to my eyes, a silver lining even to the great black cloud of a Franco-German war?' His overall attitude was one of patience: 'I see nothing for it but to sit still and wait awhile.' As for Drummond Wolff, Salisbury spent four months trying to persuade him to go on yet another mission far from home, partly in order to keep the troublesome Tory Democrat out of domestic politics. 'Wolff is getting dangerous and S. is pining to get him off to Persia,' Gwendolen noted in her diary in February 1888. After four years in Teheran, Drummond Wolff was found senior postings in Budapest and then Madrid. In all, Drummond Wolff was kept busy abroad for all but two of Salisbury's thirteen-year premiership.

On 4th February 1887, when the Franco-German war scare was at its height, a letter appeared in the *Standard* signed 'Diplomaticus', which effectively called on Salisbury to repudiate the 1839 guarantee to Belgium because it seemed likely that Germany would march through Belgium to attack France. It was intended to provoke a public debate, and stated that 'the English people should reflect, in good time, what may prove to be the nature and extent of their difficulties and responsi-bilities in the event of war between France and Germany'. Although Lord Granville had reaffirmed the 1839 Treaty of London at the time of the Franco-Prussian War in 1870, 'Diplomaticus' thought it 'unwise' to follow the same policy again, in case it landed Britain in a war against Germany and on the same side as France, which would have the effect of 'utterly vitiating and destroying the main purposes of English policy all over the world'. Instead, the anonymous author suggested that

Britain should offer Germany 'the temporary use of a right of way' through Belgium, with 'ample and adequate guarantees' from Bismarck that, at the end of the conflict, Belgian sovereignty would be restored. 'It is for the English people to perpend and pronounce,' the letter concluded. 'But it is high time they reflected on it.'

In a leading article which appeared in the same issue, the *Standard* announced that the letter's author was 'a correspondent who speaks with high authority', and who wrote 'with unprofessional terseness', but also with 'significant lucidity'. A war in which the 1839 Treaty forced Britain to side with France would strike the British people as 'utterly alien alike to their wishes and to their interests', and the right of way concept through Belgium – 'this minor trespass' – was an 'ingenious suggestion'. Both the letter and the leader were in fact written by Alfred Austin, and from a letter of 26th January it is clear that they were written at Salisbury's bidding. The editor of the *Standard*, Mudford, had wanted the leader without the letter, but Austin refused because it would be seen by foreign governments as 'an absolute communiqué'. Austin had visited Salisbury at Arlington Street on Monday 24th January and it was probably then that the suggestion was made for an article to awaken the British people to the possibility of being dragged into a European war, on what Salisbury thought was the wrong side.

Because it was the same guarantee which was to commit Britain to fighting Germany twenty-seven years later, it is worth examining the archæology of Salisbury's attitude towards the Belgian guarantee and the independence of the invasion ports on the Channel. 'England has ever watched the Scheldt with an especial jealousy,' he wrote in his 1862 *Quarterly Review* essay on Pitt the Younger. 'It has always been one of the cardinal maxims of our policy to secure that it should not fall into the hands of any power whom she had need to fear.' One of the arguments he raised against cutting the Defence Estimates in 1860 was that if it happened, 'we must publicly renounce, as beyond our strength, the guarantees that we have given to Switzerland and Belgium...and Antwerp becomes, under French auspices, a standing menace to the Thames'.

By 1887, however, his attitude had changed, primarily because it was friendly Germany rather than unfriendly France which now posed the greatest threat to Belgium. If 'Diplomaticus' also discouraged French politicians from relying on British support, so much the better. Salisbury deliberately left unanswered the questions posed by Lord Vivian, the British Ambassador in Brussels, as to future British policy in the event of a violation of Belgian neutrality. Four years later, when Stanhope asked whether a War Office intelligence officer, Colonel Chevenix Trench, should visit Belgium as a spy or an accredited agent to conduct military conversations with the Belgians, Salisbury

answered that he had preferred not as an agent, 'because I do not want to
raise undue hopes in the Belgian breast'.[18] There can be little doubt that
had Salisbury's desire for an end to the half-century-old guarantee been
realised in the late 1880s, Britain would have had considerably more
room to manoeuvre in 1914.

~

When Salisbury inherited Hatfield from his father in 1868, the 2nd
Marquess's property was sworn in at £300,000, not including certain
plate, china, carriages and horses. Eustace received £20,000 and the four
daughters annuities of £500 each, but a huge annuity of £5,000 had to be
paid to his widow, Mary, for the remainder of her life. On top of that,
Salisbury's own in-laws were a constant financial drain, especially his
brother-in-law, Edward Alderson, who finally went bankrupt with
Salisbury so much his largest creditor as 'may swamp the rest'.
Salisbury was nonetheless a generous donor to charity, so long as he was
not expected to attend the dinners given in their aid. 'Do you think it
creditable to the charities of the nineteenth century that they cannot
get on without raising money by a Lord-show?' he asked his Oxford
contemporary J.A. Shaw-Stewart, enclosing a cheque for £100 for a
hospital and demanding anonymity, explaining that 'to give myself over
to be exhibited, with other Lords, as if I was Tom Thumb or the Hirsute
Woman is more than I can stand'. When in 1890 his eldest son asked his
advice about sitting on a particular charity committee, Salisbury replied
that the problem was that 'you are perpetually furnishing hall-mark to
plate whose fineness you have no means of knowing'.[19]

Salisbury's private account book, which accounted for every penny of
the £38,809.10s.9d he spent in 1887, shows how generous he was to his
children and close family (£7,159.11s.9d), how much he spent on
pensions for his labourers (£1,748.8s.2d), and so on, all the way down to
the £33.1s.5d he paid the Liverpool Gas Company. His own clothing for
the year only cost him £120.19s.6d (i.e. 0.3 per cent of the total). Indeed,
his entire personal expenditure, including books, medicine and newspapers, amounted to less than £1,000.

Despite his supposed unclubbability, in 1887 Salisbury was paying
subscriptions to the Royal Institute, the Northbrook India Club,
Grillions, the Royal Society, the Athenæum (£8.8s), the Cecil Club, the
Conservative Club, the Zoological Institute, the Junior Carlton Club,
the Botanic Society, the City Carlton, the Oxford Historical Society and
the Carlton Club (£10.10s). He was also a member of The Club, which
had been founded in 1764 by Reynolds, Johnson, Burke and Goldsmith
and which in Salisbury's time included many of the brightest luminaries of the age, including Gladstone, Froude, Tennyson, Acton, Leighton,

Lecky, Carnarvon, Rosebery, Wolseley, Goschen, Huxley, Layard and Boehm.

The next year, in May 1888, Salisbury realised £200,000 on the sale of three acres in the Strand, showing a lack of confidence in the future of leased property and allowing the area to be developed for theatres, clubs and residential chambers. The Hotel Cecil, larger even than the Savoy, opened there in the 1890s. As well as having £22,124 in four bank accounts in February 1890, Salisbury had large investments in railway shares and debentures, a sector which he understood and in which he did well. Other more solid investment vehicles, such as India 4 per cent consols, formed the majority of his holdings. After the Overend and Guerney crash, he tended to prefer safer stocks, such as the government bonds of the settler colonies which typically paid a percentage point or so over the consol rate.

Fortunately for Salisbury, agriculture was not the major source of his income, three-quarters of which was derived from other pursuits. The fall in agricultural income in the last quarter of the nineteenth century was more than offset by the rise in urban rentals, and Salisbury's gross income of around £53,000 in 1868 rose to £60,000 by 1902, in a period of very low inflation, placing it in the second fifty of great British landowners.[20]

'According to my experience,' Salisbury complained to Dufferin in 1897, 'land is worth very little now unless it is near a town.' Fortunately for Salisbury his mother's inheritance was being turned into a city. Childwall, the original seat of the Gascoyne family, which had once been on its north-eastern edge, now formed part of the suburbs of Liverpool, and by 1889 the 2,000 houses built there brought in £10,000 per annum. The money went out in pensions, stipends, coal, the Dorset Clergy Widows and Orphans fund, missions, hospitals, Christmas gifts, Hertfordshire unemployed relief and a soup kitchen. Salisbury also clothed and shod the local Hatfield police, paid off Lord Edward Cecil's gaming debts and donated money to the Hertfordshire Militia Band, Hitchin Cricket Club and the local habitation of the Primrose League. 'Slovenly and sloppety as he was in his dress and appearance,' Lord George Hamilton wrote to his friend Curzon after Salisbury's death, 'still you could not help feeling, especially when at Hatfield, that he was in all essentials the embodiment of the *grand seigneur.*'

TWENTY-SEVEN

'Bloody Balfour'

Coercion in Ireland –
The Mitchelstown Riot –
The Special Commission –
The Fall of Parnell

March 1887 to July 1891

'Too much softness has crept into our counsels.'

'All the politics of the moment', Salisbury said in March 1887, 'are summarised in the word "Ireland".' His view of the Irish problem was neatly summed up in his 1883 article 'Disintegration':

> Possession of Ireland is our peculiar punishment, our unique affliction, among the family of nations. What crime have we committed, with what particular vice is our national character chargeable, that this chastisement should have befallen us?

Although he had fought the 1885 election on the policy of extending the same local institutions to Ireland that existed in England, an agricultural depression in the winter of 1886/7 encouraged fresh disturbances which Salisbury was determined to crush. The Liberal Unionists had forsaken their Party over Home Rule, and in Ireland he believed they could be trusted to support his policy of twenty years of 'resolute government'.

Ever the fatalist, Salisbury had no difficulty in believing that some problems simply had no solutions. 'Is it not just conceivable', he had asked in the *Quarterly Review* in 1872, 'that there is no remedy that we can apply for the Irish hatred of ourselves?' Instead of constantly trying new initiatives, he had recommended simply keeping the peace and rooting out organised crime on the other side of the St George's Channel, asking:

May it not, on the contrary, be our incessant doctoring and meddling, awakening the passions now of this party, now of that, raising at every step a fresh crop of resentments by the side of the old growth, that puts off the day when these feelings will decay quietly away and be forgotten?

By mid-January 1887, once it was clear that the law was incapable of dealing with the Nationalist MPs John Dillon and William O'Brien and their anti-rent-paying Plan of Campaign, Salisbury wanted alterations made. This in turn required a change in parliamentary procedure, owing to the ingenious obstructionism of the Irish Nationalist MPs. Clôture, by which debates could be guillotined, had been reluctantly introduced by Gladstone in 1881. In 1861, the then Lord Robert Cecil had criticised 'count-outs', when business would be closed when a quorum of one-sixteenth of the Commons were not present, as being 'habitually used as a loophole to escape from the discussion of disagreeable questions', although he admitted it could also be seen as 'the revenge of the bored upon the bores'. He had disliked Gladstone's 1881 measure, but once in Government he resorted to it to foreshorten the debate on the Queen's Speech in February 1887.

Writing to Hicks Beach on 28th February, criticising the arguments of the Irish Under-Secretary, General Sir Redvers Buller, against prosecuting a seditious printer, Salisbury said that he agreed 'that you cannot govern the Irish, or anybody else, by severity alone: but I think he is fundamentally wrong in believing that conciliation and severity must go together. The severity must come first. They must "take a licking" before conciliation would do them any good.' When Hicks Beach developed serious cataracts on his eyes and his doctors ordered him to retire before he went blind, Salisbury decided to take a risk in filling the vacant post of Chief Secretary. It was ironic that, when Rowland Winn had consulted Parnell and Power in June 1885, they had mentioned Arthur Balfour as one of the five men they would like to see appointed to the post.[1] For although Balfour seemed soulful and other-worldly – in 1879 he had published a book entitled *A Defence of Philosophic Doubt* – he actually turned out to be the toughest, most intractable Irish proconsul of modern times.

With Churchill, Carnarvon and Hicks Beach out of the way, Balfour was to be the vehicle through which Salisbury pacified Ireland after his own fashion. He carefully won the agreement of Smith, Goschen and Cranbrook before approaching Balfour, so as to be better placed to repel the inevitable charges of nepotism. This was a serious concern; in December 1883, Salisbury had persuaded Balfour to change his seat from Hertford, which was thought to be in his influence, to East Manchester, as he thought it detracted from his nephew's credibility to be thought of as 'my double'.

'We have killed Forster, blinded Hicks Beach and smashed up Trevelyan,' one Irish MP said of the appointment of the new Chief Secretary; 'what shall we not do with this weakling?' But Balfour recognised his opportunity to stake a claim as Salisbury's heir apparent if he was successful in Ireland, and accordingly mastered his brief and faithfully carried out his uncle's hardline policy. Nicknamed 'Pretty Fanny' at Cambridge and 'Clara' and 'Tiger Lily' later on, it was not long before the Irish had obligingly rechristened him 'Bloody Balfour'. 'I shall be as relentless as Cromwell in enforcing obedience to the law,' he declared, 'but at the same time I shall be as radical as any reformer in redressing grievances and especially in removing every cause for complaint in regard to the land.' Salisbury saw it as his role to advise and encourage Balfour, and to warn him when he was not going far enough in his uncompromising policy. Balfour's father, James Maitland Balfour, a very rich Tory MP, had died when his son was seven years old, and Salisbury, who was seventeen years older, acted very much as his surrogate father. 'Arthur's manner with Uncle Robert', recalled his sister-in-law, was 'so intimate, and yet almost tenderly deferential'.[2]

There was nothing tender about his governance of Ireland. Balfour's languid manner helped him in the first few difficult weeks when he had to convince the Commons that there was more to him than just a lucky nephew. When an Irish member shook his fist a few inches from Balfour's nose during one debate, the Chief Secretary 'regarded the frantic figure with no more and no less than the interest of a biologist examining through a microscope the contortions of a rare and provoked insect. There was in fact no way of getting at him.' This attribute proved invaluable as he ruthlessly pursued a policy which is summed up by one of his quips: 'There are those who talk as if Irishmen were justified in disobeying the law because the law comes to them in foreign garb. I see no reason why any local colour should be given to the Ten Commandments.'

Knowing relatively little about the Irish question at the start, Balfour worked hard at the beginning of his Secretaryship. For the first three months, Ashbourne helped him over the legal technicalities of the tough new Crimes Bill he intended to pass, closely watched over by Salisbury.[3] 'Surprise was universal,' Ashbourne recalled of the initial reaction to Balfour's appointment, 'hesitation common, dismay not uncommon, in the feelings then expressed by the then members of the Cabinet.' These feelings were shared by George Hamilton, Smith and Ashbourne himself. Balfour soon showed himself 'full of courage, energy and resource', however, to the delight of many hitherto sceptical Tories.

The day before Balfour's appointment was announced in early March, Salisbury delivered a speech at the inauguration of the National

Conservative Club, in which he likened the Irish problem to a night-mare 'where a danger or a horror presses upon you which you feel you ought to be able to dissipate but something fetters your limbs and para-lyzes your energies'. As a result, 'Our national fault is that too much softness has crept into our counsels.' Ireland, he said, could no longer be governed by 'platitudes and rosewater'. Balfour assured the Irish Viceroy, the 6th Marquess of Londonderry, that he would be consulted on all measures, but this rarely happened and on occasion Londonderry only discovered policy initiatives from the Irish newspapers.[4] Their relative positions had thus hardly changed since, twenty-two years earlier, Londonderry had been Balfour's fag at school. Just as foreign policy was decided largely from Hatfield, so Irish policy also now swung on an exclusively Cecilian axis.

Balfour introduced his Crimes Bill, formally known as the Criminal Law Amendment (Ireland) Bill, in a three-hour speech on 28th March 1887. All the ideas contained in it had been readily agreed by the Cabinet a fortnight earlier, and despite concerted opposition from Irish Nationalist MPs they were also recognised as necessary by the Conservatives and Liberal Unionists, although some amendments were forced upon the Government by the latter. Balfour's choice of a new Parliamentary Under-Secretary, Colonel Edward King-Harman, was almost a calculated affront to the Nationalists, who loathed the rich Irish landowner. The actual provisions of the Bill, which were forced through in night after night of often violent debate, obstruction and eventual clôture, were far harder for the Nationalists to stomach.

The Bill had six sections. It allowed magistrates to make preliminary examinations in private and under oath; it made boycotting, intimida-tion and resistance to eviction illegal, as well as conspiring and inciting to commit them; it allowed trials to be moved by the Attorney-General from where the alleged crime was committed to a less agitated place; it allowed the Viceroy to proclaim which part of the country the Act was to be in force; furthermore, he could simply declare any organisation illegal by special proclamation. Six months' hard labour was the maximum sentence, with the right of appeal. Nor was the Bill to be an annual measure, as with earlier emergency coercion legislation. This was to be a permanent feature of the Irish criminal law until such time as the Government chose to repeal it. Salisbury had wanted even tougher provisions in order to secure convictions 'in those parts of the county where outrage is beating the police'. He preferred either to institute courts-martial or to let a simple majority of the jury bring in verdicts, or, using an act of Henry VIII's reign for his precedent, to change the trial venues from Ireland to London. It was not quite internment, martial law or the suspension of *habeas corpus*, but it was the next best thing.

On 18th April, the day the Bill was to be given its second reading, *The*

Times published the most sensational of its 'Parnellism and Crime' series of articles, which had begun appearing on the day Balfour's appointment had been announced. This featured a facsimile of a letter the newspaper had bought for £1,780, purporting to be from 'Yours very truly, Charles S. Parnell' and written to Patrick Egan, a Fenian bomber. It said, amongst other things: 'Though I regret the accident of Lord F Cavendish's death I cannot refuse to admit that Burke got no more than his deserts.' (Thomas Burke was the Under-Secretary who had been assassinated with Cavendish in 1882.) Although Parnell denounced the letter in Parliament as 'a villainous and barefaced forgery' that same afternoon, the Government refused his initial request for a Commons Select Committee to investigate. Salisbury soon afterwards alleged in a speech that a 'gentleman who intimately knew Mr Parnell murdered Mr Burke', and concluded that Gladstone 'accepts in political brotherhood men upon whom the presumption of conniving at assassination rests'.

Salisbury was too much of a realist to believe that the letters were genuine, as some have alleged, simply because he wished they were.[5] It suited his overall strategy for Ireland whether they were real or not. He was happy to pass on the various rumours about Parnell to the Queen, and to afford *The Times* all the help he could to fight Parnell's libel action. He was ready to set up a Special Commission, on his own terms, to investigate the whole subject. This was not necessarily because he thought the letters were genuine, so much as because he realised that the lessons the British public would learn from a full investigation into the nature of Irish Nationalist politics could only work in the long-term political advantage of Unionism. Those who have condemned Salisbury for gullibility over the Parnell–*Times* controversy have missed the far subtler game he was playing, and the huge political capital he believed could be gleaned from it.

In May, Salisbury described the continual Irish opposition to every clause of Balfour's Bill as 'the dreary drip of dilatory declamation', and he told Abercorn that whatever happened, 'we are passing a Crimes Bill which will practically disarm the tenant'. Complaining that the Liberal Unionists were 'more apt at criticism than suggestion', Salisbury fought hard for every possible protection from the 'intolerable danger to which loyal jurymen are exposed'. Yet he was also keen to prevent 'harsh or unreasonable' evictions, as he told Abercorn and Balfour, knowing that some landlords were charging impossible rents to get rid of unwanted tenants.[6]

At 10 a.m. on Friday, 17th June 1887, after MPs had spent thirty-five days discussing the Bill, the guillotine fell on it, after a week's notice. The Government had a majority of 101 on the second reading, and the measure went into its committee stage. The clôture also had to be applied in July for the third reading. That month also saw the introduction of a further Irish Land Act, the provisions of which were expanded against Salisbury's wishes. It extended Gladstone's 1881 Act to over one hundred thousand leaseholders, and allowed revision of judicially fixed 'fair' rents. Chamberlain, Churchill and the Ulster Unionists, as well as many of Hartington's followers, had all demanded concessions as the price of their support. Salisbury thought them to be an unwarranted interference in what one Irish peer had called 'solemn covenants entered into by men perfectly competent to make agreements'. Although he disliked it intensely, however, and the Cabinet 'submitted rather than approved', Salisbury accepted the demands of his allies. 'It is the price we have to pay for the Union,' he explained to a Party meeting at the Carlton Club, 'and it is a heavy one.'[7] However grudgingly and hesitantly, Salisbury nonetheless paid it in full, the first experience of the many compromises he would have to make with allies in order to protect his majority.

Armed with what the nationalists sarcastically nicknamed his 'Jubilee Coercion Act', Balfour moved swiftly against the National League, which was banned under section 6 of the Act, on Friday, 19th August.[8] 'The hot weather has been too much for all of us,' Salisbury wrote to Richmond after thirteen weeks of temperatures of up to ninety-one degrees finally broke into thunderstorms. 'I wonder when these fiendish Irishmen will let me go!' Before they did, they subjected the Government to a daunting test, when on 9th September a mob of between five and eight thousand rioters attacked the policemen who were attempting to arrest William O'Brien MP in the market town of Mitchelstown in County Cork.

The crowd, incited by John Dillon, attacked the police in their barracks and threatened to burn it down. The massively-outnumbered constables opened fire, killing one man and mortally wounding two others. Balfour went on to the offensive afterwards, refusing to apologise for the killings and laying the blame squarely on the mob and its leaders. 'It was Mitchelstown that made us certain we had a man at last,' Edward Carson, the thirty-three-year-old counsel for the Irish Attorney-General, later recalled about Balfour's uncompromising stance. He was effectively the British Government's chief prosecutor and had been in Mitchelstown that day. Balfour admired Carson's bravery, a feeling which was fully reciprocated.

Writing from Royat in the South of France as Parliament's very long session, which had included a record number of midnight sittings, was finally prorogued, Salisbury told Balfour that he had 'enormously added to your reputation and influence'. To his son-in-law, Lord Wolmer, who had married Maud in 1883, he commented favourably on Balfour and 'how rapidly he has grown'. It looked as if his nepotistic gamble had paid off.[9] When in October 1887 the Mitchelstown coroner's report went against Balfour, stating that the police had in fact been in the wrong, Salisbury's response was simply to suggest legislation to reform the procedures for appointing coroners. With conditions he thought to be close to insurrection, the rights and wrongs of individual situations were only secondary considerations. Salisbury's personal views on Irish law and order had hardly altered since his *Saturday Review* days, when he had written that 'a more arbitrary Government, that was not squeamish about forms of law, or particular about hanging the wrong man occasionally, might very possibly succeed in weaning the Irish peasantry from their inveterate affection for the blunderbuss'. He saw it as a question of will, and he was determined that the Government should be seen to prevail over 'Captain Moonlight', Parnell, the 'Invincibles', the League and the secret societies.

Salisbury approved Balfour's changes in the personnel at Dublin Castle, effected after the Chief Secretary returned from a golfing holiday in early October. Balfour later reminisced how when he went out to Dublin he found the entire administration there demoralised, with 'no one daring to do their duty for fear they should be disowned and thrown over'. He excused Carson from this general obloquy, admiring the relish with which he carried out his many prosecutions, once even gaoling the Lord Mayor of Dublin. Peter O'Brien, known as 'Peter the Packer' for his distinctive way of choosing juries, was appointed as the new Irish Attorney-General. Sir Redvers Buller, whom Salisbury thought 'had reached that pitch of eminence at which men become imbecile', was sent back to the War Office, to be replaced as Under-Secretary by the tough, former Afghan Frontier Commissioner, Sir Joseph West Ridgeway. After his Castle purge, Balfour was ready to take on the forces of nationalism.

On 18th October, Gladstone declared to a large public meeting: 'I have said, and say again, "Remember Mitchelstown!"' This was precisely the stance Salisbury hoped his opponent would adopt. For all the mitigating circumstances of the case, Gladstone seemed to be apologising for the actions of the Irish mob.[10] On a visit to Oxford later that year, the town was placarded with three-foot-high black-bordered posters announcing: 'Lord Salisbury is coming. Remember Mitchelstown!' Salisbury was happy that people should, and if possible until the next general election. He appreciated how little the average Briton sympathised with violent Irish nationalism, and how much of a vote-winner his Irish policy might therefore become. 'I was delighted to see you had run Wilfrid Blunt in,' Salisbury congratulated Balfour after the poet and diarist had been arrested for defying the Crimes Act. 'The great heart of the people always chuckles when a gentleman gets into the clutches of the law.' Salisbury could see only one 'unfavourable symptom' of the otherwise favourable situation, the fact 'that Randolph is supporting us so zealously'.

A speech by Justin M'Carthy in Hull on 13th December, repeating the old allegations that bargains had been struck in June 1885 to bring down Gladstone in return for Home Rule, embarrassed but did not endanger Salisbury. 'I entreat you to give the lie', he asked a huge audience in Liverpool in mid-January 1888, 'to those who say there can be no consistency of purpose, no tenacity of resolution, in a democratic Government.' It was, of course, precisely what he himself had often said about that form of government in 1867 and afterwards, but when speaking on the stump Salisbury did not always consider himself to be absolutely on oath. He did consider it an important part of his duty to keep his nephew up to the mark. 'Do not avow a change of policy', he told Balfour on Christmas Eve, 'even to your pillow: for pillows chatter in Ireland.'

Early 1888 saw Salisbury's and Balfour's Irish policy prosper. Gladstone urged the electors of Deptford to vote for Wilfrid Blunt, despite the fact that he was in prison, but the Tory candidate won by 4,345 to 4,070 on 29th February. The Queen approved Salisbury's award of the Garter to Lord Londonderry, 'as it gave her an opportunity of expressing her strong approval' of his Government's policy in Ireland. The sentences of several Irish MPs were confirmed on appeal in April. That same month, after much work behind the scenes by Salisbury, Pope Leo XIII issued a Rescript condemning both boycotting and the Plan of Campaign. Salisbury told Dufferin that the Pontiff was 'to be looked upon in the light of a big gun, to be kept in good order and turned the right way'. A good harvest and significant reductions in the crime statistics led to Balfour being able to 'de-proclaim' various areas of Ireland as the year progressed.[11]

Balfour might have been 'Bloody', but he was proving extremely effective. This was obliquely acknowledged by the Fenians themselves when a plot to assassinate him was uncovered in America. Asked to hold Balfour's jacket during a tennis match at Hatfield, Cranborne's new wife, Alice, found a loaded revolver in his pocket. (It probably posed more of a danger to its never very practical owner than to any potential assassin.) In January 1889, the Home Secretary warned Salisbury that he had received intelligence that he 'might be an object of attention by Irish American extremists even more than Balfour'. The previous Sunday, a council meeting of the New York Fenian Brotherhood had resolved to assassinate him, but by October the threat was thought to be be over, and his extra protection at Hatfield was withdrawn. His plain-clothes detective for many years, John Sweeney, later wrote that he could quite believe that Salisbury did not know he was being protected, 'so absolute was his seeming aloofness from matters sublunary'.

At one point in December 1888, Balfour was prosecuting no fewer than eleven MPs. 'Everyone here is in high spirits,' he reported to

Salisbury. 'Rents are paid better here than they have been for <u>years</u>.' The following month, however, resistance to evictions grew more serious, with police regularly being injured by stone-throwing mobs and by the defenders of elaborately fortified houses. Salisbury suggested setting fire to them, which would be 'not so lamentable as leaving the Police to be mutilated.... Cannot more be done by way of surprise?' Refusing to extend County Councils to Ireland, Salisbury ruled out promoting any further self-government there until complete peace had returned. 'To ask the British nation in its present moral and political condition', he told Canon MacColl in April 1889, 'to execute such a transformation would be like asking the rector's cob to win the Derby. The forces are not there.'[12]

In mid-July 1889, the Parnellite MP William O'Brien brought a slander case against Salisbury for remarks he had made in a speech at Watford the previous March. In it, Salisbury, himself commenting on a speech O'Brien had made in Tipperary about the 'land-grabbers' who bought evictees' land, had said that O'Brien had recommended that they 'should be murdered, robbed, their cattle shot and ill-treated, their farms devastated'. O'Brien chose the case to be heard in the Radical stronghold of Manchester and claimed £10,000 damages.

Although Salisbury's solicitor advised that he should attempt to avoid defending the case, he made it perfectly clear to his barrister, Sir Edward Clarke QC, the Solicitor-General, that he wanted 'the question of truth or untruth fought out, no question of privilege being raised'. With Salisbury's son Robert acting as Clarke's junior, the case was heard over three days in Manchester's Civil Court, with witness after witness describing the murders and boycottings that had been committed in Tipperary after the date of O'Brien's speech. Clarke dropped the last sixteen of his witnesses after O'Brien's barrister, William Gully QC – later a Liberal Speaker of the Commons – accepted that outrages against the carpet-baggers had indeed been commonplace. The jury were out for only six minutes before returning and finding for Salisbury, who had remained in London throughout the trial. Leave to appeal was refused. 'If Lord Salisbury's account of the [O'Brien] speech was not absolutely correct in every particular', opined the (by now thoroughly anti-nationalist) *Times*, 'it was a legitimate criticism upon the general effect of such speeches.'

The papers relating to secret service activity during Balfour's term of office as Chief Secretary were originally classified under the Hundred-Year Rule, but have recently been re-classified to keep them secret in perpetuity, so even today we cannot know the undercover methods that were employed by him to combat the Fenian threat. The secret service's Bank of Ireland chequebook is available for public inspection, however, and its stubs show that by 1889 Balfour was spending twice as much as Smith, Hart Dyke, Morley and Hicks Beach had done. The widow of an informer might receive £50, the 'emigration of a witness' could cost the same, £150 would be 'sent to U.S.', presumably for undercover information about Fenian activity there.

For general correspondence the codebook is also extant; the Attorney-General was 'Maud', 'Bohemia' meant 'I have persuaded X to act with us', 'Waterloo' denoted that 'the writer had had an interview with Y, who hesitated', and 'Myrtle' meant 'I quite concur with the course you propose to adopt.' A detailed, thirty-two-page document drawn up for the Cabinet by Sir E.G. Jenkinson, the Assistant Under-Secretary for Police and Crime at Dublin Castle, was circulated in April 1889 detailing the exact inner workings of both the Irish Republican Brotherhood in Great Britain and the United Brotherhood in America, which had both been deeply penetrated by British Intelligence.[13]

Salisbury had noticed in his nephew a rare attribute which he himself possessed – 'his perfect indifference to what is said of him. Not only does he not give way to abuse, it does not even drive him in the opposite direction, which is rarer.' The stage at last came when conciliation could be appended to coercion. The nationalists had 'taken a licking', and now it was time for generosity. The voluntary land purchase scheme was augmented by £5 million, and Bills for irrigation and a light railway were introduced. Grants were also made for technical training and industrial development by the Congested Districts Board. Dillon was even released two months early, but only because he was ill, for as Salisbury sagely pointed out: 'He would have been far more formidable dead than alive, and it did not do to run the risk.'[14] In 1891, a further £33 million was made available to guarantee tenants' loans.

By late October 1889, Balfour was ready to 'unproclaim the greater part of Ireland', and Salisbury thought the 'least splashy' date on which to do it would be 1st January 1890. Crime was lower than at any point in the previous decade. In May 1890, Salisbury wrote to one of his backbenchers, Colonel Waring, that the intention behind Balfour's Land Act was 'not that it will fill the country with peasant proprietors, but that it will establish them in greater or lesser numbers in the various parts of

the country, scattered all over it, so that the present uniformity of
condition and feeling which enables agitators to turn the whole political and social force of the occupiers against the landlords will be
arrested and broken'. The idea was to create 'islands and backwaters of
honest feeling'.

Salisbury rarely passed up an opportunity to mock English sympathis-
ers of Irish nationalism. Lady Butler, whose paintings *Scotland Forever!*
of the charge of the Scots Greys at Waterloo and *Balaklava* of the roll-
call after the charge of the Light Brigade had so moved Victorian
exhibition visitors, had emigrated to the Wicklow Mountains in 1888.
When her painting *An Eviction in Ireland*, complete with departing
dragoons and grieving peasant women, was exhibited at the Royal
Academy in 1889, Salisbury was, she complained, 'pleased to be facetious about it in his speech at the Banquet, remarking on the "breezy
beauty" of the landscape, which almost made him wish he could take
part in an eviction himself'.[15]

Was it legitimate political calculation, or outrageous cynicism, or, as
Winston Churchill believed, naïve foolishness that led Salisbury to act
in the way he did over the Special Commission which investigated the
allegations made by *The Times* connecting Parnell and others of his
party with terrorism? It was Salisbury who, encouraged by Chamberlain
but few others, drove forward the movement to institute the Special
Commission in the first place. With three carefully selected judges
reporting to Parliament, this was neither a parliamentary Select
Committee nor a court of law. In effect, it was a state conspiracy trial
without a jury. Parnell, in one of those paradoxes which seem to be the
rule rather than the exception in Irish politics, was a Protestant and a
landowner, and thus a class and creed traitor in Salisbury's eyes,
notwithstanding his Anglophobic American mother. To bring down
such an eloquent enemy of England would constitute a great triumph
for Unionism, but it was by no means the only game Salisbury was
playing with the Special Commission.

Salisbury's intention was to connect in the mind of the British public
the indelible idea that if not necessarily Parnell himself, then those
around him, especially other Irish MPs, condoned and even incited
outrages, including murder. To tar the Parnellite party with the suspicion of criminality, even at one step removed, would be well worth
the embarrassment if it turned out that in the specific Parnell–Egan case
The Times had bought and published forgeries. It was crucial, therefore,
that the Commission's inquiries should range freely over the whole
question of Irish crime, and not be restricted to the specific issue of

whether the ten letters in *The Times'* possession were genuine or not. Although at different points almost everyone, including Balfour, faltered at what was admittedly a risky and ruthless enterprise, Salisbury saw the operation through to its conclusion, increasing his regard for his new ally Joseph Chamberlain in the process.

'It was resolved that the inquiry should be in no sense restricted,' Salisbury reported to the Queen after a Cabinet meeting on 23rd July 1888, 'but should be as large as possible, so as to bring out the circumstances of the conspiracy in their fullest scope.' Although a majority of the Cabinet did not want to proceed with a Bill to set up the body if it was strongly opposed by the Irish and the Opposition, Salisbury managed to steamroller the matter through, clôture having eventually to be used to set up the Special Commission. 'Lord Salisbury's own view', he told the Queen, 'was that the matter had now gone too far... and that the questions raised must now be investigated and solved.' The only other person who stuck by Salisbury throughout his persecution of Parnell, besides Chamberlain, was the Queen herself, who remembered how Irish nationalists had boycotted Prince Albert's funeral and then blown up his Dublin statue.[16]

When asked by Balfour what support the Government ought to give to *The Times*, Salisbury replied in August that if secret service evidence 'has come naturally into our hands – and still more it clearly fixes some one's guilt, we shall be fulfilling an obvious and elementary duty in facilitating the proof of it before the Commission'. *The Times* was already regularly sent important announcements at the same time as they were forwarded to Parliament, in order for it to beat the Press Association and Central News Agency wire services, but now the Government actually allowed the paper's solicitor privileged access to the secret files held in Dublin Castle on Irish MPs and others. Balfour, Smith, Cranbrook, Hartington and several others wished the Government to stay as aloof as possible from the Commission's proceedings. It was Salisbury who gave all assistance to *The Times* in order to broaden the inquiry out into a general investigation. It was also he who virtually forced the Attorney-General, Sir Richard Webster, to appear as leading counsel for *The Times*, a blatant connection of the paper's stance with that of the Government, and one which incidentally made *The Times* a supporter of Salisbury's for the rest of his career.

Webster had already appeared for *The Times* in a case in July, when a former Irish Nationalist MP, R.H. O'Donnell, had unsuccessfully sued for libel. In a stiff letter in mid-September, Salisbury pointed out that if he refused to do so again, 'the world would conclude that you retire from some motive which was not in existence last July: and which, therefore, presumably – they will think – is the discovery of a fatal flaw in *The Times'* case'. Of the question of whether 'the Government entertains undue and partisan sympathy' with *The Times*, Salisbury wrote: 'But why should we shrink from being thought to wish, or to strive to bring this guilt home <u>if it exists</u>? ... I see no reproach in the idea that we desire to bring home guilt to Parnell if he is guilty.' Salisbury did not know for sure whether Parnell was guilty or not, but he knew the investigation into Parnell's party could only result in bad publicity for it.

Sir Henry James, who was similarly backsliding, was also persuaded against his better judgment to appear against Parnell. Salisbury feared that otherwise the Irish witnesses, seeing the Government back away, would 'be convinced that P's is the winning card and they will forswear themselves like men'. By 20th September, Salisbury wrote to Balfour: 'I surmise you heard from Smith of Webster's attempt to get out of his collar. We have kept the harness tight on him – but I am afraid he shows signs of gibbing still.' In the end, both Webster and James took on the case, albeit with extreme reluctance.[17] The judges sat for 128 days in public between September 1888 and November 1889, wading through what the Liberals complained had turned into 'the bloody puddle' of murders and outrages before getting on to the specific forgery issue. MPs were examined on speeches and actions of ten years previously, and the Royal Irish Constabulary gave evidence as the case was pushed further and further away from the original forgery issue. *The Times* subpoenaed government papers which purported to link, however tangentially, Parnellite MPs with dozens of grisly murders and atrocities.

A shocked Victorian public heard, and through the agency of the illustrated papers such as *The Graphic* also saw, witnesses such as 'David Freely, farmer, and member of the Land League. After he had paid his rent, Moonlighters called for the "___ rent-payer". His son was pulled out of the house and shot dead.' A Crimean War veteran was kneecapped by Moonlighters, 'for the crime of paying his rent'. The Commission heard from a beautiful woman whose father was murdered at Lixnaw and from the deaf Jeremiah Buckley who had his ear cut off after he paid his rent. (Q: 'What sort of scissors did they use?' A: 'I don't think they were good ones.') This sort of evidence continued for weeks. The propaganda potential for Unionism was enormous and was milked mightily, and in the opinion of a recent Irish historian, the whole process 'succeeded in connecting Irish nationalism with crime in the mind of Middle England', thus justifying Balfour's coercion policy, especially against the National League, which was made to look like little more than a criminal conspiracy.

By December 1888, Sir Joseph West Ridgeway had discovered that *The Times* had bought the ten letters from none other than Richard Pigott, a notorious blackmailer, pornographer and sworn enemy of Parnell. Not only was he the forger, but he was so illiterate a forger that when on Friday, 22nd February 1889, Parnell's leading counsel, Sir Charles Russell QC, asked how to spell 'hesitancy', one of the words misspelt in the letters, Pigott said it was with an 'e' in place of the 'a'. After further incisive cross-examination, his testimony was left in ribbons. Salisbury prepared the Queen for bad news, telling her that the forger was 'evidently a thorough rogue'. Yet few could have predicted that Pigott would confess all to Labouchere and then flee the country before the cross-examination ended, promptly to shoot himself in the Hôtel des Ambassadeurs in Madrid.

The sensational collapse of the Pigott part of the inquiry – Parnell won a standing, cheering ovation from the Opposition in the House of Commons, the Freedom of the City of Edinburgh and even an invitation to Hawarden Castle – undoubtedly damaged the Government in the short term. When the talented young Liberal barrister and MP Herbert Henry Asquith, another of Parnell's barristers, subsequently mauled the integrity of *The Times'* manager, James Cameron MacDonald – 'the uncanny Scot' – Parnell's victory seemed complete.

West Ridgeway could not understand the panic that gripped Dublin Castle: 'All along we have anticipated a collapse of this part of the case with equanimity,' he wrote to Balfour. Moreover, the Commission continued to sit until November 1889, and in the intervening nine months Parnell made some damaging admissions. Salisbury was delighted when Parnell said, for example, that when in January 1881 he had told the Commons that secret conspiracies no longer existed in Ireland, 'it is possible I was endeavouring to mislead the House on that occasion.... In order to cut the ground from under the argument of the Government in support of the [Coercion] Bill.'[18]

On 3rd February 1890, *The Times* paid Parnell £5,000 in libel damages, far less than the £100,000 claimed, but hugely expensive nonetheless once legal costs were added. In all the Commission cost the newspaper over £200,000, plunging it into deficit for the first time in its history. George Buckle offered to resign, but the proprietor John Walter III refused to contemplate it. Salisbury wanted to help the paper financially, but sensibly told Smith that 'I have seen and heard nothing to make me think that the House of Commons would accept such a proposal.'

When the Commission finally submitted its Report to Parliament later that month, Salisbury found several positive avenues to follow amongst its no fewer than thirty-five volumes. Lunching at Arlington Street on 14th February, Balfour's sister Lady Rayleigh 'found Lord Salisbury's unmarried sons & daughter wild with excitement over the Report, quoting choice passages and imagining leaflets put together from it to convince the country'. Balfour was also pleased with it, on the grounds that 'in future it will be what three judges say against what Mr

Parnell says'. Rudyard Kipling summed up the popular view of the Report in his poem *Cleared*:

> If black is black or white is white, in black and white it's down,
> You're only traitors to the Queen and rebels to the Crown.
> If print is print or words are words, the learned court perpends,
> We are not ruled by murderers, but only – by their friends.

The Report attested that no fewer than seven named Irish MPs had taken part in activities which 'led to crime and outrage and persisted in it with knowledge of its effect'. Although the words 'not proven' and 'not established' appeared in many parts of the Report, so did 'criminal conspiracy' and 'encouragement of intimidation' in others. With something in it for everyone, therefore, Salisbury went on to the offensive in the House of Lords debate on 21st March 1890, speaking on the resolution to thank the Commissioners and adopt their Report. He claimed that, with regard to the Pigott letters, he had 'never attached that importance to them which it was convenient for noble Lords opposite and members of the Opposition in the other House to attach to them'. Of the Parnellite party, however, he quoted a phrase from the Ulster Tory MP Colonel Edward Saunderson, saying: 'they had their hand upon the throttle-valve of crime. When they allowed crime to go forward, it acted; when they suppressed it, it retreated; and we are unable to admit that no alliance of a tacit character existed between bodies connected by such phenomena as these.'

It was an ill-tempered debate, with Kimberley and Spencer claiming that the Commission had been political rather than judicial, Derby and Rosebery accusing Salisbury of having few Tory supporters, and other Liberals complaining that no actual apology had been made to Parnell himself. Faced with this last accusation, the imp in Salisbury that a quarter of a century earlier had made the notorious 'attorneys' quip, reappeared with yet anothing 'blazing indiscretion': 'Because one nationalist has forged the signature of the nationalist leader – that is no proof that the leader possesses every statesmanlike quality and virtue.' Salisbury had a long record of making disparaging remarks about Parnell. In October 1877 he had called him a 'great fact. You can no more shut your eyes to [him] than you can to the potato disease or the Colorado beetle.'[19] Yet to mention the vindicated hero in the same breath as a disgraced suicide was generally considered entirely unacceptable. Weeks later the Government lost a by-election in the Caernarvon Boroughs, one of a series through the summer and autumn, when a pro-Home Rule Liberal called David Lloyd George was returned. The new MP proceeded to augment his reputation as an orator with swingeing, highly personalised attacks on Salisbury.

Had the Commission known what emerged forty years after its

Report – that Parnell had taken the Irish Republican Brotherhood oath in, of all places, the library of Trinity College, Dublin, only days after being released from Kilmainham in May 1882 – Salisbury would have been almost entirely vindicated. Although there is, of course, no direct contemporary evidence for this having taken place, the circumstantial and oral evidence is good and it is credited by several distinguished Irish historians.[20] As it was, Parnell's prestige and influence were destroyed only months after his great triumph when in mid-November 1890 the news broke that he would not be contesting his citation as a co-respondent in the divorce case brought by a former Irish Nationalist MP, Captain William O'Shea, against his wife Kitty.

In Committee Room Nineteen of the House of Commons, the Irish Nationalist party tore itself apart over Parnell's future. Salisbury thought that Gladstone made a signal error in 'giving in to the nonconformist conscience' and encouraging Parnell to resign. Gladstone had known perfectly well the nature of Parnell's relationship with Kitty O'Shea, who had regularly acted as a political go-between. Despite his distaste at sitting in judgment on moral issues, his support for Dilke staying in the Privy Council being another case in point, Salisbury could not resist making a risqué joke in the House of Lords when on 25th November he mentioned fire-escapes in the debate on the Queen's Speech, after the divorce court had heard the means sometimes used by Parnell to leave his lover's bedroom. The *Annual Register* for 1890 recorded that 'the House of Lords was greatly amused but somewhat astonished' at Lord Salisbury's uncharacteristically crude sally. Parnell himself kept his dignity, and was so cold and aloof at one meeting of Irish MPs in late November that one of them remarked afterwards that 'He treated us as if *we* had all committed adultery with *his* wife.'[21]

Writing to Hartington on 2nd December, Salisbury agreed 'that our business is to sit still while Parnell is being devoured by the wolves. I am very sorry I have got to speak tomorrow. All I can do is to improve the occasion by pointing out what a nice Home Rule Parliament the aforesaid animals would make.' Speaking to a crowd of 8,000 in Hartington's constituency of Rossendale, Salisbury mocked the Irish party for attempting to appear as 'the apostles of domestic piety' while still supporting boycotting and violence. For what he called 'purely sentimental' reasons, but which probably also included the calculation that he did not want the wolves to unite, Salisbury did not attack Parnell himself: 'I care not whether Mr Parnell wins in this conflict or whether he is cast down. It may be a weakness in human nature, but perhaps I prefer the man who is fighting desperately for his life to the crew whom he made and who are turning against him.' Victorian family values could not be entirely ignored, however, and Salisbury dutifully intoned that the scandal 'has brought out an uprising in favour of domestic purity which we must all regard with the deepest satisfaction'.

As the New Year of 1891 beckoned, Salisbury could survey the political landscape with the deepest satisfaction. The disorderly scenes in Committee Room Nineteen had finally ended on 6th December when Justin M'Carthy led forty-five MPs out, leaving only twenty-seven staying behind with Parnell.[22] Obstruction was lifted, and in 1891 Balfour's Irish Land Bill reached its second reading in only a fortnight. Conservatives began to win by-elections again, and by 29th July Salisbury could announce to a banquet at the Mansion House that he had never known Ireland so peaceful. As if in echo, the following day Dillon and O'Brien were released from Galway Gaol and immediately declared their opposition to Parnell, thus encouraging yet further internecine splits. The 1,000 cases of agrarian outrage in 1886 had been halved in number by 1889. The 5,000 cases of boycotting in 1887 had fallen to almost negligible levels by January 1891. For all Gladstone's boasts of his mission to pacify Ireland, it was Balfour and Salisbury who actually achieved it, at least in the medium term.

TWENTY-EIGHT

'The Genie of Imperialism'

The Golden Jubilee – The Colonial Conference
– Great Power Diplomacy –
'Bloody Sunday' – Tithes –
Allotments – Fiscal Retaliation

May 1887 to January 1888

'Some people seem to think that no negotiation is worth having
unless the other side is very sore.'

On Tuesday, 17th May 1887, Lord Cranborne married Lady Alice Gore, the second daughter of the 5th Earl of Arran, at St Margaret's, Westminster. Schomberg McDonnell, the 5th Earl of Antrim's fifth son, who was nicknamed 'Pom', was best man. The Prince and Princess of Wales and their three daughters were present, as were the Crown Prince of Denmark, Princess Christian of Schleswig-Holstein, Princess Mary Adelaide, the Duchess of Teck, the French Pretender the Comte and Comtesse de Paris and their daughter Princess Hélène d'Orléans. Lords Lytton, Rowton, Selborne, Airlie, Cowper, Clarendon, Yarborough, Headfort, Waldegrave, Stanhope, Kenmore, Calloway, Burgley, Egerton and Alcester were there, and even Lord and Lady Derby attended. Most of the Government were present, along with the Corps Diplomatique, except Waddington, who as the representative of La République could hardly rub shoulders with the Comte de Paris. According to *The Times*, Salisbury 'was heartily cheered by the concourse collected in Parliament Square'. (He set little store by popular applause, believing crowds to be intensely fickle and just as likely to boo him later.) 'The service was very beautiful,' Salisbury reported to the Queen, 'and the bride bore herself throughout with admirable composure.'[1] It turned out to be a happy and successful marriage.

It was the Queen's turn to compose herself the following month when her subjects celebrated her fifty years on the Throne with the

Golden Jubilee. Salisbury took a predictably utilitarian attitude towards pageantry, finding most secular ceremonial inherently absurd. In his *Saturday Review* days, he had mocked the Opening of Parliament and thought the Lord Mayor's Day 'not worth keeping'. With the Crimes Bill, the Mediterranean Agreements, Lord Randolph Churchill, the Liberal Unionist alliance and Bulgaria all pending, Salisbury left the Jubilee arrangements to the Lord Steward of the Household, the Earl of Mount Edgcumbe, and a committee including the Lord Chamberlain the Earl of Lathom, and Edward Hamilton of the Treasury. The Government was frugal with public funds; Parliament only contributed £17,000 to the cost, forcing the Queen to stump up the remaining £50,000 herself. Goschen even cut the expenditure on the official firework display on Primrose Hill overlooking Regent's Park, out of concern for criticism by Churchill, Labouchere and the Irish. Only those visiting royalties not related to the Queen by blood, such as the Persian, Siamese and Hawaian, were accommodated at public expense.

In December 1886, Salisbury had told a disappointed Archbishop Benson that the Queen 'is desirous that the service should not be too long: and there should be no discourse or sermon: because at that time of year the weather is very likely to be hot; and in hot weather, her strength fails her almost entirely'. Salisbury insisted that the Queen include Gladstone in the festivities: 'He is so famous a man that many people would be shocked by any neglect of him, even when they differ from him.'[2] The harsh rules which forbade the innocent female party in a divorce suit from being presented at Court were relaxed, but Salisbury ensured this only applied to British subjects, 'on account of the risk of admitting American women of light character'.

The organisation of the Jubilee was unimpressive; there had been no State Visits since Tsar Alexander II's in 1874 and no one was quite sure how the celebrations would work. Mount Edgcumbe complained that Salisbury showed insufficient interest in the minutiæ, and his responsibilities overlapped with too many of Lathom's and Ponsonby's to prevent petty turf wars, in which Salisbury failed to support him. That the occasion was eventually a great success owed little to the Government's organisation and much to the Queen's popularity; many lessons were learnt for the Diamond Jubilee ten years later. One of the reasons Salisbury was unwilling to side with Mount Edgcumbe might have been that soon after the Jubilee, on 4th August 1887, his second son William ('Fish') married Lathom's daughter, Lady Florence Mary Bootle-Wilbraham. The Lord Chamberlain, who had been Conservative Chief Whip in the House of Lords between 1874 and 1885, was a splendid figure with a vast beard which parted in the middle, allowing him to tie it behind his head when shooting.

Salisbury only concerned himself with the political aspects of the

Jubilee. Honours had to be awarded, an imperial conference organised for the colonial premiers, and the central object of the festivities, nurturing the love and respect in which the people held the Queen, could not be allowed to be spoilt by Irish or left-wing disturbances. 'I feel so convinced of the universal execration with which the list of honours, whatever it may be, will be received,' Salisbury wrote to Smith on Easter Day, 'I think it will be best not to publish it till the very day of the Jubilee. Otherwise the wrath of the undecorated might imperil the Crimes Bill.' In the event, so many honours were distributed that it was said that one couldn't throw a stone at a dog in London without hitting a knight. Salisbury told Richmond that if he attended to all the requests he received, 'the Queen will have as many "knights" in her train as Edward III going to Crécy. But they will not be very soldierlike.' The republican paper *Reynolds News* complained that it was going to be a 'Happy and Toryous' Jubilee, but in fact the Liberal Unionists did proportionately better in the honours dole-out than the Conservatives.[3]

Although he respected the ancient rank of baronet, Salisbury had long thought the concept of knight bachelor to be inherently absurd. 'There is a false air of feudalism about it, which attaches to it the ridicule that belongs to all barefaced shams,' he had written when the Provost of Perth obtained one for simply being present at the unveiling of one of Prince Albert's statues. 'It is irredeemably associated in everybody's mind, especially in the minds of those who have read *Ivanhoe*, with tournaments and blazoned shields, and vizored helms, and all that sort of thing.' It was perhaps easier for the son of a marquess to mock 'the whole army of hospitable aldermen, science-and-art jobbers and court flunkeys' who received knighthoods, and he later sympathised with a Governor of Bombay who wanted a privy councillorship because he had 'a very strong repugnance to the dignity of a Knight Bachelor – which is usually reserved for aldermen and lawyers'.[4]

The 1887 Jubilee Honours were carefully distributed, as the Liberal *Daily News* complained, to emphasise the rewards that loyalty to the Unionist cause might engender. 'Shall I keep this man on his hind legs any longer?' Salisbury asked Akers-Douglas in March of the Tory MP for Londonderry, C.E. Lewis. 'I am rather inclined to offer his baronetcy to Ulster, as a kind of complimentary present from Arthur.' Writing to Hartington days before the Jubilee, at which the Liberal Unionist MP Sir John St Aubyn became Baron St Levan, Salisbury agreed 'that the fact that some have been made because they are Liberal Unionists should not be hidden under a bushel: and the mention of your name as Sir John St Aubyn's proposer will in his case sufficiently indicate that fact'.

On opening the People's Palace in the East End in May 1887, the Queen had heard something she described to Salisbury as 'a horrid noise

... (quite new to the Queen's ears) "booing" she believes it is called'. Salisbury was 'much grieved' to hear it: 'London contains a much larger number of the worst kind of rough than any other great town in the island; for all that is worthless, worn out, or penniless, naturally drifts to London.' He blamed the booing not on the undertow of republicanism that existed in some parts of London at the time, but exclusively on the socialists and Irish, 'very resentful men who would stick at nothing to show their fury'.

The Jubilee celebrations, which culminated in a service at Westminster Abbey at 3 p.m. on 21st June, were vast, sunny and successful. 'London went wild with excitement,' wrote the normally lugubrious Cranbrook. That morning, Lady Monkswell 'detected the bulky figure of Lord Salisbury in a privy councillor's uniform walking across from the Abbey'. He took no significant part in the proceedings, thinking it a constitutional solecism for politicians to intrude upon royal occasions. Lady Salisbury said she would like to hang Dean Bradley for putting up a high enclosure which screened the Queen in the Abbey.

The long troop of mounted princes from every European royal house, the Queen's scarlet-and-blue escort, the cheering of millions for hours, all took place exactly as the authorities had wished. Salisbury later had to apologise to the Queen for having missed seeing the procession in Hyde Park because of a traffic jam. He 'was in good time, but by some mismanagement he was involved in the block and entirely failed to pierce it. He saw Your Majesty pass, but could not get through.' He had that afternoon presented her with the painting she had commissioned of him by George Richmond, a mark that the celebrated portraitist was back in favour after he had declined to paint Prince Albert's corpse twenty-six years earlier. In 1861, Salisbury said of Richmond's works that they were 'pleasanter to look at than a photograph, though one may not be able to suppress the consciousness that it overflatters the grim human reality'. Lady Salisbury had presented the Queen with a gold coffer from 'The Women of England' at a reception in the White Dining Room at Buckingham Palace.[5]

Although Salisbury wrote fulsomely to the Queen congratulating her on the Jubilee – 'the gratitude of Your people was as manifest as it was manifestly sincere' – other more satirical feelings were vouchsafed to his friend Janetta Manners:

At last the Jubilee is pretty nearly over. It has been a terrible time – what with black Queens, Indian feudatories, and general royal festivities, on top of our ordinary work. Everything went off well – the only hitches were due to the limited education of the Chamberlain's office... [which] declined to recognise the Persian, Siamese and Japanese princes as anything else but blacks – and treated them accordingly. On the other hand the whole Court was never tired of lavishing honours on the Black Queen of Hawaii – who looks exactly like Lady Rosebery stained walnut. The Queen kissed her – and after that we all had to be very civil to her.

Another protocol problem was caused by a Mahratta Prince who stabbed a footman who served him beef.

∽

Sir Henry Holland, the Colonial Secretary, thought that the presence of all the colonial premiers in London for the Jubilee was a good pretext for holding a Colonial Conference. Although imperial unity had been a regular theme in Salisbury's speeches against Home Rule – 'a mischievous policy is attempting to sliver our Empire into atoms', he had told the Grocers' Company in May 1886 – he was no doctrinaire imperialist, and he hoped the Conference might dampen Jingoist ardour for any early political or economic federation of the Empire. Within a fortnight of the invitations being sent out in November 1886, Salisbury was showing his irritation with the 'monstrous' New Zealand Government for claiming parts of Samoa. As the distance between them was 1,600 miles, he told Sir Henry that Britain might as well claim a special interest over Tenerife, or Russia over the Sandwich Islands.[6] Part of the problem lay in Salisbury's disdain for colonists in general, born of his own grand tour of a third of a century earlier: 'You will understand the inward, though suppressed, exultation with which I send you a letter in which a colonist accused you of having snubbed him,' he once wrote to Holland.

At his speech to the opening of the Conference on 4th April 1887, Salisbury acknowledged that the British Empire 'yields to none, it is, perhaps superior to all in its greatness, in its extent, in the vastness of its population, in the magnificence of its wealth'. Nevertheless, he asked the delegates to remember its 'want of continuity. The Empire is separated into ... distant parts by large stretches of ocean; and what we are really here to do is to see how far we must acquiesce in the conditions which that separation causes, how far we can obliterate them by agreement and by organisation'. Any hope of an imperial customs union he described as 'distant and shadowy', and he obdurately prevented official discussion of the proposals by Queensland and the Cape for full-scale imperial federation. Derby, a former Colonial Secretary who was present at the speech, said Salisbury 'looked very ill: fagged, beat, and his face discoloured by eczema.... I hear frequent speculation on the possibility of his breaking down.' The speech itself he called 'sensible and unpretending', and better than Holland's dull, hour-long address.

Salisbury predicted that the Conference's results would be 'prosaic', and indeed the only actual benefit derived from it was an Australian agreement to pay £126,000 per annum for its own naval squadron. Salisbury prevented any further such conferences being held until the Diamond Jubilee ten years later. His major hope for it was articulated in his opening remarks – 'to form neither a general union nor a *Zollverein*, but a *Kriegsverein* – a combination for purposes of self-defence' – but after that he rarely attended the sessions. 'Of course I shall be delighted to come to the Colonial Conference meeting,' he wrote to Holland when the Australians were criticising France over the New Hebrides. 'I will do my best to keep my temper, but the outrecuidance of your Greater Britain is sometimes trying.'[7]

Although the New Hebrides islands were many hundreds of miles away, the Australians were angry about France's *de facto* annexation of them the previous year, in contravention of an Anglo-French agreement. However piratical Salisbury thought the French action, he was able to put it into a global context, whereas the Australians, he told Holland on 27th April, were:

> the most unreasonable people I have ever heard or dreamt of. They want us to incur all the bloodshed and the danger, and the stupendous cost of a war with France, of which almost the exclusive burden will fall on us, for a group of islands which are to us as valueless as the South Pole – and to which they are only attached by a debating-club sentiment.

He instructed Holland not to publish the Australian criticisms of France in the Blue Book account of the Colonial Conference proceedings. 'It has a bad effect on my liver to think how these Australian colonists put upon us,' he told Holland. When in October they complained that the French proposed to send convicts out to the New Hebrides, Salisbury asked how it would be any better for Britain instead to have them 'within twenty miles of <u>our</u> shores – in order to keep them from sullying Australian purity by living a thousand miles from <u>their</u> shores'.

Salisbury regarded minor colonial governorships as a reward to poor friends and an exile for potential trouble-makers. 'Have you any little island in any neglected corner of the world where you could put the Earl of Buckinghamshire as Governor?' he asked Holland in May 1887; 'in that sort of market Earls have their value: and he is an exemplary young man and he is absolutely and completely ruined.' (At twenty-seven, the Earl was rather young for a governorship, and instead solved his problems the following year by marrying an heiress.) Once Drummond Wolff's Egyptian travails were almost over, Salisbury hoped that Holland might find him another mission 'at a distance from his native land', thereby continuing to deny Churchill a parliamentary ally. As he put it to his Colonial Secretary, the plan 'will expand itself before your mind in all its seductive amplitude'. Drummond Wolff was offered

Hong Kong, which he 'indignantly refused', so he was appointed envoy to Persia instead, keeping him out of Britain for a further four years.

Salisbury enjoyed a close working relationship with Holland, and even recommended 'driving a hole into your room' in the Colonial Office to expedite communication between the Colonial and Foreign Offices, which he complained, 'reckoned by time, is about as long as the distance between London and Berlin'. The informal, almost bantering tone of his messages – 'If Germany takes Samoa, would your appetite be satisfied by our taking Tonga?' – was appreciated by Holland, who became a staunch supporter of Salisbury in Cabinet. 'Of course you have no other choice but to defend your black subjects,' Salisbury once wrote to him over incursions by slave-traders in West Africa. 'I wish you had fewer of them. They have a faculty for getting killed in the wrong place.'[8]

With 'Greater Britain' ever expanding in the late 1880s, taking on Bechuanaland in 1885, Burma and Nigeria in 1886, Somaliland and Zululand in 1887, Kenya and Sarawak in 1888, Rhodesia in 1889 and Zanzibar in 1890, there was little likelihood of the Crown having fewer black subjects. The expansion process was bound to throw up occasional international incidents, as near Lagos in June 1887 where France was pursuing claims on Lake Denham. Promising to look into it at once, Salisbury suspected that the Third Republic, which was going through one of its endemic bouts of political instability, was 'seeking a counter-irritant for their internal pains, and we are performing the part of the blister'. Although Bismarck remarked that 'the friendship of Lord Salisbury is worth more to me than twenty marshy colonies in Africa', he was not above occasionally flexing Germany's muscles, and in early May 1887 he criticised the British Consul Mr Holmwood's activities in Zanzibar and requested his removal. Salisbury was shocked by Bismarck's 'monstrousness', and told Count von Radowitz so, but German support for British reforms in Egypt was too valuable to be endangered and Holmwood was quietly reassigned.

On 18th June 1887, the European outlook took a lurch towards danger when Germany and Russia signed a secret 'Reinsurance Treaty', under the provisions of which Germany promised to recognise Russia's 'historical' rights in Bulgaria and observe benevolent neutrality should Russia attack Turkey. In return, Russia promised neutrality should France attack Germany, thereby relieving Bismarck of his perennial fear of a war on two fronts. It was additionally agreed that Alexander of Battenberg was not to be restored to the throne of Bulgaria. Salisbury sensed some kind of formal arrangement had been entered into and could not understand the aggressive attitude France continued to adopt.

'If there is any sense in Paris,' he wrote on 10th August to White, who had succeeded Layard as minister to the Porte in Constantinople, 'they must know they are running the risk of war,' and that such a war, 'whoever it began with', would end with France fighting Germany. The previous month he had listed to Lord Lyons the areas where France was encroaching on British interests. As well as wrecking the Drummond Wolff Convention on Egypt, the French were blocking Cromer's press laws there, had occupied the New Hebrides, were causing trouble over Newfoundland fishing rights, had planted the short-lived *tricoleur* in Dongarita and were also 'trying to elbow us out of at least two unpronounceable places on the West Coast of Africa'. France was thus generally going the right way about creating a situation in which Britain would exhibit no sympathy if she were once again smashed in a sudden war against Germany.

Anticipating the other half of the Reinsurance deal, a Russian attack on Turkey, Salisbury wrote to White saying, 'it would be a terrible blow to lose Constantinople. But have we not lost it already? With this sickly, sensual, terrified, fickle Sultan on the throne, have we really any arm with which we can meet [the Russian Ambassador at Constantinople] Nelidoff's threats of an invasion of Erzurum? And would it be worth our while to save him, for the purpose of preventing Germany having free elbows with France?' Believing the reform and regeneration of Turkey now to be 'a dream', Salisbury added that the Ottoman equilibrium was 'too strained and artificial to last very long: though it <u>may</u> last 'till it is upset by war'.[9]

The uneasy peace held, however, and when in October 1887 General Boulanger's coup attempt failed and he was imprisoned, Europe breathed again. Although Salisbury thought war the next spring not unlikely, he consoled himself that everyone had also thought the same thing the last spring. The best news, which Salisbury inferred from such acts as the Tsar's refusal to encompass Berlin on his annual visit to his in-laws in Copenhagen in September, was that the Reinsurance Treaty had fallen through only three months after it was signed, because of German withdrawal of support for Russian schemes to destabilise Prince Ferdinand in Bulgaria.

Taking advantage of the political uncertainty in Paris, Salisbury came to terms with France over the New Hebrides and elsewhere. It had to be concluded before the French Assembly met, so Salisbury, who negotiated everything alone with his old Constantinople colleague M. Chaudhory at Puys, acted without direct Cabinet authorisation. Such was his predominance in foreign policy-making after 1886, however, that he knew it would find retrospective approval, especially as he kept Goschen closely informed. When the *Standard* criticised the agreement along Jingoistic lines, Salisbury wrote to Austin to say that 'some people seem to think that no negotiation is worth having unless the other side is very sore'.

Lyons's ill-health finally forced him to relinquish the Paris Embassy in October 1887, and Salisbury's choice of replacement, Lord Lytton, surprised many in view of his insubordination over Afghanistan a decade earlier. But as Salisbury told one complainant, the Prince of Wales, 'His talents are of the highest order: and the faults with which he was charged as Governor-General are faults which as Ambassador he will have no opportunity of committing. Rashness in directing a military operation, and extravagance in paying for it were undoubtedly – with whatever justice – laid to his charge... policy is absolutely in the hands of the Foreign Office.' Salisbury believed that Lytton possessed the 'gift of captivating individuals' and in a country like France, 'where so much depends on impressions', that would be invaluable. The connection was made closer two months later when Lytton's daughter Elizabeth married Arthur Balfour's younger brother Gerald, the Tory MP for Leeds.

In the rest of the letter to the Prince of Wales, Salisbury ran through the scanty alternatives the Foreign Office could offer for the Paris embassy. Sir Augustus Paget was disqualified by a German wife, Lionel Sackville-West was 'not clever', Sir J. Lumley was retiring soon, William White was 'only useful at Constantinople', the French hated Sir Robert Morier and Sir Francis Ford was 'not sufficiently polished' for Paris. George Petre, Sir Horace Rumbold, Sir Vincent Corbett and Henry Stuart were all too dim and Lord Vivian was needed for St Petersburg. Monson 'has hardly ability enough – and has an awkward tendency to make things smooth by speaking well of everyone'. As his letter showed, this was clearly not a problem that afflicted Salisbury.

European diplomacy took a startling new turn when in late October 1887 Count Herbert Bismarck, the Chancellor's widely disliked eldest son and Foreign Minister of Germany, presented Malet with a proposal to protect the Sultan from Franco-Russian pressure, whilst the Austrian Chargé in London produced an identical scheme to Salisbury in London. Writing to Lumley in Rome on 28th October, Salisbury summed up the eight bases of the Bismarck *fils* plan: 'Austria and Italy have made a proposal for telling Turkey that, if she resists Russia, she will be supported, but that if she makes herself Russia's vassal, she will be invaded.... In secret [Germany] patronises and presses it; in public she stands aloof – and no doubt privately expresses her horror of it in St Petersburg.' Salisbury's own view was that 'it commits the blunder of building on the Sultan's fitful and feeble disposition', and he ordered Lumley to 'put the drag on'.

The only three significant bases of the agreement were those which bound the signatories to assist Turkey against Russia, and which also bound them to attack her if necessary. Salisbury told White he thought it all part of Bismarck's 'unscrupulous game' to isolate France, and that although the Anglo-Austrian-Italian *entente à trois* was too important to lose, he suspected 'we are merely rescuing Bismarck's somewhat endangered chestnuts'. On 4th November, the Cabinet supported Salisbury's line that the plan could not be rejected outright, but also his demand that Germany must explain exactly what she would do in an Austro-Russian war. To answer him, Bismarck sent Salisbury the text of the hitherto secret clauses of the Austro-German Treaty of 1879, which the Prime Minister promised not to show to any Cabinet member. As Salisbury wrote to the Queen, 'it sufficiently establishes that Germany must take the side of Austria in any war between Austria and Russia'. It told him that a Russian invasion of Bulgaria, if taken by Austria as a *casus belli*, would automatically involve Germany in a war against Russia.

The reasons that Salisbury looked more favourably at Herbert Bismarck's Turkish protection plan were both this new-found knowledge of the depth of German commitment to Austria and concern over the pro-Russian tendencies of Prince Wilhelm, the eldest son of the cancer-stricken Crown Prince Friedrich Wilhelm, who was himself the heir to the nonagenarian German Kaiser Wilhelm I. As Salisbury wrote to Malet on 16th November, 'between us and Prince William's perhaps unchecked rule, there only stand now three lives – one of 91, one of 73 [Bismarck was actually 72] and one menaced by a disease "that does not pardon". Without such official declaration we should have no security whatever against his taking the side of Russia in the Eastern Question.'[10]

Goschen was making a tour of Manchester speaking against Irish Home Rule and on his return, 'now that you have laid aside the oratorical shillelagh', Salisbury told him that his perusal of the Austro-German Treaty of 1879 had satisfied him that Germany was committed to helping Austria 'to the utmost' in any future war. So he proposed going ahead with the eight bases, which represented a significantly greater commitment to Italy and Austria than had the Mediterranean Agreements back in March. Goschen insisted that neither the Sultan nor the Russians were told of the Treaty, so a ninth base was drawn up specifying secrecy and the Notes were exchanged. Further to encourage British adherence, Bismarck sent Salisbury an unusually long private letter on 22nd November 1887, covering twenty quarto pages of manuscript, to reassure him that in the event of the Crown Prince's early demise, even a new Kaiser Wilhelm II would be obliged to defend Austria against Russia, 'or if England or Italy were in danger of being attacked by the armies of France'.

By stressing the defensive nature of German foreign policy and above all his fear of 'the eventuality of Germans being compelled to fight two powerful neighbours at the same time!', Bismarck hoped to encourage Salisbury to display more precision in his commitment than the Mediterranean Agreements contained, and he was partially successful. In his answer on 30th November, Salisbury gave Bismarck a *tour d'horizon* of British foreign policy, pointing out that in the event of a Franco-German war, Russia would occupy positions in the Balkans or Asia Minor which would 'compel the Sultan to assent to proposals which would make her mistress of the Bosphorus and Dardanelles'. Italy and Britain alone could not prevent this. 'All would depend therefore upon the attitude of Austria.' But Britain and Italy could not help Austria militarily on her land locked north-eastern frontier, where the Russian invasion must take place. 'Your Serene Highness has removed my apprehensions by the great frankness with which you have expressed the true situation to me,' Salisbury wrote to Bismarck, but he nonetheless still privately doubted whether a future Kaiser Wilhelm II might not alter the policy.

On the nine bases, however, Salisbury said that he was willing to sign the Tripartite Agreement. Denying to White in Constantinople that Britain had entered into any significant new undertaking from the Mediterranean Agreements – 'it is like putting a coarse sieve under a fine one' – he insisted on the Treaty of Berlin being mentioned in the text as the basis of the Agreement. When the Notes were exchanged in mid-December 1887, Salisbury had ended the European isolation that Gladstone had bequeathed him in June 1885. Within two and a half years, Austria and Italy and, if it came to war, Germany, too, were effectively committed to defending Bulgaria and Turkey against Russia. 'I think that Lord Derby and Lord Beaconsfield both acquired an exaggerated view of Turkish vitality and power,' Salisbury wrote to MacColl, 'and they both thought that my recommendations sacrificed too much of the Turkish Empire.'[11] That Empire had now been protected, albeit without its knowledge, and the guarantees Britain had accorded it in the 1878 Anglo-Turkish Convention were at last being officially underwritten by other Great Powers.

The war scares did not end, and after a particularly worrying one in late December, Salisbury wrote to Vienna blaming 'journalistic reverberation' for 'some impulse' of ill-feeling between Bismarck and the Tsar: 'No one wants war – except the officers and the publicists. But the Tsar is stupid – Prince Bismarck's nerve has become a little excitable – and there is a dark uncertain future which creates a constant state of inchoate panic.' This, he believed, was exacerbated by the 'serious and nasty element' of the huge standing armies that each potential combatant had placed in far too close proximity to one another. Salisbury confided to Chamberlain that he thought the last scare had been 'got up by Berlin to make Vienna arm'. For all his appreciation of Bismarck's Machiavellian nature, Salisbury replied positively when, on Christmas Eve, Hatzfeldt asked about the two Governments exchanging some of the secrets of their Intelligence departments. Soon afterwards, secret information as to the state of fortifications and dockyard accommodation at Calais, Dieppe, Le Havre, Cherbourg, Dunkirk and Brest was being exchanged between Britain and Germany.

Sunday, 13th November 1887 saw some of the century's most violent scenes of civil unrest in central London, when a loose alliance of socialist, anarchist and Irish republican groups converged on Trafalgar Square to protest against Balfour's Irish policy. On 19th October, the police dispersed what Cranbrook called 'roughs falsely called unemployed' from the Square after six days of occupation. Salisbury insisted on the prosecution of all speakers who incited any breach of the law and the reinforcement of the police, 'so that the roughs in passing through Hyde Park should not endanger property or molest the peaceable inhabitants'. He told the Home Secretary, Henry Matthews, that he wanted police drafted in from neighbouring counties, former policemen called up, and the swearing-in of special constables 'wherever necessary'.

Salisbury's more controversial proposal was for the railing in of the whole of Trafalgar Square, 'with gates of course'. He told the Queen that, since it was Crown property, this would be quite legal. 'I have just walked through Trafalgar Square,' he reported to her on 28th October, 'there was no sign of disorder: only about three hundred dirty people clustering around the column. The streets were in no way obstructed or disturbed, and everything was going on as normal.' Nonetheless, the Queen gave her approval to any scheme for the Square that Salisbury might have in mind. After the Cabinet of 8th November officially forbade meetings or processions in the Square, it became clear that the Metropolitan Radical Federation would defy the ban and hold a mass demonstration there the following Sunday.

Sir Charles Warren, the Chief Commissioner of the Metropolitan Police, repeated the prohibition of the meeting and had 1,500 of his constables occupy the Square early in the morning. Two squadrons of cavalry and a detachment of the Grenadier Guards were also held in readiness. Rioting broke out in the afternoon as thousands of demonstrators converged on the Square from Northumberland Avenue, Pall Mall, St Martin's Lane and the Strand. The fighting continued for hours, and resulted in over a hundred casualties, two rioters later dying of their injuries. There were a large number of arrests although no shot was fired and the Riot Act, astonishingly enough, was not read. In the course of their baton charges, two policemen were stabbed. The socialist orator and future MP, John Burns, and a Radical MP called Robert Cunninghame Graham were arrested. As one of the demonstrators, George Bernard Shaw, recorded, 'we skedaddled...on the whole, I think it was the most abjectly disgraceful defeat ever suffered by a band of heroes, outnumbering their foe by a thousand to one'. Shaw's middle-class vegetarian friend Henry Salt discovered during the rioting that his watch had been stolen, and regretted that under the circumstances he was in no position to report the matter.

The *Pall Mall Gazette* dubbed it 'Bloody Sunday' and blamed Warren for promoting class warfare by recruiting middle-class special constables especially for the occasion. 'It ended in such a decisive victory for the authorities', one commentator has written, 'that it marked the end of revolutionary heroics based on the plight of the East End poor.' Despite the victory, Salisbury and Cranbrook were angry at what they saw as Matthews's and Warren's 'half-measures', and made political capital when the subject came to be debated in Parliament in March by insisting on dividing the Houses and gaining large Government majorities against amendments calling for an investigation.[12]

Salisbury told Austin that he did not believe socialism had any political staying power. Ireland would be the next election issue, because 'the Socialism question...is in the habit of making a burst for a year or two, and then disappearing. It did so in 1839 and in 1848, and I think again in 1880.... I expect that by October 1892 socialist quackeries will either have been dropped or they will have been exposed by experience.' It is fortunate for Lord Salisbury that history judges him for his governance rather than his sooth-saying.

Nowhere was Salisbury's support for the Church of England made clearer than in the four-year struggle over his Tithe Rent-Charge Bill between 1887 and 1891. Hitherto a tithe of 10 per cent on land was payable to the owners of Church benefices, who were usually the local Anglican clergy. Although this was an ancient arrangement going back to feudal times, the long agricultural depression had made the imposition as unpopular with ordinary tithe-payers as it always had been with nonconformists. Hussars had even been sent in to quell riots against tithe-paying in Wales in the winter of 1887/8.

Salisbury's Bill was intended to replace the then system of distraint on non-payers with County Court judgments, making it easier for the clergy to receive their money. For four successive years he pressed his measure on Parliament. Landowners, who thought the charge far too high, blocked the legislation, angry at the way it made them, rather than their tenant-farmers, directly responsible for the collection of the money. The reluctance of the Conservative front bench in the House of Commons to force through the Bill against the landowning interest severely depressed Salisbury, who blamed weak leadership. As he resentfully told Hicks Beach in March 1888, he was 'confident that if he himself were leading the Commons it would pass all right'.

The 1889 session was so exhausting, Salisbury had to explain to a disappointed Archbishop Benson, 'that none but very strong men can stand it'. It was not much of an excuse, and by mid-August, when 'a complication of blunders' had brought the Bill to a discreditable end, Salisbury finally lost his patience. Writing to Lady Dorothy Nevill from Puys on 25th August 1889, Lord Lytton said that Lady Salisbury had told him that Salisbury 'was so disgusted at the mismanagement of the Tithes Bill by his lieutenants in the Commons that he would have resigned the other day if the Queen had let him'.[13] Instead he had to wait until 1891 to pass the Tithes Bill, when parliamentary obstruction could be finally overcome after the Irish split following the revelations of the O'Shea divorce case. The fact that Salisbury was willing to persevere so far was testament to the doggedness of his support for the Anglican Establishment.

Both parties hoped to win the important agricultural labourers' vote through the provision of allotments and small-holdings, on which labourers could grow their own fruit and vegetables. These would not extend to three acres and a cow, but the land would come cheaper than if bought on the open market. Powerful elements in the Conservative Party hoped to offer a comprehensive policy which might confiscate the support of the agricultural labourer from the Liberals. They reckoned, however, without Salisbury's powerful instinct for the sanctity of property and his intense dislike of setting dangerous precedents over compulsory purchase of land, which he feared would set Britain on the slippery slope towards confiscation.

When in January 1886, Balfour wrote a memorandum advocating the compulsory purchase of allotments in parishes by the Local Government Board for 'the public good', Salisbury annotated that he could 'under no circumstances consent', and struck out the whole paragraph concerning it. He would not oppose legislation 'to facilitate the holding of allotments by agricultural labourers', he stated in August, but absolutely drew the line at anything smacking of compulsory purchase, let alone for so nebulous a concept as 'the public good'. He was broadly in favour of the aim of turning the British peasant into a yeoman, in a mainland version of what the tenant-purchase schemes were trying to achieve in Ireland, but if the owners of the land did not want to sell land for allotments, Salisbury would champion their right.

When the issue resurfaced in December, and a Bill was drawn up which provided for the Sanitary Authorities in rural districts compulsorily to acquire land for re-letting as allotments to 'small-holders', Salisbury wrote his own memorandum, pointing out how such a scheme was entirely without precedent:

> Land has never been taken forcibly by Parliament from one individual merely to benefit another individual. The principle so introduced will spread. The restriction to one acre is purely artificial, and will speedily be overstepped. After this Bill passes there will be no course of precedent or accepted practice to restrain it. The extension to any class of men of the benefits of expropriation at their neighbours' expense will depend solely upon the possession of sufficient electoral power to disquiet a certain number of Conservative members.

Salisbury was angered by Conservative MPs, such as Henry Chaplin and Arthur Balfour, who supported this most un-Tory idea merely for 'electoral purposes'. He argued that property had only been expropriated, or bought at an artificially lower than market price, for public health, educational or communication reasons. By July 1887, the Government was forced to bring in a Bill permitting compulsory purchase by local councils, but Salisbury managed to limit its powers to the bare minimum, despite being almost completely alone in Cabinet. He even spoke of 'the evil of breaking up [the] Government' on the issue. After a defeat in a by-election in the rural seat of Spalding in Lincolnshire, the general pressure for legislation grew too strong for him, and Salisbury had to bow to it. He nevertheless felt 'the discredit of having adopted for electoral purposes a proposal, which is inconsistent with the rights of property as hitherto understood, and which some twelve months ago we were vehemently denouncing'.[14] For Salisbury, it was yet another instance of the Conservatives' lust for office overcoming the ancient principles of Toryism.

Another problem for the Conservative Party arose on 22nd November 1887 when the NUCCA Conference meeting in Oxford voted by a thousand to twelve in favour of a resolution calling for 'Fair Trade', the established euphemism for retaliatory Protectionism. Since the 1850s, Free Trade had been good for Britain, whose superior industrial and technological power had taken advantage of the ability to buy raw materials and sell finished products in world markets largely without paying import and export duties. But by the mid-1880s, emerging industrial nations such as Germany and America were protecting their own industries and markets behind high tariff walls, and a growing movement on the political Right in Britain argued that employment could only be protected if she reciprocated. Although it is impossible to identify a precise moment when Britain lost her global economic lead, the mid-1880s certainly saw the end of her long post-Industrial Revolution hegemony.

In his reactionary youth, Salisbury had been a Protectionist, equating Free Trade with Peelism and Protectionism with the Corn Laws which had for so long benefited the landowning classes. At the Oxford Union in February 1850 he had spoken in favour of the motion: 'That the state of the nation imperatively requires a return to the principles of protection', citing a fall in exports since 1845 and saying: 'Why all this mischief? To advance the manufacturing class!' By the time he stood for Parliament three years later, however, he had faced the fact that, as the young Cecil told his Stamford electors: 'We must submit to the new commercial system which goes by the name of Free Trade. Consequently, I do not present myself before you as a Protectionist, for, I repeat, the Protectionist party is at an end.'

Although he ridiculed 'the dogma of Free Trade' in his journalism, and the 'passion for symmetry' of the Manchester School of Richard Cobden and John Bright, Salisbury steadily evolved a stance of his own on fiscal issues, which was to be studiously undoctrinaire. When asked his views on tariff reform, his answer was: 'It all depends on the tariff: show me one and I will tell you whether I approve of it or not.' He criticised the Tory Party of 1845–6 'for having erected a mere matter of fiscal detail into a vital question'. This was the stance he adopted for the rest of his life, believing in retaliating against those countries which slapped tariffs on British goods, but otherwise keeping broadly to the Free Trade policy which he grudgingly acknowledged had been the foundation of British commercial prosperity.[15] It was a sensible, pragmatic position to take, but it was increasingly coming under threat from the clashing ideologies of Free Trade and Tariff Reform.

The foodstuff which sparked major controversies between Fair Traders and Free Traders was sugar, the import to Britain of which was free despite foreign countries paying heavy subsidies ('bounties') for its domestic production, thereby damaging the British West Indies' staple industry. The National Fair Trade League was founded in the summer of 1881, the year that eighty Tories defied the Whip to support duties on all bounty-supported foreign sugar. Salisbury brought forward the sugar question in the Lords in early July, denying categorically that he wanted to bring in protection but pleading on behalf of industries attacked by foreign tariffs. 'In spite of any formula, in spite of any cry of Free Trade,'

Salisbury told an enthusiastic audience in Bradford in mid-October 1881, 'if I saw by raising the duty on knives, or threatening to raise it, I could exercise pressure on a foreign Power, inducing it to lower rates and give relief, I should pitch orthodoxy and formulæ to the winds and exercise pressure.' It was pure retaliationism; but he thought that the Party as a whole should not embrace the Fair Trade League as 'opinion is so much divided'.[16] For him, unity and practicality mattered more than ideology.

In 1885, Salisbury ruled out any return to duties on corn, but again it was owing to the specific case that 'the amount of corn that we produce is so very short of the amount necessary to feed our people'. He urged that this it should not be a Party issue, pointing out that Pitt, Huskisson and Liverpool were Free Traders long before Bright, Cobden and Gladstone, whereas Melbourne had been a Protectionist. Salisbury's first Cabinet included seven men – Northcote, Churchill, Hamilton, Cross, Halsbury, Manners and Salisbury himself – who had spoken in favour of Protection, Fair Trade or retaliation. Lord Dunraven, the Under-Secretary for the Colonies, was actually the official spokesman for the Fair Trade League.

Salisbury was far too sensitive to the Liberal accusations of adopting policies that would lead to a 'dear loaf' to give any open encouragement to the Fair Traders before the election. In answer to a delegation of workmen from the sugar-refining industry in early August 1885, he regretfully said that he had no electoral mandate, thus offering them nothing but implicitly inviting them to campaign for a Conservative majority at the polls. He did not specifically want to introduce across-the-board retaliation, he said, so much as have the power to threaten it: 'I believe that freedom from the self-imposed trammels of particular theories is necessary if you want to deal with the world as it is.'[17]

Since many of his Liberal Unionist allies were committed Free Traders, as were several Conservative MPs, Salisbury saw his job as postponing and nullifying an issue that could only damage government unity. 'As any measure interfering with it', he told a correspondent about Free Trade in June 1887, 'must of necessity involve interfering with the cost of articles of the first necessity, I feel sure that it will never be accepted by the large centres of population in this country.' In a letter to Goschen on 18th November 1887, with his speech to the NUCCA Conference less than a week away, Salisbury asked what the Chancellor felt about fiscal retaliation, arguing that hostile tariffs invited reciprocity. He approached the question philosophically, saying that reciprocity was perfectly consistent:

> with the Free Trade theory in its most absolute form: unless it can be said that self-defence is inconsistent with a peaceful policy.... In every other department of life, wrong is averted by the danger of retaliation. Nations

have to inflict the retaliation for themselves: individuals get courts of justice to do it for them.... Why is this true as to every other evil men can inflict – and not true as to hostile tariffs?

After Goschen's detailed reply, mainly about sugar bounties, Salisbury wrote again advocating 'retaliation for the wall of tariffs which is slowly shutting us out of one market after the other', and asked him to consider reimposing the shilling duty on corn. He predictably got nowhere with his highly orthodox, Liberal Unionist Chancellor.

Speaking to the NUCCA Conference at Derby, Salisbury dismissed the Fair Trade agitation and, by implication, the resolution, as 'mainly academical and...not...within the region of practical politics'. This tough stance – Goschen had threatened to resign from the Maidstone Farmers' Club if they passed Protectionist motions and was quite capable of doing the same to the Government – was repeated by Salisbury at Derby on 19th December. With the resolution's proposer, the Sheffield MP and Fair Trade campaign leader Howard Vincent, sitting on the same platform, Salisbury said that each tariff should be dealt with simply on the merits of each individual case. He denied that he was a Protectionist, said the protection of corn was 'very unwise' and challenged the Fair Traders to produce a detailed programme because 'upon those points upon which they are precise they are not agreed, and upon those points upon which they are agreed they are not precise'.

Between 1887 and 1902, no fewer than nine Party conferences passed Protectionist resolutions; it was an issue that would grow until it split the Party apart, just as it had in 1845–6. Salisbury somehow managed, through a brilliant and dogged rearguard action in which his own retaliationist credentials and speeches were vital, to stave off the catastrophe for fifteen years. When Vincent attempted to repeat his 1887 triumph the following year, the Government got the vote postponed from the first day of the Conference 'owing to the lateness of the hour'. When only fifty of the thousand delegates were present early the next morning, a snap vote was taken on a conference motion servile to the Government even by the standards of the time, which resolved that commercial matters were receiving 'the attention of Lord Salisbury and his colleagues and are best left to their consideration'. When the Fair Traders turned up later that morning and protested at this reverse-filibuster, they were persuaded not to push their opposition to the point of open rebellion. The NUCCA Conference in Nottingham the next year found the discussion of the subject censored.

In October 1890, the United States had adopted the McKinley Tariff, a wide-reaching Protectionist measure that gave the Fair Trade movement a huge impetus. By the time the November 1891 NUCCA Conference opened in Birmingham, the Fair Traders were ready, militant and unappeasable. Despite Salisbury asking delegates not to jeopardise his alliance with the Liberal Unionists only months before a general election by making a controversy of anything that 'is not a burning question of the moment', Vincent's resolution calling for 'the extension of commerce upon a preferential basis throughout all parts of the Empire' was passed with only six dissentient votes. It was pressure such as this that encouraged Salisbury to adopt an openly retaliationist stance when the issue arose again in the 1892 general election, with disastrous results.

TWENTY-NINE

Rumours of Wars

A Reshuffle – 'Pom' McDonnell
– The Vienna Incident –
General Boulanger's War Scare – 'Europe'
– The Bering Sea Dispute –
House of Lords Reform –
Lord Wolseley's Alarms

February to July 1888

'I can sea the sea covered with white horses.'

After Balfour had taken his post as Irish Chief Secretary in March 1887, the half-blind Hicks Beach remained in the Cabinet without a portfolio, becoming steadily more resentful and self-pitying. 'If any serious importance was attached by you, or by the party, to my presence in the Cabinet at this moment,' he wrote to Salisbury in October, 'it might be my duty to yield at the cost of any private difficulties: but I have every reason to suppose that this is not the case: if it were surely office might be open to me, as it has been to others.' Salisbury answered: 'How you can imagine that an office can be "open", when its occupant has not resigned – I cannot guess.' Privately he told Smith that a 'not sweet tempered' Hicks Beach was aggrieved that he would not dismiss one of the Queen's ministers in order to make room for him.

In February 1888, the Marquess of Lansdowne, Governor-General of Canada since 1883, was promoted to the Viceroyalty of India in succession to Lord Dufferin. The President of the Board of Trade, Lord Stanley of Preston, was appointed to Ottawa in his place. As the Presidency involved little reading and most of that was in print, Salisbury hoped Hicks Beach would accept it. After a full ten days' contemplation, he did, but only on the condition that Baron Henry de Worms, the Jewish Conservative MP for Toxteth, was not his deputy. In a deft reshuffle, Sir

Henry Holland took a peerage as Baron Knutsford and de Worms became his deputy in the Colonial Office. 'He is exceedingly clever – with all the tenacity of his race', Salisbury told Holland, 'and a knowledge of the value of advertisement.' Salisbury then appointed de Worms to the first Jewish privy councillorship.

The Earl of Onslow was moved to the Under-Secretaryship of the Board of Trade, with Salisbury having twice to write to deny that he had been demoted. Salisbury did not believe the arrangement would last long, as Hicks Beach could not yet read by candlelight, but unlike the previous ministerial reconstruction it went smoothly.[1] At the same time Salisbury's 'strong bias' in favour of a Department of Agriculture was endorsed by the Cabinet, and one was set up under Henry Chaplin the following year, with the sole remit being to deal with the outbreak of disease in animals.

Dufferin, who had already been Ambassador at St Petersburg and Constantinople, succeeded Lumley at the Rome Embassy with a well-deserved marquessate, taking the additional title 'and Ava' to mark his part in the annexation of Burma. 'All the names in Burma are horribly uncouth,' he had complained to a friend, 'and would sound like names out of Offenbach's operas or The Mikado.' He had originally wanted to take Quebec for his title, but the Queen thought it might be needed for a royal relation, and anyhow his most significant service had been in the sub-continent.

Managerial politics had not blunted the sharpness of Salisbury's tongue and on one day, 9th February, he said publicly of Gladstone that 'the great majority of Conservatives would rather not have a conversation with him', which he had to semi-apologise for later, saying that he spoke 'as to a fact I observed with respect to others'. He also wrote to Smith about the Treasury's suggestion that the 'intention' of Parliament should be ascertained about the size of the secret service budget: 'I don't believe it has got an intention. At the moment the vote is put the House probably consists of fifty sleeping men who are talking of something else. How am I to attribute an aggregate intention to them? It is a mere fiction.' His temper was not improved by the 'awful smash', as Gwendolen put it, of the West Southwark by-election on 17th February, where the Gladstonian Liberals increased their majority from 100 to 1,234. Another defeat at West Edinburgh the following day worried Party managers, and Salisbury further angered them by blaming the local organisation in Southwark for inefficiency. All was forgiven, however, in the 'ecstatic delight' after the defeat at Deptford of the gaoled Wilfrid Blunt by 275 votes.[2]

February 1888 also saw a serious war scare with France. Asking Sir Evelyn Baring in Cairo not to prosecute his quarrel with Nubar Pasha, the Khedive's Francophile minister, Salisbury wrote on 17th February saying that he must 'try and manage to postpone any breach with him to a more convenient season. We are at this moment on the sharp ridge that separates the slopes towards war and peace... a very slight push either way will decide the issue.' He begged Baring to 'avoid any unnecessary cause of conflict' with France, where Boulangist candidates were winning a series of by-elections on ultra-xenophobic platforms.

> They are so unreasonable, and have so much incurable hatred of England, that I should dread any very glaring exhibition of our sovereignty in Egypt at this moment.... I do not wish our administration in Egypt to be the cause to which the long European war is to be ascribed by the future historian.

In working his way through the difficulties imposed by France's imperial inferiority complex, Salisbury was enormously helped by Waddington, who after a brief stint as Prime Minister in 1879 became Ambassador to London between 1883 and 1893. Sitting next to Lady Rayleigh at Lady Tweeddale's dinner party in March 1888, Waddington explained how his job was now merely to settle 'petty quarrels between obscure individuals of the two nations, on the Gold Coast or such places ... before the newspapers on either side begin talking about the honour of the nation etc. He has always found Lord Salisbury very pleasant to deal with in such matters.' One such problem area was Zeyla on the Somali coast, which Salisbury told Baring 'seems to be a coast without harbours, trade, produce, or strategic advantage. But as everybody else is fighting for it, I suppose we are bound to think it valuable.'

When Lord John Manners succeeded his brother as 7th Duke of Rutland in early March 1888, his son Henry became the Marquess of Granby, with the means to take over his father's Melton seat in the Commons, which he did in a matter of days. Another of Salisbury's private secretaries, Lord Walter Gordon-Lennox, the son of the Duke of Richmond, had also recently inherited a family seat, prompting Gwendolen to remark with delight that they had evidently not yet disappeared altogether. Back in 1884, Salisbury had told Janetta Manners that 'my epitaph must be: "Died of writing inane letters to empty-headed Conservative Associations." It is a miserable death to look forward to.' He offered the job of private secretary to Schomberg McDonnell, the fifth son of the Earl of Antrim and Cranborne's best man. 'The work is interesting and not too hard,' he wrote, 'the salary is £400.' 'Pom' McDonnell had wisdom and tact far beyond his twenty-six years, and as Salisbury's *homme d'affaires* he gradually became invaluable to 'The Chief'.

On top of his standard secretarial duties to do with Salisbury's correspondence, McDonnell would scan the newspapers for Salisbury, organise his diary, relay rumours and gossip, politely disabuse honours-hunters, report Commons proceedings, spot prospective problems over colonial governorships and legal appointments, liaise with the Whips, write memoranda to the Prince of Wales about what had taken place in Cabinet, undertake confidential missions to embassies, compile invitation lists, oversee charitable donations to recipients as varied as the Toronto University Library and the band of the Royal Marines, and generally carry out the duties which today occupy the attention of the Prime Minister's Private Office. An entirely typical letter from Salisbury in August 1898 illustrates the sort of tasks McDonnell would undertake for him: '1. I think clearly the Queen must have her way about the Albert Museum. People will like the sentiment. 2. Ask George Curzon what Irish title he would like. 3. Please find out whether Chaplin's son has any money of his own. 4. Is there any chance of Brodrick accepting U-Sec FO? 5. Is police protection at Windsor good enough?'[3]

Every Prime Minister needs a factotum to deal with those unavoidable and confidential matters which do not necessarily invite the closest scrutiny, and McDonnell did the job superbly. If an editor needed to be told why a particular minister was being sidelined, for example, McDonnell was the man for the task, and when an MP wrote to Salisbury to complain about his activities, Salisbury was able to reply, somewhat disingenuously: 'You might as well hold me responsible for the way in which my solicitor passes his evenings.'

A charming, tactful character, McDonnell became, along with Balfour, almost a surrogate son of Salisbury's, loved by the Cecils for his utter devotion to their father's interests. McDonnell's grandmother was a Lothian Kerr, which was taken to explain his slightly eccentric behaviour and his habit of volunteering for military duty despite not wanting to be a full-time soldier. McDonnell's discretion, efficiency and sage counsel proved invaluable to Salisbury for the rest of his life. He also developed acute political antennae which warned his master of forthcoming problems. Salisbury always took all his important decisions entirely alone, but McDonnell came as close as anyone ever did to becoming his confidential adviser.

When in late January, Bismarck had once again insisted on knowing precisely what Britain would do in the event of a Russo-German war, Salisbury replied to Hatzfeldt with his classic constitutional argument, that Parliament, not the Executive, had 'absolute authority' and it would not sanction any promises on the issue, without knowing in advance the exact *casus belli*. Keeping Bismarck guessing was part of Salisbury's peace policy, and he answered that had he the powers of the German Chancellor, or was at least in possession of a purely Conservative majority in the Commons, he could have answered more precisely.

On 3rd February 1888, Bismarck published the text of the 1879 Austro-German Alliance, to show Russia the dangers that any invasion of Bulgaria would incur. In a conversation in mid-February, Bismarck told de Worms, whom Gwendolen thought he liked for his Jewishness, intellect and ability to speak German, that Germany would not fight for Bulgaria, but 'as soon as Austria and Russia are at war, I fight France – without waiting for her to join Russia'. Gwendolen called it 'a saying which much impressed S.' When on 1st March her father had a long interview with 'Hateful Herbert' at which, as he told the Queen, 'Count Bismarck spoke the whole time', he heard how Germany's action in seeming to support Russia over Turkey in public while secretly opposing her in private, 'was not open to the charge of duplicity'.[4] Salisbury was understandably unconvinced and continued to fear for European peace.

On 6th March, Bismarck *fils* told Lady Salisbury that Kaiser Wilhelm I 'sits and cries every day and he is utterly wretched, and it seems hardly possible that he can survive the stroke. All Europe is waiting, motionless, by the deathbed of his son.' Three days later the old Kaiser died, and Salisbury told Gwendolen that evening 'that we felt as if we were just leaving harbour – this was the shock of the first great wave upon the bow'. Gwendolen asked him if he meant that he did not yet know what kind of weather he should find outside. 'Oh no,' Salisbury replied, shaking his head. 'I can see the sea covered with white horses.' Moving from a nautical to an even more prescient theatrical analogy, Gwendolen wrote the next day that at Hatfield 'everyone feels...that the curtain has risen upon a new act in the drama, and that the plot is likely to be a bloody one'.

The next few pages of Gwendolen's diary are written in code, with two pages having been removed altogether. Any clue as to which code was being employed has sadly not survived. Despite the best efforts of the Foreign Office Librarian, of the decrypters, GCHQ, and many kind readers of *The Times*' literary pages, including Bletchley Park alumni, it has proved impossible to decipher it, owing to its shortness. Something of the sense of crisis can be deduced from the vocabulary which intersperses the numbers, however:

> S's political anxiety is enormously increased by a conversation he had with 465113, 49359 – just 54461 415211 A & 55154 – is so 39751 30939 the 62818 562412 has been 60313 that 525210 the first 62041 562412 will 47651 497316 her 52062 will be 59941 60633 and yet 546410 477316. S

could hardly believe his ears and was still more horrified when he gathered that 53561I 58955. During 443513, 41463, always 39869 39869 31763 43447 and family and 48811 seems 50458 29911. From what S knows 457316 434447 336318 43168 thinks 43447. 33145 497316 anything, though this 50741 34942. He does not think that 562412 63131 58453 if she 60633. Doubtful how far 43447 45147 over 44148 40012 even now, and if he should 35234 S thinks 48355 36946 incapable 497316 424219 & 47651 – 539620.

Salisbury's initial advice to the new Empress, Queen Victoria's daughter Vicky, was 'to discourage any leaning to English notions of policy', fearing that, although the poor woman could not affect it positively, she might provide an excuse for a backlash by her son, the new Crown Prince Wilhelm. Her liberal, Anglophile and peace-loving husband Kaiser Friedrich III was dying of cancer, and Salisbury knew better than to antagonise the next Kaiser for at best a few months of diplomatic advantage. 'It is her role to be mildly Bismarckian and intensely German,' he told Malet. When in an interview with the British Ambassador she burst into tears, Salisbury called her agony 'grausam' (cruel).[5] He could hardly have been reassured when Hartington told him that at the Golden Jubilee Prince Wilhelm had asked him if it were true that he had more than once refused the premiership. When told it was, the new Crown Prince exclaimed: 'I would have taken it and gone to war!'

Early April saw what was later called 'The Chancellor Crisis' in Berlin, when Bismarck threatened to resign rather than allow the Emperor's second daughter, Moretta, to marry Alexander of Bulgaria. The implications for Germany's relations with Russia were obvious, and Salisbury feared that Bismarck would blame Queen Victoria for encouraging the match. 'He has a vast corrupt influence over the Press,' Salisbury warned the Queen, 'and can give enormous circulation to slanders.' Bismarck was reported to be in a raging mood, 'drinking stimulants all day and narcotics all night', and Salisbury advised the Queen to postpone her visit to her daughter and dying son-in-law in Germany due to take place after her Florentine holiday. Bismarck's request that Salisbury intervene, saying the proposed marriage would be an insult to the Tsar, prompted a letter to Malet to say that 'he is asking me to assist him in thwarting the wishes of his Emperor and my Queen in order to gratify the malignant feelings of the Russian Emperor. This would certainly be inconsistent with my duty and, if German co-operation can only be had at this price, we must do without it.'

The Chancellor Crisis, which Bismarck eventually won, together with the demand over Consul Holmwood the previous year, led Salisbury to wonder aloud to Malet whether 'friendship with Germany is a more uncertain staff to lean upon than friendship with France'. The major problem, 'most unhappily', as he told the Queen, was that in future, 'all Prince William's impulses, however blameable or unreasonable, will henceforth be political causes of enormous potency: and the two nations are so necessary to each other, that everything that is said to him must be very carefully weighed'.[6] Salisbury's none too subtle hint to the Queen to treat the Prince, whom she thought 'a most unnatural son', with, as Hatzfeldt had begged, 'special consideration', was understood by a monarch who had formidable powers of diplomacy and tact when she chose to employ them. The meetings with both Bismarck and Wilhelm went far better than the Duke of Rutland, who attended her, had feared. Rutland himself had a short meeting with Bismarck, who said that his army was ready 'to take the field at any moment' against both France and Russia if necessary.

On 15th June 1888, only ninety-nine days after becoming Emperor Friedrich III died. A decent, intelligent Kaiser, who had wanted to advance representative institutions in Germany, was replaced by the autocratic, vain and unstable Wilhelm II. 'I do not like the look of things in Germany. It is evident the young Emperor hates us and loves Russia,' Salisbury wrote to Sir Henry Drummond Wolff within a fortnight of the new Kaiser's accession, 'and how long the Chancellor's policy can keep that inclination from asserting itself remains to be seen.'[7]

Problems with Germany arose almost immediately, when in July 1888 Herbert Bismarck accused the British Ambassador to St Petersburg, Sir Robert Morier, of revealing to the French the operational plans of the German army, allegedly leaked to him by the Dowager Empress Friedrich. It was a transparent attempt to force him to resign his embassy and to blacken the Dowager Empress's name. Morier obtained a categorical denial from the French Marshal Bazaine, which unsurprisingly failed to convince the Germans, and Salisbury decided to take no official notice of the incident. The Prince of Wales complained to the Queen about Salisbury's attitude, and Morier himself was furious, as he told Lady Derby, about 'the slobbering way in which everybody is making up to Herbert Bismarck, who has never offered me a word of apology for this gross insult to a British ambassador'.

Yet what later became known as the 'Morier Incident' was as nothing compared to the 'Vienna Incident' two months later.[8] The first that Salisbury learnt of Kaiser Wilhelm II's refusal to see his uncle, the Prince of Wales, during their forthcoming simultaneous visits to Vienna in early October, came on 12th September in a letter from the British Ambassador there, Sir Augustus Paget. The Austrian Emperor Franz

Josef, he reported, was 'begging me to tell the Prince of Wales' to leave
Vienna before the Kaiser arrived on 3rd October, in order to avoid being
cut by the Kaiser. The Prince of Wales was 'shocked and indignant'
when informed of this gross snub. He had written to the Kaiser on 15th
August asking after his nephew's plans and had received no reply. Now,
via his equerry and the British Military Attaché in Berlin, Colonel
Swaine, he learnt that the Kaiser had deliberately intended to humiliate
him.

'What is the meaning of all this?' the Prince asked; he not only
received no reply but the Kaiser then also cut Swaine at the German
Army's autumn manoeuvres. Paget believed that the reason was that
certain remarks of the Prince, such as 'William the Great needs to learn
that he is living at the end of the nineteenth century and not in the
Middle Ages,' had been reported back to the Kaiser. It is just as possible
that the Kaiser's strange love–hate relationship with the British Royal
Family and his supposed disapproval of the Prince's louche living were
to blame. Whatever the cause, Salisbury was not about to allow an
unpleasant family row jeopardise his carefully balanced European
entente, upon which he believed the lives of millions might depend.

Salisbury arranged that the Prince of Wales should leave Vienna for
Romania the day before the Kaiser arrived in Vienna. At the concert and
diplomatic reception given in Wilhelm's honour, Salisbury instructed
Paget to 'be reserved and avoid conversation so far as you can. Any
observation about the Prince of Wales seems to me to invoke one of two
dangers. Either he will think you are apologising which will duly be
announced in the reptile press; or he will think your language implies a
reproach; in which case he will reply with an enumeration of his griefs
against the English court couched in rude language.' The twenty-nine-
year-old Kaiser's touchiness was clearly set to be a major factor in
European diplomacy for decades, and Salisbury did not wish to start off
the reign with a full-scale international incident.

After a very careful conversation with an embarrassed Hatzfeldt, one
of several during the Vienna Incident, Salisbury received a memorandum from Bismarck listing the 'grounds of offence'. Salisbury passed on
what he called this 'dubious document' to the Queen. It seemed clear to
Salisbury that the political grounds for the Kaiser's actions were at best
shaky and the personal ones could be boiled down to the way 'that the
Prince treated him as an uncle treats a nephew, instead of recognising
that he was an Emperor who, though young, had still been of age for
some time'. Salisbury asked Hatzfeldt to ask Berlin not to request a
State Visit in the near future.

The Queen's reaction to the memorandum was quintessential
Victoria. Much given to underlinings, eccentric grammar, multiple
exclamation marks and capital letters in the middle of sentences, she

let herself go about her 'hot-headed and conceited and wrong-headed' grandson in a manner usually reserved for comments about Gladstone: 'As regarding the Prince's not treating his nephew as Emperor this is really too vulgar and too absurd as well as untrue almost to be believed. We have always been very intimate with our grandson and nephew and to pretend that he is to be treated in private as well as in public as "His Imperial Majesty" is perfect madness!' Furthermore, she did not want him to visit Britain, thinking that preventing political relations from being affected by 'these miserable personal quarrels... may, at any moment, become impossible'.[9]

After another meeting with Hatzfeldt, it dawned on Salisbury that the German Ambassador had been 'simply afraid' to pass on his concerns about future visits from the Kaiser, and his 'terror' probably also extended to political questions, including Salisbury's warning to Bismarck not to attack the Sultan of Zanzibar. Salisbury ordered the Admiralty to send reinforcements to the Zanzibar Squadron immediately: 'If nobody dares tell Prince Bismarck the truth, there is no knowing what he might do.' Salisbury had a low view of German colonialist conduct in general, and at Zanzibar in particular, which Bismarck wanted to blockade. He thought the Germans 'have brought all this trouble on themselves and us by sheer brutality. The good-humoured Hans of story seems to be as extinct as the Dodo.' Salisbury was on his guard; writing to the Queen the next year he said that 'in dealing with the Bismarcks, especially on personal matters, it is necessary to be extremely careful. To get rid of a rival, they will do things of which it would be absurd to suspect any other statesman in Europe.'

Salisbury's explanation to Paget for the Vienna Incident was that the Kaiser 'must be a little off his head' and he took full responsibility for refusing to allow Paget to take the subject further. 'Nothing that has been alleged gives any kind of explanation for this extraordinary freak of temper,' he told the Ambassador.[10] On 22nd October 1888, Salisbury had personally to explain his appeasement policy to the Prince of Wales at Marlborough House, prior to the Prince leaving for three days' racing at Newmarket. In what sounds like an *ex post facto* rationalisation of the Incident, he emphasised the international aspect of attempting to allay the Tsar's suspicions of the Austrian, German and British royals meeting together, but he also dropped in the uncle–nephew issue. For all his sympathy, Salisbury nevertheless made it clear that, if the Kaiser insisted on visiting Britain, a private family row could not be allowed to 'affect the general policy of the two nations', which was to be as friendly as possible, short of an actual alliance.

The affair dragged on until May 1889, by which time the go-between, Prince Christian of Schleswig-Holstein, had managed to extract verbal assurances from the Kaiser that he had not meant to insult the Prince of

Wales, although his privately expressed explanation ascribing the whole affair to 'Uncle Bertie's imagination' scarcely helped matters. Neither did the Kaiser's crowing, when staying in the Viennese hotel that the Prince of Wales had been forced to vacate so precipitately, that he 'preferred his uncle's rooms to his company'. The Prince's private secretary, Francis Knollys, wrote animatedly to Prince Christian complaining that 'the Prince of Wales is sacrificed by Lord Salisbury to political expediency, and no one who has the <u>power</u>, has the nerve to insist on the proper reparation being granted to him'. At one level this was entirely true, but when the Kaiser made his visit to Cowes Week in early August, the two men, both in the uniform of Admirals of the Fleet, buried their differences, the Prince even putting his nephew up for membership of the Royal Yacht Squadron. Salisbury made sure he was personally present to ensure that everybody behaved themselves when the Kaiser arrived (two and a half hours late) at Osborne.[11]

The crisis in France over General Boulanger, who though technically ineligible to stand topped the poll in Marseilles on 25th March and was elected to the Assembly for the Département du Nord in mid-April, bringing about a change of government, worried Salisbury. 'If Boulanger has anything in him,' he remarked to his family, 'things may become serious at any moment.' Lytton was sending highly alarming despatches from Paris, and war rumours abounded. At some stage, and it is not known exactly when, Lady Salisbury is thought to have met Boulanger during 1888, at dinner with Eustace and Lady Frances Balfour. Although *incognitos* were ostensibly used, they clearly did not survive long, as Frances overheard Boulanger saying 'gallantly that he would send the French fleet to salute her at Beaulieu. She passed it over as one without hearing, and no further lapse occurred.' It is known that Salisbury had employed his wife for secret diplomacy before, specifically to meet Ignatiev in Paris in 1878, and it seems probable, but sadly unprovable, that ten years later he also used her to reassure Boulanger of Britain's pacific intentions.

It was in this atmosphere of suspicion and war scares that Salisbury made an important speech at Caernarvon, reaffirming his faith in the ability of the Concert of Europe so to arrange matters that peace could be preserved. Salisbury pursued Britain's interests diligently, and occasionally ruthlessly, but he never lost sight of the fact that, with a voluntary standing army which was as small as her trade and investments and strategic commitments were huge, European peace was a primary British interest in itself. 'There is all the difference in the world between good-natured, good-humoured effort to keep well with your neighbours', he told the Welsh contingent of the NUCCA, 'and that spirit of haughty and sullen isolation which has been dignified with the name of non-intervention. We are part of the community of Europe, and we must do our duty as such.'

Salisbury had long asserted, as he had written in his *Quarterly Review* essay on Poland a quarter of a century earlier, that 'in a carefully balanced structure like the European system of nations, each State has a vested right in the complete and real independence of its neighbour'. Never a Little Englander, Jingoist or isolationist, Salisbury believed in a diplomatic Concert of Europe deciding issues of peace or war together, as his hero Castlereagh had achieved at Vienna and he himself had tried unsuccessfully at Constantinople and later successfully at Berlin. Salisbury also believed in national prejudices and stereotypes, however. Men were manifestly not 'beings of the same passions' from country to country. In the *Saturday Review*, he had written about 'how hard it is to press religious liberty upon the Scotch', of how necessary strong government was to the French, and how in Germany 'it will probably be always necessary to sacrifice a good deal of practical utility to logical symmetry'. His conclusion was that 'in the face of such profound differences ... it is impossible that any universal maxims for the construction of constitutions can be safely framed'.

Although he never attempted to federate European foreign policy – preferring to use the Triple Entente to balance France and Russia, and always working against a *Dreikaiserbund* or other grouping which might threaten British interests in the Near East, Salisbury included a rare Utopian passage in his Caernarvon speech which has regularly, and even as recently as 1997 by a former Foreign Secretary at the Conservative Party Conference, been misconstrued by commentators and politicians. 'The federated action of Europe', he said, 'is our sole hope of escaping from the constant terror of war, which weighs down the spirits and darkens the prospect of every nation in this part of the world. The federation of Europe is the only hope we have.'

This remark, which referred to diplomatic rather than any federated political, economic or military action, has been regularly quoted out of context to imply that Salisbury somehow did not believe in the complete independence of the United Kingdom. It is worthwhile therefore to quote another part of the same speech, in which he depicted other European countries as 'envying our Empire, occupying our markets, encroaching upon our sphere, and whose efforts, unless we are wide awake and united and enterprising, will end in diminishing still further our means of supporting our vast industrial population'.

This was hardly the language of a man who expected the federated action of Europe to mean anything more than occasional summits such as those of Vienna, Paris or Berlin, held between independent and competing states to preserve the general peace between them, thereby also preserving their hegemony over the rest of the world except America.[12] In time even his belief in the Concert of Europe, which in 1895 he described as 'not a rapid machine' and later as 'too ponderous a machine for daily use', started to fade. 'Our first duty is towards the people of this country,' he declared in his Guildhall speech, 'to maintain their interests and their rights; our second is to all humanity.' In Salisbury's diplomacy, unlike in Gladstone's, the first duty considerably outweighed the second.

One of the highly contentious issues that divided Britain and France, the fishing rights off Newfoundland and in the Bering Sea, was not really susceptible to decision by the Concert. American and Canadian interests were also involved, and an inordinate amount of time and trouble had to be taken over these disputes. On occasion, fishery disputes even threatened the withdrawal of diplomatic representation. Without entering into the minutiæ of such a long-dead issue, the Newfoundland fisheries dispute went back to a clause in the Treaty of Utrecht of 1713 which gave France the right to a stretch of the Newfoundland coastline for the drying and packing of her fishermen's cod-catch, despite British sovereignty over the rest of the territory. As early as the Congress of Berlin, Salisbury had spotted the dangers that might arise from the growing Newfoundland resentment against what the local people increasingly saw as French government-subsidised over-fishing.

In 1886, a protectionist French Government brought in a bounty for French fishermen, allowing them to undercut Canadian prices for fish caught in Canadian waters. Squabbles turned into scuffles, until gunboats were sent and Canada appealed to the British Government to intervene with both the French and American Governments. Having spotted Chamberlain's messianic brand of imperialism as early as 1882, when he had been hawkish over the occupation of Egypt, Salisbury chose the Radical Unionist leader to be Chief Commissioner of a delegation to be sent to Washington in August 1887, with wide plenipotentiary powers to resolve the dispute. The other Commissioners were to be Sir Charles Tupper, the Canadian High Commissioner to London, and the British minister in Washington, Sir Lionel Sackville-West.[13] 'He is a very sensitive individual,' Smith told Salisbury, encouraging him to write often to Chamberlain in Washington, 'and easily influenced by attentions paid to him in an easy and natural sort of way.'

Salisbury paid them, and in one of his letters he pointed out to

Chamberlain how 'the position of England towards Canada is so unexampled – so anomalous – so eccentric – that any large measure affecting
the position of Canada may open for us wholly unexpected embarrassments'. He meant that he hoped a smaller scheme might be agreed upon
than one which might open up large-scale US–Canadian commercial
co-operation. On 15th February 1888, Chamberlain signed a Fisheries
Treaty with the United States, which was generally regarded as a
triumph for him, though it was unpopular in Newfoundland. Although
President Cleveland recommended it, the Senate subsequently rejected
it. Nonetheless, by Chamberlain's return to Britain in March 1888,
Salisbury had formed a new respect for his plenipotentiary. He took the
significant step of writing to him as 'My dear Mr Chamberlain' for the
first time. Although the absence from active politics for seven months
of a potential Churchill-supporter who was also suspected of negotiating a return to the Liberal camp might have been a prime reason for his
appointment, Salisbury was delighted by Chamberlain's temporary
success.

When a separate and further dispute over seal-fishing in the Bering
Sea blew up, and the negotiations and arbitrations continued throughout the 1890s, several aspects of Salisbury's diplomatic style were
displayed. His love of paradox was exhibited in his December 1888
letter to the Canadian Governor-General, Lord Stanley, in which he
recalled the King of Portugal, who 'once entertained me for three-
quarters of an hour with an exposition of his mode of Government. It
was summed up in the last sentence: "Whenever I wish for a conservative policy, I put a Liberal statesman in power: whenever I wish to carry
a rather startling change, I send for a Conservative." In the same way
our best chance of ordinary civility is to have a thoroughly anti-British
Administration at Washington.'

Salisbury's capacity for choosing men was exhibited in his appointment of the former Permanent Under-Secretary at the Foreign Office,
Sir Julian Pauncefote, to Washington, and in trusting and supporting
him when *en poste*. His contempt for colonists was manifest in his July
1888 remark to Lord Knutsford that 'though I hate the
Newfoundlanders I am obliged to admit the French have not a leg to
stand on'. His omnipresent sense of the past is apparent in his
December 1889 remark: 'To think that we should be paying, in hopeless
weary negotiation, the penalty of Bolingbroke's abortive intrigues a
hundred and eighty years ago!' His weakness for secret diplomacy is
evident in his private message to Pauncefote that someone should 'let it
get round to [the American Secretary of State] Blaine's ear that we were
advised by the Law Officers that, from a legal point of view, it would
not be possible for us to submit to any more seizures'.

When nothing else sufficed, Salisbury was reluctantly willing to resort to threats of force, and in May 1890 the Cabinet unanimously approved his policy to send cruisers from the China Station to protect Canadian sealing vessels from being seized by American cruisers, warning that 'the claim of the U.S. to treat the Bering Sea as if it were their own territorial waters could not be tolerated'. When in June the Americans promised to enter arbitration, 'respect our flag' and pay compensation, Salisbury's natural instinct for finding a *modus vivendi* took over, and when Canada wished to push further he had to warn Knutsford that he thought her attitude unreasonable and unjust to the Mother Country and 'that in conversation with a colonist on public affairs I find it very difficult to prevent these sentiments from peeping out'.

Another diplomatic technique Salisbury used extensively during the long and complex sealing dispute was to keep the other sides guessing his intentions for as long as possible. When the Canadian Government begged to know the exact extent of the protection British warships would give, Salisbury rationalised that '<u>unless</u> they allow it to be known, such information is worthless to them: and if they allow it to be known, it will be repeated in every newspaper throughout the Union, and will almost drive Blaine into an aggressive policy'. When Salisbury told the Queen in January 1891 that the Canadians were being unreasonable in refusing arbitration, but he had 'agreed to guarantee the cost of a Newfoundland railway as a bribe', it shed light on Salisbury's faith in the silent, unattributable *quid pro quo*. His assumption that Blaine was not negotiating for a proper outcome, 'but only for an electioneering one', fitted in perfectly with his overall view of American democracy, and his July 1891 frankness to Lord Stanley that 'the world would not be perceptibly better or worse off whether the fur seal survives or disappears' is also typical.

Some cynicism might be detected in his comment to Stanley on US–Canadian relations: 'It is of vital interest to us that they should not agree enough to unite: and yet it is perfectly certain that Canada will not remain separate to please us but only to suit herself.' His belief in direct but unattributable correspondence was also a feature of the Bering Sea arbitration question, with Stanley complaining to Pauncefote in October 1891 that Salisbury had 'resumed the practice of telegraphing to me secretly and unofficially – over the heads of the C[olonial] O[ffice] I fear – a practice which however useful in itself is very embarrassing when one has to deal with a Council such as we have here – and to whom the *ipsissima verba* cannot be given'.

Salisbury's caustic comments about people were regularly displayed too. Of one of the officials involved in the negotiations, Sir George Baden-Powell, Salisbury wrote: 'His trumpeter died in infancy and his aggressive self-consciousness makes him many enemies.' Finally, there is the tone of weary resignation he often employed: 'Oh! Why was Newfoundland created?' he wrote to Knutsford in December 1889. 'Or why have the fish not the good taste to frequent a warmer place?' In the end, in January 1897, Pauncefote and yet another American Secretary of State, Richard Olney, signed an arbitration treaty, which on 5th May passed the Senate by only forty-three votes to twenty-six, some way short of the necessary two-thirds majority.[14] This was devastating for Pauncefote, but at that point, a full decade after the fisheries and sealing questions first loomed into Salisbury's life, they dropped off his agenda of important issues.

'He never likes to keep his sword in its sheath,' Rosebery said of Salisbury when moving the appointment of a committee to propose reforms of the House of Lords on 19th March 1888. 'He is always trying its temper.... He is like the King of Hungary on his coronation, who rides to all eminences and brandishes his sword to the four corners of the globe.' Rosebery's projected committee would look into all aspects of the House of Lords, including life peerages and the possibility of striking off errant or criminal members. Surprisingly for one often seen as an ideological reactionary, Salisbury supported both these ideas. He did not, however, want a fully professionalised House of Lords, which he suspected would inevitably 'insist on sharing equally all the powers of the House of Commons'. The Lords only worked so well, he argued, because:

> only a small majority of us are devoted politicians. We are overruled...by ...the less zealous, less intense feeling of those who constitute a majority of the House. If ever men chose the House of Lords for a political career rather than the Commons, they would soon challenge the Lower House for supremacy over the initiation of legislation, the control of taxation and expenditure and the make-up of Cabinets.

Answering Rosebery's accusation that it was unfair to have a permanent Tory majority in one of the Houses of Parliament, Salisbury was on shakier ground when he argued that it was solely due to 'Gladstone's rise to power and might be regarded as temporary'. Wanting a life peerage for Cardinal Manning, he also supported 'finding some means of getting rid of "black sheep"'. Salisbury found Rosebery's ideas, whereby a certain number of peers would be elected by the rest and have powers along French senatorial lines, were 'eloquent and able but very vague. He laid down no clear policy but merely insisted that something must be done.' Salisbury had long supported the idea of life peerages, telling their Lordships back in 1869 that: 'We belong too much to one class....

With respect to a large number of questions we are all too much of one mind.'

In order to offset a maverick life peerages Bill from Lord Dunraven, the Cabinet unanimously agreed on 26th April to bring in one of its own. On 10th July, Salisbury was placed in the 'exceedingly humiliating position' of commending a life peerages Bill to the Lords, and then having to say at the end of the debate that Smith had, without his knowledge, abandoned it in the Commons because Gladstone had threatened to oppose it. The 'black sheep' Bill was also withdrawn. 'Life peerages are likely to be the creations of the imagination for some time to come,' Salisbury wrote to Akers-Douglas two days later. In April, George Curzon, heir to the Barony of Scarsdale, had tried to insert his own self-interested reform by which heirs to peerages might be allowed to renounce them. 'Poor Curzon,' Salisbury wrote of the attempt, 'I am afraid he has overworked himself for a very inadequate object. Institutions like the House of Lords must die, like all other organic beings, when their time comes: but they are not to be saved by little grafts of this kind.'

Despite Salisbury's support when Carnarvon brought in a Bill the following March to discontinue the writs of peers convicted of felonies, it failed to pass its second reading and non-judicial life peerages were not introduced for another eighty years. Salisbury had no romantic attachment to his 'sword'; his struggle for the rights and privileges of the House of Lords was strictly utilitarian, as the most effective political vehicle of his class and political creed, and a bulwark against unrestrained democracy. As he had once written in the *Saturday Review*:

> The English aristocracy is a wonderful institution, not for its power, which is nothing, nor for its achievements, which are few, but for the gigantic impression it is able to make upon weak minds. Practically, its political power has dwindled to the prerogative of occasionally obstructing a theological measure for a limited period...[but it is] one of the stock nightmares of morbid brains. It takes its place with Antichrist and irremissible sin among the dismal spectres that haunt a disturbed imagination.

Snobbery was entirely absent in his defence of the Lords; he believed their hereditary right to legislate did not depend on peers being better people, but merely coming from 'the wealthier and more educated classes', who were thus simply more likely to be 'undefiled by the taint of sordid greed' than members of the House of Commons. 'Always wealth, in some countries birth, in all countries intellectual power and culture' made up a properly functioning aristocracy, he believed, but 'it is indeed as representing the wealth of the country that its hereditary character can be in any degree justified'. That was why he promoted successful men of commerce to the peerage. Salisbury never denied that the Lords was 'a paradise of bores', made worse by the absence of anti-bore devices which were employed in the Commons, such as coughing, groaning or quorum-taking.

'A Quaker jollification, a French horse-race, a Presbyterian psalm, all are lively and exciting compared to an ordinary debate in the House of Lords,' he wrote, likening them to 'a debate in one of Madame Tussaud's showrooms'. From the early 1860s, he had hoped that instead of 'scanty attendance and microscopic division-lists and perfunctory sittings', the Lords would flex their muscles, complaining that they had not genuinely tried in recent years to exercise their great constitutional powers. 'The first condition of inducing others to believe in you', he fumed after only eight peers had turned up to a particular debate, 'is that you should entertain some sort of belief in yourself. Even a beefeater could not properly perform his part in the exalted ceremonies in which he takes a share, if he looked upon himself as a sham.' To treat the House of Lords as merely 'a place for passing an idle hour or two before dinner' would soon convert the public to that way of thinking. When the Lords failed to live up to their responsibilities, Salisbury believed their enemies were justified in 'uttering that most frightful of all insults, "I told you so"'.

Salisbury believed the House of Lords had a noble and indeed crucial constitutional function, however badly they sometimes performed it. He devoutly supported 'the check imposed upon hasty legislation by men who devote themselves to the service of their country unaffected by any of those motives which might mislead those who are less safe from the freaks of fortune, and less insensible to the fascinations of ambition or of gain'. He happily admitted the House of Lords' 'subordination to the nation', but never its subordination to the Commons. What has been called Salisbury's 'Referendal' theory of the House of Lords is best articulated in his Hackney speech on November 1880, when he said that 'its duty was to represent the permanent as opposed to the passing feelings of the English nation'.

This analysis flew in the face of the most recent constitutional thought and practice. Earl Grey's book, *Parliamentary Government* (1858) and Walter Bagehot's *The English Constitution* (1867) both represented the elected chamber as constitutionally sovereign, with the Lords relegated merely to revising and occasionally postponing legislation. Salisbury believed, and regularly stated, that it would be better not to have a House of Lords at all than one reduced to such servility. 'It has a quite peculiar political organism', Salisbury told Lord James in 1901 who had complained of its weakness ' – peculiar I fear to the lowest class of Creation. It is very difficult to stimulate it: but it is almost impossible to kill it.'

~

As early as May 1874 Salisbury had spoken of Sir Garnet Wolseley, the hero of the war against the West African kingdom of Ashanti, as 'our general of the future' and in 1878 he was sent out as Cyprus's first British Administrator. Salisbury rated Wolseley's 'strong head' highly and appreciated his indiscretions about Gladstone's personal responsibility for the death of Gordon, the doomed expedition to save whom Wolseley had commanded. Wolseley is generally credited with having been the very model for Gilbert and Sullivan's modern major-general, and the phrase 'All Sir Garnet' had already entered the language to mean spick and span, present and correct. 'It is quite true that Wolseley is an egoist and a braggart,' Disraeli had told the Queen in 1879. 'So was Nelson. Men of action when eminently successful in early life are generally boastful and full of themselves.' Salisbury would not have disagreed, but he did not hire soldiers for their social qualities; the (perhaps apocryphal) story was told of Salisbury sending Wolseley off on an expedition with the parting words called down the main staircase of the Foreign Office: 'Sir Garnet, Sir Garnet – I like success – goodbye.'[15]

Since 1885, Wolseley had been privately warning that France could land 30,000 troops on the English coast virtually unopposed in a surprise attack, an estimation that in April 1888 was supported by a top-secret memorandum produced by Colonel John Ardagh, the Assistant Adjutant-General at the War Office. This paper, 'The Defence of England: Mobilisation of the Regular and Auxiliary Forces for Home Defence', argued that a French fleet could also fire so much more shrapnel from heavy naval guns with far greater accuracy than hitherto that 'the operation of disembarkation can hardly be interfered with on the beach'.

On 27th April 1888, at a public dinner, Wolseley, who was by then Adjutant-General and a peer, described Party government as 'that curse of modern England' and claimed that certain ministers had tried to build a 'claptrap reputation' by cutting the Estimates. Considering the lengths to which Salisbury had gone to prevent Churchill doing exactly that, this was hardly fair. Wolseley's other remarks, however, to the effect that the French could capture London by surprise, were far more serious and caused widespread unease. Salisbury scathingly rebuked him on 11th May, but Wolseley reiterated his views three days later in the House of Lords, stating categorically: 'Our military forces are not organised or equipped as they should be to guarantee even the safety of the capital.' Answering him again, Salisbury admitted it was 'a very grave statement' for a senior officer to make, but that defence spending and the numbers in the armed forces had greatly increased in recent years.

Wolseley's reputation and popularity, and the support for him by the Duke of Cambridge, the long-standing and formidable Commander-in-Chief who was moreover the Queen's cousin, meant that there was no question of his being sacked, so instead a Royal Commission was appointed under Hartington to investigate the relations between the War Office, the Admiralty and the Treasury. A *de facto* standing committee of the Cabinet, the Committee of National Defence, was set up and presided over by Salisbury, which eventually formed the nucleus of the famous Committee of Imperial Defence. Salisbury was fundamentally uninterested in military matters, and it took just such a public, if hyperbolic, attack from the political Right to goad him into reforms.[16]

Salisbury had himself long feared a sudden French strike against London, thinking that it would be the best way for them to paralyse the Empire. But after much work and thought and many meetings on the subject in the summer and autumn, including memoranda from the Director of Military Intelligence, Wolseley himself, the First Lord of the Admiralty and several others, Salisbury doubted whether the surprise annihilation of the Channel fleet and the capture of London was a realistic possibility. He nonetheless wanted all the necessary plans made ready in case of 'a great naval disaster', as there would hardly be time to formulate them afterwards. Salisbury suspected that the civilian population, when ordered to clear the country of the transport and supplies necessary to help an invader, would be in two minds: 'While one half of them would be too contemptuous of the French to take a precaution ... the other half would be incapacitated by panic.' His natural pessimism given full rein, he foresaw the local population of Chatham using force to prevent rolling stock being removed, 'privateers of all sorts will try to plunder the various communal ports', and volunteers would mutiny sooner than protect London, pleading 'the necessity of defending their own locality'.

In another of his Cabinet memoranda five months later, in November 1888, Salisbury indulged yet further this apocalyptic vision of a French army, commanded by 'the kind of soldier who comes to the top in a revolution', departing from the French coast soon after nightfall,

the majority of them would be landed, say, in Pevensey Bay twelve hours later. If a Saturday night were selected for the operation, and if two or three Irish patriots were employed to cut the telegraphic wires at suitable ports after nine o'clock in the evening, a large portion of the expedition might be one day's march upon its road to London before the military authorities in that city were fully aware of what was taking place.

The war itself would not be declared until Sunday afternoon and any 'adventurer' who had unleashed this attack would be instantly a hero in France, especially if it led to 'the destruction of London'.[17]

Salisbury's recommended precautions were to complete Dover Harbour, connect the town with military stations by underground rather than overhead telegraph lines, keep craft ready to embark at an hour's notice and impose surprise mobilisations of the Royal Navy to see if it could be in fighting readiness within forty-eight hours. Although today these might seem almost paranoiac, they show how the Victorian Cabinet and General Staff were far from being the massive, immovable, phlegmatic monoliths of popular estimation, even as the Empire was approaching its apogee in terms of prestige and influence.

THIRTY

The Business of Government

County Councils – The Drinks Trade –
Votes for Women –
Sir Lionel Sackville-West –
A 'Black Man' – The Viceroy's Indian Proposals –
Diplomatic Style

August to December 1888

'A treaty is in most cases the result of an employment of force –
openly applied or covertly threatened.'

Although the Commons had to continue legislating until 7th September, the Lords rose a fortnight earlier and Salisbury took the opportunity to go to Royat in the South of France. Before he left, he delivered a speech at the Mansion House promising to evacuate Egypt – 'an unnecessary burden' – the moment it was internally stable and strong enough to repel an external foe. He also took the opportunity to compliment Tsar Alexander III. Privately Salisbury described his speech as 'a string of truths, which verge on truisms', but he reasoned that if the Tsar was seriously contemplating moving on the Bosphorus in return for allowing Bismarck to crush France, 'in the crisis of self-debate, a provocation from England might push him one way, and civility from England would have the opposite tendency'.

The Queen was unhappy about Salisbury's absence abroad and urged him to return in late August to talk to Francesco Crispi, the Italian Prime Minister, and generally to bolster the Triple Entente. But it was August, and he thought it improper to intrude on Bismarck's and Kálnoky's holidays, and anyhow, as his daughter recalled, 'Appeals for the exertion of his influence in person, whether in great things or small, always found him immovably resistant and sceptical.' He calmed the Queen by reminding her that the fundamentals of British foreign policy remained unchanged. 'France is, and must always remain, England's greatest danger,' he wrote from Royat. 'But that danger is dormant, so long as the present strained relations exist between France and her two eastern neighbours. If ever France should be on friendly terms with them, the Army and Navy Estimates would rise very rapidly.'

To Drummond Wolff in Teheran he wrote that Europe was quieter than he had known it for some time – 'it is quite phenomenal' – but he naturally appended the pessimistic footnote: 'I daresay it will all have changed before you get this.' Despite Crispi's annexation of Massowah in Abyssinia, his irritation of Germany over Zanzibar and his provoking quarrels with Greece, actions which Salisbury called Crispi's 'incurable propensity for breaking windows' and which he charitably put down to lumbago, the international scene was indeed quiet. A British fleet at Zanzibar prevented any bombardment of the Sultan by Germany or Italy, and Bismarck in return was allowed a free hand in colonising parts of Samoa, 'and a pretty pass he has made of it!'

The most important piece of domestic legislation of 1888, perhaps of the whole Parliament, was the creation of County Councils as the primary instruments of rural local government, replacing the previous arrangements under which local magistrates took *ad hoc* administrative decisions at Quarter Sessions. Salisbury has been accused of betraying the squirearchy, who tended to dominate the magistracy, in the interests of increasing local democracy, and he was keenly sensitive to the charge. 'How far do you think the class of magistrates would endure their complete deposition from the position of vantage which they have occupied for centuries – without bitterly resenting it,' he asked Lord Bath in February 1887, 'especially if those who deposed them was the party to whose friendship they thought themselves entitled to look?'[1]

Rather than giving a simple knee-jerk defence of the squires, however, Salisbury felt that if they wished to retain their powers when, as he wrote to one, 'representative bodies are the fashion of the day', they simply ought to contest the elections. The Tory squires had generally supported the 1867 Reform Act, and Salisbury, considering how he was often regarded as their champion, in fact had little respect for them. 'A squire is a dull thing,' he had written in the *Saturday Review* in 1857, 'but a squire speaking on finance is rather an amusing entertainment.' The squire in question, Sir John Tyrrell, had hailed from rural Essex, 'where the English language seems as yet to have obtained a very limited development'. Squires, he wrote, would not be converted by books or education 'any more than constant jingling will turn a penny into a half-crown'. In debates on the Indian *ryot* (peasant) in the

Commons, he was amused how 'a country gentleman can never get out of his head that a ryot is something that he ought to suppress'.

If Tory squires tended to irritate him, then those who voluntarily immersed themselves in local government fared even worse. 'Village Hampdens are, in practice, fussy, greasy sort of people, very fond of jobbing, and endowed with a preternatural thickness of cuticle in order to enable them to endure patiently the mortifications incident to a life passed in parochial contested elections.'[2] He opposed the centralisation practised in France, preferring 'the inconveniences of being governed by squabbling juntas of shopkeepers and tenant farmers' to the dangers to liberty from a strong central administration. But if, as he believed by 1868, 'pure squire Conservatism was played out', what could replace it that would not place the numerical majority in a position to raid the coffers of the rich minority via local taxation? In 1888, the country gentlemen used Smith to transmit to Salisbury their concern that County Councils would wreck their power base in the magistracy, but apart from removing authority over policing and the Poor Law from the scope of the new County Councils, Salisbury went ahead with fairly radical plans, though nothing like so radical as those he feared Gladstone would put forward should he return to office.

'The civilisation of many English counties is sufficiently backward to make it hazardous for the Crown to part with power over the police,' he explained to Chamberlain in February 1888, but otherwise 'we have acceded to your views on the County Council Bill to a great extent'. The Liberal Unionists were indeed happy with the outcome, which was considerably more far-reaching than they had expected to squeeze out of Salisbury. In his Caernarvon speech, Salisbury specifically denied that he was dethroning the squirearchy, as over the years many of their powers had been taken over by central government anyhow. He claimed that the only area of genuine independent power which the magistrates still retained was 'the liberty of repairing county bridges or not, as they like'. Large towns had already had popularly elected local bodies for sixty years, and Salisbury appreciated how impossible it was for the Justices of the Peace, who were appointed by the Lord-Lieutenant, to continue to exercise authority in local affairs. By withdrawing poor relief from the power of the new bodies, because labourers would form the majority in most of the counties, Salisbury made it a far less class-based and potentially dangerous reform than the Liberals would have passed.

Salisbury was delighted when Justices of the Peace won over half of the seats in the January 1889 County Council elections. As local aldermen were also co-opted, and made up one-third of the number of members, Salisbury realised that the County Councils were not going to be revolutionary bodies. He made an exception, however, for London's County Council, which Goschen had insisted upon being included in the Bill. The Liberals (standing as 'Progressives') defeated the Conservatives (the 'Moderates') in the first set of elections, and thereafter the London County Council (LCC) became a bugbear of Salisbury's.[3] 'I rather look to the new London County Council to play the drunken helot for our benefit,' he told Gwendolen after the elections. 'Such a body at the outset must make some portentous blunders,' he hoped, for which the Liberals would be blamed.

It was Salisbury's decision to allow the LCC to build houses in 1890, but he soon despaired of it, believing such an enormous task was too heavy for an amateur body to bear. In November 1894 he made one of his 'blazing indiscretions' when launching the Moderates' election campaign for the LCC, saying that: 'It is the place where collectivist and socialistic experiments are tried. It is the place where a new revolutionary spirit finds its instruments and collects its arms.' Considering that Lord Rosebery was its first chairman and Beatrice Webb complained that it was 'the most aristocratic local body in the world!', with Council members including the Duke of Norfolk, the Earl of Dudley, Earl Cadogan, Lord Mountmorres and the Earl of Onslow, Salisbury was exaggerating once again. His view was more justified in the longer term, however, when he complained to Onslow that once the novelty of County Councils wore off, 'it will be more and more difficult to get candidates of the "leisured" classes'.[4]

The most hazardous moment in the passing of the Local Government Bill came when the left wing of the Conservative Party threatened to support John Morley's amendments to its licensing clauses. A lifelong supporter of the drinks trade, Salisbury did not want to see local authorities in nonconformist and Temperance areas of the country penalising publicans and breweries through licensing restrictions. Calling a Party meeting at the Foreign Office, he upbraided the more independent Tory members and generally rapped knuckles successfully. Even though he asked for secrecy, a short abstract of the meeting appeared in the following morning's *Times* to the embarrassment of George Curzon, who had been elected for Southport in 1886 and who was quoted as having, albeit deferentially, disagreed with Salisbury.

Salisbury never believed that restricting the number of public houses would significantly lessen the amount of alcohol consumed nationally. When thirty-five MPs had supported a Temperance motion in June 1864, he remarked that they might as well bring in a Bill to abolish pocket-handkerchiefs 'in order to restore the over-tempted virtue of the pickpockets'. On another occasion, in a debate in the House of Lords on reducing the number of liquor licences, Salisbury confessed that he could never understand how more public houses meant a greater danger to public sobriety: 'I forget how many bedrooms I have at Hatfield, but I know that I never feel any more inclination to go to bed there than I do in Arlington Street.' The right to drink went to the heart of his libertarian beliefs. 'It is impossible for any legislation to perform', he told the House of Lords in May 1872, 'by the action of Government to ensure morality among the people.' The upper classes of 150 years before, he said, were just as drunkenly behaved 'as the lower classes are now. People did not then trust to legislative action, they resorted to civilisation and religion.'[5]

Derby assumed that Salisbury's 'eager and almost violent' support for the licensed victuallers in 1874 was because teetotallers were 'for the most part dissenters or freethinkers', and it was true that, in those areas of Wales where nonconformism was strongest, the Temperance movement most threatened the drinks trade. Derby was half right, for as Salisbury told Janetta Manners, teetotalism tended to encourage 'a rush towards Puritanism in amusements and social life'. He also disliked sudden change of any kind: 'The reformation which comes of "rushes" is more than three-quarters mere following of fashion.' Salisbury also believed in the beneficial powers of alcohol. When Gladstone suffered a bad fall in February 1881, Salisbury commented how 'Dr Kidd, Lord Beaconsfield's doctor, is fond of prescribing claret: and you may have observed that Lord Beaconsfield never tumbles.' Sound enough advice, except that two months after Salisbury wrote it, Beaconsfield died. Lady Salisbury also believed in alcohol's medicinal properties; she would administer a medication to elderly tenants at Hatfield made up of the whole family's left-over medicines all mixed together in a jug, added to an equal measure of her husband's port.

Salisbury, who was himself a prodigious tea-drinker but who also appreciated good wine, was opposed to the Sunday closing of public houses in Cornwall, as 'tending to restrict the liberty of the subject'. He built a small 'coffee-palace' in Hatfield for those teetotallers who felt they needed one, on much the same basis that he also gave land for a nonconformist chapel there. When on 23rd June 1886 Lord Fitzgerald proposed a Bill to prohibit the sale of intoxicating liquor to children under thirteen, Salisbury recalled his rowing days at Eton, when aged twelve he would pull up-river to Surley Hall and commit 'the enormity of drinking cider to quench his thirst'. He commented on the Bill that 'it was not worthy of serious opposition, because he did not suppose that anyone would pay attention to it if it were passed'. Later that year he told Janetta Manners that he considered 'the racing mania in England far more destructive – because that seems to get <u>worse</u> as civilisation advances. Yet I would not wish for Parliamentary interference even to stop that.'

When in 1890 Salisbury proposed an excise duty on beers and spirits to compensate those publicans who had been refused licences by

Temperance-dominated local authorities, a political row broke out which was fought out over twenty-five nights, the longest amount of time spent on a customs measure since the Corn Laws. The Opposition denounced the measure as 'pensioning a lot of decayed publicans', but Salisbury was adamant. With a fine disregard for mixed metaphors, one Temperance reformer accused the Prime Minister of 'throwing down an apple of discord which has burst into flames and flooded the country!' As well as the Church, Salisbury secured the influential drinks trade to the Tory cause, receiving vast contributions to the election fighting funds and even ennobling brewers. Once again his deepest-held principles and his Party's political advantage were able to merge fortuitously.

In one sense the 1889 LCC elections had indeed been revolutionary, in that women were elected for the first time, Lady Sandhurst for Brixton and Jane Cobden for Bromley. Salisbury did not oppose female suffrage, and in 1872 he told Lady Knightley that he could see no reason against it, but, typically, he did 'not consider it to be a pressingly needed reform at the present time'. Otherwise, Salisbury was contemptuously dismissive of women's political capability, believing them to vote 'on the impression or whim of the moment'. Once again his stance seems to find its genesis in religion. 'A good deal of the political battle of the future will be a conflict between religion and unbelief and the women will in that controversy be on the right side,' he told Janetta Manners in June 1884. 'When I am told my ploughmen are capable citizens, it seems to me ridiculous to say that educated women are not as capable.'

It was not until December 1888, speaking to the Primrose League in Edinburgh, that Salisbury publicly declared himself in favour of votes for women, saying that by knowledge, training and character they were obviously abundantly fit to enjoy it, and they could be as trusted as men to cast their votes 'in the direction of morality and religion'. He believed that married women should have the vote as they represented the most stable part of the community, and he anyhow assumed that in nine cases out of ten they would vote like their husbands. John Morley and Lord Rosebery, who were both against female suffrage, thought that Salisbury only supported it as a Tory counterpoise to their own cry for 'one man, one vote'. Salisbury appreciated that, although a majority of the Cabinet were probably in favour, the Party at large was definitely against female suffrage, so he resolved to leave it as an 'open' question, meaning that it would be a Liberal Government which tore itself apart over the issue, and then only after he was dead.[6]

Salisbury could be just as scornful of women as of Macedonians, reformers, philanthropists and the Irish. In his *Saturday Review* articles, he pointed out how, despite the fact that music had formed a staple of female education for centuries, there was not a single female name amongst the greatest musical masters, or amongst the greatest mathematicians or philosophers either, proving 'that women are fatally deficient in the power of close consecutive thought'. He complained that on country-house weekends, 'by the time luncheon comes, that vast range of subjects which the female mind embraces – scandal, dress, crotchet-work, and babies, is exhausted'. It is unfortunately not known what his able and intelligent wife and daughters thought about this thesis, but Lady Salisbury was a firm opponent of female suffrage. Once in November 1892 she was taken by Lady Knightley to an all-women club, and said that by the end of the evening 'the presence of none but females made her so wild she almost hugged the little boy outside who called the cabs'. Salisbury replied that he had 'never found the same enthusiasm for the maid-of-all-work at the Albemarle Club'.

Salisbury did not believe that women should be allowed to take university degrees, as an over-accomplished young woman was 'one of the most intolerable monsters in creation'. Women's colleges at Oxford, he admitted, might be useful for 'furnishing a diploma to ladies who wish to be governesses', but on Sunday mornings instead of going to church women undergraduates would, he feared, assemble in the rooms of a free-thinking don and 'as they call it "search after Truth" – that is, discuss all conceivable forms of unbelief'. If all women were educated to their highest capacity, it would furthermore 'make marriage more difficult than it is now to their unhappy victims'. He thought a strong-willed woman to be 'like a pretty man; the merit is unnatural to both, and both are certain to be ridiculously vain of it'. When women wrote articles, he did not think they ought to quote men. 'It is an honour to the person quoted,' he admonished Janetta Manners, who was guilty of it in 1884, 'but it is inappropriate to the dignity of the feminine pen. She should take no notice of the opinions of the baser sex.'

When contemplating a guest at Hatfield in the 1890s, Salisbury remarked under his breath to his daughter-in-law, Violet: 'I don't think any woman has any idea how insulted a man feels by the sight of an ugly woman.' Make-up, he believed, deceived no one but the very short-sighted. He thought that young girls very often had 'a half-conscious taste for perjury', citing the Salem witch trials, and yet also believed that 'to be favoured and flattered by a woman who is known to snub is a great distinction.... All ladies, therefore, who are in training to be leaders of fashion should, above all things, cultivate insolence.' He believed that proven adulterers should be treated harshly at Court to set a moral example, but agreed with the Queen that the upheaval involved would be 'too considerable'. He refused to invite one of his MPs, the dashing Harry Cust, to stay at Hatfield after he had reputedly fathered a child (Lady Diana Manners, later Cooper) by his former secretary Henry Manners's wife in 1892. He also flatly refused to have the Prince of Wales under his roof without the Princess also being present. His attitude was neither naïve nor strait-laced; he merely saw no reason why he should be seen condoning bad behaviour.

In September 1888, Sir Lionel Sackville-West, who had been British minister at the Washington Legation since 1881, made an astonishing error for a seasoned diplomat when he replied to a letter from a certain 'Mr Charles F. Murchison', who claimed to be an Englishman, asking whether he should vote for President Grover Cleveland, the first Democrat President since the Civil War, who was standing for re-election, or his Republican rival Benjamin Harrison. Sackville-West stupidly replied that, as Harrison was a protectionist, it would be better for Britain if Cleveland won. Six weeks later, and a fortnight before the elections, the letter, in fact written by a Republican called Osgoodley, was published in the *New York Tribune*, to Sackville-West's embarrassment.[7]

'It may possibly be necessary to recall him,' Salisbury told the Queen, admitting to 'a great repugnance to taking that course on account of the peculiar circumstances'. These were that Sackville-West was the brother of Lady Derby, Salisbury's father's widow. Fortunately the decision was made for him by the American Secretary of State, Thomas Bayard, who, responding to political pressures, sent Sackville-West his passports for interfering in American domestic politics, rather unnecessarily adding that his continued presence in America was 'detrimental to good relations of both Governments'. Sackville-West, who succeeded to his brother's peerage during the incident, had not made matters easier by telling an American interviewer how little he cared about all the fuss. When Salisbury saw him on 7th November, however, he 'seemed to be a good deal abashed'. The new Lord Sackville went home to Knole Park with a pension, and Salisbury showed his displeasure with the State Department by refusing to appoint a replacement until Pauncefote went out there five months later.

'Scotch Tories are difficult people to deal with,' Salisbury wrote to Goschen in October 1888. 'They have a strange generic resemblance to French Legitimists.' It was at a speech in Edinburgh the following month that Salisbury made yet another of his 'blazing indiscretions'. Recent jokes had gone down very well, as for instance when he had said of Irish self-government that: 'If three people are sitting upon two people and rifling their pockets, you must not say they are a group of five enjoying the blessings of self-government.' Or when he mock-admonished a crowd for booing the name of Sir George Trevelyan, who had rejoined the Gladstonian Liberals after a brief flirtation with Liberal Unionism: 'Do not hoot his name. Nothing is more useful than an instrument which is so sensitive that it will tell you every passing word of opinion, and to hoot Sir George Trevelyan is as sensible as hooting a well hung weathercock or an accurate barometer.'[8] But in Edinburgh on 30th November his sense of humour let him down.

The day before, a Conservative called Mr Gainsford Bruce had beaten Earl Compton, a Liberal, in the Holborn by-election. Bruce won by a smaller majority than the Tory Colonel Duncan had held the seat by in the 1885 general election. 'But then', explained Salisbury to a vast audience, 'Colonel Duncan was opposed to a black man, and, however great the progress of mankind has been, and however far we have advanced in overcoming prejudices, I doubt if we have yet got to the point where a British constituency will elect a black man to represent them.... I am speaking roughly and using language in its colloquial sense, because I imagine the colour is not exactly black, but at all events, he was a man of another race.' Dadhabai Naoroji, a Parsee former mathematics professor and Prime Minister of Baroda, had also sat in the Legislative Council for Bombay and had been President of the India National Congress. He thereafter called himself 'Lord Salisbury's black man'. Much was made by the Liberals of Salisbury's comment, with its suggestion that none but white Britons could represent a British constituency.

Three weeks later, after a furore in which even the Queen criticised him, Salisbury was forced into one of his unapologetic apologies, when he denied in a speech at Scarborough that 'the word "black" necessarily implies any contemptuous denunciation. Such a doctrine seems to be a scathing insult to a very large proportion of the human race.... The people whom we have been fighting at Suakim, and whom we have happily conquered, are among the finest tribes in the world, and many of them are as black as my hat.' Salisbury went on to say that he still thought 'such candidatures are incongruous and unwise. The British House of Commons, with its traditions ... is a machine too peculiar and too delicate to be managed by any but those who have been born within these isles.'[9] The National Liberal Club promptly gave a dinner in honour of Naoroji, who was elected for Finsbury at the next general election. Soon afterwards, Salisbury invited Naoroji to become a Governor of the Imperial Institute, which he graciously accepted.

By mid-1888, Salisbury had formed the opinion that Henry Matthews, the Home Secretary, was not up to the job. Matthews's position was already precarious after Bloody Sunday and because he had been a

Churchillite, but a series of unsolved, grisly murders in Whitechapel, popularly attributed to 'Jack the Ripper' after Mary Ann Nicholls was found horribly murdered on 31st August, also persuaded the Queen that he was incompetent. Salisbury had already considered moving Matthews, but was doubtful that his intended replacement, Lord Knutsford, was the right man. 'He is so amiable, he would hang nobody,' Salisbury complained. Hicks Beach, 'on the other hand, would make a very good Home Secretary, and would hang everybody', but he was still half blind. Matthews's perceived mismanagement of the Ripper investigations led the Queen to write to Salisbury on 28th October 1888, after three more women had been murdered, to complain that the Home Secretary's 'general want of sympathy with the feelings of the people are doing the Government harm'. Salisbury admitted that Matthews had not been a success, telling her: 'There is an innocence of the ways of the world which no one could have expected to find in a criminal lawyer of sixty.'

After the corpse of Mary Kelly, the Ripper's fifth victim, was found horrifically mutilated in Whitechapel on 8th November, the Queen admonished Salisbury for not having acted to light the streets and improve the detective work there. Salisbury telegraphed on 10th November that the Cabinet had that same day resolved to issue a proclamation offering a free pardon to anyone who gave evidence as to the recent murder, except of course the killer himself. The Queen was not content with this, however, and a week later she spoke to Salisbury about his plan to make Matthews a Lord Justice of Appeal, despite a blatant lack of qualification for the post, and move C.T. Ritchie, who was thought to have done well over the complicated County Councils legislation, to the Home Office. Matthews, greatly helped by the fact that he sat for a marginal Birmingham constituency, survived. By 1890 Salisbury thought it required 'an open and palpable error' to justify a bare dismissal, which would itself 'beget numberless intrigues'. Goschen, Smith and Balfour all thought it better to keep Matthews until the general election, and in 1895 he was awarded a viscountcy as a consolation for not being asked to return to office.[10]

Before he left India, Lord Dufferin drew up proposals for the Viceregal and provincial Legislative Councils. These envisaged their enlargement, the removal of restrictions on the topics they could discuss, and, most controversially, the introduction of some form of limited and indirect elections. Salisbury had hoped that Dufferin's experiment in drawing up the (by then defunct) 1883 Egyptian constitution would have dissuaded him from attempting to liberalise the Indian Councils, but he was to be disappointed. In a memorandum on what he described as the most important reform proposals since the dissolution of the East India Company in 1858, Salisbury explained how Dufferin's proposals were only the thin end of the wedge, and that giving legislative powers to elect natives as councillors in India would be a momentous step to inflict on the sub-continent, not just 'on the present, but on the future'.

Demanding that the India Secretary, Cross, must refuse even to publish Dufferin's scheme, Salisbury wrote:

> The opinion that has introduced it is not an Indian opinion – it is the mere echo of English opinion – the application to India of ideas bred in the political conflicts of this country.... The men who will be brought to the front by this plan will be... lawyers, agents, newspaper writers: not the men of business (who have not time for this work), nor the men of property (who would despise it): nor the simpler and more numerous members of the community, who would not have the requisite qualification. Now the class thus selected would be in England a very trustworthy class: but England is not ruled by conquest. In India they are the class among whom disaffection is the strongest, and they are the most competent to use the weapons which membership of a legislative Council would place in their hands to embarrass and damage the Government.... They are not to be feared, unless we put power into their hands. We shall in no way please the classes on whose goodwill the submission of India depends: we shall not reconcile our only enemies; but we shall give them arms against ourselves.

The problem with another Whig and Liberal Unionist, Lord Lansdowne, following Dufferin as Viceroy, was that such arguments had to be made again and again. Writing to Lansdowne in June 1890 to explain why the Indian Councils Bill had once again been denied parliamentary time, Salisbury admitted that it was partly due to his own firm opposition.

> I dread the impression that the Raj of the Governor-General is nearing its end: and that under the new regime there were good things to be had for those who are its earliest partisans.... I dread this question being discussed while Mr Gladstone is still a political force. He has, to my eyes, so entirely lost all sense of political responsibility, while retaining much of his old mastery over vague and philanthropic phraseology, that it would be a capital charge to the Empire if the language he is seen to use is taken as a watchword and a rallying cry by the novators in India. There is no other statesman near him, or in sight, who could effect a tenth part of the evil which will be caused by a few of his phrases of gorgeous, reckless optimism.[11]

Salisbury's refusal even to allow Dufferin's Indian proposals to be made public reflected an important aspect of his political and diplomatic method: he was addicted to secrecy to an extent that would be impossible in any modern Foreign Secretary. 'For the whole of Lord Salisbury's administrations our official records are incomplete,' wrote Eyre Crowe censoriously in January 1907, 'all the most important business having been transacted under cover of "private correspondence".' Thus the documents relating to an Anglo-German *rapprochement* in 1897 can be found in the German Foreign Ministry archives and at Hatfield, but not in the library of the British Foreign Office.

Although it understandably frustrated his officials, this secrecy allowed Salisbury to keep all the strings of his complex global policy securely in his own hands, trusting only a small coterie of subordinates with the larger picture. As his notes to his under-secretaries show, Salisbury delighted in giving as little information as possible to the House of Commons. One of the earliest examples of the political term 'leak' arises in a letter from Salisbury to Northbrook in July 1875, when he was concerned that Baron Reuter's telegraph news service was obtaining information from members of the Viceroy's staff. He insisted on all correspondence, especially from Ireland, being properly sealed and protected, and he assumed, as he told the Queen in 1888, that 'no letter is safe from being opened in France, Italy, or Germany', so he tended to use special messengers and cypher codes even for relatively mundane messages. His private office's codeword for his coming to London, for instance, was 'Omnipotent', followed by the hour of arrival. He had two postbox-sized holes cut into his huge locked desk at Hatfield, where he deposited memoranda and correspondence once he had worked on them.

For all his humiliation of Robert Lowe over the censorship of the Education Blue Books back in 1864, Salisbury took enormous care over the selection of Foreign Office papers for publication. He would regularly 'correct' documents, and even had *Hansard* retrospectively altered to make his culpability for the Carnarvon–Parnell conversation sound less direct. He was perfectly straightforward about this, telling an Under-Secretary, Edward Stanhope, after he had recorrected certain corrections to his 1876 Afghanistan correspondence, that they were 'principally in matters that would be embarrassing from the point of view of this office'. Salisbury would regularly write papers more with an eye on their publication than on what they were intended to convey to the recipient, who often privately received an accompanying handwritten letter which did not therefore need to go on file. 'I have abstained from any further action,' he wrote about the 1889 Cretan crisis for example, 'except sending to White a "Blue-Book" telegram of advice to the Turks.'[12] Such advice was not necessarily intended to be taken, but was sent in order to make the policy more defensible in Parliament.

More orthodox diplomats resented this intensely personal nature of Salisbury's diplomacy. In his memoirs, Sir Henry Layard criticised the way Salisbury transacted business, and especially how during the period

of the 1878 Anglo-Turkish Convention, the Under-Secretary of State
and the head of the Turkish Department were kept in complete ignorance of his negotiations. Only those in what Layard called Salisbury's
'secret department', which was 'composed of his private secretary and
other gentlemen who were employed in his private rooms and specially
attached to his person', were allowed to know exactly what was going
on. This was understandably resented by officials outside the charmed
circle and doubtless did, as Layard complained, 'give rise to very serious
mischief and to great inconvenience'. Especially after the Marvin incident, however, Salisbury took no chances.

Sometimes entire diplomatic *démarches* have to be pieced together from
information not in the Foreign Office papers but from elsewhere, especially
the private papers of ambassadors. Salisbury's letters were typically short,
often cynical, usually entertaining, bereft of verbosity and frequently
capable of summing up in a few often delightfully ironic sentences what
would take a less acute brain many paragraphs. After his retirement,
Salisbury kept his vast archive of documents at Hatfield, where, apart from
a brief sojourn at Christ Church, Oxford, they have remained.

'Salisbury and I have agreed to talk to each other just like private individuals,' Hatzfeldt told Holstein during the Bulgarian negotiations of
September 1886, mutually promising not to make official use of any
information given or received. It was a relationship that was to work to
both countries' advantage. In a revealing *coda* to a 'Secret and
Confidential' unnumbered telegram to Salisbury from Drummond
Wolff in May 1890, Salisbury noted to his Foreign Office private secretary, Eric Barrington, that he should have the document printed and
distributed to the Cabinet, as 'it is the only means my colleagues have
of knowing what I am doing'. Salisbury was a great burner of secret
documents, telling Dufferin in Paris in April 1895 that he had 'duly
delivered the despatch to the flames', and another trusted lieutenant,
Francis Bertie, that when it came to destroying confidential information: 'The weather is fortunately getting cold.' Salisbury's passion for
secrecy was taken to absurd lengths in June 1895 when he noted to
McDonnell on a letter from Buckle asking the names of the new
Cabinet members: 'What is the object of announcing a Cabinet?'

When a Chinese minister had asked the arms dealer Sir Ernest Cassel
whether the British Government might guarantee a Chinese loan,
Salisbury minuted to Bertie that 'the result of recent experience is that if
you wish to keep a secret you must say nothing 1. To Cabinet Ministers.
2. To Foreign Diplomatists. 3. To the War Office. A pretty prospect!' The
Queen was not sure that Lady Salisbury could be entirely trusted not to
speak of what passed at the royal interviews with her husband, and
contrasted her unfavourably in that respect with Lady Beaconsfield, who
neither knew nor wished to know any Cabinet secrets.[13]

Salisbury disliked it when ministers went on holiday without their cypher-books. 'A precautionary clause ought to have been inserted into the bill which conferred on you the liberty of travel,' he chaffed the Lord Chancellor in 1900. 'Like the five luckless men who were let out of the Bastille when it was taken, liberty evidently dazzles you.' A letter of Salisbury's to W.H. Smith of December 1885 shows how, even when ministers took their code-books with them, problems could still arise:

> My dear Smith, I telegraphed to you to ask what the politics of Fleming Canon of York were – You reply to me that the Bashi-Bazouks made difficulties but they were overdone. I fear our cyphers don't match. Can you answer my question? I rather think of him for Manchester – but I don't want to appoint a Radical.

Although Salisbury used trusted confidants like Philip Currie, William White, Julian Pauncefote and occasionally 'Pom' McDonnell to furnish him with the in-depth knowledge of foreign politics and personalities, the ultimate decisions were always taken by him alone. Even his most senior civil servants were used primarily as clerks and glorified private secretaries, rather than playing any significant part in the decision-making process. Salisbury made British foreign policy entirely by himself, helpfully inured by his peerage from the clamour of the Commons. For even a senior official at the Foreign Office to offer unsolicited political advice, Salisbury regarded as something of an impertinence.[14] 'The interpretation of the oracle is his own secret,' as Cecil Spring-Rice wrote. 'He consults it alone.' Indeed, Salisbury actively disliked 'talking things over'. 'Until my own mind is made up,' he told his daughter, 'I find the intrusion of other men's thoughts merely worrying.'

Salisbury conceived a few general, if rather cynical, rules of diplomacy which he stuck to throughout his long career at the Foreign Office. The first was that nations tended to have shorter memories than individuals, and acted according to entirely different moral precepts. 'Gratitude or indignation may last in the breasts of individuals for so long a period,' he told the House of Commons in May 1864, asking for a tough line against the Union over the Confederate ship *Georgia*, 'though even that is a rare phenomenon; but I am quite sure that you cannot find in the history of the world an instance in which these feelings have endured so long in the breasts of nations.' He cited as examples Denmark's friendship for Britain despite the Napoleonic Wars and the bad Anglo-French relations despite the Crimean alliance only a decade earlier.

Secondly, as he wrote to Northbrook in 1874 after one of the Indian princes wished to renegotiate a treaty he claimed was unjust because it was only signed under compulsion: 'If a treaty is to be impeached by that circumstance, how many of our treaties in India can stand? How many in the world generally? A treaty is in most cases the result of an employ-

ment of force – openly applied or covertly threatened.' To those Jingoes
who constantly demanded action against Russia, he emphasised that 'all
diplomatic remonstrances and threats must have a background of force',
and there was little Britain could practically do to harm Russia while her
army was only a fraction the size. He also believed that a good diplomat
acted cautiously and never attempted to squeeze the last drop of concession from his protagonist, which only made future success more difficult.

Instead, the diplomat had to walk 'the difficult, the narrow line that
separates an undue concession from that rashness which has, in more
than one case in history, been the ruin of nations as great and powerful
as ourselves'. Nor did he believe there was any point in trying to build
up pro-British parties in foreign countries. To Drummond Wolff, who
was trying to do just such a thing in Spain in 1899, he wrote that 'the
elaborate structures of influence which some diplomatists take so
much pains to build up' were merely 'waste labour'. But there was
always 'another form of influence which is as important as the other is
of little weight. "Influence" disappears: territory remains.' In the
protection and extension of British territorial ambitions, Salisbury
always sought to remind strategists that 'We are fish,' and that 'England
alone can do nothing to remedy an inland tyranny.'

Keeping his opponent guessing was a favoured pastime. When in
October 1897 Sanderson asked whether an untrue Reuter's report about
troop movements to Malta should be officially contradicted, Salisbury
minuted, 'I think not. I am hoping it will make our foreign friends
unhappy – because they cannot decide what mischief we are at.' The
diary of Sir Ernest Satow records how when in October 1897 he suggested
to Salisbury that he should counsel Japan to give way to America over
Hawaii or risk war, Salisbury 'smiled grimly saying there was no harm in
their having a little dispute about it' and Britain need only consider her
position if war actually broke out. It was cynical, but it kept the United
States occupied in an area where Britain had few interests.[15]

Salisbury's pithy red-ink annotations attained semi-mythical status
in the Foreign Office; he was a master of marginalia. When a British
trader asked the Foreign Office for help against a foreign potentate who
was ill-treating him, Salisbury jotted on the file: 'Buccaneers must
expect to rough it.' The bare line: 'Mr X beats his wife' would be affixed
to a recommendation for a vice-consul's promotion. When the Dowager
Empress of Japan died and Salisbury was asked whether Court mourning should be observed, he replied: 'Better not make a new precedent. If
there are several wives, are we to mourn them all?' 'I deeply sympathise
with your suffering at the hands of ambassadors,' Salisbury noted to
Sanderson, who as Permanent Under-Secretary was allowed to receive
the envoys of less important countries. 'If they think to alarm me by
boring you to death, they are much mistaken.' When the ambassadors

from the important countries began to bore Salisbury, he would keep himself awake by jabbing himself in the legs under the table using a dagger-shaped wooden paper knife.

'If one bored him at an interview,' recalled a Cabinet colleague, 'one knew at once as his leg began to "weg". I always wondered whether ambassadors took the hint.' All too often they did not, especially the Turkish ones who regularly had to be told white lies. Once when his assistant private secretary, Arthur Hardinge, was showing out Rustem Pasha having told him that the Prime Minister was at Hatfield, they both suddenly saw Salisbury open his door at the end of the passage and descend a back staircase. 'Rustem turned on me with a look of silent resentment,' Hardinge recalled, 'too intense to find expression in mere words.' The most trying of all the dignitaries was the octogenarian Chinese tyrant-warlord, Li Hung Chang, who brought a pipe-filler and a cluster of opium pipes along to meetings in the Foreign Office. Salisbury had 'a well known horror of tobacco, whose fumes made him very uncomfortable'.[16] (The absence of the chain-smoking Lord Randolph Churchill had been yet another happy by-product of the events of December 1886.)

The vast diplomatic receptions Salisbury was obliged to host at the Foreign Office, which the Cecils called 'packs', he enjoyed no more than the political parties he had to give at Arlington Street. When a niece asked if she could attend one of the latter, he replied that of course she could, 'if you enjoy the vexation of the Conservative Party trampling on your toes'. Lord and Lady Salisbury would receive guests at the top of the huge marble double staircase at Arlington Street. Lord Killanin, the Lord Chief Justice, said that Lady Salisbury was so expressionless on these occasions that it was like shaking hands with the village pump. Lady Brooke, later the Countess of Warwick, remembered such receptions as:

> incomparably splendid, dazzling to both eye and to the mind. It was certain that some of the Royal Family would attend. Rajahs and Maharajahs, ambassadors and foreign attachés in uniforms of infinite splendour, stalked god-like among the stately beauty of St James's. Ablaze with jewels and the sashes of countless orders, they glowed with colour and complacency.

Before 1914, Britain only had nine ambassadors (against 149 in 1997) and 125 diplomatic posts abroad, seven of which were in St Petersburg. The Foreign Office staff in London then numbered fifty-two. Never in the history of diplomacy was so much negotiated for so many by so few. By 1895, the Office had four political departments – Western, Eastern, American and Asiatic, African and Protectorates – and five administrative departments – Chief Clerk's office, Commercial, Consular, Library and Treaty. The number of despatches handled increased from 78,000 in 1878 to 102,000 in 1898 (against the 23 million received in 1997). As Pauncefote told the Royal Commission on Civil Establishments, 'one lady typewriter is employed. It is proposed to extend the system when opportunity occurs.' Soon afterwards the work became too much even for Mrs Fulcher.

Accounts differ as to whether Salisbury was popular in the Foreign Office, although all agree that the question would have produced complete indifference in him one way or the other. On becoming Under-Secretary there in 1898, the aristocratic MP for Guildford, St John Brodrick, said that Salisbury was 'worshipped', and on taking up his appointment he was advised: 'Remember he is very difficult to move, but he comes down like a bag of bricks when he does.' Salisbury routinely held up professional advancement by sending non-diplomats to key posts – Lytton to Paris, Dufferin to Rome, Drummond Wolff to Constantinople and Teheran, for instance – and he insisted on a higher turnover at embassies than had been usual. 'An occasional change of post increases the usefulness of a diplomatist,' he told the Queen in September 1888. 'If he remains too long at one post he falls under special personal influences, or gets mixed up in local quarrels.'

Salisbury thought the Foreign Office a nest of Whiggery and had a low opinion of the general level of ambassadorial competence. He was angry in 1883 when he heard that Sir Augustus Paget, whom he thought one of the only Tories there, was to be pensioned off. (In fact, Paget's career was resurrected and the next year he went off to Vienna, where he stayed until 1896, dying suddenly while staying at Hatfield three years later.) Salisbury certainly antagonised the Foreign Office by promoting men he considered able far above their places in the hierarchy. Impressed by Charles Hardinge's performance at Teheran, he promoted him to counsellor at St Petersburg, over the heads of no fewer than seventeen more senior officials. Questions were asked in Parliament, which Salisbury parried by simply stating that in his opinion Hardinge was the man best suited for the job.

When in 1888 Salisbury invited Sir Harry Johnston, the African explorer and Acting Consul of the Niger Coast Protectorate, to Hatfield to dine and sleep and discuss African affairs, a burst of jealous rage came from Clement Hill, the chief clerk of the African Department, who told Johnston that he had been at the Foreign Office since 1871 and not only had Salisbury never once asked to see him, but he 'wouldn't know me if we met in the street!' George Goschen's younger brother Edward – whom Salisbury once sent off as minister to Belgrade after a two-minute interview in which he said, 'Let's see, King Milan is there, well I suppose we'd better keep our eye upon him' – said that 'if he hates the Service as he is said to, the Service perfectly loathes him'.[17]

For the less important posts in minor countries, and especially in Latin America where he had at best a hazy geographical grasp, Salisbury could be almost skittish in his choice of envoys – 'Brown? Brown. A good old English name. Give it to Brown.' The diplomat Sir Ernest Satow, irritated at being accorded only a five-minute interview with

Salisbury, came away under the impression that Salisbury believed Uruguay and Chile had a contiguous frontier.

Salisbury thought the work of commercial attachés 'mere drudgery'. He nevertheless supported their attachment to embassies, and wrote of an official who was blocking the process that he was too 'severely orthodox and rather looks upon all trades as an old maid looks upon all men – as being a conspiracy to surprise him into some illicit favour'.[18] Salisbury was also fully capable of wielding that most potent weapon in diplomatic negotiations – silence. 'I preserved throughout the attitude of a listener,' he reported to Bigge after an audience with King Leopold II of the Belgians in January 1896. 'He made several pauses in order to give me an opportunity of breaking in and imploring him to take the lease of the Mahdi's country. But I made no sign, and at last he retired (with a shower of compliments, but) in despair.'

Salisbury was sublimely unconcerned by the complaints in the Office about his practice of not writing up reports of his meetings with ambassadors. He used to do it in the first three years of his Foreign Secretaryship, he explained to Curzon in 1896, but then Dilke had later 'made an abominable use of the knowledge' and so he had ceased. Anyhow, 'the knowledge that I abstain from it makes both Hatzfeldt and [the French Ambassador Baron] de Courcel speak more freely than they would do otherwise'. Instead he wrote to the Queen, and he told Curzon he could see some of those letters instead. 'Salisbury keeps us in the dark about his foreign policy and its ultimate objects and tendencies,' the junior diplomat Eyre Crowe told his father in 1887. When the head of the Western Department complained that he had had no knowledge of the agreement Salisbury had made over Suez and the New Hebrides, Pauncefote apologised, saying that he 'had no voice in the matter as Salisbury did it all himself'. This caused difficulties once he had retired and gaps were discovered in the records of Britain's negotiations with other Powers; Harold Nicolson was still complaining as late as 1939 of the 'considerable confusion' caused by Salisbury's diplomatic correspondence all being at Hatfield instead of in the Foreign Office library.

What Crowe complained of as 'Lord Salisbury's mania of keeping things secret and working by back-channels' meant that he could personally control and direct an integrated global policy by himself. Treating Foreign Office officials as glorified versions of the agents on his estates, and keeping his Cabinet colleagues slightly in the dark, and Parliament more so, allowed him greater freedom of action than any other Foreign Secretary since the Congress of Vienna, and far more than any since.[19] One central brain controlled all, which was alright when that brain was as subtle and fecund as Salisbury's. Only the Queen was taken fully into his counsels. 'Always tell the Queen everything,' was his advice to colleagues and – other than in the exceptional case of the Carnarvon–Parnell interview – he practised what he preached.

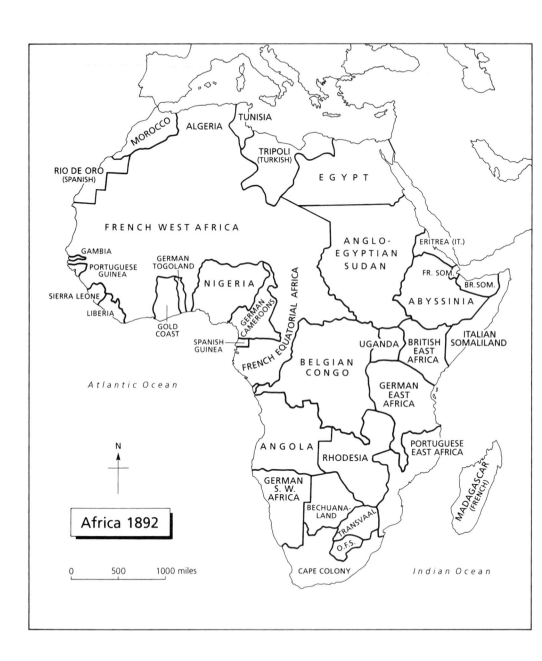

Africa 1892

MOROCCO
ALGERIA
TUNISIA
TRIPOLI (TURKISH)
EGYPT
RIO DE ORO (SPANISH)
FRENCH WEST AFRICA
ANGLO-EGYPTIAN SUDAN
ERITREA (IT.)
GAMBIA
PORTUGUESE GUINEA
GERMAN TOGOLAND
NIGERIA
FR. SOM.
BR. SOM.
SIERRA LEONE
LIBERIA
GOLD COAST
GERMAN CAMEROONS
FRENCH EQUATORIAL AFRICA
ABYSSINIA
SPANISH GUINEA
UGANDA
BRITISH EAST AFRICA
ITALIAN SOMALILAND
Atlantic Ocean
BELGIAN CONGO
GERMAN EAST AFRICA
N
ANGOLA
RHODESIA
PORTUGUESE EAST AFRICA
MADAGASCAR (FRENCH)
GERMAN S. W. AFRICA
BECHUANA-LAND
TRANSVAAL
O.F.S.
0   500   1000 miles
CAPE COLONY
Indian Ocean

THIRTY-ONE

Africa

Overall Policy – Bullying Portugal –
Zanzibar – The Sahara
– Italian Ambitions
– Cecil Rhodes

1885 to 1892

'We have been engaged in drawing lines upon maps
where no white man's foot has ever trod.'

'Africa is the subject which occupies the Foreign Office more than any
other,' Salisbury told his Guildhall audience in November 1889. It was
during his two premierships between 1885 and 1892 that many of the
major agreements were put into place which delineated which parts of
the continent fell into the spheres of influence of which European
powers. Far from being subjected to an inherently unstable scramble,
Africa was carved up in a remarkably orderly manner, without provoking war between any of the European Powers involved. It was an
admirable achievement, and much of the credit must be accorded to
Salisbury. That the British lion took so large a share was not due to
crude land-grabbing, although various commercial agents of British
policy certainly did occasionally indulge in that, but to careful negotiation and compromise with the major chancelleries of Europe. In 1889,
Salisbury had the maps of Central Asia and the Balkans taken down
from his vast room at the Foreign Office, and instead he 'curtained the
walls in aggressive profusion' with maps of Africa. More were placed 'in
crowded layers' in his study at Hatfield.

By 1914, Africa was divided up between Britain, France, Spain,
Portugal, Belgium, Turkey, Italy and Germany. A process that could so
easily have led to war never did because Bismarck and Salisbury tended
to put European considerations before African ones. Salisbury's first
object was the avoidance of war with France or Germany, and African

affairs were, at least in the period from 1885 to 1892, always seen in this light. Jingoism, which Salisbury viewed as the 'bastard brother' of patriotism, was not allowed to wreck the process of relentless but peaceful acquisition of only those areas Britain really needed.[1] The strategic imperatives were greatly eased by the fact that neither Russia nor America were involved, to Salisbury's great relief, and that Bismarck inherently regarded Germany's African colonies with something approaching disdain, primarily seeing them as means by which European tensions could be eased and domestic constituencies appeased.

By the end of the nineteenth century, nearly half of Africa's internal frontiers were made up of straight longitudinal or latitudinal lines. Whatever the morality of this process – a modern concept which would not have detained Salisbury for very long – it was clear that tribal or even geographical considerations were not paramount, so much as the general desire to find peaceful outcomes. The great energy and dynamism of Europe in the last quarter of the nineteenth century had been harnessed successfully for exploration and development rather than internecine conflict. In a speech in May 1886, Salisbury had stated that when he left the Foreign Office in 1880, 'nobody thought about Africa', but when he returned to it five years later, 'the nations of Europe were almost quarrelling with each other as to the various portions of Africa which they could obtain. I do not exactly know the cause of this sudden revolution,' but it was one he joined enthusiastically.

There were many causes for the European explosion on to the Dark Continent, amongst which were the discovery of gold and diamonds in South Africa, the opening up of eastern Africa by the Suez Canal, the evangelical impulse to abolish the slave trade and convert the heathen, national pride and the fear of being left behind, France's lust for *la gloire* after her 1871 defeat, private adventurism, the quest for new markets and raw materials, the vicious greed of King Leopold II of Belgium, Britain's need for a safe new route to India, and the invention of steamships, new medicines and advanced weaponry. With her naval superiority, historical links and adventurous explorers, missionaries and traders, Britain, which had not prospered much in Africa under Gladstone and Beaconsfield, was set fair to carve out a huge African empire under Salisbury, so long as the other Great Powers did not combine to stop her.

In June 1888, Salisbury asked to meet Harry Johnston, the thirty-year-old Acting Consul of the Niger Coast Protectorate and former leader of the Royal Society's scientific expedition to Mount Kilimanjaro. Johnston found Salisbury 'shrewd, sensible, acquainted with African questions and conditions, and retentive of memory'. He must have impressed the Prime Minister too, because the following month he was invited to stay at Hatfield. An artist, adventurer and explorer, Johnston entertained the younger Cecils in the billiards room with tales of cannibalism. During a walk in the park after church on Sunday, Salisbury spoke to Johnston and Sir Robert Morier of his plans for 'the future allotment of Africa' and archly said: 'What a pity it is that no one could put the whole African question basically before the public – in some newspaper article I mean.' Johnston later recalled, 'I had a sort of feeling that his eye rested on me for a moment before it looked ahead.'

The result, published in *The Times* on 22nd August once it was checked over by Salisbury, was a long and authoritative article by 'An African Explorer' entitled 'Great Britain's Policy in Africa'. It stated that Africa was the next New World, which must 'inevitably be exploited by the white races' and that Britain should now carefully demarcate those areas she needed, take them, and not bother overmuch about peripheral ones which were likely to provoke conflict with other European powers. The whole Nile Valley, as a strategic necessity to protect Egypt, must certainly be brought under the British *ægis*, along with enough of its hinterland to negate threats from any other Power.

'We are forced', Johnston wrote anonymously, by German, Portuguese and French ambitions, 'to extend our direct political influence over a large part of Africa', particularly as the world grew steadily more protectionist, closing market after potential market to British goods. It was a call to arms, but only in specific areas for specific purposes for specific periods, rather than a general Jingoistic appeal for unlimited territorial acquisition. Clement Hill, the Foreign Office Africa specialist, thought it 'an extraordinary proceeding' to announce Government policy in this covert way, but it had the advantage of complete deniability abroad.

Johnston's Hatfield weekend left a valuable insight into Salisbury's conversational style through the words of the Marquess of Wiltshire, the statesman in *The Gay-Dombeys*, Johnston's thinly veiled *roman à clef*, published in 1919. After an evening in which the daughter of the house acted Lord Randolph Churchill 'in a wonderful moustache' in charades – something Gwendolen Cecil did the weekend that Johnston stayed – Lord Wiltshire walks in the park with the hero, based on Johnston. Wiltshire is 'an elderly Hercules' who subjects the hero to 'a quiet, conservative businesslike cross-examination' and who displays a 'considerable sense of humour, and a little malice, an enjoyment of a joke or an incongruity, but no laugh, only a genial smile'. During their walk, Wiltshire says:

> And now, now that I am tolerably out of hearing of my excellent tenantry –
> though so quaint is our national education that I might shout out strings of

African names and they would not be a bit the wiser – now let us settle the fate of the Niger. It is, I may observe, a curious anomaly that the future weal or woe of millions of black or brown people – should you call the Falahs brown? – well then of millions of black and brown people, is being determined in a Hertfordshire beech avenue in latitude fifty-one something North, where there hasn't been the shade of a palm for – what should we say: you Evolutionists are so liberal in time – two million years?... And now to business. We've settled more or less our frontier with the Cameroons, and as regards the French....[2]

(Other than as Sir Ethelred, the 'Great Presence' in Joseph Conrad's *The Secret Agent*, and the Earl of Elveston in Lewis Carroll's *Sylvie and Bruno*, it is Salisbury's sole appearance as a fictional character. A theory has been adduced, however, that the characters Gwendolen and Cecily in *The Importance of Being Earnest*, as well as the opening of the play at ·a Hertfordshire country house and the Cecil family motto: 'Late but in Earnest', imply that Wilde was satirising the Cecils in his 1895 play.)

It was not in fact West Africa and the French that Salisbury wished to discuss with Johnston that day, but southern Africa and the Portuguese. In his article Johnston wrote, 'we have one pressing want – Delagoa Bay', the strategic port in Mozambique which he foresaw Portugal would one day be obliged to sell to Britain or lose altogether. Soon after the conversation, Johnston was sent out as Consul to Mozambique, with a brief to oppose Portuguese incursions into Nyasaland – part of modern-day Malawi. The Portuguese Government were pressing claims, with the minimum of right measured either by previous occupation or trading agreements with local chieftains, to the whole of the hinterland of Mozambique on the east coast of Africa right across to its Angolan colony on the west. This precipitated a diplomatic clash with Britain that brought the two countries to within an ace of war by Christmas 1889. Portuguese expansion into Nyasaland and along the Zambezi, which had been traversed by David Livingstone, British missionaries, Scottish anti-slavery campaigners and but few others, had forced Salisbury to consider seizing Goa from Portugal as early as New Year's Eve 1888.

'She is a most tiresome little Power,' Salisbury wrote to Lord Harrowby, his ex-Cabinet colleague and the spokesman for the Nyasaland missionaries, when Portuguese officials in Delagoa Bay refused to allow the British-owned Lakes Trading Company to import arms to protect themselves and missionaries who had been attacked by Arab slave-traders around Lake Nyasa. The Cabinet resolved that the Portuguese claim to the lower part of Lake Nyasa 'was unfounded and could not be admitted'. The friction continued, with Portugal presumed to have 'strained' rather than broken international law by her further incursions in June 1889, but enough to provoke the Cabinet resolution

that 'some sharp warning would be of value'. It was a remarkable tweak-
ing of the lion's tail by a far weaker power unsupported by any European
allies; British railway lines were torn up by Portuguese authorities,
Union Flags were hauled down in Matabeleland and British engineers
were arrested. While urging the Queen to keep her temper, Salisbury
found his own sorely tested.

By November, Salisbury was asking the War Office Intelligence
department to report on how difficult it might be, in the event of war, to
take and hold Lourenço Marques – present-day Maputo – the capital of
Portuguese Mozambique, once the Government of India had vetoed the
idea of invading Goa. On 13th December, Salisbury's patience snapped
when news reached London of a raid by Major Serpa Pinto, the
Portuguese commander on the Zambezi, against the British-protected
Makalolo tribe in the Shiré Highlands. Harry Johnston protested vigorously about the action against the tribe, which was massacred when its
leaders refused to accept Portuguese 'protection' instead of British.[3]

Salisbury instructed Lord George Hamilton to have the Cape and
Zanzibar naval squadrons coaled up and ready to sail to Mozambique.
He demanded that Portugal recall Pinto forthwith, and the threat of
military retaliation was made plain in the event of an unfavourable
answer from Lisbon. Salisbury also insisted on swift action against any
other Powers which supported Portugal. When the Portuguese reply
came, refusing not to interfere with British-protected chieftains and
using seventeenth-century land titles as the justification for Pinto's
actions, Salisbury obtained the Cabinet's permission to go to war
against 'our oldest ally'. He was keen 'to make the fall as soft for
Portugal as possible', not wanting to provoke a republican revolution
there, but when news arrived on Christmas Eve that Portuguese troops
were due to leave Goa for Mozambique on New Year's Day, Salisbury
telegraphed to Lansdowne to 'intimate to the Government at Goa –
when the occasion for doing so shall arise – that if the troops are sent it
will be necessary for us to occupy Goa'.

Salisbury was dismissive of the Portuguese historical claims, and told
the Queen on 27th December that he:

> utterly rejects the archæological arguments of the Portugese who claim
> half Africa on the supposed cession to them in 1630 of the Empire of
> Monomotapa of which event Lord Salisbury can find no account whatever,
> in this country. Nor does he consider that the existence of ruined forts
> proves any claim, but rather the contrary, since it shows that the Power
> that built these forts has abandoned them.

The other Powers would be firmly told that the Portuguese action had
been 'an invasion of Your Majesty's rights'.

On Boxing Day, Salisbury was hit by a virulent strain of Russian influenza, which at the height of the crisis left him completely debili-tated, even to the extent that it became life-threatening during the last few days of 1889. This particular virus, popularly believed to have started when thousands of Chinese corpses buried near the Yangtze had been washed into the river by freak flooding, was no respecter of the *Almanach de Gotha*, killing the King of Italy's brother, the Duke of Aosta, the Dowager Empress Augusta of Germany and very nearly the King of Spain. In Britain, it gave Hartington severe congestion of both lungs and it killed Lord Napier. Although Salisbury was unable to write until mid-January, could not visit London until February and did not feel fully better until April – and indeed never regained the complete use of his legs, walking slowly for the rest of his life – he was sitting up directing the crisis by 6th January 1890 and insisted on drafting the ulti-matum to Portugal himself.[4]

That day, HMS *Enchantress* was sent to take away Sir George Petre, the Envoy Extraordinary and Minister Plenipotentiary in Lisbon, should the Portuguese not respond positively to the ultimatum. To emphasise the threat, the Channel Squadron was sent to Tagus with sealed orders on 11th January, the day that Britain gave the Portuguese Government twenty-four hours to withdraw the Pinto expedition. Although the Portuguese Government fell, and the Lisbon mob broke their own ministers' windows as well as those of the British Legation, Salisbury's gunboat diplomacy succeeded and Nyasaland was preserved for the British sphere. The whole crisis had been conducted from Salisbury's sick-bed at Hatfield, with no Cabinet meeting called until 6th February. Portuguese requests for a return to the status quo were refused, as were their demands for international arbitration. 'As a starting point for negotiations', Salisbury told Buckle, Portugal 'calmly proposes that we should admit her right to a band of territory stretching from the East Coast of Africa to the West'.

A treaty of 20th August 1890, in which Britain acquired Lake Nyasa and the Shiré Highlands and Portugal held on to areas to the west with free international navigation of the Zambezi, fell through when the Cortes in Lisbon failed to ratify it on 21st September. 'The Portuguese Government do not seem to be amenable to anything except threats,' Salisbury lamented to the Queen. Nothing happened until British gold-miners in the Manica Plateau in Matabeleland, encouraged by Cecil Rhodes, started making unofficial inroads into areas which in the unrat-ified treaty had been designated as Portuguese. Suddenly the Portuguese returned to the negotiating table. The twenty-six-year-old King Charles had ascended the Portuguese throne on 28th December 1889, and Salisbury was 'very much disgusted by the way in which the various agents harp upon the argument that unless we give them what they want the King will lose his throne'.

Salisbury believed that it was not his duty to protect the Braganza dynasty, even though he came under pressure from the Kaiser, the Prince of Wales and Queen Victoria to do just that. He believed that the Portuguese were 'making the most of their weakness', and told Petre that his language 'should be stiff and uncompromising', pointing out that the British Government also had to placate 'a public opinion as exacting and powerful as their own'. Salisbury's typically utilitarian attitude, understandably not shared by his royal correspondents, was that 'If the [Portuguese] monarchy is so desperately weak that...our... demands will overthrow it, it is not worth saving.'

Salisbury found the Portuguese the least satisfactory negotiators of any he had dealt with, for, as he told Morier, when pressed in argument, 'instead of arguing back again, they throw themselves on their backs and scream'. He found it hard to explain to them that they had actually to colonise the areas they claimed: 'If they cannot provide settlers of their own blood, we can of ours: and we shall do so, whether we – that is Great Britain – desire it or not.' A new draft treaty was ready by mid-April 1891. It was much the same as the last one except the Manica Plateau was now placed in the British sphere. Once ratified, it established a British protectorate over Nyasaland without dethroning the Braganzas, who lasted on the Portuguese throne until 1910. Salisbury had a low opinion of the Portuguese Prime Minister, the Marquis Luis de Soveral, whom he told Bertie 'likes the society of princes and pretty women. Any other society is a duty not a pleasure and is therefore partaken of sparingly.'[5]

Before the Cortes finally ratified the Anglo-Portuguese Zambesi Agreement in June 1891, two and a half years and four Portuguese foreign ministers after the Pinto raid, yet another incident occurred. It was announced in the House of Lords on St George's Day 1891 that two ships under the command of a hot-headed baronet called Sir John Willoughby had been seized in the mouth of the Pungwé River and their Union Flags hauled down by Portuguese. Under an earlier *modus vivendi* with Portugal the river had been declared open, and Salisbury reported that he had sent three ships there to demand retribution. 'They will not be large vessels,' he announced dismissively, 'but they will be adequate for the purpose.'

If Portugal could be bullied with gunboat diplomacy in the way he had despised when it was practised (albeit less effectively) on Brazil and Japan by Lord John Russell, Salisbury knew that Germany had to be treated with a good deal more respect. The Sultan of Zanzibar – whose territory roughly covered modern-day Tanzania – had granted leases, for substantial rents, both to Sir William MacKinnon's British East Africa Company and to the German East Africa Company along his coastline. When in September 1888 a local revolt forced the Germans out of all of their coastal territories except Dar-es-Salaam, they threatened vengeance. Salisbury told Malet that British and Indian interests in Zanzibar, from where much trade was done with Bombay and other Indian ports, were too strong to allow a German blockade or bombardment. He feared that unilateral German action against the Sultan – but ostensibly against the slave trade and arms importation – might force the British out, just as the French had been edged out when they refused to take part in the chastisement of Egypt in 1882.

Only by keeping British ships alongside German and Italian ones during the operations against Arabs on the Zanzibar coast did Salisbury feel it was possible to protect the Sultan himself, limit the campaign and defend British interests. So, most reluctantly, the Royal Navy took part in the operations, ever vigilant for incursions on British rights. 'It is the extreme untrustworthiness of the present ruling powers both at Berlin and Rome', Salisbury explained to the Queen on Christmas Day 1888, which led him 'to advise a participation in the blockade as a means of control.'[6] Bismarck announced in the Reichstag on 18th January 1889 that 'we have proceeded, and shall ever proceed, solely with and in agreement with, the greatest colonial power in the world, England'.

Salisbury was unconvinced of German good intentions, and in briefing the thirty-year-old Gerald Portal, who in April 1889 left Baring's Cairo staff to be Acting Consul at Zanzibar, he warned that in Africa the German character 'shows itself in a very unamiable light, as seen in their more distant officials. They are self-willed, brutal and overbearing, but apparently without the good faith which is often found in such rugged characters.' Salisbury made no attempt to underplay Portal's difficulties: 'You have to govern an imbecile Sultan, and make him like the operation, while encouragements to revolt against you, more or less open, are being held out by both Germans and Arabs.... It requires vigilance and a scrupulous abstinence from heroic or summary methods of action.'

Salisbury appreciated that it was easier to prescribe patience and virtue 'in this foggy climate than to practise under the sun of Zanzibar', but he emphasised to the young man that he was not 'asking you to take my opinion against any which a deliberate survey of the circumstances on the spot may induce you to form'. Friction with German traders and settlers was evident in Fiji, New Guinea, the Congo and South-West Africa, and when a German naval captain steamed past the Union Flag on the island of Heligoland in the summer of 1889 without acknowledging it, Salisbury telegraphed to Malet to ask the German naval ministry for 'more respectful behaviour' in future.

Although Britain had officially banned the slave trade throughout her

Empire in 1833, it was still rife in many other parts of Africa, especially in Leopold II's personal fiefdom, the Belgian Congo. A conference in Brussels in November 1889 called for its global suppression, which Salisbury praised in public while seeking to ensure that its provisions in no way impinged on British rights or interests. Instead, the Conference's support for Britain to build a railway from Mombasa to Lake Victoria, a long-standing pet project of Salisbury's which he hoped would strengthen the British presence in Uganda, meant it actually worked in Britain's favour. Salisbury always favoured generous compensation to those Arab slave-owners whose trade in non-British territories was declared illegal by the *fiat* of the Great Powers, inspired by a Christianity they did not share.

By February 1890, Salisbury was concerned that 'the friction between Germans and Englishmen in Africa whenever they come into contact is increasing'. This was starkly proven in March when Dr Karl Peters, the deposed Chairman of the German East Africa Company, concluded a treaty with a chief called King Mwanga for a German protectorate in Uganda. Beyond Mwanga's territory lay the headwaters of the Nile in southern Sudan, and suddenly Salisbury, who held British control of the entire Nile Valley to be absolutely sacrosanct, had to face the threat of a future German presence near the river's source.[7] This danger would not manifest itself for several years, not least because King Mwanga soon turned against Peters, but it was a serious cause for concern.

Although he had not met the German Chancellor face-to-face since the Congress of Berlin, Salisbury had been dancing an intricate diplomatic minuet with Bismarck, in which mutual respect and distrust were the principal features. The Empress Friedrich did not envy Salisbury for having to deal with Bismarck, but told her mother Queen Victoria that he did it admirably, showing 'a patience, tact and sagacity which are very great'. On 20th March 1890, the Kaiser suddenly dismissed Bismarck, after twenty-eight years of guiding the destiny first of Prussia and then of Germany. When he offered him the title Prince Lauenberg as a consolation, the Iron Chancellor replied that it might prove useful if he ever needed to travel incognito. Salisbury appreciated the paradox of Bismarck's 'curious Nemesis', and in particular the way in which 'the very qualities which he fostered in the Emperor in order to strengthen himself when the Emperor Frederick should come to the throne, have been the qualities by which he has been overthrown'. The only clouds on the European horizon, Salisbury believed, were 'motionless' ones, but presented with the new regime of Kaiser Wilhelm II and Count Georg von Caprivi, who replaced Bismarck as Imperial Chancellor and Prussian Prime Minister, Salisbury decided to offer an inspired deal that an unsure Berlin keen for an easy bloodless victory might well accept.

After Bismarck had removed his 300 packing cases and more than a thousand cases of wine from Berlin to his Friedrichsruh estate, and 'Hateful Herbert' had been replaced by Baron von Marschall as German Foreign Minister, Salisbury made a startling offer. On 13th May, after failing to get an agreement on the issue of the hinterland of East Africa, he told Hatzfeldt that, if Britain were allowed to establish a sole protectorate over Zanzibar, Witu and all the neighbouring coastal and inland districts hitherto administered by Germany, Britain would cede Heligoland, an unfortified island at the mouth of the Kiel Canal, to Germany. Once a Danish possession, then owned by Hanover, it had been in British hands almost by accident since 1814. Because of its close proximity to the German coast, yet 350 miles away from Britain, it was impossible to defend in the event of war. Since the Kiel Canal had been cut in 1887, German naval strategists had shown interest in it, and the incoming post-Bismarck ministry believed it might be a popular coup to acquire it.

For Britain the advantages were obvious: in exchange for a small territorial white elephant she could immediately protect the south-eastern approaches to the Nile Valley, remove a major bone of contention with Germany, and extend British commercial interests in Zanzibar. All that, as Cranbrook noted after Salisbury mentioned the prospective deal to the Cabinet on 21st April, for 'not a valuable or useful possession' which would have fallen in the first week of any war with Germany anyhow. Admiral 'Jackie' Fisher was years later to condemn Salisbury for giving up 'the key of Germany in the North Sea when he gave Heligoland to Bismarck's threatenings'; Bismarck was not in power at the time Salisbury made the offer, nor could Heligoland possibly have been fortified without a direct provocation to Germany.[8]

In his first major foray into foreign policy after Bismarck's fall, the Kaiser had stated a desire for cross-continental territorial communications between German possessions in the Congo and East Africa. 'It is clear that his own personal intervention is shaping the course of German policy in this matter,' Salisbury wrote in a Cabinet memorandum, recommending the Heligoland deal:

> The claims of the Germans rest simply upon the doctrine of 'Hinterland', which they have to a great extent invented; and which in their arguments appear to mean, that if you have possessions in an uncivilised country, you have a right to extend those possessions to an unlimited distance inland from the sea, until you strike the frontier of another civilised country.

It was not a doctrine Bismarck had set much store by, or that Salisbury could possibly allow, but so long as the Kaiser promoted it the threat was there.

Salisbury's fears were laid to rest when, after the Admiralty grudg-

ingly gave its approval, the Cabinet agreed to his deal on 8th June.[9] There
was one other obstacle, and she proved harder to convince than
Parliament. 'It is a <u>very serious</u> question which I do not like,' the Queen
told Salisbury on 9th June, reminding him that she was also monarch of
the 2,000 Heligolanders, and 'it is a shame to hand them over to an
unscrupulous despotic Government like the German without first
consulting them.... The next thing will be to propose to give up
Gibraltar.' She refused to assent unless the wishes of the islanders were
consulted.

Salisbury replied that all those Heligolanders wishing to retain British
citizenship could do so, and none would be liable to German military
conscription, but to ask their collective opinion on the matter would
set a precedent which 'might be used by discontented persons in
Gibraltar, Malta, Cyprus and even India'. He further explained that, as
well as the protectorate over Zanzibar, various other islands and 150
miles of coastline were included in the deal, and Germany would be
abandoning all claims to the African interior behind them. Besides, the
Cabinet 'unanimously and earnestly' recommended it, and he promised
that it could set no precedent as there was 'no possible case like it'.
On 12th June, the Queen reluctantly sanctioned it, but with the
splendid parting admonition: 'Giving up what one has is always a bad
thing.'[10]

Salisbury came under a good deal of parliamentary and press criticism
once the deal was made public in mid-June 1890. Dilke rightly said that
'if Mr Gladstone had given, they would have destroyed him for giving'.
By presenting it as good for the suppression of the slave trade, and for
delimiting the exact spheres of Germany's African interests, Salisbury
managed to sell its merits. When Rosebery asked whether and by what
means the wishes of the Heligolanders had been ascertained, Salisbury
answered that it was 'confidential', at which Granville interjected:
'Confidential with the population?' On the second reading on 10th July,
Salisbury avoided the subject of the Heligolanders' wishes altogether,
and although Rosebery likened the deal to the apportionment of the
New World by the Borgia Pope Alexander VI, the Liberals did not
formally oppose it.

By August 1890, Salisbury was telling Dufferin in Rome that, with
Bismarck gone, the Germans were much more pleasant to deal with:
'but one misses the extraordinary penetration of the old man'. It did
mean, especially as neither von Caprivi nor von Marschall had any
experience in foreign affairs, Kálnoky was out of power the following
year and French leaders never lasted long enough to make their mark,
that Salisbury became the senior European statesman, despite – or
perhaps because of – Britain's lack of formal, binding Continental
alliances.

'We are perforce partners with the Germans,' Salisbury had written to Portal in November 1889, 'whose political morality diverges considerably from ours on many points.' As he told Dufferin the same month, the Mediterranean partnership was based entirely on *Realpolitik*, adding that 'Italy suspects Austria: Austria suspects Germany: and Germany thinks both her humble allies are exceedingly insubordinate. But I suppose terror of the French will keep them all together.' For all the morality of consigning a European population of Crown subjects to a foreign country for an African advantage, it turned out to be a vital part of the general African carve-up. After it, peace reigned between German and British Africa until 1914.

New areas, covering modern-day Uganda and Kenya, were swiftly ingested into the Empire, with Uganda being annexed by Rosebery, who continued Salisbury's practice of running these areas directly from the Foreign Office rather than through the Colonial Office. Germany kept Tanganyika – modern-day Tanzania – as well as Rwanda and Burundi. 'The great advantage of getting such a character as Lord Salisbury has got', Spring-Rice told a friend in 1892, 'is that one can surrender Heligoland. We've got to earn the character, in order, if necessary, to be false to it with impunity.'[11] The deal, which Salisbury had kept secret from Waddington until the last minute, was extremely unpopular in France. 'As you have given Heligoland to Germany,' the French Foreign Minister, Alexandre Ribot, facetiously inquired, 'I suppose you will not mind handing Jersey over to us?'

As soon as the interior was safeguarded, Salisbury threw himself into a scheme to help the East Africa Chartered Company finance a railway from Mombasa to the Lakes, which he believed would open up the interior to British exploration and development faster and more effectively than anything else, whilst forestalling French ambitions in the Sudan. After a long campaign he was thwarted by the Treasury, Cabinet and the House of Commons.

When in March 1892 Portal, who by then had been made Consul-General in Zanzibar, suggested extending the Protectorate there into full-scale annexation after the death of the present Sultan, Salisbury wrote a letter to explain his general preference for informal over formal empire. Firstly, he argued, to replace a local Muslim Sultanate with direct British rule would send a dangerous message to the Indian princes. Secondly, it would cost far more than 'the semi-patriarchal government which you have invented for Zanzibar', and thirdly, a stiff British code of law and administration would have to be introduced which might not sit well with the *ad hoc* local conditions, for example slavery. Instead, when the Sultan died, 'if you can find among his relatives an eligible baby sufficiently nearly related to him in blood to make a plausible successor, much of your immediate object may be gained'.[12]

Sure enough when the Sultan died in August 1896 – not, Salisbury suspected, of natural causes – a very young cousin, Hamoud, was chosen as his successor and installed as soon as British warships had bombarded the palace and ousted the pretender, Said Khalid.

Four years later, Hicks Beach again brought up the subject of simply annexing Zanzibar, but as Salisbury's reply explained: 'I have always been of opinion that the condition of a protected dependency is more acceptable to the half civilised races, and more suitable for them than direct dominion. It is cheaper, simpler, less wounding to their self-esteem, gives them more career as public officials, and spares them unnecessary contact with white men.' This last point meant that at Zanzibar, 'we have to deal with Moslems, with Arabs who hate us and our religion and our special notions with a particular hatred'. Bloodshed could be avoided by working through the puppet Sultan, who 'at his dearest will be very cheap compared to direct government from Downing Street'. Despite adding massively to the territory of the British Empire, Salisbury's promotion of the concept of 'informal' empire kept it safe from over-stretch.

Under the terms of a treaty which Palmerston had concluded with Napoleon III in 1864, Britain was not allowed to establish a sole protectorate over Zanzibar without the prior permission of France. So on 5th August 1890 Salisbury concluded an agreement which recognised the French protectorate over Madagascar, grabbed during Gladstone's premiership, as well as various mainly desert regions of western and northern Africa, including the southern Saharan border between Sir George Goldie's Royal Niger Company and French Algeria. 'The interests of this country are the interests of the Royal Niger Company,' Salisbury wrote to a correspondent that month, an unusually frank acceptance of the overlap. He was fully alive to some of the absurdities of the colonial process. 'We have been engaged in drawing lines upon maps where no white man's foot has ever trod,' Salisbury joked in his Mansion House speech the following day. 'We have been giving away mountains and rivers and lakes to each other, only hindered by the small impediment that we never knew exactly where the mountains and rivers and lakes were.'

He was hardly exaggerating; in a treaty signed with France in 1845, when Britain exchanged settlements in the Cameroons for others on the Niger, a river called the Rio del Rey was included as part of the frontier between the two. This was only altered when Salisbury discovered forty years later that no such waterway existed. Giving France the western Sahara and the Algerian hinterland as far south as Lake Chad was criti-

cised by Jingoes, and in defending the convention in the House of Lords
Salisbury made another of his gaffes. Admitting that vast tracts of terri-
tory had indeed been allocated to France, Salisbury asked their
Lordships to consider its quality as well as its quantity. 'This is what
agriculturalists would call very "light" land,' he told them, implying
that the Royal Niger Company had got much the better of the deal.
Waddington glowered from the Lords gallery, and two days later wrote
Salisbury an understandably pained letter, complaining that he had:

> diminished very much the good feeling created by the conclusion of the
> arrangement. No doubt the Sahara is not a garden, and contains, as you say,
> much 'light land', but your public reminder of the fact now, perhaps you
> will allow me to say, was hardly necessary. You might well have left us to
> find it out.[13]

Considering that they were nominally almost allies, the Italians proved
difficult over Zanzibar; indeed, in October 1888 Salisbury described
Bismarck as 'an angel of light compared to Crispi', who was only
prevented from pillaging the island by Salisbury's 'intimating pretty
plainly that force would be repelled by force'. Salisbury thought Crispi,
who had been one of Garibaldi's Thousand, a gambler desperate for
domestic popularity and willing to launch any African adventure in
order to gain it. 'In meanness, in mendacity, in treachery, in brutality,
in cynical and arrogant injustice it is impossible to surpass Crispi's
policy towards Zanzibar,' he told Goschen, adding that a war against
Italy 'would be excessively inconvenient and unpopular, though possibly not dangerous'.

At the Mansion House in November 1888, Salisbury had referred to
the wars against the Khalifa around Suakim, against the Arab slave-
traders in East Africa and against recalcitrant tribesmen on the
North-West Frontier as 'merely the surf that marks the edge of the
advancing waves of civilisation'. He felt himself beset, as he wrote to
Lytton the next month, by Turcophobes and Jingoes, 'who simply desire
to annex and object to evacuating in all cases', as well as by 'lunatics
who believe that by some magic wave of the diplomatic wand the Sudan
can be turned into a second India'. All Salisbury would do was to avoid
committing himself to a date for the eventual evacuation of Egypt,
whilst vigorously denying that Britain meant to stay permanently.

'The more I look at it,' Baring wrote to Salisbury about Egypt in June
1889, 'the more does the evacuation policy appear to me impossible
under any conditions.' He cited the Dervish danger in the Sudan, the
shift of strategic emphasis from Constantinople to Cairo, nascent

Egyptian nationalism, the weak Khedive and his weaker government, the interests of the European bondholders and the likelihood of having one day to return militarily. Although he is sometimes credited with persuading a reluctant Salisbury to stay in Egypt, in fact Baring was only preaching to one who had long been converted. Salisbury nevertheless held out the prospect of a British evacuation of Egypt as a means of thwarting French plans for an anti-British combination. 'Any mask that conceals the English power in Egypt from the eyes of the French journalist or elector is a thing to be preserved,' Salisbury wrote to Baring, pleased that yet another Egyptian Prime Minister had not been forced to resign by the Agent whose nickname in Cairo was 'Over-Baring'.

Using financial excuses, Salisbury steadily refused throughout his second ministry to authorise any large-scale attack on the Khalifa, who then controlled the Sudan. He would avenge Gordon when he was ready, but with Italy trying to establish herself in Ethiopia, Eritrea and the eastern Sudan, Salisbury was in no hurry. 'The Italians are exceedingly tiresome with their misplaced and suicidal African ambitions,' he told Baring in November 1889, 'and I have no wish that their aspirations should be gratified at the cost of any solid sacrifice on our part.' Even when, after a crushing defeat of the Khalifa at the Battle of Toski, the chance presented itself further to damage Mahdism by taking Tokar, fifty miles south of Suakim, Salisbury was sceptical. 'Step by step,' Salisbury warned Baring in March 1890, 'the imperious exactions of military necessity will lead you on into the desert.'

In August, Salisbury sent Baring to Naples to negotiate the Egyptian–Italian frontier with Crispi, whom he described to the Queen as 'rather the Randolph Churchill of Italy'. 'I feel as sure of being cheated', Salisbury told Dufferin, 'as when I have to investigate the bill of an Italian hotel-keeper.' His instructions to Baring were to 'insist on the command of all affluents of the Nile', but said that Egypt had very few visible interests in the Red Sea or eastern Sudan. When the negotiations broke down in mid-October, Salisbury reluctantly allowed Baring to take Tokar, thereby making Suakim more secure.

In Evelyn Baring, whom Salisbury ennobled as Baron Cromer before he left office in 1892, the Prime Minister had spotted one of the greatest of all Britain's imperial proconsuls. Secretary to his cousin Lord Northbrook during his Viceroyalty, Baring became Comptroller-General of Egyptian finance, and after a three-year stint as India's finance minister he was appointed British Agent and Consul-General in Egypt, serving for twenty-four years between 1883 and 1907. 'It's no good having right on your side', went a French saying in Cairo, 'if Lord Cromer is against you.' Author, linguist, bibliophile, classicist, soldier and financier, Cromer reformed every aspect of Egyptian administration, especially justice and finance and in particular the hitherto onerous land tax system, which he altered in the interests of the peasantry. Jingoes regarded him (wrongly) as responsible for the death of Gordon, Radicals suspected that he wanted to annex Egypt and the Sudan, whilst Conservatives saw him as a Liberal, when in fact he was the best kind of Whig. Salisbury admired him for his supreme competence and took him entirely into his confidence with regard to all North African questions. It was perhaps the best professional relationship that Salisbury enjoyed with any other public servant.

Salisbury told Baring that his proposed expedition to Tokar had occasioned very little opposition in Britain because 'We are thinking of nothing except strikes, and of later cantos of the epic of Kitty O'Shea.' In general Salisbury deprecated military expeditions, at least until Egypt's finances and the European situation were ripe for a full-scale reconquest of the Sudan. When Baring's military experts advised against allowing Turkish troops to garrison certain forts on the Midian coast, Salisbury's natural scepticism about experts came to the fore: 'I would not be too much impressed by what the soldiers tell you about the strategic importance of those places. It is their way. If they were allowed full scope, they would insist on the importance of garrisoning the Moon in order to protect us from Mars.'[14]

In direct contrast to Baring, Salisbury saw Cecil Rhodes as a self-seeking, chauvinistic 'prodigal son' of the type he had so long denounced. He could not help but admire Rhodes's dynamism, but the nebulous connection between his private enrichment and public ultra-Jingoism made Salisbury suspect hypocrisy. 'The Boer question will peaceably resolve itself', Johnston had written in his anonymous *Times* article, 'by the continual influx of the English into the Transvaal and the eventual mingling of the two white races.' This was Salisbury's hope, but he feared the activities of men like Rhodes would only antagonise the Boers and frustrate the process. He nonetheless appreciated the necessity of working through him.

Salisbury had long argued that what was needed to increase imperial production was not territory but capital. 'Abundance of fertile land is to be had in many places,' he had written to Sir Richard Temple in 1875. 'But, partly for want of security, partly for want of energy, and for fear of exile, or hardship, capital in most of these places is wanting.' Salisbury accepted that Rhodes could provide the energy, face the exile, endure the hardship and also provide the capital in South Africa, but it was up to the British Government to provide the security. Salisbury had managed it in Nyasaland with the Portuguese, but faced a more intractable antagonist in President Paul Kruger of the Transvaal.

Gladstone's two Conventions with the Boers certainly rankled with Salisbury, but he hoped the issue might resolve itself with the Transvaal republic gradually being effaced by immigration and territorial encroachment.

On 11th February 1888, King Lobengula of the Matabele tribe concluded a treaty with the British High Commissioner at the Cape, Sir Henry Lock, recognising only Britain in his territories between the Transvaal and the Zambezi, and on 30th September the King granted a separate concession to Rhodes, acting for De Beers, to prospect for gold in Mashonaland. As Salisbury wrote in a Cabinet memorandum later, native treaties tended to have 'this inconvenient flaw', that the potentates often made identical agreements simultaneously with several powers. To prevent this happening, Rhodes felt that a Chartered Company, along the lines of MacKinnon's British East Africa Company or Goldie's Royal Niger Company, would give him the quasi-sovereign authority he needed.

Rhodes could not have chosen a better time to arrive in London and lobby for a Chartered Company to pursue British commercial interests in southern Africa. The Zambezi convention with Portugal had been held up by the Cortes and on 20th June Portugal had declared her determination to cancel the concession to the British-owned Delagoa Railway Company, despite strong protests. 'I am afraid that the new Company which will carry civilisation into the midst of Africa will startle people a little at Berlin,' Salisbury warned Malet, but it was also intended to startle people a lot at Lisbon.

Turning down Rhodes's offer that his son Robert, then a barrister, should act for him in London, Salisbury told McDonnell: 'I know nothing of the duties of such a post. Rhodes' magnificence rather alarms me.' Nonetheless, when it became clear that nothing would be asked from the British taxpayer, and a vast territory south of the Zambezi might eventually accrue to the Empire if Rhodes were successful, without any direct Treasury outlay, responsibility or risk, Salisbury supported Rhodes's application for a Crown Charter. In a meeting on 3rd August, he told Rhodes that he could inform Germany that he did not consider the country west of Nyasa 'as coming under the head of territory in the rear of German influence', and would let him see the despatch to Berlin before it was sent. Rhodes came away with the impression that Salisbury thought that 'I was not an enterprising bagman trying to develop some extra trade but really had a higher object.'[15]

Whatever Salisbury thought of Rhodes at the time – 'a gentleman with some considerable force of character' was one rather understated description – he saw the Chartered Company as an ideal way of fighting a proxy territorial battle against the Portuguese, Germans, Boers and

Belgians without incurring any direct responsibility or expense. Objections from Free Traders, humanitarian groups and King Lobengula himself were therefore overriden, and a twenty-five-year charter was signed by Queen Victoria and sealed under Letters Patent on 29th October 1889. No northern frontier was stipulated in it, so unconcerned was Salisbury about antagonising the Portuguese who were then still claiming northern Zambesia. The Duke of Abercorn became Chairman, the Queen's son-in-law the Duke of Fife was Deputy Chairman and there were five other directors including Alfred Beit and the driving force behind it all, Cecil Rhodes. The Charter allowed the Company to run its own police force, settle territories, fly its own flag and only required it to fight the slave trade 'so far as it be practical'.

Salisbury completely repudiated Rhodes's visionary scheme of building a railway from Cairo to the Cape, to travel solely over British territory the entire way, describing it as 'a curious idea which had lately become prevalent' and pointing out in the House of Lords that it 'would mean a long tract of narrow occupation, hedged in by two white protectorates – those of Germany and Belgium – placed at a distance of three months' march from our own sea-base. I cannot imagine a more inconvenient possession.' In an echo of his famous put-down of Lord De Mauley in 1877, he said of the Jingoists' schemes: 'I think the constant study of maps is apt to disturb men's reasoning powers.... We have had a fierce conflict over the possession of a lake whose name I am afraid I cannot pronounce correctly – I think it is Lake Ngami – our only difficulty being that we do not know where it is ... there are indeed great doubts as to whether it is a lake at all or only a bed of rushes.'

There was, however, no doubt about Rhodes's act of homage to Salisbury, made at ten o'clock on the morning of Friday, 12th September 1890, where the pioneer column of the British South Africa Company police halted in Mashonaland. The headquarters was declared by the Order of the Day to be called Fort Salisbury, and it later became the capital of the 440,000 square miles of southern Africa which Rhodes named after himself. The spot itself, in Cecil Square of what is today called Harare in Zimbabwe, heard three cheers for Queen Victoria and a twenty-one-gun salute the next day, which Rhodesians afterwards celebrated as Premier Day. There is no indication that Salisbury was particularly flattered or impressed by the honour, although he did as much as he decently could to help the Company in Zambesia, that vast territory of the central basins of the Zambezi and Limpopo rivers, north of the Limpopo, west of Lake Nyasa and south of the Congo.[16]

Rhodes was an important enough figure by February 1891 that, when the Duke of Fife gave a dinner to celebrate his arrival in London, it was attended, amongst many others, by the Prince of Wales, Salisbury, Gladstone, Hartington and Abercorn. But, although he might put dukes on his board and get himself elected to the Kimberley Club, Rhodes was viewed by Salisbury with the same detached scepticism and caution with which Lord Burghley had viewed those earlier pirate-patriots, Drake and Raleigh. Admiration for their energy and successes was tempered with irritation at their capacity to complicate larger foreign policy considerations by their adventures. After a meeting in March 1891 with Salisbury, where he had tried but failed to persuade the Prime Minister to accept Cape Colony's and Queensland's schemes for imperial federation, Rhodes complained to the Prime Minister of Canada that the 'curse is that English politicians cannot see the future'. His own dream was still for British territory to stretch, as the Jingo phrase went, 'from Cairo to the Cape'.

If Salisbury had been able to see the future that Rhodes and other Jingoists had begun to pull him towards in South Africa, it is doubtful that he would have granted the Charter in the first place. Yet Rhodes did come round to appreciating Salisbury's strategic overview, and at a dinner party at George Wyndham's in 1898 he declared it 'quite extraordinary that such a man, who never travels abroad further than Dieppe or the Riviera, should have found out all the places in South Africa where an Englishman can breed, reserved them for Great Britain, and rejected all the others'.

By strong-arming Portugal in the south-east, an advantageous swap with Germany in the east, a shrewd convention with France in the west, a *laissez-faire* attitude towards Italy in the north-east, a willingness to abandon any claims in the unprofitable central and south-west, and the licensing of merchant-adventurers, Salisbury had in only seven years laid down the outlines of the division of Africa which were to last until the Great War. He could not know it, but by 1939 there was indeed an unbroken line of British-controlled territories stretching from Cairo (although still nominally under the Khedive), through the Sudan, Kenya, Tanganyika, Rhodesia and Bechuanaland and down to the Cape, though not connected by rail. The British achievement in Africa had more to do with Salisbury's patient diplomacy and foresight than any alliterative dreams of Jingoes such as Cecil Rhodes.

THIRTY-TWO

Mid-Term Crises

General Boulanger – Royal Grants
– The Two-Power Standard –
The Paris Exhibition –
The Shah's Visit – 'The "Socialist" Current' –
The Cleveland Street Scandal –
A Mid-Term Crisis – Prince Eddy in Love –
Trouble at Barings

January 1889 to December 1890

'If I were asked to define Conservative policy,
I should say it was the upholding of confidence.'

'I have become too much of a machine to know what I wish for,'
Salisbury wrote to Alfred Austin on New Year's Day 1889. 'I am grateful
for your wishes in an abstract form. When I was put together, my brain
and stomach were procured from different establishments and they do
not match. The result is that intellectually I am dead tired, and longing
for repose – but work certainly keeps one in health. But it's dreary
work.' Convinced that class war, or 'bloodless civil war' as he put it to
Smith in early February, was on the way, Salisbury rediscovered his fear
of socialism and the conviction that in the politics of the Left, 'to loot
somebody or something is the common object, under a thick varnish of
pious phrases'. It filled him with despair. 'I do not believe there is on the
earth so prosaic an animal as a politician,' he told Austin that month.
'Some ideal, some imaginative colour, may attach itself to the details of
almost any other vocation: but you cannot ennoble the cares of a
Minister, under a Parliamentary Government. I often wish I could speak
out and say what I think of it: but if I did, no one would listen to me.'

It was in the field of international power politics that, largely untram-
melled by parliamentary government, let alone democracy, Salisbury
felt he could be of most use. In a broad overview of the European

situation written for Dufferin as he took over the Rome Embassy, Salisbury explained that Germany was 'ceaselessly busy in building up diplomatic breakwaters against France and Russia' and had forced Austria to join in an intimate alliance with Italy against France and Russia. Far from being an isolationist, Salisbury thought that should France attack Italy, especially 'gratuitously by sea', Britain would come to Italy's assistance, but 'if a war were to arise out of one of Crispi's trumpery quarrels', which he was continually trying to pick with France over every issue from Tunisian school-teaching to the Suez Canal, Britain 'would certainly stand aloof'. Although she had preserved her freedom of action, Britain was in no sense isolated from the European balance of power.

The mysterious death of the Crown Prince Rudolf of Austria at Mayerling on 30th January 1889 initially led Salisbury to assume an assassination, until Queen Victoria, who had her own family information network centring on Philip of Coburg, put him right.[1] That same month Bismarck renewed his perennial offer of a full alliance, which Salisbury carefully and politely refused. 'I am afraid the Bismarcks cannot be acquitted of being intolerably bitter and vindictive,' he explained to Janetta Manners, now the Duchess of Rutland. As well as an alliance, the Germans were pressing for a visit to Britain from the Kaiser. He had not made any genuine apology to the Prince of Wales for the Vienna Incident, the Radicals and Irish were Francophile, and Germany was popularly blamed for problems in Zanzibar and atrocities in Samoa, so Salisbury told Malet to inform Wilhelm II that 'we have many desperadoes about, familiar with the idea of political murder'. He wanted the visit, 'in all friendliness', postponed, or at least downgraded from a full State occasion which might 'expose him to the risk of insult', to a yachting trip to Osborne and the Solent. But the Germans kept pressing, and when in early March Queen Victoria at last extended an invitation to visit Osborne in late July, Hatzfeldt told Salisbury that the Kaiser was 'beside himself with joy' over the prospect.

As the Kaiser had still refused to apologise for Vienna, it was arranged that everyone should now agree to believe that he had never sent the original message to the Austrians, who had somehow misinterpreted his friendly wishes. It convinced no one, but it would have to do. The visit was fixed for two or three days at Osborne, with visits to ports and arsenals but no State ball. Even this sensible arrangement failed to raise Salisbury's heavily depressed spirits, oppressed as he was by 'the dreary routine of our political life'. On 8th March, he wondered aloud to Janetta Rutland why he bothered to go on with it: 'I think the solution is to be found in one of the most amiable characteristics of human nature. I do believe politicians would be far more ready to resign office if they did not feel that their doing so would give such infinite pleasure to their adversaries.'[2]

The heavily contested Kennington by-election a week later, in which Salisbury's nephew, Philip Beresford-Hope, lost to the Gladstonian Liberal candidate by 4,069 to 3,439, raised the prospect of Salisbury eventually not having much choice in the matter of resignation, but he comforted the Queen that the canvassers there had said the major issue had not been Ireland. 'The life of the Ministry and the life of the G.O.M. are both ebbing,' he wrote to Austin afterwards, 'the question is which will ebb the fastest.' In fact, Gladstone had nearly another decade left in him.

April Fool's Day 1889 saw the curtain come down on General Boulanger's comic-opera attempts to become master of France, when, aided by the French Government, he fled to Belgium. 'If Boulanger succeeds the chances of war are considerable,' Salisbury had written in January, 'for he must amuse the French somehow.'³ After failing to mount his long-expected *coup d'état*, but merely causing political havoc in the Third Republic, Boulanger at last left the scene, only re-appearing to shoot himself on his mistress's grave in Brussels in September 1891.

A typical Cabinet agenda, taken from Saturday, 22ⁿᵈ June 1889, shows the breadth of subjects that would be covered in a normal sitting. 'The Zambezi [Portugal's cancellation of the Delagoa Railway concession]. Egypt and France. Egypt Commercial [France using conversion of the debt to discuss British evacuation]. Japan [withdrawal of most-favoured-nation status]. India and Representation [Dufferin's plans as taken up by Lansdowne]. The Berne Meeting [on labour laws]. The [Education] Code.' One issue not on that particular agenda, but which Salisbury had to deal with extensively over the following month, was the question of financial grants to the Royal Family. Salisbury wanted to replace the system whereby Parliament voted money whenever a prince or princess married, which, as he told the Queen, due to the 'deteriorating' charac-ter of the House of Commons, had become a regular opportunity for the Radicals and Irish to make 'malicious and inflammatory suggestions'.

Salisbury proposed to avoid all such debates in future by instituting a dotation fund to bestow dowries on the younger royals as and when marriages occurred. He did not want to go into the general question of Crown finances until after the Queen's death because, as he told Smith, 'the temper of the times is bitter and unscrupulous' and it would only lead to 'great confusion, very scandalous debates and a sharp measure of retrenchment'. His original plan had been to sell the royal parks to the nation for £500,000 so as to avoid having to apply to Parliament for any more money, but he was overruled in Cabinet. Salisbury's primary desire was to spare the Royal Family embarrassment from the Radicals, but he was no respecter of blue blood. Minor royals he looked upon as minor irritations; after one lady-in-waiting counted no fewer than seventy-six of them in the South of France one summer, Salisbury wrote to Lord Granby to complain how 'the coast is tiresomely full of minute royalties – persons known only to the editor of the *Almanach de Gotha*'.

The Queen was furious that the Committee for the Royal Grants should have included 'that horrible lying Labouchere and that rebel Parnell', but Salisbury soothed her, pointing out that the Government had a thirteen to ten majority there. The whole subject put the Queen in, as one of her doctors warned another, 'a vile humour', but Salisbury struck as good a deal as possible for her five Connaught and Albany grandchildren. The Liberal opposition to Salisbury's largesse if anything prejudiced the Queen further against them, as he perhaps intended all along.[4]

On 13th July 1887, the Queen had attended a garden party for 300 people at Hatfield, where her host and hostess brought up 'celebrities' such as Robert Browning and the historian W.E.H. Lecky to converse with her on the terrace. Salisbury knew exactly how to handle her, occasionally coaxing her, indulging her and sometimes blatantly trying to make her flesh creep. On the question of finding a military post in India for the Comte de Paris's son in November 1887, for example, he reminded her of the fate of the Prince Imperial in 1879. Solicitous for his health, the Queen asked Salisbury to sit down in their audiences, an almost unique honour. He was just as defensive of her, insisting that a minister be with her at all times in difficult or potentially embarrassing situations. 'If no Minister has been with her for a fortnight,' he told Ponsonby of her 1888 Berlin visit, 'it will be much more difficult to deal in discussion with any people who may make imputations against her.' As a result of their mutual respect and intimacy, a genuine bond grew between monarch and premier. 'She need not say that he knows he possesses her confidence,' she wrote to him in June 1890, 'and how anxious she is to support him in every way.'[5]

It was in 1889 that Salisbury redeemed the splendid pledge he had made to the Queen on 11th December 1888, that his Government's huge new building programme 'will place Your Majesty's fleet in a completely commanding position'. In his Guildhall speech that November he had announced that 'In a sensitive commercial community like ours, alarm is almost as destructive as danger; and what we have to provide is not only safety for our citizens, but a sense that that safety exists.' To that end, Salisbury persuaded Goschen, Smith, Stanhope and George

Hamilton to support a new Naval Defence Act which would spend an extra £20 million on the Royal Navy over the following four years. Since the Battle of Trafalgar, Britain had been content with having a fleet always one-third bigger than the world's next largest (usually France). The yardstick they were henceforth to use came to be known as the 'Two-Power Standard', by which the Royal Navy was always to be kept 'to a standard of strength equivalent to that of the combined forces of the next two biggest navies in the world'. As Hamilton later recalled, 'It was deemed impolitic to mention either France or Russia by name.'

Salisbury had been methodically holding up subsidies for a Pacific railway, Irish drainage schemes, technical education and many other proposed capital projects, so that the public finances would be healthy enough to justify the massive expenditure necessary to build ten new battleships, thirty-eight cruisers, eighteen torpedo boats and four fast gunboats. It represented the greatest peacetime expansion of British maritime power. The Royal Sovereign class battleships were to be larger and more powerful than any warships previously constructed. With a Royal Navy thus augmented, it was hoped that the Franco-Russian combination could be faced down, the Empire's communications protected, the Mediterranean fleet made a match for the Toulon fleet, French invasion fears dispelled and the Jingoes silenced.

With the rapid evolution of naval construction and armaments, especially the torpedo, it was assumed that the heavy expenditure would have to be continued by governments of whatever hue, and indeed, although Gladstone considered it 'militaristic', the Opposition pledged itself to support the programme, partly out of fear of what would happen to them at the polls if they refused. At huge cost to the Exchequer, Salisbury delivered imperial impregnability, the tangible manifestation of which could be admired at the Diamond Jubilee's Spithead Review eight years later.

One by-product of the increase in armaments was the growth in the value of shares in armaments manufacturers, some of which were held in ministers' portfolios. Lansdowne had £20,000 invested in Armstrong in the early 1890s, Salisbury himself had £750 and no fewer than twelve MPs sat on the boards of arms companies by 1898. Devonshire was chairman of the Naval Construction and Armaments Company until he joined the Government in 1895. That year, Salisbury rescinded the Liberal Government's self-denying ordinance by which ministers resigned their directorships in public companies, and by 1900 over half his ministers held them. Despite the obvious potential conflicts of interest, there was never any hint or suspicion of what has since been termed 'sleaze'. Salisbury reasoned that as he only asked gentlemen, and usually very rich ones, to join his Cabinets, they would automatically put the national interest before their own in any conflict, and he was 'perfectly happy to leave it to the consciences and good sense of individual ministers to protect the Government's reputation'.[6]

The centenary of the French Revolution fell on 14th July 1889, and France intended to commemorate it in style, commissioning a temporary 985-foot tower in the Champ de Mars designed by the engineer Alexandre Gustave Eiffel. The Revolution and its aftermath had long exercised a morbid fascination for Salisbury, and he saw no reason to celebrate an event which would have hoisted him up on to the first tumbril. He had made a close study of it, collecting a large number of books and pamphlets, and references to it cropped up regularly in his journalism and speeches. Its lessons infused his political beliefs. 'The witness of history is uniform to this,' he wrote about it in 1860, 'that Nemesis may spare the sagacious criminal, but never fails to overtake the weak, the undecided and the over-charitable fool.' Men such as Jacques Necker, the Abbé Sieyès and the Marquis de Lafayette he saw as archetypes of the weak-willed liberals he so despised:

> They believed intensely in amiable theories, they loved the sympathy and applause of their fellow men, they were kind-hearted, and charitably fancied everybody as well meaning as themselves; and therefore – so far as it can be said of any single man – they were the proximate causes of a civil convulsion which, for the horror of its calamities, stands alone in the history of the world.

It was because of what happened in France between 1789 and 1815 that Salisbury believed that 'Free institutions, carried beyond the point which the culture of the nation justifies, cease to produce freedom. There is the freedom that makes each man free; and there is the freedom, so called, which makes each man the slave of the majority.' Salisbury blamed Voltaire, Rousseau and the Encyclopædists for giving the Revolution 'that character of extravagant horror which made it an epoch', because it was 'by their writings – their infidelity and their rant about the rights of man, that the gloomy enthusiasts were inspired'. Foremost among those gloomy enthusiasts was Robespierre, a man whose character fascinated Salisbury and who exemplified his view that half-starved populations do not create revolutions themselves, but require 'the discontent of place-hunters, dependent provinces, or priests', or in this case Arras *notaires*, to start them, a truth he extended to Ireland and India.

'Until recently, revolutions were looked upon with the same kind of ignorant awe with which a savage watches an eclipse,' Salisbury commented dolefully in 1863, but 'before long, the statistics of revolutions will be as reliable as the statistics of births, deaths and marriages.'[7] On public platforms he held up the French Revolution as an unparalleled time of 'cruelty, bloodthirstiness, treachery and contempt for every human tie', so when President Carnot invited the Corps Diplomatique in Paris to celebrate its hundredth anniversary, Salisbury was adamant that Lytton should not attend. 'I do not think it will do,' he wrote to the Ambassador in January 1888, arguing that if the French Government 'wishes to go into ecstasies over her own centenary history, she will hardly induce any large portion of the world to go with her'. The German, Austrian and Italian monarchies were no more enthusiastic for what they saw as a celebration of republican regicide.

When trying to think up an excuse for Lytton's absence from the May 1889 opening ceremony of the Paris Exhibition, Salisbury mused that: 'Influenza is not in season in May and neither the plague, cholera, nor small-pox are prevalent in Paris just now. I give it up.... Could not your maiden aunt fall ill at Nice?' Whatever Lytton decided upon, 'it will not do for you ... to appear as the supporter of the rights of man and the principles of '89'. Salisbury only agreed to Australia's participation in the Exhibition because she had not been settled by 1789, 'and therefore cannot be supposed to have any corporate knowledge of what took place in that year'. The Liberal press were furious at this perceived snub to a friendly nation, but Salisbury firmly refused to let Lytton take part and put out a communiqué which said that 'it did not appear to H.M.G. appropriate to join in celebrating political events in a foreign country where differences of opinion exist regarding them'.

One man who did intend to visit Paris for the celebrations was the Shah of Persia. Nasr-el-Din wanted to visit Britain first and, despite Salisbury's reservations, the whims of the leading potentate in the project to keep Russia out of Afghanistan had to be indulged. Included in his itinerary was a visit to Hatfield, where he attended a garden party on 8th July 1889, staying that night. Despite Lady Salisbury going to great lengths to put oriental furniture in the two floors of bedrooms set aside for the Shah and his retinue, his followers insisted on sleeping on the staircase outside the room where their master slept, lying in descending order of importance. 'A coarse tyrannic face,' noted Cranbrook in his diary after a Buckingham Palace levée a few days before. He was unimpressed by the Shah's mixing up the Lord Chancellor with the Chancellor of the Exchequer, his inability to pronounce the word 'Cranbrook' and his (admittedly spectacularly ill-briefed) question to Balfour about whether or not he meant to grant Home Rule to Ireland.

London society lapped up the stories about the Shah, some of them doubtless apocryphal and others hailing from his earlier visit in 1873. When he was taken to see a model British prison, he asked to see the gallows in action. On being told that no one was due to be hanged that day, he offered one of his entourage. He failed to appreciate the opera, but vigorously applauded during the *entr'acte* tuning of the instruments. Weak tea had to be brought to him at all times of the day and night. He was popular with the British crowds, not just for his large moustache and fabled generosity, but because he publicly kissed Queen Victoria's photograph on his arrival at Windsor railway station. At one City banquet, the Shah mistook the toast-master for the deputy mayor, and congratulated him on the way everyone obeyed when he ordered them to stand and drink. Instead of arm-in-arm, he and the Lady Mayoress walked into the Guildhall hand-in-hand, which, according to one observer, looked like 'a schoolboy and schoolgirl going a-maying'.

The Shah knew no English but did speak French, and when Baroness Burdett-Coutts, the seventy-five-year-old philanthropist, was presented to him by the Prince of Wales, he exclaimed: '*Quelle horreur!*' An ugly, unruly boy was kept in his retinue as a lucky mascot, because many years before he had as a baby cried during a storm on a hunting expedition; the Shah, going outside to investigate, had narrowly missed death when the roof of the hunting lodge fell in. 'He is a true Eastern potentate in his consideration for himself and himself only,' wrote the author Augustus Hare, a regular visitor to Hatfield,

> is most unconcernedly late whenever he chooses: utterly ignores everyone he does not want to speak to: amuses himself with monkeyish and often dirty tricks ... and wipes his wet hands on the coat-tails of the gentleman next to him without compunction. He expresses his wonder that Lord Salisbury did not take a new wife, though he gave Lady Salisbury a magnificent jewelled order.

Despite Salisbury's initial doubts, the visit was a success, and Britain's month-long reception more than offset the influence of France's later hospitality during the centennial celebrations. When the Shah was shot in a Teheran mosque on 1st May 1896, it struck one of the Hatfield guests of the time, Lady Dorothy Nevill, as 'doubly hard' considering his reputation as an agnostic.[8]

In October 1889, Salisbury had told the Queen that on investigation the recent by-election losses in Peterborough and North Buckinghamshire had not been down to 'mere mismanagement', as had been originally thought, but instead, 'He fears they indicate also the existence of a

"Socialist" current.' His speech to the NUCCA at Nottingham on 26th November therefore contained several passages against 'these peddling philosophers with their petty, spiteful acts of confiscation, animated by no philanthropic spirit, but by a mere impulse of class antipathy'. He warned that 'if you allow them to have their way, the substratum and foundation of all your civilisation and prosperity and happiness will melt away'. So too would the confidence of capitalists, and 'you will be left to such support as can be obtained from the efforts of the hour and lose all the advantages of a great sovereignty.... If I were asked to define Conservative policy, I should say that it was the upholding of confidence.'

Such confidence disappeared, he argued, when property and contract rights came under attack. Salisbury believed that if one worked more than eight hours a day, 'you add nothing to the value of the work you do'. But legislation to stop a man working ten hours if he so desired 'would be an unpardonable interference with the freedom which Englishmen of all classes have established for generations'. Despite the London dock strike having lasted from 19th August to 16th September, and 50,000 people having marched in its support from the docks to Hyde Park, Salisbury was sanguine enough about labour troubles when writing to Drummond Wolff in Teheran in mid-December: 'There is a strong amount of feeling which may affect the general politics of the country, though I think the better opinion is that it will not last very long.'[9]

By no means fully recovered from his Russian influenza by the time Parliament opened on 11th February 1890, Salisbury looked frail at the eve-of-session dinner at Arlington Street. He missed the next two Cabinet meetings to stay at his brother Eustace's house at Lytchett Heath, near Poole. After at least a week's complete rest he seemed on better form to face the new session, but health worries were to reappear regularly over the next decade. 'Both Gladstone and I – for different reasons – are phenomena of very uncertain duration,' he wrote to a cousin, Edward Talbot, then vicar of Leeds.[10]

In November 1862, Salisbury had written in the *Saturday Review* that it was sometimes acceptable to tell white lies in order to help 'a fugitive who is in danger, or a friend who is in trouble'. On 18th October 1889, Salisbury met Sir Dighton Probyn VC, the Prince of Wales's Comptroller and Treasurer, at King's Cross before his 7 p.m. train left and warned him that Major the Lord Arthur Somerset, Extra Equerry to the Prince of Wales's eldest son, Prince Albert Victor, Duke of Clarence, was about to be arrested for gross indecency for his lewd conduct at a male brothel at No. 19, Cleveland Street, north of Soho. The very next day, Somerset skipped the country to France. In fact it was not until a week after his honourable discharge from the Royal Horse Guards (the Blues) had been gazetted that Scotland Yard issued the warrant.

Charles Hammond, the brothel-keeper, also fled to Belgium and thence to America, using money supplied by Arthur Newton, Somerset's solicitor. Writing to the Home Secretary, Salisbury said that he did not 'consider this to be a case in which any official application could justifiably be made' for extradition. In a subsequent trial of Newton for conspiracy to pervert the course of justice, the solicitor received a sentence of only six weeks' imprisonment and was not even struck off the rolls. The Duke of Grafton's son, the Earl of Euston, was also implicated, but successfully sued for libel. Henry Labouchere, the Radical MP for Northampton, began to investigate Salisbury's role in helping Somerset escape justice, writing in his magazine *Truth* that 'if Mr Newton is prosecuted, Lord Salisbury and several others ought also to be prosecuted'.

'If Labouchere and his myrmidons show that they can <u>prove</u> things which our police were unable to discover,' Salisbury wrote to Goschen on 20th December, 'they will have scored a point. But I gravely doubt it.' In fact, on Friday, 28th February, Labouchere made a seventy-five-minute speech in the Commons accusing the Government of 'a criminal conspiracy to defeat the ends of justice'. It was a devastating and largely accurate account of what had happened, down to the rather otiose remark that 'the Government wish to hush this matter up'. When Labouchere refused to accept the Attorney-General Sir Richard Webster's defence of Salisbury, saying that he didn't believe the Prime Minister, he was 'named' by the Speaker and suspended from the Commons for a week. His resolution for an inquiry was meanwhile defeated by 206 to 66. 'My honourable Friend was suspended for disbelieving in God,' Labouchere joked, pointing to his fellow Northampton MP Charles Bradlaugh, 'and I am suspended for disbelieving in Man.' Writing to the ubiquitous socialite Reginald Brett, the future Lord Esher, the following day, Labouchere said: 'Nothing could have suited me better than to be suspended wrongfully for not believing that august being Lord Salisbury. I dare say that in private life he is the soul of honour, but as a public man Cranmer was not in it with him.'[11]

In 1860, Salisbury had written of the campaigning MP John Roebuck: 'A Parliamentary Cato is under a terrible necessity never to let the edge of his trenchant virtue rust,' and Labouchere was another such Cato. The son of a banker and the nephew of Lord Taunton, he had gone to Eton and Trinity College, Cambridge, where he had been accused of cheating at cards and reputedly ran up debts of £6,000 in two years. After a sojourn in Latin America where he lived with a Mexican circus *artiste*, Labouchere returned to marry an actress and join the Diplomatic Service, from which he was dismissed a decade later. 'Labby' was one of the most colourful characters on the Victorian political scene and he might have justifiably thought that he had caught Salisbury out.

When Salisbury rose in the House of Lords on 3rd March, to loud cheers, he admitted meeting Probyn at King's Cross, for 'a casual interview for which I was in no way prepared, to which I did not attach the slightest degree of importance, and of which I took no notes whatever. The train started very soon afterwards.' Salisbury admitted telling Probyn 'that rumours had reached me that further evidence had been obtained, but I did not know what its character was'. This is half corroborated by Probyn's letter to Salisbury of 19th October: 'I fear what you told me last night was all too true.' Salisbury ended his short statement by saying, 'the subject is not one that lends itself to extensive treatment'. He sat down 'amid renewed cheers', fortunately without any peer wishing to go into the matter further.

Somerset's father, the Duke of Beaufort, was an important Tory magnate and political supporter of Salisbury's who occasionally attended Arlington Street dinners. He corresponded with Salisbury over twenty-five years, on the usual aristocratic subjects of cadging archdeaconries for friends, baronetcies for neighbours and honours for the mayors of towns on his estates. When he heard that Henry Matthews was about to take Glamorgan as his title on retirement, Beaufort wrote to warn Salisbury that he was already Earl of Glamorgan, so Matthews had to make do with Llandaff. (In fact, the Letters Patent for the 1645 creation never passed the Great Seal, so although Charles I had styled his ancestor as Earl of Glamorgan, it was not legally a Beaufort title.)

If Salisbury had, via a courtier, warned Beaufort's son to flee the country before a warrant was even issued, and the circumstantial evidence suggests that he did, it would have been out of general class solidarity with Somerset, as well as a desire to protect Prince Albert Victor, who would have been embarrassed at the revelation of his friend's activities.[12] Technically, Salisbury probably conspired to pervert the course of justice and committed misprision of felony, and he would not have done so without good reason. With so much of the power of the upper classes resting on their social prestige and the deference accorded them by the rest of society, Salisbury was acutely conscious of how politically dangerous such 'West End Scandals', as they were termed in *Hansard*'s index, could be. Salisbury shrugged off Labouchere's accusations, which eventually came to nothing, and Somerset lived quietly in the South of France with a companion, until his death in 1926.

April 1890 saw Salisbury on holiday at Monte Carlo, occasionally visiting the casinos there and thinking them 'a wonderful machinery for taking money out of the pockets of the fools of the earth and handing it over to the wise men!' Although he was worried about the Kaiser's choice of friends – 'He is meddling with some very sharp-edged tools indeed' – he was otherwise relatively calm about European affairs that spring. Domestically, however, he still felt, or at least professed to feel, that his ministry could fall at any time. 'The difficulty of inducing the mass of the Conservative voters to defer to the opinion of their leaders', he told Lord Bateman, 'is a very serious one, and I am sorry to say that it is meeting us in many quarters.'

It was not just the constituency rank-and-file but also MPs themselves who were expressing dissatisfaction with the Government's direction. Smith's health was failing; Balfour's eighty-clause Irish Land Purchase Bill was encountering obstruction; Salisbury's own pro-Church Tithes Bill was considered reactionary; Goschen's licensing proposals to compensate publicans had infuriated the Temperance lobby; Gladstonians had won important by-elections at St Pancras, Stoke-on-Trent and Bristol East; there was fury in the police force against Matthews over wages and pensions, and Salisbury's unapologetic reaction to the discovery of the Pigott forgeries in the Parnell libel action still rankled with many. So on 12th June Salisbury called a Party meeting at the Carlton Club to try to reassert control and propose that Bills be carried over from one session to the next, the better to defeat Irish obstructionism and get contested measures on to the Statute Book. A mutiny led by Sir John Mowbray, the veteran chairman of two standing committees, wrecked the project, and four days later, during Ascot week, absenteeism and abstentions caused the Government to come within four votes of defeat on a licensing clause of Goschen's Local Taxation Bill.

'We have had two very important foreign negotiations in London,' Salisbury reported to the Duchess of Rutland, 'a revolt of the party at home – a threatened mutiny in the police, three colleagues [Goschen, Matthews and Ritchie] full of resigning – in short a peck of troubles – and, on top of it, a Foreign Office party and a dinner at the Trinity House.' Salisbury blamed James Monro, the Metropolitan Police Chief Commissioner, for the row with Matthews, and privately admitted that 'the objection to resisting the demands of the Police with regard to wages and pensions, was not the difficulty of replacing them, but the fear of losing their votes'.

Salisbury believed the discontent voiced at the Party meeting was merely a vent for the feeling of irritation against Goschen's licensing proposals, which it was felt impossible now to drop as being 'tantamount to admitting the principle of no compensation'. Opposition continued, however, and eventually they were ditched on 23rd June, despite a 600,000-signature petition in their favour. Mid-term unpopularity had turned into a full-scale crisis, and on 24th June Cranbrook wrote to Salisbury in favour of a general jettisoning of all controversial measures. MPs lunching at the Carlton Club were even talking about 'an early dissolution of the Government', Akers-Douglas reported.[13]

Reassuring the Queen that he had no intention of resigning, and complaining to Lansdowne in India that 'passing bills will soon be a lost art', Salisbury flatly refused all calls to readmit Churchill into the Cabinet, which prepared to suspend the passage of all contested Bills. On 5th July 1890, although Salisbury said that he opposed the decision to the utmost of his power and argued that it would bring great discredit on the Government, the Cabinet, now also threatened with Hicks Beach's resignation, resolved to drop all contentious legislation for the session, including the Irish Land Bill and Salisbury's own Tithes Bill. Salisbury was only prevented from dissolving Parliament because, as he told the Queen, Gladstone's Home Rule plans meant that he must be 'kept from making even an abortive attempt to form a Government'. Instead, they would limp on, entirely free of legislative baggage. 'For the next two years which remain,' he said of his Government, 'they must get on as well as they can.'

The day after the Cabinet's decision, Salisbury's doctors insisted he take a fortnight's rest, which he postponed until after commending the Heligoland deal to the House of Lords on 10th July.[14] His first foray when he returned was a sharply worded note to Smith, who had publicly committed the Government to opposing a religious census. 'I cannot conceive what forgetfulness induced you to speak on behalf of the whole Government in the sense you did last night,' Salisbury wrote to him on 23rd July, reminding him that it was an open question which he and Cranbrook personally intended to support. A census would, Salisbury hoped, show up how few Welsh nonconformists there really were, compared to Anglicans. It was the only time there were cross words between Salisbury and his trusted Commons colleague, who replied that he had 'found that suddenly the temperature had risen to fever heat ... a man who acts as Leader must take such a responsibility as occasions arise'.

As early as April 1889, Smith's ill-health had given rise to reshuffle rumours, and some Liberals remarked upon the paradox that although the Conservatives still had a good majority and were succeeding in their Irish policy, nevertheless they were limping badly in the Commons. As neither Hartington nor Goschen would take on the Leadership of the

House, and Salisbury was disinclined to offer it to Hicks Beach or Churchill, and at forty-one Balfour was thought to be too young, Smith soldiered on through his eczema and exhaustion, despite the threat to his health from the hard work and constant late nights.[15]

Writing to Hartington in early September 1890, Salisbury took the unusual line of lauding the American constitutional process. Urging much more rigorous measures to defeat Home Ruler filibustering, Salisbury suggested that: 'A power of moving that "So and So be not heard" is wanted – the question to be decided without debate.' He advocated a body along the same lines of the US Congress Committee of Rules, which would assist the Speaker to sift out time-wasting questions and amendments and fix the amount of time devoted to the remainder. 'Unless we do something of the kind,' he warned, 'the machine will break down.' The Government was too weak to act on the matter just then, staggering along in Micawberish hope, but the proposal found a receptive ear in Hartington.

'I am very sorry the Queen will not let him marry the Teck girl,' Salisbury had written to the Duchess of Rutland of Prince Albert Victor ('Eddy') in September 1889, 'she is very nice – and an Englishwoman.' The reason neither the Queen nor the Waleses wanted Princess May of Teck to marry the man second in line to the Throne, although she was George III's great-granddaughter, was, as Balfour vouchsafed to Salisbury a year later, 'because they hate [her spendthrift father Prince Francis of] Teck and because the vision of [her mother] Princess Mary [Adelaide] haunting Marlborough House makes the Prince of Wales ill'. Nevertheless, the Queen was nervous about turning her down for her grandson, telling Balfour that there were only 'three marriageable protestant princesses at this moment in Europe', besides May of Teck and Alix of Hesse, 'all three ugly, unhealthy and idiotic'. (Alix of Hesse later became the tragic Tsarina Alexandra of Russia.)

The question of whom Prince Eddy would eventually marry, hitherto a diverting regal parlour game, was suddenly transformed into a potential international crisis when in August 1890 he fell in love with Princess Hélène d'Orléans, the daughter of the French Pretender, the Comte de Paris. When apprised of the proposed marriage by Balfour from Balmoral, and even worse of Queen Victoria's support for it, and furthermore her satisfaction at the idea of the Princess renouncing her Catholicism for the match, Salisbury was horrified. He telegraphed the same day to tell Balfour that the Comte de Paris should be immediately informed 'that marriage with a Frenchwoman will be very unpopular', that few would think the religious conversion sincere but instead a cynical means of attaining the British Throne, and as such 'all will despise her for it'. The Queen also had to be immediately acquainted with the dire foreign policy implications of any such match. These included 'great and general offence' in Germany because she was French, to the French Republic because her father claimed the non-existent French throne, and also to French royalists because she would have to become a Protestant. 'Prevent any royal consent being given,' Salisbury unequivocally instructed his nephew.

Balfour replied the next day that he feared the Queen would consent to a long engagement and wait for public opinion to 'go with the lovers!' It was a situation Salisbury could not allow to develop. His entire geopolitical system rested on close relations with the Central Powers, to counterbalance Britain's rivalry with France and Russia around the globe. A future French Queen of England could therefore cause untold complications. Balfour adopted a characteristically light-hearted tone throughout the crisis, which Salisbury was certainly in no mood to share. Enclosing Prince Eddy's letter to the Queen – which said that: 'I believe that in this case it is quite sufficient to have the sovereign's concent [sic] and that the Prime Minister need only to be told of her decision' – Balfour joked to his uncle: 'So now you know your true position in the constitution!'

On 9th September, Salisbury submitted to the Queen a long memorandum on the constitutional, political and historical circumstances surrounding the match, which contained no fewer than seventeen reasons why it could not take place. This explained that any clergyman marrying her without her parents' consent would be liable to imprisonment, that the only French consort of a British monarch since the Wars of the Roses had been Charles I's Queen Henrietta Maria, that for centuries British public opinion 'has been hostile to France', that Hélène's change of religion would 'secure the hostility of the Catholic and Royalist party' in France, and that the Act of Settlement might prohibit it anyhow as without excommunication by the Pope no other ceremony existed which could ascertain the sincerity of her new-found faith. Raising the threat of Prince Eddy disqualifying himself from inheriting the Throne because of his marriage, Salisbury managed to bring the Queen round to the seriousness of the situation.

By 16th September, when Salisbury went to the arsenic baths of La Bourboule in a renewed attempt to get rid of his eczema, Hélène's father, supported by Pope Leo XIII, had refused to allow his daughter to renounce her Catholicism. Paris might have been worth a Mass to Henri IV, but London wasn't worth an Anglican Communion to the Comte de Paris. 'I am afraid you must be dreadfully tired of writing me letters about this Royal Idyll,' Salisbury wrote to Balfour, who stayed at Balmoral throughout the crisis, pronouncing himself very relieved. A further scene then arose when the Duke of Fife announced that Prince Eddy was willing to renounce his right of succession to marry his princess, but that too was smoothed over successfully with the help of the Queen. On 3rd December 1891, as Salisbury had originally intended, Prince Eddy proposed to Princess May of Teck. Salisbury preferred a Westminster Abbey wedding: 'Spry east winds will be a considerable danger,' he said of Balfour's preference for St Paul's. 'I am not anxious to antedate the demise of the Crown.'[16]

Rather than the Queen, it was Prince Eddy himself who died of influenza the following month, on 14th January 1892, aged twenty-eight. With only Eddy's younger brother standing, as Salisbury put it, 'between us and the dynasty of King Fife', Princess May was gently passed on to Prince George, later King George V, and they were married at the Chapel Royal, St James's Palace, on 6th July 1893. For someone who did not believe that a man should marry his deceased wife's sister, Salisbury gave his blessing to a marriage with a deceased fiancé's brother. Nor did the Queen show any signs of holding a grudge against Salisbury over the failed Orléans match; she 'is wonderfully well, very cheerful, strongly anti-Gladstonian', Cranbrook reported to the Prime Minister in October.

On Sunday, 9th November 1890, Goschen received a mysterious letter from William Lidderdale, the Governor of the Bank of England. Visiting him there the next morning, the Chancellor found the Governor 'in a dreadful state of anxiety. Barings in such danger that unless aid is given, they must stop.' The merchant bank was heavily exposed to disastrous Argentinian securities and had £20 million of liabilities against £12 million of assets. It needed £4 million urgently to avoid imminent collapse. Lidderdale proposed to offer £1 million of the Bank of England's money if the Government could match it, hoping other City institutions would provide the remainder. 'If I do nothing and the crash comes I should never be forgiven,' Goschen concluded about his dilemma; 'if I act and disaster never occurs, Parliament would never forgive my having pledged the national credit to a private firm.'

Just before the Lord Mayor's banquet that evening, Goschen warned Salisbury of the situation, and after a sleepless night he returned to the City to continue negotiations. On Wednesday, 12th November, a very pessimistic Lord Rothschild visited Salisbury. He claimed that a general collapse in banking confidence could be triggered by a crash at Barings, and asked for government assistance to avert 'a catastrophe' which he thought 'would put an end to the commercial habit of transacting all business of the world by bills on London'. He warned that the crisis was

as serious as that of 1866, (when Salisbury himself had been badly hit by
the collapse of Overend and Gurney.) After the meeting, Salisbury
proposed to the Cabinet that an Act of Indemnity be passed to help the
Bank of England lend to Barings on Argentinian securities, but only if
Rothschild obtained cross-Party support from Gladstone.

Rothschild found his interview with Salisbury 'rather satisfying', and
by lunchtime on Friday, 14th November, Salisbury and Smith went even
further. With Goschen absent on a speaking tour of Scotland and incom-
municado, they agreed to bear half of any losses on Barings bills taken
on by the Bank of England in the twenty-four-hour period after 2 p.m.
that day. By 5.30 p.m. on Friday, just as the news was leaking out to the
City and press that Barings was in serious trouble, Lidderdale and
Rothschild tied up the details of the deal which rescued it: £1 million
was provided by the Bank, £3 million by a syndicate of other merchant
banks, and five other large joint-stock banks weighed in with more. By
Saturday lunchtime, over £10 million had been pledged, although only
£7.5 million was ever called upon once the news of the Government
guarantee and the formation of a rescue plan calmed the fear of Barings'
bill-holders. By 1894, Barings had managed to pay back the various
advances with interest.

In general, Salisbury was a committed non-interventionist, believing
in minimal State involvement in commerce and finance. He regularly
refused calls for government intervention in areas such as Peru, Siam
and Chile's Atcama Desert. When asked to get involved in arbitrating
quarrels in the west coast of Latin America or in regenerating
Argentinian finance, his answer was that on neither subject 'are Her
Majesty's Government in the least degree disposed to encroach on the
function of Providence'. When it came to a crisis which threatened
London's primacy in the acceptance market, however, he did not hesi-
tate to pledge large amounts of taxpayers' money, which, because it was
pledged in time, was not finally needed. 'A bank which, according to the
formal rules of the financial market, should have failed', writes the
historian of the House of Rothschild, 'was bailed out by a collective
intervention initiated by the Bank of England, underwritten at the critical juncture by the Government, and paid for by a broad coalition of
other City houses,' led by Rothschilds.[17] Salisbury's swift and decisive
action had helped Lidderdale and Rothschild to save the day.

It had been an exhausting, dangerous and difficult series of crises over
the previous two years, ones that had induced a re-emergence of his
depression and endangered his health. But at last on 17th November
1890, with the revelations of the O'Shea divorce case and the conse-

quent collapse in Parnell's influence, Salisbury could see an opportunity for regeneration. The hopelessly split Irish party at last allowed both Balfour's Irish Land Bill and even Salisbury's own Tithes Bill to be passed, just as Portugal backed down over Zambesia. On 17th December, Salisbury wrote to the former MP for York Sir Frederick Milner, who had two days earlier won a by-election in Bassetlaw, the first Conservative victory in months: 'In this weather we may say of you – "Now is the winter of our discontent made glorious summer by the sun of York". It was just the sustenance for our failing spirits that was urgently wanted.' Salisbury's 'peck of troubles' was, albeit temporarily, behind him.

THIRTY-THREE

Alliance Politics

*Visitors at Hatfield – Free Education
– The Prince of Wales in Difficulties –
The Death of W.H. Smith
– Party Organisation
– The Liberal Unionist Alliance*

January to October 1891

'The ballot is the regime of surprises.'

A curious torpor overcame British politics in the first five months of 1891. What Salisbury called 'the extraordinary mortality of Conservative members', five deaths in three weeks, had produced encouraging by-election victories. The excellent result in the Birmingham Aston seat, of a 3,000 Unionist majority when only 1,000 was expected, he described as 'rather perplexing'. Apart from a bout of neuralgia, which started painfully in his teeth and which he found it hard to shrug off, Salisbury felt better.

Foreign affairs also entered something of a lull. 'To my mind the Italian alliance is an unprofitable, and even slightly onerous corollary on the German alliance,' Salisbury wrote to Dufferin in mid-January. 'Germany and Austria are very useful friends as regards Turkey, Russia, Egypt, and even France. They value the Italian alliance greatly, because it means many battalions to them: and for their sake, we value it too.' It greatly complicated Anglo-French relations, however, and was 'no use anywhere else'. He complained that Crispi 'reproaches me like a neglected lover; [the Italian Ambassador Count] Tornielli scolds me like an injured wife. And now the Bismarcks are gone it is not so easy to keep Crispi in order as it was. I suppose there is nothing for it but patience.'[1] Salisbury did not have to exercise his preternatural patience for long, as on 31st January Crispi lost office, to be replaced by the Marchese di Rudini. The new Italian Prime Minister signed the Red Sea colonial agreement that Crispi had refused, which gave Italy a short lease on the African province of Kassala. This was the last of the major bilateral agreements by which Salisbury sliced up Africa.

It was in this positive atmosphere that Hatfield welcomed both Kaiser Wilhelm II and the Crown Prince Victor Emmanuel of Italy on two separate visits in July 1891. After the Kaiser had solicitously written to Salisbury in February about improvements that he felt should be made to British naval organisation and equipment, Salisbury asked the First Lord of the Admiralty to send 'a civil, argumentative reply – showing that in some directions we are adopting his recommendations.... It rather looks to me as if he was not "all there"!' Salisbury's attempt to minimise the amount of time the Kaiser spent in London, protesting that it was 'full of socialists', had failed, and Wilhelm II's first full State Visit as Kaiser was laid on with all possible pomp. He had managed to put the visit off the previous year, telling Hatzfeldt that he feared the crowds might boo the autocrat, and suspecting that the only reason that the Lord Mayor of London was so keen was that he might cadge a baronetcy out of it.

Salisbury described the death of Waddington's mother the day before the visit began as 'opportune', allowing the French Ambassador to be absent during the opening festivities. Fearing his absence for too long might be misconstrued, Waddington later attended the Hatfield house party, albeit in deep mourning. Unwilling to allow Britain to be too closely identified with the Triple Alliance, Salisbury encouraged the Queen to visit the French fleet in Portsmouth that August, saying, 'it is most important to persuade the French, if we can, that England has no antipathy to France nor any partisanship against her'.

After naval and military reviews, a City procession, a reception at the Italian Opera, a speech at the Mansion House and another reception at Windsor, a huge garden party was given for the Kaiser in the park at Hatfield. Because the Kaiser brought a retinue of thirteen, as well as the Prince and Princess of Wales and the Duke of Cambridge and their suites, the younger Cecils had to stay elsewhere on the estate, despite the house having sixty-five bedrooms. Years later, Lord George Hamilton remembered how it was 'a scene of unusual magnificence in the great Jacobean drawing room' on the second day of the Kaiser's stay. 'The huge room, with its blaze of electric light, was a compact mass of jewels, orders and decorations and gorgeous gowns, the cream of the splendour and ability of the two great empires.' There were sixty for dinner each night in the Marble Hall. Only Salisbury seemed entirely unimpressed and 'thankful to have got rid of foreign visitors'. He thought the Kaiser, in one of his better prophecies, 'a disturbing influence' on peace, 'mad enough for anything' and potentially 'the most dangerous enemy we had in Europe'.[2]

For the visit of the Prince of Naples a fortnight later, 4,849 people attended a garden party at Hatfield, 800 of them travelling from King's Cross in special trains. At the end of the festivities, Salisbury joked to Lytton: 'It is a great comfort to me to think that [the French President] M. Carnot has not got an heir apparent.' In commemoration of his visit, the Kaiser later gave Salisbury a 30' x 10' portrait of himself aboard ship in the uniform of a British Admiral of the Fleet. This gigantic painting, complete with swagger, flags, sword and medals, framed in gold leaf nearly a foot wide, is of the school which a French art critic once described as not so much a work of art as a declaration of war. It was hung in a place of honour in the King James drawing room until August 1914, when it was promptly consigned to an outbuilding. When in 1901 the Anglophobic Austrian Archduke Franz Ferdinand also expressed a wish to come to stay at Hatfield, McDonnell drafted a letter to Prince Metternich at their Embassy to say that the house was shut up because several of Salisbury's grandchildren had mumps. 'It is within the accepted limits of diplomatic veracity,' noted Salisbury.

'I am inclined to believe they will win,' Salisbury wrote to Lord Stanley about the Liberals' prospects at the next general election, 'but unless some heavenborn genius presents himself they cannot last.' In order to minimise the expected defeat, the Conservatives introduced free elementary education, a measure for which Chamberlain and the Radical Unionists had long been agitating. Carnarvon had predicted that the Second Reform Act would turn all elections into 'sordid auctions', but once it had passed Salisbury saw little point in being too fastidious to take part. When Austin remarked that free education should not be offered until just before a general election, Salisbury 'smiled and answered in his ironical way: "Of course not. One should never bribe till a quarter to four"', a reference to the 4 p.m. time when the polls used to close.[3] It was in this spirit that, when asked in 1888 whether Belfast should be accorded the honour of formally becoming a city, Salisbury noted: 'Better keep it back until an election is nearer.'

Although Salisbury, and later Gwendolen, tried to portray free elementary education as one of his long-term policy objectives, indeed merely the continuation of his 1885 Newport programme, it was in fact nothing of the sort. 'I should shrink before I gave every subject of the Queen, whether rich or poor,' he had actually said at Newport, 'the right to have his children educated at the public expense.' The imperative which drove Salisbury six years later, as well as the obvious desire for working-class votes, was the need to ensure that a Conservative measure left as much power as possible in the hands of the Church of

England's denominational 'Voluntary' schools, which then educated over half of all children in England and Wales. Without financial support from the Treasury this class of school was under threat, especially as the Education Department in Whitehall seemed keen to undermine religious instruction, preferring the Civic Schools, which had no religious bias and were run by elected Boards. Rather than allow Radical, non-Anglican legislation to be passed by the Liberals, Salisbury decided to take the initiative.

Salisbury had appointed Cranbrook as Lord President of the Council partly because he hoped his High Church convictions would help keep the Education Department in line. He denounced School Boards to Cranbrook as 'the most recklessly extravagant bodies in England', and wanted local authorities to have more say in the running of them, 'as having businesslike people [who] possessed ordinary common sense'. In his Nottingham speech to the NUCCA on 26th November 1889, Salisbury had turned his Newport policy on its head and argued that as the State had enforced a statutory duty on an individual to educate his children, 'You are bound to make it as easy for him as you can ... and very greatly to relieve the difficulties of the working man in that respect.'[4] Sir George Kekewich, the Secretary at the Vice-President's office (effectively the Permanent Under-Secretary for Education), described the Nottingham offer as simply 'a bribe to the working classes', and several senior Tories, including the former Chief Whip Hart Dyke, agreed.

'There is nothing new in my speech in Nottingham,' Salisbury claimed to Cranbrook in December. 'Since the compulsory law of 1876, I hold that the poor have suffered a great grievance.' It was not one Salisbury had spoken of in those terms, however, for well over a decade. Other attractions of the new policy included the fact that the Liberals could not very well oppose it, that it would help keep the Liberal Unionists content, and that some of the poorer Voluntary schools would now be saved by a regular income. 'If you choose to deal with "assisted" education yourselves,' he told a meeting of peers and bishops in the Carlton Club in March 1890, 'you may put the Voluntary Schools into a position from which no future hostile majority can dislodge them; if you choose to pass the question by, you may be pronouncing their doom.' To the Bishop of Exeter's 'twaddle' about how parental responsibility would be diminished by free education, Salisbury was characteristically dismissive: 'Does he ever object to a young man getting an exhibition at the University, because it will lessen his father's sense of parental responsibility?'[5]

In a Cabinet memorandum in November 1890, Salisbury observed that 'there is no limit to the extent to which Parliamentary liberality may go, if all children of all ages are to be taught, *gratis*, whatever their parents may desire that they should learn'. He believed that the best way to encourage labourers to send their children to school would be to pay parents ten shillings if their children attended 300 classes, with the money going direct to them rather than to the school managers, who at the time were paid it as a grant for every five- to fourteen-year-old attending Board or Voluntary schools. 'The labourer will not value a boon which only reaches him in the shape of an exemption', Salisbury wrote, 'so much as he will the solid silver which his child will appear to have earned.' Cranbrook said the scheme could never work and no one else in Cabinet supported it, but it showed how blatant was the inducement which Salisbury intended.

In early June 1891, as the Education Bill came up for its second reading, Salisbury once again complained about the way Cabinet decisions seemed to be ignored by ministers in the Commons. When Goschen explained that 'strong pressure' from Harcourt and Trevelyan had led to a particular concession, Salisbury replied that 'what the people on the other side will say … is a matter of no importance whatever'.[6] The Bill finally received Royal Assent on 5th August 1891. As with County Councils, Salisbury had interpreted a Radical measure in a Tory way, partly to avoid Gladstone passing something he feared would be worse.

Relations between Salisbury and the Prince of Wales were never particularly close. Salisbury found him morally and intellectually inferior to the Queen and privately dreaded his accession. He had taken some of the Prince's friends into his 1886 Government at his urging, but neither Londonderry nor Lord Charles Beresford, the Fourth Lord of the Admiralty, had been particularly successful appointments. It was through a third, Earl Cadogan, that Salisbury initially advised the Prince over the baccarat scandal which broke in June 1891, after Colonel Sir William Gordon-Cumming was discovered cheating while playing with the Prince and other guests at Tranby Croft, near Doncaster. Before the libel case in which the Prince was to give evidence came to court, the Queen had wanted her son to write publicly to the Archbishop of Canterbury denouncing gambling as a social evil, which Salisbury said would be hypocritical and would almost certainly backfire.

Instead, Salisbury advised the Prince, whose popularity reached its nadir during the affair despite being an innocent witness, to:

> sit still and avoid baccarat for six months and at the end of that time write a letter to some indiscreet person (who would publish it) saying that at the time of the Cumming case there had been a great deal of misunderstanding as to his views: but the circumstances of that case had so convinced him of

the evil that was liable to be caused by that game that since that time he had forbidden it to be played in his presence.

This, Salisbury thought, 'would suffice to deodorise him of all the unpleasant aroma which this case has left upon him and his surroundings'. In the meantime, Salisbury refused all calls for an official announcement on the issue, saying that the private life of the Prince of Wales was not a fit subject for parliamentary questions and thus 'we should refuse to discuss them'.[7]

Only a month after the Tranby Croft affair, Salisbury was again called in to deal with a scandal far more perilous for the Prince's reputation. Lord Charles Beresford, an old friend of the Prince and former Unionist MP for Marylebone East, was a Regency figure trapped in a Victorian moral universe. A famous philanderer, hell-raiser and commander of a naval brigade in the 1884–5 Nile Expedition, Beresford, who was also a politician, was assessed by Salisbury as 'an officer of great ability afloat; but he is too greedy of popular applause to get on in a public department'.

On 12th January 1890, Beresford called on his former friend the Prince of Wales at Marlborough House. Lady Charles Beresford had obtained a letter which had been written to Lord Charles by his mistress, Lady Brooke, reproaching him for going back to his wife. Despite its now being in the possession of George Lewis, the Beresfords' solicitor, Lady Brooke wanted it returned and had prevailed upon her admirer the Prince of Wales to get it. The Prince had personally bullied the hapless lawyer into letting him see a copy. When, after two visits from the Prince, Lady Charles refused to return or destroy the letter, he began to cut her from Marlborough House society and at social occasions in general.

Somewhat bizarrely, Lady Charles drafted her husband to fight her case against this social ostracism, and a serious scene ensued on 12th January at which the words 'blackguard' and 'coward' were used by Beresford to the Prince, who then went off to take up a naval command in the Mediterranean. The situation festered for eighteen months until 12th July 1891 when, with his wife threatening to leave England unless she was received socially by the Prince, Beresford wrote accusing him of being a blackguard who had 'instituted a species of society boycotting' against his wife. The letter contained the postscript: 'If there remained in your character a spark of chivalry, manliness or justice it would be impossible for you not to recognise how you have behaved in this painful business.' This letter was not actually sent off, but was instead taken by Lady Charles to Salisbury, as he later put it, 'apparently to obtain my advice'.

Salisbury, who regarded the whole affair as sordid and pathetic, naturally advised against the Beresfords sending the letter. He nevertheless also recognised the palpable danger to the Prince's reputation if a *modus vivendi* were not arranged before the whole story was leaked to the press. On 3rd August, Beresford wrote to Salisbury announcing his intention to return from active service and cause mayhem. By threatening what he called 'a more just way of getting right done than can duelling: and that is – publicity!', he said he would not only resign his naval command, but also call the press and wire agencies to his home in Eaton Square and give them all the details of that affair and others.

Salisbury's answer to Beresford was a model:

> You have stood in a certain relation to the anonymous Lady: and you are consequently bound, according to our social laws, so far as you can help it, not to let that relation with you be a source of inquiry or obloquy to her. It must not be your pen or voice that brings her into any disgrace because she yielded to you.... I think your proposed letter, unintentionally, sins against this law and therefore I am sure that if published it would have done you endless harm.

On the issue of social ostracism, Salisbury's sublime self-confidence and his 'Buffalo'-like disdain for Society shone through:

> The acquaintance of <u>no</u> illustrious person is necessary to one's happiness, and if any illustrious person whom you know withdraws from your intimacy, you have no reason to trouble yourself further in the matter than for his sake to regret the opportunities of engagements he has lost. Your position in society and in your profession are not affected by the friendship of anyone, however well placed.[8]

For four months it seemed that the Beresfords had taken this advice, but then in mid-December Lady Charles wrote to the Queen. Beresford meanwhile wrote to the Prince demanding an apology for his 'direct intention to damage my wife'. Salisbury met Beresford, but to no avail. 'He is a mere tool,' he told McDonnell afterwards. Advising the Prince 'to sit quite still and not answer the letter', Salisbury said that legal advice should be requested 'to determine how matters can be stopped so as to bring in the Prince least – and hurt the Beresfords the most. He deserves no quarter after this.'

Writing to Beresford himself on 23rd December, Salisbury returned the letter he had sent the Prince and asked him to submit another, suitably worded to allow the Beresfords to be once more socially received by the Prince. Over the following four days, Salisbury brokered a peace deal between the two sides, which included an exchange of civil letters (the one from the Prince apologising if Lady Charles 'should have been led to conceive an erroneous impression'), the temporary exclusion of Lady Brooke from Marlborough House, as well as a promise from the Beresfords not to execute their publicity plan. 'Lord Salisbury brought peace,' Lord Esher noted in his diary about the affair, 'whether with much honour or not may be questioned.' Protecting the Royal Family from embarrassment, whether it be political in Berlin, financial over the Royal Grants, sexual over disappointed mistresses, or even highly tangential, as over the Cleveland Street scandal, Salisbury simply saw as part of the duties of the premiership, and he carried them out impeccably.

~

The unexpected death of Henry Raikes, the Postmaster-General, on 24th August 1891 caused a series of headaches for Salisbury and Balfour, as the £2,500 per annum (non-Cabinet) post would be a promotion for no fewer than fourteen junior ministers, one of whom would be pleased by it and the other thirteen annoyed that they had been passed over. The issue was complicated by some ministers holding insecure seats which might be lost if they were re-fought, as all ministerial appointees had to be re-elected to their seats. Balfour thought that the 'slight air of ridicule which attaches to all his performances' ruled out Ashmead-Bartlett, and the selection was whittled down to three: Sir James Fergusson, Salisbury's Under-Secretary at the Foreign Office, the Tory Democrat Under-Secretary for India, Sir John Gorst, or the Financial Secretary to the Treasury, William Jackson, who had, as he told his uncle, 'middle class tact and judgment, I admit, but good of their kind'.

To Gorst's blatant request for the post, Salisbury delivered a magisterial slap-down for his past disloyalties: 'In order to secure the general support and confidence of a party, something is more necessary than ability – and that is the general confidence that the party can rely upon you to stand by them at a pinch.' Jackson turned down the post when Salisbury assured him he was more useful where he was. The final choice of Sir James Fergusson, McDonnell put down to the fact that 'the Chief dreads much offending the extreme Right in the declining years of a Parliament', and that 'many of the old boys would be very sick' if Gorst were awarded the post.

Fergusson's job went to James Lowther, the MP for Penrith, after Goschen was sounded out by Salisbury: 'Do you see any objection? He is a good linguist – and the son of a diplomatist.... The only thing I know against him is that he is my nephew: and that ought hardly to stand in his way.' Being related to Lord Salisbury – Lowther was married to his niece Mary (née Beresford-Hope) – was never a bar to office. He did the job entirely unobtrusively, recalling of Salisbury that 'it was very rarely that I ever saw him officially. He did not believe in interviews.'[9] Lowther eventually became Speaker of the House of Commons

between 1905 and 1921, serving with fairness and tact. Soon after his
appointment to the Foreign Office, however, Salisbury was seeking
Goschen's approval for a far more magisterial act of avuncular
nepotism.

During the Kaiser's visit to Hatfield in July, Lord George Hamilton had
noticed that amongst all the splendour in the Jacobean drawing room,
'in a corner of the room sat poor Smith, huddled up in evident pain with
the unmistakable stamp of death upon his face'. On 6th October 1891,
W.H. Smith died at Walmer Castle – 'a martyr to duty' thought
Hamilton – coincidentally only hours before Parnell. 'He was a straightforward, honest man,' wrote Cranbrook, 'and won the confidence of all
by character and not genius.' 'Old Morality' had been a loyal and reliable lieutenant to Salisbury, sitting, a rug over his knees, night after
night in the House of Commons for four-and-a-half sessions trying to
get the Government's business past Irish obstructionism. Popularly
believed to be the inspiration for the Rt Hon. Sir Joseph Porter in HMS
Pinafore, he once had to endure Cambridge undergraduates waving that
garment at him when he arrived there to collect his honorary degree. He
refused a GCB in 1886, however, on the grounds that as a newsagent –
albeit one worth £2 million – he was not grand enough. Salisbury solved
that problem posthumously by creating his widow Viscountess
Hambleden, with remainder to his heirs.

Salisbury found the 'distressing and quite unexpected' news of
Smith's death 'very shocking and a terrible blow'. He was in Beaulieu,
unfit to travel and deeply troubled. The Leadership of the House of
Commons was a far more powerful post then than today; whoever was
chosen would be widely seen as Salisbury's heir apparent. To the
Queen, Salisbury predicted that 'the trouble about filling up Mr Smith's
place will be very great'. As early as July, she had thought Arthur
Balfour the most conspicuously successful of all the departmental
ministers, and 'the only person' capable of succeeding the ill Smith.
Salisbury had replied that for obvious reasons he could not propose him.

The combination of uncle and nephew in the two most powerful positions in the Lords and Commons would, Salisbury feared, provoke
outrage, if not from the Conservatives themselves then at least from the
Liberal Unionists. Smith's ability to hold the coalition together in the
Commons, partly by his personal moral force, had to be replicated in
any successor. 'He was such a good, loyal, self-sacrificing man!'
Salisbury wrote to Richmond, still unable to return home. Smith and he
had had occasional tussles over legislation, aggravated by Salisbury's
low opinion of the House which Smith had to placate, but his loyalty in

the crises occasioned by Churchill, Hicks Beach and Carnarvon had rendered him invaluable.

Insofar as Salisbury really had them at all in politics, Smith had been a friend. He had provided Salisbury with more than just advice and support. According to George Hamilton, Salisbury 'did not come sufficiently into contact with influences, movements and aspirations of classes other than his own. Smith admirably supplied this deficiency.' Once the millionaire bookseller and newsagent had gone, Chamberlain became one of the very few to fill this gap in Salisbury's knowledge. Lord Newton remembered Salisbury in the 1890s as 'a severe and Olympian form, admired and respected, but remote from the interests and circumstances of the ordinary peer' – and that at a time when many peers' experiences were themselves remote from the interests and circumstances of ordinary people.

Salisbury's telegram to McDonnell from Beaulieu on 11th October illustrated the way his mind was working: 'If it seems quite clear that Mr Goschen must give way to Arthur ... would it not put Mr Goschen in a much more satisfactory position if he took the initiative previously and let it be known that he would not take the post of Leader, before I come back to England. It will make him safe from all taunts in the future.' By his not hurrying back, Salisbury hoped that a clamour for Balfour might build up, at least enough of one to protect him from the charge of nepotism once he had returned, which he did on the 12th. The line subtly put about by McDonnell, Akers-Douglas and others was that Goschen had been closely associated with the collapse of the legislative programme in 1890, whereas Balfour was a fine debater who had recently been able to lift the special powers provisions of his Crimes Act from almost every part of Ireland. 'He is awfully shocked by Smith's death,' McDonnell wrote confidentially about Salisbury to Akers-Douglas from the Beefsteak Club on 13th October; but that did not prevent him from thinking carefully about the future. [10]

'Circumstances are concurring to make Mr Balfour an inevitable choice,' Salisbury reported to the Queen after Hicks Beach had once more refused the Leadership of the House on health grounds, 'though the objections to it from many points of view are considerable,' not least of which was the inconvenience of removing Balfour from Ireland. Salisbury was still unsure about the appointment. 'I do not feel certain how the experiment will end,' he told his wife. The actual decision could not finally be made until both Goschen and Hartington acquiesced, and as Salisbury complained to Balfour on 15th October: 'Hartington is at Newmarket and all political arrangements have to be hung up until some quadruped has run faster than some other quadruped.'[11] Akers-Douglas visited Goschen to urge him to follow Hicks Beach's example and declare publicly that he was not in the running and furthermore that he would be happy to serve under Balfour. Goschen, correctly estimating that he did not have the support from the Tory backbenches necessary to challenge Balfour for the Leadership, duly did this in a speech in Cambridge.

'It will make you the target for very jealous and exacting criticism,' Salisbury wrote to Balfour on the 16th, reporting that he had still not heard back from Hartington. 'But I do not think you can avoid or refuse it as matters stand.' Salisbury was sorry that he was seeming to slight Goschen, 'but he could not hold the party together. His refusal to belong to the Carlton is of itself a fatal disqualification.' Tory backbenchers did not warm to the fastidious calculating machine, whereas Balfour's successes in Ireland were a justifiable boast they could make to their constituents as the Parliament entered its last session before dissolution. Once Hartington returned from the Cæsarevitch Stakes on 17th October and agreed to Balfour's appointment, Salisbury wrote to Goschen that evening. The letter was a masterful commiseration with Goschen for his loss of place on the *cursus honorum*:

> You possess, in our judgment, all the qualities required for a House of Commons leader at this juncture, <u>except one</u>: That you are not a member of the political party which furnishes much the largest portion of the Unionist phalanx. In opinion you are more Conservative than many of your colleagues: but for motives which I quite understand, and honour, you have not been willing yet to become a member of the Carlton. But we are on the eve of an election, when such questions assume an exaggerated importance.

The Queen wanted Balfour to combine the jobs of Leader of the House of Commons and Irish Secretary, but Salisbury delicately made the obvious point that 'the Leader of the House must be always in the House – while the Chief Secretary must occasionally be in Ireland'.[12] Writing to Hicks Beach that Balfour had accepted 'with rather a wry face', Salisbury asked for advice as to whom to appoint to Ireland. In the end, the job went to William Jackson. On Goschen's insistence, Gorst took over the Treasury job, where, Salisbury told the Queen, 'he can scarcely do any harm', and the thirty-two-year-old George Curzon, whom Salisbury described as 'a rising man of great ability, acquainted with the East', filled Gorst's post as Under-Secretary at the India Office.

Originally Salisbury had reluctantly passed over Curzon for the job, telling Hicks Beach that 'he had pledged awkwardly in regard to one or two foreign questions.... A certain amount of impenetrable apathy is necessary in the man who is to answer Labouchere.' A dearth of qualified alternatives sent him back to Curzon, but Salisbury demanded certain excisions from his forthcoming book, *Persia and the Persian Question*, in which Curzon had written about the 'black and ineffaceable' stain of the Shah's rule. Curzon paid the literary price for office without too much grumbling. 'I have no positive claims to authorship,' wrote Salisbury, 'but by eliminating your most interesting paragraphs I shall always feel I have had a negative share in a great work.' In his Guildhall speech on 9th November, Salisbury paid a fine personal tribute to Smith, describing him as 'my beloved colleague' and employing far warmer terms than he ever used about anyone outside his family.

Balfour, for all his banter and love of irony, was not such a fatalist as Salisbury. Like Chamberlain and Churchill he believed in comprehensive political programmes, constructions of reform across different political arenas which taken together implied a greater aim than just the sum of their parts. Such concepts were always anathema to Salisbury, and smacked to him of cant.[13] Nonetheless, Salisbury's personal hold on the upper echelons of the Party hierarchy had been immeasurably strengthened, and was now secure for the remainder of his career. Salisbury had used Churchill to wreck Northcote, Goschen to destroy Churchill and Akers-Douglas to persuade Goschen not to oppose Balfour. It had taken a decade, but Cecilian hegemony of the Tory Party was now firmly in place. For over a quarter of a century, at a time of ever-increasing democratisation of politics, the leadership of the Conservative Party stayed in the hands of an aristocratic uncle and his nephew. To facilitate communication between them, Salisbury had a telephone connection installed over the short distance between his house in Arlington Street and Balfour's at No. 4, Carlton Gardens.

Although Salisbury was happy to give the impression of staying aloof from the mundane matters of Whipping, Party organisation and local affairs, leaving them to Aretas Akers-Douglas and Richard Middleton, this was something of a pose, intended to increase his authority when occasionally he was required to rebuke a recalcitrant constituency chairman or encourage a reluctant candidate. In fact, Salisbury took a close personal interest in the day-to-day work of Party management both inside and outside Parliament. After the close of sitting at the House of Lords, he would regularly join Middleton at Conservative Central Office in St Stephen's Chambers in the evening. Gwendolen remembered how subordinates would withdraw and the two men would go through the constituency reports together, discussing the merits of aspirants for promotion, the winnable and unwinnable seats and the general morale of the Party. Perhaps it appealed to Salisbury's cynicism about human nature to hear the tales of grubbing hackery which 'Skipper' Middleton, the Party's brilliant Chief Agent, was able to recount.

'[Akers-]Douglas and Middleton have never put me wrong,' Salisbury used to say. He was fortunate to have two of the most formidable political operators in Tory history working for him for so long, who furthermore got on well with each other and with 'Pom' McDonnell. With elections for County Councils, School Boards and Poor Law Guardians, as well as parliamentary and borough elections, Middleton was never idle. He called Salisbury 'The Old Man' and gave him unvarnished and, in the days before sophisticated polling, uncannily accurate forecasts of election results, often predicting a by-election result to within a dozen votes. 'The ballot is the regime of surprises,' Salisbury had said in 1883, but Middleton's hand-picked lieutenants throughout the country managed to keep them to a minimum. They occasionally disagreed; 'Hopeless seats should never be fought,' was one of Salisbury's dictums, but Middleton generally demurred, thinking it gave candidates good practice and forced the Liberal to spend more. Overall, however, Salisbury deferred to Middleton's superb local knowledge, just as Middleton left national policy entirely up to 'The Old Man'.

'It is impossible to deny the fascinations that must attach to the position of wire-puller,' Salisbury had written in the *Saturday Review* a quarter of a century earlier. 'The pomp and pageantry of power have charms only for vulgar minds. The refined enjoyment of it consists in the ignorance of those over whom it is exercised. To look upon your fellow-creations as puppets, whom you are managing through the instrumentality of a great big puppet to whom they give the name of leader, must be a very gratifying position to a cynical and lazy mind.' Middleton, who like almost all the senior Party officials of the day came from Kent, had joined the navy at fifteen. He had fought slave traders off East Africa in the early 1870s, becoming Conservative agent for West Kent in 1883. By 1885, he was Chief Agent and the following year he overhauled the entire National Union, staying in the job until 1903.

Middleton organised nationwide pamphleting campaigns, registration drives, the mobilisation of volunteers and the collection of door-to-door intelligence. He spotted potential candidates, estimated the proportion of electors likely to poll, assessed local grievances, and took into account seasonal factors on the turn-out. He also raised funds, increased agents' pay, co-ordinated press campaigns and spearheaded the creation of an efficient vote-garnering organisation, which served Salisbury superbly and only began to fall apart after Middleton's retirement. He and Akers-Douglas were as adept with the stick as the carrot, and if anyone showed half the insubordination to Salisbury as he himself had shown to his Party leadership in the 1850s and 1860s, they could expect retribution. After both the 1895 and 1900 general election campaigns, Salisbury presented Middleton with cheques for £10,000 from a grateful

Party, enough to buy a large house. Liberal papers such as the *Birmingham Daily Gazette* were left bemoaning the fact that the Liberals did not have a Middleton of their own.[14]

In Akers-Douglas, Salisbury also had a lieutenant who knew his master's mind intimately. His work allowed Salisbury never to have to be in the lobby, indeed almost never to have personally to canvass the opinions of any backbencher as to policy. Salisbury could thus retain what one backbencher, Winston Churchill, called 'a certain aloofness of spirit, now considered old-fashioned'. It also allowed him to lead by example, reasonably certain that the Party would follow. It was Akers-Douglas who made sure that it did, privately keeping Salisbury in close and constant touch with the views of the Party in the Commons. As the events of August 1890 had shown, it did not always work, but overall the victories far outnumbered the reverses. It was really due to Akers-Douglas's hard work that Salisbury could look Olympian, and rule the country from outside the Commons.

'When a man says that he agrees with me in principle,' Salisbury used to remark, 'I am quite certain that he does not agree with me in practice.'[15] Akers-Douglas's aristocratic team of Whips – who included Sidney Herbert (later 14th Earl of Pembroke), Lord Arthur Hill (son of the 4th Marquess of Downshire), Lord Lewisham (later 6th Earl of Dartmouth), Lord Edmund Talbot (son of the 14th Duke of Norfolk), as well as the formidable baronet Sir William Walrond, who succeeded Akers-Douglas as Chief Whip in 1895 – persuaded, cajoled and encouraged practical support. Lady Salisbury often asked Akers-Douglas's advice as to whom she should invite to her receptions, 'who could be of use to the party'. On the reverse of one such inquiry, he noted a typically down-to-earth *aide-mémoire* to himself: 'Put Ellis on Thames Sewerage Committee.' (He did not specify whether this was as a reward or a punishment.)

Salisbury regularly wrote to congratulate Akers-Douglas on a 'splendid bit of whipping', especially after divisions in which every single Tory MP was present or paired. In May 1891, he submitted his name for a privy councillorship without asking his permission, 'because I had considerable doubt whether I should have got your leave'. The efficiency of his successor Walrond can be measured by the session of 1901, in which, out of 390 divisions, of the thirty-one ministers in the House of Commons all but six attended over 333, and no fewer than eight ministers made 386 or more. Salisbury believed in rewarding his Whips. When in 1888 Goschen wanted to abolish a Treasury sinecure traditionally reserved for ex-Whips, he blocked the move, saying that it was 'among the prizes which animate that class of superior wire puller who are the very soul of our party organisation. Starving the sheep dogs is even worse than starving the sheep.'

Although Salisbury privately thought the business of answering Conservative and Primrose League correspondence was 'useless', and suspected it cost him as much in postage as the Duke of Rutland spent on cigars, his staff dutifully replied to every letter he received. One of his assistant private secretaries recalled how Salisbury used to receive 'almost daily communications from an old gentleman belonging to the Carlton Club about some curious dreams he had had there after luncheon. He believed they foretold, if correctly interpreted, important political developments.' Someone else wrote to ask whether, because friends had told him he looked like Lord Salisbury – and the photograph he enclosed did indeed show a tall, stout, bearded man – he could perhaps secure a public appointment for his son. When Glasgow Conservative Association wrote to ask for a speaker, Salisbury complained to his private secretary that 'they seem to imagine that we keep an institution which furnishes spouters to evening parties on application – like conjurors'. Nonetheless, Conservative Central Office's increasing efficiency in every department of political organisation, especially in mobilising the 'Villadom' of suburbia, proved invaluable to Salisbury in the latter half of the 1890s.[16]

The other pillar of Salisbury's electoral success was his alliance with the Liberal Unionists. However much they might disagree with their allies, their dislike of Gladstone and Home Rule concentrated minds on both sides. The key figure was always Hartington, whose real character, insiders felt, was wholly unlike his sleepy, leisurely image. 'In spite of his blunt manner and ungrammatical sentences,' Salisbury told his daughter, 'there's no man who weighs his words more carefully than Hartington, or has more "intention" in what he says.'[17]

Salisbury quickly established a fine working relationship with Hartington, whom he found 'cordial and loyal', writing regularly on all political matters. By June 1887 he did not believe, as he told Austin, that actual fusion would take place under him. 'A new name will be wanted – it might have been Randolph's if he had the most rudimentary common sense.' But once again his prediction was wrong, as the Liberal Unionists were gradually wooed into the Government by 1895. Originally Salisbury had been willing to reconstruct the Government with Hartington and Sir Henry James, but, as he told Cranbrook, he 'naturally did not see his way to acting with Chamberlain'. Yet even 'Radical Joe' did not cause the problems originally envisaged.

Although Salisbury had privately accused Chamberlain of 'sharp practice' during the August 1886 re-election of Henry Matthews in Birmingham, relations had since greatly improved. Salisbury readily admitted to Eustace in July 1887 that various government measures were 'payment to Chamberlain ... the price at which the Crimes Bill can be passed', but it was never too high, especially as it encouraged Chamberlain not to rejoin the Liberals during his Round Table Conference with the Gladstonians.[18] Salisbury thought of Chamberlain as an 'element so uncertain' that the Liberal Unionists might crumble away, especially when the Conservatives occasionally found themselves 'in a state of decided pout' with them, but in fact the coalition held together well.

Salisbury asked Smith to remind Goschen in October 1888 that the Liberal Unionists, although comprising less than a fifth of the Unionist force in the House of Commons, enjoyed far more than a fifth of the major public appointments, citing Dufferin at Rome, Lansdowne in India, and all the various legal posts they held. Over one such, a Lordship of Appeal that was offered to Sir Henry James, Salisbury ruthlessly changed his mind when he heard that his seat would probably be lost by his Liberal Unionist successor. 'Lord Salisbury had not the courtesy to write again either to Lord Hartington or to Sir Henry James upon the subject and in no way attempted to explain matters,' James complained in an outraged memorandum, which rather pompously employed the third-person singular. In fact, Salisbury had written to Hartington to report that Smith, Goschen and Balfour all agreed that the loss of James's seat would be disastrous, so he had no other course but to offer the Appeal post to Sir James Hannen, the High Court Judge who had presided over the Parnell Special Commission. As Salisbury had admitted to Devonshire, *'force majeure electorale'* was paramount in his calculations.[19]

Another appointment, that of the undistinguished MP Evelyn Ashley to a privy councillorship in 1891, was questioned by the Queen. Cranbrook explained to her that it was because Ashley was a Liberal Unionist, 'and really to please the goodnatured Hartington'. Salisbury wrote ambiguously to Hartington to say that he was 'consoled as to Ashley by the reflection that everybody will know it is your doing'. When, in September, Lords Abergavenny and Londonderry conceived a scheme for luring the Liberal Lord Barnard over to the Tories with an earldom, Salisbury agreed with McDonnell: 'These fishermen are too fond of the harpoon. There is no danger of his becoming Radical – unless we frighten him by our eagerness. Even if he becomes Liberal Unionist – he must come to us when the Liberal Unionists break up.'

In October 1891, Chamberlain extravagantly praised Salisbury's record of social reform. The Working Class Dwellings Act of 1885, County Councils, the Technical Instruction Act of 1889, the Housing of the Working Classes Act of 1890, the Public Health Act of 1890, various Allotments Acts, the Factory and Workshops Act of 1890, free elementary education and the Shop Hours Act of 1892 all added up to a significant and far more than merely consolidatory programme of social reform. 'Lord Salisbury's Government has done far more for the solid improvement of the masses of the population', pronounced the leader of the Radical Unionists at Carmarthen, 'than any Government has done before in the present century in a similar period.'[20] Considering that Chamberlain himself had been a Cabinet minister during Gladstone's 1880–5 Government, which he denounced as 'incompetent, if not unsympathetic, in the treatment of social questions', this was high praise indeed. Although Salisbury generally did not like change, and thought it usually for the worse, if established interests were not too badly damaged he was willing to countenance it for a specific, verifiable public benefit, and also occasionally, of course, for electoral advantage.

THIRTY-FOUR

Leaving Office

The General Election – Cabinet Style

November 1891 to August 1892

'An official life contains but two happy days – the day of assuming office, and the day of leaving it.'

'Uncle Robert is rather oppressed by his Lord Mayor's speech,' wrote Frances Balfour to her sister in November 1891, 'the most difficult he says of all the year, for the foreign courts watch it so closely, and Gladstone has made Egypt a ticklish business.' The previous month Gladstone had criticised the continued 'burdensome and embarrassing' occupation of Egypt. Alighted upon by the French and anti-British Cairo press, it was taken as a Liberal pledge to evacuate, and Baring urged Salisbury to use the opportunity of his Guildhall speech to emphasise the unchanged nature of Government policy towards Egypt. 'Head bent down, irresponsive to the cheers which greeted him,' Henry Lucy thought Salisbury's pallor and whole bearing 'was that of a man wearied almost to death'.

He addressed his speech to French and Turkish audiences, and announced yet again that Britain would not leave Egypt until she was secure internally and externally. He explained that back in 1882, 'if England acted alone in this matter, it was not her fault...we cannot allow all that to be swept away as if it were last year's almanac...whatever party may be in power, the English people will never withdraw its hand from the steady and vigorous prosecution and the benefit of the humane understanding with which now it is their pride and honour to be connected'. Politicians nowadays shun the taboo word 'never', but Salisbury used it regularly, and on this occasion Baring telegraphed his thanks.

In another part of the speech, dealing with Thomas Croke, the Archbishop of Cashel, a strong Irish nationalist and supporter of land agitation, Salisbury said that 'ecclesiastical domination in purely secular affairs was a most serious evil'. When the Duke of Norfolk, Britain's leading lay Roman Catholic, wrote to complain about this, Salisbury reiterated that the clergy's 'training and Mission do not give them the slightest fitness for advising on questions of secular expediency, which are often of vast moment'. Salisbury specifically excluded the issues of education, marriage and church policy, but otherwise he was adamant. 'Parnell's <u>party</u> have not committed adultery: and the fact that Parnell did does not justify the Irish clergy in placing themselves at the head of so purely a secular movement as that for Home Rule.'

At sixty-one, Salisbury was approaching the stage in life when contemporaries and friends start to die. In November it was Lytton, and the French Government, uniquely for a foreigner, declared his a public funeral and closed all the shops along the route from the Embassy to the church and then on to St Lazare railway station. White died of influenza in Berlin *en route* to see Salisbury the next month, stalling the negotiations over Egypt in Turkey. On New Year's Day 1892, Salisbury lamented to Sir Henry Acland: 'What a year this has been – among my friends at Oxford, Beauchamp dead, Sandon [the Earl of Harrowby] laid on the shelf – and my poor dear friend Smith gone – ... And last year Carnarvon and [Canon] Liddon. It is very sad.' Salisbury's own health was not good and his great stoutness – the Sandringham scales now tipped to eighteen stone five pounds – left him wheezing and short of breath. He was also working harder than ever before, reporting to Portal in September that his average of thirteen or fourteen hours a day left too little time for food, sleep and exercise. As a result, the last tended to be sacrificed.

The death of the 7th Duke of Devonshire in December 1891 sent Hartington to the House of Lords, with Chamberlain taking his place as leader of the Liberal Unionists in the Commons. The Gladstonian candidate took Hartington's Rossendale seat by 1,225 votes in a poll of 11,000, which, along with the diminution of Hartington's effective power, and a concomitant increase in Chamberlain's in the Commons, put Salisbury in a somewhat weaker position. Expecting to lose the coming general election, Salisbury saw no reason to surrender to Chamberlain's demand for Radical legislation, such as allowing labourers to purchase artificially cheap allotments and small-holdings.

'I have a strong conviction that I can get better terms for property out of office, than I can in office, upon this point,' he told Balfour in January 1892. 'Compulsion must end in taking land at an artificially low valuation,' which could set a very dangerous precedent. Small-holdings at their real value could be bought easily enough on the open market; compulsory purchase, Salisbury believed, was merely a form of legalised plunder.[1] On Chamberlain's pressure to introduce old age pensions, Salisbury offered only a modest reinforcement of the existing benefit societies, something Chamberlain had to accept for the present. 'The only true lasting benefit which the statesman can give to the poor man', Salisbury declared at Exeter in early February, 'is so to shape matters that the greatest possible liberty for the exercise of his own moral and intellectual qualities should be offered to him by law.'

February saw Salisbury furious at Admiralty obstruction to Hamilton's naval reforms. 'The experts – the pedants', he wrote to Goschen in letter which explained much about his own running of the Foreign Office, 'have too much power. They ought to be advisers and subordinates [but instead] they are checks and colleagues.... The result is that everything which is done by the First Lord on his own initiative has to be carried out in the teeth of a stiff, silent resistance.' Salisbury wanted to institute a series of deep-seated reforms 'if ever we form a Government again', including making the First Lord of the Admiralty a Secretary of State, giving the Service departments lump sums instead of Estimates, setting up a tribunal of Cabinet ministers to determine all issues between the War Office and the Admiralty, and establishing a permanent committee for all promotions, which would vote by secret ballot.

Salisbury's doubts about the general election result represented more than his normal pessimism. On 18th March, he brought up the idea of deferring the dissolution until the autumn, but Cranbrook and others thought that the Government was too weak to last that long. As if to emphasise it, that evening eighteen Tory MPs arriving at a party at Arlington Street 'were seized immediately on their arrival by Mr McDonnell and sent back to fight the battle of Supply against obstruction'.[2] In this atmosphere of impending dissolution, every 'blazing indiscretion' of Salisbury's was picked up and magnified by the Liberals. He did not stint them. On 24th November 1891 at Birmingham, for example, explaining why parish councils had not been included in the local government reforms, when the Liberals argued that strong ones would help the rural labourer, Salisbury joked that 'If among the many duties the modern State undertakes, the duty of amusing the rural population should be included, I should rather recommend a circus or something of that kind.' This remark laid him open to the accusation that he considered agricultural labourers too stupid to appreciate anything more than a travelling circus, and that parish councils were anyhow no better than circuses.

Two speeches on Home Rule, in February and April, in which he claimed that it would 'be setting up within one and a half hours from our shores an ultra-protectionist island', a theocratic state run by the Catholic Church for which the Protestant merchants of Belfast and Londonderry would end up paying, caused another furore. 'If you fail in this trial,' he warned the Primrose League, 'one by one the flowers will be plucked from the diadem of Empire, and you will be reduced to depend on the resources of this small, over-peopled island.' By this portrayal of a future 'hostile Ireland on our flank', Salisbury brought Rosebery out of semi-retirement, to devote a large part of an Edinburgh speech in mid-May to rebutting Salisbury's remarks. In May, Harcourt called Salisbury the Mrs Malaprop of politics, who always said 'things one would rather have not said'. He cited his 1867 attacks on Disraeli, the 'Hottentot' remark, the 'black man' reference, describing the Irish as the 'hereditary and irreconcilable foes' of England and likening parish councils to circuses.[3] It was already an impressive list, and in a speech at Hastings on 12th May 1892 Salisbury added to it. Using his strongest language yet he called for tariff retaliation, but he did so in terms the Liberals easily twisted to make sound like full-scale protectionism.

Speaking to the NUCCA, which always tended to bring out his fighting spirit, Salisbury employed a series of military metaphors:

> We live in an age of war of tariffs.... In this great battle Great Britain has deliberately stripped herself of the armour and the weapons by which the battle has to be fought.... The weapon with which they all fight is admission to their own markets.... I would impress upon you that if you intend, in this conflict of commercial treaties, to hold your own, you must be prepared, if need be, to inflict upon the nations which injure you the penalty which is in your hands, that of refusing them access to your markets.

When a voice in the crowd shouted out 'Common sense at last!', Salisbury replied: 'There is a reproach in that interruption, but I have never said anything else,' which at least since his Oxford days, when he was a fully fledged Protectionist, was true.

Although Salisbury had stated that 'you cannot raise the price of food or raw material', but only on luxuries such as wine, gloves, spirits, lace and silk, the Liberals lost little time in suggesting that the Corn Laws were about to be reintroduced and the cheap loaf was in peril. Harcourt concluded that Salisbury must be 'a terrible trial to his friends' for the way he handed the Opposition such gifts. Gladstone told the well-connected diarist George Rendel that Salisbury's defect was that 'he could not restrain the violence of his tongue, yet there was always the foundation of good faith in Lord Salisbury', unlike in Disraeli, whom Gladstone never regarded 'as serious or sincere in his utterances, however vehement'.

Yet Salisbury had regularly described any return to the Corn Laws as 'impossible'. As he had told Henry Howorth, the Conservative MP for South Salford, the population of the towns 'who subsist to the extent of two-thirds on the supply of foreign corn, would never endure the artificial increase of the price of their bread, especially when they would be told that the result of that enhancement of price was to make the landed proprietors richer'.[4] Chamberlain later estimated Salisbury's 'unfortunate allusion to Fair Trade' had cost the Unionists a dozen county seats. Walter Long, secretary to the Local Government Board, certainly thought he owed his defeat in East Wiltshire entirely to that speech alone. Conversely, Fair Traders such as Howard Vincent and James Lowther argued that Salisbury's speech had prevented a Gladstonian landslide.

One thing was certain, Salisbury was not about to follow Beaconsfield's unfortunate 1880 example and stay aloof from the contest because he was a peer. 'There are still people – among our ignorant "masters"', Salisbury had told Balfour in January, 'who are taken in by the stuff about its being a breach of privilege for a Peer to interfere in a particular election.' As he went off to Beaulieu for a week's rest, he readied himself for the contest which he still hoped might be put off until October, but which the majority of his Cabinet wanted to take place in late June. On his return, he wrote to his son Edward from Hatfield about how much the family had enjoyed their new house in the South of France: 'That view comes across my mental vision as I look at the green path bathed in dingy mist and I wonder that such an emotion as patriotism exists.'

On 25th May, Salisbury, Devonshire, Balfour, Chamberlain, Middleton, Akers-Douglas and Salisbury's son-in-law, the Liberal Unionist Chief Whip Lord Wolmer – later Lord Selborne – met at Devonshire House to decide upon the date of the dissolution. The two men who had wanted to fight on and not drop the legislative programme in 1890, Salisbury and Chamberlain, also now wanted to press on with the Irish Local Government Bill and other legislation, and then go to the country in October. Everyone else urged an early poll: 'The idea of another autumn of spouting was too terrible for them,' Salisbury reported to Austin. Fear of successive defeats in the Commons and then a forced dissolution in August tipped the balance, and Salisbury had to explain to the Queen that hanging on until October 'might provoke mutiny; or at all events disgust; resentment and consequent apathy'.[5]

That evening the discussion at Arlington Street, where the family were 'seated under a blaze of electric light', turned to eloquence and gestures in political speeches. Salisbury so ridiculed them that Frances Balfour called him 'a base Saxon' (which he doubtless took as a compliment). A couple of days later, Salisbury was involved in a minor carriage accident. Cranbrook thought it 'might have involved serious issues', considering there was no obvious succession and a dissolution loomed, but Salisbury made very light of it at the next Cabinet meeting.

The electoral prospects were not good; by-elections had been running against the Government fairly regularly throughout the Parliament, except during the O'Shea divorce case. In 1891, the Opposition had won no fewer than five. Dissenters were still angry at Goschen's proposal to pay 'whisky money', i.e. compensation to licensees, and Balfour's great success against Irish land agitation actually worked against the Government, as it put the issue towards the bottom of the political agenda rather than, as in 1886, right at the top. As well as Home Rule, Gladstone's Newcastle Programme held out the offers of leasehold reform, stronger parish councils, employers' liability for workplace accidents, shorter working hours, triennial parliaments, the abolition of plural voting, and Welsh and Scottish disestablishment. It was a clear message which got through to the electorate in the long campaign. Salisbury himself blamed County Councils and free education for the alienation of traditional Tory voters: 'You may say that they can't vote against you,' he warned, 'but they won't trouble to vote for you, and they won't work for you, and you'll find it out at the polls.'[6]

Salisbury was outwardly sanguine about the change of ministry as Parliament moved towards the dissolution, telling the Queen on 3rd June that it would 'bring to the test many promises which are really hollow, and which the electorate must learn by experience to see through'. But he was showing a brave face. Late June 1892 saw him deeply irritated at Chamberlain's constant claims to have been the driving force behind the Government's social programme over the previous six years. To Howorth's complaints about it in December, he had calmly replied that Chamberlain's need to harp on about it indicated 'some proof that this is not self-evident, and requires a good deal of special pleading to make it out'. But finally on 22nd June, annoyed at the continued trumpeting and insinuations that the Tories had been forced to adopt Chamberlain's 'Unauthorised Programme' of 1885, Salisbury delivered a tactful knuckle-rap. 'If you wish to praise us on this point,' he wrote to Chamberlain, 'as may be very expedient – do it absolutely and without any unnecessary reference to the controversies of 1885.... Corns when you examine them in a microscope are very small things.' By treading on the Tories' corns, Salisbury added, 'you give them an uncomfortable feeling that they have deserted their colours'.

The Conservatives' own colours were hoisted on 28th June, the day Parliament was dissolved, in a single-column manifesto published in The Times. An open letter to 'The electors of the United Kingdom' from Salisbury said that he wished, 'as a matter of respect, to place before you a brief statement of the issues on which, in my judgment, this election turns'. Declaring that the Conservatives had no inherent aversion to change and citing their desire to examine legislation regarding trade disputes, the Poor Law and industrial accidents, Salisbury asked 'whether Parliament is to have the power of at once grappling with those questions, or whether the whole time of the next Parliament shall be devoted to a struggle over Irish government'. Other issues, such as loyalty to Ulster and anti-disestablishmentarianism were also briefly mentioned. Gladstone called the letter 'wicked' and the *Spectator* said its lack of tolerance was worthy more of a leader-writer than a statesman, but it was really only an attempt to set the political agenda for the election by putting Ireland centre-stage, and it failed.

As is common in long and close campaigns, it was not entirely ethical. The Liberals claimed that Salisbury had favoured Home Rule at the time of the Parnell–Carnarvon interview and that he favoured a tariff on imported corn, neither of which was true. 'The "assault of lies" has been something marvellous,' Salisbury told a candidate, Sir Frederick Milner. Yet Salisbury himself even went so far as to approve Wolmer's scheme for 'a system of organised heckling of Gladstonian candidates', which Balfour and Chamberlain also thought worthy of consideration.

One bombshell Salisbury and Balfour considered dropping, but eventually did not, was the revelation that Gladstone and Granville had been in negotiation with the Vatican between 1881 and 1885, in a manner that would have shocked and alienated many of their nonconformist and Low Church supporters. Although the line of communication went through W.E. Forster, Sir George Errington and Cardinal Jacobini, by 1890 McDonnell had managed to unearth the connection between Gladstone and Pope Leo XIII and Salisbury seriously considered using the information in the 1892 election campaign. The communications concerned which Catholic bishops were appointed in Ireland and involved British relations with France and Portugal. They also involved 'emphatic proffers of friendliness to the Vatican', and less than a year before the Hawarden Kite Gladstone had instructed Errington to declare that there was 'a unanimous feeling in Britain' that Ireland could 'never' be granted Home Rule. Unlike Gladstone himself, who had used the secret Berlin conversation with Waddington over Tunis in 1878 to embarrass Salisbury in 1881, it was decided not to damage the national interest for Party advantage.[7]

The election results started coming in on 4th July. The Unionist vote held up remarkably well – at 2.159 million (47 per cent) it actually outstripped the Liberal vote of 2.088 million (45.1 per cent) – and the Party won a majority of English seats. In all, 268 Conservative MPs were returned, 45 Liberal Unionists and 272 Liberals. But with the Irish Nationalists winning 81 seats, and with two Independent Labour MPs, J.W. Burns and Keir Hardie, Gladstone had a Commons majority both for government and, more worryingly for Salisbury, for Home Rule. 'These are trying moments,' the Queen wrote to her daughter Vicky, 'and it seems to me a defect in our much famed Constitution, to have to part with an admirable government like Lord Salisbury's for no question of any importance, or any particular reason, merely on account of the number of votes.'

The 'hideous moment' at Hatfield when the news of Cranborne's defeat at Darwen arrived was captured superbly by Frances Balfour and Lytton's daughter Emily. Thirty years before, Salisbury had written of the tribulations of the English stately home owner in the *Saturday Review* and described how:

> By a curious and unexplained fatality, he will find that the days which he sets apart for the enjoyment of privacy are always the days upon which Americans, who are on the point of starting home across the Atlantic by the next boat, happen to be in the neighbourhood, and are anxious above all to see the house, park and shrubberies and the homeowners' family before they go back.

Sure enough, on the very day that Cranborne's result came in, Thursday, 12th July, the Cecils had to put on a show of stiff upper lips for a party of visiting Americans:

> Almost half an hour before lunch the telegrams began to arrive. Every time the door opened there was nearly a scream of excitement. No news of Lord Cranborne. Lord Salisbury made constant excuses for going out on to the steps. He was far more nervous than she [his wife] was. The Americans arrived and we proceeded to lunch, and were half way through before the telegram arrived. Lord Salisbury read it and simply said 'Bad news from Darwen, we have lost it by two hundred.' Lady Salisbury at the other end of the table saw something was wrong, but as she was listening to a story she could not ask the news for some minutes. When at last the telegram was passed to her, she read it out and said in the calmest voice 'Oh, that is a great bore.' And Linky, who was sitting next to her, said 'Very tiresome!' They were wonderful, though you could see how much they felt it, he especially.

This atmosphere of *sang froid* dissipated the moment the Americans finally left. Salisbury retired to his room, feeling 'the ingratitude of the country'. Lady Salisbury burst into tears, blaming Lancastrians and Liberals and crying: 'Damn the Catholics! Damn the Catholics!' That evening the family were 'utterly crushed'. Salisbury did not know whether to respect Darwen's verdict or to find a new constituency for his son and 'push Jim in anywhere at once'. (He decided to hold off, and the next year advised Cranborne not to stand there again as the train journey was too long and 'the Roman Catholics are hopelessly slippery'.) The atmosphere was, in the words of one Hatfield spectator, 'as gloomy as possible'.[8] But, once the results were all in and precisely weighed, the situation did not seem so bad. Added together, Gladstone only had what Salisbury described as 'a motley majority' of around forty.

Salisbury had to decide whether or not to resign immediately or to meet Parliament, and whether to present a substantive programme if they did. The close result engendered talk of a coalition government including Chamberlain and Churchill, with a programme moderate enough to try to tempt some Liberals over. But Salisbury was in no mood to water down his Toryism yet further. Chamberlain wanted a Queen's Speech promising a wide-ranging and detailed social reform programme which the Liberals could not 'trump', but Salisbury was antipathetic. 'Though we may use phrases which will please Joe,' he told Balfour, who was conducting the negotiations,

> we must in so doing alarm a good many people who have always been with us. I fear these social questions are destined to break up our party – but why incur the danger, before the necessity has arrived: and while the party may still be useful to avert Home Rule? Of course, this danger may be averted or mitigated by a wishy washy speech – but surely that course would combine all the disadvantages.

So although Balfour might profess to Lady Salisbury to feel like a schoolboy on the first day of the holidays, in fact there was still work to be done before the Government met Parliament on 4th August.

Salisbury refused a second offer of a dukedom from the Queen, but gratefully accepted instead the right to wear the special Windsor coat which she had previously awarded to her favourite Prime Ministers, Melbourne, Aberdeen and Beaconsfield.[9] Cranbrook's viscountcy was raised to an earldom. Reporting to Devonshire that the Queen had approved his name for the Garter, Salisbury wrote in a typically blasé way about an Order he in fact highly valued: 'It is a liability you inherit – like the Lord Lieutenancy. At all events it may serve as a very slight expression of the debt which the existing – but moribund – Government owes to you.'

Salisbury refused offers to speak on platforms, not only because he was about to go abroad, but also because in the coming battle over Irish Home Rule, which must now take place according to Gladstone's timing, he did not want to preach to a sated audience. The Midlothian campaign of 1879–80, he reminded C.B. Stuart-Wortley, who had invited him to address the National Union, had taken place after three years of virtual silence from Gladstone, and was all the more powerful for it. 'If we speak to the electors too constantly when we have very little to say, they will not listen to us so readily when we have a great deal to say.' (Gladstone's majority in Midlothian had collapsed to 690 in 1892, from its 1885 figure of 4,631.)

Salisbury was bitter about the election defeat, blaming not only ingratitude, but also the 'utterly baseless and ridiculous inventions' of the Liberals, and the way that 'the votes of the South and West of

Ireland overbear and neutralise the majority which the rest of the U.K. has recorded' in his favour. Turning down an opportunity to receive an honorary degree at St Andrews University simultaneously with Gladstone, Salisbury admitted to the Marquess of Bute that 'my feelings on current events are much too strong' to enjoy being in Gladstone's company just then. Gladstone generally took Salisbury's public criticisms of him in good part, commenting in 1890 that 'His mother was very kind to me when I was a young man, and I remember Salisbury as a young fellow in a red frock rolling about on the ottoman.'[10] Gladstone felt the responsibility about to devolve upon him. 'The weight upon me is great and presses at many points,' he confided to his diary on 9th August, 'but how trifling compared with the trials of great Christians.'

Although they had occasional tea-parties together, inviting the publisher John Murray to one at Arlington Street in April 1891, Salisbury had come to believe that Gladstone had 'entirely outlived his judgment, though his eloquence to a great extent remains, and his passions have become more imperious'. Salisbury's animus was predicated primarily but not solely on Gladstone's Irish policy. He fundamentally saw Gladstone as a traitor in the great class war, the non-violent civil war which he always saw himself engaged in fighting. He regarded Gladstone as aristocratic and saw the rich, highly intelligent, High Anglican, Eton- and Christ Church-educated former reactionary Tory MP as someone who should naturally have been on his side in the struggle. Instead, as he told the Queen during the election, Gladstone's 'revolutionary appeals to the jealousy of the poor will do much harm…he is making wider and wider the dangerous antagonism between rich and poor'.

There was nothing Salisbury could do to prevent the vote of 350 to 310 on Asquith's amendment to the Address on 11th August 1892. Chamberlain's speech on that occasion had so packed the Commons that chairs had to be placed in the chamber to accommodate all the members, but it was to no avail. 'It is a saying attributed to Lord Derby', Salisbury had written in the *Saturday Review* in August 1863, 'that an official life contains but two happy days – the day of assuming office, and the day of leaving it.' At 4.45 p.m. on Friday, 12th August 1892, Salisbury went to Osborne by special train to tender his ministry's resignation. At their last meeting at 12.15 p.m. that day, the Cabinet 'cordially voted him our thanks and it was quite a merry meeting'. Eric Barrington even told Cranbrook that Salisbury showed 'indecent joy at his release'.

The Queen was in pugnacious mood and complained that Salisbury 'appeared to acquiesce too much in the result of the elections', as though the vote in the Commons the night before could just be willed away. Reluctantly writing to ask Gladstone to form a government, she said that she had accepted Salisbury's resignation 'with much regret' and, most unconstitutionally, she even took advantage of Ponsonby's temporary absence to say the same in an official statement inserted in the Court Circular. When Harcourt visited her to express the new Government's desire to make matters 'as easy and little troublesome to you as we possibly can', the Queen answered: 'How is Lady Harcourt? Terrible weather, is it not? And so oppressive.' The following year, when Gladstone inserted a sentence in the Queen's Speech saying that Irish Home Rule was intended to provide 'better government' for Ireland, she adamantly refused to allow the phrase to be read out by her representative.

So ended the 1886 to 1892 Salisbury ministry, described by no less an historian than Elie Halévy as 'perhaps one of the best England has ever known'. Another historian has described its Irish policy as 'the most repressive in the history of the Union', although the two estimations are not necessarily mutually exclusive. Even Gladstone's private secretary Edward Hamilton agreed that it had been 'a good Government – it has held well together; it has got into few scrapes; it has avoided war abroad; it has passed some very useful Liberal measures at home; and it has displayed a more than ordinary capacity for administration'.[11] He might also have added that it had divided up Africa without bloodshed and pacified Ireland from a state not far short of civil war.

Salisbury was not certain that Rosebery would agree to join the Liberal Government. 'I do not feel any confidence in the stability of his decisions,' he wrote to Cranborne. 'I think he has lost his nerve – and with it the power of deciding.' To Malet in Berlin he said that he thought Rosebery would carry on the main lines of his own foreign policy. 'What I am afraid of is a too hurried rapprochement with France, involving the abandonment of the Triple Alliance by Italy – a recon-struction of the *Dreikaiserbund* and Russia on the Bosphorus.' In a long letter written to Philip Currie on 18th August, intended for Rosebery's eyes as an *aide-mémoire* which had it been sent directly might have looked didactic, Salisbury set out his foreign policy in detail, region by region.

Rosebery was annoyed by Salisbury's avoidance of a face-to-face meeting. 'I cannot say he has acquired good manners with the Windsor uniform,' he complained to Ponsonby, 'which I thought never clothed any but chivalrous bosoms?' Instead, Salisbury made his way to Puys. 'What a luxury it is to have no boxes arriving of an evening!' he wrote from there to Knutsford on 24th August. 'I suppose one will miss it some day – at least, my friends tell me so; but at present it is a delicious change.' Although he found the experience of his second electoral defeat deeply unpleasant, Salisbury had much with which to console himself.

No government since the Great Reform Act of sixty years before had actually won a second full term in office, so his defeat was merely par for the course. The alliance with the Liberal Unionists was closer than ever, and Gladstone had been kept to a majority small enough for Salisbury to be able to argue that it did not give him a moral mandate for Irish Home Rule. The inevitable concentration of attention on the action of the House of Lords would also place Salisbury at the centre of the political stage, once he was fully rested. 'That our term of office was singularly free from quarrels among friends, or party divisions was in a large measure your work,' he wrote generously to McDonnell on 26th August 1892. After six years in office, he could now report: 'I mainly employ myself in sleeping.'[12]

One of the rare criticisms Hugh Cecil made of his father was that he was a very bad committee man. This might have been true in the sense that he occasionally joined boards and committees which he subsequently never found time to attend, but in the only political committee that mattered – the Cabinet Council, as it was then called – he excelled. Salisbury was able, at least once Randolph Churchill had been bundled off the scene, to keep his 1886–92 Cabinet united and happy. Hicks Beach put this down to his willingness, unlike Beaconsfield, to allow departmental ministers to get on with their jobs without significant interference from the Prime Minister. 'You don't jog a man's elbow when he is holding the reins,' Salisbury used to say. Although he once cynically advised the new Foreign Secretary, Lord Rosebery, to 'bring as little as possible before the Cabinet.... Nothing was ever satisfactorily settled in the Cabinet,' in fact a great deal of important work was expedited relatively quickly there. After sitting in all of Salisbury's, Ashbourne could say he 'never saw a row at Cabinet, although I have seen a reproof given', remembering in particular Lord John Manners's rebuke of Churchill for threatening to resign over a relatively minor matter.

Another factor making for harmony was Salisbury's willingness, again unlike Beaconsfield, to accept defeat when heavily outnumbered. Hicks Beach remembered how he would frequently allow himself to be overruled by small majorities against him. This was almost never pushed to a vote; indeed, Cranbrook only once recorded a vote being taken in any Cabinet in which he sat, when in July 1885 they voted by a majority to give the new Secretary of State for Scotland control over education there. Northcote complained of Salisbury's readiness to be overruled, albeit usually on domestic matters rather than foreign affairs, saying in February 1886 that: 'He has not guided his colleagues, but has thrown the question loosely before us, taken a division, and proposed himself to adopt the decision of the Cabinet whatever it might be.'

With Churchill gone, and Iddesleigh following him soon afterwards, Salisbury had no rival for the Tory leadership from 1887 until his retirement fifteen years later. As competition for the crown is often the most potent source of Cabinet discord, this also helped make for greater harmony. Cranbrook, Cross and Manners were the elder statesmen of the Party, who posed no threat. Smith was loyal and ill. Hicks Beach was ambitious but junior, as were the less talented Hamilton and Stanhope. So it was understandable if by February 1888 Gwendolen's diary was recording that Balfour and Salisbury spent dinner dwelling 'on the virtues of their Cabinet – they're all good fellows and all charming apparently. We are a happy family we are.'

Salisbury's own considerable charm was deployed to its full at Cabinet. Ashbourne was delighted 'when in Cabinet Lord Salisbury would say some of his cleverest things off-hand and in the course of casual remarks'. The Prime Minister used his sense of humour to defuse potentially difficult situations. 'If in public utterances he had command of a humour which pierces,' recalled Gwendolen, 'in his private intercourse he was a master of that which heals.' He treated his Cabinet as friends, showing interest in their health and families, inviting them regularly to Hatfield and Arlington Street, attempting to persuade rather than cajole them, arranging meetings so as not to clash with their holiday and sporting activities, even consulting them on minor Indian and Colonial judicial appointments. 'The agreement and solidarity of our Cabinet have been quite remarkable – ever since Randolph left us,' Salisbury wrote to Hamilton on leaving office in August 1892. 'We have been fortunate in having a very "straight" set of men; so that intrigue in the Cabinet was unknown. And a good deal must be attributed to the great affection in which Smith was held.'[13] Even more must be attributed to the collegiate atmosphere Salisbury encouraged, whilst all the time remaining *primus inter pares*.

THIRTY-FIVE

Opposition

The Second Irish Home Rule Bill
– Lord Rosebery – Evolution
– Dissolution

August 1892 to June 1895

'In this country we have got to look upon Budget promises as
made of the same stuff as lovers' oaths.'

Salisbury was not a good patient. Writing from La Bastide, his new
house in Beaulieu, on 3rd October 1892, after a doctor at Lucerne had
given his father a very pessimistic prognosis on his state of health,
Robert Cecil complained that he:

> wholly disbelieves all experts as such and therefore if a doctor's recommen-
> dations do not seem to him reasonable, he obeys him with the utmost
> reluctance...he is not easily convinced that anything serious is the matter
> with him, his astounding courage and unworldliness prevent him caring
> very much about the matter. On the other hand, it is really impossible to
> exaggerate his patience and fortitude.... Besides everything else he hates a
> fuss, and does not even like enforced idleness.

Salisbury used the opportunity to write a long article for the *National
Review* entitled 'Constitutional Revision', in which he tried to explain
why his Referendal theory of the House of Lords, in which it did not
throw out measures for which the Government of the day had a direct
electoral mandate, did not now apply in the specific case of Irish Home
Rule. His argument was based on the way that Gladstone's 'motley'
majority had been cobbled together out of various different elements,
making it merely a group of special interests temporarily acting
together, rather than a body which represented the settled will of the
nation on the most momentous issue of the day.

Welsh nonconformists had voted Liberal for disestablishment, he
argued, Temperance reformers had wanted the local authority liquor

licence veto, Norfolk 'peasants' and Scottish crofters had demanded agricultural reform, in Wiltshire and Oxfordshire they had voted to prevent duties on corn. 'Many constituencies voted for the Eight Hours Bill, the Lancaster people voted for vaccination; the dockyard constituencies were fired with indignation against some obscure Admiralty wrong.' So 'amid this multiplicity of interests', to argue that the British electorate had delivered a mandate for Irish Home Rule was 'to use language without meaning'. The House of Lords had therefore every right to throw it out. Furthermore, as England and Scotland had returned a majority of twenty against Home Rule, the decision depended on Ireland and Wales. As England was the 'predominant partner' in the United Kingdom, her view should be paramount.

As ingenious an argument as it was sophistic, Salisbury believed it justified him advocating total resistance, even if Gladstone should threaten 'to inject five hundred sweeps into the House of Lords' to vote for the Bill. He even hoped that the House of Lords' own procedure could be used to prevent the Liberals flooding the place. He cited precedents in which the Lords had refused to allow newly-created peers to take their seats, which he claimed could happen 'if there was any circumstance attaching to their creation which indicated an intention on the part of the Crown to encroach on the independence of the House'. In 1711, Scottish peers of British creation were prevented from sitting and voting until 1782, and in 1856, when Palmerston attempted to create a life peer by royal prerogative, 'the House decided that Lord Wensleydale ... should not be allowed to take his seat'. (It was a tenuous argument; in fact the Committee of Privileges had decided that the Crown had lost by disuse the power of creating life peerages, so the judge Sir James Parke took his seat as the hereditary Baron Wensleydale six months later.)

Once again, Salisbury was reduced to lauding America, when he pointed out that Holland, Belgium, Norway, Greece, Switzerland and the United States all had entrenched safeguards against major constitutional change, in contrast to Britain's just accepting a majority of one in both Houses. He further argued that if just three electors had voted differently in Central Finsbury, four in Ayr, ten in North Somerset and so on up to sixty-two in Cambridgeshire North, he rather than Gladstone would have won the general election. 'The decision therefore, in favour of Home Rule,' he went on to argue, 'has been given by 775 electors out of an electorate of 4,800,000.'

Numerical majorities had never impressed Salisbury, and he was not about to allow Gladstone's to force 'the surrender of a race who ... assumed their present position of danger to do our bidding, and whom we are commanding to exchange their present allegiance ... for a new, untried, sinister jurisdiction which they abhor and despise'. The article's conclusion made it clear that it was not precise logical arguments, let alone tenuous psephological ones, which guided him. These were presented to give an intellectual respectability, a smokescreen. His true argument was far removed from theories of constitutional practice. Salisbury meant to stand by the Loyalists whom his ancestor had planted in Ulster, and was fundamentally actuated not by logic, still less by parliamentary democracy, but by the far more visceral appeals of history, soil and race. 'We are to cut our country in two,' he protested, 'and, in the smaller portion, we are to abandon a minority of our own blood and religion to the power of their ancient enemies, in spite of their bitter protest against the debasing and ruinous servitude to which we propose to leave them.'

To prevent that happening, Salisbury even looked carefully at the use of the referendum. The constitutional authority Professor A.V. Dicey wrote to him from Oxford in November 1892 to draw his attention to an article which advocated its use, pointing out how its strength lay in the convenient fact that the referendum was 'at once distinctly and undeniably democratic and in practice Conservative'. Salisbury answered that he agreed 'that some form of Referendum is the only solution towards which we are tending, and indeed the only one by which a termination can be put to the entire divergence of view which has grown up between the two Houses of Parliament'.[1]

By the end of 1892, back on the Riviera and enjoying the fact that when Ritchie tried a gambling system at Monte Carlo it 'naturally failed', Salisbury showed that he had learnt the lessons of his Hastings speech when he stopped Henry Chaplin attending a Fair Trade rally in Yorkshire. He did not want to produce any programme which might split the anti-Home Rule forces before the great struggle. The Unionists had very few actual policies, and Salisbury looked forward to a spring of agitation which he did not want to 'give an awkward turn, if we avowed the poverty ostentatiously now'. He was looking forward to the struggle, so long as the Irish Tories stood firm. As he told Cranbrook: 'What I dread above all things is a so-called compromise – and if it is gilt with a bit more of the landlord's property, our Ulster friends, or some of them, might be shaky.'

The Second Irish Home Rule Bill of 1893 was different from its 1886 predecessor in that it provided for continued Irish representation at Westminster, thereby raising the question of why Irish MPs should be allowed to legislate on domestic mainland issues but English MPs could not legislate for Ireland. Salisbury argued that whilst 'a semi-detached house was habitable, a semi-detached Empire was an impossibility'. He published a pamphlet entitled *The Case Against Home Rule From an International Point of View*, which stated that the Empire's 'reputation of invincibility' would be fatally damaged, with serious consequences for British rule in India, that a future neutral or hostile Ireland would threaten Britain's ability to import food in time of war, and that 'surrender' was the wrong way to go about alleviating 'seven centuries of unbroken racial antagonism'.

Proposing the first reading of the Bill on 13th February 1893, Gladstone spoke for two-and-a-half hours. Salisbury held a meeting in his room at the Lords on 28th February attended by Devonshire, Balfour and Chamberlain to discuss their opposition. Chamberlain suggested that, if the House of Lords was intending to give way after the Bill was sent up to them a second time, it would be better to pass it with a clause requiring a referendum, which would place Gladstone in a difficult position. Salisbury said that he could not bring himself to vote for a second reading under any circumstances, but was nevertheless also in favour of inserting a referendum clause.[2] He did not want amendments to the Bill carried in the Commons, as 'every improvement to the Bill made it more difficult to resist'.

On 21st April, the day Lord Derby died – 'He had great qualities much marred by timidity of action' was Cranbrook's valediction – the second reading of the Bill was carried by 347 to 304 in the Commons. Three days later, an anti-Home Rule demonstration was held at Hatfield, where 1,600 Ulstermen had congregated, and Chamberlain was carried shoulder-high around the south court of the house. 'Salisbury did not believe in tea and buns for Fighting Ulster,' recalled a niece. 'He scorned the advice not to give champagne, he said the effects of champagne if soonest visible were most effervescent, like the liquid.' He would not, however, allow himself to be carried on anyone's shoulders, if such a thing were physically possible by then, and disappeared down a narrow passageway into the house from the west garden, which he sometimes used to escape from tiresome visitors. In May, Salisbury finally visited Ulster, giving a series of rousing speeches in Belfast and Londonderry to vast, rapturous audiences. To complaints that his oratory rarely soared to the same heights in Parliament, he answered that he 'should like to hear anyone trying to "soar" in the House of Lords'.[3]

At the end of June 1893, the Liberals began to guillotine debate on the Home Rule Bill, giving Salisbury an entirely new line of attack. His own Government had used the clôture regularly against Irish obstructionism, but now that it was being used against the Unionists he denounced it. In a speech to the Junior Constitutional Club on 7th July, he attacked the 'reckless application of the party screw', which was converting 'the ancient privilege and power of the House of Commons ... into the subtle instrument of the caprices of a single man'. Although no fewer than eighty-two parliamentary sittings had been devoted to the Bill, twenty-six of its thirty-seven clauses had still not been discussed, to the indignation of *The Times* which published the entire text of the Bill with those eleven clauses which had been debated in italics. The newspaper was not as angry as some MPs, however, and when on the last day the Committee passed the clôture resolutions, a free-for-all fist fight broke out on the mixed Conservative–Irish Nationalist Opposition benches, centring on the pugnacious Ulster Tory leader, Colonel Saunderson, who claimed to have been hit from behind.[4]

The Post Office at Hatfield was kept open on the night of 1st/2nd September 1893 to deliver the result of the Commons third reading. 'Lady Salisbury was in her best fighting mood,' Frances Balfour remembered, and:

> the light of battle shone in her eyes, which were never far away from his Lordship.... We gathered around him after dinner, and he chose the topics furthest away from all our thoughts.... As a late hour drew on, he slipped away to his room, while we waited, her Ladyship quite unweary and scorning to show any anxiety. It was past two o'clock when through the open window outside, while a heat-mist was making the summer night dark, we heard a loud shout coming nearer the house ... in a second or two Hugh burst breathless into the room, majority thirty! ... As we stood scarcely believing the size of the majority, the door at the further end opened, and framed in the light behind him stood his Lordship's massive figure. He seemed quite unconscious that on his shoulder in majestic calm sat a grey Persian cat 'Bul-Bul'.

It was the ideal result for Salisbury, a smaller majority than at the second reading and not large as to give Gladstone the moral authority to create enough peers to overcome the Lords.

In the House of Lords, Earl Spencer moved the second reading on 5th September, with the Duke of Devonshire formally opposing it. There were four days of debate; Salisbury spoke on the last, Friday, 8th September. He rose just after 10 p.m. to a prolonged cheer from the Unionist benches. For the previous half-hour the galleries and area before the Throne had been filling up in expectation of what all knew would be an historic occasion. 'The House was crowded when Lord Rosebery spoke,' recorded an eye-witness, 'it was packed when Lord Salisbury began to address it.' Salisbury had sat out the long and often dreary debate with his head bowed and legs crossed, Henry Lucy noticing the tic in his leg. When at last he had his chance to speak, Salisbury took out an envelope on which he had set out some notes, which he then proceeded to ignore throughout his speech. It was, according to one listener, 'a stately river of perfectly turned phrases', quoting earlier speeches in the debate without paraphrase.

In his peroration, Salisbury quoted Macaulay as saying that the repeal of the Act of Union would be fatal to the Empire and warned their Lordships that,

> if you allow this atrocious revolution to pass, you will be untrue to the duty which has descended to you from a splendid ancestry, you will be untrue to your highest traditions, you will be untrue to the trust that has been bequeathed to you from the past, you will be untrue to the Empire of England.

According to Archbishop Benson, who along with Cranbrook and Hugh Cecil thought Salisbury's oration good but not one of his best, Salisbury's most impressive point was that thirty-eight Irish Nationalist MPs had been described by judges over the years as being associated with organisations which mutilated cattle, withheld rents and even murdered people, yet the majority in the Commons for Irish Home Rule had only been thirty. The Lords voted against the Bill by 419 to 41, a crushing ten-to-one victory for the 'Not Contents'. Over four-fifths of all eligible peers voted in the largest turn-out in the history of the House of Lords. As over half of the 'Contents' were actually ministers on the Government payroll, Cranbrook considered it a 'grand independent testimony against the Bill'. Every bishop voted against it, as did the great majority of the thirty-six Liberal peers whom Devonshire and Salisbury had personally canvassed in the previous weeks. Salisbury left the House through a huge crowd which was singing *Rule Britannia* and letting off fireworks.[5]

The struggle was not over. The Lords had disposed of a measure on which the Government had been elected only the previous year, but Salisbury told McDonnell that he believed that the Government 'will evidently make nothing of a "Lords" agitation. The powder is wet, it won't burn. Their next move is a puzzle.' In his speech, Salisbury had turned his back on the Lord Chancellor and spoken up to the press gallery to ensure that his words were reported correctly in the papers. He expected a public campaign against the Lords, along the lines of 'Peers against People', but one that would, to continue his own metaphor, eventually fizzle out. McDonnell meanwhile had volunteered for the paramilitary force which was preparing to fight for his Ulster homeland if Home Rule passed.

Salisbury had not long to wait to discover Gladstone's policy. Pressing ahead with Bills on employers' liability for workmen's accidents and increasing powers for parish councils, the Prime Minister shrewdly promoted two issues designed to split the Unionist alliance. Over parish councils nothing could be done, and in February 1894 Devonshire voted in the same lobby as the Liberals. 'It's a pity swearing has gone out of fashion,' Salisbury told Lady Rayleigh, believing that when he had told Devonshire his views on the Parish Councils Bill, if he 'had enforced them with one or two good oaths I might have impressed him!' Lady Salisbury was dismissive of Devonshire's support for Liberal proposals during the debate, telling Frances Balfour that 'the truth is that the Duke belongs to the well-known and too common class of English politicians, the Hamlets'. Even more offensively, she said that 'We can expect nothing better from the man who betrayed Gordon.' As it turned out, this was to be one of the only serious disagreement of policy between the allies.

Over the issue of 'contracting out' over employers' accident liability, Salisbury was determined to work closely with Chamberlain, which he managed to achieve. He had long believed in the efficacy of insurance. 'If I could have my way, I should like to see insurance made universal,' he told Gwendolen, 'that is to say, that it should apply to all accidents, to whatever cause they were due ... and I would gladly see State gifts-in-aid in order to provide the machinery for carrying it out.'[6] Like Bismarck, Salisbury saw the potential for insurance to provide a non-socialist method of protecting workers.

On 3rd March 1894, after a lachrymose Cabinet meeting, Gladstone retired. As early as July 1892 he had been telling his diary that 'frankly: for the condition (now) of my senses, I am no longer fit for public life', and he disliked the idea of having to uphold Salisbury's Two-Power naval standard now that the original four-year programme had come to an end. Even his biographer and friend John Morley believed that Gladstone's refusal to address the issue of naval policy before he resigned was a 'childish duplicity', intended to leave the decision to his successors.

The Queen was naturally delighted that Gladstone had gone, but wrote to Salisbury to say that there could not be a dissolution as 'the present Government still have a majority in the House of Commons'. As she had only a year before been suggesting dissolving Gladstone's majority government, this was somewhat illogical. The truth was that she both liked the Liberal Imperialist, Lord Rosebery, who to Sir William Harcourt's fury succeeded Gladstone as Prime Minister, and did not want her spring holiday and a grandchild's wedding disturbed by a political crisis.[7]

Rosebery, the first Prime Minister in over a quarter of a century who was not either Gladstone, Disraeli or Salisbury, inherited a stronger position than is generally thought. 'I am alarmed', Salisbury told McDonnell when he heard that Gladstone was about to resign, 'at having to speak with a new Ministry which will have put forward no programme, no measures and not even a Budget.' Rosebery had a working majority, some by-election successes, a popular stance on the Empire and the opportunity to drop some of Gladstone's less popular policy positions.

Salisbury, seventeen years his senior, had always found it difficult to take the new Prime Minister entirely seriously as an opponent, and, as one MP put it, 'always treated Rosebery as the spoilt and brilliant boy whose exuberant declamation was to be smiled at rather than answered'. In the Home Rule debate, Salisbury had put Rosebery down, saying that he 'did what I often observed in speakers with a singular facility for the lighter and more humorous kind of speech. He took refuge in that in order to save himself from the necessity of expressing a grave opinion on any grave subject whatever.' On that occasion, Rosebery had gone home 'profoundly disgusted with myself', because he had stopped speaking after one hour under the misapprehension that he had been speaking for two.

Salisbury had been impressed and pleased with the way that Rosebery had broadly continued his foreign policy, as set out in his valedictory letter to Currie. The new Foreign Secretary had warned Hatzfeldt in September 1892 that he would set aside the Mediterranean Agreements, but then he had stood by them loyally. When in March 1893 Labouchere attacked Rosebery's East African policy, denouncing him as 'the high priest of Jingoism', the Conservative Party supported Rosebery.[8]

For all Salisbury's satisfaction at Rosebery's succession as Prime Minister, however, he was not above hitting hard and early. On the very day Parliament met, on 12th March, Salisbury welcomed Rosebery to the premiership and added, almost parenthetically, that as Home Rule was now in suspense – and the issue depended on England accepting it – there should be a general election on the issue. Rosebery, who had never been tested in the Commons, marched into the trap: 'The noble marquess made one remark on Irish Home Rule with which I confess myself in entire accord. He said that before Irish Home Rule is concluded by the Imperial Parliament, England as the predominant member of the partnership of the three kingdoms will have to be convinced of its justice and equity.'

The Liberal Party went into uproar over his blithely giving such a hostage to fortune. The leader of the Party which took so much of its strength from the Celtic fringe had acknowledged an English veto, when in England alone there were seventy more MPs opposed to Home Rule than supporting it. Liberal policy had been completely derailed, seemingly on the hoof, and the next day the Government suffered a crushing defeat on the Address in the Commons when the Irish Nationalist leader, John Redmond, denounced the new Prime Minister.

'It had the effect of making the Government look ridiculous,' recorded Rosebery's biographer, Lord Crewe, 'and reflected cruelly on its head.' Even years later, Crewe could not understand the 'needless fidelity' with which Rosebery had followed Salisbury's argument. 'What a pricked bubble the Rosebery is,' Chamberlain crowed to Balfour that December.

Lady Salisbury thought the new Prime Minister 'entirely inhuman', and declared herself 'delighted' when his Derby winner Ladas lost to a fifty-to-one outsider in the St Leger. On 11th April 1894, Rosebery – described as 'Salisbury's obedient pupil' by the historian A.J.P. Taylor – declared Uganda a British protectorate, to Salisbury's great approbation and in direct contravention of Gladstonian thought on African expansionism. Salisbury also approved of Rosebery's appointment of Lord Kimberley as his Foreign Secretary, primarily because he was unlikely to upset the Salisbury–Rosebery imperialist consensus.[9]

Harcourt, who believed that he should have succeeded Gladstone, was not so amenable. There was nothing consensual about his July Budget, where £4.5 million had to be found to finance, amongst other things, the continued naval construction programme. A penny increase in income tax and sixpence on the excise proved insufficient. 'In this country we have got to look upon Budget promises', Salisbury had written in the 1870s about Gladstone's pledge to abolish income tax, 'as made of the same stuff as lovers' oaths.' Salisbury had long thought a graduated income tax, by which those with higher incomes paid both proportionately as well as absolutely more, was an abomination and 'the most revolutionary of all schemes'. In the July 1894 Budget, however, Harcourt proposed, on the advice of the Chairman of the Inland Revenue, Alfred Milner, to introduce death duties which were steeply graduated on the estimated capital value of landed estates.

This left Salisbury in a dilemma: to throw out the Budget would invite an election fought on the peers' seemingly self-interested opposition to the proposals. Salisbury had studiously avoided making an issue of other Liberal class-based legislation and was keen to deny them such an election 'cry' now. On the other hand, the proposals were a deliberate challenge to the class of which he was the champion. Estates estimated to be worth over £1 million would attract an 8 per cent succession duty, as against a flat rate of 1.5 per cent for estates over £50,000 under Goschen.

Salisbury feared the graduation principle would threaten property rights, telling Gwendolen that it easily 'could be developed against an electorally impotent group', meaning the rich. He fully appreciated the need to raise revenues to pay for the new fleet, but preferred a heavy stamp duty on the leasing or selling of land where the real value had been actually realised, rather than estimated by the tax authorities.

With the agricultural depression continuing – Salisbury let his tenants off 30 per cent of their rents in December 1894 – further impositions on the aristocracy came at a difficult time, and many backbench peers were perfectly ready to throw out Harcourt's Budget altogether.

For sound strategic reasons, or, as he had once put it in a different context, *force majeure electorale*, Salisbury decided not to oppose the second reading of the Finance Bill in the Lords. It was an obvious trap from a fissured Liberal Government, and he would sidestep it. Instead, he undertook the 'silent stifling' of Tory backbench opposition to the Budget and did not even mention it in a speech to the Primrose League three days after the announcement. He bit his tongue and held out the prospect of repealing the measure when in government, something which the cost of the Boer War tragically never permitted. In the third reading of the Finance Bill in the Lords on 30th July, he confined himself to arguing that the Lords had the right to fling it out if they so desired, but on this occasion he would not divide the House against it.

He did, however, protest strenuously at the whole principle of graduation. 'Justice in political matters is to a large extent a question of conventional tradition. But this is absolutely new. It has been done in no country before. It was never done in this country before the present time.' Calling it 'a very clever device ingeniously carried out', he warned that the 8 per cent ceiling rate was not sacrosanct but would be raised by future Chancellors of the Exchequer, who would simply use it to shift the tax burden on to the rich. 'This violent revolutionary departure from former principles of finance', he told their Lordships, would 'work great injustice, and possibly it will produce great social evil'. Yet in the interests of avoiding a class-based election, and against Devonshire's more bellicose instincts, Salisbury reluctantly allowed it to go through.[10] Overall the tax burden was not too onerous for most Britons, with a basic rate of eightpence in the pound, or 3.3 per cent. In 1900, a bachelor earning £1,000 took home, after income tax and surtax, nearly £967.

Next to the Chancellorship of Oxford and the Order of the Garter, the honour which gave Salisbury greatest pride was his election to the Presidency of the British Association for the Advancement of Science. For his Presidential Address to the Association, delivered in the Sheldonian Theatre at Oxford on 8th August 1894, Salisbury chose to eschew uncontroversial topics and discuss Evolution, the greatest, most disputed scientific question of the age. He had been interested in the subject since reading Charles Darwin's *The Origin of Species* when it was published in 1859. Reviewing a book on Equatorial Africa,

Salisbury dwelt on the gorilla because 'there are difficulties in the way of disbelieving that a real link exists, or has existed – far greater difficulties, perhaps, in believing it'. Salisbury thought that there was a middle, scientific way between Creationism and Atheism, and, reviewing a book of essays by Knutsford's father in 1862, he wrote that Theology and Science should be kept as separate as possible, 'refusing alike the intrusion of Biblical arguments upon Science from the one side, and unproved generalisations from the other'.

Salisbury denied that a belief in Genesis was necessary for Christianity, arguing that its cosmogonical passages might prove 'a corrupt interpolation' or had perhaps been written 'without Divine warrant', or that that warrant only extended to the moral and spiritual inferences drawn from the tale and not to its actual scientific accuracy. Scientists, he thought, enjoyed baiting parsons with Darwinism, 'experiencing the same kind of glee as a small boy feels when he is tying a tin kettle to a dog's tail'. Anglican clergymen, he urged, should learn about Science in order to fight their antagonists on their own ground.[11] One of Salisbury's first acts as Chancellor of Oxford had been to offer Charles Darwin an honorary doctorate. As a Cabinet minister in 1866, he had recommended him for a knighthood, and in 1882 he had attended Darwin's funeral. After Alexander Beresford-Hope died in 1887, Salisbury offered Professor T.H. Huxley, the senior living Evolutionist and Darwin's intellectual successor, the vacant British Museum Trusteeship.

'Looking at what Science is and what Science has achieved,' Salisbury told the Chemical Society in February 1891, 'it is rather like an Alpine prospect in the early morning, when you see, here and there, a few peaks bathed in light, but separated from each other by depths and chasms of the unknown.' He predicted that over the forthcoming half-century, Science would produce 'achievements of which we now cannot even dream'. So impressed was Salisbury by the extent of the unknown that he was even sympathetic to the investigation of psychical phenomena.

It was on the inadequacy of Darwinism to explain everything in nature, whilst fully admitting that *The Origin of Species* had proved that animals with different characteristics could descend from common ancestors, that Salisbury based his 1894 Oxford Address. A pupil of Huxley's, Professor Henry Osborn, was present at the Sheldonian and saw it 'packed with one of the most distinguished scientific audiences ever brought together, and the address of the Marquess was worthy of the occasion'. After praising Darwin's genius and describing his book as 'the most conspicuous scientific event of the half-century', Salisbury went on to criticise the doctrine of natural selection, arguing that it was self-contradictory:

If we think of that vast distance over which Darwin conducts us, from the jellyfish lying on the primæval beach to man as we know him now; if we reflect that the prodigious change requisite to transform one into the other is made up of a chain of generations each advancing by a minute variation from the form of its predecessor, that in the course of our historical period – say three thousand years – this progressive variation has not advanced by a single perceptible step, we must admit that for a change so vast the biologists are making no extravagant claim when they demand for its accomplishment many hundred million years. But if for the purpose of their theory organic life must have existed more than a hundred million years, then it must have been in a state of vapour. The jellyfish would have been dissipated in a steam long before he had a chance of displaying the 'advantageous variation' which was to make him the ancestor of the human race.

Salisbury's argument, which no less an authority than Lord Kelvin commended as 'thoroughly scientific', was that because the earth was cooling at a recognised rate, it would have been too hot for Man's ancestors to survive if Darwin's rate of evolution was as slow as he described. 'In natural selection the law of chance takes the place of the cattle-breeder or the pigeon fancier,' Salisbury went on to argue, getting his distinguished audience to laugh at his picture of an 'advantageously varied' bride at one end of the primæval forest looking for but never actually finding her equally 'advantageously varied' bridegroom at the other. Salisbury was keen to make 'a survey not of our knowledge, but of our ignorance. We live in a bright small oasis of knowledge, surrounded on all sides by a vast unexplained region of impenetrable mystery.'

Ranging over the unsolved problems of chemistry, magnetism, electricity, astronomy, physics and atomic theory, Salisbury concluded that: 'Whether you believe that Creation was the work of design or of inconscient law, it is equally difficult to imagine how this random collection of dissimilar materials came together.' After a long and intellectually rigorous Address, Salisbury came down in favour of the view that the proofs of intelligent and benevolent design were so common in Nature that there had to be 'one everlasting Creator and Ruler'. Professor Huxley, in the last public appearance of his life, predictably took issue with Salisbury's Address – which had even contained a reference to Evolution as a 'comforting word' – and defended the Darwinian thesis he had spent his life propounding, but he veiled his 'unmistakable and vigorous protest in the most gracious and dignified vote of thanks'. Privately Huxley thought Salisbury's speech 'an awful hash' and wished he 'could have shown up the rottenness of the theory'.[12] It is hard to think of many other Prime Ministers capable of delivering such an Address on so important yet entirely non-political a subject, and hugely impressing Kelvin and all but the confirmed Darwinians in the audience.

Writing to Lord Granby from Puys on 23rd September, Salisbury was sanguine about the political prospects. 'The general movement of opinion in the country is I think in our direction.... Everybody who has anything to lose is steadily making for our camp – though the process is a slow one: and they bring with them each man a certain member of the proletariat whom they influence.' The increasing enmity between Rosebery's Liberal Imperialists and Harcourt's disappointed Gladstonian Liberals encouraged Salisbury enormously. He was hoping to 'reap an unmixed advantage from the pulverisation of the dishonest combination which calls itself the Liberal party'. To that end he greatly exaggerated the threat that the Liberals posed to the Constitution. 'Physical force, no doubt, could overthrow the House of Lords,' he told an Edinburgh audience on 30th October, 'but I should be surprised to see the people of this island applying physical force in order to ensure that their own wishes should be subjected to those of the south and west of Ireland.'

Rosebery, cruelly described by the *Spectator* as 'a butterfly Prime Minister, ephemeral in his essence', who only amounted to 'an iridescent flutter of a sterile epoch', was hardly given a chance to be much more, so fundamentally split was his Party by the time of Gladstone's departure. In the three years of Liberal Government between Salisbury's long ministries, the Cabinet managed to disagree over the annexation of Uganda, the evacuation of Egypt, the Naval Estimates, Kimberley's Foreign Secretaryship, Home Rule, death duties and an Anglo-Belgian African treaty, with the second man in the Government, Sir William Harcourt, differing from Rosebery over each issue. Early in 1895 the sorely-tried Rosebery's delicate health broke, under a combination of influenza, insomnia, Cabinet splits and virulent attacks from his Radical and Irish allies.

When at the end of October the Queen, back from her holidays and alarmed at a 'disloyal' speech from Rosebery implying that the next election might be fought on the issue of the veto powers of the House of Lords, asked if the Unionists were 'fit for a Dissolution <u>now</u>', Salisbury's initial reaction was to say yes. It would have been bad advice, likely to have made the election turn as much on the royal prerogative itself as on the rights of the House of Lords, and Devonshire, Argyll, Chamberlain, Balfour and James all persuaded the Queen that Salisbury was wrong. By 12th November, Salisbury himself wrote back to admit that on reflection 'such a course would be inexpedient <u>now</u>', but implying that it might not be soon.[13]

Meanwhile, Salisbury and Chamberlain engaged in a bout of shadow-boxing over the latter's scheme for a series of social reforms, to be originated in the House of Lords and sent to the House of Commons to embarrass and wrong-foot the Liberal Government. Chamberlain suggested no fewer than nine areas where the Unionists could propose popular, progressive legislation, from labour exchanges and immigration controls via technical instruction and cheaper railway travel, to working-class housing and workmen's accident compensation. Salisbury was predictably unimpressed with the Temperance and shop-keepers' hours suggestions, but he described the other seven proposals as 'salutary in themselves'. He pointed out that time was not pressing, however, that they had no Commons majority, that the Lords was 'a checking – not an originating – chamber', that several issues 'required wary walking', and so on, but he by no means dismissed the ideas altogether.[14]

The Unionist alliance, which Salisbury had feared might crack after Gladstone's departure, in fact only solidified, although it was not until 1912 that the two Parties formally merged. Chamberlain appeared at a purely Conservative gathering at Edgbaston for the first time in January 1894, and Goschen did finally become a member of the Carlton Club. At the local level there were difficulties over the division of constituencies, especially over Leamington and Hythe in March 1895, but nationally Devonshire was prepared to follow Salisbury's lead.[15]

In April 1895, with a dissolution looming, Chamberlain, who was still publicly pursuing his Radical agenda, especially over death duties and Welsh disestablishment, began vigorously to press for a Liberal Unionist candidate to contest Leamington, rather than a Conservative. As a result, he was made the subject of a series of disobliging articles in *The Times* and the *Standard*. The Constitutional Club even postponed a dinner in his honour. An anonymous article by Curzon in the *New Review* particularly bruised his feelings, and Salisbury was asked to soothe them. For all Salisbury's concern that the alliance should hold firm, he also felt for Tories in Leamington, who he said because of the alliance 'belong to a political tribe which happen what may can never win'.

Chamberlain's opinions betrayed, Salisbury told his son-in-law Lord Wolmer, 'a very common defect of earnest men – he cannot believe in the earnestness of the other side'. There might even have been a slight frisson of pleasure at Chamberlain's discomfiture. 'I think some of our people are ungrateful to him – but after all his policy has been very peculiar,' Salisbury wrote to Akers-Douglas on 16th April. 'To sit upon the fence for nine years is an unprecedented achievement: but he can hardly complain because we will not hold his legs to prevent him tumbling upon either side.'

Salisbury thought Chamberlain should be above the 'folly' of assuming that he was personally behind the *Standard*'s attacks on him and he also ridiculed Chamberlain's thin skin: 'I have known one distinguished statesman who went half-mad whenever he was caricatured in *Punch*: and another who wished to resign his office because he was <u>never</u> caricatured in *Punch*.... But I never met anyone before who was disturbed by articles in the *Standard*; except the foreign ambassadors.' He had forgotten poor Iddesleigh, but it did astonish Salisbury how, as he told Balfour, a man like Chamberlain, 'who has been exposed to the brickbats of political life for twenty years', could possibly mind what was said about him in the newspapers or anywhere else.[16] The man who in 1883 had famously accused him of neither toiling nor spinning was now tasting his own medicine, and Salisbury did not see it as any part of his duty to sweeten it.

May 1895 saw a return to 'oriental bestiality', as the newspapers described it, when the Turks semi-officially repressed the Armenian Christians in Asian Turkey with a ferocity reminiscent of the Bashi-Bazouks exactly twenty years before. When on 11th May Rosebery's Government, along with France and Russia, demanded that the Christian minorities should be allowed to take part in the administration of their provinces proportionately to their numbers, Salisbury warned that mere words, unsupported by any action or threat of it, would only exacerbate the situation. It was advice that was before long to be thrown back at him.

On the night of Friday, 21st June, a motion to censure Henry Campbell-Bannerman, the Secretary for War, over an alleged shortage in cordite, by reducing his salary from £5,000 per annum to £4,900, was passed in the Commons by 132 votes to 125. This was hard on Rosebery, because defence expenditure had been one of his few strong suits, and, as he complained to the Queen, the Unionist front bench had been privately assured that the small-arms ammunition reserves were quite adequate, a fact which was disregarded by Campbell-Bannerman's opponent, St John Brodrick, in the debate.

Instead of pressing for a dissolution, Rosebery preferred to resign the next day and let Salisbury be Prime Minister when the elections came, just as Gladstone had done ten years earlier. So on Sunday, 23rd June, the Queen sent her assistant private secretary, Arthur Bigge, to Hatfield to invite Salisbury to form a government, asking him to find places in it for Cross, Halsbury and Goschen. Salisbury told Bigge that they would have been included anyhow, as 'He did not believe in throwing over old friends', not out of any sentimentality but because it destroyed confidence and encouraged 'general trip up'. Salisbury let Bigge have an outline of his ministry straightaway, saying that he would either become Foreign Secretary or supervise the armed forces from the Lord Presidency of the Council. Balfour would be Leader of the House of Commons and he would invite the Liberal Unionists to join the government at noon the next day. He added that he would dissolve as soon as he decently could after taking office.[17]

Chamberlain and Devonshire visited Arlington Street on Monday the 24th, having previously communed together at Devonshire House. Salisbury started the proceedings by asking the obvious question: would the Liberal Unionists be prepared to enter a coalition government? Devonshire said that they would if they received certain assurances as to policy. Salisbury replied that he could not foresee difficulties, unless the Liberal Unionists wished to alter the status of the Established Church. He added that with the exception of Balfour, who was also present and had to be Leader of the House, they could take any four Cabinet places and arrange them virtually however they liked. This time Salisbury did not offer the premiership to Devonshire, but mentioned either the Foreign Secretaryship or the Lord Presidency of the Council, saying that he himself would take whichever post Devonshire declined. Devonshire decided upon the latter, generously citing Salisbury's mastery of foreign affairs as his reason.

Chamberlain was then offered the pick of the rest, and he surprised the two Tories by opting for one of the more junior Cabinet posts, the Colonial Secretaryship. Salisbury, wondering whether to infer from this that Chamberlain did not genuinely mean to join at all, suggested the far more prestigious Home Office. Balfour added that the Chancellorship of the Exchequer was also vacant. When Chamberlain repeated that he genuinely wanted the Colonial Office, Salisbury postponed the discussion until the following day, to give him another chance to think it over.

This was Salisbury's first indication that, for all the social reforms that Chamberlain had urged and for which the Home Office would have been the ideal post, 'imperial policy evidently lies nearer his heart', as Gwendolen noted to Maud. With her acute political sense she predicted that Chamberlain and her father would 'end up being the Cabinet allies – their minds jump together so on many points'. Wolmer believed that the two men could never become intimate 'because their stories, friends, tastes and natures were so different', but Salisbury admired Chamberlain's tough, forthright personality and, as he told Violet Maxse, who married his son Edward, he liked Chamberlain's absence of cant. Salisbury had once publicly compared Chamberlain to the mediæval revolutionary leader Jack Cade but he now admired him, partly because his old protagonist had never been to public school, let alone university, and was entirely unacquainted with Latin and Greek. 'Joe' was not therefore 'mixed up with the kind of people whose education had given them pretensions which always severely tried him'. Furthermore, Salisbury said, he 'liked looking at' Chamberlain's pretty American third wife Mary, whom he nicknamed 'the puritan maid'.[18]

On 25th June, the conference at Arlington Street resumed, this time with Hicks Beach, Goschen, Halsbury and Akers-Douglas also in attendance. They heard that Rosebery had told Bigge that, since Salisbury had brought his Government down, it was his duty to carry on without a dissolution. Devonshire complained to an ill Henry James, for whom he obtained the Duchy of Lancaster, that Salisbury 'is extraordinarily precipitate in his arrangements and assumes off-hand that everybody will take offices which they do not want'. By the end of the meeting Goschen had accepted the Admiralty, and Salisbury had discovered that Chamberlain's choice of the Colonial Office arose out of neither modesty nor calculation but from imperial conviction. Hicks Beach's being a convinced monometallist, a believer in gold as the ultimate guarantor of currency value rather than both gold and silver, did not prevent Salisbury, who had bimetallist sympathies, appointing him Chancellor of the Exchequer. As he had told Goschen in 1892: 'What am I that I should receive a bimetallic deputation? My opinions are unorthodox – and my ignorance is profound.'

Salisbury's reason for haste in ministry-making was that the parliamentary authority of the Government to spend money was due to run out on 10th July, so a further Army vote had to be taken immediately and a further Ways and Means Bill had to be passed quickly also. Without a ministry neither would be possible. Salisbury also feared that before they left office the Liberals might appoint Sir Redvers Buller instead of Wolseley as the Duke of Cambridge's successor as Commander-in-Chief.[19] So on Tuesday, 25th June 1895, Salisbury went to Windsor to kiss hands as Prime Minister for the third time, telling the Queen that he had but one policy: 'Dissolution'.

THIRTY-SIX

Problems with Non-Alignment

*A Landslide – The Armenian Massacres
– The Cowes Incident – Walmer Castle –
Venezuela: The Problem*

June to December 1895

'Our ships will not surmount the mountains of Taurus.'

Salisbury began his third premiership with an unattractive spat. 'My father is mad to get into the War Office to see if he cannot get around the money difficulty,' wrote Gwendolen. Sir Edward Hamilton believed that Salisbury wished to halt all military expenditure and payments on contracts until he was certain there would be a majority in Parliament to pass the Army vote before Parliament was dissolved on 8th July. 'Uncle Robert is depressed,' wrote Lady Rayleigh in her diary on 25th June, the day he became Prime Minister, 'he thinks he ought to have found some way of carrying on the business of the country without having money voted by Parliament.'

It was not Salisbury's only unconstitutional thought that day. In the morning he had sent McDonnell to ask the outgoing Secretary for War, Henry Campbell-Bannerman, whether he would be willing to hand over the seals of office to Salisbury immediately, because his successor, Lord Lansdowne, was in Scotland for his mother's funeral. Campbell-Bannerman refused to hand his seals over without Rosebery's permission, which Rosebery indignantly refused to give, saying, quite properly, that seals were surrendered to the Sovereign from whom they were received. It was an embarrassing error of judgment on Salisbury's part, prompted in part by his impatience over formalities when he thought serious issues were at stake.

Kimberley thought that Salisbury had sent McDonnell 'very much as he might have sent his footman'. Gladstone remarked that 'Lord Salisbury was imbued with less [*sic*] constitutional principles than any other public man,' but somehow blamed Disraeli for the fact. Even the

normally loyal Cranbrook thought it 'needless and requiring explanation, must be wrong for party purposes'. Rosebery complained of the
rudeness and 'want of constitutional etiquette', and Campbell-
Bannerman stood on his dignity and protested to the Queen about his
'scandalous treatment'. In his original conversation, McDonnell had
told Campbell-Bannerman that direct transfer of seals had 'frequently
occurred', but, other than Randolph Churchill, the only precedent
anyone could think of was in 1780, when Sir Evan Nepean had been
admitted to Lord North's bedchamber to ask for his seals. North had
given him the key to the closet in which they were kept, turned over
and gone back to sleep.[1] Of McDonnell's apologetic memorandum on
the incident for the Palace, in which he casuistically tried to explain
that he had not in fact asked Campbell-Bannerman for the seals but
only if he would mind being asked for them, the Queen noted: 'It was
quite wrong and Lord Salisbury's fault.'

After this inauspicious start, matters improved. Wolseley was
appointed Commander-in-Chief, despite the Queen's canvassing for her
son Arthur, Duke of Connaught. Redvers Buller remained Adjutant-
General, Lord Roberts took over Wolseley's post as Commander-
in-Chief in Ireland and Connaught stayed in command at Aldershot.
Nor did the Liberals try to disturb the Supply arrangements before the
dissolution. Cabinet-making was more fraught, as the Liberal
Unionists' adhesion meant that senior Conservatives had to be moved
aside or denied promotion. Knutsford, who was seventy, offered up his
right to a place and became a viscount, leaving active politics without
rancour. Matthews did not offer up anything, but was nevertheless not
reappointed and became Viscount Llandaff. Cranbrook, aged eighty-one,
and Rutland, aged seventy-three, retired. Edward Stanhope had died in
1893.
    Salisbury had a miserable time explaining their rejection to the junior
ministers. William Jackson, Sir James Fergusson, Sir William Hart Dyke
and Ellis Ashmead-Bartlett all had to defer their ambitions. Only the
last, an American *arriviste*, resented it publicly, despite picking up a
consolation knighthood. Salisbury appointed George Curzon his Under-
Secretary at the Foreign Office, despite Curzon believing himself
qualified for the India Secretaryship, to which Cross gave up his claims
in favour of Lord George Hamilton. The thirty-six-year-old Curzon
insisted on the compensation of becoming the youngest privy councillor in living memory, explaining that it might offset his constituents'
disappointment that he had not been awarded a Cabinet post. Salisbury
told the Queen that he found government-making with two parties like

'a Chinese Puzzle' and hoped that she would be tolerant, which she was, even though Goschen's appointment to the Admiralty and Brodrick's to the Under-Secretaryship at the War Office were announced publicly before she had approved them.

There were over a hundred applicants for the fifty-eight government places. 'My wretched father has been filling up the interstices of his time by writing the *coup de grâce* letters to the shelved,' Gwendolen wrote to Maud; 'the poor man has been going through such misery as I believe only a tender-hearted Prime Minister is called upon to suffer.' As before in 1885, Salisbury forgot to ask Ashbourne to be Irish Chancellor. 'I hope you will forgive me and consent all the same,' he wrote much later, adding: 'I hope you are not as sensitive as Campbell-Bannerman.' The Cabinet, as Asquith later admitted, had a 'wealth of talent and capacity'. Edward Hamilton counted no fewer than six people capable of being Prime Minister in Salisbury, Devonshire, Goschen, Hicks Beach, Balfour and Chamberlain. Of the 'swollen' Cabinet, eight came from the upper and eleven from the middle class. By early July, Salisbury had finally finished when he appointed the Duke of Bedford as Master of the Horse, 'though I imagine he does not know more of the noble animal than I do'.[2]

The Unionist Government went into the July 1895 general election campaign singularly light on policies. Confident of victory against a disunited Liberal Party and keen not to encourage Liberal Unionist dissent, Salisbury placed vague commitments on agricultural relief, working-class housing and small-holdings and a revision of the Poor Law on his very short agenda. There was no formal manifesto. As for the Liberals, Rosebery spoke on the House of Lords during the campaign, Harcourt on Temperance and the 'local veto' against licensed victuallers, Morley about Home Rule, and others offered Welsh disestablishment and help for Scottish crofters. Their lack of co-ordination, let alone mutual personal regard, was obvious to all.

At one point in the campaign, Rosebery facetiously suggested that if Salisbury truly believed that the House of Lords better represented the country, then he should abolish the Commons and 'abide contentedly by the unbiased, the patriarchal, and the mellow wisdom of the House of Lords'. Sarcasm was not enough, however; the agricultural depression was telling and Rosebery and Gladstone were no match for Salisbury at the apogee of his powers. The demoralisation of the Liberals showed in the fact that 132 Unionist seats went unopposed, as against only forty in the previous election. In the *Campaign Guide* produced by Conservative Central Office, the Party proudly boasted that under

Salisbury 'national expenditure per head had been <u>reduced</u>', which was then considered a vote-winner. There were the usual accusations, one of the more bizarre of which was that Salisbury had stated that English fishermen were 'in a low state of civilisation', which he indignantly rebutted.

Salisbury won his second landslide victory. The Conservatives took 340 seats, giving them an absolute Commons majority for the first time in twenty-one years, and with the 71 Liberal Unionists they had a combined majority of 159 over the 177 Liberals and 82 Nationalists. Morley, Harcourt and Asquith lost their seats, with Lady Salisbury 'rejoicing' at the last: 'I always thought him an offensive prig.' Her son Hugh was elected for Greenwich, allowing him to begin a career of political controversy, which he described as 'one of the privileges of civilised life'. In a turnout of 3.866 million, far lower than the 4.598 million who voted in 1892, the Unionists won 1.899 million votes (49.1 per cent), the Liberals 1.765 million (45.6 per cent) and the Nationalists 157,000 (4.0 per cent). The Independent Labour Party, polling over 44,000 votes (1.1 per cent), fielded twenty-eight candidates but failed to win any seats.

Salisbury had triumphed, but had the election been called before Rosebery resigned it is hard to believe that he would have been so generous to the Liberal Unionists in the formation of the Government, however cheaply he believed he had bought Chamberlain. 'My impression is that Chamberlain's interest in the Colonies is entirely theoretic,' Salisbury told Wolmer on appointing him Chamberlain's Under-Secretary, 'and that when he gets into the office he will leave the practical work entirely to you.'³ It was to prove one of his worst predictions.

The 1895 Cabinet threatened to be considerably less personally and politically congenial than Salisbury's previous all-Tory ones had been, at least since Churchill's resignation. With nineteen members it was much larger than the fifteen who sat around the Cabinet table in 1886; Gladstone condemned the number as hopelessly unwieldy. It also had a radically different social composition, with only eight upper-class members and eleven from the middle class, against the ten upper- to five middle-class mix of nine years earlier. There were also now four Liberal Unionists in Cabinet (five if Goschen is counted). To reflect this, Salisbury arranged that Devonshire, as the Liberal Unionist Party leader, should sit directly across the table from him. Balfour sat on Salisbury's left, with Chamberlain next to Balfour. What Goschen called 'the quartet' spoke on all important matters, while departmental ministers generally restricted themselves to their specific briefs.

Two conflicting insider views of Salisbury's 1895 to 1902 Cabinets come from Lord James of Hereford and Lord George Hamilton. The former thought that the Cabinet was a highly effective instrument of government, especially as 'extraordinary unanimity has been maintained'. This was because Salisbury 'keeps complete control over the discussions of the Cabinet, but he is very tolerant and mitigates any warmth in argument by a current of good humour'. Chamberlain, who would occasionally state that his views were more Radical than the majority of the Cabinet's, nevertheless 'has always yielded his opinion to the majority. Especially he seems desirous to show his accord with Arthur Balfour, his leader in the House of Commons.'

In choosing the times and dates for Cabinets, which Salisbury said was a matter 'on which, in my experience of Cabinets, there is the gravest discussion', the Prime Minister used to defer to Devonshire. He would suggest a date and then 'say with a smile, "Does that happen to be a sacred day, Duke?", in case the date should coincide with the Derby or Ascot'. Devonshire's sporting and social engagements tended to clash with the Disraelian idea of Saturday Cabinets. 'The struggle between the Saturdayites and the non-Saturdayites in the Cabinet is severe,' Salisbury told Balfour in 1895, but it was soon decided in the Duke's favour. 'I suggest for the next Reform Bill that Parliament should only sit on rainy days,' Salisbury wrote to Halsbury, who sat on his right in Cabinet.

A less cosy view came from Hamilton, who in one of his letters to Curzon in September 1900 denounced the Cabinet as 'a most effete organisation. This is mainly the Chief's fault. He won't press for a decision, he does not keep people to the point, and all sorts of irrelevant trivialities are discussed *ad nauseam* to the exclusion of affairs of real importance.' Set against those criticisms, however, is the admission that 'if he will give his attention to any subject, he can grasp all its features and idiosyncrasies quicker than any man I ever dealt with, and he is the greatest master of compact and expressive language in politics'. Where Hamilton castigated time-wasting and irrelevance, others might have seen courtesy and an infinite capacity for taking pains with Cabinet colleagues, something that had served Salisbury well ever since Churchill's departure in 1886. Salisbury fully appreciated how important it was to suffer his Cabinet ministers gladly.

The first crisis Salisbury faced on his return to office was the resumption of massacres inflicted by the Turks on their Armenian population. The Armenians were too geographically remote for British warships to be able to offer direct protection, yet racially proud enough to refuse to submit to Ottoman oppression in the way other religious and ethnic groups of Asia Minor had in the past. It proved a disastrous combination. In 1889, Salisbury had told Gladstone that he had 'always found the Sultan, personally, a humane man', and blamed him for being 'more weak than wilful in his Government'. By 1895 he had changed his mind, but he was unsure whether direct pressure on the Porte would help matters on the ground. Archbishop Benson was exasperated by Salisbury's attempts to dampen down agitation over the Armenians' plight, as the prelate put it, 'lest our utterances in the House of Lords should exasperate the feeling between Kurds and Armenian peasants!'[4]

Yet Salisbury genuinely believed, as he told Devonshire, that 'any representations from us about the goings on in Armenia induces, not a mitigation of abuses, but a more furious attempt to frighten the wretched creatures from crying out'. Salisbury's primary interest in Turkey was whether Russia or the Mediterranean entente would predominate there. 'The next chapter of European history', he told Sanderson, would be the one in which Turkey fell into a Russian orbit, 'and we are trying to recoup ourselves by making good our title to whatever scraps of the Turkish Empire we can lay hands on'.[5] He was also realistic about the level of aid Britain could deliver on the ground to the landlocked Armenians. 'Our ships will not surmount the mountains of Taurus,' he told his Guildhall audience in November 1896.

Four major factors made this situation different from earlier Eastern Question crises. The first was that France and Russia had signed a mutual defence pact during Rosebery's premiership. The death of Tsar Alexander III on 1st November 1894 and two months later of Nikolai de Giers, who was replaced by Prince Lobanov-Rostovsky, had given a new impetus to Russian foreign policy, and on 10th June 1895 the French Foreign Minister, Gabriel Hanotaux (a biographer of Cardinal Richelieu), hinted broadly at the existence of an alliance in a speech in the Assembly. A second major difference was that Salisbury now led a stable government with an overall Conservative majority in the Commons. A third was his greater personal distrust of the Sultan than in 1889. The circumstantial evidence suggested that the massacres were centrally orchestrated to terrorise the Armenians, rather than spontaneous and ungovernable outbreaks of viciousness by their Muslim neighbours in Anatolia.

Salisbury told White in 1891 that the Sultan 'hates us', for the simple reason that in Egypt and India 'we have shown that we can govern Mahometans so as to make them prosperous and contented'. When the following year Salisbury received a porcelain service from the Sultan's private factory, he told Rutland, who had often complained his policy was anti-Turkish: 'What we have done to merit these favours I cannot conceive. Perhaps the Sultan is only animated by a very fine spirit of irony.'

The fourth and last great change, and one that infuriated Salisbury, was what he saw as the Admiralty's cowardice over forcing the Dardanelles. The last time the narrow straits between the Aegean and the Sea of Marmora had been navigated against Turkish opposition had been in 1807. A carefully considered memorandum by the Director of Military Intelligence, General E.F. Chapman, and the Director of Naval Intelligence, Captain Cyprian Bridge, written on 18th March 1892, had argued that without French neutrality it would be too risky to send a squadron through the Dardanelles. Alternatively, the French Toulon fleet would have to be neutralised before the Royal Navy's Mediterranean fleet could advance into the Black Sea.

This drew Salisbury's bitter ire and sarcasm, and in a memorandum of 7th June 1892 he had asked why, if it could not do its job in either defending or threatening Constantinople, Britain needed a Mediterranean fleet at all. Clearly the Government had been 'enormously overrating the utility of our fleet for any purpose except that of bare coast defence at home', and the loss of Constantinople to Russia was now an 'absolute certainty, according to the opinion of those two distinguished officers because we may not stir a finger to prevent it'. As a result, the entire basis of British foreign policy would need 'to be speedily and avowedly revised'.

Within days of taking office again in 1895, Salisbury tried to encourage Germany to show an interest in the Armenian issue, while making it clear to the Russians that Britain would not support so 'ridiculous' an idea as actual Armenian autonomy. Coercion ideas considered by Salisbury ranged from placing three gunboats – one each from Britain, France and Russia – under the Sultan's palace windows, 'to the less romantic but more lucrative resource of confiscating the proceeds of the Smyrna customs house', as he suggested to Lascelles in St Petersburg, concluding that 'we must consider how we are to get out of the very boggy line of policy into which our finer feelings have beguiled us'. Those finer feelings were even then being orchestrated by Canon MacColl at huge 'indignation' meetings against Turkey held up and down the country. Much as he liked MacColl personally, he would not allow him to come and discuss the question, as 'You carry a flag – and your coming would give an occasion to many unfounded references.' In September 1896, he wrote to tell McColl: 'You might turn this Government out, and then ten other Governments after it, but you will not be able to accomplish a result which Austria, Russia, Germany, France and Turkey are determined to prevent.'

On 12th August 1895, Lascelles reported an 'unqualified refusal' from Prince Lobanov-Rostovsky to any coercive act against Turkey, either by Russia or any other Power. Salisbury's schemes of taking Jeddah on the Red Sea and toppling the Sultan came to nothing because the Russians were attempting their own *rapprochement* with the Porte, and were beginning to feel concerned about their own revolutionary and national- ist Armenian populations which were seeking independence.[6] Within days the Sultan, emboldened by Russia, rejected the Note that Rosebery along with Russia and France had sent back on 11th May. Abdul Hamid II was once again calling the British Government's bluff.

At the opening of Parliament, Salisbury stated that Turkish indepen- dence existed only 'by reason of the agreement of other Powers that they will not interfere with it', and that sooner or later Europe must tire of making appeals to Turkey for the better government of her minori- ties. It was a speech laden with implied threat, a mere five months after he had in Opposition attacked Rosebery's diplomacy of empty threats. Both domestically and internationally, Salisbury was attacked for not following up these heavy hints with action, but his critics could not know how aggressively he was pushing for a tough response, be it the occupation of Mytilene and Scanderoon, the blockade of Smyrna or even, until it was discovered to be hardly navigable, the sending of the navy up the River Tigris.

Salisbury believed the time had finally come to use force against Turkey, and perhaps even to accept the offer Tsar Nicholas I had made back in 1853 for an agreed partition. To that end, he sent McDonnell to Constantinople in late September 1895 to discuss the situation with Currie, who had been Ambassador there since 1893. He asked Goschen to keep the Mediterranean fleet at Lemnos (in Turkish waters) because Currie 'attributes to it much effect on the Sultan's mind'. Yet what had worked in 1878 the Admiralty experts did not think could work again, because it was known that Turkey had strengthened the defences along the Dardanelles. Goschen was supported by the majority of the Cabinet, as well as the First Sea Lord, Admiral Sir Frederick Richards, when he refused to accede to Salisbury's request that Currie be put in overall charge of the disposition of the Mediterranean fleet. 'If our ships are always to be kept wrapped in silver paper for fear of their paint getting scratched,' Salisbury complained to the Queen, 'I shall find it difficult to go on defending the Naval Estimates in Parliament.'

When on 6th November, at Goschen's insistence, the nine battleships of the Mediterranean fleet left Lemnos for Salonika, outside Turkish waters, Salisbury's effort to force the Sultan to agree to meaningful reforms collapsed. Although the Sultan had agreed to some on 17th October, when threatened by the fleet, once it had been removed he knew the pressure was off. On 28th November, Salisbury made a veiled resignation threat, telling Goschen: 'I am administering a policy in which I entirely disbelieve, and which I fear may lead to much disgrace.' But his bluff was called just as effectively by Goschen as it had been by the Sultan. In a long letter to Goschen on 3rd December, he then brought up the fear that because the Russian Black Sea fleet had not been demobilised after its autumn manoeuvres, a sudden assault on Constantinople might be in the offing. In which case Currie should certainly be given overall control of the British fleet, because if he was able to 'act immediately he would have a fair chance of seeing the British arrive there first'. If attempts were made to cut telegraph wires, to refer home for instructions might waste valuable time.

As to the policy of keeping Russia out of Constantinople, Salisbury assured Goschen that he was no 'bigot', but 'our fame and prestige are so tied up with it', rightly or wrongly, that when the blow fell it 'will be tremendous.... I do not envy the Foreign Secretary who is in office when the surprise of Constantinople happens. I hope it may not be me.' Quoting Mephistopheles in Goethe's *Faust*, Salisbury then accused the Admiralty of being *'der Geist der stets verneint'* ('the spirit who always says no'). But Goschen was unmoved, as was Admiral Richards, who even walked out of one meeting rather than commit his ships.

When in mid-December Austria also interposed a veto on coercing the Sultan, Salisbury finally accepted defeat. Throughout the winter of 1895 and into 1896 the massacres continued, with tens of thousands of Armenians being killed over eighteen months. Salisbury, to his intense chagrin, had to take overall responsibility for a combination of his predecessor's impotent demands and his colleagues' refusal to coerce Turkey. He had been beaten by the experts he so despised and forced to reappraise his entire foreign policy. Worse, the enormously expensive fleet whose keels he had laid in 1889 had proved worthless – he called it 'absolutely useless' – and the result was the continued genocide of Christians whom he had made public statements about trying to protect.

So deeply did Salisbury feel this humiliation that 'the episode was one to which he never would refer in his home circle', Gwendolen recalled, 'or encourage reference to in his presence'. To make matters worse, there were subsequent indications that had the fleet been sent up the Dardanelles in the autumn of 1895 the Turks would not have resisted and the massacres could indeed have been stopped. Though not so terrible as the genocides committed in 1904 and again in 1915–16, the 1895–6 outbreak was a tragedy that might have been avoided had Salisbury's will prevailed. For the first time his judgment in a foreign policy matter was overruled by his Cabinet, with the sceptics led by the Liberal Unionist George Goschen.[7]

The mutual jealousies of the Powers had condemned the Armenian Christians, and Salisbury fatalistically told Balfour that coercing the Sultan would probably have proved useless anyhow, as 'if we grilled him alive, that would not enable him to keep his disorganised and demoralised empire in order'. Enclosing to Balfour – who had shown his uncle hardly any support – a letter from Chamberlain he had received on Christmas Day 1895, Salisbury commented that 'Randolph at his wildest could not have made a madder suggestion'. The letter from Chamberlain's home, Highbury, which Salisbury said he had read 'with perfect dismay', suggested that Salisbury should attempt to draw the United States into the Armenian question as an Anglo-Saxon counterbalance to the Franco-Russian combination. A solution less likely to appeal to Salisbury, who was on the verge of a showdown with President Cleveland over Venezuela, could hardly be conceived. Having never served with Chamberlain in government before, Salisbury was unprepared for his visions and enthusiasms, another of which, in South Africa, was only days later to embroil his ministry in its greatest embarrassment.

In Hicks Beach's opinion, the 1895–6 Armenian crisis was the one foreign policy issue on which Salisbury was more bellicose than his colleagues. This could not be advertised publicly however, so Salisbury had to endure a great deal of ill-informed criticism for his coldheartedness and even suspected cowardice, when it was in fact his Cabinet's caution that had been responsible for the inaction. The Liberal MP David Lloyd George made Salisbury the butt of his impassioned, even histrionic attacks on the Government's Armenian policy, saying that the Sultan used Salisbury's protests for his cigarette paper and that British honour was being cast away in 'the mean, sordid, craven spirit of a hucksterer'.[8] Although Salisbury claimed in 1896 that 'There is no such thing as a fixed policy, because policy like all organic entities is always in the making,' his policy during the crisis was solidly in favour of drastic unilateral action. Instead, the crisis tolled the knell on the Mediterranean Agreements, which were originally based on the alternative protection or coercion of Turkey.

'Words are quite inadequate to describe the horrors,' Salisbury wrote to the Queen on 15th January 1896. 'But England's strength lies in her ships, and ships can only operate on the seashore or the sea. England alone can do nothing to remedy an inland tyranny; and the other Powers will not move.' For all his insistence on a foreign policy based on national interest rather than moral ethics, Salisbury made no attempt to underestimate the atrocities. Addressing the Nonconformist Unionist Association on 31st January, he spoke of 'horrors to the like of which Europe has not listened since the days of Genghiz Khan and Tamerlane'.

Despite having achieved little in dealing with the issue himself, Rosebery launched a blistering attack on Salisbury in the debate on the Queen's Speech on 11th February 1896, recalling the Knightsbridge Barracks banquet speech of July 1878 when Salisbury had set out his hopes for good Turkish government on his return from the Congress of Berlin. 'By a strange irony of fortune it devolves on the noble Marquess, who partly blew that bubble then, to prick that bubble today,' declared Rosebery. 'This is where we stand as a result of "Peace with Honour" – in an elaborate impotence, elaborately declared.' In fact, Salisbury had merely followed the policy to which Rosebery had already pledged Britain. Wishing to avoid Lord John Russell's mistake of encouraging insurgents only to disappoint them later, Salisbury told the House of Lords that he wanted to raise no false hopes in the Armenian breast, but it was too late. Of the fit of morality in which the British public opinion had indulged itself, Salisbury told Lascelles to let the Kaiser know 'that these philanthropic tempests are as much a recurring feature of our political climate as the Tourments is in the Alps or the Typhoon in the China Seas. I came into office in the middle of one of these hurricanes.'

Nor could he see an end in sight, unless, as he told Currie in September 1896, 'the growing penury of the [Ottoman] Empire reduces some ruined Turk to cut the Sultan's throat'. Writing that month in the phlegmatic style he always adopted with Devonshire, he predicted: 'I suppose we are to have an "atrocity autumn". But with five Powers distinctly against us on the sentimental question we can't be expected to do much in the way of dethroning the Assyrian.' He admitted to Gwendolen that he held out very little hope for the Armenians after the Cabinet overruled his plan, but somewhat callously admitted: 'I feel very little sympathy with a race which allows itself to be slaughtered with clubs to the number of five thousand, almost without resistance.

Occasionally Salisbury's exasperation with his British critics would show, as in this reply of 24th October 1896 to his High Church friend and cousin Bishop Talbot of Rochester, who had written exhorting him to use 'the stick or the threat of it' to enforce reforms in Turkey:

What stick? Bombard Yildiz? Our experts assure us that we could not force the Dardanelles without the loss of several ironclads. They may be wrong – but that is what two or three successive 'Sea-Lords' have told us. When you have done it the Sultan would retire to Br [sic] which your guns will not reach. You cannot go after him – for he has 200,000 men in and around Constantinople, besides a good many more within reach; and you would be sorely puzzled to land 50,000. People talk of stopping the customs at Smyrna. They are already the security for loans; you would only hurt the bondholders.... I have argued on the assumption that the other Powers would remain neutral during an attack on Turkey. I am concerned to say that I have adopted this hypothesis, not because I believe it to be true or possible, but for facility of calculation; just as in physics we calculate the action of forces in a vacuum, though a vacuum is actually unobtainable.[9]

The Franco-Russian alliance gave added impetus to Devonshire's responsibility to overhaul the co-ordination of the armed services. He was the obvious choice, having been Secretary of State for War in 1866 and 1882–5, and possessing the social rank necessary to impress the often mutually antagonistic leaders of the two Services. An *ad hoc* Colonial Defence Committee had existed for a short time in 1878, which Salisbury had briefly revived in 1885 without giving it significant teeth. In 1890, he had set up a Joint Naval and Military Defence Committee for inter-Service disputes, but that too had failed to work efficiently.

The Queen thought that Salisbury did 'not understand military matters', which was a legitimate and significant criticism of a Prime Minister who presided over two significant wars and countless small conflicts. He tended to assume, as he told Goschen in discussions about whether civilians should sit on the new Joint Defence Committee, that 'professional men are always narrow-minded'. As Balfour complained years later, Salisbury's mind did not 'bite' on military questions as it did on most others. Ever since turning down his father's offer to join the Hertfordshire Militia, interest in matters military had been a lacuna in his statesmanship. The new Cabinet Defence Committee set up in 1895 did not even feature the Prime Minister himself, had no Foreign Office or Colonial Office members, no permanent secretariat or even a precise definition of its functions. It did not even take minutes. Hoping to stop it becoming another unwieldy body like the India Council, Salisbury effectively emasculated it, with ill results that became obvious four years later. It was not until after his uncle's death that Balfour set up the altogether more impressive Committee for Imperial Defence.[10]

Writing from his yacht, the *Hohenzollern*, on 12th July 1895, Kaiser Wilhelm II congratulated his grandmother on 'the reappearance of the Conservatives with the Marquess at their head', saying that confidence in British foreign policy had been 'greatly strengthened again' as a result. Yet within a month Salisbury had, entirely accidentally, damaged Anglo-German relations by failing to take his own advice about how to treat the Kaiser – 'like a jealous woman who insists on the undivided devotion of all her admirers'. Before sending Sir Frank Lascelles to Berlin, Salisbury also told him that in dealing with the Kaiser it would be his job 'to convince him of our polygamous tendencies', but that this had to be done sensitively.

When the Kaiser visited Cowes, staying in the Solent on board his yacht, Salisbury was invited to stay at Osborne. An audience took place on board the *Hohenzollern* on Monday, 5th August, at which no notes were taken, but at which, although Gwendolen later denied it, the circumstantial evidence suggests that Salisbury brought up his favoured scheme for the dismemberment of Turkey between the Powers. The Kaiser, understandably, saw very little advantage for Germany in any partition of the Ottoman Empire, except for the risk of war with Russia in defence of Austria, and if indeed it was made he must have turned the offer down.

The (largely worthless) memoirs of the heavy-drinking Baron Hermann von Eckardstein, the counsellor of the German Embassy in London, claim that Salisbury arrived an hour late for the interview, 'hurried panting' up the ladder and then engaged the Kaiser in a conversation which 'ended in a heated altercation'. Eckardstein's recall can be judged from the fact that although he claims to have arranged the meeting, he dated it on 8th August, when Salisbury was in London all day. While Salisbury (at well over eighteen stone) doubtless was breathless as he climbed up the yacht's ladder, it is impossible to believe that someone so well versed in the diplomatic arts, and so conscious of the Kaiser's caprice, allowed his voice to be raised, especially over the refusal of a speculative proposal of his own.

On the following day, at 3.30 p.m., as he was about to attend the Queen at Osborne, Salisbury was informed by telephone that the Kaiser would see him at four o'clock. 'I thought it was a civility,' he explained to the Queen soon afterwards, 'and replied that I had to attend on your Majesty. I had no idea his Majesty was waiting in to receive me.' Salisbury assumed the summons was a mere 'Court *politesse* of farewell', of the type the social buffalo in him had always found absurd, whereas in fact the Kaiser had indeed wanted a second opportunity to discuss important affairs. When Salisbury sent a note of excuse and explanation to the Kaiser, and the next morning returned to London, His Imperial Highness was furious. The Vienna snubber considered himself snubbed. 'It originated in a lapse of manners on Lord Salisbury's part,' admitted Gwendolen in the unpublished fifth volume of her father's life, but one which was 'aggravated in its effects on this occasion by the telephone'.

It was not an intentional snub, as the Kaiser's certainly had been, but it had equally unfortunate results. Even though Salisbury wrote to apologise, the Kaiser took Salisbury's refusal to see him as a personal insult, and later claimed that he had suggested the conversation should be resumed when the two men met at the first interview. It showed the perennial danger of unrecorded interviews, and when fifteen years later *The Times* correspondent in Berlin, Valentine Chirol, attempted to check the story after having been shown a highly suspect record of the conversation by the Kaiser, Salisbury's former assistant private secretary Ian Malcolm merely told him how 'it showed the expediency of having a third person present when talking to the Emperor'.[11] Nevertheless, a gaffe by Salisbury, this time social and political rather than oratorical, had given the Germans an excuse – however petty – to pursue a new, more anti-British stance. Had the Kaiser not used that pretext, of course, he would doubtless have found another one.

Salisbury had first visited Walmer Castle, the official residence of the Lord Warden of the Cinque Ports, in August 1837, when his mother visited the Duke of Wellington there. His sisters Mildred and Blanche had sat on either side of the seven-year-old boy in church and pinched him mercilessly. When Earl Granville died in April 1891, Salisbury offered the vacant post to Lord George Hamilton, who thought that he could not afford it, so he then successfully offered it to the very rich W.H. Smith instead, with the hardly encouraging words: 'It is a white elephant of the whitest kind.' On Smith's death that October, Salisbury offered it to Goschen, who refused it, already having a house in Kent. Explaining to Akers-Douglas that it ought to be offered to a Liberal Unionist 'to stop scandalous mouths', he then persuaded Lord Dufferin to take it on.

By late 1895 Dufferin, an Irish landlord who had been Ambassador in Paris throughout his Wardenship, had also tired of the £700 per annum it cost to run, so Salisbury sold the Chalet Cecil in Puys and devoted the proceeds to taking on Walmer himself. 'I think I shall hate it,' Lady Salisbury remarked. 'Tinsel picturesqueness and false sentiment about the old Duke of Wellington!' Salisbury appreciated its associations with his hero Pitt the Younger, but the Queen declared it the most uncomfortable house she had ever stayed in and Lady Salisbury agreed. Her husband's typically utilitarian plan for the bedroom where the Iron Duke had died – to 'lock up the relics' and convert the room into a study – brought such protests from local residents that it had to be stopped.

At his installation as Lord Warden at Dover on 15th August 1896, large crowds came to applaud Salisbury; a sign, so the *Illustrated London News* believed, of his increasing popularity, despite his adamant refusals to court it. After three proclamations by the Seneschal of the Court and a nineteen-gun salute followed by a banquet, Salisbury had to be entertained by the celebrated painter Lady Butler, whose husband commanded South-East District. Taking him to a window to see the town from Dover Castle, she 'moralised, à la Ruskin, on the ugliness of the coal smoke which was smudging the view'. When she took him back to the sofa and observed that at least she had the consolation that the coalfields of England were finite, Salisbury shouted: 'What?!' with what she later described as 'a bound that nearly broke the back of that settee. I don't think he said anything more to me that day.'[12]

'Great Britain has just now her hands very full in other quarters of the globe,' the American Ambassador in London, T.F. Bayard, wrote to his Secretary of State, Richard Olney, on 1st December 1894, and so 'the other European nations are watching each other like pugilists in the ring'. It seemed an ideal time for America to tweak the British lion's tail, then a popular activity for American administrations. 'England's necessity', as President Grover Cleveland's biographer later wrote, 'was America's opportunity.' With Britain facing a hostile Franco-Russian alliance, an increasingly unfriendly Germany and the collapse of the Mediterranean Agreements because of her inability to force the Straits, Washington considered it an ideal time to take up the case of Venezuela, which for half a century had claimed more than half of the colony of British Guiana, land on which Crown subjects had lived and worked for generations.

In 1887, the Venezuelans had seized a British ship and imprisoned the captain until Salisbury sent part of the navy's West Indies squadron to 'demand satisfaction', which it swiftly got. The situation became far more serious when, in late July 1895, Olney ordered Bayard to give Britain a 'jolt' by demanding that Britain submit the boundary dispute to 'impartial arbitration', invoking the 1823 Monroe Doctrine which had declared that European powers could not acquire new colonies in the Western Hemisphere.

At a meeting on 7th August, Bayard read Salisbury a long despatch from Olney which reiterated the history of the dispute, quoted at length from the Monroe Doctrine, stated the (somewhat tenuous) American interests involved, demanded a reply before the President's State of the Union speech to Congress, and even included the potentially bellicose phrase that the United States considered 'the controversy is one in which both its honour and its interests are involved'. There were also some gratuitously rude remarks about how the 4,000-mile distance from London meant that 'any permanent political union' between London and British Guiana was 'unnatural and inexpedient'. As Olney well knew, many British dependencies lay at far greater distances than that.

At the end of this lecture, Salisbury politely thanked Bayard, expressed surprise that such an insignificant subject as Venezuela could have so exercised the Administration, and said that as a reply would involve much labour and time the Americans were not to expect it too soon. Although the whole of the rest of the Cabinet except Salisbury was keen on appeasing America, Chamberlain – who believed that there might be gold in the disputed region – was all for belligerence. He thought Washington should be told not to interefere, and that Britain was also a great American power, with a greater territorial area even than the United States itself.

Although Salisbury's answer to the United States was ready by 27th November, Pauncefote did not deliver it to Olney until after President Cleveland's speech on 2nd December, so that the President could only announce that they had asked Britain for 'a definite answer'. Salisbury's answer was definite, and came in two parts. The first accepted the principle of the Monroe Doctrine, as Britain had done for over half a century, but argued that it did not apply to British Guiana any more than to Canada or the British West Indies or any other British possession in the Western Hemisphere, and the Venezuelan issue was thus 'a controversy with which the United States have no apparent practical concern'.

The second part gave a history of the dispute since 1796, and stated that whilst Britain was willing to discuss ceding land on one side of the Line that had been surveyed by the Royal Geographical Society naturalist Robert Schomburgk in 1841-3, on the other side 'Her Majesty's Government cannot in justice to the inhabitants offer to surrender to foreign rule' Crown subjects, especially as the Venezuelan claims were 'based on the extravagant pretensions of Spanish officials in the last century and involving the transfer of large numbers of British subjects ... to a nation ... whose political system is subject to frequent disturbance, and whose institutions as yet too often afford very inadequate protection to life and property'.[13]

Bayard privately admitted the last point to Cleveland, saying that Salisbury's answers were 'good in temper and moderate in tone' and that moreover the Venezuelans were 'wholly unreliable'. Olney, however, was unimpressed with Salisbury's argument that British Guiana predated the very existence of the Venezuelan republic, and wrote an aggressive first draft of a message for Cleveland to deliver to a special meeting of Congress, most of which was fortunately erased.[14] What remained was menacing enough, however. On 17th December 1895, Cleveland announced that it was 'the duty of the United States to resist by any means in its power... the appropriation by Great Britain of any lands...which after investigation we have determined of right belong to Venezuela'. The Senate chamber rang with applause and Cleveland won unanimous support for a purely American commission to investigate Venezuela's claims. He had sounded, as Pauncefote reported to Salisbury, 'the note of war'.

The German and French press joined the American in paroxysms of excitement about Britain's international isolation and her inevitable humiliation. Canada looked to her military preparedness in the event of war with America. Sanity was only restored by the heavy discounting of prices on the New York Stock Exchange on 20th December, which hit the otherwise very bellicose Americans where it tended to hurt them most. Nevertheless, the excitable American 'yellow' press still called for war with Britain, as did ex-President Harrison. The Irish Nationalist MP John Redmond even wrote to New York's *World* newspaper to say that Irish sentiment would be supporting America in the coming conflict.

Throughout it all, Salisbury stayed perfectly calm, telling Goschen the day after Cleveland's speech that he supposed 'the American conflagration will fizzle away', and then informing the Queen that, since nothing had been officially received from Washington, he would simply ignore it altogether and 'if we remained quiet, this feeling would shortly disappear'. He preferred not to raise the political temperature by even summoning the Cabinet during the Christmas Recess. Privately calling it 'Cleveland's electioneering dodge', Salisbury decided simply to sit the crisis out. He did not assume that America was necessarily bluffing, however, and indeed less than three years later she went to war with Spain over Cuba.

Salisbury told the Austrian Chancellor in January 1896 that 'my countrymen have their special peculiarities', one of which was that they would never again fight the Americans. But did he truly believe it? Salisbury had no sympathy with the increasingly popular concept that there was some form of romantic, special relationship between the two English-speaking peoples. He treated America in the same way as he did France, Germany or Russia, strictly according to the exigencies of *Realpolitik*. Although he told Chamberlain that the Venezuelan crisis was 'blowing out', he was not so sanguine about the long-term future of Anglo-American relations. 'A war with America – not this year but in the not distant future – has become something more than a possibility,' he wrote to Hicks Beach on the issue of Naval Estimates on 2nd January 1896, arguing that it was probably more likely than the Russian and French fleets combining to sink the British.

Late 1895 and early 1896 found Salisbury heavy with foreboding about the international situation. The Armenian atrocities had caused a dangerous Black Sea standoff with Russia in which Austria had offered nothing but diplomatic support, and precious little of that. The Admiralty had denied him the traditional final resort of British

Governments regarding the Straits. A minor border dispute had been taken up by an electioneering President Cleveland and turned into a full-scale war scare. Germany seemed to be taking every opportunity to demonstrate her unfriendliness. France, now allied to Russia and sabre-rattling over Siam, had also denounced a Congolese treaty in August 1894 and, as Salisbury warned Chamberlain, in Africa she might be about to try to 'sell us a property she has already sold to someone else'. Belgium was disinclined to be helpful in the region, and after a meeting with King Leopold II, Salisbury could only report that 'much of our time was passed in elaborately complimenting each other'.

Most pressing of all, President Kruger of the Transvaal had closed the drifts of the Vaal River to Cape Colony trade, in direct defiance of the 1884 London Convention, and only the threat of war that November had managed to get them reopened. The Pretorian paper *De Volkstem* had denounced 'this hateful British intervention', and future clashes threatened. To the north, the Mombasa-to-Lake Victoria railway had still not been built, and, as a result, Salisbury warned the House of Lords, 'four – if not five – other Powers were now steadily advancing to the upper reaches of the Nile'. Halfway through December, rumours about Salisbury's health persuaded the *Daily Telegraph* to update his obituary. 'Both at home and abroad there are heavy clouds,' Salisbury wrote to Cranbrook on 19th December 1895 about the new year in prospect; 'it will be full of rumours of wars, if not of wars.' This time his powers of prediction did not fail him.

THIRTY-SEVEN

'Splendid Isolation'

The Jameson Raid – The Kruger Telegram
– The Poet Laureate – 'Splendid Isolation'
– Venezuela: The Solution

December 1895 to January 1896

'No-one seems to have anticipated this mad move of Jameson's.'

Defending his preference for informal empire in a debate on the Mombasa railway on 14th February 1895, Salisbury had praised Cecil Rhodes, Prime Minister of Cape Colony since 1890, a director of De Beers Mines and managing director of the British South Africa Company, for having 'laid the foundations of a splendid empire' in southern Africa, and all without having to go to the Government for financial help. Of the Boers he made his worst-ever prediction, that 'by friendly and peaceful, and yet by irresistible force, they will be compelled to fall into line and join the great unconscious confederation that is growing up'.

Salisbury did not comment on the toughness, leadership and general bloody-mindedness of Paul Kruger, a Voortrekker of the 1830s, leader of the Boers since 1877 and President of the Transvaal since 1883, who saw the increasing British immigration into his republic to work the goldfields as an eventual political threat to Boer domination of the territory that their fathers had made the exodus from the British Cape Colony to claim. After gold was discovered on the Rand in the mid-1880s, the Transvaal was transformed from a poor, backward, puritanical regime into a rich but equally backward and puritanical one. As they saw themselves increasingly swamped by outsiders, whom they dubbed 'Uitlanders', the Afrikaners protected their political paramountcy by setting ever more restrictive qualifications for the franchise and employing blatant gerrymandering to ensure that the Transvaal parliament, the Volksraad, remained under Boer domination.

The Uitlanders' demands for citizenship and rights fell on cussedly deaf ears, and various nasty incidents between them and the Transvaal police force were highlighted by the British press and turned into a series of *causes célèbres*. Encouraging Uitlander resistance was Rhodes in Cape Town, whose comment: 'I would annex the planets if I could' summed up his attitude towards the small republic, which, along with its sister-state the Orange Free State to its south, was obstinately obstructing his plans for a British South Africa. The victory of his physician, Chartered Company administrator and close friend Dr Leander Starr Jameson over the Matabele, and the death of King Lobengula in January 1894, had only encouraged Rhodes in these schemes. Rather than wait for events to take their course, while pressing all the time for political rights to be extended to the Uitlanders, Rhodes and Chamberlain decided to push the process forward.

A small but strategic piece of land called the Pitsani Strip, part of the Bechuanaland Protectorate, was ceded by the Colonial Office to the British South Africa Company in early November 1895. Adjacent to the Transvaal, it was the perfect place from which the Chartered Company's private army, officially designated the Bechuanaland police force, could launch an attempted coup against the Pretoria Government, hoping to raise the Uitlanders in Johannesburg against their Boer oppressors. Unfortunately for the scheme, the Uitlanders themselves proved keener to dig for gold than fight for political representation in a country most would leave once they struck it rich. They would grumble about their lot, but only a small proportion were willing to risk open rebellion. Yet although any such raid would be in complete contravention of international law, and would strictly speaking be an invasion, it was thought in certain parts of the Colonial Office that with the British colonies of Natal and Cape Colony in support, and with no practical direct foreign intervention probable, a Rhodes-inspired rising might have a chance of success if correctly timed.

It did not and it was not. On Boxing Day 1895, Chamberlain wrote to Salisbury from Highbury:

> I have received private information that a rising in Johannesburg is imminent and will probably take place in the course of the next few days. The state of the Transvaal has been threatening trouble of this kind for some time, and I have given secret instructions to [the Cape Colony High Commissioner] Sir Hercules Robinson, after consulting him by letter, how to act in an emergency. The War Office has arranged that two regiments, one from Bombay and one from Barbados, shall call at the Cape about the middle of January. I think the outbreak will be at the end of this month, but we have of course our usual garrison at the Cape and Rhodes has the Bechuanaland police. There is nothing more to be done but to watch the event, which we have done nothing to provoke. If the rising is successful, it ought to turn to our advantage.

Although this important letter makes it clear that Salisbury was aware of the likelihood of an Uitlander uprising before one occurred, it made no mention of Dr Jameson's raid into Transvaal territory, which Chamberlain also knew was likely to happen, although not precisely when. The fact that Chamberlain had to tell Salisbury of the secret instructions to Robinson – telegraphed that same day and instructing him to co-operate with Rhodes – implies that the Prime Minister knew nothing of them. Nevertheless, Salisbury's acquiescence in the plan to 'watch the event', but do nothing to hinder the rising, might be considered to be complicitous.[1] Above all, Chamberlain's claim that the Government had not helped to provoke the rising does not sit well with the Colonial Office's donation to Rhodes of the crucial Pitsani Strip only a few weeks beforehand.

By Sunday, 29th December, Chamberlain had lost hope in a successful outcome, telling Salisbury: 'I think the Transvaal business is going to fizzle out. Rhodes has miscalculated the feeling of the Johannesburg capitalists.' At 5.30 p.m. he sent a very tentative warning to Rhodes not to force the issue, telling Robinson to let Rhodes know that he might have to repudiate the action if it now went ahead. It was too late. Jameson, observing that Clive of India would have done it, launched a raid into the Transvaal from Pitsani on 29th December, riding at the head of 500 armed men. Rhodes's half-hearted order to halt was ignored, and was probably sent with the prior arrangement that it should be ignored anyhow. On 2nd January 1896, after a desultory shoot-out which left seventeen Raiders dead and fifty-five wounded, the fiasco was over. Jameson surrendered to 1,500 Boers at Doornkop, and his force was disarmed and taken into custody. The Johannesburg Uitlanders had not only not risen, but Mark Twain, who was touring South Africa at the time, observed the panic that gripped them as they rushed for the trains to escape the city.

Chamberlain had not kept Salisbury fully informed of what his South African specialist, Edward Fairfield, was reporting, but it is doubtful that in such a murky affair Salisbury wanted to be told on the record precisely what was going on anyhow. In Salisbury's defence, it must be pointed out that at the time he considered the Venezuelan and Armenian issues to be more pressing, and left policy in what he thought were Chamberlain's capable hands. His overall sympathies were evident from the reply he sent Chamberlain on Monday, 30th December, when, unbeknownst to him, Jameson's men were galloping towards Johannesburg:

It is evident that sooner or later that State must be mainly governed by Englishmen: though we cannot yet precisely discern what their relations to the British Crown or the Cape Colony would be. I am not sorry that at this stage the movement is only partially successful. If we get to actual fighting, it will be very difficult to keep the Cape forces – or our own – out of the fray. In such a case we should have an angry controversy with Germany. Of course Germany has no rights in this affair, and must be resisted if the necessity arises: but still it would be better if the revolution which transfers the Transvaal to British rulers were entirely the result of action of internal forces, and not of Cecil Rhodes' intervention, or of ours.

For all his sympathy with its ultimate purpose, Salisbury had no prior knowledge of Jameson's Raid, and would have stopped it if he could. Neither Chamberlain, nor Rhodes, and certainly not Jameson, had a particle of Salisbury's preternatural patience.

When the news of the Raid reached London during the night of Monday, 30th December, Chamberlain acted swiftly. To increase his chances of plausibly denying that he had foreknowledge of what by then he rightly suspected would be a catastrophe, he left his servants' annual ball at Highbury at 12.50 a.m. on Tuesday, 31st December, and got back to London by 4 a.m. Once at the Colonial Office he ordered Robinson to denounce the Raid and to warn Rhodes that the British South Africa Company's Charter would be in jeopardy if it turned out – as he well knew it would – that the Cape premier had been involved. *The Times* even criticised Chamberlain for acting so aggressively against the Raid, but it was Rhodes's timing, not the plan itself, to which Chamberlain took exception.[2] When on 31st December, J.H. Hofmeyr, the Afrikaner leader in the Cape parliament, asked the High Commissioner to issue a proclamation calling on all British subjects not to aid Jameson, Robinson complied.

Rhodes, claiming to have tried to have stopped Jameson, nevertheless offered Robinson his resignation the next day. Arranging to meet Chamberlain at the Foreign Office, Salisbury wrote: 'Fortunately no harm seems to have been done in the Transvaal – except to Rhodes' reputation. If filibustering fails, it is always disreputable – Hatzfeldt is coming to me tomorrow and no doubt will utter dark and mysterious threats. But I don't think he will venture to offer any formal remonstrance.' Had the Raid succeeded, Salisbury would have been delighted, but he took the reverse philosophically and hoped to minimise the international ill-effects, especially with regard to Germany.

Seeing Hatzfeldt on Wednesday, 1st January 1896, Salisbury asked the German Ambassador, 'as a friend', to say nothing 'which could be construed into a threat, as that would make everything impossible to him'. Salisbury's good personal relations with Hatzfeldt were crucial during this crisis; anyone less sympathetic might easily have made the situation very hazardous. The day before the interview, Salisbury told Devonshire that having known Hatzfeldt well for ten years and finding him trustworthy, 'I speak more freely to him than to the other ambassadors.' So Salisbury related what had happened and read Robinson's telegram ordering Jameson to desist, leaving Hatzfeldt feeling 'quite amiable'.³ His master in Berlin, however, was not.

The twenty-fifth anniversary of his grandfather's foundation of the Second Reich fell on 1ˢᵗ January 1896, and Kaiser Wilhelm II marked it by announcing: 'The German Empire has become a World Empire [*Weltreich*].' On 20ᵗʰ December, he had told Colonel Swaine that Britain was isolated, had her hands full with France over Siam, America over Venezuela and all Europe over Egypt, and 'everywhere you stand alone'. He ordered Hatzfeldt to request his passports and leave Britain should there be the slightest indication that the Government had had any prior knowledge of the Raid. Salisbury recognised the Kaiser's mood and wrote to Devonshire on New Year's Eve to say: 'He is very susceptible, and imperious: and he would resent bitterly anything like personal remonstrance. He is more than usually resentful... because our Royal Family, who belong to an older generation, have given him more lectures and hints than he thinks a German Emperor, whatever his age, ought to receive.' Fortunately for Anglo-German relations, however, no actual evidence had yet come to light connecting Chamberlain with the Raid; though much was suspected, nothing could be proved.

On 2ⁿᵈ January, Salisbury wrote to Wolmer to 'congratulate you on Jameson having fizzed out'. It meant, as he hinted to Hatzfeldt, that Rhodes would fall, which would prove 'an escape from diplomatic difficulties'.⁴ Putting a brave face on the disaster was not enough, however. The Kaiser was keen to make an issue of it, not least to help along his domestic campaign for large-scale naval construction. With 900 million Marks invested in the Transvaal, Germany felt she had an interest in the republic remaining independent. So on 3ʳᵈ January the Kaiser sent a public telegram which congratulated Kruger on the way that 'you and your own people, by your own energy against the armed bands which have broken into your country as disturbers of the peace, have succeeded in re-establishing peace, and defending the independence of the country against attack from without'. This implied challenge to British suzerainty brought the private response from Salisbury that 'the Germans' only idea of a diplomatic approach is to stamp heavily on your toes'. In fact, only Prince Hohenlohe's threat of resignation had got the telegram toned down from an even more deliberately offensive wording. 'The driving force was not reflection,' von Holstein recalled in his memoirs, 'but the Kaiser's whim', along with a desire to avenge Salisbury's perceived snub at Cowes.

Several accounts have survived of the dinner party at Hatfield at which Salisbury was acquainted of the Kaiser's telegram, along with an unconfirmed Intelligence report that German marines would be landed at Delagoa Bay in Portuguese East Africa to march to Pretoria's defence. Queen Victoria's third daughter, Princess Christian of Schleswig-

Holstein, was present when the red box from the Foreign Office was brought to the Prime Minister's table, a rare event that meant something both important and pressing had occurred. Indeed the last time it had happened was also when royalty was being entertained at Hatfield, on the night of Churchill's resignation nine years earlier. Salisbury asked Princess Christian's permission to open the box; he then read the single sheet of paper inside, briefly wrote on it and shut and locked the box, which was taken back to the Foreign Office.

Accounts differ as to what Salisbury then told the expectant company. According to Ian Malcolm, Salisbury's assistant private secretary, who was present, he 'said casually to H.R.H., with a shrug of his massive shoulders "What cheek, Madame, what cheek!"' His daughter-in-law Violet, who claimed to have been at his table, recorded that in 'a conversational voice' Salisbury told the Princess about the telegram and added: 'I have ordered a naval squadron to proceed at once to South Africa.' A third, more colourful, account has the Princess asking, 'What answer have you sent?', and Salisbury replying, 'I have sent no answer. I have sent ships.'

A flying squadron was indeed sent to Delagoa Bay, as, in Gwendolen's phrase, 'a not too invidious gesture of national self-assertion'.[5] Soon afterwards Salisbury told the Prince of Wales that, had marines indeed been sent by the Kaiser, a war would undoubtedly have broken out with Germany, but fortunately Portugal refused to afford them passage. 'Though I share the great indignation of the people against Germany,' the Queen wrote to him on 8th January, 'do, I entreat you, do all you can to pour oil on the flames.' (She presumably meant water.) Salisbury tried to lessen the deluge of British press abuse that greeted the Kruger telegram, which even affected Germans doing business in the City, by contacting senior editors and asking them to tone down their anti-German leading articles.

Salisbury thrived in such international crises, differentiating as he did between the burdens of decision and those of responsibility. A passage from his daughter's biography relates how, standing at an open door about to go for a walk, he once told his family how he could not understand a recent guest's condolences on his 'burden of responsibility'. When his remark drew protests, he elaborated further:

> I should understand if they spoke of the burden of decision – I feel it now, trying to make up my mind whether or no to take a greatcoat with me. I feel it is exactly the same way, but no more, when I am writing a despatch upon which peace or war may depend. Its degree depends upon the materials for decision that are available and not in the least upon the magnitude of the results which may follow. With the results I have nothing to do.'

The first major speech by a Cabinet minister after the Kruger telegram was delivered by Balfour in Manchester on 15th January. His notes bear the annotation 'Approved by Lord Salisbury, January 11th'. 'Without attempting to excuse the inexcusable,' Balfour said about the Raid, 'it is plain that difficulties <u>must</u> arise with a State whose inhabitants are arbitrarily divided between those who pay and those who govern.' Simply because the Raid had been an embarrassing fiasco, the British Government – which vehemently insisted that it had no foreknowledge of it – was not about to give up its campaign for the rights of the Uitlanders.[6]

On that basis, Salisbury supported the idea of Kruger visiting London for direct negotiations. At that stage he believed that a *modus vivendi* could be reached over the Uitlanders' political rights, and there was always the chance, as he told Chamberlain, that 'he will emulate the fate of Clarence and be drowned in turtle soup', the staple *hors d'oeuvre* at diplomatic dinners. The long-term effect of the Kruger telegram affair, as he and Balfour privately admitted at the end of the year, was a profound sense of Germany's untrustworthiness in foreign affairs. No official notice was taken of the telegram, because it was not an official document addressed to the British Government, but the Cabinet unanimously agreed not to allow the Transvaal to alter its treaty status *vis-à-vis* the Crown, which they interpreted as suzerainty.

Despite Chamberlain thinking that 'an act of vigour' was required 'to soothe the wounded vanity of the nation', adding, 'it does not matter which of our numerous foes we defy but we ought to defy someone', Salisbury kept British policy pacific, at a time when it might easily have slipped towards war. 'It was [a] matter of common knowledge that the "Uitlanders" were meditating an attempt to revolt this winter,' Salisbury told Devonshire on 4th January, 'but no one seems to have anticipated this mad move of Jameson's.' He did not at the time know that his Colonial Secretary had indeed anticipated and even connived in it, right up to the moment that he realised that it was about to go off at half-cock. 'I don't think it particularly criminal,' Cranborne wrote to his younger brother Edward about the Raid four years later, echoing his father's view, 'but its conduct and the general atmosphere of intrigue and suspicions were odious.' In the intricate historical debate over Salisbury's personal culpability, a prime piece of evidence has until now been missed.

Writing from Hatfield on 19th January 1896, only a fortnight after the Raid, Lady Frances Balfour described to Gerald Balfour's wife, Lady Elizabeth ('Betty'), the jolly mood at Hatfield. Salisbury had told her how on leaving the Cabinet meeting that day Chamberlain had 'said it was curious that he *and* Jameson both appeared to be the popular heroes of the minute', even though he had tried to halt the Raid as soon as he had heard of it. The family then joked about whether, in the light of the

Kruger telegram, Jameson's portrait should be painted over the huge one given by the Kaiser. Salisbury said he hoped that the Grand Jury being assembled to try Jameson would throw the case out. Then Frances asked Salisbury directly why he had not known about the Raid beforehand, considering how bad Boer–British relations were. With absolutely no reason to lie to his nephew's wife in such private company, Salisbury answered that: 'He could not account for this, except by saying that we thought we knew for certain that there was to be a revolution this year in Johannesburg, but "raiding" we did not know of.'[7]

If 'we' is taken to mean the Government (except for Chamberlain and perhaps Selborne), this rings true. In Salisbury's case there was no 'smoking gun' this time. Had he known about Jameson's plan he would have put a stop to it, not out of obedience to international law or the inviolability of the Transvaal's borders, but purely to avoid damaging Anglo-German relations. As ever, *Realpolitik* rather than strict ethics guided his steps. After a mild private rebuke from Queen Victoria, the Kaiser replied that his telegram had been intended to show that 'I was standing up for law, order and obedience to a sovereign whom I revere and adore.' Kruger's response to such pusillanimity, made to the German Consul-General in Pretoria, was predictably withering: 'The old woman just sneezed and you ran away.'

January 1896 also saw the effective termination of the Mediterranean Agreements, because although Salisbury was willing to stick to the original status quo policy, he would not extend them into an alliance with Austria and Italy, and nor could he now guarantee Constantinople, once the Admiralty had pulled back from the idea of fighting the Russo-French alliance in the Black Sea and Mediterranean simultaneously. Retreating from Balkan commitments was the inevitable concomitant of such a strategic blow as Goschen's Admiralty forced upon Salisbury, and Egypt and Cyprus were in future to be relied upon to protect the route to India.

To the Queen, Salisbury explained once again how the Agreements, which had served Britain well for nine years but in the changed circumstances of Europe now committed her too far, had 'contained no promise to go to war...in accordance with the well-known policy of England, and carefully avoided all references to active measures'.[8] Once again he argued that in a Constitution such as Britain's, 'Parliament and people would not be guided in any degree' by prearranged treaties, but could only decide to go to war according to the situation as it stood at the time. So in January 1896 Salisbury cut loose from the nebulous bonds which connected Britain to Italy – which he privately described as a 'sturdy beggar' – and Austria, which he told Monson was 'the one power which does not hate us'.

~

Jingoism might have been responsible for Anglophobia, imperial over-stretch and the Boer War, but it also spawned some truly dreadful poetry. On 1st January 1896, Salisbury's pet propagandist, Alfred Austin, was appointed Poet Laureate in succession to Tennyson, who had died three years earlier and who had himself inherited it from Wordsworth. The tiny Austin was nicknamed 'Alfred the Little' to differentiate him from Tennyson. It was entirely Salisbury's doing, and when asked why he demeaned the post by such an absurd appointment answered: 'No one else applied for the laurel crown,' and Austin had so wanted it. Balfour, who unlike his uncle appreciated the arts and could not think of a worse poet than Austin except Lewis Morris, suggested Rudyard Kipling, who was sounded out but who turned it down, as he did Salisbury's offer of a knighthood three years later.

Balfour and others suspected Salisbury had chosen Austin as a private, disobliging joke against the literary establishment. He prided himself on his Philistinism, echoing the great Lord Burghley, who, when ordered by Elizabeth I to give Edmund Spenser a pension for having written *The Faerie Queen*, expostulated: 'What? A hundred pounds for a song!' Austin was fortunate that the serious poets of the day had ruled themselves out – Swinburne was a pagan, William Morris a socialist, Ruskin principally wrote prose, and Oscar Wilde announced that Swinburne was actually already Laureate, and 'the fact that his appointment to this high post has not been degraded by official confirmation renders his position all the more unassailable'.

Ten days after his appointment, Austin published a poem in *The Times* eulogising *Jameson's Ride*, one of the stanzas of which read:

> So we forded and galloped forward,
> As hard as our beasts could pelt,
> First eastward, then trending northward,
> Right over the rolling veldt.

In another stanza he rhymed 'madmen' with 'bad men'. Even Salisbury had to admit to the Queen that it was 'a pity that this effusion was his first performance'. Another of Austin's effusions, *Why England is Conservative*, ended with the lines:

> Though the throats of envy rage and rail,
> Be fair proud England proud fair England still!

The month after Austin's appointment, the Oxford Union passed the motion: 'That Lord Salisbury has been unwise in reviving the Laureateship', and Austin, almost universally ridiculed by the literary world, wrote to the *Critic* to say that the Queen had appointed him on the advice of 'Her First Minister' who 'doubtless acted in conformity with what he believed to be the preponderant genuine literary opinion of his fellow countrymen'. The pomposity of the five-foot hack knew few bounds. The Prince of Wales enjoyed teasing Salisbury about Austin's 'trash', but allowed him to stay on as Poet Laureate when he became King, on the understanding that everyone knew Austin was unpaid and that the appointment had had nothing to do with him.[9]

The series of diplomatic and actual rebuffs which had afflicted British foreign policy in the first half of the 1890s – Rosebery's abandoned Congo treaty with Belgium, the French conquest of Madagascar, Franco-Russo-German co-operation in the Far East, the Venezuelan embarrassments, the Armenian massacres, the Franco-Russian alliance and finally the Jameson debacle and Kruger telegram – prompted a national debate about whether Britain was too isolated diplomatically, and, if so, what could be done about it. Balfour was particularly fearful of what he called 'our national isolation', believing that in any future war America would take British trade, Germany some of her colonies and France her influence in the East, 'and possibly even in India'.

Over 9th and 10th January 1896, *The Times* ran a series of comments from the European press about British isolation, and in a wide-ranging Cabinet meeting held on 11th January, the first since the Raid, it was agreed to sign a convention with France over Siam and generally 'to settle as many questions with France as possible'. The Raiders were being brought back to Britain for trial, but Rhodes's Charter would not be withdrawn, although his military force would be placed under Crown control with a commander who 'could be trusted not to lend himself to such expeditions as that of Dr Jameson'. The Kruger telegram would be ignored, as Salisbury had a verbal assurance from Hatzfeldt that it did not presage any encroachments on British rights. Over Venezuela, after a long discussion, the Cabinet agreed to accept arbitration over 'large stretches of virgin forest', but refused to hand over British subjects 'to so detestable a government as Venezuela'.[10] 'The Queen cannot help feeling that our isolation is dangerous,' she declared on 14th January, when Hatzfeldt repeated the old offer of an anti-French compact. Salisbury had to reiterate his constitutional objections, repeating that when the crisis came, 'Parliament and people would not be guided in any degree by the fact that the Government had some years before signed a secret agreement to go to war.'

The whole debate took on a fresh impetus once a Canadian politician gave it a memorable soubriquet. During a debate in Ottawa, a minister called George Foster said: 'The great Mother Empire stands splendidly isolated in Europe.' Later on in the same debate a Liberal opponent, Sir Richard Cartwright, attacked 'this same subject of splendid isolation', arguing that it was not splendid at all, but dangerous. Foster's speech was reported in *The Times* on 18th January, and speaking to a banquet at the Hotel Metropole three days later, Chamberlain quoted from it, saying to loud cheers that the Empire 'stands secure in the strength of her own resources...in the abundant loyalty of her children from one end of the Empire to another'.[11] A sub-editor at *The Times* chose the phrase 'Splendid Isolation' for a sub-heading in the report of the speech, and thus was a label born, one that has unfairly affixed itself to Salisbury's foreign policy.

Just as George Curzon was tagged for life by the 'accursed doggerel' about considering himself a 'superior person', so Salisbury, who had long despised and denounced what he called the 'sterile' and 'dangerous' policy of isolation, was stuck with a label for his non-aligned but heavily engaged foreign policy, which was far more complex, subtle and intelligent than crude isolationism. The avoidance of joining entangling alliances or European power blocs, which Salisbury considered an inherent threat to peace, while insisting on complete freedom of manoeuvre in all circumstances, was by no means the same as the Little England isolationism of which he often still stands accused.

Under the Treaty of London's guarantee of 1839, Britain was committed to go to war with any power which invaded Belgium. She had promised in 1855 to defend Sweden and Norway against Russia in a treaty which remained in force, as was the Tripartite Treaty of 1856 in which any breach of the Treaty of Paris was declared a *casus belli*. Other promises to Greece in 1863 and Luxembourg in 1867 had been made, and in 1878 Salisbury's Cyprus Convention guaranteed Turkey's Asian territories against Russia. A series of bilateral agreements had also peacefully divided up Africa, and various alliances with Portugal dating back to 1373 and 1815 were also theoretically in force.

Far from being unattached to the continent of Europe, therefore, Britain was heavily pledged there, only not to the inherently unstable Great Power blocs which were growing up. Even with those, Salisbury had spent nine years observing the Mediterranean Agreements. In March 1896, he summed up his policy to Lascelles: 'I certainly wish to be good friends with Germany: as good friends as we were in 1892. That is to say, that we wish to lean to the Triple Alliance without belonging to it. But in 1892, as now, we were free from any engagement to go to war under any contingencies whatever.'

If a disinclination to be drawn into a general European conflagration, with its potentially unlimited cost in terms of blood and treasure, without any say over the *casus belli*, was 'splendid isolation', then Salisbury would have to have pleaded guilty. As he also told Lascelles, however, Britain could take advantage of 'our insular position which makes the burdensome conditions of an alliance unnecessary for our safety', and so Germany's heavy-handed overtures, only weeks after the Kruger telegram, were turned down. Salisbury's oft-repeated excuse, that under a democratic constitution no promise to fight could necessarily be upheld, was both a dig at democracy and something of a smokescreen.

Salisbury appreciated how Britain was always intimately involved in the European balance of power and could not stand isolated, splendidly or ignominiously, apart from it. In joining neither the Triple Alliance nor the Franco-Russian axis, Salisbury hoped that Britain could squeeze out more concessions than if she were a fully paid-up member of either. Instead of being the guarantors of peace that they claimed, Salisbury could see how the European Great Power blocs were creating the very climate of suspicion and rivalry under which a great war could start.

Salisbury's contention that public opinion was 'the great oracle' whose pronouncements were ambiguous was certainly valid with regard to Turkey. In 1877, the *vox populi* declared Constantinople to be worth fighting for, but twenty years later it vociferously denounced Turkey as a potential enemy. Salisbury's oft-expressed opinion that, as he put it to Monson in February 1896, 'in this country it was impossible to take any engagement involving an obligation to go to war', was not constitutionally accurate so much as a convenient use of one feared phenomenon – democracy – to defeat another, international entanglement.

Salisbury had denounced isolationism as 'foolish' since writing in *Bentley's Quarterly Review* in the late 1850s. Reviewing the second volume of Leopold von Ranke's *The History of England* for the *Saturday Review* in March 1861, he had pointed out the effect that the Thirty Years' War had had on British politics: 'Spite of indifference to foreign examples and foreign influence which Englishmen are very fond of professing, they have always been singularly sensitive to the reflex action of political events abroad.' This did not mean that Britain should preach to her neighbours about their internal affairs, which he called 'a superstructure of brag', or that she should fight for causes that did not intimately concern her. Opposing the calls for war against China in July 1862, he wrote: 'It is our duty to protect British property and British lives, and to concern ourselves with nothing else.' If the loss of the Chinese tea and silk trade would turn out to be less expensive to Britain than the loss of blood and treasure involved in intervention, war was indefensible.[12]

Isolation, or even worse a situation in which the other Powers combined against Britain to strip her of trade and colonies, was in fact Salisbury's worst fear. It was his staple criticism of the 1880–5 Liberal Government that Britain was left isolated in Europe and, as he put it in the House of Lords in February 1885, 'that boasted Concert of Europe, of which we used to hear so much, now appears to be a Concert of Europe against England'. No Power that needed to protect its communications to India via the Mediterranean, and which had important outposts in Gibraltar, Malta, Cyprus and Egypt, could ever be entirely isolated from the antagonisms and power politics of the Continent. Yet that never meant to Salisbury that Britain needed to be irrevocably dragged into them, so much as tangentially and diplomatically involved, with national interest as her sole criterion. 'Lord Salisbury has no reason to think that England runs at present any special danger of being isolated,' he had reassured the Queen in August 1888. The very term 'isolation' was consistently used by him as something to be strenuously avoided rather than implying anything desirable, let alone splendid.[13]

'If we take the *beau rôle* and protest to the last in favour of the integrity of Siam,' Salisbury had told Chamberlain in September 1895 about the country which comprises modern-day Thailand, 'France will some day pick a quarrel with Siam – and carry it off under our nose. On the other hand, if we play the base *rôle*, we may be able to partition Siam before the last stage is reached. There is our choice.' With the public thought to be unwilling to fight France over Siam, and the perceived need quickly to settle as many questions with France, on 15th January 1896 Salisbury concluded an agreement covering Siam, the delimitation of territory in the Lower Niger and relations with Tunis. Although France obtained territory in Siam, both she and Britain pledged to leave the richest and most fertile portion of the country intact, and to guarantee her against any third Power.

Britain's interests were protected by the Convention, and by another secret agreement the following year in which she agreed to assist Siam against any Power attempting to take territory in the South Malay states. The January 1896 Mekong Agreement was a holding operation to avoid the 'very awkward *impasse*' that would arise should France take Bangkok, and as a result Siam was to remain one of the very few countries of the world never colonised by Europeans.[14] It did, however, involve Salisbury making two agreements to go to war with unnamed powers in unknown circumstances, which entirely contradicted what he was simultaneously telling Monson and the Queen about the constitutional impossibility of a German alliance.

With France satisfied, Salisbury could look towards settling the Venezuelan problem with greater confidence. 'We are contending for men – not for land,' he told Chamberlain, 'for the rights of settlers whom we have encouraged to invest in such property.' In mid-January 1896, Salisbury sent the appropriately named Lord Playfair to Bayard to say privately that the dispute 'should not be allowed to drift, but be promptly settled by friendly co-operation', suggesting a conference of all European colonial powers to confirm the Monroe Doctrine. In return, a Court of Arbitration composed of American, British and Venezuelan commissioners could settle a frontier not far from the existing Schomburgk Line, which already roughly divided the Venezuelan and British settlements. Olney turned the offer down.

Salisbury was undecided whether America was attempting merely to win 'justice' for Venezuela, or whether she ultimately wanted an excuse to invade Canada. Writing to Devonshire on 16th January he asked: 'If the quarrel rests not on a passing question like Venezuela but on permanent grounds – then it is bound to come, in a few years. If it is granted that it must come, the question arises – have we any interest in delaying it?' He was 'rather sceptical' that America actually desired war with Britain, but 'until a new President is elected we cannot fairly tell'. His letter implied that Britain would not only fight for Canada, but would not allow America to dictate the timetable towards war once he had ascertained that that was her ultimate object.

By 11th February, the Cabinet had agreed to try to pursue a general arbitration scheme rather than accept the all-American Commission. As Salisbury reported to the Queen, the arrangements would be so organised 'without running the risk of putting the vital interest of your Majesty's Empire at the disposal of a foreigner, who may be partial or eccentric in his views'.[15] Meanwhile, Harcourt helpfully remembered that Queen Elizabeth I had given the whole of Venezuela to one of his ancestors, and he thought he had the title deeds to the country somewhere at Malwood, his house in Hampshire.

Salisbury was highly sceptical about arbitrations in general and those involving America in particular. He had opposed the post-Civil War arbitrations over seized ships, even to the point of considering resignation over the *Alabama* dispute in 1866. As he told Devonshire in February 1896, in a case like Venezuela where the arbitrators themselves 'will probably be an enemy in disguise', any title other than occupation must be very 'shadowy' and 'only partially applicable', considering how much of the land was virgin forest. Otherwise 'there is nothing to guide an arbitration but general expediency'. He saw great future dangers for the Empire in the general use of a process by which, as he complained to Pauncefote in March, 'issues in which the litigant states are most deeply interested will be decided by the vote of one man, and that man a foreigner'. With no jury or court of appeal, the foreigner would be bound to be credited with bias: 'Nations cannot afford to run such a risk.'

Pauncefote nevertheless drew up some Heads of Agreement for an arbitration treaty, which was signed in February 1896. Salisbury was convinced that it was all due to 'a jingo flare-up' in America for electioneering purposes, and because Olney wanted 'a splash of some kind before the [political] conventions'. Under the Treaty, five jurists were appointed, comprising of two British High Court judges, two Americans and a Russian, Frédéric de Martens. The tribunal sat in Paris until 3rd October 1899, when they handed down a final Award loosely based on the Schomburgk Line, but with two British areas going to Venezuela which were big enough to look impressive on the map but which only contained a handful of inhabitants.

Salisbury has been accused of appeasing America over Venezuela, but it had been his proposal which, in Cleveland's biographer's estimation, 'enabled America to abandon her independent study of the Venezuelan boundary and opened the way to a peaceful settlement'. Salisbury had been keen to avert an unnecessary crisis, and continued to humour America over the Hay–Pauncefote Panama Canal Treaty and over Alaskan–Canadian border disputes. By deflecting friction with America, he ensured that he could concentrate on more pressing and significant Asian and African questions.

'The United States will do all the mischief they can without going to war,' he had predicted to the Queen, in answer to a worried letter from the Queen-Regent of Spain in May 1896. When this proved to be wrong, and America fought Spain in 1898, Salisbury declared British neutrality and encouraged all other European nations not to side with Spain. When it was discovered that the American secret service had been operating in Canada against a Spanish naval officer, Lieutenant Carranza, and Pauncefote suggested he be expelled despite his denials of espionage, Salisbury took the view that it was best to drop the matter rather than either expel the Spanish spy or remonstrate with America.[16] With quite enough problems in the eastern hemisphere, Salisbury did not need to add to them in the west. He felt a certain degree of tail-tweaking had to be endured but, as his letter to Devonshire demonstrated, any serious threat from the country he had long despised would undoubtedly have met stern resistance, whatever the European dangers.

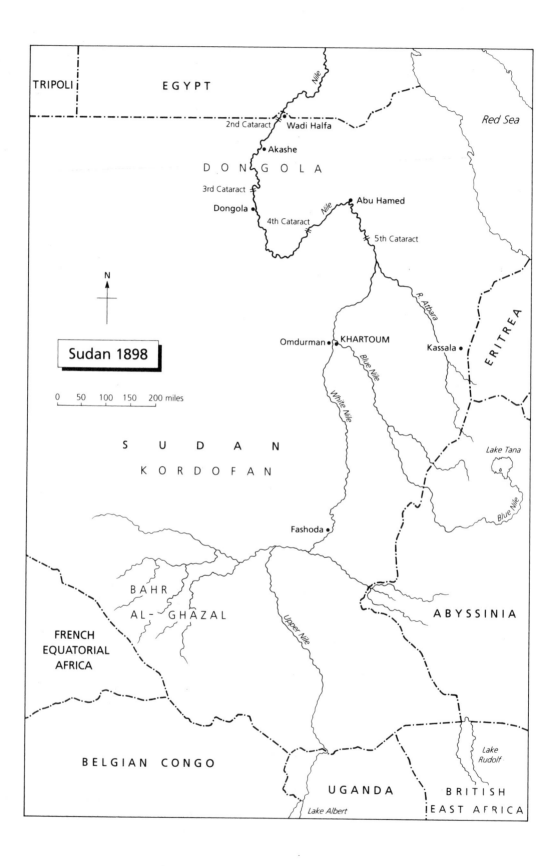

THIRTY-EIGHT

Great Power Politics

The Jameson Aftermath – The March on Dongola
– The Balmoral Conversations –
The 'Wrong Horse' Speech
– Crisis on Crete – Gerald Balfour –
The Transvaal

February 1896 to May 1897

'Similarity of political faith is no more an indication of a useful ally
than similarity of religious faith would be.'

'The art of round, uncompromising, abusive denial is a very valuable art
to possess,' Salisbury had written in the *Saturday Review* in December
1863. 'It is very difficult to disbelieve in the sincerity of a man who has
really contrived to work himself up into a rage. But he should not work
his powers in that respect too hard.' It is likely that, although he had no
actual prior knowledge of the Raid itself, Salisbury was involved in the
successful Government cover-up of Chamberlain's role, which
remained solid until January 1946, fifty years after the Raid and long
after the deaths of all the major participants. 'Englishmen will never
quarrel with a minister for holding the scale of justice a little awry in
their favour,' Salisbury had written in 1863. 'But it must be only a little
awry.' After Jameson had surrendered at Doornkoop on 2nd January
1896, Chamberlain had telegraphed Kruger asking for mercy for the
captured Raiders. Rhodes resigned from the premiership of Cape Colony
on the 6th and Kruger handed over most of the Raiders to the British
authorities by the 7th, and was thanked by Queen Victoria the next day.[1]
Meanwhile, seventy-two members of Johannesburg's Uitlander organisation, the Reform Committee, were arrested for treason and taken to
Pretoria.

On 21st January, Jameson sailed from Durban and was cheered by the
crowd outside Bow Street Magistrates Court when he was bailed on 25th

February. During the trial, Rhodes's solicitor, Bourchier F. Hawksley, refused to produce the cablegrams that had passed between Rhodes in Cape Town and his London agents, Dr Rutherfoord Harris and Rochfort Maguire, back in November and December 1895.[2] According to a May 1897 letter from Hawksley to Rhodes, which was not made public until 1978, these 'compromising cables' consisted of 'true reports of what had passed' between Harris and the Colonial Office officials, including Chamberlain, concerning the projected uprising in Johannesburg. They proved that the British Government 'had influenced the action of those in South Africa' who undertook the Raid. The most damaging of the cables probably showed that Chamberlain had allowed Rhodes's troops on to the Pitsani Strip in anticipation of the rising. On 20th December 1895, Chamberlain had even told his Assistant Under-Secretary Edward Fairfield to see Rochfort Maguire, an All Souls' Fellow, to encourage Rhodes to 'hurry up', because of the worsening Venezuelan situation, just as Rhodes was considering postponing the rising for lack of support.[3]

When Sir Graham Bower, the Imperial Secretary to the High Commissioner, Sir Hercules Robinson, urged Rhodes to slow down his preparations, Rhodes was able to answer that he was being disloyal to his chief, Chamberlain, 'who is hurrying me up'. The cablegrams, if published, would show, Hawksley advised Rhodes, that Chamberlain 'has deceived the House of Commons and the country, if not also his colleagues in the Cabinet'. In order to allow Rhodes to blackmail Chamberlain into not abrogating the Charter of the South Africa Company, copies of the 2nd August to 20th December 1895 telegrams were given to Chamberlain by Hawksley on 6th June 1896. Rhodes also hoped to block a parliamentary Select Committee inquiry into the Raid, but he failed in that. Chamberlain read Hawksley's file, including the implication that the Pitsani Strip had been handed to the South Africa Company on 18th October 1895 with the express purpose of facilitating the Company's military intervention in the Transvaal, rather than for its overt purpose of protecting a railway.[4] They were, of course, only cables by others about him rather than from Chamberlain himself; nonetheless, he knew his career was on the line.

Chamberlain decided to come clean to Salisbury on or soon after 6th June 1896, showing him Hawksley's copy file and offering his resignation. A total dearth of evidence about this vital moment permits only speculation. It is not even known whether Chamberlain showed Salisbury all of the cablegrams, which numbered over fifty. Did Salisbury refuse to accept Chamberlain's proffered resignation because of Chamberlain's popularity, knowing how it would destabilise the Government? Did he think that Chamberlain had even acted wrongly anyhow? In the days before records were kept at Cabinet, it is not even known whether the ceding of the Pitsani Strip had been sanctioned at Cabinet level, although it seems not. Salisbury would also have wanted to protect his son-in-law and Chamberlain's Under-Secretary, Wolmer – who had the prevous year become the 2nd Earl of Selborne – whose position would also have become untenable if Chamberlain resigned.

Did Salisbury wish to deny the Liberals the satisfaction of bringing down the man who had done most to defeat Irish Home Rule? Was he finding Chamberlain a useful ally in Government, as Gwendolen had predicted, despite their occasional disagreements over foreign affairs? Or did he fear the damage the popular, Jingoist ex-minister might wreak from the backbenches? Unfortunately, such was the comprehensive nature of the cover-up that not a hint remains as to what was going through Salisbury's mind at the time. From his track record as a political pugilist and as someone who was willing to cut constitutional corners, we can make an informed guess as to his response to Chamberlain's admission of complicity, which was to act decisively and aggressively in support of his Colonial Secretary. By endorsing Chamberlain's threat to withdraw the Charter from Rhodes if Hawksley's file ever saw the light of day, Salisbury effectively blackmailed the blackmailers.

The most pressing task was to destroy all copies of the cablegrams. Hawksley had one set, which disappeared either when Rhodes's papers were burnt by his executors on his death in 1902, or at Hawksley's own death. The copies Chamberlain took to show Salisbury have, not surprisingly, never come to light. Finally the Eastern and South African Telegraph Company had a copy set, which also disappeared. Between 1871 and 1892 Sir Robert Herbert had been Permanent Under-Secretary at the Colonial Office, and on his retirement he had become a director of the Eastern and South African Telegraph Company. An expansionist in imperial policy who liked 'vigorous' methods and had a 'slightly cynical mind', Herbert was ideally placed to purloin them, although there is no actual evidence that he did.

A grandson of the 1st Earl of Carnarvon, educated at Eton and Balliol, a fellow of All Souls and a former premier of Queensland, a member of Grillions and The Club, and Chancellor of the Order of St Michael and St George, Herbert personified the British imperial Establishment. His career after the cablegrams incident is also instructive. He was offered (and refused) a directorship of the British South Africa Company by Rhodes in 1898, was briefly recalled to the Colonial Office in 1900 by Chamberlain and went on later to help Chamberlain in the tariff reform campaign. Of the missing cablegrams, Hawksley had told Rhodes: 'We are absolutely in the dark as to how or why this is. It is impossible that their absence is an accident as might have been assumed if one or two important or unimportant could not be produced...whether this is through Sir Robert Herbert or not I do not know.' Nor can we today, but although the evidence must be circumstantial, it also looks likely that they were taken away and destroyed by the Telegraph Company director.

Although Salisbury, Chamberlain, Hawksley, Rhodes, Robinson, Fairfield, Harris, Maguire, Sir Robert Meade the Permanent Under-Secretary at the Colonial Office, possibly Bower, probably Herbert, the Cable Office telegraphist and Frank Newton, the Resident Commissioner at Mafeking, all knew what the cablegrams contained, and others who guessed the truth included Flora Shaw, the Colonial correspondent of *The Times*, Moberly Bell, the paper's assistant manager, Sir Alfred Beit, Rhodes's partner, and Earl Grey, no one incriminated anyone else for half a century. When the Empire needed to cover up the traces of its skulduggery, it managed to do so with impressive efficiency. Historians differ as to whether there were originally fifty-four or fifty-one telegrams in all, but only forty-six were ever submitted to the Select Committee, none of them particularly incriminating. The rest have never been found.

Salisbury ensured that Chamberlain himself was appointed to the Select Committee and he also insisted that only documents which the Select Committee specifically demanded by name should be passed on. The scapegoats eventually chosen were two of the junior officials on the spot, Bower and Newton. The latter was knighted in 1919 and later became the South African High Commissioner in London, dying in May 1948 still silent about the events. Bower, who had been Robinson's private secretary from 1880 to 1884 and had been Imperial Secretary to the High Commissioner since 1884, was packed off to be Colonial Secretary of Mauritius. He also stayed silent until his death in 1933, but wrote a memorandum in 1904 which was made public on the fiftieth anniversary of the Raid in January 1946, making clear both Chamberlain's and Robinson's personal complicity in the schemes, including Robinson's direct orders to Bower to 'allow the troops to come down to Pitsani'.[5]

Jameson and Willoughby eventually received fifteen-month sentences and four other officers between five and seven months, all without hard labour. In Cabinet, Salisbury took the view that as much leniency as possible should be shown to the British army officers involved. At a party held at the time, Salisbury approached Edward Carson, Jameson's barrister, and joked: 'I wish you'd brought "Dr Jim" with you.' Of Willoughby and the others, whom Lansdowne thought should be forced to retire, Salisbury wrote in September:

> Is it not very harsh to inflict military punishment on them for the error of believing him [Jameson] and therefore obeying his orders? Put the matter the other way. Suppose H.M.G. had resolved [to invade] the Transvaal....

Suppose Willoughby had replied to Jameson 'I don't believe you: this is an attack on a friendly state. Your orders are *ultra vires* and invalid' and had refused to move. Suppose that in consequence a critical military operation had failed...he would have been very severely and very justly punished.

While admitting it was a difficult case, Salisbury told Lansdowne: 'I greatly doubt about the "retirement" of those men,' and although he said the whole matter 'makes wary walking', he was adamant in their support. As he had put it during the Eastern Question crisis of 1878: 'If our ancestors had cared for the rights of other people, the British Empire would not have been made.'

The Select Committee continued to sit throughout 1897, although Jameson had been released from Holloway Gaol through ill-health in December 1896, having served hardly any of his sentence. (He lived to become premier of Cape Colony himself from 1904 to 1908 and did not die until 1917.) Although it was embarrassing for the Government, Salisbury stuck to the official line, complaining of 'the monstrous libels which have been invented against Chamberlain, and for which proof has to a certain extent been manufactured'.[6] He was fortunate that no one questioned him closely on the 'certain extent' to which it had not been.

Salisbury was strengthened in his attitude by great public sympathy for the Raiders. Rhodes appeared six times before the Committee in February and March 1897, being cross-examined by Harcourt and Labouchere, and he readily admitted to supporting the Uitlanders' aspirations. He claimed that the Raid took place without his orders but he continued to refuse to hand over the Company's London–Cape Town cable communications. Jameson's evidence on 26th March stuck to this script, exculpating Chamberlain, Robinson, Rhodes and the Chartered Company into the bargain. One of Harris's counsel was none other than Salisbury's son Robert, who for the rest of his life somewhat naïvely believed Harris's claim that neither he nor Chamberlain knew anything about the Raid.

When the Committee, chaired by the Tory former minister William Jackson, severely reprimanded Bower and Newton in July 1897, the Cabinet agreed that 'they should be removed from South Africa, and employed in some less notable portion of the Queen's dominions'. Salisbury wanted Jameson's five co-conspirators to have their army commissions restored to them once they left prison, but he recognised the impossibility of persuading the majority of the Cabinet to sanction this. 'Throughout the whole crisis,' claimed the Conservative *Campaign Guide* at the next general election, 'the attitude of the British Government was firm, judicious and correct.' This was untrue, but Salisbury had ridden out another storm, if not with much credit, then at least with great tenacity.[7] As the *Guide* put it: 'The moral rights of the question were with the Uitlander; but legally and technically they and their allies were hopelessly in the wrong.' Salisbury had never been a man to let legal and technical questions stand in his way.

On 1st March 1896, Emperor Menelik II of Ethiopia defeated the Italian Governor of Eritrea, General Baratieri, at the Battle of Adowa, killing 5,000 men and capturing all his guns and stores. When the news reached Rome, Crispi's ministry fell, and in London fears grew that a regenerated Mahdist movement under the Khalifa might capture the Italian stronghold of Kassala and once again threaten Egypt. The new Italian Prime Minister, the Marchese di Rudini, begged Salisbury for a diversionary Anglo-Egyptian attack on the Dervishes to protect Kassala. Salisbury knew he was fortunate in the two men he had to rely upon in Egypt; Cromer and Kitchener. He allowed Cromer complete control over Egyptian internal affairs, making it a rule not to 'jog his arm' unless absolutely necessary. Once when on holiday in France he answered an urgent telegram from Cromer asking for instructions with the words: 'Do as you like.'

In 1884, Herbert Horatio Kitchener of the Royal Engineers had accompanied Wolseley's expedition to relieve Gordon, and from 1886 he was Governor of the eastern Sudan. When he was wounded in the Sudan in January 1888, Salisbury told Cromer that although he had never met Kitchener, 'I feel as if I know him well. He is a very gallant and efficient officer, though a headstrong subordinate.' In fact they had met, when on 1st September 1878 Salisbury had commissioned Kitchener to make a one inch to one mile survey of Cyprus. When they met again over a decade later, Edward Cecil recalled that his father 'was much impressed with him. That I clearly remember, for my father was not often impressed.'[8] Although Kitchener had blurted out that if made Sirdar (Commander-in-Chief of the Anglo-Egyptian Army) he intended to retake Khartoum eventually – exactly the 'Forward' policy the Cabinet feared the soldiers were pressing on Cromer – Salisbury said that he could 'deal with a man who has the courage of his opinions and can wait'. In 1892, Kitchener was appointed Sirdar, but with the clear understanding that no expedition to Dongola would be undertaken until the Cabinet was ready.

Salisbury reiterated to Cromer that finance and politics, not his military advisers, must dictate the timing and extent of the reconquest of the Sudan, and that he must be patient. To listen to experts, he warned, would mean that 'step by step the imperious exaction of military necessity will lead you on into the desert'. For his part, Cromer believed that Salisbury was rather like 'a steersman of a surf-boat lying outside the mouth of an African river. He has to wait for a high wave to carry him over the bar.'⁹ The massacre at Adowa was just such a high wave, enabling him to argue for an Anglo-Egyptian expedition to be sent to Dongola. It was explained to the other Great Powers that such action was necessary for the defence of Egypt and to protect the exposed Italian position at Kassala. After two Cabinet meetings on 11ᵗʰ and 12ᵗʰ March, which Wolseley also attended, Salisbury telegraphed Cromer to say that the Government wanted to use the same military effort to help the Italians as well as 'to plant the Egyptian foot farther up the Nile'.

Although Salisbury claimed to the Prince of Wales that Cromer fully concurred in the decision, in fact the Consul-General was sceptical, especially once the French and Russians voted against the £500,000 cost of the expedition being paid out of the £2 million General Reserve Fund of the Caisse de la Dette Publique, the international body which virtually controlled the Egyptian economy. When Kitchener received the order to advance, he danced a jig, and a column set out three days later. In fact, the Cabinet had not finally agreed to march to Dongola at all, but only to Akashe, but once Cromer pointed out that the enterprise was not worth undertaking otherwise, Salisbury helped to alter the expedition's ultimate objective to Dongola. 'I could have wished our Italian friends had less capacity for being beaten,' Salisbury wrote to Cromer, 'but it would not have been safe, either from an African or European point of view, to sit quite still while they were being crushed.' Salisbury ensured that he, rather than the War Office, had overall control of the expedition, with Kitchener reporting directly to Cromer rather than to Lansdowne.

Salisbury told the Queen that Khartoum itself was 'the ultimate object', but more time and money were required before that goal could be attained.¹⁰ McDonnell had to write to the Prince of Wales that the rumours of a Cabinet split and Lansdowne's resignation were untrue, but Salisbury also had to admit to the Queen in late April that his colleagues, especially Hicks Beach and Chamberlain, were not prepared to send the British expeditionary force that Cromer and Kitchener believed necessary for the task. In fact, Egyptian *fellaheen* (peasant) troops under British officers proved good enough.

April's news that Kitchener had purchased 5,000 camels also worried Salisbury, who feared that it might 'operate on the Sirdar's mind as a powerful temptation to go on to Berber – and possibly to Khartoum'. In fact, only 2,000 had been bought, but as Salisbury told Cromer on 1ˢᵗ May, there were some in the Cabinet who 'fear that Kitchener meditates an expedition into the wilderness at the head of a string of camels'. Cromer had in February himself written to Sanderson that Kitchener might turn out to be 'a Jamesonian type', so it was a justifiable concern. Gladstone opposed the expedition, even going so far – in a much derided line – as to describe the Dervishes as 'a people rightly struggling to be free'.

One of the British officers Kitchener chose to accompany him as an *aide de camp* was Salisbury's son, Lord Edward Cecil of the Grenadier Guards. It was a shrewd move, allowing the Sirdar a direct line of communication to the Prime Minister. 'All shall be known at home by the proper people,' Edward wrote in his diary over a particular *bêtise* of the War Office during the Dongola campaign. On 7th June, he was mentioned by Kitchener in his despatches on the successful capture of Dongola. Five days later, Salisbury announced in the House of Lords that the town was not the Government's final objective.

Financial considerations forced the Cabinet to decide on 31st July not to advance beyond Merowe and the final £750,000 that the expedition cost was paid by Hicks Beach out of the British Exchequer, with the Chancellor denouncing 'impotent foreign spite' in a debate. One result of the Powers' financial boycott of the expedition was that the advance could only be seen in terms of an Anglo-Egyptian, rather than an international, victory. As Salisbury told the Queen in September, 'the question of going forward to Khartoum is purely a question of money. If it is to be done, it must be done with English money.' With the first stage successful and paid for, Salisbury began saving up for the second stretch of Kitchener's reconquest of the Sudan.[11]

In the meantime, a railway would be built from Wadi Halfa to Abu Hamed, which was also in Anglo-Egyptian hands and which, when the Nile was low, could only otherwise be supplied by camel. As Salisbury reported to Cromer, he 'had to give my approval at the end of a moment's notice, when the train by which K was to go away was already overdue. I need not say that I was very glad to do so.' Salisbury thought that the 230-mile railway across the desert was equally important for the protection of the territory already reconquered as well as to provide a base for a further advance to the south. Although Salisbury thought men like Sir Edward Hamilton and what he called 'the Gladstonian garrison of the Treasury' had a bad effect on Hicks Beach's mind, he managed to squeeze the money out of the Exchequer, although £2 million for a giant reservoir scheme of Cromer's had to be refused.

In September 1896, Salisbury expressed his irritation at the way Suakim and Tokar had to be garrisoned exclusively by forces from India when the crew of a battleship from the Mediterranean fleet could do the job just as well: 'It is like a man who has a large balance at the bank borrowing a thousand pounds from Shylock.' In an obvious reference to Rhodes in the House of Lords in January 1897, Salisbury said that 'if any millionaires who spent their money in supporting raids and invasions would come forward with an offer to carry the [Dongola] expedition further the Government might not be deaf to their entreaties'.[12]

(The Emperor Menelik, whose victory had provided the excuse for the march on Dongola, survived. He used to eat pages of the Bible to cure illness, his doctors feeding them to him page by page. One day in December 1913, trying to recover from a stroke, he expired a few chapters into the Book of Kings.)

'What a strange spectacle Europe is presenting,' Salisbury wrote to an acquaintance, Canon Gordon, in late August 1896, 'a perfectly unknown future depending upon the will of three or four men. It is very remarkable that in spite of the progress of democratic ideas, the weight of individual personalities, for good or evil, is greater than ever. Now every turn in the humours of the Emperor Nicholas or the Emperor William, or the Sultan of Turkey, is watched and interpreted – the fate of many thousands of lives depends on them.' Only days before that was written, forty Armenian revolutionaries had bombed and robbed the Ottoman Bank in Pera and escaped by boat, leaving their countrymen to a swift and terrible retribution. Around seven thousand were massacred by Muslim mobs as the Turkish police looked on. The secretary of the British Legation in Constantinople reported how he now found it easy to visualise what the St Bartholomew's Day massacre must have been like.

So when the new Tsar, Nicholas II, confirmed his willingness to visit Balmoral in September 1896 to celebrate Queen Victoria's becoming as the longest-reigning British monarch, Salisbury decided to reciprocate the offer that his great-grandfather Nicholas I had made to Seymour in 1853 for an agreed partition of Turkey. Together the Tsar and the Queen-Empress reigned over half the world's land mass, and if Salisbury could establish a *modus vivendi* between the two empires, based on the dethroning of Abdul Hamid II, the inherently destabilising Eastern Question might at last be resolved.

When, in August, Hicks Beach had become concerned about the brevity of the fifty-three-year period after which Cyprus's revenue would revert to the Sultan, Salisbury reassured him that it did not much matter, 'for the Ottoman Empire will be in atoms long before that date ... whatever the future two generations hence have in store it cannot be a mere continuation of the present ineffective set of compromises'. To replace them, Salisbury held a conversation with the Tsar at Balmoral at 7 p.m. on Sunday, 27th September 1896, which lasted until 8.30 p.m. and in which he found his interlocutor 'conciliatory, straightforward, and honest'. According to a 'VERY SECRET' memorandum Salisbury drew up for the senior members of the Cabinet, the Tsar said that he had no objections to pressurising the Sultan into reforms, or to Britain remaining in Egypt. When Salisbury then brought up Nicholas I's proposal to dismember Turkey, however, the Tsar changed the subject to 'the absurdity of Russia even trying to obtain' India, and his support for the status quo in Persia. Over China, Salisbury assured the Tsar that Britain had no intentions to hamper Russian trade, which was accepted 'with great apparent satisfaction'.

This otherwise cordial global overview only reached difficulties when the Tsar, 'thoroughly in earnest', said that the Straits ought to be navigable by Russian warships and the Dardanelles should be in Russian hands, likening the present situation to a man not owning the key of the room in which he lived. Russia did not want Constantinople or any other Turkish territory, he claimed, 'she only wanted the door, and the power of fortifying it' against an attack such as that launched on the Crimea. Salisbury could not accept this, although he 'admitted the theory that Turkish rule at Constantinople was a bulwark to our Indian Empire could not be maintained'. Any alteration must be made, Salisbury implied, as part of a general dismemberment of the Ottoman Empire, which would also involve France, Austria and Italy. After some talk about how much the Tsar disliked his 'nervous' and ill-mannered cousin the Kaiser, who 'would poke him in the ribs, and slap him on the back like a schoolboy', the conversation ended, leaving Salisbury with the impression 'that if we give him the Straits he will help us, and will consider favourably proposals for compensation'. It was agreed that they would speak again two days later.

By the time of the second conversation, on the evening of Tuesday the 29th, the Russian Ambassador, Georges de Staal, had arrived to pour cold water on Salisbury's visionary if cynical partition scheme. The Tsar stated that dethroning the Sultan was 'too great a risk to run'. For Christian countries such as Russia and Britain to oust the world's foremost Muslim might bring chaos, a possible Muslim revolt in Russia and the prospect of the Great Powers being forced to rule Turkey in perpetuity. Furthermore, whomever was chosen by the Powers as the new Sultan would soon be assassinated. Salisbury ended the conversation by holding out the possibility of Russian control of the Straits, but only as part of a general settlement 'after the Turkish Empire had disappeared'.[13] It was a *quid pro quo* for which the Russians were not yet ready, but at least it had been proposed. Salisbury did not blame the Tsar personally for the rebuff, saying at the Mansion House soon afterwards that if Russia and Austria did not act against Turkey in a way that might end in a European war, they were only 'pursuing a selfishness which is much to be praised, and which ought to be implemented by all. The selfishness is, in truth, only the selfishness of trustees.'

'It is, I think, a superstition of an antiquated diplomacy that there should be any necessary antagonism between Russia and Great Britain,'

Salisbury reiterated in his Guildhall speech of 9th November 1896. His only mention of 'splendid isolation' was in his remark that it was unfair to expect Austria and Russia to show, in their attitude to Turkey, 'the same emotional and philanthropic spirit with which you, in your splendid isolation, are able to examine all the circumstances'. As Gwendolen pointed out, there was a 'characteristic touch of ironic rebuke to the self-righteousness of his compatriots', which when quoted, as it often has been, entirely out of context, sounded as though Salisbury was actually praising isolation as splendid. Irony is sadly inadmissible in politics at discourse, as too liable to misinterpretation.

Salisbury indulged in no such linguistic subtleties in the Queen's Speech debate on 19th January 1897. The massacres of Turkish Christians had continued, despite the twenty years that had passed since the rainy day on which Abdul Hamid II's vaunted Constitution had been saluted with cannonfire. Philip Currie reported from Constantinople that the Sultan was probably not personally implicated but was, at best, incapable of preventing the horrors. Salisbury was not so sure, telling a cleric in February 1898 that the lives of Armenians were 'valueless' to the Sultan and 'To order them to be exterminated is to him no more than it is to an English gentleman to order his rabbits to be shot.' With British power firmly established in Egypt, Salisbury felt the time had come for some brutal frankness about what, in a speech at Dover the previous April, he had called Europe's 'gangrene in the south-eastern extremity', of which it was 'no part of England's duty' to excise without support from the other Great Powers.

'I do not know that I can sum up the present trend of English policy better than by saying we are engaged in slowly escaping from the dangerous errors of 1848 to 1856,' Salisbury wrote privately in August 1896, blaming Palmerston for believing 'that foreign policy should follow your political proclivities' and thus supporting liberal France against autocratic Russia and Austria:

> Such a policy is obviously unsound – similarity of political faith is no more indication of a useful ally than similarity of religious faith would be. Politics is a matter of business; our alliances should be those who are most likely to help or not to hinder the interests of which we as a Government are the trustees.... But Palmerston would be governed by common sympathies instead of common interests. He made war with Russia; he insulted Austria; and he ostentatiously made friends with France.

With Tory Turcophilia dead, after twenty years of earnest pressure resulting in next to no reforms, and the route to India now no longer dependent on the south-eastern European balance of power, Salisbury felt able in his speech on the Address to commit what at the time was assumed to be another 'blazing indiscretion', but was in fact an attempt to jolt the public and signal a radical new departure in foreign policy. 'The parting of the ways was in 1853, when the Emperor Nicholas' proposals were rejected,' Salisbury baldly informed the House of Lords as Parliament opened. 'Many members of the House will keenly feel the nature of the mistake that was made when I say that we put all our money on the wrong horse.' He went on to defend Beaconsfield's pro-Turkish policy as merely upholding Palmerston's, by protecting Constantinople while trying to press reforms on to Turkey. But even after his rare analogy from the turf, which ensured that it became known as the 'Wrong Horse' speech, Salisbury rubbed in the message again, saying that without reforms, which he privately had accepted would now not be forthcoming, 'the doom of the Turkish Empire cannot be very long postponed'.

By publicly announcing regret at the failure of Nicholas I's 1853 initiative, Salisbury was only repeating in public what he had for decades been saying in private, and had thought ever since he himself had opposed the Crimean War. But this denunciation of forty-three years of British foreign policy-making, for twelve of which he had himself personally been responsible, was nonetheless astonishing. He was attempting to alert the public to the fact that the whole crux of British Near Eastern policy had shifted from Constantinople to Egypt. For Salisbury, Beaconsfield's policy of being prepared to fight for Turkish integrity was over, the Mediterranean Agreements were moribund, the Straits were (according to the Admiralty) unforceable, Russia posed no real threat to India's North-West Frontier, the Franco-Russian alliance made incursions into the Black Sea too dangerous for Britain, and an Austro-Russian *rapprochement* in the Balkans was coming anyhow, and was indeed signed on 8th May.

These new factors demanded new strategic thinking on the part of the British Parliament, press and public, and Salisbury was keen to initiate it. The Dongola expedition had highlighted how highly he prized possession of the Nile, if possible right to its source. The protection and reinforcement of India would now take place via the Suez Canal. Salisbury's 'Wrong Horse' speech confirmed to Italy and Austria that the Agreements really were moribund, reassured the public that war would not be fought for Turkey, and warned Turkey that she could no longer count on British protection. 'By lying, by delay, by the connivance of subordinates, by crafty use of the differences which always exist among the Powers,' Salisbury wrote of the Sultan to Currie after the speech, 'he knows that as long as his ultimate supreme authority is not affected he will always be able to render futile the most imposing scheme of reforms.' After twenty years of cajoling, Salisbury's huge patience had finally snapped, and Turkish independence and integrity were henceforth to be left up to the mutual forbearance of

Russia and Austria. Harcourt approved of Salisbury's speech, correctly interpreting it as indicating one of the most important foreign policy changes in four decades.

The Liberal politician G.W.E. Russell set up the Forward Movement to attack Salisbury's policy of not saving the Armenians, accusing him of having 'handed back more than a million of liberated Christians to Turkish slavery in 1878', and being 'the weak man with the strong style' who had promised much in his 1895 Guildhall speech and then delivered nothing. Salisbury was unimpressed and merely remarked that 'Armenia is not alone. In many parts of Asia and Africa the most appalling sufferings are being inflicted by human fiendishness and superstitions. It is fortunate that owing to natural impediments we do not fully hear of or appreciate such things in England, or I am afraid the injudicious exhibition of our powerless sympathy would tend to re-intensify the human suffering that goes on.' Such sympathy, as he told Rutland in November 1898, he blamed on Gladstone's 'mad philanthropy' which had placed 'an eternal enmity between the Turks and us'. As a result, by not antagonising Turkey, the Kaiser 'thinks he can slip into our shoes.... I doubt his getting more than a few tradesmen's orders.' This was another dud prediction, for by 1913 Germany was conducting military conversations with Turkey, which duly fought against the Allies.

'The Eastern Question makes me regret the death of Offenbach,' Salisbury had said at The Club a month after his speech, 'it would have afforded him so much material.'[14] Instead, almost as a *coda* to the Question, a dispute arose over Crete, which in the tense state of *fin de siècle* international relations developed into yet another crisis.

On the Turkish-owned island of Crete, the Greek Christians outnumbered Muslims by seven to one and were demanding the political incorporation of the island into Greece. In 1889, fighting had broken out between the two communities. The Greek Prime Minister, M. Tricoupis, threatened to intervene, which had brought a swift response from Salisbury, who refused to allow it and supported his decision with the mobilisation of the Mediterranean fleet. 'When I first came to the Foreign Office in 1878,' Salisbury reminisced to Monson in November 1889, 'I believed strongly in the Greeks.' The pro-Greek clauses in the Treaty of Berlin were 'largely, if not entirely due to my urgent pressure' against Beaconsfield's Turcophile sentiments. 'Now that I know Greece better – I regret what I did: for I see that while European statesmen are labouring to extinguish every cause of conflagration, the policy of Greece is to threaten, at each crisis, to kindle a European war, unless she is bought off. She is the blackmailer of Europe.'

Salisbury was never attached to the philhellenism so common amongst Victorians such as Gladstone, a renowned Classicist. In the *Quarterly Review*, Salisbury had ridiculed 'the modern theory that the territorial limits of a country ought to be settled according to its literary history', so that just because Aeschylus wrote in Attica and Pindar about the Games of Morea, twenty-five centuries later the government of either place should be altered. Such romances could never have had any part to play in Salisbury's foreign policy. 'The Greeks have magnificent dreams and splendid recollections,' Salisbury told the Queen in 1891, 'but after seventy years of independence their exchequer is nearly bankrupt, their public men and their tribunals are corrupt, and their punishment of crime is rendered so uncertain by political favouritism that brigandage is beginning to rear its head again.' Salisbury treated philhellenism amongst educated Britons as, in his daughter's words, 'a psychological problem – incomprehensible and definitely irritating'. Salisbury had even deprecated the allied victory over the Turkish fleet at Navarino in 1827, which, 'by forming an artificial and premature freedom upon Greece, had resulted in the product of two "sick men" instead of one'.

When in the spring of 1896 the Greeks made further attempts to encourage a Cretan revolt, Salisbury did not wish to see the Turks send troops to crush the Greek Christians, as their counterparts were doing to Armenians in inaccessible parts of the Turkish Empire. Unlike the Armenians behind 'the mountains of Taurus', Crete was fortunately entirely at the mercy of the Royal Navy. Yet when in June and July Austria and Germany proposed blockading Crete, both to prevent Greece arming the insurgents and Turkey reinforcing her garrison, Salisbury told de Staal that this was unfair to Turkey. A 'watching' flotilla of twenty-six warships, mostly British, kept order as best it could in the Cretan ports and seaboard, although inter-communal fighting did take place further inland. Meanwhile, the Athenian mob demanded direct military intervention in support of the Greek population on the island.

By mid-January 1897, Salisbury had formulated a compromise whereby Crete would be largely autonomous, under neither Greek nor Turkish direct rule but as a 'privileged province' under Ottoman suzerainty. On 24th January, he circularised the Great Powers to that effect, saying both Turkey and Greece should withdraw their troops and irregulars forthwith. The situation was complicated by the Kaiser's support for his brother-in-law, King George I of Greece. But events simply overtook Salisbury's good intentions when in early February the leaders of the Greek insurgents overthrew Berovitch Pasha, the Ottoman Governor, and Prince George of Greece sailed from Athens's Piraeus harbour to Crete with a flotilla of torpedo boats. These were successfully intercepted by the 'watching flotilla', but in mid-February

Colonel Vassos, King George's *aide de camp*, managed to land west of Canea with 2,000 volunteers and formally annex the island in the name of his master.

Greece and Turkey immediately prepared for full-scale war on their Macedonian and Thessalonian frontiers. Watching closely were those other populations under Turkish suzerainty in Europe, the Serbians, Bulgarians and Montenegrins, who Salisbury feared would rise up the moment Crete won its independence, and thereby, in his warning to the Queen, 'break up the Turkish Empire and bring on a general war.' For all his desire to dismember that institution himself, Salisbury recognised it had to be done carefully with Great Power consensus at the top, not as a result of a general scramble for autonomy from below.

Salisbury decided to let the events on the ground make absolutely no difference to his original intentions. He ignored the large philhellenic public meetings being held in London, and, after 'anxious and prolonged' discussion, he overruled the Liberal Unionists in the Cabinet, who, he told the Queen, 'wished for an absolute abandonment of any policy hostile to the demands of Greece'.[15] Instead, he stuck to his original Circular proposals to the Great Powers, which they accepted in late February 1897. Mass meetings against this policy were held in Hyde Park and Trafalgar Square, but entirely failed to move him. The Byron Society met in St James's Hall, and 100 Radical MPs signed a letter of support to King George, but neither affected him one iota. Balfour complained privately that his uncle 'never thinks of Parliament or English opinion: he only thinks of his foreign governments'.

Harcourt challenged the Government to debate its Cretan policy seven times between February and the Easter Recess, aiming to aggravate its internal disagreements. Despite frayed tempers and occasional strong words, Salisbury held to his policy, even persuading the Cabinet in mid-March to blockade Crete to force the Greeks to accept his Circular. Despising what he described to Goschen as 'the caprices of Parliament', Salisbury even called for Piræus to be blockaded and the navy to be so positioned at Volo on the Macedonian frontier as to prevent a Græco-Turkish war.[16] When Goschen refused to extend the blockade to Volo, because he said it had not been sanctioned by the Cabinet, Salisbury said he 'distinctly remembered' mentioning Volo at the meeting, although he admitted that his voice 'might have been low' at the time. All the ministers who were still in London agreed with Goschen's version of events, and Salisbury grumbled that 'the result of this mode of conducting public business will be that for three days or more, at least, the Greeks will be able to send troops and munitions of war to the Macedonian frontier'. To Hatzfeldt he complained of the 'unshakeable' pro-Greek sympathies of his colleagues, mentioning both Goschen and Balfour as opponents of his policy.[17]

Although Harcourt attacked Salisbury for dithering, it was in fact the Cabinet which prevented him from pursuing a more actively anti-Greek line. Long and hard-fought Cabinet meetings culminated in a major clash on Tuesday, 23rd March 1897, when Hicks Beach and Chamberlain came out against coercing Greece into not fighting Turkey, and Devonshire and Lansdowne eventually sided with Salisbury in favour of it. Suffering from influenza, Salisbury called the Cabinet to his library at Arlington Street, where, his health breaking, he finally won agreement to blockade Greece herself, in concert with the other Powers, in order to prevent a Græco-Turkish war breaking out on the Macedonian frontier. Salisbury left for Beaulieu three days later, stopping in Paris for an interview with Gabriel Hanotaux, the French Foreign Minister, who, he told Goschen, 'met every suggestion with a universal optimism which implied that he was not letting me see to the bottom of his sack'.

Lady Salisbury reported to Henry James, now Lord James of Hereford, that the day in Paris had left her husband 'rather knocked up and weak', and that he needed his time in the South of France to recuperate, particularly by watching the Duchess of Devonshire 'amusing herself' losing money at Monte Carlo. With his innate taste for historical parallels, Salisbury likened the problem of 'how to exclude the Turk from all kind of power in the provinces of the Turkish Empire, while strenuously maintaining its independence and integrity', to the way the Long Parliament had needed to maintain perfect loyalty in their language while waging war against King Charles I.[18] Lunching with the Queen at her Cimiez holiday home, Salisbury told her that 'the time was coming when we should have to break away from Germany and Austria, but not quite yet'.

For all his efforts, however, war between Greece and Turkey did break out in April 1897. 'It has been a great game of bluff,' Salisbury told Sanderson, 'but it has failed, and now I think everybody had better go home and agree to say nothing about it.' He did not believe Turkey's attack through Thessaly would be successful, but this proved to be another of his bad predictions, as by mid-May she was occupying Thessaly and Epirus and was almost in a position to threaten a thoroughly panicked Athens. The fourth Greek government since February was soon imploring the Concert of Europe for protection, and the Bulgarians and Serbs quietened down at the sight of the Turkish successes.

'The Greeks are a contemptible race,' was Salisbury's estimation, 'and I have no doubt will turn on the King and blame him for the policy which they themselves, the Greek mobs, forced upon him.' HMS *Nile* was sent to Piraeus to spirit King George away should that happen. Salisbury was equally conscious that Britain could hardly assist Turkey in repressing the Greek Christians on Crete. 'It will take a lot of white-

As Chancellor of Oxford University, by George Richmond, 1870-2

Tsar Nicholas II, with whom
Salisbury hoped to partition
Turkey before dinner at Balmoral

The Chinese Viceroy visits Hatfield
in August 1896
From left to right: three unidentified
Chinamen, Salisbury, 'Pharoah' the
dog, Li Hung Chang, George Curzon,
Francis Bertie

Salisbury with his grandchildren Robert (later the 5th Marquess)
and Beatrice (later Lady Harlech), about 1895

God Save the Queen: Queen Victoria Arriving at St Paul's Cathedral by John Charlton.
Salisbury can be seen in blue on the left of the Queen's third mounted postilion

President Paul Kruger of the
Transvaal, an intractable foe

Sir Alfred Milner in Johannesburg, October 1900. "We have to
act upon a moral field prepared for us by him and his Jingo
supporters", Salisbury complained of his High Commissioner

Cecil Rhodes: "I would annex the planets if I could"

General Sir Redvers Buller, whose
defeats earned him the nickname "Sir
Reverse"

Crowds celebrating the relief of Mafeking on the night of 18th May 1900. Salisbury's son Edward was Baden-Powell's Chief of Staff during the siege

Field-Marshal Lord Roberts: Commander-in-Chief in South Africa

General the Lord Kitchener, victor of Omdurman and Roberts's Chief of Staff and successor in South Africa

Lord Salisbury at Walmer Castle, 1896

wash to justify the spectacle of the Seaforth Highlanders fighting by the side of the Bashi-Bazouk,' he told Lady Randolph Churchill. Instead of allowing a Carthaginian peace to be imposed on Greece, Salisbury let the Porte know that Britain would not be party to any arrangement which put under the Sultan's rule any Christian community not already under it before the war. The Turkish army was prevented from entering Athens and instead Greece was allowed to regain Thessaly and Epirus, paying a large indemnity and accepting an autonomous Crete not unified with Greece. In order to coerce Turkey into yielding Thessaly, which had been Turkish as recently as 1881, Salisbury went so far as to propose to St Petersburg that an Anglo-Russian flotilla should be sent to anchor off Yildiz to bully the Sultan. Three days after this imaginative offer was presented to Russia, the Sultan agreed to the Great Powers' insistence on the suspension of hostilities.

In a speech to the Junior Constitutional Club, Salisbury admitted his lack of sympathy for Greece, 'due, no doubt, to the misuse of my school days'. He did not add that, when the Foreign Office had complained that the proposed new Governor of Crete knew no Greek, he had retorted: 'So much the better. He will hear fewer lies.' He did however virtually say that sympathetic though he was for the Turkish Christians their plight could not be allowed to threaten general European peace. Salisbury had a very limited view of Britain's ability to affect the policy of the other Great Powers, telling Balfour that 'the utmost we have is a slight negative influence by which we prevent them from flying at each other's throats'. He never lost sleep over political crises. Talking to Lady Rayleigh in May 1897, he said that no mental pain, no anxiety, public or private, ever interfered with his sleep, but 'Of course, you could not sleep with a toothache.'[19]

In the decade after 1886, when he had said they needed to 'take a licking' before they could enjoy the blessings of benevolent government, Salisbury's views on the Irish had not perceptibly softened. 'There must be something in the Irish atmosphere that sends people mad,' he wrote of an English judge's decisions in November 1892, and two months later, in a letter of complaint to Halsbury about another judge, he wrote: 'The sight of the shillelagh and the whisky of his youth were too much for Matthew. He gave a wild hurroo and became a Galway boy again.' When Brodrick drew up a memorandum in October 1894 which was intended to limit the demands of the Nationalists through a generous land scheme, Salisbury promptly buried the idea by saying that no one had the authority to speak for the Nationalist Party, and even if they had, no one in it 'could be trusted to adhere to any such arrangement'.

When Salisbury appointed his nephew, Gerald Balfour, Arthur's younger brother, to the Chief Secretaryship for Ireland in early July 1895, he did not realise the extent to which the forty-two-year-old former Cambridge don was committed to a new form of constructive, engaged Unionism. 'I have heard that Gerald Balfour has a very complicated Land Bill on the anvil,' Salisbury wrote to the Viceroy, Lord Cadogan, in early October. 'We must not give too much of our Parliamentary time to Ireland next year.' Gerald Balfour's stance was made apparent in mid-October, when in a speech at Leeds he candidly admitted that 'the Government would, of course, be very glad if they were able by kindness to kill Home Rule'. It was his first major policy speech as Chief Secretary, and it provoked uproar amongst Nationalists. Although he swiftly said that his words had been taken out of context, in the way politicians sometimes do, it was in fact an accurate description of his policy, and the first instalment of his attempt to kill Home Rule by kindness was embodied in his generous 1896 Irish Land Bill.

As well as providing £36 million for land purchases, this comprehensive measure effectively abolished the earlier arrangements whereby prospective tenant buyers were initially forced to pay rents at a higher rate in order to provide security against default. Salisbury disliked the Bill from the start. He complained to Cadogan that it reminded him of the 1887 Act, which had contained 'some very bad provisions – but they were the price of obtaining the votes of the Liberal Unionists, and of the left wing of our party, for the Crimes Act. We have no such costly favour to purchase now: and I trust we shall pay no such price.' Gerald Balfour, supported by his brother and much of the Cabinet, had other ideas, and resolved on a wide-reaching, conciliatory Bill which would increase the number and value of purchase applications and attempt to create a class of peasant proprietors in Ireland with enough of a stake in their property to encourage them to oppose Home Rule.

Salisbury had little time for such schemes, which struck him as Utopian, costly and ultimately doomed. In a speech in late January 1896, he said that Home Rule was 'sleeping the sleep of the unjust' and that Ireland would soon 'forget her Home Rule delusions'. He drew an analogy between the Protestant landlords of Ulster and the oppressed British Uitlanders in South Africa. It was a provocative speech which did not make Gerald Balfour's work any easier – and was probably not intended to. Writing to his son Edward on 24th July 1896, Salisbury described the new Land Act as 'a discreditable bit of work: the less said of it the better'. In the same letter, he complained of Arthur Balfour's support for Gerald, which, because of his earlier success as Chief Secretary, lent the brothers great authority. It was not the elder Balfour's sole misdemeanour:

There is a gruesome story of Conan Doyle's where the hero meets a young lady who is a mesmerist and has the power of making people do what she likes, if they have once submitted to her. As he declines to fall in love with her she punishes him by making him talk nonsense in his lectures, hit his dearest friend between the eyes, rob a bank, and try to throw vitriol on his lady love. Arthur must have met some mesmerist of the kind. He who never made a blunder, for the last six weeks has made nothing else.

When the Irish Finance Commission reported in 1896 that Irish tax rates were proportionately higher than in the rest of the United Kingdom, and deserved a rebate of around £750,000, Salisbury was furious. 'I quite feel for your embarrassment over the Irish Finance Commission,' he wrote to Cadogan in Dublin. 'It is a very ugly and treacherous blow: a Parthian arrow from the defeated Home Rulers. We must undoubtedly face the movement: but face it by resisting it.' He told Cadogan that if Ireland were accorded a special reduction in taxation, it must mean higher taxation for the mainland, which was certain to be unpopular. All Salisbury's contempt for the Irish spilled out at the prospect:

> The Irish peasant, by drinking more than other people, has paid what he considers an excessive contribution to the Exchequer. If a penny was put on the English taxpayer this inconvenience might be remedied. The Irish peasant might get his whisky proportionately cheaper....Do you imagine that such a proposal would bring peace? – that the British taxpayer would be so patient that he would increase his own burden in order that the Irish peasant might get drunk more easily?

It was more the argument of a *Saturday Reviewer* than a Prime Minister.

At the beginning of August 1896, the Liberal MP Sir Charles Hobhouse noted in his diary that Walter Long had told him that Salisbury 'had done what he could to get the Irish Land Bill wrecked in the House of Lords'. Later that month, after Salisbury had refused to speak in the Bill's support and Lord Londonderry had heavily amended it in the Commons, Arthur Balfour told his close friend Lady Elcho: 'It has been a baddish business and I fear some of the blame (to put it mildly) must rest in very high quarters (this is for your ear alone).' Speaking to his sister, Lady Rayleigh, the following July, Balfour did not put it at all mildly and said that their uncle had entirely let Gerald down. He even 'indicated that if this sort of thing were to occur again, they could not go on working together'. Salisbury had effectively sabotaged his own Government's measure, one proposed by his nephew. He did not, however, blame Gerald for the early release of some Fenian 'Dynamitards' in October 1896, which he put down to 'a demon called "Home Office routine"'.[20]

In March 1897, a deputation from the Irish Landowners' Convention visited Salisbury to demand a Royal Commission on the workings of the Irish Land Commission, which they believed was biased against them. He said that they should reveal the unfairness of the land courts in 'a blaze of publicity', adding that 'unless an injured class cries out and shows fight, it immediately goes to the wall'. Identifying entirely with the landlords, Salisbury overruled the Balfours and agreed to a Commission, and then proceeded to distance himself from his nephew's local government proposals as well. The Irish Government was left in the hapless position of attempting to defend the independence of its Land Courts in the face of the active hostility of the Prime Minister. When Sir Edward Fry's Royal Commission corroborated the Irish Landowners' Convention case against the Land Courts in January 1899, Salisbury took the side of their leader, Abercorn (who farmed 76,500 Irish acres), against Cadogan and Balfour. It took all of Ashbourne's tact to stop Cadogan resigning.

One Irish scheme that Salisbury did approve was the idea, after the Duke of York's successful visit there in August 1897, of a permanent Royal residence in Ireland. As he told Cadogan: 'I cannot help wishing that we might compass an Irish Sandringham. I do not expect any magical results from it: but it would remove the appearance of a Royal Boycott which Ireland now presents and I think the presence of the Duke of York occasionally, in the character of an Irish country gentleman, would have a favourable effect on the public opinion, and the conduct, both of landlords and tenants.' Salisbury managed to squeeze £200,000 out of Hicks Beach for the idea, which he insisted should be a proper residence: 'A Royal Hotel would be no good at all – besides lending itself slightly to ridicule.' Salisbury told Cadogan that he could consult the Yorks themselves before submitting the proposal to the Queen and the Prince of Wales, on the grounds that: 'I once knew a young lady who received many proposals: but she always made a rule of declining even to discuss one if the lover had consulted the parents first.' It soon became clear, however, that none of the Royal Family liked the idea, much to Cadogan's dismay, who thought it 'a great disappointment to the loyal men in Ireland'.[21]

In February 1898, Gerald Balfour presented the Irish Local Government Bill, designed to create county and district councils throughout Ireland, which were to be democratically elected triennially. These were to have fiscal and other powers, and Nationalists understandably saw them as a major step on the way towards Home Rule. Irish Unionists put up with it because the Irish Government linked relief from taxation with local government reforms, although they had severe doubts about the result of extending democratic self-determination to Ireland at the local level. Salisbury shared their misgivings in full, believing the proposals – which were being forced upon him by the Liberal Unionists and his own left wing – to be potentially disastrous for the Union.

Sure enough, in the first elections in March 1899, the Nationalists won 551 county seats, against 125 Unionists (86 of whom were in Ulster). Salisbury's view was further corroborated later that year when Nationalist-dominated councils proceeded to fly the Irish tricolour, declare for Home Rule and pass resolutions in support of the Boers. Gerald Balfour ended the longest Chief Secretaryship since the 1840s full of bitterness at the lack of support his uncle had shown him. 'The so-called Prime Minister disliked Irish affairs and understood nothing of them,' he complained to his sister Lady Rayleigh, and although their uncle had agreed the outlines of his policy before his inaugural speech at Leeds, he afterwards 'would give no help in carrying it through'. The depth of Salisbury's cynicism about the Emerald Isle can be deduced from his remark to Violet Cecil of March 1903, when after his retirement he was told yet another Irish Land Bill was in the offing: 'Why should we pay a huge sum to pacify Ireland? What is the use of a pacified Ireland to us?'[22]

In early March 1896, the Cabinet had to decide on the tricky question of Kruger visiting London to negotiate over the Uitlanders. The Transvaal President wanted assurances from Chamberlain before he came, which the Cabinet could not give. They answered his offers by making it clear that under no circumstances would Article IV of the 1884 Convention, which prevented the Transvaal from making treaties with outside powers without British consent, be reconsidered. Furthermore, they made it clear that the Uitlander franchise would be urged upon Kruger if he turned up. Gold had been found in the Witwatersrand back in 1886, meaning that many Uitlanders had been resident for ten years. The new proposal to restrict the Volksraad franchise only to citizens of fourteen years' residence – a piece of blatant gerrymandering – was clearly going to lead to trouble in the future.[23] Since the backdown over the Vaal River drifts, the British Government believed that only by standing up to Kruger could anything be obtained from him.

Neither Salisbury nor Chamberlain intended to allow the Jameson embarrassment to tie their hands when it came to future rigorous dealing with the Transvaal. In an almost calculated rebuff to Kruger in July 1896, Chamberlain recommended that the Governor of Cape Colony and High Commissioner of South Africa Sir Hercules Robinson, who had been talking of retiring because of an attack of the dropsy, be granted a peerage. A month later, after Robinson was made Baron

Rosmead, the dropsy suddenly disappeared and he blithely announced his intention of carrying on. Salisbury, who had informed the Queen that Robinson's fortune was 'adequate' to the honour, likened his medical condition to that of Pope Sixtus V, who feigned feebleness at the 1585 Conclave to win the votes of the older cardinals who hoped to succeed him, and promptly regained his vigour once elected.

September 1896 saw the Volksraad pass laws banning any publications 'in conflict with public morals or dangerous to the order and peace of the Republic'. Three months later, this was deemed to include the English-language Johannesburg weekly paper *The Critic*, whose editor appealed directly to Chamberlain, but the following March the daily paper the *Star* was also suppressed. On 12th December, Chamberlain vigorously protested against the Transvaal's new immigration law, which required that visas needed to be periodically renewed, thus allowing the Transvaal to refuse entry to British subjects. Salisbury believed this contravened Article XIV(a) of the 1884 Convention, and he was supported by the Crown law officers in his contention. Not surprisingly, Kruger's own legal experts disagreed.

The underlying fear which led to increasingly serious clashes with the Transvaal over the next three years was neatly summed up in a letter Selborne wrote to Chamberlain in October 1896. Pessimistic that Rhodes's drive to the north, which had so far unearthed few significant mineral deposits, could redress the geopolitical balance against the Boer republic, especially after the revolts of the Ndebele and Shona tribes, Selborne predicted that 'In a generation the South African Republic [i.e. Transvaal] will by its wealth and population dominate Southern Africa. South African politics must revolve around the Transvaal, which will be the only possible market for the agricultural produce or the manufacturers of Cape Colony and Natal.' To prevent this and to invigorate the two British colonies, Chamberlain suggested that Rosmead should be replaced by Alfred Milner, then Chairman of the Board of the Inland Revenue. Salisbury had originally wanted Sir Harry Johnston as British Governor of Cape Colony and High Commissioner for South Africa, whom he thought 'an absurd little man to look at but he is a born governor of men'. Milner was eventually chosen in January 1897, partly because Johnston, in Salisbury's estimation, was 'very far from being a constitutional ruler'. In fact, it turned out to be the autocratic Milner who was the archetypal 'prodigal son' of Empire.

Milner was reared partly in Germany (he was one-quarter German) and educated at Tübingen, King's College, London, and Balliol, taking a first and winning the Hertford, Craven, Eldon and Derby scholarships and becoming President of the Oxford Union. He was then successively a fellow of New College, an Inner Temple barrister, assistant editor of the *Pall Mall Gazette*, private secretary to Goschen, a founder of the

Liberal Unionist Association, Under-Secretary for Finance in Egypt and then Chairman of the Inland Revenue in 1892, aged only thirty-eight. A fanatical imperialist of unbending will, his analysis of the South African situation closely approximated to Selborne's, that time was no longer on the side of the British Empire. The Boers had only settled the Transvaal after their treks in the 1830s, but already British policy-makers could see the threat they posed in a region where they wanted unchallenged paramountcy for the Crown.

Article IV of the 1884 London Convention had specifically stated that the Transvaal 'will conclude no Treaty or engagement with any state or nation other than the Orange Free State, nor with any native tribe to the eastward or westward of the Republic, until the same has been approved by H.M.G.' Nevertheless, Kruger had signed extradition treaties with Portugal in 1893 and Holland in 1895, which he had deliberately failed to submit to Britain for approval. As Chamberlain fumed against the Volksraad's blatantly anti-British Banishment of Aliens Act and Prevention of Immigration of Aliens Act, the Transvaal was buying arms from Germany in bulk and smuggling them through Portuguese-owned Delagoa Bay on the Mozambique coast. In early April 1897, Chamberlain warned Salisbury that the Transvaal had 'a stock of artillery, rifles and ammunition of all sorts enough to furnish a European army'. With only one battery at the Cape, and reinforcements taking between six and eight weeks to arrive, the War Office informed the Cabinet that it could not guarantee the defence of Cape Colony or Natal, which were consequently 'at the mercy of the Boers'.

Although Salisbury was perfectly content for fresh forces to be sent, and for £200,000 from the Budget to be earmarked for transporting them, he told Chamberlain from La Bastide on 16th April 1897 that it would be better politically if they went to defensive positions in Natal such as Laing's Nek, because no one could find fault with them for 'defending such an important point in the face of Kruger's excessive armaments'. At this stage, however, he was not contemplating actual hostilities, and told Chamberlain bluntly that he would look 'with something like dismay to a Transvaal war'.

Salisbury's reasons were, as ever, to be found in the European rather than the African balance of power. In a long letter to Sanderson on 21st April, he went into some detail about why, despite a willingness to engage in brinkmanship with Kruger, he did not favour war. The seventeen-year-old Queen Wilhelmina of Holland was likely to marry soon, and if it was to someone under the Kaiser's influence a Dutch–German *Kriegsverein* might enable him to enlist Dutch sailors into his growing navy. 'His great ambition is to have a fleet: but until he gets a maritime population he cannot have a fleet,' wrote Salisbury, who thought the Germans were not natural sailors. Any adventurous policy against the

Boers in the Transvaal would turn French, German and Dutch as well as the rest of European opinion against Britain.[24] Nonetheless, Milner, whom Salisbury had had to stay at Hatfield four years earlier and whose intellect he admired, went out to South Africa, and at his very first meeting with the Cape statesman John X. Merriman he made clear his intention to engineer a clash with the Transvaal.

THIRTY-NINE

Apogee of Empire

The Diamond Jubilee – Jingoism
– Honours – Bishop-Making
– The Munshi

June 1897

'No more tobacconists I entreat you.'

With massacres in Turkey, skirmishes in the Sudan, Venezuelan disputes with America, Cretan disturbances, Russian expansionism in China, and a looming confrontation in southern Africa which might involve Germany, all was not quiet on the international scene by June 1897. Nevertheless, the British Empire had far more to celebrate than to bemoan, and that month's sixtieth anniversary of Queen Victoria's accession gave it the ideal opportunity for the greatest outpouring of national celebration in British peacetime history.

Salisbury was unbeguiled by pomp and circumstance, taking a predictably utilitarian view of all ceremonial occasions which depended upon romance and a touch of whimsy. As a journalist he had delighted in those 'ludicrous inconsistencies' that were sure 'to spoil any bit of pageantry we attempt in England'. There was a touch of impish pleasure when he described how 'some malignant spell broods over our most solemn ceremonials and inserts into them some feature which makes them all ridiculous'. But, for all his mockery, Salisbury fully appreciated the significance of ceremonial. 'In spite of the march of intellect,' he wrote in mock-lament in the *Saturday Review* in 1863, discussing the Prince of Wales's forthcoming wedding, 'the philosopher must confess with regret that the people, both high and low, are still passionately fond of shows.' When the ceremony was held in Windsor due to the Queen's mourning, he complained that a royal marriage was the Londoner's 'one chance of seeing a great royal show, and to deprive him of it is stripping the naked'. Salisbury was fully alive to what he called 'the political importance of conciliating popular feeling on an occasion of national rejoicing such as this'.

When it came to his own chance to stage-manage a great occasion of national rejoicing, Salisbury was not about to pass up the opportunity of milking it for all its political and imperial symbolism. In a *Saturday Review* article in 1861, he had emphasised how much of the Stuarts' initial popularity had been dissipated because 'not a single pulse in their characters beat in unison with the feelings of the nation', whereas despite being just as arbitrary, despotic and religiously inflexible, Elizabeth I was loved because she never failed to identify herself with the nation. What worked for Good Queen Bess could be made to work for Queen Victoria. Salisbury had been present at the State Opening of Parliament in 1854 when there had been 'a plentiful sprinkling' of hissing from the crowd, but by 1897 she was at the height of her popularity. The Diamond Jubilee would be the opportunity for Crown, Empire and People (and the Unionist Party) to be seen to fuse together in an extravaganza of patriotism and imperial pride.

The sixtieth anniversary of the Queen's accession was marked across the Empire by a vast number of street parties, balls, receptions, speeches, statue unveilings, military parades, bonfires, illuminations and church services. They culminated in a great procession through London and a huge open-air church service outside St Paul's Cathedral, the nature of which had been the result of a good deal of negotiation due to the Queen's lumbago. The previous November, Salisbury had thought it possible for the Queen, who found long walks difficult, to be driven in a carriage up the steps of St Paul's Cathedral to hear the *Te Deum* inside. 'This is a grand idea,' agreed Bigge, 'but what would the parsons say?' The Cathedral clergy did not mind, but the idea was dropped from worries about whether the horses could turn the carriage around once inside.

Having established that her lumbago would keep the Queen in her carriage, McDonnell came up with the idea of uncoupling it from the horses outside and having her pulled up the steps by naval ratings instead. 'It would be a magnificent spectacle and would afford the Queen the minimum of discomfort,' he wrote. But the Queen said that nothing would induce her to try it, and by late November it was agreed that the *Te Deum* would be heard at the foot of the West steps.[1] The question then arose of what to do with the large statue of Queen Anne directly in front of the Cathedral, which would block the view down Fleet Street as the Queen's carriage arrived. Proposals that it could be temporarily moved were also dismissed by the Queen, on the grounds that 'it might some day be suggested that <u>my</u> statue should be moved, which I would much dislike!'

Taking the Golden Jubilee of 1887 as its template – except that this time the Government would pick up the whole bill – the subject was hardly brought up at all in Cabinet, except to agree on legislation closing the metropolitan police courts for the day. In one central aspect, however, there was to be a major change from the Golden Jubilee, which had been essentially a family event, bringing to Britain several crowned heads of Europe. Salisbury and the Queen together determined that the Diamond Jubilee of 1897 would be a specifically imperial, rather than purely national or dynastic occasion. They wished the Empire to be the central theme, presented as the greatest achievement of the long reign. The units which marched and rode in the procession – such as the Canadian Hussars, Trinidad Light Horse and Cape Mounted Rifles – were specially chosen to emphasise this. The Kaiser's telegram to Kruger had made this decision easier to take.

So in mid-December 1896 Salisbury informed the Austrian and German Ambassadors that no other monarchs would be invited. Even the King of Siam, who had already announced his intention to attend, was politely turned away. It was instead to be the colonial Prime Ministers who would be lionised, with places in the procession for some and special seats outside St Paul's for others. Wilfred Laurier of Canada was knighted on the morning of the procession. Indian princes were also encouraged to attend, and they outdid each other in their splendour. Salisbury was amused by the way that Hicks Beach and Harcourt 'weep over their crowned heads', but instead of a parade of royalties he thought that 'a great naval review would be a most fitting mode of celebration'.[2]

'Politics seem peaceful in Arlington Street which I am thankful to say,' Lady Salisbury wrote to Frances Balfour in mid-February 1897, 'and I hope that...we shall be able to give our undivided attention to the many extraordinary ways of celebrating the Queen's long reign, each one of which seems foolisher than another.' When the Mayor of Coventry wanted to present the Queen with a bicycle, a curious choice of gift for a seventy-eight-year-old Queen-Empress with lumbago, Salisbury worried about her accepting 'mere advertisements from pushing tradesmen of various kinds', let alone from people who were 'on the hunt for knighthoods'. One such, Thomas Lipton the tea magnate, who donated no less than £25,000 to the Princess of Wales's project to give London's poor a banquet, duly received his knighthood the following year.

The 'hunt' was definitely on, and Salisbury was fortunate to have a second Jubilee list to exploit. Although personally disgusted by what he called the 'rage for distinctions', he fully appreciated their value. Salisbury warned Devonshire how jealously the Palace watched their doling out of honours to political supporters and tried to keep the new baronetcies down to 1887 proportions. The Queen did not want the artist George Watts to be made a privy councillor on the grounds that 'he makes pictures on order for private customers', but Salisbury thought that he could not think of a better way in which 'a proper tribute to Art could be more innocuously paid'.[3] Watts, who had twice refused a baronetcy, eventually received the newly founded Order of Merit in 1902 instead.

Salisbury thought Devonshire's peerage suggestions 'a rum lot' and likely to excite 'the jealousies down there' (meaning the House of Commons), but he accommodated them as best he could. Occasionally he jibbed; 'Please let your baronet or baronets be as presentable as possible,' he asked Devonshire after Frederick Wills, the rich Liberal Unionist MP for Bristol North and director of Imperial Tobacco, received one. 'No more tobacconists I entreat you.' The idea of a special Jubilee medal to be struck for mayors, provosts and municipal worthies was, as Salisbury told the Queen, promoted in the hope that 'it would tend to console them' for the lack of other honours available. Although Arthur Balfour found them dull, and thought conversing with them 'just like talking to constituents', all eleven colonial Prime Ministers were appointed privy councillors. Good news even came from South Africa, where Kruger magnanimously released the last two Jameson Raiders held at Pretoria, Messrs Woolls-Sampson and Davies, who had refused to petition for their liberty but were given it anyhow as a gesture of goodwill.[4]

On Monday, 21st June, the day before the procession, Salisbury moved a Humble Address in Parliament, congratulated the Queen and came as close as he ever did to acknowledging that the democratic revolution had at least been peaceful. He described the Queen's reign as:

> a period of great political change. The impulse of democracy, which began in another century in other lands, has made itself fully felt in our time, and vast changes in the centre of power and incidence of responsibility have been made almost imperceptibly without any disturbance or hindrance in the progress of the prosperous development of the nation.

He went on, to loud cheers, to speak of 'a grateful and adoring people', and the debt they owed 'to the moderation, the self-controlling influence of the Queen, from whom, legally, all power flows'.

Although crowned heads were not invited, princes and grand dukes and other royalties flooded in from Prussia, Naples, Russia, Hesse, Austria, Saxony, Württemberg, Luxembourg and Bavaria, and Salisbury met them on the evening of the 21st at a State Banquet at Buckingham Palace. The *Illustrated London News* showed him properly attired in privy councillor uniform, complete with cocked hat, buckled shoes and breeches, being presented to the Queen. Only a few months earlier, however, he had turned up at the Palace wearing the trousers of an Elder

Brother of Trinity House, an admiral's sword and a 'hiatus between vest and trousers'. When questioned by his family, Salisbury admitted the wrong trousers, said that he had found the sword at Walmer, denied the hiatus, and said that the Prince of Wales could not have noticed as he 'had carefully hidden behind the Lord Chancellor'. On another occasion, at the opening of the Law Courts in the Strand, a Frenchman asked what uniform Salisbury was wearing. When told it was that of 'le frère aîné de la Trinité', he exclaimed: 'Mon dieu! Quelle distinction!'[5]

On Tuesday, 22nd June, Salisbury wore Full Dress uniform, Royal Household pattern, something the Duke of Wellington also wore on grand occasions, complete with the blue riband, garter and star of the Order of the Garter. He and his wife took their seats on the bottom step in front of St Paul's Cathedral, eight people in from the right, to watch the procession, cocked hat tucked under his left arm. The members of the Cabinet who sat behind him wore the privy councillor's uniform, which years earlier he had described as 'Something between the dresses of a postilion and a buffoon.'

When his family left Arlington Street at half past nine that morning, soon after the band of the 1st Battalion of the Border Regiment had struck up outside, his blue brougham had been 'at once recognised and met with a very hearty reception'. It was as nothing compared with the tumultuous applause enjoyed by the Queen after she left Buckingham Palace at a quarter past eleven, having pressed a button which sent a telegraph message to the Empire: 'From my heart I thank my beloved people. May God bless them.'

Salisbury was proud of London and what he called its rambling, 'prosaic chaos', arguing that although Baron Haussmann's Paris was more magnificent, its architecture was the product of autocracy rather than of ancient liberties. As the procession wound its way along the festooned six-mile route, the Rhodesian Horse were 'applauded vociferously' because of the Jameson Raid, and the poor Cypriots were mistaken for Turks because of their fezes and hissed for the Armenian massacres. The Papal Nuncio shared a carriage with the Emperor of China's representative, who carried a fan and excited some ribald comments from the crowd. A large phalanx of princes rode behind the Queen's carriage. Their wives, travelling in their own carriages behind, gloried in names as exotic as their husbands' uniforms. The eleventh carriage of the procession, for example, contained the Hereditary Princess of Saxe-Meiningen, the Princess Frederick Charles of Hesse, the Princess Adolph of Schaumburg-Lippe and the Hereditary Princess of Hohenlohe-Langenburg.

Gladstone did not attend what the St James' Gazette unkindly described as 'the celebration of everything which he has so long striven to destroy'. His fifth child, Mary, watched the trotting troops from a window in Piccadilly and evinced a suitably Gladstonian moral from the spectacle, that it 'made one hold one's breath to think of the responsibilities they implied'. Meanwhile, the nonconformist press and *Daily News* complained that only Rosebery and Harcourt had been invited to St Paul's, and not the whole ex-Cabinet. Yet it was neither responsibilities nor reproaches that occupied the crowds that day, only wild celebrations. The Jubilee has since been interpreted by historians as, in the words of one, 'the response of an insecure and uncertain people'. If so, such feelings must have been very deeply sublimated, because at the time only mass celebration, happiness and enormous pride were evident from the public response.

Two thousand five hundred beacons were lit between Caithness and Land's End. Every town and major village held parties. Manchester voted £10,000 for decorations and gave a breakfast party for 100,000 children. Every tenth prisoner in Hyderabad was freed. A special 10oz galosh with 4½" heels was invented to help short people watch the processions. The Civil Service lining Constitution Hill, the Balaclava veterans in Ludgate, women who 'became inarticulate and hysterical in their excitement', the peers who sat in stands in front of the National Gallery, the millions lining the route and waving from every window, all celebrated in the shining sun the existence of an Empire on which they were assured (though never by Salisbury) that it would never set.

The sun was too much for some; although the sailors in their broad-brimmed straw hats managed to pull their naval guns the whole distance, some of the colonial infantry fell by the wayside. Earl Howe fell off his horse when the procession got south of the river, which Salisbury later agreed with the Queen 'was not an adequate reason for giving him the ribbon of the [newly founded Royal] Victorian Order'. Salisbury refused the Order on the grounds that having carefully avoided recommending any Cabinet colleagues for honours, to accept one for himself would put him 'in an entirely false position'.

'From what point did you see the procession?' the Queen asked the Bishop of Winchester afterwards, then she recollected that he had been on the steps of St Paul's with the clergy. 'I was unfortunate,' she said. 'I had a very bad place and saw nothing.' Sir Arthur Sullivan rejected Alfred Austin's first attempt at a Jubilee hymn as unworthy of his music. The second was hardly any better, including the line: "'Tis thou hast dower'd our queenly Throne with sixty years of blessing', so the Bishop of Wakefield wrote one instead. On 24th June, the Princess of Wales hosted a banquet for 400,000 of London's deserving poor at which 700 tons of food was consumed.

The same day, the Prince of Wales sailed past twenty-one battleships, fifty-three cruisers, thirty destroyers and twenty-four torpedo boats – twenty-five miles of beflagged, floating confidence. No better advertisement could possibly have been devised to show how Salisbury's Two-Power Standard ensured that Britannia ruled the waves. Goschen was understandably proud of the fact that, entirely without drawing on ships from the Pacific, Mediterranean, North American or any other but the Home Squadron, 128 vessels could be presented at the Spithead Naval Review, manned by 56,000 sailors.

The Jubilee was denounced by the Left, both at the time and since, as a tasteless confidence trick on the British people. Keir Hardie, the first Labour MP, wrote that 'the soldiers are there because they are paid for coming, and nine out of every ten of them will heartily curse the whole affair as a disagreeable and irksome additional duty'. According to this pitiless analysis, the statesmen only attended 'because Empire means trade, and trade means profit, and profit means power over the common people'. Yet, watching the film footage of the spectacular cavalcade and its delirious spectators, one is struck even a century later by the grandeur of the event. The actual sight of the individuals on the film reels, with their bowlers and boaters, their stiff collars, slicked hair and waving handkerchiefs, shows only the happy response of a populace bursting with legitimate pride at the longevity of their Queen and the breadth of her Empire.

Even the tophatted boy in an Eton collar who in the newsreel is nonchalantly leaning by an open French window on the corner of St James's Street and Piccadilly reading a newspaper, stops and takes notice when the royalties go past. The grand lady in her white dress next door curtseys to the Queen-Empress's carriage. Queen Victoria never visited her Empire, so it had come to her. The last word can go to Salisbury's son Robert, who half a century later looked back on the Diamond Jubilee as 'the climax of the Victorian age. England had never been so powerful.... Her fleet was unconquerable and, since there was then no danger from the air, naval supremacy appeared to guarantee the safety of all her Dominions.'[6]

Those whom the gods have chosen for Nemesis they first make hubristic, and Salisbury was acutely conscious of the threat of Jingoism. At the height of all this boisterous but sincere self-congratulation, indeed begun on the very day of the procession itself, was written a poem by none other than the Empire's first poet, Rudyard Kipling, which sounded a severe note of restraint. Appearing in *The Times* on 17th July and entitled *Recessional* – itself a title which confounded Jingoistic expectations – it spoke of a post-Jubilee period when: 'The tumult and the shouting dies: The Captains and the Kings depart.' The third stanza struck many as almost fatalistic:

> Far-called, our navies melt away;
> On dune and headland sinks the fire:
> Lo, all our pomp of yesterday
> Is one with Nineveh and Tyre!
> Judge of the Nations, spare us yet,
> Lest we forget – lest we forget!

The Times' editorial accompanying the poem emphasised how 'the most dangerous and demoralising temper into which a state can fall is one of boastful pride', a sentiment with which Salisbury fully concurred. Within a few months he had identified the Jingoism which the two Jubilees, especially the last, had unleashed, as a serious political problem. He saw the strident support for the expansion of the Empire, 'wider still yet wider' in Arthur Benson's later phrase, regardless of any other diplomatic or strategic considerations, as noble Imperialism's bastard brother, and the bane of his foreign policy. Imperial chauvinism, my empire right or wrong, struck him as a form of insanity, and he used to complain to his officials during Jingoistic outbreaks that it was like having 'a huge lunatic asylum at one's back'. Sceptical, pragmatic and anti-determinist, Salisbury had absolutely no sense of Britain possessing any kind of Manifest Destiny such as Americans were then claiming for the United States. 'I am an utter unbeliever that anything that is violent will have permanent results,' he would regularly aver.

'They are very patriotic men and the warmth of their patriotism sometimes clouds their appreciation of details; but they exist in all countries,' Salisbury had said in his 'Wrong Horse' speech. 'Now, my belief is that a well working arbitration system would be an invaluable bulwark to defend the Minister from the Jingoes.' The following month, talking privately to Lady Rayleigh, he said that the 'English were liable to fancies', whether it be fear of the Russians in Afghanistan or the trade of Hong Kong threatened by Russia in northern China. 'Of course, if we assumed we had a right to the whole world not already subject to European races, there <u>was</u> a cause for alarm!'[7]

Yet this, or something very like it, was the subliminal message many took away from the Diamond Jubilee, which in that sense operated as something of a Pandora's Box for Salisbury. For all his criticisms of the messianic, Jingoistic view of Empire, which his private secretary thought was 'most distasteful to him', Salisbury also believed, as he told the House of Lords the following November, that 'to keep our trade, our industries alive we must open new sources of consumption in the more untrodden portions of the earth'. One of Salisbury's many contradictions was that, whilst despising the Jingoes, he pursued an agenda that they admired, and won the support of clerkdom and villa Toryism for articulating their ultra-patriotic views, while he continued to mock what he called 'Jingo-fever'.[8]

Chamberlain amused Frances Balfour at dinner 'by complaining how Uncle Robert would tell him his colonies were useless possessions, and when Joe comes to him with some scheme of development he would crush it, "especially", said Joe, "if he thinks it annoys"'. A speech Salisbury delivered to the Constitutional Club in mid-December 1898 shows how conscious he was of the danger of imperial over-extension, a phenomenon that was indeed to pose a serious threat to the Empire when Chamberlain's son was Prime Minister four decades later:

> The more our Empire extends, the more our imperial spirit grows, the more we must urge on all who have to judge that those things are matters of business and must be considered upon business principles. The dangerous temptation of the hour is that we should consider rhapsody an adequate compensation for calculation.

Salisbury blamed Gladstone for having 'awakened the slumbering genius' of Jingoism when he promoted Irish Home Rule, but whoever was responsible, and Beaconsfield and Salisbury must themselves be prime contenders with their 1878–80 'Forward' policy, by 1900 Jingoism was well entrenched politically, not least in the Victorian League, British Empire League, Imperial Federation League, Imperial South African League, Navy League, National Service League, China Association and League of the Empire. Salisbury viewed these overwhelmingly pro-Unionist organisations as a distinctly mixed blessing, and stopped Edward VII becoming the Patron of the Navy League on the grounds that he could not constitutionally belong to any organisation whose object was to compel his own Government to follow a certain course of political conduct.

In June 1900, Salisbury wrote to Archbishop Temple asking the Primate to cut four lines from an archiepiscopal letter which referred to Salisbury speaking of 'constantly expanding territories'. He argued that with Africa 'now all "pegged out"', the expansion of the Queen's dominions there could only be at the expense of another Power. 'I think the Church's language must be less jingo,' he implored, despite it only having been a *précis* of his own speech that the Primate had wanted to circulate.

Jingoistic newspapers, he complained, did infinite harm to Britain's relations with Germany and Russia, and he particularly blamed them for making the Venezuelan crisis more dangerous than it otherwise might have been. Papers such as the *Daily Mail*, which apropos of the Sudanese campaign had opined in February 1896 that 'a little blood letting is good for a nation that tends to excess of luxury', played on fears of unemployment through foreign protectionism, and took a super-patriotic line which Salisbury complained made his foreign policy harder to pursue. By 1901, the circulation of the *Daily Mail* reached one million, and Salisbury quipped that Alfred Harmsworth had 'invented a paper for those who could read but not think and then another [the *Daily Mirror*] for those who could see photographs but not read'. He worried whether the press's special correspondents, rather than the Foreign Office, were taking over the reins of diplomacy, with the result that there was 'a raw state of irritation' between the governing classes of countries, which tended to make 'any advances on the part of either Government impracticable'.[9] There was an element of ingratitude in this stance, as the Harmsworth papers were staunch supporters of Unionism in general and Salisbury in particular.

Salisbury did not sell honours, but neither did he go out of his way to disabuse rich men of the notion that they could be bought. A large contribution to the Conservative Party's fighting fund, or the nursing and contesting of an expensive seat in a general election campaign, were certainly not allowed to weigh against the prospects of an honours-hunter. The 'rage for distinctions' disgusted him, and it confirmed him in his low estimation of human nature, but he used it as a political tool like every other Prime Minister, and far less venally than most. When in December 1888 it was proposed that Sir Hercules Robinson, the Governor of Cape Colony since 1880, be given a peerage to stop him resigning to take up various lucrative directorships, Salisbury wrote to Knutsford: 'Quite impossible to make such a bargain. We had better hang up a tariff of prices at the Herald's College – as they do in the bedrooms of an hotel.'

'Directly man has satisfied his most elementary material wants,' Salisbury had written in the *Saturday Review* in 1864, 'the first aspiration of his amiable heart is for the privilege of being able to look down upon his neighbours.' In his early career he was predictably censorious about the use Lord John Russell made of the honours system, and the way that lord-lieutenancies, baronetcies and other honours were directed towards those who won costly county seats for the Liberal Party. 'What is bribery if these appointments are not?' he asked of the Prime Minister. 'As sole stopcock of the fountain of honour, he appears to believe that he is at liberty to direct its grateful stream into whatever channel will produce most return to himself.' Despite occasional qualms about the applicants' social, financial or moral suitability, Salisbury nevertheless acted in much the same way once he himself became the 'sole stopcock'.

Fighting elections was getting progressively more expensive, and after the 1883 Corrupt Practices Act forced a cut in local expenditure, political parties needed larger funds held centrally for campaigning. The

Conservatives' general election fund for 1880 raised between £30,000 and £50,000, the 1895 election required over £60,000 and by 1906 somewhere between £80,000 and £120,000 was being spent by the Party. This effectively meant that industrialists needed to be honoured and that more honours had to be doled out than in previous years. Salisbury was nonetheless very careful about not devaluing the currency, and not weakening the prestige of his Order by sub-standard entrants into the House of Lords.

In November 1885, a surprised Carnarvon complained to Harrowby that 'Salisbury is so extremely chary of giving away honours that I know it is vain to ask for any' for his clients and supporters. Carnarvon found this 'a very odd mental phenomenon in a man who I should have thought would not have cared a pin's head about such matters'. In fact, Salisbury well understood the way the honours system reflected social change, and cared deeply about it, whilst all the time adopting a bantering tone on the subject in his correspondence with colleagues. In September 1885, he even employed his only recorded pun, when he told Randolph Churchill in answer to a request for a CB for the Commander-in-Chief of Bombay: 'Unluckily "Baths' are running dry just at present: and unless the cholera will help us, I do not know what we are to do.'

The applications made to Salisbury, via the Whips or through Schomberg McDonnell, were often blush-makingly blatant. 'You may think it advisable to recommend HM to be graciously pleased to confer a peerage upon me,' suggested Sir H.M. Havelock Allan. 'It would be very pleasant to me to be made a baronet,' remarked Sir John Aird MP. 'It would be of assistance to me in this severe fight if I could receive some recognition of my service in Parliament during the last 12 years in the shape of an hereditary honour,' wrote Claud Alexander, who enclosed his *curriculum vitæ* to remind Salisbury that he had twice been President of the Hull Chamber of Commerce.[10] When in August 1885 Robert Richardson-Gardener, MP for Windsor since 1866, wrote to Salisbury to complain that his constituency 'has cost me a small fortune and that I have never received the slightest help or favour from the party', he found that he received none from Salisbury either, because in 1868 he had ejected those of his tenants who had failed to vote for him. 'By recent experience I am convinced that my "work" is refusing baronetcies,' Salisbury told Janetta Manners the following February, 'at least I have been doing little else the last three months – so I feel blessed and shall seek no other blessedness.'

In May 1886, describing William Pitt the Younger's methods of bringing about the Act of Union, he tongue-in-cheek told the Grocers' Company: 'We are often told that he carried the Union by bribery. Well, I believe he did give a certain number of honours and titles to people who supported him. Of course in these days, you know we are so pure, no such things are ever done.' Yet if they were not done by him they certainly were by Northcote, who via the former minister David Plunket verbally offered Sir Edward Guinness a baronetcy if he would stand for the City of Dublin in the 1885 general election, a promise Salisbury was later called upon to redeem.

In his short 'Caretaker' ministry, Salisbury doled out, as Gladstone afterwards ascertained from the Garter King of Arms, no fewer than thirteen peerages, seventeen baronetcies, twenty-three privy councillorships and twenty knighthoods, not a bad haul for the Party faithful in only six months. Yet as he told his brother Eustace, the only thing wrong with Cardinal Richelieu's dictum that patronage made one ingrate and twenty malcontents, was that 'perhaps the last figure is too small'. He lamented to Stanhope in May 1891: 'If it were only possible to decorate people in secret – it would be so much easier.' The archive at Hatfield is full of the laments of disappointed would-be baronets complaining of their ill-treatment at Salisbury's hands.

The Liberal Unionist alliance imposed a huge new burden on Salisbury, who appreciated the need to reward his new allies, at least until they would condescend to accept office. He likened himself to the publisher Spenlow in *David Copperfield*, protesting that in the Liberal Unionists he was 'tied to a remorseless Jawkins as a partner', who sucked honours from him that he would have otherwise liked to have awarded to Tories. He also often pointed out to colleagues the 'grumbles' of the Queen and Ponsonby at the inflated size of the lists. Occasionally Salisbury would baulk, as in May 1887 when Hartington wanted to honour a man named Dunbar who was seventy-four and whose son was a keen Gladstonian who had fought against the Unionists at the previous election. 'I should mind less if he had not done so in Scotland (Dumfries),' Salisbury told Hartington, 'but the Scotch Conservatives are an exacting and cross grained case – and I am afraid I should have a mutiny.'[11]

The importunities of mayors and local dignitaries were a particular bugbear, especially during jubilees, with Salisbury never attaching much weight to the argument they tended to proffer, that in honouring them the Government was thereby honouring their locality, thinking it 'somewhat circuitous' reasoning. 'I have refused swarms of Jubilee Mayors on the grounds that the list was closed and could not be reopened,' he told Balfour, who wanted a knighthood for the Mayor of his Manchester constituency in November 1887, 'and I am afraid, if I reopen it now, I shall have the whole pack at my heels again.' Because Balfour emphasised that 'it would be a good move politically; and I am sure it will make an enormous difference to my personal comfort!!', an exception was nonetheless made.

By 1898, Salisbury was perfectly willing to grant the Lord Mayor of

London a baronetcy 'on party grounds', but he did not want to set the precedent of Lord Mayors always receiving baronetcies merely for doing their job. 'Mayors are very numerous and very ambitious,' he told his son-in-law Selborne, who wanted a knighthood for Winchester's worthy in 1901, 'and it is difficult to define the kind of merit which should gratify their aspirations.... Municipal honours have been granted with excessive frequency – but that circumstance is rather reason for <u>not</u> extending the area of distribution. The late Queen had the greatest objections to them except to mark her personal presence.'

Salisbury held up the creation of an Order of Merit in 1888 because in 'the present acrimony of party politics, and the absence of any fixed majority', the Queen's pet project to recognise excellence in the arts and sciences would 'add materially' to Goschen's and Smith's difficulties in the House of Commons. He feared that the Order would inevitably become politicised, and managed to get its institution postponed until a fortnight before he retired in 1902.

In the meantime, Salisbury busily annotated his objections to the hordes of honours-seekers who besieged him. In response to the demand of Major Dickson, MP for Dover, for the KCMG in March 1888, Salisbury told McDonnell: 'All he has done is to own a channel steamer. No reply.' To a request for a knighthood from a civil servant in June 1889: 'This is a man of no note at all,' and later: 'I think some element of distinction is desirable,' otherwise knighthoods would merely become 'a mode of discharging departmental debts'. By February 1889, he was telling Londonderry that the requests were coming in 'thick and fast. I wish we could imitate James I and charge £8,000 each for them.' He was delighted when deaths, such as that of Lord Malmesbury in May 1889, released KCBs for his disposal, something he complained never happened regularly enough. The Order of the Bath was, he declared, 'a positive elixir of life – a prophylactic against influenza and all other epidemics. Nobody dies who is either KCB or CB. I shall bring it under the notice of the hospitals.' On another occasion he likened himself to 'the cashier of a bank on which there is a run. I pay in as small coin as I can.' To Lord Knutsford he vouchsafed the rule: 'When you are recommending for an honour the first thing you have to ask yourself is – whom will it disgust?'[12]

The nonconformist and Radical press was outraged when, in his first ministry, Salisbury continued Beaconsfield's practice of awarding peerages to brewers and self-made men. Henry Allsopp, a large-scale Burton brewer and Deputy Chairman of the Great Northern Railway, only had a modest Worcestershire seat but was nevertheless created Baron Hindlip. Sir Charles Mills, a banker, became Baron Hillingdon. These two creations were violently criticised at the time as a surrender to plutocracy, but they marked the opening of the House of Lords to new commercial, industrial and financial interests, not necessarily supported by the hitherto-crucial ownership of land. In all, 23 per cent of Salisbury's peerage creations went to businessmen. This revolution did not extend to John Robinson MP for Nottingham, however, who, as McDonnell explained to Salisbury in November 1891, was a staunch political supporter, very popular, the founder of the Small Owners Allotment Association, 'esteemed by the Duke of Portland' and the landed proprietor of Worksop Manor, but whose 'money was made by the turf as well as by brewing'. The reply was immediate: 'Knighthood impossible. S.'

'I wish I had more baksheesh to give you,' wrote Salisbury to Lord George Hamilton prior to his August 1892 resignation honours list. 'But I am cleared out. I look upon my own list of honours with such horror that I have arranged to be across the water before it is published.' He did not, however, exchange peerages for cash in the manner of which Gladstone was guilty. In 1891, the Liberal Chief Whip, Arnold Morley, and the Chief Liberal Party agent, Francis Schnadhorst, persuaded Gladstone to permit two men, Sydney Stern and James Williamson, to buy peerages. Both Liberal MPs, Stern specialised in Portuguese finance and Williamson made oil-cloth, and neither would have been so much as considered had not large amounts of money changed hands. When Rosebery became Prime Minister in 1894, he only agreed to honour the deal once he had written assurance from Gladstone of it, and in the subsequent resignation honours Rosebery reluctantly allowed Stern to become Lord Wandsworth and Williamson Lord Ashton.[13] In contrast, Salisbury turned down honours for several large contributors to Tory funds, including John Malcolm of Poltallock, who had spent £100,000 on Tory politics, and Sir George Elliot, who since 1868 had spent £120,000.

The Tories did have two honours scandals of their own, but Salisbury was personally innocent of any wrong-doing in both. When in 1899 a financier called Thomas Hooley – who in his time had bought and sold the Dunlop, Schweppes, Bovril and Singer companies – went bankrupt, the official receiver asked the Conservative Party for the return of £10,000 which had been donated the previous year. Middleton returned the money immediately, but at the hearing in the Court of Bankruptcy Hooley claimed that he had paid £30,000 to join the Carlton Club and £50,000 for a jubilee baronetcy, which he never received. Furthermore, he had done the deal through the former Conservative Solicitor-General, Sir William Marriott QC MP, who had taken a 20 per cent 'commission', something which Marriott could not deny under oath.

Fortunately, Middleton had returned the £50,000 cheque without cashing it once he heard about the strings attached, and the *Spectator* congratulated Salisbury on his 'vigilance' in not considering awarding the baronetcy. It was all very embarrassing nevertheless, and the correspondence between Salisbury and Devonshire in 1898 bristles with warnings from the former about the dangers of another Hooley debacle. He was against another large-scale contributor, Horace Farquahar, getting a peerage after only three years as a Liberal Unionist MP, but it went through, helped by the support of Devonshire and the Prince of Wales.

The nearest Salisbury ever got to admitting that some honours could be bought came in a letter to Devonshire of May 1898, commenting on the remarks of James Wanklyn, the Liberal Unionist MP for Bradford, who was 'publicly denouncing honours given with regard to pecuniary contributions to party funds – which he calumniously asserts to have been the case with Ripley. But I am afraid there is no doubt that [James Fortescue] Flannery's merits are of that complexion – so it will not do to nominate him at this moment. We should have something of a scandal.'[14] Fortescue Flannery, a shipbuilder and Conservative MP, nonetheless received a knighthood the following year.

Another request for a peerage in 1898 came from John Jacob Astor, the New York property magnate, whom Salisbury had encouraged to subscribe to Party funds since July 1895. 'My impression is that there is no instance of creating an alien a peer unless he is of Royal blood,' Salisbury minuted to McDonnell. Astor contributed the huge sum of £20,000 to the 1900 election campaign fund, but he did not receive his peerage, despite constant pressure, until 1916.

'I am distressed at being obliged to lay so large a list before Her Majesty,' Salisbury told Ponsonby on returning to power in 1895. 'If she comments on it, pray remind her that this is a Coalition Government; that we have an exceptional number of supporters, and consequently an exceptional number of candidates for honours.' Between 1895 and his own retirement in 1902, Salisbury was responsible for forty-four new hereditary creations, including two from the Law. This average of six per year was more than Balfour's five, but fewer than Campbell-Bannerman's nine, or Asquith's eleven, let alone Lloyd George's outrageous sixteen. Baronetcies were more plentifully provided, but Salisbury always had to turn away far more than he could satisfy. 'If Mr Foster is distressed at not obtaining a baronetcy this year pray assure him that he belongs to a noble army of martyrs,' Salisbury told the Marquess of Granby in December 1896. 'I have never myself experienced the exquisite joy of becoming a baronet: but it must be a felicity of a very rare order – to judge by the enthusiasm with which this prize is pursued.'

An idea of Middleton's in 1894 to raise money from Indian princes did appeal to Salisbury, who readily agreed to become the president of an Indian Carlton Club which 'The Skipper' wanted to set up. The Rajah of

Bobilli had sent a large cheque after the 1892 general election, and in November 1894 Middleton sent a well-connected Englishman, Mr Turner, out to India to call on various princes, armed with a letter from Salisbury about how 'Radicalism has turned its eyes towards India, and is trying to place individual rights and liberties there as elsewhere, at the mercy of a mere numerical majority,' emphasising that the Unionist Party and the princes, in both opposing nationalism, were 'natural allies'.

Turner returned saying that the rajahs really wanted peerages for their financial support, something Salisbury knew to be out of the question. By November 1895, however, Middleton had a draft constitution for the Imperial Loyalty League of India, in which cash levels were set down for the vice-presidencies. McDonnell found this 'a little crude', and Salisbury agreed, specifying that they should put 'no price in writing'. After Salisbury wrote to the Maharajah of Darbhanga, the cheques started arriving. 'No Englishman is a match for an intriguing Hindoo,' complained Lord George Hamilton to Salisbury from the India Office, lamenting that the princes would expect something tangible in return, but the Indian Carlton Club was nonetheless founded and helped to fill the Party's war chest.[15]

Although Salisbury did not mind accepting foreign donations, he was, as he told Brodrick in February 1901, strongly opposed to the policy of allowing British subjects to accept foreign decorations, especially once the Kaiser started to deluge Britons with a 'shower of orders'. When Wolseley had been offered the Order of the Red Eagle after a successful visit to Berlin in 1886, Salisbury told him via Ponsonby and Ambassador Malet that 'Foreign Secretaries must refuse these applications or hide their eyes like the Verginé di Padover'. He was equally averse to Britain honouring foreigners, only agreeing to give Admiral von der Goltz an honorary GCMG in March 1891 'merely as a matter of policy', and discouraging Lord George Hamilton's suggestion to give the Sultan of Muscat the KCMG just because the French had awarded him the Grand Cordon of the Légion d'Honneur.

As well as industrialists, Salisbury was keen that peerages should be available to callings not usually represented in the House of Lords. He was the first Prime Minister to ennoble a journalist, when, in 1895 and on the Queen's suggestion, Sir Algernon Borthwick MP, the editor and proprietor of the *Morning Post*, was made Baron Glenesk. 'It had, however, better be done after the General Election,' Salisbury told Bigge. 'The House of Lords will be a good deal discussed at the hustings.' Salisbury also wanted to ennoble Sir Joseph Lister, the President of the Royal Society and the Royal College of Surgeons, explaining to the Queen 'that he wished to bring into the House of Lords men of science and art'.

Back in 1891, Salisbury had proposed the artist Sir Frederick Leighton and the physicist Sir William Thomson for peerages. As he told the Queen: 'It is very desirable to give the feeling that the House of Lords contains something beside rich men and politicians...the more the House of Lords can be provided, as occasion serves, with the elements of eminence of different kinds, the greater will be its moral authority.' Nevertheless, when the dying painter Sir John Millais was suggested in 1896, Salisbury blocked the idea, as he did not want to set a precedent for Presidents of the Royal Academy automatically to receive peerages.

Salisbury drew the line at ennobling poor men, turning down the application for Lord Aberdeen's son, Arthur Gordon, to be made a peer 'on the ground of his not being rich enough'. (Gladstone later made him Lord Stanmore.) Professor Thomas Huxley was also considered too poor properly to sustain an hereditary honour, but Salisbury put him up for the Privy Council instead, telling the Queen that he 'has no sympathy with his opinions, but thinks that his great intellectual and scientific eminence deserves recognition'. Huxley thus became the first Crown adviser on science, and he was surprised that 'a Tory and Church Government should have delighted to honour the worst famed heretic in the three kingdoms'.[16]

Other extraneous factors could influence Salisbury on his choice of honours. When in 1885 Carnarvon asked for a peerage for an Irish politician, Arthur MacMurrough Kavanagh, who had been born legless, Salisbury wrote to say he preferred to honour someone called Bates as: 'He would please the Orange men a great deal more.... And he has two arms and two legs.' The Lord Lieutenancy of Cardiganshire could not go to a man called Davies in June 1888 because he was 'a tough nonconformist: and though in any other part of the country that might not be an insuperable difficulty, in Wales at this moment such an appointment would be taken as an olive-branch to the dis-establishers'. Wives could also raise problems. To the proposal for a colonial order for ladies along the lines of the all-male Order of the Indian Empire, Salisbury wrote to Knutsford in January 1891 that: 'The lady question is always a difficult one. Men who have made themselves, have rarely taken the trouble to make their wives at the same time.'

This problem had come to a head in May 1888 when, on Alfred Rothschild's advice, Hartington had put the art collector Sir Richard Wallace up for a peerage. Unfortunately, Lady Wallace had borne Sir Richard a son in 1840 without the preliminary precaution of a wedding, which did not take place until 1871. Salisbury was perfectly content with ennobling Wallace, who had been a Unionist MP between 1874 and 1884, but he told Hartington that: 'The only trouble is the wife. Can one recommend a lady to be made a Peeress, who cannot be presented at Court?' It was one of Salisbury's very rare acts of prudery, but the answer was no. (Lady Wallace nevertheless still bequeathed her art collection at Hertford House in Manchester Square, to the British nation.)[17]

Salisbury used to joke that the English clergy could be divided into two mutually exclusive categories: those who were fit to be made bishops but unwilling, and those who were willing but unfit. There seems to have been an exceptionally high episcopal mortality rate during his term of office, and in all he distributed no fewer than thirty-eight diocesan mitres, more than any other Prime Minister before or since. 'I declare they die to spite me,' he said.

His policy was simple and generally fair; overcoming his partisan High Churchmanship was his lifelong fear of 'civil war' in the Church of England, so his appointments were intended to reflect the three great schools of thought in the Church, the Low, Broad and High. He did not always find this easy, and would occasionally go on a 'hunt for a Low Churchman.... Will no one find me one?' He found the dearth of impressive Evangelicals 'very embarrassing', but did not discriminate against them, as they sometimes suspected he did. 'I am not, as you know, a free agent in such matters,' he told the Duke of Richmond in October 1895. 'Every appointment in the Church is more or less the result of a negotiation.... I wish all Bishops were appointed like the apostle Mathias, by lot.'

When he joined Disraeli's Government in February 1874, Salisbury had been more concerned about the Prime Minister's policy for the appointment of bishops than any other aspect of government, and when he himself became Prime Minister he took the process very seriously indeed. 'I am obeying no theological predilections of my own,' he protested to Ponsonby over an appointment in February 1890. 'In the advice I have tendered to H.M. on these subjects, I have tried to put aside all individual bias – and to think chiefly of this – how can we best keep the Church together at a critical time, at the same time selecting efficient men for Bishops.' The Queen, he felt, too often thought of the efficiency of the candidates and not enough about the importance of keeping the Evangelical, Broad and High Church groups content. Because in Salisbury's opinion the High Church was supported by a majority of Anglican clergy and the Low by a majority of laity, 'The exasperation on both sides is equal.'

Salisbury was a consummate juggler of sees, keen to promote men 'of moderate temper and views'. Neither Ritualists nor ultra-Protestants were favoured, due to their propensity to irritate the other, for, as Salisbury told Hicks Beach in October 1889, 'I am convinced that the mass of English Churchmen are moderate men – caring little for a man's views so [long as] extremes are avoided.' Not only did Salisbury attempt to find balance across the Church generally, he also tried to pursue it in each diocese as well, not wishing any area to become exclusive to any particular section of the Church. Because the Bishop of Peterborough was a Low Churchman in May 1901, for example, Salisbury told McDonnell that the Low Churchman Dr Barlow of Islington would not be a suitable choice for its Dean.

Occasionally the delicate process of prelate-making could go awry. All administrations have their tales, often apocryphal, about the wrong man being appointed to places or honours through misunderstandings, but in the case of the Rev. William Page-Roberts, Canon of Canterbury, it seems to be true. In late 1898, Devonshire suggested Page-Roberts to Salisbury for a bishopric, but Salisbury mistook his name for that of the entirely unsuitable John Page Hopps, a religious journalist who had denounced the Government, and so the post went to someone else.[18]

In a *Saturday Review* article in 1863, Salisbury had taken a typically undeferential attitude towards the episcopate: 'That a man has become a Bishop shows that he knows how to get on in the world, and to recommend himself to those above him,' adding that when the bishops all agreed upon something, 'It is an admirable index of tea-table opinion.' He complained of the way the Church had made Sundays so dull, almost forcing the working classes to 'prefer the pot-house'. The journalist Henry Lucy found Salisbury 'snappish' towards the Bench of Bishops in the House of Lords, and quoted his remark to the Bishop of Winchester in a June 1901 debate on the liquor laws, 'The object you are seeking to obtain is trivial in the extreme. You are purposing to introduce the maximum of disturbance with a minimum of result.' When Sir William Houldsworth recommended the Rev. H. Webb-Peploe for a bishopric, Salisbury annotated: 'A mere windbag' to McDonnell and left it at that. On leaving the Foreign Office for lunch at the Athenæum Club one day, Salisbury was asked by the doorman whether he would like to take an umbrella for the short walk in case it rained. He declined, 'saying that he could not trust the Bishops there and he might lose it'.

The *Saturday Review* article had been inspired by the bishops' campaign against Sunday excursion trains. Thirty-six years later, the Archbishop of Canterbury, Frederick Temple, along with the Bishop of Winchester, suggested to the Queen that she should protest against the publication of Sunday editions of the *Daily Telegraph* and the *Daily Mail*. Perhaps the Rev. Faithfull's rigid Sabbatarianism played a part in forming Salisbury's more liberal views on the matter. 'The upper class and the lower class are in the main averse to a rigid observance of the Sunday: the middle class support it,' he told the Queen in a memorandum in May 1899. The excursion trains had been permitted, as was the sale of food on a Sunday, so Salisbury advised the Queen against taking sides in the Sunday newspaper controversy. 'By their vast numbers they are evidently a luxury valued by the lower classes. If these classes learn that high social influences are directed against them, I should dread to see your Majesty's name mixed up in it.' He suggested she tell the prelates that pronouncing on Sabbatarianism 'does not fall within the ordinary range of your Majesty's duties'. The Queen replied that it was not the religious consideration but the loss of relaxation time of the newspaper staff and distributors that most concerned her. She was worried that the staff of the *Daily Telegraph* would be exploited by having to produce a Sunday edition. Salisbury replied that behind the moderates on this issue were 'a huge fanatical body', and so it was best left alone.

The delicate negotiations between the anti-Tractarian Queen and her Tractarian Prime Minister over episcopal appointments came to a head in July 1888, when Salisbury had hoped to appoint Canon Henry Liddon, the great Tractarian and, in Salisbury's opinion, 'so much the most brilliant member of the clergy of the Established Church', to the see of Oxford, 'the intellectual centre of the Church'. As the Queen wrote to Ponsonby: 'Bishop of Oxford he must never be. He might ruin and taint all the young men as Pusey and others did before him.' Randall Davidson, her long-standing domestic chaplain and now Dean of Windsor, agreed with her, but for obvious reasons this stance was not vouchsafed to Salisbury himself. Instead, the Queen raised health grounds for not promoting Liddon, which Salisbury respectfully disputed. 'She fears Lord Salisbury is <u>rather</u> narrow and old-fashioned, or his advisers are. Really it is very tiresome,' the Queen wrote to Davidson in January 1890. Liddon was finally, in April 1890, offered St Albans instead, which he refused, dying five months later.

That September, the Queen and Salisbury clashed over Davidson himself, whom she wanted to translate to Winchester, because it 'borders on Windsor and includes Osborne'. Salisbury wanted to offer Rochester or Worcester to Davidson, with the Bishop of Rochester going to Winchester. Salisbury thought Davidson, a Broad Churchman who was only forty-two, 'able but not, as yet, distinguished', and the see of Winchester, which carried with it a seat on the Bench of Bishops in the House of Lords, too great a promotion for him. He considered Davidson needed a stint in an ordinary see first. The Queen, meanwhile, urged Archbishop Benson to write to Salisbury contradicting Salisbury's view that the High and Low Church parties would be offended by so conspicuous a promotion of a Broad Churchman. 'I think a letter from you, as from <u>yourself</u> and <u>without mentioning</u> me, to Lord Salisbury,' she wrote 'would have great weight.' Salisbury nevertheless won. When in 1890 the Archiepiscopate of York – a great political as well as religious post –

came up, Salisbury refused to have Brooke Westcott, whom the Queen had pushed into Durham, because of the 'Socialist tendencies of the speeches he has made since he became a bishop'. After Salisbury's 'eloquent and safe' candidate William Magee died in office only two months later of influenza, he accepted one of the Queen's other choices, William Maclagan, who stayed in the post for seventeen years.

On 11th October 1896, Edward Benson, the Archbishop of Canterbury, died suddenly while staying at Hawarden. Salisbury plumped for the seventy-five-year-old Frederick Temple, Bishop of London, whom he told the Queen was the obvious successor despite his age. It would be a slur if he were passed over, he argued, but if Temple refused on grounds of age, 'the fact that it has been offered to him should be allowed to transpire'. The seventy-seven-year-old Queen thought Temple's age 'far too advanced to undertake such an arduous position', and instead wanted Davidson. She believed Temple to be 'not gentlemanlike and does not possess any of the social qualities.... He has even a strong provincial accent in speaking and preaching.' Salisbury nevertheless insisted, and eventually she allowed Salisbury to make the offer and professed herself 'disappointed' when Temple accepted with alacrity.

In general, Salisbury's problem was that the best potential bishops refused his offers. His first would-be episcopal appointment, William Inge, Provost of Worcester College, Oxford, turned down the see of Salisbury 'in terms', the Prime Minister reported to the Queen, 'which would have been unnecessarily strong if he had been asked to go to Sierra Leone'. It went to the third choice. Of a Scottish minister called Dr Story, Salisbury said: 'He has the legs of a Bishop, I wish he were an episcopalian, I would make him one.' He employed almost passionate language when he pressed the bishopric of London on to Davidson in February 1901, saying:

> The period is critical – the moral authority of a powerful Bishop is grievously needed by the Church and there is no Bishop on the bench that can speak with the authority which you possess.... I am sure the time is <u>very</u> critical: and if you feel forced to decline I fear the Church may have much to suffer.[19]

Davidson did decline, on health grounds, but accepted the post of Archbishop of Canterbury on Temple's death nearly two years later, a position he then held for a quarter of a century.

It was in an almost impish, end-of-term mood that Salisbury appointed his last bishop in November 1901, completely reversing his policy of placating all sects of the Church by choosing for the Worcester see someone who was bound to cause controversy. Charles Gore was Canon of Westminster and the leader of the Anglo-Catholics. He was Superior of the Community of the Resurrection at Mirfield and a

controversial essayist and author. Extreme Protestants believed his to
be the most outrageous Anglican episcopal appointment since the
Reformation, and vowed to block it. In January 1902, the Church
Association actually forced Gore's consecration to be postponed when
it raised doctrinal objections at the confirmation ceremony. When the
Vicar-General rejected these, an appeal was made to the Court of King's
Bench, and Gore was only finally consecrated a month later. The
parting religious shot of Salisbury's premiership was thus a brazen tease
of the ultra-Protestants, whom he had regularly denounced in his
Saturday Review days but whom he had had to appease during his thirteen years of prelate-making.

All of Salisbury's tact was required for the row which broke out
between the Queen and senior members of her Household over the role
of her favourite Indian servant, Abdul Karim, known as the 'Munshi'
(meaning 'teacher'). Although she never visited India, Queen Victoria
took special pride and interest in her Empire there, and learnt much
about it from her Muslim servant. Despite his paunch and lowly background, the Munshi had become the symbol of India for the Queen. By
the late 1890s, he had taken the place in the Queen's platonic affections
once occupied by John Brown, although he was loathed by the gentlemen of the Royal Household for his mendacity and uncouth
assertiveness. Salisbury had managed to block the Munshi's requests,
made via the Queen, for a diplomatic post for his journalist friend
Raffiuddin Ahmed, blaming Foreign Office 'prejudice'. By July 1897
members of the Household, using the Queen's doctor, Sir James Reid, as
their mouthpiece, were alleging that the secret telegrams arriving in the
Queen's red boxes were being perused by the Munshi.

Salisbury, who had long been obsessed with secrecy, received from
the Queen the contradictory excuses that the Munshi 'does not read
English fluently enough to be able to read anything of importance' and
that he 'only helps her to read words that she cannot read'. She blamed
ill-natured India Office gossip and disrespectful courtiers for the
rumours.[20] In September, Salisbury personally investigated the allegations made against both the Munshi and Raffiuddin Ahmed and cleared
both men.

When in January 1898 the Queen told Salisbury that she wanted
Raffiuddin Ahmed to be awarded the Jubilee medal, saying that if
'clergymen, <u>actors</u>, artists, besides of course soldiers and sailors'
received it, so should someone who wrote loyal articles in the
Nineteenth Century periodical, Salisbury discussed the matter with Sir
Edward Bradford, the Police Commissioner. Bradford had been secretary

of the political and secret departments of the India Office and entertained unfavourable opinions of Raffiuddin and his capacity for mischief. Salisbury warned the Queen that Raffiuddin 'associates with people who are certainly disloyal' and came down on the side of Sir Arthur Bigge, who thought that the two Indians were a potential source of leaks. But he never exerted pressure on the Queen, not thinking the issue important enough to incur her displeasure.

Salisbury suspected that the Queen rather enjoyed the rows which the Munshi provoked in her circle: 'She could always get rid of him, but ... he believes she really likes the emotional excitement, as being the only form of excitement she can have.' Salisbury was certainly not about to endanger his close working relationship with her over this, however, especially as by March 1898 she was writing reams of memoranda about the 'bitter, ungenerous and ... racial feeling' against the two men, which she believed was prompted entirely 'out of dislike to a native being treated as a gentleman!' Getting Raffiuddin invited to a Court Ball became something of an obsession with her and in December 1898, in a letter she asked Salisbury to burn, she begged him to intimate to the visiting Lord Hopetoun not to allow 'any attempt to poison his mind against the poor, most shamefully maligned Munshi'. Her eyesight failing, she asked him in a postscript: 'Pray write with as black ink as you can [on] these private questions,' so that not even her children – who sided with the Household – would need to read them to her.[21]

By April 1899, the senior members of the Royal Household were prepared to resign en masse sooner than accept the Munshi's presence on holiday at Cimiez in the South of France. Another appeal was made to Salisbury, who tactfully explained to the Queen that the French were 'such odd people' that they might make jokes at her expense were her Indian servant to attend. For a while this had the desired effect, but the man was to remain an irritating nuisance until the Queen's death. After it, Edward VII ordered the Munshi's papers burned in the presence of Queen Alexandra and Princess Beatrice, with a further conflagration on the Munshi's own death in 1909.

FORTY

Choosing his Ground

Imperial Federation – A French Convention
– Port Arthur – Anglo-German Relations –
The 'Dying Nations' Speech
– The Death of Gladstone –
Curzon as Viceroy – The Battle of Omdurman

July 1897 to September 1898

'"Eat and be eaten" is the great law of political as of animated nature.'

Discussing Imperial Federation with Lord Pembroke at Grillions Club one evening in late May 1897, Salisbury remarked: 'It lends itself more to peroration than argument.' Salisbury knew that there was little economic sense in federating the Empire, and thus inevitably putting up protective tariffs against non-imperial produce. Between 1883 and 1892, Britain's exports to foreign countries rose from £215 million to £291 million, whereas to the Empire they fell from £90 million to £81 million. By 1902, her imports amounted to £421 million from foreign countries and only £107 million from the Empire. So whilst he was content to leave it as an open question for the future, and even as an ultimate goal to be invoked when winding up speeches, Salisbury was not about to risk Britain's powerful global trading position for a Jingoist pipe-dream.

He was happy to receive deputations from various pressure groups, such as the Imperial Federation League, which wanted 'closer and more substantial union', but he preferred not to call another Colonial Conference on the lines of the 1887 one, arguing that it was up to the colonies themselves to devise a workable scheme. To an Australian correspondent in 1889 he wrote that federation 'involves a considerable sacrifice on the part of England and the independence which she at present possesses'. Moreover, it would mean a modification of the

Constitution, and should one-man-one-vote ever be instituted, the Asians and Africans rather than the Anglo-Saxons would soon dominate. The threat to British sovereignty, he believed, heavily outweighed any possible economic advantages of welding the Empire into a single superstate. Salisbury was even doubtful about the creation of the Imperial Institute, preferring instead to strengthen the oriental chairs at the University of London.

Although he sometimes seemed to give the impression that he was a supporter of their federation schemes, Salisbury was always more lukewarm on the subject than his supporters guessed. When two deputations advocating federation arrived on two consecutive days, Salisbury explained to Stanhope how 'Having them on the same day would be very tedious and might be thought disrespectful – as if I was poking fun at them.' They were not however put off by his clear message that 'the time has not yet come', and continued to agitate and organise at constituency level.

Despite his misgivings, a second Colonial Conference had to be held at the time of the Diamond Jubilee, but Salisbury left it to Chamberlain to open. As in 1887 it produced little that was substantive. The 1862 Treaties with Germany and Belgium which prevented the United Kingdom negotiating preferential customs agreements with Australia and Canada were denounced, and Salisbury agreed to cancel them that summer. Otherwise little progress was made along the lines of a 'Council of the Empire', or indeed any of the other schemes Chamberlain hoped to promote. Telling Lady Rayleigh in October that he 'thinks we shall be hated as long as we go on adding to our territories as we do', Salisbury recognised that some of the most recent annexations were more of a burden than a boon. The amount of trade with those territories annexed since 1880 only comprised 2.5 per cent of Britain's overall total by 1901. Salisbury's line – not to rush Providence in the creation of imperial unity – could only hold so long as the Unionists had someone of his undoubted gravity and record to propound it. Conservative Central Office's *Campaign Guide* for the 1900 election could state that a 'complete customs union... is as yet impracticable',[1] but as soon as Salisbury went the issue started to tear the Party apart.

It also took all of Salisbury's powers of diplomacy to steer a course between Chamberlain's espousal of the 1897 Workmen's Compensation Bill and the conservatism of Lord Londonderry, spokesman for the coal-owners, and Lord Wemyss of the Defence of Liberty and Property League. Salisbury's support of Chamberlain's measure, which established the principle of automatic compensation for industrial accidents as a charge upon the employer, was a brave stand, especially as Londonderry had threatened to resign his presidency of the Northern Union of Conservative Associations in protest. 'When property is in question I am guilty, like [Wemyss], of erecting individual liberty as an idol,' Salisbury admitted during the second reading in July 1897, 'but when you pass from liberty to life, in no well-governed state, in no state governed according to the principles of common humanity, are the claims of mere liberty allowed to endanger the lives of the citizens.'[2]

Salisbury tended to take the Lord Chancellor, Lord Halsbury's advice on purely legal matters, but whenever they interfered with his political arrangements, politics came first. In August 1897, Salisbury wanted to shuffle Sir Edward Clarke QC off to the Mastership of the Rolls because of the criticisms of Government policy which the former Solicitor-General was making from the backbenches. Salisbury knew that Halsbury held a low opinion of Clarke's judicial capacity, but rationalised the problem in a somewhat blasé manner:

> We shall not keep him off the Bench: and if we take him young, he may have some time to learn some Law. Besides, as Master of the Rolls he cannot hang anybody by mistake: a misadventure which might happen if you delay his promotion so that he may take a common law judgeship.

When Halsbury baulked at the prospect of having someone he considered unqualified in so eminent a position, Salisbury wrote again to complain that:

> It is at variance with the unwritten law of our party system: and there is no clearer statute in that unwritten law, than the rule that party claims should always weigh heavily in the disposal of legal appointments....It would be a breach of the tacit covenant on which politicians and lawyers have worked the British Constitution together for the last two hundred years. Perhaps it is not an ideal system. Some day no doubt the Master of the Rolls will be appointed by a competitive examination in Law Reports. But it is our system for the present: and we shall give our party arrangements a wrench if we throw it aside.

He went on to cite Lords Coleridge, Chelmsford and Romilly as senior judges who could only boast 'a very slender garment of legal knowledge to keep them warm'. He got his way, but in the event Clarke refused the Rolls in order to retain his capacity to criticise the Government, which he did so regularly that his constituency association deselected him three years later.[3] A vain egotist, Clarke was accorded that most delicious of all valedictory privileges: he wrote his own *Times* obituary.

The Conventions made with France in 1890 delineating various West African spheres of influence began to break down seven years later, and in July 1897 the Cabinet agreed to send ships and men to the Niger River 'to take formal possession of the points in the territory of the Royal Niger Company which the French explorers are endeavouring to occupy'. By September, Salisbury thought the Niger situation could threaten war with France and complained to Goschen: 'I am yoked there together with Chamberlain and [Sir George] Goldie – and both of them "pull".' Salisbury considered Goldie, the Chairman of the Royal Niger Chartered Company, a 'perfect nuisance', telling Selborne that 'his knowledge of foreign relations must have been acquired in a music-hall'. Salisbury was unwilling to countenance a war against France over various near-worthless mosquito-ridden possessions in West Africa, a part of the world he considered of infinitely less importance than southern Africa or the Nile Valley.

Salisbury did not see the Franco-Russian alliance as an immediate threat, telling Goschen in early September that it was overall beneficial 'for us – and for peace. It is a decided check to the Emperor William, who, if he had elbow-room, would certainly be nasty for us.... I am always glad to see him "hobbled".' As for French incursions on Niger Company territory, Salisbury told Sanderson there was a third option between war and acquiescence:

> what Bismarck used to call Versumpfung [stagnation]. We should maintain our present argumentative position. We should steadily refuse to recognise any of their robberies. So far as we had strength to do so we should cut off all supplies from them. We should make a <u>defensive</u> alliance on carefully guarded terms with [the local chieftain] Samory...they will soon find the hardship so intolerable that they will offer reasonable terms. I quite agree that our party would break from us rather than admit a simple acquiescence. I think they would be right.

Of the 'cranky' Goldie, Salisbury feared he was watching the creation of yet another 'prodigal son' along the lines of Browne, Lytton, Frere, Warren, and now Milner.[4]

Although Chamberlain clashed with the Foreign Office over the Niger, Salisbury never allowed the situation to develop into one that threatened war. Speaking to Esher in late January 1898, Chamberlain said that over China and West Africa he and Salisbury 'had a strong difference of opinion. He believes we are at the parting of the ways, and that we must stand fast for Imperial expansion now or never, whatever the result.' It was a tribute to Salisbury's powers of diplomacy that

Chamberlain did not desert the Unionist coalition during his lifetime, although he did resign from it the month after Salisbury's death.

Although Salisbury thought the French 'are such liars', he rather admired the way that unlike every other European nation who feared Britain, 'even those out of danger from our fleet', France did not. West Africa held few strategic or economic enticements for Salisbury, who ever since the Cabinet had refused him leave to force the Straits two years before had seen the Suez Canal as the crucial possession. As he told Currie in October 1897, 'the only policy' available to Britain was now 'to strengthen our position on the Nile (to its source)'. In order to be given a free hand in Egypt and the Nile Valley, Salisbury was willing to countenance a deal with France which would offer her territory on both sides of the Niger, a free hand in the New Hebrides, and other agreements over Tripoli, Morocco and China. British control over the Nile Valley, however, was sacrosanct. A whole year before the Fashoda Crisis, Salisbury was writing to Lansdowne about 'the diplomatic difficulties which might be interposed if any French explorer reaches the Nile before we have taken Khartoum'. He was under no illusions 'that by destroying the Dervish power we are killing the defender who is holding the Valley for us now'.[5]

Unusual foresight was displayed at Salisbury's annual Guildhall speech on 9th November 1897 when he warned of the effect of a great European war:

> You notice that on all sides the instruments of destruction, the piling up of arms, are becoming larger and larger. The powers of concentration are becoming greater, and the instruments of death more active and are improving with every year; and every nation is bound, for its own safety's sake, to take part in this competition.... the one hope that we have to prevent this competition from ending in a terrible effort of mutual destruction which will be fatal to Christian civilisation – the one hope we have is that the Powers may gradually be brought together, to act together on a friendly spirit on all questions of difference which may arise, until at last they shall be welded in some international constitution which shall give to the world as a result of their great strength a long spell of unfettered trade and continued peace.

Rather like Imperial Federation, however, these musings were matters which lent themselves more to peroration than argument. They nevertheless inspired his son Robert, who was to dedicate his life to the League of Nations, for which he received the Nobel Peace Prize in 1937.

Salisbury used the debate on the Queen's Speech on 8th February 1898 to warn against imperial overreach and to inveigh against the Jingoism which he believed was making his diplomatic work harder by the year. He pointed out how in China and the North-West Frontier 'we have no desire for an increase in territory which would only be an increase in burden', and stated that:

I have a strong belief that there is a danger of the public opinion of this country undergoing a reaction from the Cobdenic principles of thirty or forty years ago, and believing that it is our duty to take everything we can, to fight everybody, and to make a quarrel of every dispute. That seems to me a very dangerous doctrine, not merely because it might incite other nations against us…but there is a more serious danger, that is lest we overtax our strength. However strong you may be, whether you are a man or a nation, there is a point beyond which your strength will not go. It is madness; it ends in ruin if you allow yourself to pass beyond it.[6]

It was brave, so soon after the Jubilee, to warn against crossing what he called 'the difficult, narrow line that separates an undue concession from that rashness which has, in more than one case in history, been the ruin of nations as great and powerful as ourselves'.

The rebuke was intended as much against some of his colleagues in the Cabinet as the Jingoist leader-writers in the press. For over the following months and years Salisbury found his conduct of foreign affairs increasingly challenged by a growing number of ministers who were worried about what they perceived as Britain's isolation. They had won their first major victory over the Dardanelles, but it was over policy towards China that a significant attempt was made to wrest overall control of foreign affairs from Salisbury. The most dangerous manifestation of this came in Chamberlain's attempts to explore the possibility of a German alliance behind Salisbury's back, in a manner which Asquith was later to characterise as 'touting for allies in the highways and byways of Europe'.

Jingoes who believed that Britain should be scrambling for China just as strenuously as she had for Africa were outraged by the Kaiser's seizure of Kiachow Bay on the North China coast on 28th November 1897, in revenge for the murder of two German missionaries. It was when a Russian fleet steamed into the Chinese harbour of Port Arthur on 18th December, however, obliging British warships to vacate the area, that they became apoplectic. Back in August 1896, Salisbury had wondered aloud whether Russia would have gone to war with Britain had she attempted to stop her taking Port Arthur, concluding: 'Such speculations are hazardous because they depend on the force of passing paroxysms of passion.' He had remembered how Palmerston's refusal to fight Prussia and Austria over Schleswig-Holstein in 1864 had been rewarded with a Commons majority of seventy in 1865, whereas Beaconsfield's support of 'a very forward policy' in 1879 had resulted in Gladstone winning a majority of 120 the following year.

Salisbury was determined not to overreact to the Russian seizure of what was nonetheless a strategically vital part of China. 'I quite agree with you that "the public" will require some territorial or cartographic consolation in China,' he wrote to Chamberlain on 30th December. 'It will not be useful, and will be expensive: but as a matter of pure sentiment we shall have to do it.' He telegraphed the Chinese authorities in Peking not to concede a formal lease over Port Arthur to Russia, otherwise 'Her Majesty's Government will be compelled to consider that [the] Chinese government acquiesce in the dismemberment of their Empire'. It failed to deter them, and on 23rd March Russia obtained a twenty-five-year lease on Port Arthur and also on Talienwan on the Liaotung Peninsula. Furthermore, she won the right to connect both places to the Trans-Siberian railway.

After a perfunctory protest to Peking, Britain decided to reverse her decision not to take a lease on Wei-hai-wei, another Chinese port. 'Russian negotiations are as long as Russian winters, and longer,' Salisbury told Brodrick of his inability to stop St Petersburg's actions, 'but that is hardly our fault.' He was further hampered by another serious onset of influenza, with the result that Balfour had to take his place in Cabinet. He was present, however, at the meeting on 25th March where it was decided 'not worthwhile to promote a war with Russia in order to keep her out of Port Arthur'. Pausing only officially to deny 'the sensational paragraphs' which had appeared in the press about his impending retirement, Salisbury left for Beaulieu and recuperation. *The Times* reported him as wearing a heavy overcoat and a muffler and walking quickly to the carriage. 'Although unmistakably bearing signs of his recent illness, he appeared to be in best of spirits,' and even raised his hat to the crowd of people waving their hats, umbrellas and handkerchiefs as his train left for Dover.

Salisbury had appeased Russia over China in a way that would have wrecked Gladstone had he tried it.[7] Salisbury believed that the Empire was beginning to become over-extended and, as he explained from Beaulieu about the Russians: 'I don't think we carry guns enough to fight them and the French together.' His pacific policy came under sustained criticism, and not just from the Opposition. Sir Ellis Ashmead-Bartlett was the first to break ranks, complaining in Parliament that Britain was being 'steadily pushed downhill', and unless she returned to her 'ancient alliances' she could not, 'against an armed Europe, stand alone'. Anonymous articles started appearing in the *Contemporary Review*

('The Failure of our Foreign Policy'), the *Fortnightly Review* ('Where Lord Salisbury has Failed') and elsewhere, running from April to June 1898. All had the sub-text that a German alliance was urgently needed.

The occupation of Wei-hai-wei (variously pronounced 'wi-hi-wi' by the Government and 'woe-woe-woe', 'wee-hee-wee' and 'way-hay-way' by the Opposition) was an acknowledgment of the demise of the British policy of protecting the integrity and independence of the Celestial Empire. Salisbury attempted to portray the action as an encouragement to the Chinese, who otherwise 'would give themselves up to despair, and believe that the domination of one foreign power was a destiny from which it was impossible for them to escape'. The criticism continued, with Lord Charles Beresford denouncing the withdrawal of British ships from the environs of Port Arthur as 'one of the most humiliating things that had happened in English history'.[8]

Stung by such criticism, which was repeated *sotto voce* by Bertie, George Wyndham and the diplomat Edward Goschen, and louder by the 4th Earl Grey, Dilke, the China Association and *The Times*, and in Harcourt's remark at Cambridge that 'The English people do not want to go to war, but they do not like being snubbed all round the world,' the Government decided to demand an extension of its territory on the Chinese mainland adjacent to Hong Kong island. On 9th June 1898, a Convention was signed for a ninety-nine-year lease, to commence on 1st July, over all the land between Mirs Bay and Deep Bay including Lantao Island. Signed in quadruplicate in Peking, it was declared to be 'necessary for the proper defence and protection of the Colony'.[9]

War with Russia had been averted, but throughout the first half of 1898 the impression had been given that Salisbury's policy of having no military alliances on the Continent had been a source of British weakness rather than strength. During one of his enforced absences from the Foreign Office from influenza, a serious problem developed when Chamberlain indulged his passion for amateur diplomacy and personally tried to resurrect the idea of an Anglo-German alliance. On 29th March 1898 – the day after Salisbury had left for France and a wide-ranging naval law had been passed in Berlin – Chamberlain met Hatzfeldt at Alfred Rothschild's house, ostensibly to discuss colonial grievances and China. Hatzfeldt was astonished when, instead, Chamberlain suggested that Britain should join a full alliance with the Central Powers, clearly directed against Russia and France. Although Chamberlain stressed the private and unofficial nature of their discussion, Hatzfeldt understandably assumed, and told Berlin, that this was an official Government offer.

Germany's Foreign Secretary, Count Bernhard von Bülow, suspected that it was only a ploy to protect Britain should she wind up with a war against France over West Africa, and he furthermore thought that she wanted to goad Germany into a war against Russia. Once Germany's naval construction plans were fulfilled, he calculated that far better terms could be squeezed out of Britain. If anything, the German Foreign Office saw China as an area in which Russian expansionism could be syphoned off without danger, rather than as a potential area for conflict. It was not until 9th April that Balfour informed Salisbury, via Cranborne, of Chamberlain's *ad hoc* activities, which had been followed up by a second conversation with Hatzfeldt. Balfour had spoken to Hatzfeldt about a *rapprochement* himself on 5th April, but in far more restrained language than Chamberlain had used.

The talks had been further complicated by the activities of Baron Hermann von Eckardstein, the counsellor at the German Embassy in London, who had single-handedly attempted to keep the idea of an Anglo-German alliance afloat, simultaneously exaggerating to each side the enthusiasm of the other. Eckardstein, who had married the heiress daughter of Sir Blundell Maple MP, the race-horse owner and Tottenham Court Road furniture magnate, had his own social and political motives for wanting an Anglo-German alliance, and misrepresented Berlin's views to Chamberlain and vice versa.

Salisbury was enjoying his rest in the South of France, especially as 'the coast is happily deserted of Royalties'. He had brushed off criticisms made in *The Times* of his holding both great offices of state, telling McDonnell that it was 'all nonsense supposing that the Prime Minister's office in itself adds much to the burden. It is only severe when it involves the lead of the House of Commons.'[10] McDonnell meanwhile shot down a press *ballon d'essai* that Salisbury was about to resign and be replaced by Devonshire. The news about Chamberlain's activities drew forth an unmistakable broadside from the convalescing premier, intended as much to discourage Balfour from interfering with his policy as anyone else:

> The one object of the German Emperor since he has been on the throne has been to get us into a war with France. I never can make up my mind whether this is part of Chamberlain's object or not. The indications differ from month to month.... France acts as if she meant to draw us into a German alliance: which I look to with some dismay, for Germany will blackmail us heavily.

In Salisbury's opinion, the British public would not fight either for Germany in Alsace-Lorraine or for Austria on her north-eastern frontier. Talk of a genuine offensive and defensive alliance was therefore meaningless.

Balfour took refuge in ridiculing Chamberlain's actions, writing to Salisbury on 14th April that 'the general outline of their amateur diplomacy is perhaps worth putting on record. Among the minor actors in it are one H. Chaplin, Alfred Rothschild, and Eckardstein – the principal roles being filled by Hatzfeldt and Chamberlain – a very motley "cast"!' The bantering tone did not disguise the fact that the moment Salisbury's back was turned, through illness and absence, Balfour had permitted Chamberlain to wreak havoc with British foreign policy. It was a weakness Chamberlain had also noted. Ironically enough, the Liberals were regularly attacking Salisbury for being too pro-German. When, during a speech at Wrexham given by David Lloyd George the previous September, a heckler shouted, 'What about German-made goods?', his response was: 'I will deal with that when I come to Lord Salisbury's foreign policy. That is made in Germany.'

By the end of April 1898, Chamberlain had sent Salisbury 'the notes of some very curious conversations I have had with the German Ambassador and Baron Eckardstein. You will see that in every case the interviews were sought by the Germans and the initiative was taken by them.' He ended by affirming that he was 'a strong partisan of the alliance under present circumstances'. Salisbury's private reply, on 2nd May, was to tell Chamberlain that he had seen Hatzfeldt that afternoon, whose 'business was evidently to throw cold water' on the whole project.[11] Salisbury was happy to have a closer friendship and understanding with Germany, but was not about to follow Chamberlain down the path of an alliance, even had the Germans themselves desired it, which at the time they did not.

A more public rebuke to Chamberlain was encoded in Salisbury's famous 'Dying Nations' speech, delivered as Grand Master of the Primrose League to its Grand Habitation in the Albert Hall on 4th May. Despite being no Evolutionist, Salisbury had long applied the theory of natural selection to international relations, believing that the survival of civilisations went to the fittest. Three decades earlier he had written in the *Saturday Review* that: '"Eat and be eaten" is the great law of political as of animated nature. The nations of the earth are divided into the sheep and the wolves – the fat and defenceless against the hungry and strong.' Countries like Italy, Flanders and India which were 'soft', 'meek' and 'effeminate' were invaded by tougher races. Writing to Lytton in May 1877, Salisbury had looked forward to the day when Turkey was dismembered, saying how absurd it would be 'if we go on treating and respecting the Turkish Empire as a living organism, when everybody else was treating it as a carcass'.

It was in the same frank mood that Salisbury addressed the Primrose League after Lady Blythswood had presented the champion banner to the Rochdale Habitation. After an extensive *tour d'horizon* of foreign policy, taking in the Sudan, Rhodes, Zanzibar, 'those fetish orgies in West Africa, in Ashanti, and in Benin' to which 'the sword of England has put a final stop', and the 'great result' of taking Wei-hai-wei, 'which we can defend, in place of Port Arthur, which we could not', Salisbury made his central point: 'We know that we shall maintain against all comers that which we possess, and we know, in spite of the jargon about isolation, that we are amply competent to do so.' To refer to Chamberlain and others' fears over isolation as 'jargon' was only the first shock of the speech. He then said:

> You may roughly divide the nations of the world as the living and the dying. On one side you have great countries of enormous power growing in power every year, growing in wealth, growing in dominion, growing in the perfection of their organisation. Railways have given to them the power to concentrate upon any one point the whole military force of their population.... Science has placed in the hands of those armies weapons ever growing in their efficacy of destruction.

There were also 'dying' nations, mired in disorganisation and decay, misgovernment and corruption, and 'the living nations will gradually encroach on the territory of the dying, and the seeds and causes of conflict among civilised nations will speedily appear'. The speech caused a massive outcry in those nations which perceived themselves as approaching the mortuary slab – Spain, Portugal, China and Turkey. America and Germany were generally held to be 'living' nations; France and Italy were unsure.[12] Britain's declaration of neutrality in the Spanish–American War which had broken out the previous month, and her active discouragement of any European nation from supporting Spain, suddenly became intelligible to all, and America's swift naval victories and her invasion of Cuba and annexation of the Philippines also seemed to justify Salisbury's thesis.

Chamberlain would not take the implied criticism of his 'jargon' lying down. To the Birmingham Liberal Unionist Party annual meeting just over a week later, he said: 'We must not reject the idea of our alliance with those Powers whose interests most nearly approximate to our own.' At present, 'we have had no allies – I am afraid that we have had no friends'. Speaking of Russia he commended as wise the proverb: 'Who sups with the Devil must have a long spoon.' His message was that in order to be able 'seriously to injure Russia', let alone maintain an Open Door policy in China, Britain had to join the Central Powers. The press let fly at Chamberlain's hostile references to Russia, especially to 'injuring' a friendly power. Prices fell on the Stock Exchange on the expectation of further trouble. Harcourt denounced what he called the 'Birmingham foreign policy' in the Commons and Morley described the speech as 'flagitious'.

Salisbury kept his own counsel, telling the House of Lords when questioned on his speech that he thought his colleague had been quoted out of context. He simultaneously telegraphed Sir Claude Macdonald in Peking to say that the wire reports of what became known as the 'Long Spoon' speech were 'malignant and unfair', putting all the fuss down to the fact that Baron Reuter was Russian.[13] Fortunately, any further embarrassments were avoided when attention was drawn away by Parliament rising for the Whitsun Recess and the death of Gladstone on 19th May.

'The most distinguished political name in this century', Salisbury announced in the House of Lords on 20th May 1898, 'has been withdrawn from the roll of the living.' Moving a proposal for a memorial to Gladstone, Salisbury spoke of his 'rare and splendid gifts and his devoted labours to Parliament'. His short valediction mentioned how 'men recognised in him a man guided…in all the steps that he took, in all the efforts that he made, by a high moral ideal', and as such they revered 'the memory of a great Christian statesman'. At the Westminster Abbey funeral on Saturday, 28th May, Salisbury impressed several observers with the evident depth of his mourning. The son of Archbishop Benson recorded him in his skull-cap with a 'huge, shabby, tear-stained and a heavy brooding look, most impressive'. As a pall-bearer, along with the Prince of Wales, Balfour, Harcourt, Kimberley, the Dukes of York and of Rutland, and two others, Salisbury carried his old opponent to his grave.

Reporting the occasion to the Queen, who had complained how she 'regrets the extraordinary fuss made about it', Salisbury wrote that 'the music was very fine. Outside there were great crowds, but the effect was made almost ridiculous by the rows of cameras which lined the pavement and the roofs.' Salisbury had 'strongly advised' the Queen not to issue a public appreciation of Gladstone in the *Gazette*, but she wrote a letter of condolence to Gladstone's widow in her own hand. 'What a good life and what a beautiful death,' Lady Salisbury wrote to Mary Gladstone, a far cry from the 'old hypocrite' and 'Murderer of Gordon' remarks that were once common parlance at Hatfield. Yet within a fortnight, Arthur Balfour was telling Lady Rayleigh how, in private conversation, Gladstone 'could be the prosiest bore at times'.[14]

~

The appointment of George Curzon to succeed Lord Elgin as Viceroy of India, formally announced on 11th August 1898, was one of Salisbury's more inspired choices. Curzon had written to propose himself on 11th April; and Salisbury never minded self-propelled thrust in a politician if it was justified by ability, which in Curzon's case it was. Since becoming Under-Secretary at the Foreign Office in 1895, Curzon had been employed not on the grand diplomacy to which he aspired, but on mundane matters such as minor customs and commercial disputes, the treatment of British prisoners abroad, the import of gin and rum into the Niger Coast Protectorate, and the choice of a vice-consul for Fez. He used to complain that, although he asked his Chief for instructions, he was 'never helped in the least degree', or even told what sort of answer to make to any of the hundreds of questions that were put to him in the Commons. Even on subjects on which he was an acknowledged expert, such as Indo-Chinese railways, Curzon sometimes only heard of deputations to Salisbury when he read about them in *The Times* the next morning.

Nevertheless, when Lord Elgin came to retire in 1898, Salisbury praised Curzon's 'great ability' to the Queen, saying that although he would have preferred Hicks Beach, who had refused it, he wanted Curzon for the Empire's foremost proconsular post. 'His only fault is occasional rashness of speech in the House of Commons; but he would have no temptation to that error at Calcutta. He has now a strong physique.' This last point is doubtful; the thirty-nine-year-old was in fact a martyr to backache, but the job was his once Salisbury had assured the Queen that Curzon was capable of making the Indians, in her words, 'of course feel that we are masters, but it should be done kindly and not offensively, which alas! is so often not the case'. Once again, Salisbury exacted a literary sacrifice from Curzon for office. He deemed it inappropriate for the new Viceroy to publish his forthcoming work, *On the Indian Frontier*, so the £1,500 advance had to be repaid to the publisher and the book never appeared. *The Times* described it as 'an interesting appointment', but such was Curzon's genius as an administrator that it turned out to be one of Salisbury's best, even though his former junior minister was soon to clash with him over policy towards Persia and China.

Welcoming St John Brodrick to Curzon's post at the Foreign Office, Salisbury said: 'I think the obligation of running out to the division bell (which would make me mad) is imposed with undiscriminating severity. On some occasions, surely, it is not of first rate importance whether the majority is one hundred or one hundred and one.' Curzon's suggestion that his friend and fellow Soul George Wyndham should take Brodrick's place as Under-Secretary at the War Office, Salisbury dismissed with the words: 'I don't like poets.'[15]

The situation in South Africa, where Chamberlain and Kruger had been unable to agree on the nature, or even the existence, of British 'suzerainty' over the Transvaal, came to a head on 16th April 1898, when the Transvaal Government simply rejected the British definition outright. Salisbury then began thinking in terms of an agreement with Portugal, which owned Delagoa Bay in Mozambique, that might remove the republic's capacity to import arms in the event of war with Britain. Soon after negotiations began in May, Hatzfeldt stepped in to inform Salisbury that Germany could not accept any alternative in Delagoa Bay's status without her concurrence. Salisbury now took control of the negotiations from his Assistant Under-Secretary, Francis Bertie. He hoped soon to give the order for Kitchener to march on the Khalifa's army in the Sudan, a move likely to inflame French protests, and he did not want to be faced with a general Great Power combination against Britain.

Emphasising that Hatzfeldt should not continue to deal directly with Chamberlain, Salisbury examined the possibility of an Anglo-German treaty which would cut out any third power from taking advantage of the near-bankruptcy of the 'dying nation' Portugal. In late August, another bout of influenza sent Salisbury to Contreville in France to recuperate, from where he wrote to Balfour, who was conducting the day-to-day negotiations with Hatzfeldt. 'If the Germans take to being punctilious they are quite intolerable,' he said, adding that he was nonetheless satisfied with the overall result. Two days later, on 30th August, an Anglo-German Convention was signed, with a secret clause in which Britain and Germany agreed to oppose the intervention of any third power in Mozambique, Angola or Port Timor, and set out the way they would split the Portuguese empire between them in the event of its collapse.

The Convention also provided for simultaneous loans to Lisbon on the security of Timor and Portugal's African possessions, which in the event were not needed as Portugal managed to raise the money elsewhere. Germany meanwhile renounced all her interests in Delagoa Bay and promised neutrality in a future Anglo-Transvaal war, a result that Alfred Milner believed eliminated 'formally and forever Germany as a political influence in the Transvaal'.

In a memorandum of 5th September, Balfour called the deal 'a complete defensive alliance with Germany against any power desiring to intervene in Mozambique or Angola'.[16] Part of the reason Salisbury was wrongly believed to have pursued 'splendid isolation' is because few people knew about the many secret treaties he concluded. Not only had he tried to pursue Concert of Europe solutions over Armenia and Crete, but when his fears about Chinese nationalism were realised in the Boxer Rising two years later, he also attempted to co-ordinate a joint international response to that. These were not the actions of an isolationist.

The other Iberian 'dying nation', Spain, was in a more bellicose mood than her neighbour. Sore at Britain's unfriendly neutrality during her disastrous war against America, in August 1898 she began to build batteries which when completed would eventually command the British anchorage at Gibraltar. Salisbury telegraphed Drummond Wolff, by then British Ambassador in Madrid, to tell him that the construction must cease, and 'we would shrink from no consequences in order to avoid such a result; and though we must leave it to you to communicate our views in the manner least likely to wound Spain's susceptibilities, please understand that no room for misconception should be left as to the settled policy of this country'. Salisbury considered the blockade of Algeçiras as the best response to the Spanish sabre-rattling, but did not think an impending war with Spain important enough to cut short his rest-cure in Schlucht.[17] He was right; threatened with this naked gunboat diplomacy, Spain backed down and halted construction. In return, Salisbury signed a secret treaty on 16th March 1899 committing Britain to go to war with any power that attacked Algeçiras. As Gibraltar would have been threatened by any such attack it would probably have engendered war with Britain anyhow, but once again it was hardly the response of a dogmatic isolationist.

On 2nd September 1898, three days after the Anglo-German loan convention was signed, and just as the Spanish had resolved to step back from a confrontation, Kitchener won a famous victory over the Khalifa at the Battle of Omdurman. In the debate on the Queen's Speech in February, Salisbury had called Mahdism 'barbarous, cruel, unscrupulous, inconsistent with any idea of civilisation which one can entertain'. He authorised Cromer to extinguish it as soon as he could raise the finance. This at last came in June 1898, when Parliament agreed to treat its November 1896 loan of £800,000 as a gift instead, and generously to advance a further £750,000 to finish the job. On 27th July,

Cromer attended a Cabinet meeting to set out his plans for the settlement of the Nile Valley after the fall of Khartoum. It was resolved to hoist both the Union and the Egyptian Flags over the city simultaneously, to remind the Khedive that his sovereignty there 'must be in conjunction with the British Government'. Salisbury likened the situation to that of Marlborough's joint command over the British and German contingents, 'without treading on the independent rights of the allied Governments', during the War of Spanish Succession.

A 'Most Confidential' letter in red ink from McDonnell to the Prince of Wales disclosed what else the Cabinet had resolved at that meeting. The Intelligence reports that a French expedition under Captain Jean-Baptiste Marchand was making its way to the White Nile meant that Cromer was informed that, 'After the victory, the Sirdar will probably send an expedition of gunboats with a small force, which will ... go up the White Nile to Fashoda ... further action will be left to the officer in command. Both the British and Egyptian flags will be hoisted at suitable places and no others will be permitted.'

The Khalifa's army of around sixty thousand tribesmen obligingly made a frontal attack on the 8,200 British and 17,600 Egyptian and Sudanese troops in the Sirdar's army at Omdurman, near Khartoum. Hardly a Dervish made it to within 300 yards of the Allied lines. It was, as one of the participants later wrote, 'the most signal triumph ever gained by the arms of science over barbarians'. The loss of around sixteen thousand men to Western modern weaponry destroyed the Khalifa's power in the Sudan, although he personally escaped the field. Only fifty-one of Kitchener's men were killed and a further 382 were wounded. On 12th September, Salisbury acknowledged Cranbrook's congratulations:

> I cannot claim any share in it except that I insisted upon the employment of Kitchener, much against the grain of the great men in London. But it was a wonderful display of tenacity and foresight on the part of Kitchener and Cromer. The 'butcher's bill' is ghastly. The only consolation is that they were sustaining the worst and cruellest Government in the world. I hope it will calm some of the feverish aspirations on the back benches. A slaughter of sixteen thousand ought to satisfy the Jingoes for at least six months. Some people say that the strange outburst of unreasoning desire for war which showed itself last winter and spring was due to the intoxication of the Jubilee. If that was so, the victory at Khartoum may even do harm.

It was a characteristically downbeat assessment from a man who never gloried in carnage. His son, Brevet-Major Lord Edward Cecil, had been with the Sirdar and entered Khartoum with him after the battle, trying to identify the place where Gordon had fallen in 1885. Salisbury was keen to get back from the Hotel Altenburg in Münster to the

Foreign Office, and once he did he wrote to Rutland to say: 'I am very pleased that it has happened during our administration that the dark disgrace of Gordon's death has been wiped out.'[18] Salisbury supported the award of a peerage to Kitchener. Less pleasing for him was the task of apologising for Kitchener's draconian measures against the defeated Dervishes. Not only were many of the enemy wounded left to die, but more of the Khalifa's followers were later found in Khartoum and killed in cold blood.

In February 1899, the Queen complained to Salisbury about the desecration of the Mahdi's corpse, all of which bar its 'unusually large and shapely' skull had been dug up and flung into the Nile on Kitchener's orders. She ordered that the skull at least be given a decent burial. Salisbury explained to the House of Lords that 'certain steps had to be taken with a view to the possibility of the revival of fanatical feeling in the country'. These steps had not been a question of policy or ethics, but of 'taste', he explained, 'and taste varies in different countries at different times'. It was not until November 1899 that the Khalifa himself was killed along with a large number of his emirs, in a battle against General Sir Reginald Wingate. A contrite Kitchener reported to the Queen that the Khalifa's remains 'were respectfully buried by the survivors of his bodyguard'.[19]

~

In his 1888 Guildhall speech, Salisbury had described the various frontier wars then being fought as 'but the surf that marks the edge and the advance of the wave of civilisation'. It was this quotation that Winston Churchill chose for the front cover of his first book, *The Story of the Malakand Field Force*, published in 1898. Having read it, Salisbury asked to meet the twenty-four-year-old son of his former protagonist. At 4 p.m. on Tuesday, 5th July 1898, the great English tribal leader of the nineteenth century met his counterpart of the twentieth. 'The Great Man, Master of the British world, the unchallenged leader of the Conservative Party, a third time Prime Minister and Foreign Secretary at the height of his career,' Churchill later recorded in *My Early Life*, 'received me at the appointed hour, and I entered for the first time that spacious room overlooking Horse Guards Parade in which I was afterwards for so many years from time to time to see much grave business done in Peace and War.'

Salisbury got up to meet his young visitor at the door with 'old-world courtesy' and 'a charming gesture of welcome and salute', as he conducted him to a small sofa in the middle of his vast room. In a meeting which took longer than scheduled, Salisbury told him of his admiration for the subject matter and style of his book, adding, 'I myself have been able to form a truer picture of the kind of fighting that has been going on in these frontier valleys from your writings than from any other documents which it has been my duty to read.' By the end of the month, Salisbury had helped Churchill get attached as a supernumerary lieutenant to the 21st Lancers, with whom he charged at the Battle of Omdurman. Churchill's record of that campaign, *The River War*, had the following dedication:

THIS BOOK IS INSCRIBED TO
THE MARQUESS OF SALISBURY KG
UNDER WHOSE WISE DIRECTION
THE CONSERVATIVE PARTY HAVE LONG ENJOYED POWER
AND THE NATION PROSPERITY
DURING WHOSE ADMINISTRATIONS THE
REORGANISATION OF EGYPT HAS BEEN MAINLY ACCOMPLISHED
AND UPON WHOSE ADVICE HER MAJESTY DETERMINED
TO ORDER THE RECONQUEST OF THE SOUDAN

Salisbury's absence in Germany in the first half of September 1898 not only coincided with the Battle of Omdurman, but also with renewed rioting in Candia on Crete on 6th September and the assassination of the Empress of Austria at Lake Geneva four days later. In Candia, Muslim irregulars killed the British Vice-Consul and 800 Christian Cypriots. Salisbury gave the British admiral on the spot permission to execute the ringleaders without reference home. The stabbing of Elizabeth of Austria – the anarchist Luigi Lucheni had wanted to kill King Umberto of Italy but could not afford the fifty-lire train fare to Rome – was only the latest in a string of tragedies to hit the Hofburg Palace. Franz Josef's son, the Crown Prince Rudolf, had shot himself at Mayerling. His sister-in-law Sophia burned to death at a charity bazaar in Paris. His brother, the Emperor Maximilian of Mexico, was shot by firing squad. His cousin Ludwig of Bavaria drowned himself. A further five close relations died by fire, suicide, drowning, shooting and in a hunting accident. His nephew Archduke Franz Ferdinand's ill-fated visit to Sarajevo in June 1914 was therefore really only in line with family destiny. 'Fortune seems never tired of pursuing the Emperor of Austria,' was Salisbury's comment to the Queen, adding that the assassination of his wife seemed to have been undertaken out of 'a bastard sort of ambition – a diseased love of notoriety'.

Salisbury arrived back at Dover on the afternoon of 21st September, refreshed and in good health. He now faced his greatest international crisis since 1878, one for which he had been carefully preparing for over a year. Following the instructions that had been sewn into his jacket and were only to be opened after the Khalifa's defeat, Kitchener had taken a flotilla southwards down the White Nile. On 18th September 1898, he arrived at Fashoda, and, as Salisbury suspected, he found the French *tricoleur* flying there and the intrepid Captain Marchand already in possession.

FORTY-ONE

The Fashoda Crisis

The Marchand Expedition –
Parisian Politics – Triumph

September to November 1898

'All this weeping does not sound very soldierly.'

'There is nothing dramatic in the success of a diplomatist,' Salisbury had written of Lord Castlereagh in 1862. 'His victories are made up of a series of microscopic advantages: of a judicious suggestion here, or an opportune civility there: of a wise concession at one moment, and a far-sighted persistence at another; of sleepless tact, immovable calmness, and patience that no folly, no provocation, no blunders can shake.' Salisbury's diplomacy over the Fashoda Crisis employed all those qualities and justifies his reputation as a Foreign Secretary of the Castlereaghan stamp.

When in the spring of 1898, Gwendolen expressed surprise over the mildness of Salisbury's reaction to the Port Arthur crisis, her father had answered that with Kitchener about to march on Khartoum, 'In six months' time we shall be on the verge of war with France; I can't afford to quarrel with Russia now.' Salisbury understood how events taking place on the northern coast of China would reverberate thousands of miles away on the mud-flats of the White Nile. Salisbury's appeasement policy over Port Arthur must be seen in terms of what Gwendolen called 'the approaching crisis in the Nile Valley, which made friendliness with Russia a precautionary necessity'.

Ever since her refusal to participate in Gladstone's occupation of Egypt in 1882, France had looked for a way to exercise influence in the area of the Upper Nile. Control of the river's headwaters in the Bahr al-Ghazal region effectively meant control of Egypt, whose agriculture and economy so depended on them. Control of Egypt in turn meant control of the Suez Canal, Britain's principal line of communication with India. Possession of Fashoda, an abandoned mud-brick fort on the west bank of the White Nile, therefore had huge strategic implications.

'We must <u>occupy</u> Fashoda,' the leading French advocate of a Nile policy, Major Monteil, wrote to the Under-Secretary of the Colonies, André Lebon, in March 1894, but his own expedition was forced to turn back before it reached its objective. Although France considered Bahr al-Ghazal as being *res nullius* (belonging to none), Britain argued that it was actually the Khedive's, and in the House of Commons on 8th March 1895 the Liberal Under-Secretary at the Foreign Office, Sir Edward Grey, had unambiguously warned that any French expedition to territories 'over which our claims [as lessees of the Khedive] have been so long known – would be an unfriendly act and would be so regarded by us', a statement repeated by Curzon the following year. Undeterred, Captain Marchand, a veteran of various West African campaigns, was given written instructions by the Quai d'Orsay on 30th November 1895 to proceed to Bahr al-Ghazal and claim Fashoda for France. He did not leave Marseilles until 25th June 1896, by which time Salisbury had authorised Kitchener's advance on Dongola. 'The Nile Valley is in the diplomatic market,' Salisbury wrote to Cromer that April, 'and, considering how much Egypt depends on the Nile, we can hardly keep her from bidding at the sale.'

The epic journey of Captain Marchand and his ten French officers and NCOs, accompanied by a small number of Senegalese soldiers and bearers, covered more than two thousand miles from the West African coast, and traversed almost every kind of African terrain and conditions. Out of communication with France, they struggled manfully to reach Fashoda before the British. At one point the expedition had to carry its 100-horsepower steamer, the *Faidherbe*, for 120 miles over bush and mountain. It was a remarkable feat of leadership and endurance. Meanwhile, having received Intelligence reports that Marchand was on his way, Salisbury decided that Britain should send a secret expedition of her own by an only slightly shorter eastern route.

Salisbury chose Major J.A.L. Macdonald, a Royal Engineer who had been involved in the preliminary survey for the Uganda railway, to lead it. As the Mahdists then controlled the Nile around Omdurman and Khartoum, it had to start via Uganda, and take a route of no less than seventeen hundred miles. Ostensibly intended purely to map the sources of the Juba River, its true objective, to beat Marchand to Fashoda, was verbally explained to Macdonald at a secret meeting in the Foreign Office. Macdonald was further ordered to ignore 'any claims or pretensions which may be advanced on the ground of prior treaties or occupation'. Salisbury kept the Cabinet in the dark about the Macdonald expedition, only informing Hicks Beach of his real intentions because he needed £35,000 for 'sending an expedition to the east bank of the Nile to make friends with the tribes before the French get there from the west'. With only a handful of people knowing the real reason for the expedition, Salisbury had high hopes for it, but Macdonald soon ran into provisioning difficulties, and in September 1897 his force of Sudanese bearers and soldiers mutinied, wrecking any British hopes of beating Marchand.[1]

During the following month, October 1897, Salisbury put a brave face on what he told Lansdowne would be 'the diplomatic difficulties which might be interposed if any French explorer reaches the Nile before we have taken Khartoum', predicting that the Anglo-Egyptian claim to own the whole Nile Basin would attract 'a very lively protest from the French…. The diplomatic question will be interesting and difficult: but the increase of those qualities conferred by the French adventurers' "effective occupation" will not be serious.' The irony was not lost on him that 'by destroying the Dervish power we are killing the defender who is holding the Valley for us now'. Salisbury was keen to focus the area of contention with France down to the Nile Basin alone, so over what he called the 'jostlings' with France in the rest of Africa, Asia and Australasia he was happy to come to arrangements in 1897. Chamberlain and the Jingoist press ascribed this desire to find accommodations over Siam, Tunis, Madagascar and Niger to appeasement, as usual failing to appreciate the far subtler stategy Salisbury was pursuing.

An important letter to Philip Currie of 19th October 1897 lays bare Salisbury's overall strategic thinking at this crucial period:

> I confess that since, some two years back, the Cabinet refused me leave to take the Fleet up the Dardanelles because it was impracticable, I have regarded the Eastern question as having very little serious interest for England…. On the other hand our interest in Egypt is getting stronger… the idea that the Turkish Empire is on the point of dissolution has been dissipated: and the Concert of Europe has decisively shown that it can never be trusted with even the slenderest portion of Executive authority…. There is only one policy which it seems to me is left to us by the Cabinet decision to which I have referred – to strengthen our position on the Nile to its source; and to withdraw as much as possible from all responsibility at Constantinople.

Gwendolen remembered how, at a dinner party at Arlington Street in December 1897, her brother-in-law Lord Selborne argued that France must not be allowed to occupy a particular disputed territory. 'You are perfectly right – the French haven't a leg to stand upon,' said Salisbury, but in a lowered voice as he sank back into his armchair he added, 'but I mean to let them have their way all the same.' This, he explained, was because:

The first rule in negotiation was to select beforehand the one point which all others must subserve. That, in this instance...was to secure the Nile Valley.... If you want to understand my policy at this moment in any part of the world – in Europe, Asia, or the South Seas – you would have constantly to remember that.

Nor was Salisbury over-legalistic about the precise rights of the situation. 'We have two titles to rest upon in the Sudan,' he wrote to Earl Cadogan just before the debate on the Queen's Speech in early February 1898,

Conquest – and the former possession of Egypt. We are equally entitled to use both claims. 'Conquest' is much the most convenient – because it gets rid of the Caisse and the Mixed Courts and sundry other troubles. We were forced – partly by the course public discussions have taken – to rely more upon the Egyptian claim, at first. But I lose no chance of referring to the 'conquest' ground when I can. It was with a view to this policy that we hoisted the two flags.[2]

On 10th July 1898, unbeknownst to anyone in the outside world, Marchand arrived at the former Egyptian fort of Fashoda, after a two-year cross-continental voyage carrying champagne, claret, a mechanical piano, fresh uniforms and *haricots verts* seeds. On 3rd September, the day after the Battle of Omdurman, Kitchener opened an envelope from Salisbury containing his secret instructions. These ordered him to proceed 400 miles south to Fashoda and claim it in the name of the Khedive. Taking five gunboats, 100 Highlanders, a staff which included Colonel Wingate and Lord Edward Cecil, four machine-guns and 2,500 Sudanese troops, he arrived there on 18th September.

At their meeting aboard Kitchener's gunboat the following day, the two soldiers made their formal protestations about each other's 'illegal' presence, and then left the politicians to decide what should be done about the two nations claiming the same territory. They behaved impeccably towards one another, drank whisky and champagne, and congratulated each other on their achievements. Kitchener was particularly impressed with the Frenchmen's *haricots verts*. Although Kitchener refused Marchand the right to send telegrams, he did leave him some French newspapers, which plunged the French officers into despair because they contained the latest news about the Dreyfus Affair.[3] Once he had returned north, Kitchener reported to London that the position of Marchand, unable to communicate with the outside world except through him, was 'as impossible as it is absurd', but the focus had now moved away from what was happening on the Nile to what was taking place between Paris and London.

Although Salisbury did not believe France to be generally corrupt, but only 'partially' so, like most other Englishmen he was disgusted by the injustice meted out to Captain Alfred Dreyfus. 'I am afraid matters will go badly in France,' he told Rutland on 24th September (before the news arrived of what Kitchener had found at Fashoda), 'it is inconceivable that an army, with such traditions, can have reached such a pitch of degradation that forgery is the ordinary recourse of the Intelligence Department. It is a fearful result of competitive examination.' His fear was that the French Government, the seventh since 1893, might try to use the Fashoda incident to reunite a country torn apart by *L'Affaire*.

When the news of Marchand's predicament arrived in Paris, relayed by the British Ambassador, Sir Edward Monson, to the French Foreign Minister, Théophile Delcassé, nothing had been heard of the explorer since the previous December. Delcassé anxiously asked Monson if there had been any bloodshed, and when told that there had not, asked if he might communicate *en clair* with Marchand via Kitchener, who was by then back at Omdurman, having left 600 men at Fashoda guarding the British and Egyptian flags he had hoisted there. The French colonial party, led by Georges Trouillot, the Colonial Minister, and right-wing papers such as *Le Gaulois*, demanded that, as a typical headline put it, 'Marchand Cannot be Disavowed or Recalled!' Salisbury wrote to Devonshire on 27th September that, with the problems caused by the nationalist Dowager Empress of China and now the Fashoda Crisis, the most powerful factors in foreign affairs were 'the caprices of a Chinese Aunt and a Paris mob'.

The *Daily News* had that day attacked the Prime Minister for 'the widespread belief prevailing on the continent that Lord Salisbury's squeezability is unlimited'. They too had misunderstood how much the Nile Basin mattered to Salisbury. As Sir Almeric Fitzroy, the Clerk of the Privy Council, who had plenty of opportunity to study Salisbury at close quarters, put it during the opening stage of the crisis: 'The idea of a section of the British public that Lord Salisbury's resolution is in need of strengthening, shows very little knowledge of the sagacious states-manship that is often masked by the play of his placable and pessimistic intelligence.'

The Queen declared herself 'much worried about this terrible Fashoda deadlock – but quite agrees that we cannot yield'. In his conversations with the French Ambassador, Baron de Courcel, Salisbury made it perfectly clear that he had no intention of yielding. 'Khartoum and Fashoda will rally the popular sentiment as much as Trafalgar and Salamanca,' Harcourt warned Morley, as Rosebery declared that no British Government which gave way over Fashoda could last a week. With Monson writing long and aerated despatches about the mood in Paris, Salisbury calmly negotiated his way through the crisis, letting Delcassé know via the Austrian Chargé d'Affaires of 'the absolute impossibility of our abating one iota of our claim'.[4] This was not merely the traditionally tough opening shot of a campaign; this time Salisbury meant it.

In a long conversation with de Courcel at the Foreign Office on 12th October, Salisbury argued that 'no right or title of occupation could be created by the secret expedition across unknown and unexplored wastes, at a distance from the French border, by Monsieur Marchand and a scanty escort', whereas Kitchener's victory at Omdurman had convincingly re-established Khedival sovereignty over the Sudan, which Egypt had ruled before the Mahdi's revolt in 1881. He also pointed out that Marchand had not the necessary supplies to return westward, and as he could not navigate the Nile without British permission he was effectively stuck at Fashoda. Salisbury then offered the food, escort and arms necessary to go back, on the condition that he returned straight to French territory. No agreement was reached.

Although Monson predicted a military coup in Paris, and 'a government of generals who might even welcome war with England if they could in this way stave off the "revision" of the Dreyfus case', Salisbury did not budge. De Courcel then offered a compromise which would allow France a small outlet on the Nile, for which Marchand would vacate Fashoda. As Delcassé told his wife, 'All we have is arguments, and they have soldiers on the spot.' Martial passions were being stirred in France, although a backlash against war was also beginning to manifest itself. Jealous of office, Hanotaux publicly announced that 'nobody knew where Fashoda was or cared three straws about the Marchand expedition', and that furthermore Bahr al-Ghazal was simply 'a country inhabited by monkeys and black men worse than monkeys'.

On 25th October, after a long discussion, the British Cabinet agreed with Salisbury's stance that de Courcel should be told that 'so long as the French flag flew at Fashoda, it was impossible that this Government could enter upon any territorial discussion'. That same day the French Government was on the verge of collapse, prompting Salisbury to remark that 'in such a confused situation an ultimatum was hardly necessary'. With an aggressive Germany, France could not risk a full-scale war with Britain, although a significant proportion of her ultra-nationalist press was clamouring for it. On 27th October, Salisbury made a judicious concession, which, however tiny, allowed the French to retreat with some dignity intact. After Marchand's retreat, Salisbury told de Courcel, there could be 'a discussion upon the frontier in those regions', but he could promise nothing more than that. De Courcel's advice to Delcassé was to order an immediate and unconditional withdrawal from Fashoda, in the hope that Salisbury would then grant '*une petite négotiation sur le Bahr al-Ghazal*'.

On 28th October, Delcassé begged Monson for some definite concession over access to the Nile saying that he 'anxiously' wished to remain in office. Salisbury's reply to these and other such pleadings was merely to say: '*Oui, oui, vous avez raison, mais il faut vous en aller.*' Nor did he believe French intimations that Russia would support her. On discovering that the Tsar had personally refused to extend the alliance beyond Europe, Salisbury said: 'I thought as much. The Tsar's ministers never give anything for nothing.'[5] With his interest in, and knowledge of, the French Revolution, Salisbury diagnosed France's internal state as very much like 'the early days of the Directory – allowing for milder times. But there is no Bonaparte on the horizon yet.'

At a Cabinet meeting on 28th October, Salisbury refused to accede to Chamberlain's and Goschen's demands to present France with a definite ultimatum. Instead, orders were sent to mobilise the Mediterranean fleet, and the next day part of the Channel fleet was ordered to Gibraltar to put further pressure on the French at Toulon. Without ever categorically demanding the withdrawal of Marchand from Fashoda, let alone sending an ultimatum, Salisbury forced the French Government to give way. Delcassé's agents in England reported that the British Cabinet was 'obdurate and unanimous', and a strategic leak to the *Pall Mall Gazette* to that effect might also have helped tip the French hand. The Queen took a far softer line, warning Salisbury that 'a war for so miserable and small an object is what I could hardly bring myself to consent to'. She thought the sacrifice of many thousands of lives 'too horrible and wrong. We must try to save France from humiliation.' Her answer was to offer France communal access to the Nile and a generous delimitation of the French frontier at Bahr al-Ghazal.

In 1862, Salisbury had written of Castlereagh that 'a willingness on good cause to go to war is the best possible security for peace', and he had further calculated that the Third Republic was in no position to engage in a naval duel with Britain. Delcassé believed that the Toulon fleet would be sunk in a fortnight in any clash with the Royal Navy, and, as Salisbury suspected but could not have known for certain, the French Government never seriously considered fighting over Fashoda. Instead, on 3rd November, Delcassé instructed de Courcel to tell the British Government that 'in view of the precarious situation and state of health of Marchand and his companions, the Government had decided to leave Fashoda'.[6] It was as good an excuse as any, and not chosen before Delcassé had privately (and untruthfully) told Monson that Marchand had gone to Fashoda 'on his own initiative and in an excess of zeal', rather than under Government instructions.

Salisbury announced the news at a banquet at the Mansion House given in honour of Kitchener on 4th November. He had been greeted with cheers by the thousands who had lined the streets to see the Sirdar, the only politician amongst Curzon, Rosebery, Lansdowne and

Harcourt to be so honoured by the crowd. In his speech proposing
Kitchener's health, Salisbury was able to announce that: 'I received
from the French ambassador this afternoon the information that the
French Government had come to the conclusion that the occupation of
Fashoda was of no sort of value to the French republic,' at which *The
Times'* reporter noted loud cheers and some laughter, before Salisbury
continued, 'and they have resolved that that occupation must cease,' at
which there was renewed cheering. Later on he added: 'I daresay that we
shall have many discussions in the future; but the cause of controversy
of a singularly acute and somewhat dangerous character has been
removed and we cannot but congratulate ourselves.' He was right, and
even the Liberal attacks over his foreign policy – Lloyd George had
called Salisbury 'a kind of india rubber dummy' – temporarily abated.

That weekend, Chamberlain came to stay at Hatfield. 'You should
have seen the two walking yesterday,' Frances Balfour wrote to Betty.
'Uncle Robert in his Spanish poncho, with a shawl like a bolster round
his neck, and the most shapeless of wideawakes [broad-rimmed, low-
crowned, soft felt hats]. Joe in a bowler, with a long close-fitting grey
coat, a huge cigar in his mouth, no shoulders, and "dissenter" written
from his eyebrows to his toe.' When asked by his family why the French
had delayed so long before capitulating, Salisbury answered that they
could not make up their minds until they had heard from Marchand
how absolutely untenable the position was. Frances overheard
Chamberlain say to Salisbury that the Marchand expedition should
be allowed to come down the Nile to Cairo 'as a sort of triumphal
procession for us', but Salisbury 'laughed and said something
about their return via Abyssinia', the return route they did
eventually take. Salisbury had in fact already mentioned the Nile
course to de Courcel, who 'almost resented the suggestion as a great
insult'. As Salisbury told Devonshire, 'It is impossible to fathom the
eccentric depths of French feeling.'[7] His wife was yet more phlegmatic, remaining at Beaulieu throughout the crisis but writing to
relatives about her plans to disguise herself and escape back to Britain in
the event of hostilities.

It was to soothe French feeling that Salisbury dedicated his speech at
the Guildhall on 9th November. In the *Saturday Review* in 1863, he had
ridiculed the 'prodigious expenditure upon a bad dinner' and the Prime
Minister's traditional speech which 'shall seem to discuss the political
situation of the moment and yet shall make no indiscreet revelation of
the actual state of affairs'. Little had changed in the intervening thirty-
five years. Wearing his Garter star and looking remarkably well,
Salisbury arrived at the Guildhall to 'prolonged and enthusiastic cheering'. The tables were decked with orchids and other exquisite flowers.
The Salisburys processed to their places headed by trumpeters and the

loving cup was passed from lip to lip. After the meal the Queen's health was toasted, then the Prince of Wales's, then 'The Navy, Army and Reserve Forces', 'Their Excellencies the Foreign Ministers', and the Lord Mayor proposed 'Her Majesty's Ministers'.

As Salisbury rose to reply there was more cheering. He gave his audience a wide-ranging overview of the international situation. He expressed his condolences over the assassination of the Empress of Austria, 'one whose life had in no respect and in no one's judgment furnished any ground for so terrible a fate'. He complimented the Concert of Europe for according Crete its autonomy under the Sultan's suzerainty. Of Fashoda he paid tribute to 'the great judgment and common sense displayed by the French Government in circumstances of unusual difficulty', and said that their action had 'relieved Europe of a very dangerous and threatening storm'. He repeated his belief that 'You see nations who are decaying ... there are always neighbours.... And that is the cause of war.' He even managed to fit in an indiscretion when he described the American annexation of Spain's Philippines possessions as 'a grave and serious event, which may not conduce to the interests of peace, though I think that in any event it is likely to conduce to the interests of Great Britain'. Then there were more toasts, to 'The Judges and the Bar of England', 'The Lord Mayor and the Sheriffs', 'The Lord Chancellor' and 'The Houses of Parliament'. Apart from irritation at the cheers which greeted his mention of the Egyptian protectorate over the Sudan, the French press expressed general satisfaction with his remarks. The British press was also happy, the *Fortnightly Review* admitting that it was 'at Fashoda that Lord Salisbury has really retrieved himself'.[8]

If such bloodless victories were to be preserved, however, Salisbury knew that a closer relationship with Germany needed to be cultivated. To that end he wrote to the Queen on 17th November asking her to look favourably on any intimation from the Kaiser that he would like an invitation to Britain. He had been the first foreign head of state to congratulate the Queen after Omdurman and, as Salisbury pointed out, 'Matters have much changed during the last twelve months, and he has shown himself disposed to be friendly to this country. The attitude of France makes it desirable that the world should believe in an understanding between Germany and England.' Salisbury was not willing to countenance a formal one, which he feared might pitch Britain into just such an intervention on the Continent which his diplomacy was designed to avert, but he did not mind if the Quai d'Orsay suspected that such an alliance did exist.

In the House of Lords on 7th February 1899, Salisbury described 'Conquest' as the 'most useful, simple and salutary' of the two titles of right for the Anglo-Egyptian condominium in the Sudan. The following month he even partially admitted that the Macdonald expedition had been sent because he had been 'anxious to establish our military power at some station of the Upper Nile'. What in March 1898 would have seemed like provocation, by March 1899 looked like great foresight. On 21st March, Salisbury agreed a Convention with a new French Ambassador, Paul Cambon, over the boundary between the British and French spheres of influence in Africa, with Britain abandoning a claim for a corridor through French territory to Nigeria, and the watersheds of the Congo and the Nile fixed as the boundary between the British zone of influence and the French. 'It keeps the French entirely out of the Nile Valley, and restores most of the Egyptian province of Darfur,' he told the Queen.

Beaconsfield would have presented the coup to her in a much more flowery way, but when she saw Salisbury at Cimiez in the South of France a week later, the Queen heartily congratulated him on gaining the 'entire possession of the Valley of the Nile', urging that he now conclude an agreement with Russia over Chinese railways too. Salisbury hoped, as he told Curzon the next month, that in Anglo-French relations 'a mutual temper of apathetic tolerance may be cultivated on both sides, without sacrificing the interests of either... anything like a hearty goodwill between the two nations will not be possible'.[9] When Marchand received an emotional reception in France on his return, Salisbury was predictably unimpressed. 'All this weeping does not seem very soldierly,' he told Admiral Maxse, the Crimean War hero whose daughter Violet had married his son Edward in June 1894.

The Fashoda Crisis left a strongly Anglophobic feeling in France; it deeply influenced, amongst many others, the eight-year-old Charles de Gaulle. It did not prevent the Entente Cordiale being promulgated in 1904, however. By his careful diplomacy in isolating France, then his granite resolve in refusing to treat with her, then allowing her a last-minute, tiny, face-saving let-out whilst all the time refusing to menace her with an ultimatum, Salisbury had won his greatest victory. It was one he had been planning for many months, if not years. In his autobiography, *My Early Life*, Winston Churchill paid tribute to Salisbury's far-sightedness and single-mindedness during the late 1890s, and in particular the way in which:

> He allowed the British China fleet to be ordered out of Port Arthur by the Russians. He put up with the mockery of the Liberal Opposition of those days somewhat incongruously directed upon his pusillanimity. When the Olney Note about Venezuela – virtually an ultimatum – arrived from the United States, he sent the soft answer which turned away wrath. He confined his purposes to the British Empire. He kept the board clear for the Sudan and the Transvaal.[10]

The Sudan had been conquered, Gordon had been avenged and the French had been excluded from the Nile. One of Gladstone's two great blots on Britain's imperial escutcheon had therefore been wiped clean. Now it was the turn of the Transvaal.

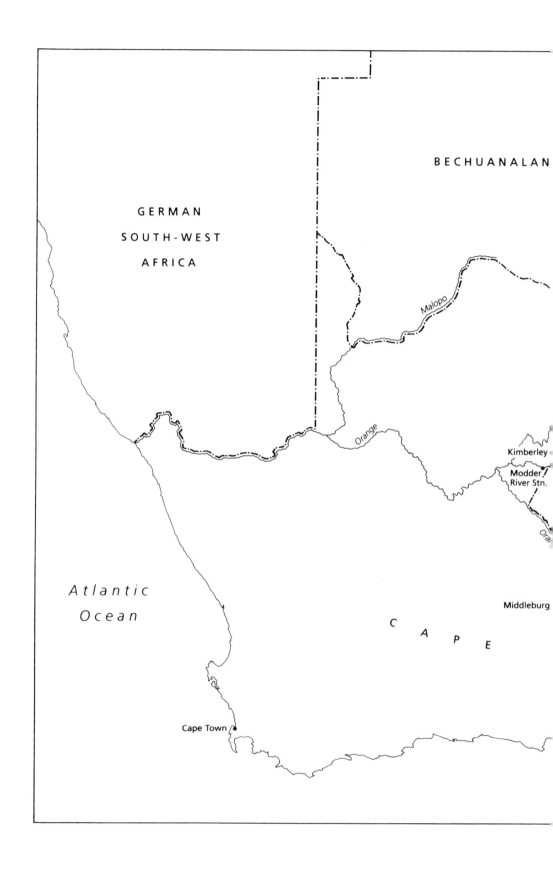

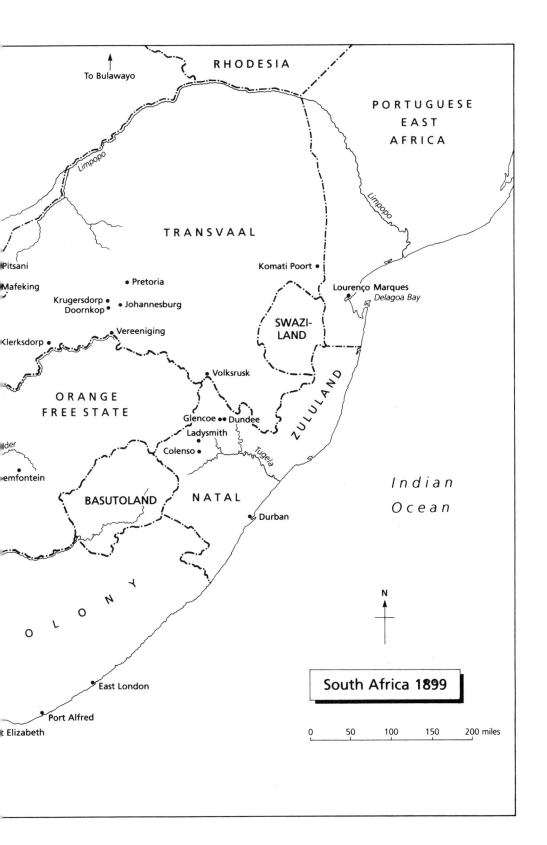

To Bulawayo

RHODESIA

PORTUGUESE
EAST
AFRICA

Limpopo

TRANSVAAL

Limpopo

Pitsani

Mafeking

Komati Poort

Lourenço Marques
Delagoa Bay

Krugersdorp
Doornkop

Pretoria

Johannesburg

SWAZI-
LAND

Klerksdorp

Vereeniging

ORANGE
FREE STATE

Volksrusk

ZULULAND

Glencoe Dundee
Ladysmith

Colenso

Tugela

der

emfontein

*Indian
Ocean*

BASUTOLAND

NATAL

Durban

OLONY

N

East London

Port Alfred

Elizabeth

South Africa 1899

| 0 | 50 | 100 | 150 | 200 miles |

FORTY-TWO

The Outbreak of the Boer War

Sir Alfred Milner – Appeasing Germany
– The 'Uitlanders' – Lady Salisbury's Illness
– Exasperation with the Transvaal
– The Aliens Bill – British Objectives
– The Boer Ultimatum

December 1898 to October 1899

'The real point to be made good to South Africa is that we not the
Dutch are Boss.'

Eighteen ninety-nine found Salisbury feeling his sixty-nine years. The
previous October he had told McDonnell that he could not 'venture the
expedition to Portsmouth on a winter evening' for a speaking engagement. Instead, he bought a Humber tricycle with raised handlebars and
Dunlop tyres (serviced by the British Pattison Hygienic Saddle
Company of New Bond Street). He wore a purple velvet poncho when
out cycling along the Mall and down Birdcage Walk in the mornings. In
March 1901, he was given the run of Buckingham Palace's gardens,
which disappointed the breakfast parties given by Harry Cust in
Delahaye Street and Clinton Dawkins in Queen Anne's Gate which
were discreetly arranged to view what even Lady Rayleigh had to admit
was 'a most amusing spectacle'.

The tricycle had a step on the back for a footman to stand on when it
went downhill, but at Hatfield enormous effort went into constructing
zig-zag paths to reduce the undulating parkland to tolerably level tracks.
Nearly five hundred tons of gravel had to be removed for one cutting
which was a hundred yards long and ten feet deep. 'He thoroughly enjoys
his exercise,' noted Lord Balcarres during a visit to Hatfield, 'and is
always in terror lest he be ambushed by some of the numerous grandchildren who all think him fair game. Recently at Beaulieu two of them
were found by their mother on a wall above his Lordship's favourite

walk, where they were awaiting his arrival with two huge jugs of water.'

His obesity led to other health complications, which depressed him but about which, beyond some occasional tricycling, he seems to have done very little. Bronchitis reappeared regularly and failing eyesight also bothered him. In December, Lady Rayleigh recorded how he 'sighed a good deal over his lot in life – he liked to live alone with quantities of books – instead of that he had to be always entertaining visitors'. His consolation was sleep: 'Nirvana is my ideal.' A defeat for female suffrage on the London County Council evoked a rare self-pitying remark to Frances Balfour: 'You mind too much. I have been beaten all my life, and do not mind now.' She recorded 'a certain pathos in the voice' as he said it.

The cause of his fall in spirits was not his own ill-health, however, but that of his wife. In May 1897, she had undergone an operation then called 'tapping for dropsy', after a long and debilitating illness. A weak pumping action in her heart led to an abnormal and painful accumulation of fluid in tissue spaces – today known as oedema – which required an operation to drain off. Although Salisbury had a lift installed for her, and the Queen invited her to drive on the smooth paths of Buckingham Palace's gardens rather than the jolting streets, she never fully recovered her strength. Her doctor, Sir William Broadbent, was in almost constant attendance, and her artist friend, Sir Edward Burne-Jones, sent her a drawing, but even the mountain air of Schlucht afforded her only temporary remission. Just as Salisbury, whose distrust of experts led him to blame the doctors for not diagnosing her early enough, began to allow himself some shafts of optimism in late 1898, she suffered a stroke.

'The three years' fight for her cure or relief never slackened,' remembered their daughter Gwendolen, on whom much of the burden fell. 'There was an unceasing search for new treatments, new remedies, fresh advice' about a life-threatening disease which today is controlled by aspirin. 'The possibility of failure was never admitted,' recalled Gwendolen, although it must have lain at the back of Salisbury's mind; dropsy had been the disease which killed his mother. 'The sympathy with which he constantly enveloped her never suggested to onlookers any expectation of it for himself. He refused to admit there was any call for it,' despite the fact that it involved an undoubted strain upon his own health. When she was in the South of France trying to recuperate, he was forced to stay in London working, but every morning, 'his one query is whether any letter has arrived from Lady Salisbury in Beaulieu'.[1]

'War, in whatever form it comes, is a horrible and barbarous thing. It must produce slaughter and rapine; it must often reduce the free to dependence, and the prosperous to ruin; it must frequently condemn proud and renowned nationalities to insignificance or to extinction.' So wrote Salisbury in his essay on Poland in the *Quarterly Review* in April 1863, and so he had long believed. The Afghan, Zulu, Ashanti and other 'little wars' in which he had been involved were but the almost accidental by-products of imperialism. Yet it was also under Salisbury's premiership that a full-scale war broke out in 1899 involving the British Empire in a bitter, expensive, thirty-one-month struggle with a white nation – albeit not a Great Power – which did indeed produce all the results he had listed in the *Quarterly Review* three and a half decades earlier. Was this reversal of his pacific policy because, as A.J.P. Taylor has pronounced, 'Salisbury was dragged into war by Chamberlain; and Chamberlain was dragged into war by Milner,' or had imperial *hubris*, stoked up by the Fashoda success, gone to his head? Or did he fully approve of the war which took so much of the sheen off British imperialism and led to an unwelcome re-examination of many hitherto accepted assumptions?

Salisbury had formed a low opinion of the Boers when he had come into close contact with them half a century earlier. He had written to his father from Cape Town in November 1851 that 'few of the Boers know what "free institutions" mean: they are as degraded a set of savages as any white men in the world: many of them can't read – few of them can write'. In his *Saturday Review* journalism in 1860, he had suggested that the Boers had only trekked out of British jurisdiction because 'They could stand the loss of their nationality but not the loss of their slaves.' The Transvaal republic which they had set up was 'their last retreat', somewhere they could 'maltreat the natives to the utmost of their hearts' content'.

It was the humiliation of the British military defeat at Majuba Hill in 1881, and the Gladstone Government's subsequent 'lamentable' Conventions signed in 1881 and 1884, which Salisbury called 'that attempt at the Quakerization of Mankind', which infuriated him. At the unveiling of a bust of Beaconsfield at the Pall Mall Club in May 1883, Salisbury recalled how his late Chief had 'repudiated with indignant emphasis the conduct of a Ministry that was suing for peace [and] trailing the standard of England in the dust'. This was no synthetic outrage. In a letter to the Lord Mayor of London in September 1885, after he had become Prime Minister, he wrote: 'I quite appreciate the sinister character of the neighbourhood of the Boers. We owe those difficulties to the retreat after Majuba Hill, and it may be that some day or other that that terrible blunder will have to be repaired.'

This could not be achieved in the short term, and in February 1887 Salisbury made one of his indiscretions when he wrote to a correspondent that 'In their heart of hearts MPs have made up their minds to abandon South Africa if it ever threatens to cost them any considerable expense again.' When the letter became public, the price of South African stocks plunged in the City and, under pressure from Sir Henry Holland, Salisbury had to explain to Parliament that he had merely been 'speaking of the heart of hearts of the ordinary MPs and not that exalted body of Her Majesty's Ministers'.[2]

By September 1891, Salisbury was even sceptical about the idea of forcing the Transvaal to extend the suffrage to all white immigrants, telling Holland, by then Lord Knutsford, that Sir Henry Lock, the South African High Commissioner who proposed it, 'must be a little off his head. Universal suffrage exercised mainly by a floating population of mining adventurers can not be an ideal form of government.' Two months later, the Cabinet decided not to extend self-government to Natal, where, as he told the Queen, 'the native population exceeds the white population in the proportion of ten to one' and where he feared that these natives 'would remain practically at the mercy of a ministry chosen by the small majority of colonists', little different from the harsh settler regimes which he had personally witnessed misgoverning New Zealand and the Cape in the early 1850s.

The Transvaal was in no sense a democracy. No Catholic or Jew was allowed to vote or hold office. Every Boer was compelled to own a rifle, no non-Boer was allowed to. Johannesburg, with 50,000 mainly Uitlander inhabitants, was not even allowed an unelected municipal council. English was banned in all official proceedings. Judges were appointed by Kruger, who controlled all the government monopolies from jam to dynamite. By far the largest proportion of the tax burden was carried by the Uitlanders, yet no open-air public meetings were permitted. Newspapers could be closed down arbitrarily without any reason given. Above all, full citizenship was almost impossible to gain for non-Boers. Pretoria ran a tight, tough, quasi-police state.

In the immediate aftermath of the Jameson Raid, Salisbury was unconvinced about the desirability of President Kruger visiting Britain, believing that once the President had discovered that Germany would not fight for the Transvaal, he would find it was 'not worth his while to come here to be pressed about Uitlanders' votes'. In a somewhat cynical display of Realpolitik, Salisbury told Selborne that 'There are consolations in every trouble. If there is a permanent strain between the South African Republic [Transvaal] and the Cape Colony, there is no immediate danger of their combining in the immediate future to set themselves up as the United States of South Africa.'[3] As it was, Cecil Rhodes's machinations and the suspicions they inevitably raised in Pretoria made this highly unlikely. For all his public appreciation of Rhodes's work, Salisbury's private view was not dissimilar from Mark Twain's, who said of the great adventurer: 'I admire him, I frankly confess it; and when his time comes, I shall buy a piece of the rope for a keepsake.'

In November 1898, Salisbury's policy of not unnecessarily antagonising Kruger was tested when Lord Harris, the Chairman of Consolidated Goldfields, asked him how the British Government would respond to his company granting the Transvaal's request for a £2 million loan. On this occasion, Salisbury's *laissez-faire* beliefs neatly dovetailed with his strategic overview. 'I do not think it is wise for us either to interfere with the business of English bankers – or on the other [hand] to endorse Kruger's policy,' he told Harris and Chamberlain. His Colonial Secretary disagreed, and told Lord Rothschild, who was also involved, that he and Harris 'should not advance a sixpence to the Transvaal Government without satisfactory guarantees of some effective reform in administration', i.e. towards the Uitlanders' demands over education, city improvements, sanitation, policing and above all the franchise.[4]

The following week, Kitchener and Milner, who were home on leave, visited Hatfield. Milner told Frances Balfour, and therefore probably also Salisbury, 'that he thought Rhodesia would never be like the Rand, but it has enough gold to be worth settling and working. The fatal point in South Africa now is the Transvaal – the corruption and mismanagement are such that they cannot be tolerated indefinitely. We shall have to interfere sooner or later.' One of the other guests that day was Violet, Lady Edward Cecil, whom Milner married after her husband's death.

Later that month, Chamberlain, who substantially agreed with Milner's analysis, sent a letter which belies his reputation as someone who was continually attempting to criticise and subvert Salisbury's foreign policy:

> In wishing you and yours a merry Christmas I hope I may be allowed to congratulate you most heartily on your management of Foreign Affairs during the last twelve months and on the great success which has attended it. Crete, West Africa and Egypt – not to mention our relations with the United States – constitute a real triumph and meanwhile Germany has been comparatively friendly and Russia is on her best behaviour.[5]

Soon all of that was to be jeopardised by their South African adventure, which provoked huge hostility to Britain amongst all the Great Powers. By creating the ideal international climate in which Britain could act against the Transvaal without giving any other Powers the opportunity to intervene – despite constant rumours of anti-British coalitions – Salisbury's diplomacy was as much responsible for the Boer War as Chamberlain's agitation in favour of the Uitlanders' rights.

As the year 1899 progressed, British policy-makers became convinced that British paramountcy in southern Africa, so crucial for the future development and protection of the Empire, was under growing threat. The two Boer republics were asserting their independence in a way both offensive to Anglo-Saxon pride and damaging to British interests in the region. This racial antagonism between Boer and Briton was, it was felt in Cape Town, Pretoria and London, leading inexorably towards a clash.

As Chamberlain had been closely involved in the London Convention negotiations between Kruger and Derby in 1884, he was accepted as the specialist, and as Liberal Unionist leader in the Commons he had a far stronger voice in the Cabinet than his post as Colonial Secretary implied. He and Salisbury were genuinely outraged at the way Pretoria treated the Uitlanders. Calling them 'strangers' and 'aliens', the Transvaal Government repeatedly raised the residency period requirements for the franchise and ignored their petitions. The Uitlanders themselves found that, despite their refusal to rebel during the Jameson Raid, they were subjected to higher taxes, poorer school provision, a corrupt administration, heavy-handed policing, and a series of private and state monopolies that grossly inflated their cost of living.[6] All this was humiliating for the British Government, which saw itself as their champion as so many of the Uitlanders were British born.

'I do not know whether Rhodes can keep a secret,' Salisbury told Chamberlain in January 1899, 'but if so his reputation belies him.' Salisbury insisted that the British response to Kruger should be co-ordinated through official channels, primarily the Cabinet, Chamberlain and Milner, rather than thrust along by the machinations of the Chartered Company and South African monopoly capitalists. He was relatively relaxed about the perennial prospect of a combination of powers against England. Of one such rumour, that France was planning to invade Egypt, he told Brodrick that the other Great Powers 'may back her if she chooses to go first – but it will be a purely sentimental backing. No one can tell what the French Chamber may do next November: but they will get no assistance for an attack on England.' To be on the safe side, Salisbury ordained that there would be no let-up in the heavy defence expenditure programme he had instituted in 1889, and which Rosebery had continued. Of the Tsar's calls for peace and disarmament, Salisbury stated in the debate on the Address on 7th February 1899 that 'while these efforts for peace are being prosecuted we must obey the proverb and prepare for war'.[7]

Although the situation with Germany over Samoa never actually threatened war, it went some way towards cooling the friendlier relations Salisbury had tried to engender at the time of the Delagoa Bay agreement. Back in March 1889, Salisbury had wanted to end the joint Anglo-American-German sovereignty over the islands, and either partition them up or at least divide them into defined spheres of influence. 'Samoa matters very little to us,' he told Malet at the time, 'and I strongly demur to an arrangement under which, for Samoa's sake, we shall quarrel either with the Germans or the Americans once a month.' The situation he called 'furor consularis', whereby two of the consuls

could outvote the third, continued however. By April 1899, with no
prospect of agreement over the islands, Salisbury wrote tongue in cheek
to Chamberlain that 'the question is how are we to work an impossible
tri-dominion? – or to get rid of it. I see no issue except to draw lots and
divide the islands. But that would be undignified.'

Salisbury's seeming reluctance to appease the Kaiser over Samoa led
to an extraordinary, almost pathetic letter of complaint from Wilhelm II
to his grandmother in late May. 'Lord Salisbury cares for us no more
than for Portugal, Chile or the Patagonians,' bemoaned the Kaiser, going
on to mention the Prime Minister's 'high-handed treatment' of
Germany, which was all 'on account of a stupid island which is a
hairpin to England compared to the thousands of square miles she is
annexing right and left unopposed every year'. Salisbury's response to
the Queen, affixed to a memorandum refuting the allegations, was to
ascribe the Kaiser's anger to 'his outspoken desire' for an Anglo-French
war, which was now unlikely to be gratified. Salisbury ended his letter
with a typically understated rebuke to the Queen's grandson: 'He
entirely concurs with your Majesty in thinking that it is quite new for a
Sovereign to attack in a private letter the Minister of another Sovereign;
especially one to whom he is so closely related. It is not a desirable
innovation, and might produce some confusion.'8 The Queen's laconic
and accurate comment to her daughter Vicky, the Kaiser's widowed
mother, about his threat not to visit Britain while Salisbury was Prime
Minister was: 'I think he will have to wait a long time.'

The Queen replied to her grandson, enclosing Salisbury's uncompromising memorandum, 'which will show you are under a misapprehension', and adding that she 'never personally attacked or
complained of Prince Bismarck, though I knew well what a bitter
enemy he was to England and all the harm he did'. She ended by inviting him to Osborne. The Kaiser was unappeased. After a yachting
competition in Kiel later that month, the Ulster Tory MP Colonel
Saunderson found 'the All-Highest' 'much incensed against England
about Samoa. Lord Salisbury has evidently succeeded in roughing him
up to an extraordinary extent.' For all the ill-feeling, however, Germany
was not about to interfere in the Transvaal again.

Salisbury offered Germany a deal which gave her paramountcy in
Samoa, a part of the world that was utterly unimportant to the development of the British Empire. In 1886 he had warned Currie that Bismarck
was interested in Samoa and by encouraging the British client there,
King Mahietoa, 'if we do not look out...we shall force him into a
menacing position on a matter upon which we are not prepared to resist
him in the end: and the result will be a discreditable "skedaddle"'.
Instead, in 1899 Britain effected a fairly creditable exit, and helped to buy
German non-intervention in southern African affairs into the bargain.

In March 1899, after a British subject, Mr Edgar, was shot dead in a drunken brawl by a Boer policeman who subsequently escaped punishment, 21,684 Uitlanders signed a petition of reproach. This time they addressed it not to Kruger, but to Queen Victoria. Chamberlain's Cabinet memorandum on the subject argued that it could not be ignored, otherwise 'British influence in South Africa will be severely shaken'. An ultimatum on the other hand would be likely to lead to war. Instead, Chamberlain enclosed a draft despatch 'intended as a protest, and still more as an appeal to public opinion'. This acknowledged that the British Government recognised the Transvaal's right to manage its own internal affairs, but only under the terms of the 1881 and 1884 Conventions. It then went into detail about how the Uitlanders were treated as second-class non-citizens, despite the enormous contribution they made to the country's prosperity. It mentioned in particular education costs, the liquor laws, the lack of political representation, bias in local government, police brutality, arbitrary arrests, the partiality of the courts, press censorship, government corruption, the expulsion laws and the precedence given to Afrikaans over English, even in mainly Uitlander schools.

The draft despatch was discussed at a Cabinet meeting on 2nd May. Balfour believed that the Boers would sooner fight than accept a constitution of one (white) man, one vote. Salisbury, and to a lesser extent Hicks Beach and Lansdowne, agreed. The Prime Minister declared himself 'uncomfortable' with the despatch and critical of Milner, who was furnishing Chamberlain with highly coloured accounts of Uitlander distress. The Cabinet agreed that the situation in the Transvaal was 'so unsatisfactory as to be almost intolerable', but Balfour managed to get the despatch held up for a week.

On 4th May, Milner sent Chamberlain what later became known as the 'Helot Despatch' because of its equation of the Uitlanders with the slaves of Classical Greece. Written with deliberate sensationalism for eventual publication, the High Commissioner reported that: 'The spectacle of thousands of British subjects kept permanently in the position of helots, constantly chafing under undoubted grievances, and calling vainly to H.M.G. for redress' was one that undermined British prestige around the globe. Milner warned that the Transvaal was arming quickly, acting in close conjunction with the Orange Free State whilst propagating 'a ceaseless stream of malignant lies about the intentions of the British Government'. All he wanted, Milner protested, was 'to obtain for the Uitlanders in the Transvaal a fair share of the Government of the country which owes everything to their exertion'.

Salisbury was unused to his new role of champion of the democratic and civil rights of workers, but on 9th May he and Balfour withdrew their objections to Chamberlain's despatch, which was sent off. In Cabinet a week later, Chamberlain expressed the hope that negotiations with the Transvaal might be brought to a satisfactory conclusion, and at the end of the month, after a second Uitlander petition had been published, Kruger met Milner for a conference at Bloemfontein. 'Three Royal functions and two public dinners in four days,' Salisbury replied to Brodrick on 31st May as the Conference began, 'with a North-East wind, naturally gave me a touch of the "flu". But I am about again.'

On 5th June, the Bloemfontein Conference broke up in failure and mutual recrimination. Kruger had tried to haggle over the extent of Uitlander franchise, offering a seven-year residency qualification and five seats in the thirty-five-seat Volksraad. When Milner demanded more, Kruger told him: 'I am not ready to hand over my country to strangers. There is nothing else now to be done.' For his part, Milner privately called Kruger 'a frock-coated neanderthal'.[9] Later that month, Chamberlain published Milner's 'Helot Despatch' in a Blue Book, raising the temperature of the dispute still further.

When on 10th June the leading article in the pro-Unionist *Daily Telegraph* called for an ultimatum against the Transvaal, Salisbury was secretly informed via McDonnell by its proprietor Sir Edward Levy-Lawson, later 1st Baron Burnham, that Chamberlain had instigated it. Salisbury saw Levy-Lawson on the 13th and an hour later he also saw Buckle. According to Buckle's report to Arthur Walter, *The Times'* Chief Proprietor, Salisbury 'thinks the Government must go on and apply steady and increasing pressure to Kruger: but that there is no need to hurry, and that anything approaching to an ultimatum should be delayed for as long as possible'. Salisbury added that he had information that Kruger was coming under great pressure from the Cape Dutch leaders, the Orange Free State, the German and Dutch Governments and some of his own supporters to make enough concessions to avoid war. Buckle noted that the difference between Salisbury and Chamberlain did not seem to be over the importance of slow pressure being exerted on the Transvaal, so much as the likelihood of eventual war, with Salisbury for once being optimistic.

Salisbury was very concerned about the domestic unpopularity of a war, telling the Queen on 13th May that 'it was recognised by all members of the Cabinet that any actual breach with the Transvaal would not be cordially supported here, and would divide the Colonial community at Cape Town into two hostile camps. For those reasons war would be very much to be deprecated.' Nonetheless, the Cabinet were unanimous in their decision 'to maintain firmly their language and protests towards President Kruger', and 'the future must be shaped very much by his action'. Salisbury found it hard to believe that a tiny country of 410,000 Boers could seriously be considering taking on the might of the British Empire at such a pitch of its fame. Intelligence sources nevertheless continued to suggest that the republics were arming to the maximum extent possible.

'Chamberlain is trying to frighten Kruger,' Salisbury told Frances Balfour, but she noted how it was said 'rather in a voice as if he thought it was an experiment not going to succeed'. Telling Milner on 21st June that a British ultimatum backed up by a reinforcement of 10,000 men would force a 'complete climb-down' and 'surrender' by Kruger, Chamberlain added that if he was wrong, a war, however 'deplorable', would 'at least enable us to put things on a sound basis for the future better than even the best-devised constitution can'.[10] It was a view entirely reciprocated by Milner, but not yet by Salisbury, Balfour or Hicks Beach, who were still keen to balance the books and not take on the open-ended financial commitment of a full-scale war. The policy of 'steady and continued pressure', but without reinforcements or an ulti-matum, was therefore adhered to throughout June 1899.

On 6th July, Lady Salisbury suffered another stroke. 'The cough under which Lady Salisbury has suffered has produced a slight effusion at the base of the brain,' Salisbury reported to McDonnell from Walmer Castle. One of her doctors, Sir Douglas Williams, 'refused as yet to say how the matter will turn – but my fears far outweigh my hopes'. Although she recovered her power of speech, she could not use her right arm and other limbs were also occasionally rendered powerless. During this crucial period in Anglo-Transvaal relations, Salisbury cared more for her than for politics. 'Poor Salisbury!' George Hamilton wrote to Curzon in India on 14th July. 'I do not know what he will do without her; and Kruger's, as well as other foreign difficulties, just now require his very closest attention.' They did not immediately get it. By 19th July, Lady Salisbury was slightly better, but at best permanently convales-cent. 'I found Uncle Robert sitting on the ramparts, looking very weary and low,' Frances wrote to Betty Balfour from Walmer. Septic poisoning was found, Lady Salisbury's lungs were affected and she had occasional 'imaginings'. As her husband cancelled his speaking engagements, he thanked one friend for his 'kind expression in regard of my great sorrow – which is indeed hard to bear'.

Hatzfeldt noticed a new irritability in Salisbury around this time. In his reports to von Holstein, the Ambassador omitted to mention the exasperation that Salisbury had expressed to him privately about the Kaiser's recent remarks to the Queen. When Hatzfeldt, with reference to French envy of Britain in Egypt, 'urged him to express his opinion by pointing out the great uncertainty of the future', Salisbury tersely answered that: 'England would be obliged to act according to her motto: "Dieu et mon droit".' When Salisbury claimed that the Anglo-German agreement on Portugal had been concluded by Balfour rather than him, and Hatzfeldt understandably pointed out that it had in fact largely been negotiated by the Prime Minister, Salisbury merely shrugged his shoulders.[11]

'The general feeling of the Cabinet was one of indignation with the Transvaal,' McDonnell wrote in his regular report to the Prince of Wales after a briefing from Salisbury, 'but it is also evident that the majority of H.M.'s ministers are determined to move very warily and not to take any hurried action.' The terms of a new franchise offer from Kruger were about to be received and Salisbury, still suspecting that a war would be unpopular, favoured 'very circumspect action'. Meanwhile, he was receiving secret memoranda about the large orders for weapons and ammunition that the Transvaal had placed in Europe, and how the Orange Free State had also begun arming rapidly after the collapse of the Bloemfontein talks. Intelligence reports asserted that these arms were still being smuggled in through Delagoa Bay, over which the Portuguese had retained customs rights.

On 18th July, McDonnell told the Prince that private information from non-official sources suggested that Kruger was about to propose a seven-year residency qualification pre-dated to 1890, which Salisbury believed might be 'a satisfactory solution'. Most Cabinets were now devoted solely to the Transvaal issue. Chamberlain initially saw Kruger's offer as acceptable, writing to Salisbury to say: 'I am really sanguine that the crisis is over,' and calling it 'a triumph of moral pressure – accompanied by special service officers and three batteries of artillery'. Salisbury could not have communicated this sentiment to the Queen in his conversation with her that day, because writing in her journal at Windsor that evening she concluded that 'the country, as well as the Cabinet, excepting perhaps Mr Chamberlain, were against a war'.[12]

In fact, Chamberlain was in favour of accepting the seven-year residency compromise, even though he had originally wanted it to be only five. He told Milner that 'no one would dream of fighting over two years in qualification period', and ordered him to accept it as a basis of settlement. Milner was angry at the compromise, but fully appreciated the danger of being seen as wanting war at any price. With even *The Times* proclaiming the crisis over, it was now Salisbury who insisted on the pressure being kept up on Kruger, even to the extent of threatening troop movements near the northern Transvaal. On 19th July 1899, he wrote an important letter to Chamberlain showing how he wanted to squeeze yet more out of the retreating Boers if possible:

> It was not easy to persuade – as you succeeded in persuading – Kruger that we were in earnest. The moment he attained to that belief, the risk to himself was evidently more than he cared to run ... above all it is necessary to guard against backsliding.... I most earnestly press you to think of the advantage of keeping up the pressure from the Northern side.

By this Salisbury meant sending a brigade to reinforce the Matabeleland town of Bulawayo, which he pointed out would be free of the parliamentary pressures of Natal and Cape Colony, a healthier place to station an army, and in constant communication with the disaffected Uitlander population in Johannesburg. Far from being a dove, as he later made out and seemed to imply to the Queen, Salisbury adopted a particularly hawkish stance at precisely the time that Kruger was coming to the conclusion that Britain was more interested in humiliating the Transvaal than in winning democratic rights for her Uitlander subjects. The Cabinet's decision to accept Kruger's seven-year franchise offer, but also to demand a Tribunal of Arbitration and another Milner–Kruger conference, was also largely down to Salisbury, who saw Kruger's concessions as a starting point for negotiations, when in Pretoria they were regarded as a best and final offer.[13]

On 27th July, Selborne reported to Milner a conversation which makes it quite clear that Kruger had assessed the situation correctly:

> Last Sunday [23rd July] I had it all out with the PM at Walmer. I was wholly pleased with the result. He said he meant to secure full effective (as distinct from pedantic) compliance with your Bloemfontein demands as a minimum, and he added 'of course the real point to be made good to South Africa is that we not the Dutch are Boss,' but he added rather testily 'I will go my own pace. I will not be hurried by anyone, not by all the English in South Africa.' He has got a great desire to send a brigade to Bulawayo as pressure but the War Office are very averse. He is altogether in favour of continuing steadily the military preparations.

When, four days later, Selborne, whose correspondence with Milner makes it clear that both men cordially envisaged war, took Salisbury a despatch accusing the Transvaal Government of bad faith, and proposing a joint inquiry into the franchise law and another conference between Milner and Kruger, he was told: 'Do not alter a word.'

Salisbury sent occasional notes to Hicks Beach implicitly criticising Milner – 'Does not this remind you of all that happened with Bartle Frere in 1879?' – but, as with the Sudan the previous year, it was he himself who drove forward the tough stance. In the House of Lords debate on the Transvaal on 28th July, unencumbered by any personal responsibility like Chamberlain, Salisbury denounced the 1881 Anglo-Boer Convention, saying, 'I resisted it to the utmost of my power,' and that it had 'in my eyes almost the most dangerous fault a policy can have – it was an optimistic policy'. Salisbury said that since 1881 the policy of the Transvaal had been to 'reduce the English to the condition of almost a conquered, certainly of a subjugated race'. Only if the Afrikaners 'show a real desire to eliminate the racial inequality' between Briton and Boer could there now be peace.

Then came a very thinly veiled threat: 'If this country has to make exertions in order to secure the most elementary justice for British subjects, I am quite sure we will not reinstate a state of things which will bring back the old difficulties.... I do not think President Kruger has sufficiently considered this.' Should the Transvaal not concede enough to avert a war, he was warning, it would end in her annexation, and just to re-emphasise the seriousness of the situation, he wound up with the words: 'We have put our hands to the plough, and we do not intend to withdraw them from it.' It was Salisbury's first public statement since his wife's stroke and there had been considerable speculation that Salisbury might let Chamberlain down, reverting to the appeasement tack he had followed at Port Arthur. But the commentators misunderstood his policy, just as Salisbury failed to appreciate how little Kruger would allow himself to be pushed.[14]

Between 1870 and 1891, the European population of South Africa had leapt from fewer than a quarter of a million to over six hundred thousand. Without a proper census the exact numbers could not be known, but the Boers felt themselves swamped by the Uitlanders, many of whom tended to live a very different and more hedonistic life than the People of the Book. Nominal suzerainty was one thing; but this dispute over Uitlander rights was now being seen by both sides as a question of overall British supremacy, something to which the voortrekkers and their descendants refused to accede.

One embarrassment for Salisbury in his demands for the Uitlanders' immigration rights was the tough Aliens Exclusion Bill that he had himself attempted to introduce in 1894, designed to exclude undesirable immigrants. For someone so keen to promote emigration, it was understandable if he simultaneously, as he put it in a letter in 1887, had serious objections to 'the immigration of pauperised foreigners into this country'. In May 1898, his new Aliens Bill received its second reading in the Lords. When Lord Monkswell said that it would have refused entry to the Huguenots in Tudor times, Salisbury answered that all countries had the right to refuse access to persons 'likely to become a public charge', as well as 'idiots, lunatics, and persons suffering from any dangerous infections, or contagious diseases'. He complained that a Commission had sat for five years on the subject, but although it had 'printed as much evidence as would cover half an acre of land', nothing concrete had been done.

The legislation was intended to cut the number of very poor Polish and Russian Jews who were escaping Tsarist pogroms and arriving in London's East End in the 1890s. 'These destitute aliens are concentrated on particular portions of the community,' Salisbury told the House of Lords, 'upon particular parishes, and they weigh down the natives where the rates are already a heavy burden.' To protestations that London's Jewish community helped to take care of its co-religionists, Salisbury pointed out that in 1897 the parish of St George's-in-the-East relieved 980 aliens, of whom 908 were Polish and Russian Jews: 'Now, that seems to me to dispose of the contention that the Jewish community relieves them all.'

Salisbury was at pains to point out that it was to help the already overburdened indigenous East Enders that he wanted the powers 'to refuse to have the destitute, the abjectly destitute often, of other countries thrust upon our shores to add to the obligations with which we have to deal.... The rates are rising, rising, rising, and many philanthropic members of the community think there is no better way in which they can spend their time than in discovering new modes by which new rates can be laid upon the ratepayer.' The Bill passed by 81 to 19.[15] Nevertheless, in 1900 a total of 135,000 would-be immigrants landed, of whom half were refused entry. The Home Office estimated that the majority of the remainder settled permanently, many of them in Whitechapel, Stepney and St George's-in-the-East. Of a London population of around four million, this was relatively insignificant, and proportionately nothing like so serious as the huge Uitlander influx into the Transvaal which Salisbury was effectively demanding should be allowed to continue unchecked.

'War is an uncertain hazard and seldom produces as much good as its direct and necessary evil,' Salisbury had told Northbrook about the prospects of war with Burma in August 1875, adding, 'we cannot afford to lower our tone before the Burmese however slightly.' His attitude towards the Transvaal was similar; he would have much preferred Pretoria to have backed down and accepted British hegemony in southern Africa, and he expected that a campaign of steady pressure would eventually achieve that. Milner's desire for a clash did not commend itself to him, not least because he refused to believe that the public wanted an expensive war. But the alternative, to let the Transvaal go its own way, possibly to grow into a long-term threat to British paramountcy in the region, further strengthened by the added prestige of having successfully faced down the Empire's demands, was an even worse prospect.

On 1st August, the Cabinet, despite 'several divergent opinions' which manifested themselves during a long discussion, agreed by a good majority to reinforce Natal in order to offset the danger of a surprise attack from the Transvaal. Responding privately to criticism from Hicks Beach, who along with Balfour was proving recalcitrant, Salisbury said that 'the moment has passed' when Chamberlain could be restrained, and protested that even if he had wanted to, 'I do not know enough of the details of his game.' It was hardly an excuse, even though Salisbury was spending every spare moment at Walmer tending to his wife and, as George Hamilton told Curzon, 'though very plucky and apparently cheerful, feels very much the weight of this impending blow'.

In fact, Salisbury generally approved of his Colonial Secretary's policy of keeping up constant pressure on the Transvaal, something the Natal reinforcements was intended to augment, although he wanted to move at a slower, more cautious pace to help bring public opinion along with them.[16] Selborne, who was a close friend of Milner's as well as a political ally, wrote from the Colonial Office on 11th August that: 'It has been a case of moods, nothing else, with our chief [Chamberlain], and a certain resentment on the part of the Prime Minister that he was being hustled. There was never any real danger of the Cabinet budging from their position.'

It was a position which it required military force to substantiate, and on 12th August the Cabinet was aghast to learn from Lansdowne that it would cost nearly £1 million to place the First Army Corps on the Transvaal frontier. In a letter to Chamberlain, Salisbury said that he did not doubt the 'futility' of the War Office – a department he had long despised – but thought it 'uncivil' to criticise it just as they were limbering up for a war. Writing of 'the scandal which will certainly be created by the conditions of our military preparedness', Salisbury thought it best not to incur any serious extra expenditure 'until it is quite clear that we are going to war'.

On the same day on which the Cabinet met, the Pretoria Government contacted Conyngham Greene, the British Agent there, to ask whether the British Government would waive the demand for a joint inquiry if they liberalised the franchise law and increased the number of seats in the Volksraad represented by the Rand, where most of the Uitlanders lived and worked. Greene met Jan Christian Smuts, the Transvaal's Attorney-General, who offered what became known as the 'Smuts Proposals'. The seven-year retrospective franchise qualification would be dropped to the five years that Milner had originally demanded at Bloemfontein. It was agreed that an arbitration process would be set up to ascertain the facts of the franchise issue. No fewer than ten out of the Volksraad's thirty-six seats would be reserved to the Rand. In return, Smuts asked for the British Government to drop its interference with the Transvaal's internal affairs outside the terms of the Conventions and also tacitly to drop the claim of suzerainty. Under pressure from Cape Afrikaners, Kruger had made serious concessions and now offered a scheme which might have averted war, if London was prepared to acknowledge his country's complete independence from the Crown.

Once again Chamberlain was jubilant, writing to Salisbury on 16th August that the Smuts Proposals amounted to a climbdown, 'which, as far as I can see, is really complete this time'. At the same point he ordered Milner, who wanted the Proposals to be ignored, to get them down on paper, as they 'evidently constitute an immense concession and even a considerable advance on your Bloemfontein proposals', which had only mentioned seven seats for the Rand. That day Salisbury wrote to the Queen from Walmer to say that he 'still thinks a war improbable'. He was more concerned that the Dreyfus Affair – 'the disgraceful incidents in which France is now involved' – might encourage the extreme parties in France to unite the country by declaring war on Britain.

The following day, 17th August, Salisbury wrote to Chamberlain that Milner's insistence on what the High Commissioner called 'steadily turning the screw' was 'a little alarming and he seems to me unnecessarily suspicious and pedantic in his adherence to form.... It looks as if he had been spoiling for the fight with some glee, and does not like putting his clothes on again.' Chamberlain tended to agree, reporting to Salisbury: 'I am sanguine that the crisis is over.'[17] The Smuts Proposals were officially handed to Greene in writing on 19th August, and formally submitted to London on the 22nd, along with a verbal intimation that English and not just Afrikaans might be used in the Volksraad and that further details about the franchise proposals were negotiable. Hicks Beach, who saw Milner as just another Frere, wrote to Salisbury on the 24th to say that he hoped the High Commissioner and the Uitlanders 'will not be allowed to drag us into war'. As Chancellor he had to find the money to transport regiments to South Africa, to pay £45 per horse and re-clothe the army in khaki, yet somehow not to increase overall taxation.

Sitting next to Salisbury at dinner at Osborne that evening, the Queen's Lady-in-Waiting, Lady Lytton, recorded how Salisbury was confident that 'Kruger will go on for his own people pretending not to give in but will not go to war as it would put an end to himself.' This over-confident assessment was echoed by Chamberlain in a widely reported speech at Highbury delivered on 26th August. In the grounds of his home, the Colonial Secretary told a large crowd: 'Mr Kruger procrastinates in his replies. He dribbles out reforms like water from a squeezed sponge ... the knot must be loosened or else we shall have to find our ways of untying it.... The sands are running down in the glass.' For all his liberal mixture of metaphors, the point was made. McDonnell greatly deprecated Chamberlain's speech, as likely to make Kruger 'think that Lord Salisbury is hanging back and that Joe is trying to force him on by violent speeches: which is not the case'. He predicted to Curzon that Britain would be at war within a month. But as it took more than a month for troops to reach the South African ports, Salisbury wanted negotiations to continue for as long as possible, especially as he still did not believe that public opinion was yet fully behind the Goverment.

It was at this time that Salisbury employed a classical allusion which came to be misunderstood. Livy described how the Sibyl of Cumæ offered to sell Tarquin of Rome nine books of oracles. When he refused, she burned three and offered the rest to him at the same price. When he refused again, she burned another three, after which Tarquin, by now thoroughly rattled, bought the remaining three at the same price originally charged for all nine. Chamberlain, who was no classicist, deduced from Salisbury's reference to this that if Britain was put to the huge expense of military preparations by Kruger merely playing for time, the terms for an eventual settlement might rise rather than fall. What Salisbury actually meant was that, should the Transvaal's obstinacy lead to war, Britain would not lower her demands upon victory.

In their official reply to the Smuts Proposals, Salisbury and Chamberlain decided on 28th August to accept the proposed franchise concession and the principle of arbitration, but also to continue to demand a joint inquiry and to draw up a Note to be sent to Pretoria, which was subsequently dubbed a 'penultimatum'. This threatened that if the Transvaal's reply 'is not prompt and satisfactory, and if it becomes necessary to despatch further troops, H.M.G. will feel justified in withdrawing previous suggestions for compromise and will formulate their own demands for a settlement', i.e. send an ultimatum. By refusing to abandon the right to intervene in the Transvaal's affairs, but instead reasserting their rights under the 1881 and 1884 Conventions and giving no guarantees, the two men believed that they were boxing Kruger into a corner. In fact, they were merely confirming his suspicions.

They were also on exceedingly tricky ground legally. Derby had struck out the Preamble to the 1881 Pretoria Convention in the original documents used in the 1884 negotiations. In July 1894, the British Government's Law Officers reported that: 'We are of opinion that the suzerainty has been abandoned,' because the 1884 London Convention amounted to a new and separate treaty, rather than merely an amendment to the 1881 Pretoria Convention. Milner privately admitted in May 1897 that the 1884 Convention 'is such a wretched instrument that even an impartial court would ... render it perfectly useless to us'; something with which Chamberlain, again privately, agreed. It was Salisbury who, following the reasoning first adopted by Rosebery's Colonial Under-Secretary Sydney Buxton, attempted to promote the view that the 1881 Preamble 'had not been extinguished, and that the suzerainty still existed'. Contrary to his withering remarks in Parliament about it in the early 1880s, Salisbury now wanted to try to give the concept of suzerainty some teeth. He saw it as a useful, but not vital, part of Britain's case. For as he admitted to W. T. Stead in September 1899: 'I do not think that we have done anything that we should not have done, if the word had never been uttered.'[18]

No Cabinet was called before the Note was sent off to Milner on 28th August, and Hicks Beach was furious that, holiday period or no, they had not had a chance to debate the tough, even peremptory wording, which naturally lost nothing in the re-telling to Kruger by Milner. In March 1902, with the war almost over, Salisbury admitted to Hicks Beach that it had been 'a very grave mistake' not to have had more general discussion of the Note which accepted Smuts's proposals so partially, conditionally and ungraciously.

Salisbury was keen, in a letter to Chamberlain on 29th August, to find 'contrivances for shortening the four months which the extraordinary futility of the War Office interposes between us and effective action'. Ideas about fortifying the Natal frontier, building a pier at Durban and dredging the harbour there occurred to him. The following day, he told Hicks Beach that the troops had to come from Britain rather than India, at greater expense and length of time, because the ones from India 'are so riddled by venereal and other complaints that they are comparatively unfit for service. This is pleasant, if true.' It was indeed true, and it seriously impaired the military efficiency of the Indian army that over half the 71,000 British troops stationed in India in the 1890s had at some stage been admitted for VD treatment, and at no time were fewer than 3,000 incapable of undertaking military duties as a result of sexually transmitted diseases.

Salisbury argued that, whatever happened, the Natal frontier needed reinforcing, because 'if the Boers submit, and we do not go to war, they will be intensely bitter' and therefore almost as dangerous. 'At present I understand the Boers' offer in effect to be – the Bloemfontein demands: <u>but</u> a renunciation of the suzerainty in exchange. This does not seem a possible solution.'[19] Salisbury was playing something of a double game here, letting some ministers such as Balfour, Hicks Beach and Lansdowne think that he was against a war, whilst letting Chamberlain reject the Smuts Proposals in such a way as almost to encourage one. As Britain's powerful and long-serving Prime Minister and Foreign Secretary, Salisbury must bear overall responsibility for the situation.

The famous letter which Salisbury sent Lansdowne on 30th August 1899 should therefore be read in the light of his joint direction of policy with Chamberlain, with Milner only acting in an advisory rather than an executive capacity after the Bloemfontein Conference. Of Milner's reported request for troops, which Salisbury had fully supported, the Prime Minister wrote:

> His view is too heated, if you consider the intrinsic significance and importance of the things which are in controversy. But it recks little to think of that now. What he has done cannot be effaced. We have to act upon a moral field prepared for us by him and his jingo supporters. And therefore I see before us the necessity for considerable military effort – and all for people whom we despise, and for territory which will bring no profit and no power to England.

Ordering Lansdowne to alter the tenor of the army's autumn manoeuvres, from 'the technical conditions of continental warfare' towards 'that of a military fire brigade', Salisbury repeated how keen he was to reinforce the Natal garrison, because in the Cape Colony 'our force is so small that if we scatter it we shall come to grief'.[20]

Salisbury's strictures against Milner were not wholly fair; overall policy was made in London, not Cape Town, and he personally approved every communication to Kruger before it was sent, often bearing his own amendments. Salisbury's intransigence had actually won a series of concessions from Kruger, and if the issue really had been about Uitlanders' rights – and the phrase 'people whom we despise' implies that it was not – a compromise solution might have been found. Certainly by late August the political distance between the two sides was very narrow indeed. But the two obstinate bearded old patriarchs, Salisbury and Kruger, both knew that this struggle was actually about ultimate regional paramountcy, about showing who was 'Boss' in South Africa. Salisbury would have preferred a peaceful outcome, but if sweeping away the shame of Majuba Hill took a war, as it had with the death of Gordon – another Gladstonian legacy – then so be it. As Lady Randolph Churchill had warned her husband in vain, Lord Salisbury believed in vengeance.

Writing of the supposed aimlessness of the Foreign Office that month, George Hamilton told Curzon that: 'The position, reputation, and intellectual subtlety of its chief made it possible for him to carry on this form of diplomacy with an authority and apparent success that a lesser man could not attempt.'[21] Yet, far from being aimless, Salisbury had managed to maintain the international status quo which the previous year had allowed him to subdue the Sudan and occupy Fashoda without any foreign intervention. By timely strategic concessions to Germany and Russia he had bought a free hand in South Africa, despite the deep international unpopularity of British action against the Transvaal. That all this was taking place when, as he told the Queen on 12th August, his wife was 'still exceeding weak', only adds to his achievement. Although the impatient junior members of his Government might refuse to recognise it, Salisbury had isolated his next victim in 1899 just as successfully as he had isolated France in 1898.

Salisbury's objectives in South Africa were very different from those in other parts of the world, such as China, Latin America, West Africa, Turkey, Morocco and Siam, where he only hoped to maintain an 'Open Door' policy. Ideas for a form of federation, a Union of South Africa under the British Crown, had been current for over thirty years, and it was hoped that equal political rights would eventually, through sheer weight of numbers, bring the Afrikaner-majority areas into the British orbit. Although the Boers were fanatically jealous of their independence, British policy-makers were guilty of treating their obstinacy no differently from those of the black African tribes which had eventually succumbed to their colonial impulse. On 2nd September 1899, Pretoria responded to the British Note of 28th August by withdrawing the Smuts Proposals and reverting to an offer of a seven-year retrospective franchise and four additional seats in the Volksraad. It refused to accept that Britain enjoyed any suzerainty and was non-committal about the idea of a further Kruger–Milner conference. The 'sponge' had been squeezed dry.

Chamberlain wrote to Salisbury that day, asking whether they should raise their terms, or 'confine our ultimatums to the franchise question'. The issue had moved from whether there would be a war, to how to find the best *casus belli* to unite British and colonial opinion behind one. Meanwhile, in South Africa on 4th September, Jan Smuts sent a top-secret memorandum to the Transvaal Executive to show how the Boers also nursed their own imperialist ambitions:

South Africa stands on the eve of a frightful blood-bath out of which our Volk shall come ... either as ... hewers of wood and drawers of water for a

hated race, or as victors, founders of a United South Africa, of one of the
great empires [*rijken*] of the world... an Afrikaans republic in South Africa
stretching from Table Bay to the Zambezi.

'Salisbury is low and depressed,' George Hamilton told Curzon on 6th
September, 'he now has a very heavy load of responsibilities.' He never-
theless managed to find time to write to the General Manager of the
London, Chatham and Dover Railway to request that, when Lady
Salisbury was moved from Walmer to Hatfield in an invalid saloon, it
should undergo as little shunting as possible when the train was
coupled and decoupled. He also found a £200 per annum pension for
Alfred Austin, although Balfour insisted on requesting the money from
Parliament solely in Austin's capacity as Poet Laureate rather than as a
recognition of his poetic talents. Over old age pensions, long a desideratum of Chamberlain's, Salisbury was predictably lukewarm. 'I think
any measure in favour of those who are not in real poverty would be
very unjust,' he wrote to Hicks Beach, who feared the unquantifiable
and potentially vast expense involved in the scheme. 'But I think some
relaxation of the rigour of the Poor Law in favour of old people would be
... both just and wise.' A weekly payment to septuagenarians and older
was Salisbury's preferred option, with the alternative to go further later.
In the event, the massive cost of the Boer War put a stop to all advances
on the issue, despite support for it from Chamberlain, Balfour and
Chaplin.[22]

With war looking increasingly likely, Chamberlain circulated a
memorandum to the Cabinet on 7th September which argued that the
casus belli must be widened beyond the franchise question, from the
refusal to prosecute Mr Edgar's murderer to the general 'reduction of
Englishmen in the Transvaal to the position of an inferior race, little
better than that of the Kaffirs and Indians'. What Chamberlain called
'the Oligarchy in Pretoria' wished to dissolve the British connection and
substitute a Boer-dominated United States of South Africa, and it could
no longer be tolerated. He estimated that there were 430,000 Britons in
South Africa, 410,000 Afrikaners and 3,160,000 blacks, the latter being
'interested spectators, with a preference for the English as their masters,
but ready to take the side of the strongest'. He briefly mentioned
approvingly Salisbury's Sibylline Books policy of increasing the terms
until Pretoria cracked. He emphasised how it was no longer simply a
South African issue, because the outcome now affected imperial prestige, 'and with it the estimate formed of our power and influence in our
Colonies and throughout the world'.[23] The success of the tiny Transvaal
would have hugely negative global consequences for the Empire as a
whole.

In a reply memorandum, Salisbury denied having mentioned the
Sibylline Books in a context which implied that 'in the course of these

negotiations a time would come when it would be necessary or expedient that we should increase our demands'. He said that it was 'an entire mistake', and claimed that he had been merely speaking 'of the course we should feel justified in taking <u>after</u> any war'. Completely denying that he had said 'anything in favour of increasing our demands so long as peace remained', he repudiated the construction Chamberlain had placed on his words and added: 'I cannot conceive any advantage in such a course.' As for the *casus belli*, Salisbury believed that concentrating on minor grievances such as the demands for an inquiry and arbitration, rather than the central franchise grievance, would be wrong because 'they are certainly not of sufficient importance to sustain a war'.

When the Cabinet finally met the next day, for the first time since Chamberlain had despatched the 28th August Note, they considered the two memoranda and a despatch from Milner warning of demoralisation amongst the Uitlanders should London falter. When the Bloemfontein Conference had broken down in June, there were only 9,500 British troops in the whole of South Africa. By early September this had only been brought up to 12,000. So at the Cabinet meeting held at 12.30 p.m. on Friday, 8th September, in Salisbury's room in the Foreign Office over-looking St James's Park, it was agreed to send out an extra 10,000 troops. Chamberlain later reported to Milner that there had been 'no difference of opinion on any important subject' at this crucial meeting. If some members such as Hicks Beach and Balfour had agreed to dispatch the troops in the hope that Kruger would capitulate, they gravely miscalculated.

A draft despatch from Chamberlain to Kruger, the second 'penultimatum', was considered sentence by sentence by the Cabinet. Salisbury left it 'very moderate in tone', but it still adhered strongly to the demands for franchise and constitutional reform. As nobody wished to force the pace until the battalions had arrived at Cape Town and Durban, nothing in the way of an ultimatum was approved. Before the Cabinet ended, Salisbury gave an 'emphatic warning' about what Goschen later called 'the big character of the job before us'. It was probably this occasion which Ashbourne remembered many years later, at which Salisbury made the 'grim statement' that: 'We must remember, this is the first occasion we have gone to war with people of Teutonic race.' Salisbury feared that the sending of troops would precipitate a Boer attack, and he was right, yet not to send them would have been equally perilous. At 2.50 p.m., the meeting, one of the longest of Salisbury's career, broke up with war now the likeliest outcome.

It had to be staved off for another five weeks to give Kruger a chance to back down, but more importantly to give the new troops a chance to be deployed.[24] Salisbury refused Chamberlain's request to recall Parliament and call out the Reserves. The Transvaal was fully armed and ready, so nothing useful would be gained from precipitating the clash. 'We must prepare for war as the most probable alternative,' he told Chamberlain. 'But I do not quite go with you in the matter of pace.' Salisbury did not believe that they could hold all the most exposed parts of Natal, especially if, as seemed likely, the Orange Free State joined the Transvaal.

The very next day, Salisbury wrote again at length about how to prepare the right political ground for the ultimatum, when finally they were ready to send it. 'Public opinion here is not very irritable,' he told Chamberlain, 'and will take little count of a month's delay just now.' As for Milner's reports of the Uitlanders' demands, Salisbury admitted that they were 'no doubt rabid: but as they must come to us – because they have no one else to go to – their wrath does not matter much'. His other reason for delaying the outbreak of hostilities was to try subtly to alter the *casus belli*:

> I want to get away from the franchise issue, which will be troublesome in debate – and to make the break on a proposal to revise or denounce the [1884] Convention on the ground that it has not been carried out as we were promised: and because it has been worked out to benefit not the people of the Transvaal with whom we were contracted, but a very limited minority of them who are hostile to the rest. A proposal to revise it would of course be refused by the Boers; and it might then be formally denounced.

These are not the words of a man who, as some historians have suggested, was dragged into war by Chamberlain and Milner, but rather one who sympathised with the ultimate object of making Britain paramount in South Africa by whatever means necessary. The almost contemptuous reference to the Uitlanders' fears, on top of the remarks about them in his letter to Lansdowne three weeks before, shows Salisbury's true priorities. His 'emphatic warning' at the crucial 8th September Cabinet meeting was not an attempt to warn the Cabinet against war, so much as to leave no one in any doubt of the profound implications of what was about to take place.

On 22nd September, the Cabinet agreed to its third penultimatum to Pretoria via Milner, but one that would not give the Transvaal an excuse to attack: 'H.M.G. are now compelled to consider the situation afresh, and to formulate their own proposals for a final settlement.' Afterwards, Chamberlain told Milner that the Cabinet was 'unanimous and resolved to see the matter through', but the public would not be told about the preparations that were being made.[25] It was all to be done at Salisbury's careful and steady pace, not at the speed desired by Milner, Rhodes or the Jingoes.

Late September saw Salisbury personally scotch two private peace initiatives. The first was undertaken by Devonshire, working through the Pretoria branch of Rothschilds, who said that the British Government was anxious for peace and had no designs on the Transvaal's territorial integrity. If Pretoria would grant the Uitlanders a five-year franchise without suzerainty conditions, Devonshire personally guaranteed there would be no further demands. When Salisbury found out about this four days later, he told Lord Rothschild that 'he cannot but deprecate very earnestly any further communications of this kind with Pretoria'. It is not known what, if anything, passed between Salisbury and Devonshire on the subject, but nothing more was heard from him on these lines. Similarly, when Montague White, the Transvaal's Consul-General in London, privately met Salisbury's private secretary, Eric Barrington, to say that 'the Boer Government would jump at any chance of a pacific solution', Salisbury merely wrote: 'I doubt' in red ink at the bottom of the report, effectively closing the matter.[26] He was in part concerned about going behind Chamberlain's back, but if he had truly yearned for peace it is doubtful Salisbury would have personally administered the *coup de grâce* to both initiatives quite so decisively.

At Cabinet on 29th September, the wording of an actual ultimatum was agreed, as were the calling up of the Reserves and the summoning of Parliament for 17th October, once the troops had safely disembarked in South Africa. Salisbury still hoped that the Boers would take the offensive first. If that happened, as Chamberlain told a still-doubting Hicks Beach, 'the Lord will have delivered them into our hands – at least as far as diplomacy is concerned'.[27]

Salisbury's diplomacy was predicated by the need to retain a free hand in South Africa. To achieve this, he refused to be drawn into rows with Russia or Germany over China, telling Brodrick that although the Chinese plains might well be as valuable economically as the Nile Valley, 'the only question to me [is] which are we able to take. The superiority of the African over the Chinese adventure was that, as we have shown, the African was possible, the Chinese was not.' As for a correspondent who had asserted to Brodrick that control of the Yangtze River engendered control of the provinces on each side of it, Salisbury had a ready analogy, telling his Under-Secretary that: 'This is as good as saying that occupying the Humber would of itself give you the command of Lincolnshire and Yorkshire – only that the Chinese provinces are much larger.' When a British official named Fleming was murdered in China in September 1899, Salisbury told Sir Claude Macdonald, the British minister at Peking, that 'in the present circumstances of the world we cannot afford naval demonstrations', but he might punish China by withholding excise revenue instead.

For so intelligent a man, Lord Curzon displayed little perspicacity when in September he outlined a 'Forward' policy for India which involved challenging Russia over the Seistan province and maintaining British influence in Central Persia at all costs.[28] In the delicate international situation that a Transvaal war was about to produce, Salisbury hardly needed any further commitments or quarrels, an attitude which Curzon, with the characteristically Calcutta-based view of so many viceroys, entirely failed to appreciate and increasingly came to rail against.

In a letter to Lord Courtney on 2nd October, Salisbury said that his own 'general view of the situation, taken broadly, is sufficiently expressed in a letter signed "Englishman" in today's *Times*'. With his track record for inspiring anonymous newspaper articles, it might easily be that the pithy letter originated from him, although there is no evidence for this and 'Englishman' does describe himself as a Gladstonian Liberal. 'The one aim of the Boer leaders in all the South African states is the establishment of a Republic in which they would be supreme,' wrote 'Englishman', in much the same terms as Salisbury was then writing to the Queen. According to 'Englishman''s analysis, the Boers had never forgotten or forgiven the British for taking possession of the Cape in 1814, and in 'Oom Paul' Kruger they thought they had a man who could recapture it. 'President Kruger will never give equal rights to Englishmen,' the letter continued, 'it cannot be finally or thoroughly settled without war sooner or later.'

Two letters written by Salisbury on 5th October show how much he agreed. The first, to his former private secretary Henry Manners, now Marquess of Granby, asked him to move the address for the Queen's Speech debate in the House of Lords when Parliament met on the 17th:

> Public affairs are getting exciting. At first I thought K[ruger] was merely honestly trying to stand up for his rights and would be satisfied if they could be secured. But now I feel convinced that the Dutch leaders in Transvaal, Free State and [Cape] Colony, have got an understanding together and have agreed to make a long pull and a strong pull to restore Dutch supremacy in South Africa. If that is their view, war must come: and we had better take it at a time when we are not quarrelling with anyone else.

In an almost identical letter to Courtney three days after his first, Salisbury admitted that 'of course I cannot produce evidence which would convict Kruger of conspiracy in a Court of Law. In political life you have to guess facts by the help of such indications as you can get.' He was however convinced that Kruger aimed at 'a renunciation of suzerainty' and 'a restoration of South Africa to the Dutch race'. Had Salisbury had the evidence of Smuts's secret memorandum to the Transvaal Executive, he could indeed have indicted the Boer leadership for just such a conspiracy.

After a conversation with Rosebery and Rothschild, Sir Edward Hamilton assessed the situation correctly when he noted in his diary that Salisbury was 'prepared to face war sooner than not get out of Kruger terms that will secure good government at Johannesburg and make the Boers feel that we are and must be the paramount power in South Africa'. Rothschild actually believed, despite Chamberlain being the Liberals' bogey-man, that in fact 'Lord Salisbury has taken an even stronger line than Chamberlain lately.'[29]

In the evening of 9th October, after a game of billiards, Milner received an ultimatum from F.W. Reitz, the State Secretary of the Transvaal, threatening war at 5 p.m. on Wednesday, 11th October, unless various demands were met. In one of the bravest, if most foolhardy, documents of the nineteenth century, Pretoria demanded 'that the troops on the borders of this Republic shall be instantly withdrawn', 'that all reinforcements of troops which have arrived in South Africa since 1st June 1899, shall be removed' and even 'that Her Majesty's troops which are now on the high seas shall not be landed at any port in South Africa'. The Boers needed to strike before the reinforcements arrived, hoping also for foreign intervention and for the Unionist Government to fall if they could hold out. They were convinced that their independence was in mortal danger, so the tiny Boer republics decided to challenge the largest Empire the world has ever seen. If they expected Britain to come to terms after some initial defeats, as Gladstone had done in 1881, they failed to appreciate that in Salisbury they had to deal with a very different type of politician, one for whom imperial prestige was a tangible, treasured asset.

Salisbury was happy enough with the Boer ultimatum, pausing only to warn Chamberlain that the Government must not be seen as 'doing work for the capitalists' such as Rhodes and Beit in fighting the Boers. The next morning he replied: 'Her Majesty's Government have received with great regret the South African Republic's peremptory demands conveyed in your telegram of October 9th... the conditions demanded by them are such as H.M.G. deem it impossible to discuss.'[30] Salisbury agreed with Cranbrook that it had been 'an ultimatum of astonishing insolence', but at least it had not arrived for a month after the key 8th September Cabinet meeting. By being the recipient of the ultimatum rather than its sender, Salisbury had also won something of a diplomatic coup.

FORTY-THREE

'The Possibilities of Defeat'

War – The Death of Lady Salisbury
– 'Black Week' – A Peace Offer –
The Relief of Mafeking

October 1899 to May 1900

'We seek no goldfields. We seek no territory.'

'The mere fact that a rebellion can be crushed', Salisbury had written about the American Civil War in 1862, 'is generally no sort of guarantee that it will not be attempted.' Now that the Boers had attempted their rebellion against the Crown's suzerainty, Salisbury would have done well to have re-read another of his old *Saturday Review* articles about the American War of Independence. 'It was a wealthy Empire against a famished, unarmed distracted dependency,' but because the army had no 'tolerable commander', it 'was twice out-manoeuvred, surrounded and taken prisoner by the ill-drilled and ill-formed militiamen of Washington'. Apart from the fact that the Transvaal had been arming for just such a struggle ever since before the Jameson Raid, the similarities with the opening stages of the Boer War were uncanny. The experiences of more than eight decades of small wars around the globe since Waterloo had not prepared the British army for a completely different type of warfare, against mounted Boer farmers who were crack shots and knew the country.

The complacency with which the military authorities regarded the outbreak of hostilities was breathtaking. Balfour told his sister Lady Rayleigh on 24th September that the War Office 'thinks the mobilisation will be successful, and that the war does not present great strategic diffi- culties and will be short'. In fact, the Boer War followed the classic pattern of most modern British wars, including the Napoleonic, Crimean, Indian Mutiny, Zulu, Afghan, First and Second World Wars – of humiliating initial defeats followed by national arousal and exertion before ultimate victory.

The Boer War produced far greater bitterness in domestic politics than any event since the Great Reform Bill. 'Pro-Boer' became a term of violent abuse and the Liberal Party, already split, was plunged into yet deeper schism. The war did for British social cohesion what the Dreyfus Affair was doing in France; 'it divided families and ruptured the ideological solidarity, and the competent reputation of the ruling class'.[1] The future use of the particularly vicious dumdum bullets, a soft-nosed round which expanded on impact, had been attacked by the Irish Nationalist MPs John Dillon and Michael Davitt in mid-July 1899, and as the war progressed the Irish Nationalist members came out vocally in support of the Boers, further embittering parliamentary dialogue.

Victorian regard for individual liberty meant that conscription was out of the question, so the whole war was fought on a volunteer basis. Despite Queen Victoria's exhortations to Salisbury, non-whites were not employed in significant fighting roles during the conflict. He had the previous year supported the idea of allowing black officers in the Indian army, but the Cabinet had rejected it because 'white British soldiers might not obey colonial officers in moments of difficulty'. Back in 1885, Salisbury had suggested that the Zulus could be employed to fight the Boers, as importing a British army to do the job would be too expensive. This time, however, only a large-scale mobilisation of British troops was trusted to do the job. As they embarked for South Africa, the troops were each handed a copy of *Songs for England*, the war poetry of Alfred Austin. On the long journey south they could savour the sentiments of poems such as *Pax Britannica*, with the verse:

> Slowly as stirs a lion from her bed,
> Lengthened her limbs and crisps her mane, She rose,
> Then shook out all her strength, and flashing, said,
> 'Where are my foes?'

Salisbury had long complained about the small size of Britain's standing army, writing to Sir Frederick Roberts, a favoured general: 'The fact that Providence is generally on the side of the big battalions is a nuisance for the only country whose institutions do not allow her to possess that luxury.'[2] There were only 12,000 British troops in South Africa when the Boers attacked. Very soon, however, with offers of aid and volunteers flooding in from Canada, Australia and New Zealand, Britain started to recruit and deploy an army which by the end of the conflict, two years eight months later, had grown to a staggering total of 365,693 Imperial and 82,242 South African troops. They fought an estimated 87,000 Boers, only half of whom were in the field at any one time.

If the total numbers of imperial servicemen involved was huge, the numbers that died were comparatively small. The Empire lost only

7,774 killed in action, nearly 10 per cent of them officers. A further 16,168 died of wounds or disease, mainly the latter. Around 7,000 Boer soldiers died in the war, although around twenty thousand of their women and children also perished through disease.[3] The total numbers killed in action on both sides, fewer than 15,000 over nearly three years, were comparable to the monthly losses on the Western Front a decade and a half later.

Unlike his hero William Pitt the Younger during the Napoleonic Wars, or Palmerston at the time of the Crimean War, Salisbury did not regard his role as a wartime Prime Minister as being to give a boost to national morale, so much as to oversee the running of the war and ensure no foreign countries intervened. Declaring that the war was no business of any other Great Power, he ordered part of the Channel fleet to the Mediterranean in mid-October, in order to discourage any disagreeable naval demonstrations by France. 'He entirely shares your Majesty's burning indignation at the gross and monstrous injustice which has been perpetrated in France,' Salisbury had written to the Queen the previous month when a fresh condemnation of Dreyfus was passed by five judges' votes to two. 'It is perfectly horrible; and gives the impression that truth and justice are no longer regarded as of any serious consequence.' The Dreyfus Affair was extremely useful for Britain in keeping France preoccupied and her society divided, although Salisbury also feared a demagogue emerging who might try to reunite the country by championing the Transvaal and avenging Fashoda.

On 14th October, Salisbury signed a treaty with Portugal, which, like the 1887 Mediterranean Agreements and the 1898 Anglo-German Convention, had clauses that were to be kept secret. The Foreign Office itself had no knowledge of the negotiations while they were being conducted between Salisbury and the Marquis de Soveral, the Portuguese minister in London. By reaffirming Britain's 1373 alliance with Portugal and promising to protect Portugal's colonies, Salisbury prevented Portugal from formally declaring her neutrality, which would have allowed the Transvaal to import munitions through Delagoa Bay. The Transvaal's only point of access to the sea was closed for the duration of the war.[4]

Armed with a memorandum on the concept of suzerainty, in which Salisbury admitted that it 'is a very vague word, and I do not think it is capable of any precise legal definition', ministers met Parliament on Tuesday, 17th October, for the first time since war had been declared. The best Salisbury could affirm in his memorandum was that 'a certain controlling power is retained' by the Paramount Power under the 1881 and 1884 Conventions, and he hoped to move the argument on to stronger ground once he addressed the House of Lords. 'Potentates who are going to war are apt to use the most popular topics they can hit upon to stir up the martial ardour of their people,' he had written in the *Saturday Review* in 1861, 'without disquieting themselves by the inquiry whether those are exactly the most prominent topics in their own minds.'

The House of Lords was packed when Salisbury stood up. He defended Chamberlain, raised a laugh at the expense of Lord Kimberley, and displayed great candour when he admitted that 'It may be that the word suzerainty has no meaning.... But my impression is not that it does not mean nothing, but that it means a number of things from which you can take your choice ... it is still true that, having been put into the Treaty, it has obtained an artificial value and meaning which prevents us from entirely abandoning it.' Britain would not do that, as otherwise she might intimate that 'the ideas which have come to be associated with it are ideas which we repudiate and abandon altogether'. Having thus disposed of the 'suzerainty' issue, Salisbury got down to the more visceral reasons why the war had to be fought.

Although he stated that the Transvaal had 'issued a defiance so audacious that I can hardly depict it adequately without using stronger words than are suited to this assembly', and in so doing they liberated him from 'the necessity of explaining to the people of England why we are at war', Salisbury nevertheless did go on to enumerate Britain's war aims. 'There must be no doubt that the Sovereign of England is paramount; there must be no doubt that the white races will be put upon an equality, and that due precaution will be taken for the philanthropic and kindly and improving treatment of those countless indigenous races of whose destiny, I fear, we have been too forgetful.' Of the three stated war aims – British paramountcy, Uitlanders' equal rights and 'kindly' government for blacks – few of his listeners could doubt which was personally the most important to Salisbury, especially once he added: 'The moment has arrived for deciding whether the future of South Africa is to be a growing and increasing Dutch supremacy or a safe, perfectly established supremacy of the English Queen.'[5]

In the House of Commons 135 MPs, including a Conservative and a Liberal Unionist, voted against the Government over its negotiation of the crisis. Sir Edward Clarke attacked the Government but abstained, the Liberal Imperialists who looked to Rosebery as their leader voted with the Government, and Henry Campbell-Bannerman, the new Liberal leader in the Commons, himself abstained but privately encouraged his supporters to vote against the Government. At the time, Cranborne believed that the war did not have universal support, telling his brother Edward that 'the sentiment of the thing is only of music hall intensity in the lower orders'. It was, paradoxically enough, only when the army began to suffer serious reverses that the war became truly popular. Answering a criticism from Lord Loch that the proclamation calling out the Reserves had come too late, Salisbury told the Queen, with some logic, that if the proclamation had come out sooner, the Boer ultimatum would have come sooner also.

Meanwhile, Salisbury had to face the first of a series of resignation threats from Hicks Beach over the enormous increases in expenditure involved. The Chancellor, who wanted no tax increases and no old age pensions for anyone who was not destitute, complained that the War and Colonial Offices were incurring huge expenditure without the Treasury having any real say in the matter. Salisbury answered that Hicks Beach's resignation, which would be misunderstood as a protest against the war itself rather than just its financing, would be 'injurious' to the Government, Party and country. So often was the same threat made in the course of the war, and so often did Salisbury placate him, that he joked that he kept a special drawer in his desk for Hicks Beach's resignation letters.

When the Queen telegraphed to say that she hoped that the cost of the war would not fall on the working classes, Salisbury answered that: 'It would not be fair on the richer classes, who in the elections are in a small minority. The policy of the country is decided by the working classes, and of course they don't pay the income tax.' As the first working-class minister did not enter the Cabinet until 1924, this was an exaggeration, but a sixpence duty on beer was indeed temporarily withheld from the Budget. In contrast to her reservations during the Fashoda Crisis, the Queen was enthusiastic about the Boer War, telling Salisbury how she was 'shocked at the shameful want of patriotism of the Opposition'. Such was the support for the Transvaal in France that she decided to holiday that year at Bordighera on the Italian Riviera, rather than at Cimiez.[6]

'Complete success has crowned our arms in the first serious engagement of the war in South Africa,' crowed *The Times* on 21st October about the victory, at best pyrrhic, of Sir Penn Symons at Talana Hill the day before. It was the last such good news for a long time, as that same day the Battles of Elandslaagte and Glencoe saw heavy losses, and the town of Dundee was abandoned to the Boers, who found forty days' military supplies for 5,000 men stored there. At Elandslaagte some Boers hoisted a white flag and then suddenly started firing after the fighting had stopped. It was the first indication that they would sometimes not observe the rules of warfare, which created a great deal of bitterness in the British army and soon led to reprisals.

'As you can imagine this war is a matter of great anxiety to me both on private and public grounds,' Salisbury wrote to Austin on 21st

October, alluding to his son Edward who had gone out to serve under Colonel Robert Baden-Powell at Mafeking and was now being besieged there. On 2nd November, Ladysmith, the main British supply base for the Cape Colony, also came under siege. By tying up troops in the three great sieges of Ladysmith, Mafeking and also Kimberley, the Boers probably made a serious tactical error. Had they pushed through to Durban and taken the other major South African ports before the British reinforcements landed, they could possibly have dealt a knock-out blow. In a war that was to become synonymous with British military incompetence, the errors were not all made by the British generals.

Before Parliament was prorogued on 27th October, the Battle of Rietfontein had cost the life of Colonel Wilford, the third colonel killed in the war, and Kruger laid formal claim to Bechuanaland and West Griqualand, just as the Orange Free State annexed part of Cape Colony. On 30th October, 'Mournful Monday', General Joubert defeated Sir George White at the Battle of Ladysmith and forced 860 men to surrender. On the same day, Lieutenant-Colonel Carleton, commanding officer of the Dublin Fusiliers, was forced to surrender at Nicholson's Nek. It seemed a relief to hard-pressed British arms that General Sir Redvers Buller, the Commander-in-Chief of the army in South Africa, landed at Cape Town the following day.

In late October, Salisbury had received from Monson in Paris reports that the Russians and French were plotting a combination to take advantage of Britain's embarrassments in South Africa. So when it was reported that a French fleet had sailed through the Suez Canal and was heading towards Madagascar, and Curzon telegraphed that he suspected 'an intrigue on the Persian Gulf', Salisbury sent for the French Ambassador. Telling him that Britain was 'very hard up for coal in South Africa', he requested that the French ships should not ask to buy any from British stations in the region. Knowing that France only had Madagascar as a coaling station, this was, as Lord Esher wrote to his son, 'a rather ingenious way of hampering their movements'.

To dispel any doubts about foreign intervention, Salisbury devoted a passage of his Guildhall speech at the Lord Mayor's Banquet to the subject. To cheers he stated that international law opposed any intervention, and in any case 'we should not accept of an interference by anybody'. The speech became famous for a phrase he used about Britain's war aims, and in particular in rebutting the accusation that the war was primarily being fought for the pecuniary advantage of the South African capitalists:

England as a whole would have no advantage from the possession of gold mines, except so far as her Government conferred the blessings of good government upon those who had the prosecution of that industry.... But that is the limit of our interest.... We seek no goldfields. We seek no territory. What we desire is equal rights for men of all races and security for our fellow-subjects and for the Empire.... We do not allow any other considerations to cross our path.[7]

The 'goldfields' remark was perhaps an echo of Disraeli's Guildhall peroration of November 1876: 'Peace is especially an English policy.... She covets no cities and no provinces,' and it was essentially accurate. The British State as such had no intention of nationalising the private concerns which exploited the Rand, but of course the supply of gold was undoubtedly an important consideration for British policy-makers. As *The Times* pointed out five days later: 'Though we covet no goldfields we shall not allow the territory that happens to contain them to renew in a more formidable shape the dangers that now confront us.' The paper went on to praise Lord George Hamilton for dispelling the 'monstrous delusion' that everything would be the same after the war.

Salisbury's Guildhall speech also included a fine compliment to General Buller, of whom he said: 'My confidence in the British soldier is only equalled by my confidence in Sir Redvers Buller.' The day before, Salisbury had written to Lansdowne on the question of whether Lords Grenfell or Kitchener should command the advance to relieve White in Ladysmith, saying that although Kitchener was a fine general, 'I have not seen him at work <u>under</u> another soldier who is in some sense a rival.... My advice – my very earnest advice – is to leave the matter entirely to Buller.' Salisbury's belief in trusting the man on the spot, however, indeed his (never great) faith in British generalship itself, was on the wane. When Richmond sent him a present of kippers on 11th November, he thanked him, appending the note: 'What a mess White has got himself into in Natal!' The next month this exasperation turned to sarcastic fury as defeat piled upon defeat. Discussing some of Salisbury's indifferent military and political appointments, Balfour opined: 'My explanation is that at the back of his mind there is a feeling that all men are equal, by which he means, equally incompetent.'[8]

'I fear now it is only a question of weeks,' George Hamilton wrote to Curzon about Lady Salisbury's health on 2nd November. 'Salisbury also has a son at Mafeking, and the burden of anxiety and responsibility is, I am sorry to say, telling visibly upon him.' At 2.45 p.m. on Monday, 20th November 1899, Georgina, Lady Salisbury, died. She had been very ill ever since her stroke in July, and except for a few lucid intervals she had been drowsy and practically unconscious for the final fortnight. In complete contrast to his usual fatalism, her husband had been defiantly optimistic, hailing 'the slightest sign of improvement as evidence of solid hope'. In the last six weeks, as Hugh Cecil told Frances Balfour, 'Even when there was hope of her life there was little of her mind, and one can't regret that she did not live mindless.'

Salisbury was present when the end came. 'They did not dare tell Lord Salisbury until half an hour before the end that she was dying,' McDonnell reported to Curzon, 'and she passed away quite quietly in her sleep. Poor old man; it is sad to see him; after all the warning he has had you would suppose he would have been prepared for the blow; but to the last day he clung to the hope that she would get better: and he was absolutely broken-hearted.' His foremost emotional mainstay, closest friend and confidante, his anchor against depression, had gone. As George Hamilton recorded, Georgina Salisbury was 'capable, clever, courageous, and dedicating herself heart and soul to the furtherance of her husband's views. They were a most devoted couple.'

'My dear wife died this afternoon from failure of the heart's action,' Salisbury telegraphed the Queen. 'She suffered no pain as far as we could see. I trust your Majesty will excuse me during this week.' In fact, a serious bout of influenza laid Salisbury so low immediately afterwards that he could not even attend the funeral, which was conducted by their son William, rector of Hatfield, on a misty November day. The Salisburys had personally selected the site of her grave, near their daughter Fanny, in the family burial ground behind the church. 'Her active sense of humour', read *The Times*' obituary, 'served as a valuable corrective to his natural inclination to see things more or less *en noir*.' Edward was the only one of her children not present; they had heard nothing from Mafeking for over two months. Weeks later a letter from Robert was allowed through the Boer lines which told Edward that 'It was not so much that she died as that she slowly ceased to live.'

Family, friends and politicians watched Salisbury very closely over the following weeks. 'He bears it wonderfully,' Robert told Edward. 'His own care seems to be to try to lessen the blow to us.' On 1st December, McDonnell reported to Curzon: 'He <u>looks</u> tired and old, white and unhappy; but he is still full of vigour.' Gwendolen wrote to Edward's wife Violet in Cape Town:

I have only realised now how terribly my father has felt that long strain of anxiety... he is so utterly selfless that it is difficult to know which are his true feelings and which those he wishes us to see. I know that his greatest anxiety is lest our lives should be darkened – but I know too that there is a smile and a tone of voice which will never be there again. He speaks of my mother quite naturally as if she were still alive or had been dead a long time.[9]

Gwendolen proceeded to dedicate herself to her father, taking over the Hatfield duties she was *de facto* performing during her mother's illness. She adored him and never married, admitting to Lady Rayleigh that she had something of a father-fixation, of which he had never had an inkling. After his death she wrote a fine four-volume life of him, which ends in 1892. During the Boer War she flung herself into Violet's campaign to send the sick and wounded supplies not provided by the War Office. Robert Cecil good-naturedly complained that she had turned Arlington Street into a government office. Another occasion found the Prime Minister, having climbed over bundles of nightshirts and towels, sitting on a soap box and announcing that the house smelt like a grocer's shop.

The press, sensing that Salisbury might take his wife's death as an opportunity to resign, almost unanimously called upon him to carry on. McDonnell put this down in part to the simple fact that 'The sober-minded men in the country are frightened at Joe's recklessness.' At Lady Salisbury's memorial service on 25th November at the Chapel Royal, St James's Palace, Sir Almeric Fitzroy noticed how Chamberlain 'paid the rite the compliment of the most engrossed attention'. The Colonial Secretary – once again taking advantage of Salisbury's temporary incapacity – was also busily promoting his former scheme of a German alliance. He had visited the German Foreign Secretary and soon-to-be Reich Chancellor, Count Bernhard von Bülow, on the afternoon of 22nd November. Von Bülow thought Chamberlain, who was sixty-three, looked no more than fifty with his 'cold eyes', very long and very strong Havana cigar, trademark orchid in buttonhole and gold-rimmed monocle. The Kaiser was in Britain for a State Visit and, after conversations with both him and von Bülow, Chamberlain made a speech at Leicester, where, fighting off a heavy cold, he announced that there should be 'a new triple alliance between the Teutonic race and the two great branches of the Anglo-Saxon race'.[10]

This offer of an Anglo-American-German alliance, a 'potent influence in the future of the world', was made in a particularly anti-French tone, but it was shot down by von Bülow on 11th December in a speech to the Bundesrath about German naval expenditure, to Chamberlain's lasting chagrin. The backlash in the press against the Colonial Secretary, led by the *Economist*, was privately echoed by McDonnell, who found it 'fantastic' that he should implicitly threaten France while Britain had 70,000 men tied up in South Africa. Writing to the Reich Chancellor, Prince von Hohenlohe-Schillingsfürst in Berlin, Hatzfeldt voiced his suspicion that Chamberlain was pursuing, out of personal ambition, 'the object of precipitating a rupture with Lord Salisbury and of unseating him, in order to take his place'. Meanwhile Salisbury, as soon as he was out of deep mourning, politely put paid to any German alliance proposals.

On 8th December, as the second item on their agenda after old age pensions, the Cabinet considered measures to be taken 'assuming that we are successful in the war'. The discussion centred on forming a small, separate, land-locked, mainly Dutch colony within the Empire. The same day, Field Marshal Lord Roberts, the Commander-in-Chief in Ireland, wrote to Lansdowne proposing himself for Buller's command. Salisbury, who was then nearly seventy, told Lansdowne emphatically that Roberts's age, sixty-seven, 'rendered it doubtful whether so heavy a task should be imposed on him'. The events of the next seven days, known to history as 'Black Week', soon changed Salisbury's mind.

The series of defeats began on 10th December with the ambush of General Sir William Gatacre at Stormberg, where 700 men surrendered. The next day, Lieutenant-General Lord Methuen's 1st Division was repulsed by Piet Cronje at Magersfontein and thus failed to relieve Kimberley. Methuen lost 210 killed, 675 wounded and 63 missing, against negligible Boer losses, after he attacked frontally in mass formation at dawn in the rain. On 15th December, Buller was routed by Louis Botha at the Battle of Colenso, thus also failing to relieve Ladysmith. Buller made every possible error; the total British killed, wounded and captured numbered 1,119 to the Boers' fifty. Major-General Lyttelton later reported that there had been 'no proper reconnoitring of the ground, no certain information as to any ford by which to cross the river, no proper artillery preparation, no satisfactory targets for the artillery'. He might have added that Buller imposed no proper skirmishing order, lost eleven guns and, despite the seven Victoria Crosses awarded in the futile battle, which was all over by 11 a.m., had been completely outmanoeuvred in the first engagement which he had commanded for twelve years.

Salisbury later insisted that it was not Colenso which cost Buller his job but the defeatist message he sent to Lansdowne immediately after the battle. Tired, angry and in pain, Buller telegraphed that he was not strong enough to relieve White, adding: 'My view is that I ought to let Ladysmith go, and occupy good positions for the defence of Natal.' Salisbury had initially been responsible for promoting Buller, despite his reputation for Radical ideas about land ownership in Ireland when he was Under-Secretary there in the late 1880s. By splitting his South African expeditionary force into three columns, each one of which suffered reverses, Buller had subsequently fallen into every available Boer trap. There is a school of thought which portrays Buller as a scapegoat, sacrificed to deflect attention from the inadequacies of Lansdowne and the War Office. It is true that there were deficiencies in training, logistics, administration and the quality of recruits for which the War Office and the Cabinet Defence Committee (which Devonshire had chaired since 1895) must bear some of the blame. Salisbury also thought that Lansdowne was 'quite overdone and the work beyond him'. The generalship of the largest force Britain had sent overseas since the Crimean War was also desperately poor, however, and Buller's was among the worst.[11]

Salisbury had at least learnt the lesson of the Zulu War, and acted ruthlessly and swiftly. The Cabinet Defence Committee considered Buller's telegram and decided to replace him with Roberts, leaving Buller in charge of the army in Natal. Salisbury insisted that Kitchener joined Roberts as his Chief of Staff, a combination Lansdowne correctly predicted the public would approve. Roberts was told the news at the same time as that of his only son's mortal wounding at Colenso. 'Our loss is grievous,' he wrote to Queen Victoria with the stiffest of imperial upper lips, 'but our boy died the death he would have chosen.'

It was on 18th December, at the close of Black Week, that Queen Victoria famously told Balfour, who was explaining the defeats to her at Windsor: 'Please understand that there is no one depressed in this house: we are not interested in the possibilities of defeat; they do not exist.' Sydney Holland, the son of Lord Knutsford and a friend of Robert Cecil at the parliamentary Bar, was staying at Hatfield during Black Week and recorded how Salisbury's views were identical: '"All will come right" was his attitude – and he seemed quite unable to appreciate any feeling of anxiety or worry about the ultimate result.' Salisbury wrote to Balfour on 18th December of Buller's 'abominable cheek' in countermanding an order from Wolseley. On the question of the use of coloured troops he added: 'I think we have got beyond the zones of sentiment now – and can do as we like.' Although Chaplin and Long strongly agreed, blacks were still not employed for active duties *en masse*, partly because arming natives was thought inherently dangerous and partly because it was feared it would only stiffen Boer resistance. When the policy was relaxed later on, the socialist leader Keir Hardie pronounced in a speech in January 1902: 'We are breaking faith with every nation in Europe by arming the blacks to fight against white men.'

Of the Queen's desire to give Roberts's vacant Irish post to her son Arthur, Duke of Connaught, Salisbury also withdrew any objections he might have had, telling his nephew: 'I think we have passed the stage of caring whether the Nationalists hate Royalty or not.'[12] The next month he had another opportunity for abusing the Emerald Isle, telling Rutland that he had 'no doubt that the [Orange] Free Staters will in the next generation live so comfortably under British rule as the Highlanders did after Culloden. The Irish are exceptionally difficult to assimilate, owing to their religion, and perhaps to their vile climate.'

On 19th December, Salisbury wrote to Balfour again, urging him not to allow Buller's friend, Sir Arthur Bigge, to influence the Queen in his favour. 'Bigge is very dangerous in that respect,' he warned. 'As for Buller he is inconceivable. We must have a Committee of Inquiry that such excellent fooling may not be lost to the world.' If there was to be a public row between Buller and the Government, Salisbury needed to ensure that the Queen was on the right side. He went down to Windsor three days later and, according to the Queen's journal, he 'lamented the loss of life, and the mistakes that had been made, and was especially alarmed at Sir R. Buller having changed his mind so often'. In this the Prime Minister was supported by Roberts, whom she saw just prior to his departure for the Cape. Meanwhile, Hugh Cecil was getting exasperated at people who argued that Black Week had somehow been a 'special judgment' on Britain for her weak Christian faith. 'The natural causes are evident,' he wrote to Frances Balfour, 'incompetent Generals and the like. Then how about our success at Omdurman? Were we less sinful a year ago?' As though Black Week had not been bad enough, Alfred Austin published a poem entitled *Spartan Mothers*, in which he wrote of the British soldier that:

> Should he fall
> By ridge or wall,
> And lie 'neath some green Southern sod, –
> 'Who dies for England, sleeps with God.'

When Balfour suggested blockading Delagoa Bay, through which Milner and Buller suspected contraband arms were still passing to the Transvaal, Salisbury demurred on grounds of expense, lack of reliable Intelligence, and the domestic and international ramifications of blockading the port of a friendly nation. On Christmas Day, he received the news from Hicks Beach that the war had already cost closer to £21.5 million than the £10 million originally estimated, and the shortfall would have to be financed by increases in income tax and liquor duties 'and either tobacco, tea or sugar, perhaps all three'. Income tax went up to a shilling in the pound in the next Budget, and duties on tobacco, beer and spirits were also increased. That same day Salisbury pronounced himself 'horrified' by reports that Milner now also wished to abandon Kimberley.

On 29th December, Salisbury told Balfour that he had, in the course of reading a biography of Wellington, 'Come across a letter from him to [William Wellesley-]Pole which begins "I am beginning to agree with you that every gallant officer is a fool." The type remains unchanged to this day.'[13] (Buller had won the Victoria Cross in the Zulu War.) Salisbury's attitude towards soldiers in general and generals in particular had long been sardonic. Discussing duelling in the *Saturday Review* in 1862, he had written that the 'theory that when a man is insulted, he is bound to give his insulter the opportunity of putting a bullet into him into the bargain was, in a less civilised age, prevalent in certain classes of society, and may possibly still lurk in some military brains, in which, as is frequently the case in such organisations, the reasoning faculty is inordinately minute'.

Salisbury had predicted in 1864 that the Maori and Ashanti campaigns would not be inscribed on the banners of the regiments involved, because the British army with its 'poker-like attitudes' was entirely unfitted for 'a bush war with savages'. In 1879, he had agreed with Beaconsfield that all the generals of the Afghan War except Roberts were 'utterly worthless', and save for Wolseley, Roberts and Kitchener he thought little of military men. Even Wolseley – whom one of his former staff officers Edward Cecil thought 'as full of vanity and susceptible to flattery as a passée beauty' – had embarrassed him politically in 1888.

The late-Victorian General Staff was full of martinets, each with their own cliques and petty jealousies, political mentors and gargantuan ambitions. Some generals like Roberts carefully nurtured their own public images as well. They fought inter-departmental campaigns against one another at least as diligently as they fought the Queen's enemies, and were masters of intrigue and recrimination. None of this would have much mattered had they not also had hopelessly outdated notions of how to wage war. Admitting to von Bülow that the war was not going 'too well at present', the former Commander-in-Chief, the Duke of Cambridge, stated that one of the compensations was that at least 'it is giving the British nobility the opportunity of showing that they still know how to die, and I am glad of that'.[14]

The Battle of Spion Kop on 24th January 1900 gave them yet another opportunity. Perhaps the most incompetent general of the war, Lieutenant-General Sir Charles Warren, a fifty-nine-year-old on the retired list, the soldier Salisbury had recalled from Bechuanaland and the police commissioner who failed to catch Jack the Ripper or prevent Bloody Sunday, took twenty-six hours to cross the Tugela River, allowing the Boers to reinforce their positions tenfold. He sent his troops forward without machine-guns, sandbags or a field telegraph unit, and with only twenty picks and shovels to entrench 2,000 men. The

Lancashire Brigade were ordered to halt on the wrong hill peak in thick fog, where they were massacred from three sides and above once it lifted. Although Warren was the slowest, another general, Sir Leslie Rundle, fully deserved the nickname 'Sir Leisurely Trundle' for his equally dilatory approach to soldiering. Nor was it long before Buller was called 'Sir Reverse'.

Balfour's own contribution was to make two singularly ill-contrived speeches in East Manchester on 8th and 9th January, the first statement to the nation by any senior minister since Black Week. Instead of admitting any Government errors, he defended Lansdowne and the War Office and blamed the British people and Parliament for the lack of military preparation. Neither Balfour nor Salisbury seemed fully to appreciate the anxious national mood, for, as Brodrick wrote to Violet Cecil that month, 'the country is on fire and flame against the Government.... We are a proud nation and bad at taking lessons.' Although Salisbury admitted privately to Austin that 'it is an anxious time – and for us one of great pressure', not least because he had still heard nothing of his son in Mafeking, he was not about to share this anxiety publicly, partly out of his natural reserve and stiff upper lip, and partly out of fear of damaging national morale.

Instead, in the Queen's Speech debate in the House of Lords on 30th January 1900, Salisbury badly misinterpreted the public mood and gave them phlegmatic irony when they wanted explanations and defiance. Replying to Lord Kimberley, who had complained about the Transvaal's successful importations of munitions, Salisbury asked: 'How on earth were we to know it? I believe, as a matter of fact – though I do not give this as official – that the guns were generally introduced in boilers and locomotives, and the munitions of war were introduced in pianos.... You cannot see through a deal board. We had no means of knowing the extent of the preparations, although everybody knew they existed to a certain extent.' Salisbury then blamed the 'ridiculously small' secret service budget, as though he had not been in power for twelve of the previous fifteen years. He also blamed Gladstone's 1881 and 1884 Conventions for the disastrous situation, an excuse which had also stretched thin by 1900.

Salisbury went on to argue that on each of the four occasions in the century when Britain had sent out expeditionary forces – the Walcheren expedition of 1809, the Peninsular War, the Crimea and now in South Africa – 'the opening of these was not prosperous, and on each occasion the Government of the day and the officers in command were assailed with the utmost virulence of popular abuse'. Yet it was not his Government that was to blame, he stated, but the Constitution. 'I do not believe in the perfection of the British Constitution as an instrument of war,' he told their Lordships. 'It is evident that there is something in your machinery that is wrong.... The art of war has been studied on the continent of Europe with a thoroughness and self-devotion that no other science has commanded, and at the end of the day we find ourselves surrounded by five great military Powers, and yet on matters of vital importance we pursue a policy wholly different from those military powers.' He explained that he was not actually advocating conscription, however, and even essayed the joke: 'I am pointing out that in this matter we enjoy splendid isolation.'

Salisbury also blamed other factors for Black Week, including the lack of conscription and a national military ethos, the lack of military experts in Parliament, too much promotion by seniority, Treasury parsimony and low funding of the Intelligence department. It was his contention, however, that 'I do not think the British Constitution as at present worked is a good fighting machine' which caused the most outrage. He went on:

> I have stated that it is unequalled for producing happiness, prosperity, and liberty in time of peace; but now, in time of war, when Great Powers with enormous forces are looking at us with no gentle or kindly eye on every side, it becomes us to think whether we must not in some degree modify our arrangement in order to enable ourselves to meet the dangers that at any moment may arise.

Yet beyond that bald statement he proposed no actual reforms to deal with the problem. The Prince of Wales told his sister Vicky that the speech had been 'simply deplorable' and 'painful' to his colleagues and supporters. His vitality had gone, his voice was indistinct and he had aged considerably, said the Prince, who had never been a particular admirer of Salisbury's.

Salisbury's speech was the oratorical equivalent of one of his burly shoulder-shrugs, and Rosebery, who was not expecting to speak in the debate, got up and dealt Salisbury a series of heavy blows. In a fiery address, the Liberal Imperialist said that the nation 'will have to be inspired by a loftier tone and by a truer patriotism than we have heard from the Prime Minister tonight'. Salisbury's insouciance angered some of his own supporters, and Lord Esher wrote to his son after the debate that: ' We may want a change badly a few months hence, if things go steadily wrong.'

Although Salisbury's patriotism was never in doubt, it seemed almost as though, with the diplomatic side of the issue settled and the purging of the senior commanders completed, he regarded the war, in the words of one historian, 'with a kind of sardonic detachment'.[15] When the Permanent Under-Secretary of the Treasury, Sir Francis Mowat, offered to resign over the criticisms made of his department, Salisbury had to return to the House of Lords on 1st February to say that he was 'blaming a system' rather than any individuals, and that the idea that he might be blaming Hicks Beach was nothing short of 'idiotic'. The secret service fund was more than trebled from £15,000 to £50,000.

When Kruger and Steyn threatened that, if any of the Cape Colony rebels were punished, reprisals would be visited on the British prisoners of war, the Cabinet on 2nd February decided to reply 'that if any British prisoners were treated in any different way to the usage of nations, the two Presidents would be held responsible'. The threat worked. The next day, Saturday, 3rd February, saw a day of National Intercession, on which prayers were said in church for the troops in South Africa. Salisbury, on whose seventieth birthday it fell, had originally turned the idea down as 'peculiar' and unprecedented, fearing it might smack of defeatism, and he only relented once the Queen had worked out a compromise formula for the services with the Archbishop of Canterbury.

At lunch at Arlington Street the next day, Salisbury was 'full of the stupidity of our officers. He proposed we should advertise for brains – "a little cowardice not objected to!"' Because the Germans compelled the entire *Junker* class to become officers, he said, they got a good cross-section of intelligence into the army, 'whereas here the clever members of the upper classes are very apt to go into other professions'. (His own refusal half a century earlier to serve in his father's yeomanry regiment was a case in point.) He told Lady Rayleigh that he would like 'to hang White for getting shut up in Ladysmith', but when asked whose fault it was that so many military stores were also stuck there, he changed the subject.

Although, when writing to the Queen, Salisbury accepted full responsibility for appointing Buller, in the House of Lords he was less forthcoming. 'I am shut off from discussing those questions altogether,' he answered a specific attack from Kimberley on military policy on 15th February. He held out the prospect of better news soon and added that: 'No military advantage is now to be obtained by taking a gloomy view.' Of Kimberley's speech he said: 'A more gloomy collection of lugubrious vaticinations I never heard.' It was uninspiring leadership, but he was at last proved correct about the upturn, for that same day General French's cavalry rode into Kimberley, finally lifting the 124-day siege. When Sanderson suggested sending an *en clair* telegram to all the major British embassies, Salisbury minuted: 'Much better not. Too emotional for F.O.'[16] It was the first of a series of victories as Roberts's great flanking march advanced towards Pretoria. On 18th February, General Cronje was surrounded at Paardeburg in the bend of the Modder River, and nine days later, on the anniversary of Majuba Hill, he and 4,000 of his men were starved into surrender by Roberts.

On 15th February, the Queen had written to Salisbury a letter 'to be burnt' (thus guaranteeing its careful preservation) continuing her campaign for Sikhs, Gurkhas and Zulus to be employed in the war. 'Is it obstinacy on Lord Lansdowne's part or timidity on Lord George Hamilton's, overruled by his Council?' she asked, adding that Devonshire was also 'growing very apathetic'. Salisbury had to answer that the India Office, War Office, Natal and Indian Governments could not be overriden in their opposition, although 'this ineradicable race prejudice is deeply to be regretted'. When she later insisted that he 'put his foot down' on the matter, Salisbury replied that it would bring his ministry down if he did.

For all his dislike of Whitehall bureacracy, Salisbury considered deep-seated reform of the War Office too difficult a task to be undertaken in wartime. He must however bear ultimate responsibility for a War Office that by 1899 was in no proper state to fight the Boer War efficiently. When in December 1898 the department had been particularly dilatory about sending out three medical officers to Cairo, it had taken the Queen, Cromer and Salisbury himself finally to get the matter expedited. He contented himself with the observation that the Americans in Cuba and French in Madagascar 'have failed far more conspicuously' in their medical arrangements than had the British in Egypt. It was not an answer he himself would have been satisfied with in his caustic younger days.

Salisbury told the Queen that Stanhope, Stanley and Gathorne-Hardy had all been criticised over War Office reform, and Lord Lansdowne was only the latest victim: 'It is obvious that the subject-matter is one of colossal difficulty.' Watching Salisbury during Lord Dunraven's questioning of Lansdowne over home defence in February 1900, Henry Lucy noticed how the Prime Minister sat 'in his favourite attitude, his head sunk on his chest, his clenched fists dug into the cushions of the bench supporting his ponderous figure. The pose has special advantages, inasmuch as it implies close attention, whilst affording opportunity for decently dropping asleep.'

At dinner at Arlington Street on 17th February, Salisbury laughed at Buller's attempts to surprise the Boers and cross the Tugela River. He told Lady Rayleigh that his huge wagon train could cover only five miles a day because the good-natured Buller allowed his officers to take far too much luggage. He was exaggerating, and sometimes Balfour would gently kick other family members under the table 'to accentuate his absurdities'. Balfour told his confidants that he felt like a Chief of Staff to a delightful but infuriating old general, who was getting 'more and more impossible to do business with.... Witty and suspicious – he never believes what he is told.'

The truth was that, at seventy, Salisbury, who was often ill and who, according to his son Robert, never truly recovered from his wife's death, was feeling tired and anxious. His heart was no longer really in the job. 'I cannot imagine what has happened to Lord Salisbury,' wrote Esher on 22nd February. 'His speeches show much weariness and entire misunderstanding of the people's mood.'[17] Only two days before, Salisbury had defeated Lord Wemyss's proposal for compulsory military service, using the argument that it would drive young men to America in order to escape the draft. It was generally considered a regrettable line to have adopted. When Lord Teynham asked what would happen to the Boer republics after the war was won, Salisbury answered: 'Does it not occur to my noble friend that it is a little premature to ask such a question?', which, however logical, also did not inspire confidence. Two days later, Salisbury took pleasure in expelling the pro-Boer French pretender, Louis Philippe Robert, Duc d'Orléans, from Britain, after it emerged that he had written to congratulate the cartoonist Adolphe Willette on his vicious caricatures of Queen Victoria in the French press.

It took Buller's relief of Ladysmith from its four-month siege on 28th February 1900 to dispel the mood of national tension which the Government had been so mishandling. Church bells were rung, flags were flown, schoolchildren were given a half-day off school, Stock Exchange trading was suspended, Kruger was burnt in effigy and the young ladies of Newnham College, Cambridge, danced and sang around a bonfire. 'The further progress of the war', Salisbury confidently predicted to the Queen, 'will no longer be accompanied by the anxiety which has attached to it hitherto.'[18] He was right, and the relief of Ladysmith is generally seen as the moment the tide of the war turned in Britain's favour.

The series of defeats had encouraged at least two serious attempts at joint action by the other Great Powers to take advantage of Britain's preoccupation in South Africa. France, Germany and Russia secretly discussed the possibilities, but the Kaiser told Sir Frank Lascelles, the British Ambassador to Berlin, that Her Majesty's Government would be a set of 'unmitigated noodles' if they cared a farthing about them. Salisbury agreed, and calmed Brodrick, who still feared a sudden French attack on Egypt, by saying that it was 'an impossibility – so say our generals – who let us trust know more about it than of the capabilities of Northern Natal'. Despite his confidence that France would get only 'a purely sentimental backing' from St Petersburg, a Russian general called Sakharov was in fact sent to Paris in July to conduct secret military conversations, but they eventually came to nothing.

This is not to suggest that the Russians were not acutely conscious of the strength of their position. On 2nd November, Tsar Nicholas II wrote to his sister to say:

I do like knowing that it lies solely with me in the last resort to change the course of the war in Africa. The means is very simple – telegraph an order for the whole Turkestan army to mobilize and march to the frontier. That's all. The strongest fleet in the world can't prevent us from settling our scores with England precisely at her most vulnerable point.[19]

That the Tsar never did this is a tribute both to his own pacific nature and to Salisbury's policy of not provoking Russia, however much Curzon wished he would.

On 5th March, the two Boer Presidents telegraphed Salisbury to say that they would sue for peace if the 'incontestable independence of both Republics' was admitted. Their attempts to involve Germany, France, Holland and America had come to nothing, and the war in the field was now clearly being lost. Salisbury told the Queen that this 'remarkable message' was only intended to encourage the pro-Boer element in Britain who 'are not many, but they are noisy'. After a Cabinet on 10th March, at which the peace overtures were unanimously rejected, Salisbury replied officially in four pithy paragraphs why peace was impossible: 'The British Empire has been compelled to confront an invasion which has entailed upon the Empire a costly war and the loss of thousands of precious lives. This great calamity has been the penalty which Great Britain has suffered for having in recent years acquiesced in the existence of the two Republics.' To a letter from the Kaiser offering to mediate, which to Salisbury looked suspiciously like a desire to intervene, the Queen replied that Britain 'will resist all interference'. This impressed Salisbury, who wrote to thank her, as 'it would not have been *convenable* for me to use such strong language'.

The Transvaal's offer had nonetheless aroused the organisations and individuals who opposed the war. The Quakers redoubled their efforts for peace and the South African Conciliation Committee presented an appeal to Salisbury not to annex the republics now that victory was in sight. Labouchere predicted that the British people 'will soon see that they have been fooled into this war by the vilest body of financiers that ever existed in this world, and that the opportunity has been taken to lay hold of the territory and gold, which Lord Salisbury himself boasted we did not wish for'. Even Lord Rosebery was tempted to make the Delphic public utterance that: 'Some of the greatest peaces in the world's history have begun with an apparently casual meeting of two travellers in a neutral area.'

On 14th March, Salisbury scotched any hopes of clandestine meetings with Kruger in Holland when he read out 'in tones of unusual emphasis and alertness' the terms demanded by the Boers and the reply he had given. One spectator described Salisbury's reply as having been recited with 'a lofty scorn it was unnecessary to conceal'.[20] The following day, Roberts, who had captured Bloemfontein on the 13th, proclaimed the British alternative to peace. Any Boer who laid down his arms and took an oath of neutrality would be allowed to return to his farm, this amnesty applying to all but the Boer political leaders who were accused of starting the war and having ordered the abuse of the white flag. Thousands of Boers took up the offer, although a number subsequently reneged on their oaths and rejoined the commandos.

Two more defeats in late March and early April – when Christiaan De Wet ambushed Major-General Robert Broadwood at Sannah's Post and the Royal Irish surrendered at Reddersburg – further infuriated Salisbury. On 6th April, the Cabinet, in Salisbury's words, 'resolved to telegraph their sense of the deep evil, in various ways, which these successive displays of carelessness would produce; and to urge on Lord Roberts, without mentioning any names, that the officers who were responsible for those mishaps ought to be superseded'. The Queen thought that it should be up to Roberts to decide, but Salisbury reiterated after a further Cabinet meeting three days later that: 'The successive loss of so many bodies of men in consequence of the officers taking no precautions against ambush amounts to a scandal. These repeated exhibitions of negligence are most injurious to the service and require severer notice than they have received.' That same day, Roberts relieved Gatacre of his command and sent him back to England. Speaking to Lady Rayleigh on 12th April, Salisbury was 'very angry still at the stupidity of our officers – will not hear of sympathy with Gatacre ... saying truly enough that the pity should be given to those whom his mistakes have sent prisoners to Pretoria'.

Salisbury went down to Hatfield in mid-April, hoping for his first holiday in twenty months, but, as he told Francis Bertie, 'it is only half a holiday as the boxes still come'. He had been taking morning constitutional walks in Green Park, and at 9.20 a.m. Edward Hamilton would pass him every day, 'creeping or waddling along with a cloak hung around his shoulders, and hardly ever recognised'. The only moving film which exists of Salisbury dates from around this time. It consists of fifteen grainy seconds of the enormous bulk of his back, as he moves along a reception line at a garden party greeting the papal nuncio and a man in a fez, holding a black shiny top hat and certainly not deigning to acknowledge the presence of the camera.[21]

A problem which had been rumbling since mid-March, when Lansdowne had produced a Cabinet memorandum criticising the accuracy of almost every line of Buller's tendentious official report of his period as Commander-in-Chief, erupted the next month. Buller had even included in his official report lines such as: 'Had any attention been paid to my advice there would have been no Ladysmith to relieve.' On 17th April, he wrote to Lansdowne to say that he 'deeply resented the cruel, and, as I thought, quite uncalled-for sneer' contained in the telegram which the War Secretary had sent replacing him with Roberts back on 18th December 1899. Lansdowne then allowed Roberts's despatch about the Spion Kop disaster, which named Buller and Warren as having been largely responsible, to be published in the press. The Queen went incandescent about this breach of security, initially assuming the despatch had been stolen, and demanded to know from Salisbury: 'What has caused this lamentable want of discretion and judgment', which she considered 'cruel and very injurious towards Sir R. Buller who did relieve Ladysmith'.

Salisbury telegraphed the Queen who was staying at Dublin's Viceregal Lodge to say that he too was 'puzzled' and explained that Lansdowne must have 'entirely misunderstood the decision of the Cabinet' that the despatch should be kept secret. Cabinet meetings were not minuted and Lansdowne was unrepentant, saying that he had been unable to construct a clear decision 'from the materials afforded by Devonshire's yawns, and casual interjections around the table'. When the Queen asked Salisbury to repudiate Lansdowne's action, he replied:

> If I did so publicly, he would certainly resign. Probably the other three Liberal Unionists would take the same course, and perhaps some others; and a change of Government or a dissolution must necessarily follow. It would be a great responsibility to bring about these events in the very crisis of war.[22]

So Lansdowne stayed, but the Buller issue continued to bedevil the Government. Salisbury had no intention of bowing to the Queen's instruction that he 'must insist on no discussion being entered into now as to the conduct of the Generals'. If they were primarily responsible for the defeats, Salisbury saw no reason why they, rather than the War Office and his Government, should not be made the scapegoats.

Salisbury was proud when both Cranborne (in command of 4th Battalion of Bedfordshire Regiment) and also McDonnell went out to fight in South Africa, but he was merely amused when the fifty-two-year-old Duke of Norfolk resigned from the Postmaster-Generalship to join the colours. 'We shall have old Cross going next,' he said of the seventy-seven-year-old Lord Privy Seal. Answering an invitation in late April from Archbishop Temple to speak at Exeter Hall about missions, a subject of which he protested he knew nothing, Salisbury added: 'I suppose that in these days when a Postmaster-General goes to the front as an infantry lieutenant, we must not talk about incongruity.'[23]

He himself was accused of gross incongruity in his annual speech to the Grand Habitation of the Primrose League at the Albert Hall on 9th

May 1900. Compulsory conscription was impossible, he conceded, but instead he called for 'an armed people', saying that the League should take the lead and 'foster the creation of rifle clubs', which could recreate 'the skill and fame of ancestors many centuries ago, who by their practice in archery raised this country to its high level of military glory'. Labouchere, reminding his listeners of an earlier Salisbury gaffe, asserted that circuses would be about as useful for winning the Boer War as rifle clubs. The *Naval and Military Record* also ridiculed the idea, and Salisbury's call was written off as an absurd eccentricity. One of his remarks that day proved prophetic, however, when he said that in the new century then looming, 'the dangers which we will have to meet in external affairs will occupy a considerably larger place than they have done in the periods of the century that has passed by'.[24]

Early May brought an improvement on late March and April. On the 3rd, Roberts resumed his march to Pretoria from Bloemfontein, and the next day Major-General Bryan Mahon's column struck out to relieve Mafeking. Buller resumed his advance a week later and even out-manoeuvred a Boer force from Biggarsberg. Meanwhile, Colonel Robert Baden-Powell's small contingent in Mafeking continued to beat off Boer attacks. The best news of the war, indeed the most popularly celebrated news of the reign, came on 17th May 1900 when Mahon finally relieved Mafeking, ending its 217-day siege.

It is no mean achievement for a family when even its black sheep is a war hero. Financially incontinent and a keen but bad baccarat player in the Grenadier Guards, Edward – nicknamed 'Nigs' – was also charming and a famed raconteur. 'Dear Papa, I write as a younger son always ought to write to his father, for money,' he once began a letter in 1883, begging that it be sent quickly, 'unless you wish me to be detained here for attempting to fly from my creditors'. Eventually Salisbury's patience with paying his son's gambling debts ran out, and in April 1891, the month that Edward became aide-de-camp to Lord Wolseley, he wrote this admonition:

> Of the people who game there are two sorts – the people who are very fond of it, but who are quite cool at the table, and can stop when they please – and the people who, at first at least, are not very fond of it, but who get excited at it, and lose their heads. To these last – and I am afraid, you belong to them – the taste for gambling is one of the extremest danger.

When, a month later, he paid £1,126.8s.6d into Edward's account at Cox's Bank, Salisbury informed his son that it was money that had originally been earmarked for his unmarried sister Gwendolen.

Nevertheless, the debts began mounting again, reaching £2,000 by May 1894.

The next month, Edward married Violet Maxse at St Saviour's Church in Chelsea, the ceremony being taken by his brother William. Of Salisbury's five children who married, all but Edward chose the offspring of earls. He married the daughter of Admiral Frederick Maxse, a Crimean War hero but an atheist and Radical parliamentary candidate, who had moreover separated from his wife. His daughter Violet was equally free-thinking and unconventional; there were six poets at her wedding including Oscar Wilde and Wilfrid Blunt. The political representation was also eclectic; the marriage register was signed by Salisbury, Balfour, Asquith, Morley and Chamberlain. Blunt recorded how at the reception, 'the crowd was immense, and I found myself for ten minutes flattened like a herring between Lord Salisbury and a tall Dutch clock. Truly matrimony makes strange pew fellows.' Lady Salisbury was unconvinced about Violet, as she told Nelly:

> It will be good for Nigs to have a clever wife and one accustomed to take care of expense and I hope he will convert her. I don't believe in pious Pagans – and my only objection (real) to the Souls, is their heathenry. The world, the flesh and the devil are far too strong to be conquered by anything but the three creeds! 'Art', 'refinement' and 'intellect' are all bosh without them and will never keep you straight.

Unlike his own father, Salisbury did not disapprove of his son marrying into the middle class. Of his Maxse in-laws he gave Edward some sage advice: 'Their characters are a matter of infinitely less importance than hers. You are not going to marry them.' He paid off his son's debts yet again and settled £1,000 per annum on him, and promised another £1,000 per annum upon his own death. With Violet contributing £400 per annum and Edward drawing £200 per annum in army pay, they would be comfortable but not flush. 'For many years of my married life I had much less,' Salisbury recalled, 'and I do not think I was less happy than I have been since I was richer. Plenty of people in our rank of life have had similar experience. But it will require a certain amount of sustained effort, and of contempt for the opinion of other people.' Unfortunately the couple turned out ill-suited, and the marriage was unhappy.

On 3rd July 1899, Colonel Baden-Powell had been ordered to attend the Commander-in-Chief at the War Office, where Wolseley ordered him to leave immediately for Mafeking, hold it in the coming war and if possible conduct raids into the Transvaal using the town as his base. He was also told to take Major Lord Edward Cecil of the Grenadier Guards as his Chief Staff Officer. Unlike Wolseley and Kitchener, Baden-Powell did not appreciate the advantages of having the Prime Minister's son on his staff, and jibbed that he had to take someone who knew neither him nor southern Africa. In his autobiography years later, he complained that 'If you make a man responsible for a job you must, if you would be fair to him, let him choose his own tools.'[25] The staff were told to make their way to Cape Town under assumed names and without even informing their families, something they found very amusing at Hatfield. When Edward sailed on 8th July, Violet went too.

Soon after arriving in South Africa – leaving Violet at Cape Town, where she stayed in Rhodes's home, Groote Schuur – Cecil proved his worth by giving the profiteering contractors Julius Weil & Co. his signature on a contract for £500,000 to supply the necessary stores to take them through what he and Baden-Powell correctly estimated would be a long siege. The Cape authorities had refused to underwrite the stockpiling, and only with the Prime Minister's son's signature on the sale document would Weil & Co. part with the huge amount of stores. Although Cecil had nothing like that amount in the world – and indeed Salisbury himself would have been hard put to find it in the unlikely event of Parliament turning down a grant – it ensured that the town was well provisioned for the coming onslaught.

During that epic siege of Empire, Cecil distinguished himself as Baden-Powell's effective second-in-command. He imposed the death penalty for suspected spies, looters and any man found near the women's *laager* at night, as well as for 'anyone, white or native, who trespasses in a field'. He had to oversee the provision of rations, which out of military necessity were more generous and varied for the defending troops than the native civilians. When Weil's stores finally ran out, dogs and horses were eaten, but even though the official figure for those who died of starvation was 478, there was only one recorded case of cannibalism. With 700 regular troops and 300 local volunteers, 1,000 white civilians and 7,000 non-combatant natives, Baden-Powell kept 3,000 Boer troops tied down for over seven months. By the use of homing pigeons and native runners they managed to keep in irregular touch with the outside world, and as the months passed gradually learnt that they were becoming national heroes.

It was not all summary punishment and starvation; they held concerts and gymkhanas – 'Lady Sarah Wilson has kindly consented to present the prizes' – and Cecil set up the Mafeking Cadet Corps for boys between the ages of nine and fifteen. Known as 'Scouts', they wore khaki uniforms with forage caps and were drilled and used as orderlies and messengers. Baden-Powell later wrote that Cecil's success in the experiment at Mafeking 'led me to go into it further'.[26] When in December 1899, Lady Sarah Wilson, Randolph Churchill's sister, was captured by the Boers, Cecil had chivalrously insisted on a deal being done with the Boer general, J.P. Snyman. He told Baden-Powell that 'it was unseemly for an Englishwoman to be left in the hands of the Boers and transported to Pretoria by the rough coach, exposed to possible insults and to certain discomforts'. She was instead exchanged for a train-wrecker and horse-thief named Petrus Viljon, and remained an ornament to the garrison for the rest of the siege.

'Our news from Mafeking is very contradictory,' Salisbury wrote to Frances Balfour in April 1900, 'but there is fair grounds for hoping that it is only the blacks who are starving.' Despite this gallows humour, Salisbury was hugely gratified when the news arrived that the siege had finally been raised. In the Mafeking lottery, Cecil had drawn 6th August and 3rd November 1900 for the day on which the relief would finally happen, and was as unlucky in that as in the rest of his gambling. It actually came on 17th May, and when the news reached London the following day the nation went spontaneously wild with joy. At 9.20 p.m. the Lord Mayor announced at the Mansion House that the town had been relieved, and that night millions of people emptied on to the streets for what was later described as 'the most wonderful and harmless saturnalia of the century'.

Across the country patriotic songs were sung at the top of voices, and a contemporary remembered 'dancing, jumping, screaming in a delirium of unrestrained joy'. The verb 'to maffick' temporarily entered the vocabulary, to mean crazy public rejoicing. Crossing class boundaries, such extravagant celebrations showed how pent up had been the national tension. When the crowd reached the War Office, they were amused to find the bulletin posted outside the door still reported 'No News'.[27] Winston Churchill believed that the Mafeking celebrations were even greater than those of Armistice Night 1918, for the reason that 'there were too many ghosts about the streets after Armageddon'. The writer Rebecca West, who witnessed both, believed that they were even greater than those of V-E Day in 1945.

Mafeking might have been relieved, but Lady Edward Cecil was not. It meant the interruption of the close relationship, more probably the affair, that she had been conducting with Milner. On hearing the news that her husband had been freed, she went to bed with a headache and received a note there from Milner which simply read: 'There is nothing at all that I can say to you. I think you know what I should like to say. God ever bless you and give you all good and don't write. It is not a day for writing.' All she said about her reunion with her husband at Mafeking on 29th June was that 'it was a poignant meeting', before Cecil went off up-country to administer a portion of the occupied Transvaal, leaving her at Groote Schuur to ride and dine with Milner almost every day.

Back at Hatfield, Gwendolen recorded how the town's inhabitants dressed up as soldiers, sailors, nurses 'and heaven knows what', and marched through the parish up to the house with torches, bands and flags on the night of 20th May. They paraded to the north front, shouting and cheering. Gwendolen found it 'thrilling'. Salisbury made a short speech from the north steps and then everyone marched to the Red Lion field nearby, where an enormous bonfire was lit by Edward's four-and-a-half-year-old son George. It had been he who, along with his cousin Mary Alice ('Moucher', later Duchess of Devonshire), had two days earlier dashed around the house yelling the news: 'Mafeking is relieved; three cheers for Baden-Powell and God Save the Queen!' Gwendolen reported that 'Even my father was impressed' with the spontaneous happiness and pride the town had shown.[28] For someone who had once had sleepwalking nightmares about mobs marching on his home with flaming torches, this manifestation of the democratic will was infinitely preferable.

Of course, Alfred Austin commemorated the Relief with a poem in *The Times*. When Frances Balfour teased Salisbury, asking what he thought of the misrhyming of ''Gainst death could wrestle' with 'Gallant young Cecil!', the Prime Minister answered that he had 'thought it best not to read the poem of his Poet Laureate'. Eleanor Balfour's reaction to Austin's effusion was merely 'Pah!' To the Queen, Salisbury called the Relief 'a most blessed termination of a long and wearing anxiety', and wrote to Edward: 'I suppose the others have told you of all the rejoicings here.... Don't bother about repaying the £1,000. I am sensible that you must pay for the luxury of going through an eight month siege.'

When Edward finally returned to Hatfield on 18th December, the town once again erupted into celebration. The local fire brigade encircled his carriage carrying torches. It was uncoupled and pulled up to the house by the Hatfield brewery-men in their white linen jackets. The whole town 'had decorated itself nobly for the occasion ... every house had made an effort to express, by gay devices and flags, the popular feeling of joy at the home-coming of the House of Cecil from the war'.[29] As the carriage was drawn up at the steps in the great courtyard, where Salisbury stood with his family and guests, 'thousands of faces, illumined by the torches' watched as he proudly greeted his son with a simple handshake. After very brief speeches from Salisbury and Lord Edward, there were refreshments for all-comers in the park, where young George lit another great bonfire, 'as the disturbed peacocks shrieked angrily'.

FORTY-FOUR

Resolution

*False Dawn – Curzon
– The Boxer Rebellion –
The 'Khaki' Election –
The Unionist Alliance*

May to October 1900

'Every seat lost to the Government is a seat gained to the Boers.'

If the Boers had hoped that the relief of Mafeking might make Salisbury look upon peace proposals more favourably, they were swiftly and cruelly disabused. Speaking at the City of London Conservative Association's annual banquet at Cannon Street Hotel on 29th May 1900, he declared that no long-term security was 'within our reach so long as we leave a shred of real independent government to either republic'. He also repudiated the pledge he had given in his Guildhall speech the previous November about seeking no territory. To great cheering he announced: 'Because we declared that it was not greed of territory that led us into war, we therefore bound ourselves never to annex any territory is a most ridiculous contention.' The cheers turned to laughter when he added the analogy: 'I might tell you that in coming here tonight I had no intention of going to Brighton, but I do not bind myself for all time that I shall not go to Brighton.' After the toast, given by the Master of the Rolls, Salisbury stood up again to announce that he had just been informed that Lord Roberts had taken Johannesburg, at which the orchestra struck up the National Anthem and, as *The Times* reported the next day, there was an 'extraordinary outburst of enthusiasm' among the 300 diners present.

A week later, on 5th June, Roberts also captured Pretoria and released the British prisoners of war held there. Kruger fled to Portuguese and Dutch protection and formal resistance ended. The war was far from over, however, because the Boers switched from fighting pitched battles towards making hit-and-run commando raids. On 31st May, Piet De Wet captured a battalion of Irish Yeomanry and its commanding officer, Lieutenant-Colonel Spragge, and on 7th June his brother, the military genius Christiaan De Wet, won a victory at Roodewal. Generals Botha and De La Rey also remained in the field.

Salisbury blamed what he called 'race arrogance' for these defeats. Back in 1862 he had written about the 'old contempt for semi-barbarous enemies which has so often led English troops into calamity'.[1] Now, twenty-eight years later, he wrote to his former private secretary and Iddesleigh's younger son, Lord Northcote, now Governor of Bombay:

> It interests me that you are struck with the 'damned nigger' element in the British society of Bombay. It is bad enough in official and military circles here. I look upon it as not only offensive and unworthy but as representing what is now, and will be in a highly magnified proportion, a serious political danger. But I preach in the wilderness. It belongs to that phase of British temper which in the last few months has led detachment after detachment of British troops into the most obvious ambuscades – mere arrogance.... It is painful to see the dominant race deliberately going over into the abyss.

Taking a Prussian proclamation from the Franco-Prussian War for his precedent, Roberts announced on 16th June that he would raze those farms which were closest to the places where railway lines had been sabotaged. This harsh and arbitrary policy, fully supported by Salisbury, forced Boer women and children from their homesteads and towards the refugee camps which the British were setting up. By 20th June, the last formidable body of Boers in the Cape Colony north of the Orange River surrendered, finally ending the fighting there.

The great harshness with which Salisbury proposed to treat those Boer soldiers who had reneged on their neutrality oath is reminiscent of the man who decades earlier had, albeit anonymously, recommended occasionally hanging Irish priests. Writing to Brodrick on 2nd July, he suggested that 'every [Crown] colonist taken in arms' should be sent to Bermuda for penal servitude for life, and any who could be proved to have taken life should suffer death: 'I do not see that we can go further than this.' The difficulty was 'with the çi devant citizens of the two republics, who it appears can only be treated as prisoners of war. I can think of nothing but "confiscating" i.e. giving to somebody else the property of those you catch.' As for those who were now taking the oath of neutrality, Salisbury believed there was no way of holding them to it, 'unless you see your way to making on them some personal mark – brand, tattoo, or what you like to recognise a prisoner who has broken his oath'. Humanitarian considerations prevailed, however, and the Boers were not branded.

Meanwhile, the war was progressing well and, on 21st July, Roberts began his advance towards Komati Poort, moving up through the west Transvaal. He instituted a new strategy of 'sweeping' the veldt with flying columns of mounted infantry, burning farms and smashing all organised resistance. On the 27th, he sent Lansdowne a telegraph reporting that, although the Boer High Command wanted to prolong the war 'to the bitter end', many of their troops now wished it over. Despite rumours reaching the Foreign Office of a foreign combination against Britain, Salisbury was ready to make a joke at Lord Wemyss's expense in the House of Lords over his scare story of a French invasion of Britain. When Wemyss claimed that 'reliable sources' had told him, 'England should be strong and unassailable in the month of November next,' Salisbury answered: 'I believe there is to be a great collection of shooting stars in the early part of November. That is the only peculiarity in the month of November that I know of that we need apprehend.'[2]

One problem Salisbury did apprehend was the escalating cost of the war. 'I know of one suicide we shall hear of,' he announced to his family one evening in July 1900. When everyone looked up anxiously, he said: 'Beach! The money is pouring out like water.' In 1900, the British economy grew more slowly than at any time since the late eighteenth century, and the costs of the war forced both increased government borrowing and a rise in direct and indirect taxation. Hicks Beach, an orthodox financier, loathed what he had to do, especially to pay for a war he had considered to be avoidable. Hoping to finance the war through traditional methods, he retrenched and suspended the Sinking Fund, whilst sticking rigidly to Free Trade principles and gradually increasing income tax from 8d in the pound to 1s.2d. By the end of the war in 1902, the National Debt stood at over £800 million.

One result of the financial squeeze, as Salisbury tried to explain to the Viceroy in August 1900, was that Curzon's great schemes of expansion and confrontation in Persia had to be shelved:

> I hope the effect of paying that disagreeable Income Tax may have the effect of inducing our countrymen to believe that, in Empire as well as in everything else, we must cut our coat according to our cloth. It is obvious that our fighting power in the Persian Gulf ... must be confined to the sea coast. In the rest of Persia we could only fight at the cost of efforts which would swallow up twice or thrice as much income tax as the Transvaal. For, after all, you must divide victories by taxation if you wish to know in solid figures the real worth of Empire.[3]

This logic entirely failed to appease Curzon, whose private criticisms of Salisbury became louder and more insistent. Curzon was exasperated at the way South African policy constantly headed the national agenda. On the flimsiest of evidence, such as the French request for a coaling station from the Sultan of Muscat, he presented a conspiracy theory for a Franco-Russian plot against British interests in the Persian Gulf, which Salisbury politely disregarded. 'I do not suppose that Lord Salisbury will be persuaded to lift a little finger to save Persia,' Curzon complained self-pityingly to his closest Cabinet ally, George Hamilton. 'We are slowly – no, I think I may say swiftly – paving the way for the total extinction of our influence in that country.'

Curzon's worries about Britain's waning influence at Teheran left the Prime Minister entirely unmoved. 'Appointing a new consul to a Persian district', he told Brodrick the following November, 'is like thrusting a poker into a dull fire.' It is evident from the letters between Curzon and Brodrick that there was more than simply patriotism to their desire that the top job in politics should become vacant. 'Was ever such a Cabinet known?' Curzon complained to his friend in July 1899. 'Four years without a change.' Salisbury did not believe in reshuffling his Cabinet during a Parliament, thinking that the longer a minister stayed in a department, the better he could master its complexities against his civil servants.

Back in 1896, Curzon had written to Salisbury begging him to take no notice of a newspaper report saying that he opposed an appointment of Salisbury's, adding 'if there is a suspicion calculated to wound, it is that of disloyalty'. Yet by June 1900 such was the Viceroy's self-regard that he was writing to Clinton Dawkins, the Finance member of his Council, to say that in Persia he was trying 'to foresee changes and to anticipate it by prompt action', but was only 'snubbed' by Salisbury. 'I am only joining a band of good men and true,' he added. It seems not to have occurred to Curzon that, just as the British army was fighting the grim Battle of Diamond Hill in South Africa, policy-makers in London had more important things on their minds than playing a costly Great Game against the phantom Russian threat in central Persia.

The following month, the Viceroy wrote to Brodrick to complain about 'that strange, powerful, inscrutable, brilliantly obstructive dead-weight at the top'. In a letter to Dawkins from Simla on 29th August 1900, he even seemed to imply that Salisbury was jealous of him, writing: 'I think from all that I hear that he is himself losing his former vigour, and deprecates in others that in which he formerly excelled himself.... He regards as dangerous jingoism the effort to save from total ruin our waning influence in Persia.' Yet that same month Salisbury had gone into some detail explaining to Curzon precisely why he thought his fears were exaggerated. He almost apologised for controlling Curzon so closely, but 'In old time the Indian Government was a law unto itself, and treaties did not matter much. But the Suez Canal and the Electric Telegraph have altered all that: and as you are well aware, our character for hubris all over the continent is a bad one.' As for the war, Salisbury readily admitted that it 'has been a bad investment. The total expense will about represent another penny on the Income Tax in perpetuity; or a little more.'

This letter brought further abuse from Curzon, who told Brodrick that in China, Persia, Morocco, Egypt, 'or any place in the world', Salisbury had shown 'no prescience, and therefore no policy'. He was adept enough at handling immediate crises like Venezuela, he would grant, 'But the future to him is anathema.' Salisbury's own estimation of Curzon was that 'He always wants me to negotiate with Russia as if I had five hundred thousand men at my back, and I have not.' Yet he took a great deal of trouble with his errant former Under-Secretary, and admitted in October 1900 that his feeling with respect to French activity in the Persian Gulf 'is very similar to that experienced by the owner of a large expanse of very precious china when contemplating the evolutions of a highly muscular housemaid'. Britain could simply not exercise the military weight in inland Persia which Russia could bring to bear.[4]

As for Germany, which was 'in mortal terror of Russia', Salisbury told Curzon that she would never stand by Britain when it came to the crunch, 'but is always rather inclined to curry favour with Russia by throwing us over'. With such a serious imperial commitment being made to South Africa, simultaneously to take on a 'Forward' policy such as the Viceroy desired in Persia would have been a perilous undertaking, as Curzon would doubtless have appreciated had he been in any other post. 'I want to get forwarder,' Curzon wrote to Lansdowne in April 1901, warning that otherwise, 'we are presently drifting merrily towards another Port Arthur'.

The Viceroy spent six months planning his magnificent Durbar of January 1903, which Salisbury dubbed the 'Curzonisation'. He excluded *Onward Christian Soldiers* from the ceremony not because the hymn might offend Hindus and Muslims but on the grounds that the lines: 'Crowns and Thrones may perish / Kingdoms rise and wane' was subversive of the image of the Raj he wished to convey. When the Financial Secretary to the War Office, Lord Stanley (later 17th Earl of Derby), was preparing to visit India, Salisbury joked that if Curzon should proclaim himself King-Emperor at the Durbar, Stanley was to declare that the proposal had not received the approval of the Government. Three weeks after the Durbar, at which Curzon reviewed 40,000 troops, Salisbury told Violet Cecil that he had dreamt that he had been transported to the Curzonisation and was 'very upset' at finding himself there.

In the summer of 1900, as Britain was fully militarily committed in South Africa, a terrifying insurrection broke out in the Shandong province of China and swiftly spread across the northern part of the country. The secret Yi He Tuan organisation, or 'Society of Righteous Harmonious Fists', was a fanatical sect dedicated to martial arts and the expulsion of all foreigners from the Celestial Kingdom. Its devotees, known as 'Boxers', formed the nucleus of a pan-Chinese nationalist uprising, which in mid-June 1900 attacked Peking, assassinated Baron Klemens von Kettler, the German Ambassador, and besieged the foreign Legations. The Dowager Empress of China, Tzu Hsi, nominally opposed them but covertly gave the Boxers her moral support.

At first Salisbury seemed to underestimate the gravity of the situation, describing the Boxers as 'a mere mob' to Queen Victoria. 'Russia, not China, seems to me the greatest danger of the moment,' he informed her. Deeply pessimistic about retaining influence even in the Yangtze Basin once Russia's Trans-Siberian railway was completed, Salisbury had only the previous year told Chamberlain that 'If you consider the position of the Russians ethically, it is as bad as can be. Negotiating with them is like catching soaped eels.' Now, however, the Russians and the British were, in theory at least, on the same side as the Germans, Japanese and Americans in needing to get an international force to Peking to relieve their Legations.[5]

Salisbury had long opposed the policy of the 'Forward' school of imperialists in the China Association, as also proposed by Jingoes, the British community in Shanghai, parts of the British press and the Acting Consul-General in Shanghai, Pelham Warren. Not only did he believe that imperial resources were quite stretched enough by the Boer War, but any overt expansionism would, he feared, irritate the local anti-Boxer Chinese warlords, create further xenophobia in the southern and central areas so far unaffected by the rebellion, and above all give Germany and Russia an excuse to extend their presence, probably at the expense of British interests in the Yangtze Basin. Having been officially advised that the Boxers were 'badly organised, destitute of leaders and armed with only agricultural implements, and occasionally bows and arrows', Salisbury stood out against overreacting to events. When a small Allied Marine relief force under the British Admiral E.H. Seymour was repulsed by Chinese troops thought to be loyal to the Empress, Salisbury insisted that it should not be taken as a *casus belli* against the whole Chinese Empire. He even told Betty Balfour that von Kettler's death had been 'poetical justice', saying: 'It's all the fault of Germany. They began all this trouble.'

In early July, the seriousness of the situation was brought home to Salisbury by an article in the *Daily Mail*, based on a Reuters' report, which stated that the Peking Legations had fallen and that all the inhabitants there, including the British Ambassador Sir Claude Macdonald, had been massacred. The Queen pronounced herself haunted by the spectre and demanded to know what was being done. People swiftly equated it with the Cawnpore massacre during the Indian Mutiny and the massacre at the Kabul Legation in 1879. The Dean of St Paul's 'so annoyed' Salisbury by suggesting a national memorial service in his Cathedral before the news was even verified. Salisbury himself kept his head, just as he had during Black Week, and told Frances Balfour that he doubted the news was true and had not given up hope. As he told the Queen: 'We are urging troops forward with all rapidity in our power, but we cannot diminish the distance.'

Throughout the crisis, Salisbury insisted on regarding the uprising as an isolated act of anarchy, rather than a deliberate warlike act on behalf of the Peking Government which would justify a formal declaration of war. In Cabinet he attempted to play down the demands of the Jingoist ministers who wanted to widen and deepen the conflict, especially by involving Germany in a closer alliance than he was willing to contemplate. 'We are drifting in this Chinese matter,' Lord George Hamilton complained to Curzon on 27th July, 'and everyone in the Cabinet knows it.' Yet, soon after the war party in the Cabinet got reinforcements sent to China, Hamilton was complaining loudly to the Viceroy for the way 'the hysterical element in Shanghai' had forced the decision, which turned out to be largely unnecessary.[6]

More hysterical still, and far more distasteful, was the speech Kaiser Wilhelm II gave at Bremerhaven on 27th July 1900. Bidding farewell to Field Marshal Count Alfred von Waldersee, whom Salisbury had agreed could command the overall international military force in China, the Kaiser told him and his troops that when they made contact with the Boxer enemy:

> No pardon will be given, and prisoners will not be taken. Any one who falls into your hands falls to your sword! Just as the Huns under their King Etzel created for themselves one thousand years ago a name which men still respect, you should give the name of German such cause to be remembered in China for one thousand years that no Chinaman, no matter if his eyes be slit or not, will dare to look a German in the face.

By the time von Waldersee arrived in China on 12th September, the international force had relieved the Legations, which had not fallen after all, although sixty-five of the defenders had been killed. In the fierce fighting, the Boxers' belief that they were immune to foreigners' bullets had proved over-sanguine. Soon after the relief of the Legations, the allies occupied the Forbidden City and expelled the Empress's Court from Peking. Salisbury was delighted by the result, but philosophical about the cause of the rise in Chinese nationalism, telling Cranbrook: 'I have passed some time in trying to persuade my countrymen that bluffing with the Chinese was a dangerous amusement: but I did not anticipate such a very striking confirmation of my views.' To Violet Cecil he later ascribed the problem to 'a mad Empress', Chinese viceroys in German pay, 'Germans afraid of Russia' and 'a stupid English ambassador'.

Salisbury's *sang froid* did not go down well in Cabinet, and the Boxer crisis did much to bring the anti-isolationist elements together in condemnation of Salisbury's cautious, non-aligned foreign policy. Goschen, Devonshire, Selborne and George Hamilton all more or less supported Chamberlain's far more 'Forward' approach, and to a lesser extent Balfour and Lansdowne sympathised with him too. Although Chamberlain readily admitted to Salisbury that China would not be an electoral issue, and the constituencies cared no more about it 'than they do about Ashanti', he nevertheless believed that it afforded Britain the perfect opportunity for closer co-operation with Germany.

Chamberlain saw only weakness and isolation arising from Salisbury's refusal to contemplate a German entente or alliance, and the Cabinet was swinging behind him in the silent hope that Salisbury could be dislodged from the Foreign Office after the next election. Goschen's two letters to Chamberlain of 1st and 2nd September are entirely typical of the correspondence between leading Cabinet members during this period. Enclosing Salisbury's proposed reply to a letter from the Kaiser asking for more support for von Waldersee, Goschen wrote:

> It makes one despair. A *non possumus* in every direction. It is quite possible the Emperor has some designs that are not clear: but we shall not thwart them by standing aloof.... If some policy is forced on Salisbury, which he disapproves of, it breaks down in the execution.... The difficulty lies not in any one step we might jointly persuade Salisbury to take, but in his whole attitude in this question.... Pressure on Salisbury does not produce any real change of attitude, though he may take some small step.... Absolute isolation is playing the devil.

Quite unperturbed by the growing opposition in his Cabinet, Salisbury refused to see China as a significant enough reason to alter what must always be primarily a European power bloc grouping, and dismissed the rivalries between the Great Powers in China as 'a sort of diplomatic cracker that has produced a great many detonations, but I think the smoke of it has now floated into the distance'. His stance on India's opium trade with China was similarly insouciant. He did not permit its increase, owing to its growing unpopularity, but nor was he about to deprive the Government of India of its £1 million per annum in tax revenue by abolishing it. He also denied, on the same principle he applied to public houses, that the more opium was produced, the more would be consumed.

Although Salisbury came under great Cabinet criticism for his cautious handling of the Boxer Rebellion, and was later forced into a limited agreement with Germany in October 1900, he was finally proved right in his doubts about how far Germany could be relied upon to provide a counterpoise to Russia in the Far East. When Manchuria was effectively annexed by Russia in the New Year, the Anglophobic von Waldersee did nothing, and constantly leaned towards Russia in the region. It is one of the great ironies of his career that just as Salisbury's stance was being vindicated, just as his cool nerve was required more than ever before in international affairs, the forces in the Cabinet – led by the Liberal Unionists Devonshire, Chamberlain, Goschen, Selborne and Lansdowne – combined against him to wrest overall control of foreign policy from him. At the moment that Salisbury most needed his fellow Tories' support, Balfour cleaved to the new grouping, privately denouncing his uncle's 'apathy'.[7]

August 1900 witnessed a series of optimistic telegrams from Roberts in South Africa. 'I am thankful to say war is practically confined to Transvaal,' read one on 18th August about a huge sweep eastwards. 'I trust they will have [a] successful, if not final, result.' By the end of the month, he was reporting that 'the Boers are completely demoralised and, were it not for the very difficult nature of the country, could soon be brought to terms'. This was what Salisbury wished to hear, in contrast to the views of his Chief of Staff, whose uncommunicative despatches once prompted Salisbury to minute: 'Why does Kitchener never tell us anything except the record of every Boer cow his troops have caught by the hind leg?' With the war seemingly on the verge of being won, and in the sixth year of the Parliament, Salisbury's mind turned to capitalising on the patriotic mood through a general election. Balfour, Chamberlain and others had wanted to go to the polls in June, immediately after the relief of Mafeking, but Salisbury had considered this to be taking almost indecent Party advantage. He preferred to win the war outright first. Nor was he absolutely certain of electoral victory, even after Mafeking Night. 'There is a voting strength that does not shout,' he told Balfour, adding, 'You are like Joe, who again is like Randolph. You don't care the least for <u>character</u>. We could not dissolve with our work unfinished without loss of character.'

By 3rd September, however, once Roberts had formally annexed the Transvaal, the argument had changed. The Commander-in-Chief was writing of ultimate victory as certain, but only after the guerilla war was won. 'Enemy are now chiefly in small bodies, cropping up everywhere,' read a typical telegram. Salisbury now convinced himself that another great electoral victory would, as he told his son Edward in August, destroy the Boers' 'last hope of something turning up'.[8] The decision to call what was nicknamed the 'Khaki' Election, because it took place in wartime with so many Unionist MPs on active service, has been described as the first example of the electoral opportunism which today we take for granted. There is no doubt that Salisbury fully appreciated the advantages of going to the polls with the Liberal Party in utter disarray over the war. But, as Devonshire told a Yorkshire audience in September, it was like a cricket captain who, having won the toss, of course chose whether to bat or field according to the likelihood of victory. Anything else 'the English people would think it very odd indeed'.

Salisbury explained to the Queen that there were plenty of precedents for dissolving in the sixth year of a Parliament, that MPs were canvassing already, 'and cannot be got together for the work of the House', and, much more convincingly, with critical points having been reached in the South African War and in the campaign against the Boxer Rising in China, the future Government 'will act with much more confidence if they are fully acquainted with the views of the electors'. Salisbury was also concerned about the unity of his Cabinet surviving without a fresh electoral mandate. On 26th August, Lansdowne had threatened to resign over the criticisms of the War Office, and Hicks Beach's threats arrived perennially. Writing to Lansdowne about a hypothetical future dissolution, Salisbury emphasised to the Liberal Unionist how: 'We must face it together. It would have the worst effect if discussions about future resignations, etc., etc. were to be encouraged and get abroad just now. It would give the impression that we were falling to pieces.'

On 11th September, Roberts telegraphed Lansdowne to ask permission for Kitchener and himself to return home in a month's time: 'War will then be practically at an end, and it is unlikely that any extensive military operations will have to be conducted.' Buller had captured Lydenburg and Major-General Reginald Pole-Carew was on his way to take Komati Poort, so, Roberts believed, the 'duty entrusted to me is, I may say, finished'. This was to prove absurdly optimistic, but it was in this mood that Parliament was dissolved and the general election fought. Back in 1896, Salisbury had written to Wolmer about how Olney and the Democrats had used the Venezuelan issue because 'just now when platforms are being drawn up, candidates selected, it would suit their purpose to have a jingo flare-up'.[9] When it came to jingo flare-ups, however, Salisbury's Khaki Election could even teach the Yankee Democrats a trick or two. The Queen happily agreed to a dissolution on 25th September and Salisbury went off on holiday to Schlucht, where the mountain air and comparative rest had done him a great deal of good in the past.

On his return, he received Akers-Douglas's advice and predictions. 'Our great effort has been, and must be, to keep the war in the foreground,' opined his former Chief Whip, now First Commissioner for Works, whilst the Liberals must try to ignore the war and their own divisions over it, and concentrate on old age pensions and other social issues. Akers-Douglas predicted a Unionist majority of between 100 and 120. The Government's record on social legislation included the Workmen's Compensation Act of 1897, which made employers pay for the consequences of industrial accidents for the first time, and the Small Dwellings Acquisition Act of 1899, which provided for help for workers to buy their own homes. It was not much, hence the need to concentrate on the war. Only with the greatest reluctance did Salisbury agree to issue any sort of manifesto at all, wanting to have his hands free after the election and telling Devonshire frankly that anyhow he had 'nothing to say'. When finally a somewhat lacklustre call to arms was published in *The Times* on 24th September, Chamberlain found it 'most depressing'. Nonetheless, the Colonial Secretary flung himself into the campaign, hitting new heights of populism when he announced: 'Every seat lost to the Government is a seat gained to the Boers.'

On the eve of the third landslide victory of his career, Salisbury still managed to see things *en noir*. Advising Wolmer on whether to accept Chamberlain's offer of the Cape Governorship on Milner's retirement, he wrote:

> Your principal duty will be persuading Dutchmen. If you can imagine yourself sitting for a constituency of which [the Cape Afrikaner leader William] Schreiner and Rhodes are the principal types of electors I fancy you can represent the life you will lead with tolerable fidelity.... I am afraid of going on for pessimism gets hold of my pen and guides it.

At the same time he told Curzon: 'Our whole attention here has been engrossed by this interminable war,' and he could not yet draw a moral from the duration of the Boers' resistance. Had new weapons enormously increased the odds in favour of defence over offence? 'Or are our officers very inferior to what they used to be?' Salisbury concluded: 'If we had an army of Red Indians, we should have been in many respects better off.'[10]

As the first election results started coming in, with Lewisham and the Strand declaring on 28th September, Salisbury was faced with a delicate royal problem. The Queen sincerely believed that her son Arthur, Duke of Connaught, should succeed Wolseley as Commander-in-Chief of the British army rather than Lord Roberts. Wolseley's term of office was due to expire on 31st October 1900 and ever since late June Lansdowne had made it clear that, judged on their military merits, there was no comparison between the two candidates. Salisbury decided to tell the Queen that 'democratic rancour' made it impossible to appoint Connaught, adding that only Roberts could get Cabinet support. He added that after Roberts's presumably short tenure, 'there is no other officer who can compete with the claims of His Royal Highness'.

Expressing herself 'much surprised' at his proposal, the Queen grudgingly gave in, showing a rare *aperçu* of constitutional propriety when she admitted: 'as my ministers think otherwise I suppose I cannot object'. She did, however, object to Salisbury's suggestion that Kitchener should become Commander-in-Chief in India after the war, 'and swears nothing will induce her to accept, because she thinks his manners are too ferocious'. As Salisbury told Lansdowne the next day: 'This is her riposte to my objection to Connaught excluding Roberts, for she knows I value Kitchener.' In the end, the resurgence of fighting meant that Kitchener had to stay in South Africa, and he did not become Commander-in-Chief in India until after the Queen's death.[11] (Connaught never became Commander-in-Chief, because the post was abolished after Roberts's retirement in 1904.)

Conservative Central Office's official *Campaign Guide* for the Khaki Election had more than a whiff of gunpowder to it. Gladstone was blamed for the 1881 Majuba Hill debacle, the lowest point in 'a serious war, costly in blood and treasure, and unusually ferocious in the insults, spoliation and miseries inflicted by a semi-civilised and brutal enemy'. An enemy, moreover, who in the present conflict was responsible for 'the treacherous misuse of the white flag which has cost us so many valuable lives'. The war itself was blamed on 'a deep-seated determination to oust Great Britain from South Africa and to organise a United States of South Africa as a Dutch-speaking state'. To prevent this, 'their defeat must be followed by the disappearance of the Boer states as separate political entities', and the extirpation of 'the anti-British combination and conspiracy'. It quoted *Daily News* reports about ill-treated Uitlander refugees and spoke of 'Boer brutality, and of unspeakable insults and foul language used to Englishwomen, for resenting which one man was stabbed'. Another man had his arm broken with the butt end of a rifle for refusing to take off his hat and sing the Transvaal national anthem. The *Guide* concluded that: 'The great lesson of the war has been the reality of the great danger from which the British Empire has been saved by the firmness of the Unionist Government.'

The first chapter covered 'Foreign Policy', 'The Transvaal and the War', 'The Unity and Integrity of the Empire' and 'Imperial Defence and the Conduct of the War', and it was very much on those issues that the Conservative high command hoped to fight the election. The *Guide* boasted that between 1886 and 1891 Salisbury had brought 2,069,000 square miles and 19.987 million people 'under the British flag', only ceding Heligoland with its three-quarters of a square mile and population of 2,000. It was not all khaki, however. The *Guide* devoted 190 pages to home affairs and 226 to issues such as labour problems, disestablishment, land law reform, liquor laws, taxation and the franchise.

Under 'Miscellaneous', the Party announced that it was against the payment of jurors, that Ritualism was not a party question, that the Post Office workers' grievances were largely unjustified, that the inspection and registration of boilers would be enforced, that it was in favour of a closed period for trout-fishing and that the Deceased Wife's Sister Act would be inapplicable to marriages in the colonies unless the couple went there on purpose to evade the British law. It was also claimed that the opium trade with China did not need to be abolished because opium did not harm a Chinaman as much as a European. Of female suffrage it simply stated: 'This thorny subject is mentioned only to show that it has not been forgotten.' The even thornier issue of Free versus Fair Trade was relegated to only one paragraph in the 500-page publication.

Once again a relatively low turn-out, at 74.6 per cent the lowest poll since 1886, helped the Unionists. Because the Liberals failed to contest 163 Unionist seats, whereas only twenty-two of their own went uncontested, they started off at an inbuilt disadvantage. Despite having done so badly in the opening stages of the war, it was thought that only Salisbury's ministry would prosecute it to a victorious conclusion and then impose a tough peace. After a string of adverse by-election results before the war, Salisbury was effectively saved by the Liberal split and the military defeats, and what he called the 'Jingo hurricane' which had been unleashed. The Unionists won 1,797,444 votes (51.1 per cent), against the Liberals' 1,568,141 (44.6 per cent), the Irish Nationalists polled 90,076 (2.5 per cent) and the Labour Party, 63,304 (1.8 per cent). This relatively tight result in terms of votes cast nevertheless led to 402 Unionists, 184 Liberals, 82 Irish Nationalists and 2 Labour MPs being elected. A majority of 134, it was only sixteen seats short of Salisbury's 1895 landslide. The Liberals even failed to win a majority of Scottish seats for the first time since 1832.[12]

A leaflet put out by Cranborne thanking the people of Rochester for electing him illustrated the unabashed way the Unionists milked the patriotic mood. It displayed coloured photographs of Salisbury, Devonshire, Balfour and Chamberlain, the Royal Standard and Union Flag, the crests of the Cecils and the city of Rochester, and featured a letter from Lady Cranborne which read: 'Gentlemen, in the absence of my husband in South Africa, I hope you will allow me on his behalf, to express my warmest thanks to you for again returning him to represent your City in Parliament.' In his election address, Cranborne had confined himself to stating that he was 'for maintaining and strengthening the Empire', annexing the Boer republics, 'a firm but circumspect policy in China', an increase in the army and navy, 'the liberty of the individual', 'security of capital', 'the interests of Religion' and the general welfare of the city of Rochester. 'In home politics I am a Conservative,' he wrote, somewhat otiosely. 'I rejoice at the splendid imperial feeling of our Colonies at this crisis.' Rarely can a ministry have entered another period of government burdened by fewer concrete pledges.

For the first time since Palmerston in 1865 an incumbent government had won a general election, yet still Salisbury managed to look on the dark side. Thanking Granby for his congratulations on 6th October he wrote: 'I confess I look forward to the future with some misgiving. I had secretly indulged the hope that we should be beaten at this election. A spell in Opposition is so good for bracing up the Conservative fibre of our party.' To Cranbrook a fortnight later, as the last results came in, he took this pessimism a stage further:

> I am not sure whether I can consider the omens as altogether favourable. The phenomenon is without example that a party should twice dissolve, at an interval of five years, and in each case bring back a majority of more than one hundred and thirty. What does it mean? I hope the causes are accidental and temporary. But it may mean that the Reform Bill, digging down deeper and deeper into the population, has come upon a layer of pure combativeness. If this is the case I am afraid the country has evil times before it. Of course I recognise the justice of the verdict the country has just given: but that the love of justice should have overborne the great law of the pendulum I confess puzzles and bewilders me.

To Curzon he pronounced himself 'afraid that the real interpretation of a rather inscrutable phenomenon is that the English party system is breaking up. By what shall we be governed in the future? A fortuitous concourse of groups?' The mass electorate that Salisbury had fought against bringing into existence in 1867 had given him a double endorsement. Yet still he did not recant on his distrust of democracy, now fearing that it meant unrestrained Jingoism. The Queen laboured under no such misgivings, telling Salisbury that 'the Elections have really been beyond expectation favourable'.[13]

Even as the results of his third landslide victory were still coming in, a Cabinet combination against Salisbury forced him to conclude an agreement with Germany over China which he, Hicks Beach, Sanderson and Bertie all viewed with extreme reluctance. Concerned at the lack of German co-operation against Russia in the Far East, Goschen, Chamberlain, Hamilton, Lansdowne and Balfour all demanded that Salisbury agree with Hatzfeldt a convention that would maintain Chinese integrity and the 'Open Door' policy on the Yangtze. 'I do not think the agreement is necessary,' Salisbury told Brodrick on 8th October, 'but it seemed a consistent part of the policy of pleasing the Germans to which so many of our friends are attached.' So on 16th October a document was signed which Salisbury managed to water down to an agreement that Britain and Germany would 'consult to protect their interests' if any other Powers attempted to demand special rights from China. Once again Baron von Eckardstein was in the background, feeding rumours to Cabinet ministers of a possible Franco-Russo-German combination designed to cut Britain out of Yangtze trade.

'As to Germany I have less confidence in her than you,' Salisbury told Curzon, explaining his reservations the very day after the Convention was signed. 'She is in mortal terror on account of that long undefended frontier of hers on the Russian side. She will therefore never stand by us against Russia; ... I have no wish to quarrel with her, but my faith in her is infinitesimal.' Salisbury, who believed that the Russian Government was inherently stable and not liable to a *coup de tête*, felt less apprehensive about her than the Viceroy and almost all the Cabinet except Hicks Beach. As well as Russia, France was angry about the Anglo-German Convention and Salisbury worried whether: 'It may at any moment be a case of Kruger all over again. Whether he thought that we should yield, or that he could win, we cannot tell: but in a reckless fit he forced us into war. The French chamber is full of Krugers.'[14]

Salisbury was finding it increasingly difficult to recognise people, partly through failing eyesight, partly because so many Victorian parliamentarians wore beards, and partly through an underlying lack of interest in other people, especially those who inhabited the House of Commons. The stories are as legion as many of them are apocryphal: about how he failed to recognise his Chief Whip, Sir William Walrond; how at Hatfield he mixed up two vice-consuls bound for Asia Minor with a couple of landscape gardeners; how he mistook his eldest son for a visitor; how he spent half an hour walking up and down a garden conversing happily with 'a delightful sporting peer' under the impression he was Field-

Marshal Lord Roberts. Picking up a photograph of Edward VII at Sandringham one day in June 1901, Salisbury was heard to remark: 'Poor Buller, what a mess he made of it.' When later the same day he also failed to recognise Arthur Winnington-Graham, the Bishop of London, whom he had only appointed three months earlier, the King lost no time in informing the slighted divine. One story which can be authenticated was of how he discreetly inquired at a breakfast party the identity of a man sitting near him, only to be told it was W.H. Smith, his faithful lieutenant with whom he had served in successive ministries for over a decade. Salisbury's unconvincing explanation was that he always sat opposite Smith in Cabinet, so he 'never learnt what his profile looked like'.

He worked out a mnemonical code with his family to help him remember the names of guests he feared he would not recognise. When two visitors arrived at Hatfield in November 1894, Lady Rayleigh was primed to say: 'Oh! Uncle Robert' for Mrs Ogilvy, and: 'See! Uncle Robert' for Mr Cooper. Should these devices fail and Salisbury flounder, there were many complaints, especially from politicians. Arthur Griffith-Boscawen, a tariff reformer and MP for Tonbridge, complained that Salisbury did not know by sight one Tory MP in ten. Walter Long, who had not been recognised by Salisbury even though he was President of the Board of Agriculture, complained that he wished he was on the backbenches again so little did Salisbury consult with anyone other than Devonshire, Chamberlain, Balfour and Hicks Beach. (He might well have been relegated to the backbenches anyhow, had Salisbury taken heed of the 80,000-signature petition calling for his dismissal collected by the Canine Defence League; however, the Prime Minister 'was amused by this agitation' and gave the petition to Long as a souvenir.)

In order to help rectify this distance between Leader and led, Balfour occasionally arranged dinners at Downing Street. At one such, Salisbury sat next to Mr Muntz, MP for Tamworth, and talked stock-breeding and crop rotation. 'I think I have done them all,' he told his host at the end of one such evening. 'But there is one I have not identified who, you said, made mustard.' Salisbury drew the line at spending time at the Carlton Club, however, saying 'that if he did he would only get into a corner between Sir William Blank and Sir Henry Asterisk and never escape'.

Salisbury was slowing down. He had a lift installed in the Foreign Office to save himself climbing the stairs, and in the large-scale Government reshuffle after the Khaki victory, an alliance of Balfour, Akers-Douglas and the Queen decided that they would, in as diplomatic a manner as possible, press him to give up the department of state he loved.[15]

~

Although it was never called by the name 'Coalition', the alliance between Conservatives and Liberal Unionists in office after June 1895 was precisely that, and for seven years at least it was to bely Disraeli's famous dictum that 'England does not love coalitions.' Salisbury's coalition was kept intact by his willingness occasionally to defer to Devonshire and Chamberlain, take them into his confidence and not act without hearing their views. The consideration Salisbury showed Devonshire can be seen from a typical letter, written on the approach of 1894's Glorious Twelfth:

> My dear Devonshire,
>
> As one of those who has not the happiness to shoot grouse, I am wholly impartial as to the date on which [the] Evicted Tenants [Bill] should be taken in our House. I only desire the greatest happiness of the greatest number. But some Peers tell me that, from the grouse point of view, it is desirable that the division should be taken on a Friday: as that will interfere <u>least</u> with country house parties, bent on slaughter.... If the Irish Peers have any of the eloquence of their race we ought to take two nights about the debate: if so – the second reading should be <u>moved</u> on Thursday 16th.

Salisbury appreciated Devonshire's lugubrious wisdom, as well as his habit of resolving Cabinets in favour of the status quo and against policy innovations, employing the admonition: 'Far better not.'

Salisbury treated Chamberlain with equal civility, so much so that C.A. Vince, Chamberlain's chief constituency agent, remembered his master saying how much he appreciated the way that the Prime Minister, 'unlike Mr Gladstone, gave him reasonable opportunity of expressing his views on any important point of policy, before the final decision was taken. He had found, in short, that his position, as a Liberal member of a Unionist administration, was far more comfortable and required less sacrifice of independence than his former position, as a Radical member of a Liberal administration.' Salisbury and Chamberlain admired each other's courage and strength, and what might have been the most combustible combination in the Cabinet, because of their utterly different backgrounds and opinions and the sharp language each had employed against the other in the past, never produced the expected explosion.

Goschen was harder work for Salisbury, who found his new First Lord of the Admiralty 'decidedly stiff' at times, and, as he complained to Balfour, 'too much of a martinet and doesn't understand the advantages of fighting in open order'. Nevertheless, he expended a good deal of charm on the former financier. Even at the height of their disagreements over Armenia in December 1895, he would write to Goschen in the following bantering style:

> You have put me in a serious dilemma. I feel it is a rude thing to send a man's letter back to him. But through some secretarial mistake your note has arrived in a condition from which only the Higher Criticism of Germany could extract any continuous meaning.... My exegetical skill is a good deal baffled – but at least I can see that something has dropped out.

Salisbury had little problem adapting himself to the conditions of give and take made necessary by coalition government. In late November 1895, he publicly told a group of hop-growers that they should not hold out any great hopes for protection of their industry: 'That is, I am aware, very cold comfort ... but it comes from the construction of the Government.' The convention soon developed whereby no promotion involving a parliamentary vacancy was to be granted without the Cabinet having a chance at least to be informed, and Salisbury ensured that Devonshire and Chamberlain were made privy to information on matters far beyond those which touched their duties as Lord President of the Council and Colonial Secretary. When he had to disappoint Chamberlain, Salisbury expended maximum charm in so doing. On removing a proposed Bill on colonial rinderpest from the 1897 Queen's Speech, he explained: 'George Hamilton had already secured a niche for the bubonic plague – and I thought, if we had both contagious diseases we might provoke irreverent remarks.'

Haggling over honours was a potential source of dissension, which Salisbury also sought to diffuse by generosity, patience and good humour. The 1896 New Year's List saw him explaining to Devonshire how a number of senior Tories, who but for the presence of the Liberal Unionists in the Government might have expected office, had to be appeased. 'You have not quite got your fair share this time,' he admitted to the Duke, 'but the pressure from various other quarters was enormous. You must set it off against the glut of Law Officers you carried away in September.' Salisbury was generally unimpressed with the quality of Devonshire's honours proposals, telling the Duke the following May that they would have to wait to see whether Sir John Muir's fraud lawsuit went against him, 'before he is put forward as one whom the Queen delighteth to honour'.

The Unionist alliance grew ever closer during Salisbury's term of office. In the reshuffle after the 1900 general election, Salisbury ensured that Henry James's vacant seat in the Cabinet was taken by another Liberal Unionist, Lord Selborne, and they increased their overall representation in the Government by one under-secretary. 'The Unionist Party is like two men in one pair of trousers,' Salisbury said in August 1901, but at least under his leadership they marched in the same direction.[16]

FORTY-FIVE

Reconstruction

The 'Hotel Cecil' –
The Death of Queen Victoria

October 1900 to January 1901

'In August and September, remember to give good places to your relations.'

'The taste for jobs is, in truth, a very curious feature in political human nature,' Salisbury had written in the *Saturday Review* in 1862. 'It is like the taste for poisoning, or the taste for throwing logs on the railway. The temptation is so small, and the risk incurred so serious, that it is difficult for anyone who is not actually engaged in jobbing to conceive the state of mind under which the offence is perpetrated.' A wholesale reshuffle of the Government was generally recognised, in the light of the Boer War reverses, to be a prerequisite for national regeneration, and Salisbury did not shrink from the unpleasant task of easing out those he thought superfluous to Unionism's requirements.

The man asked to make the greatest sacrifice was Salisbury himself. He had recognised, as he told McDonnell back in 1898, that 'the work of the Foreign Office is very heavy and is getting heavier. When I first became Foreign Secretary in 1878 there was no Egypt – except diplomatic – no West Africa – no Uganda – no Zanzibar – no China to speak of.' Now the Foreign Office had to deal with all of these and much more. In Salisbury's obituary in *The Times*, the story was told of a bishop who remonstrated with him over the indifference he was showing towards the chairmanship of a commission, which in the bishop's opinion was 'extremely important'. 'My lord,' retorted Salisbury with unaccustomed vanity, 'in this country there are only two extremely important appointments; one is that of Prime Minister, the other that of Foreign Secretary. For all the rest any fairly competent person will do equally well.'

In a covering note on the file concerning the moves of Balfour, the Queen and Akers-Douglas to ease Salisbury out of the Foreign Office in

October 1900, Akers-Douglas wrote: 'I was negotiator, and was successful: but it was a difficult and unpleasant mission.' Salisbury did not make it any easier for them. 'If the Queen wishes it, I will gladly come up to Balmoral after the elections,' he wrote to her on 4th October, 'but I am afraid it will excite some attention, as I have not been there often.' She replied that perhaps he should see Sir Arthur Bigge first. At their meeting in London on 13th October, Bigge reported that Salisbury was 'looking very well and in good spirits' and he even joked that he did not know whether it was the Queen's intention 'that he should continue at the head of the Government'.

Salisbury then said that his doctors had advocated less work, and 'outside opinion' favoured his leaving the Foreign Office, but as he felt himself strong enough to carry on, 'he is ready to do whatever is most agreeable to the Queen', thereby firmly putting the onus on her to remove him. He added that his only possible successor would be Lansdowne, with whom the Queen had crossed swords over the Duke of Connaught, the Spion Kop despatches and the War Office's lacklustre performance in South Africa. The War Office was notorious as a graveyard for Victorian political reputations, and Salisbury generously did not hold Lansdowne's tenure of it against him. 'A War Minister must find his reward in his conscience or his salary,' Salisbury had written in 1862, 'he must not look for fame.' He added that Brodrick, to whom the Queen also took exception, must replace Lansdowne at the War Office.

As Akers-Douglas told Balfour on 18th October, the Queen 'shrinks from having to ask him to go', so his two closest colleagues took the task upon themselves. Balfour, from Whittinghame, wrote to Akers-Douglas at Balmoral to say: 'I do very earnestly hope that the Queen will not insist upon Lord Salisbury keeping both offices.' He added that it took no doctor to convince his family that the work, 'whenever it gets really serious, is too much for him'. Couching the letter entirely in terms of Salisbury's age and health, Balfour told the former Chief Whip that if the Queen wanted to keep his uncle as Prime Minister, 'I feel sure she would be well advised not to insist on his being also Foreign Minister.' The Queen then sent Akers-Douglas to Hatfield. 'I do not relish the job as I fear Lord Salisbury may resent it, but the Queen insists,' he reported to Balfour. Akers-Douglas was not even allowed to tell Salisbury that the Queen 'thinks he ought to go'. Trying to 'evade the keen sight of the Press detectives', Akers-Douglas made the journey south, and on 21st October was hugely relieved to discover, as he broached the subject, that Salisbury himself now wanted to give up the double office due to family pressure on him. The Queen, who therefore escaped having to express any opinion on the matter when Salisbury went up to Balmoral, was greatly relieved.

To ensure continued Cecilian input into foreign policy-making,

Cranborne was appointed Lansdowne's Under-Secretary.[1] Furthermore, all telegrams and despatches had to be submitted to Salisbury before Lansdowne was allowed to send them off. The promotion of Lansdowne, whom many considered to have failed at the War Office, surprised the political world, which correctly interpreted it as a typically perverse move by Salisbury. Even usually loyal Unionist MPs criticised the appointment, but it was later vindicated when Lansdowne went on to become a good Foreign Secretary, albeit one dedicated to reversing Salisbury's non-alignment policy.

Goschen had wanted to retire even before the elections, but Salisbury had persuaded him to stay until they were over. As Salisbury's secretary laconically scrawled on the back of his resignation letter: 'Accepts viscountcy: would have liked an earldom.' Taking Goschen's place at the Admiralty was Lord Selborne, another opponent of Salisbury's non-alignment policy, as was St John Brodrick who became War Secretary after Lord Roberts refused the post.

Lord James believed Balfour was behind the removal of the Home Secretary, Sir Matthew White Ridley, and the President of the Local Government Board, Henry Chaplin. 'I hope a peerage will dispose of Ridley,' Salisbury told Balfour on 21st October. A well-deserved viscountcy did the trick. His place was taken by C.T. Ritchie, whose own post of President of the Board of Trade was filled by Gerald Balfour. Salisbury had been unimpressed by Arthur's younger brother, telling Bigge at their original post-election meeting that he had been an unsatisfactory Chief Secretary of Ireland and had been personally responsible for the loss of Sir David Plunket's University seat in Dublin in 1895. He was originally earmarked for demotion to Scottish Secretary, with Lord Balfour of Burleigh (who 'does not make mistakes') going to the Admiralty.

As it turned out, Salisbury relented. He liked appointing Scots to ministries, telling Lady Rayleigh they almost always had a certain amount of prudence and common sense. 'In making appointments I can count on a Scotchman not falling below a certain level, they may not be very clever, but they are safe not to be stupid. There is a strong resemblance between the Scotch and the Jews. They both begin as fighters, then become very religious and finally are devoted to money-making.' (Salisbury was fond of semi-jocular racial stereotyping, as his earlier generalisations about Montenegrins, Greeks, Portuguese, Spaniards, Boers, Irishmen, Americans and Italians attest.)

Hicks Beach, who told Arthur Balfour (though significantly not Salisbury) that he would not mind leaving the Exchequer, stayed there partly because of the Queen's professed 'terror' of what he might do at the Home Office. Also staying in place were Ashbourne, Halsbury, Devonshire, Chamberlain, Cadogan, George Hamilton, Akers-Douglas and Balfour himself. It nevertheless rated as one of the most extensive reshuffles in British political history, with no fewer than eight people changing Cabinet posts.[2] When Salisbury saw the Queen at Balmoral on 23rd October, he received great encouragement for this wholesale reconstruction. She told him that Balfour of Burleigh was 'too ponderous' for the Admiralty and agreed to Salisbury's suggestion of Selborne instead. Salisbury explained that he intended to take Cross's place as Lord Privy Seal himself. They both regretted Cross's retirement, but agreed that 'he had aged a good deal, and didn't like his present office'. The spectacle of two people of seventy and eighty-one disqualifying people from high office on grounds of age has its comic side.

George Wyndham, who was thought too young to become War Secretary, instead became Chief Secretary for Ireland outside the Cabinet. According to his colourful account, he was appointed at Hatfield with the advice 'Beware of Healy' from Salisbury, accompanied by Gwendolen's rendition of *The Wearing of the Green* on the piano. Despite what Salisbury called 'the disadvantage of being very deaf and also a little priggish', Brodrick was confirmed at the War Office. Thus armed with the Queen's support, Salisbury sat down at Balmoral over the next two days to wield the butcher's blade.

His letter to Cross on the 24th made it quite clear that Salisbury wanted the veteran former Tory Democrat's resignation because he needed his place: 'The prime ministership must be joined to some office; it cannot stand alone. I am afraid therefore that an inevitable consequence of the change is that I should take the office that you now hold.... I have to thank you sincerely for having so long held an office which brought with it no emolument, and of which the duties were uninteresting.' In case Cross thought he might be able to appeal to the Queen, Salisbury added that she also agreed to the necessity of it. Like Goschen, Cross bid for an earldom but was knocked down to a viscountcy. The £2,000 per annum salary for the Lord Privy Seal had been abolished in 1884, but was revived for Salisbury because the job of Prime Minister did not officially exist. It was a relatively small amount, less than that received by a manager of a minor railway company and roughly that allotted to the secretaries of successful companies, but Salisbury did not see why he should work *gratis*.

The sacking of Chaplin was long overdue, though still deeply resented by him when it happened. Salisbury told the Queen that the President of the Local Government Board 'was of no use and he wished he would retire', but instead he expected promotion to the War Office. Whatever happened, Chaplin could not be allowed to stay where he was, as Salisbury feared that he would dilute the forthcoming Housing Bill. When Salisbury got back to London on 26th October, there was 'a painful scene' when he asked for Chaplin's resignation. For all his image as a high-spending owner of 23,000 Lincolnshire acres who cared more for hunting than politics, Chaplin was furious when Salisbury made him return to his estates. Despite a kind letter – 'I am afraid therefore that we cannot ask you to renew your association with us at our start on this new voyage' – and the offer of a peerage (which was haughtily refused), Chaplin wrote a peeved letter to the chairman of his constituency association protesting that his sacking was 'without precedent'. He even considered refusing to resign, but thought it a 'more dignified and proper course' to accede to Salisbury's demand.[3] Walter Long replaced Chaplin, his own place as President of the Board of Agriculture being taken by the former Financial Secretary to the Treasury, R.W. Hanbury.

Having carried out what he called his 'evictions' and made his promotions, Salisbury told Devonshire of all the changes and his 'weary journey to the Arctic part of Scotland'. He wrote of Chaplin that 'no amount of hinting, however broad, could raise in him the slightest suspicion that he was considered inefficient'. He did not like to increase the number in the Cabinet to twenty, but Londonderry was appointed Postmaster-General, the position vacated by the valiant Norfolk.

Salisbury decided to continue to house himself at the Foreign Office. 'I only want one room,' he told Akers-Douglas, who as Commissioner for Works arranged ministerial accommodation. 'Before you do it obtain Lansdowne's consent personally; for the Foreign Office staff, who are very cliquish, will prevent it if they can.' They could not, and for the rest of his premiership Salisbury made his office in three large reception rooms in the building he had occupied for so long. 'It was in one sense a relief – in another painful – to sever my connection with a department in which I have served some fifteen years,' Salisbury told his old friend the Duke of Rutland, 'but I think the sense of relief predominates, especially as the labour was becoming physically more than I could face.' Nevertheless, as Lord Esher noted in his journal, although Lansdowne readily gave his consent to Salisbury staying at the Foreign Office, he was 'aware that ill-natured critics will say that Lord Salisbury remains there as Mayor of the Palace'. As it was connected to the Colonial Office, India Office and Home Office, Salisbury had access to principal centres of power 'without the necessity of running the gauntlet of prying reporters'.[4]

Some ministers fared badly at Salisbury's hands, such as T.W. Russell, who was unceremoniously sacked from the Secretaryship of the Local Government Board because of his outspokenly pro-nationalist views on Ireland and to appease the demands of Irish landlords led by the Duke of Abercorn and Colonel Saunderson. Others fared better, such as Cadogan who was offered, but refused, a marquessate for his Viceroyalty of Ireland. When Cadogan had offered to resign in April

1899, after his daughter Lady Sophie Scott had sensationally eloped with a friend of her husband, Salisbury had sympathetically turned it down out of hand, saying that although high character was required from a Viceroy and his wife, 'I have never heard of responsibility being carried further,' and if it had been he could name two ambassadors, a viceroy and a governor-general whose careers would have had to have been interrupted. Cadogan stayed in Dublin until 1902.

Instead of a smaller, younger Cabinet, Salisbury had installed one that was larger and slightly older. The *National Review* called it Salisbury's 'first-rate joke on the nation', executed with a huge parliamentary majority and a blithe disregard for public opinion. The major criticism that was levelled, however, was not over the Cabinet's size or average age, but the large number of Salisbury's relations who had found their way into senior ministerial positions. Back in October 1898, G.C.T. Bartley had written to Salisbury complaining that in the Tory Party, 'all honours, emoluments and places are reserved for the friends and relations of the favoured few'. By 1900, with the announcement of the new Government, the extent of his nepotism caused an outcry.

Salisbury's nephew, Arthur Balfour, was First Lord of the Treasury and Leader of the House of Commons. Another nephew, Gerald Balfour, was President of the Board of Trade. A third, Evelyn Cecil, became the Prime Minister's parliamentary private secretary. Salisbury's nephew-in-law, James Lowther, was Chairman of the Commons' Ways and Means Committee. His son-in-law, Lord Selborne, was First Lord of the Admiralty and his eldest son, Lord Cranborne, was Under-Secretary at the Foreign Office, which Hugh Cecil, another son and an MP, called 'only a stipendiary' but which was an acknowledged route to higher office. Rosebery scored a palpable hit in the House of Lords when he congratulated Salisbury 'on being the head of a family with the most remarkable genius for administration that has ever been known'.

The situation worsened when Labouchere nicknamed the new Government 'the Hotel Cecil', after the vast hotel built on the Cecils' original land south of the Strand – on the site presently occupied by Shell-Mex House – where the Government occasionally held large official dinners. At 9s.6d per night for a double room it was considered hugely luxurious, despite its having been built by a famous fraudster who went by the (under the circumstances unfortunate) name of Jabez Balfour. Echoing the criticisms of the former Tory MP Sir Henry Howorth, and the sitting MP Thomas Gibson Bowles, G.C.T. Bartley put down a motion in December censuring the Prime Minister for nepotism. (It was, incidentally, the first occasion the word 'Prime Minister' appeared on a parliamentary order paper.) Salisbury's answer was defiant, telling Balfour that:

> exactly the same number of 'relations' (minus Jim) were in the Government in July 1895 as there are now. The arrangement has therefore been before the country during two general elections without provoking any adverse comment. Herbert Gladstone may pair off with Jim. No doubt one or two have been promoted. But they cannot be treated as a class apart who can be employed but not promoted, like second division clerks.

Salisbury added that he genuinely wanted to appoint the best people; it just so happened that he knew more about the qualities of his own family than about strangers.[5] McDonnell, now back from South Africa and in Salisbury's employ, was cruder, telling Akers-Douglas: 'In the words of Charles II, I value Howorth not at the weight of a turd.... Tommy Bowles may and probably will be troublesome. But he doesn't carry enough guns.' In fact, as the Irish leader John Redmond was to complain in a debate in July 1902, a large number of Tory MPs privately disliked the nepotistic arrangements but did not have the courage to denounce them publicly.

Salisbury had often engaged in and even eulogised nepotism. He had anonymously commended the 'great merit' of his elder brother's book of essays in the *Saturday Review*, as well as his brother-in-law's biography of Georgina's father. In 1885, Salisbury had obtained a Scottish Prison Commissionership for the son-in-law of his Hatfield agent, and the following year a CB for his brother-in-law, who was a general. In 1887, he had obtained the bishopric of Calcutta for Robert Milman, his wife's first cousin, and in December 1898 he had helped Captain Middleton's son get an army commission after he had failed the medical examination.

In the *Quarterly Review* in October 1860, he had written that: 'Until human hearts shall work with the strict regularity and singleness of purpose of a steam-engine, it is likely that men who have the disposal of offices will do a great turn to their own friends, if they can.' With his 'Hotel Cecil' appointments forty years later, Salisbury could and did. He was not entirely consistent, however, and in criticising Lord John Russell's jobbery for a cousin in August 1863, he had denounced 'the traditional Whig tendency to nepotism' and had written: 'If there were such a thing as a Downing Street Almanac, in the place where the garden operations suitable to the season are usually described it would contain the memorandum – "In August and September, remember to give good places to your relations".'[6] Salisbury himself had merely waited an extra month.

At his Guildhall speech on 9th November 1900, Salisbury referred to 'events that are not quite yet concluded' in South Africa and gloried in the reliefs of Kimberley, Ladysmith and Mafeking. He mourned those who had fallen both in battle and 'under the fell and pitiless stroke of disease', and defended the War Office as best he could. Privately, however, as Brodrick learned from the Queen, Salisbury was highly critical of the advice Wolseley had been giving the Cabinet, and he was delighted when on 29th November, Kitchener took over from Roberts as Commander-in-Chief in South Africa and Roberts returned home to become Commander-in-Chief of the British army. He was still fatalistic, however, telling Violet Cecil a week later that 'He didn't believe our army would ever get any better unless we were invaded.'

Accounts differ as to the effect that relinquishing the Foreign Office had on Salisbury. Esher's journal records how at the three Cabinets before the reshuffle, Salisbury had sat in 'a crumpled heap – like [*Bleak House*'s decrepit] Grandpa Smallweed – evidently wearied out. Since giving up the Foreign Office he is brisk and attentive. A changed man.' It was not a total makeover, however. Selborne remembered how, at his first Cabinet meeting in November 1900, Ritchie had put forward a proposal for a new Bill and warned the Cabinet that it would lead to a great deal of discussion and waste of time. At this Salisbury, who had been sitting with his eyes shut, suddenly opened them and asked: 'Isn't that just what we want?'[7]

Salisbury's first major speech since the Election was delivered to 700 NUCCA members at the Hotel Metropole on 18th December. He marvelled at the revolution in the Party's fortunes in London, which in his youth had always been a Radical stronghold. He permitted his audience a moment of sweet triumphalism when he pointed out that there had never been an occasion, 'since the time of the Great Reform Bill, where a ministry has twice referred its conduct to the judgment of the constituencies and has twice been returned.... It has been a very great change.' But then came the warning: 'If you observe that the villas outside London are the principal seedplots of Conservatism,' he told them, the principal seedplots of Radicalism were to be found in the bad housing of the working class. This was 'a scandal to our civilisation', and his listeners 'must not allow yourselves to be frightened away from the remedies of social ills by the fact that they are made a cover or pretence for attacks upon property and other institutions'.

~

The invasion of Cape Colony from the Orange Free State by General P.H. Kritzinger on 16th December brought the Government up sharply after their hubristic pre-election assumptions that the war was as good as over. Salisbury told Brodrick on the 19th that 'if Kitchener wants more men he must have them. If the Treasury resists, we must appeal to the Cabinet: but the situation is critical.' Salisbury also now wanted to return to the policy of strategic farm-burning, thus denying the Boers places of supply, information and recuperation. 'I should prefer to see a complete protection of [railway] lines and bridges,' Salisbury told Brodrick, 'and then you ought to be able to destroy food, with flying columns of considerable strength. You will not conquer these people until you have starved them out. The supply of fighting men from our own territory is probably unlimited.'[8] As he had said of the two Boer republics in the House of Lords the same month, 'We can never allow, and never have allowed, that any shred of independence can be left.'

It was a harsh, scorched-earth policy, but Salisbury was furious that the war had gone on so long and cost so much. He still blamed the generals, saying in mid-January that rather than hold an inquiry, 'gibbeting the incompetent officers is the best disciplinary punishment you can inflict on them'. When Violet Cecil said that Buller looked like a strong man, he answered: 'Do you think that a pig has any particular fixity of purpose?' To her retort that at least Sir George White was a gentleman, Salisbury replied: 'That is one quality I believe to be unnecessary for a general,' adding that he preferred the businesslike head of Lord Roberts, who had risen up through the ranks from private to Field Marshal, to any noble heart.

By October 1900, Salisbury had discovered yet another scapegoat for the defeats. The Army Selection Board, he told Hicks Beach, had been set up as 'a natural reaction from the failings which attended the Duke of Cambridge's nominations. But we must not keep that terrifying figure always before us. No despot, no royal jobber, could have made worse selections than were made by this Board, and their shortcomings have been more the cause of our disasters than any other cause.' His conclusion was that the Hartington Commission had gone too far in 'belittling the Commander-in-Chief' and the post should be boosted in the future. (Balfour in fact abolished it.)

Back in July 1887, Salisbury had commended to a colleague Beaconsfield's dictum: 'Never admit anything', saying: 'I believe the advice to be sound as such admissions are always used against you.' By January 1901, he considered that an official inquiry into the conduct of the war, if properly conducted, could usefully shift the blame for the blunders away from the Government and on to the generals, where he thought it belonged. His views were only reinforced when he read the letters Akers-Douglas had been receiving from his son on active service about the bungling of the High Command at the Battles of Modder River and Magersfontein. On 4th January 1901, Salisbury wrote to Balfour to say that Kimberley could chair the Inquiry which could fully investigate the war, and that this was 'essential if we are to get out of a rather awkward corner'. Once asked whether it was advisable for the Tory Party to wash its dirty linen in public, Salisbury answered: 'Is it not better to wash it than to wear it?'[9] The Queen initially believed the Inquiry could only help the Boers and foreign countries, but Salisbury and Balfour brought her round reluctantly to endorse the idea. Her approval, in January 1901, was one of the last official acts of her life.

The death of Queen Victoria in the early evening of Tuesday, 22nd January 1901, came as a huge personal blow to Salisbury. Her Coronation was one of his earliest memories, and although they had had their differences in the period up to his becoming Beaconsfield's Foreign Secretary in 1878, the subsequent twenty-two years had cemented a fine working relationship, and even friendship. She had been a stalwart supporter in the Irish Home Rule Bill struggles of 1886–93, and by 1898 the Prince of Wales was writing to his sister Vicky: 'Mama seems to think her present Government cannot do wrong.' For all her occasional great obstinacy, Salisbury had been able to humour her along the paths he wanted her to follow. 'It is easy to see that she is very fond of him,' Violet Cecil noted at one of their tea parties in the South of France, 'indeed I never saw two people get on better, their polished manners and deference to and esteem for each other were a delightful sight and one not readily to be forgotten.' On holidays there they would go to church together, and the woman they nicknamed 'The Widow' would occasionally even arrive for lunch with the Cecils at Beaulieu with only the scantiest of notice.

'My lord,' Queen Elizabeth I had said to Salisbury's gouty ancestor, Lord Burghley, who was allowed to sit during audiences, 'we make use of you, not for your bad legs, but for your good brain.' Salisbury, who was Victoria's first Prime Minister to be her junior in age, was also accorded the very rare privilege of being allowed to sit in the Queen's presence. He was in turn protective of her, turning down the Marquess of Lothian's request that she open the Forth Bridge because he did not wish her to venture 'on a structure so entirely novel in its character until the stability had been ascertained by experience'. They thought alike on many issues. 'It never entered his head to recommend to your

Majesty to give back the Elgin Marbles,' Salisbury assured her in December 1890. 'It is the fancy of a few fanatics.' Salisbury could be gently humorous at the Queen's expense in private. When in 1896 she asked that the ugly Lord Waldegrave, a Lord in Waiting, should be promoted to Captain of the Yeomen so that he might cease to offend her æsthetic sense, Salisbury told McDonnell that 'my gracious Sovereign, who is a slave of the eye', did not appreciate the 9th Earl's 'peculiar style of manly beauty.... And to that *aller höchster Befehl* [highest possible command] I shall probably obey.'[10] He did.

As the Queen's eyesight deteriorated, huge handwriting had to be adopted so that she could continue to read letters from Salisbury. Subjects as mundane as Lord Belper becoming an (unpaid) assistant private secretary at the Home Office required lettering an inch high, sometimes fitting only ten words to the page. From 1897, Salisbury had many of the Queen's scrawled letters to him deciphered by Gwendolen. Enclosing some pages of royal hieroglyphics to Halsbury in May 1898, Salisbury wrote: 'It is quite possible that some member of your able staff is adept at deciphering handwriting. If so, he may be able to tell you what it is your gracious Sovereign wants you to do.... I hope I may be able to report 1. That you understand it. 2. That you will give effect to it.' As to what it actually was that the Queen wanted, Salisbury was satisfied to be left in the dark.[11]

Salisbury considered it his duty during the Boer War to protect the Queen as much as possible from anything which might cause her anxiety. She was deftly shielded from the worst excesses of the Anglophobia of the European press, and when in October 1900 the Duke of York begged Salisbury to bring up the issue of his visiting Canada and Australia, he answered that having twice attempted to mention it at Balmoral, to bring it up a third time would be 'at the cost of inflicting great anxiety upon her, which at her age and in addition to the sorrows and worries which have accumulated upon her during the present year would be most prejudicial'. He even once told Frances Balfour, somewhat melodramatically, that 'The War killed her, but she never flinched.'[12] By early November 1900, Queen Victoria was eighty-one, ill, exhausted, feeling 'wretched' and enduring restless nights. After dinner on 16th December, the Queen's doctor, Sir James Reid, spoke to Salisbury about his fears. He had given her twelve grains of Trianol to help her sleep. The Christmas card Salisbury received from her that year was shakily scrawled 'VRI', above the forbidding augury: 'The Old Year dies; God beckons those we love.'

The Cabinet Defence Committee was sitting on the evening of 22nd January 1901, when Lord Halsbury called Salisbury out to tell him the news. In his panegyric in the House of Lords, moving an address of condolence to King Edward VII on Friday, 25th January, Salisbury spoke of the country's 'deep and heartfelt feeling – a feeling deeper than I ever remember – of sorrow at the singular loss'.[13] The scene of mourning peers and peeresses impressed the diarist Lady Monkswell, who thought Salisbury's voice quite shaky at first, and who wondered whether 'he purposely avoided too moving an address for fear he himself should break down'. Salisbury said of the Queen something that might equally have applied to himself:

> It was always a dangerous matter to press on her any course of the expediency of which she was not thoroughly convinced.... She had an extraordinary knowledge of what her people would think – extraordinary because it could not have come from any personal intercourse. I have said for years that when I knew what the Queen thought I knew pretty certainly what view her subjects would take, and especially the middle classes of her subjects. Such was the extraordinary penetration of her mind.[14]

In January 1896, the very religious Lady Erroll had commiserated with Queen Victoria on the death of Prince Henry of Battenberg: 'Oh Ma'am, we shall see him soon, just think, Ma'am, you will see all those who have gone before, you will meet Abraham.' 'I will not meet Abraham. Certainly not,' the Queen answered firmly, without any further explanation. Whichever Old Testament prophets Her Majesty permitted to converse with her in the Next World, Salisbury was present at her very choral funeral at St George's Chapel, Windsor.

In July 1902, Bishop Boyd-Carpenter of Ripon informed Salisbury that, in a conversation they had held at Osborne shortly before her death, the Queen had said that she considered him as having 'an equal place with the highest among her ministers, not excepting Disraeli'. It was a fine compliment considering her well-known regard for Beaconsfield, and Salisbury replied with a heartfelt encomium:

> The late Queen was always most indulgent to me, both in hours of political difficulty – which in my long service under her were not infrequent – and also in the more trying periods of personal sorrow. She always displayed a sympathy, a consideration, and a wisdom, which, if my life ran to ten times its probable span, I never could forget.[15]

FORTY-SIX

'Methods of Barbarism'

King Edward VII – The Boer War:
The Second Phase – Anglo-German Relations –
The Concentration Camps –
The Taff Vale Judgment

January to December 1901

'I realised that we were in the face of a Jingo hurricane.'

Just as the 1st Earl of Salisbury had managed the smooth transition from the Tudor to Stuart dynasties in 1603, so his descendant arranged the details of the transition from the House of Hanover to that of Saxe-Coburg-Gotha three centuries later. Relations between Salisbury and the new King were professional but never close. Although they had served together on the 1884 Royal Commission on the Housing of the Working Classes, in March 1891 Salisbury had prevented the then Prince of Wales sitting on a Royal Commission to examine industrial relations, thinking the subject too controversial. Salisbury had generally taken the Queen's side in disputes, had turned down the Prince's (terrible) advice to meet Rhodes in the aftermath of the Jameson Raid, and had not invited him to the Balmoral talks with the Tsar in September 1896. Although back in 1875 he had insisted on the Prince visiting India, in 1888 he had not supported him over the Vienna Incident. He had, however, been generally in favour of the Prince being allowed to see selected Foreign Office despatches.

When the Queen descended on La Bastide for tea having given hardly any warning, the Cecils, who revered her, were flustered but honoured. When the Prince did the same, and stayed until the evening in April 1896, they were merely irritated. Hatfield was tacitly barred to him because of his habit of corridor-creeping, unless Princess Alexandra was also of the party. Salisbury also disliked having to give honours to those of the Prince's friends he considered worthless, such as Sir Thomas Lipton.

The two men occasionally chafed one another good-naturedly. Inviting the Prince to the Queen's birthday dinner on 21st May 1898, Salisbury explained that it had to be held at the Hotel Cecil rather than Arlington Street because 'My main drain has suddenly broken loose – and if I asked Your Royal Highness and the Corps Diplomatique to dine at my house, it would be at the risk of giving typhoid fever to the whole of that distinguished assemblage.' As Prince Albert was thought to have died of typhoid in 1861, and the Prince of Wales had himself very nearly succumbed to it in 1871, it was perhaps a quip in questionable taste. Nonetheless, in February 1899 the Prince was anxious that Salisbury should join the Marlborough Club, which he had founded at No. 52, Pall Mall, 'as it is free from political bores, and the food is particularly good'. Although he found his membership of the Athenæum and two Carltons more than enough, Salisbury accepted 'very happily'.

The Prince was much put out in April 1900 when Salisbury failed to record a parliamentary vote of congratulation, after a fifteen-year-old anarchist called Sipido shot at him at Brussels' Gare du Nord. When his brother the Duke of Edinburgh had escaped assassination at the hands of an Irish gunman in New South Wales in 1868, there had been such a vote, but Salisbury explained that on this occasion it would have involved recalling the House of Lords for a special sitting and 'it was not even known that the pistol contained a bullet which the extreme youth of the culprit rendered doubtful'.[1]

The night before the Queen died, Violet Cecil recorded in her diary: 'Lord Salisbury is very unhappy. The break for him is fearful and he hates the Prince of Wales.' 'Hates' was probably too strong a word, but he was certainly worried that a man with so rackety a private life was about to succeed to the Throne. The Queen had told Salisbury that she feared her son would turn out like her uncle George IV, and, having been involved in proffering advice during both the Tranby Croft and Beresford scandals, Salisbury needed little convincing.

The new King's Council made their act of homage at the Banqueting House in St James's on 24th January 1901. About one hundred and fifty privy councillors attended in uniform. 'Some curious old fossils,' noted Esher. When the Council had assembled, Devonshire as its Lord President sent Salisbury off to fetch the King. 'I went in to see him,' related Salisbury back at Hatfield. 'He was very much upset. We had a long talk alone. He broke down.' Once he was ready to face the Council, the new King-Emperor spoke briefly and a cushion was placed at his right hand for the Royal dukes to kiss his hand on bended knee. The Duke of Cambridge, at eighty-one, was allowed to perform it standing up. Another cushion was placed at his left hand where the Duke of Devonshire and then Salisbury performed the same ceremony. The King gave Salisbury a signal not to kneel down if he did not wish, but he insisted on going down on one knee like everyone else. 'I was rather offended,' an ungrateful Salisbury said later. 'He raised Lord Salisbury very tenderly and respectfully,' thought Esher. When the Prime Minister and Balfour returned to Hatfield they related the proceedings to the family at dinner, after the servants had left. 'I am quite tired of breaking the Third Commandment,' Salisbury said, about his time spent bowing down before false gods.

To his surprise, except over the single issue of honours, Salisbury found the new King easy enough to deal with, and was soon commenting on his good behaviour. 'I think we shall have to call him Edward the Confessor Number Two,' he told Violet.[2] On 14th February, the King had to make a declaration to Parliament under a formula prescribed by William and Mary, in which he renounced various Catholic rites as 'superstitious and idolatrous'. Salisbury considered this oath 'scurrilous' and 'a stain on the Statute Book', and tried to get the Cabinet to scratch it, but out of fear of provoking a Protestant backlash it was allowed to stay there until 1910.[3] The new reign also prompted *Whitaker's Almanac* to write to Salisbury to ask whether he thought the change of monarch meant that he was now heading a new ministry. He minuted to McDonnell: 'I think Whitaker must be left to settle this his own way. I should be puzzled to say whether this is my third or fourth administration. It is a highly metaphysical question.'

Less metaphysical was Christiaan De Wet's 'invasion' of Cape Colony between 10th and 28th February 1901. Although these attacks were little more than raids in force, they emphasised how the Boer War was still far from over. 'Sir Alfred Milner had been a very unfortunate choice,' Salisbury told his family on 10th February, 'a man who put himself at the head of a party. It was the loyal Cape Colonists who had forced on the war.' He then went on 'to rail at the stupidity' of the War Office's cavalry remount department's purchasing policy. When asked why Hicks Beach had not spent more on war preparations, Salisbury said that he would have resigned and only Hanbury could have taken his place, with whom Salisbury found it awkward to work. Salisbury's scapegoating of Hicks Beach, Knutsford's supposedly 'pro-Boer' Colonial Office, Milner, General White, the Army Selection Board, Gatacre, Buller and even on one occasion poor long-dead Carnarvon was an unattractive and uncharacteristic exercise in blame-shifting. He sometimes also privately described the conflict as 'Joe's war'.

In the House of Lords a few days later, he was utterly unbending: 'We must be the masters, otherwise if they retain any portion of their independence it is perfectly obvious that the first purpose to which they would put the power granted them could be to accumulate new forces, new armaments, and prepare once a fitting occasion arises, for the same attack which we had to meet eighteen months ago.' On 28ᵗʰ February, Kitchener held peace talks at Middleburg with Louis Botha, which, although they proved abortive partly because of Milner's hostility, at least showed that the Boers were willing to parley. The Cabinet decided to oppose Kitchener's proposal to give an amnesty to those Afrikaners from Natal and Cape Colony who rebelled against the Crown. By 17ᵗʰ March, Salisbury was telling Lady Rayleigh that the war could drag on for some time yet. He doubted whether 'we shall get much out of the gold mines, great damage has been done to the machinery by the Boers, and Cecil Rhodes and his clique will do all they can to cheat the Government'. Kitchener had wanted specially taxed revenues from the goldmines to be spent on the Transvaal after the war, an idea of which Salisbury approved. It was all a far cry from his famous 'We seek no goldfields' pronouncement of November 1899.

Salisbury squarely blamed Jingoism for the Empire's discontents, speaking to Lady Rayleigh of 'the present passion for Imperialism as if it were a sort of zone of poisonous atmosphere we have got into ... he thought it began here and spread to the colonies and that it followed naturally on our two jubilees'. Equally morbidly he told her that the ethics of suicide needed revision. In the light of the abilities of doctors to extend the painful lives of cancer-sufferers, he said of euthanasia that it was 'absurd to call it murder, it was nowhere forbidden in the Bible and he believed the early Christians went against it because the Romans approved it'.⁴ To Violet Cecil he was equally iconoclastic five days later, saying that he did not believe such a thing as 'policy' really existed: 'The Press and historians talk nonsense,' he said.

On 20ᵗʰ March 1901, *The Times* announced that 'within the next few days ... the country can congratulate Lord Salisbury and itself upon the fact that he has been Prime Minister for a longer period than any other statesman during the last seventy years', beating Gladstone's twelve years and 137 days in the office. Far from celebrating, Salisbury caught a bad cold, after which he suffered a fall in his bedroom which left him weak and depressed. 'He is evidently very gloomy about his own condition,' recorded Violet, especially once the family had engaged a nurse to keep an eye on him, because he could not abide people fussing over him.

In South Africa, Kitchener had erected 8,000 blockhouses and 3,700 miles of wire mesh to hamper the commandos' movement, while General French was undertaking huge sweeps of the eastern Transvaal. Fulfilling the Cecil family motto, Salisbury's Government might have got round to prosecuting the war late, but it was certainly being done in earnest. By the end of it, over half the Boer male population of military age had been taken prisoner. Meanwhile, Salisbury had to go to La

Bastide for further recuperation, writing to McDonnell from there on 1st May that he would be 'shirking' a speech to the Primrose League because 'I am not fitted to speak on military matters.' It was one of a number of such admissions that were only meant in ironic jest from a Prime Minister who had had to preside over a long and draining war, but nonetheless contained more than a grain of truth. A fortnight later, he was speaking to the NUCCA about the way that the Boers had been stockpiling arms for years in readiness for their invasion: 'It has now become an ordinary thing when you open your paper in the morning to see that so many hundreds of thousands of rounds of ammunition have been dug out of the ground. Well, they did not grow there.'

For all his private blaming of Milner and Chamberlain for the outbreak of war, Salisbury appreciated how popular the High Commissioner now was, and how necessary it was to co-ordinate the arrangements for final victory with him. He gave friendly advice to the Liberal Unionist proconsul, such as this estimation of the Conservatives, which summed up everything he had felt since 1867 about the Party he had led since 1885:

> It is a Party shackled by tradition; all the cautious people, all the timid, all the unimaginative, belong to it. It stumbles slowly and painfully from precedent to precedent with its eyes fixed on the ground. Yet the Conservative Party is the Imperial Party. I must work with it – who indeed am just such a one myself – but you must work with it if you are to achieve even a part of your object.[5]

When Milner embarked for London for discussions about the eventual peace, the King suggested that Salisbury should send his carriage to meet him at Waterloo Station. 'It would have been rather a bumptious proceeding on my part in any case,' Salisbury told Chamberlain, 'but the King's idea seems to have been that my carriage, empty, was to meet him. With all deference to H.M., I think this would have been a bit of bad manners on my part, and therefore inadmissible.' Salisbury suggested that both he and the Colonial Secretary went to greet Milner at the station. So, at 2.30 p.m. on 24th May 1901, Salisbury, with Chamberlain, Roberts, Lansdowne and Balfour following him, shook Milner's hand as he alighted from the train. He then took Milner and Chamberlain by open landau to Marlborough House, where the King bestowed a barony upon the High Commissioner.

Salisbury invited Milner to attend the Cabinet meeting of 14th June at which it was agreed to confirm the courts-martial death sentences for those Cape Colony rebels who had taken the neutrality oath and were subsequently captured in the field. Five days later, Milner circulated a memorandum to the Cabinet which went even further, proposing: 'At whatever cost these [Boer commandos] must be hunted down, or hunted out', by establishing 'settled areas' in which anyone found with un-licensed arms was automatically liable to the death penalty. At a subsequent Cabinet on 21st June, Milner expanded his idea, suggesting that the areas should include larger towns, railways and mining concerns. Although the Cabinet approved Milner's general plans, it left the overall military policy in Kitchener's hands and pointed out that the present expenditure rate of £1.25 million per week 'could not be indefi-nitely continued'. A large house party for Milner at Hatfield two days later included Violet Cecil. Sir Harry Johnston, who also stayed that month, reported that Salisbury 'had obviously lost much interest in worldly affairs', though he showed curiosity in the Okapi antelope, the five-horned giraffe and many other natural historical discoveries of Johnston's recent expedition to Uganda.[6]

From almost the moment Salisbury had relinquished the Foreign Office to Lansdowne, his non-alignment policy had begun to come under threat. In January 1901, Chamberlain and Devonshire held meetings at Chatsworth with Baron von Eckardstein, a friend of the German-born Duchess, without Salisbury's and Hatzfeldt's knowledge. Ever up to his old tricks, Eckardstein encouraged both Holstein in Berlin and the two Liberal Unionist leaders to believe that the other side was keen for an alliance. As before, the attempt came to nothing, but the general desire to end Britain's perceived 'isolation' did result in a proposal in March from Lansdowne, another Liberal Unionist, to come to an agreement with Germany to contain Russia in the Far East. 'The Germans want to push us into the water and then steal our clothes,' Bertie warned Salisbury, who needed no such promptings to try to obstruct progress.

Salisbury denied that Germany was outstripping Britain commer-cially, telling the annual banquet of the Associated Chambers of Commerce in March 1901 that he recognised 'the spectre of Germany' existed, but denying that British trade had somehow grown decadent. 'I am inclined rather to attribute it to the national pessimism which attends as its Nemesis upon all great success,' he argued, uncharacteris-tically, concluding that the commercial classes should all be taught French and German, and possibly Spanish, 'before they think of Latin and Greek'.

On the day Milner arrived in London, 24th May, Salisbury received a memorandum from Lansdowne on the advantages of a proposed Anglo-German entente. The following day, Lansdowne visited an ill Hatzfeldt to discuss proposals. Each was led by Eckardstein to believe the other had initiated the offer, so they both asked a high price for each other's friendship. There was an element of farce to the proceedings, and

Salisbury effectively ended them with an important memorandum of
29ᵗʰ May 1901. Although Lansdowne had instructed Sanderson to draw
up a draft treaty of alliance, and Brodrick had even asked Kitchener to
look into how Britain could help Germany in a continental war,
Salisbury squashed the scheme, writing:

> I do not see how, in common honesty, we could invite other nations to rely
> upon our aid in a struggle, which must be formidable and probably
> supreme, when we have no means whatever of knowing what may be the
> humour of our people in circumstances which cannot be foreseen.

He went on to describe Britain's lack of allies as 'a danger in whose existence we have no historical reason for believing'.

The following month, Salisbury pooh-poohed the fears of Selborne,
yet another Liberal Unionist, who thought that the French might
launch a surprise attack on the south coast: 'What have the French to
get by going to war in this piratical fashion? The utmost they can do
would be to confiscate a couple of P&O steamers.' Yet again he had
defended his non-alignment policy, but the opposition from the influential Liberal Unionist voices in his Cabinet, as well as now from Arthur
Balfour and Brodrick, was becoming too great, and his capacity to hold
up the Cabinet's desire to join a European bloc was weakening by the
month.

If Salisbury had needed any further evidence for his distrust of
Germany, it came days after his resignation, when in August 1902 the
Secretary of the Admiralty, Hugh Arnold-Forster, submitted a confidential Cabinet memorandum after a visit to Kiel and Wilhelmshaven, in
which he reported that the massive expansion programme of the
German navy could not be directed against France or Russia, as wars
against both must be decided on land. 'Against England alone is such a
weapon as the modern German Navy necessary,' concluded Arnold-
Forster, and Britain must therefore henceforth consider Germany not as
a possible, but as a 'probable' future enemy. As the Imperial Chancellor,
Theobald Bethmann-Hollweg, himself put it in July 1912: 'We Germans
are too strong, too parvenu, and simply too repulsive to be liked.'⁷

On 14ᵗʰ June 1901, the Liberal leader in the Commons, Sir Henry
Campbell-Bannerman, spoke to the National Reform Union and coined
a bold phrase which seemed unpatriotically to castigate British troops
in the field: 'When is a war not a war? When it is carried on by methods
of barbarism in South Africa.' Although the phrase provoked outrage at
the time, being taken as encouraging the Boer and criticising the imperial fighting man, he had pointed to a real tragedy, for no fewer than

twenty thousand Boer women and children died in what were called 'concentration' camps, set up by the British authorities in South Africa. When the King asked him whether he should reprimand Campbell-Bannerman for the speech, Salisbury advised against, saying that 'it might have a bad effect' if the fact were publicised.

Despite subsequent propaganda, by Joseph Goebbels amongst others, the British did not invent concentration camps. The 'recconcentrado' camps had been used by the Spanish in Cuba to intern guerillas two years earlier. Nor were they anything like the extermination camps of Nazi Germany, being set up for the refuge of the Boers who had flooded into them for food, shelter, clothing and above all physical protection when the men left their homesteads to fight. Once the harsh home-stead-burning policy was adopted, there was often no alternative accommodation on the veldt. Blatant lies about the British putting fish-hooks into bully beef and ground glass into food, and of pigs devouring the corpses of children, were officially taught in South African schools as late as the 1940s, such was the bitterness caused by the memory of the camps. A myth of deliberate British cruelty was devised and even persists to this day, despite a wealth of well-documented evidence – including no fewer than fourteen Blue Books which go into great detail on the subject – showing clearly how the tragically high levels of mortality happened.

'Seeing the unprotected state of women now living in the Districts,' Kitchener wrote to his generals from Pretoria on 21st December 1900 about moving the Boer population into camps, 'this course is desirable to ensure their not being insulted or molested by natives.' With the men away in their commando units, the Boer women and children living on isolated farms, and those whose farms had been burned for providing intelligence and succour to the enemy, flocked into the camps, vastly more people than the Royal Army Medical Corps (RAMC) could ever have expected. Both the soldier–politician Jack Seely and Leopold Amery's *The Times History of the War* mention 'the tender mercy of the Kaffirs' as a primary reason why the British took in the Boer women, children and elderly, despite the fact that in so doing they relieved Pretoria of all responsibility for them and placed a huge load on the already greatly overstretched resources of the British authorities. 'The high rate of mortality in the camps has been mainly due to the deplorable state of starvation and sickness in which large numbers of people arrived at the camps,' recorded Milner in one memorandum, 'and which rendered them easy victims to the attack of epidemic diseases.' Living cheek-by-jowl in the camps only exacerbated this deeply unsatis-factory state of affairs.

The sites of the refuge camps were hastily selected according to the strategic imperatives of the situation, and some were ill-chosen on health grounds. Many of the Boers had only the most rudimentary understanding of modern science and hygiene, and they obstinately refused to change their habits when living in close proximity in the camps. Urine and slops were often thrown out of hut and tent doors, for example. As the families of Afrikaners who fought for the British had to live next to hard-line Boers, as well as those who had fought against the British and then changed sides, internecine hatreds abounded. By October 1901, there were 118,000 white inmates and 43,000 coloured, far more than the civil authorities could provide for, especially as the outlying camps were regularly cut off from supplies and communications by Boer attacks, to the extent that the official standard diet of a pound of meal and a pound of meat per person per day sometimes fell dramatically. (Women whose husbands were with commando units disgracefully received shorter rations than those whose husbands were not.)[8]

There were a few isolated cases of starvation, but epidemics of measles, pneumonia and cholera caused by far the largest number of fatalities. (British staff at the camps died also, including superintendents and doctors.) Dysentery, diphtheria and whooping cough were diseases which killed ordinary civilians outside the camps during the war, and the RAMC, which had originally expected to have to deal with 40,000 soldiers, ended up instead caring for over two hundred thousand soldiers and in all around two hundred thousand civilian refugees as well. As a general rule, the Boers could leave the camps whenever they wished, and occupants were encouraged to go out to work and stay with friends and relatives if at all possible. Attendance was normally voluntary, although in practice many of the Boers had little alternative to living in them.

Entry and exit regulations tended to vary according to the danger posed by local commando units of course, but the inmates were not prisoners. 'As the railways were continually cut,' Winston Churchill reminisced in My Early Life, 'it was difficult to supply those camps with all the necessities of life.' It was not all unmitigated horror, either; in some there were musical societies, reading rooms, home industries, games and sports. No less than £23 in prizes were distributed at the Vereening Camp athletics meeting in June 1901. Voluntary schools were established in all the camps, and nearly twice as many Boer children received regular schooling during the war than before it.

Infant mortality rates were very high in peacetime South Africa at the end of the nineteenth century. In Cape Colony, they were lower than the Transvaal and Orange Free State, yet infant deaths still averaged between 147 and 214 per thousand there in the years before the war. Antidotes to typhoid, dysentery, pneumonia, bronchitis, whooping cough, diphtheria and malaria had not yet been discovered in 1900.

Antiseptics were in their infancy and dieticians had not yet heard of vitamins. Even in peacetime, typhoid killed around one in five children, and diphtheria and pneumonia generally killed one in three; so with the deprivations of wartime it could only be worse. As those rich enough to live outside the camps tended to do so, only the poorest Boers, generally the most ignorant and superstitious, remained.

These people often believed in their own quack remedies, a distressingly large number of which involved animal dung. Pigs' manure was used as medicine for a child in Krugersdorp Camp, for example; goat droppings in oil were taken medicinally at Pietersburg Camp; goat dung was put on a measles rash in Middleburg Camp; a cow-dung bath was employed to fight rheumatism, and at another camp the British nurses found boiled and strained horse dung being eaten by a mother and child, not out of hunger, but for its supposed medicinal properties.[9]

In all, around 4,000 Boer adults and 16,000 children died in the camps – the 26,370 women and 1,421 children commemorated in the Women's Monument at Bloemfontein is Afrikaner propaganda. Some 12,000 coloureds also perished. The period of highest mortality came in the winter of 1901/2. With an average camp population of 114,000 in 1902, this was tragically high. British soldiers were also dying of disease at an alarming rate, and accounted for almost as many deaths as among Boer civilians. Out of the 4,667 cases of enteric fever diagnosed amongst soldiers over three months at Bloemfontein, for example, no fewer than 891 proved fatal. The RAMC was prepared for 4 per cent of the army being ill at any one time, but was soon faced with an actual figure of nearly 10 per cent. Vast amounts of money were spent on the camps, no less than £112,000 in the period for 13th March to 30th June 1901. It cannot be sustained that the camps were part of the deliberate use of 'methods of barbarism' against the Boers, so much as a terrible, unexpected by-product of guerilla war.

In a General Order of 6th October 1900, General Louis Botha commanded his men to 'Do everything in your power to prevent the burghers laying down their arms. I will be compelled, if they do not listen to this, to confiscate anything moveable and also to burn down their farms.' As well as Botha, Generals Smuts and De La Rey also burnt the farms of Boers who had surrendered, adding to the refugee problem. Indeed, in the plans drawn up by President Steyn and General De Wet for the invasion of Cape Colony, the captured women and children were also to be housed in similar camps. Furthermore, when in December 1901 Kitchener wrote to De Wet to say that he was more than willing to send 'all women and children at present in our camps' to wherever the Boer general specified, no reply was received.

Salisbury's attitude towards the tragedy was at best detached. Although as Prime Minister he must bear the ultimate responsibility for what happened, he left the arrangements to deal with the problem up to Kitchener and Milner. In an article in the *Saturday Review* written during the American Civil War, he had argued that the Federal burning of towns 'is a direct act of war upon non-combatants' and 'to burn down private houses is a complete return to all the worst practices of barbarous times'. Nevertheless, by July 1900 he was writing to Brodrick, in the same letter as he had suggested the branding of Boer prisoners: 'Could you not put your concentration camps much nearer Cape Town? A female uprising is not to be dreaded and the further the Boer families are taken from their homes the more they will feel it.'

Lloyd George was predictably virulent on the question, accusing the Government on 17th June 1901 of 'a deliberate and settled policy' of 'extermination' against women and children. In fact Kitchener was not genocidal, so much as uninterested. It was the British campaigner Emily Hobhouse who awoke the conscience of a section of the British people to what was going on, sending reports of the horrors back home and blaming 'Crass male ignorance, stupidity, helplessness and muddling'. She also denounced war, 'in all its destructiveness, cruelty, stupidity and nakedness'. She found the conditions in the camps varied enormously, depending on the superintendent, supply of fuel and water, attitude of the local populance and date of foundation.

An element of callousness towards the Boer suffering was also evident in Salisbury's letter of 14th November 1901 to Canon MacColl, who had written to say that the farm-burning policy might lose the Unionists the next general election. 'War is a terrible thing,' Salisbury replied.

> The Boers should have thought of its horrible significance when they invaded the Queen's dominions without a cause. The detailed measures of the war must be adopted in conformity with the opinions of the Generals to whom we trust our policy.... I agree with you that the horrors of Concentration Camps followed on this decision – almost of necessity. The huddling together of so many human beings, especially women and children, could not but cause a great mortality; particularly among a people so dirty as the Boers. The question whether it will dispose the election against us in 1905 or 1906 is not a question which can aid us now – though I dare say you are right.[10]

For all the harshness of those observations, ten days after sending that letter, Salisbury wrote to Brodrick trying to relax the farm-burning policy. 'In view of the present state of opinion here, and the probable effect later on the memories of the Boers of unwise measures', he suggested that it ought to be laid down that guilt over wrecking railways or telegraphs 'must be established by some degree of proof', rather than 'simply presumed from proximity'.

When the all-female Fawcett Commission visited the (white) camps between August and December 1901, they confirmed Emily Hobhouse's general impressions, and made ten important and useful recommendations for reform. Once these practical suggestions, to do with the sterilisation of linen and so on, were put into effect by the authorities, the death rate in the camps fell to 2 per cent, lower than that of contemporary Glasgow. The Fawcett Commission's report also blamed the lack of hygiene practised by the average Boer woman, saying she 'has a horror of ventilation.... It is not easy to describe the pestilential atmosphere of the tents ... the Saxon word "stinking" is the only one which is appropriate.' When the Boer women abused them on their tours, the plucky Fawcett ladies reminded them how they themselves had treated the Zulu and Basuto women in defeat.

Another explanation given for the sheer size of the catastrophe was that:

> Europeans, hardened by the frequent recurrence of epidemics in Europe, enjoy a certain immunity from infection, which appears to be lost by the South African Dutch, owing perhaps to the long sojourn in that country and to the complete isolation of their homes. The variation of temperature was also a potent factor in the production of disease. It was often as much as 90 degrees Fahrenheit and provided, especially for children and aged persons, the very conditions most conducive to the germination of diseases.

As each new batch of refugees arrived, new viruses and new strains of old viruses were introduced into the camps.

'The black spot – the one black spot – in the picture is the frightful mortality in the concentration camps,' Milner admitted to Chamberlain in December 1901, telling another correspondent it was 'a sad fiasco', because the soldiers had swept up the Boer population 'higgledy piggledy into a couple of dozen camps', who once they were there had 'no idea how to make close cohabitation tolerable'.[11] Once railway-wrecking and other transport difficulties had made the supply of the camps 'impossible', and serious shortages developed, the epidemics naturally began. It was undoubtedly a severe black mark on Salisbury's war premiership, as well as on Milner's gubernatorial record, but it was also a grim presage of the nature of Total War of which the new century was to witness so much.

In June 1901, Tsar Nicholas II sent a letter about the war to Edward VII, in which he argued that 'a small people are desperately defending their country'. To help the King answer it, Salisbury submitted a memorandum, in which he politely suggested that the Tsar was:

evidently unaware that the war was begun and elaborately prepared for many previous years by the Boers, and was unprovoked by any single act on the part of England of which the Boers according to international law had any right to complain. It was preceded a few days before by an ultimatum from the Boers forbidding England to send a single soldier into any part of the vast expanse of South Africa. If England had submitted quietly to this outrage no portion of her dominions throughout the world would have been safe.

He wondered whether, if Sweden had invaded Russia in three places, the Tsar would have abstained from defence. 'It's not "extermination" that we seek: it is security against a future attack.' Salisbury added that Russia had now been fighting in the Caucasus for a quarter of a century. He also claimed that 'the unexampled leniency with which [the Government] have applied the laws of war to their prisoners has materially lengthened the campaign'. When the following month the King asked whether he should send a commiserative telegram to Kruger on his wife's death, Salisbury counselled against it.

On 18th July, Edouard Lippert, an envoy of Kruger's, visited Rosebery at his house in Berkeley Square to discuss peace, on the basis of 'a federal states of South Africa'. Rosebery communicated the proposals to Salisbury, only to be told that 'it is wisest to adhere to the beaten roads of negotiation'. Salisbury was unwilling to sideline Milner and Chamberlain, which was the obvious intention of the Boers, and on 31st July he wrote to Rosebery more fully:

> I most entirely and earnestly share your desire that this terrible drain of life and money should cease, but we have to take care lest in trying to arrest it we could only succeed in prolonging it.... If such a negotiation was known to be on foot, it could be widely read on the Boer side as proof that we are exhausted and disposed to give in. I do not see how it is possible to guard against the danger.

He wrote again on 11th August, telling Rosebery that the Boer demands of amnesty for the Cape Colony rebels would create 'intense resentment among those Colonials who have not rebelled', and adding that any peace proposals should be addressed directly to Kitchener or Milner. He then showed the correspondence to Balfour and Chamberlain, telling the former that 'the whole affair is so foolish that I think [the anti-war journalist W.T.] Stead must be at the bottom of it'.[12] Rosebery was undeterred, and at a speech at Chesterfield in December he called for a meeting, perhaps at 'a wayside inn', which might produce peace.

On 7th August, Kitchener proclaimed that all Boers captured after 15th September would suffer banishment after the war. Five days later, Kritzinger was driven out of Cape Colony. On 3rd September, however, Smuts crossed the border into the Colony and proceeded to inflict serious damage on the 17th Lancers at Elands River Poort four days later. The war was clearly far from over, and to a memorandum from Hicks Beach demanding economies, Salisbury argued that the Government was insufficiently homogeneous to accept them. 'After the beginning of the year,' Salisbury wrote to Hicks Beach on 14th September,

> when I saw how blindly the heads of our defensive departments surrendered themselves to the fatal guidance of their professional advisers, I realised that we were in the face of a Jingo hurricane, and were driving before it under bare poles. But when that justification has ceased to operate, I am not sanguine of the cohesion of the Government.

Back in January, Sir Edward Hamilton at the Treasury had warned the Cabinet that the war was taking twice as long and costing twice as much as had been thought likely the previous year. Now Hicks Beach was insisting that significant savings had to be made in areas unrelated to the war effort. Salisbury relied on Hicks Beach's loyalty not to break up the Government, saying: 'I think it is the duty of all of us – I have certainly made it my own – not to do anything which might bring about that catastrophe <u>while the war lasts</u>. When it has ceased, we shall return to the guidance of ordinary rules.' Salisbury's fear that Brodrick would resign sooner than carry out War Office economies against Kitchener and Milner was balanced by the fear that Hicks Beach might resign rather than preside over large-scale borrowing and tax increases. 'In the matter of war finance,' Salisbury urged Hicks Beach, 'our difficulties may be intensely disagreeable, but they are hardly perplexing. If the worst comes to the worst, it is legitimate to borrow in order to pay your bills in war.'

One project that had to be dropped was Curzon's pet idea for a subsidised railway from Seistan in Persia to Quetta in Baluchistan, or even on to the Persian Gulf. Writing to warn him that Parliament would simply not authorise it, Salisbury told a deeply frustrated Viceroy: 'In the last generation we did much what we liked in the East by force or threats, by squadrons and tall talk. But we have now "allies' – French, German, Russian: and the day of free, individual, coercive action is almost passed by. For years to come, Eastern advance must depend largely on payment: and I fear that in that race England will seldom win.'

Salisbury feared a 'parliamentary explosion' about the cost of the war and also begged Brodrick to try 'to snip down expenses. It seems to me we ought to do things more economically – but of course I am far too ignorant to be able to say how.' Brodrick's answer came in the form of a memorandum stating that he was responsible for feeding 314,000 men and 244,000 horses and mules in South Africa, not including the Boer prisoners who had been sent overseas. The war was now costing £5.5 million per month. By March 1902, the Government was running a very considerable deficit, forcing large increases in duties and income tax.[13] By the end of the war, it was estimated to have cost Britain £223 million, which, as well as the men and horses and munitions, paid for the 1,374,000 tons of equipment and stores and the 1,027 ships engaged in provisioning them. This completely reversed the careful husbandry of public expenditure of the post-Gladstonian period, and Salisbury bequeathed an unenviable financial legacy to his successor.

War fatigue was widespread by October 1901; even the *Primrose League Gazette* admitted that in working-class areas, 'the idea is there that the war ought to have been over by now'. Kitchener warned Roberts that his policy of having 'to catch every man in the field' was prolonging the conflict, and reported that the Boers 'are as far as I can judge, more irreconcilable and fanatical than ever'. Despite Cape Colony being under martial law there were still occasional guerilla actions taking place.

By October 1901, Milner had lost patience with Kitchener and wanted him removed from the South African command. Calling the Commander-in-Chief a 'dictator of very strong views and strong character', words that also applied to himself, Milner blamed Kitchener for not setting up the protected areas properly and for ignoring the problem in the concentration camps. The Cabinet split between supporters of Milner (Chamberlain, Selborne, Long and Ashbourne) and supporters of Kitchener (Lansdowne, James, Hanbury, Brodrick, Balfour of Burleigh, Hamilton and Akers-Douglas). Salisbury was decisive in resolving the matter in Kitchener's favour on 26th November, when he told Chamberlain that there was no evidence anyone else would do any better, let alone a Milner appointee, and that recalling Kitchener might provoke resignations from the Government.

'England is, I believe, the only country in which, during a great war, eminent men write and speak publicly as if they belonged to the enemy,' Salisbury complained in November about the pro-Boer movement. Yet he remained confident that the majority of Britons supported the idea of the war being fought through to final victory, however long that might take. Writing to Cranbrook on 22nd December, he admitted that: 'This unhappy war has lasted much longer than we expected. Its continuance is very sad and wearisome: but I have no doubt that it was forced upon us, and that we had no choice in respect to it. I agree with you that the nation has in no way changed its view in regard to it.'[14]

On 22nd July 1901, the House of Lords handed down what was called the Taff Vale Judgment, establishing that a trade union could be sued as a corporate body. The railwaymen's union then lost an action, and had to pay £23,000 in damages and costs for holding an official strike. This judgment acted as a superb recruiting-sergeant for the Labour Representation Committee, a body which had been founded on 27th February 1900 to increase the voice of organised labour in Parliament. It led the trade unions to politicise themselves, drove the nascent Labour movement into an electoral pact with the Liberals, and alienated many traditionally Tory working-class areas, such as Lancashire, from the Unionists.

Salisbury had long feared the political power of organised labour. In an article entitled 'Our Future Rulers' in 1859, he had focused on the violence with which the closed shop was enforced in Sheffield, where a man had been shot for refusing to join the saw-grinders' union and three fork-grinders blown up for not joining theirs. Of the criminals responsible, Salisbury had written: 'These men, if the suffrage be widely extended, must, in virtue of their numerical superiority, become our masters. Long live our future rulers!' In an identically entitled article five years later, he predicted that universal suffrage would lead to trade unions combining for political as opposed to merely industrial ends, and he raised the spectre of 'a voluntary organisation, huge in its extent, despotic in its government, and raising at its will large amounts of taxation'. This organisation would, he warned, be 'irresistible ... when the trade unions have it all their own way at Westminster'.

It was not really until the Dock Strike of 1889, which won the right to the 'docker's tanner' (sixpence per hour), that organised labour found its feet. Although Keir Hardie was elected for West Ham in 1892, and turned up to Parliament wearing his cloth cap, the process of converting working-class Liberals to voting Labour was long and hard. Balfour's report of a Cabinet discussion on the coal strike in early May 1901 shows how the Government had become almost unhinged on the issue: 'The Cabinet was strongly of opinion that to yield to pressure of such a character would be the end not only of this Government, but of any Government, and all Government.' So when the Taff Vale Judgment was handed down, Salisbury was in no mood to soften it. A memorandum of May 1902 by the Home Secretary C.T. Ritchie admitted that the decision had been 'unexpected in point of law', but that it was just and therefore 'must stand'.[15] It was a fateful decision, and gave British syndicalism its greatest moral boost since the transportation of the Tolpuddle Martyrs. Far from ending in failure, like that of so many politicians, Salisbury's career was ending in an almost dangerous surfeit of success.

FORTY-SEVEN

A Weary Victory

The Anglo-Japanese Alliance –
Coronation Honours – The Education Bill –
Peace at Vereeniging – Retirement –
Death

January 1902 to August 1903

'Bob's your uncle.'

'By predilection I am an old Tory,' Salisbury wrote to Canon MacColl on 6th September 1901, 'and would have rejoiced if we had been able to maintain the friendship with Russia which existed in 1815. But ... other statesmen are acutely watching the chessboard of Europe: and they ... can offer enlargement of Russian territory on the Chinese, the Persian, and the Turkish frontier, and we cannot do so.... I wish it were otherwise: but wishing is no good.' It was in order to discourage Russian enlargement in the Far East that Salisbury's Government concluded Britain's first peacetime alliance for a century, ending her perceived 'isolation' and committing her to go to war in some future, unforeseen circumstances. Salisbury's own isolation in the Cabinet meant that he no longer had the power to prevent an entente about which he was deeply sceptical.

The genesis of the Anglo-Japanese alliance lay in unofficial conversations which Sir Claude MacDonald, now British Ambassador to Tokyo, held with Count Hayishi, the Japanese Ambassador in London, while on leave. On 31st July 1901, Lansdowne officially offered Hayishi an 'understanding', and both Governments then got down to considering concrete proposals. Lansdowne wished to ease Britain's extended position in the Far East; he feared a possible Russo-Japanese deal that would damage British interests in the Far East, and he despaired of coming to any meaningful arrangement with Germany. An agreement with Japan to protect each other's Chinese and Korean interests could be mutually beneficial, and would include a promise to fight if either country were attacked by more than one Great Power.

Salisbury had never held too high an opinion of Japan or the Japanese. 'The moderation which arises from a sense of justice is unknown to an Asiatic,' he had written in the *Saturday Review* in July 1863. 'He only knows the moderation that springs from fear, still less would he appreciate the waiver of strict right to which a European might consent from generosity, or from the chivalrous consideration which, among Western nations, the strong are induced to exhibit towards the weak.' During the Japanese revolution that year, Salisbury argued that Britain should refrain from making acquisitions there, even if France and Russia did. By 1889, he was describing Japan's as a 'mushroom civilisation', which would decay as rapidly as it grew.

Writing to Ernest Satow when he took up the Tokyo Embassy in 1895, Salisbury said that the strategic and military interest being shown in Japan by experts was hugely overestimated: 'She may no doubt be of use in hindering Russia from getting an ice-free port. But how long would her obstruction be effective?' Once Russia had obtained Port Arthur and seemed to be looking for more concessions from Peking, however, Salisbury began to look more favourably on an Anglo-Japanese combination. By July 1899, he was writing to Brodrick about a proposal of financial assistance to Japan, saying that he was 'earnestly in favour of our offer not being mutilated'.

When in March and April 1901, Japan objected to Russia declaring a protectorate over Manchuria, and forced the withdrawal of the draft of the Sino-Russian treaty containing it, Britain was impressed with her resolution. Salisbury preferred to defer discussion, disliking the idea of acting without German support in the Far East, but Lansdowne's conversations with Hayishi culminated in an agreement in mid-August to discuss actual proposals. Just as Britain was considering her first full peacetime alliance in decades, Lansdowne blithely went on holiday for seven weeks, leaving Francis Bertie and Hayishi to draw up the treaty.[1] Hicks Beach wanted to make a global settlement directly with Russia herself, rather than recruit Japan to oppose her, but as Salisbury told Lansdowne, 'She will pretend to consider it – will waste time in colourable negotiations – and when she has arranged matters to her liking will decline any co-operation with us.' Negotiations over China had dragged on in St Petersburg over eighteen months up to March 1897. 'Russian negotiations are as long as Russian winters, and longer, but that is not our fault,' he told Brodrick.

On 10th October, Hayishi produced a draft treaty. In the meantime, a memorandum from Selborne had warned the Cabinet that the navy's battleships were severely outgunned by the combined Franco-Russian fleets in the Far East, but if the Japanese fleet was added to the British total they would enjoy an easy superiority. On 25th October, Salisbury answered Lansdowne's request for comments with the positive words: 'I agree generally with the despatch and the draft treaty.' Apart from some slight rewording 'in view of our relations with Germany', Salisbury was content to go ahead, and failed to raise his traditional constitutional objections to all alliances *per se*.

By 19th December, Salisbury could report to the King that the differences with Japan were 'more with respect to the details than the substance'. They were over Britain's need to station a naval force in Japanese waters, whether to extend the geographical limit of the treaty to India and Siam, and if it should apply if Japan turned out to be the clear aggressor. On this last point Salisbury jibbed, and wrote a Cabinet memorandum on 7th January 1902, which turned out to be his last major foreign policy statement.

> There is no limit: and no escape. We are pledged to war, though the conduct of our ally may have been followed in spite of our strongest remonstrances.... I feel sure that such a pledge will not be sanctioned by Parliament, and I think in the interests of the Empire it ought not to be taken.

Japan's formal promise to follow a non-aggressive policy Salisbury dismissed as 'a sentiment; not a stipulation', and added: 'We cannot rely on the goodwill, or the prudence, or the wise policy of the present Government of Japan, however conspicuous at present those qualities may be.'[2]

It was fitting that his last major policy statement should be in favour of continuing his non-alignment stance, but the great majority of the Cabinet supported the five-year alliance, especially once Russia had shown herself to be unamenable to compromise in Persia and elsewhere. The Anglo-Japanese Alliance was finally signed on 30th January 1902, a full six months after it was first mooted. Hicks Beach later told Gwendolen that, had her father still been Foreign Secretary, it would not have been concluded at all. Far from it not being sanctioned, however, the alliance sailed through Parliament. It gave Cranborne, as Under-Secretary at the Foreign Office, the opportunity for making one of the most splendidly arrogant remarks of the era, when in answer to Dilke's criticism about the length of time the treaty had taken to conclude, he said: 'It is not for us to seek treaties; we grant them.'[3]

~

Opinion differed about Salisbury's physical state in early 1902. He had made a private decision, vouchsafed only to Balfour, McDonnell and close family members, to resign as soon as the war ended. This was partly on health grounds and partly because of his realisation that in foreign policy, to use his own analogy regarding Randolph Churchill, the first fiddle wanted to play a different tune from the rest of the orchestra. He was also very conscious of his declining powers. Sir Almeric Fitzroy, the Clerk of the Privy Council, thought that Salisbury 'vigorously pummelled' Earl Spencer in the Lords debate on the King's Speech on 16th January, but Winston Churchill wrote to Rosebery about the same occasion that 'Sarum was very pathetic and really ought not to be allowed.' At the end of the month, Lady Rayleigh recorded that her uncle 'showed, I thought, very slight lapses of memory, but brilliant as ever'.

Lansdowne was irritated by the way Salisbury sometimes stayed up at Hatfield 'in spite of urgent public affairs'. He enjoyed attending the annual Sheriffs Dinner, where 'his mordant humour played over every topic, and he excited the Duke [of Devonshire] to unwonted hilarity'. Overall, however, as Lady Rayleigh recorded on another visit in February: 'He seemed well, but with very little life or go.' The deaths of his wife and then the Queen were followed in February 1902 by that of his old friend and colleague the Marquess of Dufferin and Ava, who, two days before he died, wrote this letter to Salisbury:

> Being, as the doctors seem to say, on my death-bed, I desire, while I have my wits about me ... to thank you for the great kindness and consideration which you have never failed to show me since the time you started me in my diplomatic career, for having kept the Italian embassy so long for me, and for innumerable acts of kindness. I do not think you ever knew how much I liked you from the time you were a thin, little lower boy at Cookesley's, even then writing, as my tutor used to say, such clever essays. This is all I have strength to say. Good-bye and God bless you. Ever yours, Dufferin and Ava.[4]

On the issue of Coronation honours, Salisbury geared himself up for a clash over the King's wish to ennoble the shady financier Sir Ernest Cassel and the flashily rich Glaswegian grocer and yachtsman Sir Thomas Lipton. 'I have always felt that in Lipton's case the exercise of Royal Prerogative has to be seriously dreaded,' Salisbury had told Granby in September 1901. Five months later, McDonnell returned from a forty-minute meeting with the King to report that Edward VII believed that with regard to his Coronation honours, 'the initiative in the matter should rest with himself rather than with the Prime Minister!', and that 'no more suitable men can be found' than Cassel and Lipton. McDonnell hardly needed to warn Salisbury that 'if it should be carried out the scandal which would ensue would be positively dangerous'.

Salisbury replied that he did not like the King's ideas about who should be receiving the Orders of the Garter, Thistle and St Patrick, but 'no great notice would be taken of them. But the peerages! Neither would be a good nomination – but the second [Lipton] is impossible. I could not accept the responsibility of that creation. The man – and his name and vocation, are moreover ridiculous. I think we shall come to blows over that.' Salisbury also opposed the foundation of the Order of Merit, believing the country had quite enough orders and decorations as it was. He also suspected that the King 'wanted his reign to be remembered in connection with orders', an ambition he thought absurd.

Salisbury despised the coterie of parvenus who surrounded the King, whom he believed had tended to lower the social tone of the monarchy since the Queen's death. He had resigned over a point of principle in defence of his social order before, and he now seemed quite prepared to do so again. In 1901, he had told Granby about the plans to ennoble unsuitable friends of the King: 'I have not at any time during the present year communicated to any human being my intentions in any contingency.' The King, furious, had to withdraw in the face of Salisbury's adamant refusal to allow a man he considered unworthy into the House of Lords, and the most Lipton received was a baronetcy and Cassel a privy councillorship. Furthermore, Lord Haddington, whom McDonnell thought too 'fond of his whisky and his *amours*', had to wait until Salisbury had retired before he got his Thistle and Lord Hawkesbury, a Radical Home Ruler, did not get the earldom of Liverpool until after Salisbury's death. March 1902 saw the King and Salisbury agreeing on something, however, when the State Visit to Ireland was postponed, after Irish Nationalist MPs had cheered when it was announced in the Commons that Lord Methuen had been captured by General De La Rey at the Battle of Tweebosch.

When McDonnell warned Salisbury that he would be expected to give a dinner on 30th May to celebrate the King's Birthday, but that most of the interesting and important people were already being entertained officially elsewhere, Salisbury answered: 'I am painfully aware of it. I shall get nothing but the sweepings, but please draft a list.'[5] It was of just such occasions that Salisbury now fervently wished to be free, and it was about this time that he seems to have decided to resign after the Coronation on 26th June, always assuming the Boers had surrendered by then.

'What people always forget when they talk of "the strongest government of modern times"', Salisbury wrote to the Bishop of Rochester in December 1901,

> is that we are a coalition Government: that at least four, possibly more of our most important members, are still Liberals on all internal questions. They may postpone their special views on this or that internal question for the moment in order not to hinder the work of the Government, in regard to some external matter: but this tolerance cannot be counted on to last beyond the day ... we never have any security that the congenital division of the Cabinet will not declare itself. This circumstance makes any reliance on our assured majority simply futile.

On no issue was this estimation of his ministry's weakness – despite its defeating an Opposition censure motion in January 1902 by a majority of 210 – more true than over Education.

Salisbury had never believed in over-educating the working classes. In the *Quarterly Review* in October 1860, he wrote that it was hard to induce the working man to send his children to school because, 'though his neighbour's child has learned the heights of all the mountains, and the length of all the rivers, and the breadth of the straits in the world, these acquirements have not helped the boy much, for he is now above his work and objects to scaring crows'. Although it meant that occasionally a child might get a clerkship, nonetheless 'in ninety-nine cases out of one hundred the boys must fail and must return sullen and discontented men to the plough-tail'. If they did manage to enter vocations better than domestic service or agricultural labour, such as serving in a shop, these occupations became overcrowded and, as he wrote in September 1884, 'The inevitable result is that the masters do just what they please and in a time of depression when profits are falling every month, their impulse is to screw the last farthing's worth out of their shop-people.'

It was therefore not a reactionary desire to keep the working classes in perpetual ignorance that animated Salisbury, so much as the hope of preventing exploitation and job dissatisfaction. Just as the Chancellor of Oxford did not believe in an Oxford education for women, Roman Catholics, Dissenters, agnostics, Jews or atheists, but had to concede their admission, so he did not really believe in teaching the working classes much more than reading, writing, arithmetic and religion, but also recognised that the times had changed against him.

The free education Salisbury had introduced in 1891 had not saved the Church of England's Voluntary Schools as he had hoped, and they were steadily losing out to the Board Schools, a process he believed was encouraged by the Education department. Salisbury was determined, on returning to office in 1895, to protect the denominational schools against the State. An Education Bill was fashioned in June 1896 to give the poorer Voluntary Schools increased aid from the Treasury, whilst exempting them from paying rates. As a *quid pro quo* it allowed some powers to new, elected local authority education committees. The Bill ran into huge opposition. From the Left, the Liberals, School Boards, nonconformists, National Union of Teachers and others attacked it for subsidising Anglicanism. Meanwhile on the Right, the pro-Church faction, which included Cranborne, rejected any secular supervision over Church schools whatsoever. Over a thousand amendments were tabled of which many were bitterly fought over. It took five days for one thirteen-word clause to be carried.

Eventually, Salisbury had to bow to Cabinet pressure to drop the measure, which he did most reluctantly, refusing to chair the Party meeting held at the Foreign Office which announced its cancellation. Much of the blame was put on the Vice-President of the Council, Sir John Gorst, effectively the Education minister in the Commons. 'I do not see how Gorst can be got rid of – except by the vulgar device of turning him out,' Salisbury wrote to Devonshire, the President of the Council. 'There is no apparent prospect of any vacancy into which he can be pitchforked.' Devonshire – who had told Gorst of the Cabinet's decision to drop the Bill by stalking into his room, standing with his back to the fire, and saying: 'Well, Gorst, your damned Bill's dead' – could not think of a suitable method either, so he stayed until Balfour became Prime Minister in 1902, when he was offered (and refused) the Governorship of the Isle of Man.

Salisbury's distrust of experts is evident from his letter to Balfour of November 1896, as he picked over the wreckage of the Bill.

> There are three forces contending for the mastery on the educational field. 1. The Economists. 2. The Religionists. 3. The Educationists.... The Department of course consists only of Educationists. They think neither of Economy, nor Religion: all they aim at is to press Education: and they have shown that that instinct is not limited either in respect of cost, or of the character of the subjects taught.

He also regretted the advances made by education since Forster's 1870 Education Act:

> Where the three Rs were enough twenty years ago, now you must have French, pianoforte playing and trigonometry; and no doubt German and astronomy will come next. Where £150 a year was sufficient for a teacher he must have £300 now: and that will not be the limit of his rewards. The educationist is one of the daughters of the horse leech: and if you let him

suck according to his will, he will soon have swallowed the slender increase of sustenance you are now tendering to the Voluntary schools.... You had much better give no grant at all, and let the money go to build an ironclad.

When, late in 1901, the Education issue re-emerged, Salisbury was as keen as ever to defend Church interests. As he told the King after a two-hour Cabinet on the subject in November: 'The difficulty lies in this: that many of the Voluntary Schools are ruined: that they can only be saved by contributions in some form by the State: that the Exchequer at the present time is not in a condition to give contributions from the taxes: and that contributions from the Rates raise the religious difficulty in its acutest form.'[6] With nonconformists refusing to pay their rates if any portion of them went to teach Anglican doctrine, the issue was politically explosive, especially as Chamberlain, a Unitarian, was the third most powerful man in the Government after Salisbury and Balfour.

Yet Salisbury was insistent, and, as he warned Devonshire in January 1900, he would not accept any measure which aided undenominational religion out of the public funds and refused the same aid to denominational religion. His other great concern was that the ratepayer should not be badly hit. By January 1901, a great deal of Cabinet time was being devoted to a new Education Bill of Balfour's, and the differences of opinion between ministers was very marked. Devonshire came close to resignation in February 1902, and the Bill was continually drafted and re-drafted to reflect the differences of opinion in Cabinet. When finally it was introduced by Balfour in March, it ran into all the problems inherent in any hybrid measure. Salisbury started to jib at the extra costs being put on the ratepayers and he became even more unhappy in October when Balfour failed to oppose an amendment which made the school manager rather than the parish priest responsible for children's religious education. Salisbury told his family that if he had known that Balfour 'meant to take power from the clergyman, he would have put off his resignation a year to prevent it'.

Hugh Cecil, MP for Greenwich and a leader of a small but boisterous parliamentary group nicknamed 'the Hughligans' (which included Winston Churchill), vigorously opposed the amendment along with Cranborne. Salisbury told Rutland in retirement that he would not go to London to vote for Balfour's Bill: 'I am still puzzled to understand why it was thought expedient to administer a gratuitous affront to the clergy.'[7] Right at the beginning of his career he had opposed the abolition of the Church Rate; in his stentorian support of the rights and privileges of the Church of England, he stayed absolutely consistent throughout his half-century in politics.

~

'The store of Boer soldiers appears to be very like the widow's cruse,' Salisbury wrote to his son Edward, who had gone back to Egypt as Military Secretary to the Sirdar in February, 'the more you kill or take, the more there are.' However he ended the letter with uncharacteristic optimism: 'Financially the war is a great nuisance: but I think from every other point of view it has done good.' Kitchener estimated that there were no more than 5,000 Boer soldiers left in the field, but Smuts was still capable of besieging Ooklep for a month in early April. Salisbury had disagreed with Chamberlain over the venue for the negotiations once the Boers eventually sued for peace. He wanted them held at Cape Town rather than London, so that the vexed question of an amnesty could be decided between Milner and Kitchener, thus relieving the Government of the accusation that it had let down the men on the spot. When finally the Boer leaders arrived in Pretoria on 12th April, Salisbury objected to Kitchener meeting them on a Sunday as 'an admission of precipitancy', and he insisted that he should only meet them with witnesses present. In a handwritten note he added: 'The only instruction we can give at this time is a negative one – that is to say – that they are not to listen to any proposals which do not accept the annexation of the Colonies as final.'

Although they had waited many months for the news, Salisbury was still irritated with St John Brodrick for dragging him down to London for a Cabinet on 12th April to discuss peace negotiations before he had any definite reports from Kitchener. 'Lord S. doesn't believe in "fidgeting about Peace",' Violet Cecil recorded. 'He nearly collapsed when St. John suggested that he should stay in London, so as to be ready in case anything happened!' Balfour later said that it was worth the bother of the whole Cabinet assembling just to see Salisbury's face when Brodrick admitted he had no further news. 'Lord S. merely said that if St John was so keen he'd better stay in London himself.'[8]

Milner distrusted all negotiations, preferring to win the war simply by killing or capturing every last Boer soldier. On 21st April, he urged Chamberlain to guard against 'the thoughtless generosity of the national temperament', adding, 'If I am once more represented as the evil genius, who always prevents peace and reconciliation, I can't help it. I know I am right.' The Boer delegates left Pretoria unwilling to accept Kitchener's terms, and the war continued, as huge 'drives' through the north-east Orange River Colony and western Transvaal flushed out more resisters.

On 7th May 1902, Salisbury delivered his last public speech, reassuring the Primrose League that he would not be responsible for any peace treaty which could let anyone 'challenge the complete supremacy of our Sovereign'. He included an exhortation against the idea of over-hasty colonial federation:

> We have no power by legislation to affect the flow of opinion and of affection which has so largely risen between the mother country and her daughter states.... The tendency of human beings, and of statesmen ... is ... to think that because their own wretched lives are confined to some sixty or seventy years, therefore it is open to them to force an anticipation of the results which the natural play of forces and affections and the alteration of the judgment and the mutual feelings of the various peoples in the world will bring before us.

He had identified the drive for imperial federation as a bacillus that would damage the coalition he was preparing to hand over to his nephew, and he was keen to use his authority to combat it.

On 15th May, the Boer delegates returned to meet Kitchener and Milner to discuss peace terms again. Salisbury, Chamberlain and Selborne were the hawks in the Cabinet, holding out for as tough a settlement as Milner wanted. Milner himself felt let down by Kitchener, whom he feared would let the Boers off too lightly. Salisbury seems to have sympathised, and Violet Cecil wrote to Milner on 17th May that the Prime Minister 'is saying openly and to gossips (therefore on purpose) that K. would make any peace to get out of the country'. The terms which were signed at Vereeniging, fifty miles south of Pretoria, on 31st May 1902, provided for the Boers to hand over all their arms, 'and desist from any further resistance to the authority of H.M. King Edward VII, whom they recognise as their lawful sovereign'.

'The policy of emptying the pockets of beaten powers is not noble,' Salisbury had written in 1878 of Italy's plans to take advantage of a Russian defeat of Austria, 'but it has been profitable before and may be again.' Yet at the end of the Boer War the peace terms were relatively magnanimous. All Boer soldiers would be allowed home immediately with no property confiscated; there was to be a general amnesty for all Cape rebels, except some leaders, but permanent disenfranchisement; the Afrikaans language was to be taught in both the republics; licensed firearms would be allowed to farmers; the military administration would be turned over to civilians as soon as possible; and no decision would be taken on enfranchising the blacks until self-government was introduced. (This made a mockery of Chamberlain's statement: 'We cannot consent to purchase a shameful peace by leaving the Colonial population in the position in which they stood before the war.') No special taxes would be introduced to defray war expenses and a commission would be set up with £6 million to pay off the Transvaal's pre-war debts and oversee the rebuilding of the region through loans made regardless of which side the recipient had fought on.

'Heartiest congratulations upon the glorious news,' Salisbury telegraphed Milner on 1st June. In fact, Milner was unhappy with the terms,
believing that he could have obtained unconditional surrender, but the
Cabinet and Colonial Office, and crucially Chamberlain, had supported
Kitchener's more generous approach. Later that month, Salisbury said
that he saw no objection to Chamberlain's proposal to raise Milner's
barony to a viscountcy.

In a leader celebrating the peace in *The Times* on 2nd June, Salisbury
was congratulated on the 'sagacious and conciliatory diplomacy' by
which he had avoided war with 'our American cousins' over Venezuela,
and which had meant that, 'except perhaps to some extent in China, our
rivals have not extracted from us any substantial concessions by the
diplomatic pressure usually applied to a Power embarrassed by war'.[9] In
this atmosphere of mutual congratulation, Salisbury advised the King to
leave the choice of a national day of Thanksgiving up to the archbishops, but suggested a Sunday because any day when the public houses
were open 'might be injurious to public order'.

Sir Almeric Fitzroy recalled the atmosphere in the House of Lords on
2nd June when Salisbury announced that the peace treaty had been
signed:

> The benches were thronged, the steps of the Throne invisible, and the
> galleries crowded with ladies, who in many places looked as if they were
> climbing on each other's backs. Lord Salisbury first rose to pass an
> eulogium on the late Lord Pauncefote, and then, amid loud cheers, to make
> the formal announcement of Peace, the terms of which he read in clear and
> impassive tones.... Lord Rosebery had the sense of the great assembly with
> him when he offered his hearty, unstinted and unreserved congratulations
> to the Government on the announcement.

In his speech congratulating the army on 5th June, Salisbury had to pick
his words carefully. A number of observers mentioned how halting his
speech was on the occasion and uncharitably put it down to his age. It
was more likely to have been due to his belief that incompetent soldiering had been responsible for the early string of unnecessary defeats.
When soon afterwards a family conversation got round to the judicial
execution of Admiral Byng during the Seven Years' War, Salisbury told
Lady Rayleigh he wished Buller had lived in those days.

On the same day that he had to eulogise the army, Salisbury reported
to the King that the Cabinet agreed that there was to be a formal inquiry
into the conduct of the war. The King remonstrated, but although
Salisbury promised that 'every effort will be made to make the inquiry
innocuous', held *in camera* and kept within 'the narrowest possible
limits', the Government were publicly committed to it. Although
Salisbury himself would by then have liked to have escaped holding it

altogether, other Cabinet ministers felt themselves honour bound and had threatened to resign over it. Never a believer in 'open' government, Salisbury feared that Lansdowne might fare badly, especially if the Inquiry turned out to be like John Roebuck's intrusive and explosive parliamentary investigation into the conduct of the Crimean War.[10] The Commission, which reported in August 1903, in fact did little harm to anyone's reputation.

On 24th June 1902, only forty-eight hours before the Coronation, it was announced that the King had suddenly been taken ill with acute peritonitis and required an immediate operation. Salisbury had to look into the question of establishing a Regency in case of the King's incapacity, and the Coronation ceremony had to be postponed until 9th August. This meant a bonanza for London's poor when the food for the Coronation banquets was distributed to them instead. Paupers in soup-kitchens were served with 2,500 quails, 300 legs of mutton, *consommé de faison aux quenelles*, Dover sole poached in Chablis, as well as oysters, prawns and snipe.

Salisbury had intended to retire immediately after the Coronation, and he saw no reason to delay his resignation just because the ceremony had been postponed. 'I will never consent to be in politics the Dowager Lord Salisbury,' he had said in 1898. When he caught himself dropping off to sleep during a Cabinet meeting, he told Selborne that he had 'looked upon that lapse as a warning that it was time to go'. Cranbrook had not believed the rumours in autumn 1901 that Salisbury was about to resign, because 'he will stick to the ship till in smooth water', but with the war won and the new reign well advanced, the time had come. Even Gwendolen had to admit that 'there was a slackening of energy and mental vigour during the last two years of office'.

In his *Saturday Review* articles, Salisbury had mocked politicians who clung on to office, likening them to outgoing tenants who have no interest in making non-urgent repairs. An old Prime Minister, he contended, 'will be disinclined to sow any new harvest of future fame'. He had written of Lord John Russell and Palmerston how 'It is not until they open their mouths to speak, that the way in which old age has hit them becomes apparent. Their intellects have evaporated in very harmless but very attenuated twaddle.' That fate was not for him. Although most senior ministers thought the Prime Minister should retire – as most senior ministers usually do – he was in no sense eased out. Salisbury is the one great exception to Enoch Powell's famous dictum that all political lives, unless they are cut off in midstream at a happy juncture, end in failure. He lent a spirit of grandeur, stability and *sang froid* to governance which the British public admired.[11] He had won two wars and three landslide election victories, and his stock never stood higher than at the moment he left office.

~

Salisbury's final task was to ensure his nephew's smooth succession to his premiership. Earlier in the year a Jingo press campaign, spearheaded by the *National Review* edited by Violet Cecil's brother Leopold Maxse, clamoured for Chamberlain to succeed Salisbury instead of Balfour. (Violet told friends that, apart from Chamberlain, only she and Leo were really capable of running the country ' – and sometimes I'm not sure about Leo'.) In February 1902, Fitzroy believed that the bulk of Tory MPs might even hail Chamberlain 'with enthusiasm', such was his popularity during the war. But as McDonnell told Curzon, 'the King is the trump card', and he was solidly for Balfour. On 3rd July, McDonnell wrote to his friend that 'by the time this reaches you [Salisbury] will have retired into private life. Poor old man! He has never recovered from the blow of his wife's death: he would have gone eighteen months ago if it had not been for the war: all work has become a burden to him, and he longs for rest.'[12]

Four days later, on the afternoon of Monday, 7th July, Chamberlain left the Colonial Office in a cab heading for the Athenæum Club. His horse shied in Whitehall, slipped and fell. Chamberlain was pitched forward and his head went through a glass window, leaving a 3½-inch cut from forehead to right temple. The next day, Tuesday the 8th, he spent in Charing Cross Hospital. He went home on the 9th having lost a pint of blood, and his doctors insisted he convalesce for a fortnight. Although it has been alleged that Salisbury grasped this opportunity to slip his nephew into the premiership, McDonnell's letter to Curzon predating the accident disproves this. In fact, by allowing Chamberlainites later to claim sharp practice, it actually worked against Balfour's interests.

The key player in the resignation was McDonnell, who had only very recently left Salisbury's employ to become permanent secretary at the Office of Works in succession to Lord Esher, a move George Hamilton spotted as a preliminary to Salisbury's retirement. As McDonnell related after Salisbury's death: 'Just before the Coronation he was so broken and ill that I pressed his resignation upon the King with a fervour that was almost indecent: for I felt that the strain of attending the ceremony would probably kill him.' On the evening of Wednesday, 9th July, McDonnell presented Salisbury with a 'startling' proposal for a lightning coup in which Balfour should kiss hands as Prime Minister immediately after Salisbury resigned.

In a long letter to McDonnell the following morning, Thursday, 10th July, Salisbury explained why he could not go along with this:

> Remember that I have a bad character for nepotism, and that any steps taken to control the succession to my office will be judged in the light of that reputation. Do you not think that our strictest secrecy up to one o'clock on Friday – and then the substitution of Arthur for me within the space of one hour, will raise a fierce outcry in the party, and outside it? I have no doubt that left to themselves they will prefer Arthur, but that is quite a different thing to having him forced upon them in such a fashion that they will have no time either to resist or to discuss. Add to this (the outside critic will say) that a time has been selected when the other candidate, Mr Chamberlain, is *hors de combat* for a week: and when the King is not yet able to attend to business. I fear the arrangement will be denounced as an intrigue – and in very vigorous language. When it is disclosed that my interview with the King was not due to any summons from him or from his secretary, but from you only, who had just ceased to be my secretary, the impression will be strengthened that this has not been entirely fair play.

So Salisbury stated that he would like to receive a letter from Sir Francis Knollys, the King's private secretary, 'written in language that can be published if necessary', asking him to call on the King to give up his seals. 'Otherwise I shall be, not unreasonably, suspected of having arranged the whole affair in order to ensure Arthur's succession – and the partisans of Devonshire and Chamberlain, who are quite numerous enough to make themselves heard, will be very indignant.' Perhaps remembering the Iddesleigh debacle, Salisbury was also very keen that 'My colleagues and Middleton ought not to see it first in the newspaper.'[13]

So McDonnell instead arranged that Salisbury should be summoned to the Palace by Knollys the next day, which gave him an opportunity to write to his senior Cabinet colleagues that evening. He turned down as 'embarrassing' the idea of holding a farewell Cabinet meeting. The gravamen of the letters he wrote from Downing Street to Hicks Beach, Halsbury, Chamberlain and Devonshire can be summed up by the one he wrote to the last:

> After some communication with the King, I have arranged to wait upon him tomorrow: and give him my seals. As my strength has considerably diminished of late, I had contemplated this step for some time: but as long as the war lasted I was apprehensive that it might be misconstrued to indicate some division in the Cabinet, and therefore might have a prejudicial effect. In taking my official leave of you, I desire to thank you most warmly for your kindness and forbearance which during the last seven years has enabled us to carry through a difficult experiment with very fair success.[14]

In none of the letters did he so much as allude to the succession.

At 1 p.m. on Friday, 11th July 1902, Lord Salisbury delivered up his seals of office to King Edward VII. He had spent twenty-one years in ministerial office since becoming Secretary of State for India in 1866, serving as Prime Minister for thirteen years and 252 days, the fourth-longest premiership after Walpole, Pitt the Younger and Liverpool. The King awarded him the Grand Cross of the Royal Victorian Order, the only honour, except the Garter and the Windsor Coat, that he accepted in his whole career. With characteristic insouciance he slipped it into his pocket without bothering to open the box when the King handed it to him, and it was only when he got back to Hatfield that he was embarrassed to discover that the insignia had been especially encrusted in diamonds in his honour. He sheepishly wrote to thank the King for 'this magnificent decoration', adding his regret 'that by accident I omitted to express my appreciation at the time of receiving it'.

No public announcement was made until after the weekend, giving Balfour the opportunity – after the King had called for him in the afternoon – to visit Chamberlain on his sickbed. As Salisbury's farewell letter written the night before had for some reason not yet arrived, Chamberlain was woken to receive Balfour not even knowing that Salisbury had resigned. He did know, however, that the Liberal Unionists were very much the junior partners in the Unionist alliance, however personally popular he was with Tory MPs, so he had little alternative but to give Balfour 'the fullest assurance of his support'. Balfour then went straight to Devonshire, who said that he also 'saw no difficulty' in the arrangement, especially as Chamberlain had already assented to it. Devonshire was rueful about the tempo of the proceedings, telling Lansdowne: 'I cannot say that I am quite pleased at not having been consulted at all in the matter,' but he agreed to take Salisbury's place as Leader of the House of Lords. As he was the second minister in the Government by seniority, Devonshire rather regretted not being given a fourth opportunity to turn down the premiership.

On 11th July, Salisbury received a letter from Chamberlain, written by Mary, which expressed his 'sincere gratitude for all the kindness you have shown him. The years that he has worked with you and under you have been very full ones and he has always relied on your kindness and sympathy.' Chamberlain's biographer has detected in this a reference to Salisbury's action in protecting Chamberlain over the Jameson Raid telegrams six years before.

Balfour went back to the Palace the following day, Saturday, 12th July, to kiss hands as Prime Minister. The rest of the Cabinet were not consulted and the process was all over in little more than twenty-four hours. It was not quite McDonnell's sudden coup, but a very similar Cecilian variation on the theme. When Lady Rayleigh saw her brother Arthur Balfour at Downing Street on the night of Friday the 11th, he told her that their uncle had resigned and he would be Prime Minister, saying: 'It would not have been much by itself but combined with getting the Education Bill through the Commons it was very heavy.' The speed and ease with which Balfour inherited Salisbury's premiership inspired the popular phrase: 'Bob's your uncle.'

Like Napoleon III, being his uncle's nephew was both Balfour's making and his undoing. Some, including Lord George Hamilton in his memoirs, depicted Salisbury's handing over of power in July 1902 in terms of a poisoned chalice; just as the 'temporary popularity' afforded by the Sudanese and South African campaigns had evaporated, Salisbury's 'successor has to face the accumulated effects of seven years of internal simmering and dissatisfaction'. If true, this was not apparent at the time, as since October 1900 the Unionists had only lost two seat in by-elections, winning one and retaining nine. Only after Balfour took over did the hitherto safe Tory seat of North Leeds fall to the Liberals, the first of twenty-two which were lost before the catastrophic 1906 general election. The new Prime Minister quickly recognised how hard it was to step into such giant shoes, and his niece recorded how 'often when speaking of the past, he would date not in terms of his own career, but say "that was before (or after) Uncle Robert went"'.

Gwendolen thought her father's 'spirits are pretty good' on relinquishing office, and when the public was finally informed on Monday, 14th July, Balfour summoned all Unionist MPs to a meeting at the Foreign Office, which unanimously acclaimed him as the new Leader. Austen Chamberlain read out a loyal message full of 'pride and pleasure' from his father, and Devonshire pledged the Liberal Unionists' renewed support for the coalition. Jingoists such as Leo Maxse resented 'the jobbed premiership', but it produced hardly a ripple at the time.

A few people presciently, and saw Salisbury's departure as a turning point in Tory and, indeed in British fortunes. Wilfrid Blunt believed it 'marked the end of the Victorian era' and poetically likened his disappearance to the fall of the fifteen-centuries-old, 300-foot campanile of St Mark's in Venice on 14th July. Sir Edward Hamilton saw the resignation as 'the loss of a great national asset. He occupies ... an European position of his own. There was a general feeling that so long as he was at the helm the country was safe.' Alfred Austin, of course, wrote some suitably oleaginous verses:

> Great, wise and good, too near for men to know
> 'Till years shall pass, how good, how wise, how great,

And Time shall scan, with vision clear if slow
This modest master-servant of the State.

Thanking Austin for them, Gwendolen reported that down at Hatfield her father was 'full of the things to be done, charged about the place, to which he has not been able to give attention before!'[15]

With his last great supporter gone, Hicks Beach took the opportunity to resign as well. Cadogan and Collings also retired from the Government, and Gorst went less willingly. McDonnell was awarded a knighthood; he stayed at the Office of Works until 1912. When the Great War broke out, he joined the 5th Cameron Highlanders as a major, aged fifty-three, and died of wounds received in Flanders in 1915.

Of the hundreds of letters he received on his retirement, Salisbury pronounced George Buckle's the most affecting. For that reason, and because it places Salisbury's premierships in their overall historical context, it bears extensive repetition:

> You are indeed happy in the political end to which you come. You leave your country, after long service, victorious at the end of a hard-fought war with the fruits of victory duly garnered in a satisfactory peace, prosperous and wealthy in spite of all her serious efforts, on good terms with all her powerful neighbours, on better terms with those we specially desire to be our friends than we have ever been; and you leave your Party at the height of prosperity, with a majority (and apparently an assured majority) such as you can never have dreamed of in your early political career. The destructive movements you dreaded have lost ground; the principles you contended for are in the ascendant. Finally you are able to hand over your proud position to your pupil and nephew.
>
> What English minister has ever quitted from power in such auspicious circumstances? Not Mr Gladstone, broken in the attempt to reverse what he supported in his prime; not Lord Beaconsfield, dying in unlooked-for Opposition, not Sir Robert Peel, or Lord Derby, Lord Grey or Lord Melbourne. Lord Palmerston in recent years furnishes the only possible parallel; but his good fortune at the close was not nearly as striking as yours.

Buckle was referring to the fact that Palmerston's majority in the 1865 election held three months before his death had been eighty, whereas Salisbury's was 134.

Curzon's letter – 'such promotion as I have enjoyed, I owe to you; such wisdom, if any, I have learned, has been acquired in the same school. Believe me that I can never forget my debt of gratitude to so great an exemplar, or to my first patron' – sits somewhat ill with his constant campaigning for Salisbury's retirement. No longer Prime Minister, Salisbury gave a Coronation garden party for 2,000 people at Hatfield on 19th July, for which special trains were laid on and after which Buckle said 'none could mistake the expression of relief on the ex-Prime Minister's countenance'. Salisbury missed the Coronation itself on the advice of his doctor, Sir Richard Powell, who had been Queen Victoria's physician-in-ordinary.

On the day of the Coronation, 9th August 1902, Salisbury wrote two letters. The first was to Lord Northcote to say that with his influenza attacks, 'I thought I had much better resign and get out of the way: especially as since the death of the last Queen politics have lost their zest for me. I am glad that my resignation has come about at a time when it will be easy for Arthur to take up the running.' The second was to Curzon, which contained a more doleful view of the future. It was not quite *après moi le déluge*, but it included a definite presentiment of Armageddon:

> It may be a misconception, but I cannot resist the impression that we are near some great change in public affairs, in which the forces which contend for the mastery among us will be differently ranged and balanced. If so, it is certainly expedient that younger men should be employed to shape the policy which will no longer depend upon the judgments formed by the experience of past times. The times will be very difficult. The large aggregations of human forces which lie around our Empire seem to draw more closely together, and to assume almost unconsciously a more and more aggressive aspect. Their junction, in menacing and dangerous masses, may be deferred for many years, or may be precipitated with little notice at any moment.[16]

After being deferred for twelve years, almost to the day, the junction of menacing masses was indeed precipitated with little notice, and engulfed the Empire in exactly the way Salisbury had long feared.

After his retirement, Salisbury went to Homburg and Lucerne to recuperate and try to heal a leg he had hurt while out tricycling the previous year. Instead he bruised it afresh, and it developed into an ulcer which laid him up for nearly a month and never properly healed. This left him depressed, but as Eleanor Cecil wrote back to Hatfield, 'he is never cross or irritable or difficult and only says long afterwards that he hasn't liked a thing'. Above all he disliked being fussed over. At Frankfurt railway station a plush saloon carriage was made ready for him, 'but he walked straight through it and sat down in a small carriage reserved for the servants and wouldn't stir out of it. We had to soothe a 6'4" station master in broken German.'

'I think he misses the work, misses the grindstone on which to sharpen his mind,' Gwendolen recorded in November, 'of course lethargy must come with so great a weight as he carries about.' By Christmas, Salisbury was slowing down physically, but he was mentally alert until the very end and keen to keep up with political news. In January, he even attended a meeting of Hertfordshire County Council in his capacity as an honorary alderman, the discussion dying away as he entered the chamber. Once it had resumed, he 'was ingenuously surprised at the debate he heard and the stupidity of the Hertfordshire magnates'. That month, Violet Cecil recorded Salisbury blaming the Boer War on Carnarvon (who had died nine years before it broke out) on the grounds that 'He became imbued with the idea that he was a great colonial statesman and Empire builder and [in 1877] he annexed the Transvaal without reflection. If any one man may be said to be responsible for this war, it is Carnarvon.'[17]

In April 1903, Salisbury took possession of a new motor-car, in which he was ably driven by Gwendolen. He had bought his first one the previous October, which a one-eyed Hatfield electrician who spoke no French had somehow navigated from Paris to Beaulieu. For his new car, long asphalt tracks were laid out through the Park, and whenever it encountered a seemingly insurmountable obstacle, Salisbury 'had but one word "go on" ... as an invalid [he] enjoyed the new game of rapid motion'. He also took great pleasure playing with his grandchildren, who would sit on his knee and dive their fingers into his beard. Although he very nearly died of congestion of the kidneys in early June, a fortnight later he was better and laughing 'at everyone in turn, especially Arthur'.

Balfour was not giving his supporters much to laugh about. On 10th June, he told the House of Commons à propos of tariff reform: 'I should consider that I was but ill-performing my duty ... if we were to profess a settled conviction when no settled conviction exists.' It was no rallying cry. His nephew's increasing problems over Imperial Preference worried Salisbury, who took a strongly anti-Chamberlain stance. As George Hamilton acknowledged to Balfour, Salisbury had had a latent power of 'preventing awkward questions being pushed by his colleagues into an inconvenient position of prominence'. Once he had gone, the tariff reform controversy reappeared with a vengeance.

Salisbury's attitude was that rather than binding the Empire closer, Imperial Preference could mean 'the loss of our colonies, because the country is asking what good are they to us. In his own manner he says our mistake is having an empire!' Any party that proposed to put a permanent tax upon food, he believed, would 'ultimately be knocked to pieces'. In the last weeks of his life, Salisbury was angry with Balfour for allowing a dual Party leadership to develop with Chamberlain, saying that as Prime Minister he should assert himself more, and that unless he did, it 'would bring any party thus conducted to real political disaster'.[18] Before he had resigned he told McDonnell that 'Things will be in a very fluid state after my disappearance,' and he was very soon proved right. Less than a month after his death, Chamberlain, Devonshire, Ritchie, Balfour of Burleigh and George Hamilton had all resigned from the Unionist Government. Three years later, the Unionists were annihilated in the January 1906 general election, when they won only 156 seats against the Liberals' 399.

Salisbury's health had ebbed with the century, and by 1903 there was little left. In 1894, he had told Lady Rayleigh that he thought 'the petition in the Litany against sudden death must refer euphemistically to hanging or execution. Sudden death was otherwise so much to be desired.' When his end came it was not sudden, but nor was it painful. On Monday, 10th August, he suffered a mild heart attack as a result of a fall from his chair, but this time he did not seem to rally from it. When Gwendolen, who along with Maud stayed at their father's bedside throughout his last illness, asked Sir Richard Powell what her father was dying of, he answered that there was no single cause: 'It was just that the machine was worn out.' Salisbury had the opportunity to bid farewell to McDonnell and Hicks Beach just before he died, and Balfour made it to his bedside and was also recognised by him before the end.

Late on the night of Friday, 21st August, Salisbury slipped out of consciousness, and he sank slowly on Saturday afternoon. That day his half-sister, Lady Galloway, was buried at Hatfield church and one of the mourners recalled how:

> we all sat down in the great hall to a luncheon which stood ready, but the lord of the palace was dying upstairs, as we all knew, and the funeral baked meats stuck in our throats. I doubt whether any of us had the courage to eat more than a few mouthfuls. Then I went on for my walk alone and wandered an hour in the park, where children were playing as if nothing momentous were taking place in the great house. The deer were lying out in a cool place in the open and rabbits were busy nibbling under the great oaks, and the ownership of it all was passing from one Cecil to another, as Robert Lord Salisbury died at sunset.

Salisbury breathed his last shortly after nine o'clock on the evening of Saturday, 22nd August 1903, surrounded by Arthur Balfour and all his children except Edward, who had embarked from Egypt three days before. His son William, rector of Hatfield, read aloud the prayers for the dying, including 'Depart, O Christian soul'. 'I wish you could have seen him after death,' McDonnell told Curzon. 'I never saw anything more beautiful than the expression of rest on his face.'[19]

~

The funeral was delayed until the end of August in order to allow time for Edward to reach England. True to form, Salisbury had turned down the offer of a public funeral and resting place in Westminster Abbey, agreeing to have a memorial service there but wishing the interment to be at Hatfield, where he would lie with his wife in the family burial plot behind the parish church. At the Abbey, Balfour told Chamberlain of his increasing doubts about a Government commitment to introduce taxes on food – an action of which his uncle would have approved. The memorial service, reported the *Fortnightly Review*,

> passed almost unnoticed. There was no crowding, no throng of eager sight-seers, outside Westminster Abbey; a few policemen were dotted about the precincts, but they were scarcely needed. Indifferently, the passers-by on foot, or on the roof of omnibuses, turned their heads as the solemn note of the bell crossed the rattle of Victoria Street, and now and again some faint strain of Schubert or Chopin was wafted through the windows of the great Minster. But men and women went by upon their own occasions, casual, inattentive, not pausing to remember that there was a solemn ceremony of one who had been a Prince among his peers, who had sat in council with Emperors and Kings, who had swayed the destinies of a quarter of the human race, and who had gone to his rest after being three times Prime Minister of England. *Sic transit gloria.*

Judging by his caustic remarks about the crowds and cameras outside Gladstone's funeral service, it was doubtless the farewell Salisbury would have preferred.

Alfred Austin published a poem in *The Times*, in which 'cathedral dome' was rhymed with 'stately home', and one particularly glutinous stanza read:

> Aves loud and vehement
> Never were his quest or choice;
> All he cared for was assent
> Whispered by the still small voice,
> And being loved and understood
> By the just, and wise and good.[20]

In fact, of course, being loved and understood by the good, any more than the just and the wise, had always been of supreme unconcern to that most self-confident of statesmen, who gloried in his perversity and always regarded *bien pensant* wisdom as likely to be humbug.

He was buried in Hatfield churchyard in 'mellow sunshine' at 3.30 p.m. on Monday, 31st August 1903. Hatfield's shops closed, the church flag of St George flew at half-mast, and the 650 family, household servants, estate-workers and friends took their places for a service conducted by the Archbishop of Canterbury and the Rev. Lord William Cecil. *Abide With Me* and *Praise, My Soul, The King of Heaven*, written by his favourite schoolmaster, Henry Lyte, were sung. The coffin, adorned with a large wreath of white orchids, stephanotis, gardenias and lilies of the valley, was carried down the nave and out towards the grave on the shoulders of a dozen tenants, as the church organ played Handel's death march from *Saul*.

Robert Arthur Talbot Gascoyne-Cecil, 3rd Marquess of Salisbury, was interred in silence, save for the cawing of startled rooks. From the church could be heard the strains of *O God our Help in Ages Past*, 'as the shadows in the waning glory of the summer afternoon lengthened and deepened'.[21] Thirty-five members of the family then walked past the grave, each lady as she withdrew dropping a single white blossom into the grave.

The Legacy

'Whatever happens will be for the worse, and therefore it is in our
interest that
as little should happen as possible.'

'It's difficult enough to go around doing what is right
without going around trying to do good.'

'Hostility to Radicalism, incessant, implacable hostility,
is the essential definition of Conservatism.'

'The use of Conservatism was to delay changes 'till they became
harmless.'

In his seventy-three-page review of a biography of Lord Castlereagh in
January 1862, Salisbury had written with ironic satisfaction of 'the just
Nemesis which generally decrees that partisans shall be forced to do in
office precisely that which they most loudly decried in opposition'.
Salisbury's own career abounds with such contradictions, and the sacri-
fices principle must occasionally make to power.

Here is a man who denounced the arms race but inaugurated the
Two-Power Naval Standard; a paternalist landowner who was also a
free-market ideologue; a High Tory who sat at the same Cabinet table as
Joseph Chamberlain; a leader of 'the stupidest party' who reviewed
works of German philosophy and lectured at Oxford on Evolution;
someone who feared change, yet eagerly embraced electric lighting,
telephones, automobiles and telegraphy; a supporter of the right of a
minority of Americans to secede from a Union, but not a majority of
Irishmen; a believer in small government who created new Whitehall
departments; the denouncer of Robert Lowe for tampering with Blue
Books in the Education department, who then happily embroidered
them himself once at the Foreign Office; a statesman who professed
outrage at the deposing of a Bulgarian prince, yet who himself plotted to
oust an Amir, a Khedive and a Sultan.

Here is also a man who mocked pageantry, yet oversaw Lytton's and

Curzon's Delhi Durbars and the Golden and Diamond Jubilees; who opposed the invasion of Egypt, yet never evacuated it; who spoke for the squirearchy, yet introduced County Councils; who loathed Eton, yet sent his children there; who fought the Boer War over the very franchise rights he had resigned rather than extend to his fellow-countrymen. Here is a peace-monger who believed in low taxation but presided over a war that cost £233 million; an opponent of proconsular 'prodigal sons' who appointed Lytton to India and Milner to the Cape; a supporter of giving women the franchise but not a university education.

Salisbury opposed Lord John Russell's bullying gunboat diplomacy, yet practised it himself against Spain, Greece and Portugal. He believed in economic non-intervention, but agreed to bail out Barings. He criticised Palmerston's nepotism and jobbery, and appointed so many members of his own family to his Government that it was nicknamed the 'Hotel Cecil'. He declared parliamentary 'count-outs' were inimical to free speech, and then employed the clôture. He wrote movingly about the ill-treatment of women and children during the American Civil War, yet was Prime Minister when concentration camps were constructed in South Africa. He condemned 'race arrogance', but stated that no black man could sit at Westminster. He denounced Gladstone's Irish Land Acts as crimes against the sanctity of property, and led a Unionist Government which passed four comprehensive measures of its own. He leaked Cabinet discussions in 1867, yet helped force Lord Derby out of the Foreign Office for leaking them in 1878.

Salisbury opposed British interference in the internal affairs of foreign countries, yet went to Constantinople to try to force reforms on the Sultan. He spoke up for two-member constituencies as a bulwark for minorities at the time of the Second Reform Act, yet was instrumental in virtually abolishing them in the Third. He wanted to partition the Ottoman Empire, yet was ready to go to war for its integrity. He described nonconformist chapels as 'objectionable buildings', yet donated land for the erection of one at Hatfield. He despised Jingoism, yet was Prime Minister during the Diamond Jubilee, Mafeking Night and the 'Khaki' Election, its three most extreme manifestations. 'Too honest a Tory for his Party and his time', he lied to the House of Lords over the *Globe*'s revelations in 1878, encouraged Carnarvon not to tell the whole truth about his interview with Parnell, and very likely helped Lord Arthur Somerset evade the law by skipping the country.

Salisbury's detractors of course ascribe these many paradoxes and contradictions to simple hypocrisy, but in fact they were the result of three overlapping phenomena. The first was the maturing of his opinions from the rigid, ideological, sometimes reactionary High Toryism of his twenties and thirties into the more empirical High Toryism which emerged after his 1867 resignation. He never reneged on his earlier beliefs, but he did recognise how some subtlety and flexibility were required to promote them. If he was to achieve anything for his country and class, he would have to temper his *Saturday Review* prejudices with the pragmatism of the practical minister. They nevertheless remained the foundation of his principles for the whole of his career; they were the lodestar by which he was guided, even if, after 1867, he permitted himself more room to tack as political circumstances dictated.

The second major factor was that after 1886, when the Liberal Unionists entered his *de facto* coalition, and especially after 1895 when they came in *de jure*, he had to make compromises with his political allies. In accommodating Hartington and Chamberlain, a certain amount of watering-down of his Tory policy was inevitable, but it proved a price well worth paying, inaugurating almost two decades of Unionist domination. 'It is one of the most painful disenchantments of office to find how much of one's discretion has been mortgaged by one's predecessors,' Salisbury told the Duke of Buckingham, the Governor of Madras, in 1878, and in his time allies performed an identical function.

The third factor was the 'vast, impersonal forces' of History, which were making Salisbury's world increasingly difficult to sustain, but against which he fought an impressive lifelong rearguard action. Urbanisation, industrialisation, the rise of middle-class self-confidence, massive population growth, syndicalisation, the collapse of land prices and revenues, all led to the loosening of aristocratic political control as the nineteenth century progressed, and all were out of his power significantly to affect, let alone to control. The position of the aristocracy in late-Victorian Britain was rather like that of a family firm which has gone public; although the turnover, profits and market capitalisation of the company had increased enormously, their influence on the future direction had diminished proportionately.

Salisbury has collected a myriad of detractors, although he has also attracted praise from some unlikely quarters. Shortly before he died, Clement Attlee was invited to Chequers by Harold Wilson and asked whom he thought the best Prime Minister of his lifetime. Without hesitation Attlee replied 'Salisbury.' Overall, however, the historical verdict has so far been ungenerous. His inaction in the 1895–6 Armenian crisis has even been described as 'one of the most discreditable blunders ever committed by an Anglo-Saxon statesman'. (In fact, the Cabinet and Admiralty had prevented Salisbury from taking the very active measures he had wanted.) The socialist leader Henry Hyndman called Salisbury's policy 'quite Venetian in its subtlety and patriotic unscrupulousness', which he would not necessarily have taken as an insult.

The Irish MP T.P. O'Connor said that Salisbury was a 'not very attractive personality, for he is lumbering, uncouth, ponderous beyond the ordinary, black in visage, pale in cheek, heavy and awkward in frame; he strikes one as a very rough piece of Nature's carving – not in the least like the delicate and more refined material out of which we suppose aristocrats to be composed'. Once again this analysis would hardly have discomposed the Great Marquess, who had a rhinocerine hide for criticism. When in 1869 he was attacked for speaking of Gladstone's 'arrogant will', he expressed himself puzzled to Canon MacColl: 'If anyone said of me that I had an arrogant will I do not think I should regard it as a severe censure.'

The *Morning Post* called him 'The Prime Minister of Despair' and a *Times Literary Supplement* review of his biography described him as 'strange, profound, aloof, unlovable' with a 'slightly brutal streak in his character'. Historians have complained that his achievements were generally negative, in the sense that they tended to prevent change both at home and abroad. There is more than a little truth in all these analyses, nor would he have particularly dissented from the historian Paul Smith's opinion that 'In an age of democratic politics centred largely on social issues, Salisbury seems to belong to a distant and antipathetic tradition, the last grand aristocratic figure of a political system that died with Victoria, or even before, a great whale irretrievably beached on the receding shore of the nineteenth century.' For a man who showed unconcealed pleasure when he overheard a workman in Pall Mall saying, 'There goes the Old Buffer!', this would have sounded almost like praise and fitted in perfectly with his fatalistic streak.[1]

Then there are the historians who complain that Salisbury was 'too much obsessed with Great Power Politics', left Britain dangerously isolated, never developed an overarching doctrine, failed to answer the Irish Question, left no distinctive political legacy and 'made no bid for the credit of a settled plan' in international relations. In most cases, of course, Salisbury is being accused of failing to do something he thought either undesirable or impossible. To blame a self-proclaimed fatalist and empiricist for not imposing ideological solutions is self-evidently absurd. Salisbury's legacy lies in what he said and did; all overarching political programmes and doctrines he regarded as dangerous cant. As he himself said of Palmerston's statesmanship, the 'most difficult and most salutary [thing] for Parliament to do' was often 'to do nothing'. It was only with the greatest difficulty that his colleagues persuaded him even to issue general election manifestos.

After reading the first two of Gwendolen's four-volume biography of Salisbury, the socialist intellectual Harold Laski thought him: 'not quite honest, a rasping tongue, all the absence of manners of the English country gentleman, just enough scholarship to be a spider among flies, and a sufficient income to appear generous to poor relations'. This is about as spiteful and unfair as the criticism has got, except perhaps from his own Iago, his brother Eustace, whose fraternal vitriol in his *Apologia* included the accusation that Salisbury looked 'upon politics as a question of personal ambition, rather than of principles'.

Even Salisbury's principled 1867 stand against the advent of mass democracy has been belittled by one of his former MPs, Alfred Baumann, who wrote in 1927 that 'there was no question of principle involved; it was merely a matter of detail, of clauses and schedules'. The assumption that great principles cannot be contained in a Bill's clauses and schedules must cast doubt on Baumann's own worth as a parliamentarian. The Second Reform Act ushered in the modern democratic era, and Salisbury's stand against it was, in the context of the time, as logical and principled as it was ultimately doomed. The case for the prosecution can conclude with the remark of the Duchess of Devonshire to Herbert Asquith's wife Margot: 'We both married angels; when Hartington dies he will go straight to Heaven.' At this she pointed her finger up above her head. 'And when Mr Asquith dies he will go straight there too.' She then turned her finger downwards with a diving movement to the floor and beyond – 'Not so Lord Salisbury.'[2]

'In men of genius, as a rule, the imagination or the passions are too strongly developed to suffer them to reach the highest standard of practical statesmanship,' wrote Salisbury in his *Quarterly Review* essay on his hero Lord Castlereagh. 'They follow some poetical ideal, they are under the spell of some fascinating chapter of past history, they are the slaves of some talismanic phrase which their generation has taken up, or they have made for themselves a system to which all men and all circumstances must be bent.' Salisbury's distinctive philosophy of Toryism was based on the opposite creed; one that viewed with intense scepticism any concept of liberty not steeped in precedent, which considered the inherent or inalienable rights of peoples or nations as 'a folly and chimera', and secular schemes for the improvement of Mankind as hopelessly utopian. Despairing of projects based upon lofty ideals rather than practical, day-to-day experience, Salisbury has been criticised for not providing any spiritual 'uplift'. But once again he believed the duty of statesmen was to provide good governance and to leave morality and 'uplift' to the Church. 'When great men get drunk with a theory,' he wrote about political theorists, 'it is the little men who have the headache.' The bloody experience of much of the twentieth century has more than borne him out.

'All absolute dogmas in human affairs are a mistake,' Salisbury told Lytton in September 1877 over the question of interfering with India's trade to relieve famine. 'Trade finds its level in the long run – but the

Hindu starves in a very short run.' Salisbury's instinctive distrust of all
metaphysics not covered by Anglican doctrine led him to denounce the
'cloudy metaphysical speculations' of German philosophers, and state
that 'all the civilisation of modern Europe is due to the spirit of scepticism'. His scientific experiments underlined this trust in the rational
and quantifiable; dewy-eyed romance played no part in his Toryism, as
it did in that of Bolingbroke, Burke or Beaconsfield.

'Nothing can be certain 'till it happens' was one of his watchwords.
'One of the difficulties about great thinkers is that they so often think
wrong' was another. 'A gram of experience is worth a ton of theory' was
yet another. Once when asked a particularly hypothetical question by
his family, he answered: 'I will wait until I *am* a tiger!'[3] Writing to
Sanderson about Crete in 1897, he said of a proposed scheme: 'It is
better to deal with it practically not theoretically: that is, to avoid
laying down any doctrine, but to let things in practice go on as they are.'
He took this Tory empiricism to its logical conclusion when he even
denied the existence of 'policy'.

'I do not think that the charge of being socialistic will have any
weight with the House of Commons,' Salisbury told a correspondent
about encouraging Irish emigration to southern Africa in 1887. 'If it is
convinced that the measure is likely to answer, it never troubles itself
about the school of thought from which the measure is drawn.' Lord
Wemyss's accusation that his housing proposals were collectivist also
cut little ice. Such pragmatism came to an apogee when he discussed
with Lady Rayleigh how to stop the Athanasian Creed being read out in
churches, which, although he subscribed to it himself, he believed
alienated many of the cultivated, university-educated people whom the
Church needed to retain. 'Why can't it be sung?' was Salisbury's solution. 'That way no-one would know what it was about!'[4]

Salisbury's critics were right when they accused him of habitually
cutting corners. He was contemptuous of rules and, as the *Globe* incident in 1878 showed, perfectly willing to lie in what he regarded as the
national interest. Frederick Dolman, the editor of the *Junior Liberal
Review*, was only slightly exaggerating when in a pamphlet in 1884 he
accused Salisbury of being 'manifestly deficient of the slightest appreciation of the most elementary of the political ethics'. In his struggle to
protect the privileges of Church and property, Salisbury felt that with
democracy increasingly stacking the odds against them, every weapon
at hand was permissible, and the invention of a few new ones essential.

The key to Salisbury's philosophy of Toryism was his innate fatalism,
itself partly a factor of his depression. 'I have for so many years entertained a firm conviction that we were going to the dogs that I have got
to be quite accustomed to the expectation,' he wrote to Henry Acland a
week before Disraeli introduced his Second Reform Bill. Walking with

Gwendolen on a mountain in the French Riviera one summer's day, Salisbury morbidly contemplated the end of civil society. His daughter recalled how his voice and manner 'grew heavily oppressed, and his eyes – looking out upon the sunlit sea beneath him – seemed to be filled with a vision of gloom as he dwelt with unforgettable emphasis on the tragedy which would be involved in such a catastrophe'. This was no pose, but the comprehensible reaction of a rich, devoutly Anglican aristocrat in an age of increasing democratisation, atheism and secularisation, moreover someone who had witnessed human nature in unpleasant forms, both at school and in the settler colonies. He was a congenital depressive, and an Englishman – he always described himself as English rather than British – whose country's power had waxed so much that he knew it could only now wane.

It was not all pessimism; there was a healthy admixture of realism too. Just over a decade after his death, the reversal of his non-alignment policy led to British involvement in an Armageddon which cost the lives of five of his nine beloved grandsons, including the nineteen-year-old George who as a young boy had lit the Mafeking bonfire. The secularisation of modern society would also have justified his 'vision of gloom'. Holding out little hope for mankind meant he was rarely disappointed in it, but occasionally he could provide some 'uplift', as when he wrote this moral in a tenant's autograph album: 'Confidence of success is almost success, and obstacles often fall by themselves before a determination to overcome them.'

In no area was his fatalism more pronounced than in the assumption that democracy would eventually lead to the extinction of the power and wealth of his own class. In attempting to channel and civilise the forces of democracy in the thirty-five years after the Second Reform Act, Salisbury did an astonishingly successful job, especially in helping so to draft the 1884 Reform Act that it worked to the Conservatives' eventual advantage. Although he denied the very existence of 'the people', saying that they 'as an acting, deciding, accessible authority are a myth', he always feared them *en masse* because 'an emotion will shoot electrically through a crowd which might have appealed to each man by himself in vain'. The emotion he most feared was envy, which he thought would eventually lead to the many imposing a confiscatory taxation regime upon the few. He regarded social reforms such as free elementary education and old age pensions as the ever-increasing danegeld that the haves were forced to pay the have-nots in order to protect their property rights and stave off revolution.

'We are on an inclined plane leading from the position of Lord Hartington to that of Mr Chamberlain and so on to the depths over which [the socialist] Mr Henry George rules supreme,' Salisbury warned in a classic thin-end-of-the-wedge speech in Dorchester in January 1884.

Ten years later, he likened Henry George's and Keir Hardie's demands for land nationalisation to 'a Plantagenet or Tudor sovereign's views on the subject of benevolences, or a Highland chief's notions as to his neighbour's cattle'. Socialism for him was merely a form of legalised theft. This view has since been described as 'unreasoning' and 'dangerous', but it was sincerely held.[5] 'If English workers are promised an elysium of high wages and little work, as a result of pillaging other classes in the community,' Salisbury wrote in the *Quarterly Review*, 'it would be too much to expect that they should be keen-sighted enough to see through the delusion and refuse the tempting bait.' Salisbury took it for granted that the proletarianisation of British culture and society would inevitably follow.

'I reckon myself as no higher in the scale of things than a policeman,' he said of his political rôle, 'whose utility would be gone if the workers of mischief disappeared.' The primary vehicle through which the policeman would defeat the mischief-workers had to be the Conservative Party, an institution officially born in the same year as Salisbury himself. Although he carefully avoided last ditches after 1867, Salisbury engaged in a lifelong struggle against what he saw as the forces of atheism and political progressivism, becoming a master of patient obstructionism. He preferred 'careful and tentative reform' to 'ethereal doctrines and high-flying theories', and only accepted change when it was forced upon him or when, as with free education and County Councils, the Radicals threatened to pass something more comprehensive. He intensely disliked doing it, and subsequently blamed those two measures for his defeat in the 1892 general election. That year he told Lady Rayleigh: 'The use of Conservatism was to delay changes 'till they became harmless.'[6]

This was as true in foreign affairs as in domestic politics. Writing to Dufferin about the defence of Persia in December 1879, Salisbury said that 'Whatever happens will be for the worse, and therefore it is in our interest that as little should happen as possible.' He wanted 'to provide halting places where the process of change may rest awhile'. With the British Empire's global position, Salisbury was acutely conscious of the envy it excited and the dangers it faced, an attitude which precluded him from feeling the imperial hubris that gripped so many of his contemporaries. It was this profound sense that the Empire must avoid fighting a major continental war which led Salisbury to adopt his policy of non-aligned but full engagement with the Great Powers. Together he and Bismarck appreciated the dangers of war; it was only when both men had quitted the scene that the Great European Peace of 1871–1914 came to an end.

Even as he took High Toryism to its loftiest altitudes, Salisbury was keen not to seem to oppose all change *per se*. 'The axioms of the last age are the fallacies of the present,' he wrote, 'the principles which save one generation may be the ruin of the next.' As he told the Primrose League in November 1888, 'Remember that the problems of the age are changing as we live, that the things for which we fought when we were young no longer remain to be fought about when we are old.' Salisbury instinctively disliked any political change that was not gradual, consensual and also, if possible, compensatory to the losers. In December 1883, he told a Watford audience that:

> My idea of a Conservative policy, though I do not exclude the necessity of organic change when that necessity is clearly proved, is to entertain those measures which are directly for the benefit of the nation, and not to be perpetually improving the machine by which these measures are to be passed.

He went further, saying that although organic change 'is sometimes inevitable, we regard it as an evil, and we do not desire to give it any assistance we can avoid ... it occupies time and energies which are wanted for other purposes'.[7]

Salisbury believed that everything 'respectable and aristocratic' was 'singularly impatient of change', and he saw no reason to apostatise. He took great solace from the study of history, and in particular, as Gwendolen recorded, he enjoyed:

> The proved futility of theorists to whatever school of thought they might belong; the worthlessness of forecasts based on logical calculation; the evil which has repeatedly been wrought by the best intended policies; the hopeless incongruity between aim and result which dominates history.

This sometimes even led him, as in his estimation of the Paris Commune, to conclude that sometimes the 'perils of change are so great, the promise of the most hopeful theories is so often deceptive, that it is frequently the wiser part to uphold the existing state of things, if it can be done, even though in point of argument it should be utterly indefensible'.[8] In other words, there were circumstances in which it was best to leave ill alone, where an attempt at reform, however well meaning, will only make matters worse.

Paul Smith has written of Salisbury's political philosophy that 'It is an intellectual and sophisticated Toryism which employs an apparatus of close empirical reasoning to support the conclusions at which it is programmed by instinctive predilection to arrive.... It is, in short, Toryism for the clever man.' As Salisbury wrote in his classic attack on democracy in the *Quarterly Review* in July 1861, welcoming the implosion of the 'ideal republic' across the Atlantic: 'It is only in the wreck of all ideals, and the collapse of all fantastic hopes, that sober cynical Truth can make her prosaic accents heard.' His warnings about both the

Paris Commune and German hyper-nationalism, the forerunners of the two creeds which have wrought so much misery in the twentieth century, implies that Salisburyian Toryism had something to say to ages other than his own.

Nowhere did his sense of restraint, scepticism and utilitarianism serve Salisbury better than in his foreign policy. 'A diplomatist's glory is the most ephemeral of all forms of that transient reward,' he wrote in his Castlereagh essay. 'There is nothing in the achievement which appeals to the imagination: nothing which art can illustrate, or tradition retain, or history portray.' Salisbury's own realism allowed him to distinguish between the chimera and cant so often present in diplomacy, and as one contemporary foreign critic complained, 'He never in his life said a flattering thing without adding a pin-prick.'

Salisbury did not believe in going too deeply into hypothetical situations during negotiations. When the Foreign Office was discussing the outlines of an African deal with Germany in July 1895, he told Sanderson: 'I have some doubt of the policy of discussing disagreeable contingencies which are purely hypothetical. It reminds me of the anxious couple who broke off their intended marriage, because they could not agree as to the second name of their (future) third son.' The belief that the British Empire could coexist peacefully with its neighbours without needing to align itself with one or other of the Great Power blocs expired with Salisbury. The Entente Cordiale with France was concluded barely a year after his death, thereby linking British fortunes to those of a country which turned out to be in faster relative decline during the first half of the twentieth century, especially in the all-important military sphere, than even Britain herself.

Salisbury was left utterly cold by the emotional antipathies and sympathies which countries like Greece, France or Turkey could evoke in his compatriots. It was a strength in his diplomacy that, except for his bias against America as the home of democracy and plutocracy, he felt no particular predilection for or against the various foreign Powers. He lived for part of the year in France, read and spoke fluent German, and wished for friendship with Russia, but he always applied cold logic to Britain's relations with all of them, treating them as rivals and potential enemies to be dealt with on the strictly rational precepts of strategy and *Realpolitik*. Hatzfeldt was right when he reported to Berlin that Salisbury 'is a man who in general cherishes no sympathies for any other nation, and in the transaction of business is moved by purely English considerations'.

In his four Foreign Secretaryships, Salisbury scored many notable triumphs with relatively few reverses. Sir Edward Grey later put this down to his natural willingness to compromise, 'the caution which springs from strength'. Yet no part of the world where Salisbury was criticised for making concessions – Madagascar, Samoa, northern China, Panama, Venezuela, Heligoland, Siam, Alaska, Timor, the Sahara – was ever likely to have been important to the development of the British Empire. As Cecil Rhodes himself remarked, Salisbury pegged out Britain's imperial ground carefully, and only that which was left over was negotiable. The man whom Hanotaux called the '*tête dominant*' of post-Bismarckian European statesmen was largely responsible for partitioning Africa, usually through bilateral agreements, without occasioning a European conflict. When the situation required toughness however, as at Fashoda, he was perfectly ready to fight.

Salisbury presided over many crises which could easily have led to a general European conflagration, especially in the Balkans and the Near East, and he worked hard to ensure that none did. Part of his secret lay in his preternatural patience. '*Sero sed serio*' certainly applied to this Cecil. As the Khalifa and Kruger discovered, his vengeance might have been long awaited, but once he was ready it came in earnest. When he did fight a major war, as in the Sudan and South Africa, it was only after he had carefully manoeuvred Britain into a position where she could act without any outside interference. In the course of his premierships he added the Central and East African Protectorates, Nigeria, New Guinea, Rhodesia, Upper Burma, Wei-hai-wei, Zanzibar and Pemba, the Transvaal and the Orange River Colony to the dominion of the British Crown, comprising over two and a half million square miles and over forty-four million inhabitants (not including the Anglo-Egyptian condominium in the Sudan). All this despite the fact that he was never a doctrinaire imperialist.[9]

'No tinge of that enthusiastic temper which leads men to overhunt a beaten enemy, to drive a good cause to excess, to swear allegiance to a formula, or to pursue an impracticable ideal, ever threw its shadow upon Lord Castlereagh's serene, impassive intelligence.' The same can be said of the author as of his subject; the *Pax Salisburiana* blessed Europe between his joining the Foreign Office in 1878 and his leaving office in 1902. Of course, in a diplomatic career of over two decades there were occasional setbacks and errors. His high hopes for reform in Asiatic Turkey, so confidently proclaimed on his return from Berlin in 1878, were never implemented, for example. Yet, if as his critics suggest he was 'obsessed' with Great Power politics, it was only because it was a war against another Great Power, or combination of them, which posed the greatest danger to Britain. Small wars were 'mere surf' to him; it was the great conflict between the European Powers which he foresaw, feared and was determined to avoid.

When Salisbury privately recommended the partition of Turkey to the Kaiser at Cowes and to the Tsar at Balmoral, he was turned down both times. If one of the remarkable things about the First World War is that it did not break out earlier, Salisbury is largely responsible for that achievement. That no great Anglo-Russian conflict took place in the last quarter of the nineteenth century, as seemed probable when Salisbury sat down to pen his famous April 1878 Circular, especially considering the many areas where the two other empires impinged on one another, is also largely down to him. An Anglo-French war was also at times a distinct possibility, but Salisbury knew how and when to 'turn away wrath'.

For all the early defeats of the Boer War, fewer British troops fell in the thirty-one months of that conflict than in the first thirty-one minutes of the Somme Offensive. Counterfactual history can never be much more than a diverting parlour game, but if Salisbury had had Gladstone's political longevity and had also stayed in office until he was eighty-four, he would have been Prime Minister in 1914. Could he have prevented the Great War from breaking out? His 'Diplomaticus' attempt in 1889 to escape from the 1839 guarantee to Belgium suggests that he saw the dangers posed by a German Schlieffen Plan even before it was drawn up. He certainly recognised the dangers to peace personified in Kaiser Wilhelm II.[10] We cannot know, but must suspect, that Salisbury would have made more strenuous efforts to prevent the cataclysm.

In a critique written in March 1902 about the proposed alliance with Japan, Salisbury cast doubt on whether Britain would go to war with Germany if she violated Belgian sovereignty, concluding that 'our treaty obligations will follow our national inclinations and not precede them'. By 1914, of course, the German Imperial Navy had become the great threat, and Salisbury's strictures about the protection of the Scheldt would have applied as directly to the Kaiser's navy as it had to that of Napoleon III. Yet it is hard not to agree with Algernon Cecil, Salisbury's nephew, that the 1914 crisis would have been dealt with very differently by his uncle than it was by the Asquith Government:

A private letter to Berlin might have either indicated at what point Austrian polemics must encounter British opposition; a private letter to St Petersburg have conveyed how long mobilisation must be restrained before the claims of Russian prestige could count upon British support; and a Circular terminating in a Congress, with the British Foreign Secretary this time as honest broker, have sufficed to reconcile the claims of peace and honour for another quarter of a century.

Nowhere has Salisbury's legacy been more virulently condemned than over Ireland. 'Those who frustrated Gladstone in 1886 and for years afterwards', one reviewer wrote in *The Times Literary Supplement* after twenty-nine people were killed in a bomb blast in 1998, 'are in a real sense the authors of the trail of blood that leads all the way to the streets of Omagh.' This is as contentious as it is hypothetical. What can be said with relative certainty is that had an unpartitioned Ireland won Home Rule, any Dublin legislature would have soon been faced with a full-scale revolt in the north. As Randolph Churchill had warned in May 1886: 'Ulster will fight; Ulster will be right,' and a civil war would probably have resulted in far more bloodshed than was ever seen in the Easter Rising, or even during the Troubles. The Duke of Cambridge, the Commander-in-Chief of the British army, openly intimated that it would under no circumstances put down a Protestant revolt in Ulster against Irish Home Rule.

Because it never happened we cannot ascertain the precise lengths to which the Ulstermen would have been willing to go in 1886. Certainly, by 1912, three-quarters of all Ulster Protestants over the age of fifteen had signed a covenant to use 'all means which may be found necessary to defeat Home Rule', and 90,000 men joined the Ulster Volunteer Force the following year. Perhaps Salisbury prevented a civil war; we cannot know. From a selfish strategic point of view, had a self-governing Ireland stayed neutral in the First World War – as she did in the Second – the 170,000 Irishmen who fought against the Kaiser in the British army would probably not have served.

In the May 1904 Commons debate over the erection of a memorial to Salisbury near the west door of Westminster Abbey, the Irish Nationalist leader John Redmond struck a discordant note amongst all the eulogies when he described Salisbury as 'a man who all through his career was the consistent and the vehement opponent of every exten-sion of the liberties of the Irish people'. This can hardly be denied. Yet Salisbury's major argument, that Home Rule would 'be a sentence of exile or ruin' for the Protestant minority in the south of Ireland, was later proved accurate in almost every detail. Between 1911 and 1926, but especially after the withdrawal of the British army and disbandment of the Royal Irish Constabulary in early 1922, the twenty-six counties that became the Irish Free State witnessed the exodus of no less than 34 per cent of their Protestant population. As the historian of these terrible events attests, the Protestants were 'menaced, boycotted, frightened, plundered or deprived of their land'.

This horrific outbreak of ethnic cleansing has been described as 'a transformation as thorough as those of the Cromwellian plantations, or the Williamite confiscations', and represents the only post-seventeenth-century mass displacement of any native group in the British Isles. Protestant homes, churches and public buildings were burnt down, as were many great houses, such as Palmerston in County Kildare, Castle Boro in County Wexford and Dersart Court in County Kilkenny. Massacres took place, for example fourteen Protestants were killed in West Cork on a single day in April 1922, and there was a flood of refugees. The Free State Government was not directly involved, but it was just such an outbreak of mass religious and ethnic sectarianism of which Salisbury had warned, and which he halted Home Rule in order to prevent.[11]

Writing to Balfour about a proposal that the mastership of Trinity College, Cambridge, should no longer be confined to clergymen, Salisbury said: 'Intrinsically I doubt the clerical qualification being of much value – but a great number of people cling to it still: and innovations on such a point must not come from us.' Salisbury believed in the political fitness of Radicals proposing radical measures and of Conservatives opposing them. So when historians complain that Salisbury was 'not a Peel' and was thus incapable of the 'imaginative' action of supporting Gladstone's Home Rule policy, believing that if he had, Ireland might have been kept 'permanently within the British connection', they entirely miss the point. Salisbury was proud of not being yet another Tory apostatiser; he exulted in it. He had no wish to be 'imaginative', but merely true to his principles.

Disraeli said that 'England does not love coalitions', but she liked the Unionist one well enough to entrust it with power for sixteen of the nineteen years after 1886. Somehow Salisbury managed to incorporate High Tories, Whigs, Radical Imperialists, Fair Traders, Tory Democrats, Free Traders, Jingoes, Liberal Unionists and Tariff Reformers in his coalition ministries. He deployed tremendous personal qualities, not least of humour and forbearance, to achieve this, and unlike Gladstone before him or Balfour afterwards, Salisbury was able to keep Chamberlain and Devonshire inside his ministries.

More of a natural rebel than an orthodox Party man, Salisbury had found it hard to understand the anguish felt by the Liberal Unionists over leaving their Party. If the Conservative Party abandoned its principles, he told his family, 'I should walk for the last time down the steps of the Carlton Club without casting a glance of a regret behind me.' Salisbury believed that there was a large penumbra of floating voters amongst the British electorate, whom he told MacColl inhabited 'the zone of temporary adherents, who fall away in times of rebuke'. Gladstone's messianic Home Rule campaign, undertaken without so much as a word of warning or consultation with his Party, was just such a time. Even when the Liberals did include Home Rule in their election cry, Salisbury refused to accept they had a real mandate for it. 'How can a man give you a clear answer if he only has one answer to give and you ask him ten questions at the same moment?' he asked before the 1895 election campaign got under way. Even after he had won it, he still maintained that 'When the great oracle speaks, we are never quite certain what the great oracle said.'

A believer in small government and minimal public spending (except on armaments), Salisbury did not measure his Government's success by the number of new laws placed on the Statute Book.[12] In the 1900 session, only 174 statutory instruments were passed by Parliament. 'There is no evidence upon which he can be credited with the paternity of any measure introduced while he was Prime Minister,' boasted Gwendolen of her father's time in office.[13] When the leading theatre managers visited Salisbury to ask for a special government department for the arts to be set up, he refused because it would open up 'an indefinite vista of expense'. He only agreed to create the Scottish and Agriculture Departments when it was demonstrated to his satisfaction that there was an overwhelming need for each, and even then he limited them to the smallest possible bureaucracy and powers.

Although Salisbury did not believe his administrations should be judged according to Liberal criteria, they did initiate some social reform. The first factory inspections of adult workers and compulsory accident compensation were introduced under Salisbury, and the problem of working-class housing was eased by his 1885 and 1890 initiatives. Nor did free primary education come as a result of Attlee's Welfare State, but under the most right-wing Tory Prime Minister in modern history. The reason Salisbury did not make more of these achievements was that he knew that, by so doing, he would enter into a 'sordid auction' for votes in which he could never outbid the Left. It would also encourage the advent of what he called 'an age when every man is profoundly sensible of the duty of mending his neighbours' ways'. Salisbury was a devout believer in *noblesse oblige*, as his treatment of the Hatfield tenantry showed, but he also thought that the working man should insure himself against accident and illness. Charity should never, he told an audience when opening a convalescent home near Bradford in October 1877, 'diminish the sense of freedom, independence and self-help which is an essential portion of the character of the British working man'.

Libertarianism was a mainspring of his political thought. 'Sobriety is a very good thing and philanthropy is a very good thing,' he once wrote, 'but freedom is better than either.'[14] When in the last few weeks of his life a measure was discussed to prevent children entering public houses, Salisbury told his family that he 'cannot bear grandmotherly legislation'. The spirit of tyranny, he had warned the Primrose League in May 1889, was usually dressed in the garments of an angel of light:

> It may wear the appearance of some religious movement or pretend to the authority of some great moral effect. But underneath that cloak there is concealed that steady enemy of human liberty – the desire of men, whenever they may grasp a bit of power, to force others to conform their ideas to their own.

Salisbury made a sharp distinction between the general philosophy of Toryism and the short-term practical needs of the Conservative Party. After 1867, he recognised that the interests of the former were not always best realised through the vehicle of the latter. When forced, as over his nephew's Irish Land Act or the campaign for allotments, to choose between Toryism and Conservatism, he unerringly adhered to the former. As his remarks to Milner and others demonstrated, Salisbury was acutely conscious of the Conservative Party's failings, principally its traditional willingness to ditch its principles when the prospect of office beckoned.

'I always associate the names of Gladstone, Beaconsfield and Salisbury as the three giants of the late Victorian era,' a Glamorganshire MP, Sir Alfred Thomas, said in the May 1904 debate. Posterity has not agreed. There was no cult of Salisbury as there was – and to an extent still is – of the other two. Gladstone and Disraeli were glorified in hundreds of commemorative busts and mugs and plates; Salisbury had only two busts and a plate that was misspelt. Plays and films are regularly written featuring Gladstone and Disraeli; Salisbury almost never appears on the screen or boards, and was even portrayed as clean-shaven in a BBC drama about Cecil Rhodes. Questions are set in history examinations about the famous duo, but rarely feature Salisbury's longer period in office. Yet Salisbury was, in A. J. P. Taylor's estimation, 'a character as Dr Johnson was a character and on the same scale'. His wit was the equal of Disraeli's, relying on high irony rather than mere paradox.

The reason that, despite being Prime Minister for over thirteen and a half years at the height of British imperial prestige, Salisbury has been largely ignored by biographers and school *curricula* alike is that his is seen as an essentially negative message, providing no 'uplift'. He wrote of Castlereagh that he was 'A practical man of the highest order, who yet did not by that fact forfeit his title to be considered a man of genius.' Practical men of the highest order are not necessarily loved, however, especially when they go so far out of their way to avoid being embarrassed by popular applause. There could never be a 'People's Robert' as

Gladstone was 'The People's William'. Salisbury did not believe 'the people' even existed, he despised populist cant, and few apart from his wife ever presumed to use his Christian name. The populace admired and trusted Salisbury, but since he entirely lacked (and despised) the common touch, he could never be taken to their bosom as the other two arch-exhibitionists were. Yet, if Gladstone and Disraeli won the people's hearts, Salisbury won their votes.

What Winston Churchill called Salisbury's 'caustic, far-ranging common sense', allied to an intellect as fine as that of any British Prime Minister and a talent for ruthlessness when the occasion demanded, made him the third triumvir of late-Victorian politics, fully the equal of Gladstone and Disraeli. Together these three men guided the destiny of Great Britain for a third of a century. Salisbury's memorial service might not have attracted the attention of passers-by, and he was never given the mythification accorded to his fellow triumvirs, but History should not be so gullible and inattentive.

Salisbury was a natural leader to whose authority men yielded. He had an entirely self-contained personality. 'With the possible exception of his wife,' recalled Gwendolen, 'I am unable to fix upon any individual whose character or opinion left any trace upon his own.' It helped that, unusually for a Tory leader, Salisbury's place was utterly secure; no one posed a threat to his position at any time after Churchill's fall in 1886. If anything, Salisbury was too successful. His foreign and imperial policy successes unconsiously spawned Jingoism; his 'Khaki' victory in 1900 made all the more painful his nephew's huge defeat five years later. His stifling of the debate over tariff reform meant it erupted with all the more vigour once he had gone. The Taff Vale Judgment so damaged trade unionism that it created a backlash which helped create the Labour Party.

Despite transforming their fortunes, Salisbury is regularly excluded from the Conservative Party's pantheon of heroes. Platform speakers will regularly invoke the legacies of Disraeli and Churchill, Pitt and Peel, Thatcher and Macleod, but they tend to omit Salisbury. Between 1846 and his coming to power in 1885, the Conservatives had only formed one majority government, yet over the next two decades they were in office for all but three years. Salisbury might have despised democracy, but he certainly made it work for the Tories, discovering in the new suburbia and lower-middle classes a whole new area of support for his brand of Tory Unionism. In the course of his career he turned the Party from a disaffected, marginalised pressure group into the popular, natural Party of government. Yet it is to the mantras of Disraeli's 'One Nation' and Randolph Churchill's 'Tory Democracy' that much of the Conservative Party still defers. Some of Disraeli's novels are always in print, while only a small selection of Salisbury's journalism and speeches has ever been published. Despite being described by the Tory historian Robert Blake as 'the most formidable intellectual figure that the Conservative Party has ever produced', Salisburyian Toryism has found few followers in the modern Party.

When Gwendolen was writing her father's biography, which ends in 1892 and which was not helped along by her being thrown downstairs by a stone-deaf cook suffering from anæmic hysteria, her brother Hugh advised that 'one must beware of unrelieved panegyric – a thread of criticism greatly adds to the effect'. Salisbury's willingness to cut constitutional corners, his *à la carte* attitude to obeying the law, his occasional ruthlessness and morbidity, the Orissa famine of 1866, his ignorance of and lack of interest in matters military, and of course his inability to prevent terrible fatalities amongst Boer women and children in the concentration camps have all been held against him. 'Africa was created to plague the Foreign Office,' he once said, and the 1899-1902 South African War has certainly plagued his reputation, even though it was not he who started it, but he who succeeded in winning it. Against all these criticisms must be set the testimony of Winston Churchill, that:

> Lord Salisbury, for all his resistance to modern ideas, and perhaps in some way because of it, played a greater part in gathering together the growing strength for a time of trial which few could foresee and none could measure, than any other historic figure that can be cited.

Early in life Salisbury recognised that the institutions he cherished were coming under grave threat. The Established Church, the British Empire, the House of Lords, High Tory and High Church Oxford, Crown prerogatives, the rights of property, the landed aristocracy, the Act of Union – all that he regarded as the very foundations of English governing society – were being subjected to increasing pressures from within and strains from without. In some cases the threats proved exaggerated, in others illusory, the result of his depression. Overall, however, subsequent events have proved his analysis correct; the twentieth century was a disastrous time for the institutions by which Salisbury set store. His was consciously a lifelong rearguard action.

Because, as his daughter Gwendolen wrote, 'he was essentially a fighting animal', Salisbury's response was to fight with every weapon at his disposal. A true Tory to the marrow, he believed in 'hostility to Radicalism, incessant, implacable hostility'. If Radical schemes could not be halted altogether, they might at least be postponed for as long as possible. In the course of fighting this rearguard action he was instrumental in bringing into being the modern Conservative Party, equipping it with a creed and an organisation which in the century after his retirement has helped to keep it in office for 70 per cent of the time.

The period of fifty years 'was something in the life of a nation', said young Salisbury when trying to hold up John Bright's abolition of the Church Rate.[15] On 22nd August 1853, he wrote his Stamford constituents an open letter, thanking them for electing him to Parliament for the first time, and pledging to them 'a zealous and undeviating adherence to the Conservative principles which have gained for me the honour of your support'. When he died, fifty years later to the day, the greatest Tory of them all had fully redeemed his pledge.

In 1898, Salisbury divided the world between the 'Living' countries, which were growing in power, unity and prestige, and the 'Dying' ones which, over time, began to forfeit first their integrity and eventually their independence. In the century since his death, his own country has passed from the first category to the second. As Kipling predicted, all the pomp of her imperial yesterday 'is one with Nineveh and Tyre'. His countrymen can, however, take solace from the knowledge that in Robert Gascoyne-Cecil, the great Marquess of Salisbury, they had a leader who brought Britain to a pitch of greatness never seen before or since.

Chapter Notes

A refers to the papers of the 3rd Marquess of Salisbury at Hatfield House

ed. Bahlman refers to Dudley W.R. Bahlman's editions of the diaries of Sir Edward Hamilton

BL refers to the British Library Manuscripts

BQR refers to *Bentley's Quarterly Review*

ed. Buckle refers to the 2nd and 3rd series of G.E. Buckle's edition of *The Letters of Queen Victoria*

C refers to the papers of the 3rd Marquess of Salisbury at Hatfield House

Cecil, G refers to the four published and fifth unpublished volumes of Lady Gwendolen Cecil's *Life of Robert, Marquis of Salisbury*

D refers to the papers of the 3rd Marquess of Salisbury at Hatfield House

E refers to the papers of the 3rd Marquess of Salisbury at Hatfield House

F refers to the papers of the 3rd Marquess of Salisbury at Hatfield House

FO refers to the Foreign Office Papers at the Public Record Office

FP refers to the Family Papers at Hatfield House

FR refers to the *Fortnightly Review*

Hansard references are all to the 3rd Series unless otherwise stated

HH refers to papers at Hatfield House.

HP refers to Lord Beaconsfield's Hughenden Papers at the Bodleian Library in Oxford

ILN refers to the *Illustrated London News*

NR refers to the *National Review*

OIOC refers to the Oriental and India Office Collection of the British Library

PRO refers to the Public Record Office at Kew

QR refers to the *Quarterly Review*

RA refers to the Royal Archives at Windsor Castle

Rayleigh refers to the diary of Evelyn, Lady Rayleigh

SR refers to the *Saturday Review*

TLS refers to the *Times Literary Supplement*

ed. Vincent refers to Prof. John Vincent's editions of the diaries of the 15th Earl of Derby

One: Early Life [pp 5–21]

  1 Cecil, G I 1

  2 Grant Duff *Notes* II 29, HH Wellington to 2nd Marchioness 250 10/7/1837, HH McD/381

  3 Hare *Story* I 72–7, Cecil, D. *Cecils* 218, Cecil, E. *Apologia* 8–9, Oman *Heiress* 218

4 Cecil, G I 19–20, Oman *ibid.* 286, FP XIII 85, Cecil, A. *Secretaries* 280, SR XV 272, FP XIII 181, SR XI 190

5 FP XIII 289–93 & 308, Lady Gwendolen Cecil Papers: Box 2

6 SR IX 83, Meyrick *Memoirs* 85, FP XIII 329–31, FP XIV 99, D75/127 & D74/132

7 Rockley Papers 29/8/1867, D75/444, FP XIV 191 & 203, D75/157, FP XIV 231–3, *Lincoln, Rutland and Stamford Mercury* 19/8/1853

Two: Rebellions [pp 22–36]

1 FP XIV 314, D75/191, Cecil, D. *Cecils* 222, Cecil, G I 114, FP XIV 149, Cecil, Viscount *Way* 39, SR XVII 102

2 SR XIX 751, ed. Cartwright *Journals* 186, Hutchinson *Oxford* xii, Cecil, A. *Secretaries* 281, Rayleigh 1/11/1894, V. Milner Papers 8/F2/1/47

3 Lady Gwendolen Cecil Papers Box 2, QR 112 236–70, Benson Papers 78/296, SR XVII 406, SR XI 119, FP XIV 106, Cowling *Doctrine* 364, SR XIX 300, HH Lady Salisbury's memorandum Family Box 1/4

4 Hansard 132 c711–14, FP XIV 329, Mowbray *Seventy* 94, Dennis *House* 168, Cecil, G I 49

5 SR XIII 439, Meyrick *Memoirs* 19, Hansard 138 c1601–4

6 *Lincoln, Rutland and Stamford Mercury* 27/3/1857, Cecil, E. *Apologia* 15–16, Rockley Papers *passim*, E14/15 & 16, Cecil, G I 59, E1/37

7 Butler *Cecils* 183, ed. Ellis *Thatched* 65, Hamilton, G. *Parliamentary* II 315, Hare *Life* 16, Tilley and Gaselee *Foreign Office* 141, V. Milner Papers 14/F63/6, Ribblesdale *Impressions* 173–4

8 Warwick *Afterthoughts* 51, Rose *Cecils* 46, Gower *Grill* 95–6, Egremont *Balfour* 121, Lytton *Blessed* 213, SR XI 43, FP XIV 101

Three: Journalism: Foreign Policy [pp 37–50]

For a complete list of all Salisbury's journalism see Michael Pinto-Duschinsky, *The Political Thought of Lord Salisbury* 1967, 157–88

1 Cowling *Doctrine* 363, Cecil, G I 71, SR XV 545, SR III 556

2 SR XII 450, Pinto-Duschinsky *Political* 24, Mason *Salisbury, Law Beresford-Hopes* 215, BL 44416/84

3 *Review of Reviews* XVII 233, SR XVII 215, Shannon *Crisis* 41, SR XVI 270, SR XVI 17, SR XVIII 437

4 SR XVII 707, SR XVII 129, SR XV 228, SR XVIII 407

5 SR XVIII 741, Malcolm *Vacant* 4, SR IX 11, SR XVI 17, SR XII 146, SR IX 99

6 SR XVI 242, SR II 209, SR XVII 95, SR XV 346, SR XIII 72, SR XV 552

7 SR XVI 716, QR 115 236–87, Hansard 175 c1289–90, SR XII 75

8 SR XIV 667, Hansard 173 c872, SR XVI 108, SR XI 563, SR XV 132, SR XIV 200, SR XIV 359, Cecil, G I 170, SR III 203, FP XIV 101

9 SR III 253, SR XVI 41, SR XII 460, SR III 458, SR IV 18, Jackson *Forster* 90, Cecil, G I 170, SR XIII 671, SR XIV 8, SR XII 267

10 SR XII 528, SR XVI 577, SR XVII 248, SR XIV 330, SR XIX 532, D67/72, Selborne Papers 5/67

Four: Journalism: Domestic Policy [pp 51–67]

1 SR XVII 69, SR XVII 101, SR V 402, SR XIII 506, SR XIV 533, SR XX 631, SR XII 585

2 SR XV 395, SR III 34, SR XX 411, SR XIV 558, SR XIV 399, SR XIII 552, SR XIII 484, SR XII 580, SR VIII 390, SR XII 585, SR XVII 523, SR XX 4, SR XIX 363, SR XVIII

386, SR XVI 541, SR XV 395, SR XVII 774, SR XVII 402

3 BL 46617/186, SR XV 789, SR XV 40, SR XVII 550, SR V 193, SR XI 78, SR XVIII 358

4 SR XVIII 530, SR XIX 689, SR XVII 63–90, QR 110 247–88, SR XV 303, SR XVIII 292, SR XIII 92, SR XI 364

5 SR XVI 693, Pinto-Duschinsky *Political* 87, SR III 361, SR XIX 251, SR XVI 199, SR XIII 153, SR XIII 733, SR XI 470, SR III 240, QR 110 247–88, SR VIII 222, SR XII 404, SR XVIII 584, SR XVI 715, SR XX 479, BQR I 355

6 SR XIII 644, SR XIII 125, SR XVII 130, SR XI 553, SR XIX 429, SR VIII 677, SR XV 45, SR XVI 664, SR XVIII 555, *The Times* 4/4/1871

7 SR XI 161, SR XIV 287, SR IX 178, SR XI 161, SR XV 453, SR XVIII 378, SR VII 270, ed. Russell, G. *MacColl* 110, SR XI 161, SR XVI 147, SR XII 226, QR 107 514–54, SR XIX 330

8 SR XIV 472, QR 109 212–47, SR XII 89, SR XVII 399, SR XVI 105, SR XIII 410, SR XX 352, SR XVII 612

Five: Politics [pp 68–82]

1 FP XV 75, SR III 152

2 Devonshire Papers 340.2564, ed. Buckle II 5, Morier Papers 25B/1, QR 123 559, SR V 193–7, Cowling *Doctrine* 370, Monypenny & Buckle *Disraeli* VI 332, FP XV 79, 84–7, SR VII 661, SR XVI 684, NR Nov. 1931 660, SR X 837, Cowling *ibid.* 376

3 Hansard 149 c512–15, *Lincoln, Rutland and Stamford Mercury* 6/5/1859, FP XV 119, BQR I 29, SR VII 272

4 FP XV 127, SR VIII 12, SR VII 709, Cecil, G I 123, Genesis ch.16 v.12, Hansard 157 c386–93, ed. Russell, G. *MacColl* 267, QR 108 568–605, SR VII 557, SR XVIII 260, ILN 29/8/1903

5 FP XV 145–8, 155–9, Cecil, G I 97, QR 107 514–54, FP XV 201, D31/3, White *Inner* II 3, Ward, W. *Oxford* 229, Hansard 175 c1030–4, ed. Vincent 18/12/1863, 27/1/1864, 19/2/1864, 6/5/1864, D27/170, Otter *Woodard* 110, 116–17, 237

6 Winter *Lowe* 190–1, SR XV 433, SR XIII 515 & 545, Hansard 174 c912, SR XVII 490, SR XVII 465, ed. Buckle 2nd Series I 171, Gathorne-Hardy, A. *Cranbrook* I 173, ed. Vincent 240

7 BL 50063/65, 71–5, 83–4, 92–4, SR XIX 523, 14th Derby Papers 163/7

Six: Secretary of State for India [pp 83–98]

1 Lawrence Papers 4/16 & 21, Cecil, G I 107, D72/12, Lawrence Papers F90/27/96

2 SR XIII 695, SR XV 66

3 SR XVI 137, Lawrence Papers F90/28/103 & 106, Gopal *British Policy* 61–2

4 White *Inner* II 73, Hansard 189 c808–14

5 Cowling *1867* 117, BL 50063/Diary 5/2/1866, 8/3/1866, 25/3/1866, Hearnshaw *Principles* 276

6 Briggs *People* 248, White *Inner* II 50–1, BL 60899/20, M'Carthy *History* III 328, Hardinge *Carnarvon* I 343, Winter *Lowe* 231, ed. Burghclere *Lady's* 101

7 Hardinge *ibid.* I 345, BL 60899/25 & 26

8 ed. Vincent 290, BL 60899/27 & 28, D71/2, Hardinge *ibid.* I 346, Cowling *1867* 150–1

9 14th Derby Papers 920 DER/14/163/7, Cowling *ibid.* 148, BL 60889/29, Gathorne-Hardy, A. *Cranbrook* I 199, Peel Papers K6/10

10 Cowling *ibid.* 155–6, Hardinge *ibid.* I 348, ed. Vincent 290, ed. Buckle 2nd Series I 399, Whibley *Manners* II 123

11 PRO 30/6/173, ed. Buckle 2nd Series I 402–3
12 Rutland Papers 4/3/67, ed. Vincent 292, Hardinge *Carnarvon* I 350, Whibley *Manners* II 126, BL 60899/34
13 ed. Cartwright *Journals* 162, Trevelyan *Bright* 377, Hamilton, G. *Parliamentary* II 315, BL 60899/43
14 D78/9, D31/7 & 8, Otter *Woodard* 195
15 Hansard 188 c1539, *The Times* 24/8/1903, D75/209, Balfour, F. *Ne* II 91

Seven: Life Outside Politics [pp 99–115]

1 SR XVII 249, Rockley Papers 7/9/1867, Shannon *Disraeli* 24, QR 123 533–65
2 Southgate *Leadership* 103, Cowling *1867* 161, Smith, P. Review of Marsh 871
3 Denison *Leaves* 25/2/1868, D31/15 & 17,
4 ed. Buckle 2nd Series I 519, D31/19, Bright *Diaries* 315, Lytton Papers E218/5/11, ed. Johnson *Cranbrook* 86
5 C6/4, Barker *Railway* 89–90, ed. Blake *Salisbury* 255ff, BL 44414/94
6 D31/20, HH 2M: Dowager Lady Salisbury's memoir 68, Selborne Papers 5/13
7 ed. Coleridge *Coleridge* II 156, Hansard 193 c88–90, Lucy *Memories* 120, Lambeth Palace Papers 1865/99
8 Hardinge *Carnarvon* I 341n, SR XXVI 702, E1/36, Hansard 208 c479, Fitzmaurice *Granville* I 540, Houghton Papers 22/113
9 Rose *Cecils* 32, ed. Brett *Esher* II 263, Cecil, D. *Cecils* 256, Cecil, Viscount *Way* 13, Balfour, F. *Ne* II 87
10 Rose *ibid.* 28–9, Jusserand *Befell* 30, Cecil, D. *ibid.* 261
11 Hare *Story* IV 77, TLS 10/4/1953, Beckson *London* 116, Dugdale, B. *Family* 106
12 Cornwallis-West *Reminiscences* 97, SR XIII 11, Hamilton, G. *Parliamentary* I 74, Hare *Solitary* 19, St Helier *Memories* 266
13 Cecil of Chelwood Papers 51/30, Milner, V. *Picture* 80, F1/12, A76/2, Ashbourne Papers 88/1, Balfour, F. *Ne* II 341, ed. Johnson *Cranbrook* 746
14 Cecil, G II 14, ed. Blake *Salisbury* 262–7, Cecil, D. *Cecils* 249, Rose *Cecils* 66
15 SR XVI 352, SR XIX 660, Milner,V. *Picture* 81, Balfour, F. *Ne* II 265
16 Balfour, F. *ibid.* II 310, D42/161, Cecil, G III 3, Butterfield 'Alterations'
17 RA PS/GV/L 2314/87, Lady Gwendolen Cecil Papers Box 2, Forwood *Recollections* 174, Cecil, G III 8
18 SR XIV 371, Rosebery *Churchill* 70, Cecil, G II 12 & III 3, D42 & 43 *passim*
19 Packenham *Dieppe* 78–94 & 152, V. Milner Papers 65/c708/8, Cecil, Viscount *Way* 39, Cecil, G II 17
20 Bentley *Ritualism* 74, Longford *Victoria* 440

Eight: The Politics of Opposition [pp 116–33]

1 ed. Vincent 345, Gathorne-Hardy, A. *Cranbrook* I 294, Rockley Papers *passim*
2 ed. Johnson *Cranbrook* 106, 117, ed. Vincent 53, ed. Burghclere *Lady's* 238
3 Weston *Lords* 59, Hansard 197 c83–5, *Spectator* 26/6/1869
4 ed. Johnson *Cranbrook* 260, D87/852, C6/26, Mason, J. *Election passim*, Mowbray *Seventy* 252–3
5 D65/36, Hansard 175 c1029–34, BL 43519/5, Crewe *Rosebery* I 58, *The Times* 12/10/1872
6 Balfour, A. *Opinions* 34, QR 129 540–56, QR 130 256–86
7 Hansard 202 c80–1, ed. Vincent 60, QR 166 569
8 SR XVI 377, SR XVIII 588, Meyrick *Memoirs* 84, Schreuder *Scramble* 308, FP XIV 15, Rockley Papers July 1921

9 Rockley Papers *passim*, SR XIII 401, Cecil, E. *Apologia* 16
10 ed. Vincent 55 & 340, D72/20
11 ed. Drus *Kimberley* 5/8/1871, ed. Vincent 84, Hansard 208 c474–81, Hardinge *Carnarvon* II 24
12 *The Times* 29/11/1872, ed. Vincent 111, 107, Hansard 211 c1493–4, Rockley Papers *passim*
13 *The Times* 18/10/1873, Houghton Papers 22/106, Rose *Cecils passim*
14 Hardinge *Carnarvon* II 60, Cecil, G II 46, ed. Vincent 6/2/74
15 Rockley papers, E1/36, *The Times* 12/2/1874, D75/213, SR XIV 37
16 ed. Johnson *Cranbrook* 198, Cecil, E. *Apologia* 31–2, D42/97, D75/215, ed. Cartwright *Journals* 257, ed. Buckle 2nd Series II 320, ed. Vincent 63

Nine: A Careful Start [pp 134–48]

1 Gopal *British Policy* 103–4, Northbrook Papers F86/16/18 & 1, Mallet *Northbrook* 82–3
2 Marsh *Church* 158–92, *The Times* 11/10/1872, Holland *Devonshire* I 132–3, Bentley *Ritualism passim*
3 Tait Papers 203/230, HP B/xii/F/2/a
4 Bentley *Ritualism* 68, ed. Vincent 175
5 Hansard 221 c78–80, D31/33, Walsh, W. *Secret History* 70
6 E1/36, D 31/34, ed. Johnson *Cranbrook* 217, QR 108 277, Hansard 221 c1358–9
7 Rockley Papers *passim*, Cecil, G II 62, ed. Vincent 176, Hansard 222 c1253
8 Mallet *Northbrook* 90–2, Hyam *Imperial* 165
9 Woodham-Smith *Nightingale* 541
10 ed. Buckle 3rd Series II 101, FO 65/1097, Judd *Empire* 81, D40/32, ed. Vincent 269, HP B/xx/Ce/63, Shannon *Disraeli* 278, BL 45779
11 Knutsford *Black and White* 218, D72/48, *The Times* 24/8/1903
12 D40/12, Lawrence Papers vol. 3/42
13 RA VIC T6/100, D87/20
14 ed. Ponsonby *Life* 72–3, Moore *Liberalism* 16–22, Hough *Edward* 156
15 Mallet *Northbrook* 107–11, Northbrook Papers *passim*
16 Northbrook Papers vol. 12/1/5/8 & vol. 11/1/12/60, Duthie *Pragmatic* 476, SR X 695, SR XI 228, SR IV 330
17 Lowe *Reluctant* I 78, Northbrook Papers C/144/12/50 & 11, vol. 11/1/20/40, Gopal *British Policy* 75
18 F1/ I, D40/15 & 59

Ten: Senior Plenipotentiary [pp 149–68]

1 D45/237, D72/43, SR XIV 643, SR XII 480
2 QR 111 201–38, ed. Vincent 339, D72/51
3 D72/52, Cecil, G II 91–3, Monypenny & Buckle *Disraeli* VI 87, D40/214
4 ed. Vincent 345, D72/57, D40/297, BL 49688/24–5
5 D72/73 & 61, Cecil, G II 177, 15th Derby Papers 17/2/7, HH Lady Salisbury's Constantinople Diary *passim*
6 Lady Gwendolen Cecil Papers Box 1, *Annual Register* 6/1/1880, D 72/75, Elliot *Revolutions* 291
7 ed. Zetland *Letters* II 95, D72/81, D 31/50, ed. Vincent 351
8 Gathorne-Hardy, A. *Cranbrook* I 381, Elliot *Revolutions* 296–8, Cecil, G II 110, 15th Derby Papers 16/2/7, D31/53, D72/84
9 Cecil of Chelwood Papers 51/1, D45/253, D31/55, Hardinge *Carnarvon* II 347,

FO 358/1, Lady Gwendolen Cecil Papers Box 1
  10 D72/90 & 86, Rockley Papers, ed. Vincent 356
  11 Cecil, G II 124, D73/101, D72/97
  12 Butler, E. *Cecils* 204, ed. Bahlman 70, *Punch* 20/1/1877, D72/106, D31/62 & 59, Lucy *Two Parliaments* 174, How *Salisbury* 120

Eleven: Cabinet Crises [pp 169–87]

  1 *The Times* 12/2/1877, ed. Johnson *Cranbrook* 305, ed. Zetland *Letters* II 105, Hardinge *Carnarvon* II 350
  2 D40/341 & 344, Cecil, G III 115
  3 D72/112, ed. Curtius *Hohenlohe* II 188, E/36, Cecil, G II 34
  4 RA VIC H 12/200, ed. Vincent 384, Cecil, G II 133, ed. Zetland *Letters* II 108, Cecil, Viscount *Way* 300
  5 D31/69, FO 358/2
  6 ed. Vincent 392–3, Hardinge *Carnarvon*: 1879 memorandum
  7 Hardinge *ibid.* II 357, ed. Vincent 410n, D40/410, 382, 388, Morier Papers 24A/2
  8 D40/444, 427, Hardinge *ibid.* II 359
  9 RA VIC B 52/11, ed. Vincent 422–3
  10 D40/476, D31/75
  11 Iddesleigh Papers 50019/53, D56/133, Hurst *Chamberlain* 41, ed. Vincent 463
  12 ed. Ramm *Correspondence* I 65, Lady Gwendolen Cecil Papers Box 2, ed. Johnson *Cranbrook* 347, Monypenny & Buckle *Disraeli* VI 210, D82/102, ed. Vincent 416, Cecil, A. *Secretaries* 293
  13 ed. Vincent 479–82, RA VIC B 54/49, ed. Johnson *ibid.* 347, *The Times* 3/1/1878, D31/80
  14 ed. Johnson *ibid.* 348, Hardinge *Carnarvon* 372–3, Smith, P. *Disraeli* 192, Powell, J. *Art* 184–5, Wellesley *Recollections* 144, Monypenny & Buckle *Disraeli* VI 219, ed. Vincent 490
  15 Hansard 237 c53, ed. Vincent 486–7
  16 Cecil, G II 191, BL 49688/24, ed. Vincent 488–90, Hardinge *Carnarvon* II 35–7
  17 ed. Vincent 493–4, D31/80, Cecil, G II 193
  18 ed. Vincent 517, 508, 503, D56/141
  19 BL 50063A/302, Cecil, G II 213, ed. Vincent 532–3, Monypenny & Buckle *Disraeli* VI 262, Lady Gwendolen Cecil Papers Box 2, BL 50063A/307

Twelve: The Congress of Berlin [pp 189–209]

  1 RA Add VIC A 36/804, Temperley & Penson *Foundations* 372–80, FO 244/314, Cecil, G II 232, ed. Buckle 2nd Series II 369
  2 D 87/51
  3 W.H. Smith Papers PS6/108, D87/67 & 75
  4 Cecil, G II 273, D 87/80 & 83
  5 How *Salisbury* 147–9, Cecil, A. *Secretaries* 299–300, SR XIV 590, ed. Howard, C. 'Cabinet Journal' 12, 16, 47, 19–20, *The Globe* 31/5/1878, D87/78
  6 BL 51228/21, Lowe *Reluctant* I 35, Gauld 'Anglo-Austrian' 108–12, ed. Howard, C. *ibid.* 16, 13, 9
  7 FO 28/2899/1, FO 78/2905, ed. Curtius *Hohenlohe* II 206–7, Medlicott *Congress* 44–6, ed. Howard, C. *ibid.* 22
  8 Russell, G. *Collections* 218, Medlicott *ibid.* 39, Lee *Cyprus* 88, Cecil, A. *Secretaries* 301
  9 Rayleigh 27/1/1902, Penson 'Principles' 87, Whitman *Bismarck* 252, ed. Brett *Esher* I 54

10 Lord Edward Cecil Papers Box 1, RA VIC A 49/1, ed. Zetland *Letters* I 190, RA VIC A 50/44

11 FO 78/290, Cecil, G II 201, Egremont *Balfour* 48, Monypenny & Buckle *Disraeli* VI 332, ed. Howard, C. 'Cabinet Journal' 27

12 Lee *Cyprus* 90–1, FO 364/3/5, *The Times* 24/8/1903, Tilley & Gaselee *Foreign* 139, Hansard 240 c1061, 1569–70, 1614

13 Medlicott *Congress* 52–3, FO 78/2899, Cecil, G II 283

14 FO 363/4/33, Cecil, G II 286, BL 50019/79, E1/36

15 FO 363/4/59 & 30, ed. Howard, C. 'Cabinet Journal' 18, FO 363/2

16 Cecil, G II 291–2, Lee *Cyprus* 102, FO 363/1/part 1

17 FO 27/2311, BL 50019/99, RA VIC J 86/154

18 Hansard 242 c378–9, Shannon *Disraeli* 304, Lee *Cyprus* 123, Traill *Salisbury* 178, SR XVI 718, *The Times* 18/10/1879

19 Lee *ibid.* 110, Seton-Watson 501, D42/145, ed. Howard, C. 'Cabinet Journal' 40, ed. Cartwright *Journals* 325, *The Times* 17/7/1878

20 Houghton Papers 22/107

21 Hansard 239 c833–4, Wilson, Harold *The Governance of Britain* 1976, 72

22 Cecil, G II 221, Hansard 241 c1787–1812, SR XIII 230, Russell, G. *Some* 52

23 Rockley Papers, ed. Johnson *Cranbrook* 380, ed. Ramm *Correspondence* I 72, *The Times* 24/8/1903, Lang *Northcote* II 108, Monypenny & Buckle *Disraeli* VI 246, 262

24 Cecil, G II 302–3

Thirteen: Lytton as Viceroy [pp 212–24]

1 D40/9 & 18, James, A. *Roberts* 78–9

2 D40/125, 83, 85, Mallet *Northbrook* 106–7

3 D40/28, 91, 110, 125, 149

4 D40/ 131, 102, 104, 301, 226, 291, 132, 217, 240, *Annual Register* 1/1/1877, Balfour, B. *Lytton* II 32

5 ed. Vincent 333, D 45/258, *The Times* archive at Texas Recip 11, D40/369

6 D29/56, D45/255, Cecil, G II 152–3, Hansard 234 c1564–6

7 D40/393, 422, 67, D72/122

8 D40/311, 303, 452, 495, 450, 476, *The Times* 12/10/1877

9 D40/548, 527, 536, ed. Vincent 443, 15th Derby Papers 920/17/2/7

10 D56/189, BL 50019/12, Lytton Papers E/218/5/57, D29/69

11 Gathorne-Hardy, A. *Cranbrook* II 102, Duthie 'Pragmatic' 475–95, Cowling 'Lytton' 79, Lowe *Reluctant* I 80, FO 65/1022

Fourteen: 'Beaconsfieldism' [pp 225–41]

1 BL 49688/24–5, Beach *Beach* I 23, 15th Derby Papers 920/12/3/2, Lawrence Papers F90/27/144

2 St Aldwyn Papers 2455/PCC/23/21 & 40, HP B/xx/Ce/112, Knutsford *Black* 225, ed. Johnson *Cranbrook* 399, D56/200

3 FO 633/2, D56/204, 200, 196, Shannon *Disraeli* 352, BL 51228/71

4 D87/112, D29/78, Lowe *Reluctant* I 33

5 D56/179, D84/128, W.H. Smith Papers PS 6/347, Lee *Cyprus* 159–61, FO 358/4, D87/119

6 ed. Ramm *Correspondence* I 99, HP XX/Ce/308, *The Times* 5/8/1879, D87/150, 144, W.H. Smith Papers PS6/385

7 D87/154, Cecil, D. *Cecils* 234, Medlicott *Congress* 43

8 HP 72/1/8, *The Times* 18/10/79, Monypenny & Buckle *Disraeli* VI 491, Medlicott *ibid.* 386–8

9 Dugdale, B. *Family* 43–4, Gladstone, Viscount *Thirty* 52 & 144, D87/161& 163

10 Cecil, G II 319, *The Times* 13/10/1881, Lee *Cyprus* 152,

11 Cecil, G II 377–8, ed. Zetland *Letters* II 260, *The Times* 28/1/1880, 20/2/1880, 23/2/1880, ed. Johnson *Cranbrook* 434–9 & 441

12 *The Times* 10/12/1879, ed. Howard, C. 'Cabinet Journal' 10/8/1878, BL 51228/161, Aldcroft *Economy* 4–5

13 I/36, HP 93/2/32, Howard 'Splendid' 82, Cecil, Viscount *Way* 20, ed. Zetland *Letters* II 264, Cecil, G II 280, Mitchell *Cross* 96, ed. Vincent 220

14 Richmond Papers 869/46, ed. Johnson *Cranbrook* 446–7, ed. Bahlman 116

Fifteen: The Dual Leadership [pp 242–61]

1 HP 93/2/46, Marsh *Discipline* 7, BL 50063A 28/4/80

2 Gathorne-Hardy, A. *Cranbrook* II 153, *The Times* 7/9/1880, ed. Bahlman 34

3 Monypenny & Buckle *Disraeli* VI 595, BL 50063A/327 & 366, Gorst *Fourth* 135, Shannon *Disraeli* 390, Southgate *Leadership* 101, BL 49688/33

4 Foster *Randolph* 75, Gorst *ibid.* 139–40, Chaplin Papers D3099/1/13/10

5 BL 49688/72, *The Times* 20/11/1880, D29/133

6 Schreuder *Scramble* 221–2 & 434, Hansard 277 c334–5 & 260 c314, ed. Johnson *Cranbrook* 472, *Daily Telegraph* 4/11/1998, ed. Bahlman 131

7 Cecil, G III 1–2, Balfour, F. *Ne* I 347, D81/652, Rayleigh 29/1/1889, HH 4M 387/6

8 *The Times* 12/10/1881, Chamberlain, A. *Down* 256, Lucy *Salisbury* 422–4, Huntly *Milestones* 151

9 C7/358, 303, Ribblesdale *Impressions* 172–3

10 Curzon *Modern* 34–6, Balfour, F. *Burleigh* 89–93, Lucy *Later* 325, Hamilton G. *Parliamentary* I 98

11 SR XV 584, V. Milner Papers 14/F63/39, Wolff *Rambling* II 266, James, R. *Churchill* 155n1

12 BL 49688/24, D87/167, Taylor *Essays* 119, Sichel *Disraeli* 326, Balfour, F. *Burleigh* 89–93

13 HP 93/2/16, Bigham *Prime* 308, Cecil, A. *Secretaries* 288, V. Milner Papers 14/F63/26

14 BL 50063A/374, Churchill, W. *Randolph* I 228, D56/227, Richmond Papers 870/9

15 Rockley Papers 30/11/1882, Dugdale, B. *Balfour* I 318, Hamilton, G. *Parliamentary* II 255, BL 50021/137–8, BL 50032/43–4, ed. Johnson *Cranbrook* 476

16 Morier Papers Box 11/5, *The Times* 31/5/1881, Burne Papers 951/12/125, ed. Bahlman 138–9

17 *The Times* 2/6/1881, Lowe *Reluctant* I 31

18 *The Times* 2/12/1881, HP B/xx/Ce/148, Curtis *Coercion* 9, *The Times* 27/10/1880

19 Hansard 264 c254–70, QR 151 536, D56/225 & 222, Rockley Papers 23/12/1880

20 ed. Powell, J. *Liberal* 156, Hardinge *Carnarvon* III 143, Ashbourne A1/1, ed. Johnson *Cranbrook* 480

21 ed. Bahlman 178, *The Times* 25/10/1881, 13/11/1881, 14/11/1881, BL 94688/54

Sixteen: Reaching the Nadir [pp 262–78]

1 BL 48632/27, *The Times* 21 & 23/3/1882, ed. Williams, R.H. *Salisbury–Balfour* xii, Cecil, G III 44

2 Richmond Papers 871/4, ed. Bahlman 251, *The Times* 13 & 14/4/1882

3 ed. Bailey, J. *Diary* 319, *Daily Telegraph* 12/3/1996, ed. Johnson *Cranbrook* 491

4 Chilston *Smith* 175, Cecil, G III 50, Hansard 271 c1579, Balfour, F. *Ne* 349

5 Robinson & Gallagher 123–5, Medlicott *Bismarck* 32–3

6 *The Times* 8/8/1882, D56/239 & 241

7 *The Times* 25/5/1882, Weston *Referendal* 102–7, Curtis *Coercion* 9, 31

8 Hansard 273 c1328–37, D56/236, Gathorne-Hardy, A. *Cranbrook* II 180

9 SR XIV 294, Churchill, W. *Randolph* I 229, *Punch* 19/8/1882, Cranbrook Papers A43/T501/298/337, D87/169

10 *The Times* 29 & 16/3/1883, ed. Johnson *Cranbrook* 514, D56/241

11 National Sound Archive, Rayleigh 7/2/1896, Churchill, W. *Randolph* I 281

12 *The Times* 29/3/1883, 2/4/1883, Churchill, W. *ibid.* I 245, FR May 1883 197

13 Richmond Papers 871/20, ed. Bahlman 474, D56/249

14 ed. Ramm *Correspondence* I 105, QR 156 559–95, Southgate *Leadership* 105, Marsh *Discipline* 11, Fforde *Conservatism* 43

15 SR XX 449, D56/234, 252, Primrose League Papers MSS 1/1, Pugh *Tories* 16

16 Robb, J. *Primrose* 40, 80, Pugh *ibid.* 27, 108, Wooff *Rambling* II 271, Fforde *Conservatism* 32

Seventeen: Opposition and Renewal [pp 279–94]

1 C7/232, V. Milner Papers 14/F67, *The Times* 31/10/1895, 1/12/1880, 23/11/1882, 28/11/1882, 14/6/1883, SR V 298

2 SR XIX 243, ed. Johnson *Cranbrook* 521n4, 4th Hansard 70 c1285, SR IX 107, *The Times* 23/10/1862

3 *The Times* 5/5/1891, 17/10/1882, FO 800/26/45, SR XVII 403, Otter *Woodard* 264, QR 117 283, HH Secretary's Notebook 609

4 D42/193, SR XIV 66, D70/156, FO 800/1/204, SR XI 392, SR XVIII 259

5 Cannadine *Decline* 450, SR XV, Selborne Papers 29/119, A/113, Marder *Naval* 77

6 Kunze 'Housing' 251, Wohl *Slum* 226, ed. Blake *Salisbury* 273, NR II no. 9 301–16

7 Chamberlain Papers 6/4i/12, Pullar *Harris* 75, BL 58779/87–9, *Daily News* 29/10/1883, *Pall Mall Gazette* 25/10/1883

8 Hansard 284 c1686–90, Wohl *Slum* 237, D29/151

9 Hansard 300 c648–53, Dilke Papers 43876/14 & 6, 43938/136–7, Kunze 'Housing' 255, Wohl *ibid.* 239, Butler *Cecils* 217

10 ed. Blake *Salisbury* 277 & n5, 281, 288, Dilke Papers 43937/200, *Standard* 6/12/1883, Metcalf *London* 147

11 Benson Papers 147/21–2, *The Times* 25/6/1890, E/56, RA VIC S 26/142 Knollys Memo. Feb. 1884, SR XIX 556, Morrah *Oxford* 237

12 *Nineteenth Century* 1906 207, Shannon *Disraeli* 2, Kennedy, J.M. *Tory Democracy* 1911 118

13 James, R. *Churchill* 142–3, Balfour, A. *Chapters* 159–60

14 ed. Johnson 535, ed. Bahlman 612, James *ibid.* 144–8, E1/180

15 Churchill, R. *Churchill* I 59, Cairns Papers XI, Bagenal *Tory* 94

16 Hansard 285 c1008–10, *The Times* 5/6/1884, 17/4/1884, 18/4/1884, 31/1/1884, 12/3/1884, Greaves *Persia* 63

Eighteen: Provoking Constitutional Crisis [pp 295–307]

1 BL 60899/4, Weston 'Mediation' 8, Hansard 290 c468–9, BQR I 29, Balfour, F. *Ne* II 421

2 ed. Russell, G. *MacColl* 92, ed. Bahlman 649 & 652, BL 60899/5, Crewe *Rosebery* I 206

3 BL 60899/7, ed. Bahlman 652–3

4 *The Times* 23 & 25/7/1884, Balfour, F. *Ne* I 409

5 D41/38, Austin Papers 24/7/1884

6 *The Times* 1/10/1884, D86/222, D85/186, ed. Bahlman 693, Cecil, G III 115

7 *The Times* 2 & 13/10/1884, Gardiner *Harcourt* I 500–1, Cecil, G III 116

8 Rayleigh 2/4/1900, D56/262, ed. Russell, G. *MacColl* 279

9 For the version of which I thank the late Rt Hon. J. Enoch Powell.

10 Balfour, F. *Ne* I 387, ed. Johnson *Cranbrook* 542, *The Times* 22/10/1884, SR XVI 509

11 Weston 'Mediation' 296, Fair 'Carnarvon' 97–116, BL 60899/61, Hardinge *Carnarvon* III 115–16, ed. Bahlman 715, BL 60899/64, Fair 'Royal' 100

12 ed. Russell, G. *MacColl* 102–11, D29/158, BL 60899/66, D66/42

13 Cecil of Chelwood Papers 53/1, ed. Bahlman 733, ed. Ramm *Correspondence* II 284–5, Hardinge *Carnarvon* III 118, Weston *Referendal* 296–322

14 Cecil of Chelwood Papers 53/5, ed. Ramm *ibid.* II 287, V. Milner Papers 14/F63/19, ed. Gordon, P. *Red* I 280

15 Jackson *Hartington* 177–8, Marsh *Chamberlain* 178–80, Lawrence & Elliot 'Elections' 18–28, Cecil, G III 122–4, ed. Johnson *Cranbrook* 545, BL 44488/150 & 164, Gathorne-Hardy, A. *Cranbrook* II 203, BL 43676/42–6, ed. Bahlman 741, BL 43876/23

16 Jackson, A. *Ulster* 27, James Papers M45/91, Cecil, E. *Apologia* 37–40

Nineteen: The Path to the Premiership [pp 308–20]

1 C7/116, Cecil, G III 98, Cromer *Egypt* I 589

2 eds Cooke, A. & Vincent, J. *Carlingford* 72, Hansard 294 c1311, *Punch* 26/2/1885

3 HH Secretary's Notebook 536, PRO 30/67/4/78, SR XIV 640, SR IX 279

4 Koss *Press* 329, C7/251, *The Times* archive PHL/2/262, D40/420, C7/107, Texas *The Times* archive Recip/11/93

5 Austin Papers 29/11/82, Koss *ibid.* I 12, Stead Papers 1/63, MacDonagh, M. *The Reporters' Gallery* 1920 418

6 Selborne Papers 5/29, D87/485, Koss *ibid.* 300 & 272, Austin Papers 15/6/84 & 28/2/1889, Austin *Autobiography* II 177

7 Lowe *Reluctant* I 88, *The Times* 22/4/1885 & 6/5/1885, ed. Bahlman 857

8 ed. Johnson *Cranbrook* 557, 530, BL 50064/15. For the version of which I thank Hubert Picarda QC.

9 SR XVII 367, SR XVI 142, QR 111 516–61, SR IX 348, Rosebery *Churchill* 145

10 ed. Ponsonby *Life* 72–3, Reid *Ask* 35, SR XVII 675, RA VIC H47/73

11 RA VIC B30/133, Cecil, G III 184, ed. Vincent 481

12 Bell Papers 227/214, ed. Bahlman 401, Longford *Victoria* 550

13 D29/165, D56/264, Curtis *Coercion* 28, *The Times* 19/3/1885, St Aldwyn Papers 2455/PCC/30

Twenty: 'Elijah's Mantle' [pp 321–37]

1 SR IX 201, Whibley *Manners* II 307, BL 50063A/424 & 422, Kimberley Papers C4263/84, Butler, E. *Cecils* 219, St Aldwyn Papers 2455/PCC/30, D87/172

2 Curtis *Coercion* 29, D82/109, BL 50063A/425, D56/265, Whibley *ibid.* II 308, Woolf *Rambling* II 271, Cecil, G III 135

3 E/180, D56/267, D87/172, ed. Bahlman 883, ed. Johnson *Cranbrook* 559, Lang *Northcote* II 212

4 D87/173, ed. Johnson *ibid.* 560–1, 50063A/426, Whibley *Manners* II 308

5 Gathorne-Hardy, A. *Cranbrook* II 215, Greaves *Persia* 32, Churchill, W. *Randolph* I 416, 421, Chilston *Whip* 45, E1/36, Rockley Papers, James, R. *Churchill* 182–3, ed. Bahlman 885, Rosebery *Churchill* 42, 69

6 ed. Bahlman 885–6, Butler *Cecils* 222, D87/177

7 Churchill, W. *Randolph* I 407, F1/QVI, D56/272, D87/178, D32/1

8 D87/180, Whibley *Manners* II 311, F1/QVI, ed. Bahlman 888

9 Churchill, W. *Randolph* I 395, Rosebery *Churchill* 13–14, E/180, Lang *Northcote* II 214, ed. Bahlman 889-90, F1/QVI

10 ed. Bahlman 893, ed. Johnson *Cranbrook* 563, D87/187, Whibley *Manners* II 313

11 Brown, B. *Tariff* 62, D22/159, Hamilton, G. *Parliamentary* I 276, Cooke, A. & Malcolmson *Ashbourne* xv

12 D31/106-7, Curtis *Coercion* 39, NR IV 721-40, Hardinge *Carnarvon* III 155, Cecil, G III 155

13 Cecil, G III 149, Hardinge *ibid.* III 156-9

14 ed. Wolfe, H. *Personalities* 135, Whibley *Manners* II 313, Selborne Papers 5/1, James, R. *Churchill* 189

15 Rose *Cecils* 46 & 50, McDonnell Papers D4091/A/3/1/2/10, BL 49690/92, Stead Papers 1/63

16 Ribblesdale *Impressions* 37, Jusserand *Befell* 109, SR XII 209, SR XVI 727

17 ed. Vincent 235, Cecil, G I 46, Dolman *Criticism passim*, ed. Williams, R.H. *Salisbury–Balfour* vii, Churchill, W. *Randolph* I 499

Twenty-one: The 'Caretaker' Ministry [pp 339–57]

1 D87/225, 202, 189, *Spectator* 27/6/1885

2 ed. Johnson *Cranbrook* 569, Lowe *Reluctant* I 75, D87/205

3 D85/194, James, R. *Churchill* 202

4 D87/222, 236, FO 364/1, Lowe *Reluctant* I 91

5 FO 51228/183, D57/2, D86/235

6 D56/279, D44/198, BL 51228/175, Interview with Lord Salisbury 5/2/1998, Hatfield Estate Newsletter, Nov.1996, Butler, E. *Cecils* 214, Cecil, G III 213-14

7 D56/277, RA VIC B 36/57, Gathorne-Hardy, A. *Cranbrook* II 286

8 D87/213, D31/112, D87/198

9 Marsh *Discipline* 103n29, Hansard 299 c1351-5, ed. Johnson *Cranbrook* 570

10 Cecil of Chelwood Papers 53/9, Curtis *Coercion* 43, D31/114, Hardinge *Carnarvon* III 173

11 Hansard 313 c104, O'Day *Parnell* 72, Curtis *ibid.* 44, ed. Cooke, A.B. *Ashbourne* xvi

12 D31/90, SR XIV 102, SR XII 444, Kee *Parnell* 477-8

13 E/180, Curtis *Coercion* 22, Hardinge *Carnarvon* III 151

14 Hardinge *ibid.* III 164-5, Rosebery *Churchill* 20-1, Hansard 298 c1658, O'Day *Parnell* 54, Curtis *ibid.* 23

15 Hardinge *ibid.* III 178-81, James, R. *Churchill* 208n2, Churchill, W. *Randolph* I 450

16 ed. Johnson *Cranbrook* 572, Ashbourne Papers B25/12, Kee *Parnell* 480, Curtis *Coercion* 52-3, Cecil, G III 157

17 Richmond Papers 871/45, ed. Ponsonby *Life* 199-200, D29/169, C7/195

18 D87/242 & 240, Lowe *Reluctant* I 99, Smith *White* 22-3, Hardinge *Europe* 82, SR XV 232

19 *Daily News* 26/9/85, Smith *ibid.* 21, BL 51228/201, BL 44178

20 D32/187, Lowe *Reluctant* I 100–1, D87/259 & 248, A39/140, D87/237, Medlicott 'Powers' 74–5, Smith *ibid.* 24–5, Cecil, G III 245, D54/58

21 Lowe *ibid.* I 102, D87/282, 265, Cecil, G III 248–50, D87/271, D87/250

22 D54/66, D87/283, Cecil, G III 254–5

23 *The Times* 8/10/1885, Curzon *Eloquence* 35, C7/207

24 ILN 17/10/1885, Curtis *Coercion* 59, Jackson, A. *Ulster* 37, Hardinge *Carnarvon* III 195, Healy *Letters* I 213 & 225, O'Brien, R. *Life of Parnell* 1898 II 104–5, O'Shea *Parnell* 25

Twenty-two: The 'Hawarden Kite' [pp 358–75]

1 *The Times* 5/11/1885, *Pall Mall Gazette* 3/11/1885, O'Connor *Old* II 21, Chilston *Whip* 175, Curtis *Coercion* 63

2 ed. 'B.B.' *Hatfield Letters* 2, Matthew, H.C.G. *Gladstone 1875–98* 148, Hardinge *Europe* 86, *The Times* 23/11/1885, C7/230, Hardinge *Carnarvon* III 197, *The Times* 28/11/1885

3 R. Churchill Papers RCHL/11186, Simon 'Disestablishment' 791–2

4 D31/144, D82/85, D87/287 & 285

5 D87/295, D31/150, D76/236, Curtis *Coercion* 68

6 BL 44769/256, *Annual Register* 1871 105–6, Jenkins, R. *Gladstone* 555, Cecil, G III 150, *The Times* 12/12/1885

7 ed. Russell, G. *MacColl* 126, O'Day *Parnell* 126, Hansard 208 c479, SR IX 215, SR XVI 569, Curtis *Coercion.* 67, Thorold *Labouchere* 244

8 BL 49692/7, Churchill, W. *Randolph* I 449

9 D82/115, HH Balfour Letters 2/60–1, D87/298, BL 49692/11, Cecil, G III 280

10 ed. Brett *Esher* I 119, Curtis *Coercion* 74, *The Times* 24/11/1885 & 30/11/1888, ed. Blake *Salisbury* 223, James, R. *Churchill* 229, Cecil, G III 180

11 Hardinge *Carnarvon* III 209–10, Curtis *ibid.* 75, D31/162, Churchill, W. *Randolph* I 525, Gopal *British Policy* 141, 15th Derby Papers 12/3/2

12 D87/310, Curzon Papers F112/371, D31/168

13 D31/177 & 175, D87/317, Ashbourne Papers A1/1, Lady Gwendolen Cecil Papers Box 2, D31/152, Curtis *Coercion* 48

14 Benson *Benson* II 107, D29/181, Chilston *Smith* 202, D87/318, ed. Howard, C. 'Osborne' 216, Hardinge *Carnarvon* III 219

15 D87/325 & 321, Churchill, W. *Randolph* II 37

16 D70/117, Viscount Harcourt Journal 26/1/1886, Rosebery *Churchill* 44, ed. Buckle 3rd Series I 19, ed. Johnson *Cranbrook* 593, Curzon Papers F112/371

17 ed. Buckle 3rd Series I 23–6, RA QVJ: 28/1/1886 insert, D87/333

18 Butler *Cecils* 226, Rayleigh 10/2/1901, ed. Brett *Esher* I 121

19 ed. Ramm *Correspondence* II 424, ed. Buckle 3rd Series I 34, RA VIC C37/203, D89/339

Twenty-three: Apotheosis [pp 376–93]

1 Chilston *Whip* 65, F1/QVI, Longford *Victoria* 609ff, ed. Howard, C. 'Osborne' 217, ed. Buckle 3rd Series I 45, ed. Johnson *Cranbrook* 596

2 James, R. *Churchill* 274, Askwith *James* 168, Bardon *Ulster* 376, ed. O'Day *Reactions* 340, Cooke, A. & Vincent, J. *Passion passim*

3 Churchill, R. *Churchill* I 72, R. Churchill Papers 1/12/1416a, Leach *Devonshire* 375, *The Times* 14/11/1881

4 RA VIC D44/6, D29/297, BL 49688/112, Cecil, G III 298

5 Longford *Victoria* 613, ed. Johnson *Cranbrook* 605, *The Times* 15/4/1886, F1/QVI, National Sound Archives, BL 46238/127

6 *The Times* 11/5/1886, F1/QVI, ed. Buckle 3rd Series I 117

7 Jenkins, R. *Gladstone* 553, 4 Hansard 37 c202, NR Nov. 1892, Jackson *Ulster* 117, *The Times* 17/5/1886

8 ed. Johnson *Cranbrook* 607, Smith, P. *Conscience* 236, Jenkins *ibid.* 555, Dugdale, B. *Balfour* I 102, Hansard 295 c649, Brabourne Papers U951/C174/7, D44/23 & 243

9 Hardinge *Carnarvon* III 247–8, 223–6, Chilston *Whip* 61, ed. Johnson *ibid.* 610, *The Times* 11/6/1886, Hansard 325 c1179, Churchill, W. *Randolph* I 447

10 Hamilton, G. *Parliamentary* I 163–4, Cooke & Vincent *Governing* 126, SR XVII 336, F1/QVI, Gladstone, Viscount *Thirty* 400, ed. Vincent 78

11 SR IX 178, V. Milner Papers 14/F63/1, SR XIX 329, Lubenow *Politics* 302–3, SR XV 326

12 D44/36, D31/182, *The Times* 19/6/1886, Hardinge *Carnarvon* III 226

13 HH Secretary's Notebook 569–70, E/Box 180, BL 49600/73

14 *The Times* 30/6/1886, D31/193 & 187, Brabourne Papers U95/C174/8

15 Green, E.H.H. *Crisis* 126, ed. Blake *Salisbury* 225, D87/350, ed. Matthew, H. *Diaries* XI 583, Jenkins R. *Gladstone* 556, Chilston *Whip* 84, ed. Ramm *Correspondence* II 458

16 St Aldwyn Papers 2455/PCC/69/25 & 27, 15th Derby Papers: 1886 diary, Jackson *Whigs* 242, James R. *Churchill* 249, Devonshire Papers 340.7019, ed. Buckle 3rd Series I 165

Twenty-four: Enduring Randolph [pp 394–406]

1 Churchill, R. *Churchill* I 77, ed. Johnson *Cranbrook* 817, ed. Blake *Salisbury* 229, ed. Buckle 3rd Series I 166, D79/21, D31/196, D29/204, O'Callaghan *High* 142

2 ed. Johnson *ibid.* 614–15, D66/45, ed. Buckle 3rd Series I 667

3 ed. Johnson *ibid.* 620–1, Rockley Papers 15/8/1886, D29/206, Austin Papers 14/8/1886, Balfour, F. *Ne* II 73, D29/207

4 Lowe *Reluctant* I 105–6, ed. Buckle 3rd Series I 201, D29/216, D87/363–70

5 FO 343/2, ed. Dugdale, E.T.S. *Documents* I 251–70, D29/222, ed. Rich *Holstein* II 300

6 Morier Papers 24/A/2, Churchill, W. *Randolph* II 159–62, ed. Dugdale, *ibid.* IV 866, ed. Buckle 3rd Series I 211

7 D87/401, ed. Buckle 3rd Series I 220, D87/399, James, R. *Churchill* 273, Rosebery *Churchill* 49–50

8 D87/421 & 414, ed. Rich *Holstein* II 370

9 Cecil, G III 325, James, R. 277, Lubenow *Parliamentary* 166, Rosebery *Churchill* 113, R. Churchill Papers RCHL 1991, O'Connor *Old* II 113–14

10 Rockley Papers 18/11/1886, *The Times* Archives PHL 2/259 & 85, BL 49688/129

11 D87/416, D29/234, 231

12 D29/237, Cecil, G III 326–7, IV 29

13 ed. Buckle 3rd Series I 229, R. Churchill Papers 9248/18/2163, Hamer *Army* 96, ed. Bahlman 50, Cornwallis-West *Reminiscences* 143

Twenty-five: Breaking Randolph [pp 407–22]

1 HH Churchill Letters 351, D29/245, Churchill, R. *Churchill* I 184, D70/119

2 SR XII 369, Hansard 204 c1364–5, Churchill, R. *ibid.* I 84, Hamilton, G. *Parliamentary* II 49–50, Rosebery *Churchill* 32, St Aldwyn Papers, 2455/PCC/69/42, Balfour, F. *Ne* II 76, Hamilton, G. *ibid.* II 49

3 Churchill Papers 9248/18/2194

4 HH Churchill Letters 355, Chilston *Smith* 225, Rosebery *Churchill* 54–7, Churchill, R. *Churchill* I 84, Halsbury Papers 56371/31

5 *The Times* 23/12/1886, Churchill, R. *ibid.* I 85, Koss *Press* 296, Cecil, G III 353–4, Rosebery *ibid.* 103

6 Mosley *Curzon* 36, ed. Gwynn *Spring-Rice* I 43, Cooke 'Ireland' 334, ed. Ellis *Thatched* 60–1

7 ed. Brett *Esher* I 129, Hamer *Army* 99, Lees-Milne *Enigmatic* 74, Asquith *Autobiography* I 62, Cecil, G III 325, Churchill, R. *Churchill* I 86, E1/37, Churchill, W. *Randolph* II 262, ed. Howard *Chamberlain* 235

8 Churchill Papers 9248/18/*passim*, Chilston *Whip* 100, Foster, R. *Churchill* chs 7 & 8, Devonshire Papers 340.2070, ed. Brett *Esher* I 129, ed. Howard *ibid.* 235

9 Stead Papers 1/63, Viscount Harcourt Journal 24/12/1886, Churchill Papers 9248/18/2196–7

10 ed. Brett *Esher* I 130, W.H. Smith Papers P59/205, *Morning Post* 25/12/1886, D29/245

11 BL 50073/113, Chilston *Whip* 99–102, Redesdale *Memoirs* II 685, D77/2, Esher Papers 1/3

12 *The Times* Archive PHL/2/261, Chilston Papers U/564/C/375/1a, Middleton Papers U/564/Cpl 8, D32/3, ed. Buckle 3rd Series I 236, Hurst *Chamberlain* 42–3, Gathorne-Hardy, A. *Cranbrook* II 280

13 D87/424, James, R. *Churchill* 310, ed. Colson *Goschen* 87, D77/7

14 E1/37, Gathorne-Hardy, A. *Cranbrook* II 271, D29/251, Balfour, F. *Ne* II 76, D87/426, Devonshire Papers 340.2078, Middleton Papers U/564/Cpl 8

15 Balfour, F. *ibid.* II 296, Devonshire Papers 340.2083, E1/37, D9/183, D87/428, ed. Buckle 3rd Series I 247

16 James, R. *Churchill* 311

Twenty-six: Reconstruction at Home and Abroad [pp 425–41]

1 Austin Papers 4/1/1887, *Standard* 4/1/1887, D56/283, ed. Buckle 3rd Series I 252, Lambeth Palace Papers 1870/5, Koss *Press* 302

2 D56/289, 288, 430, 285–7, Austin Papers 5/1/1887, Balfour, F. *Ne* II 79, Cooke 'Ireland' 335, Hardinge *Carnarvon* II 339–44, Monypenny & Buckle *Disraeli* VI 70–2, D40/234, D45/247, Cecil, G II 83, D31/44, Marsh 'Ottoman' 67, D40/203, D55/112

3 R. Churchill Papers 9248/19/2335, Gathorne-Hardy, A. *Cranbrook* II 275, D56/293, Lang *Northcote* II 282, D56/292, Devonshire Papers 340.2097, Crewe *Rosebery* I 297

4 Lang *ibid.* I xxi, D56/293, Lucy *Eight* 194

5 *The Times* 19/1/1887, A46/10, D87/437

6 Churchill, P. *Jennie* 161, R. Churchill Papers 9248/19/2330, Onslow Papers 173/28/4, D87/469, Hardinge *Carnarvon* III 235

7 James, R. *Churchill* 311, ed. Buckle 3rd Series I 383, PRO WO 110/8

8 V. Milner Papers VM8/F2/2/16, Chamberlain Papers 11/30/10, D87/568

9 Rockley Papers 8/1/1887, ed. Buckle 3rd Series I 255

10 D87/445–54, Lowe *Reluctant* I 94, ed. Buckle 3rd Series I 265, FO 364/1

11 Howard 'Splendid' 50–1, Crowe *Crowe* 83, Grenville, J.A.S. *Salisbury* 12, Cecil, G IV 19, Morier Papers Box 32/2, Taylor *Mastery* 314

12 ed. Buckle 3rd Series I 271, D87/440, Lowe *Reluctant* I 94–7 & 109, D32/188, D67/458

13 Taylor *Bismarck* 176, BL 51229/10, D87/463

14 Hansard 313 c38, D87/475

15 D87/443, ed. Buckle 3rd Series I 295, D44/201, D32/190, Smith *White* 68

16 Austin Papers 7/3/1888, Lady Gwendolen Cecil Papers: diary 6/3/1888, D57/7, Lowe *Reluctant* I 116–17, C7/391–4, O'Conor Papers 5/5/2, FO 364/1, Cecil, G IV 65, D87/531 & 509, D84/163, Austin Papers 8/3/1887, FO 800/1/63

17 D86/249, D87/464

18 Cecil, A. *Secretaries* 353–4, Stanhope Papers U/1590/6308, Cecil, G IV 55–62, SR XVIII 407, QR 107 529, QR 111 116–61, HH Austin Letters 281, *Standard* 4/2/1887

19 D29/277, D32/191, Cecil, G IV 47, 43, 44, D86/252

20 ed. Blake *Salisbury* 225 & 278, Thompson, F.M.L. *Landed* 307, HH 4th Marquess Papers 387/10, *The Times* 7/5/1888, Offer *Property* 157, HH 3M Personal Account books, D78/18, E/2, D70/187, Smith *White* 74, Marlowe *Cromer* 120, Curzon Papers F111/162/259

Twenty-seven: 'Bloody Balfour' [pp 442–58]

1 E/Box 180, ed. Buckle 3rd Series I 9, D87/437, SR XV 646, O'Callaghan *High* 100, QR 133 588–93, Curtis *Coercion* vii

2 Gerald Balfour Papers D 433/2/28/4, ed. 'B.B.' *Hatfield Letters* 79, Curtis *ibid.* 175, ed. Williams, H.R. *Salisbury–Balfour* vii–xxiv, Young, K. *Balfour* 105, SR XI 527, Cecil, G III 47

3 Cooke 'Ireland' 337, Churchill, W. *Contemporaries* 194, Stewart *Carson* 1

4 Rayleigh March 1887 *passim*, *The Times* 7/3/1887, Jackson, A. *Saunderson* 104, Ashbourne 'Journal' A1/1

5 Curtis *Coercion* 179, D29/284, *The Times* 18 & 21/4/1887, Koss *Press* 297, Churchill, W. *Contemporaries* 290, Shannon *Balfour* 37

6 C7/373–9, D87/501–7

7 Cecil, G. *Biographical* 91–2, BL 49822/49–50, D87/524, ed. Johnson *Cranbrook* 677, Marsh *Chamberlain* 276–7, McDowell *Conservatism* 116, Jackson, A. *Ulster* 133, Hansard 315 c1674

8 ed. Johnson *ibid.* 680–1, Curtis *Coercion* 185, D87/533

9 BL 49688/147, Selborne Papers 5/3, Rayleigh 20/5/1924, Dugdale *Balfour* I 147

10 *The Times* 19/10/1887, BL 49688/149

11 Rayleigh 3/5/1888, Marsden *Tunis* 257, D79/28, ed. Johnson *Cranbrook* 694, Atlay *Acland* 452, Chilston *Whip* 61, BL 49688/155

12 BL 49689/31, ed. Williams, R.H. *Salisbury–Balfour* xi, ed. O'Day *Reactions* 352, HH 5M Appreciation of Balfour, HH Llandaff Letters 205, Egremont *Balfour* 93

13 ed. Russell, G. *MacColl* 137, BL 49689/42

14 HH Cabinet Prints Box 1, PRO 30/60/13/1

15 Butler, E. *Autobiography* 199, Jackson *Saunderson* 109

16 ed. Buckle 3rd Series I 431–2, O'Callaghan *Franchise* 95, ed. O'Day *Reactions* 102–24

17 Egremont *Balfour* 91, BL 49689, Davies, A.J. *We* 234, Koss I 312

18 ed. Buckle 3rd Series I 498, Kee *Parnell* 528, *The Graphic* 11/3/1889

19 *The Times* 12/10/1877, Hansard 342 c1357–69, ed. Johnson *Cranbrook* 757, O'Callaghan *High* 99–100, Rayleigh 15/2/90, D70/196, Crewe *Rosebery* II 358, Hammond *Gladstone* 594

20 Bew *Conflict* 2n, Maume 'Parnell' 363–70, *An Phlobacht* 8/3/1930

21 ed. Brett *Esher* I 146, Hammond *Gladstone* 631, Cecil, G III 398, 'B.B.' *Hatfield Letters* 36

22 Churchill, W. *Contemporaries* 294, *The Times* 4/12/1890, Devonshire Papers 340.2260

Twenty-eight: 'The Genie of Imperialism' [pp 459–77]

1 *The Times* 18/5/1887, D87/513

2 ed. Buckle 3rd Series I 280, ed. Johnson *Cranbrook* 659, D87/478, Lant *Insubstantial* 40, Benson Papers 48/4, Kuhn 'Jubilees' 111, Pinto-Duschinsky *Political* 96

3 *Reynolds News* 12/6/1887, Richmond Papers 873/5, ed. Johnson *ibid.* 666, Lant *ibid.* 49, D70/129

4 14th Derby Papers 920/163/7, SR XVIII 320, *Daily News* 20/6/1887, Maclean *Recollections* 126

5 ed. Buckle 3rd Series I 327–30, Stirling, A.M.W. *The Richmond Papers* 1976 53, ed. Collier *Monkswell* I 136, ed. Johnson *Cranbrook* 671, Hudson *Jubilee* 16, D87/511, Devonshire Papers 340.2138, Chilston Papers U564/C18/21

6 Stanhope Papers U1590/O/308, *The Times* 31/5/1886, Grenville *Foreign* 20, D48/299

7 Knutsford *Black* 217, 15th Derby Papers 920/1881 diary, Brown *Tariff* 97, D32/77, Blakeley *Colonial* 158n

8 D32/27, 35, 19, 16, 28, 15

9 D84/168, Smith *White* 76–7, Aydelotte *Bismarck* 21, D32/70

10 D44/207, D84/175, Cecil, G IV 80, D87/562, D84/173, D29/276

11 D41/49, Lowe *Reluctant* I 118–19, Eyck *Bismarck* 297, Cecil, G IV 73

12 ed. MacKenzie *Webb* I 150, ed. Johnson *Cranbrook* 687, ed. Buckle 3rd Series I 359, Austin Papers 2/12/1887

13 Marsh *Discipline* 167–8, Nevill *Five* 245–6, D70/194, D87/703, Benson Papers 54/432, HH Lady Gwendolen Cecil Papers: diary 16/3/1888, C7/353, Smith, P. *Conscience* 237

14 Marsh *ibid.* 160, ed. Johnson *Cranbrook* 673–4, HH Cabinet Prints Box 1, C76/299, BL 49688/82

15 ed. Cowling *Conservative* 29, SR XIII 637, SR X 586, *Lincoln, Rutland and Stamford Mercury* 26/8/1853, Morrah *Oxford* 128–37

16 D85/186, *Bradford Observer* 13/10/1881, ed. Johnson *Cranbrook* 482, ed. Bahlman 151, Marsh *Discipline* 27, D29/142

17 *The Times* 6/8/1885, Brown *Tariff* 63–79, *The Times* 24/11/1887, ed. Seldon *Tory* 232, C7/382

Twenty-nine: Rumours of Wars [pp 478–97]

1 D32/42, HH Lady Gwendolen Cecil Papers: diary 13/2/1888, D87/590, Onslow Papers 173/28/6, D70/135

2 HH Lady Gwendolen Cecil Papers: diary 2/3/1888 & 24/2/1888, D70/137, ed. Matthew *Diaries* XII 98, Hansard 322 c113–18, ed. Johnson *Cranbrook* 692, Lyall *Dufferin* II 192

3 McDonnell Papers D/4091/A/3/1/3/11, Koss *Press* 456, D42/54, D70/142, HH Lady Gwendolen Cecil Papers: diary 15/3/1888

4 D81/586, HH Lady Gwendolen Cecil Papers: diary 15/2/1888, D87/581 & 512

5 A46/204, HH Lady Gwendolen Cecil Papers: diary 9/3/1888 & 15/3/1888, D44/203

6 D87/613, D44/204, D87/610 & 496

7 D86/256, 636, 619, 625

8 Magnus *Edward* 206–13, Morier Papers Box 16/1

9 RA VIC T9/110–11, FO 343/1/95, Magnus *ibid.* 207, Heffer *Power* 70

10 D57/11, ed. Buckle 3rd Series I 440–1, D87/706, D70/172

11 ed. Buckle 3rd Series I 521, Magnus *Edward* 210–13, RA VIC T9/158, Pakula *Uncommon* 515

12 *The Times* 11/4/1888, SR XVI 420, HH Lady Gwendolen Cecil Papers: diary 4/4/1888, Balfour, F. *Ne* II 180–5

13 Marsh *Chamberlain* 281–2, D87/535, Devonshire Papers 340.2669, ed. Russell, G. *MacColl* 282

14 D32/80–115, 16th Derby Papers 20/10, 20/4, 17/4, ed. Johnson *Cranbrook* 821, HH Cabinet Prints Boxes 1 & 2, Mowat *Pauncefote* 147–8, D87/782, ed. Buckle 3rd Series I 606/7, D58/16

15 Weston *Referendal* 4n54, SR XX 44, SR XVII 547, SR XII 113, SR XV 228, BQR January 1860, Wells, J. *The House of Lords* 1997 200–4, SR VII 190, Lady Gwendolen Cecil Papers: diary 28/3/1888 & 20/3/1888, D70/150, ed. Buckle 3rd Series I 394–5, D87/603, Hansard 323 c1561, Wynne *Irishman* 157, Cecil of Chelwood Papers 53/9, D45/243, ed. Cartwright *Journals* 260

16 ed. Buckle 3rd Series I 414, Hansard 326 c103–8, Johnson *Committee* 23, *The Times* 15/3/1888

17 HH Cabinet Prints Box 1 6/11/1888, 18/6/1888, 29/6/1888, 17/4/1888, Stanhope Papers U1590/D/308

Thirty: The Business of Government [pp 498–515]

1 D82/120, D86/254, Cecil, G IV 107, D44/206–7

2 SR XVI 489, SR VIII 616, SR III 197, C76/302

3 QR II 429, Dunbabin *County* 226, Lynd *1880s* 169–70, Lady Gwendolen Cecil Papers: diary 15/2/1888, Rayleigh 29/1/1889

4 Onslow Papers 173/7/71, Gibbon & Bell *London* 97n, Rayleigh 3/3/1897, *The Times* 8/11/1894, Fforde *Conservatism* 61, Cadogan Papers 514

5 Hansard 211 c89–90, Harrison *Drink* 336, SR XVII 709, *The Times* 22/6/1888, ed. Johnson *Cranbrook* 709

6 Gibbon & Bell *London* 245, Escott *Journalism* 236, Rose *Cecils* 319, Hansard 307 c185, D48/235, C7/118, ed. Vincent 168

7 A/46/85, Mowat *Pauncefote* 112–16, D87/646, Devonshire Papers 340.2721, ed. Bahlman 86, ed. Vincent 21/12/1888, *The Times* 21/12/1888, *Primrose League Gazette* 15/12/1888, C7/371, ed. Cartwright *Journals* 231

8 *The Times* 30/11/1888, ed. Jennings *Anecdotal History* 428, Milner *Picture* 85, Egremont *Balfour* 113, ed. Buckle 3rd Series I 288, SR XIX 251, SR XIX 758, SR XVIII 111, SR XVI 726, SR IV 238

9 *The Times* 21/12/1888, Masani *Dadabhai* 265–7, Lucy *Eight* 114–15, *The Times* 1/12/1888

10 Southgate *Leadership* 134, RA VIC A78/78, ed. Buckle 3rd Series I 616, 447–9, 15th Derby Papers 16/2/7, D87/752, D87/648, F1/QV II, *The Times* 1/12/1888

11 FO 800/146/279, BL 51264, Cecil, G IV 194–6

12 Penson *Methods* 93, Stanhope Papers U1590/O/308, A46/42, FO 800/26, Crowe, S. *Crowe* 83, Chirol *Fifty* 291

13 BL 63013/83 & 201, Offer *Property* 22 & 17, Dufferin Papers D1071/B/C/250/35, FO 60/513, ed. Rich *Holstein* II 302, BL 38937/84, Penson *ibid.* 91, E1/27, Steiner 'Last' 59, ed. Johnson *Cranbrook* 658, Lowe *Reluctant* I 12

14 ed. Buckle 3rd Series III 25, Cecil, G II 233, IV 282, III 202, Steiner *Foreign* 9, W.H. Smith Papers 19/41, ed. Wilson *British* 120–1

15 PRO 30/33/16/1, FO 800/2/116, Hart, N. *Foreign* 91, Taylor *Mastery* 357, PRO 30/67/5/80, 4th Hansard 53 c43–4

16 Malcolm *Vacant* 7, Hardinge *Europe* 87, St Aldwyn Papers PCC/69, Gilmour *Curzon* 125, Cecil, G III 210–18, FO 800/2/5, Tilley & Gaselee 140–1, ed. Collier *Monkswell* II 22

17 Rose *Cecils* 51, ed. Howard, C. *Goschen* 9 & 18, D87/638, Midleton *Records* 106, Mowat *Pauncefote* 59–61, Tilley & Gaselee *ibid.* 140–1, Wynne *Irishman* 175, RA VIC A 67/5a

18 Hardinge *Europe* 81–2, Cecil, G III 207–16, Steiner *Foreign* 217, Bigham *Prime* 307, Johnston, H. *Story* 217, Hardinge *Diplomacy* 68

19 Crowe, *Crowe* 84–7, Nicolson *Diplomacy* 194, PRO 30/33/15/14

Thirty-one: Africa [pp 517–35]

1 TLS 28/10/1926 & 3/12/1931, Gooch, G.P. *Recent Revelations of European Diplomacy* 1940 355, Lowe, C.J. *Foreign* 23, Cecil, G V 233 & IV 254

2 Johnston, H. *Gay-Dombeys* 169–92, *The Times* 22/8/1888, ed. Wilson, K. *British* 130, Judd *Empire* 102, Blake *Rhodesia* 78

3 ed. Johnson *Cranbrook* 752, D87/696 & 687, D66/47, *Sunday Telegraph* 12/2/1995

4 D87/722–3, ed. Buckle 3rd Series I 538 & 556–7, Gathorne-Hardy, A. *Cranbrook* II 328, D29/340

5 BL 63013/26, Morier Papers 24/B/5, D60/19 & 20, D87/770 & 726, Blake *Rhodesia* 80

6 ed. Buckle 3rd Series I 459, D87/660, Jeal *Livingstone* 379–87, Hansard 352 c1129-30

7 D32/82, Oliver *Johnston* 139, D44/213, D61/22

8 ed. Johnson *Cranbrook* 764, Sanderson *Nile passim*, Gillard *African passim*, Taylor *Mastery* 330, ed. Dugdale E.T.S. *Documents* II 31–2, Rayleigh 4/9/1910, D81/735, Ponsonby, F. *Empress* 393

9 HH Cabinet prints Box 1, Cecil, G IV 284–5

10 *The Times* 24/8/1903, A46/104, D87/747, A45/928, ed. Buckle 3rd Series I 612–15

11 Gathorne-Hardy, A. *Cranbrook* II 318, ed. Johnson *Cranbrook* 775, D60/25, Crewe *Rosebery* II 359

12 St Aldwyn Papers 2455/PCC/69/117, D61/29, Portal Papers 5113/87

13 D83/126, Cross *Political* 160, 16th Derby Papers 20/5, Cecil, G IV 255 & 318, D87/762

14 Cromer *Egypt* II 75–7n, Zetland *Cromer* 139, A45/50–5, FO 633/56, Marlowe *Cromer* 108, ed. Johnson *Cranbrook* 745

15 Rhodes Papers Afr. 6/1, Marlowe *ibid.* 89, C7/436, *The Times* 27/8/1888

16 D87/787, Blake *Rhodesia* 41, 53 & 74–5, ed. Johnson *Cranbrook* 727

Thirty-two: Mid-Term Crises [pp 536–53]

1 Palmer *Twilight* 265, Geiss *German* 58, W.H. Smith Papers PS 14/11

2 D48/312, Cecil, G IV 124, D87/672, D44/209

3 Marsh *Chamberlain* 315, D70/183, D86/256, D87/680

4 D70/189 & 697, Rutland Papers 6/4/1896, ed. Buckle 3rd Series I 509 & 384, D70/186, ed. Johnson *Cranbrook* xxxvi & 738–9, D70/176, D87/592

5 ed. Buckle 3rd Series I 617 & 337, A46/176, D87/560, ed. Johnson *ibid.* 675

6 Searle *Corruption* 44–6, Marder *Naval* 27, *Birmingham Post* 26/5/1888, FO 800/25/195, *Star* July 1889 *passim*, D87/686, D40/5 & 4, D32/41

7 SR XVI 54, SR XI 78, FP XIV 103, SR IX 312

8 ed. Nevill *Reminiscences* 299, Cornwallis-West *Reminiscences* 214, Wolff *Rambling* 355ff, Hare *Solitary* 229, Warwick, Earl of *Memoirs* 107, Warwick, F. *Ebb* 181, Rose *Cecils* 52, Lucy *Wilderness* 171, ed. Johnson *Cranbrook* 740, Cecil, G IV 142, A45/91

9 D86/256, *The Times* 27/11/1889, D87/715, D87/670, BL 49689/142, Hamilton, G. *Parliamentary* II 106–7, D87/658, Marder *Naval* 123 & 143, HH Cabinet Prints Box 4, Hansard 333 c1171

10 D80/52, D70/195, ed. Johnson *Cranbrook* 753–8

11 Hyde, H.M. *Cleveland* 231, Pearson *Labouchere* 214, ed. Johnson *ibid.* 759n3, Hansard 341 c1534–72, *Truth* 2/1/1890, PRO DPP 1/95/1

12 Hansard 341 c1618–19

13 D29/353, Rayleigh 21/6/1890, C7/466, ed. Buckle 3rd Series I 573–4, D70/199, Marsh *Discipline* 174

14 D87/757, ed. Johnson *Cranbrook* 774, ed. Buckle 3rd Series I 618–19

15 BL 49689/89, Gooch *Courtney* 289, ed. Buckle 3rd Series I 490, D70/207–8

16 BL 49689/166 & 93, ed. Bahlman 173, D87/763, Cadogan Papers RC/55, Young *Balfour* 123–4, Devonshire Papers 340.2245

17 Spinner *Goschen* 147–9, ed. Bahlman 127, 134–5, Ferguson *Banker* 866–70, Ziegler *Barings* 249, D70/260, Davis *Mammon* 264

Thirty-three: Alliance Politics [pp 554–70]

1 Dufferin Papers D1071/H/NI/1, D87/793 & 801

2 16th Derby Papers 20/7, Hamilton, G. *Parliamentary* II 137, Cecil, G IV 368, D70/210, ed. Johnson *Cranbrook* 804, Smith *White* 153, ed. Buckle 3rd Series II 64–5

3 Austin *Autobiography* II 214–15, Marsh *Chamberlain* 331, 16th Derby Papers 20/7

4 Sutherland *Education* 284–5, Lady Gwendolen Cecil Papers: diary 13/2/1888, ed. Johnson *Cranbrook* 735, D29/289, Marsh *Discipline* 169

5 D70/159, ed. Howard *Chamberlain* 288, D29/335, Sutherland *ibid.* 287

6 HH Salisbury to Goschen 7/6/1891, ed. Johnson *Cranbrook* 800–1, 805, 781, 793, D87/798, HH Cabinet Prints Box 1

7 Devonshire Papers 340.2387, Plumptre *Edward* 116, Cadogan Papers RC/65

8 E1/19, Hough *Edward* 177, D87/580, Magnus *Edward* 232–7

9 Ullswater *Commentaries* I 219, Chilston Papers U564/C24/17,

10 Hamilton, G. *Parlimentary* II 253 & I 81, Newton *Lansdowne* 456–7, Richmond Papers 873/39, ed. Buckle 3rd Series II 49–50, ed. Johnson *Cranbrook* 810

11 BL 49689/14, ed. Buckle 3rd Series II 76, Cecil, G V 219, D87/821, Egremont *Balfour* 101

12 RA VIC B44/89, Marsh *Discipline* 214, BL 49689/143, Chilston *Whip* 225, *Standard* 16/10/1891

13 *The Times* 10/11/1891, ed. Buckle 3rd Series II 78

14 *Birmingham Daily Gazette* 18/9/1896, ed. Johnson *Cranbrook* 583, Marsh *Discipline* 189–93, Hanham *Elections* 358, Cecil, G III 197, Baumann *Victorians* 65, SR XVII 212, Sandars *Studies* 161 & 167

15 ed. Smart, N. *Robert Bernays' Diary* 1998 211, Chilston *Whip* 35, Mackenzie *Political* 266–7, *The Times* 20/3/1896

16 Hardinge *Europe* 78–83, Chilston Papers U564/C19/5, Chilston *ibid.* 95, Coetzee 'Villa' 29–47

17 ed. Brett *Esher* I 125, Davis *Unionist* 105, Hurst *Chamberlain* 361 & 366

18 Hurst *ibid.* 362, Rockley Papers 18/4/1887, ed. Buckle 3rd Series I 172, Gathorne-Hardy, A. *Cranbrook* 285, D87/523

19 Devonshire Papers 340.2261 & 2459, James Papers M45/437, BL 49689/38, D70/171, ed. Blake *Salisbury* 232

20 ed. Howard, C. *Chamberlain* 277, Chilston *Whip* 230, Southgate *Leadership* 132, ed. Johnson *Cranbrook.* 802, Devonshire Papers 340.2272

Thirty-four: Leaving Office [pp 571–83]

1 BL 49690, ed. Johnson *Cranbrook* 816, D61/26, Lucy *Wilderness* 377, HH Hatfield Letters 8/11/1891

2 Rayleigh 19/3/1892, Hamer *Army* 74–5, *The Times* 3/2/1892

3 Cecil, G III 176, Crewe *Rosebery* 390, Butler, R.A. *The Conservatives* 1977 215, How *Salisbury* 192, ed. Blake *Salisbury* 284

4 HH Secretary's Notebook 533, Chilston *Whip* 241, ed. Hamer *Rendel* 100, Brown, B. *Tariff* 79–80, Langer *Diplomacy* 79

5 D87/858, Austin Papers 13/7/1892, Garvin *Chamberlain* II 538–9, BL 49690/1, Chilston *Whip* 242, Green *Crisis* 5

6 Cecil, G IV 401–2, James, R. *Rosebery* 231, ed. Seldon *Fall* 218, *The Times* 31/5/1892, Southgate *Leadership* 131, ed. Johnson *Cranbrook* 824, Balfour, F. *Ne* II 215

7 ed. Bahlman 333, ed. Ramm *Correspondence* I 406–13, BL 49690/22, D70/211, ed. Williams, R.H. *Salisbury–Balfour* 460–3, *Spectator* 2/7/1892, *The Times* 28/6/1892, ed. Johnson *ibid.* 827, Carter *Office* 82, HH Secretary's Notebook 537–8

8 HH 4M 387/12, HH Hatfield Letters 11/7/1892, Balfour, F. *Ne* II 207, Lutyens *Blessed* 134–40, SR XVI 727, Longford *Victoria* 518

9 ed. Buckle 3rd Series III 134, BL 49690/65 & 55

10 Asquith, Earl of *Memoirs* I 119, Bryce *Studies* 456, HH Secretary's Notebook 576, 583, 579, ed. Matthew *Diaries* XIII 57, C7/475

11 ed. Bahlman 169, Gardiner *Harcourt* II 185, ed. Hutchinson, H. *West* 52, ed. Johnson *Cranbrook* 833, SR XVI 270, Grigg *Lloyd George* 130n3, D87/865 & 863, ed. Buckle 3rd Series II 126, D55/121

12 McDonnell Papers D4091/A/3/1/1/8, Marsh *Discipline* 220, D32/140, Devonshire Papers 304.2969, ed. Bahlman 173, James, R. *Rosebery* 255, ed. Ponsonby, H. *Life* 276, D44/218

13 Marsh *Discipline* 145, Ashbourne Papers A/1/1, HH Lady Gwendolen Cecil Papers: diary 20/2/1888, Robinson & Gallagher *Africa* 260, BL 50063A/437, ed. Buckle 3rd Series I 45, Cecil, G III 169–70 & II 237, Beach *Beach* II 360

Thirty-five: Opposition [pp 584–600]

1 HH Secretary's Notebook 595, NR XX 289–300, HH Hatfield Letters 77

2 Garvin *Chamberlain* II 577, Cecil, G V 4, *The Times* 27/5/1893, BL 51075, Cranbrook Papers HA43/T501/263, BL 49690/70 & 68

3 Cecil, G V 4, Balfour, F. *Ne* II 124

4 ed. Johnson *Cranbrook* 29/7/1893, *The Times* 22/8/1893, 8/7/1893, Rayleigh 18/5/1893, Jenkins, R. *Gladstone* 604

5 Lucy *Home Rule* 249, Weston *Referendal* 118, Benson *Benson* II 539, Lucy *Peeps* 276, Balfour, F. *Ne* II 55

6 Cecil, G V 9, Devonshire Papers 340.2532 & 2539, ed. Blake *Salisbury* 241, Marsh *Discipline* 232, Marsh *Chamberlain* 352–3, McDonnell Papers D40–91/A/3/1/2/4 & 8, Rayleigh 6/3/1894

7 Baumann *Victorian* 79, ed. Buckle 3rd Series II 369, Longford *Victoria* 665, ed. Matthew *Diaries* XIII 438 & 43

8 Wilson *C-B* 238, ed. Matthew *ibid.* XIII 196, Crewe *Rosebery* II 431–2

9 ed. Buckle 3rd Series II 376, Taylor *Essays* 115, Crewe *ibid.* 444, C51/15

10 4th Hansard 27 c1222–9, Cecil, G V 11–15, Marsh *Discipline* 232–3, Lady Gwendolen Cecil Papers: diary 4/4/1888, Weston *Referendal* 147, ed. Vincent 286, Lytton Papers E/218/5

11 SR XIX 467, SR XVIII 386, SR XIII 503, SR XI 506

12 Desmond *Huxley* 223–5 & 315n25, *The Times* 24/8/1903, ed. Huxley, L. *Huxley* II 376–7, Cecil, G V 22, How *Salisbury* 218, Rayleigh 9/8/1894, 'B.B.' *Hatfield Letters* 29 & 17, *The Times* 25/2/1891, C7/4/6

13 ed. Buckle 3rd Series II 443–8, Rutland Papers 23/9/1894

14 Chamberlain Papers JC/11/30/13 & 18, JC/5/67/22–3, Marsh *Chamberlain* 357 & 236, ed. Boyce *Power* 20–2, *The Times* 31/10/1894, Cecil, G V 19

15 Cecil, G III 300–2, Balfour, F. *Ne* II 149, Sandars Papers C723/172, Selborne Papers 5/25, Marsh *Discipline* 238, Chelwood Papers 58/43, Chilston Papers U564/C18/37

16 BL 49690/105, Chilston Papers U564/C18/42, Chilston *Whip* 266, ed. Boyce *Power* 24–6, Marsh *ibid.* 239

17 RA VIC C40/20, Chamberlain Papers 5/67/26, Cecil, G V 57 & 75–6

18 NR CIII 796–801, Chamberlain Papers JC 6/6/D/2, Selborne Papers 1894 191–3

19 ed. Buckle 3rd Series II 526, Cecil, G V 30, Chamberlain Papers 6/6/10/3, ed. Bahlman 303

Thirty-six: Problems with Non-Alignment [pp 601–18]

1 *The Times* 29/6/1895, ed. Bahlman 303, PRO 30/6/3/1, RA VIC C 40/85–6, Rayleigh 26/6/1895, Lambeth Palace MS 2851/86, Wilson *C-B* 211

2 Butler, R.A. *The Conservatives* 1977 83, Asquith, Earl of *Fifty* I 273, Hamilton, G. *Parliamentary* II 251, Ashbourne Papers B131/27, Cecil, G V 34, Benson Papers 2851/92, ed. Bahlman *ibid.* 304, RA VIC C 40/20, Rayleigh 29/6/1895, PRO 30/67/3/46, Devonshire Papers 340.2626

3 Selborne Papers 5/31, Cecil of Chelwood Papers 51/38–49, Conservative Central Office *Guide* 1895 114–24, Weston *Referendal* 135

4 FO 800/1/36, Devonshire Papers 340.2243, Benson Papers: diary 28/6/1889, BL 44508/233, Cecil, G V 73

5 Salt *Eastern* 90, Cecil, G V 78–82 & 62, Marsh *Ottoman* 73–83, HH Cabinet Prints Box 2, D84/185

6 Lowe *Mediterranean* 91, Marder *Naval* 242–6, Cecil, G V 79–86

7 BL 49690/133, Cecil, G V 93, *The Times* 24/8/1903, Chamberlain Papers 11/30/25

8 *North Wales Observer* 21/1/1898, BL 800/9/32, Crewe *Rosebery* II 516, 4th Hansard 307 c55–8, ed. Buckle 3rd Series III 23, *The Times* 1/2/1896, Lowe *Mediterranean* 41, Greaves *Persia* 218, Chamberlain Papers JC 5/67/36, BL 49690/136, Cecil, G V 58

9 Stephenson *Talbot* 126–7, Cecil, G V 106, Devonshire Papers 340.2694, Mackintosh 'Committee' 492, BL 44503/229, Southgate *Leadership* 137, ed. Buckle 3rd Series I 582, BL 49690/119, Devonshire Papers 340.2657, Grenville, J.A.S.

Salisbury 18, PRO CAB 37/40/64, Lowe *Reluctant* I 7, Hamer *Army* 164, Dugdale, B. *Balfour* 365, Judd *Empire* 148–9

10 RA QV E63/35, Chirol *Fifty* 288–93, Grenville *ibid.* 40–2, Cecil, G V 68–72, Eckardstein *Ten* 57–9

11 RA VIC I 60/119, Rose *Cecils* 44, FO 800/1/150, Chilston *Whip* 211, ed. Buckle 3rd Series II 548, ed. Johnson *Cranbrook* 797, Chilston Papers U564/C18/33, ed. Buckle 3rd Series II 363, Balfour, F. *Ne* II 272

12 Butler, E. *Autobiography* 262, ILN 22/8/1896, Nicolson *Mary* 173

13 McElroy *Cleveland* II 178–88, Cecil, G V 112–14, D87/538, Mowat *Pauncefoote* 178–82

14 St Aldwyn Papers 2455/PCC/111, McElroy *ibid.* II 189ff, ed. Boyce *Power* 28n, Cecil, G V 117–18

Thirty-seven: 'Splendid Isolation' [pp 619–33]

1 Pakenham *Boer* 26–8, Garvin *Chamberlain* III 78, Van der Poel *Jameson* 79, Chamberlain Papers 5/67/4 & 40, Judd *Empire* 160, 4th Hansard 30 c701

2 *The Times* 1/1/1896, Blake 'Jameson' 328–37, Chamberlain Papers 5/67/35, Cecil, G V 140, Van der Poel 82

3 Chamberlain Papers 5/67/37–8 & 42, Devonshire Papers 340.2674, Selborne Papers 79/81, Selborne Papers: unpublished memoir 191–3, HH Chamberlain Telegrams 6–8

4 Cecil, G V 144, ed. Dugdale, E.T.S. *Documents* II 381 & 388, Selborne Papers 5/33, FO 64/1351

5 Cecil, G V 149, Magnus *Edward* 253, NR CIII 796–801, Malcolm *Vacant* 11, ed. Rich *Holstein* I 161–3, Pakula, H. *Uncommon* 247–8, ed. Dugdale *ibid.* II 303

6 Dugdale, B. *Balfour* I 224–5, ed. Buckle 3rd Series III 13 & 20, Cecil, G V 148–50 & I 118–19, Devonshire Papers 340.2674

7 'B.B.' *Hatfield Letters* 39, Violet Milner Papers 66/c710/60, Devonshire Papers 340.2676, Chamberlain Papers 5/67/39 & 42, F1/11, Cecil, G V 175, Longford *Raid* 79–80

8 ed. Buckle 3rd Series III 22, Walters *Mediterranean* 267, Penson 'New Course' 133, Grenville 'Goluchowski' 340–69

9 Middlemas *Edward* 121, Crowell *Austin* 20, *The Times* 11/1/1896, ed. Buckle 3rd Series III 24, Rayleigh 2/1/1896, Beckson *London* 102–69, Birkenhead *Kipling* 384, ed. Hutchinson, H. *West* 65

10 RA VIC A 72/45, Rayleigh 31/12/1895, Howard, C. *Splendid* 36, Howard, C. *Casus* 134

11 *The Times* 22/1/1896, Howard 'Splendid' 14–15, ed. Buckle 3rd Series III 21

12 SR XIV 97, SR XIII 733, SR XI 251, FO 800/9/32, Howard, C. *Casus* 58, Hansard 109 c9088, TLS 21/8/1967

13 Howard, C. *Casus* xii, 70–9, Dawson *Cambridge* III 261, Hargreaves 'Yangtze' 62–75, ed. Buckle 3rd Series I 437, FO 120/721/17

14 BL 49209/99, Howard, C. *Casus* 17, Marsden *Tunis* 252, *The Times* 22/1/1896, Klein 'Siam' 119–39

15 RA VIC A 72/61, McElroy *Cleveland* II 199–200, Cecil, G V 121, Devonshire Papers 340.2680

16 Mowat *Pauncefote* 210–11, ed. Buckle 3rd Series III 45, Judd *Empire* 145, McElroy *ibid.* II 202, BL 49690/174, D72/25, Selborne Papers 5/45, James *Olney* 248, Devonshire Papers 340.2683

Thirty-eight: Great Power Politics [pp 635–58]

1 F1/11, St Aldwyn Papers 2455/PCC/69/119, ed. Boyce *Power* 33

2 F1/11, Rayleigh 14/5/1896

3 Drus, E. 'Complicity' 581–93, Blake 'Jameson' *passim*, Rhodes House Papers Afr S/647/229ff, SR XVI 745 & 16

4 Rhodes House Library Afr S.63, NR December 1934, Garvin *Chamberlain* III 106–8, Pakenham *Boer* 29, Drus, E. 'Complicity' 589–90, *The Times* 8/5/1905, Goodfellow *Africa* 34, Van der Poel *Jameson* 262

5 FO 800/146/273, HH Cabinet Prints Box 2, F1/11, Wheatcroft *Randlords* 187, Marsh *Chamberlain* 391–2, Wodehouse, C. 'Missing' June & July 1962

6 Conservative Central Office *Guide* 52–3, Taylor *Essays* 178, Marjoribanks *Carson* 256, Cecil, Viscount *Way* 62, Bower Papers S.1279/30, F1/11, Rhodes Papers t.5.123, E1/121, Rhodes Papers S 1647/235 & 223

7 Jefferson 'Conversations' 216–22, HH Cabinet Prints Box 2, Milner *Picture* 191, Cecil, G V 216 & 104, ed. Buckle 3rd Series III 85, St Aldwyn Papers 2455/PCC/69/115, BL 63178/30

8 Cecil, E. *Leisure* 175–83, Zetland *Cromer* 350, Raymond 'Cromer'181, D56/189

9 Cromer Papers 633/86, Shibeika *Sudan* 324, Morley *Gladstone* III 144, Midleton 'Reaction' 214

10 ed. Buckle 3rd Series III 37, Hansard 38 c1113, F1/11, Shibeika *ibid.* 359, Marlowe *Cromer* 200–2

11 ed. Buckle 3rd Series III 85, Cecil, G V 168, Lord Edward Cecil Papers: Box 1, Zetland *Cromer* 226, BL 56371/63

12 Pollock *Kitchener* 106, Magnus *Kitchener* 102–3

13 Lascelles Papers 800/9, 4th Hansard 45 c219, Salt *Imperialism* 141, Cecil, G V 107, 217, 226–7

14 Grant Duff *Notes* II 186, Whibley *Manners* II 278, Bryce Papers C.198/107, Russell, G. 'Armenia', *The Times* 25/9/1896, Gardiner *Harcourt* II 440, Cecil, G V 105, H. Gooch *Cambridge* IX 775–6, Marder *Naval* 273, Marlowe *Cromer* 137

15 ed. Buckle 3rd Series III 133, Cecil, G V 178, 186, 99, Monson Papers S.593/1, ed. Johnson *Cranbrook* 745, D87/700, Cecil, G IV 131–2

16 4th Hansard 47 c745, ed. Dugdale, E.T.S. *Documents* II 455, Cecil, G V 181–9, Rayleigh 133, FO 800/2/143

17 FO 800/2/12, Cecil, G V 192–5, F1/11, ed. Buckle 3rd Series III 148 & 151

18 Rayleigh 15/5/1897, BL 49690/200, FO 800/2/149, Cecil, G V 197–200, ed. Buckle 3rd Series III 113 & 155

19 Chamberlain Papers JC 11/30/76 & 68, F1/11, Marais *Kruger* 128–9, ed. Buckle 3rd Series III 56

20 Rutland Papers 20/10/1896, Rayleigh 28/7/1897, ed. Ridley *Letters* 141, V. Milner Papers 65/C 708/19, *The Times* 1/2/1896, Cadogan Papers 756 & 731, *Leeds Mercury* 17/10/1895, PRO 30/67/27, BL 56371/51

21 Cadogan Papers 1226 & 1185, ed. O'Day *Reactions* 361, Gailey 'Rhetoric' 117

22 V. Milner Papers 8/F2/2/32, Rayleigh 3/1/1901, Gailey *ibid.* 54, ed. O'Day *ibid.* 362, Cadogan Papers 1472 & 971, Jackson *Ulster* 155

23 Whates *Third* 171, Chamberlain Papers 5/67/56

24 Newton *Lansdowne* 145–6, FO 800/146/263, ed. Boyce *Power* 50, Chamberlain Papers JC 11/30/77

Thirty-nine: Apogee of Empire [pp 659–81]

1 RA VIC R45/6, F/15, SR XI 252, ed. Vincent 118, SR XV 823, SR XV 256, SR XI 140

2 RA VIC R45/42 & 8, Pakula *Uncommon* 574n, Kuhn 'Jubilee' 164, Lant *Pageant* 229

3 RA VIC R46/8, Devonshire Papers 340.2705, Longford *Victoria* 686, ed. Buckle 3rd Series III 125, Balfour, F. *Ne* II 148

4 Holt *Boer* 60, Rayleigh 19/5/1897, RA VIC R46/4, Devonshire Papers 340.2739

5 Fitzroy *Memoirs* I 24, SR XVI 609, Rayleigh 3/3/1897, ILN 19 & 26/6/1897, 4th Hansard 50 c417–21

6 Cecil, Viscount *Way* 77, National Film and Television Archive for 22/6/1897, Judd *Empire* 139–40, *Labour Leader* 19/6/1897, *The Times* 23/6/1897, F1/III, Guedella *Hundred* 183–7, Morris, J. *Pax* 1–11, *Annual Register* 22/6/1897, Balfour, F. *Ne* II 282, Chapman *Jubilees passim*, Lant *Pageant* 243, Longford *Victoria* 687, ed. Buckle 3rd Series III 184, *The Noncomformist* 24/6/1897, Rayleigh 2/7/1897

7 Mee, A. *Salisbury* 39, *The Times* 17/7/1897, Newsome, G. in *Kipling Journal* Sept. 1990, FO 800/111

8 Malcolm *Vacant* 11, 4th Hansard 25 c151 & 45 c32–4, Rayleigh 3/3/1897

9 Langer *Diplomacy* 85, ed. Russell, G. *MacColl* 283, Temple Papers 38/398, Chilston *Whip* 86, *The Times* 17/12/1898, ed. 'B.B.' *Hatfield Letters* 44, Selborne Papers 26/123

10 E/180, Hanham 'Sale' 282, BL 60663, SR XXI 7, SR XVIII 83

11 Devonshire Papers 340.2129, Rockley Papers 15/8/1886, BL 44351/305, Hanham *ibid.* 372–5, 281, E1/149, *The Times* 31/5/1886

12 D32/138 & 117, D79/29, D87/587, Selborne Papers 26/130, BL 49688/157

13 Hanham *Elections* 375, Hanham 'Sale' 277–9, HH Cabinet Prints Box 4, Thompson, F. *Landed* 293, Cannadine *Decline* 199–200, *Daily News* 6/2/1886, Lant *Pageant* 191

14 Devonshire Papers 340.2766 & 2788, Heffer *Power* 68, Searle *Corruption* 86–90, Pinto-Duschinsky *Finance* 37, Hanham 'Sale' 288–9

15 McGill 'Glittering' 89, E130/543, Davies *We* 168, Rutland Papers 26/12/1896, ed. Buckle 3rd Series II 582

16 Desmond *Huxley* 210–13, ed. Buckle 3rd Series II 135 & 85, Devonshire Papers 340.2270, James Papers M45/860, D87/832, Reid *Ask* 170, RA VIC A 72/1, FO 800/2/150, FO 343/1/56, PRO 30/67/7/351

17 Devonshire Papers 340.2179, D32/100, Lubenow *Parliamentary* 177–9, Devonshire Papers 340.2181

18 Blunt *Diaries* 307, ed. Pethica *Diary* 196, Bell Papers 227/61 & 68, Richmond Papers 873/40, PRO 30/67/3, Cecil, G III 194–5, Steele *Salisbury passim*

19 Palmer *Mitred* 112–24, Davidson Papers IV 71, Balfour, F. *Ne* I 113, Bell Papers 227/126, ed. Buckle 3rd Series I 426, SR XV 345, Tait Papers 96/13, HH Add Misc 2, Lucy *Peeps* 432, PRO 30/67/3/55

20 F1/III, Reid *Ask* 147, RA VIC A 73/68, ed. Buckle 3rd Series I 569, Anand *Indian passim*

21 Pope-Hennessy, James *Queen Mary* 1959 346, Reid *ibid.* 154–5, F1/III, Ahmed, R. *Nineteenth Century* vol CCIX October 1898

Forty: Choosing his Ground [pp 682–700]

1 Lowe *Reluctant* I 4–5, Rayleigh 19/10/1897, St Aldwyn Papers 2455/PCC/69/113, HH Secretary's Notebook 591, Stanhope Papers U1590/O/308, Denison *Struggle* 149–50, C7/458, Grant Duff *Notes* I 219

2 4th Hansard 51 c1436–7, ed. Vincent *Crawford* 42

3 F1/11

4 FO 800/2/79, Cecil, G V 239, Selborne Papers 5/49, F1/11

5 Cecil, G V 237, 242, Lowe *Reluctant* II 107–8, Rayleigh 143, Chamberlain Papers 11/30/106, ed. Brett *Esher* I 210

6 4th Hansard 53 c43–4

7 Lucy *Peeps* 228, Dugdale, B. *Balfour* I 254, PRO 30/67/3/62, A106/51 & 33, Chamberlain Papers 11/30/111, Austin Papers 17/8/1896, Lowe *Reluctant* I 8

8 Lucy *Unionist* 211, 4th Hansard 57 c1514–21, 4th Hansard 54 c303, Kennedy, A.L. *Old* 276

9 Langer *Diplomacy* 487, *The Times* 9/5/1898, Blunt *Diaries* 29/3/1898, ed. Howard, C. *Goschen* 17

10 McDonnell Papers D4091/A/3/1/3/9, Geiss *German* 87–8, Lucy *Peeps* 169, Garvin *Chamberlain* III 259–60, Kennedy, P. 'World' 606, Koch 'Alliance' 378–92

11 Chamberlain Papers 5/67/91 & 11/30/117–18, BL 49691/6,4 & 2, *Wrexham Advertiser* 20/10/1897, Dugdale, B. *Balfour* I 257, FO 64/1436

12 Rayleigh 13/5/1898, Garvin *Chamberlain* III 281, *The Times* 5/5/1898, D40/399, SR III 481

13 A106/33, *The Times* 14/5/1898, Howard, C. *Casus* 143

14 BL 46238/131, F1/III, Lees-Milne *Enigmatic* 115, Huntly *Milestones* 306, Rayleigh 7/6/1898, ed. Buckle 3rd Series III 250, 4th Hansard 80 c80–2 20/5/1898

15 Avon Papers at Birmingham University 20/1/12, Midleton *Records* 108, F1/III, ed. Buckle 3rd Series III 251 & 266, Mosley *Curzon* 61–3, Bonar Law Papers 18/6/136, FO 30/67/4/23

16 Howard, C. *Isolation* 44 & 77–88, Steiner *Foreign* 27 & 38–9, Marais *Kruger* 216, Crowe *Crowe* 120, Egremont *Balfour* 139, ed. Buckle 3rd Series III 262, Chamberlain Papers 11/30/133, F1/Box II, Selborne Papers 191–3/89, PRO CO 417/244

17 Howard, C. *Casus* 21, ed. Buckle 3rd Series III 264, BL 49691/27

18 Rutland Papers 24/9/98, Cecil, E. *Leisure* 183, Cecil of Chelwood Papers 51/19, Gathorne-Hardy, A. *Cranbrook* II 368, Rayleigh 20/6/1904, Ziegler *Omdurman* 216, F1/II, PRO 78/5050

19 ed. Buckle 3rd Series III 425, 4th Hansard 72 c601, Magnus *Kitchener* 144–5, F1/III, Ziegler *ibid. passim*, Churchill, W. *Early* 179

Forty-one: The Fashoda Crisis [pp 701–11]

1 *History Today* July 1998, TLS 17/11/1921, Bates *Fashoda passim*, Marlowe *Cromer* 209, Turton 'Macdonald' 35–52, Shibeika *Sudan* 259, Rodd *Memoirs* II 232, Taylor *Essays* 131, Cecil, G. *Biographical* 58, Cecil, G V 213

2 Cadogan Papers 521, Cecil, G V 230 & 245, FO 800/146/277

3 FO 800/2/66, ed. Buckle 3rd Series III 261, F1/II, Chamberlain Papers 5/67/97

4 ed. Buckle 3rd Series III 294, ed. Brett *Esher* I 221, Howard *Casus* 144, F1/III, Fitzroy *Memoirs* I 1, *Daily News* 27/9/1898, Devonshire Papers 340.2780, Rayleigh 16/5/1898

5 Midleton *Records* 109, Cecil, A. *Secretaries* 307, ed. Buckle 3rd Series III 299–301 & 306, F1/II, Brown, R. *Fashoda* 112, Monson Papers C594/88

6 Bates *Fashoda* 159, ed. Buckle 3rd Series III 305, F1/III, ed. Brett *Esher* I 221–2, Brown *ibid.* 113

7 Devonshire Papers 340.2783, ed. 'B.B.' *Hatfield Letters* 44–8, *Bradford Observer* 25/10/1898, Whates *Third* 188, *The Times* 5/11/1898

8 FR LXIV 1002, *The Times* 10 & 11/11/1898, Fitzroy *Memoirs* I 4, SR XVI 633

9 Monger *Isolation* 10, Andrew *Delcassé* 94, ed. Buckle 3rd Series III 351–5 & 312, Rayleigh 3/12/1898, 4th Hansard 48 c1298

10 Churchill, W.. *Early* 109, Maxse Papers 371/9

Forty-two: *The Outbreak of the Boer War* [pp 714–39]

1 ed. Pethica *Diary* 187, Cranbrook Papers HA43/T501/263, Cecil, G V 176, ed. Lutyens *Diary* 106, Rayleigh 28/7/1897, 7/12/1898 & 19/3/1901, RA VIC A73/71, Interview with 6ᵗʰ Marquess of Salisbury 5/2/1998, ed. Vincent *Crawford* 65, Balfour, F. *Ne* II 155, Steiner *Foreign* 25, Taylor *Cold* 37, BQR October 1859, QR 113 448–83

2 Schreuder *Scramble* 292, D29/173, C7/202, *The Times* 10/5/1883, SR IX 251

3 Johnston, H. *Life* 155, Shearman 'Mistaken' 487ff, Selborne Papers 5/39, Cecil, G V 342, D87/828

4 Chamberlain Papers 11/30/138, Drus 'Documents' 171, Marais *Kruger* 229, ed. Vincent *Crawford* 48

5 Chamberlain Papers 11/30/138, Wrench *Milner* 196, Rayleigh 7/12/1898

6 Smith, I. *Origins* 417, Schreuder *Gladstone and Kruger* 363, Marsh *Chamberlain* 374, TLS 16/2/1896

7 4ᵗʰ Hansard 66 c31–4, PRO 30/67/4/143, Chamberlain Papers 5/67/105

8 ed. Buckle 3ʳᵈ Series III 379, 239, 375 & 341, Chamberlain Papers 11/30/156, D44/210

9 Smith *Origins* 272–89, F1/12, FO 30/67/4/175, Command Paper 934 no. 78, Marais *Kruger* 269, HH Cabinet Prints Box 3, Jackson, A. *Saunderson* 134, ed. Buckle 3ʳᵈ Series III 381

10 ed. Headlam *Milner* III 400 & 444, Balfour, F. *Ne* II 292, ed. Buckle 3ʳᵈ Series III 382–4, F1/12, *The Times* Archive TNL/WFA/3/1/32, Koss *Press* 394

11 Bülow *Memoirs* I 414–15, James Papers M45/1024, ed. "B.B." *Hatfield Letters* 49, Marsh *Discipline* 283, McDonnell Papers D4091/A/2/1/4/3

12 ed. Buckle 3ʳᵈ Series III 387, Chamberlain Papers 11/30/160, FF F1/12, HH Cabinet Prints 3

13 Marsh *Discipline* 284, Porter, A. *Origins* 19, Chamberlain Papers 5/67/114

14 4ᵗʰ Hansard 75 c661–4, Beach *Beach* II 106n, ed. Boyce *Power* 91–2, Lucy *Unionist* 303, ed. Dugdale, E.T.S. *Documents* III 89–90

15 4ᵗʰ Hansard 58 c285, C76/343, Smith, I *Origins* 47, HH Cabinet Prints Box 4

16 Curzon Papers F111/158, St Aldwyn Papers 2455/PCC/169/170, F1/12, RA VIC A 75/75, Porter 'Salisbury' 3–4

17 Chamberlain Papers 11/30/164 & 166 & 5/67/115–16, Balfour, F. *Ne* II 294, ed. Boyce *Power* 92, Pakenham *Boer* 82–3

18 Stead Papers 1/63, Porter, A. *Origins* 86, Smith, I. *Origins* 174, PRO CO 291/26, Marlowe *Milner* 86, Curzon Papers F111/14/5, *The Times* 28/8/1899, 4ᵗʰ Hansard 75 c664, Smith *ibid.* 358, ed. Lutyens *Diary* 148, HH Hicks Beach Letters 325

19 St Aldwyn Papers 2455/PCC/69/171, Chamberlain Papers 5/67/117, Fraser *Chamberlain* 204, Smith *ibid.* 358, ed. Headlam *Milner* I 483

20 FO 800/146/290, Newton *Lansdowne* 150–7, Pakenham *Boer* 94, Marais *Kruger* 318, Smith *ibid.* 410, Porter, A. *Origins* 237

21 Curzon Papers F111/158/132, Smith *ibid.* 413, Pakenham *ibid.* 101

22 Marsh *Discipline* 268, St Aldwyn Papers 2455/PCC/69/174, Rayleigh 24/9/1899, Pakenham *ibid.* 416–23, Chamberlain Papers 11/30/169, Smith *ibid.* 367, Marais *Kruger* 318

23 HH Cabinet Prints Box 3, Smith *ibid.* 367, Marais *ibid.* 318

24 Pakenham *Boer* 92–4, ed. Buckle 3ʳᵈ Series III 395, F1/12, Smith *ibid.* 366–7, Ashbourne Papers A1/1

25 F1/12, Drus 'Documents' 181–2, Chamberlain Papers 5/67/124 & 11/30/178

26 HH Cabinet Prints Box 3, Jackson, P. *Devonshire* 300

27 Marais *Kruger* 322, F1/12, ed. Buckle 3rd Series III 401

28 Steiner *Foreign* 234–5, PRO 30/67/4

29 BL 48675/70, Gooch *Courtney* 376–7, *The Times* 2/10/1899

30 ed. Buckle 3rd Series III 404–5, Chamberlain Papers 5/67/129, Marais *Kruger* 331

Forty-three: 'The Possibilities of Defeat' [pp 740–65]

1 Raphael, F. *The Necessity of Anti-Semitism* 1997 188, Taylor *Essays* 183, Rayleigh 24/9/1899, SR IX 279, SR XIV 463

2 16th Derby Papers 4/5, F1/II, Longford *Victoria* 554, Wilkinson *Thirty-Five* 229

3 Belfield *Boer* x, Pakenham *Boer* 572, ed. Maurice *Official* IV Appendix , Roberts Papers 7101/23/80/7

4 Crowe *Crowe* 158 & 85, Howard, C. *Isolation* 57, ed. Brett *Esher* I 240–1, ed. Buckle 3rd Series III 397

5 4th Hansard 77 c16–22, SR XII 292, Fitzroy *Memoirs* I 20, HH Cabinet Prints Box 3

6 F1/III, ed. Buckle 3rd Series III 409, HH Hicks Beach Letters 331, NR November 1931 662, St Aldwyn Papers 2455/PCC/69/180

7 *The Times* 15 & 10/11/1899, Smith, I. *Origins* 408–11, Pakenham *Boer* 388, ed. Brett *Esher* I 241, Austin Papers 21/10/1899, Rayleigh 31/5/1922, Rose *Cecils* 201

8 Rayleigh 24/9/1899, Richmond Papers 873/45, Newton *Lansdowne* 160, FO 800/146/296

9 Milner, V. *Picture* 165 & 123, Rockley Papers 16/11/1899, Balfour, F. *Ne* II 308, ed. Buckle 3rd Series III 421, 'B.B.' *Hatfield Letters* 51, Cecil, D. *Cecils* 264, ed. Lutyens *Lytton* 147, Curzon Papers F111/158/*passim*

10 Bülow *Memoirs* I 307 & 334, *The Times* 1/12/1899, Koch *Anglo-German* 378–92, Curzon Papers F111/14/31, Fitzroy *Memoirs* I 25, *The Economist* 9/12/1899, BL 48675/106, Devonshire Papers 340.2108

11 Marsh *Discipline* 291–3, Milner, V. *Picture* 216, ed. Buckle 3rd Series III 445, Regan *Blunders* 26–37, Stanhope Papers U1590/O/308, Powell, G. *Buller* 152–3, Holt *Boer* 135, James, A. *Roberts* 262–5, F1/12, RA VIC A 75/83, Williams *Defending* 8

12 BL 49691/48 & 77, Cecil, G III 191, ed. Buckle 3rd Series III 440, Pakenham *Boer* 244

13 BL 49691/88, HH Hicks Beach Letters 334, Whibley *Manners* II 261, Selborne Papers 5/59, HH Cabinet Prints Box 3, ed. 'B.B.' *Hatfield Letters* 56

14 Bülow *Memoirs* I 307, SR XVII 74, SR XIII 494

15 Pakenham *Boer* 246, Ashbourne Papers B8/1, ed. Brett *Esher* I 254, 4th Hansard 78 c26–39, Austin Papers 15/1/1900, Egremont *Balfour* 142, ed. 'B.B' *Hatfield Letters* 57, Milner,V. *Picture* 157

16 Bertie Papers 63014/5, 4th Hansard 75 c45 15/2/1900, ed. Buckle 3rd Series III 485, F1/12, HH Hicks Beach Letters 338, Rayleigh 4/2/1900, Temple Papers 33/103–4, 4th Hansard 78 c237

17 ed. Brett *Esher* I 257–8, Rayleigh 18/2/1900, Lucy *Unionist* 334–5, V. Milner Papers 8/F2/1/73–4, ed. Buckle 3rd Series III 321 & 487, F1/III

18 RA QV A76/3a, Rayleigh 23/3/1900, 4th Hansard 79 c771 & c547

19 Greaves *Persia* 15, HH Cabinet Prints Box 3, PRO 30/67/4, Hargreaves 'Yangtze' 62

20 4th Hansard 80 c700–2, Fitzroy *Memoirs* I 36–7, ed. Buckle 3rd Series III 503 & 509, ed. Headlam *Milner* I 562–3, F1/12

21 ed. Bahlman 388, BL 63014/14, ed. Buckle 3rd Series III 526 & 523

22 ed. Buckle 3rd Series III 533–41, F1/III, BL 49835 & 49691, HH Cabinet Prints Box 3

23 Temple Papers 38/381, Midleton *Records* 108

24 *The Times* 10/5/1900, Hewison *Almonds* 105, Marder *Naval* 77

25 Baden-Powell *Varsity* 199, Cecil of Chelwood Papers 55/13 & 10, 51/44 & 51/20, Pakenham *Boer* 90, Rose *Cecils* 194, V. Milner Papers 65/708/10

26 Lord Edward Cecil Papers: Mafeking Records vols I & II, Gardner *Mafeking* 40 & 65, Hamilton, A. *Mafeking* 46, Grinell-Milne *Baden-Powell* 179, Warwick, P. *Black* 35–8, Pakenham *ibid.* 403

27 Price *Jingo* ch. 4, Churchill, W. *Contemporaries* 298, Wilson, Lady *South* 153, ed. Marshall *Cambridge* 53, Lord Edward Cecil Papers: Mafeking Records vols I & II, 'B.B.' *Hatfield Letters* 59, Gardner *Mafeking* 102–5

28 Milner, V. *Picture* 194–5, Gardner *ibid.* 199

29 *Daily Mail* 19/12/1900, Balfour, F. *Ne* II 326, Rose *Cecils* 3, ed. Buckle 3rd Series III 553

Forty-four: Resolution [pp 766–83]

1 SR XIV 97, *The Times* 30/5/1900

2 4th Hansard 86 c1458–78, PRO 30/67/5, HH Cabinet Prints Box 3

3 Curzon Papers vol. III/159/59/204, F1/12, ed. Seldon *Fall* 213, Balfour, F. *Ne* II 335 & 327, Aldcroft *Economy* 5, Gilmour *Curzon* 202

4 Ronaldshay *Curzon* I 282–3 & 254, Dilks *Curzon* 31, Curzon Papers F111/18/104 & F111/158/43, Nicolson *Mary* 37, PRO 30/67/4/104, BL 50073/247–9, Hopkirk *Game* 505

5 V. Milner Papers 8/F2/2/15 & 8/F2/1/66, Hyam *Imperial* 192, Cohn 'Representing' 208, ed. Borden, H. *Robert Laird Borden* 1938 905, FO 800/145/200, Ronaldshay *ibid.* II 206, Curzon Papers F111/181/125

6 Curzon Papers F111/159/175, Balfour, F. *Ne* II 328–31, ed. Buckle 3rd Series III 570–1, HH Secretary's Letterbook 66, A/106/65, Bertie Papers 63013/183, Hargreaves 'Yangtze' 62–75, PRO 30/67/5

7 HH Secretary's Notebook 502, Amery *Chamberlain* IV 140–1, Smith, P. *Conscience* 240, Taylor *Essays* 124, Steiner *Foreign* 27, Chamberlain Papers 11/30/198, Hargreaves 'Yangtze' 71, Cranbrook Papers HA/43/T501/263

8 V. Milner Papers 65/C708/21, Balfour, F. *Ne* II 335 & 326, 'B.B.' *Hatfield Letters* 65, Midleton *Records* 217, HH Cabinet Prints Box 3

9 HH Cabinet Prints Box 3, ed. Buckle 3rd Series III 586, Selborne Papers 5/45, Holland *Devonshire* 278, ed. Blake *Salisbury* 7

10 Curzon Papers F111/160/274a, Selborne Papers 5/61, Southgate *Leadership* 148, Newton *Lansdowne* 186, *The Times* 24/9/1900, Chilston Papers U564/C23/1, Pakenham *Boer* 464

11 F1/III, HH Lansdowne Letters 579, ed. Buckle 3rd Series III 594, HH Cabinet Prints Box 3

12 ed. Seldon *Fall* 219, Price, R. *Imperial* 98–9, Conservative Central Office *Campaign Guide passim*

13 Rutland Papers 6/10/1900, Gathorne-Hardy, A. *Cranbrook* II 374, Beach *Beach* II 153, Curzon F111/159/250, F1/III

14 Curzon Papers F111/159/249, PRO 30/57/106, Grenville 'Abortive' 203–4, Hargreaves 'Yangtze' 74, Monger *Isolation* 19–20, Taylor *Mastery* 393, PRO 30/67/5, Steiner *Foreign* 40

15 Lucy *Eight* 279, ed. David, Edward *Inside Asquith's Cabinet* 1977 2/11/1896, Raymond *Nineties* 63, *Pall Mall Gazette* 3/11/1893, NR November 1931 665, Midleton *Records* 111, Griffith-Boscawen *Fourteen* 129, Chilston *Whip* 172, Rayleigh 29/11/1894

16 V. Milner Papers 8/F2/1/98, Chilston Papers U 564/C21, Devonshire Papers 340.2765 & 2671, Steiner *Foreign* 24–5, BL 49690/135 & 99, *The Times* 340.2766 23/11/1895, Amery *Chamberlain* IV 456, Chamberlain Papers 11/30/69, Balfour, F. *Ne* II 270

Forty-five: Reconstruction [pp 784–95]

1 RA VIC A 76/50, 47 & 50, Chilston *Whip* 287–92, Chilston Papers U564/C22/20 & U564/C21, ed. Buckle 3rd Series III 603 & 600, McDonnell Papers D4091/A/3/1/3/9, SR XIV 11

2 Rayleigh 23/10/97, ed. Brett *Esher* I 267, BL 49691/106, ed. Buckle 3rd Series III 604, Hargreaves 'Yangtze' 75, ed. Vincent *Crawford* 62, Askwith *James* 259–60, Steiner *Foreign* 46–8, Lucas *Saunderson* 305, Newton *Lansdowne* 191

3 Londonderry *Chaplin* 175, BL 51264, Cross *Political* 171, ed. Buckle 3rd Series III 611, RA QVJ: 23/10/1900 (insert), Lucy *Later* 414, Healy *Leaders* II 446

4 ed. Brett *Esher* I 267–8, Rutland Papers 8/11/1900, Chilston *Whip* 293, PRO 30/67/5, Selborne Papers 5/63, Devonshire Papers 340.2841 & 2845

5 BL 49691/110, Cadogan Papers 1555, Rose *Cecils* 71, ed. Boyce *Power* 4, Stanhope Papers U/590/O 308, Cross *Political* 172, NR December 1900 462–3, ed. Williams, R.H. *Salisbury–Balfour* xix

6 Curzon Papers F111/159/175, Balfour, F. *Ne* II 328–31, ed. Buckle 3rd Series III 570–1, HH Letterbook 66, A/106/65, Bertie Papers 63013/183, Hargreaves 'Yangtze' 62–75, PRO 30/67/5

7 Amery *Chamberlain* IV 140–1, Smith *Conscience* 240, Taylor *Essays* 124, Steiner *Foreign* 27, Chamberlain Papers 11/30/198, Hargeaves 'Yangtze' 71, Cranbrook Papers HA/43/T501/263

8 Le May *Victorian* 97, SR XVI 270, QR 108 569, E1/121, SR XIII 105, Cecil, E. *Apologia* 40, 4th Hansard 110 c757–8, Chilston Papers U564/C24/37

9 Milner, V. *Picture* 221, ed. Brett *Esher* I 270, V. Milner Papers 8/F2/1/39, PRO 30/67/13, *The Times* 10/11/1900

10 PRO 30/67/6/313, *The Times* 19/12/1900

11 NR November 1931 660, St Aldwyn Papers 2455/PCC/69/185, BL 49691/112, Chilston *Whip* 283, Chilston Papers U564/C22/17, Stanhope Papers U1590/O/308, V. Milner Papers: diary 28/1/1901, PRO 30/67/6/333

12 BL 56371/104, RA VIC A 68/7, Ponsonby, F. *Recollections* 40, Milner, V. *Picture* 229–31, D87/775

13 Balfour, F. *Ne* II 347, RA GV/A 1A/23, Steiner *Foreign* 202, Chelwood Papers 51/22, Rose *Cecils* 53, D87/775

14 4th Hansard 89 c7–11, ed. Collier *Monkswell* II 78, Balfour, F. *ibid.* II 343, Reid *Ask* 198

15 Boyd-Carpenter *Some* 236–7, V. Milner Papers 8/F2/1/228

Forty-six: 'Methods of Barbarism' [pp 796–811]

1 Magnus *Edward* 265–6, RA VIC T 10/87

2 Milner, V. *Picture* 236, 231, V. Milner Papers 8/F2/1/57–60, ed. Brett *Esher* I 276–7

3 Balfour, F. *Ne* II 351, Braye *Fewness* 490–2, Magnus *Edward* 292

4 Rayleigh 19/3/1901, 4th Hansard 89 c46, Selborne Papers 5/51, Rayleigh 11/2/1901

5 Milner Papers Box 43, McDonnell Papers 4091/A/3/1/5/1, V. Milner Papers 8/F2/1/79

6 F1/12, Johnston, H. *Story* 379, HH Steward's book, HH Cabinet Prints Box 4, Milner Papers 214/27, ed. Headlam *Milner* II 248-9, ILN 1/6/1901, Chamberlain Papers 11/30/202

7 Arnold-Forster Papers 50287, Selborne Papers 26/124, Koch 'Alliance' 387-9, SR XV 512, Cecil, G IV 118, Gooch & Temperley *Foundations* 518-20, Steiner *Foreign* 28-49, Grenville 'Abortive' 201-3, FO 46/545, Geiss *German* 94, *The Times* 14/3/1901, Howard *Splendid* 39-40, Jackson *Devonshire* 300

8 ed. Headlam *Milner* II 225ff, Martin *Concentration passim*, Seely *Adventure* 74, ed. Amery, L. *War* V 66-7, Magnus *Edward* 293, HMSO Command Papers 608, 694, 789, 793, 819, 853, 893, 902, 934, 936, 939, 942, 1161 & 1163

9 HMSO Command Papers 819, 934, 1163 & 893, Martin *ibid.* 36, 53, 20-5, 30, Churchill, W. *Early* 369-70, *Heidelberg News* (South Africa) 3/12/1937

10 ed. Russell, G. *MacColl* 231, 4th Hansard 95 c573-83, ed. Headlam *Milner* II 229, 197, 293, V. Milner Papers 8/F2/1/121-2, Milner, V. *Picture* 224, HH Cabinet Prints Box 3, F1/12, PRO 30/67/5, SR XVI 355, HMSO Command Paper 902 123, Walker *History* 498

11 ed. Headlam *ibid.* 229-30, Rayleigh 3/12/1908, PRO 30/67/8/471, ed. Maurice *Official* IV 659-66, Pakenham *Boer* 494-518

12 Sandars Papers c734/81-8, James, R. *Rosebery* 428-9, F1/12, Magnus *Edward* 306, RA VIC R 22/29

13 Southgate *Leadership* 149, F1/12, HH Cabinet Prints Box 4, PRO 30/67/8/459, Curzon Papers F111/160/274a, St Aldwyn Papers 2455/PCC/69/191, Beach *Beach* II 152-3

14 Cranbrook Papers HA43/T501/263, Surridge *Managing* 144-7, Chamberlain Papers 11/30/216, Patriotic *Truth* 4, Powell, G. *Buller* 199, HH Cabinet Prints Box 4, *Primrose League Gazette* 1/10/1901, Belfield *Boer* 141

15 HH Cabinet Prints Box 4, F1/12, Cranbrook Papers HA43/T501/263, SR XIX 68, SR XVIII 470, SR VIII 577

Forty-seven: A Weary Victory [pp 812-33]

1 Steiner, Z. 'Anglo-Japanese' 27-36, F1/12, PRO 30/67/4, FO 800/1/40, SR XVI 76, ed. Russell, G. *MacColl* 282

2 HH Cabinet Prints Box 4, PRO CAB 37/60, F1/12, Nish, I. *Anglo-Japanese passim*, PRO FO 46/547/302, FO 277

3 Rodd, R. *Memoirs* II 275-6, ed. Gwynn *Spring-Rice* I 353, Beach *Beach* II 312, HH Cabinet Prints Box 4

4 Fitzroy *Memoirs* I 72-80, Curzon Papers F111/161/60, Rayleigh 27/1/1902, Churchill, R. *Churchill* Companion vol. II Part 1 114

5 Rutland Papers 9/9/1901, Searle *Corruption* 90-1, Heffer *Power* 24-5, Rayleigh 27/7/1902

6 F1/12, BL 49690/180, Sykes *Tariff* 29, Dugdale *Balfour* I 323, Mackintosh *Echoes* 40, Devonshire Papers 340.2694, RA VIC A 73/16, Marsh *Discipline* 251-2, *The Times* 13/6/1895, QR 108 579-80

7 Scöllgen, Gregor *Imperialismus und Gleichgewicht: Deutschland, England und die Orientalische Frage 1817-1914* 1993 150, Rutland Papers 12/2/1903, *Punch* 24/7/1901, Egremont *Balfour* 151, ed. Seldon *Fall* 220, F1/12, HH Cabinet Prints Box

4, Fitzroy *Memoirs* I 73 & 67–8, Southgate *Leadership* 149, Devonshire Papers 340.2818, Smith *Conscience* 237

8 V. Milner Papers 8/F2/1/161 & 65/C708/22, HH Cabinet Prints Box 4

9 *The Times* 2/6/1902, Milner Papers 186/73, F1/12, HH Cabinet Prints Box 4, ed. Headlam *Milner* II 342, *The Times* 8/5/1902

10 F1/12, Magnus *Edward* 296, Heffer *Power* 120–1, Pakenham *Boer* 563–9, ed. Headlam *Milner* II 350–1, RA VIC R 22/97 & 94, Fitzroy *Memoirs* I 88–9, Newton *Retrospection* 116

11 Ullswater *Commentaries* I 320, Baumann *Victorians* 83, Lucy *Later* 127, Balfour, F. *Ne* II 371, V. Milner Papers 8/F2/1/197

12 Curzon Papers F111/14/65 & 53, Fitzroy *Memoirs* I 76, Askwith *James* 267–8, Balfour, F. *ibid.* II 363, Rayleigh 26 & 30/6/1902

13 McDonnell Papers D4091/A/3/1/5/3, Curzon Papers F111/161/222, Amery, J. *Chamberlain* IV 449, Shannon *Crisis* 308, Clarke *Hope* 21

14 Devonshire Papers 340.2883, McDonnell Papers D/4091/A/3/1/5/4, BL 56371/132, St Aldwyn Papers 2455/PCC/69/193, Chamberlain Papers 11/30/232

15 Lady Gwendolen Cecil Papers: Box 1, RA VIC/ADD C 7/Honours, ed. Bahlman 419–20, Blunt *Diaries* 444, Cecil of Chelwood Papers 53/17, Amery *Chamberlain* IV 453–7, Rayleigh 12/7/1902, Dugdale, B. *Balfour* I 318, Hamilton, G. *Parliamentary* II 255, Jackson, P. *Whigs* 322, 'B.B.' *Hatfield Letters* 75, E1/40, Ashbourne Papers B9/21, Austin, A. *Autobiography* II 180

16 Curzon Papers F111/161/266, 225 & 230, Rayleigh 30/7/1902, E1/27, HH Hicks Beach Letters 373, RA VIC W 36/18, *The Times* 24/8/1903, Curzon Papers F111/182/127, Richmond Papers 873/51, Gathorne-Hardy, A. *Cranbrook* II 378

17 V. Milner Papers 8/F2/2/17 & 12, Curzon Papers F111/14, HH Letterbooks 76, Maxse Papers 435/4 & 15

18 Beach *Beach* II 195, Marsh *Chamberlain* 575, Hamilton, G. *Parliamentary* II 323, Curzon Papers F111/162/182 & 259, Egremont *Balfour* 179, V. Milner Papers 8/F2/1/160, Balfour, F. *Ne* II 374

19 Rayleigh 1/11/1894, Curzon Papers F111/14/96, Blunt *Diaries* 482–4

20 *The Times* 3/8/1903, Marsh *Chamberlain* 575, Rempel *Unionists* 55, HH Letterbooks 61, Egremont *Balfour* 180, Curzon Papers F111/14/91

21 *The Times* 1/9/1903, Rutland Papers 31/8/1903, Balfour, F. *Ne* II 397, Curzon Papers F111/162/238, HH Newspaper Cuttings Book

The Legacy [pp 834–52]

1 Patten, C. *East and West* 1998 294, BQR I 1–32, Curzon *Modern* 61, ed. Smith *Salisbury* 1, Lynd, H., *1880s passim*, TLS 10/4/1953, D41/14, Fyfe *O'Connor* 166–7, Wilson, Harold *The Governance of Britain* (1976) 31n, Davis, Stearns *A Short History of the Near East* (1923) 358n, Hyndman *Adventurous* 207, Taylor *Essays* 127

2 Asquith, M. *Autobiography* 207, Baumann *Victorians* 68, 73–6, Cecil, E. *Apologia* 25–6, ed. Howe, Mark *The Holmes–Laski Letters* (1953) 384, Penson 'Principles' 106, ed. Smith, P. *ibid.* 105–8, Southgate *Leadership* 224, *The Spectator* 24/4/1999, Steele, David *Salisbury passim*, Raymond *Nineties* 67

3 Cecil, G IV 88, D40/496, Cecil, D. *Cecils* 237, D82/48, Pinto-Duschinsky *Political* 12, Cowling *Doctrine* 371, QR 111 201–38

4 Rayleigh 16/5/1894, C7/347, Marsh *Discipline* 11, Cecil, D. *ibid.* 237, Pinto-Duschinsky *ibid.* 73–86, 59, FO 800/2/14

5 Smith, F. *Reform* 74, NR XXIV 457, Garvin *Chamberlain* I 462, Christie, O.F. *Democracy* 4, Butler, E. *Cecils* 215, Smith, P. *Disraeli* 179, Lady Gwendolen Cecil Papers: letter 3/12/1921

6 Rayleigh 5/2/1892, Shannon *Crisis* 251, Cecil, G III 167

7 ed. Lucy *Speeches* 102, *The Times* 5/6/12/1883, Hansard 196 c1192–203, *The Times* 1/12/1888, QR 109 531–65, Lowe *Reluctant* I 84

8 Kedourie 'Tory' *passim*, Cecil, G III 20, *The Times* 24/8/1903, 3rd Hansard 284 c1689, SR VIII 133

9 Uzoigwe *Africa* 6, Rodgers & Moyle 32, Gooch, G.P. *Recent* 355, *The Times* 30/7/1909, Pinto-Duschinsky *Political* 137, Gillard 'Defence' 248 & 283

10 Kennedy, P. *Diplomacy* 376, Cecil, G III 167, QR 111 201–38, ed. Smith, P. *Salisbury* 3 10 4th Hansard 112 c813, BL 39137, Penson 'Principles' 105

11 Hart 'Experience' 81–99, McDowell *Unionists* 136, Jackson, A. *Ulster* 195, Jenkins, R. *Gladstone* 564, TLS 18/9/1898

12 *The Times* 25/11/1882

13 4th Hansard 30 c32 & 36 c51, Cecil, G III 301, ed. Russell, G. *MacColl* 279–80, Vincent *Disraeli* 52–6, QR 127 538–61

14 Marsh *Discipline* 128, *The Times* 11/10/1877, SR XIII 305

15 Hansard 161 c1509–11, SR XIII 678, Lady Gwendolen Cecil Papers: Box 2 10/4/1908 & 15/6/1921, ed. Blake *Salisbury* 245, Taylor *Essays* 122, 4th Hansard 135 c49–57, BQR I 1–32, *Lincoln, Rutland and Stamford Mercury* 26/8/1853, Churchill, W. *Early* 383 & 179

Bibliography

Archives

OIOC denotes the Oriental and India Office Collections of the British Library
PRONI denotes the Public Record Office of Northern Ireland in Belfast

Acland, Sir Henry (Bodleian Library, Oxford)
Ampthill, 1st Baron (Public Record Office)
Arnold-Forster, H.O. (British Library)
Ashbourne, 1st Baron (House of Lords Record Office and PRONI)
Asquith, 1st Earl of Oxford and (Bodleian Library, Oxford)
Austin, Alfred (Bristol University Library)
Baden-Powell, 1st Baron (National Army Museum)
Balfour, 1st Earl of (British Library)
Balfour, 2nd Earl of (British Library)
Beaconsfield, 1st Earl of (Bodleian Library, Oxford)
Bell, Bishop George (Lambeth Palace Library)
Benson, Archbishop Edward (Bodleian Library, Oxford, Lambeth Palace Library and
    Trinity College, Cambridge)
Bertie, 1st Viscount (Public Record Office and British Library)
Bower, Sir Graham (Rhodes House Library)
Brabourne, 1st Baron (Centre for Kentish Studies)
Bryce, 1st Viscount (Bodleian Library, Oxford)
Burdett, Sir Henry (Bodleian Library, Oxford)
Burne, Sir Owen (OIOC)
Cadogan, 5th Earl (House of Lords Record Office)
Cairns, 1st Earl (Public Record Office)
Cambridge, HRH Duke of (Royal Archives, Windsor)
Campbell, Sir George (OIOC)
Campbell-Bannerman, Sir Henry (British Library)
Carnarvon, 4th Earl (Public Record Office and British Library)
Carson, 1st Baron (PRONI)
Cecil, Lord Edward (Bodleian Library, Oxford)
Cecil, Lord Eustace (by kind permission of Lord Rockley)
Cecil, Lady Gwendolen (by kind permission of Lord Salisbury)
Cecil of Chelwood, 1st Viscount (British Library)
Chamberlain, Sir Austen (Birmingham University Library)
Chamberlain, Joseph (Birmingham University Library)
Chaplin, 1st Viscount (PRONI)
Chilston, 1st Viscount (Centre for Kentish Studies)

Malet, Sir Edward (Public Record Office)
Maxse, Admiral Frederick (West Sussex Record Office)
Maxse, Leopold (West Sussex Record Office)
Middleton, Richard (Centre for Kentish Studies and Bodleian Library, Oxford)
Midleton, 8th Viscount (Surrey History Service)
Midleton, 1st Earl of (Public Record Office and British Library)
Milner, 1st Viscount (Bodleian Library, Oxford)
Milner, Violet, Lady (Bodleian Library, Oxford)
Monkswell, 2nd Baron (Bodleian Library, Oxford)
Monson, Sir Edmund (Bodleian Library, Oxford)
Montgomery, Sir Robert (OIOC)
Morier, Sir Robert (Balliol College, Oxford)
National Film and Television Archive National Sound Archive (British Library)
Nightingale, Florence (British Library)
Northbrook, 1st Earl of (OIOC)
O'Conor, Sir Nicholas (Churchill Archives Centre, Cambridge)
Onslow, 4th Earl of (Surrey History Service)
Oxford Union Society
Paget, Lord Augustus (British Library)
Pauncefote, 1st Baron (by kind permission of Mrs Diana Makgill)
Peek, Sir Henry (by kind permission of Sir William Benyon)
Peel, General Jonathan (Balliol College, Oxford)
Portal, Sir Gerald (Rhodes House Library)
Primrose League (Bodleian Library, Oxford)
Quickswood, 1st Baron (by kind permission of Lord Salisbury)
Rayleigh, Evelyn, Lady (by kind permission of Lord Rayleigh)
Rhodes, Cecil (Rhodes House Library)
Richmond 6th Duke of (West Sussex Record Office)
Ripon, 1st Marquess of (British Library)
Ritchie, 1st Baron (British Library)
Roberts, 1st Earl (National Army Museum)
Rockley, 1st Baron (kind permission of Lord Rockley)
Rutland, 6th, 7th and 8th Dukes of (by kind permission of the late Duke of Rutland)
St Aldwyn, 1st Earl (Gloucester Record Office)
Salisbury, 2nd, 3rd, 4th and 5th Marquesses of (by kind permission of Lord Salisbury)
Sandars, John (Bodleian Library, Oxford)
Sanderson, 1st Baron (Public Record Office)
Satow, Sir Ernest (British Library)
Saunderson, Col Edward (PRONI)
Selborne, 1st Earl of (Lambeth Palace Library)
Selborne, 2nd Earl of (Bodleian Library, Oxford)
Simmons, Sir John (Public Record Office)
Smith, W.H. (by kind permission of Lord Hambleden)
Stanhope, Edward (Centre for Kentish Studies)
Stanmore, 1st Baron (British Library)
Stead, W.T. (Churchill Archives Centre, Cambridge)
Tait, Archbishop (Lambeth Palace Library)
Temple, Archbishop (Lambeth Palace Library)
Temple, Sir Richard (OIOC)
Tenterden, 3rd Baron (Public Record Office)
Times, The (Times Newspapers Ltd Archive and University of Texas at Austin)
Victoria, HM Queen (Royal Archives, Windsor Castle)

Walpole, Sir Horatio (OIOC)
White, Sir William (Public Record Office)
Wodehouse, Sir Philip (OIOC)
Wolseley, 1st Viscount (British Library)

Newspapers and Journals

Bentley's Quarterly Review
Contemporary Review
Daily Chronicle
Daily News
Daily Telegraph
Fortnightly Review
Globe
Graphic
Illustrated London News
Irish Times
Lincoln, Rutland and Stamford Mercury
Londonderry Sentinel
Morning Chronicle
Morning Post
National Review
Pall Mall Gazette
Primrose League Gazette
Punch
Quarterly Review
Review of Reviews
Reynolds News
St James' Gazette
Saturday Review
Spectator
Standard
Star
The Times
The Times Literary Supplement
Truth

Salisbury Biographies and Studies

Bagenal, P.H., *The Tory Policy of the Marquess of Salisbury* 1885
eds Blake, Robert, and Cecil, Hugh, *Lord Salisbury: The Man and his Policies* 1987
Cecil, Lady Gwendolen, *The Life of Robert, Marquess of Salisbury* 4 vols, 1921, 1931 and 1932
—— *Biographical Studies of the Life and Political Character of Robert, 3rd Marquess of Salisbury* 1948
Dolman, Frederick, *A Record of the Career and a Criticism of the Character of the Marquis of Salisbury* 1884
Grenville, J.A.S., *Lord Salisbury and Foreign Policy* 1964
How, F.D., *The Marquess of Salisbury* 1902

Howard, Christopher H.D., *Splendid Isolation: A Study of Ideas concerning Britain's International Position and Foreign Policy during the Latter Years of the 3rd Marquess of Salisbury 1967*

Jeyes, S.H., *Life and Times of Lord Salisbury* 4 vols 1895–6

Kennedy, A.L., *Lord Salisbury 1830–1902: Portrait of a Statesman* 1953

ed. Lucy, Sir Henry, *Speeches of Rt Hon. Marquess of Salisbury* 1885

Marsh, Peter, *The Discipline of Popular Government: Lord Salisbury's Domestic Statecraft 1881–1902* 1978

Mee, Arthur, *Lord Salisbury: The Record Premiership of Modern Times* 1901

Pinto-Duschinsky, Michael, *The Political Thought of Lord Salisbury* 1967

Rodgers, Edward, and Moyle, Edmund, *Lord Salisbury* 1902

Salisbury, Lord, *Essays of the Late Marquess of Salisbury* 2 vols, 1905

—— *Evolution – A Retrospect* 1894

Shannon, Richard, *The Age of Salisbury 1881–1902* 1996

ed. Smith, Paul, *Lord Salisbury on Politics: A Selection from his Articles in the Quarterly Review 1860–1883* 1972

Smith, W. Brooke, *Lord Salisbury* 1902

Steele, David, *Salisbury: A Political Biography* 1999

Taylor, Robert, *Lord Salisbury* 1975

Traill, H.D., *The Marquis of Salisbury* 1892

Primary Published Sources and Autobiographies

(All books were published in Britain unless otherwise stated)

Argyll, Dowager Duchess of, *George Douglas, 8th Duke of Argyll* 2 vols, 1906

Argyll, Duke of, *Passages from the Past* 2 vols, 1907

Asquith, Earl of Oxford and, *Fifty Years of Parliament* vol. 1, 1926

—— *Memories and Reflections* 2 vols, 1928

Asquith, Margot, *The Autobiography of Margot Asquith* 2 vols, 1920 and 1922

Austin, Alfred, *The Autobiography of Alfred Austin* 2 vols, 1911

Baden-Powell, Lord, *Lessons from the Varsity of Life* 1933

ed. Bahlman, Dudley W.R., *The Diary of Sir Edward Walter Hamilton 1880–85* 2 vols, 1972

—— *The Diary of Sir Edward Walter Hamilton 1885–1906* 1993

ed. Bailey, John, *The Diary of Lady Frederick Cavendish* 1927

Balfour, A.J., *Chapters of Autobiography* 1930

—— *Opinions and Argument* 1927

Balfour, Lady Betty, *Letters of the 1st Earl of Lytton* 2 vols, 1906

Balfour, Lady Frances, *Ne Obliviscaris: Dinna Forget* 2 vols, 1930

Barclay, Sir Thomas, *Thirty Years: Anglo-French Reminiscences 1876–1906* 1914

ed. 'B.B.' [Lady Elizabeth Balfour], *Hatfield Letters 1883–1903* (privately printed)

ed. Bassett, A. Tilney, *Gladstone to His Wife* 1936

Blunt, W.S., *My Diaries 1884–1914* 2 vols, 1919–20

ed. Borden, Henry, *Robert Laird Borden: His Memoirs* 1938

ed. Boyce, D.G., *The Crisis of British Power: The Imperial and Naval Papers of the 2nd Earl of Selborne 1895–1910* 1990

—— *The Crisis of British Unionism: The Domestic Political Papers of the 2nd Earl of Selborne 1885–1922* 1987

Braye, Lord, *Fewness of my Days* 1927

ed. Brett, Maurice V., *The Journals and Letters of Reginald, Viscount Esher* 2 vols, 1934

Bridges, J.A., *Reminiscences of a Country Politician* 1906

ed. Bright, Philip, *The Diaries of John Bright* 1930

Brookfield, A.M., *Annals of a Chequered Life* 1930

ed. Brooks, David, *The Destruction of Lord Rosebery: From the Diary of Sir Edward Hamilton 1894–1895* 1986

ed. Buckle, G.E., *The Letters of Queen Victoria* 2nd and 3rd Series, 6 vols, 1930–2

Bülow, Prince von, *Memoirs* 4 vols, 1931

ed. Burghclere, Lady, *A Great Lady's Friendships: Letters to Mary, Marchioness of Salisbury, Countess of Derby 1862–90* 1933

Burnaby, Frederick, *A Ride to Khiva* 1876

Butler, Elizabeth, *An Autobiography* 1922

Campbell, Sir George, *Memoirs of My Indian Career* 2 vols, 1893

Carpenter, Bishop W. Boyd, *Some Pages of My Life* 1911

ed. Cartwright, Julia, *Journals of Lady Knightley of Fawsley 1856–1884* 1915

Cecil, Lord Edward, *The Leisure of an Egyptian Official* 1921

Cecil, Lord Eustace, *Apologia Pro Vitâ Suâ* (privately printed) 1901

—— *Impressions of Life* 1865

Cecil, Evelyn, *On the Eve of the War* 1900

Cecil of Chelwood, Viscount, *A Great Experiment* 1941

—— *All the Way* 1949

Chamberlain, Sir Austen, *Down the Years* 1935

—— *Politics from Inside* 1936

Chamberlain, Joseph, *Home Rule and the Irish Question* 1887

ed. Childers, Spencer, *The Life and Correspondence of Hugh C.E. Childers 1827–1896* 2 vols, 1901

Chirol, Sir Valentine, *Fifty Years in a Changing World* 1927

Churchill, Winston S., *My Early Life* 1930

Clarke Sir E., *The Story of My Life* 1918

ed. Cohen, Morton, *The Letters of Lewis Carroll* 2 vols, 1979

ed. Collier E.C.F., *A Victorian Diarist: Extracts from the Journals of Mary, Lady Monkswell* 2 vols, 1944–6

Cooke, A.B., and Malcomson A.P.W., *The Ashbourne Papers 1869-1913* (Belfast) 1974

Cooke A.B., and Vincent, John, *Lord Carlingford's Journal* 1971

Cornwallis-West, Mrs, *The Reminiscences of Lady Randolph Churchill* 1908

ed. Crispi, Thomas Palamenghi, *The Memoirs of Francesco Crispi* vols 2 and 3, 1912

Cross, Lord, *A Political History* 1903

ed. Curtius, Frederich, *Memoirs of Prince Hohenlohe* 2 vols, 1906

ed. David, Edward, *Inside Asquith's Cabinet* 1977

Denison, John Evelyn, *Leaves from my Journal when Speaker of the House of Commons* 1899

Drummond Wolff, Sir Henry, *Rambling Recollections* 2 vols, 1908

ed. Drus, Ethel, *A Journal of Events During the Gladstone Ministry 1868–74 by John, 1st Earl of Kimberley* (Camden Miscellany) 1958

Dugdale, Blanche, *Family Homespun* 1940

Dunraven, Earl of, *Past Times and Pastimes* 2 vols, 1922

Eckardstein, Baron Hermann von, *Ten Years at the Court of St James* 1921

Elliot, Sir Henry, *Some Revolutions and Other Diplomatic Experiences* 1922

ed. Ellis, Jennifer, *Thatched with Gold: The Memoirs of Mabell, Countess of Airlie* 1962

Fitzroy, Sir Almeric, *Memoirs* 2 vols, 1925

ed. Foot, M.R.D., *Gladstone's Midlothian Speeches 1879* 1971

Forwood, Sir William, *Recollections of a Busy Life* 1910

ed. Gordon, Peter, *The Red Earl: The Papers of the 5ᵗʰ Earl Spencer* 2 vols, 1981 and 1986

Gower, George Leveson, *Mixed Grill* 1947

Gladstone, Viscount, *After Thirty Years* 1928

Grant Duff, Sir Mountstuart, *Notes from a Diary 1886–1901* 2 vols, 1901

Griffith-Boscawen, A.S.T., *Fourteen Years in Parliament* 1907

ed. Hamer, F.E., *The Personal Papers of Lord Rendel* 1931

Hamilton, Lord Frederick, *The Vanished Pomps of Yesterday* 1919

Hamilton, Lord George, *Parliamentary Reminiscences and Reflections 1868–1885* 1916

—— *Parliamentary Reminiscences and Reflections 1886–1906* 1922

Hardinge, Sir Arthur, *A Diplomatist in Europe* 1927

Hardinge, Lord, *Old Diplomacy* 1947

Hare, Augustus, *The Story of My Life* vols 4 and 6, 1900

—— *In My Solitary Life* 1953

ed. Headlam, Cecil, *The Milner Papers* vol 1, 1931, vol 2, 1933

Healy, Timothy Michael, *Letters and Leaders of My Day* 2 vols, 1928

ed. Howard, C.H.D., *Joseph Chamberlain: A Political Memoir 1880–1892* 1953

—— *The Diary of Edward Goschen 1900–1914* 1980

Huntly, Marquess of, *Milestones* 1926

ed. Hutchinson, Horace, *The Private Diaries of Rt Hon. Sir Algernon West* 1922

Hyndman, Henry, *The Record of an Adventurous Life* 1911

ed. Jennings, Louis J., *Speeches of Lord Randolph Churchill 1880–88* 2 vols, 1889

ed. Johnson, Nancy E., *The Diary of Gathorne Hardy, later Lord Cranbrook 1866–1892* 1981

Johnston, Sir Harry, *The Story of My Life* 1923

Jusserand, J.J., *What Me Befell* 1933

Kebbel, T.E., *Lord Beaconsfield and Other Tory Memories* 1907

ed. Kebbel, T.E., *Selected Speeches of the Late Earl of Beaconsfield* 2 vols, 1882

Knutsford, Viscount, *In Black and White* 1926

Lake, Henry, *Personal Recollections of Lord Beaconsfield* 1891

Loftus, Lord Augustus, *Diplomatic Reminiscences* vol. 2, 1894

Long, Walter, *Memories* 1923

Lucy, Sir Henry W., *Later Peeps at Parliament* 1905

—— *A Diary of the Salisbury Parliament 1886–1892* 1892

—— *A Diary of the Unionist Parliament 1895–1900* 1901

—— *A Diary of Two Parliaments 1874–85* 2 vols, 1885

—— *A Diary of the Home Rule Parliament 1892–95* 1896

—— *Memories of Eight Parliaments* 1908

—— *Sixty Years in the Wilderness* 1909

—— *The Balfourian Parliament 1900–1905* 1906

eds Mackail, J.W., and Wyndham, Guy, *Life and Letters of George Wyndham* 2 vols, 1925

eds MacKenzie, Norman and Jeanne, *The Diary of Beatrice Webb* vols 1–3, 1982–4

Mackintosh, Sir Alexander, *Echoes of Big Ben* 1945

Maclean, J.M., *Recollections of Westminster and India* 1902

Malcolm, Ian, *Vacant Thrones* 1931

ed. Masterman, Lucy, *Mary Gladstone: Her Diaries and Letters* 1930

ed. Matthew, H.C.G., *The Gladstone Diaries* vols 5–14, 1978–94

Maxwell, Sir Herbert, *Evening Memories* 1932
Meyrick, Frederick, *Memoirs of Life at Oxford* 1905
Midleton, Earl of, *Records and Reactions 1856–1939* 1939
Milner, Viscountess, *My Picture Gallery 1886–1901* 1951
Morley, John, *Recollections* 2 vols, 1917
Mowbray, Sir John, *Seventy Years at Westminster* 1890
Nevill, Lady Dorothy, *Under Five Reigns* 1910
ed. Nevill, Ralph, *The Reminiscences of Lady Dorothy Nevill* 1906
Newton, Lord, *Retrospection* 1941
O'Connor, T.D., *Memoirs of an Old Parliamentarian* 2 vols, 1929
Oxford Essays 1858
Pease, Sir Alfred E., *Elections and Recollections* 1932
ed. Pethica, James, *Lady Gregory's Diaries 1892–1902* 1996
Ponsonby, Sir Frederick, *Recollections of Three Reigns* 1957
ed. Ponsonby, Sir Frederick, *Letters of the Empress Frederick* 1928
ed. Ponsonby, Lord, *Henry Ponsonby: His Life from His Letters* 1942
ed. Ponsonby, Magdalen, *Mary Ponsonby: A Memoir, Some Letters and a Journal* 1927
Powell, John, *Liberal By Principle: The Politics of John Wodehouse, 1st Earl of Kimberley 1843–1902* 1996
Radziwill, Princess, *Those I Remember* 1914
ed. Ramm, Agatha, *The Political Correspondence of Mr Gladstone and Lord Granville 1876–1886* 2 vols, 1962
Redesdale, Lord, *Memoirs* 2 vols, 1915
Ribblesdale, Lord, *Impressions and Memories* 1927
eds Rich, Norman, and Fisher, M.H., *The Holstein Papers: The Memoirs, Diaries and Correspondence of Friedrich von Holstein 1937–1909* 4 s, 1955–63
eds Ridley, Jane, and Percy, Clayre, *The Letters of Arthur Balfour and Lady Elcho 1885–1917* 1992
ed. Robson, Brian, *Roberts in India: The Military Papers of Field Marshal Lord Roberts 1876–1893* 1993
Rodd, Sir James Rennell, *Social and Diplomatic Memoirs 1902–19* 3 vols, 1925
Russell, Sir Charles, *The Opening Speech for the Defence* 1889
Russell, G.W.E., *Collections and Recollections* 1899
St Helier, Lady *Memories*
Sandars, J.S., *Studies of Yesterday, by a Privy Councillor* 1928
ed. Scott, Sir Ernest, *Lord Robert Cecil's Gold Fields Diary* (Melbourne) 1935
Seely, J.E.B., *Adventure* 1930
Selborne, Earl of, *Memorials: Part II Personal and Political 1865–1898* 2 vols, 1898
Temple, Sir Richard, *The Story of My Life* vol 1 1896
—— *Letters and Character Sketches from the House of Commons* 1912
Tollemache, Hon. Lionel, *Talks with Mr Gladstone* 1901
Tupper, Sir Charles, *Recollections of Sixty Years* 1914
Ullswater, Viscount, *A Speaker's Commentaries* vol 1 1925
ed. Vincent, John, *The Crawford Papers: The Journals of David Lindsay, 27th Earl of Crawford and 10th Earl of Balcarres 1871–1940* 1984
—— *Disraeli, Derby and the Conservative Party: Journals and Memoirs of Edward Henry, Lord Stanley 1848–1869* 1978
—— *The Later Derby Diaries, Home Rule, Liberal Unionism and Aristocratic Life in Late Victorian England* 1981
—— *The Diaries of Edward Henry Stanley, 15th Earl of Derby: Between September 1869 and March 1878* 1994

Waddington, Mary King, *Letters of a Diplomat's Wife 1883–1900* 1904
Warwick, Frances Countess of, *Life's Ebb and Flow* 1929
—— *Afterthoughts* 1931
ed. Wellesley, Frederick, *Recollections of a Soldier-Diplomat* 1944
West, Sir Algernon, *Recollections 1832–1886* 2 vols, 1899
White, William, *The Inner Life of the House of Commons* 2 vols, 1897
Wilkinson, Henry Spenser, *Thirty-Five Years 1874–1909* 1933
ed. Williams, Robin Harcourt, *The Salisbury–Balfour Correspondence 1869–1892* 1988
Wilson, Lady Sarah, *South African Memories* 1909
ed. Zetland, Marquis of, *The Letters of Disraeli to Lady Bradford and Lady Chesterfield* 2 vols, 1929

Biography

Aberdeen and Temair, Marchioness of, *Edward Marjoribanks* 1909
Alderson, Charles, *Selections from the Charges and Other Detached Papers of Baron Alderson* 1858
Alexander, Michael, and Anand, Sushila, *Queen Victoria's Maharajah: Duleep Singh 1838–93* 1980
Amery, Julian, *The Life of Joseph Chamberlain 1901–1903* 1951
Anand, Sushila, *Indian Sahib: Queen Victoria's Dear Abdul* 1996
Arnold-Forster, M., *Hugh Oakley Arnold-Forster: A Memoir* 1910
Askwith, Lord, *Lord James of Hereford* 1930
Atlay, J.B., *Sir Henry Wentworth Acland* 1903
Balfour, Lady Frances, *A Memoir of Lord Balfour of Burleigh* 1925
Battiscombe, Georgina, *Queen Alexandra* 1969
—— *Shaftesbury: A Biography of the 7th Earl 1801–1885* 1974
Beach, Lady Victoria, *The Life of Sir Michael Hicks Beach* 2 vols, 1932
Benson, Arthur C., *The Life of Edward White Benson* 2 vols, 1900
Bew, Paul, *Charles Stewart Parnell* 1980
Birkenhead, Lord, *Rudyard Kipling* 1978
Blake, Robert, *Disraeli* 1966
Blunden, Margaret, *The Countess of Warwick* 1967
Bradford, Sarah, *Disraeli* 1985
Bryce, James, *Studies in Contemporary Biography* 1903
Busch, Briton Cooper, *Hardinge of Penshurst* (Indiana University) 1980
Busch, Dr Moritz, *Bismarck: Some Secret Pages of His History* 3 vols, 1898
Cecil, Lord David, *Melbourne* 1955
—— *The Cecils of Hatfield House* 1973
Chilston, 3rd Viscount, *Chief Whip: The Political Life and Times of Aretas Akers-Douglas, 1st Viscount Chilston* 1961
—— *W.H. Smith* 1965
Churchill, Peregrine, and Mitchell, Julian, *Jennie: Lady Randolph Churchill* 1974
Churchill, Randolph, *Winston S. Churchill* vol. 1, 1966, vol. 2, 1967
—— *Derby: A Life of the 17th Earl* 1959
Lord Randolph Churchill 2 vols, 1906
Coleridge, E.H., *The Life and Correspondence of John Duke, Lord Coleridge* 2 vols, 1904
ed. Colson, Percy, *Lord Goschen and His Friends: The Goschen Letters* 1946

Corti, Egon, *Alexander von Battenberg* 1954
Crankshaw, Edward, *Bismarck* 1981
Crewe, Marquess of, *Lord Rosebery* 2 vols, 1931
Crosby, Travis L., *The Two Mr Gladstones* 1997
Crowe, Sibyl, and Corp, Edward, *Our Ablest Civil Servant: Sir Eyre Crowe 1864– 1924* 1994
Crowell, Norton B., *Alfred Austin, Victorian* 1955
Darnley, Gillian *Octavia Hill* 1990
Dasent, Arthur Irwin, *John Thadeus Delane* 2 vols, 1908
Dennis, Ravenscroft G., *The House of Cecil* 1914
Desmond, Adrian, *T.H. Huxley: Evolution's High Priest* 1997
Dharmapala, Mahajana, *The Administration of Sir John Lawrence in India 1864–69* 1952
Dilks, David, *Curzon in India* vol. 1, 1969, vol. 2, 1970
Drew, Mary, *Catherine Gladstone* 1920
Dugdale, Blanche, *Arthur James Balfour* 2 vols, 1936
Edwards, H. Sutherland, *Sir William White* 1902
Egremont, Max, *A Life of Arthur James Balfour* 1980
Elliot, Hon. Arthur, *The Life of George Joachim Goschen, 1st Viscount Goschen 1831–1907* 2 vols, 1911
Eyck, Erich, *Bismarck and the German Empire* 1950
Fisher, John, *Paul Kruger* 1974
Fitzmaurice, Lord Edmond, *The Life of Granville George Leveson Gower, 2nd Earl Granville* 2 vols, 1905
Foster, R.F., *Lord Randolph Churchill: A Political Life* 1988
Fraser, Peter, *Joseph Chamberlain* 1966
Froude, J.A., *Life of Lord Beaconsfield* 1914
Fyfe, Hamilton, *T.P. O'Connor* 1934
Gardiner, A.G., *The Life of Sir William Harcourt* 2 vols, 1929
Garvin, J.L., *Life of Joseph Chamberlain* 3 vols, 1932–3
Gathorne-Hardy, A.E., *Gathorne Hardy, 1st Earl of Cranbrook: A Memoir* 2 vols, 1910
Gilmour, David, *Curzon* 1994
Gooch, G.P., *Life of Lord Courtney* 1920
Goschen, Viscount, *The Life and Times of George Joachim Goschen* 2 vols, 1903
Grigg, John, *The Young Lloyd George* 1973
Grinnell-Milne, Duncan, *Baden-Powell at Mafeking* 1957
ed. Gwynn, Stephen, *The Letters and Friendships of Sir Cecil Spring Rice* 2 vols, 1929
Gwynn, Stephen, and Tuckwell, G.M., *Life of Rt Hon. Sir Charles W. Dilke MP* 2 vols 1917
Hamer, David A., *John Morley* 1968
Hamilton, Keith, *Bertie of Thame* 1990
Handover, P.M., *The Second Cecil: The Rise to Power of Sir Robert Cecil, later 1st Earl of Salisbury 1563–1604* 1959
Hardinge, Sir A., *The Life of Henry Herbert, 4th Earl Carnarvon* 3 vols, 1925
Haslip, Joan, *Abdul Hamid II* 1958
Heuston, R.F.V., *Lives of the Lord Chancellors 1885–1940* 1964
Hinchcliff, Peter, *Frederick Temple, Archbishop of Canterbury: A Life* 1998
Hobhouse, L.T., and Hammond, J.L., *Lord Hobhouse: A Memoir* 1905
Holland, Bernard, *The Life of Spencer Compton, 8th Duke of Devonshire* 2 vols, 1911
Hough, Richard, *Edward and Alexandra: Their Private and Public Lives* 1992

Jackson, Alvin, *Colonel Edward Saunderson* 1995
Jackson, Patrick, *The Last of the Whigs: A Political Biography of Lord Hartington, later Eighth Duke of Devonshire 1833–1908* 1994
—— *Education Act Forster* 1997
ed. Jagger, Peter J., *Gladstone* 1998
James, Andrew, *Lord Roberts* 1954
James, J. *Richard Olney*
James, Robert Rhodes, *Lord Randolph Churchill* 1959
—— *Rosebery* 1963
Jeal, Timothy, *Baden-Powell* 1989
—— *Livingstone* 1973
Jenkins, Roy, *Gladstone* 1995
—— *Sir Charles Dilke: A Victorian Tragedy* 1958
Johnston, Alexander, *The Life and Letters of Sir Harry Johnston* 1929
Johnston, Joseph, *Life and Letters of Henry Parry Liddon* 1904
Jones, W.D., *Lord Derby and Victorian Conservatism* 1956
Kee, Robert, *The Laurel and the Ivy: The Story of Charles Stewart Parnell and Irish Nationalism* 1993
Lang, Andrew, *The Life, Letters and Diaries of Sir Stafford Northcote, 1st Earl of Iddesleigh* 2 vols, 1890
Lang, Theo, *My Darling Daisy* 1966
Law, W. and I., *The Book of the Beresford-Hopes* 1925
Lee, Sir Sidney, *King Edward VII* 2 vols, 1925
Lees-Milne, James, *The Enigmatic Edwardian: The Life of Reginald, 2nd Viscount Esher* 1986
Londonderry, Marchioness of, *Henry Chaplin: A Memoir* 1926
Longford, Elizabeth, *Victoria R.I.* 1964
Lucas, Reginald, *Colonel Saunderson: A Memoir* 1908
Lucy, Sir Henry, *W.E. Gladstone: A Study from Life* 1895
Lutyens, Lady Emily, *A Blessed Girl* 1953
ed. Lutyens, Mary, *Lady Lytton's Court Diary 1895–1899* 1961
Lyall, Sir Alfred, *The Life of the Marquess of Dufferin and Ava* 2 vols, 1905
Mackay, Ruddock F., *Balfour: Intellectual Statesman* 1985
Magnus, Philip, *Gladstone* 1954
—— *King Edward VII* 1964
—— *Kitchener* 1958
Mallet, Bernard, *The Life of Lord Northbrook* 1909
Manners, Lady, *Lady Gwendolen Cecil* (privately printed) 1946
Marjoribanks, Edward, *The Life of Lord Carson* vol I 1937
Marlowe, John, *Milner: Apostle of Empire* 1976
—— *Cromer in Egypt* 1970
Marsh, Peter T., *Joseph Chamberlain: Entrepreneur in Politics* 1994
Martin, Patchett, *A Life and Letters of Robert Lowe, Viscount Sherbrooke* 2 vols, 1893
Martin, Ralph G., *Lady Randolph Churchill* 2 vols, 1969 and 1972
Masani, R.P., *Dadabhai Naoroji* 1939
Matthew, H.C.G., *Gladstone 1809–1874* 1986
—— *Gladstone 1875–1898* 1995
Maurois, André *Disraeli* 1927
Maxwell, Sir Herbert, *Life and Times of Rt Hon. William Henry Smith MP* 2 vols, 1893

McDonald, J.G., *Rhodes: A Life* 1927

McElroy, Robert, *Grover Cleveland: The Man and the Statesman* 2 vols, 1923

Melville, Col C.H., *The Life of General Sir Redvers Buller* 2 vols 1923

Middlemas, Keith, *The Life and Times of Edward VII* 1972

Mitchell, Dennis J., *Cross and Tory Democracy* 1991

Monypenny, W.F., and Buckle, G.E., *The Life of Benjamin Disraeli, Earl of Beaconsfield* 6 vols, 1910–24

Morley, John, *The Life of William Ewart Gladstone* 3 vols, 1903

Mosley, Leonard, *Curzon: The End of an Epoch* 1961

Mowat, R.B., *Life of Lord Pauncefote* 1929

Murray, D.L., *Disraeli* 1927

Newton, Lord, *Lord Lansdowne* 1929

—— *Lord Lyons* 1913

Nicholls, David, *The Lost Prime Minister: A Life of Sir Charles Dilke* 1995

Nicolson, Harold, *Lord Carnock* 1930

Nicolson, Nigel, *Mary Curzon* 1977

O'Brien, R. Barry, *Life of Charles Stewart Parnell 1846–1891* 2 vols, 1898

—— *John Bright* 1910

—— *The Life of Lord Russell of Killowen* 1901

O'Brien, Terence, *Milner* 1979

O'Broin, Leon, *The Prime Informer* 1971

Oliver, Roland, *Sir Harry Johnston and the Scramble for Africa* 1957

Oman, Carola, *The Gascoyne Heiress* 1968

O'Shea, Katherine, *Charles Stewart Parnell: His Love Story and Political Life* 2 vols, 1914

Otter, Sir John, *Nathaniel Woodard* 1925

Pakula, Hannah, *An Uncommon Woman: The Empress Frederick* 1996

Palmer, Alan *Twilight of the Habsburgs: The Life and Times of Emperor Francis Joseph* 1994

Pears, Sir Edwin, *Life of Abdul Hamid* 1917

Pearson, Hesketh, *Labby: The Life and Character of Henry Labouchere* 1936

Petrie, Sir Charles, *Walter Long and His Times* 1936

Plumptre, George, *Edward VII* 1995

Pollock, John, *Kitchener* vol. 1, 1998

Powell, Geoffrey, *Buller: A Scapegoat?* 1994

Powell, J. Enoch, *Joseph Chamberlain* 1977

Ramm, Agatha, *Sir Robert Morier* 1973

Reid, Michaela, *Ask Sir James: The Life of Sir James Reid, personal physician to Queen Victoria* 1996

Reid, T. Wemyss, *The Life of Rt Hon. William Edward Forster* 2 vols, 1888

—— *Memoirs and Correspondence of Lyon Playfair* 1899

Ronaldshay, Lord, *The Life of Lord Curzon* 3 vols, 1928

Rose Kenneth, *Superior Person: A Portrait of Curzon and his Circle in Late Victorian England* 1969

—— *The Later Cecils* 1975

Rosebery, Lord, *Lord Randolph Churchill* 1906

Russell, G.W.E., *Dr Liddon* 1905

ed. Russell, G.W.E., *Malcolm MacColl: Memories and Correspondence* 1914

St Aubyn, Giles, *The Royal George: the Life of HRH Prince George, Duke of Cambridge 1819–1904* 1963

Saintsbury, George, *The Earl of Derby* 1892

Shannon, Richard, *Gladstone: Peel's Inheritor 1809–1865* 1982
—— *Gladstone: Heroic Minister 1865–1898* 1999
Sichel, Walter, *Disraeli: A Study in Personality and Ideas* 1904
Smith, Paul, *Disraeli: A Brief Life* 1996
Spinner, Thomas J., *George Joachim Goschen: The Transformation of a Victorian Liberal* 1973
Steele, David, *Palmerston and Liberalism 1855–1865* 1991
Stephen, Leslie, *Life of Henry Fawcett* 1886
Stephenson, G., *Edward Stuart Talbot 1844–1934* 1936
Stewart, A.T.Q., *Edward Carson* 1981
Stirling, A.M.W., *The Richmond Papers* 1926
Taylor, A.J.P., *Bismarck* 1955
Thorold, Algar, *Labouchere: The Life of Henry Labouchere* 1913
Trevelyan, G.M., *The Life of John Bright* 1913
—— *Grey of Fallodon* 1937
Vincent, John, *Disraeli* 1990
Weintraub, Stanley, *Disraeli: A Biography* 1993
Wheatcroft, Geoffrey, *The Randlords: The Men Who Made South Africa* 1985
Whibley, Charles, *Lord John Manners and his Friends* vol. 2, 1925
Whitman, Sidney, *Personal Reminiscences of Prince Bismarck* 1902
Wilson, John, *C-B: A Life of Sir Henry Campbell-Bannerman* 1973
Winter, James, *Robert Lowe* 1976
ed. Wolfe, Humbert, *Personalities: a Selection from the Writings of A.A. Baumann* 1936
Woodham-Smith, Cecil, *Florence Nightingale* 1950
Worsfold, Basil, *Sir Bartle Frere* 1923
Wrench, John Evelyn, *Alfred Milner: The Man of No Illusions* 1958
Wynne, Maud, *An Irishman and his Family: Lord Morris and Killanin* 1937
Young, Kenneth, *Arthur James Balfour* 1963
Zetland, Marquis of, *Lord Cromer* 1932

Secondary Sources

Aronson, Theo, *Prince Eddy and the Homosexual Underworld* 1994
Adonis, Andrew, *Making Aristocracy Work 1884–1914* 1993
Aldcroft, Derek, and Richardson, Harry, *The British Economy 1879-1939* 1969
ed. Amery, Leopold, *The Times History of the South African War* 7 vols, 1902–9
Anderson, Pauline, *The Background of Anti-English Feeling in Germany 1890–1902* (Washington) 1939
Andrew, Christopher, *Delcassé and the Making of the Entente Cordiale* 1968
Argyll, The 9th Duke of, *Imperial Federation* 1885
Arnstein, Walter L., *The Bradlaugh Case* 1965
Auerbach, Erna, and Adams, C. Kingsley, *Paintings and Sculpture at Hatfield House* 1971
Ausubel, Herman, *In Hard Times* 1960
Aydelotte, William, *Bismarck and British Colonial Policy: The Problem of South-West Africa 1883–85* (Pennsylvania) 1937
Balfour, Sebastian, *The End of the Spanish Empire 1898–1923* 1997
Ballhatchet, Kenneth, *Race, Sex and Class Under the Raj 1793–1905* 1980
Bardon, Jonathan, *A History of Ulster* 1992

Bartlett, C.J., *The Global Conflict* 1984
Bateman, John, *The Great Landowners of Great Britain* 1878
Bates, Darrell, *The Fashoda Incident of 1898* 1984
Baumann, Arthur A., *The Last Victorians* 1927
Beckson, Karl, *London in the 1890s* 1992
Belfield, Eversley, *The Boer War* 1993
Beloff, Max, *Britain's Liberal Empire 1897–1921* 1969
Bentley, James, *Ritualism and Politics in Victorian Britain* 1978
Bevington, M.M., *The Saturday Review 1855–1868* (Columbia) 1941
Bew, Paul, *Land and the National Question in Ireland 1858–82* 1978
—— *Conflict and Conciliation in Ireland 1890–1910* 1987
Bigham, Clive, *The Prime Ministers of Britain 1721–1921* 1923
Black, Eugene C., *The Social Politics of Anglo-Jewry 1880–1920* 1988
Blake, Robert, *A History of Rhodesia* 1977
Blakeley, Brian, *The Colonial Office 1868–92* (Duke University) 1972
Blunt, Wilfrid Scawen, *Gordon at Khartoum* 1911
Bogdanor, Vernon, *The People and the Party System* 1981
Boyce, D.G., *The Irish Question and British Politics 1868–1986* 1988
eds Boyce, D.G., and O'Day, Alan, *Parnell in Perspective* 1991
Briggs, Asa, *Victorian People* 1955
Brown, B.H., *The Tariff Reform Movement 1881–95* (New York) 1943
Brown, R.G., *Fashoda Reconsidered* 1969
Busch, Briton Cooper, *Britain and the Persian Gulf 1894–1914* (Berkeley) 1967
Butler, Ewan, *The Cecils* 1964
Butler, J., *The Liberal Party and the Jameson Raid* 1968
Campbell, A.E., *Great Britain and the United States 1895–1903* 1960
Cannadine, David, *The Decline and Fall of the British Aristocracy* 1990
Carr-Gomm, Francis Culling, *Handbook of the Administrations of Great Britain in the Nineteenth Century* 1901
Carroll, Lewis, *Sylvie and Bruno* 1889
Carter, Byrum E., *The Office of Prime Minister* 1956
Cecil, Algernon, *Facing the Facts in Foreign Policy* 1941
—— *British Foreign Secretaries 1807–1916* 1927
Cecil, Evelyn, *On the Eve of War* 1900
Cecil, Hugh, *Conservatism* 1912
Chapman, Caroline, and Raben, P., *Queen Victoria's Jubilees* 1977
Christie, O.F., *The Transition to Democracy* 1934
—— *The Transition from Aristocracy* 1928
Churchill, Winston S., *The River War* 1899
—— *Great Contemporaries* 1935
Clammer, David, *The Zulu War* 1973
Clarke, Peter, *Hope and Glory: Britain 1900–1990* 1996
Clements, Paul H., *The Boxer Rebellion* (New York) 1915
Coetzee, Frans, *For Party or Country* 1990
Coleman, Bruce, *Conservatism and the Conservative Party in the Nineteenth Century* 1991
Conservative Central Office *The Campaign Guide* 1892
—— *The Campaign Guide* 1895
—— *The Campaign Guide* 1900
Cook, Edward T., *The Rights and Wrongs of the Transvaal War* 1901
Cooke, A.B., and Vincent, John, *The Governing Passion: Cabinet Government and Party Politics in Britain 1885–86* 1974

Cowling, Maurice, *1867, Disraeli, Gladstone and Reution: The Passing of the Second Reform Bill* 1967

—— *Religion and Public Doctrine in England* vol. 1, 1980

—— ed. Cowling, Maurice, *Conservative Essays* 1978

Cromer, Earl of, *Modern Egypt* 2 vols, 1908

Curtis, L.P., *Coercion and Conciliation in Ireland 1880–1892* (Princeton) 1963

Curzon, Lord, *Modern Parliamentary Eloquence* 1913

Davies, A.J., *We, the Nation: The Conservative Party and the Pursuit of Power* 1995

Davis, Lance E., and Huttenback, Robert A., *Mammon and the Pursuit of Empire: The Political Economy of British Imperialism 1860–1912* 1986

Davison, Roderic, *Reform in the Ottoman Empire 1856–1876* 1963

Dawson, W.H., *The Cambridge History of British Foreign Policy* vol. 3, 1923

Denison, Col George, *The Struggle for Imperial Unity* 1909

Disraeli, Benjamin, *Coningsby* 1844

—— *Lothair* 1870

ed. Dugdale, E.T.S., *German Diplomatic Documents* 4 vols, 1928

Eddy, J., and Schreuder, D., *The Rise of Colonial Nationalism* 1988

Escott, T.H.S., *The Story of British Diplomacy* 1908

Ewing, Thomas, *Mr Gladstone and Ireland or Lord Salisbury and the Orange Faction* 1886

Feinstein, C.H., *National Income, Expenditure and Output of the UK 1855–1965* 1972

Ferguson, Niall, *The World's Banker: The History of the House of Rothschild* 1998

Feuchtwanger, E.J., *Disraeli, Democracy and the Tory Party* 1968

Fforde, Matthew, *Conservatism and Collectivism 1886–1914* 1990

Fisher, Trevor, *Scandal: The Sexual Politics of Late Victorian Britain* 1995

Foot, Sir Dingle, *British Political Crises* 1976

Foster, R.F., *Paddy and Mr Punch* 1993

Francis, Mark, and Morrow, John, *A History of British Political Thought in the Nineteenth Century* 1994

Friedberg, Aaron L., *The Weary Titan: Britain and the Experience of Relative Decline 1895–1905* (Princeton) 1988

Gailey, Andrew, *Ireland and the Death of Kindness* 1987

Gardner, Brian, *Mafeking: The Making of a Victorian Legend* 1966

Geiss, Immanuel, *German Foreign Policy 1871–1914* 1976

Gibbon, Ioan, and Bell, Reginald, *History of the London County Council* 1939

Gollin, Alfred, *Balfour's Burden: Arthur Balfour and Imperial Preference* 1965

Gooch, G.P., and Ward A.W., *The Cambridge History of British Foreign Policy* vol. 3, 1923

Goodfellow, C.F., *Great Britain and the South African Confederation 1870–81* 1966

Gopal, S., *British Policy in India 1858–1905* 1965

Gorst, Harold E., *The Fourth Party* 1906

Greaves, Rose L., *Persia and the Defence of India 1884–1892: A Study in the Foreign Policy of 3rd Marquess of Salisbury* 1959

Green, E.H.H., *The Crisis of Conservatism 1880–1914* 1995

Gretton, R.H., *Imperialism and Mr Gladstone* 1923

Guadalla, Philip, *The Hundred Years* 1936

Guttsman, W.L., *The British Political Elite* 1963

ed. Gwynn, Stephen, *Lord Curzon: The Personal History of Walmer Castle and its Lords Warden* 1927

Hamer, William S., *The British Army: Civil–Military Relations 1885–1905* 1970

Hamilton, Angus, *The Siege of Mafeking* 1900

Hammond, J.L., *Gladstone and the Irish Nation* 1964

Hanham, H.J., *Elections and Party Management: Politics in the Time of Gladstone and Disraeli* 1959

Hardie, Frank, *The Political Influence of the British Monarchy 1868–1952* 1970

Hargreaves, J.C., *Prelude to the Partition of West Africa* 1963

Harrison, Brian, *Drink and the Victorians* 1994

Harrison, Henry, *Parnell, Joseph Chamberlain and Mr Garvin* 1938

Hart, Neil, *The Foreign Secretary* 1973

Hearnshaw, F.J.C., *The Political Principles of Some Notable Prime Ministers of the Nineteenth Century* 1926

Heffer, Simon, *Power and Place: The Political Consequences of Edward VII* 1998

Hewison, H.H., *Hedge of Wild Almonds: South Africa, the Pro-Boers and the Quaker Conscience 1890–1910* 1989

Himmelfarb, Gertrude, *Poverty and Compassion: The Moral Imagination of the Late Victorians* 1991

Hollingsworth, L.W., *Zanzibar under the Foreign Office 1890–1913* 1953

Holt, Edgar Crawshaw, *The Boer War* 1958

Hopkirk, Peter, *The Great Game: On Secret Service in High Asia* 1990

Hoppen, K.T., *Elections, Politics and Society in Ireland 1832–1885* 1984

Horn, Pamela, *High Society: The English Social Elite 1880–1914* 1992

Howard, Christopher, *Britain and the Casus Belli 1822–1902: A Study of Britain's International Position from Canning to Salisbury* 1974

Hudson, Roger, *The Jubilee Years 1887–1897* 1996

Hughes, Judith M., *Emotion and High Politics: Personal Relations at the Summit in Late Nineteenth Century Britain and Germany* (Berkeley) 1983

Hurst, Michael, *Joseph Chamberlain and Liberal Reunion: The Round Table Conference of 1887* 1967

Hutcheson, John A., *Leopold Maxse and the National Review 1893–1914* (New York) 1989

Hutchinson, William, *The Oxford Movement* 1906

Hyam, Ronald, *Britain's Imperial Century 1815–1914* 1976

Hyde, H. Montgomery, *The Cleveland Street Scandal* 1976

ed. Ingram, Edward, *Allan Cunningham: Eastern Questions in the Nineteenth Century* vol 2, 1993

Iremonger, L., *The Fiery Chariot* 1970

Jackson, Alvin, *The Ulster Party: Irish Unionists in the House of Commons 1884–1911* 1989

Jay, R., *Joseph Chamberlain: A Political Study* 1981

Jelavich, Barbara, *The Ottoman Empire, the Great Powers and the Straits Question 1870–1887* 1973

Jenkins, Roy, *The Chancellors* 1998

Jenkins, T.A., *Disraeli and Victorian Conservativism* 1996

ed. Jennings, George Henry, *An Anecdotal History of the British Parliament* 1899

Johnson, F.A., *Defence by Committee: The British Committee for Imperial Defence 1885–1959* 1960

Johnston, Sir Harry, *The Gay-Dombeys* 1919

Jones, Andrew, *The Politics of Reform 1884* 1972

Jones, Raymond, *The Nineteenth Century Foreign Office* 1971

Judd, Denis, *Empire: The British Imperial Experience from 1765 to the Present* 1996

—— *Balfour and the British Empire* 1968

Kennedy, A.L., *Old Diplomacy and New 1876–1922* 1923

Kennedy, Paul, *The Rise of Anglo-German Antagonism* 1980

—— *The Realities Behind Diplomacy* 1981

Keown-Boyd, Henry, *A Good Dusting: A Centenary Review of the Sudan Campaigns 1883–1899* 1986

—— *The Fists of Righteous Harmony: A History of the Boxer Uprising in China in the Year 1900* 1991

Koss, Stephen, *The Pro-Boers: The Anatomy of an Anti-War Movement* (Chicago) 1973

—— *The Rise and Fall of the Political Press in Britain* 1981

Kubicek, Robert, *The Administration of Imperialism: Joseph Chamberlain at the Colonial Office* (Duke University) 1969

Langer, W.L., *The Diplomacy of Imperialism 1890–1902* 1956

Lant, Jeffrey L., *Insubstantial Pageant* 1979

Lee, Dwight E., *Great Britain and the Cyprus Convention of 1878* (Massachusetts) 1934

Lee, E., *Wives of the Prime Ministers* 1917

Le May, G.H.L., *The Victorian Constitution* 1979

Liberal Publication Department, The, *Six Years of Tory Government 1886–1892* 1892

Lloyd, Trevor, *The General Election of 1880* 1968

Longford, Elizabeth, *The Jameson Raid* 1960

Loughlin, James, *Gladstone, Home Rule and the Ulster Question of 1886–1892* 1986

Lowe, C.J., *The Reluctant Imperialists: British Foreign Policy 1878–1902* 2 vols, 1967

—— *Salisbury and the Mediterranean* 1962

Lubenow, W.C., *Parliamentary Politics in the Home Rule Crisis* 1988

Lutyens, Mary, *The Lyttons in India* 1979

Lynd, Helen Merrell, *England in the 1880s* 1968

Lyons, F.S.L., and Hawkins, R.A., *Ireland Under the Union* 1980

MacColl, Malcolm, *The Eastern Question* 1877

Mackenzie, John M., *The Partition of Africa* 1983

—— *Propaganda and Empire* 1984

—— *Imperialism and Popular Culture* 1986

Mackenzie, R.T., *British Political Parties* 1955

Mallet, Bernard, *British Budgets 1887–1913* 1913

Marais, J.S., *The Fall of Kruger's Republic* 1961

Marder, Arthur, *British Naval Policy 1880–1905* 1941

Marriot, J.A.R., *The Eastern Question* 1917

Marsden, Arthur, *British Diplomacy and Tunis 1875–1902* 1979

Marsh, Peter, *The Conscience of the Victorian State* 1979

—— *The Victorian Church in Decline* 1969

Marshall, P.J., *The Cambridge Illustrated History of the British Empire* 1996

Martin, A.C., *The Concentration Camps* (Cape Town) 1958

Marvin, Charles, *The Public Offices* 1879

ed. Massingham, Hugh, *The Great Victorians* 1932

Matthew, H.C.G., *The Liberal Imperialists: The Ideas and Politics of a Post-Gladstonian Elite* 1973

ed. Maurice, Maj.-Gen. Sir Frederick, *The Official History of the War in South Africa* 4 vols, 1906–10

M'Carthy, Justin, *History of Our Own Time* 3 vols, 1882

McDowell, R.B., *British Conservatism 1832–1914* 1959

—— *Crisis and Decline: The Fate of the Southern Unionists* 1997

McKenzie, Robert, and Silver, Allan, *Angels in Marble: Working Class Conservatives in Urban England* 1968

Medlicott, W.N., *The Congress of Berlin and After* 1938

Metcalfe, Priscilla, *Victorian London* 1972

Monger, George, *The End of Isolation: British Foreign Policy 1900–1907* 1963

Moore, R.J., *Liberalism and Indian Politics 1872–1922* 1966

Morrah, Herbert A., *The Oxford Union 1823–1923* 1923

Morris, Jan, *Pax Britannica* 1968

Moulton, Edward C., *Lord Northbrook's Indian Administration 1872–1876* 1969

Munro, H.H., *The Westminster Alice* 1902

Newsome, David, *The Victorian World Picture* 1997

Nish, Ian H., *The Anglo-Japanese Alliance* 1966

O'Callaghan, Margaret, *British High Politics and a Nationalist Ireland* 1994

ed. O'Day, Alan, *Reactions to Irish Nationalism 1865–1914* 1987

O'Day, Alan, *Parnell and the First Home Rule Episode* 1986

Offer, Avner, *Property and Politics 1870–1914* 1981

O'Leary, Cornelius, *The Elimination of Corrupt Practices in British Elections 1868–1911* 1962

Packenham, Simona, *Sixty Miles from England: The English at Dieppe 1814–1914* 1967

Pakenham, Thomas, *The Boer War* 1979

—— *The Scramble for Africa* 1991

Palmer, Bernard, *High and Mitred* 1992

Parsons, Neil, *King Khama, Emperor Joe and the Great White Queen* 1998

Patriotic Association, The, *The Truth about the Conduct of the War* 1901

Penson, Lilian, *Foreign Affairs Under Lord Salisbury* 1962

Pinto-Duschinsky, Michael, *British Political Finance 1830–1980* (Washington) 1981

Porter, Andrew, *The Origins of the South African War* 1980

Porter, Bernard, *Critics of Empire* 1968

—— *Plots and Paranoia* 1989

Powell, John, *Art, Truth and High Politics* 1996

Price, Richard, *An Imperial War and the British Working Class* 1972

—— *The Jingo Crowd*

Pugh, M., *The Tories and the People 1880–1935* 1985

Quinton, Anthony, *The Politics of Imperfection*, 1978

Ramsden, John, *An Appetite for Power* 1998

Raymond, E.T., *Portraits of the Nineties* 1921

Regan, Geoffrey, *Military Blunders* 1991

Rempel, Richard, *Unionists Divided* 1972

Robb, Janet, *The Primrose League 1883–1906* (New York) 1942

Robinson, Ronald, and Gallagher, John, *Africa and the Victorians* 1961

ed. Robson, Robert, *Ideas and Institutions in Victorian Britain* 1967

ed. Rogers, Alan, *The Making of Stamford* 1965

Rosebery, Lord, *Miscellanies: Literary and Historical* 2 vols, 1921

Russell, G.W.E., *Prime Ministers and Some Others* 1918

Saab, Ann Pottinger, *Gladstone, Bulgaria and the Working Classes 1856–1878* 1991

Salt, Jeremy, *Imperialism, Evangelism and the Ottoman Armenians 1876–1896* 1993

Schreuder, D.M., *The Scramble for Southern Africa 1877–95* 1980

—— *Gladstone and Kruger* 1969

Scott, J.W. Robertson, *The Life and Death of a Newspaper: The Pall Mall Gazette* 1950

Seaman, L.C.B., *Victorian England: Aspects of English and Imperial History 1837–1901* 1973

Searle, Geoffrey R., *The Quest for National Efficiency* 1971
—— *Corruption in British Politics 1895–1930* 1987
—— *Entrepreneurial Politics in Mid-Victorian Britain* 1993
—— *Country Before Party* 1995
ed. Seldon, A., *How Tory Governments Fall: The Tory Party in Power Since 1783* 1996
Shannon, Catherine, *Arthur J. Balfour and Ireland 1874–1922* (Catholic University of America Press, USA) 1988
Shannon, Richard, *The Age of Disraeli 1868–81: The Rise of Tory Democracy* 1992
—— *Gladstone and Bulgarian Agitation 1876* 1963
—— *The Crisis of Imperialism 1865–1915* 1976
Shibeika, Mekki, *British Policy in the Sudan 1882–1902* 1952
Shiell, Anthony George, *Camps of Refuge* 1901
Smith, Colin L., *The Embassy of Sir William White at Constantinople 1886–91* 1957
Smith, Iain R., *The Origins of the South African War 1899-1902* 1996
Smith, Jeremy, *The Taming of Democracy: The Conservative Party 1880–1924* 1997
Southgate, Donald, *The Conservative Leadership 1832–1932* 1974
Spiers, Edward, *The Late Victorian Army* 1992
Stead, W.T., *The Truth About the War* 1900
Steele, Edward, *Irish Land and British Politics: Tenant-Right and Nationality 1865–1870* 1974
Steiner, Zara, *The Foreign Office and Foreign Policy 1898–1914* 1969
Surridge, Keith, *Managing the South African War 1899-1901* 1998
Sutherland, Gillian, *Policy-Making in Elementary Education 1870–1895* 1973
ed. Sutherland, Gillian, *Studies in the Growth of Nineteenth Century Government* 1972
Sykes, Alan, *Tariff Reform in British Politics 1903–1913* 1979
Taylor, A.J.P., *The Struggle for Mastery in Europe* 1954
—— *From the Boer War to the Cold War* 1995
—— *Essays in English History* 1977
Temperley, Harold, and Penson, Lillian, *Foundations of British Foreign Policy* 1938
Thompson, George Carslake, *Public Opinion and Lord Beaconsfield 1875–1880* 2 vols, 1886
Thompson, F.M.L., *English Landed Society in the Nineteenth Century* 1963
ed. Thompson, J.A., and Meijia, Arthur, *Edwardian Conservatism: Five Studies in Adaptation* 1988
Thornton A.P., *For the File on the Empire* 1968
Tidrick, Kathryn, *Empire and the English Character* 1990
Tilley, Sir John, and Gaselee, Stephen, *The Foreign Office* 1933
—— *The Times: The Tradition Established 1841–1884* 1939
—— *The Twentieth Century Test 1884–1912* 1941
—— *The Truth about the Conduct of the Tranvaal War* 1902
Uzoigwe, G.N., *Britain and the Conquest of Africa: The Age of Salisbury* (Ann Arbour) 1974
Van der Poel, Jean, *The Jameson Raid* 1951
ed. Vincent, John, and Stenton, M., *McCalmont's Parliamentary Poll Book: British Election Results 1832–1918* 1971
Walker, E.A., *A History of South Africa* 1957
Walsh, Walter, *The Secret History of the Oxford Movement* 1899
ed. Ward, A.W., *The Cambridge Modern History* vols XI and XII, 1920
Ward, W.R., *Victorian Oxford* 1965

Warwick, Peter, *Black People and the South African War: 1899–1902* 1980

West, Rebecca, *1900* 1982

Weston, Corinne Comstock, *The House of Lords and Ideological Politics: Lord Salisbury's Referendal Theory and the Conservative Party 1846–1922* (American Philosophical Society) 1995

Whates, H.R., *The Third Salisbury Administration 1895–1900* 1901

Williams, Richard, *The Contentious Crown* 1997

Williams, R.H., *Defending the Empire* 1991

Wilson, Keith, *The Policy of the Entente* 1985

ed. Wilson, Keith, *British Foreign Secretaries and Foreign Policy* 1987

ed. Wohl, A.S., *The Bitter Cry of Outcast London* 1970

Wohl, A.S., *The Eternal Slum: Housing and Social Policy in Victorian London* 1977

Ziegler, Philip, *The Sixth Great Power: Barings 1762–1929* 1988

—— *Omdurman* 1973

Articles

IHR stands for the Institute of Historical Research
EHR stands for *The English Historical Review*

Andrew, Christopher, 'France and the Making of the Entente Cordiale' *Historical Journal* x, 1967

Barker, T.C., 'Lord Salisbury, Chairman of the Great Eastern Railway 1868–72', in ed. Marriner, Shiela, *Business and Businessmen* 1978

Berrington, Hugh, 'Partisanship and Dissidence in the Nineteenth Century House of Commons', *Parliamentary Affairs* xxi 4, Autumn 1968

Blake, Robert, 'The Jameson Raid and the Missing Telegrams', in ed. Lloyd-Jones, Hugh, *History and Imagination* 1981

Bloch, Michael, 'Great Britain and the First Hague Peace Conference August 1898–July 1899', Unfinished Cambridge PhD thesis 1980

Brailey, Nigel, 'Protection or Partition: Ernest Satow and the 1880s Crisis in Britain's Siam Policy', *Journal of Southeast Asian Studies* 29,1, March 1998

Brooks, Sydney, 'Lord Salisbury', *North American Review* no. 175, 1902

Brumpton, P.R., 'Lord Salisbury at the India Office', Leeds University PhD 1994

Butterfield, W., 'Alterations in and about Hatfield House since 1868' (privately printed) 1908

Cecil, Lord Hugh, 'The Life of Gladstone', *Nineteenth Century* cccxlix, March 1906

Cecil, Hugh, 'Lord Robert Cecil: A Nineteenth Century Upbringing', *History Today* February 1975

—— 'Introduction' to ed. Harcourt Williams, *The Salisbury–Balfour Correspondence 1869–92* 1988

Cecil, Lord Robert, 'Lord Salisbury', *Monthly Review* xiii, October 1903

Chadwick, Mary Elizabeth, 'The Electoral System in the United Kingdom as set up by the Third Reform Act', University College, London, PhD 1977

Chamberlain, Joseph, 'Labourers' and Artisans' Dwellings', *Fortnightly Review* xxxv, December 1883

Churchill, Randolph, 'Elijah's Mantle', *Fortnightly Review* cxcvii May 1883

Coetzee, Frank, 'Villa Toryism Reconsidered: Conservatism and Suburban Sensibilities in Late-Victorian Croydon', *Parliamentary History* 1, 1997

Cohn, Bernard, 'Representing Authority in Victorian India', in ed. Hobsbawm, Eric, *The Invention of Tradition* 1983

Cooke, Alistair, 'The Great Lord Salisbury', *Salisbury Review* Autumn 1982

Cooke, A.B., and Vincent, John, 'Ireland and Party Politics 1885–87: An Unpublished Conservative Memoir', *Irish Historical Studies* 1968/9

Cornford, James, 'The Transformation of Conservatism in the Late Nineteenth Century', *Victorian Studies* vii, September 1963

Cornish, Martyn, 'The Importance of the Dreyfus Affair in Late-Victorian Britain', *Franco-British Studies* no. 22, Autumn 1996

Cowling, Maurice, 'Lytton, the Cabinet and the Russians, August to November 1878', *EHR* lxxvi, 1961

Davis, Peter, 'The Liberal Unionist Party and the Irish Policy of Lord Salisbury's Government 1886–1892', *Historical Journal* xviii, 1975

Drus, Ethel, 'Select Documents from the Chamberlain Papers Concerning Anglo-Transvaal Relations 1896–1899', IHR *Bulletin* xxvii, 1954

—— 'The Question of Imperial Complicity in the Jameson Raid', *EHR* lxviii, October 1953

Dunbabin, J.P.D., 'The Politics of the Establishment of County Councils', *Historical Journal* 6, 1963

Duthie, John Lowe, 'Lord Salisbury, the Forward Group and Anglo-Afghan Relations 1874–78', *Journal of Imperial and Commonwealth History* viii, May 1980

—— 'Pragmatic Diplomacy or Imperial Encroachment? British Policy Towards Afghanistan 1874–1879', *International History Review* v, November 1983

Escott, T.H.S., 'The Marquess of Salisbury', *Fortnightly Review* ccxii, August 1884

—— 'Lord Salisbury and Journalism', *Contemporary Review* cxxi, February 1922

Eustance, Claire, 'Protests from Behind the Grille: Gender and the Transformation of Parliament 1867–1918', *Parliamentary History* 16, 1997

Fair, John D., 'Royal Mediation in 1884: A Reassessment', *EHR* lxxxviii, 1973

—— 'The Carnarvon Diaries and Royal Mediation in 1884', *EHR* cvi, 1991

Fraser, P., 'The Liberal Unionist Alliance: Chamberlain, Hartington and the Conservatives 1886–1904', *EHR* lxxvii, 1962

Frisby, Alfred, 'Has Conservatism Increased in England Since the Last Reform Bill?', *Fortnightly Review* December 1881

Gailey, Andrew, 'Unionist Rhetoric and Irish Local Goverment Reform 1895–9', *Irish Historical Studies* xxiv, 1984/5

Gauld, W.A., 'The Anglo-Austrian Agreement of 1878', *EHR* xli, 1926

Gillard, D.R., 'Salisbury's African Policy and the Heligoland Offer of 1890', *EHR* lxxv, October 1960

—— 'Salisbury and the Indian Defence Problem 1885–1902', in eds Bourne, Kenneth, and Watt, Donald Cameron, *Studies in International History* 1967

—— 'Salisbury', in ed. Wilson, Keith, *British Foreign Secretaries and Foreign Policy* 1987

Green, E.H.H., 'The Age of Transition: British Politics 1880–1914', *Parliamentary History* 16, 1997

Grenville, J.A.S., 'Lansdowne's Abortive Project of 12 March 1901 for a Secret Agreement with Germany', IHR *Bulletin* xxvii, 1954

—— 'Goluchowski, Salisbury, and the Mediterranean Agreements 1895–1897', *Slavonic and East European Review* 36, 1957–8

Hanham, H.J., 'British Party Finance 1868–80', IHR *Bulletin* xxvii, 1954

—— 'The Sale of Honours in Late Victorian England', *Victorian Studies* viii, March 1960

Hargreaves, J.D., 'Lord Salisbury, British Isolation and the Yangzte Valley June–Sept 1900', IHR *Bulletin* xxx, 1957

Hart, Peter, 'The Protestant Experience of Reution in Southern Ireland', in eds English, Richard, and Walker, Graham, *Unionism in Modern Ireland* 1996

Howard, Christopher, 'Splendid Isolation', *History* xlvii, February 1962

—— 'The Policy of Isolation', *Historical Journal* 1967

Eds. Howard, Christopher, and Gordon, Peter, 'The Cabinet Journal of Dudley Ryder, Viscount Sandon 11th May–10th August 1878', IHR *Bulletin* special supplement no. 10, November 1974

—— 'The First Balmoral Journal of Dudley Ryder, Viscount Sandon 6th–14th November 1879', IHR *Bulletin* xlx, May 1977

—— 'The Osborne Journals, Second Balmoral Journal and Notes of Events of Dudley Ryder, Viscount Sandon 1879-86', IHR *Bulletin* l, no. 122, November 1977

Humphreys, R.A., 'Anglo-German Rivalries and the Venezuelan Crisis of 1895', *Transactions of the Royal Historical Society* 5th series 17, 1967

Hurst, Michael, 'Always Splendid and Never Isolated: Lord Salisbury and the Public Scene 1830–1903', *The Historian* no. 47, 1995

Jefferson, Margaret, 'Lord Salisbury and the Eastern Question 1890–98', *Slavonic and Eastern European Review* 39, 1960/1

—— 'Lord Salisbury's Conversations with the Tsar at Balmoral, 27 and 29 September 1896', *Slavonic and Eastern European Review* 39, 1960–1

Johnson, Lawrence, 'Lord Derby: Man, Statesman and Victorian', Temple University, New Jersey PhD, 1974

Johnson, R.A., 'The Penjdeh Incident 1885', *Archives* 24, 100, 1999

Jones, Adrian, and Bentley, Michael, 'Salisbury and Baldwin', in ed. Cowling, Maurice, *Conservative Essays* 1978

Jones, Raymond Arthur, 'The Administration of the British Diplomatic Service and Foreign Office 1848–1906', PhD 1986

Kedourie, Elie, 'Tory Ideologue: Salisbury as a Conservative Intellectual', *Encounter* June 1972

Kelly, J.B., 'Salisbury, Curzon and the Kuwait Agreement of 1899', in eds Bourne, Kenneth, and Watt, Donald Cameron, *Studies in International History* 1967

Kennedy, Paul M., 'German World Policy and the Alliance Negotiations with England 1897–1900', *Journal of Modern History* 45, 1973

Klein, Ira, 'Salisbury, Rosebery and the Survival of Siam', *Journal of British Studies* viii, 1968

Knatchbull-Hugessen, E.H., 'My Oxford Days', in ed. Yates, Edmund, *Time* 1879

Koch, H.W., 'The Anglo-German Alliance Negotiations: Missed Opportunity or Myth?', *History* 54, 1969

Kubicek, Robert V., 'The Randlords in 1895: A Reassessment', *Journal of British Studies* x, May 1972

Kuhn, William M., 'Queen Victoria's Jubilees and the Invention of Tradition', *Victorian Poetry* 25, 1987

Kunze, Neil, 'Lord Salisbury's Ideas on Housing Reform 1883–85', *Journal of Canadian History* viii, no. 3, December 1973

—— 'Late Victorian Periodical Editors and Politicians', *Victorian Periodicals Review* no. 2, Summer 1987

Lacy, George, 'Some Boer Characteristics', *North American Review* clxx, January 1900

Lawrence, Jon, and Elliot, Jane, 'Parliamentary Elections Reconsidered: An Analysis of Borough Elections 1885–1910', *Parliamentary History* 16, 1997

Lieven, Anatole, 'Salisbury: A Model for Imperialists', *National Interest* no. 53, Fall 1998

Louis, W. Roger, 'Sir Percy Anderson's Grand Strategy 1883–1896', *EHR* 81, no. 319, April 1966

Low, Sidney, 'The Rise of the Suburbs', *Contemporary Review* lx, October 1891

Lowry, Donal, 'When the World Loved the Boers', *History Today* May 1999

Mackintosh, John P., 'The Role of the Committee for Imperial Defence before 1914', *EHR* lxxvii, 1962

Mahajan, Sneh, 'The Defence of India and the End of Isolation: A Study in the Foreign Policy of the Conservative Government 1900–1905', *Journal of Imperial and Commonwealth History* January 1982

Marsh, Peter, 'Lord Salisbury and the Ottoman Massacres', *Journal of British Studies* x, May 1972

Mason, J.F.A., 'The Election of Lord Salisbury as the Chancellor of the University of Oxford', *Oxoniensia* xxix–xxx 1964–5

—— 'The 3rd Marquess of Salisbury and the Saturday Review', IHR *Bulletin* xxxiv May 1961

Matthew, H.C.G., 'Learning from Gladstone', *Prospect* August 1998

Maume, Patrick, 'Parnell and the IRB Oath', *Irish Historical Studies* xxix, May 1995

McGill, B., 'Glittering Prizes and Party Funds in Perspective 1882–1931', IHR *Bulletin* lv, 1982

Medlicott, W.N., 'The Mediterranean Agreements of 1887', *Slavonic and Eastern European Review* 5, 1926/7

—— 'The Powers and the Unification of the Two Bulgarias', *EHR* liv, 1939

—— 'Lord Salisbury and Turkey', *History* xii, 1927–8

Milner, Lady, 'Footnotes to Chamberlain's Life', *National Review* December 1934

Munson, J.E.B., 'The Unionist Coalition and Education 1895–1902', *Historical Journal* 1977

O'Callaghan, Margaret, 'Franchise Reform, First Past the Post and the Strange Case of Unionist Ireland', *Parliamentary History* 16, 1997

—— 'Parnellism and Crime: Constructing a Conservative Strategy of Containment 1887–91', in ed. McCartney, Donal, *Parnell: The Politics of Power* 1991

Otte, Thomas, 'Great Britain, Germany and the Far Eastern Crisis of 1897–8', *EHR* cx, no. 439, November 1995

—— 'Eyre Crowe and British Foreign Policy: A Cognitive Map', in eds Otte, T.G., and Pagedas, Constantine A., *Personalities, War and Diplomacy* 1997

—— 'Cabinet Government and Foreign Policy 1895–1900', Paper read at IHR on 20th March 1996

Papadopolous, 'Lord Salisbury and the Projected Anglo-German Alliance of 1898', IHR *Bulletin* xxvi, 1953

Penson, Lillian, 'The Principles and Methods of Lord Salisbury's Foreign Policy', *Cambridge Historical Journal* v, 1935

—— 'The New Course in British Foreign Policy 1892–1902', *Transactions of the Royal Historical Society* 4th series xxv, 1943

—— 'Obligations by Treaty: Their Place in British Foreign Policy 1898–1914', in ed. Sarkissian, A.O., *Studies in Diplomatic History* 1961

Porter, Andrew, 'Lord Salisbury, Mr Chamberlain and South Africa 1895–9', *Journal of Imperial and Commonwealth History* i, October 1972

Price, Richard N., 'Society, Status and Jingoism: The Social Roots of Lower-Middle Class Patriotism', in ed. Crossick, G., *The Lower Middle Class in Britain 1870–1914* 1977

Quinault, R.E., 'The Fourth Party and Conservative Opposition to Bradlaugh 1880–1888', *EHR* xci, 1976

Rafiuddin, Ahmad, 'The Battle of Omdurman and the Mussulman World', *Nineteenth Century* cclx, October 1898

Raymond, John, 'Cromer: The Proconsul', *History Today* March 1960

Rempel, Richard, 'Lord Hugh Cecil's Parliamentary Career: Promise Unfulfilled', *Journal of British Studies* xi, May 1972

Russell, G.W.E., 'Armenia and the Forward Movement', *Contemporary Review* lxxi, January 1897

Ryan, A.P., 'The Marquis of Salisbury', *History Today* April 1951

Sanderson, George N., 'England, Italy, the Nile Valley and the European Balance 1890–91', *Historical Journal* VII, 1964

—— 'The Anglo-German Agreement of 1890 and the Upper Nile', *EHR* lxxviii 1963

Savage, David Cockfield, 'The General Election of 1886 in Great Britain and Ireland', King's College, London, PhD 1958

Searight, Sarah, 'Steaming Through Africa', *History Today* July 1998

Shearman, Thomas G., 'Mistaken Sympathy with Republics', *North American Review* April 1900

Simon, Alan, 'Church Disestablishment as a Factor in the General Election of 1885', *Historical Journal* xviii, 1975

Smith, Jeremy, 'Conservative Ideology and Representations of the Union with Ireland 1885–1914', in eds Francis, Martin, and Zweiniger-Bargielowska, Ina, *The Conservatives and British Society 1880–1990* 1996

Smith, Paul, Review of Marsh, Peter, *Discipline of Popular Government*, *EHR* 95, 1980

Stead, W.T., 'The Marquis of Salisbury', *Review of Reviews* xvii, Jan–June 1898

Steiner, Zara, 'Great Britain and the Creation of the Anglo-Japanese Alliance', *Journal of Modern History* xxxi, March 1959

—— 'The Last Years of the Old Foreign Office 1898–1905', *Historical Journal* 6, 1963

Surridge, Keith, 'The Military Critique of the South African War 1899–1902', *History* October 1997

Thornton, A.P., 'British Policy in Persia 1858–90', *EHR* lxix, 1954

Turton, E.R., 'Lord Salisbury and the Macdonald Expedition', *Journal of Imperial and Commonwealth History* v, October 1976

Walters, Eurof, 'Lord Salisbury's Refusal to Revise and Renew the Mediterranean Agreements', *Slavonic and East European Review* 29, 1950–1

Weston, Corinne C., 'Disunity on the Front Bench 1884', *EHR* cvi, 1991

—— 'Salisbury and the Lords 1868–95', *Historical Journal* xxv, 1982

—— 'The Royal Mediation in 1884', *EHR* lxxxii, 1967

Wilson, Keith, 'Drawing the Line at Constantinople: Salisbury's Statements of Primat Der Innenpolitik', in ed. Wilson, Keith, *British Foreign Secretaries and Foreign Policy* 1987

—— 'Constantinople or Cairo: Lord Salisbury and the Partition of the Ottoman Empire 1886–1897', in ed. Wilson, Keith, *Imperialism and Nationalism in the Middle East: the Anglo-Egyptian Experience 1882–1982* 1983

Wodehouse, C.M., 'The Missing Telegrams and the Jameson Raid', *History Today* xii, nos 6 and 7, June and July 1962

Index